Fifth Edition

501

FRENCH VERBS

fully conjugated in all the tenses
and moods in a new easy-to-learn
format, alphabetically arranged

by

Christopher Kendris

B.S., M.S., Columbia University
M.A., Ph.D., Northwestern University
Diplômé, Faculté des Lettres, Sorbonne

Former Chairman
Department of Foreign Languages
Farmingdale High School
Farmingdale, New York

and

Theodore Kendris

B.A., Union College
M.A., Northwestern University
Ph.D., Université Laval

Former *Chargé de cours*
Université Laval
Québec, Canada

 EDUCATIONAL SERIES, INC.

All inquiries should be addressed to:
Barron's Educational Series, Inc.
250 Wireless Boulevard
Hauppauge, New York 11788
http://www.barronseduc.com

Library of Congress Catalog Card No. 2003040395

International Standard Book No. 0-7641-2429-3

Library of Congress Cataloging-in-Publication Data
Kendris, Christopher.
    501 French verbs fully conjugated in all the tenses in a new easy-to-learn format /
alphabetically arranged by Christopher Kendris and Theodore Kendris.—5th ed.
        p.   cm.
    ISBN 0-7641-2429-3
    1. French language—Verb—Tables.   I. Title: Five hundred and one
French verbs fully conjugated in all the tenses in a new easy-to-learn format.
II. Title: Five hundred one French verbs fully conjugated in all the tenses
in a new easy-to-learn format.   III. Kendris, Theodore.   IV. Title.
PC2271.K378 2003
448.2′421—dc21   2003040395

PRINTED IN CANADA
9 8 7 6

Contents

To St. Sophia Greek Orthodox Church
of Albany, New York

and

Yolanda, Alex, Tina, Fran, Bryan, Daniel, Matthew, Andrew, Athena,
Tom, Donna, Amanda, Laura, Thomas, Mary Ann, Hilda, Arthur,
Karen, George, Christopher, Matthew, Delores, Faith,
Demetra, Stephanie, Tony, Toni, LC, Mike, Dot, MJ, Nick, Bob, Katie,
Brett, Ellen, Connor, Hannah, Anne, Marie, Jean-Claude, Pierrette, Kamal,
Sabrina, Thierry, René, Nathalie, Pierre, Jocelyne, Tillie, Richard, Alice,
Elizabeth, Katherine

With love

About the Authors

Dr. Christopher Kendris has worked as interpreter and translator of French for the
U.S. State Department at the American Embassy in Paris. He earned his B.S. and M.S.
degrees at Columbia University in the City of New York, where he held a New York State
Scholarship, and his M.A. and Ph.D. degrees at Northwestern University in Evanston,
Illinois, where he held a Teaching Assistantship and Tutorial Fellowship during four years.
He also earned two diplomas with *Mention très Honorable* at the Université de Paris (en
Sorbonne), Faculté des Lettres, École Supérieure de Préparation et de Perfectionnement
des Professeurs de Français à l'Étranger, and at the Institut de Phonétique, Paris. In
1986 he was one of 95 teachers in the United States awarded a Rockefeller Foundation
Fellowship for Teachers of Foreign Languages in American High Schools. He has taught
French at the College of the University of Chicago as visiting summer lecturer, at Colby
College, Duke University, Rutgers—The State University of New Jersey, and the State
University of New York at Albany. He was Chairman of the Department of Foreign
Languages and Supervisor of 16 foreign language teachers on the secondary level at
Farmingdale High School, Farmingdale, New York, where he was also a teacher of all
levels of French and Spanish, and prepared students for the New York State French and
Spanish Regents, SAT exams, and AP tests. Dr. Kendris is the author of 22 school and
college books, workbooks, and other language guides of French and Spanish. He is
listed in *Contemporary Authors* and the *Directory of American Scholars*.

Dr. Theodore Kendris earned his B.A. degree in Modern Languages at Union College,
Schenectady, New York, where he received the Thomas J. Judson Memorial Award for
modern language study. He went on to earn his M.A. degree in French Language and
Literature at Northwestern University, Evanston, Illinois, where he held a Teaching
Assistantship. He earned his Ph.D. degree in French Literature at Université Laval in
Quebec City, where he studied the Middle Ages and Renaissance. While at Université
Laval he taught French writing skills as a *chargé de cours* in the French as a Second
Language program and, in 1997, he was awarded a doctoral scholarship by the *Fondation
de l'Université Laval*. He has also taught in the Department of English and Foreign Lan-
guages at the University of St. Francis in Joliet, Illinois.

iv

Preface to the Fifth Edition

This anniversary edition has been updated to take into account the many technological advances that have taken place over the past several years. Increased globalization and social changes have also made it necessary to ensure that *501 French Verbs* will continue to provide the guidance that students and travelers like you have come to expect. We have therefore added to the related words and expressions (listed, along with English meanings, at the bottom of each entry). We hope that you will take advantage of the section on verb drills and tests with answers explained, beginning on page 622. You will need a lot of practice in French verb forms and tenses in a variety of tests to determine your strengths and weaknesses and to make some things clearer in your mind. You should also review the section on definitions of basic grammatical terms, with examples. Many students who study a foreign language do not understand certain grammatical terms. If you know what they are, what they are called, and how they are used in the grammatical structure of a sentence, you will be able to communicate better in French.

In your spare time, especially if you are planning a trip abroad, consult the two sections on travel vocabulary in the back pages. One section, which begins on page 568, contains thirty practical situations you may find yourself in while visiting a French-speaking country or region of the world. The other section, which begins on page 599, gives you many popular phrases, words, expressions, abbreviations, signs, and notices in French and English in one alphabetical listing. This allows you to look in one place instead of two for an entry. Also, cognates and near-cognates in both languages are given in a single entry.

On page 566 there is a simple system of transcription of sounds to help you pronounce French words effectively. Pay attention to page 568, which explains the reasons for the use of hyphens in the sound transcriptions. And, if you can't remember the French verb you need to use, don't forget to refer to the index of English–French verbs, which starts on page 503.

We hope that you will make full use of all the features of this new edition and that you will enjoy your exploration of French language and culture.

C.K. and T.K.

Introduction

This self-teaching book of 501 commonly used French verbs for students and travelers provides fingertip access to correct verb forms.

Verb conjugations are usually found scattered in French grammar books and they are difficult to find quickly when needed. Verbs have always been a major problem for students no matter what system or approach the teacher uses. You will master French verb forms if you study this book a few minutes every day, especially the pages before and after the alphabetical listing of the 501 verbs.

This book has been compiled in order to help make your work easier and at the same time to teach you French verb forms systematically. It is a useful book because it provides a quick and easy way to find the full conjugation of many French verbs.

The 501 verbs included here are arranged alphabetically by infinitive at the top of each page. The book contains many common verbs of high frequency, both reflexive and non-reflexive, which you need to know. It also contains many other frequently used verbs which are irregular in some way. Beginning on page 515 you can find an additional 1,100 French verbs that are conjugated in the same way as model verbs among the 501. If the verb you have in mind is not given among the 501, consult this list.

The subject pronouns have been omitted from the conjugations in order to emphasize the verb forms. You can find the subject pronouns on page xxxii. Turn to that page now and become acquainted with them.

The first thing to do when you use this book is to become familiar with it from cover to cover—in particular, the front and back pages where you will find valuable and useful information to make your work easier and more enjoyable. Take a minute right now and familiarize yourself with the following features:

(a)   On page viii there is an explanation of which verbs are conjugated with *avoir* or *être* to form a compound tense. Study page viii and refer to it frequently until you master those verbs.

(b)   On page ix you will find how to form a present participle regularly in French and we give you examples. We also give you the common irregular present participles.

(c)   On page ix we do the same for past participles, with examples. The present and past participles of each verb are at the top of the page where verb forms are given for a particular verb.

(d)   On page xii you will find the principal parts of some important verbs, which, in French, are called *Les temps primitifs*. This is useful because if you know these you can easily form all the tenses and moods from them.

(e)   On pages x and xi there are two tables showing the derivation of tenses of a typical verb conjugated with *avoir* and another conjugated with *être*. These are presented as in a picture so that you can see what tenses are derived from the principal parts.

(f)   On pages xiii and xiv a sample English verb conjugation gives you an idea of the way a verb is expressed in the English tenses. Many people do not know one tense from another because they have never learned the use of verb tenses in a systematic and organized way—not even in English! How can you know, for example, that you need the conditional form of a verb in French when you want to say "*I would go* to the movies if . . ." or the pluperfect tense in French if you want to say "*I had gone* . . ."? The sample English verb conjugation with the names of the tenses and their numerical ranking will help you to distinguish one tense from another so that you will know what tense you need to express a verb in French.

(g) Beginning on page xv is a summary of meanings and uses of French verb tenses and moods as related to English verb tenses and moods. That section is very important and useful because the seven simple tenses are separated from the seven compound tenses. The name of each tense is given in French and English starting with the present indicative, which is called tense number one, because it is the tense most frequently used. A number is assigned to each tense name so that you can fix each one in your mind and associate the tense names and numbers in their logical order. There is a brief explanation of what each tense is, and when you use it, and there are examples using verbs in sentences in French and English.

(h) On page xxvi is a summary of all the fourteen tenses in French with English equivalents, which have been divided into the seven simple tenses and the seven compound tenses. After referring to that summary frequently, you will soon know that tense number 1 is the present indicative, tense number 2 is the imperfect indicative, and so on.

(i) On page xxvii you are shown how to form the seven simple tenses for regular verbs and here, again, the same number has been assigned to each tense name. We also explain how each compound tense is based on each simple tense in the table on page xxviii and on page xxix. Try to see these two divisions as two frames, two pictures, with the seven simple tenses in one frame and the seven compound tenses in another frame. Place them side by side in your mind, and you will see how tense number 8 is related to tense number 1, tense number 9 to tense number 2, and so on. If you study the numerical arrangement of each of the seven simple tenses and associate the tense number with the tense name, you will find it very easy to learn the names of the seven compound tenses, how they rank numerically according to use, how they are formed, and when they are used. Spend at least ten minutes every day studying these preliminary pages to help you understand better the fourteen tenses in French.

Finally, in the back pages of this book there are useful indexes, an additional 1,100 French verbs that are conjugated like model verbs among the 501, many examples of verbs used in idiomatic expressions and simple sentences, as well as verbs that require certain prepositions. If you refer to these each time you look up verb tense forms for a particular verb, you will increase your knowledge of French vocabulary and French idioms by leaps and bounds.

Consult the table of contents to find the page numbers of new features in the appendixes of this book; for example, explanations and examples of orthographically changing verbs (verb forms that change in spelling), French verbs used in weather expressions and in proverbs, as well as a summary of the sequence of verb tenses and a note about the subjunctive.

We sincerely hope that this book will be of some help to you in learning and using French verbs.

Christopher Kendris and Theodore Kendris

Verbs Conjugated with *avoir* or *être* to Form a Compound Tense

(a) Generally speaking, a French verb is conjugated with *avoir* to form a compound tense.

(b) All reflexive verbs, for example, *se laver*, are conjugated with *être*.

(c) The following is a list of common non-reflexive verbs that are conjugated with *être*. The five verbs marked with asterisks (*) are conjugated with *avoir* when used with a direct object.

1. **aller** to go
   Elle est allée au cinéma.
2. **arriver** to arrive
   Elle est arrivée à une heure.
3. ***descendre** to go down, come down
   Elle est descendue vite. *She came down quickly.*
   BUT: ***Elle a descendu la valise.** *She brought down the suitcase.*
4. **devenir** to become
   Elle est devenue docteur.
5. **entrer** to enter, go in, come in
   Elle est entrée dans l'école.
6. ***monter** to go up, come up
   Elle est montée vite. *She went up quickly.*
   BUT: ***Elle a monté l'escalier.** *She went up the stairs.*
7. **mourir** to die
   Elle est morte hier.
8. **naître** to be born
   Elle est née hier.
9. **partir** to leave
   Elle est partie vite.
10. ***passer** to go by, to pass by
    Elle est passée chez moi. *She came by my house.*

BUT: ***Elle m'a passé le sel.** *She passed me the salt.*

AND: ***Elle a passé un examen.** *She took an exam.*

11. ***rentrer** to go in again, to return (home)
    Elle est rentrée tôt. *She returned home early.*
    BUT: ***Elle a rentré le chat dans la maison.** *She brought (took) the cat into the house.*
12. **rester** to remain, to stay
    Elle est restée chez elle.
13. **retourner** to return, to go back
    Elle est retournée à sa place.
14. **revenir** to come back
    Elle est revenue hier.
15. ***sortir** to go out
    Elle est sortie hier soir. *She went out last night.*
    BUT: ***Elle a sorti son mouchoir.** *She took out her handkerchief.*
16. **tomber** to fall
    Elle est tombée.
17. **venir** to come
    Elle est venue ce matin.

Formation of the Present and Past Participles in French

Formation of the present participle in French

The present participle is regularly formed in the following way. Take the "**nous**" form of the present indicative of the verb you have in mind, drop the ending **-ons** and add **-ant**. That ending is the equivalent to *-ing* in English. Examples:

chantons, chantant   **vendons, vendant**   **allons, allant**
finissons, finissant   **mangeons, mangeant**   **travaillons, travaillant**

Common irregular present participles

The three common irregular present participles are: **ayant** from **avoir**; **étant** from **être**; **sachant** from **savoir**.

Formation of the past participle in French

The past participle is regularly formed from the infinitive:

-er ending verbs, drop the **-er** and add **é:**   **donner, donné**
-ir ending verbs, drop the **-ir** and add **i:**   **finir, fini**
-re ending verbs, drop the **-re** and add **u:**   **vendre, vendu**

Common irregular past participles

INFINITIVE	PAST PARTICIPLE	INFINITIVE	PAST PARTICIPLE
apprendre	**appris**	naître	**né**
asseoir	**assis**	offrir	**offert**
avoir	**eu**	ouvrir	**ouvert**
boire	**bu**	paraître	**paru**
comprendre	**compris**	permettre	**permis**
conduire	**conduit**	plaire	**plu**
connaître	**connu**	pleuvoir	**plu**
construire	**construit**	pouvoir	**pu**
courir	**couru**	prendre	**pris**
couvrir	**couvert**	promettre	**promis**
craindre	**craint**	recevoir	**reçu**
croire	**cru**	revenir	**revenu**
devenir	**devenu**	rire	**ri**
devoir	**dû, due**	savoir	**su**
dire	**dit**	suivre	**suivi**
écrire	**écrit**	taire	**tu**
être	**été**	tenir	**tenu**
faire	**fait**	valoir	**valu**
falloir	**fallu**	venir	**venu**
lire	**lu**	vivre	**vécu**
mettre	**mis**	voir	**vu**
mourir	**mort**	vouloir	**voulu**

Tables Showing Derivation of Tenses of Verbs Conjugated with *avoir* and *être*

Derivation of Tenses of Verbs Conjugated with *avoir*

INFINITIF	PARTICIPE PRÉSENT	PARTICIPE PASSÉ	PRÉSENT DE L'INDICATIF	PASSÉ SIMPLE
donner	**donnant**	**donné**	**je donne**	**je donnai**

FUTUR	IMPARFAIT DE L'INDICATIF	PASSÉ COMPOSÉ	PRÉSENT DE L'INDICATIF	PASSÉ SIMPLE
donner**ai**		**ai** donné		donn**ai**
donner**as**	donn**ais**	**as** donné	donne	donn**as**
donner**a**	donn**ais**	**a** donné	donne**s**	donn**a**
donner**ons**	donn**ait**	**avons** donné	donne	donn**âmes**
donner**ez**	donn**ions**	**avez** donné	donn**ons**	donn**âtes**
donner**ont**	donn**iez**	**ont** donné	donn**ez**	donn**èrent**
	donn**aient**		donn**ent**	

CONDITIONNEL		PLUS-QUE-PARFAIT DE L'INDICATIF	IMPÉRATIF	IMPARFAIT DU SUBJONCTIF
donner**ais**		**avais** donné	donne	donn**asse**
donner**ais**		**avais** donné	donn**ons**	donn**asses**
donner**ait**		**avait** donné	donn**ez**	donn**ât**
donner**ions**		**avions** donné		donn**assions**
donner**iez**		**aviez** donné	PRÉSENT DU	donn**assiez**
donner**aient**		**avaient** donné	SUBJONCTIF	donn**assent**
			donne	
		PASSÉ ANTÉRIEUR	donne**s**	
		eus donné	donne	
		eus donné	donn**ions**	
		eut donné	donn**iez**	
		eûmes donné	donn**ent**	
		eûtes donné		
		eurent donné		

FUTUR ANTÉRIEUR	CONDITIONNEL PASSÉ	PASSÉ DU SUBJONCTIF	PLUS-QUE-PARFAIT DU SUBJONCTIF
aurai donné	**aurais** donné	**aie** donné	**eusse** donné
auras donné	**aurais** donné	**aies** donné	**eusses** donné
aura donné	**aurait** donné	**ait** donné	**eût** donné
aurons donné	**aurions** donné	**ayons** donné	**eussions** donné
aurez donné	**auriez** donné	**ayez** donné	**eussiez** donné
auront donné	**auraient** donné	**aient** donné	**eussent** donné

Derivation of Tenses of Verbs Conjugated with *être*

INFINITIF	PARTICIPE PRÉSENT	PARTICIPE PASSÉ	PRÉSENT DE L'INDICATIF	PASSÉ SIMPLE
arriver	**arrivant**	**arrivé**	**j'arrive**	**j'arrivai**

FUTUR	IMPARFAIT DE L'INDICATIF	PASSÉ COMPOSÉ	PRÉSENT DE L'INDICATIF	PASSÉ SIMPLE
arriver**ai**		**suis** arrivé(e)		arriv**ai**
arriver**as**	arriv**ais**	**es** arrivé(e)	arriv**e**	arriv**as**
arriver**a**	arriv**ais**	**est** arrivé(e)	arriv**es**	arriv**a**
arriver**ons**	arriv**ait**	**sommes** arrivé(e)s	arriv**e**	arriv**âmes**
arriver**ez**	arriv**ions**	**êtes** arrivé(e)(s)	arriv**ons**	arriv**âtes**
arriver**ont**	arriv**iez**	**sont** arrivé(e)s	arriv**ez**	arriv**èrent**
	arriv**aient**		arriv**ent**	

CONDITIONNEL		PLUS-QUE-PARFAIT DE L'INDICATIF	IMPÉRATIF	IMPARFAIT DU SUBJONCTIF
arriver**ais**		**étais** arrivé(e)	arriv**e**	arriv**asse**
arriver**ais**		**étais** arrivé(e)	arriv**ons**	arriv**asses**
arriver**ait**		**était** arrivé(e)	arriv**ez**	arriv**ât**
arriver**ions**		**étions** arrivé(e)s		arriv**assions**
arriver**iez**		**étiez** arrivé(e)(s)	PRÉSENT DU	arriv**assiez**
arriver**aient**		**étaient** arrivé(e)s	SUBJONCTIF	arriv**assent**
			arriv**e**	
		PASSÉ ANTÉRIEUR	arriv**es**	
		fus arrivé(e)	arriv**e**	
		fus arrivé(e)	arriv**ions**	
		fut arrivé(e)	arriv**iez**	
		fûmes arrivé(e)s	arriv**ent**	
		fûtes arrivé(e)(s)		
		furent arrivé(e)s		

FUTUR ANTÉRIEUR	CONDITIONNEL PASSÉ	PASSÉ DU SUBJONCTIF	PLUS-QUE-PARFAIT DU SUBJONCTIF
serai arrivé(e)	**serais** arrivé(e)	**sois** arrivé(e)	**fusse** arrivé(e)
seras arrivé(e)	**serais** arrivé(e)	**sois** arrivé(e)	**fusses** arrivé(e)
sera arrivé(e)	**serait** arrivé(e)	**soit** arrivé(e)	**fût** arrivé(e)
serons arrivé(e)s	**serions** arrivé(e)s	**soyons** arrivé(e)s	**fussions** arrivé(e)s
serez arrivé(e)(s)	**seriez** arrivé(e)(s)	**soyez** arrivé(e)(s)	**fussiez** arrivé(e)(s)
seront arrivé(e)s	**seraient** arrivé(e)s	**soient** arrivé(e)s	**fussent** arrivé(e)s

Principal Parts of Some Important Verbs
(*Les temps primitifs de quelques verbes importants*)

The principal parts of a verb are very important to know because from them you can easily form all the tenses. See the following pages where two tables are given, one showing the derivation of tenses of a verb conjugated with **avoir** and the other with **être**. Note that the headings at the top of each column are the same as the following headings.

INFINITIF	PARTICIPE PRÉSENT	PARTICIPE PASSÉ	PRÉSENT DE L'INDICATIF	PASSÉ SIMPLE
aller	allant	allé	je vais	j'allai
avoir	ayant	eu	j'ai	j'eus
battre	battant	battu	je bats	je battis
boire	buvant	bu	je bois	je bus
craindre	craignant	craint	je crains	je craignis
croire	croyant	cru	je crois	je crus
devoir	devant	dû, due	je dois	je dus
dire	disant	dit	je dis	je dis
écrire	écrivant	écrit	j'écris	j'écrivis
être	étant	été	je suis	je fus
faire	faisant	fait	je fais	je fis
lire	lisant	lu	je lis	je lus
mettre	mettant	mis	je mets	je mis
mourir	mourant	mort	je meurs	je mourus
naître	naissant	né	je nais	je naquis
ouvrir	ouvrant	ouvert	j'ouvre	j'ouvris
porter	portant	porté	je porte	je portai
pouvoir	pouvant	pu	je peux *or* je puis	je pus
prendre	prenant	pris	je prends	je pris
recevoir	recevant	reçu	je reçois	je reçus
savoir	sachant	su	je sais	je sus
venir	venant	venu	je viens	je vins
vivre	vivant	vécu	je vis	je vécus
voir	voyant	vu	je vois	je vis
voler	volant	volé	je vole	je volai

Tip

In the present indicative (*présent de l'indicatif*) and the simple past (*passé simple*) columns above, only the 1st person singular (**je**) forms are given just to get you started. If you cannot recall the remaining verb forms in the *présent de l'indicatif* and the *passé simple* of the verbs listed above in the first column under infinitive (*infinitif*), please practice them by looking them up in this book, where the infinitive form of the verb is listed alphabetically at the top of each page from page 1 to 501. When you find them, say them aloud at the same time you practice writing them in French. This is a very useful exercise to do.

Sample English Verb Conjugation

INFINITIVE   **to go—aller**
PRESENT PARTICIPLE   **going**   *PAST PARTICIPLE*   **gone**

Tense no.	The seven simple tenses
1 *Present Indicative*	I go, you go, he (she, it) goes; we go, you go, they go
	or: I do go, you do go, he (she, it) does go; we do go, you do go, they do go
	or: I am going, you are going, he (she, it) is going; we are going, you are going, they are going
2 *Imperfect Indicative*	I was going, you were going, he (she, it) was going; we were going, you were going, they were going
	or: I went, you went, he (she, it) went; we went, you went, they went
	or: I used to go, you used to go, he (she, it) used to go; we used to go, you used to go, they used to go
3 *Passé Simple*	I went, you went, he (she, it) went; we went, you went, they went
	or: I did go, you did go, he (she, it) did go; we did go, you did go, they did go
4 *Future*	I shall (will) go, you will go, he (she, it) will go; we shall (will) go, you will go, they will go
5 *Conditional*	I would go, you would go, he (she, it) would go; we would go, you would go, they would go
6 *Present Subjunctive*	that I may go, that you may go, that he (she, it) may go; that we may go, that you may go, that they may go
7 *Imperfect Subjunctive*	that I might go, that you might go, that he (she, it) might go; that we might go, that you might go, that they might go

Tense no.	The seven compound tenses
8 *Passé Composé*	I have gone, you have gone, he (she, it) has gone; we have gone, you have gone, they have gone
	or: I went, you went, he (she, it) went; we went, you went, they went
	or: I did go, you did go, he (she, it) did go; we did go, you did go, they did go
9 *Pluperfect or Past Perfect Indicative*	I had gone, you had gone, he (she, it) had gone; we had gone, you had gone, they had gone
10 *Past Anterior*	I had gone, you had gone, he (she, it) had gone; we had gone, you had gone, they had gone
11 *Future Perfect or Future Anterior*	I shall (will) have gone, you will have gone, he (she, it) will have gone; we shall (will) have gone, you will have gone, they will have gone
12 *Conditional Perfect*	I would have gone, you would have gone, he (she, it) would have gone; we would have gone, you would have gone, they would have gone
13 *Past Subjunctive*	that I may have gone, that you may have gone, that he (she, it) may have gone; that we may have gone, that you may have gone, that they may have gone
14 *Pluperfect or Past Perfect Subjunctive*	that I might have gone, that you might have gone, that he (she, it) might have gone; that we might have gone, that you might have gone, that they might have gone
Imperative (Command)	Go! (sing.) Let's go! Go! (pl.)

A Summary of Meanings and Uses of French Verb Tenses and Moods as Related to English Verb Tenses and Moods

A verb is where the action is! A verb is a word that expresses an action (like *go*, *eat*, *write*) or a state of being (like *think*, *believe*, *be*). Tense means time. French and English verb tenses are divided into three main groups of time: past, present, and future. A verb tense shows if an action or state of being took place, is taking place, or will take place.

French and English verbs are also used in three moods (or modes). Mood has to do with the *way* a person regards an action or a state. For example, a person may merely make a statement or ask a question—this is the Indicative Mood, which we use most of the time in French and English. A person may say that he *would do* something if something else were possible or that he *would have done* something if something else had been possible—this is the conditional tense. A person may use a verb *in such a way* to indicate a wish, a fear, a regret, a supposition, or something of this sort—this is the Subjunctive Mood. The Subjunctive Mood is used in French much more than in English. A person may command that something be done—this is the Imperative Mood. (There is also the Infinitive Mood, but we are not concerned with that here.)

There are six tenses in English: Present, Past, Future, Present Perfect, Past Perfect, and Future Perfect. The first three are simple tenses. The other three are compound tenses and are based on the simple tenses. In French, however, there are fourteen tenses, seven of which are simple and seven of which are compound.

In the pages that follow, the tenses and moods are given in French and the equivalent name or names in English are given in parenthesis. Each tense name has been numbered for easy reference and recognition. Although some of the names given in English are not considered to be tenses (there are only six), they are given for the purpose of identification as they are related to the French names. The comparison includes only the essential points you need to know about the meanings and uses of French verb tenses and moods as related to English usage.

The examples serve to illustrate their meanings and uses. See page xxvii for the formation of the seven simple tenses for regular verbs.

THE SEVEN SIMPLE TENSES

Tense No. 1   Le Présent de l'Indicatif
(Present Indicative)

This tense is used most of the time in French and English. It indicates:

(a) An action or a state of being at the present time.
   EXAMPLES:
   1. Je **vais** à l'école maintenant. I *am going* to school now.
   2. Je **pense**; donc, je **suis**. I *think*; therefore, I *am*.

(b) Habitual action.

EXAMPLE:

1. Je **vais** à la bibliothéque tous les jours.
2. I *go* to the library every day, or I *do go* to the library every day.

(c) A general truth, something which is permanently true.

EXAMPLES:

1. Deux et deux **font** quatre. Two and two *are* four.
2. Voir c'**est** croire. Seeing *is* believing.

(d) Vividness when talking or writing about past events. This is called the *historical present.*

EXAMPLE:

Marie-Antoinette **est** condamnée à mort. Elle **monte** dans la charrette et **est** en route pour la guillotine.

Marie-Antoinette *is* condemned to die. She *gets* into the cart and *is* on her way to the guillotine.

(e) A near future.

EXAMPLE:

Il **arrive** demain. He *arrives* tomorrow.

(f) An action or state of being that occurred in the past and *continues up to the present.* In English, this tense is the Present Perfect, which is formed with the present tense of *to have* (*have* or *has*) plus the past participle of the verb you are using.

EXAMPLES:

1. Je **suis** ici depuis dix minutes.
   I *have been* here for ten minutes. (I am still here at present)
2. Elle **est** malade depuis trois jours.
   She *has been* sick for three days. (She is still sick at present)
3. J'**attends** l'autobus depuis dix minutes.
   I *have been waiting* for the bus for ten minutes.

NOTE: In this last example the formation of the English verb tense is slightly different from the other two examples in English. The present participle (*waiting*) is used instead of the past participle (*waited*).

NOTE ALSO: For the formation of this tense for regular verbs see page xxvii.

Tense No. 2 L'Imparfait de l'Indicatif
(Imperfect Indicative)

This is a past tense. It is used to indicate:

(a) An action that was going on in the past at the same time as another action.

EXAMPLE:

Il **lisait** pendant que j'**écrivais**. He *was reading* while I *was writing*.

(b) An action that was going on in the past when another action occurred.

EXAMPLE:

Il **lisait** quand je suis entré. He *was reading* when I came in.

(c) An action that a person did habitually in the past.

EXAMPLE:

Nous **allions** à la plage tous les jours. We *used to go* to the beach every day.

OR:

We *would go* to the beach every day.

(d) A description of a mental or physical condition in the past.

EXAMPLES :

(mental condition)   Il **était** triste quand je l'ai vu.
He *was* sad when I saw him.

(physical condition)   Quand ma mère **était** jeune, elle **était** belle.
When my mother *was* young, she *was* beautiful.

(e) An action or state of being that occurred in the past and *lasted for a certain length of time* prior to another past action. In English, it is usually translated as a pluperfect tense and is formed with *had been* plus the present participle of the verb you are using. It is like the special use of the **Présent de l'Indicatif** described in the above section (Tense No. 1) in paragraph (f), except that the action or state of being no longer exists at present.

EXAMPLE:

J'**attendais** l'autobus depuis dix minutes quand il est arrivé.

I *had been waiting* for the bus for ten minutes when it arrived.

NOTE: For the formation of this tense for regular verbs see page xxvii.

Tense No. 3   Le Passé Simple
(Past Definite or Simple Past)

This past tense is not ordinarily used in conversational French or in informal writing. It is a literary tense. It is used in formal writing, such as history and literature. You should be able merely to recognize this tense when you see it in your French readings. It should be noted that French writers use the **Passé Simple** less and less these days. The **Passé Composé** (Tense No. 8) is taking its place in literature, except for **avoir** and **être**, which you must know in this tense.

EXAMPLES:

(a) Il **alla** en Afrique. He *went* to Africa.
(b) Il **voyagea** en Amérique. He *traveled* to America.
(c) Elle **fut** heureuse. She *was* happy.
(d) Elle **eut** un grand bonheur. She *had* great happiness.

NOTE: For the formation of this tense for regular verbs see page xxvii.

Tense No. 4   Le Futur
(Future)

In French and English this tense is used to express an action or a state of being which will take place at some time in the future.

EXAMPLES:

(a) J'**irai** en France l'été prochain.
I *shall go* to France next summer.
OR:
I *will go* to France next summer.

(b) J'y **penserai**.
I *shall think* about it.
OR:
I *will think* about it.

(c) Je **partirai** dès qu'il arrivera.
I *shall leave* as soon as he arrives

(d) Je te **dirai** tout quand tu seras ici.
I *shall tell* you all when you are here.

If the action of the verb you are using is not past or present and if future time is implied, the future tense is used when the clause begins with any of the following conjunctions: **aussitôt que** (as soon as), **dès que** (as soon as), **quand** (when), **lorsque** (when), and **tant que** (as long as).
NOTE: For the formation of this tense for regular verbs see page xxvii.

Tense No. 5   Le Conditionnel Présent
(Conditional)

The Conditional is used in French and English to express:

(a) An action that you would do if something else were possible.
EXAMPLE:
Je **ferais** le travail si j'avais le temps.
I *would do* the work if I had the time.

(b) A conditional desire. This is the Conditional of courtesy in French.
EXAMPLES:
J'**aimerais** du thé. I *would like* some tea.
Je **voudrais** du café. I *would like* some coffee.

(c) An obligation or duty.
EXAMPLE:
Je **devrais** étudier pour l'examen. I *should* study for the examination.
OR: I *ought* to study for the examination.

NOTE (1): The French verb **devoir** plus the infinitive is used to express the idea of *should* when you mean *ought to.*

NOTE (2): When the Conditional of the verb **pouvoir** is used in French, it is translated into English as *could* or *would be able.*
EXAMPLE:
Je **pourrais** venir après le dîner. I *could come* after dinner.
OR: I *would be able* to come after dinner.

NOTE: For the formation of this tense for regular verbs see page xxvii.

Tense No. 6   Le Présent du Subjonctif
(Present Subjunctive)

The Subjunctive Mood is used in French much more than in English. It is disappearing in English, except for the following major uses:

(a) The Subjunctive is used in French and English to express a command.
EXAMPLE:
Soyez à l'heure! *Be* on time!
NOTE: In English, the form in the Subjunctive applies mainly to the verb *to be*. Also, note that all verbs in French are not in the Subjunctive when expressing a command. See **L'Impératif** on pages xxv–xxvi.

(b) The Subjunctive is commonly used in English to express a condition contrary to fact.
EXAMPLE:
If I *were* you, I would not do it.
NOTE: In French the Subjunctive is not used in this instance. Instead, the **Imparfait de l'Indicatif** is used if what precedes is *si* (*if*). Same example in French: Si j'**étais** vous, je ne le ferais pas.

(c) The Present Subjunctive is used in French and English after a verb that expresses some kind of insistence, preference, or suggestion.
EXAMPLES:
1. Je préfère qu'il **fasse** le travail maintenant. I prefer that *he do* the work now.
2. J'exige qu'il **soit** puni. I demand that *he be* punished.

(d) The Subjunctive is used in French after a verb that expresses doubt, fear, joy, sorrow, or some other emotion. Notice in the following examples that the Subjunctive is not used in English but it is in French.
EXAMPLES:
1. Je doute qu'il **vienne**.
   I doubt that he *is coming*.   OR: I doubt that he *will come*.
2. Je suis heureux qu'il **vienne**.
   I'm happy that he *is coming*.
3. Je regrette qu'il **soit** malade.
   I'm sorry that he *is* sick.
4. J'ai peur qu'il ne **soit** malade.
   I'm afraid that he *is* sick.
NOTE: After a verb that expresses fear (used in the affirmative), you should add *ne* before the verb that is in the subjunctive. If the statement is negative, do not add *ne*.

(e) The Present Subjunctive is used in French after certain conjunctions. Notice, however, that the Subjunctive is not always used in English.
EXAMPLES:
1. Je resterai **jusqu'à ce qu'il vienne**.
   I shall stay until he *comes*.
2. **Quoiqu'elle soit** belle, il ne l'aime pas.
   Although she *is* beautiful, he does not love her.
3. Je l'explique **pour qu'elle comprenne**.
   I'm explaining it *so that she may understand*.
4. Je partirai **à moins qu'il ne vienne**.
   I shall leave unless he *comes*.
NOTE: After a verb that expresses the possibility of an obstacle (or of a precaution), you may add *ne* before the verb that is in the subjunctive.

(f) The Present Subjunctive is used in French after certain impersonal expressions that show a need, doubt, possibility or impossibility. Notice, however, that the Subjunctive is not always used in English in the following examples:

1. Il est urgent qu'il **vienne**.
   It is urgent that he *come*.
2. Il vaut mieux qu'il **vienne**.
   It is better that he *come*.
3. Il est possible qu'il **vienne**.
   It is possible that he *will come*.
4. Il est douteux qu'il **vienne**.
   It is doubtful that he *will come*.
5. Il est nécessaire qu'il **vienne**.
   It is necessary that he *come*. OR: He must come.
6. Il faut qu'il **vienne**.
   It is necessary that he *come*. OR: He must come.
7. Il est important que vous **fassiez** le travail.
   It is important that you *do* the work.
8. Il est indispensable qu'elle **fasse** le travail.
   It is required that she *do* the work.

NOTE: For the formation of this tense for regular verbs see page xxviii.
See also the note about the Subjunctive which begins on page 560.

Tense No. 7 L'Imparfait du Subjonctif
(Imperfect Subjunctive)

L'Imparfait du Subjonctif is used for the same reasons as the **Présent du Subjonctif**—that is, after certain verbs, conjunctions, and impersonal expressions which were used in examples above under the section, **le Présent du Subjonctif**. The main difference between these two is the time of the action. If present, use the **Présent du Subjonctif** (Tense No. 6). If the action is related to the past, the **Imparfait du Subjonctif** (this tense) is used, provided that the action was *not* completed. If the action was completed, the **Plus-que-parfait du Subjonctif** is used. See below under the section, **Plus-que-parfait du Subjonctif** (Tense No. 14).

Since the Subjunctive Mood is troublesome in French and English, you may be pleased to know that this tense is rarely used in English. It is used in French, however, but only in formal writing and in literature. For that reason, you should merely be familiar with it so you can recognize it when you see it in your French readings. In conversational French and in informal writing, **l'Imparfait du Subjonctif** is avoided. Use, instead, the **Présent du Subjonctif**.

Notice that the **Imparfait du Subjonctif** is used in French in both of the following examples, but is used in English only in the second example (b):

EXAMPLES:

(a) Je voulais qu'il **vînt**. I wanted him to come.
(action not completed; he did not come while I wanted him to come)
NOTE: The Subjunctive of **venir** is used because the verb that precedes is one that requires the Subjunctive *after* it—in this example it is **vouloir**. In conversational French and informal writing, the **Imparfait du Subjonctif** is avoided. Use, instead, the **Présent du Subjonctif**: Je voulais qu'il **vienne**.

(b) Je le lui expliquais **pour qu'elle le comprît**.

I was explaining it to her *so that she might understand it*.

(action not completed; the understanding was not completed at the time of the explaining)

NOTE: The Subjunctive of **comprendre** is used because the conjunction that precedes is one that requires the Subjunctive *after* it—in this example it is **pour que**. In conversational French and informal writing, the **Imparfait du Subjonctif** is avoided. Use, instead, the **Présent du Subjonctif**: Je le lui expliquais pour qu'elle le **comprenne**.

NOTE: For the formation of this tense for regular verbs see page xxviii.
See also the note about the Subjunctive which begins on page 560.

THE SEVEN COMPOUND TENSES

Tense No. 8   Le Passé Composé
(Past Indefinite or Compound Past)

The past tense is used in conversational French, correspondence, and other informal writing. The **Passé Composé** is used more and more in literature these days and is taking the place of the **Passé Simple** (Tense No. 3). It is a compound tense because it is formed with the **Présent de l'Indicatif** (Tense No. 1) of *avoir* or *être* (depending on which of these two auxiliaries is required to form a compound tense) plus the past participle. See page viii for the distinction made between verbs conjugated with *avoir* or *être*.

EXAMPLES:
1. Il **est allé** à l'école. He *went* to school.
2. Il **est allé** à l'école. He *did go* to school.
3. Il **est allé** à l'école. He *has gone* to school.
4. J'**ai mangé** dans ce restaurant beaucoup de fois.
   I *have eaten* in this restaurant many times.

NOTE: In examples 3 and 4 in English the verb is formed with the Present tense of *to have* (*have* or *has*) plus the past participle of the verb you are using. In English, this form is called the Present Perfect.

5. J'**ai parlé** au garçon. I *spoke* to the boy. OR: I *have spoken* to the boy.
   OR: I *did speak* to the boy.

Tense No. 9   Le Plus-que-parfait de l'Indicatif
(Pluperfect or Past Perfect Indicative)

In French and English this tense is used to express an action which happened in the past *before* another past action. Since it is used in relation to another past action, the other past action is expressed in either the **Passé Composé** (Tense No. 8) or the **Imparfait de l'Indicatif** (Tense No. 2) in French. This tense is used in formal writing and literature as well as in conversational French and informal writing. The correct use of this tense is strictly observed in French. In English, however, too often we neglect to use it correctly. It is a compound tense because it is formed with the **Imparfait de l'Indicatif** of *avoir* or *être* (depending on which of these two auxiliaries is required to form a compound tense) plus the past participle. See page viii for the distinction made between verbs conjugated with *avoir* or *être*. In English, this tense is formed with the Past Tense of *to have* (*had*) plus the past participle of the verb you are using.

EXAMPLES:

(a) Je me suis rappelé que j'**avais oublié** de le lui dire.
I remembered that I *had forgotten* to tell him.

NOTE: It would be incorrect in English to say: I remembered that I *forgot* to tell him. The point here is that *first* I forgot; then, I remembered. Both actions are in the past. The action that occurred in the past *before* the other past action is in the Pluperfect. And in this example it is *I had forgotten* (**j'avais oublié**).

(b) J'**avais étudié** la leçon que le professeur a expliquée.
I *had studied* the lesson which the teacher explained.
NOTE: *First* I studied the lesson; then, the teacher explained it. Both actions are in the past. The action that occurred in the past *before* the other past action is in the Pluperfect. And in this example it is *I had studied* (**j'avais étudié**). If you say **J'ai étudié la leçon que le professeur avait expliquée**, you are saying that you *studied* the lesson which the teacher *had explained*. In other words, the teacher explained the lesson first and then you studied it.

(c) J'étais fatigué ce matin parce que je n'**avais** pas **dormi**.
I was tired this morning because I *had* not *slept*.

Tense No. 10   Le Passé Antérieur
(Past Anterior)

This tense is similar to the **Plus-que-parfait de l'Indicatif** (Tense No. 9). The main difference is that in French it is a literary tense; that is, it is used in formal writing, such as history and literature. More and more French writers today use the **Plus-que-parfait de l'Indicatif** instead of this tense. Generally speaking, the **Passé Antérieur** is to the **Plus-que-parfait** what the **Passé Simple** is to the **Passé Composé**. The **Passé Antérieur** is a compound tense. In French, it is formed with the **Passé Simple** of *avoir* or *être* (depending on which of these two auxiliaries is required to form a compound tense—see page viii) plus the past participle. In English, it is formed in the same way as the Pluperfect or Past Perfect. This tense is ordinarily introduced by conjunctions of time: **après que**, **aussitôt que**, **dès que**, **lorsque**, **quand**.

EXAMPLE:
Quand il **eut mangé** son dessert, il partit. When he *had eaten* his dessert, he left.

NOTE: In conversational French and informal writing, the **Plus-que-parfait de l'Indicatif** is used instead: Quand il **avait mangé** son dessert, il est parti. The translation into English is the same.

Tense No. 11   Le Futur Antérieur
(Future Perfect or Future Anterior)

In French and English this tense is used to express an action which will happen in the future *before* another future action. Since it is used in relation to another future action, the other future action is expressed in the simple Future in French, but not always in the simple Future in English. In French, it is used in conversation and informal writing as well as in formal writing and in literature. It is a compound tense because it is formed with the **Futur** of *avoir* or *être* (depending on which of these two auxiliaries is required to form a compound tense—see page viii) plus the past participle of the verb you are using. In English, it is formed by using *shall have* or *will have* plus the past participle of the verb you are using.

EXAMPLES:
(a) Elle arrivera demain et j'**aurai fini** le travail.
She will arrive tomorrow and I *shall have finished* the work.

NOTE: First, I shall finish the work; then, she will arrive. The action that will occur in the future *before* the other future action is in the **Futur Antérieur**.

(b) Quand elle arrivera demain, j'**aurai fini** le travail.
When she arrives tomorrow, I *shall have finished* the work.

NOTE: The idea of future time here is the same as in example (a) above. In English, the Present tense is used (*When she arrives . . .*) to express a near future. In French, the **Futur** is used (**Quand elle arrivera . . .**) because **quand** precedes and the action will take place in the future. Study Tense No. 4 on page xviii.

Tense No. 12   Le Conditionnel Passé
(Conditional Perfect)

This is used in French and English to express an action that you *would have done* if something else had been possible; that is, you would have done something *on condition* that something else had been possible. It is a compound tense because it is formed with the **Conditionnel Présent** of *avoir* or *être* plus the past participle of the verb you are using. In English, it is formed by using *would have* plus the past participle. Observe the difference between the following examples and the one given for the use of the **Conditionnel Présent** which was explained and illustrated in Tense No. 5 above.

EXAMPLES:
(a) J'**aurais fait** le travail si j'avais étudié.
I *would have done* the work if I had studied.

(b) J'**aurais fait** le travail si j'avais eu le temps.
I *would have done* the work if I had had the time.

NOTE: Review the **Plus-que-parfait de l'Indicatif** which was explained above in Tense No. 9 in order to understand the use of *if I had studied* (**si j'avais étudié**) and *if I had had the time* (**si j'avais eu le temps**).

NOTE FURTHER: The French verb **devoir** plus the infinitive is used to express the idea of *should* when you mean *ought to*. The past participle of **devoir** is **dû**. It is conjugated with **avoir**.

EXAMPLE:
J'**aurais dû** étudier.
I *should have* studied. OR: I *ought to have* studied.

Tense No. 13   Le Passé du Subjonctif
(Past or Perfect Subjunctive)

This tense is used to express an action which took place in the past in relation to the present time. It is like the **Passé Composé**, except that the auxiliary verb (*avoir* or *être*) is in the **Présent du Subjonctif**. The Subjunctive is used (as was noted in the previous sections of verb tenses in the Subjunctive) because what precedes is a certain verb, a certain conjunction, or a certain impersonal expression. The **Passé du Subjonctif** is also used in relation to a future time when another action will be completed. This tense is rarely used in English. In French, however, this tense is used in formal writing and in literature as well as in conversational French and informal writing. It is a compound tense because it is formed with the **Présent du Subjonctif** of *avoir* or *être* as the auxiliary plus the past participle of the verb you are using.

EXAMPLES:
(a) A past action in relation to the present
Il est possible qu'elle **soit partie**.
It is possible that she *may have left*. OR: It is possible that she *has left*.
Je doute qu'il **ait fait** cela.
I doubt that he *did* that.

(b) An action that will take place in the future

J'insiste que vous **soyez rentré** avant dix heures.
I insist that you *be back* before ten o'clock.

See also the note about the Subjunctive which begins on page 560.

Tense No. 14   Le Plus-que-parfait du Subjonctif
(Pluperfect or Past Perfect Subjunctive)

This tense is used for the same reasons as the **Imparfait du Subjonctif** (Tense No. 7)—that is, after certain verbs, conjunctions, and impersonal expressions which were used in examples previously under le **Présent du Subjonctif**. The main difference between the **Imparfait du Subjonctif** and this tense is the time of the action in the past. If the action was *not* completed, the **Imparfait du Subjonctif** is used. If the action was completed, this tense is used. It is rarely used in English. In French, it is used only in formal writing and in literature. For that reason, you should merely be familiar with it so you can recognize it in your readings in French literature. In conversational French and in informal writing, this tense is avoided. Use, instead, the **Passé du Subjonctif** (Tense No. 13).

This is a compound tense. It is formed by using the **Imparfait du Subjonctif** of *avoir* or *être* plus the past participle. This tense is like the **Plus-que-parfait de l'Indicatif**, except that the auxiliary verb (*avoir* or *être*) is in the **Imparfait du Subjonctif**. Review the uses of the Subjunctive mood in Tense No. 6.

EXAMPLES:

(a) Il était possible qu'elle **fût partie**.
It was possible that she *might have left*.

NOTE: Avoid this tense in conversational and informal French. Use, instead, **le Passé du Subjonctif**:
Il était possible qu'elle **soit partie**.

(b) Je ne croyais pas qu'elle **eût dit** cela.
I did not believe that she *had said* that.

NOTE: Avoid this tense in conversational and informal French. Use, instead, **le Passé du Subjonctif**:
Je ne croyais pas qu'elle **ait dit** cela.

(c) Je n'ai pas cru qu'elle **eût dit** cela.
I did not believe that she *had said* that.

NOTE: Avoid this tense in conversational and informal French. Use, instead, **le Passé du Subjonctif**:
Je n'ai pas cru qu'elle **ait dit** cela.

(d) J'ai craint que vous ne **fussiez tombé**.
I was afraid that you *had fallen*.

NOTE: Avoid this tense in conversational and informal French. Use, instead, **le Passé du Subjonctif**:
J'ai craint que vous ne **soyez tombé**.

NOTE: After a verb that expresses fear (used in the affirmative), you should add *ne* before the verb that is in the subjunctive. If the statement is negative, do not add *ne*.

See also the note about the Subjunctive which begins on page 560.

L'Impératif
(Imperative or Command)

The Imperative Mood is used in French and English to express a command or a request. It is also used to express an indirect request made in the third person, as in (e) and (f) below. In both languages it is formed by dropping the subject pronoun and using the present tense. There are a few exceptions in both languages when the **Présent du Subjonctif** is used.

EXAMPLES:

(a) **Sortez!** Get out!

(b) **Entrez!** Come in!

(c) **Buvons!** Let's drink!

(d) **Soyez** à l'heure! *Be* on time! (Subjunctive is used)

(e) Dieu le **veuille!** May God *grant* it! or *God willing!* (Subjunctive is used)

(f) Qu'ils **mangent du** gâteau! Let them *eat* cake! (Subjunctive is used)

(g) **Asseyez-vous!** Sit down!

(h) **Levez-vous!** Get up!

(i) **Ne vous asseyez pas!** Don't sit down!

(j) **Ne vous levez pas!** Don't get up!

NOTE: The Imperative is not a tense. It is a mood.

NOTE FURTHER: If you use a reflexive verb in the Imperative, drop the subject pronoun but keep the reflexive pronoun. Example: **Lavez-vous!** Wash yourself! See also examples (g) through (j).

Summary of verb tenses and moods in French with English equivalents

Les sept temps simples *The seven simple tenses*		**Les sept temps composés** *The seven compound tenses*	
Tense No.	Tense Name	Tense No.	Tense Name
1	**Présent de l'indicatif** *Present indicative*	8	**Passé composé**
2	**Imparfait de l'indicatif** *Imperfect indicative*	9	**Plus-que-parfait de l'indicatif** *Pluperfect indicative*
3	**Passé simple** *Past definite or Simple past*	10	**Passé antérieur** *Past anterior*
4	**Futur** *Future*	11	**Futur antérieur** *Future perfect*
5	**Conditionnel** *Conditional*	12	**Conditionnel passé** *Conditional perfect*
6	**Présent du subjonctif** *Present subjunctive*	13	**Passé du subjonctif** *Past subjunctive*
7	**Imparfait du subjonctif** *Imperfect subjunctive*	14	**Plus-que-parfait du subjonctif** *Pluperfect subjunctive*

The imperative is not a tense; it is a mood.

Formation of the Tenses

In French there are seven simple tenses and seven compound tenses. A simple tense means that the verb form consists of one word. A compound tense is a verb form that consists of two words (the auxiliary verb and the past participle). The auxiliary verb is also called a helping verb and in French it is any of the seven simple tenses of **avoir** or **être**.

FORMATION OF THE SEVEN SIMPLE TENSES FOR REGULAR VERBS

Tense No. 1   Présent de l'Indicatif
(Present Indicative)

-er verbs: drop **-er** and add **e, es, e; ons, ez, ent**

-ir verbs: drop **-ir** and add **is, is, it; issons, issez, issent**

-re verbs: drop **-re** and add **s, s, -; ons, ez, ent**

Tense No. 2   Imparfait de l'Indicatif
(Imperfect Indicative)

For **-er, -ir, -re** verbs, take the "**nous**" form in the present indicative of the verb you have in mind, drop the ending **-ons** and add: **ais, ais, ait; ions, iez, aient**

Tense No. 3   Passé Simple
(Past Definite or Simple Past)

For all **-er** verbs, drop **-er** and add **ai, as, a; âmes, âtes, èrent**
For **-ir** and **-re** verbs, drop the ending of the infinitive and add **is, is, it; îmes, îtes, irent**

Tense No. 4   Futur
(Future)

Add the following endings to the whole infinitive, but for **-re** verbs drop **e** in **-re** before adding the future endings, which are: **ai, as, a; ons, ez, ont**. Note that these endings are based on the present indicative of **avoir**.

Tense No. 5   Conditionnel
(Conditional)

Add the following endings to the whole infinitive, but for **-re** verbs drop **e** in **-re** before adding the conditional endings, which are: **ais, ais, ait; ions, iez, aient**. Note that these endings are the same as those for the imperfect indicative (Tense No. 2).

Tense No. 6   Présent du Subjonctif
(Present Subjunctive)

Drop **-ant** ending of the present participle of the verb you have in mind and add **e, es, e**; **ions, iez, ent**

Tense No. 7   Imparfait du Subjonctif
(Imperfect Subjunctive)

There is a shortcut to finding the forms of this difficult tense. Go straight to the 3d person, singular, **passé simple** tense of the verb you have in mind. If the ending is **-a**, as in **parla (parler)**, drop **-a** and add **-asse, -asses, -ât; assions, -assiez, -assent**. If the ending is **-it**, as in **finit (finir)** or **vendit (vendre)**, drop **-it** and add **-isse, -isses, -ît; -issions, -issiez, -issent**. If you find the ending **-ut**, as in many irregular **-re** verbs **(lire/lut)**, drop **-ut** and add **-usse, -usses, -ût; -ussions, -ussiez, -ussent**. Note the accent mark (ˆ) on **-ât, -ît**, and **-ût**.

NOTE:
(a) For the forms of irregular verbs, *e.g.*, **avoir, être, faire, aller,** and many others, turn to the page where the verb you have in mind is given in this book. All verbs are listed alphabetically at the top of each page.
(b) For the uses of the seven simple tenses, see pages xv–xxi.
(c) For the formation of the seven compound tenses and their uses, see pages xxi–xxv and the section below.

FORMATION OF THE SEVEN COMPOUND TENSES

An Easy Way to Form the Seven Compound Tenses in French

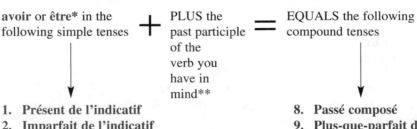

avoir or être* in the following simple tenses **+** PLUS the past participle of the verb you have in mind** **=** EQUALS the following compound tenses

1. Présent de l'indicatif	8. Passé composé
2. Imparfait de l'indicatif	9. Plus-que-parfait de l'indicatif
3. Passé simple	10. Passé antérieur
4. Futur	11. Futur antérieur
5. Conditionnel	12. Conditionnel passé
6. Présent du subjonctif	13. Passé du subjonctif
7. Imparfait du subjonctif	14. Plus-que-parfait du subjonctif

* To know if avoir or être is required, see page viii.
** To know how to form a past participle, see page ix.

Each compound tense is based on each simple tense. The fourteen tenses given on page xxviii are arranged in a logical order, which is numerical.

Here is how you form each of the seven compound tenses:

Tense number 8 is based on Tense number 1 of **avoir** or **être**; in other words, you form the **passé composé** by using the auxiliary **avoir** or **être** (whichever is appropriate) in the **présent de l'indicatif** plus the past participle of the verb you have in mind. Examples: **j'ai parlé**; **je suis allé(e)**.

Tense number 9 is based on Tense number 2 of **avoir** or **être**; in other words, you form the **plus-que-parfait de l'indicatif** by using the auxiliary **avoir** or **être** (whichever is appropriate) in the **imparfait de l'indicatif** plus the past participle of the verb you have in mind. Examples: **j'avais parlé**; **j'étais allé(e)**.

Tense number 10 is based on Tense number 3 of **avoir** or **être**; in other words, you form the **passé antérieur** by using the auxiliary **avoir** or **être** (whichever is appropriate) in the **passé simple** plus the past participle of the verb you have in mind. Examples: **j'eus parlé**; **je fus allé(e)**.

Tense number 11 is based on Tense number 4 of **avoir** or **être**; in other words, you form the **futur antérieur** by using the auxiliary **avoir** or **être** (whichever is appropriate) in the **futur** plus the past participle of the verb you have in mind. Examples; **j'aurai parlé**; **je serai allé(e)**.

Tense number 12 is based on Tense number 5 of **avoir** or **être**; in other words, you form the **conditionnel passé** by using the auxiliary **avoir** or **être** (whichever is appropriate) in the **conditionnel** plus the past participle of the verb you have in mind. Examples: **j'aurais parlé**; **je serais allé(e)**.

Tense number 13 is based on Tense number 6 of **avoir** or **être**; in other words, you form the **passé du subjonctif** by using the auxiliary **avoir** or **être** (whichever is appropriate) in the **présent du subjonctif** plus the past participle of the verb you have in mind. Examples: **que j'aie parlé**; **que je sois allé(e)**. This tense is like the **passé composé** (tense number 8), except that the auxiliary verb **avoir** or **être** is in the present subjunctive.

Tense number 14 is based on Tense number 7 of **avoir** or **être**; in other words, you form the **plus-que-parfait du subjonctif** by using the auxiliary **avoir** or **être** (whichever is appropriate) in the **imparfait du subjonctif** plus the past participle of the verb you have in mind. Examples: **que j'eusse parlé**; **que je fusse allé(e)**.

If you ever expect to know or even recognize the meaning of any of the seven compound tenses, or to know how to form them, you certainly have to know **avoir** and **être** in the seven simple tenses. If you do not, you cannot form the seven compound tenses—and they are the easiest to form. This is one perfect example to illustrate that learning French verb forms is a cumulative experience because in order to know the seven compound tenses, you must first know the forms of **avoir** and **être** in the seven simple tenses. They are found on pages 61 and 206 in this book.

To know which verbs are conjugated with **avoir** or **être** to form the seven compound tenses, see page viii. To understand the uses of the seven simple tenses, see pages xv–xxi. To understand the uses of the seven compound tenses, see pages xxi–xxv. To know the translation of all fourteen tenses into English, see pages xiii–xiv.

A Note about the *passé surcomposé* verb tense

There is another verb tense in French but it is rarely used. It is called *le passé surcomposé*. It gets its name from the fact that the auxiliary (helping) verb is already stated in a *passé composé* form. In other words, it is "extra" passé composé, just as **surchauffé** means "overheated" or **surnatural** means "supernatural." The *surcomposé* contains two auxiliary verbs and it is used in the subordinate clause when the verb of the main clause is in a compound tense. Examples: **j'ai eu** (*I have had*, or, *I had*); **j'ai été** (*I have been*, or *I was*). To change the compound form into a *surcomposé*, the past participle of the verb you have in mind is stated with the double helping verb. Examples: **Mon ami est arrivé quand j'ai eu fini la leçon** / *My friend arrived when I ("have had") finished the lesson.* The verb form in the subordinate clause with a double helping verb (**j'ai eu fini**) is what makes the form *surcomposé*. In English, some people call it *double* or *super compound*. It has also been used in other compound tenses with **avoir** or **être** as the helping verb. Nowadays, one hardly ever hears this unusual verb form, but it's worth being aware of in case you come across it in your readings in French literature.

Alphabetical Listing of 501 French Verbs Fully Conjugated in All the Tenses and Moods

Subject Pronouns

(a) The subject pronouns for all verb forms on the following pages have been omitted in order to emphasize the verb forms, which is what this book is all about.

(b) The subject pronouns that have been omitted are, as you know, as follows:

singular	*plural*
je *or* **j'**	**nous**
tu	**vous**
il, **elle**, **on**	**ils**, **elles**

(c) You realize, of course, that when you use a verb form in the Imperative (Command) you do not use the subject pronoun with it, as is also done in English. Example: **Parlez!** *Speak!* If you use a reflexive verb in the Imperative, drop the subject pronoun but keep the reflexive pronoun. Example: **Lavez-vous!** *Wash yourself!*

Abbreviations

adj.   adjectif (adjective)
adv.   adverbe (adverb)
ant.   antérieur (anterior)
art.   article
comp. computer
cond. conditionnel (conditional)
def.   défini (definite)
dir.   direct
e.g.   for example
f. or *fem.*   féminin (feminine)
fam.   familiar
fut.   futur (future)
i.e.   that is, that is to say
imp.   imparfait (imperfect)
ind.   indicatif (indicative)
inf.   infinitif (infinitive)
m. or *masc.*   masculin (masculine)

n.   nom (noun)
obj.   objet (object)
p.   page
pp.   pages
part.   participe (participle)
pl.   pluriel (plural)
plpf.   plus-que-parfait (pluperfect)
pr. or *prés.*   présent (present)
prep.   préposition (preposition)
pron.   pronom (pronoun)
qqch   quelque chose (something)
qqn   quelqu'un (someone, somebody)
refl.   reflexive
s. or *sing.*   singulier (singular)
subj.   subjonctif (subjunctive)
v.   verbe (verb)

to lower, to reduce, to humiliate, to humble

The Seven Simple Tenses		The Seven Compound Tenses	
Singular	Plural	Singular	Plural

1 présent de l'indicatif

		8 passé composé	
abaisse	abaissons	ai abaissé	avons abaissé
abaisses	abaissez	as abaissé	avez abaissé
abaisse	abaissent	a abaissé	ont abaissé

2 imparfait de l'indicatif

		9 plus-que-parfait de l'indicatif	
abaissais	abaissions	avais abaissé	avions abaissé
abaissais	abaissiez	avais abaissé	aviez abaissé
abaissait	abaissaient	avait abaissé	avaient abaissé

3 passé simple

		10 passé antérieur	
abaissai	abaissâmes	eus abaissé	eûmes abaissé
abaissas	abaissâtes	eus abaissé	eûtes abaissé
abaissa	abaissèrent	eut abaissé	eurent abaissé

4 futur

		11 futur antérieur	
abaisserai	abaisserons	aurai abaissé	aurons abaissé
abaisseras	abaisserez	auras abaissé	aurez abaissé
abaissera	abaisseront	aura abaissé	auront abaissé

5 conditionnel

		12 conditionnel passé	
abaisserais	abaisserions	aurais abaissé	aurions abaissé
abaisserais	abaisseriez	aurais abaissé	auriez abaissé
abaisserait	abaisseraient	aurait abaissé	auraient abaissé

6 présent du subjonctif

		13 passé du subjonctif	
abaisse	abaissions	aie abaissé	ayons abaissé
abaisses	abaissiez	aies abaissé	ayez abaissé
abaisse	abaissent	ait abaissé	aient abaissé

7 imparfait du subjonctif

		14 plus-que-parfait du subjonctif	
abaissasse	abaissassions	eusse abaissé	eussions abaissé
abaissasses	abaissassiez	eusses abaissé	eussiez abaissé
abaissât	abaissassent	eût abaissé	eussent abaissé

Impératif
abaisse
abaissons
abaissez

Words and expressions related to this verb

abaisser le store   to pull down the (venetian) blind, shade

abaisser les yeux   to cast one's eyes down, to look down

un abaissement   abasement, lowering

abaisser qqn   to humiliate someone

See also **s'abaisser** and **baisser.**

abaisser la valeur de qqch   to bring down the value of something

un abaisse-langue   tongue depressor

un rabais   reduction

vendre au rabais   to sell at a discount

> Consult the sections on verbs used in idiomatic expressions, verbs with prepositions, and the list of over 1,100 verbs conjugated like model verbs in the back pages.

s'abaisser

Part. pr. **s'abaissant**   Part. passé **abaissé**

to humble oneself, to lower oneself, to condescend, to slope

The Seven Simple Tenses		The Seven Compound Tenses	
Singular	Plural	Singular	Plural
1 présent de l'indicatif		**8 passé composé**	
m'abaisse	**nous abaissons**	**me suis abaissé(e)**	**nous sommes abaissé(e)s**
t'abaisses	**vous abaissez**	**t'es abaissé(e)**	**vous êtes abaissé(e)(s)**
s'abaisse	**s'abaissent**	**s'est abaissé(e)**	**se sont abaissé(e)s**
2 imparfait de l'indicatif		**9 plus-que-parfait de l'indicatif**	
m'abaissais	**nous abaissions**	**m'étais abaissé(e)**	**nous étions abaissé(e)s**
t'abaissais	**vous abaissiez**	**t'étais abaissé(e)**	**vous étiez abaissé(e)(s)**
s'abaissait	**s'abaissaient**	**s'était abaissé(e)**	**s'étaient abaissé(e)s**
3 passé simple		**10 passé antérieur**	
m'abaissai	**nous abaissâmes**	**me fus abaissé(e)**	**nous fûmes abaissé(e)s**
t'abaissas	**vous abaissâtes**	**te fus abaissé(e)**	**vous fûtes abaissé(e)(s)**
s'abaissa	**s'abaissèrent**	**se fut abaissé(e)**	**se furent abaissé(e)s**
4 futur		**11 futur antérieur**	
m'abaisserai	**nous abaisserons**	**me serai abaissé(e)**	**nous serons abaissé(e)s**
t'abaisseras	**vous abaisserez**	**te seras abaissé(e)**	**vous serez abaissé(e)(s)**
s'abaissera	**s'abaisseront**	**se sera abaissé(e)**	**se seront abaissé(e)s**
5 conditionnel		**12 conditionnel passé**	
m'abaisserais	**nous abaisserions**	**me serais abaissé(e)**	**nous serions abaissé(e)s**
t'abaisserais	**vous abaisseriez**	**te serais abaissé(e)**	**vous seriez abaissé(e)(s)**
s'abaisserait	**s'abaisseraient**	**se serait abaissé(e)**	**se seraient abaissé(e)s**
6 présent du subjonctif		**13 passé du subjonctif**	
m'abaisse	**nous abaissions**	**me sois abaissé(e)**	**nous soyons abaissé(e)s**
t'abaisses	**vous abaissiez**	**te sois abaissé(e)**	**vous soyez abaissé(e)(s)**
s'abaisse	**s'abaissent**	**se soit abaissé(e)**	**se soient abaissé(e)s**
7 imparfait du subjonctif		**14 plus-que-parfait du subjonctif**	
m'abaissasse	**nous abaissassions**	**me fusse abaissé(e)**	**nous fussions abaissé(e)s**
t'abaissasses	**vous abaissassiez**	**te fusses abaissé(e)**	**vous fussiez abaissé(e)(s)**
s'abaissât	**s'abaissassent**	**se fût abaissé(e)**	**se fussent abaissé(e)s**

Impératif
abaisse-toi; ne t'abaisse pas
abaissons-nous; ne nous abaissons pas
abaissez-vous; ne vous abaissez pas

Words and expressions related to this verb
s'abaisser   to decline, to go down
s'abaisser à   to stoop to
s'abaisser devant qqn   to humble oneself before someone
Le taux de chômage s'est abaissé.   The unemployment rate declined.

See also **abaisser** and **baisser**.

Consult the sections on verbs used in idiomatic expressions, verbs with prepositions, and the list of over 1,100 verbs conjugated like model verbs in the back pages.

to daze, to deafen, to stun, to bewilder, to stupefy

The Seven Simple Tenses		The Seven Compound Tenses	
Singular	Plural	Singular	Plural
1 présent de l'indicatif		8 passé composé	
abasourdis	**abasourdissons**	**ai abasourdi**	**avons abasourdi**
abasourdis	**abasourdissez**	**as abasourdi**	**avez abasourdi**
abasourdit	**abasourdissent**	**a abasourdi**	**ont abasourdi**
2 imparfait de l'indicatif		9 plus-que-parfait de l'indicatif	
abasourdissais	**abasourdissions**	**avais abasourdi**	**avions abasourdi**
abasourdissais	**abasourdissiez**	**avais abasourdi**	**aviez abasourdi**
abasourdissait	**abasourdissaient**	**avait abasourdi**	**avaient abasourdi**
3 passé simple		10 passé antérieur	
abasourdis	**abasourdîmes**	**eus abasourdi**	**eûmes abasourdi**
abasourdis	**abasourdîtes**	**eus abasourdi**	**eûtes abasourdi**
abasourdit	**abasourdirent**	**eut abasourdi**	**eurent abasourdi**
4 futur		11 futur antérieur	
abasourdirai	**abasourdirons**	**aurai abasourdi**	**aurons abasourdi**
abasourdiras	**abasourdirez**	**auras abasourdi**	**aurez abasourdi**
abasourdira	**abasourdiront**	**aura abasourdi**	**auront abasourdi**
5 conditionnel		12 conditionnel passé	
abasourdirais	**abasourdirions**	**aurais abasourdi**	**aurions abasourdi**
abasourdirais	**abasourdiriez**	**aurais abasourdi**	**auriez abasourdi**
abasourdirait	**abasourdiraient**	**aurait abasourdi**	**auraient abasourdi**
6 présent du subjonctif		13 passé du subjonctif	
abasourdisse	**abasourdissions**	**aie abasourdi**	**ayons abasourdi**
abasourdisses	**abasourdissiez**	**aies abasourdi**	**ayez abasourdi**
abasourdisse	**abasourdissent**	**ait abasourdi**	**aient abasourdi**
7 imparfait du subjonctif		14 plus-que-parfait du subjonctif	
abasourdisse	**abasourdissions**	**eusse abasourdi**	**eussions abasourdi**
abasourdisses	**abasourdissiez**	**eusses abasourdi**	**eussiez abasourdi**
abasourdît	**abasourdissent**	**eût abasourdi**	**eussent abasourdi**

Impératif
abasourdis
abasourdissons
abasourdissez

Words and expressions related to this verb
assourdir   to deafen, to deaden a sound, to muffle
s'assourdir   to soften the sound of a consonant, to unvoice a consonant
abasourdissant, abasourdissante   astounding, amazing
sourd, sourde   deaf

devenir sourd   to become deaf
faire la sourde oreille   to turn a deaf ear, not to listen
être sourd à   to be deaf to
la surdité   deafness
un abasourdissement   amazement, astonishment, bewilderment

The *s* in **abasourdir** is pronounced as if it were written *z*.

abattre

Part. pr. **abattant** Part. passé **abattu**

to dishearten, to strike down, to cut down, to knock down, to slaughter

The Seven Simple Tenses		The Seven Compound Tenses	
Singular	Plural	Singular	Plural
1 présent de l'indicatif		**8 passé composé**	
abats	abattons	ai abattu	avons abattu
abats	abattez	as abattu	avez abattu
abat	abattent	a abattu	ont abattu
2 imparfait de l'indicatif		**9 plus-que-parfait de l'indicatif**	
abattais	abattions	avais abattu	avions abattu
abattais	abattiez	avais abattu	aviez abattu
abattait	abattaient	avait abattu	avaient abattu
3 passé simple		**10 passé antérieur**	
abattis	abattîmes	eus abattu	eûmes abattu
abattis	abattîtes	eus abattu	eûtes abattu
abattit	abattirent	eut abattu	eurent abattu
4 futur		**11 futur antérieur**	
abattrai	abattrons	aurai abattu	aurons abattu
abattras	abattrez	auras abattu	aurez abattu
abattra	abattront	aura abattu	auront abattu
5 conditionnel		**12 conditionnel passé**	
abattrais	abattrions	aurais abattu	aurions abattu
abattrais	abattriez	aurais abattu	auriez abattu
abattrait	abattraient	aurait abattu	auraient abattu
6 présent du subjonctif		**13 passé du subjonctif**	
abatte	abattions	aie abattu	ayons abattu
abattes	abattiez	aies abattu	ayez abattu
abatte	abattent	ait abattu	aient abattu
7 imparfait du subjonctif		**14 plus-que-parfait du subjonctif**	
abattisse	abattissions	eusse abattu	eussions abattu
abattisses	abattissiez	eusses abattu	eussiez abattu
abattît	abattissent	eût abattu	eussent abattu

Impératif
abats
abattons
abattez

Words and expressions related to this verb
l'abattage *m.*   slaughtering of animals
un abattoir   slaughterhouse
rabattre   to pull down, to turn down, to knock down, to beat down
un rabat-joie   killjoy, "wet blanket"; (**des rabat-joie**)

un abatteur   slaughterer of animals
à bas!   down with! **à bas les devoirs!**   down with homework!
un abat-jour   lampshade
un abat-son   louver

See also **battre, se battre**, and **combattre**.

Consult the sections on verbs used in idiomatic expressions, verbs with prepositions, and the list of over 1,100 verbs conjugated like model verbs in the back pages.

The Seven Simple Tenses		The Seven Compound Tenses	
Singular	Plural	Singular	Plural
1 présent de l'indicatif		8 passé composé	
abolis	**abolissons**	**ai aboli**	**avons aboli**
abolis	**abolissez**	**as aboli**	**avez aboli**
abolit	**abolissent**	**a aboli**	**ont aboli**
2 imparfait de l'indicatif		9 plus-que-parfait de l'indicatif	
abolissais	**abolissions**	**avais aboli**	**avions aboli**
abolissais	**abolissiez**	**avais aboli**	**aviez aboli**
abolissait	**abolissaient**	**avait aboli**	**avaient aboli**
3 passé simple		10 passé antérieur	
abolis	**abolîmes**	**eus aboli**	**eûmes aboli**
abolis	**abolîtes**	**eus aboli**	**eûtes aboli**
abolit	**abolirent**	**eut aboli**	**eurent aboli**
4 futur		11 futur antérieur	
abolirai	**abolirons**	**aurai aboli**	**aurons aboli**
aboliras	**abolirez**	**auras aboli**	**aurez aboli**
abolira	**aboliront**	**aura aboli**	**auront aboli**
5 conditionnel		12 conditionnel passé	
abolirais	**abolirions**	**aurais aboli**	**aurions aboli**
abolirais	**aboliriez**	**aurais aboli**	**auriez aboli**
abolirait	**aboliraient**	**aurait aboli**	**auraient aboli**
6 présent du subjonctif		13 passé du subjonctif	
abolisse	**abolissions**	**aie aboli**	**ayons aboli**
abolisses	**abolissiez**	**aies aboli**	**ayez aboli**
abolisse	**abolissent**	**ait aboli**	**aient aboli**
7 imparfait du subjonctif		14 plus-que-parfait du subjonctif	
abolisse	**abolissions**	**eusse aboli**	**eussions aboli**
abolisses	**abolissiez**	**eusses aboli**	**eussiez aboli**
abolît	**abolissent**	**eût aboli**	**eussent aboli**

Impératif
abolis
abolissons
abolissez

Sentences using this verb and words related to this verb
Le législateur a soumis un projet de loi abolissant la peine de mort.
Les abolitionnistes veulent éliminer toutes les armes nucléaires.
l'abolition *f.* abolition
l'abolitionnisme *m.* abolitionism
abolitionniste abolitionist

Want to learn more idiomatic expressions that contain verbs? Check out pages 530–542.

The subject pronouns are found on the page facing page 1.   **5**

absoudre

Part. pr. absolvant　　　**Part. passé absous (absoute)**

to absolve

The Seven Simple Tenses		The Seven Compound Tenses	
Singular	Plural	Singular	Plural
1 présent de l'indicatif		**8 passé composé**	
absous	absolvons	ai absous	avons absous
absous	absolvez	as absous	avez absous
absout	absolvent	a absous	ont absous
2 imparfait de l'indicatif		**9 plus-que-parfait de l'indicatif**	
absolvais	absolvions	avais absous	avions absous
absolvais	absolviez	avais absous	aviez absous
absolvait	absolvaient	avait absous	avaient absous
*3 passé simple		**10 passé antérieur**	
absolus	absolûmes	eus absous	eûmes absous
absolus	absolûtes	eus absous	eûtes absous
absolut	absolurent	eut absous	eurent absous
4 futur		**11 futur antérieur**	
absoudrai	absoudrons	aurai absous	aurons absous
absoudras	absoudrez	auras absous	aurez absous
absoudra	absoudront	aura absous	auront absous
5 conditionnel		**12 conditionnel passé**	
absoudrais	absoudrions	aurais absous	aurions absous
absoudrais	absoudriez	aurais absous	auriez absous
absoudrait	absoudraient	aurait absous	auraient absous
6 présent du subjonctif		**13 passé du subjonctif**	
absolve	absolvions	aie absous	ayons absous
absolves	absolviez	aies absous	ayez absous
absolve	absolvent	ait absous	aient absous
*7 imparfait du subjonctif		**14 plus-que-parfait du subjonctif**	
absolusse	absolussions	eusse absous	eussions absous
absolusses	absolussiez	eusses absous	eussiez absous
absolût	absolussent	eût absous	eussent absous

*Tense Nos. 3 and 7 of this verb
　are rarely used.

Impératif
absous
absolvons
absolvez

Words and expressions related to this verb
une absolution absolution (of a sin)
donner l'absolution à un pécheur to absolve
　a sinner (of his sins)
une absoute recitation of prayers for the dead
absolument absolutely; **Je le veux**
　absolument I really insist upon it.

une confiance absolue complete confidence
un refus absolu absolute (flat) refusal
absolument pas! certainly not!
absolument rien! absolutely nothing!

The *b* in **absoudre** is pronounced as if it were written *p*. See also **résoudre**.

Get acquainted with what preposition goes with what verb on pages 543–553.

The Seven Simple Tenses		The Seven Compound Tenses	
Singular	Plural	Singular	Plural

1   présent de l'indicatif

m'abstiens	nous abstenons	me suis abstenu(e)	nous sommes abstenu(e)s
t'abstiens	vous abstenez	t'es abstenu(e)	vous êtes abstenu(e)(s)
s'abstient	s'abstiennent	s'est abstenu(e)	se sont abstenu(e)s

8   passé composé *(heading listed above right column)*

2   imparfait de l'indicatif   **9   plus-que-parfait de l'indicatif**

m'abstenais	nous abstenions	m'étais abstenu(e)	nous étions abstenu(e)s
t'abstenais	vous absteniez	t'étais abstenu(e)	vous étiez abstenu(e)(s)
s'abstenait	s'abstenaient	s'était abstenu(e)	s'étaient abstenu(e)s

3   passé simple   **10   passé antérieur**

m'abstins	nous abstînmes	me fus abstenu(e)	nous fûmes abstenu(e)s
t'abstins	vous abstîntes	te fus abstenu(e)	vous fûtes abstenu(e)(s)
s'abstint	s'abstinrent	se fut abstenu(e)	se furent abstenu(e)s

4   futur   **11   futur antérieur**

m'abstiendrai	nous abstiendrons	me serai abstenu(e)	nous serons abstenu(e)s
t'abstiendras	vous abstiendrez	te seras abstenu(e)	vous serez abstenu(e)(s)
s'abstiendra	s'abstiendront	se sera abstenu(e)	se seront abstenu(e)s

5   conditionnel   **12   conditionnel passé**

m'abstiendrais	nous abstiendrions	me serais abstenu(e)	nous serions abstenu(e)s
t'abstiendrais	vous abstiendriez	te serais abstenu(e)	vous seriez abstenu(e)(s)
s'abstiendrait	s'abstiendraient	se serait abstenu(e)	se seraient absttenu(e)s

6   présent du subjonctif   **13   passé du subjonctif**

m'abstienne	nous abstenions	me sois abstenu(e)	nous soyons abstenu(e)s
t'abstiennes	vous absteniez	te sois abstenu(e)	vous soyez abstenu(e)(s)
s'abstienne	s'abstiennent	se soit abstenu(e)	se soient abstenu(e)s

7   imparfait du subjonctif   **14   plus-que-parfait du subjonctif**

m'abstinsse	nous abstinssions	me fusse abstenu(e)	nous fussions abstenu(e)s
t'abstinsses	vous abstinssiez	te fusses abstenu(e)	vous fussiez abstenu(e)(s)
s'abstînt	s'abstinssent	se fût abstenu(e)	se fussent abstenu(e)s

Impératif
abstiens-toi; ne t'abstiens pas
abstenons-nous; ne nous abstenons pas
abstenez-vous; ne vous abstenez pas

Words and expressions related to this verb

s'abstenir de to abstain from	**faire abstinence de** to abstain from
l'abstinence *f.* abstinence	**un abstentionniste** abstentionist
l'abstention *f.* abstention	**s'abstenir de faire** to refrain from doing
abstinent, abstinente abstinent	

The *b* in **s'abstenir** is pronounced as if it were written *p*.

How are you doing? Find out with the verb drills and tests with answers explained on pages 622–673.

The subject pronouns are found on the page facing page 1.   **7**

to accept

The Seven Simple Tenses		The Seven Compound Tenses	
Singular	Plural	Singular	Plural
1 présent de l'indicatif		**8 passé composé**	
accepte	acceptons	ai accepté	avons accepté
acceptes	acceptez	as accepté	avez accepté
accepte	acceptent	a accepté	ont accepté
2 imparfait de l'indicatif		**9 plus-que-parfait de l'indicatif**	
acceptais	acceptions	avais accepté	avions accepté
acceptais	acceptiez	avais accepté	aviez accepté
acceptait	acceptaient	avait accepté	avaient accepté
3 passé simple		**10 passé antérieur**	
acceptai	acceptâmes	eus accepté	eûmes accepté
acceptas	acceptâtes	eus accepté	eûtes accepté
accepta	acceptèrent	eut accepté	eurent accepté
4 futur		**11 futur antérieur**	
accepterai	accepterons	aurai accepté	aurons accepté
accepteras	accepterez	auras accepté	aurez accepté
acceptera	accepteront	aura accepté	auront accepté
5 conditionnel		**12 conditionnel passé**	
accepterais	accepterions	aurais accepté	aurions accepté
accepterais	accepteriez	aurais accepté	auriez accepté
accepterait	accepteraient	aurait accepté	auraient accepté
6 présent du subjonctif		**13 passé du subjonctif**	
accepte	acceptions	aie accepté	ayons accepté
acceptes	acceptiez	aies accepté	ayez accepté
accepte	acceptent	ait accepté	aient accepté
7 imparfait du subjonctif		**14 plus-que-parfait du subjonctif**	
acceptasse	acceptassions	eusse accepté	eussions accepté
acceptasses	acceptassiez	eusses accepté	eussiez accepté
acceptât	acceptassent	eût accepté	eussent accepté

Impératif
accepte
acceptons
acceptez

Words and expressions related to this verb
acceptable   acceptable, satisfactory
une acceptation   acceptance
accepter une invitation   to accept an invitation
l'acception *f.*   sense, meaning

Want to learn more idiomatic expressions that contain verbs? Look at pages 530–542.

to acclaim, to applaud, to cheer

The Seven Simple Tenses		The Seven Compound Tenses	
Singular	Plural	Singular	Plural
1 présent de l'indicatif		8 passé composé	
acclame	acclamons	ai acclamé	avons acclamé
acclames	acclamez	as acclamé	avez acclamé
acclame	acclament	a acclamé	ont acclamé
2 imparfait de l'indicatif		9 plus-que-parfait de l'indicatif	
acclamais	acclamions	avais acclamé	avions acclamé
acclamais	acclamiez	avais acclamé	aviez acclamé
acclamait	acclamaient	avait acclamé	avaient acclamé
3 passé simple		10 passé antérieur	
acclamai	acclamâmes	eus acclamé	eûmes acclamé
acclamas	acclamâtes	eus acclamé	eûtes acclamé
acclama	acclamèrent	eut acclamé	eurent acclamé
4 futur		11 futur antérieur	
acclamerai	acclamerons	aurai acclamé	aurons acclamé
acclameras	acclamerez	auras acclamé	aurez acclamé
acclamera	acclameront	aura acclamé	auront acclamé
5 conditionnel		12 conditionnel passé	
acclamerais	acclamerions	aurais acclamé	aurions acclamé
acclamerais	acclameriez	aurais acclamé	auriez acclamé
acclamerait	acclameraient	aurait acclamé	auraient acclamé
6 présent du subjonctif		13 passé du subjonctif	
acclame	acclamions	aie acclamé	ayons acclamé
acclames	acclamiez	aies acclamé	ayez acclamé
acclame	acclament	ait acclamé	aient acclamé
7 imparfait du subjonctif		14 plus-que-parfait du subjonctif	
acclamasse	acclamassions	eusse acclamé	eussions acclamé
acclamasses	acclamassiez	eusses acclamé	eussiez acclamé
acclamât	acclamassent	eût acclamé	eussent acclamé

Impératif
acclame
acclamons
acclamez

Words and expressions related to this verb
l'acclamation *f.*   acclamation, cheering
nommer par acclamation   to name by
   acclamation
réclamer   to demand, to ask for

une réclame   advertisement, commercial
élire par acclamation   to elect by acclamation
se faire acclamer   to be cheered, hailed
une réclamation   complaint

It's important that you be familiar with the subjunctive. See pages 560–565.

accompagner   Part. pr. **accompagnant**   Part. passé **accompagné**
to accompany

The Seven Simple Tenses		The Seven Compound Tenses	
Singular	Plural	Singular	Plural
1 présent de l'indicatif		**8 passé composé**	
accompagne	accompagnons	ai accompagné	avons accompagné
accompagnes	accompagnez	as accompagné	avez accompagné
accompagne	accompagnent	a accompagné	ont accompagné
2 imparfait de l'indicatif		**9 plus-que-parfait de l'indicatif**	
accompagnais	accompagnions	avais accompagné	avions accompagné
accompagnais	accompagniez	avais accompagné	aviez accompagné
accompagnait	accompagnaient	avait accompagné	avaient accompagné
3 passé simple		**10 passé antérieur**	
accompagnai	accompagnâmes	eus accompagné	eûmes accompagné
accompagnas	accompagnâtes	eus accompagné	eûtes accompagné
accompagna	accompagnèrent	eut accompagné	eurent accompagné
4 futur		**11 futur antérieur**	
accompagnerai	accompagnerons	aurai accompagné	aurons accompagné
accompagneras	accompagnerez	auras accompagné	aurez accompagné
accompagnera	accompagneront	aura accompagné	auront accompagné
5 conditionnel		**12 conditionnel passé**	
accompagnerais	accompagnerions	aurais accompagné	aurions accompagné
accompagnerais	accompagneriez	aurais accompagné	auriez accompagné
accompagnerait	accompagneraient	aurait accompagné	auraient accompagné
6 présent du subjonctif		**13 passé du subjonctif**	
accompagne	accompagnions	aie accompagné	ayons accompagné
accompagnes	accompagniez	aies accompagné	ayez accompagné
accompagne	accompagnent	ait accompagné	aient accompagné
7 imparfait du subjonctif		**14 plus-que-parfait du subjonctif**	
accompagnasse	accompagnassions	eusse accompagné	eussions accompagné
accompagnasses	accompagnassiez	eusses accompagné	eussiez accompagné
accompagnât	accompagnassent	eût accompagné	eussent accompagné

Impératif
accompagne
accompagnons
accompagnez

Words and expressions related to this verb
une compagnie company, theatrical troupe
raccompagner quelqu'un to see someone
  out, see someone off
un animal de compagnie (animal domestique)
  a pet
Il vaut mieux être seul qu'en mauvaise
  compagnie! It's better to be alone than in bad
  company!

s'accompagner de to be accompanied by
un accompagnement accompanying,
  accompaniment (music)
un accompagnateur, une accompagnatrice
  accompanist (music)
un compagnon, une compagne companion

Get acquainted with what preposition goes with what verb on pages 543–553.

to accord, to grant, to reconcile, to admit

The Seven Simple Tenses		The Seven Compound Tenses	
Singular	Plural	Singular	Plural
1 présent de l'indicatif		8 passé composé	
accorde	accordons	ai accordé	avons accordé
accordes	accordez	as accordé	avez accordé
accorde	accordent	a accordé	ont accordé
2 imparfait de l'indicatif		9 plus-que-parfait de l'indicatif	
accordais	accordions	avais accordé	avions accordé
accordais	accordiez	avais accordé	aviez accordé
accordait	accordaient	avait accordé	avaient accordé
3 passé simple		10 passé antérieur	
accordai	accordâmes	eus accordé	eûmes accordé
accordas	accordâtes	eus accordé	eûtes accordé
accorda	accordèrent	eut accordé	eurent accordé
4 futur		11 futur antérieur	
accorderai	accorderons	aurai accordé	aurons accordé
accorderas	accorderez	auras accordé	aurez accordé
accordera	accorderont	aura accordé	auront accordé
5 conditionnel		12 conditionnel passé	
accorderais	accorderions	aurais accordé	aurions accordé
accorderais	accorderiez	aurais accordé	auriez accordé
accorderait	accorderaient	aurait accordé	auraient accordé
6 présent du subjonctif		13 passé du subjonctif	
accorde	accordions	aie accordé	ayons accordé
accordes	accordiez	aies accordé	ayez accordé
accorde	accordent	ait accordé	aient accordé
7 imparfait du subjonctif		14 plus-que-parfait du subjonctif	
accordasse	accordassions	eusse accordé	eussions accordé
accordasses	accordassiez	eusses accordé	eussiez accordé
accordât	accordassent	eût accordé	eussent accordé

Impératif
accorde
accordons
accordez

Words and expressions related to this verb

un accord   agreement, consent
d'accord   agreed, okay
mettre d'accord   to reconcile
se mettre d'accord   to come to an agreement
l'accord entre le sujet et le verbe   subject-verb agreement
une concordance   similarity, concordance

un accordage   tuning (music)
un accordéon   accordion (music)
un, une accordéoniste   accordionist
s'accorder   to be on good terms; to come to terms, to agree
cordialement   cordially, heartily
donner son accord   to agree, consent

Consult the sections on verbs used in idiomatic expressions, verbs with prepositions, and the list of over 1,100 verbs conjugated like model verbs in the back pages.

The subject pronouns are found on the page facing page 1.

to run to, to run up to, to come (go) running to

The Seven Simple Tenses		The Seven Compound Tenses	
Singular	Plural	Singular	Plural
1 présent de l'indicatif		**8 passé composé**	
accours	accourons	ai accouru	avons accouru
accours	accourez	as accouru	avez accouru
accourt	accourent	a accouru	ont accouru
2 imparfait de l'indicatif		**9 plus-que-parfait de l'indicatif**	
accourais	accourions	avais accouru	avions accouru
accourais	accouriez	avais accouru	aviez accouru
accourait	accouraient	avait accouru	avaient accouru
3 passé simple		**10 passé antérieur**	
accourus	accourûmes	eus accouru	eûmes accouru
accourus	accourûtes	eus accouru	eûtes accouru
accourut	accoururent	eut accouru	eurent accouru
4 futur		**11 futur antérieur**	
accourrai	accourrons	aurai accouru	aurons accouru
accourras	accourrez	auras accouru	aurez accouru
accourra	accourront	aura accouru	auront accouru
5 conditionnel		**12 conditionnel passé**	
accourrais	accourrions	aurais accouru	aurions accouru
accourrais	accourriez	aurais accouru	auriez accouru
accourrait	accourraient	aurait accouru	auraient accouru
6 présent du subjonctif		**13 passé du subjonctif**	
accoure	accourions	aie accouru	ayons accouru
accoures	accouriez	aies accouru	ayez accouru
accoure	accourent	ait accouru	aient accouru
7 imparfait du subjonctif		**14 plus-que-parfait du subjonctif**	
accourusse	accourussions	eusse accouru	eussions accouru
accourusses	accourussiez	eusses accouru	eussiez accouru
accourût	accourussent	eût accouru	eussent accouru

Impératif
accours
accourons
accourez

Words and expressions related to this verb
accourir vers qqn   to go (come) running toward someone
J'ai accouru vers la pauvre vieille dame pour l'aider à se relever   I went running up to the poor old lady to help her get on her feet.
courir   to run

See also **courir.**

concourir   to compete
encourir   to incur
secourir   to aid, help
la course et la marche   running and walking
la course au pouvoir   the race for power

This verb is conjugated with either **avoir** or **être** to form the compound tenses.

to hang (up), to hook (on a hanger, nail, *e.g.*, a coat)

The Seven Simple Tenses		The Seven Compound Tenses	
Singular	Plural	Singular	Plural
1 présent de l'indicatif		**8 passé composé**	
accroche	accrochons	ai accroché	avons accroché
accroches	accrochez	as accroché	avez accroché
accroche	accrochent	a accroché	ont accroché
2 imparfait de l'indicatif		**9 plus-que-parfait de l'indicatif**	
accrochais	accrochions	avais accroché	avions accroché
accrochais	accrochiez	avais accroché	aviez accroché
accrochait	accrochaient	avait accroché	avaient accroché
3 passé simple		**10 passé antérieur**	
accrochai	accrochâmes	eus accroché	eûmes accroché
accrochas	accrochâtes	eus accroché	eûtes accroché
accrocha	accrochèrent	eut accroché	eurent accroché
4 futur		**11 futur antérieur**	
accrocherai	accrocherons	aurai accroché	aurons accroché
accrocheras	accrocherez	auras accroché	aurez accroché
accrochera	accrocheront	aura accroché	auront accroché
5 conditionnel		**12 conditionnel passé**	
accrocherais	accrocherions	aurais accroché	aurions accroché
accrocherais	accrocheriez	aurais accroché	auriez accroché
accrocherait	accrocheraient	aurait accroché	auraient accroché
6 présent du subjonctif		**13 passé du subjonctif**	
accroche	accrochions	aie accroché	ayons accroché
accroches	accrochiez	aies accroché	ayez accroché
accroche	accrochent	ait accroché	aient accroché
7 imparfait du subjonctif		**14 plus-que-parfait du subjonctif**	
accrochasse	accrochassions	eusse accroché	eussions accroché
accrochasses	accrochassiez	eusses accroché	eussiez accroché
accrochât	accrochassent	eût accroché	eussent accroché

Impératif
accroche
accrochons
accrochez

Words and expressions related to this verb

accrocher son manteau   to hang up one's coat
un accrocheur, une accrocheuse   leech (a person who clings, "hangs on" to another person, and is difficult to shake off)
un accroche-plat   plate hanger
un accroche-coeur   curl of hair against the temple of one's head (kiss curl); **des accroche-coeurs**

Accroche-toi!   Hang on! Hang in there!
décrocher   to unhook, to pick up the receiver of a telephone; **raccrocher**   to hang up
décrocher une bonne place   to land a soft job
le décrochage   unhooking
un crochet   hook, hanger
crocheter   to hook in, to pick a lock
faire du crochet   to crochet

Use the EE-zee guide to French pronunciation on pages 566 and 567.

The subject pronouns are found on the page facing page 1.
                                                                        13

to increase, to make greater, to enlarge

The Seven Simple Tenses		The Seven Compound Tenses	
Singular	Plural	Singular	Plural
1 présent de l'indicatif		**8 passé composé**	
accrois	accroissons	ai accru	avons accru
accrois	accroissez	as accru	avez accru
accroît	accroissent	a accru	ont accru
2 imparfait de l'indicatif		**9 plus-que-parfait de l'indicatif**	
accroissais	accroissions	avais accru	avions accru
accroissais	accroissiez	avais accru	aviez accru
accroissait	accroissaient	avait accru	avaient accru
3 passé simple		**10 passé antérieur**	
accrus	accrûmes	eus accru	eûmes accru
accrus	accrûtes	eus accru	eûtes accru
accrut	accrurent	eut accru	eurent accru
4 futur		**11 futur antérieur**	
accroîtrai	accroîtrons	aurai accru	aurons accru
accroîtras	accroîtrez	auras accru	aurez accru
accroîtra	accroîtront	aura accru	auront accru
5 conditionnel		**12 conditionnel passé**	
accroîtrais	accroîtrions	aurais accru	aurions accru
accroîtrais	accroîtriez	aurais accru	auriez accru
accroîtrait	accroîtraient	aurait accru	auraient accru
6 présent du subjonctif		**13 passé du subjonctif**	
accroisse	accroissions	aie accru	ayons accru
accroisses	accroissiez	aies accru	ayez accru
accroisse	accroissent	ait accru	aient accru
7 imparfait du subjonctif		**14 plus-que-parfait du subjonctif**	
accrusse	accrussions	eusse accru	eussions accru
accrusses	accrussiez	eusses accru	eussiez accru
accrût	accrussent	eût accru	eussent accru

Impératif
accrois
accroissons
accroissez

Words related to this verb
un accroissement growth, increase, accumulation, accretion
une accrue increase, accretion
s'accroître to accrue, to increase
accroître son pouvoir to increase one's power
accroître sa production to increase one's production

See also **croître** and **décroître**.

Want to learn more idiomatic expressions that contain verbs? Look at pages 530–542.

to greet, welcome

The Seven Simple Tenses		The Seven Compound Tenses	
Singular	Plural	Singular	Plural
1 présent de l'indicatif		**8 passé composé**	
accueille	accueillons	ai accueilli	avons accueilli
accueilles	accueillez	as accueilli	avez accueilli
accueille	accueillent	a accueilli	ont accueilli
2 imparfait de l'indicatif		**9 plus-que-parfait de l'indicatif**	
accueillais	accueillions	avais accueilli	avions accueilli
accueillais	accueilliez	avais accueilli	aviez accueilli
accueillait	accueillaient	avait accueilli	avaient accueilli
3 passé simple		**10 passé antérieur**	
accueillis	accueillîmes	eus accueilli	eûmes accueilli
accueillis	accueillîtes	eus accueilli	eûtes accueilli
accueillit	accueillirent	eut accueilli	eurent accueilli
4 futur		**11 futur antérieur**	
accueillerai	accueillerons	aurai accueilli	aurons accueilli
accueilleras	accueillerez	auras accueilli	aurez accueilli
accueillera	accueilleront	aura accueilli	auront accueilli
5 conditionnel		**12 conditionnel passé**	
accueillerais	accueillerions	aurais accueilli	aurions accueilli
accueillerais	accueilleriez	aurais accueilli	auriez accueilli
accueillerait	accueilleraient	aurait accueilli	auraient accueilli
6 présent du subjonctif		**13 passé du subjonctif**	
accueille	accueillions	aie accueilli	ayons accueilli
accueilles	accueilliez	aies accueilli	ayez accueilli
accueille	accueillent	ait accueilli	aient accueilli
7 imparfait du subjonctif		**14 plus-que-parfait du subjonctif**	
accueillisse	accueillissions	eusse accueilli	eussions accueilli
accueillisses	accueillissiez	eusses accueilli	eussiez accueilli
accueillît	accueillissent	eût accueilli	eussent accueilli

Impératif
accueille
accueillons
accueillez

Words and expressions related to this verb

accueillir chaleureusement   to give a warm welcome

accueillir froidement   to give a cool reception

faire bon accueil   to give a warm welcome

l'accueil *m.*/**le bureau d'accueil**   reception desk

un accueil   welcome, reception;

un accueil chaleureux   warm welcome

accueillant, accueillante   hospitable;

l'accueil des touristes   accommodating the tourists

For other words and expressions related to this verb, see **cueillir**.

Grammar putting you in a tense mood? Review the definitions of basic grammatical terms with examples on pages 674–688.

The subject pronouns are found on the page facing page 1.   **15**

accuser
to accuse

Part. pr. **accusant** Part. passé **accusé**

The Seven Simple Tenses		The Seven Compound Tenses	
Singular	Plural	Singular	Plural
1 présent de l'indicatif		**8 passé composé**	
accuse	accusons	ai accusé	avons accusé
accuses	accusez	as accusé	avez accusé
accuse	accusent	a accusé	ont accusé
2 imparfait de l'indicatif		**9 plus-que-parfait de l'indicatif**	
accusais	accusions	avais accusé	avions accusé
accusais	accusiez	avais accusé	aviez accusé
accusait	accusaient	avait accusé	avaient accusé
3 passé simple		**10 passé antérieur**	
accusai	accusâmes	eus accusé	eûmes accusé
accusas	accusâtes	eus accusé	eûtes accusé
accusa	accusèrent	eut accusé	eurent accusé
4 futur		**11 futur antérieur**	
accuserai	accuserons	aurai accusé	aurons accusé
accuseras	accuserez	auras accusé	aurez accusé
accusera	accuseront	aura accusé	auront accusé
5 conditionnel		**12 conditionnel passé**	
accuserais	accuserions	aurais accusé	aurions accusé
accuserais	accuseriez	aurais accusé	auriez accusé
accuserait	accuseraient	aurait accusé	auraient accusé
6 présent du subjonctif		**13 passé du subjonctif**	
accuse	accusions	aie accusé	ayons accusé
accuses	accusiez	aies accusé	ayez accusé
accuse	accusent	ait accusé	aient accusé
7 imparfait du subjonctif		**14 plus-que-parfait du subjonctif**	
accusasse	accusassions	eusse accusé	eussions accusé
accusasses	accusassiez	eusses accusé	eussiez accusé
accusât	accusassent	eût accusé	eussent accusé

Impératif
accuse
accusons
accusez

Words and expressions related to this verb

accuser réception de qqch to acknowledge receipt of something
une accusation accusation, charge, indictment
porter une accusation contre to bring charges against

un accusateur, une accusatrice accuser;
l'accusateur public public prosecutor
s'accuser de to accuse oneself of
un accusé de réception
acknowledgment/confirmation of receipt

Consult the sections on verbs used in idiomatic expressions, verbs with prepositions, and the list of over 1,100 verbs conjugated like model verbs in the back pages.

The Seven Simple Tenses		The Seven Compound Tenses	
Singular	Plural	Singular	Plural

1   présent de l'indicatif

		8 passé composé	
achète	achetons	ai acheté	avons acheté
achètes	achetez	as acheté	avez acheté
achète	achètent	a acheté	ont acheté

2   imparfait de l'indicatif

		9 plus-que-parfait de l'indicatif	
achetais	achetions	avais acheté	avions acheté
achetais	achetiez	avais acheté	aviez acheté
achetait	achetaient	avait acheté	avaient acheté

3   passé simple

		10 passé antérieur	
achetai	achetâmes	eus acheté	eûmes acheté
achetas	achetâtes	eus acheté	eûtes acheté
acheta	achetèrent	eut acheté	eurent acheté

4   futur

		11 futur antérieur	
achèterai	achèterons	aurai acheté	aurons acheté
achèteras	achèterez	auras acheté	aurez acheté
achètera	achèteront	aura acheté	auront acheté

5   conditionnel

		12 conditionnel passé	
achèterais	achèterions	aurais acheté	aurions acheté
achèterais	achèteriez	aurais acheté	auriez acheté
achèterait	achèteraient	aurait acheté	auraient acheté

6   présent du subjonctif

		13 passé du subjonctif	
achète	achetions	aie acheté	ayons acheté
achètes	achetiez	aies acheté	ayez acheté
achète	achètent	ait acheté	aient acheté

7   imparfait du subjonctif

		14 plus-que-parfait du subjonctif	
achetasse	achetassions	eusse acheté	eussions acheté
achetasses	achetassiez	eusses acheté	eussiez acheté
achetât	achetassent	eût acheté	eussent acheté

Impératif
achète
achetons
achetez

Words and expressions related to this verb

faire un achat   to make a purchase
un achat électronique   electronic purchase
  (Internet)
un achat en ligne   on-line purchase
un achat   purchase; **acheter qqch à qqn**   to
  buy something from someone

un acheteur, une acheteuse   buyer, purchaser
achetable   purchasable; **racheter**   to ransom;
  to buy back
acheter comptant   to buy in cash; **acheter à
  crédit**   to buy on credit

Taking a trip? Check out the popular words, phrases, and expressions for travelers on pages
599–621.

The subject pronouns are found on the page facing page 1.

achever

Part. pr. achevant   **Part. passé achevé**

to achieve, to finish, to complete, to end

The Seven Simple Tenses		The Seven Compound Tenses	
Singular	Plural	Singular	Plural
1 présent de l'indicatif		**8 passé composé**	
achève	achevons	ai achevé	avons achevé
achèves	achevez	as achevé	avez achevé
achève	achèvent	a achevé	ont achevé
2 imparfait de l'indicatif		**9 plus-que-parfait de l'indicatif**	
achevais	achevions	avais achevé	avions achevé
achevais	acheviez	avais achevé	aviez achevé
achevait	achevaient	avait achevé	avaient achevé
3 passé simple		**10 passé antérieur**	
achevai	achevâmes	eus achevé	eûmes achevé
achevas	achevâtes	eus achevé	eûtes achevé
acheva	achevèrent	eut achevé	eurent achevé
4 futur		**11 futur antérieur**	
achèverai	achèverons	aurai achevé	aurons achevé
achèveras	achèverez	auras achevé	aurez achevé
achèvera	achèveront	aura achevé	auront achevé
5 conditionnel		**12 conditionnel passé**	
achèverais	achèverions	aurais achevé	aurions achevé
achèverais	achèveriez	aurais achevé	auriez achevé
achèverait	achèveraient	aurait achevé	auraient achevé
6 présent du subjonctif		**13 passé du subjonctif**	
achève	achevions	aie achevé	ayons achevé
achèves	acheviez	aies achevé	ayez achevé
achève	achèvent	ait achevé	aient achevé
7 imparfait du subjonctif		**14 plus-que-parfait du subjonctif**	
achevasse	achevassions	eusse achevé	eussions achevé
achevasses	achevassiez	eusses achevé	eussiez achevé
achevât	achevassent	eût achevé	eussent achevé

	Impératif
	achève
	achevons
	achevez

Words and expressions related to this verb
achever de faire qqch   to finish doing something
s'achever   to come to an end, to close, to be fulfilled
un idiot achevé, une idiote achevée   a complete idiot
un achèvement   completion, end, conclusion; **l'achèvement du travail**   completion of the work

Soak up some verbs used in weather expressions on pages 557 and 558.

to acquire, to obtain

The Seven Simple Tenses		The Seven Compound Tenses	
Singular	Plural	Singular	Plural
1 présent de l'indicatif		8 passé composé	
acquiers	**acquérons**	**ai acquis**	**avons acquis**
acquiers	**acquérez**	**as acquis**	**avez acquis**
acquiert	**acquièrent**	**a acquis**	**ont acquis**
2 imparfait de l'indicatif		9 plus-que-parfait de l'indicatif	
acquérais	**acquérions**	**avais acquis**	**avions acquis**
acquérais	**acquériez**	**avais acquis**	**aviez acquis**
acquérait	**acquéraient**	**avait acquis**	**avaient acquis**
3 passé simple		10 passé antérieur	
acquis	**acquîmes**	**eus acquis**	**eûmes acquis**
acquis	**acquîtes**	**eus acquis**	**eûtes acquis**
acquit	**acquirent**	**eut acquis**	**eurent acquis**
4 futur		11 futur antérieur	
acquerrai	**acquerrons**	**aurai acquis**	**aurons acquis**
acquerras	**acquerrez**	**auras acquis**	**aurez acquis**
acquerra	**acquerront**	**aura acquis**	**auront acquis**
5 conditionnel		12 conditionnel passé	
acquerrais	**acquerrions**	**aurais acquis**	**aurions acquis**
acquerrais	**acquerriez**	**aurais acquis**	**auriez acquis**
acquerrait	**acquerraient**	**aurait acquis**	**auraient acquis**
6 présent du subjonctif		13 passé du subjonctif	
acquière	**acquérions**	**aie acquis**	**ayons acquis**
acquières	**acquériez**	**aies acquis**	**ayez acquis**
acquière	**acquièrent**	**ait acquis**	**aient acquis**
7 imparfait du subjonctif		14 plus-que-parfait du subjonctif	
acquisse	**acquissions**	**eusse acquis**	**eussions acquis**
acquisses	**acquissiez**	**eusses acquis**	**eussiez acquis**
acquît	**acquissent**	**eût acquis**	**eussent acquis**

Impératif
acquiers
acquérons
acquérez

Words and expressions related to this verb
s'acquérir   to accrue; to improve; to be gained or obtained
une acquisition   acquisition, purchase; **faire l'acquisition de**   to acquire
un acquit   receipt; release
acquis, acquise   acquired
conquérir   to conquer
tenir quelque chose pour acquis   to take something for granted

Get acquainted with what preposition goes with what verb on pages 543–553.

The subject pronouns are found on the page facing page 1.   **19**

admettre

to admit

The Seven Simple Tenses		The Seven Compound Tenses	
Singular	Plural	Singular	Plural
1 présent de l'indicatif		**8 passé composé**	
admets	admettons	ai admis	avons admis
admets	admettez	as admis	avez admis
admet	admettent	a admis	ont admis
2 imparfait de l'indicatif		**9 plus-que-parfait de l'indicatif**	
admettais	admettions	avais admis	avions admis
admettais	admettiez	avais admis	aviez admis
admettait	admettaient	avait admis	avaient admis
3 passé simple		**10 passé antérieur**	
admis	admîmes	eus admis	eûmes admis
admis	admîtes	eus admis	eûtes admis
admit	admirent	eut admis	eurent admis
4 futur		**11 futur antérieur**	
admettrai	admettrons	aurai admis	aurons admis
admettras	admettrez	auras admis	aurez admis
admettra	admettront	aura admis	auront admis
5 conditionnel		**12 conditionnel passé**	
admettrais	admettrions	aurais admis	aurions admis
admettrais	admettriez	aurais admis	auriez admis
admettrait	admettraient	aurait admis	auraient admis
6 présent du subjonctif		**13 passé du subjonctif**	
admette	admettions	aie admis	ayons admis
admettes	admettiez	aies admis	ayez admis
admette	admettent	ait admis	aient admis
7 imparfait du subjonctif		**14 plus-que-parfait du subjonctif**	
admisse	admissions	eusse admis	eussions admis
admisses	admissiez	eusses admis	eussiez admis
admît	admissent	eût admis	eussent admis

Impératif
admets
admettons
admettez

Words and expressions related to this verb
admis, admise   admitted, accepted
une admission   admission, admittance
l'admissibilité *f.*   acceptability
se faire admettre dans un club   to be admitted to a club
admissible   acceptable

See also **commettre, mettre, permettre, promettre, remettre,** and **soumettre.**

Want to learn more idiomatic expressions that contain verbs? Look at pages 530–542.

The Seven Simple Tenses		The Seven Compound Tenses	
Singular	Plural	Singular	Plural

1   présent de l'indicatif

		8 passé composé	
admire	admirons	ai admiré	avons admiré
admires	admirez	as admiré	avez admiré
admire	admirent	a admiré	ont admiré

2   imparfait de l'indicatif

		9 plus-que-parfait de l'indicatif	
admirais	admirions	avais admiré	avions admiré
admirais	admiriez	avais admiré	aviez admiré
admirait	admiraient	avait admiré	avaient admiré

3   passé simple

		10 passé antérieur	
admirai	admirâmes	eus admiré	eûmes admiré
admiras	admirâtes	eus admiré	eûtes admiré
admira	admirèrent	eut admiré	eurent admiré

4   futur

		11 futur antérieur	
admirerai	admirerons	aurai admiré	aurons admiré
admireras	admirerez	auras admiré	aurez admiré
admirera	admireront	aura admiré	auront admiré

5   conditionnel

		12 conditionnel passé	
admirerais	admirerions	aurais admiré	aurions admiré
admirerais	admireriez	aurais admiré	auriez admiré
admirerait	admireraient	aurait admiré	auraient admiré

6   présent du subjonctif

		13 passé du subjonctif	
admire	admirions	aie admiré	ayons admiré
admires	admiriez	aies admiré	ayez admiré
admire	admirent	ait admiré	aient admiré

7   imparfait du subjonctif

		14 plus-que-parfait du subjonctif	
admirasse	admirassions	eusse admiré	eussions admiré
admirasses	admirassiez	eusses admiré	eussiez admiré
admirât	admirassent	eût admiré	eussent admiré

Impératif
admire
admirons
admirez

Words and expressions related to this verb

une admiration   admiration, wonder
admirativement   admiringly
admiratif, admirative   admiring
un admirateur, une admiratrice   admirer
un mirage   mirage, illusion
un miroir   mirror

See also **mirer.**

remplir quelqu'un d'admiration   to fill someone with admiration
être admirable de courage   to show great courage
admirablement   admirably, wonderfully
être en admiration devant   to be filled with admiration for

to worship, to adore

The Seven Simple Tenses		The Seven Compound Tenses	
Singular	Plural	Singular	Plural
1 présent de l'indicatif		8 passé composé	
adore	adorons	ai adoré	avons adoré
adores	adorez	as adoré	avez adoré
adore	adorent	a adoré	ont adoré
2 imparfait de l'indicatif		9 plus-que-parfait de l'indicatif	
adorais	adorions	avais adoré	avions adoré
adorais	adoriez	avais adoré	aviez adoré
adorait	adoraient	avait adoré	avaient adoré
3 passé simple		10 passé antérieur	
adorai	adorâmes	eus adoré	eûmes adoré
adoras	adorâtes	eus adoré	eûtes adoré
adora	adorèrent	eut adoré	eurent adoré
4 futur		11 futur antérieur	
adorerai	adorerons	aurai adoré	aurons adoré
adoreras	adorerez	auras adoré	aurez adoré
adorera	adoreront	aura adoré	auront adoré
5 conditionnel		12 conditionnel passé	
adorerais	adorerions	aurais adoré	aurions adoré
adorerais	adoreriez	aurais adoré	auriez adoré
adorerait	adoreraient	aurait adoré	auraient adoré
6 présent du subjonctif		13 passé du subjonctif	
adore	adorions	aie adoré	ayons adoré
adores	adoriez	aies adoré	ayez adoré
adore	adorent	ait adoré	aient adoré
7 imparfait du subjonctif		14 plus-que-parfait du subjonctif	
adorasse	adorassions	eusse adoré	eussions adoré
adorasses	adorassiez	eusses adoré	eussiez adoré
adorât	adorassent	eût adoré	eussent adoré

Impératif
adore
adorons
adorez

Sentences using this verb and words related to it
   Claudette adore danser avec les beaux garçons. Elle adore mettre tous ses bijoux avant d'aller au bal. Elle est adorable, gracieuse, et danse adorablement.

une adoration adoration, worship	**adorable** adorable, charming, delightful
adorablement adorably	**un village adorable** delightful village
un adorateur, une adoratrice adorer, worshipper	**une robe adorable** lovely dress

Taking a trip? Check out the popular words, phrases, and expressions for travelers on pages 599–621.

The Seven Simple Tenses		The Seven Compound Tenses	
Singular	Plural	Singular	Plural
1 présent de l'indicatif		**8 passé composé**	
adresse	adressons	ai adressé	avons adressé
adresses	adressez	as adressé	avez adressé
adresse	adressent	a adressé	ont adressé
2 imparfait de l'indicatif		**9 plus-que-parfait de l'indicatif**	
adressais	adressions	avais adressé	avions adressé
adressais	adressiez	avais adressé	aviez adressé
adressait	adressaient	avait adressé	avaient adressé
3 passé simple		**10 passé antérieur**	
adressai	adressâmes	eus adressé	eûmes adressé
adressas	adressâtes	eus adressé	eûtes adressé
adressa	adressèrent	eut adressé	eurent adressé
4 futur		**11 futur antérieur**	
adresserai	adresserons	aurai adressé	aurons adressé
adresseras	adresserez	auras adressé	aurez adressé
adressera	adresseront	aura adressé	auront adressé
5 conditionnel		**12 conditionnel passé**	
adresserais	adresserions	aurais adressé	aurions adressé
adresserais	adresseriez	aurais adressé	auriez adressé
adresserait	adresseraient	aurait adressé	auraient adressé
6 présent du subjonctif		**13 passé du subjonctif**	
adresse	adressions	aie adressé	ayons adressé
adresses	adressiez	aies adressé	ayez adressé
adresse	adressent	ait adressé	aient adressé
7 imparfait du subjonctif		**14 plus-que-parfait du subjonctif**	
adressasse	adressassions	eusse adressé	eussions adressé
adressasses	adressassiez	eusses adressé	eussiez adressé
adressât	adressassent	eût adressé	eussent adressé

Impératif
adresse
adressons
adressez

Words and expressions related to this verb
une adresse   address; skill, adroitness
adresser qqn à   to refer someone to
adresser la parole à   to direct your words to,
  to speak to
s'adresser à   to apply to, to talk to

un tour d'adresse   feat of skill
avec adresse   skillfully
dresser   to tame, to erect
redresser   to straighten up
une adresse électronique   e-mail address

Consult the sections on verbs used in idiomatic expressions, verbs with prepositions, and the list of over 1,100 verbs conjugated like model verbs in the back pages.

The subject pronouns are found on the page facing page 1.

to happen, to occur, to come to pass

The Seven Simple Tenses	The Seven Compound Tenses
Singular Plural	Singular Plural
1 présent de l'indicatif **il advient**	8 passé composé **il est advenu**
2 imparfait de l'indicatif **il advenait**	9 plus-que-parfait de l'indicatif **il était advenu**
3 passé simple **il advint**	10 passé antérieur **il fut advenu**
4 futur **il adviendra**	11 futur antérieur **il sera advenu**
5 conditionnel **il adviendrait**	12 conditionnel passé **il serait advenu**
6 présent du subjonctif **qu'il advienne**	13 passé du subjonctif **qu'il soit advenu**
7 imparfait du subjonctif **qu'il advînt**	14 plus-que-parfait du subjonctif **qu'il fût advenu**

Impératif
Qu'il advienne!
Let it come to pass!

Words and expressions related to this verb

Il advint que . . . It came to pass that . . .
Advienne que pourra . . . Come what may . . .
dans un proche avenir in the near future
À l'avenir soyez à l'heure! In the future be on time!
une aventure adventure
Voilà ce qu'il advint That's what happened.

l'avenir *m.* (from **à + venir**) future
à l'avenir in the future, from this moment on
prédire l'avenir to predict the future
l'avènement *m.* advent
l'avent *m.* advent (ecclesiastical term)
aventurer to venture
quoiqu'il advienne whatever may happen

This is an impersonal verb used in the 3rd person singular only.

to annoy, to irritate, to pester, to vex

The Seven Simple Tenses		The Seven Compound Tenses	
Singular	Plural	Singular	Plural
1 présent de l'indicatif		8 passé composé	
agace	agaçons	ai agacé	avons agacé
agaces	agacez	as agacé	avez agacé
agace	agacent	a agacé	ont agacé
2 imparfait de l'indicatif		9 plus-que-parfait de l'indicatif	
agaçais	agacions	avais agacé	avions agacé
agaçais	agaciez	avais agacé	aviez agacé
agaçait	agaçaient	avait agacé	avaient agacé
3 passé simple		10 passé antérieur	
agaçai	agaçâmes	eus agacé	eûmes agacé
agaças	agaçâtes	eus agacé	eûtes agacé
agaça	agacèrent	eut agacé	eurent agacé
4 futur		11 futur antérieur	
agacerai	agacerons	aurai agacé	aurons agacé
agaceras	agacerez	auras agacé	aurez agacé
agacera	agaceront	aura agacé	auront agacé
5 conditionnel		12 conditionnel passé	
agacerais	agacerions	aurais agacé	aurions agacé
agacerais	agaceriez	aurais agacé	auriez agacé
agacerait	agaceraient	aurait agacé	auraient agacé
6 présent du subjonctif		13 passé du subjonctif	
agace	agacions	aie agacé	ayons agacé
agaces	agaciez	aies agacé	ayez agacé
agace	agacent	ait agacé	aient agacé
7 imparfait du subjonctif		14 plus-que-parfait du subjonctif	
agaçasse	agaçassions	eusse agacé	eussions agacé
agaçasses	agaçassiez	eusses agacé	eussiez agacé
agaçât	agaçassent	eût agacé	eussent agacé

Impératif
agace
agaçons
agacez

Words and expressions related to this verb
un agacement   irritation
Cela est agaçant!   That's irritating!
agacer les nerfs de qqn   to get on someone's nerves
s'agacer   to get annoyed, irritated
Cela m'agace!   It's getting on my nerves!
Tu m'agaces!   You're getting on my nerves!

Going away? Don't forget to check out the practical situations for travelers on pages 568–598.

The subject pronouns are found on the page facing page 1.

to act, to behave, to take effect

The Seven Simple Tenses		The Seven Compound Tenses	
Singular	Plural	Singular	Plural
1 présent de l'indicatif		**8 passé composé**	
agis	agissons	ai agi	avons agi
agis	agissez	as agi	avez agi
agit	agissent	a agi	ont agi
2 imparfait de l'indicatif		**9 plus-que-parfait de l'indicatif**	
agissais	agissions	avais agi	avions agi
agissais	agissiez	avais agi	aviez agi
agissait	agissaient	avait agi	avaient agi
3 passé simple		**10 passé antérieur**	
agis	agîmes	eus agi	eûmes agi
agis	agîtes	eus agi	eûtes agi
agit	agirent	eut agi	eurent agi
4 futur		**11 futur antérieur**	
agirai	agirons	aurai agi	aurons agi
agiras	agirez	auras agi	aurez agi
agira	agiront	aura agi	auront agi
5 conditionnel		**12 conditionnel passé**	
agirais	agirions	aurais agi	aurions agi
agirais	agiriez	aurais agi	auriez agi
agirait	agiraient	aurait agi	auraient agi
6 présent du subjonctif		**13 passé du subjonctif**	
agisse	agissions	aie agi	ayons agi
agisses	agissiez	aies agi	ayez agi
agisse	agissent	ait agi	aient agi
7 imparfait du subjonctif		**14 plus-que-parfait du subjonctif**	
agisse	agissions	eusse agi	eussions agi
agisses	agissiez	eusses agi	eussiez agi
agît	agissent	eût agi	eussent agi

Impératif
agis
agissons
agissez

Words and expressions related to this verb

faire agir to set in motion, to call into action
bien agir to behave well; **mal agir** to behave badly
agir sur to bear upon, to influence, to act upon

agir contre to sue, to take action against
faire agir la loi to put the law into effect
un agitateur, une agitatrice agitator
agiter to rouse, to stir up; to agitate, to shake
réagir to react

Get acquainted with what preposition goes with what verb on pages 543–553.

to be the matter, to be a question of

The Seven Simple Tenses		The Seven Compound Tenses	
Singular	Plural	Singular	Plural
1 présent de l'indicatif **il s'agit**		8 passé composé **il s'est agi**	
2 imparfait de l'indicatif **il s'agissait**		9 plus-que-parfait de l'indicatif **il s'était agi**	
3 passé simple **il s'agit**		10 passé antérieur **il se fut agi**	
4 futur **il s'agira**		11 futur antérieur **il se sera agi**	
5 conditionnel **il s'agirait**		12 conditionnel passé **il se serait agi**	
6 présent du subjonctif **qu'il s'agisse**		13 passé du subjonctif **qu'il se soit agi**	
7 imparfait du subjonctif **qu'il s'agît**		14 plus-que-parfait du subjonctif **qu'il se fût agi**	

Impératif
[not in use]

Common idiomatic expressions using this verb
Hier, le petit Michel est entré dans la maison en pleurant.
—De quoi s'agit-il?! s'exclame sa mère.
—Il s'agit . . . il s'agit . . . de mon vélo. Quelqu'un a volé mon vélo!

s'agir de   to have to do with, to be a matter of
De quoi s'agit-il?   What's the matter? What's up?
Voici ce dont il s'agit   This is what it's about.
Il s'agit de mon vélo   It's about my bike.

Note that this verb is impersonal and is used primarily in the tenses given above.

Want to learn more idiomatic expressions that contain verbs? Check out pages 530–542.

aider

to aid, to help, to assist

The Seven Simple Tenses		The Seven Compound Tenses	
Singular	Plural	Singular	Plural
1 présent de l'indicatif		**8 passé composé**	
aide	aidons	ai aidé	avons aidé
aides	aidez	as aidé	avez aidé
aide	aident	a aidé	ont aidé
2 imparfait de l'indicatif		**9 plus-que-parfait de l'indicatif**	
aidais	aidions	avais aidé	avions aidé
aidais	aidiez	avais aidé	aviez aidé
aidait	aidaient	avait aidé	avaient aidé
3 passé simple		**10 passé antérieur**	
aidai	aidâmes	eus aidé	eûmes aidé
aidas	aidâtes	eus aidé	eûtes aidé
aida	aidèrent	eut aidé	eurent aidé
4 futur		**11 futur antérieur**	
aiderai	aiderons	aurai aidé	aurons aidé
aideras	aiderez	auras aidé	aurez aidé
aidera	aideront	aura aidé	auront aidé
5 conditionnel		**12 conditionnel passé**	
aiderais	aiderions	aurais aidé	aurions aidé
aiderais	aideriez	aurais aidé	auriez aidé
aiderait	aideraient	aurait aidé	auraient aidé
6 présent du subjonctif		**13 passé du subjonctif**	
aide	aidions	aie aidé	ayons aidé
aides	aidiez	aies aidé	ayez aidé
aide	aident	ait aidé	aient aidé
7 imparfait du subjonctif		**14 plus-que-parfait du subjonctif**	
aidasse	aidassions	eusse aidé	eussions aidé
aidasses	aidassiez	eusses aidé	eussiez aidé
aidât	aidassent	eût aidé	eussent aidé

Impératif
aide
aidons
aidez

Sentences using this verb and words related to it

Tous les soirs Roger aide son petit frère à faire sa leçon de mathématiques. Ce soir, le petit frère lui demande:—Après cette leçon, veux-tu m'aider à écrire une composition?
—Aide-toi et le ciel t'aidera, lui répond son grand frère.

aider qqn à faire qqch   to help someone do something
s'aider   to help oneself; to help each other
une aide   aid, assistance, help; **à l'aide de** with the help of

un aide-mémoire   handbook, memory aid
Aide-toi et le ciel t'aidera   God helps those who help themselves.
Je peux vous aider?   May I help you?
s'entraider   to help each other

Note that **se servir** should be used when speaking of food or drink: **Sers-toi!** (Help yourself!) **Servez-vous!** (Help yourself/yourselves!) See also **servir** and **se servir**.

The Seven Simple Tenses		The Seven Compound Tenses	
Singular	Plural	Singular	Plural
1 présent de l'indicatif		**8 passé composé**	
aime	aimons	ai aimé	avons aimé
aimes	aimez	as aimé	avez aimé
aime	aiment	a aimé	ont aimé
2 imparfait de l'indicatif		**9 plus-que-parfait de l'indicatif**	
aimais	aimions	avais aimé	avions aimé
aimais	aimiez	avais aimé	aviez aimé
aimait	aimaient	avait aimé	avaient aimé
3 passé simple		**10 passé antérieur**	
aimai	aimâmes	eus aimé	eûmes aimé
aimas	aimâtes	eus aimé	eûtes aimé
aima	aimèrent	eut aimé	eurent aimé
4 futur		**11 futur antérieur**	
aimerai	aimerons	aurai aimé	aurons aimé
aimeras	aimerez	auras aimé	aurez aimé
aimera	aimeront	aura aimé	auront aimé
5 conditionnel		**12 conditionnel passé**	
aimerais	aimerions	aurais aimé	aurions aimé
aimerais	aimeriez	aurais aimé	auriez aimé
aimerait	aimeraient	aurait aimé	auraient aimé
6 présent du subjonctif		**13 passé du subjonctif**	
aime	aimions	aie aimé	ayons aimé
aimes	aimiez	aies aimé	ayez aimé
aime	aiment	ait aimé	aient aimé
7 imparfait du subjonctif		**14 plus-que-parfait du subjonctif**	
aimasse	aimassions	eusse aimé	eussions aimé
aimasses	aimassiez	eusses aimé	eussiez aimé
aimât	aimassent	eût aimé	eussent aimé

Impératif
aime
aimons
aimez

Words and expressions related to this verb

amour *m.* love; **une chanson d'amour**
   love song (song of love)
aimer bien qqn to like somebody
aimer (à) faire qqch to enjoy doing
   something
aimer mieux to prefer, to like better
s'entr'aimer to love each other
l'amabilité *f.* kindness

aimable friendly, amiable, pleasant
un amant lover; **une amante** lover;
   amoureux, amoureuse de in love with;
   tomber amoureux, amoureuse to fall in
   love
Veuillez avoir l'amabilité de . . . Please be so
   kind as to . . .

ajouter
to add

Part. pr. **ajoutant**   Part. passé **ajouté**

The Seven Simple Tenses		The Seven Compound Tenses	
Singular	Plural	Singular	Plural
1 présent de l'indicatif		**8 passé composé**	
ajoute	ajoutons	ai ajouté	avons ajouté
ajoutes	ajoutez	as ajouté	avez ajouté
ajoute	ajoutent	a ajouté	ont ajouté
2 imparfait de l'indicatif		**9 plus-que-parfait de l'indicatif**	
ajoutais	ajoutions	avais ajouté	avions ajouté
ajoutais	ajoutiez	avais ajouté	aviez ajouté
ajoutait	ajoutaient	avait ajouté	avaient ajouté
3 passé simple		**10 passé antérieur**	
ajoutai	ajoutâmes	eus ajouté	eûmes ajouté
ajoutas	ajoutâtes	eus ajouté	eûtes ajouté
ajouta	ajoutèrent	eut ajouté	eurent ajouté
4 futur		**11 futur antérieur**	
ajouterai	ajouterons	aurai ajouté	aurons ajouté
ajouteras	ajouterez	auras ajouté	aurez ajouté
ajoutera	ajouteront	aura ajouté	auront ajouté
5 conditionnel		**12 conditionnel passé**	
ajouterais	ajouterions	aurais ajouté	aurions ajouté
ajouterais	ajouteriez	aurais ajouté	auriez ajouté
ajouterait	ajouteraient	aurait ajouté	auraient ajouté
6 présent du subjonctif		**13 passé du subjonctif**	
ajoute	ajoutions	aie ajouté	ayons ajouté
ajoutes	ajoutiez	aies ajouté	ayez ajouté
ajoute	ajoutent	ait ajouté	aient ajouté
7 imparfait du subjonctif		**14 plus-que-parfait du subjonctif**	
ajoutasse	ajoutassions	eusse ajouté	eussions ajouté
ajoutasses	ajoutassiez	eusses ajouté	eussiez ajouté
ajoutât	ajoutassent	eût ajouté	eussent ajouté

Impératif
ajoute
ajoutons
ajoutez

Sentences using this verb and words related to it

Si vous aimez faire un ragoût délicieux, ajoutez-y quelques petits oignons, du sel, du poivre, et une gousse d'ail pour obtenir une saveur piquante. Il y a d'autres assaisonnements et condiments que vous pouvez y ajouter aussi. Un assaisonnement ajoute du piquant dans votre ragoût.

un ajout addition (of words in a manuscript or page proofs)
ajouter foi à to add credence to, to give credence to

jouter to tilt, to joust; to dispute, to fight
une joute contest, tournament
rajouter to add more
un rajout an addition

Use the EE-zee guide to French pronunciation on pages 566 and 567.

30

The Seven Simple Tenses		The Seven Compound Tenses	
Singular	Plural	Singular	Plural
1 présent de l'indicatif		**8 passé composé**	
vais	allons	suis allé(e)	sommes allé(e)s
vas	allez	es allé(e)	êtes allé(e)(s)
va	vont	est allé(e)	sont allé(e)s
2 imparfait de l'indicatif		**9 plus-que-parfait de l'indicatif**	
allais	allions	étais allé(e)	étions allé(e)s
allais	alliez	étais allé(e)	étiez allé(e)(s)
allait	allaient	était allé(e)	étaient allé(e)s
3 passé simple		**10 passé antérieur**	
allai	allâmes	fus allé(e)	fûmes allé(e)s
allas	allâtes	fus allé(e)	fûtes allé(e)(s)
alla	allèrent	fut allé(e)	furent allé(e)s
4 futur		**11 futur antérieur**	
irai	irons	serai allé(e)	serons allé(e)s
iras	irez	seras allé(e)	serez allé(e)(s)
ira	iront	sera allé(e)	seront allé(e)s
5 conditionnel		**12 conditionnel passé**	
irais	irions	serais allé(e)	serions allé(e)s
irais	iriez	serais allé(e)	seriez allé(e)(s)
irait	iraient	serait allé(e)	seraient allé(e)s
6 présent du subjonctif		**13 passé du subjonctif**	
aille	allions	sois allé(e)	soyons allé(e)s
ailles	alliez	sois allé(e)	soyez allé(e)(s)
aille	aillent	soit allé(e)	soient allé(e)s
7 imparfait du subjonctif		**14 plus-que-parfait du subjonctif**	
allasse	allassions	fusse allé(e)	fussions allé(e)s
allasses	allassiez	fusses allé(e)	fussiez allé(e)(s)
allât	allassent	fût allé(e)	fussent allé(e)s

Impératif
va
allons
allez

Words and expressions related to this verb
Comment allez-vous? Je vais bien, je vais mal, je vais mieux.
aller à la pêche   to go fishing
aller à la rencontre de quelqu'un   to go to meet someone
aller à pied   to walk, to go on foot

aller au fond des choses   to get to the bottom of things
Ça va?   Is everything O.K.? **Oui, ça va!**
le va et vient   coming and going (people, cars, etc.)
un pis-aller   last resort

Want to learn more idiomatic expressions that contain verbs? Look at pages 530–542.

Can't recognize an irregular verb form? Check out pages 526–529.

to go away

The Seven Simple Tenses		The Seven Compound Tenses	
Singular	Plural	Singular	Plural
1 présent de l'indicatif		**8 passé composé**	
m'en vais	nous en allons	m'en suis allé(e)	nous en sommes allé(e)s
t'en vas	vous en allez	t'en es allé(e)	vous en êtes allé(e)(s)
s'en va	s'en vont	s'en est allé(e)	s'en sont allé(e)s
2 imparfait de l'indicatif		**9 plus-que-parfait de l'indicatif**	
m'en allais	nous en allions	m'en étais allé(e)	nous en étions allé(e)s
t'en allais	vous en alliez	t'en étais allé(e)	vous en étiez allé(e)(s)
s'en allait	s'en allaient	s'en était allé(e)	s'en étaient allé(e)s
3 passé simple		**10 passé antérieur**	
m'en allai	nous en allâmes	m'en fus allé(e)	nous en fûmes allé(e)s
t'en allas	vous en allâtes	t'en fus allé(e)	vous en fûtes allé(e)(s)
s'en alla	s'en allèrent	s'en fut allé(e)	s'en furent allé(e)s
4 futur		**11 futur antérieur**	
m'en irai	nous en irons	m'en serai allé(e)	nous en serons allé(e)s
t'en iras	vous en irez	t'en seras allé(e)	vous en serez allé(e)(s)
s'en ira	s'en iront	s'en sera allé(e)	s'en seront allé(e)s
5 conditionnel		**12 conditionnel passé**	
m'en irais	nous en irions	m'en serais allé(e)	nous en serions allé(e)s
t'en irais	vous en iriez	t'en serais allé(e)	vous en seriez allé(e)(s)
s'en irait	s'en iraient	s'en serait allé(e)	s'en seraient allé(e)s
6 présent du subjonctif		**13 passé du subjonctif**	
m'en aille	nous en allions	m'en sois allé(e)	nous en soyons allé(e)s
t'en ailles	vous en alliez	t'en sois allé(e)	vous en soyez allé(e)(s)
s'en aille	s'en aillent	s'en soit allé(e)	s'en soient allé(e)s
7 imparfait du subjonctif		**14 plus-que-parfait du subjonctif**	
m'en allasse	nous en allassions	m'en fusse allé(e)	nous en fussions allé(e)s
t'en allasses	vous en allassiez	t'en fusses allé(e)	vous en fussiez allé(e)(s)
s'en allât	s'en allassent	s'en fût allé(e)	s'en fussent allé(e)s

Impératif
va-t'en; ne t'en va pas
allons-nous-en; ne nous en allons pas
allez-vous-en; ne vous en allez pas

Common idiomatic expressions using this verb
This verb also has the following idiomatic meanings: to move away (from one residence to another), to die, to pass away, to steal away.

Monsieur et Madame Moreau n'habitent plus ici. Ils s'en sont allés. Je crois qu'ils sont maintenant à Bordeaux.

Madame Morel est gravement malade; elle s'en va.

Le cambrioleur s'en est allé furtivement avec l'argent et les bijoux.

Going away? Don't forget to check out the practical situations for travelers on pages 568–598.

The Seven Simple Tenses		The Seven Compound Tenses	
Singular	Plural	Singular	Plural
1 présent de l'indicatif		**8 passé composé**	
amène	amenons	ai amené	avons amené
amènes	amenez	as amené	avez amené
amène	amènent	a amené	ont amené
2 imparfait de l'indicatif		**9 plus-que-parfait de l'indicatif**	
amenais	amenions	avais amené	avions amené
amenais	ameniez	avais amené	aviez amené
amenait	amenaient	avait amené	avaient amené
3 passé simple		**10 passé antérieur**	
amenai	amenâmes	eus amené	eûmes amené
amenas	amenâtes	eus amené	eûtes amené
amena	amenèrent	eut amené	eurent amené
4 futur		**11 futur antérieur**	
amènerai	amènerons	aurai amené	aurons amené
amèneras	amènerez	auras amené	aurez amené
amènera	amèneront	aura amené	auront amené
5 conditionnel		**12 conditionnel passé**	
amènerais	amènerions	aurais amené	aurions amené
amènerais	amèneriez	aurais amené	auriez amené
amènerait	amèneraient	aurait amené	auraient amené
6 présent du subjonctif		**13 passé du subjonctif**	
amène	amenions	aie amené	ayons amené
amènes	ameniez	aies amené	ayez amené
amène	amènent	ait amené	aient amené
7 imparfait du subjonctif		**14 plus-que-parfait du subjonctif**	
amenasse	amenassions	eusse amené	eussions amené
amenasses	amenassiez	eusses amené	eussiez amené
amenât	amenassent	eût amené	eussent amené

Impératif
amène
amenons
amenez

Sentences using this verb and words related to it

Aujourd'hui ma mère a amené ma petite soeur chez le dentiste. Quand elles sont entrées chez lui, le dentiste leur a demandé:—Quel bon vent vous amène ici?

amener une conversation   to direct, lead a   **des propos peu amènes**   unkind words
   conversation   **un exemple bien amené**   well-introduced
amène   pleasant, agreeable   example

See also **emmener** and **mener**.

How are you doing? Find out with the verb drills and tests with answers explained on pages 622–673.

The subject pronouns are found on the page facing page 1.   **33**

amuser

Part. pr. **amusant**   Part. passé **amusé**

to amuse, to entertain

The Seven Simple Tenses		The Seven Compound Tenses	
Singular	Plural	Singular	Plural
1 présent de l'indicatif		**8 passé composé**	
amuse	amusons	ai amusé	avons amusé
amuses	amusez	as amusé	avez amusé
amuse	amusent	a amusé	ont amusé
2 imparfait de l'indicatif		**9 plus-que-parfait de l'indicatif**	
amusais	amusions	avais amusé	avions amusé
amusais	amusiez	avais amusé	aviez amusé
amusait	amusaient	avait amusé	avaient amusé
3 passé simple		**10 passé antérieur**	
amusai	amusâmes	eus amusé	eûmes amusé
amusas	amusâtes	eus amusé	eûtes amusé
amusa	amusèrent	eut amusé	eurent amusé
4 futur		**11 futur antérieur**	
amuserai	amuserons	aurai amusé	aurons amusé
amuseras	amuserez	auras amusé	aurez amusé
amusera	amuseront	aura amusé	auront amusé
5 conditionnel		**12 conditionnel passé**	
amuserais	amuserions	aurais amusé	aurions amusé
amuserais	amuseriez	aurais amusé	auriez amusé
amuserait	amuseraient	aurait amusé	auraient amusé
6 présent du subjonctif		**13 passé du subjonctif**	
amuse	amusions	aie amusé	ayons amusé
amuses	amusiez	aies amusé	ayez amusé
amuse	amusent	ait amusé	aient amusé
7 imparfait du subjonctif		**14 plus-que-parfait du subjonctif**	
amusasse	amusassions	eusse amusé	eussions amusé
amusasses	amusassiez	eusses amusé	eussiez amusé
amusât	amusassent	eût amusé	eussent amusé

Impératif
amuse
amusons
amusez

Sentences using this verb and words related to it

   Cet acteur sait bien jouer son rôle. Il amuse les spectateurs. C'est un comédien accompli. Il est amusant, n'est-ce pas?

amusant, amusante amusing
un amuseur amuser, entertainer
un amuse-gueule, un amuse-bouche tidbit, titbit, snack
une amusette diversion, pastime, idle pleasure

un amusement amusement, entertainment
Tes remarques ne m'amusent pas Your remarks don't amuse me.
C'est pour l'amusement des enfants It's for the children's entertainment.
le museau muzzle, snout

See also **s'amuser.**

to have a good time, to amuse oneself, to enjoy oneself

The Seven Simple Tenses		The Seven Compound Tenses	
Singular	Plural	Singular	Plural
1 présent de l'indicatif		**8 passé composé**	
m'amuse	**nous amusons**	**me suis amusé(e)**	**nous sommes amusé(e)s**
t'amuses	**vous amusez**	**t'es amusé(e)**	**vous êtes amusé(e)(s)**
s'amuse	**s'amusent**	**s'est amusé(e)**	**se sont amusé(e)s**
2 imparfait de l'indicatif		**9 plus-que-parfait de l'indicatif**	
m'amusais	**nous amusions**	**m'étais amusé(e)**	**nous étions amusé(e)s**
t'amusais	**vous amusiez**	**t'étais amusé(e)**	**vous étiez amusé(e)(s)**
s'amusait	**s'amusaient**	**s'était amusé(e)**	**s'étaient amusé(e)s**
3 passé simple		**10 passé antérieur**	
m'amusai	**nous amusâmes**	**me fus amusé(e)**	**nous fûmes amusé(e)s**
t'amusas	**vous amusâtes**	**te fus amusé(e)**	**vous fûtes amusé(e)(s)**
s'amusa	**s'amusèrent**	**se fut amusé(e)**	**se furent amusé(e)s**
4 futur		**11 futur antérieur**	
m'amuserai	**nous amuserons**	**me serai amusé(e)**	**nous serons amusé(e)s**
t'amuseras	**vous amuserez**	**te seras amusé(e)**	**vous serez amusé(e)(s)**
s'amusera	**s'amuseront**	**se sera amusé(e)**	**se seront amusé(e)s**
5 conditionnel		**12 conditionnel passé**	
m'amuserais	**nous amuserions**	**me serais amusé(e)**	**nous serions amusé(e)s**
t'amuserais	**vous amuseriez**	**te serais amusé(e)**	**vous seriez amusé(e)(s)**
s'amuserait	**s'amuseraient**	**se serait amusé(e)**	**se seraient amusé(e)s**
6 présent du subjonctif		**13 passé du subjonctif**	
m'amuse	**nous amusions**	**me sois amusé(e)**	**nous soyons amusé(e)s**
t'amuses	**vous amusiez**	**te sois amusé(e)**	**vous soyez amusé(e)(s)**
s'amuse	**s'amusent**	**se soit amusé(e)**	**se soient amusé(e)s**
7 imparfait du subjonctif		**14 plus-que-parfait du subjonctif**	
m'amusasse	**nous amusassions**	**me fusse amusé(e)**	**nous fussions amusé(e)s**
t'amusasses	**vous amusassiez**	**te fusses amusé(e)**	**vous fussiez amusé(e)(s)**
s'amusât	**s'amusassent**	**se fût amusé(e)**	**se fussent amusé(e)s**

Impératif
amuse-toi; ne t'amuse pas
amusons-nous; ne nous amusons pas
amusez-vous; ne vous amusez pas

Sentences using this verb and words related to it
  Il y a des élèves qui s'amusent à mettre le professeur en colère. Est-ce que vous vous amusez dans la classe de français? Moi, je m'amuse beaucoup dans cette classe.
  Hier soir je suis allé au cinéma et j'ai vu un film très amusant. Je me suis bien amusé. Mon amie, Françoise, s'est bien amusée aussi.
  Que faites-vous pour vous amuser?

Amuse-toi bien!   Have a great time!   **s'amuser de**   to make fun of
s'amuser à + inf.   to enjoy oneself + pres. part.   **s'amuser avec**   to play with

See also **amuser**.

annoncer

Part. pr. **annonçant**   Part. passé **annoncé**

to announce

The Seven Simple Tenses		The Seven Compound Tenses	
Singular	Plural	Singular	Plural
1 présent de l'indicatif		**8 passé composé**	
annonce	annonçons	ai annoncé	avons annoncé
annonces	annoncez	as annoncé	avez annoncé
annonce	annoncent	a annoncé	ont annoncé
2 imparfait de l'indicatif		**9 plus-que-parfait de l'indicatif**	
annonçais	annoncions	avais annoncé	avions annoncé
annonçais	annonciez	avais annoncé	aviez annoncé
annonçait	annonçaient	avait annoncé	avaient annoncé
3 passé simple		**10 passé antérieur**	
annonçai	annonçâmes	eus annoncé	eûmes annoncé
annonças	annonçâtes	eus annoncé	eûtes annoncé
annonça	annoncèrent	eut annoncé	eurent annoncé
4 futur		**11 futur antérieur**	
annoncerai	annoncerons	aurai annoncé	aurons annoncé
annonceras	annoncerez	auras annoncé	aurez annoncé
annoncera	annonceront	aura annoncé	auront annoncé
5 conditionnel		**12 conditionnel passé**	
annoncerais	annoncerions	aurais annoncé	aurions annoncé
annoncerais	annonceriez	aurais annoncé	auriez annoncé
annoncerait	annonceraient	aurait annoncé	auraient annoncé
6 présent du subjonctif		**13 passé du subjonctif**	
annonce	annoncions	aie annoncé	ayons annoncé
annonces	annonciez	aies annoncé	ayez annoncé
annonce	annoncent	ait annoncé	aient annoncé
7 imparfait du subjonctif		**14 plus-que-parfait du subjonctif**	
annonçasse	annonçassions	eusse annoncé	eussions annoncé
annonçasses	annonçassiez	eusses annoncé	eussiez annoncé
annonçât	annonçassent	eût annoncé	eussent annoncé

Impératif
annonce
annonçons
annoncez

Words and expressions related to this verb
une annonce   announcement, notification
demander par annonce   to advertise for
un annonceur   advertiser, announcer, speaker
un annoncier, une annoncière   advertising
   manager

See also **prononcer**.

s'annoncer bien   to look promising;
   Cela s'annonce bien   That looks promising
les petites annonces d'un journal   newspaper
   classified advertisements
s'annoncer   to announce (introduce) oneself

Note that **annoncer** can also mean to predict (weather, event): **J'ai amené mon parapluie parce qu'ils avaient annoncé de la pluie.**

36

The Seven Simple Tenses		The Seven Compound Tenses	
Singular	Plural	Singular	Plural
1 présent de l'indicatif		**8 passé composé**	
aperçois	apercevons	ai aperçu	avons aperçu
aperçois	apercevez	as aperçu	avez aperçu
aperçoit	aperçoivent	a aperçu	ont aperçu
2 imparfait de l'indicatif		**9 plus-que-parfait de l'indicatif**	
apercevais	apercevions	avais aperçu	avions aperçu
apercevais	aperceviez	avais aperçu	aviez aperçu
apercevait	apercevaient	avait aperçu	avaient aperçu
3 passé simple		**10 passé antérieur**	
aperçus	aperçûmes	eus aperçu	eûmes aperçu
aperçus	aperçûtes	eus aperçu	eûtes aperçu
aperçut	aperçurent	eut aperçu	eurent aperçu
4 futur		**11 futur antérieur**	
apercevrai	apercevrons	aurai aperçu	aurons aperçu
apercevras	apercevrez	auras aperçu	aurez aperçu
apercevra	apercevront	aura aperçu	auront aperçu
5 conditionnel		**12 conditionnel passé**	
apercevrais	apercevrions	aurais aperçu	aurions aperçu
apercevrais	apercevriez	aurais aperçu	auriez aperçu
apercevrait	apercevraient	aurait aperçu	auraient aperçu
6 présent du subjonctif		**13 passé du subjonctif**	
aperçoive	apercevions	aie aperçu	ayons aperçu
aperçoives	aperceviez	aies aperçu	ayez aperçu
aperçoive	aperçoivent	ait aperçu	aient aperçu
7 imparfait du subjonctif		**14 plus-que-parfait du subjonctif**	
aperçusse	aperçussions	eusse aperçu	eussions aperçu
aperçusses	aperçussiez	eusse aperçu	eussiez aperçu
aperçût	aperçussent	eût aperçu	eussent aperçu

Impératif
aperçois
apercevons
apercevez

Words and expressions related to this verb
sans s'en apercevoir without taking any notice (of it)
la perception perception, collection (tax)
perceptiblement perceptibly
à peine perceptible scarcely perceptible
un aperçu glimpse, glance, outline

s'apercevoir de to become aware of, to notice
la perceptibilité perceptibility
perceptif, perceptive perceptive
entr'apercevoir to glimpse
percevoir to perceive, to sense

Consult the sections on verbs used in idiomatic expressions, verbs with prepositions, and the list of over 1,100 verbs conjugated like model verbs in the back pages.

apparaître

Part. pr. **apparaissant**   Part. passé **apparu**

to appear

The Seven Simple Tenses		The Seven Compound Tenses	
Singular	Plural	Singular	Plural
1 présent de l'indicatif		8 passé composé	
apparais	**apparaissons**	**ai apparu**	**avons apparu**
apparais	**apparaissez**	**as apparu**	**avez apparu**
apparaît	**apparaissent**	**a apparu**	**ont apparu**
2 imparfait de l'indicatif		9 plus-que-parfait de l'indicatif	
apparaissais	**apparaissions**	**avais apparu**	**avions apparu**
apparaissais	**apparaissiez**	**avais apparu**	**aviez apparu**
apparaissait	**apparaissaient**	**avait apparu**	**avaient apparu**
3 passé simple		10 passé antérieur	
apparus	**apparûmes**	**eus apparu**	**eûmes apparu**
apparus	**apparûtes**	**eus apparu**	**eûtes apparu**
apparut	**apparurent**	**eut apparu**	**eurent apparu**
4 futur		11 futur antérieur	
apparaîtrai	**apparaîtrons**	**aurai apparu**	**aurons apparu**
apparaîtras	**apparaîtrez**	**auras apparu**	**aurez apparu**
apparaîtra	**apparaîtront**	**aura apparu**	**auront apparu**
5 conditionnel		12 conditionnel passé	
apparaîtrais	**apparaîtrions**	**aurais apparu**	**aurions apparu**
apparaîtrais	**apparaîtriez**	**aurais apparu**	**auriez apparu**
apparaîtrait	**apparaîtraient**	**aurait apparu**	**auraient apparu**
6 présent du subjonctif		13 passé du subjonctif	
apparaisse	**apparaissions**	**aie apparu**	**ayons apparu**
apparaisses	**apparaissiez**	**aies apparu**	**ayez apparu**
apparaisse	**apparaissent**	**ait apparu**	**aient apparu**
7 imparfait du subjonctif		14 plus-que-parfait du subjonctif	
apparusse	**apparussions**	**eusse apparu**	**eussions apparu**
apparusses	**apparussiez**	**eusses apparu**	**eussiez apparu**
apparût	**apparussent**	**eût apparu**	**eussent apparu**

Impératif
apparais
apparaissons
apparaissez

Words and expressions related to this verb

apparemment   apparently
apparent, apparente   apparent
contre toute apparence   contrary to all
   appearances
l'apparition d'un livre   the appearance
   (publication) of a new book; **vient de
   paraître**   just published

une apparition   apparition
une apparence   appearance
en apparence   in appearance, seemingly
sauver les apparences   to save face, to keep
   up appearances
juger d'après les apparences   to judge by
   appearances

See also **paraître**, **disparaître**, and **reparaître**.

Grammar putting you in a tense mood? Review the definitions of basic grammatical terms with examples on pages 674–688.

The Seven Simple Tenses		The Seven Compound Tenses	
Singular	Plural	Singular	Plural

1 présent de l'indicatif

appartiens	appartenons		
appartiens	appartenez		
appartient	appartiennent		

8 passé composé

ai appartenu	avons appartenu
as appartenu	avez appartenu
a appartenu	ont appartenu

2 imparfait de l'indicatif

appartenais	appartenions
appartenais	apparteniez
appartenait	appartenaient

9 plus-que-parfait de l'indicatif

avais appartenu	avions appartenu
avais appartenu	aviez appartenu
avait appartenu	avaient appartenu

3 passé simple

appartins	appartînmes
appartins	appartîntes
appartint	appartinrent

10 passé antérieur

eus appartenu	eûmes appartenu
eus appartenu	eûtes appartenu
eut appartenu	eurent appartenu

4 futur

appartiendrai	appartiendrons
appartiendras	appartiendrez
appartiendra	appartiendront

11 futur antérieur

aurai appartenu	aurons appartenu
auras appartenu	aurez appartenu
aura appartenu	auront appartenu

5 conditionnel

appartiendrais	appartiendrions
appartiendrais	appartiendriez
appartiendrait	appartiendraient

12 conditionnel passé

aurais appartenu	aurions appartenu
aurais appartenu	auriez appartenu
aurait appartenu	auraient appartenu

6 présent du subjonctif

appartienne	appartenions
appartiennes	apparteniez
appartienne	appartiennent

13 passé du subjonctif

aie appartenu	ayons appartenu
aies appartenu	ayez appartenu
ait appartenu	aient appartenu

7 imparfait du subjonctif

appartinsse	appartinssions
appartinsses	appartinssiez
appartînt	appartinssent

14 plus-que-parfait du subjonctif

eusse appartenu	eussions appartenu
eusses appartenu	eussiez appartenu
eût appartenu	eussent appartenu

Impératif
appartiens
appartenons
appartenez

Words and expressions related to this verb
appartenir à to belong to, to pertain to, to appertain to
Il appartient que ... It is fitting that ...
appartenir à qqn de + inf. to behoove someone to; **Il lui appartient de dire la vérité.**
une appartenance appurtenance; **appartenant, appartenante** appertaining, belonging

un sentiment d'appartenance feeling of belonging
A TOUS CEUX QU'IL APPARTIENDRA TO WHOM IT MAY CONCERN
s'appartenir to be independent
appartenir à qqn de faire qqch to be up to someone to do something

Get acquainted with what preposition goes with what verb on pages 543–553.

appeler

to call, to name, to appeal

The Seven Simple Tenses		The Seven Compound Tenses	
Singular	Plural	Singular	Plural
1 présent de l'indicatif		**8 passé composé**	
appelle	appelons	ai appelé	avons appelé
appelles	appelez	as appelé	avez appelé
appelle	appellent	a appelé	ont appelé
2 imparfait de l'indicatif		**9 plus-que-parfait de l'indicatif**	
appelais	appelions	avais appelé	avions appelé
appelais	appeliez	avais appelé	aviez appelé
appelait	appelaient	avait appelé	avaient appelé
3 passé simple		**10 passé antérieur**	
appelai	appelâmes	eus appelé	eûmes appelé
appelas	appelâtes	eus appelé	eûtes appelé
appela	appelèrent	eut appelé	eurent appelé
4 futur		**11 futur antérieur**	
appellerai	appellerons	aurai appelé	aurons appelé
appelleras	appellerez	auras appelé	aurez appelé
appellera	appelleront	aura appelé	auront appelé
5 conditionnel		**12 conditionnel passé**	
appellerais	appellerions	aurais appelé	aurions appelé
appellerais	appelleriez	aurais appelé	auriez appelé
appellerait	appelleraient	aurait appelé	auraient appelé
6 présent du subjonctif		**13 passé du subjonctif**	
appelle	appelions	aie appelé	ayons appelé
appelles	appeliez	aies appelé	ayez appelé
appelle	appellent	ait appelé	aient appelé
7 imparfait du subjonctif		**14 plus-que-parfait du subjonctif**	
appelasse	appelassions	eusse appelé	eussions appelé
appelasses	appelassiez	eusses appelé	eussiez appelé
appelât	appelassent	eût appelé	eussent appelé

Impératif
appelle
appelons
appelez

Sentences using this verb and words related to it

Madame Dubois va appeler le médecin parce qu'elle ne va pas bien aujourd'hui.
—**As-tu appelé le docteur, chérie? lui demande son mari.**
—**Non, mon chéri—répond sa femme. Je souffre. Veux-tu l'appeler, s'il te plaît?**

une appellation   appellation; **un appel**
    appeal, call
en appeler à qqn   to appeal to someone
rappeler   to call back, to remind, to recall
appellation contrôlée   French government
    approval of the quality of a wine or cheese

un appel   call; **appel téléphonique**
    telephone call; **faire l'appel**   to call the roll
faire un appel de phares   to flash the high
    beams (of a vehicle)

See also s'**appeler** on p. 41.

to be named, to call oneself

The Seven Simple Tenses		The Seven Compound Tenses	
Singular	Plural	Singular	Plural
1 présent de l'indicatif		8 passé composé	
m'appelle	nous appelons	me suis appelé(e)	nous sommes appelé(e)s
t'appelles	vous appelez	t'es appelé(e)	vous êtes appelé(e)(s)
s'appelle	s'appellent	s'est appelé(e)	se sont appelé(e)s
2 imparfait de l'indicatif		9 plus-que-parfait de l'indicatif	
m'appelais	nous appelions	m'étais appelé(e)	nous étions appelé(e)s
t'appelais	vous appeliez	t'étais appelé(e)	vous étiez appelé(e)(s)
s'appelait	s'appelaient	s'était appelé(e)	s'étaient appelé(e)s
3 passé simple		10 passé antérieur	
m'appelai	nous appelâmes	me fus appelé(e)	nous fûmes appelé(e)s
t'appelas	vous appelâtes	te fus appelé(e)	vous fûtes appelé(e)(s)
s'appela	s'appelèrent	se fut appelé(e)	se furent appelé(e)s
4 futur		11 futur antérieur	
m'appellerai	nous appellerons	me serai appelé(e)	nous serons appelé(e)s
t'appelleras	vous appellerez	te seras appelé(e)	vous serez appelé(e)(s)
s'appellera	s'appelleront	se sera appelé(e)	se seront appelé(e)s
5 conditionnel		12 conditionnel passé	
m'appellerais	nous appellerions	me serais appelé(e)	nous serions appelé(e)s
t'appellerais	vous appelleriez	te serais appelé(e)	vous seriez appelé(e)(s)
s'appellerait	s'appelleraient	se serait appelé(e)	se seraient appelé(e)s
6 présent du subjonctif		13 passé du subjonctif	
m'appelle	nous appelions	me sois appelé(e)	nous soyons appelé(e)s
t'appelles	vous appeliez	te sois appelé(e)	vous soyez appelé(e)(s)
s'appelle	s'appellent	se soit appelé(e)	se soient appelé(e)s
7 imparfait du subjonctif		14 plus-que-parfait du subjonctif	
m'appelasse	nous appelassions	me fusse appelé(e)	nous fussions appelé(e)s
t'appelasses	vous appelassiez	te fusses appelé(e)	vous fussiez appelé(e)(s)
s'appelât	s'appelassent	se fût appelé(e)	se fussent appelé(e)s

Impératif
appelle-toi; ne t'appelle pas
appelons-nous; ne nous appelons pas
appelez-vous; ne vous appelez pas

Sentences using this verb and words related to it
—**Bonjour, mon enfant. Comment t'appelles-tu?**
—**Je m'appelle Henri.**
—**As-tu des frères et des soeurs?**
—**Oui, j'ai deux frères et trois soeurs. Ils s'appellent Joseph, Bernard, Thérèse, Paulette, et Andrée.**

For other words and expressions related to this verb, see **appeler, rappeler,** and se **rappeler.**

Note: The *l* in **s'appeler** is doubled (*ll*) when stress falls on the syllable.

Don't miss orthographically changing verbs on pages 554–556.

apporter
Part. pr. **apportant**   Part. passé **apporté**

to bring, to bear

The Seven Simple Tenses		The Seven Compound Tenses	
Singular	Plural	Singular	Plural
1 présent de l'indicatif		**8 passé composé**	
apporte	apportons	ai apporté	avons apporté
apportes	apportez	as apporté	avez apporté
apporte	apportent	a apporté	ont apporté
2 imparfait de l'indicatif		**9 plus-que-parfait de l'indicatif**	
apportais	apportions	avais apporté	avions apporté
apportais	apportiez	avais apporté	aviez apporté
apportait	apportaient	avait apporté	avaient apporté
3 passé simple		**10 passé antérieur**	
apportai	apportâmes	eus apporté	eûmes apporté
apportas	apportâtes	eus apporté	eûtes apporté
apporta	apportèrent	eut apporté	eurent apporté
4 futur		**11 futur antérieur**	
apporterai	apporterons	aurai apporté	aurons apporté
apporteras	apporterez	auras apporté	aurez apporté
apportera	apporteront	aura apporté	auront apporté
5 conditionnel		**12 conditionnel passé**	
apporterais	apporterions	aurais apporté	aurions apporté
apporterais	apporteriez	aurais apporté	auriez apporté
apporterait	apporteraient	aurait apporté	auraient apporté
6 présent du subjonctif		**13 passé du subjonctif**	
apporte	apportions	aie apporté	ayons apporté
apportes	apportiez	aies apporté	ayez apporté
apporte	apportent	ait apporté	aient apporté
7 imparfait du subjonctif		**14 plus-que-parfait du subjonctif**	
apportasse	apportassions	eusse apporté	eussions apporté
apportasses	apportassiez	eusses apporté	eussiez apporté
apportât	apportassent	eût apporté	eussent apporté

Impératif
apporte
apportons
apportez

Sentences using this verb and words related to it

    Hier soir, j'ai dîné dans un restaurant français. Quand le garçon m'a apporté mon repas, je lui ai dit:—Apportez-moi du pain, aussi, s'il vous plaît et n'oubliez pas de m'apporter un verre de vin rouge.

    —Tout de suite, monsieur—il m'a répondu. Voulez-vous que je vous apporte l'addition maintenant ou après le dîner? Aimez-vous la salade que je vous ai apportée?

un apport   something brought; **un apport dotal**   wife's dowry
un apporteur   a person who brings something (usually news); **un apporteur de bonnes nouvelles**
    bearer of good news

See also **porter** and **supporter.**

The Seven Simple Tenses		The Seven Compound Tenses	
Singular	Plural	Singular	Plural

1 présent de l'indicatif		8 passé composé	
apprends	apprenons	ai appris	avons appris
apprends	apprenez	as appris	avez appris
apprend	apprennent	a appris	ont appris

2 imparfait de l'indicatif		9 plus-que-parfait de l'indicatif	
apprenais	apprenions	avais appris	avions appris
apprenais	appreniez	avais appris	aviez appris
apprenait	apprenaient	avait appris	avaient appris

3 passé simple		10 passé antérieur	
appris	apprîmes	eus appris	eûmes appris
appris	apprîtes	eus appris	eûtes appris
apprit	apprirent	eut appris	eurent appris

4 futur		11 futur antérieur	
apprendrai	apprendrons	aurai appris	aurons appris
apprendras	apprendrez	auras appris	aurez appris
apprendra	apprendront	aura appris	auront appris

5 conditionnel		12 conditionnel passé	
apprendrais	apprendrions	aurais appris	aurions appris
apprendrais	apprendriez	aurais appris	auriez appris
apprendrait	apprendraient	aurait appris	auraient appris

6 présent du subjonctif		13 passé du subjonctif	
apprenne	apprenions	aie appris	ayons appris
apprennes	appreniez	aies appris	ayez appris
apprenne	apprennent	ait appris	aient appris

7 imparfait du subjonctif		14 plus-que-parfait du subjonctif	
apprisse	apprissions	eusse appris	eussions appris
apprisses	apprissiez	eusses appris	eussiez appris
apprît	apprissent	eût appris	eussent appris

Impératif
apprends
apprenons
apprenez

Common idiomatic expressions using this verb

A l'école j'apprends à lire en français. J'apprends à écrire et à parler. Ce matin mon maître de français m'a dit:—Robert, apprends ce poème par coeur pour demain.

La semaine dernière j'ai appris un poème de Verlaine. Pour demain j'apprendrai la conjugaison du verbe *apprendre*.

apprendre par coeur   to memorize
apprendre à qqn à faire qqch   to teach somebody to do something
apprendre qqch à qqn   to inform someone of something; to teach someone something
apprendre à faire qqch   to learn to do something
un apprentissage   apprenticeship

See also **comprendre, entreprendre, se méprendre, prendre, reprendre,** and **surprendre.**

to approach, to come near, to bring near

The Seven Simple Tenses		The Seven Compound Tenses	
Singular	Plural	Singular	Plural
1 présent de l'indicatif		8 passé composé	
approche	approchons	ai approché	avons approché
approches	approchez	as approché	avez approché
approche	approchent	a approché	ont approché
2 imparfait de l'indicatif		9 plus-que-parfait de l'indicatif	
approchais	approchions	avais approché	avions approché
approchais	approchiez	avais approché	aviez approché
approchait	approchaient	avait approché	avaient approché
3 passé simple		10 passé antérieur	
approchai	approchâmes	eus approché	eûmes approché
approchas	approchâtes	eus approché	eûtes approché
approcha	approchèrent	eut approché	eurent approché
4 futur		11 futur antérieur	
approcherai	approcherons	aurai approché	aurons approché
approcheras	approcherez	auras approché	aurez approché
approchera	approcheront	aura approché	auront approché
5 conditionnel		12 conditionnel passé	
approcherais	approcherions	aurais approché	aurions approché
approcherais	approcheriez	aurais approché	auriez approché
approcherait	approcheraient	aurait approché	auraient approché
6 présent du subjonctif		13 passé du subjonctif	
approche	approchions	aie approché	ayons approché
approches	approchiez	aies approché	ayez approché
approche	approchent	ait approché	aient approché
7 imparfait du subjonctif		14 plus-que-parfait du subjonctif	
approchasse	approchassions	eusse approché	eussions approché
approchasses	approchassiez	eusses approché	eussiez approché
approchât	approchassent	eût approché	eussent approché

Impératif
approche
approchons
approchez

Words and expressions related to this verb
s'approcher de qqn ou qqch   to approach someone or something
se rapprocher de   to come closer to
rapprocher   to bring closer, nearer
reprocher qqch à qqn   to reproach someone with something; **un reproche**   reproach; **faire des reproches à**   to reproach; **sans reproche**   without blame, blameless
proche   close, near; **la pharmacie la plus proche**   the nearest pharmacy
prochain, prochaine   next; **la semaine prochaine**   next week; **la prochaine fois**   the next time

Consult the sections on verbs used in idiomatic expressions, verbs with prepositions, and the list of over 1,100 verbs conjugated like model verbs in the back pages.

The Seven Simple Tenses		The Seven Compound Tenses	
Singular	Plural	Singular	Plural
1 présent de l'indicatif		**8 passé composé**	
approuve	**approuvons**	**ai approuvé**	**avons approuvé**
approuves	**approuvez**	**as approuvé**	**avez approuvé**
approuve	**approuvent**	**a approuvé**	**ont approuvé**
2 imparfait de l'indicatif		**9 plus-que-parfait de l'indicatif**	
approuvais	**approuvions**	**avais approuvé**	**avions approuvé**
approuvais	**approuviez**	**avais approuvé**	**aviez approuvé**
approuvait	**approuvaient**	**avait approuvé**	**avaient approuvé**
3 passé simple		**10 passé antérieur**	
approuvai	**approuvâmes**	**eus approuvé**	**eûmes approuvé**
approuvas	**approuvâtes**	**eus approuvé**	**eûtes approuvé**
approuva	**approuvèrent**	**eut approuvé**	**eurent approuvé**
4 futur		**11 futur antérieur**	
approuverai	**approuverons**	**aurai approuvé**	**aurons approuvé**
approuveras	**approuverez**	**auras approuvé**	**aurez approuvé**
approuvera	**approuveront**	**aura approuvé**	**auront approuvé**
5 conditionnel		**12 conditionnel passé**	
approuverais	**approuverions**	**aurais approuvé**	**aurions approuvé**
approuverais	**approuveriez**	**aurais approuvé**	**auriez approuvé**
approuverait	**approuveraient**	**aurait approuvé**	**auraient approuvé**
6 présent du subjonctif		**13 passé du subjonctif**	
approuve	**approuvions**	**aie approuvé**	**ayons approuvé**
approuves	**approuviez**	**aies approuvé**	**ayez approuvé**
approuve	**approuvent**	**ait approuvé**	**aient approuvé**
7 imparfait du subjonctif		**14 plus-que-parfait du subjonctif**	
approuvasse	**approuvassions**	**eusse approuvé**	**eussions approuvé**
approuvasses	**approuvassiez**	**eusses approuvé**	**eussiez approuvé**
approuvât	**approuvassent**	**eût approuvé**	**eussent approuvé**

Impératif
approuve
approuvons
approuvez

Words and expressions related to this verb
approuver qqn de faire qqch to approve of someone's doing something
acheter à condition to buy on approval
avec approbation approvingly
la désapprobation disapproval, disapprobation

J'approuve votre décision de continuer l'étude de la langue française.
l'approbation *f.* approval
un approbateur, une approbatrice approver
désapprouver to disapprove, to disapprove of

See also **éprouver** and **prouver**.

Soak up some verbs used in weather expressions on pages 557 and 558.

to pull up, to pull out, to uproot

The Seven Simple Tenses		The Seven Compound Tenses	
Singular	Plural	Singular	Plural
1 présent de l'indicatif		**8 passé composé**	
arrache	arrachons	ai arraché	avons arraché
arraches	arrachez	as arraché	avez arraché
arrache	arrachent	a arraché	ont arraché
2 imparfait de l'indicatif		**9 plus-que-parfait de l'indicatif**	
arrachais	arrachions	avais arraché	avions arraché
arrachais	arrachiez	avais arraché	aviez arraché
arrachait	arrachaient	avait arraché	avaient arraché
3 passé simple		**10 passé antérieur**	
arrachai	arrachâmes	eus arraché	eûmes arraché
arrachas	arrachâtes	eus arraché	eûtes arraché
arracha	arrachèrent	eut arraché	eurent arraché
4 futur		**11 futur antérieur**	
arracherai	arracherons	aurai arraché	aurons arraché
arracheras	arracherez	auras arraché	aurez arraché
arrachera	arracheront	aura arraché	auront arraché
5 conditionnel		**12 conditionnel passé**	
arracherais	arracherions	aurais arraché	aurions arraché
arracherais	arracheriez	aurais arraché	auriez arraché
arracherait	arracheraient	aurait arraché	auraient arraché
6 présent du subjonctif		**13 passé du subjonctif**	
arrache	arrachions	aie arraché	ayons arraché
arraches	arrachiez	aies arraché	ayez arraché
arrache	arrachent	ait arraché	aient arraché
7 imparfait du subjonctif		**14 plus-que-parfait du subjonctif**	
arrachasse	arrachassions	eusse arraché	eussions arraché
arrachasses	arrachassiez	eusses arraché	eussiez arraché
arrachât	arrachassent	eût arraché	eussent arraché

Impératif
arrache
arrachons
arrachez

Common idiomatic expressions using this verb and words related to it
arracher qqch des mains de qqn   to grab something out of someone's hands
faire qqch d'arrache-pied   to do something without interruption
s'arracher à   to tear oneself away from
un arrache-clou   nail puller (extractor) (**des arrache-clous**)
s'arracher les yeux   to have a violent quarrel (to scratch each other's eyes out)
d'arrache-pied   relentlessly

How are you doing? Find out with the verb drills and tests with answers explained on pages
622–673.

The Seven Simple Tenses		The Seven Compound Tenses	
Singular	Plural	Singular	Plural
1 présent de l'indicatif		8 passé composé	
arrange	arrangeons	ai arrangé	avons arrangé
arranges	arrangez	as arrangé	avez arrangé
arrange	arrangent	a arrangé	ont arrangé
2 imparfait de l'indicatif		9 plus-que-parfait de l'indicatif	
arrangeais	arrangions	avais arrangé	avions arrangé
arrangeais	arrangiez	avais arrangé	aviez arrangé
arrangeait	arrangeaient	avait arrangé	avaient arrangé
3 passé simple		10 passé antérieur	
arrangeai	arrangeâmes	eus arrangé	eûmes arrangé
arrangeas	arrangeâtes	eus arrangé	eûtes arrangé
arrangea	arrangèrent	eut arrangé	eurent arrangé
4 futur		11 futur antérieur	
arrangerai	arrangerons	aurai arrangé	aurons arrangé
arrangeras	arrangerez	auras arrangé	aurez arrangé
arrangera	arrangeront	aura arrangé	auront arrangé
5 conditionnel		12 conditionnel passé	
arrangerais	arrangerions	aurais arrangé	aurions arrangé
arrangerais	arrangeriez	aurais arrangé	auriez arrangé
arrangerait	arrangeraient	aurait arrangé	auraient arrangé
6 présent du subjonctif		13 passé du subjonctif	
arrange	arrangions	aie arrangé	ayons arrangé
arranges	arrangiez	aies arrangé	ayez arrangé
arrange	arrangent	ait arrangé	aient arrangé
7 imparfait du subjonctif		14 plus-que-parfait du subjonctif	
arrangeasse	arrangeassions	eusse arrangé	eussions arrangé
arrangeasses	arrangeassiez	eusses arrangé	eussiez arrangé
arrangeât	arrangeassent	eût arrangé	eussent arrangé

Impératif
arrange
arrangeons
arrangez

Sentences using this verb and words related to it

J'aime beaucoup un joli arrangement de fleurs. Aimez-vous les fleurs que j'ai arrangées dans ce vase? Les Japonais savent bien arranger les fleurs. Quand mon père apporte des fleurs à ma mère, nous les arrangeons dans un joli vase.

arranger qqch   to arrange, contrive something
arranger l'affaire   to straighten out a matter
s'arranger   to come to an agreement

arranger qqn   to accommodate, suit someone;
Ça m'arrange bien   That suits me fine; **Ça s'arrangera**   It will turn out all right.

Want to learn more idiomatic expressions that contain verbs? Look at pages 530–542.

The subject pronouns are found on the page facing page 1.

arrêter

Part. pr. **arrêtant**   Part. passé **arrêté**

to arrest, to stop (someone or something), to halt

The Seven Simple Tenses		The Seven Compound Tenses	
Singular	Plural	Singular	Plural
1 présent de l'indicatif		**8 passé composé**	
arrête	arrêtons	ai arrêté	avons arrêté
arrêtes	arrêtez	as arrêté	avez arrêté
arrête	arrêtent	a arrêté	ont arrêté
2 imparfait de l'indicatif		**9 plus-que-parfait de l'indicatif**	
arrêtais	arrêtions	avais arrêté	avions arrêté
arrêtais	arrêtiez	avais arrêté	aviez arrêté
arrêtait	arrêtaient	avait arrêté	avaient arrêté
3 passé simple		**10 passé antérieur**	
arrêtai	arrêtâmes	eus arrêté	eûmes arrêté
arrêtas	arrêtâtes	eus arrêté	eûtes arrêté
arrêta	arrêtèrent	eut arrêté	eurent arrêté
4 futur		**11 futur antérieur**	
arrêterai	arrêterons	aurai arrêté	aurons arrêté
arrêteras	arrêterez	auras arrêté	aurez arrêté
arrêtera	arrêteront	aura arrêté	auront arrêté
5 conditionnel		**12 conditionnel passé**	
arrêterais	arrêterions	aurais arrêté	aurions arrêté
arrêterais	arrêteriez	aurais arrêté	auriez arrêté
arrêterait	arrêteraient	aurait arrêté	auraient arrêté
6 présent du subjonctif		**13 passé du subjonctif**	
arrête	arrêtions	aie arrêté	ayons arrêté
arrêtes	arrêtiez	aies arrêté	ayez arrêté
arrête	arrêtent	ait arrêté	aient arrêté
7 imparfait du subjonctif		**14 plus-que-parfait du subjonctif**	
arrêtasse	arrêtassions	eusse arrêté	eussions arrêté
arrêtasses	arrêtassiez	eusses arrêté	eussiez arrêté
arrêtât	arrêtassent	eût arrêté	eussent arrêté

Impératif
arrête
arrêtons
arrêtez

Sentences using this verb and words related to it

L'agent de police a arrêté les voitures pour laisser les piétons traverser la rue. Il a crié:— Arrêtez! Arrêtez!

un arrêt   halt, stop, arrest; **sans arrêt**   continually
arrêt d'autobus   bus stop
un arrêté ministériel   decree
arrêter qqn de faire qqch   to stop someone from doing something
une arrestation   arrest, apprehension; **être en état d'arrestation**   to be under arrest
arrêter un jour   to set a date; **arrêter un marché**   to make a deal

See also **s'arrêter.**

to stop (oneself, itself), to pause

The Seven Simple Tenses		The Seven Compound Tenses	
Singular	Plural	Singular	Plural
1 présent de l'indicatif		**8 passé composé**	
m'arrête	**nous arrêtons**	**me suis arrêté(e)**	**nous sommes arrêté(e)s**
t'arrêtes	**vous arrêtez**	**t'es arrêté(e)**	**vous êtes arrêté(e)(s)**
s'arrête	**s'arrêtent**	**s'est arrêté(e)**	**se sont arrêté(e)s**
2 imparfait de l'indicatif		**9 plus-que-parfait de l'indicatif**	
m'arrêtais	**nous arrêtions**	**m'étais arrêté(e)**	**nous étions arrêté(e)s**
t'arrêtais	**vous arrêtiez**	**t'étais arrêté(e)**	**vous étiez arrêté(e)(s)**
s'arrêtait	**s'arrêtaient**	**s'était arrêté(e)**	**s'étaient arrêté(e)s**
3 passé simple		**10 passé antérieur**	
m'arrêtai	**nous arrêtâmes**	**me fus arrêté(e)**	**nous fûmes arrêté(e)s**
t'arrêtas	**vous arrêtâtes**	**te fus arrêté(e)**	**vous fûtes arrêté(e)(s)**
s'arrêta	**s'arrêtèrent**	**se fut arrêté(e)**	**se furent arrêté(e)s**
4 futur		**11 futur antérieur**	
m'arrêterai	**nous arrêterons**	**me serai arrêté(e)**	**nous serons arrêté(e)s**
t'arrêteras	**vous arrêterez**	**te seras arrêté(e)**	**vous serez arrêté(e)(s)**
s'arrêtera	**s'arrêteront**	**se sera arrêté(e)**	**se seront arrêté(e)s**
5 conditionnel		**12 conditionnel passé**	
m'arrêterais	**nous arrêterions**	**me serais arrêté(e)**	**nous serions arrêté(e)s**
t'arrêterais	**vous arrêteriez**	**te serais arrêté(e)**	**vous seriez arrêté(e)(s)**
s'arrêterait	**s'arrêteraient**	**se serait arrêté(e)**	**se seraient arrêté(e)s**
6 présent du subjonctif		**13 passé du subjonctif**	
m'arrête	**nous arrêtions**	**me sois arrêté(e)**	**nous soyons arrêté(e)s**
t'arrêtes	**vous arrêtiez**	**te sois arrêté(e)**	**vous soyez arrêté(e)(s)**
s'arrête	**s'arrêtent**	**se soit arrêté(e)**	**se soient arrêté(e)s**
7 imparfait du subjonctif		**14 plus-que-parfait du subjonctif**	
m'arrêtasse	**nous arrêtassions**	**me fusse arrêté(e)**	**nous fussions arrêté(e)s**
t'arrêtasses	**vous arrêtassiez**	**te fusses arrêté(e)**	**vous fussiez arrêté(e)(s)**
s'arrêtât	**s'arrêtassent**	**se fût arrêté(e)**	**se fussent arrêté(e)s**

Impératif
arrête-toi; ne t'arrête pas
arrêtons-nous; ne nous arrêtons pas
arrêtez-vous; ne vous arrêtez pas

Sentences using this verb and words related to it
   Madame Dumont **s'est arrêtée** devant une pâtisserie pour acheter une belle tarte aux cerises. Deux autres dames **se sont arrêtées** derrière elle et les trois sont entrées dans le magasin.

s'arrêter de faire qqch   to desist from doing something
s'arrêter de fumer   to stop smoking

See also **arrêter.**

sans s'arrêter   without stopping
Madame Martin s'est arrêtée pour se reposer   Mrs. Martin stopped to rest.

Use the EE-zee guide to French pronunciation on pages 566 and 567.

arriver

Part. pr. **arrivant**   Part. passé **arrivé(e)(s)**

to arrive, to happen

The Seven Simple Tenses		The Seven Compound Tenses	
Singular	Plural	Singular	Plural
1 présent de l'indicatif		8 passé composé	
arrive	**arrivons**	**suis arrivé(e)**	**sommes arrivé(e)s**
arrives	**arrivez**	**es arrivé(e)**	**êtes arrivé(e)(s)**
arrive	**arrivent**	**est arrivé(e)**	**sont arrivé(e)s**
2 imparfait de l'indicatif		9 plus-que-parfait de l'indicatif	
arrivais	**arrivions**	**étais arrivé(e)**	**étions arrivé(e)s**
arrivais	**arriviez**	**étais arrivé(e)**	**étiez arrivé(e)(s)**
arrivait	**arrivaient**	**était arrivé(e)**	**étaient arrivé(e)s**
3 passé simple		10 passé antérieur	
arrivai	**arrivâmes**	**fus arrivé(e)**	**fûmes arrivé(e)s**
arrivas	**arrivâtes**	**fus arrivé(e)**	**fûtes arrivé(e)(s)**
arriva	**arrivèrent**	**fut arrivé(e)**	**furent arrivé(e)s**
4 futur		11 futur antérieur	
arriverai	**arriverons**	**serai arrivé(e)**	**serons arrivé(e)s**
arriveras	**arriverez**	**seras arrivé(e)**	**serez arrivé(e)(s)**
arrivera	**arriveront**	**sera arrivé(e)**	**seront arrivé(e)s**
5 conditionnel		12 conditionnel passé	
arriverais	**arriverions**	**serais arrivé(e)**	**serions arrivé(e)s**
arriverais	**arriveriez**	**serais arrivé(e)**	**seriez arrivé(e)(s)**
arriverait	**arriveraient**	**serait arrivé(e)**	**seraient arrivé(e)s**
6 présent du subjonctif		13 passé du subjonctif	
arrive	**arrivions**	**sois arrivé(e)**	**soyons arrivé(e)s**
arrives	**arriviez**	**sois arrivé(e)**	**soyez arrivé(e)(s)**
arrive	**arrivent**	**soit arrivé(e)**	**soient arrivé(e)s**
7 imparfait du subjonctif		14 plus-que-parfait du subjonctif	
arrivasse	**arrivassions**	**fusse arrivé(e)**	**fussions arrivé(e)s**
arrivasses	**arrivassiez**	**fusses arrivé(e)**	**fussiez arrivé(e)(s)**
arrivât	**arrivassent**	**fût arrivé(e)**	**fussent arrivé(e)s**

Impératif
arrive
arrivons
arrivez

Sentences using this verb and words related to it

Paulette est arrivée à la gare à deux heures. Le train pour Paris arrivera à trois heures. Elle passera une heure dans la salle d'attente. Après quelques minutes, elle voit beaucoup de personnes qui courent frénétiquement. Elle n'arrive pas à comprendre ce qui se passe.
—**Qu'est-ce qui arrive?** elle demande.
—**Il y a eu un accident!** on lui répond.

arriver à faire qqch   to succeed in + pres. part.; to manage to do something
arriver à   to happen to; **Cela n'arrive qu'à moi!**   It's just my luck! That would happen to me!
J'arrive!   I'm coming!

Want to learn more idiomatic expressions that contain verbs? Look at pages 530–542.

The Seven Simple Tenses		The Seven Compound Tenses	
Singular	Plural	Singular	Plural

1 présent de l'indicatif

m'assieds	**nous asseyons**	**me suis assis(e)**	**nous sommes assis(es)**
t'assieds	**vous asseyez**	**t'es assis(e)**	**vous êtes assis(e)(es)**
s'assied	**s'asseyent**	**s'est assis(e)**	**se sont assis(es)**

8 passé composé appears beside présent de l'indicatif.

2 imparfait de l'indicatif   **9 plus-que-parfait de l'indicatif**

m'asseyais	**nous asseyions**	**m'étais assis(e)**	**nous étions assis(es)**
t'asseyais	**vous asseyiez**	**t'étais assis(e)**	**vous étiez assis(e)(es)**
s'asseyait	**s'asseyaient**	**s'était assis(e)**	**s'étaient assis(es)**

3 passé simple   **10 passé antérieur**

m'assis	**nous assîmes**	**me fus assis(e)**	**nous fûmes assis(es)**
t'assis	**vous assîtes**	**te fus assis(e)**	**vous fûtes assis(e)(es)**
s'assit	**s'assirent**	**se fut assis(e)**	**se furent assis(es)**

4 futur   **11 futur antérieur**

m'assiérai	**nous assiérons**	**me serai assis(e)**	**nous serons assis(es)**
t'assiéras	**vous assiérez**	**te seras assis(e)**	**vous serez assis(e)(es)**
s'assiéra	**s'assiéront**	**se sera assis(e)**	**se seront assis(es)**

5 conditionnel   **12 conditionnel passé**

m'assiérais	**nous assiérions**	**me serais assis(e)**	**nous serions assis(es)**
t'assiérais	**vous assiériez**	**te serais assis(e)**	**vous seriez assis(e)(es)**
s'assiérait	**s'assiéraient**	**se serait assis(e)**	**se seraient assis(es)**

6 présent du subjonctif   **13 passé du subjonctif**

m'asseye	**nous asseyions**	**me sois assis(e)**	**nous soyons assis(es)**
t'asseyes	**vous asseyiez**	**te sois assis(e)**	**vous soyez assis(e)(es)**
s'asseye	**s'asseyent**	**se soit assis(e)**	**se soient assis(es)**

7 imparfait du subjonctif   **14 plus-que-parfait du subjonctif**

m'assisse	**nous assissions**	**me fusse assis(e)**	**nous fussions assis(es)**
t'assisses	**vous assissiez**	**te fusses assis(e)**	**vous fussiez assis(e)(es)**
s'assît	**s'assissent**	**se fût assis(e)**	**se fussent assis(es)**

Impératif
assieds-toi; ne t'assieds pas
asseyons-nous; ne nous asseyons pas
asseyez-vous; ne vous asseyez pas

Common idiomatic expressions using this verb and words related to it

Quand je voyage en train, je m'assieds toujours près d'une fenêtre si c'est possible.
Une fois, pendant un voyage, une belle jeune fille s'est approchée de moi et m'a demandé:
—Puis-je m'asseoir ici? Est-ce que cette place est libre?
—Certainement, j'ai répondu—asseyez-vous, je vous en prie.
Elle s'est assise auprès de moi et nous nous sommes bien amusés à raconter des histoires drôles.

asseoir qqn   to seat someone
rasseoir   to seat again, to reseat; **se rasseoir**   to sit down again
s'asseoir à califourchon   to sit astride

See also **seoir.**

to assist (at), to be present (at), to attend

The Seven Simple Tenses		The Seven Compound Tenses	
Singular	Plural	Singular	Plural
1 présent de l'indicatif		8 passé composé	
assiste	assistons	ai assisté	avons assisté
assistes	assistez	as assisté	avez assisté
assiste	assistent	a assisté	ont assisté
2 imparfait de l'indicatif		9 plus-que-parfait de l'indicatif	
assistais	assistions	avais assisté	avions assisté
assistais	assistiez	avais assisté	aviez assisté
assistait	assistaient	avait assisté	avaient assisté
3 passé simple		10 passé antérieur	
assistai	assistâmes	eus assisté	eûmes assisté
assistas	assistâtes	eus assisté	eûtes assisté
assista	assistèrent	eut assisté	eurent assisté
4 futur		11 futur antérieur	
assisterai	assisterons	aurai assisté	aurons assisté
assisteras	assisterez	auras assisté	aurez assisté
assistera	assisteront	aura assisté	auront assisté
5 conditionnel		12 conditionnel passé	
assisterais	assisterions	aurais assisté	aurions assisté
assisterais	assisteriez	aurais assisté	auriez assisté
assisterait	assisteraient	aurait assisté	auraient assisté
6 présent du subjonctif		13 passé du subjonctif	
assiste	assistions	aie assisté	ayons assisté
assistes	assistiez	aies assisté	ayez assisté
assiste	assistent	ait assisté	aient assisté
7 imparfait du subjonctif		14 plus-que-parfait du subjonctif	
assistasse	assistassions	eusse assisté	eussions assisté
assistasses	assistassiez	eusses assisté	eussiez assisté
assistât	assistassent	eût assisté	eussent assisté

Impératif
assiste
assistons
assistez

Common idiomatic expressions using this verb

    Lundi prochain j'assisterai à une conférence de musiciens. L'année dernière j'ai assisté à la même conférence et il y avait beaucoup de monde.

assistance *f.*   assistance, help; attendance; audience
assister à   to be present at, to attend
les services de l'Assistance publique   health and social security services
les assistants   those present; spectators

Want to learn more idiomatic expressions that contain verbs? Look at pages 530–542.

to assure, to ensure, to insure, to guarantee

The Seven Simple Tenses		The Seven Compound Tenses	
Singular	Plural	Singular	Plural
1 présent de l'indicatif		8 passé composé	
assure	assurons	ai assuré	avons assuré
assures	assurez	as assuré	avez assuré
assure	assurent	a assuré	ont assuré
2 imparfait de l'indicatif		9 plus-que-parfait de l'indicatif	
assurais	assurions	avais assuré	avions assuré
assurais	assuriez	avais assuré	aviez assuré
assurait	assuraient	avait assuré	avaient assuré
3 passé simple		10 passé antérieur	
assurai	assurâmes	eus assuré	eûmes assuré
assuras	assurâtes	eus assuré	eûtes assuré
assura	assurèrent	eut assuré	eurent assuré
4 futur		11 futur antérieur	
assurerai	assurerons	aurai assuré	aurons assuré
assureras	assurerez	auras assuré	aurez assuré
assurera	assureront	aura assuré	auront assuré
5 conditionnel		12 conditionnel passé	
assurerais	assurerions	aurais assuré	aurions assuré
assurerais	assureriez	aurais assuré	auriez assuré
assurerait	assureraient	aurait assuré	auraient assuré
6 présent du subjonctif		13 passé du subjonctif	
assure	assurions	aie assuré	ayons assuré
assures	assuriez	aies assuré	ayez assuré
assure	assurent	ait assuré	aient assuré
7 imparfait du subjonctif		14 plus-que-parfait du subjonctif	
assurasse	assurassions	eusse assuré	eussions assuré
assurasses	assurassiez	eusses assuré	eussiez assuré
assurât	assurassent	eût assuré	eussent assuré

Impératif
assure
assurons
assurez

Words and expressions related to this verb
assurer qqn de qqch   to assure someone of something; **sûr, sûre**   sure
assurable   insurable, assurable; **sûrement**   surely; **sûrement pas**   certainly not
rassurer   to reassure; **la sûreté**   safety
se rassurer   to be reassured
assuré, assurée   certain

See also **s'assurer.**

How are you doing? Find out with the verb drills and tests with answers explained on pages 622–673.

The subject pronouns are found on the page facing page 1.

s'assurer

Part. pr. s'assurant   **Part. passé assuré(e)(s)**

to make sure, to assure oneself, to insure oneself

The Seven Simple Tenses		The Seven Compound Tenses	
Singular	Plural	Singular	Plural
1 présent de l'indicatif		**8 passé composé**	
m'assure	nous assurons	me suis assuré(e)	nous sommes assuré(e)s
t'assures	vous assurez	t'es assuré(e)	vous êtes assuré(e)(s)
s'assure	s'assurent	s'est assuré(e)	se sont assuré(e)s
2 imparfait de l'indicatif		**9 plus-que-parfait de l'indicatif**	
m'assurais	nous assurions	m'étais assuré(e)	nous étions assuré(e)s
t'assurais	vous assuriez	t'étais assuré(e)	vous étiez assuré(e)(s)
s'assurait	s'assuraient	s'était assuré(e)	s'étaient assuré(e)s
3 passé simple		**10 passé antérieur**	
m'assurai	nous assurâmes	me fus assuré(e)	nous fûmes assuré(e)s
t'assuras	vous assurâtes	te fus assuré(e)	vous fûtes assuré(e)(s)
s'assura	s'assurèrent	se fut assuré(e)	se furent assuré(e)s
4 futur		**11 futur antérieur**	
m'assurerai	nous assurerons	me serai assuré(e)	nous serons assuré(e)s
t'assureras	vous assurerez	te seras assuré(e)	vous serez assuré(e)(s)
s'assurera	s'assureront	se sera assuré(e)	se seront assuré(e)s
5 conditionnel		**12 conditionnel passé**	
m'assurerais	nous assurerions	me serais assuré(e)	nous serions assuré(e)s
t'assurerais	vous assureriez	te serais assuré(e)	vous seriez assuré(e)(s)
s'assurerait	s'assureraient	se serait assuré(e)	se seraient assuré(e)s
6 présent du subjonctif		**13 passé du subjonctif**	
m'assure	nous assurions	me sois assuré(e)	nous soyons assuré(e)s
t'assures	vous assuriez	te sois assuré(e)	vous soyez assuré(e)(s)
s'assure	s'assurent	se soit assuré(e)	se soient assuré(e)s
7 imparfait du subjonctif		**14 plus-que-parfait du subjonctif**	
m'assurasse	nous assurassions	me fusse assuré(e)	nous fussions assuré(e)s
t'assurasses	vous assurassiez	te fusses assuré(e)	vous fussiez assuré(e)(s)
s'assurât	s'assurassent	se fût assuré(e)	se fussent assuré(e)s

Impératif
assure-toi; ne t'assure pas
assurons-nous; ne nous assurons pas
assurez-vous; ne vous assurez pas

Sentences using this verb and words related to it
   Pour s'assurer que la porte était bien fermée, Madame Lafontaine l'a fermée à clef. Puis elle a fermé toutes les fenêtres pour avoir de l'assurance et un sentiment de sécurité.
   Assurément, elle a raison. Il y a des cambrioleurs dans le voisinage.

assurément assuredly
assurance *f.* assurance, insurance
un assureur insurer
s'assurer de la protection de qqn to secure someone's protection

l'assurance-vie *f.* life insurance, life assurance
l'assurance automobile *f.* car insurance

See also **assurer.**

The Seven Simple Tenses		The Seven Compound Tenses	
Singular	Plural	Singular	Plural
1 présent de l'indicatif		8 passé composé	
atteins	**atteignons**	**ai atteint**	**avons atteint**
atteins	**atteignez**	**as atteint**	**avez atteint**
atteint	**atteignent**	**a atteint**	**ont atteint**
2 imparfait de l'indicatif		9 plus-que-parfait de l'indicatif	
atteignais	**atteignions**	**avais atteint**	**avions atteint**
atteignais	**atteigniez**	**avais atteint**	**aviez atteint**
atteignait	**atteignaient**	**avait atteint**	**avaient atteint**
3 passé simple		10 passé antérieur	
atteignis	**atteignîmes**	**eus atteint**	**eûmes atteint**
atteignis	**atteignîtes**	**eus atteint**	**eûtes atteint**
atteignit	**atteignirent**	**eut atteint**	**eurent atteint**
4 futur		11 futur antérieur	
atteindrai	**atteindrons**	**aurai atteint**	**aurons atteint**
atteindras	**atteindrez**	**auras atteint**	**aurez atteint**
atteindra	**atteindront**	**aura atteint**	**auront atteint**
5 conditionnel		12 conditionnel passé	
atteindrais	**atteindrions**	**aurais atteint**	**aurions atteint**
atteindrais	**atteindriez**	**aurais atteint**	**auriez atteint**
atteindrait	**atteindraient**	**aurait atteint**	**auraient atteint**
6 présent du subjonctif		13 passé du subjonctif	
atteigne	**atteignions**	**aie atteint**	**ayons atteint**
atteignes	**atteigniez**	**aies atteint**	**ayez atteint**
atteigne	**atteignent**	**ait atteint**	**aient atteint**
7 imparfait du subjonctif		14 plus-que-parfait du subjonctif	
atteignisse	**atteignissions**	**eusse atteint**	**eussions atteint**
atteignisses	**atteignissiez**	**eusses atteint**	**eussiez atteint**
atteignît	**atteignissent**	**eût atteint**	**eussent atteint**

Impératif
atteins
atteignons
atteignez

Words and expressions related to this verb
atteindre le but/la cible   to hit the target
atteindre à   to reach
une atteinte   reach; attack
hors d'atteinte   beyond reach
être atteint (atteinte) de   to suffer from

Consult the sections on verbs used in idiomatic expressions, verbs with prepositions, and the list of over 1,100 verbs conjugated like model verbs in the back pages.

to wait, to wait for, to expect

The Seven Simple Tenses		The Seven Compound Tenses	
Singular	Plural	Singular	Plural
1 présent de l'indicatif		**8 passé composé**	
attends	attendons	ai attendu	avons attendu
attends	attendez	as attendu	avez attendu
attend	attendent	a attendu	ont attendu
2 imparfait de l'indicatif		**9 plus-que-parfait de l'indicatif**	
attendais	attendions	avais attendu	avions attendu
attendais	attendiez	avais attendu	aviez attendu
attendait	attendaient	avait attendu	avaient attendu
3 passé simple		**10 passé antérieur**	
attendis	attendîmes	eus attendu	eûmes attendu
attendis	attendîtes	eus attendu	eûtes attendu
attendit	attendirent	eut attendu	eurent attendu
4 futur		**11 futur antérieur**	
attendrai	attendrons	aurai attendu	aurons attendu
attendras	attendrez	auras attendu	aurez attendu
attendra	attendront	aura attendu	auront attendu
5 conditionnel		**12 conditionnel passé**	
attendrais	attendrions	aurais attendu	aurions attendu
attendrais	attendriez	aurais attendu	auriez attendu
attendrait	attendraient	aurait attendu	auraient attendu
6 présent du subjonctif		**13 passé du subjonctif**	
attende	attendions	aie attendu	ayons attendu
attendes	attendiez	aies attendu	ayez attendu
attende	attendent	ait attendu	aient attendu
7 imparfait du subjonctif		**14 plus-que-parfait du subjonctif**	
attendisse	attendissions	eusse attendu	eussions attendu
attendisses	attendissiez	eusses attendu	eussiez attendu
attendît	attendissent	eût attendu	eussent attendu

Impératif
attends
attendons
attendez

Common idiomatic expressions using this verb

J'attends l'autobus depuis vingt minutes. Hier j'ai attendu dix minutes. Quand il arrivera, je m'attendrai à trouver une place libre.

faire attendre qqch à qqn to make someone wait for something; to keep someone waiting for something
en attendant meanwhile, in the meantime
Cela peut attendre! It can wait!
l'attente *f.* wait, waiting

une salle d'attente waiting room
s'attendre à to expect; **Je ne m'attendais pas à gagner** I wasn't expecting to win.
J'attends l'autobus depuis vingt minutes! I have been waiting for the bus for 20 minutes!

56

to attract, to allure

The Seven Simple Tenses		The Seven Compound Tenses	
Singular	Plural	Singular	Plural

1 présent de l'indicatif

attire	attirons	**8 passé composé**	
attires	attirez	ai attiré	avons attiré
attire	attirent	as attiré	avez attiré
		a attiré	ont attiré

2 imparfait de l'indicatif

		9 plus-que-parfait de l'indicatif	
attirais	attirions	avais attiré	avions attiré
attirais	attiriez	avais attiré	aviez attiré
attirait	attiraient	avait attiré	avaient attiré

3 passé simple

		10 passé antérieur	
attirai	attirâmes	eus attiré	eûmes attiré
attiras	attirâtes	eus attiré	eûtes attiré
attira	attirèrent	eut attiré	eurent attiré

4 futur

		11 futur antérieur	
attirerai	attirerons	aurai attiré	aurons attiré
attireras	attirerez	auras attiré	aurez attiré
attirera	attireront	aura attiré	auront attiré

5 conditionnel

		12 conditionnel passé	
attirerais	attirerions	aurais attiré	aurions attiré
attirerais	attireriez	aurais attiré	auriez attiré
attirerait	attireraient	aurait attiré	auraient attiré

6 présent du subjonctif

		13 passé du subjonctif	
attire	attirions	aie attiré	ayons attiré
attires	attiriez	aies attiré	ayez attiré
attire	attirent	ait attiré	aient attiré

7 imparfait du subjonctif

		14 plus-que-parfait du subjonctif	
attirasse	attirassions	eusse attiré	eussions attiré
attirasses	attirassiez	eusses attiré	eussiez attiré
attirât	attirassent	eût attiré	eussent attiré

Impératif
attire
attirons
attirez

Common idiomatic expressions using this verb and words related to it

attirant, attirante attractive
le tirage drawing, pulling; printing of a
   publication
premier tirage first printing
à gros tirage large number of copies printed
une attraction attraction

tirer to pull
un tirage limité limited number of copies
les attraits *m.* charms, beauty
Do not confuse **un tirage** with **un triage**,
   which means sorting, selecting.

See also **retirer, se retirer,** and **tirer.**

Use the EE-zee guide to French pronunciation on pages 566 and 567.

attraper

to catch

The Seven Simple Tenses		The Seven Compound Tenses	
Singular	Plural	Singular	Plural
1 présent de l'indicatif		**8 passé composé**	
attrape	attrapons	ai attrapé	avons attrapé
attrapes	attrapez	as attrapé	avez attrapé
attrape	attrapent	a attrapé	ont attrapé
2 imparfait de l'indicatif		**9 plus-que-parfait de l'indicatif**	
attrapais	attrapions	avais attrapé	avions attrapé
attrapais	attrapiez	avais attrapé	aviez attrapé
attrapait	attrapaient	avait attrapé	avaient attrapé
3 passé simple		**10 passé antérieur**	
attrapai	attrapâmes	eus attrapé	eûmes attrapé
attrapas	attrapâtes	eus attrapé	eûtes attrapé
attrapa	attrapèrent	eut attrapé	eurent attrapé
4 futur		**11 futur antérieur**	
attraperai	attraperons	aurai attrapé	aurons attrapé
attraperas	attraperez	auras attrapé	aurez attrapé
attrapera	attraperont	aura attrapé	auront attrapé
5 conditionnel		**12 conditionnel passé**	
attraperais	attraperions	aurais attrapé	aurions attrapé
attraperais	attraperiez	aurais attrapé	auriez attrapé
attraperait	attraperaient	aurait attrapé	auraient attrapé
6 présent du subjonctif		**13 passé du subjonctif**	
attrape	attrapions	aie attrapé	ayons attrapé
attrapes	attrapiez	aies attrapé	ayez attrapé
attrape	attrapent	ait attrapé	aient attrapé
7 imparfait du subjonctif		**14 plus-que-parfait du subjonctif**	
attrapasse	attrapassions	eusse attrapé	eussions attrapé
attrapasses	attrapassiez	eusses attrapé	eussiez attrapé
attrapât	attrapassent	eût attrapé	eussent attrapé

Impératif
attrape
attrapons
attrapez

Common idiomatic expressions using this verb
—**Si tu ne veux pas attraper un rhume, mets ton manteau parce qu'il fait froid dehors.**
—**Je n'ai pas le temps maintenant, maman—je dois attraper l'autobus.**

attraper un rhume   to catch cold
attraper qqn à qqch   to catch someone at something (to surprise)
s'attraper   to be catching, infectious

une attrape   trick
un attrape-mouche   flypaper (sticky paper to catch flies), fly trap
une trappe   trap

Get acquainted with what preposition goes with what verb on pages 543–553.

to augment, to increase

The Seven Simple Tenses		The Seven Compound Tenses	
Singular	Plural	Singular	Plural
1 présent de l'indicatif		**8 passé composé**	
augmente	augmentons	ai augmenté	avons augmenté
augmentes	augmentez	as augmenté	avez augmenté
augmente	augmentent	a augmenté	ont augmenté
2 imparfait de l'indicatif		**9 plus-que-parfait de l'indicatif**	
augmentais	augmentions	avais augmenté	avions augmenté
augmentais	augmentiez	avais augmenté	aviez augmenté
augmentait	augmentaient	avait augmenté	avaient augmenté
3 passé simple		**10 passé antérieur**	
augmentai	augmentâmes	eus augmenté	eûmes augmenté
augmentas	augmentâtes	eus augmenté	eûtes augmenté
augmenta	augmentèrent	eut augmenté	eurent augmenté
4 futur		**11 futur antérieur**	
augmenterai	augmenterons	aurai augmenté	aurons augmenté
augmenteras	augmenterez	auras augmenté	aurez augmenté
augmentera	augmenteront	aura augmenté	auront augmenté
5 conditionnel		**12 conditionnel passé**	
augmenterais	augmenterions	aurais augmenté	aurions augmenté
augmenterais	augmenteriez	aurais augmenté	auriez augmenté
augmenterait	augmenteraient	aurait augmenté	auraient augmenté
6 présent du subjonctif		**13 passé du subjonctif**	
augmente	augmentions	aie augmenté	ayons augmenté
augmentes	augmentiez	aies augmenté	ayez augmenté
augmente	augmentent	ait augmenté	aient augmenté
7 imparfait du subjonctif		**14 plus-que-parfait du subjonctif**	
augmentasse	augmentassions	eusse augmenté	eussions augmenté
augmentasses	augmentassiez	eusses augmenté	eussiez augmenté
augmentât	augmentassent	eût augmenté	eussent augmenté

Impératif
augmente
augmentons
augmentez

Words and expressions related to this verb
augmentation *f.*   increase, augmentation; **augmentation de salaire**   increase in salary
l'augmentation de la mémoire vive   RAM increase (computer)
une augmentation des impôts   tax increase
augmenter une douleur   to aggravate a pain
augmenter les prix   to increase prices

Grammar putting you in a tense mood? Review the definitions of basic grammatical terms with examples on pages 674–688.

to advance, to go forward

The Seven Simple Tenses		The Seven Compound Tenses	
Singular	Plural	Singular	Plural
1 présent de l'indicatif		**8 passé composé**	
avance	avançons	ai avancé	avons avancé
avances	avancez	as avancé	avez avancé
avance	avancent	a avancé	ont avancé
2 imparfait de l'indicatif		**9 plus-que-parfait de l'indicatif**	
avançais	avancions	avais avancé	avions avancé
avançais	avanciez	avais avancé	aviez avancé
avançait	avançaient	avait avancé	avaient avancé
3 passé simple		**10 passé antérieur**	
avançai	avançâmes	eus avancé	eûmes avancé
avanças	avançâtes	eus avancé	eûtes avancé
avança	avancèrent	eut avancé	eurent avancé
4 futur		**11 futur antérieur**	
avancerai	avancerons	aurai avancé	aurons avancé
avanceras	avancerez	auras avancé	aurez avancé
avancera	avanceront	aura avancé	auront avancé
5 conditionnel		**12 conditionnel passé**	
avancerais	avancerions	aurais avancé	aurions avancé
avancerais	avanceriez	aurais avancé	auriez avancé
avancerait	avanceraient	aurait avancé	auraient avancé
6 présent du subjonctif		**13 passé du subjonctif**	
avance	avancions	aie avancé	ayons avancé
avances	avanciez	aies avancé	ayez avancé
avance	avancent	ait avancé	aient avancé
7 imparfait du subjonctif		**14 plus-que-parfait du subjonctif**	
avançasse	avançassions	eusse avancé	eussions avancé
avançasses	avançassiez	eusses avancé	eussiez avancé
avançât	avançassent	eût avancé	eussent avancé

Impératif
avance
avançons
avancez

Sentences using this verb and words related to it

Le docteur a dit au petit garçon:—Ouvre la bouche et avance la langue.
Le garçon n'a pas ouvert la bouche et il n'a pas avancé la langue.
Le docteur a insisté:—Ouvrons la bouche et avançons la langue!

une avance   advance; **faire des avances à qqn**
   to make advances to somebody
à l'avance, d'avance   in advance, beforehand
arriver en avance   to arrive early
s'avancer   to advance (oneself)
l'avant *m.*   front

Ta montre avance   Your watch is fast.
avancer une théorie   to promote a theory
Comment avance le travail?   How is the
   work coming along?
en avant   ahead, in front
devancer   to arrive ahead

The Seven Simple Tenses		The Seven Compound Tenses	
Singular	Plural	Singular	Plural
1 présent de l'indicatif		**8 passé composé**	
ai	**avons**	**ai eu**	**avons eu**
as	**avez**	**as eu**	**avez eu**
a	**ont**	**a eu**	**ont eu**
2 imparfait de l'indicatif		**9 plus-que-parfait de l'indicatif**	
avais	**avions**	**avais eu**	**avions eu**
avais	**aviez**	**avais eu**	**aviez eu**
avait	**avaient**	**avait eu**	**avaient eu**
3 passé simple		**10 passé antérieur**	
eus	**eûmes**	**eus eu**	**eûmes eu**
eus	**eûtes**	**eus eu**	**eûtes eu**
eut	**eurent**	**eut eu**	**eurent eu**
4 futur		**11 futur antérieur**	
aurai	**aurons**	**aurai eu**	**aurons eu**
auras	**aurez**	**auras eu**	**aurez eu**
aura	**auront**	**aura eu**	**auront eu**
5 conditionnel		**12 conditionnel passé**	
aurais	**aurions**	**aurais eu**	**aurions eu**
aurais	**auriez**	**aurais eu**	**auriez eu**
aurait	**auraient**	**aurait eu**	**auraient eu**
6 présent du subjonctif		**13 passé du subjonctif**	
aie	**ayons**	**aie eu**	**ayons eu**
aies	**ayez**	**aies eu**	**ayez eu**
ait	**aient**	**ait eu**	**aient eu**
7 imparfait du subjonctif		**14 plus-que-parfait du subjonctif**	
eusse	**eussions**	**eusse eu**	**eussions eu**
eusses	**eussiez**	**eusses eu**	**eussiez eu**
eût	**eussent**	**eût eu**	**eussent eu**

Impératif
aie
ayons
ayez

Common idiomatic expressions using this verb

avoir . . . ans   to be . . . years old
avoir à + inf.   to have to, to be obliged to + inf.
avoir besoin de   to need, to have need of
avoir chaud   to be (feel) warm (persons)
avoir froid   to be (feel) cold (persons)
avoir sommeil   to be (feel) sleepy

avoir qqch à faire   to have something to do
avoir de la chance   to be lucky
avoir faim   to be hungry
avoir soif   to be thirsty
Vous avez raison   You are right.
les avoirs *m.*   belongings, assets, possessions

For more popular uses of **avoir** see pages 531–533.

Can't recognize an irregular verb form? Check out pages 526–529.

The subject pronouns are found on the page facing page 1.

baisser

Part. pr. baissant   **Part. passé baissé**

to lower, to sink

The Seven Simple Tenses		The Seven Compound Tenses	
Singular	Plural	Singular	Plural
1 présent de l'indicatif		**8 passé composé**	
baisse	baissons	ai baissé	avons baissé
baisses	baissez	as baissé	avez baissé
baisse	baissent	a baissé	ont baissé
2 imparfait de l'indicatif		**9 plus-que-parfait de l'indicatif**	
baissais	baissions	avais baissé	avions baissé
baissais	baissiez	avais baissé	aviez baissé
baissait	baissaient	avait baissé	avaient baissé
3 passé simple		**10 passé antérieur**	
baissai	baissâmes	eus baissé	eûmes baissé
baissas	baissâtes	eus baissé	eûtes baissé
baissa	baissèrent	eut baissé	eurent baissé
4 futur		**11 futur antérieur**	
baisserai	baisserons	aurai baissé	aurons baissé
baisseras	baisserez	auras baissé	aurez baissé
baissera	baisseront	aura baissé	auront baissé
5 conditionnel		**12 conditionnel passé**	
baisserais	baisserions	aurais baissé	aurions baissé
baisserais	baisseriez	aurais baissé	auriez baissé
baisserait	baisseraient	aurait baissé	auraient baissé
6 présent du subjonctif		**13 passé du subjonctif**	
baisse	baissions	aie baissé	ayons baissé
baisses	baissiez	aies baissé	ayez baissé
baisse	baissent	ait baissé	aient baissé
7 imparfait du subjonctif		**14 plus-que-parfait du subjonctif**	
baissasse	baissassions	eusse baissé	eussions baissé
baissasses	baissassiez	eusses baissé	eussiez baissé
baissât	baissassent	eût baissé	eussent baissé

Impératif
baisse
baissons
baissez

Common idiomatic expressions using this verb

baisser la voix   to lower one's voice
baisser les yeux   to look down, cast one's eyes down
baisser les bras   to admit defeat, to give in

See also abaisser and s'abaisser.

se jeter tête baissée dans qqch   to do something blindly, headlong
se baisser   to bend (stoop) down
rabaisser   to depreciate, to humble, to lower
un rabais   discount

Going away? Don't forget to check out the practical situations for travelers on pages 568–598.

to balance, to sway, to swing, to weigh, to throw away

The Seven Simple Tenses		The Seven Compound Tenses	
Singular	Plural	Singular	Plural
1 présent de l'indicatif		8 passé composé	
balance	balançons	ai balancé	avons balancé
balances	balancez	as balancé	avez balancé
balance	balancent	a balancé	ont balancé
2 imparfait de l'indicatif		9 plus-que-parfait de l'indicatif	
balançais	balancions	avais balancé	avions balancé
balançais	balanciez	avais balancé	aviez balancé
balançait	balançaient	avait balancé	avaient balancé
3 passé simple		10 passé antérieur	
balançai	balançâmes	eus balancé	eûmes balancé
balanças	balançâtes	eus balancé	eûtes balancé
balança	balancèrent	eut balancé	eurent balancé
4 futur		11 futur antérieur	
balancerai	balancerons	aurai balancé	aurons balancé
balanceras	balancerez	auras balancé	aurez balancé
balancera	balanceront	aura balancé	auront balancé
5 conditionnel		12 conditionnel passé	
balancerais	balancerions	aurais balancé	aurions balancé
balancerais	balanceriez	aurais balancé	auriez balancé
balancerait	balanceraient	aurait balancé	auraient balancé
6 présent du subjonctif		13 passé du subjonctif	
balance	balancions	aie balancé	ayons balancé
balances	balanciez	aies balancé	ayez balancé
balance	balancent	ait balancé	aient balancé
7 imparfait du subjonctif		14 plus-que-parfait du subjonctif	
balançasse	balançassions	eusse balancé	eussions balancé
balançasses	balançassiez	eusses balancé	eussiez balancé
balançât	balançassent	eût balancé	eussent balancé

Impératif
balance
balançons
balancez

Words and expressions related to this verb
une balançoire see-saw, swing
une balance weight scale
la balance des pouvoirs the balance of powers
le balancement balancing, rocking

Il a balancé la fleur par la vitre de l'auto
He tossed the flower out of the car window.
faire pencher la balance to favor someone
balancer le pour et le contre to weigh the pros and cons

Consult the sections on verbs used in idiomatic expressions, verbs with prepositions, and the list of over 1,100 verbs conjugated like model verbs in the back pages.

The subject pronouns are found on the page facing page 1.   **63**

balayer
to sweep

Part. pr. **balayant**   Part. passé **balayé**

The Seven Simple Tenses		The Seven Compound Tenses	
Singular	Plural	Singular	Plural
1 présent de l'indicatif		**8 passé composé**	
balaye	balayons	ai balayé	avons balayé
balayes	balayez	as balayé	avez balayé
balaye	balayent	a balayé	ont balayé
2 imparfait de l'indicatif		**9 plus-que-parfait de l'indicatif**	
balayais	balayions	avais balayé	avions balayé
balayais	balayiez	avais balayé	aviez balayé
balayait	balayaient	avait balayé	avaient balayé
3 passé simple		**10 passé antérieur**	
balayai	balayâmes	eus balayé	eûmes balayé
balayas	balayâtes	eus balayé	eûtes balayé
balaya	balayèrent	eut balayé	eurent balayé
4 futur		**11 futur antérieur**	
balayerai	balayerons	aurai balayé	aurons balayé
balayeras	balayerez	auras balayé	aurez balayé
balayera	balayeront	aura balayé	auront balayé
5 conditionnel		**12 conditionnel passé**	
balayerais	balayerions	aurais balayé	aurions balayé
balayerais	balayeriez	aurais balayé	auriez balayé
balayerait	balayeraient	aurait balayé	auraient balayé
6 présent du subjonctif		**13 passé du subjonctif**	
balaye	balayions	aie balayé	ayons balayé
balayes	balayiez	aies balayé	ayez balayé
balaye	balayent	ait balayé	aient balayé
7 imparfait du subjonctif		**14 plus-que-parfait du subjonctif**	
balayasse	balayassions	eusse balayé	eussions balayé
balayasses	balayassiez	eusses balayé	eussiez balayé
balayât	balayassent	eût balayé	eussent balayé

Impératif
balaye
balayons
balayez

Sentences using this verb and words related to it
—**Marie, as-tu balayé les chambres?**
—**Non, madame.**
—**Et pourquoi pas?**
—**Parce que je n'ai pas de balai, je n'ai pas de balayette, et je ne suis pas balayeuse. Voilà pourquoi!**

un balai broom; **une balayette** small brush, whiskbroom; **un balayeur, une balayeuse** sweeper
un balai d'essuie-glace windshield wiper blade

Verbs ending in -*ayer* may change y to *i* before mute *e* or may keep y.

64

to build, to construct

The Seven Simple Tenses		The Seven Compound Tenses	
Singular	Plural	Singular	Plural
1 présent de l'indicatif		8 passé composé	
bâtis	**bâtissons**	**ai bâti**	**avons bâti**
bâtis	**bâtissez**	**as bâti**	**avez bâti**
bâtit	**bâtissent**	**a bâti**	**ont bâti**
2 imparfait de l'indicatif		9 plus-que-parfait de l'indicatif	
bâtissais	**bâtissions**	**avais bâti**	**avions bâti**
bâtissais	**bâtissiez**	**avais bâti**	**aviez bâti**
bâtissait	**bâtissaient**	**avait bâti**	**avaient bâti**
3 passé simple		10 passé antérieur	
bâtis	**bâtîmes**	**eus bâti**	**eûmes bâti**
bâtis	**bâtîtes**	**eus bâti**	**eûtes bâti**
bâtit	**bâtirent**	**eut bâti**	**eurent bâti**
4 futur		11 futur antérieur	
bâtirai	**bâtirons**	**aurai bâti**	**aurons bâti**
bâtiras	**bâtirez**	**auras bâti**	**aurez bâti**
bâtira	**bâtiront**	**aura bâti**	**auront bâti**
5 conditionnel		12 conditionnel passé	
bâtirais	**bâtirions**	**aurais bâti**	**aurions bâti**
bâtirais	**bâtiriez**	**aurais bâti**	**auriez bâti**
bâtirait	**bâtiraient**	**aurait bâti**	**auraient bâti**
6 présent du subjonctif		13 passé du subjonctif	
bâtisse	**bâtissions**	**aie bâti**	**ayons bâti**
bâtisses	**bâtissiez**	**aies bâti**	**ayez bâti**
bâtisse	**bâtissent**	**ait bâti**	**aient bâti**
7 imparfait du subjonctif		14 plus-que-parfait du subjonctif	
bâtisse	**bâtissions**	**eusse bâti**	**eussions bâti**
bâtisses	**bâtissiez**	**eusses bâti**	**eussiez bâti**
bâtît	**bâtissent**	**eût bâti**	**eussent bâti**

Impératif
bâtis
bâtissons
bâtissez

Words and expressions related to this verb
un bâtiment   building, edifice, ship; **un bâtisseur**   builder
bâtir   to baste (sewing term; when basting food, use **arroser**); **du fil à bâtir**   basting thread
un bâtiment de guerre   warship
rebâtir   to rebuild
bâtir des châteaux en Espagne   to build castles in the air
bâtir sur le sable   to build on sand

battre
to beat, to hit, to strike

Part. pr. **battant**   Part. passé **battu**

The Seven Simple Tenses		The Seven Compound Tenses	
Singular	Plural	Singular	Plural
1 présent de l'indicatif		8 passé composé	
bats	battons	ai battu	avons battu
bats	battez	as battu	avez battu
bat	battent	a battu	ont battu
2 imparfait de l'indicatif		9 plus-que-parfait de l'indicatif	
battais	battions	avais battu	avions battu
battais	battiez	avais battu	aviez battu
battait	battaient	avait battu	avaient battu
3 passé simple		10 passé antérieur	
battis	battîmes	eus battu	eûmes battu
battis	battîtes	eus battu	eûtes battu
battit	battirent	eut battu	eurent battu
4 futur		11 futur antérieur	
battrai	battrons	aurai battu	aurons battu
battras	battrez	auras battu	aurez battu
battra	battront	aura battu	auront battu
5 conditionnel		12 conditionnel passé	
battrais	battrions	aurais battu	aurions battu
battrais	battriez	aurais battu	auriez battu
battrait	battraient	aurait battu	auraient battu
6 présent du subjonctif		13 passé du subjonctif	
batte	battions	aie battu	ayons battu
battes	battiez	aies battu	ayez battu
batte	battent	ait battu	aient battu
7 imparfait du subjonctif		14 plus-que-parfait du subjonctif	
battisse	battissions	eusse battu	eussions battu
battisses	battissiez	eusses battu	eussiez battu
battît	battissent	eût battu	eussent battu

Impératif
bats
battons
battez

Sentences using this verb and words related to it

Notre femme de chambre est dans la cour. Elle est en train de battre les tapis. Elle les bat tous les samedis. Samedi dernier, pendant qu'elle battait les tapis, mon frère jouait au tennis et il a battu son adversaire.

battre des mains   to clap, to applaud
battre la campagne   to scour the countryside
le battant   leaf, flap (of a table)
une porte à deux battants   double door
une batte   bat, beater

le battement   banging (of a door); throbbing, flutter, beating
un batteur   whisk, beater
le battage   beating

See also **abattre, se battre,** and **combattre.**

Review the Subjunctive clearly and simply on pages 560–565.

66

The Seven Simple Tenses		The Seven Compound Tenses	
Singular	Plural	Singular	Plural
1 présent de l'indicatif		**8 passé composé**	
me bats	nous battons	me suis battu(e)	nous sommes battu(e)s
te bats	vous battez	t'es battu(e)	vous êtes battu(e)(s)
se bat	se battent	s'est battu(e)	se sont battu(e)s
2 imparfait de l'indicatif		**9 plus-que-parfait de l'indicatif**	
me battais	nous battions	m'étais battu(e)	nous étions battu(e)s
te battais	vous battiez	t'étais battu(e)	vous étiez battu(e)(s)
se battait	se battaient	s'était battu(e)	s'étaient battu(e)s
3 passé simple		**10 passé antérieur**	
me battis	nous battîmes	me fus battu(e)	nous fûmes battu(e)s
te battis	vous battîtes	te fus battu(e)	vous fûtes battu(e)(s)
se battit	se battirent	se fut battu(e)	se furent battu(e)s
4 futur		**11 futur antérieur**	
me battrai	nous battrons	me serai battu(e)	nous serons battu(e)s
te battras	vous battrez	te seras battu(e)	vous serez battu(e)(s)
se battra	se battront	se sera battu(e)	se seront battu(e)s
5 conditionnel		**12 conditionnel passé**	
me battrais	nous battrions	me serais battu(e)	nous serions battu(e)s
te battrais	vous battriez	te serais battu(e)	vous seriez battu(e)(s)
se battrait	se battraient	se serait battu(e)	se seraient battu(e)s
6 présent du subjonctif		**13 passé du subjonctif**	
me batte	nous battions	me sois battu(e)	nous soyons battu(e)s
te battes	vous battiez	te sois battu(e)	vous soyez battu(e)(s)
se batte	se battent	se soit battu(e)	se soient battu(e)s
7 imparfait du subjonctif		**14 plus-que-parfait du subjonctif**	
me battisse	nous battissions	me fusse battu(e)	nous fussions battu(e)s
te battisses	vous battissiez	te fusses battu(e)	vous fussiez battu(e)(s)
se battît	se battissent	se fût battu(e)	se fussent battu(e)s

Impératif
bats-toi; ne te bats pas
battons-nous; ne nous battons pas
battez-vous; ne vous battez pas

Sentences using this verb and words related to it
   Ecoutez! Nos voisins commencent à se battre. Ils se battent toujours. La dernière fois ils se sont battus à coups de poings. Il y a toujours un grand combat chez eux.

For other words and expressions related to this verb, see **abattre, battre,** and **combattre.**

Enjoy verbs in French proverbs on page 559.

Soak up some verbs used in weather expressions on pages 557 and 558.

The subject pronouns are found on the page facing page 1.   **67**

bavarder
Part. pr. **bavardant** Part. passé **bavardé**

to chat, to chatter, to babble, to gossip

The Seven Simple Tenses		The Seven Compound Tenses	
Singular	Plural	Singular	Plural
1 présent de l'indicatif		8 passé composé	
bavarde	bavardons	ai bavardé	avons bavardé
bavardes	bavardez	as bavardé	avez bavardé
bavarde	bavardent	a bavardé	ont bavardé
2 imparfait de l'indicatif		9 plus-que-parfait de l'indicatif	
bavardais	bavardions	avais bavardé	avions bavardé
bavardais	bavardiez	avais bavardé	aviez bavardé
bavardait	bavardaient	avait bavardé	avaient bavardé
3 passé simple		10 passé antérieur	
bavardai	bavardâmes	eus bavardé	eûmes bavardé
bavardas	bavardâtes	eus bavardé	eûtes bavardé
bavarda	bavardèrent	eut bavardé	eurent bavardé
4 futur		11 futur antérieur	
bavarderai	bavarderons	aurai bavardé	aurons bavardé
bavarderas	bavarderez	auras bavardé	aurez bavardé
bavardera	bavarderont	aura bavardé	auront bavardé
5 conditionnel		12 conditionnel passé	
bavarderais	bavarderions	aurais bavardé	aurions bavardé
bavarderais	bavarderiez	aurais bavardé	auriez bavardé
bavarderait	bavarderaient	aurait bavardé	auraient bavardé
6 présent du subjonctif		13 passé du subjonctif	
bavarde	bavardions	aie bavardé	ayons bavardé
bavardes	bavardiez	aies bavardé	ayez bavardé
bavarde	bavardent	ait bavardé	aient bavardé
7 imparfait du subjonctif		14 plus-que-parfait du subjonctif	
bavardasse	bavardassions	eusse bavardé	eussions bavardé
bavardasses	bavardassiez	eusses bavardé	eussiez bavardé
bavardât	bavardassent	eût bavardé	eussent bavardé

Impératif
bavarde
bavardons
bavardez

Sentences using this verb and words related to it

Aimez-vous les personnes qui bavardent tout le temps? Je connais un homme qui est bavard. Sa femme est bavarde aussi. Elle aime à parler avec abondance. Moi, je n'aime pas le bavardage. Je ne bavarde pas parce que je n'aime pas perdre mon temps.

le bavardage chitchat, chattering, talkativeness	**perdre son temps à bavarder** to waste one's time babbling
bavard, bavarde talkative, loquacious, garrulous	**la bave** drool, dribble
	baver to drool

Try the verb drills and verb tests with answers explained on pages 622–673.

to bless, to consecrate

The Seven Simple Tenses		The Seven Compound Tenses	
Singular	Plural	Singular	Plural
1 présent de l'indicatif		8 passé composé	
bénis	**bénissons**	**ai béni**	**avons béni**
bénis	**bénissez**	**as béni**	**avez béni**
bénit	**bénissent**	**a béni**	**ont béni**
2 imparfait de l'indicatif		9 plus-que-parfait de l'indicatif	
bénissais	**bénissions**	**avais béni**	**avions béni**
bénissais	**bénissiez**	**avais béni**	**aviez béni**
bénissait	**bénissaient**	**avait béni**	**avaient béni**
3 passé simple		10 passé antérieur	
bénis	**bénîmes**	**eus béni**	**eûmes béni**
bénis	**bénîtes**	**eus béni**	**eûtes béni**
bénit	**bénirent**	**eut béni**	**eurent béni**
4 futur		11 futur antérieur	
bénirai	**bénirons**	**aurai béni**	**aurons béni**
béniras	**bénirez**	**auras béni**	**aurez béni**
bénira	**béniront**	**aura béni**	**auront béni**
5 conditionnel		12 conditionnel passé	
bénirais	**bénirions**	**aurais béni**	**aurions béni**
bénirais	**béniriez**	**aurais béni**	**auriez béni**
bénirait	**béniraient**	**aurait béni**	**auraient béni**
6 présent du subjonctif		13 passé du subjonctif	
bénisse	**bénissions**	**aie béni**	**ayons béni**
bénisses	**bénissiez**	**aies béni**	**ayez béni**
bénisse	**bénissent**	**ait béni**	**aient béni**
7 imparfait du subjonctif		14 plus-que-parfait du subjonctif	
bénisse	**bénissions**	**eusse béni**	**eussions béni**
bénisses	**bénissiez**	**eusses béni**	**eussiez béni**
bénît	**bénissent**	**eût béni**	**eussent béni**

Impératif
bénis
bénissons
bénissez

Words and expressions related to this verb
de l'eau bénite   holy (blessed) water; **du pain bénit**   holy (blessed) bread
le bénitier   holy water font
une bénédiction   blessing
dire le bénédicité   to say grace (before a meal)

Do not confuse **bénir** with **blesser,** which means *to wound.*

Consult the sections on verbs used in idiomatic expressions, verbs with prepositions, and the list
of over 1,100 verbs conjugated like model verbs in the back pages.

blâmer

Part. pr. blâmant **Part. passé blâmé**

to blame

The Seven Simple Tenses		The Seven Compound Tenses	
Singular	Plural	Singular	Plural
1 présent de l'indicatif		**8 passé composé**	
blâme	blâmons	ai blâmé	avons blâmé
blâmes	blâmez	as blâmé	avez blâmé
blâme	blâment	a blâmé	ont blâmé
2 imparfait de l'indicatif		**9 plus-que-parfait de l'indicatif**	
blâmais	blâmions	avais blâmé	avions blâmé
blâmais	blâmiez	avais blâmé	aviez blâmé
blâmait	blâmaient	avait blâmé	avaient blâmé
3 passé simple		**10 passé antérieur**	
blâmai	blâmâmes	eus blâmé	eûmes blâmé
blâmas	blâmâtes	eus blâmé	eûtes blâmé
blâma	blâmèrent	eut blâmé	eurent blâmé
4 futur		**11 futur antérieur**	
blâmerai	blâmerons	aurai blâmé	aurons blâmé
blâmeras	blâmerez	auras blâmé	aurez blâmé
blâmera	blâmeront	aura blâmé	auront blâmé
5 conditionnel		**12 conditionnel passé**	
blâmerais	blâmerions	aurais blâmé	aurions blâmé
blâmerais	blâmeriez	aurais blâmé	auriez blâmé
blâmerait	blâmeraient	aurait blâmé	auraient blâmé
6 présent du subjonctif		**13 passé du subjonctif**	
blâme	blâmions	aie blâmé	ayons blâmé
blâmes	blâmiez	aies blâmé	ayez blâmé
blâme	blâment	ait blâmé	aient blâmé
7 imparfait du subjonctif		**14 plus-que-parfait du subjonctif**	
blâmasse	blâmassions	eusse blâmé	eussions blâmé
blâmasses	blâmassiez	eusses blâmé	eussiez blâmé
blâmât	blâmassent	eût blâmé	eussent blâmé

Impératif
blâme
blâmons
blâmez

Words and expressions related to this verb

être blâmé (blâmée) to be blamed
le blâme blame
blasphémer to blaspheme

se blâmer to blame oneself
blâmable blameworthy, blamable
le blasphème blasphemy

Want to learn more idiomatic expressions that contain verbs? Look at pages 530–542.

70

The Seven Simple Tenses		The Seven Compound Tenses	
Singular	Plural	Singular	Plural
1 présent de l'indicatif		**8 passé composé**	
blanchis	**blanchissons**	**ai blanchi**	**avons blanchi**
blanchis	**blanchissez**	**as blanchi**	**avez blanchi**
blanchit	**blanchissent**	**a blanchi**	**ont blanchi**
2 imparfait de l'indicatif		**9 plus-que-parfait de l'indicatif**	
blanchissais	**blanchissions**	**avais blanchi**	**avions blanchi**
blanchissais	**blanchissiez**	**avais blanchi**	**aviez blanchi**
blanchissait	**blanchissaient**	**avait blanchi**	**avaient blanchi**
3 passé simple		**10 passé antérieur**	
blanchis	**blanchîmes**	**eus blanchi**	**eûmes blanchi**
blanchis	**blanchîtes**	**eus blanchi**	**eûtes blanchi**
blanchit	**blanchirent**	**eut blanchi**	**eurent blanchi**
4 futur		**11 futur antérieur**	
blanchirai	**blanchirons**	**aurai blanchi**	**aurons blanchi**
blanchiras	**blanchirez**	**auras blanchi**	**aurez blanchi**
blanchira	**blanchiront**	**aura blanchi**	**auront blanchi**
5 conditionnel		**12 conditionnel passé**	
blanchirais	**blanchirions**	**aurais blanchi**	**aurions blanchi**
blanchirais	**blanchiriez**	**aurais blanchi**	**auriez blanchi**
blanchirait	**blanchiraient**	**aurait blanchi**	**auraient blanchi**
6 présent du subjonctif		**13 passé du subjonctif**	
blanchisse	**blanchissions**	**aie blanchi**	**ayons blanchi**
blanchisses	**blanchissiez**	**aies blanchi**	**ayez blanchi**
blanchisse	**blanchissent**	**ait blanchi**	**aient blanchi**
7 imparfait du subjonctif		**14 plus-que-parfait du subjonctif**	
blanchisse	**blanchissions**	**eusse blanchi**	**eussions blanchi**
blanchisses	**blanchissiez**	**eusses blanchi**	**eussiez blanchi**
blanchît	**blanchissent**	**eût blanchi**	**eussent blanchi**

Impératif
blanchis
blanchissons
blanchissez

Common idiomatic expressions using this verb and words related to it

le blanc   white
le blanc d'oeil   the white of the eye
la bille blanche   white billiard ball
du vin blanc   white wine
la blanchisserie   laundry
   (store where clothes are washed)

carte blanche   unlimited privileges and authority
blanc comme neige   as white as snow
Blanche-Neige   Snow White
un chèque en blanc   blank check
un verre de blanc   a glass of white wine
le blanchissage   washing

Taking a trip? Check out the popular words, phrases, and expressions for travelers on pages 599–621.

The subject pronouns are found on the page facing page 1.   **71**

to harm, to hurt, to injure, to wound, to offend

The Seven Simple Tenses		The Seven Compound Tenses	
Singular	Plural	Singular	Plural
1 présent de l'indicatif		**8 passé composé**	
blesse	blessons	ai blessé	avons blessé
blesses	blessez	as blessé	avez blessé
blesse	blessent	a blessé	ont blessé
2 imparfait de l'indicatif		**9 plus-que-parfait de l'indicatif**	
blessais	blessions	avais blessé	avions blessé
blessais	blessiez	avais blessé	aviez blessé
blessait	blessaient	avait blessé	avaient blessé
3 passé simple		**10 passé antérieur**	
blessai	blessâmes	eus blessé	eûmes blessé
blessas	blessâtes	eus blessé	eûtes blessé
blessa	blessèrent	eut blessé	eurent blessé
4 futur		**11 futur antérieur**	
blesserai	blesserons	aurai blessé	aurons blessé
blesseras	blesserez	auras blessé	aurez blessé
blessera	blesseront	aura blessé	auront blessé
5 conditionnel		**12 conditionnel passé**	
blesserais	blesserions	aurais blessé	aurions blessé
blesserais	blesseriez	aurais blessé	auriez blessé
blesserait	blesseraient	aurait blessé	auraient blessé
6 présent du subjonctif		**13 passé du subjonctif**	
blesse	blessions	aie blessé	ayons blessé
blesses	blessiez	aies blessé	ayez blessé
blesse	blessent	ait blessé	aient blessé
7 imparfait du subjonctif		**14 plus-que-parfait du subjonctif**	
blessasse	blessassions	eusse blessé	eussions blessé
blessasses	blessassiez	eusses blessé	eussiez blessé
blessât	blessassent	eût blessé	eussent blessé

Impératif
blesse
blessons
blessez

Sentences using this verb and words related to it
   Ma soeur est tombée sur un rocher qui l'a blessée au visage. Ce fut* une blessure grave.

blesser à mort   to wound mortally
une blessure   wound, injury
une parole blessante   a cutting word
See also se **blesser.**

être blessé à la jambe (au bras)   to be injured
   in the leg (in the arm)

   *The verb form **fut** is the **passé simple** of **être.**

Do not confuse **blesser** with **bénir,** which means *to bless*.

to hurt oneself, to injure oneself, to wound oneself

The Seven Simple Tenses		The Seven Compound Tenses	
Singular	Plural	Singular	Plural
1 présent de l'indicatif		8 passé composé	
me blesse	nous blessons	me suis blessé(e)	nous sommes blessé(e)s
te blesses	vous blessez	t'es blessé(e)	vous êtes blessé(e)(s)
se blesse	se blessent	s'est blessé(e)	se sont blessé(e)s
2 imparfait de l'indicatif		9 plus-que-parfait de l'indicatif	
me blessais	nous blessions	m'étais blessé(e)	nous étions blessé(e)s
te blessais	vous blessiez	t'étais blessé(e)	vous étiez blessé(e)(s)
se blessait	se blessaient	s'était blessé(e)	s'étaient blessé(e)s
3 passé simple		10 passé antérieur	
me blessai	nous blessâmes	me fus blessé(e)	nous fûmes blessé(e)s
te blessas	vous blessâtes	te fus blessé(e)	vous fûtes blessé(e)(s)
se blessa	se blessèrent	se fut blessé(e)	se furent blessé(e)s
4 futur		11 futur antérieur	
me blesserai	nous blesserons	me serai blessé(e)	nous serons blessé(e)s
te blesseras	vous blesserez	te seras blessé(e)	vous serez blessé(e)(s)
se blessera	se blesseront	se sera blessé(e)	se seront blessé(e)s
5 conditionnel		12 conditionnel passé	
me blesserais	nous blesserions	me serais blessé(e)	nous serions blessé(e)s
te blesserais	vous blesseriez	te serais blessé(e)	vous seriez blessé(e)(s)
se blesserait	se blesseraient	se serait blessé(e)	se seraient blessé(e)s
6 présent du subjonctif		13 passé du subjonctif	
me blesse	nous blessions	me sois blessé(e)	nous soyons blessé(e)s
te blesses	vous blessiez	te sois blessé(e)	vous soyez blessé(e)(s)
se blesse	se blessent	se soit blessé(e)	se soient blessé(e)s
7 imparfait du subjonctif		14 plus-que-parfait du subjonctif	
me blessasse	nous blessassions	me fusse blessé(e)	nous fussions blessé(e)s
te blessasses	vous blessassiez	te fusses blessé(e)	vous fussiez blessé(e)(s)
se blessât	se blessassent	se fût blessé(e)	se fussent blessé(e)s

Impératif
blesse-toi; ne te blesse pas
blessons-nous; ne nous blessons pas
blessez-vous; ne vous blessez pas

Sentences using this verb and words related to it
     Madame Leblanc est tombée dans la rue et elle s'est blessée au genou. Ce fut* une blessure légère, heureusement.

se blesser de to take offense at   **se blesser pour un rien** to be easily offended

For other words and expressions related to this verb, see **blesser**.

     *The verb form **fut** is the **passé simple** of **être**.

Do not confuse **blesser** and **se blesser** with **bénir**, which means *to bless*.

boire   Part. pr. **buvant**   Part. passé **bu**

to drink

The Seven Simple Tenses		The Seven Compound Tenses	
Singular	Plural	Singular	Plural
1 présent de l'indicatif		8 passé composé	
bois	buvons	ai bu	avons bu
bois	buvez	as bu	avez bu
boit	boivent	a bu	ont bu
2 imparfait de l'indicatif		9 plus-que-parfait de l'indicatif	
buvais	buvions	avais bu	avions bu
buvais	buviez	avais bu	aviez bu
buvait	buvaient	avait bu	avaient bu
3 passé simple		10 passé antérieur	
bus	bûmes	eus bu	eûmes bu
bus	bûtes	eus bu	eûtes bu
but	burent	eut bu	eurent bu
4 futur		11 futur antérieur	
boirai	boirons	aurai bu	aurons bu
boiras	boirez	auras bu	aurez bu
boira	boiront	aura bu	auront bu
5 conditionnel		12 conditionnel passé	
boirais	boirions	aurais bu	aurions bu
boirais	boiriez	aurais bu	auriez bu
boirait	boiraient	aurait bu	auraient bu
6 présent du subjonctif		13 passé du subjonctif	
boive	buvions	aie bu	ayons bu
boives	buviez	aies bu	ayez bu
boive	boivent	ait bu	aient bu
7 imparfait du subjonctif		14 plus-que-parfait du subjonctif	
busse	bussions	eusse bu	eussions bu
busses	bussiez	eusses bu	eussiez bu
bût	bussent	eût bu	eussent bu

Impératif
bois
buvons
buvez

Sentences using this verb and words related to it

—**Michel, as-tu bu ton lait?**
—**Non, maman, je ne l'ai pas bu.**
—**Bois-le tout de suite, je te dis.**
—**Tous les jours je bois du lait. N'y a-t-il pas d'autres boissons dans la maison?**
—**Si, il y a d'autres boissons dans la maison mais les bons garçons comme toi boivent du lait.**

(Note that **si** is used instead of **oui** for "yes" in answer to a question in the negative.)

boire à la santé de qqn   to drink to someone's health
une boisson   drink; **boisson gazeuse**   carbonated drink
un buveur, une buveuse   drinker; **une buvette**   bar
un buvard   ink blotter; **boire un coup**   to have a drink
abreuver   to water an animal
un breuvage   beverage

74

The Seven Simple Tenses		The Seven Compound Tenses	
Singular	Plural	Singular	Plural
1 présent de l'indicatif		**8 passé composé**	
bouge	bougeons	ai bougé	avons bougé
bouges	bougez	as bougé	avez bougé
bouge	bougent	a bougé	ont bougé
2 imparfait de l'indicatif		**9 plus-que-parfait de l'indicatif**	
bougeais	bougions	avais bougé	avions bougé
bougeais	bougiez	avais bougé	aviez bougé
bougeait	bougeaient	avait bougé	avaient bougé
3 passé simple		**10 passé antérieur**	
bougeai	bougeâmes	eus bougé	eûmes bougé
bougeas	bougeâtes	eus bougé	eûtes bougé
bougea	bougèrent	eut bougé	eurent bougé
4 futur		**11 futur antérieur**	
bougerai	bougerons	aurai bougé	aurons bougé
bougeras	bougerez	auras bougé	aurez bougé
bougera	bougeront	aura bougé	auront bougé
5 conditionnel		**12 conditionnel passé**	
bougerais	bougerions	aurais bougé	aurions bougé
bougerais	bougeriez	aurais bougé	auriez bougé
bougerait	bougeraient	aurait bougé	auraient bougé
6 présent du subjonctif		**13 passé du subjonctif**	
bouge	bougions	aie bougé	ayons bougé
bouges	bougiez	aies bougé	ayez bougé
bouge	bougent	ait bougé	aient bougé
7 imparfait du subjonctif		**14 plus-que-parfait du subjonctif**	
bougeasse	bougeassions	eusse bougé	eussions bougé
bougeasses	bougeassiez	eusses bougé	eussiez bougé
bougeât	bougeassent	eût bougé	eussent bougé

Impératif
bouge
bougeons
bougez

Words and expressions related to this verb
avoir la bougeotte   to be on the move; to be restless, to move about restlessly; to be fidgety;
   La terre a bougé   The ground shook.
ne pas bouger   not to make a move; **Personne n'a bougé**   Nobody moved.

Get acquainted with what preposition goes with what verb on pages 543–553.

Don't miss orthographically changing verbs on pages 554–556.

The subject pronouns are found on the page facing page 1.

bouillir
to boil

Part. pr. bouillant   **Part. passé bouilli**

The Seven Simple Tenses		The Seven Compound Tenses	
Singular	Plural	Singular	Plural
1 présent de l'indicatif		**8 passé composé**	
bous	bouillons	ai bouilli	avons bouilli
bous	bouillez	as bouilli	avez bouilli
bout	bouillent	a bouilli	ont bouilli
2 imparfait de l'indicatif		**9 plus-que-parfait de l'indicatif**	
bouillais	bouillions	avais bouilli	avions bouilli
bouillais	bouilliez	avais bouilli	aviez bouilli
bouillait	bouillaient	avait bouilli	avaient bouilli
3 passé simple		**10 passé antérieur**	
bouillis	bouillîmes	eus bouilli	eûmes bouilli
bouillis	bouillîtes	eus bouilli	eûtes bouilli
bouillit	bouillirent	eut bouilli	eurent bouilli
4 futur		**11 futur antérieur**	
bouillirai	bouillirons	aurai bouilli	aurons bouilli
bouilliras	bouillirez	auras bouilli	aurez bouilli
bouillira	bouilliront	aura bouilli	auront bouilli
5 conditionnel		**12 conditionnel passé**	
bouillirais	bouillirions	aurais bouilli	aurions bouilli
bouillirais	bouilliriez	aurais bouilli	auriez bouilli
bouillirait	bouilliraient	aurait bouilli	auraient bouilli
6 présent du subjonctif		**13 passé du subjonctif**	
bouille	bouillions	aie bouilli	ayons bouilli
bouilles	bouilliez	aies bouilli	ayez bouilli
bouille	bouillent	ait bouilli	aient bouilli
7 imparfait du subjonctif		**14 plus-que-parfait du subjonctif**	
bouillisse	bouillissions	eusse bouilli	eussions bouilli
bouillisses	bouillissiez	eusses bouilli	eussiez bouilli
bouillît	bouillissent	eût bouilli	eussent bouilli

Impératif
bous
bouillons
bouillez

Words and expressions related to this verb

faire bouillir   to boil
le bouillon   broth; bubble
une bulle *(ewn bewl)*   bubble, blister
faire des bulles   to blow bubbles
la bouillabaisse   fish soup (chowder)

le bouillonnement   bubbling, boiling
faire donner un bouillon   to bring to boil
une bulle de savon   soap bubble
une bouilloire   kettle
réduire en bouillie   to beat to a pulp

Use the EE-zee guide to French pronunciation on pages 566 and 567.

See the summary of sequence of tenses with **si** (*if*) clauses on page 560.

The Seven Simple Tenses		The Seven Compound Tenses	
Singular	Plural	Singular	Plural
1 présent de l'indicatif		8 passé composé	
brosse	**brossons**	**ai brossé**	**avons brossé**
brosses	**brossez**	**as brossé**	**avez brossé**
brosse	**brossent**	**a brossé**	**ont brossé**
2 imparfait de l'indicatif		9 plus-que-parfait de l'indicatif	
brossais	**brossions**	**avais brossé**	**avions brossé**
brossais	**brossiez**	**avais brossé**	**aviez brossé**
brossait	**brossaient**	**avait brossé**	**avaient brossé**
3 passé simple		10 passé antérieur	
brossai	**brossâmes**	**eus brossé**	**eûmes brossé**
brossas	**brossâtes**	**eus brossé**	**eûtes brossé**
brossa	**brossèrent**	**eut brossé**	**eurent brossé**
4 futur		11 futur antérieur	
brosserai	**brosserons**	**aurai brossé**	**aurons brossé**
brosseras	**brosserez**	**auras brossé**	**aurez brossé**
brossera	**brosseront**	**aura brossé**	**auront brossé**
5 conditionnel		12 conditionnel passé	
brosserais	**brosserions**	**aurais brossé**	**aurions brossé**
brosserais	**brosseriez**	**aurais brossé**	**auriez brossé**
brosserait	**brosseraient**	**aurait brossé**	**auraient brossé**
6 présent du subjonctif		13 passé du subjonctif	
brosse	**brossions**	**aie brossé**	**ayons brossé**
brosses	**brossiez**	**aies brossé**	**ayez brossé**
brosse	**brossent**	**ait brossé**	**aient brossé**
7 imparfait du subjonctif		14 plus-que-parfait du subjonctif	
brossasse	**brossassions**	**eusse brossé**	**eussions brossé**
brossasses	**brossassiez**	**eusses brossé**	**eussiez brossé**
brossât	**brossassent**	**eût brossé**	**eussent brossé**

Impératif
brosse
brossons
brossez

Sentences using this verb and words related to it
—**Henriette, as-tu brossé tes souliers?**
—**Non, maman, je ne les ai pas brossés.**
—**Et pourquoi pas, ma petite?**
—**Parce que je n'ai pas de brosse.**

une brosse   brush; **brosse à chaussures**   shoebrush; **brosse à dents**   toothbrush; **brosse à
ongles**   nailbrush
donner un coup de brosse   to brush
le brossage brushing

See also **se brosser.**

If you don't know the French verb for an English verb you have in mind, try the index on pages
503–514.

The Seven Simple Tenses		The Seven Compound Tenses	
Singular	Plural	Singular	Plural
1 présent de l'indicatif		8 passé composé	
me brosse	nous brossons	me suis brossé(e)	nous sommes brossé(e)s
te brosses	vous brossez	t'es brossé(e)	vous êtes brossé(e)(s)
se brosse	se brossent	s'est brossé(e)	se sont brossé(e)s
2 imparfait de l'indicatif		9 plus-que-parfait de l'indicatif	
me brossais	nous brossions	m'étais brossé(e)	nous étions brossé(e)s
te brossais	vous brossiez	t'étais brossé(e)	vous étiez brossé(e)(s)
se brossait	se brossaient	s'était brossé(e)	s'étaient brossé(e)s
3 passé simple		10 passé antérieur	
me brossai	nous brossâmes	me fus brossé(e)	nous fûmes brossé(e)s
te brossas	vous brossâtes	te fus brossé(e)	vous fûtes brossé(e)(s)
se brossa	se brossèrent	se fut brossé(e)	se furent brossé(e)s
4 futur		11 futur antérieur	
me brosserai	nous brosserons	me serai brossé(e)	nous serons brossé(e)s
te brosseras	vous brosserez	te seras brossé(e)	vous serez brossé(e)(s)
se brossera	se brosseront	se sera brossé(e)	se seront brossé(e)s
5 conditionnel		12 conditionnel passé	
me brosserais	nous brosserions	me serais brossé(e)	nous serions brossé(e)s
te brosserais	vous brosseriez	te serais brossé(e)	vous seriez brossé(e)(s)
se brosserait	se brosseraient	se serait brossé(e)	se seraient brossé(e)s
6 présent du subjonctif		13 passé du subjonctif	
me brosse	nous brossions	me sois brossé(e)	nous soyons brossé(e)s
te brosses	vous brossiez	te sois brossé(e)	vous soyez brossé(e)(s)
se brosse	se brossent	se soit brossé(e)	se soient brossé(e)s
7 imparfait du subjonctif		14 plus-que-parfait du subjonctif	
me brossasse	nous brossassions	me fusse brossé(e)	nous fussions brossé(e)s
te brossasses	vous brossassiez	te fusses brossé(e)	vous fussiez brossé(e)(s)
se brossât	se brossassent	se fût brossé(e)	se fussent brossé(e)s

Impératif
brosse-toi; ne te brosse pas
brossons-nous; ne nous brossons pas
brossez-vous; ne vous brossez pas

Sentences using this verb and words related to it
—Tina Marie, est-ce que tu t'es brossée?
—Non, maman, je ne me suis pas brossée.
—Et pourquoi pas? Brosse-toi vite!
—Parce que je n'ai pas de brosse à habits, je n'ai pas de brosse à cheveux, je n'ai pas de brosse à chaussures. Je n'ai aucune brosse. Je n'ai pas de brosse à dents, non plus.
—Quelle fille!

se brosser les dents, les cheveux, etc.   to brush one's teeth, hair, etc.

For other words and expressions related to this verb, see **brosser.**

If you want to see a sample English verb fully conjugated in all the tenses, check out pages xiii and xiv.

The Seven Simple Tenses		The Seven Compound Tenses	
Singular	Plural	Singular	Plural

1   présent de l'indicatif

		8 passé composé	
brûle	brûlons	ai brûlé	avons brûlé
brûles	brûlez	as brûlé	avez brûlé
brûle	brûlent	a brûlé	ont brûlé

2   imparfait de l'indicatif

		9 plus-que-parfait de l'indicatif	
brûlais	brûlions	avais brûlé	avions brûlé
brûlais	brûliez	avais brûlé	aviez brûlé
brûlait	brûlaient	avait brûlé	avaient brûlé

3   passé simple

		10 passé antérieur	
brûlai	brûlâmes	eus brûlé	eûmes brûlé
brûlas	brûlâtes	eus brûlé	eûtes brûlé
brûla	brûlèrent	eut brûlé	eurent brûlé

4   futur

		11 futur antérieur	
brûlerai	brûlerons	aurai brûlé	aurons brûlé
brûleras	brûlerez	auras brûlé	aurez brûlé
brûlera	brûleront	aura brûlé	auront brûlé

5   conditionnel

		12 conditionnel passé	
brûlerais	brûlerions	aurais brûlé	aurions brûlé
brûlerais	brûleriez	aurais brûlé	auriez brûlé
brûlerait	brûleraient	aurait brûlé	auraient brûlé

6   présent du subjonctif

		13 passé du subjonctif	
brûle	brûlions	aie brûlé	ayons brûlé
brûles	brûliez	aies brûlé	ayez brûlé
brûle	brûlent	ait brûlé	aient brûlé

7   imparfait du subjonctif

		14 plus-que-parfait du subjonctif	
brûlasse	brûlassions	eusse brûlé	eussions brûlé
brûlasses	brûlassiez	eusses brûlé	eussiez brûlé
brûlât	brûlassent	eût brûlé	eussent brûlé

Impératif
brûle
brûlons
brûlez

Sentences using this verb and words related to it
—**Joséphine, avez-vous brûlé les vieux papiers que je vous ai donnés?**
—**Oui, madame, et je me suis brûlée. J'ai une brûlure aux doigts.**

une brûlure   burn
un brûleur   burner, roaster
brûler d'amour   to be madly in love
brûler de faire qqch   to be eager to do
something

brûler un feu rouge   to pass through a red
traffic light
une crème brûlée   a crème brûlée (dessert)

It's important that you be familiar with the Subjunctive. See pages 560–565.

to hide

The Seven Simple Tenses		The Seven Compound Tenses	
Singular	Plural	Singular	Plural
1　présent de l'indicatif		**8　passé composé**	
cache	cachons	ai caché	avons caché
caches	cachez	as caché	avez caché
cache	cachent	a caché	ont caché
2　imparfait de l'indicatif		**9　plus-que-parfait de l'indicatif**	
cachais	cachions	avais caché	avions caché
cachais	cachiez	avais caché	aviez caché
cachait	cachaient	avait caché	avaient caché
3　passé simple		**10　passé antérieur**	
cachai	cachâmes	eus caché	eûmes caché
cachas	cachâtes	eus caché	eûtes caché
cacha	cachèrent	eut caché	eurent caché
4　futur		**11　futur antérieur**	
cacherai	cacherons	aurai caché	aurons caché
cacheras	cacherez	auras caché	aurez caché
cachera	cacheront	aura caché	auront caché
5　conditionnel		**12　conditionnel passé**	
cacherais	cacherions	aurais caché	aurions caché
cacherais	cacheriez	aurais caché	auriez caché
cacherait	cacheraient	aurait caché	auraient caché
6　présent du subjonctif		**13　passé du subjonctif**	
cache	cachions	aie caché	ayons caché
caches	cachiez	aies caché	ayez caché
cache	cachent	ait caché	aient caché
7　imparfait du subjonctif		**14　plus-que-parfait du subjonctif**	
cachasse	cachassions	eusse caché	eussions caché
cachasses	cachassiez	eusses caché	eussiez caché
cachât	cachassent	eût caché	eussent caché

Impératif
cache
cachons
cachez

Sentences using this verb and words related to it
　—Pierre, qu'est-ce que tu as caché derrière toi?
　—Rien, papa.
　—Ne me dis pas ça. Tu caches quelque chose.
　—Voilà, papa, c'est un petit chat que j'ai trouvé dans le parc.

une cache, une cachette　hiding place
la cache　cache (computer)
un cachet　seal, mark
un cachetage　sealing
cacheter　to seal up

le cache-cache　hide-and-seek
le vin cacheté　vintage wine
cacher qqch à qqn　to hide something from
　someone
un cache-nez　muffler

See also **se cacher.**

The Seven Simple Tenses		The Seven Compound Tenses	
Singular	Plural	Singular	Plural
1 présent de l'indicatif		**8 passé composé**	
me cache	**nous cachons**	**me suis caché(e)**	**nous sommes caché(e)s**
te caches	**vous cachez**	**t'es caché(e)**	**vous êtes caché(e)(s)**
se cache	**se cachent**	**s'est caché(e)**	**se sont caché(e)s**
2 imparfait de l'indicatif		**9 plus-que-parfait de l'indicatif**	
me cachais	**nous cachions**	**m'étais caché(e)**	**nous étions caché(e)s**
te cachais	**vous cachiez**	**t'étais caché(e)**	**vous étiez caché(e)(s)**
se cachait	**se cachaient**	**s'était caché(e)**	**s'étaient caché(e)s**
3 passé simple		**10 passé antérieur**	
me cachai	**nous cachâmes**	**me fus caché(e)**	**nous fûmes caché(e)s**
te cachas	**vous cachâtes**	**te fus caché(e)**	**vous fûtes caché(e)(s)**
se cacha	**se cachèrent**	**se fut caché(e)**	**se furent caché(e)s**
4 futur		**11 futur antérieur**	
me cacherai	**nous cacherons**	**me serai caché(e)**	**nous serons caché(e)s**
te cacheras	**vous cacherez**	**te seras caché(e)**	**vous serez caché(e)(s)**
se cachera	**se cacheront**	**se sera caché(e)**	**se seront caché(e)s**
5 conditionnel		**12 conditionnel passé**	
me cacherais	**nous cacherions**	**me serais caché(e)**	**nous serions caché(e)s**
te cacherais	**vous cacheriez**	**te serais caché(e)**	**vous seriez caché(e)(s)**
se cacherait	**se cacheraient**	**se serait caché(e)**	**se seraient caché(e)s**
6 présent du subjonctif		**13 passé du subjonctif**	
me cache	**nous cachions**	**me sois caché(e)**	**nous soyons caché(e)s**
te caches	**vous cachiez**	**te sois caché(e)**	**vous soyez caché(e)(s)**
se cache	**se cachent**	**se soit caché(e)**	**se soient caché(e)s**
7 imparfait du subjonctif		**14 plus-que-parfait du subjonctif**	
me cachasse	**nous cachassions**	**me fusse caché(e)**	**nous fussions caché(e)s**
te cachasses	**vous cachassiez**	**te fusses caché(e)**	**vous fussiez caché(e)(s)**
se cachât	**se cachassent**	**se fût caché(e)**	**se fussent caché(e)s**

Impératif
cache-toi; ne te cache pas
cachons-nous; ne nous cachons pas
cachez-vous; ne vous cachez pas

Sentences using this verb and words related to it

   J'ai un petit chien que j'appelle Coco. Quelquefois je ne peux pas le trouver parce qu'il se cache sous mon lit ou derrière l'arbre dans le jardin. La semaine dernière il s'est caché sous le chapeau de mon père. Il aime jouer à cache-cache. Il est très intelligent.

une cache, une cachette hiding place	**le cache-cache** hide-and-seek
un cachet seal, mark	**le vin cacheté** vintage wine
un cachetage sealing	**un cachot** cell, prison; dungeon
se cacher de qqn to hide from someone	**en cachette de qqn** behind someone's back
cacheter to seal up	

See also **cacher.**

to break

The Seven Simple Tenses		The Seven Compound Tenses	
Singular	Plural	Singular	Plural
1 présent de l'indicatif		8 passé composé	
casse	cassons	ai cassé	avons cassé
casses	cassez	as cassé	avez cassé
casse	cassent	a cassé	ont cassé
2 imparfait de l'indicatif		9 plus-que-parfait de l'indicatif	
cassais	cassions	avais cassé	avions cassé
cassais	cassiez	avais cassé	aviez cassé
cassait	cassaient	avait cassé	avaient cassé
3 passé simple		10 passé antérieur	
cassai	cassâmes	eus cassé	eûmes cassé
cassas	cassâtes	eus cassé	eûtes cassé
cassa	cassèrent	eut cassé	eurent cassé
4 futur		11 futur antérieur	
casserai	casserons	aurai cassé	aurons cassé
casseras	casserez	auras cassé	aurez cassé
cassera	casseront	aura cassé	auront cassé
5 conditionnel		12 conditionnel passé	
casserais	casserions	aurais cassé	aurions cassé
casserais	casseriez	aurais cassé	auriez cassé
casserait	casseraient	aurait cassé	auraient cassé
6 présent du subjonctif		13 passé du subjonctif	
casse	cassions	aie cassé	ayons cassé
casses	cassiez	aies cassé	ayez cassé
casse	cassent	ait cassé	aient cassé
7 imparfait du subjonctif		14 plus-que-parfait du subjonctif	
cassasse	cassassions	eusse cassé	eussions cassé
cassasses	cassassiez	eusses cassé	eussiez cassé
cassât	cassassent	eût cassé	eussent cassé

Impératif
casse
cassons
cassez

Sentences using this verb and words related to it
—Jean, c'est toi qui as cassé mon joli vase?
—Non, maman, c'est Mathilde.
—Mathilde, c'est toi qui as cassé mon joli vase?
—Non, maman, c'est Jean.
—Quels enfants!

une casse breakage, damage
un casse-croûte snack
un casse-noisettes, un casse-noix nutcracker
casser la croûte to have a snack
un casse-pieds a bore, a pain in the neck

un cassement de tête puzzle, worry
un casse-tête puzzle
concasser to crush (cereal, sugar lumps, stones)

See also **se casser.**

to break (a part of one's body, *e.g.*, leg, arm, nose)

The Seven Simple Tenses		The Seven Compound Tenses	
Singular	Plural	Singular	Plural
1 présent de l'indicatif		**8 passé composé**	
me casse	**nous cassons**	**me suis cassé(e)**	**nous sommes cassé(e)s**
te casses	**vous cassez**	**t'es cassé(e)**	**vous êtes cassé(e)(s)**
se casse	**se cassent**	**s'est cassé(e)**	**se sont cassé(e)s**
2 imparfait de l'indicatif		**9 plus-que-parfait de l'indicatif**	
me cassais	**nous cassions**	**m'étais cassé(e)**	**nous étions cassé(e)s**
te cassais	**vous cassiez**	**t'étais cassé(e)**	**vous étiez cassé(e)(s)**
se cassait	**se cassaient**	**s'était cassé(e)**	**s'étaient cassé(e)s**
3 passé simple		**10 passé antérieur**	
me cassai	**nous cassâmes**	**me fus cassé(e)**	**nous fûmes cassé(e)s**
te cassas	**vous cassâtes**	**te fus cassé(e)**	**vous fûtes cassé(e)(s)**
se cassa	**se cassèrent**	**se fut cassé(e)**	**se furent cassé(e)s**
4 futur		**11 futur antérieur**	
me casserai	**nous casserons**	**me serai cassé(e)**	**nous serons cassé(e)s**
te casseras	**vous casserez**	**te seras cassé(e)**	**vous serez cassé(e)(s)**
se cassera	**se casseront**	**se sera cassé(e)**	**se seront cassé(e)s**
5 conditionnel		**12 conditionnel passé**	
me casserais	**nous casserions**	**me serais cassé(e)**	**nous serions cassé(e)s**
te casserais	**vous casseriez**	**te serais cassé(e)**	**vous seriez cassé(e)(s)**
se casserait	**se casseraient**	**se serait cassé(e)**	**se seraient cassé(e)s**
6 présent du subjonctif		**13 passé du subjonctif**	
me casse	**nous cassions**	**me sois cassé(e)**	**nous soyons cassé(e)s**
te casses	**vous cassiez**	**te sois cassé(e)**	**vous soyez cassé(e)(s)**
se casse	**se cassent**	**se soit cassé(e)**	**se soient cassé(e)s**
7 imparfait du subjonctif		**14 plus-que-parfait du subjonctif**	
me cassasse	**nous cassassions**	**me fusse cassé(e)**	**nous fussions cassé(e)s**
te cassasses	**vous cassassiez**	**te fusses cassé(e)**	**vous fussiez cassé(e)(s)**
se cassât	**se cassassent**	**se fût cassé(e)**	**se fussent cassé(e)s**

Impératif
casse-toi . . . ; ne te casse pas . . .
cassons-nous . . . ; ne nous cassons pas . . .
cassez-vous . . . ; ne vous cassez pas . . .

Sentences using this verb and words related do it
     Pendant les vacances d'hiver, nous sommes allés faire du ski dans les montagnes. Mon père s'est cassé le bras, ma mère s'est cassé la jambe, et moi, je me suis cassé le pied.

se casser la tête   to rack one's brains
se casser le nez   to find nobody answering the door
casser la tête à qqn   to annoy someone;   **un casse-cou**   daredevil, reckless person

See also **casser.**

How are you doing? Find out with the verb drills and tests with answers explained on pages 622–673.

to cause, to chat

The Seven Simple Tenses		The Seven Compound Tenses	
Singular	Plural	Singular	Plural
1 présent de l'indicatif		**8 passé composé**	
cause	causons	ai causé	avons causé
causes	causez	as causé	avez causé
cause	causent	a causé	ont causé
2 imparfait de l'indicatif		**9 plus-que-parfait de l'indicatif**	
causais	causions	avais causé	avions causé
causais	causiez	avais causé	aviez causé
causait	causaient	avait causé	avaient causé
3 passé simple		**10 passé antérieur**	
causai	causâmes	eus causé	eûmes causé
causas	causâtes	eus causé	eûtes causé
causa	causèrent	eut causé	eurent causé
4 futur		**11 futur antérieur**	
causerai	causerons	aurai causé	aurons causé
causeras	causerez	auras causé	aurez causé
causera	causeront	aura causé	auront causé
5 conditionnel		**12 conditionnel passé**	
causerais	causerions	aurais causé	aurions causé
causerais	causeriez	aurais causé	auriez causé
causerait	causeraient	aurait causé	auraient causé
6 présent du subjonctif		**13 passé du subjonctif**	
cause	causions	aie causé	ayons causé
causes	causiez	aies causé	ayez causé
cause	causent	ait causé	aient causé
7 imparfait du subjonctif		**14 plus-que-parfait du subjonctif**	
causasse	causassions	eusse causé	eussions causé
causasses	causassiez	eusses causé	eussiez causé
causât	causassent	eût causé	eussent causé

Impératif
cause
causons
causez

Sentences using this verb and words related to it

   Quand je voyage, j'aime beaucoup causer avec les passagers. Est-ce que vous causez avec vos voisins dans la salle de classe? En français, bien sûr! Je connais un garçon qui n'est pas très causant.

causant, causante talkative	**une cause célèbre** famous trial
causatif, causative causative	**une causerie** chat, informal talk
une cause cause, reason	**causeur, causeuse** talkative
causer de la pluie et du beau temps to chat	**une causeuse** love seat
about the weather	**causer de la peine à qqn** to hurt someone
une causette chat (Internet)	

Want to learn more idiomatic expressions that contain verbs? Look at pages 530–542.

84

to yield, to cede

The Seven Simple Tenses		The Seven Compound Tenses	
Singular	Plural	Singular	Plural
1 présent de l'indicatif		8 passé composé	
cède	cédons	ai cédé	avons cédé
cèdes	cédez	as cédé	avez cédé
cède	cèdent	a cédé	ont cédé
2 imparfait de l'indicatif		9 plus-que-parfait de l'indicatif	
cédais	cédions	avais cédé	avions cédé
cédais	cédiez	avais cédé	aviez cédé
cédait	cédaient	avait cédé	avaient cédé
3 passé simple		10 passé antérieur	
cédai	cédâmes	eus cédé	eûmes cédé
cédas	cédâtes	eus cédé	eûtes cédé
céda	cédèrent	eut cédé	eurent cédé
4 futur		11 futur antérieur	
céderai	céderons	aurai cédé	aurons cédé
céderas	céderez	auras cédé	aurez cédé
cédera	céderont	aura cédé	auront cédé
5 conditionnel		12 conditionnel passé	
céderais	céderions	aurais cédé	aurions cédé
céderais	céderiez	aurais cédé	auriez cédé
céderait	céderaient	aurait cédé	auraient cédé
6 présent du subjonctif		13 passé du subjonctif	
cède	cédions	aie cédé	ayons cédé
cèdes	cédiez	aies cédé	ayez cédé
cède	cèdent	ait cédé	aient cédé
7 imparfait du subjonctif		14 plus-que-parfait du subjonctif	
cédasse	cédassions	eusse cédé	eussions cédé
cédasses	cédassiez	eusses cédé	eussiez cédé
cédât	cédassent	eût cédé	eussent cédé

Impératif
cède
cédons
cédez

Sentences using this verb and words related to it
   Hier soir j'ai pris l'autobus pour rentrer chez moi. J'ai pris la dernière place libre. Après quelques minutes, une vieille dame est entrée dans l'autobus et j'ai cédé ma place à cette aimable personne.

céder à   to give up, give in, yield to
accéder à   to accede to, to comply with
concéder à   to concede to, to grant
décéder   to pass away

céder le pas à qqn   to give way to someone
céder qqch à qqn   to let somebody have something

NOTE: The Académie française now allows the accent grave (`) in the future (e.g., **je cèderai**) and conditional (e.g., **je cèderais**) of this verb.

to cease

The Seven Simple Tenses		The Seven Compound Tenses	
Singular	Plural	Singular	Plural
1 présent de l'indicatif		8 passé composé	
cesse	cessons	ai cessé	avons cessé
cesses	cessez	as cessé	avez cessé
cesse	cessent	a cessé	ont cessé
2 imparfait de l'indicatif		9 plus-que-parfait de l'indicatif	
cessais	cessions	avais cessé	avions cessé
cessais	cessiez	avais cessé	aviez cessé
cessait	cessaient	avait cessé	avaient cessé
3 passé simple		10 passé antérieur	
cessai	cessâmes	eus cessé	eûmes cessé
cessas	cessâtes	eus cessé	eûtes cessé
cessa	cessèrent	eut cessé	eurent cessé
4 futur		11 futur antérieur	
cesserai	cesserons	aurai cessé	aurons cessé
cesseras	cesserez	auras cessé	aurez cessé
cessera	cesseront	aura cessé	auront cessé
5 conditionnel		12 conditionnel passé	
cesserais	cesserions	aurais cessé	aurions cessé
cesserais	cesseriez	aurais cessé	auriez cessé
cesserait	cesseraient	aurait cessé	auraient cessé
6 présent du subjonctif		13 passé du subjonctif	
cesse	cessions	aie cessé	ayons cessé
cesses	cessiez	aies cessé	ayez cessé
cesse	cessent	ait cessé	aient cessé
7 imparfait du subjonctif		14 plus-que-parfait du subjonctif	
cessasse	cessassions	eusse cessé	eussions cessé
cessasses	cessassiez	eusses cessé	eussiez cessé
cessât	cessassent	eût cessé	eussent cessé

Impératif
cesse
cessons
cessez

Sentences using this verb and words related to it
—Robert, cesse de parler, s'il te plaît! Tu es trop bavard dans cette classe.
—Oui, monsieur. Je cesse de parler. Je me tais.

une cesse   cease, ceasing; **cesser de faire qqch**   to stop doing something
sans cesse   constantly
incessant   incessant, ceaseless
cesser de se voir   to stop seeing each other; **Il n'a pas cessé de neiger depuis hier**   It has not stopped snowing since yesterday.
cesser le feu   to cease fire; **un cessez-le-feu**   cease-fire

For **je me tais,** see **se taire.** See also **bavarder.**

The Seven Simple Tenses		The Seven Compound Tenses	
Singular	Plural	Singular	Plural
1 présent de l'indicatif		8 passé composé	
change	changeons	ai changé	avons changé
changes	changez	as changé	avez changé
change	changent	a changé	ont changé
2 imparfait de l'indicatif		9 plus-que-parfait de l'indicatif	
changeais	changions	avais changé	avions changé
changeais	changiez	avais changé	aviez changé
changeait	changeaient	avait changé	avaient changé
3 passé simple		10 passé antérieur	
changeai	changeâmes	eus changé	eûmes changé
changeas	changeâtes	eus changé	eûtes changé
changea	changèrent	eut changé	eurent changé
4 futur		11 futur antérieur	
changerai	changerons	aurai changé	aurons changé
changeras	changerez	auras changé	aurez changé
changera	changeront	aura changé	auront changé
5 conditionnel		12 conditionnel passé	
changerais	changerions	aurais changé	aurions changé
changerais	changeriez	aurais changé	auriez changé
changerait	changeraient	aurait changé	auraient changé
6 présent du subjonctif		13 passé du subjonctif	
change	changions	aie changé	ayons changé
changes	changiez	aies changé	ayez changé
change	changent	ait changé	aient changé
7 imparfait du subjonctif		14 plus-que-parfait du subjonctif	
changeasse	changeassions	eusse changé	eussions changé
changeasses	changeassiez	eusses changé	eussiez changé
changeât	changeassent	eût changé	eussent changé

Impératif
change
changeons
changez

Common idiomatic expressions using this verb

   Je vais changer de vêtements maintenant parce que je prends le train pour Paris, et là, je vais changer de train pour aller à Marseille.

changer d'avis   to change one's mind
changer de route   to take another road
un changement soudain   a sudden change
une pièce/un pneu de rechange   spare part/tire

échanger   to exchange
Plus ça change, plus c'est la même chose!
   The more it changes, the more it remains the same!

Want to learn more idiomatic expressions that contain verbs? Look at pages 530–542.

The subject pronouns are found on the page facing page 1.   **87**

chanter
to sing

Part. pr. **chantant**   Part. passé **chanté**

The Seven Simple Tenses		The Seven Compound Tenses	
Singular	Plural	Singular	Plural
1 présent de l'indicatif		**8 passé composé**	
chante	chantons	ai chanté	avons chanté
chantes	chantez	as chanté	avez chanté
chante	chantent	a chanté	ont chanté
2 imparfait de l'indicatif		**9 plus-que-parfait de l'indicatif**	
chantais	chantions	avais chanté	avions chanté
chantais	chantiez	avais chanté	aviez chanté
chantait	chantaient	avait chanté	avaient chanté
3 passé simple		**10 passé antérieur**	
chantai	chantâmes	eus chanté	eûmes chanté
chantas	chantâtes	eus chanté	eûtes chanté
chanta	chantèrent	eut chanté	eurent chanté
4 futur		**11 futur antérieur**	
chanterai	chanterons	aurai chanté	aurons chanté
chanteras	chanterez	auras chanté	aurez chanté
chantera	chanteront	aura chanté	auront chanté
5 conditionnel		**12 conditionnel passé**	
chanterais	chanterions	aurais chanté	aurions chanté
chanterais	chanteriez	aurais chanté	auriez chanté
chanterait	chanteraient	aurait chanté	auraient chanté
6 présent du subjonctif		**13 passé du subjonctif**	
chante	chantions	aie chanté	ayons chanté
chantes	chantiez	aies chanté	ayez chanté
chante	chantent	ait chanté	aient chanté
7 imparfait du subjonctif		**14 plus-que-parfait du subjonctif**	
chantasse	chantassions	eusse chanté	eussions chanté
chantasses	chantassiez	eusses chanté	eussiez chanté
chantât	chantassent	eût chanté	eussent chanté

Impératif
chante
chantons
chantez

Sentences using this verb and words related to it

Madame Chanteclaire aime bien chanter en jouant du piano. Tous les matins elle chante dans la salle de bains et quelquefois elle chante quand elle dort. Elle donne des leçons de chant.

une chanson song
chansons! fiddlesticks! nonsense!
C'est une autre chanson! That's another story!
chanson d'amour love song
Si ça vous chante . . . If you are in the mood for it . . .

chanson de geste epic poem
un chant carol, chant, singing
le chantage blackmail
chanteur, chanteuse singer
enchanter to enchant
Enchanté! Pleased to meet you!

to burden, to charge, to load

The Seven Simple Tenses		The Seven Compound Tenses	
Singular	Plural	Singular	Plural
1 présent de l'indicatif		**8 passé composé**	
charge	chargeons	ai chargé	avons chargé
charges	chargez	as chargé	avez chargé
charge	chargent	a chargé	ont chargé
2 imparfait de l'indicatif		**9 plus-que-parfait de l'indicatif**	
chargeais	chargions	avais chargé	avions chargé
chargeais	chargiez	avais chargé	aviez chargé
chargeait	chargeaient	avait chargé	avaient chargé
3 passé simple		**10 passé antérieur**	
chargeai	chargeâmes	eus chargé	eûmes chargé
chargeas	chargeâtes	eus chargé	eûtes chargé
chargea	chargèrent	eut chargé	eurent chargé
4 futur		**11 futur antérieur**	
chargerai	chargerons	aurai chargé	aurons chargé
chargeras	chargerez	auras chargé	aurez chargé
chargera	chargeront	aura chargé	auront chargé
5 conditionnel		**12 conditionnel passé**	
chargerais	chargerions	aurais chargé	aurions chargé
chargerais	chargeriez	aurais chargé	auriez chargé
chargerait	chargeraient	aurait chargé	auraient chargé
6 présent du subjonctif		**13 passé du subjonctif**	
charge	chargions	aie chargé	ayons chargé
charges	chargiez	aies chargé	ayez chargé
charge	chargent	ait chargé	aient chargé
7 imparfait du subjonctif		**14 plus-que-parfait du subjonctif**	
chargeasse	chargeassions	eusse chargé	eussions chargé
chargeasses	chargeassiez	eusses chargé	eussiez chargé
chargeât	chargeassent	eût chargé	eussent chargé

Impératif
charge
chargeons
chargez

Common idiomatic expressions using this verb

Je connais une dame qui charge son mari de paquets chaque fois qu'ils vont faire des emplettes. Une fois quand je les ai vus en ville, il a chargé sa femme de malédictions.

une charge   a load, burden
chargé d'impôts   heavily taxed
un chargé d'affaires   envoy
Je m'en charge   I'll take care of it.
télécharger   to download (computer)

charger de malédictions   to curse
charger de louanges   to overwhelm with praises
un chargeur de batterie   battery charger
décharger   to unload

Grammar putting you in a tense mood? Review the definitions of basic grammatical terms with examples on pages 674–688.

to hunt, to pursue, to chase, to drive out

The Seven Simple Tenses		The Seven Compound Tenses	
Singular	Plural	Singular	Plural
1 présent de l'indicatif		8 passé composé	
chasse	chassons	ai chassé	avons chassé
chasses	chassez	as chassé	avez chassé
chasse	chassent	a chassé	ont chassé
2 imparfait de l'indicatif		9 plus-que-parfait de l'indicatif	
chassais	chassions	avais chassé	avions chassé
chassais	chassiez	avais chassé	aviez chassé
chassait	chassaient	avait chassé	avaient chassé
3 passé simple		10 passé antérieur	
chassai	chassâmes	eus chassé	eûmes chassé
chassas	chassâtes	eus chassé	eûtes chassé
chassa	chassèrent	eut chassé	eurent chassé
4 futur		11 futur antérieur	
chasserai	chasserons	aurai chassé	aurons chassé
chasseras	chasserez	auras chassé	aurez chassé
chassera	chasseront	aura chassé	auront chassé
5 conditionnel		12 conditionnel passé	
chasserais	chasserions	aurais chassé	aurions chassé
chasserais	chasseriez	aurais chassé	auriez chassé
chasserait	chasseraient	aurait chassé	auraient chassé
6 présent du subjonctif		13 passé du subjonctif	
chasse	chassions	aie chassé	ayons chassé
chasses	chassiez	aies chassé	ayez chassé
chasse	chassent	ait chassé	aient chassé
7 imparfait du subjonctif		14 plus-que-parfait du subjonctif	
chassasse	chassassions	eusse chassé	eussions chassé
chassasses	chassassiez	eusses chassé	eussiez chassé
chassât	chassassent	eût chassé	eussent chassé

Impératif
chasse
chassons
chassez

Sentences using this verb and words related to it
   Avez-vous jamais chassé des papillons? Tout le monde aime chasser de temps en temps. Les chasseurs aiment chasser. Les chats aiment chasser les souris. Et les garçons aiment chasser les jolies jeunes filles.

pourchasser   to chase, pursue
un chasse-neige   snowplow
tirer la chasse d'eau   to flush the toilet

Pronounce out loud this tongue twister as fast as you can: **Le chasseur, sachant* chasser sans son chien, chassera.** (The hunter, knowing how to hunt without his dog, will hunt.)
*Sachant is the pres. part. of **savoir**.

to look for, to search, to seek

The Seven Simple Tenses		The Seven Compound Tenses	
Singular	Plural	Singular	Plural

1 présent de l'indicatif		8 passé composé	
cherche	cherchons	ai cherché	avons cherché
cherches	cherchez	as cherché	avez cherché
cherche	cherchent	a cherché	ont cherché

2 imparfait de l'indicatif		9 plus-que-parfait de l'indicatif	
cherchais	cherchions	avais cherché	avions cherché
cherchais	cherchiez	avais cherché	aviez cherché
cherchait	cherchaient	avait cherché	avaient cherché

3 passé simple		10 passé antérieur	
cherchai	cherchâmes	eus cherché	eûmes cherché
cherchas	cherchâtes	eus cherché	eûtes cherché
chercha	cherchèrent	eut cherché	eurent cherché

4 futur		11 futur antérieur	
chercherai	chercherons	aurai cherché	aurons cherché
chercheras	chercherez	auras cherché	aurez cherché
cherchera	chercheront	aura cherché	auront cherché

5 conditionnel		12 conditionnel passé	
chercherais	chercherions	aurais cherché	aurions cherché
chercherais	chercheriez	aurais cherché	auriez cherché
chercherait	chercheraient	aurait cherché	auraient cherché

6 présent du subjonctif		13 passé du subjonctif	
cherche	cherchions	aie cherché	ayons cherché
cherches	cherchiez	aies cherché	ayez cherché
cherche	cherchent	ait cherché	aient cherché

7 imparfait du subjonctif		14 plus-que-parfait du subjonctif	
cherchasse	cherchassions	eusse cherché	eussions cherché
cherchasses	cherchassiez	eusses cherché	eussiez cherché
cherchât	cherchassent	eût cherché	eussent cherché

Impératif
cherche
cherchons
cherchez

Sentences using this verb and words related to it
—Monsieur, monsieur, j'ai perdu mon livre de français. J'ai cherché partout et je n'arrive pas à le trouver.
—Continue à chercher parce que demain je donnerai un examen.

se chercher   to look for one another
chercheur   seeker, investigator, researcher
aller chercher   to go and get
chercher à   to attempt to, try to
aller chercher qqn ou qqch   to go get someone or something

rechercher   to investigate, to seek, to look for again
faire des travaux de recherches   to carry out research work
envoyer chercher   to send for
un moteur de recherche   search engine (Internet)

The subject pronouns are found on the page facing page 1.   **91**

to cherish

The Seven Simple Tenses		The Seven Compound Tenses	
Singular	Plural	Singular	Plural
1 présent de l'indicatif		8 passé composé	
chéris	chérissons	ai chéri	avons chéri
chéris	chérissez	as chéri	avez chéri
chérit	chérissent	a chéri	ont chéri
2 imparfait de l'indicatif		9 plus-que-parfait de l'indicatif	
chérissais	chérissions	avais chéri	avions chéri
chérissais	chérissiez	avais chéri	aviez chéri
chérissait	chérissaient	avait chéri	avaient chéri
3 passé simple		10 passé antérieur	
chéris	chérîmes	eus chéri	eûmes chéri
chéris	chérîtes	eus chéri	eûtes chéri
chérit	chérirent	eut chéri	eurent chéri
4 futur		11 futur antérieur	
chérirai	chérirons	aurai chéri	aurons chéri
chériras	chérirez	auras chéri	aurez chéri
chérira	chériront	aura chéri	auront chéri
5 conditionnel		12 conditionnel passé	
chérirais	chéririons	aurais chéri	aurions chéri
chérirais	chéririez	aurais chéri	auriez chéri
chérirait	chériraient	aurait chéri	auraient chéri
6 présent du subjonctif		13 passé du subjonctif	
chérisse	chérissions	aie chéri	ayons chéri
chérisses	chérissiez	aies chéri	ayez chéri
chérisse	chérissent	ait chéri	aient chéri
7 imparfait du subjonctif		14 plus-que-parfait du subjonctif	
chérisse	chérissions	eusse chéri	eussions chéri
chérisses	chérissiez	eusses chéri	eussiez chéri
chérît	chérissent	eût chéri	eussent chéri

Impératif
chéris
chérissons
chérissez

Words and expressions related to this verb
cher, chère   dear; expensive
Ça coûte cher!   That costs a lot!
chéri, chérie   darling, dear
chèrement   dearly
renchérir   to go up in cost, to make a higher bid

acheter cher   to buy at a high price
vendre cher   to sell at a high price
Vous me le paierez cher!   You will pay dearly for it!
un renchérissement   increase

Taking a trip? Check out the popular words, phrases, and expressions for travelers on pages 599–621.

to choose, to select, to pick

The Seven Simple Tenses		The Seven Compound Tenses	
Singular	Plural	Singular	Plural
1 présent de l'indicatif		**8 passé composé**	
choisis	**choisissons**	**ai choisi**	**avons choisi**
choisis	**choisissez**	**as choisi**	**avez choisi**
choisit	**choisissent**	**a choisi**	**ont choisi**
2 imparfait de l'indicatif		**9 plus-que-parfait de l'indicatif**	
choisissais	**choisissions**	**avais choisi**	**avions choisi**
choisissais	**choisissiez**	**avais choisi**	**aviez choisi**
choisissait	**choisissaient**	**avait choisi**	**avaient choisi**
3 passé simple		**10 passé antérieur**	
choisis	**choisîmes**	**eus choisi**	**eûmes choisi**
choisis	**choisîtes**	**eus choisi**	**eûtes choisi**
choisit	**choisirent**	**eut choisi**	**eurent choisi**
4 futur		**11 futur antérieur**	
choisirai	**choisirons**	**aurai choisi**	**aurons choisi**
choisiras	**choisirez**	**auras choisi**	**aurez choisi**
choisira	**choisiront**	**aura choisi**	**auront choisi**
5 conditionnel		**12 conditionnel passé**	
choisirais	**choisirions**	**aurais choisi**	**aurions choisi**
choisirais	**choisiriez**	**aurais choisi**	**auriez choisi**
choisirait	**choisiraient**	**aurait choisi**	**auraient choisi**
6 présent du subjonctif		**13 passé du subjonctif**	
choisisse	**choisissions**	**aie choisi**	**ayons choisi**
choisisses	**choisissiez**	**aies choisi**	**ayez choisi**
choisisse	**choisissent**	**ait choisi**	**aient choisi**
7 imparfait du subjonctif		**14 plus-que-parfait du subjonctif**	
choisisse	**choisissions**	**eusse choisi**	**eussions choisi**
choisisses	**choisissiez**	**eusses choisi**	**eussiez choisi**
choisît	**choisissent**	**eût choisi**	**eussent choisi**

Impératif
choisis
choisissons
choisissez

Sentences using this verb and words related to it
   **Hier soir j'ai dîné dans un restaurant français avec des amis. J'ai choisi du poisson.
Raymond a choisi de la viande et Joseph a choisi une omelette.**

un choix   choice; **faire un bon choix**   to make a good choice
faire choix de   to make choice of; **faire un mauvais choix**   to make a bad choice
l'embarras du choix   too much to choose from; **un choix de poèmes**   a selection of poems
Il n'y a pas grand choix   There's not much choice.
savoir choisir ses amis   to know how to choose one's friends
au choix   optional, elective

The subject pronouns are found on the page facing page 1.   **93**

chuchoter

Part. pr. **chuchotant**   Part. passé **chuchoté**

to whisper

The Seven Simple Tenses		The Seven Compound Tenses	
Singular	Plural	Singular	Plural
1 présent de l'indicatif		**8 passé composé**	
chuchote	chuchotons	ai chuchoté	avons chuchoté
chuchotes	chuchotez	as chuchoté	avez chuchoté
chuchote	chuchotent	a chuchoté	ont chuchoté
2 imparfait de l'indicatif		**9 plus-que-parfait de l'indicatif**	
chuchotais	chuchotions	avais chuchoté	avions chuchoté
chuchotais	chuchotiez	avais chuchoté	aviez chuchoté
chuchotait	chuchotaient	avait chuchoté	avaient chuchoté
3 passé simple		**10 passé antérieur**	
chuchotai	chuchotâmes	eus chuchoté	eûmes chuchoté
chuchotas	chuchotâtes	eus chuchoté	eûtes chuchoté
chuchota	chuchotèrent	eut chuchoté	eurent chuchoté
4 futur		**11 futur antérieur**	
chuchoterai	chuchoterons	aurai chuchoté	aurons chuchoté
chuchoteras	chuchoterez	auras chuchoté	aurez chuchoté
chuchotera	chuchoteront	aura chuchoté	auront chuchoté
5 conditionnel		**12 conditionnel passé**	
chuchoterais	chuchoterions	aurais chuchoté	aurions chuchoté
chuchoterais	chuchoteriez	aurais chuchoté	auriez chuchoté
chuchoterait	chuchoteraient	aurait chuchoté	auraient chuchoté
6 présent du subjonctif		**13 passé du subjonctif**	
chuchote	chuchotions	aie chuchoté	ayons chuchoté
chuchotes	chuchotiez	aies chuchoté	ayez chuchoté
chuchote	chuchotent	ait chuchoté	aient chuchoté
7 imparfait du subjonctif		**14 plus-que-parfait du subjonctif**	
chuchotasse	chuchotassions	eusse chuchoté	eussions chuchoté
chuchotasses	chuchotassiez	eusses chuchoté	eussiez chuchoté
chuchotât	chuchotassent	eût chuchoté	eussent chuchoté

Impératif
chuchote
chuchotons
chuchotez

Common idiomatic expressions using this verb and words related to it
un chuchoteur, une chuchoteuse   whisperer
chuchoter à l'oreille de qqn   to whisper in someone's ear
souffler   to prompt (in a stage whisper)
le chuchotement   whispering
une chuchoterie   a conversation in whispering tones so that others may not hear

Get acquainted with what preposition goes with what verb on pages 543–553.

to combat, to fight

The Seven Simple Tenses		The Seven Compound Tenses	
Singular	Plural	Singular	Plural
1 présent de l'indicatif		8 passé composé	
combats	combattons	ai combattu	avons combattu
combats	combattez	as combattu	avez combattu
combat	combattent	a combattu	ont combattu
2 imparfait de l'indicatif		9 plus-que-parfait de l'indicatif	
combattais	combattions	avais combattu	avions combattu
combattais	combattiez	avais combattu	aviez combattu
combattait	combattaient	avait combattu	avaient combattu
3 passé simple		10 passé antérieur	
combattis	combattîmes	eus combattu	eûmes combattu
combattis	combattîtes	eus combattu	eûtes combattu
combattit	combattirent	eut combattu	eurent combattu
4 futur		11 futur antérieur	
combattrai	combattrons	aurai combattu	aurons combattu
combattras	combattrez	auras combattu	aurez combattu
combattra	combattront	aura combattu	auront combattu
5 conditionnel		12 conditionnel passé	
combattrais	combattrions	aurais combattu	aurions combattu
combattrais	combattriez	aurais combattu	auriez combattu
combattrait	combattraient	aurait combattu	auraient combattu
6 présent du subjonctif		13 passé du subjonctif	
combatte	combattions	aie combattu	ayons combattu
combattes	combattiez	aies combattu	ayez combattu
combatte	combattent	ait combattu	aient combattu
7 imparfait du subjonctif		14 plus-que-parfait du subjonctif	
combattisse	combattissions	eusse combattu	eussions combattu
combattisses	combattissiez	eusses combattu	eussiez combattu
combattît	combattissent	eût combattu	eussent combattu

Impératif
combats
combattons
combattez

Words and expressions related to this verb
un combat   fight, struggle
hors de combat   out of the fight
combattant, combattante   fighting
un non-combattant, une non-combattante
   noncombatant

un combat aérien   aerial combat
combatif, combative   pugnacious, aggressive

For other words and expressions related to this verb, see **abattre**, **battre**, and **se battre**.

Consult the sections on verbs used in idiomatic expressions, verbs with prepositions, and the list of over 1,100 verbs conjugated like model verbs in the back pages.

The subject pronouns are found on the page facing page 1.   **95**

commander

Part. pr. **commandant**   Part. passé **commandé**

to command, to order

The Seven Simple Tenses		The Seven Compound Tenses	
Singular	Plural	Singular	Plural
1 présent de l'indicatif		**8 passé composé**	
commande	commandons	ai commandé	avons commandé
commandes	commandez	as commandé	avez commandé
commande	commandent	a commandé	ont commandé
2 imparfait de l'indicatif		**9 plus-que-parfait de l'indicatif**	
commandais	commandions	avais commandé	avions commandé
commandais	commandiez	avais commandé	aviez commandé
commandait	commandaient	avait commandé	avaient commandé
3 passé simple		**10 passé antérieur**	
commandai	commandâmes	eus commandé	eûmes commandé
commandas	commandâtes	eus commandé	eûtes commandé
commanda	commandèrent	eut commandé	eurent commandé
4 futur		**11 futur antérieur**	
commanderai	commanderons	aurai commandé	aurons commandé
commanderas	commanderez	auras commandé	aurez commandé
commandera	commanderont	aura commandé	auront commandé
5 conditionnel		**12 conditionnel passé**	
commanderais	commanderions	aurais commandé	aurions commandé
commanderais	commanderiez	aurais commandé	auriez commandé
commanderait	commanderaient	aurait commandé	auraient commandé
6 présent du subjonctif		**13 passé du subjonctif**	
commande	commandions	aie commandé	ayons commandé
commandes	commandiez	aies commandé	ayez commandé
commande	commandent	ait commandé	aient commandé
7 imparfait du subjonctif		**14 plus-que-parfait du subjonctif**	
commandasse	commandassions	eusse commandé	eussions commandé
commandasses	commandassiez	eusses commandé	eussiez commandé
commandât	commandassent	eût commandé	eussent commandé

Impératif
commande
commandons
commandez

Common idiomatic expressions using this verb

Hier soir mes amis et moi avons dîné dans un restaurant chinois. Nous avons commandé beaucoup de choses intéressantes.

un commandant commanding officer
une commande an order
commander à qqn de faire qqch to order someone to do something
recommander to recommend; **recommander à qqn de faire qqch** to advise someone to do something
décommander un rendez-vous to cancel a date, an appointment

Try the verb drills and verb tests with answers explained on pages 622–673.

96

to begin, to start, to commence

The Seven Simple Tenses		The Seven Compound Tenses	
Singular	Plural	Singular	Plural
1 présent de l'indicatif		**8 passé composé**	
commence	commençons	ai commencé	avons commencé
commences	commencez	as commencé	avez commencé
commence	commencent	a commencé	ont commencé
2 imparfait de l'indicatif		**9 plus-que-parfait de l'indicatif**	
commençais	commencions	avais commencé	avions commencé
commençais	commenciez	avais commencé	aviez commencé
commençait	commençaient	avait commencé	avaient commencé
3 passé simple		**10 passé antérieur**	
commençai	commençâmes	eus commencé	eûmes commencé
commenças	commençâtes	eus commencé	eûtes commencé
commença	commencèrent	eut commencé	eurent commencé
4 futur		**11 futur antérieur**	
commencerai	commencerons	aurai commencé	aurons commencé
commenceras	commencerez	auras commencé	aurez commencé
commencera	commenceront	aura commencé	auront commencé
5 conditionnel		**12 conditionnel passé**	
commencerais	commencerions	aurais commencé	aurions commencé
commencerais	commenceriez	aurais commencé	auriez commencé
commencerait	commenceraient	aurait commencé	auraient commencé
6 présent du subjonctif		**13 passé du subjonctif**	
commence	commencions	aie commencé	ayons commencé
commences	commenciez	aies commencé	ayez commencé
commence	commencent	ait commencé	aient commencé
7 imparfait du subjonctif		**14 plus-que-parfait du subjonctif**	
commençasse	commençassions	eusse commencé	eussions commencé
commençasses	commençassiez	eusses commencé	eussiez commencé
commençât	commençassent	eût commencé	eussent commencé

Impératif
commence
commençons
commencez

Common idiomatic expressions using this verb
   —**Alexandre, as-tu commencé tes devoirs pour la classe de français?**
   —**Non, maman, pas encore. Je vais faire une promenade maintenant.**
   —**Tu ne vas pas faire une promenade parce qu'il commence à pleuvoir.**
   Commence à faire tes devoirs tout de suite!

commencer à + inf.   to begin + inf.   **pour commencer**   to begin with
le commencement   the beginning   **commencer par**   to begin by
au commencement   in the beginning   **recommencer à**   to begin again + inf.
du commencement à la fin   from beginning to   **un recommencement**   a new start
end

Get acquainted with what preposition goes with what verb on pages 543–553.

The subject pronouns are found on the page facing page 1.   **97**

to commit

The Seven Simple Tenses		The Seven Compound Tenses	
Singular	Plural	Singular	Plural
1 présent de l'indicatif		8 passé composé	
commets	**commettons**	**ai commis**	**avons commis**
commets	**commettez**	**as commis**	**avez commis**
commet	**commettent**	**a commis**	**ont commis**
2 imparfait de l'indicatif		9 plus-que-parfait de l'indicatif	
commettais	**commettions**	**avais commis**	**avions commis**
commettais	**commettiez**	**avais commis**	**aviez commis**
commettait	**commettaient**	**avait commis**	**avaient commis**
3 passé simple		10 passé antérieur	
commis	**commîmes**	**eus commis**	**eûmes commis**
commis	**commîtes**	**eus commis**	**eûtes commis**
commit	**commirent**	**eut commis**	**eurent commis**
4 futur		11 futur antérieur	
commettrai	**commettrons**	**aurai commis**	**aurons commis**
commettras	**commettrez**	**auras commis**	**aurez commis**
commettra	**commettront**	**aura commis**	**auront commis**
5 conditionnel		12 conditionnel passé	
commettrais	**commettrions**	**aurais commis**	**aurions commis**
commettrais	**commettriez**	**aurais commis**	**auriez commis**
commettrait	**commettraient**	**aurait commis**	**auraient commis**
6 présent du subjonctif		13 passé du subjonctif	
commette	**commettions**	**aie commis**	**ayons commis**
commettes	**commettiez**	**aies commis**	**ayez commis**
commette	**commettent**	**ait commis**	**aient commis**
7 imparfait du subjonctif		14 plus-que-parfait du subjonctif	
commisse	**commissions**	**eusse commis**	**eussions commis**
commisses	**commissiez**	**eusses commis**	**eussiez commis**
commît	**commissent**	**eût commis**	**eussent commis**

Impératif
commets
commettons
commettez

Words and expressions related to this verb
commettre un péché   to commit a sin
être commis à   to be committed to
commis aux soins de   to be placed under the care of
se commettre   to commit oneself

commettre qqch à qqn   to entrust something to someone
commettre qqn à qqn   to entrust someone to someone, to place someone under someone's care

See also **mettre, permettre, promettre, remettre, soumettre,** and **transmettre.**

Soak up some verbs used in weather expressions on pages 557 and 558.

The Seven Simple Tenses		The Seven Compound Tenses	
Singular	Plural	Singular	Plural
1 présent de l'indicatif		8 passé composé	
compare	comparons	ai comparé	avons comparé
compares	comparez	as comparé	avez comparé
compare	comparent	a comparé	ont comparé
2 imparfait de l'indicatif		9 plus-que-parfait de l'indicatif	
comparais	comparions	avais comparé	avions comparé
comparais	compariez	avais comparé	aviez comparé
comparait	comparaient	avait comparé	avaient comparé
3 passé simple		10 passé antérieur	
comparai	comparâmes	eus comparé	eûmes comparé
comparas	comparâtes	eus comparé	eûtes comparé
compara	comparèrent	eut comparé	eurent comparé
4 futur		11 futur antérieur	
comparerai	comparerons	aurai comparé	aurons comparé
compareras	comparerez	auras comparé	aurez comparé
comparera	compareront	aura comparé	auront comparé
5 conditionnel		12 conditionnel passé	
comparerais	comparerions	aurais comparé	aurions comparé
comparerais	compareriez	aurais comparé	auriez comparé
comparerait	compareraient	aurait comparé	auraient comparé
6 présent du subjonctif		13 passé du subjonctif	
compare	comparions	aie comparé	ayons comparé
compares	compariez	aies comparé	ayez comparé
compare	comparent	ait comparé	aient comparé
7 imparfait du subjonctif		14 plus-que-parfait du subjonctif	
comparasse	comparassions	eusse comparé	eussions comparé
comparasses	comparassiez	eusses comparé	eussiez comparé
comparât	comparassent	eût comparé	eussent comparé

Impératif
compare
comparons
comparez

Words and expressions related to this verb

comparer à   to compare to (when some
  equality exists between the two compared)
comparer avec   to compare with (when one is
  considered to be of a higher degree than the
  rest)
sans comparaison   without comparison

une comparaison   comparison
comparativement   comparatively
comparatif, comparative   comparative
par comparaison avec   comparatively to
comparable à   comparable to
en comparaison de   in comparison with

For an explanation of meanings and uses of French and English verb tenses and moods, see pages
xv–xxvi.

The subject pronouns are found on the page facing page 1.   **99**

comprendre

Part. pr. **comprenant**   Part. passé **compris**

to understand

The Seven Simple Tenses		The Seven Compound Tenses	
Singular	Plural	Singular	Plural
1 présent de l'indicatif		**8 passé composé**	
comprends	comprenons	ai compris	avons compris
comprends	comprenez	as compris	avez compris
comprend	comprennent	a compris	ont compris
2 imparfait de l'indicatif		**9 plus-que-parfait de l'indicatif**	
comprenais	comprenions	avais compris	avions compris
comprenais	compreniez	avais compris	aviez compris
comprenait	comprenaient	avait compris	avaient compris
3 passé simple		**10 passé antérieur**	
compris	comprîmes	eus compris	eûmes compris
compris	comprîtes	eus compris	eûtes compris
comprit	comprirent	eut compris	eurent compris
4 futur		**11 futur antérieur**	
comprendrai	comprendrons	aurai compris	aurons compris
comprendras	comprendrez	auras compris	aurez compris
comprendra	comprendront	aura compris	auront compris
5 conditionnel		**12 conditionnel passé**	
comprendrais	comprendrions	aurais compris	aurions compris
comprendrais	comprendriez	aurais compris	auriez compris
comprendrait	comprendraient	aurait compris	auraient compris
6 présent du subjonctif		**13 passé du subjonctif**	
comprenne	comprenions	aie compris	ayons compris
comprennes	compreniez	aies compris	ayez compris
comprenne	comprennent	ait compris	aient compris
7 imparfait du subjonctif		**14 plus-que-parfait du subjonctif**	
comprisse	comprissions	eusse compris	eussions compris
comprisses	comprissiez	eusses compris	eussiez compris
comprît	comprissent	eût compris	eussent compris

Impératif
comprends
comprenons
comprenez

Sentences using this verb and expressions related to it

Je ne comprends jamais le prof de biologie. Je n'ai pas compris la leçon d'hier, je ne comprends pas la leçon d'aujourd'hui, et je ne comprendrai jamais rien.

faire comprendre à qqn que . . .   to make it clear to someone that . . .
la compréhension   comprehension, understanding
Ça se comprend   Of course; That is understood.
y compris   included, including
service compris   service included (no tip necessary)

See also **apprendre, entreprendre, se méprendre, prendre, reprendre,** and **surprendre.**

Want to learn more idiomatic expressions that contain verbs? Look at pages 530–542.

to count, to intend, to expect to

The Seven Simple Tenses		The Seven Compound Tenses	
Singular	Plural	Singular	Plural
1 présent de l'indicatif		**8 passé composé**	
compte	comptons	ai compté	avons compté
comptes	comptez	as compté	avez compté
compte	comptent	a compté	ont compté
2 imparfait de l'indicatif		**9 plus-que-parfait de l'indicatif**	
comptais	comptions	avais compté	avions compté
comptais	comptiez	avais compté	aviez compté
comptait	comptaient	avait compté	avaient compté
3 passé simple		**10 passé antérieur**	
comptai	comptâmes	eus compté	eûmes compté
comptas	comptâtes	eus compté	eûtes compté
compta	comptèrent	eut compté	eurent compté
4 futur		**11 futur antérieur**	
compterai	compterons	aurai compté	aurons compté
compteras	compterez	auras compté	aurez compté
comptera	compteront	aura compté	auront compté
5 conditionnel		**12 conditionnel passé**	
compterais	compterions	aurais compté	aurions compté
compterais	compteriez	aurais compté	auriez compté
compterait	compteraient	aurait compté	auraient compté
6 présent du subjonctif		**13 passé du subjonctif**	
compte	comptions	aie compté	ayons compté
comptes	comptiez	aies compté	ayez compté
compte	comptent	ait compté	aient compté
7 imparfait du subjonctif		**14 plus-que-parfait du subjonctif**	
comptasse	comptassions	eusse compté	eussions compté
comptasses	comptassiez	eusses compté	eussiez compté
comptât	comptassent	eût compté	eussent compté

Impératif
compte
comptons
comptez

Common idiomatic expressions using this verb
  Je compte aller en France l'été prochain avec ma femme pour voir nos amis français.

la comptabilité   bookkeeping, accounting
comptable   accountable
le comptage   counting
payer comptant   to pay cash
compter faire qqch   to expect to do something
compter sur   to count (rely) on; **Puis-je y compter?**   Can I depend on it?

escompter   to discount; **un escompte**   a discount
donner sans compter   to give generously
sans compter . . .   to say nothing of . . .
le comptoir   counter (in a store)

Want to learn more idiomatic expressions that contain verbs? Look at pages 530–542.

The subject pronouns are found on the page facing page 1.   **101**

concevoir

Part. pr. **concevant**   Part. passé **conçu**

to conceive

The Seven Simple Tenses		The Seven Compound Tenses	
Singular	Plural	Singular	Plural
1 présent de l'indicatif		**8 passé composé**	
conçois	concevons	ai conçu	avons conçu
conçois	concevez	as conçu	avez conçu
conçoit	conçoivent	a conçu	ont conçu
2 imparfait de l'indicatif		**9 plus-que-parfait de l'indicatif**	
concevais	concevions	avais conçu	avions conçu
concevais	conceviez	avais conçu	aviez conçu
concevait	concevaient	avait conçu	avaient conçu
3 passé simple		**10 passé antérieur**	
conçus	conçûmes	eus conçu	eûmes conçu
conçus	conçûtes	eus conçu	eûtes conçu
conçut	conçurent	eut conçu	eurent conçu
4 futur		**11 futur antérieur**	
concevrai	concevrons	aurai conçu	aurons conçu
concevras	concevrez	auras conçu	aurez conçu
concevra	concevront	aura conçu	auront conçu
5 conditionnel		**12 conditionnel passé**	
concevrais	concevrions	aurais conçu	aurions conçu
concevrais	concevriez	aurais conçu	auriez conçu
concevrait	concevraient	aurait conçu	auraient conçu
6 présent du subjonctif		**13 passé du subjonctif**	
conçoive	concevions	aie conçu	ayons conçu
conçoives	conceviez	aies conçu	ayez conçu
conçoive	conçoivent	ait conçu	aient conçu
7 imparfait du subjonctif		**14 plus-que-parfait du subjonctif**	
conçusse	conçussions	eusse conçu	eussions conçu
conçusses	conçussiez	eusses conçu	eussiez conçu
conçût	conçussent	eût conçu	eussent conçu

Impératif
conçois
concevons
concevez

Words and expressions related to this verb
concevoir des idées to form ideas
concevable conceivable
une conception concept, idea
un concepteur, une conceptrice designer

ainsi conçu written as follows
Je ne peux même pas concevoir . . . I just can't even imagine . . .

Consult the sections on verbs used in idiomatic expressions, verbs with prepositions, and the list of over 1,100 verbs conjugated like model verbs in the back pages.

The Seven Simple Tenses		The Seven Compound Tenses	
Singular	Plural	Singular	Plural

1 présent de l'indicatif		8 passé composé	
conclus	concluons	ai conclu	avons conclu
conclus	concluez	as conclu	avez conclu
conclut	concluent	a conclu	ont conclu

2 imparfait de l'indicatif		9 plus-que-parfait de l'indicatif	
concluais	concluions	avais conclu	avions conclu
concluais	concluiez	avais conclu	aviez conclu
concluait	concluaient	avait conclu	avaient conclu

3 passé simple		10 passé antérieur	
conclus	conclûmes	eus conclu	eûmes conclu
conclus	conclûtes	eus conclu	eûtes conclu
conclut	conclurent	eut conclu	eurent conclu

4 futur		11 futur antérieur	
conclurai	conclurons	aurai conclu	aurons conclu
concluras	conclurez	auras conclu	aurez conclu
conclura	concluront	aura conclu	auront conclu

5 conditionnel		12 conditionnel passé	
conclurais	conclurions	aurais conclu	aurions conclu
conclurais	concluriez	aurais conclu	auriez conclu
conclurait	concluraient	aurait conclu	auraient conclu

6 présent du subjonctif		13 passé du subjonctif	
conclue	concluions	aie conclu	ayons conclu
conclues	concluiez	aies conclu	ayez conclu
conclue	concluent	ait conclu	aient conclu

7 imparfait du subjonctif		14 plus-que-parfait du subjonctif	
conclusse	conclussions	eusse conclu	eussions conclu
conclusses	conclussiez	eusses conclu	eussiez conclu
conclût	conclussent	eût conclu	eussent conclu

Impératif
conclus
concluons
concluez

Words and expressions related to this verb
la conclusion   conclusion
en conclusion   in conclusion
exclure   to exclude
exclu, exclue excluded
un film en exclusivité   a first-run motion
  picture
See also **inclure**.

inclure   to enclose, to include (**part. passé:
  inclus, incluse**); **une photo ci-incluse**
  a photo enclosed herewith; **jusqu'à la
  page 100 incluse**   up to and including
  page 100

Soak up some verbs used in weather expressions on pages 557 and 558.

to lead, to drive, to conduct, to manage

The Seven Simple Tenses		The Seven Compound Tenses	
Singular	Plural	Singular	Plural
1 présent de l'indicatif		8 passé composé	
conduis	conduisons	ai conduit	avons conduit
conduis	conduisez	as conduit	avez conduit
conduit	conduisent	a conduit	ont conduit
2 imparfait de l'indicatif		9 plus-que-parfait de l'indicatif	
conduisais	conduisions	avais conduit	avions conduit
conduisais	conduisiez	avais conduit	aviez conduit
conduisait	conduisaient	avait conduit	avaient conduit
3 passé simple		10 passé antérieur	
conduisis	conduisîmes	eus conduit	eûmes conduit
conduisis	conduisîtes	eus conduit	eûtes conduit
conduisit	conduisirent	eut conduit	eurent conduit
4 futur		11 futur antérieur	
conduirai	conduirons	aurai conduit	aurons conduit
conduiras	conduirez	auras conduit	aurez conduit
conduira	conduiront	aura conduit	auront conduit
5 conditionnel		12 conditionnel passé	
conduirais	conduirions	aurais conduit	aurions conduit
conduirais	conduiriez	aurais conduit	auriez conduit
conduirait	conduiraient	aurait conduit	auraient conduit
6 présent du subjonctif		13 passé du subjonctif	
conduise	conduisions	aie conduit	ayons conduit
conduises	conduisiez	aies conduit	ayez conduit
conduise	conduisent	ait conduit	aient conduit
7 imparfait du subjonctif		14 plus-que-parfait du subjonctif	
conduisisse	conduisissions	eusse conduit	eussions conduit
conduisisses	conduisissiez	eusses conduit	eussiez conduit
conduisît	conduisissent	eût conduit	eussent conduit

Impératif
conduis
conduisons
conduisez

Sentences using this verb and words related to it

—Savez-vous conduire?

—Oui, je sais conduire. Je conduis une voiture, je dirige un orchestre, et hier j'ai conduit quelqu'un à la gare. Attendez, je vais vous conduire à la porte.

—Merci, vous êtes très aimable.

un conducteur, une conductrice driver
la conduite conduct, behavior
induire to induce
induire en to lead into

conduire une voiture to drive a car
se conduire to conduct (behave) oneself
un permis de conduire driver's license
enduire to coat, spread

See also **déduire, introduire, produire, réduire, reproduire, séduire,** and **traduire.**

104

to know, to be acquainted with, to make the acquaintance of

The Seven Simple Tenses		The Seven Compound Tenses	
Singular	Plural	Singular	Plural
1 présent de l'indicatif		**8 passé composé**	
connais	connaissons	ai connu	avons connu
connais	connaissez	as connu	avez connu
connaît	connaissent	a connu	ont connu
2 imparfait de l'indicatif		**9 plus-que-parfait de l'indicatif**	
connaissais	connaissions	avais connu	avions connu
connaissais	connaissiez	avais connu	aviez connu
connaissait	connaissaient	avait connu	avaient connu
3 passé simple		**10 passé antérieur**	
connus	connûmes	eus connu	eûmes connu
connus	connûtes	eus connu	eûtes connu
connut	connurent	eut connu	eurent connu
4 futur		**11 futur antérieur**	
connaîtrai	connaîtrons	aurai connu	aurons connu
connaîtras	connaîtrez	auras connu	aurez connu
connaîtra	connaîtront	aura connu	auront connu
5 conditionnel		**12 conditionnel passé**	
connaîtrais	connaîtrions	aurais connu	aurions connu
connaîtrais	connaîtriez	aurais connu	auriez connu
connaîtrait	connaîtraient	aurait connu	auraient connu
6 présent du subjonctif		**13 passé du subjonctif**	
connaisse	connaissions	aie connu	ayons connu
connaisses	connaissiez	aies connu	ayez connu
connaisse	connaissent	ait connu	aient connu
7 imparfait du subjonctif		**14 plus-que-parfait du subjonctif**	
connusse	connussions	eusse connu	eussions connu
connusses	connussiez	eusses connu	eussiez connu
connût	connussent	eût connu	eussent connu

Impératif
connais
connaissons
connaissez

Common idiomatic expressions using this verb and words related to it
    —**Connaissez-vous quelqu'un qui puisse m'aider? Je suis touriste et je ne connais pas cette ville.**
    —**Non, je ne connais personne. Je suis touriste aussi.**
    —**Voulez-vous aller prendre un café? Nous pouvons faire connaissance.**

la connaissance   knowledge, understanding, acquaintance; **à ma connaissance**   as far as I know
connaisseur, connaisseuse   expert
se connaître   to know each other, to know oneself
faire connaissance   to get acquainted; **avoir des connaissances en**   to be knowledgeable in
See also **méconnaître** and **reconnaître**.

to conquer

The Seven Simple Tenses		The Seven Compound Tenses	
Singular	Plural	Singular	Plural
1 présent de l'indicatif		8 passé composé	
conquiers	conquérons	ai conquis	avons conquis
conquiers	conquérez	as conquis	avez conquis
conquiert	conquièrent	a conquis	ont conquis
2 imparfait de l'indicatif		9 plus-que-parfait de l'indicatif	
conquérais	conquérions	avais conquis	avions conquis
conquérais	conquériez	avais conquis	aviez conquis
conquérait	conquéraient	avait conquis	avaient conquis
3 passé simple		10 passé antérieur	
conquis	conquîmes	eus conquis	eûmes conquis
conquis	conquîtes	eus conquis	eûtes conquis
conquit	conquirent	eut conquis	eurent conquis
4 futur		11 futur antérieur	
conquerrai	conquerrons	aurai conquis	aurons conquis
conquerras	conquerrez	auras conquis	aurez conquis
conquerra	conquerront	aura conquis	auront conquis
5 conditionnel		12 conditionnel passé	
conquerrais	conquerrions	aurais conquis	aurions conquis
conquerrais	conquerriez	aurais conquis	auriez conquis
conquerrait	conquerraient	aurait conquis	auraient conquis
6 présent du subjonctif		13 passé du subjonctif	
conquière	conquérions	aie conquis	ayons conquis
conquières	conquériez	aies conquis	ayez conquis
conquière	conquièrent	ait conquis	aient conquis
7 imparfait du subjonctif		14 plus-que-parfait du subjonctif	
conquisse	conquissions	eusse conquis	eussions conquis
conquisses	conquissiez	eusses conquis	eussiez conquis
conquît	conquissent	eût conquis	eussent conquis

Impératif
conquiers
conquérons
conquérez

Words and expressions related to this verb
conquérir l'affection de qqn   to win someone's affection
conquérir une femme   to win over a woman; **conquérir un homme**   to win over a man
la conquête   conquest; **la conquête du pouvoir**   conquest of power
avoir un air conquérant   to seem pretentious
Guillaume le Conquérant   William the Conqueror

Conquer your fear of the Subjunctive. See pages 560–565.

to advise, to counsel, to recommend

The Seven Simple Tenses		The Seven Compound Tenses	
Singular	Plural	Singular	Plural
1 présent de l'indicatif		**8 passé composé**	
conseille	conseillons	ai conseillé	avons conseillé
conseilles	conseillez	as conseillé	avez conseillé
conseille	conseillent	a conseillé	ont conseillé
2 imparfait de l'indicatif		**9 plus-que-parfait de l'indicatif**	
conseillais	conseillions	avais conseillé	avions conseillé
conseillais	conseilliez	avais conseillé	aviez conseillé
conseillait	conseillaient	avait conseillé	avaient conseillé
3 passé simple		**10 passé antérieur**	
conseillai	conseillâmes	eus conseillé	eûmes conseillé
conseillas	conseillâtes	eus conseillé	eûtes conseillé
conseilla	conseillèrent	eut conseillé	eurent conseillé
4 futur		**11 futur antérieur**	
conseillerai	conseillerons	aurai conseillé	aurons conseillé
conseilleras	conseillerez	auras conseillé	aurez conseillé
conseillera	conseilleront	aura conseillé	auront conseillé
5 conditionnel		**12 conditionnel passé**	
conseillerais	conseillerions	aurais conseillé	aurions conseillé
conseillerais	conseilleriez	aurais conseillé	auriez conseillé
conseillerait	conseilleraient	aurait conseillé	auraient conseillé
6 présent du subjonctif		**13 passé du subjonctif**	
conseille	conseillions	aie conseillé	ayons conseillé
conseilles	conseilliez	aies conseillé	ayez conseillé
conseille	conseillent	ait conseillé	aient conseillé
7 imparfait du subjonctif		**14 plus-que-parfait du subjonctif**	
conseillasse	conseillassions	eusse conseillé	eussions conseillé
conseillasses	conseillassiez	eusses conseillé	eussiez conseillé
conseillât	conseillassent	eût conseillé	eussent conseillé

Impératif
conseille
conseillons
conseillez

Words and expressions related to this verb
conseiller qqch à qqn   to recommend something to someone
conseiller à qqn de faire qqch   to advise someone to do something
un conseiller (un conseilleur), une conseillère (une conseilleuse)   counselor, adviser
un conseil   counsel, advice; **sur le conseil de**   on the advice of
déconseiller   to advise, warn against; **déconseiller qqch à qqn**   to advise someone against
    something

We recommend that you try the verb drills and tests with answers explained on pages 622–673.

to consent, to agree

The Seven Simple Tenses		The Seven Compound Tenses	
Singular	Plural	Singular	Plural
1 présent de l'indicatif		8 passé composé	
consens	consentons	ai consenti	avons consenti
consens	consentez	as consenti	avez consenti
consent	consentent	a consenti	ont consenti
2 imparfait de l'indicatif		9 plus-que-parfait de l'indicatif	
consentais	consentions	avais consenti	avions consenti
consentais	consentiez	avais consenti	aviez consenti
consentait	consentaient	avait consenti	avaient consenti
3 passé simple		10 passé antérieur	
consentis	consentîmes	eus consenti	eûmes consenti
consentis	consentîtes	eus consenti	eûtes consenti
consentit	consentirent	eut consenti	eurent consenti
4 futur		11 futur antérieur	
consentirai	consentirons	aurai consenti	aurons consenti
consentiras	consentirez	auras consenti	aurez consenti
consentira	consentiront	aura consenti	auront consenti
5 conditionnel		12 conditionnel passé	
consentirais	consentirions	aurais consenti	aurions consenti
consentirais	consentiriez	aurais consenti	auriez consenti
consentirait	consentiraient	aurait consenti	auraient consenti
6 présent du subjonctif		13 passé du subjonctif	
consente	consentions	aie consenti	ayons consenti
consentes	consentiez	aies consenti	ayez consenti
consente	consentent	ait consenti	aient consenti
7 imparfait du subjonctif		14 plus-que-parfait du subjonctif	
consentisse	consentissions	eusse consenti	eussions consenti
consentisses	consentissiez	eusses consenti	eussiez consenti
consentît	consentissent	eût consenti	eussent consenti

Impératif
consens
consentons
consentez

Words and expressions related to this verb

consentir à faire qqch   to agree to do something
le consentement   consent, approval
consentant, consentante   agreeable, willing

consentir à qqch   to consent to something
consentir au mariage   to consent to marriage
donner son consentement   to give one's consent, agreement

See also **sentir**.

Grammar putting you in a tense mood? Review the definitions of basic grammatical terms on pages 674–688.

to construct, to build

The Seven Simple Tenses		The Seven Compound Tenses	
Singular	Plural	Singular	Plural
1 présent de l'indicatif		**8 passé composé**	
construis	construisons	ai construit	avons construit
construis	construisez	as construit	avez construit
construit	construisent	a construit	ont construit
2 imparfait de l'indicatif		**9 plus-que-parfait de l'indicatif**	
construisais	construisions	avais construit	avions construit
construisais	construisiez	avais construit	aviez construit
construisait	construisaient	avait construit	avaient construit
3 passé simple		**10 passé antérieur**	
construisis	construisîmes	eus construit	eûmes construit
construisis	construisîtes	eus construit	eûtes construit
construisit	construisirent	eut construit	eurent construit
4 futur		**11 futur antérieur**	
construirai	construirons	aurai construit	aurons construit
construiras	construirez	auras construit	aurez construit
construira	construiront	aura construit	auront construit
5 conditionnel		**12 conditionnel passé**	
construirais	construirions	aurais construit	aurions construit
construirais	construiriez	aurais construit	auriez construit
construirait	construiraient	aurait construit	auraient construit
6 présent du subjonctif		**13 passé du subjonctif**	
construise	construisions	aie construit	ayons construit
construises	construisiez	aies construit	ayez construit
construise	construisent	ait construit	aient construit
7 imparfait du subjonctif		**14 plus-que-parfait du subjonctif**	
construisisse	construisissions	eusse construit	eussions construit
construisisses	construisissiez	eusses construit	eussiez construit
construisît	construisissent	eût construit	eussent construit

Impératif
construis
construisons
construisez

Sentences using this verb and words related to it

—**Je vois que vous êtes en train de construire quelque chose. Qu'est-ce que vous construisez?**

—**Je construis une tour comme la Tour Eiffel. Aimez-vous ce bateau que j'ai construit?**

un constructeur   a manufacturer, builder, constructor
une construction   construction, building
reconstruire   to reconstruct, to rebuild; **en construction**   under construction

For an explanation of meanings and uses of French and English verb tenses and moods, see pages xv–xxvi.

to contain

The Seven Simple Tenses		The Seven Compound Tenses	
Singular	Plural	Singular	Plural
1 présent de l'indicatif		8 passé composé	
contiens	contenons	ai contenu	avons contenu
contiens	contenez	as contenu	avez contenu
contient	contiennent	a contenu	ont contenu
2 imparfait de l'indicatif		9 plus-que-parfait de l'indicatif	
contenais	contenions	avais contenu	avions contenu
contenais	conteniez	avais contenu	aviez contenu
contenait	contenaient	avait contenu	avaient contenu
3 passé simple		10 passé antérieur	
contins	contînmes	eus contenu	eûmes contenu
contins	contîntes	eus contenu	eûtes contenu
contint	continrent	eut contenu	eurent contenu
4 futur		11 futur antérieur	
contiendrai	contiendrons	aurai contenu	aurons contenu
contiendras	contiendrez	auras contenu	aurez contenu
contiendra	contiendront	aura contenu	auront contenu
5 conditionnel		12 conditionnel passé	
contiendrais	contiendrions	aurais contenu	aurions contenu
contiendrais	contiendriez	aurais contenu	auriez contenu
contiendrait	contiendraient	aurait contenu	auraient contenu
6 présent du subjonctif		13 passé du subjonctif	
contienne	contenions	aie contenu	ayons contenu
contiennes	conteniez	aies contenu	ayez contenu
contienne	contiennent	ait contenu	aient contenu
7 imparfait du subjonctif		14 plus-que-parfait du subjonctif	
continsse	continssions	eusse contenu	eussions contenu
continsses	continssiez	eusses contenu	eussiez contenu
contînt	continssent	eût contenu	eussent contenu

Impératif
contiens
contenons
contenez

Common idiomatic expressions using this verb and words related to it

contenir ses émotions   to contain (dominate) one's emotions

être content (contente)   to be content, satisfied

être content (contente) des autres   to be content (satisfied) with others

se contenir   to contain oneself, to dominate (control) oneself

un contenant   container

le contenu   contents

être content (contente) de soi   to be self-satisfied

avoir l'air content   to seem pleased

See also **obtenir, retenir,** and **tenir.**

Want to learn more idiomatic expressions that contain verbs? Look at pages 530–542.

to relate, to narrate

The Seven Simple Tenses		The Seven Compound Tenses	
Singular	Plural	Singular	Plural
1 présent de l'indicatif		**8 passé composé**	
conte	contons	ai conté	avons conté
contes	contez	as conté	avez conté
conte	content	a conté	ont conté
2 imparfait de l'indicatif		**9 plus-que-parfait de l'indicatif**	
contais	contions	avais conté	avions conté
contais	contiez	avais conté	aviez conté
contait	contaient	avait conté	avaient conté
3 passé simple		**10 passé antérieur**	
contai	contâmes	eus conté	eûmes conté
contas	contâtes	eus conté	eûtes conté
conta	contèrent	eut conté	eurent conté
4 futur		**11 futur antérieur**	
conterai	conterons	aurai conté	aurons conté
conteras	conterez	auras conté	aurez conté
contera	conteront	aura conté	auront conté
5 conditionnel		**12 conditionnel passé**	
conterais	conterions	aurais conté	aurions conté
conterais	conteriez	aurais conté	auriez conté
conterait	conteraient	aurait conté	auraient conté
6 présent du subjonctif		**13 passé du subjonctif**	
conte	contions	aie conté	ayons conté
contes	contiez	aies conté	ayez conté
conte	content	ait conté	aient conté
7 imparfait du subjonctif		**14 plus-que-parfait du subjonctif**	
contasse	contassions	eusse conté	eussions conté
contasses	contassiez	eusses conté	eussiez conté
contât	contassent	eût conté	eussent conté

Impératif
conte
contons
contez

Sentences using this verb and words related to it

   Notre professeur de français nous conte toujours des histoires intéressantes. Son conte favori est *Un coeur simple* de Flaubert.

un conte   a story, tale
un conte de fées   fairy tale
un conte à dormir debout   cock-and-bull story
See also **raconter.**

un conteur, une conteuse   writer of short stories
Contez-moi vos malheurs   Tell me about your troubles.

Use the EE-zee guide to French pronunciation on pages 566 and 567.

The subject pronouns are found on the page facing page 1.   **111**

continuer

Part. pr. **continuant**   Part. passé **continué**

to continue

The Seven Simple Tenses		The Seven Compound Tenses	
Singular	Plural	Singular	Plural
1 présent de l'indicatif		**8 passé composé**	
continue	continuons	ai continué	avons continué
continues	continuez	as continué	avez continué
continue	continuent	a continué	ont continué
2 imparfait de l'indicatif		**9 plus-que-parfait de l'indicatif**	
continuais	continuions	avais continué	avions continué
continuais	continuiez	avais continué	aviez continué
continuait	continuaient	avait continué	avaient continué
3 passé simple		**10 passé antérieur**	
continuai	continuâmes	eus continué	eûmes continué
continuas	continuâtes	eus continué	eûtes continué
continua	continuèrent	eut continué	eurent continué
4 futur		**11 futur antérieur**	
continuerai	continuerons	aurai continué	aurons continué
continueras	continuerez	auras continué	aurez continué
continuera	continueront	aura continué	auront continué
5 conditionnel		**12 conditionnel passé**	
continuerais	continuerions	aurais continué	aurions continué
continuerais	continueriez	aurais continué	auriez continué
continuerait	continueraient	aurait continué	auraient continué
6 présent du subjonctif		**13 passé du subjonctif**	
continue	continuions	aie continué	ayons continué
continues	continuiez	aies continué	ayez continué
continue	continuent	ait continué	aient continué
7 imparfait du subjonctif		**14 plus-que-parfait du subjonctif**	
continuasse	continuassions	eusse continué	eussions continué
continuasses	continuassiez	eusses continué	eussiez continué
continuât	continuassent	eût continué	eussent continué

Impératif
continue
continuons
continuez

Sentences using this verb and words related to it
—**Allez-vous continuer à étudier le français l'année prochaine?**
—**Certainement. Je compte étudier cette belle langue continuellement.**

la continuation continuation
continuel, continuelle continual
continuellement continually
continuer à + inf. to continue + inf.

continuer de + inf. to continue (persist) in;
Cet ivrogne continue de boire This
drunkard persists in drinking (habit).

Get acquainted with what preposition goes with what verb on pages 543–553.

to constrain, to restrain, to compel

The Seven Simple Tenses		The Seven Compound Tenses	
Singular	Plural	Singular	Plural

1   présent de l'indicatif

contrains	contraignons	
contrains	contraignez	
contraint	contraignent	

8   passé composé

ai contraint	avons contraint
as contraint	avez contraint
a contraint	ont contraint

2   imparfait de l'indicatif

contraignais	contraignions
contraignais	contraigniez
contraignait	contraignaient

9   plus-que-parfait de l'indicatif

avais contraint	avions contraint
avais contraint	aviez contraint
avait contraint	avaient contraint

3   passé simple

contraignis	contraignîmes
contraignis	contraignîtes
contraignit	contraignirent

10   passé antérieur

eus contraint	eûmes contraint
eus contraint	eûtes contraint
eut contraint	eurent contraint

4   futur

contraindrai	contraindrons
contraindras	contraindrez
contraindra	contraindront

11   futur antérieur

aurai contraint	aurons contraint
auras contraint	aurez contraint
aura contraint	auront contraint

5   conditionnel

contraindrais	contraindrions
contraindrais	contraindriez
contraindrait	contraindraient

12   conditionnel passé

aurais contraint	aurions contraint
aurais contraint	auriez contraint
aurait contraint	auraient contraint

6   présent du subjonctif

contraigne	contraignions
contraignes	contraigniez
contraigne	contraignent

13   passé du subjonctif

aie contraint	ayons contraint
aies contraint	ayez contraint
ait contraint	aient contraint

7   imparfait du subjonctif

contraignisse	contraignissions
contraignisses	contraignissiez
contraignît	contraignissent

14   plus-que-parfait du subjonctif

eusse contraint	eussions contraint
eusses contraint	eussiez contraint
eût contraint	eussent contraint

Impératif
contrains
contraignons
contraignez

Words and expressions related to this verb

se contraindre à faire qqch   to constrain oneself from doing something
avoir l'air contraint   to have a constrained expression (on one's face)
parler sans contrainte   to speak freely
contraint, contrainte   constrained, forced

être contraint (contrainte) à faire qqch   to be constrained to doing something
la contrainte   constraint
tenir qqn dans la contrainte   to hold someone in constraint

Check out the principal parts of some important French verbs on page xii.

The subject pronouns are found on the page facing page 1.

contredire
to contradict

Part. pr. **contredisant**   Part. passé **contredit**

The Seven Simple Tenses		The Seven Compound Tenses	
Singular	Plural	Singular	Plural
1 présent de l'indicatif		**8 passé composé**	
contredis	contredisons	ai contredit	avons contredit
contredis	contredisez	as contredit	avez contredit
contredit	contredisent	a contredit	ont contredit
2 imparfait de l'indicatif		**9 plus-que-parfait de l'indicatif**	
contredisais	contredisions	avais contredit	avions contredit
contredisais	contredisiez	avais contredit	aviez contredit
contredisait	contredisaient	avait contredit	avaient contredit
3 passé simple		**10 passé antérieur**	
contredis	contredîmes	eus contredit	eûmes contredit
contredis	contredîtes	eus contredit	eûtes contredit
contredit	contredirent	eut contredit	eurent contredit
4 futur		**11 futur antérieur**	
contredirai	contredirons	aurai contredit	aurons contredit
contrediras	contredirez	auras contredit	aurez contredit
contredira	contrediront	aura contredit	auront contredit
5 conditionnel		**12 conditionnel passé**	
contredirais	contredirions	aurais contredit	aurions contredit
contredirais	contrediriez	aurais contredit	auriez contredit
contredirait	contrediraient	aurait contredit	auraient contredit
6 présent du subjonctif		**13 passé du subjonctif**	
contredise	contredisions	aie contredit	ayons contredit
contredises	contredisiez	aies contredit	ayez contredit
contredise	contredisent	ait contredit	aient contredit
7 imparfait du subjonctif		**14 plus-que-parfait du subjonctif**	
contredisse	contredissions	eusse contredit	eussions contredit
contredisses	contredissiez	eusses contredit	eussiez contredit
contredît	contredissent	eût contredit	eussent contredit

Impératif
contredis
contredisons
contredisez

Words and expressions related to this verb

se contredire to contradict oneself, to contradict each other (one another)
un contredit contradiction; **sans contredit** unquestionably
une contradiction contradiction

contradictoire contradictory
contradicteur, contradictrice contradictor
contradictoirement contradictorily
en contradiction avec inconsistent with

See also **dire, interdire, maudire, médire,** and **prédire.**

It's important that you be familiar with the Subjunctive. See pages 560–565.

114

The Seven Simple Tenses		The Seven Compound Tenses	
Singular	Plural	Singular	Plural
1　présent de l'indicatif		8　passé composé	
convaincs	**convainquons**	**ai convaincu**	**avons convaincu**
convaincs	**convainquez**	**as convaincu**	**avez convaincu**
convainc	**convainquent**	**a convaincu**	**ont convaincu**
2　imparfait de l'indicatif		9　plus-que-parfait de l'indicatif	
convainquais	**convainquions**	**avais convaincu**	**avions convaincu**
convainquais	**convainquiez**	**avais convaincu**	**aviez convaincu**
convainquait	**convainquaient**	**avait convaincu**	**avaient convaincu**
3　passé simple		10　passé antérieur	
convainquis	**convainquîmes**	**eus convaincu**	**eûmes convaincu**
convainquis	**convainquîtes**	**eus convaincu**	**eûtes convaincu**
convainquit	**convainquirent**	**eut convaincu**	**eurent convaincu**
4　futur		11　futur antérieur	
convaincrai	**convaincrons**	**aurai convaincu**	**aurons convaincu**
convaincras	**convaincrez**	**auras convaincu**	**aurez convaincu**
convaincra	**convaincront**	**aura convaincu**	**auront convaincu**
5　conditionnel		12　conditionnel passé	
convaincrais	**convaincrions**	**aurais convaincu**	**aurions convaincu**
convaincrais	**convaincriez**	**aurais convaincu**	**auriez convaincu**
convaincrait	**convaincraient**	**aurait convaincu**	**auraient convaincu**
6　présent du subjonctif		13　passé du subjonctif	
convainque	**convainquions**	**aie convaincu**	**ayons convaincu**
convainques	**convainquiez**	**aies convaincu**	**ayez convaincu**
convainque	**convainquent**	**ait convaincu**	**aient convaincu**
7　imparfait du subjonctif		14　plus-que-parfait du subjonctif	
convainquisse	**convainquissions**	**eusse convaincu**	**eussions convaincu**
convainquisses	**convainquissiez**	**eusses convaincu**	**eussiez convaincu**
convainquît	**convainquissent**	**eût convaincu**	**eussent convaincu**

Impératif
convaincs
convainquons
convainquez

Words and expressions related to this verb
convaincre qqn de qqch　to convince
　(persuade) someone of something
se laisser convaincre　to allow oneself to be
　persuaded

d'un ton convaincu　in a convincing tone
convaincant, convaincante　convincing
se convaincre　to convince oneself, to realize

See also **vaincre.**

How are you doing? Find out with the verb drills and tests with answers explained on pages
622–673.

convenir

Part. pr. **convenant**   Part. passé **convenu**

to suit, to be suitable, to be appropriate, to agree, to acknowledge

The Seven Simple Tenses		The Seven Compound Tenses	
Singular	Plural	Singular	Plural
1 présent de l'indicatif		**8 passé composé**	
conviens	convenons	ai convenu	avons convenu
conviens	convenez	as convenu	avez convenu
convient	conviennent	a convenu	ont convenu
2 imparfait de l'indicatif		**9 plus-que-parfait de l'indicatif**	
convenais	convenions	avais convenu	avions convenu
convenais	conveniez	avais convenu	aviez convenu
convenait	convenaient	avait convenu	avaient convenu
3 passé simple		**10 passé antérieur**	
convins	convînmes	eus convenu	eûmes convenu
convins	convîntes	eus convenu	eûtes convenu
convint	convinrent	eut convenu	eurent convenu
4 futur		**11 futur antérieur**	
conviendrai	conviendrons	aurai convenu	aurons convenu
conviendras	conviendrez	auras convenu	aurez convenu
conviendra	conviendront	aura convenu	auront convenu
5 conditionnel		**12 conditionnel passé**	
conviendrais	conviendrions	aurais convenu	aurions convenu
conviendrais	conviendriez	aurais convenu	auriez convenu
conviendrait	conviendraient	aurait convenu	auraient convenu
6 présent du subjonctif		**13 passé du subjonctif**	
convienne	convenions	aie convenu	ayons convenu
conviennes	conveniez	aies convenu	ayez convenu
convienne	conviennent	ait convenu	aient convenu
7 imparfait du subjonctif		**14 plus-que-parfait du subjonctif**	
convinsse	convinssions	eusse convenu	eussions convenu
convinsses	convinssiez	eusses convenu	eussiez convenu
convînt	convinssent	eût convenu	eussent convenu

Impératif
conviens
convenons
convenez

Common idiomatic expressions using this verb

convenir à to please, to suit (conjugated with avoir); **Cela lui a convenu** That suited him.

convenir de qqch to agree on something (conjugated with **être**); **Ils sont convenus d'aller au cinéma** They agreed to go to the movies.

J'en conviens I agree to it.

Ce n'est pas convenable That's not appropriate.

Faites ce qui convient Do what is suitable.

convenir de faire qqch to agree to do something; **Mon père et moi, nous avons convenu de venir chez vous à 8 h. du soir** My father and I agreed to come to your place at 8 in the evening.

Il faut convenir que vous avez raison Admittedly, you are right (One must admit that you are right).

Cela ne me convient pas That does not suit me.

See also **devenir, prévenir, revenir, se souvenir,** and **venir.**

The Seven Simple Tenses		The Seven Compound Tenses	
Singular	Plural	Singular	Plural
1 présent de l'indicatif		8 passé composé	
corrige	corrigeons	ai corrigé	avons corrigé
corriges	corrigez	as corrigé	avez corrigé
corrige	corrigent	a corrigé	ont corrigé
2 imparfait de l'indicatif		9 plus-que-parfait de l'indicatif	
corrigeais	corrigions	avais corrigé	avions corrigé
corrigeais	corrigiez	avais corrigé	aviez corrigé
corrigeait	corrigeaient	avait corrigé	avaient corrigé
3 passé simple		10 passé antérieur	
corrigeai	corrigeâmes	eus corrigé	eûmes corrigé
corrigeas	corrigeâtes	eus corrigé	eûtes corrigé
corrigea	corrigèrent	eut corrigé	eurent corrigé
4 futur		11 futur antérieur	
corrigerai	corrigerons	aurai corrigé	aurons corrigé
corrigeras	corrigerez	auras corrigé	aurez corrigé
corrigera	corrigeront	aura corrigé	auront corrigé
5 conditionnel		12 conditionnel passé	
corrigerais	corrigerions	aurais corrigé	aurions corrigé
corrigerais	corrigeriez	aurais corrigé	auriez corrigé
corrigerait	corrigeraient	aurait corrigé	auraient corrigé
6 présent du subjonctif		13 passé du subjonctif	
corrige	corrigions	aie corrigé	ayons corrigé
corriges	corrigiez	aies corrigé	ayez corrigé
corrige	corrigent	ait corrigé	aient corrigé
7 imparfait du subjonctif		14 plus-que-parfait du subjonctif	
corrigeasse	corrigeassions	eusse corrigé	eussions corrigé
corrigeasses	corrigeassiez	eusses corrigé	eussiez corrigé
corrigeât	corrigeassent	eût corrigé	eussent corrigé

Impératif
corrige
corrigeons
corrigez

Sentences using this verb and words related to it

   Dans la classe de français nous corrigeons toujours nos devoirs en classe. Le (La) prof de français écrit les corrections au tableau.

une correction correction; **la correction** accuracy, correctness; **recorriger** to correct again	**corrigible** corrigible; **incorrigible** incorrigible
	incorrectement inaccurately, incorrectly
	la correction automatique automatic correction (comp.)
corriger qqn de to correct someone of	
se corriger de to correct one's ways	**un correcteur, une correctrice** proofreader

Enjoy verbs in French proverbs on page 559.

corrompre

Part. pr. **corrompant**   Part. passé **corrompu**

to corrupt

The Seven Simple Tenses		The Seven Compound Tenses	
Singular	Plural	Singular	Plural
1 présent de l'indicatif		8 passé composé	
corromps	**corrompons**	**ai corrompu**	**avons corrompu**
corromps	**corrompez**	**as corrompu**	**avez corrompu**
corrompt	**corrompent**	**a corrompu**	**ont corrompu**
2 imparfait de l'indicatif		9 plus-que-parfait de l'indicatif	
corrompais	**corrompions**	**avais corrompu**	**avions corrompu**
corrompais	**corrompiez**	**avais corrompu**	**aviez corrompu**
corrompait	**corrompaient**	**avait corrompu**	**avaient corrompu**
3 passé simple		10 passé antérieur	
corrompis	**corrompîmes**	**eus corrompu**	**eûmes corrompu**
corrompis	**corrompîtes**	**eus corrompu**	**eûtes corrompu**
corrompit	**corrompirent**	**eut corrompu**	**eurent corrompu**
4 futur		11 futur antérieur	
corromprai	**corromprons**	**aurai corrompu**	**aurons corrompu**
corrompras	**corromprez**	**auras corrompu**	**aurez corrompu**
corrompra	**corrompront**	**aura corrompu**	**auront corrompu**
5 conditionnel		12 conditionnel passé	
corromprais	**corromprions**	**aurais corrompu**	**aurions corrompu**
corromprais	**corrompriez**	**aurais corrompu**	**auriez corrompu**
corromprait	**corrompraient**	**aurait corrompu**	**auraient corrompu**
6 présent du subjonctif		13 passé du subjonctif	
corrompe	**corrompions**	**aie corrompu**	**ayons corrompu**
corrompes	**corrompiez**	**aies corrompu**	**ayez corrompu**
corrompe	**corrompent**	**ait corrompu**	**aient corrompu**
7 imparfait du subjonctif		14 plus-que-parfait du subjonctif	
corrompisse	**corrompissions**	**eusse corrompu**	**eussions corrompu**
corrompisses	**corrompissiez**	**eusses corrompu**	**eussiez corrompu**
corrompît	**corrompissent**	**eût corrompu**	**eussent corrompu**

Impératif
corromps
corrompons
corrompez

Sentences using this verb and words related to it

corrompre qqch to corrupt something;
Je connais un élève qui corrompt la prononciation de la langue française
I know a student who corrupts the pronunciation of the French language.
corruptible corruptible
se laisser corrompre to allow oneself to be corrupted

corrompre qqn to corrupt someone; **Les spectacles ignobles à la télévision corrompent la jeunesse de ce pays** The disgraceful shows on television corrupt the youth of this country.
la corruption corruption
un corrupteur, une corruptrice corrupter

See also **interrompre** and **rompre**.

Can't recognize an irregular verb form? Check out pages 526–529.

to put to bed, to lay, to flatten

The Seven Simple Tenses		The Seven Compound Tenses	
Singular	Plural	Singular	Plural
1 présent de l'indicatif		**8 passé composé**	
couche	couchons	ai couché	avons couché
couches	couchez	as couché	avez couché
couche	couchent	a couché	ont couché
2 imparfait de l'indicatif		**9 plus-que-parfait de l'indicatif**	
couchais	couchions	avais couché	avions couché
couchais	couchiez	avais couché	aviez couché
couchait	couchaient	avait couché	avaient couché
3 passé simple		**10 passé antérieur**	
couchai	couchâmes	eus couché	eûmes couché
couchas	couchâtes	eus couché	eûtes couché
coucha	couchèrent	eut couché	eurent couché
4 futur		**11 futur antérieur**	
coucherai	coucherons	aurai couché	aurons couché
coucheras	coucherez	auras couché	aurez couché
couchera	coucheront	aura couché	auront couché
5 conditionnel		**12 conditionnel passé**	
coucherais	coucherions	aurais couché	aurions couché
coucherais	coucheriez	aurais couché	auriez couché
coucherait	coucheraient	aurait couché	auraient couché
6 présent du subjonctif		**13 passé du subjonctif**	
couche	couchions	aie couché	ayons couché
couches	couchiez	aies couché	ayez couché
couche	couchent	ait couché	aient couché
7 imparfait du subjonctif		**14 plus-que-parfait du subjonctif**	
couchasse	couchassions	eusse couché	eussions couché
couchasses	couchassiez	eusses couché	eussiez couché
couchât	couchassent	eût couché	eussent couché

Impératif
couche
couchons
couchez

Words and expressions related to this verb
C'est l'heure du coucher   It's time for bed.
le coucher et la nourriture   bed and board
au coucher du soleil   at sunset
découcher   to sleep somewhere other than in one's own bed
coucher à l'hôtel   to sleep in a hotel

See also **se coucher.**

accoucher de   to give birth to a child; **Elle a accouché d'une fille**   She has given birth to a girl.
recoucher   to put back to bed
Ils couchent ensemble   They sleep together.

Taking a trip? Check out the popular words, phrases, and expressions for travelers on pages 599–621.

The subject pronouns are found on the page facing page 1.   **119**

se coucher

to go to bed, to lie down

The Seven Simple Tenses		The Seven Compound Tenses	
Singular	Plural	Singular	Plural
1 présent de l'indicatif		**8 passé composé**	
me couche	nous couchons	me suis couché(e)	nous sommes couché(e)s
te couches	vous couchez	t'es couché(e)	vous êtes couché(e)(s)
se couche	se couchent	s'est couché(e)	se sont couché(e)s
2 imparfait de l'indicatif		**9 plus-que-parfait de l'indicatif**	
me couchais	nous couchions	m'étais couché(e)	nous étions couché(e)s
te couchais	vous couchiez	t'étais couché(e)	vous étiez couché(e)(s)
se couchait	se couchaient	s'était couché(e)	s'étaient couché(e)s
3 passé simple		**10 passé antérieur**	
me couchai	nous couchâmes	me fus couché(e)	nous fûmes couché(e)s
te couchas	vous couchâtes	te fus couché(e)	vous fûtes couché(e)(s)
se coucha	se couchèrent	se fut couché(e)	se furent couché(e)s
4 futur		**11 futur antérieur**	
me coucherai	nous coucherons	me serai couché(e)	nous serons couché(e)s
te coucheras	vous coucherez	te seras couché(e)	vous serez couché(e)(s)
se couchera	se coucheront	se sera couché(e)	se seront couché(e)s
5 conditionnel		**12 conditionnel passé**	
me coucherais	nous coucherions	me serais couché(e)	nous serions couché(e)s
te coucherais	vous coucheriez	te serais couché(e)	vous seriez couché(e)(s)
se coucherait	se coucheraient	se serait couché(e)	se seraient couché(e)s
6 présent du subjonctif		**13 passé du subjonctif**	
me couche	nous couchions	me sois couché(e)	nous soyons couché(e)s
te couches	vous couchiez	te sois couché(e)	vous soyez couché(e)(s)
se couche	se couchent	se soit couché(e)	se soient couché(e)s
7 imparfait du subjonctif		**14 plus-que-parfait du subjonctif**	
me couchasse	nous couchassions	me fusse couché(e)	nous fussions couché(e)s
te couchasses	vous couchassiez	te fusses couché(e)	vous fussiez couché(e)(s)
se couchât	se couchassent	se fût couché(e)	se fussent couché(e)s

Impératif
couche-toi; ne te couche pas
couchons-nous; ne nous couchons pas
couchez-vous; ne vous couchez pas

Sentences using this verb and words related to it
—**Couche-toi, Hélène! Il est minuit. Hier soir tu t'es couchée tard.**
—**Donne-moi ma poupée pour coucher ensemble.**

le coucher du soleil sunset
une couche a layer
une couchette bunk, cot
Le soleil se couche The sun is setting.
se recoucher to go back to bed

se coucher tôt to go to bed early
Comme on fait son lit on se couche! You've made your bed; now lie in it!
un sac de couchage sleeping bag
un couche-tard night owl

See also **coucher.**

The Seven Simple Tenses		The Seven Compound Tenses	
Singular	Plural	Singular	Plural
1 présent de l'indicatif		8 passé composé	
couds	cousons	ai cousu	avons cousu
couds	cousez	as cousu	avez cousu
coud	cousent	a cousu	ont cousu
2 imparfait de l'indicatif		9 plus-que-parfait de l'indicatif	
cousais	cousions	avais cousu	avions cousu
cousais	cousiez	avais cousu	aviez cousu
cousait	cousaient	avait cousu	avaient cousu
3 passé simple		10 passé antérieur	
cousis	cousîmes	eus cousu	eûmes cousu
cousis	cousîtes	eus cousu	eûtes cousu
cousit	cousirent	eut cousu	eurent cousu
4 futur		11 futur antérieur	
coudrai	coudrons	aurai cousu	aurons cousu
coudras	coudrez	auras cousu	aurez cousu
coudra	coudront	aura cousu	auront cousu
5 conditionnel		12 conditionnel passé	
coudrais	coudrions	aurais cousu	aurions cousu
coudrais	coudriez	aurais cousu	auriez cousu
coudrait	coudraient	aurait cousu	auraient cousu
6 présent du subjonctif		13 passé du subjonctif	
couse	cousions	aie cousu	ayons cousu
couses	cousiez	aies cousu	ayez cousu
couse	cousent	ait cousu	aient cousu
7 imparfait du subjonctif		14 plus-que-parfait du subjonctif	
cousisse	cousissions	eusse cousu	eussions cousu
cousisses	cousissiez	eusses cousu	eussiez cousu
cousît	cousissent	eût cousu	eussent cousu

Impératif
couds
cousons
cousez

Words and expressions related to this verb
recoudre to sew again, to sew up
la couture sewing; dressmaking
la couture à la machine machine sewing
découdre to unstitch, to rip up some sewing
une machine à coudre sewing machine
un couturier, une couturière fashion designer

la haute couture high fashion
décousu, décousue unstitched, unsewn; incoherent **Mon professeur d'algèbre explique les leçons d'une manière décousue.**

Want to learn more idiomatic expressions that contain verbs? Look at pages 530–542.

The subject pronouns are found on the page facing page 1.

to cut, to switch off

The Seven Simple Tenses		The Seven Compound Tenses	
Singular	Plural	Singular	Plural
1 présent de l'indicatif		8 passé composé	
coupe	coupons	ai coupé	avons coupé
coupes	coupez	as coupé	avez coupé
coupe	coupent	a coupé	ont coupé
2 imparfait de l'indicatif		9 plus-que-parfait de l'indicatif	
coupais	coupions	avais coupé	avions coupé
coupais	coupiez	avais coupé	aviez coupé
coupait	coupaient	avait coupé	avaient coupé
3 passé simple		10 passé antérieur	
coupai	coupâmes	eus coupé	eûmes coupé
coupas	coupâtes	eus coupé	eûtes coupé
coupa	coupèrent	eut coupé	eurent coupé
4 futur		11 futur antérieur	
couperai	couperons	aurai coupé	aurons coupé
couperas	couperez	auras coupé	aurez coupé
coupera	couperont	aura coupé	auront coupé
5 conditionnel		12 conditionnel passé	
couperais	couperions	aurais coupé	aurions coupé
couperais	couperiez	aurais coupé	auriez coupé
couperait	couperaient	aurait coupé	auraient coupé
6 présent du subjonctif		13 passé du subjonctif	
coupe	coupions	aie coupé	ayons coupé
coupes	coupiez	aies coupé	ayez coupé
coupe	coupent	ait coupé	aient coupé
7 imparfait du subjonctif		14 plus-que-parfait du subjonctif	
coupasse	coupassions	eusse coupé	eussions coupé
coupasses	coupassiez	eusses coupé	eussiez coupé
coupât	coupassent	eût coupé	eussent coupé

Impératif
coupe
coupons
coupez

Common idiomatic expressions using this verb
  Ce morceau de pain est trop grand. Je vais le couper en deux.

un coupon coupon	**découper** to cut out
une coupure cut, gash, crack	**entrecouper** to interrupt
couper les cheveux en quatre to split hairs	**couper la fièvre** to reduce the fever
se faire couper les cheveux to have one's hair cut	**une coupe (de cheveux)** haircut
Aïe! Je me suis coupé le doigt! Ouch! I cut my finger!	**une coupe croisée** crosscut

How are you doing? Find out with the verb drills and tests with answers explained on pages 622–673.

The Seven Simple Tenses		The Seven Compound Tenses	
Singular	Plural	Singular	Plural
1 présent de l'indicatif		**8 passé composé**	
cours	courons	ai couru	avons couru
cours	courez	as couru	avez couru
court	courent	a couru	ont couru
2 imparfait de l'indicatif		**9 plus-que-parfait de l'indicatif**	
courais	courions	avais couru	avions couru
courais	couriez	avais couru	aviez couru
courait	couraient	avait couru	avaient couru
3 passé simple		**10 passé antérieur**	
courus	courûmes	eus couru	eûmes couru
courus	courûtes	eus couru	eûtes couru
courut	coururent	eut couru	eurent couru
4 futur		**11 futur antérieur**	
courrai	courrons	aurai couru	aurons couru
courras	courrez	auras couru	aurez couru
courra	courront	aura couru	auront couru
5 conditionnel		**12 conditionnel passé**	
courrais	courrions	aurais couru	aurions couru
courrais	courriez	aurais couru	auriez couru
courrait	courraient	aurait couru	auraient couru
6 présent du subjonctif		**13 passé du subjonctif**	
coure	courions	aie couru	ayons couru
coures	couriez	aies couru	ayez couru
coure	courent	ait couru	aient couru
7 imparfait du subjonctif		**14 plus-que-parfait du subjonctif**	
courusse	courussions	eusse couru	eussions couru
courusses	courussiez	eusses couru	eussiez couru
courût	courussent	eût couru	eussent couru

Impératif
cours
courons
courez

Sentences using this verb and words related to it
   Les enfants sont toujours prêts à courir. Quand on est jeune on court sans se fatiguer. Michel a couru de la maison jusqu'à l'école. Il a seize ans.

le courrier courier, messenger, mail
le courrier électronique e-mail, electronic mail
un coureur, une coureuse runner
faire courir un bruit to spread a rumor
courir une course to run a race
courir le monde to roam all over the world

accourir vers to come running toward
courir les rues to run about the streets
par le temps qui court these days, nowadays
parcourir to go through, to travel through, to cover (distance)
recourir à to turn to (for help)
faire les courses to do the shopping

See also **accourir**.

coûter

Part. pr. **coûtant**   Part. passé **coûté**

to cost

The Seven Simple Tenses		The Seven Compound Tenses	
Singular	Plural	Singular	Plural
1 présent de l'indicatif		8 passé composé	
il coûte	**ils coûtent**	**il a coûté**	**ils ont coûté**
2 imparfait de l'indicatif		9 plus-que-parfait de l'indicatif	
il coûtait	**ils coûtaient**	**il avait coûté**	**ils avaient coûté**
3 passé simple		10 passé antérieur	
il coûta	**ils coûtèrent**	**il eut coûté**	**ils eurent coûté**
4 futur		11 futur antérieur	
il coûtera	**ils coûteront**	**il aura coûté**	**ils auront coûté**
5 conditionnel		12 conditionnel passé	
il coûterait	**ils coûteraient**	**il aurait coûté**	**ils auraient coûté**
6 présent du subjonctif		13 passé du subjonctif	
qu'il coûte	**qu'ils coûtent**	**qu'il ait coûté**	**qu'ils aient coûté**
7 imparfait du subjonctif		14 plus-que-parfait du subjonctif	
qu'il coûtât	**qu'ils coûtassent**	**qu'il eût coûté**	**qu'ils eussent coûté**

Impératif
[not in use]

Sentences using this verb and words related to it
—**Combien coûte cette table?**
—**Elle coûte dix mille euros.**
—**Et combien coûte ce lit?**
—**Il coûte dix mille euros aussi.**
—**Ils coûtent joliment cher!**

coûteusement   expensively, dearly
coûte que coûte   at any cost
coûteux, coûteuse   costly, expensive
Cela coûte joliment cher   That costs a pretty penny.
coûter cher, coûter peu   to be expensive, inexpensive

coûter à qqn   to cost someone;
   Cela lui en a coûté la vie   That cost him his life.
Coûter les yeux de la tête   To be very expensive.
le coût de la vie   the cost of living

This verb is generally regarded as impersonal and is used primarily in the third person singular and plural.

124

The Seven Simple Tenses		The Seven Compound Tenses	
Singular	Plural	Singular	Plural
1 présent de l'indicatif		8 passé composé	
couvre	couvrons	ai couvert	avons couvert
couvres	couvrez	as couvert	avez couvert
couvre	couvrent	a couvert	ont couvert
2 imparfait de l'indicatif		9 plus-que-parfait de l'indicatif	
couvrais	couvrions	avais couvert	avions couvert
couvrais	couvriez	avais couvert	aviez couvert
couvrait	couvraient	avait couvert	avaient couvert
3 passé simple		10 passé antérieur	
couvris	couvrîmes	eus couvert	eûmes couvert
couvris	couvrîtes	eus couvert	eûtes couvert
couvrit	couvrirent	eut couvert	eurent couvert
4 futur		11 futur antérieur	
couvrirai	couvrirons	aurai couvert	aurons couvert
couvriras	couvrirez	auras couvert	aurez couvert
couvrira	couvriront	aura couvert	auront couvert
5 conditionnel		12 conditionnel passé	
couvrirais	couvririons	aurais couvert	aurions couvert
couvrirais	couvririez	aurais couvert	auriez couvert
couvrirait	couvriraient	aurait couvert	auraient couvert
6 présent du subjonctif		13 passé du subjonctif	
couvre	couvrions	aie couvert	ayons couvert
couvres	couvriez	aies couvert	ayez couvert
couvre	couvrent	ait couvert	aient couvert
7 imparfait du subjonctif		14 plus-que-parfait du subjonctif	
couvrisse	couvrissions	eusse couvert	eussions couvert
couvrisses	couvrissiez	eusses couvert	eussiez couvert
couvrît	couvrissent	eût couvert	eussent couvert

Impératif
couvre
couvrons
couvrez

Sentences using this verb and words related to it

Avant de quitter la maison, Madame Champlain a couvert le lit d'un dessus-de-lit. Puis, elle a couvert son mari de caresses et de baisers.

un couvert place setting (spoon, knife, fork, *etc.*)
acheter des couverts to buy cutlery
mettre le couvert to lay the table
une couverture blanket
Le temps se couvre The sky is overcast.
découvrir to discover, disclose, uncover

recouvrir to cover
se couvrir to cover oneself, to put on one's hat
le couvre-feu curfew
un couvre-lit bedspread (**des couvre-lits**)
un dessus-de-lit bedspread (**des dessus-de-lits**)

See also **découvrir.**

to fear, to be afraid

The Seven Simple Tenses		The Seven Compound Tenses	
Singular	Plural	Singular	Plural
1　présent de l'indicatif		**8　passé composé**	
crains	craignons	ai craint	avons craint
crains	craignez	as craint	avez craint
craint	craignent	a craint	ont craint
2　imparfait de l'indicatif		**9　plus-que-parfait de l'indicatif**	
craignais	craignions	avais craint	avions craint
craignais	craigniez	avais craint	aviez craint
craignait	craignaient	avait craint	avaient craint
3　passé simple		**10　passé antérieur**	
craignis	craignîmes	eus craint	eûmes craint
craignis	craignîtes	eus craint	eûtes craint
craignit	craignirent	eut craint	eurent craint
4　futur		**11　futur antérieur**	
craindrai	craindrons	aurai craint	aurons craint
craindras	craindrez	auras craint	aurez craint
craindra	craindront	aura craint	auront craint
5　conditionnel		**12　conditionnel passé**	
craindrais	craindrions	aurais craint	aurions craint
craindrais	craindriez	aurais craint	auriez craint
craindrait	craindraient	aurait craint	auraient craint
6　présent du subjonctif		**13　passé du subjonctif**	
craigne	craignions	aie craint	ayons craint
craignes	craigniez	aies craint	ayez craint
craigne	craignent	ait craint	aient craint
7　imparfait du subjonctif		**14　plus-que-parfait du subjonctif**	
craignisse	craignissions	eusse craint	eussions craint
craignisses	craignissiez	eusses craint	eussiez craint
craignît	craignissent	eût craint	eussent craint

Impératif
crains
craignons
craignez

Sentences using this verb and words related to it

　　Le petit garçon **craint** de traverser le parc pendant la nuit. Il a raison parce que c'est dangereux. Il a des **craintes.**

une **crainte**　fear, dread	**craintif, craintive**　fearful
craindre pour sa vie　to be in fear of one's life	**craintivement**　fearfully
sans crainte　fearless	**avec crainte**　fearfully

Use the EE-zee guide to French pronunciation on pages 566 and 567.

The Seven Simple Tenses		The Seven Compound Tenses	
Singular	Plural	Singular	Plural
1 présent de l'indicatif		8 passé composé	
crée	**créons**	**ai créé**	**avons créé**
crées	**créez**	**as créé**	**avez créé**
crée	**créent**	**a créé**	**ont créé**
2 imparfait de l'indicatif		9 plus-que-parfait de l'indicatif	
créais	**créions**	**avais créé**	**avions créé**
créais	**créiez**	**avais créé**	**aviez créé**
créait	**créaient**	**avait créé**	**avaient créé**
3 passé simple		10 passé antérieur	
créai	**créâmes**	**eus créé**	**eûmes créé**
créas	**créâtes**	**eus créé**	**eûtes créé**
créa	**créèrent**	**eut créé**	**eurent créé**
4 futur		11 futur antérieur	
créerai	**créerons**	**aurai créé**	**aurons créé**
créeras	**créerez**	**auras créé**	**aurez créé**
créera	**créeront**	**aura créé**	**auront créé**
5 conditionnel		12 conditionnel passé	
créerais	**créerions**	**aurais créé**	**aurions créé**
créerais	**créeriez**	**aurais créé**	**auriez créé**
créerait	**créeraient**	**aurait créé**	**auraient créé**
6 présent du subjonctif		13 passé du subjonctif	
crée	**créions**	**aie créé**	**ayons créé**
crées	**créiez**	**aies créé**	**ayez créé**
crée	**créent**	**ait créé**	**aient créé**
7 imparfait du subjonctif		14 plus-que-parfait du subjonctif	
créasse	**créassions**	**eusse créé**	**eussions créé**
créasses	**créassiez**	**eusses créé**	**eussiez créé**
créât	**créassent**	**eût créé**	**eussent créé**

Impératif
crée
créons
créez

Sentences using this verb and words related to it

Madame Imbert, professeur de mathématiques, est une drôle de créature. Tout ce qu'elle fait manque d'originalité. Quelle misérable créature!

drôle de créature   funny, queer person
la création   creation; **depuis la création du monde**   since the creation of the world
la créativité   creativity; **la récréation** recreation

une créature   creature
recréer   to create again; **récréer**   to enliven
un créateur, une créatrice   creator

Going away? Don't forget to check out the practical situations for travelers on pages 568–598.

crier

Part. pr. **criant** Part. passé **crié**

to shout, to cry out

The Seven Simple Tenses		The Seven Compound Tenses	
Singular	Plural	Singular	Plural
1 présent de l'indicatif		**8 passé composé**	
crie	crions	ai crié	avons crié
cries	criez	as crié	avez crié
crie	crient	a crié	ont crié
2 imparfait de l'indicatif		**9 plus-que-parfait de l'indicatif**	
criais	criions	avais crié	avions crié
criais	criiez	avais crié	aviez crié
criait	criaient	avait crié	avaient crié
3 passé simple		**10 passé antérieur**	
criai	criâmes	eus crié	eûmes crié
crias	criâtes	eus crié	eûtes crié
cria	crièrent	eut crié	eurent crié
4 futur		**11 futur antérieur**	
crierai	crierons	aurai crié	aurons crié
crieras	crierez	auras crié	aurez crié
criera	crieront	aura crié	auront crié
5 conditionnel		**12 conditionnel passé**	
crierais	crierions	aurais crié	aurions crié
crierais	crieriez	aurais crié	auriez crié
crierait	crieraient	aurait crié	auraient crié
6 présent du subjonctif		**13 passé du subjonctif**	
crie	criions	aie crié	ayons crié
cries	criiez	aies crié	ayez crié
crie	crient	ait crié	aient crié
7 imparfait du subjonctif		**14 plus-que-parfait du subjonctif**	
criasse	criassions	eusse crié	eussions crié
criasses	criassiez	eusses crié	eussiez crié
criât	criassent	eût crié	eussent crié

Impératif
crie
crions
criez

Words and expressions related to this verb
un cri a shout, a cry
pousser un cri to utter a cry
crier à tue-tête to shout one's head off
un crieur hawker
un crieur de journaux newsboy
décrier to decry, criticize

un criailleur, une criailleuse nagger
un criard, une criarde someone who constantly shouts, nags, scolds; screecher
un portrait criant de vérité a portrait strikingly true to life

Want to learn more idiomatic expressions that contain verbs? Look at pages 530–542.

croire
to believe

The Seven Simple Tenses		The Seven Compound Tenses	
Singular	Plural	Singular	Plural
1 présent de l'indicatif		**8 passé composé**	
crois	croyons	ai cru	avons cru
crois	croyez	as cru	avez cru
croit	croient	a cru	ont cru
2 imparfait de l'indicatif		**9 plus-que-parfait de l'indicatif**	
croyais	croyions	avais cru	avions cru
croyais	croyiez	avais cru	aviez cru
croyait	croyaient	avait cru	avaient cru
3 passé simple		**10 passé antérieur**	
crus	crûmes	eus cru	eûmes cru
crus	crûtes	eus cru	eûtes cru
crut	crurent	eut cru	eurent cru
4 futur		**11 futur antérieur**	
croirai	croirons	aurai cru	aurons cru
croiras	croirez	auras cru	aurez cru
croira	croiront	aura cru	auront cru
5 conditionnel		**12 conditionnel passé**	
croirais	croirions	aurais cru	aurions cru
croirais	croiriez	aurais cru	auriez cru
croirait	croiraient	aurait cru	auraient cru
6 présent du subjonctif		**13 passé du subjonctif**	
croie	croyions	aie cru	ayons cru
croies	croyiez	aies cru	ayez cru
croie	croient	ait cru	aient cru
7 imparfait du subjonctif		**14 plus-que-parfait du subjonctif**	
crusse	crussions	eusse cru	eussions cru
crusses	crussiez	eusses cru	eussiez cru
crût	crussent	eût cru	eussent cru

Impératif
crois
croyons
croyez

Sentences using this verb and words related to it

Est-ce que vous croyez tout ce que vous entendez? Avez-vous cru l'histoire que je vous ai racontée?

Croyez-m'en!   Take my word for it!
se croire   to think oneself; to consider oneself
Paul se croit beau   Paul thinks himself handsome.
croyable   believable

incroyable   unbelievable
croire à qqch   to believe in something
croire en qqn   to believe in someone
croire en Dieu   to believe in God

Get acquainted with what preposition goes with what verb on pages 543–553.

The subject pronouns are found on the page facing page 1.   **129**

croître

Part. pr. croissant   **Part. passé crû (crue)**

to grow, to increase

The Seven Simple Tenses		The Seven Compound Tenses	
Singular	Plural	Singular	Plural
1 présent de l'indicatif		**8 passé composé**	
croîs	croissons	ai crû	avons crû
croîs	croissez	as crû	avez crû
croît	croissent	a crû	ont crû
2 imparfait de l'indicatif		**9 plus-que-parfait de l'indicatif**	
croissais	croissions	avais crû	avions crû
croissais	croissiez	avais crû	aviez crû
croissait	croissaient	avait crû	avaient crû
3 passé simple		**10 passé antérieur**	
crûs	crûmes	eus crû	eûmes crû
crûs	crûtes	eus crû	eûtes crû
crût	crûrent	eut crû	eurent crû
4 futur		**11 futur antérieur**	
croîtrai	croîtrons	aurai crû	aurons crû
croîtras	croîtrez	auras crû	aurez crû
croîtra	croîtront	aura crû	auront crû
5 conditionnel		**12 conditionnel passé**	
croîtrais	croîtrions	aurais crû	aurions crû
croîtrais	croîtriez	aurais crû	auriez crû
croîtrait	croîtraient	aurait crû	auraient crû
6 présent du subjonctif		**13 passé du subjonctif**	
croisse	croissions	aie crû	ayons crû
croisses	croissiez	aies crû	ayez crû
croisse	croissent	ait crû	aient crû
7 imparfait du subjonctif		**14 plus-que-parfait du subjonctif**	
crûsse	crûssions	eusse crû	eussions crû
crûsses	crûssiez	eusses crû	eussiez crû
crût	crûssent	eût crû	eussent crû

Impératif
croîs
croissons
croissez

Words and expressions related to this verb

un croissant   crescent (shape of moon); name of a pastry in crescent shape: **Au petit déjeuner, les Français aiment prendre un café et un croissant** / For breakfast, French people like to have coffee and a croissant (crescent shaped roll).

la croissance   growth; **un accroissement**   increase

crescendo   crescendo (progressive increase in intensity of sound in music; an Italian word related to **croître**).

See also **accroître** and **décroître**.

Consult the sections on verbs used in idiomatic expressions, verbs with prepositions, and the list of over 1,100 verbs conjugated like model verbs in the back pages.

to gather, to pick

The Seven Simple Tenses		The Seven Compound Tenses	
Singular	Plural	Singular	Plural
1 présent de l'indicatif		8 passé composé	
cueille	cueillons	ai cueilli	avons cueilli
cueilles	cueillez	as cueilli	avez cueilli
cueille	cueillent	a cueilli	ont cueilli
2 imparfait de l'indicatif		9 plus-que-parfait de l'indicatif	
cueillais	cueillions	avais cueilli	avions cueilli
cueillais	cueilliez	avais cueilli	aviez cueilli
cueillait	cueillaient	avait cueilli	avaient cueilli
3 passé simple		10 passé antérieur	
cueillis	cueillîmes	eus cueilli	eûmes cueilli
cueillis	cueillîtes	eus cueilli	eûtes cueilli
cueillit	cueillirent	eut cueilli	eurent cueilli
4 futur		11 futur antérieur	
cueillerai	cueillerons	aurai cueilli	aurons cueilli
cueilleras	cueillerez	auras cueilli	aurez cueilli
cueillera	cueilleront	aura cueilli	auront ceuilli
5 conditionnel		12 conditionnel passé	
cueillerais	cueillerions	aurais cueilli	aurions cueilli
cueillerais	cueilleriez	aurais cueilli	auriez cueilli
cueillerait	cueilleraient	aurait cueilli	auraient cueilli
6 présent du subjonctif		13 passé du subjonctif	
cueille	cueillions	aie cueilli	ayons cueilli
cueilles	cueilliez	aies cueilli	ayez cueilli
cueille	cueillent	ait cueilli	aient cueilli
7 imparfait du subjonctif		14 plus-que-parfait du subjonctif	
cueillisse	cueillissions	eusse cueilli	eussions cueilli
cueillisses	cueillissiez	eusses cueilli	eussiez cueilli
cueillît	cueillissent	eût cueilli	eussent cueilli

Impératif
cueille
cueillons
cueillez

Sentences using this verb and words related to it
Je vois que tu cueilles des fleurs. As-tu cueilli toutes les fleurs qui sont dans ce vase?

un cueilleur, une cueilleuse gatherer, picker
la cueillaison, la cueillette gathering, picking
un cueilloir basket for picking fruit;
  instrument for picking fruit on high branches

Cueillez, cueillez votre jeunesse (Ronsard)
  Seize the day (Horace: *Carpe diem*).

For other words related to this verb, see **accueillir** and **recueillir**.

Grammar putting you in a tense mood? Review the definitions of basic grammatical terms with examples on pages 674–688.

to cook

The Seven Simple Tenses		The Seven Compound Tenses	
Singular	Plural	Singular	Plural
1　présent de l'indicatif		8　passé composé	
cuis	cuisons	ai cuit	avons cuit
cuis	cuisez	as cuit	avez cuit
cuit	cuisent	a cuit	ont cuit
2　imparfait de l'indicatif		9　plus-que-parfait de l'indicatif	
cuisais	cuisions	avais cuit	avions cuit
cuisais	cuisiez	avais cuit	aviez cuit
cuisait	cuisaient	avait cuit	avaient cuit
3　passé simple		10　passé antérieur	
cuisis	cuisîmes	eus cuit	eûmes cuit
cuisis	cuisîtes	eus cuit	eûtes cuit
cuisit	cuisirent	eut cuit	eurent cuit
4　futur		11　futur antérieur	
cuirai	cuirons	aurai cuit	aurons cuit
cuiras	cuirez	auras cuit	aurez cuit
cuira	cuiront	aura cuit	auront cuit
5　conditionnel		12　conditionnel passé	
cuirais	cuirions	aurais cuit	aurions cuit
cuirais	cuiriez	aurais cuit	auriez cuit
cuirait	cuiraient	aurait cuit	auraient cuit
6　présent du subjonctif		13　passé du subjonctif	
cuise	cuisions	aie cuit	ayons cuit
cuises	cuisiez	aies cuit	ayez cuit
cuise	cuisent	ait cuit	aient cuit
7　imparfait du subjonctif		14　plus-que-parfait du subjonctif	
cuisisse	cuisissions	eusse cuit	eussions cuit
cuisisses	cuisissiez	eusses cuit	eussiez cuit
cuisît	cuisissent	eût cuit	eussent cuit

Impératif
cuis
cuisons
cuisez

Sentences using this verb and words related to it
　　Qui a cuit ce morceau de viande? C'est dégoûtant! Il est trop cuit. Ne savez-vous pas faire cuire un bon morceau de viande? Vous n'êtes pas bon cuisinier.

la cuisine　kitchen	**un cuiseur**　pressure cooker
cuisinier, cuisinière　cook	**trop cuit**　overcooked, overdone
faire cuire à la poêle　to pan fry	**la cuisson**　cooking (time)
Il est cuit　He's done for; His goose is cooked.	**bien cuit**　well done
une cuisinière　kitchen range (stove)	

Would you rather go to a French restaurant? Check out page 578 and the other practical situations for travelers on pages 568–598.

132

The Seven Simple Tenses		The Seven Compound Tenses	
Singular	Plural	Singular	Plural
1 présent de l'indicatif		**8 passé composé**	
danse	**dansons**	**ai dansé**	**avons dansé**
danses	**dansez**	**as dansé**	**avez dansé**
danse	**dansent**	**a dansé**	**ont dansé**
2 imparfait de l'indicatif		**9 plus-que-parfait de l'indicatif**	
dansais	**dansions**	**avais dansé**	**avions dansé**
dansais	**dansiez**	**avais dansé**	**aviez dansé**
dansait	**dansaient**	**avait dansé**	**avaient dansé**
3 passé simple		**10 passé antérieur**	
dansai	**dansâmes**	**eus dansé**	**eûmes dansé**
dansas	**dansâtes**	**eus dansé**	**eûtes dansé**
dansa	**dansèrent**	**eut dansé**	**eurent dansé**
4 futur		**11 futur antérieur**	
danserai	**danserons**	**aurai dansé**	**aurons dansé**
denseras	**danserez**	**auras dansé**	**aurez dansé**
dansera	**danseront**	**aura dansé**	**auront dansé**
5 conditionnel		**12 conditionnel passé**	
danserais	**danserions**	**aurais dansé**	**aurions dansé**
danserais	**danseriez**	**aurais dansé**	**auriez dansé**
danserait	**danseraient**	**aurait dansé**	**auraient dansé**
6 présent du subjonctif		**13 passé du subjonctif**	
danse	**dansions**	**aie dansé**	**ayons dansé**
danses	**dansiez**	**aies dansé**	**ayez dansé**
danse	**dansent**	**ait dansé**	**aient dansé**
7 imparfait du subjonctif		**14 plus-que-parfait du subjonctif**	
dansasse	**dansassions**	**eusse dansé**	**eussions dansé**
dansasses	**dansassiez**	**eusses dansé**	**eussiez dansé**
dansât	**dansassent**	**eût dansé**	**eussent dansé**

Impératif
danse
dansons
dansez

Sentences using this verb and words related to it
  René: **Veux-tu danser avec moi?**
  Renée: **Je ne sais pas danser.**
  René: **Je suis bon danseur. Je vais t'apprendre à danser. Viens! Dansons!**

danser de joie   to dance for joy
une soirée dansante   evening dancing party
un thé dansant   dancing at teatime (usually 5 o'clock); tea dance
Quand le chat n'est pas là les souris dansent   When the cat's away the mice will play.

un danseur, une danseuse   dancer
une danse   dance; **un bal**   ball (dance)
danseur, danseuse de claquettes   tap dancer
la danse macabre   dance of death

Want to learn more verbs used in proverbs and sayings? Take a look at page 559.

The subject pronouns are found on the page facing page 1.   **133**

to deceive, to disappoint

The Seven Simple Tenses		The Seven Compound Tenses	
Singular	Plural	Singular	Plural
1 présent de l'indicatif		**8 passé composé**	
déçois	décevons	ai déçu	avons déçu
déçois	décevez	as déçu	avez déçu
déçoit	déçoivent	a déçu	ont déçu
2 imparfait de l'indicatif		**9 plus-que-parfait de l'indicatif**	
décevais	décevions	avais déçu	avions déçu
décevais	déceviez	avais déçu	aviez déçu
décevait	décevaient	avait déçu	avaient déçu
3 passé simple		**10 passé antérieur**	
déçus	déçûmes	eus déçu	eûmes déçu
déçus	déçûtes	eus déçu	eûtes déçu
déçut	déçurent	eut déçu	eurent déçu
4 futur		**11 futur antérieur**	
décevrai	décevrons	aurai déçu	aurons déçu
décevras	décevrez	auras déçu	aurez déçu
décevra	décevront	aura déçu	auront déçu
5 conditionnel		**12 conditionnel passé**	
décevrais	décevrions	aurais déçu	aurions déçu
décevrais	décevriez	aurais déçu	auriez déçu
décevrait	décevraient	aurait déçu	auraient déçu
6 présent du subjonctif		**13 passé du subjonctif**	
déçoive	décevions	aie déçu	ayons déçu
déçoives	déceviez	aies déçu	ayez déçu
déçoive	déçoivent	ait déçu	aient déçu
7 imparfait du subjonctif		**14 plus-que-parfait du subjonctif**	
déçusse	déçussions	eusse déçu	eussions déçu
déçusses	déçussiez	eusses déçu	eussiez déçu
déçût	déçussent	eût déçu	eussent déçu

Impératif
déçois
décevons
décevez

Words and expressions related to this verb

décevoir la confiance de qqn   to deceive
   someone's confidence (trust)
décevant, décevante   disappointing, deceptive
être déçu   to be disappointed
décevoir les espoirs de qqn   to disappoint
   someone's hopes

la déception   disappointment; **la tromperie**
   deceit
Vous m'avez déçu   You have disappointed me.
Quelle déception!   What a disappointment!

Consult the sections on verbs used in idiomatic expressions, verbs with prepositions, and the list
of over 1,100 verbs conjugated like model verbs in the back pages.

to rip, to tear, to rend

The Seven Simple Tenses		The Seven Compound Tenses	
Singular	Plural	Singular	Plural
1 présent de l'indicatif		**8 passé composé**	
déchire	**déchirons**	**ai déchiré**	**avons déchiré**
déchires	**déchirez**	**as déchiré**	**avez déchiré**
déchire	**déchirent**	**a déchiré**	**ont déchiré**
2 imparfait de l'indicatif		**9 plus-que-parfait de l'indicatif**	
déchirais	**déchirions**	**avais déchiré**	**avions déchiré**
déchirais	**déchiriez**	**avais déchiré**	**aviez déchiré**
déchirait	**déchiraient**	**avait déchiré**	**avaient déchiré**
3 passé simple		**10 passé antérieur**	
déchirai	**déchirâmes**	**eus déchiré**	**eûmes déchiré**
déchiras	**déchirâtes**	**eus déchiré**	**eûtes déchiré**
déchira	**déchirèrent**	**eut déchiré**	**eurent déchiré**
4 futur		**11 futur antérieur**	
déchirerai	**déchirerons**	**aurai déchiré**	**aurons déchiré**
déchireras	**déchirerez**	**auras déchiré**	**aurez déchiré**
déchirera	**déchireront**	**aura déchiré**	**auront déchiré**
5 conditionnel		**12 conditionnel passé**	
déchirerais	**déchirerions**	**aurais déchiré**	**aurions déchiré**
déchirerais	**déchireriez**	**aurais déchiré**	**auriez déchiré**
déchirerait	**déchireraient**	**aurait déchiré**	**auraient déchiré**
6 présent du subjonctif		**13 passé du subjonctif**	
déchire	**déchirions**	**aie déchiré**	**ayons déchiré**
déchires	**déchiriez**	**aies déchiré**	**ayez déchiré**
déchire	**déchirent**	**ait déchiré**	**aient déchiré**
7 imparfait du subjonctif		**14 plus-que-parfait du subjonctif**	
déchirasse	**déchirassions**	**eusse déchiré**	**eussions déchiré**
déchirasses	**déchirassiez**	**eusses déchiré**	**eussiez déchiré**
déchirât	**déchirassent**	**eût déchiré**	**eussent déchiré**

Impératif
déchire
déchirons
déchirez

Words and expressions related to this verb
déchirer qqn à belles dents   to tear someone
   apart
déchirer le voile   to discover the truth
une déchirure   laceration, tear
une déchiqueteuse de papier   paper shredder

déchirer en lambeaux   to tear into shreds
se déchirer   to tear each other apart
un déchirement   tearing; **un déchirement du
   coeur**   heartbreak
déchiqueter   to cut to pieces

Grammar putting you in a tense mood? Review the definitions of basic grammatical terms on
pages 674–688.

décider

to decide

Part. pr. **décidant**   Part. passé **décidé**

The Seven Simple Tenses		The Seven Compound Tenses	
Singular	Plural	Singular	Plural
1 présent de l'indicatif		**8 passé composé**	
décide	décidons	ai décidé	avons décidé
décides	décidez	as décidé	avez décidé
décide	décident	a décidé	ont décidé
2 imparfait de l'indicatif		**9 plus-que-parfait de l'indicatif**	
décidais	décidions	avais décidé	avions décidé
décidais	décidiez	avais décidé	aviez décidé
décidait	décidaient	avait décidé	avaient décidé
3 passé simple		**10 passé antérieur**	
décidai	décidâmes	eus décidé	eûmes décidé
décidas	décidâtes	eus décidé	eûtes décidé
décida	décidèrent	eut décidé	eurent décidé
4 futur		**11 futur antérieur**	
déciderai	déciderons	aurai décidé	aurons décidé
décideras	déciderez	auras décidé	aurez décidé
décidera	décideront	aura décidé	auront décidé
5 conditionnel		**12 conditionnel passé**	
déciderais	déciderions	aurais décidé	aurions décidé
déciderais	décideriez	aurais décidé	auriez décidé
déciderait	décideraient	aurait décidé	auraient décidé
6 présent du subjonctif		**13 passé du subjonctif**	
décide	décidions	aie décidé	ayons décidé
décides	décidiez	aies décidé	ayez décidé
décide	décident	ait décidé	aient décidé
7 imparfait du subjonctif		**14 plus-que-parfait du subjonctif**	
décidasse	décidassions	eusse décidé	eussions décidé
décidasses	décidassiez	eusses décidé	eussiez décidé
décidât	décidassent	eût décidé	eussent décidé

Impératif
décide
décidons
décidez

Words and expressions related to this verb
une décision decision; **prendre une décision** to make (come to) a decision
décidément decidedly
décider de faire qqch to decide to do something; **J'ai décidé de partir** I decided to leave.
se décider à faire qqch to make up one's mind, to resolve to do something; **Le docteur Malaise s'est décidé à faire l'opération.**
Décidez-vous! Make up your mind!

Get acquainted with what preposition goes with what verb on pages 543–553.

136

The Seven Simple Tenses		The Seven Compound Tenses	
Singular	Plural	Singular	Plural
1 présent de l'indicatif		8 passé composé	
découvre	**découvrons**	**ai découvert**	**avons découvert**
découvres	**découvrez**	**as découvert**	**avez découvert**
découvre	**découvrent**	**a découvert**	**ont découvert**
2 imparfait de l'indicatif		9 plus-que-parfait de l'indicatif	
découvrais	**découvrions**	**avais découvert**	**avions découvert**
découvrais	**découvriez**	**avais découvert**	**aviez découvert**
découvrait	**découvraient**	**avait découvert**	**avaient découvert**
3 passé simple		10 passé antérieur	
découvris	**découvrîmes**	**eus découvert**	**eûmes découvert**
découvris	**découvrîtes**	**eus découvert**	**eûtes découvert**
découvrit	**découvrirent**	**eut découvert**	**eurent découvert**
4 futur		11 futur antérieur	
découvrirai	**découvrirons**	**aurai découvert**	**aurons découvert**
découvriras	**découvrirez**	**auras découvert**	**aurez découvert**
découvrira	**découvriront**	**aura découvert**	**auront découvert**
5 conditionnel		12 conditionnel passé	
découvrirais	**découvririons**	**aurais découvert**	**aurions découvert**
découvrirais	**découvririez**	**aurais découvert**	**auriez découvert**
découvrirait	**découvriraient**	**aurait découvert**	**auraient découvert**
6 présent du subjonctif		13 passé du subjonctif	
découvre	**découvrions**	**aie découvert**	**ayons découvert**
découvres	**découvriez**	**aies découvert**	**ayez découvert**
découvre	**découvrent**	**ait découvert**	**aient découvert**
7 imparfait du subjonctif		14 plus-que-parfait du subjonctif	
découvrisse	**découvrissions**	**eusse découvert**	**eussions découvert**
découvrisses	**découvrissiez**	**eusses découvert**	**eussiez découvert**
découvrît	**découvrissent**	**eût découvert**	**eussent découvert**

Impératif
découvre
découvrons
découvrez

Sentences using this verb and words related to it
    Ce matin j'ai couvert ce panier de fruits et maintenant il est découvert. Qui l'a découvert?

un découvreur   discoverer
une découverte   a discovery, invention
un découvert   overdraft
se découvrir   to take off one's clothes; to take off one's hat
See also **couvrir.**

aller à la découverte   to explore
Découvrir saint Pierre pour couvrir saint Paul   To rob Peter to pay Paul.

Enjoy more verbs in French proverbs and sayings on page 559.

décrire
to describe

The Seven Simple Tenses		The Seven Compound Tenses	
Singular	Plural	Singular	Plural
1 présent de l'indicatif		8 passé composé	
décris	décrivons	ai décrit	avons décrit
décris	décrivez	as décrit	avez décrit
décrit	décrivent	a décrit	ont décrit
2 imparfait de l'indicatif		9 plus-que-parfait de l'indicatif	
décrivais	décrivions	avais décrit	avions décrit
décrivais	décriviez	avais décrit	aviez décrit
décrivait	décrivaient	avait décrit	avaient décrit
3 passé simple		10 passé antérieur	
décrivis	décrivîmes	eus décrit	eûmes décrit
décrivis	décrivîtes	eus décrit	eûtes décrit
décrivit	décrivirent	eut décrit	eurent décrit
4 futur		11 futur antérieur	
décrirai	décrirons	aurai décrit	aurons décrit
décriras	décrirez	auras décrit	aurez décrit
décrira	décriront	aura décrit	auront décrit
5 conditionnel		12 conditionnel passé	
décrirais	décririons	aurais décrit	aurions décrit
décrirais	décririez	aurais décrit	auriez décrit
décrirait	décriraient	aurait décrit	auraient décrit
6 présent du subjonctif		13 passé du subjonctif	
décrive	décrivions	aie décrit	ayons décrit
décrives	décriviez	aies décrit	ayez décrit
décrive	décrivent	ait décrit	aient décrit
7 imparfait du subjonctif		14 plus-que-parfait du subjonctif	
décrivisse	décrivissions	eusse décrit	eussions décrit
décrivisses	décrivissiez	eusses décrit	eussiez décrit
décrivît	décrivissent	eût décrit	eussent décrit

Impératif
décris
décrivons
décrivez

Sentences using this verb and words related to it

Quel beau paysage! Je le décrirai dans une lettre à mon ami. Je ferai une description en détail.

une description   description
indescriptible   indescribable
écrire   to write
proscrire   to proscribe

prescrire   to prescribe, stipulate
une prescription   prescription (medical prescription: **une ordonnance**)

See also **écrire.**

How are you doing? Find out with the verb drills and tests with answers explained on pages 622–673.

to decrease, to diminish

The Seven Simple Tenses		The Seven Compound Tenses	
Singular	Plural	Singular	Plural
1 présent de l'indicatif		8 passé composé	
décrois	**décroissons**	**ai décru**	**avons décru**
décrois	**décroissez**	**as décru**	**avez décru**
décroît	**décroissent**	**a décru**	**ont décru**
2 imparfait de l'indicatif		9 plus-que-parfait de l'indicatif	
décroissais	**décroissions**	**avais décru**	**avions décru**
décroissais	**décroissiez**	**avais décru**	**aviez décru**
décroissait	**décroissaient**	**avait décru**	**avaient décru**
3 passé simple		10 passé antérieur	
décrus	**décrûmes**	**eus décru**	**eûmes décru**
décrus	**décrûtes**	**eus décru**	**eûtes décru**
décrut	**décrurent**	**eut décru**	**eurent décru**
4 futur		11 futur antérieur	
décroîtrai	**décroîtrons**	**aurai décru**	**aurons décru**
décroîtras	**décroîtrez**	**auras décru**	**aurez décru**
décroîtra	**décroîtront**	**aura décru**	**auront décru**
5 conditionnel		12 conditionnel passé	
décroîtrais	**décroîtrions**	**aurais décru**	**aurions décru**
décroîtrais	**décroîtriez**	**aurais décru**	**auriez décru**
décroîtrait	**décroîtraient**	**aurait décru**	**auraient décru**
6 présent du subjonctif		13 passé du subjonctif	
décroisse	**décroissions**	**aie décru**	**ayons décru**
décroisses	**décroissiez**	**aies décru**	**ayez décru**
décroisse	**décroissent**	**ait décru**	**aient décru**
7 imparfait du subjonctif		14 plus-que-parfait du subjonctif	
décrusse	**décrussions**	**eusse décru**	**eussions décru**
décrusses	**décrussiez**	**eusses décru**	**eussiez décru**
décrût	**décrussent**	**eût décru**	**eussent décru**

Impératif
décrois
décroissons
décroissez

Words and expressions related to this verb
le décroît de la lune   waning of the moon
la décroissance   decrease
être en décroissance   to be diminishing
une décrue   decrease (water level)
décroissant, décroissante   decreasing,
   diminishing

un croissant   crescent shaped roll; crescent (of
   the moon)
la croissance   increase, growth
croître   to grow, to increase

See also **accroître** and **croître.**

Consult the sections on verbs used in idiomatic expressions, verbs with prepositions, and the list
of over 1,100 verbs conjugated like model verbs in the back pages.

déduire

Part. pr. **déduisant**   Part. passé **déduit**

to deduce, to infer, to deduct

The Seven Simple Tenses		The Seven Compound Tenses	
Singular	Plural	Singular	Plural
1 présent de l'indicatif		**8 passé composé**	
déduis	déduisons	ai déduit	avons déduit
déduis	déduisez	as déduit	avez déduit
déduit	déduisent	a déduit	ont déduit
2 imparfait de l'indicatif		**9 plus-que-parfait de l'indicatif**	
déduisais	déduisions	avais déduit	avions déduit
déduisais	déduisiez	avais déduit	aviez déduit
déduisait	déduisaient	avait déduit	avaient déduit
3 passé simple		**10 passé antérieur**	
déduisis	déduisîmes	eus déduit	eûmes déduit
déduisis	déduisîtes	eus déduit	eûtes déduit
déduisit	déduisirent	eut déduit	eurent déduit
4 futur		**11 futur antérieur**	
déduirai	déduirons	aurai déduit	aurons déduit
déduiras	déduirez	auras déduit	aurez déduit
déduira	déduiront	aura déduit	auront déduit
5 conditionnel		**12 conditionnel passé**	
déduirais	déduirions	aurais déduit	aurions déduit
déduirais	déduiriez	aurais déduit	auriez déduit
déduirait	déduiraient	aurait déduit	auraient déduit
6 présent du subjonctif		**13 passé du subjonctif**	
déduise	déduisions	aie déduit	ayons déduit
déduises	déduisiez	aies déduit	ayez déduit
déduise	déduisent	ait déduit	aient déduit
7 imparfait du subjonctif		**14 plus-que-parfait du subjonctif**	
déduisisse	déduisissions	eusse déduit	eussions déduit
déduisisses	déduisissiez	eusses déduit	eussiez déduit
déduisît	déduisissent	eût déduit	eussent déduit

Impératif
déduis
déduisons
déduisez

Words and expressions related to this verb
une déduction deduction, inference; allowance
déductif, déductive deductive
se déduire to be deduced

une réduction reduction
réduire to reduce
à prix réduit at a reduced price
déductible deductible

See also **conduire**, **introduire**, **produire**, **réduire**, **reproduire**, **séduire**, and **traduire.**

It's important that you be familiar with the Subjunctive. See pages 560–565.

The Seven Simple Tenses		The Seven Compound Tenses	
Singular	Plural	Singular	Plural
1 présent de l'indicatif		**8 passé composé**	
défais	défaisons	ai défait	avons défait
défais	défaites	as défait	avez défait
défait	défont	a défait	ont défait
2 imparfait de l'indicatif		**9 plus-que-parfait de l'indicatif**	
défaisais	défaisions	avais défait	avions défait
défaisais	défaisiez	avais défait	aviez défait
défaisait	défaisaient	avait défait	avaient défait
3 passé simple		**10 passé antérieur**	
défis	défîmes	eus défait	eûmes défait
défis	défîtes	eus défait	eûtes défait
défit	défirent	eut défait	eurent défait
4 futur		**11 futur antérieur**	
déferai	déferons	aurai défait	aurons défait
déferas	déferez	auras défait	aurez défait
défera	déferont	aura défait	auront défait
5 conditionnel		**12 conditionnel passé**	
déferais	déferions	aurais défait	aurions défait
déferais	déferiez	aurais défait	auriez défait
déferait	déferaient	aurait défait	auraient défait
6 présent du subjonctif		**13 passé du subjonctif**	
défasse	défassions	aie défait	ayons défait
défasses	défassiez	aies défait	ayez défait
défasse	défassent	ait défait	aient défait
7 imparfait du subjonctif		**14 plus-que-parfait du subjonctif**	
défisse	défissions	eusse défait	eussions défait
défisses	défissiez	eusses défait	eussiez défait
défît	défissent	eût défait	eussent défait

Impératif
défais
défaisons
défaites

Common idiomatic expressions using this verb and words related to it

défaire un lit to strip a bed
défaire une malle, une valise, etc. to unpack
a trunk, suitcase, etc.
une défaite (military) defeat
avoir le visage défait to look pale
défaire les boutons to unbutton, to undo the
buttons

défaire la table to clear the table
se défaire de qqch to rid oneself of
something
se défaire d'une habitude to break a habit
le défaitisme defeatism
des cheveux défaits dishevelled hair

See also **faire** and **satisfaire.**

Taking a trip? Check out the popular words, phrases, and expressions for travelers on pages
599–621.

The subject pronouns are found on the page facing page 1.   **141**

défendre
Part. pr. **défendant**   Part. passé **défendu**

to defend, to forbid, to prohibit

The Seven Simple Tenses		The Seven Compound Tenses	
Singular	Plural	Singular	Plural
1 présent de l'indicatif		**8 passé composé**	
défends	défendons	ai défendu	avons défendu
défends	défendez	as défendu	avez défendu
défend	défendent	a défendu	ont défendu
2 imparfait de l'indicatif		**9 plus-que-parfait de l'indicatif**	
défendais	défendions	avais défendu	avions défendu
défendais	défendiez	avais défendu	aviez défendu
défendait	défendaient	avait défendu	avaient défendu
3 passé simple		**10 passé antérieur**	
défendis	défendîmes	eus défendu	eûmes défendu
défendis	défendîtes	eus défendu	eûtes défendu
défendit	défendirent	eut défendu	eurent défendu
4 futur		**11 futur antérieur**	
défendrai	défendrons	aurai défendu	aurons défendu
défendras	défendrez	auras défendu	aurez défendu
défendra	défendront	aura défendu	auront défendu
5 conditionnel		**12 conditionnel passé**	
défendrais	défendrions	aurais défendu	aurions défendu
défendrais	défendriez	aurais défendu	auriez défendu
défendrait	défendraient	aurait défendu	auraient défendu
6 présent du subjonctif		**13 passé du subjonctif**	
défende	défendions	aie défendu	ayons défendu
défendes	défendiez	aies défendu	ayez défendu
défende	défendent	ait défendu	aient défendu
7 imparfait du subjonctif		**14 plus-que-parfait du subjonctif**	
défendisse	défendissions	eusse défendu	eussions défendu
défendisses	défendissiez	eusses défendu	eussiez défendu
défendît	défendissent	eût défendu	eussent défendu

Impératif
défends
défendons
défendez

Sentences using this verb and words related to it
Le père: Je te défends de fumer. C'est une mauvaise habitude.
Le fils: Alors, pourquoi fumes-tu, papa?

une défense defense
DÉFENSE DE FUMER SMOKING
   PROHIBITED
défendable justifiable
défendre qqch à qqn to forbid someone
   something

se défendre to defend oneself
défensif, défensive defensive
défensivement defensively
se défendre d'avoir fait qqch to deny having
   done something

Want to learn more idiomatic expressions that contain verbs? Check out pages 530–542.

142

to lunch, to have lunch, breakfast

The Seven Simple Tenses		The Seven Compound Tenses	
Singular	Plural	Singular	Plural
1 présent de l'indicatif		**8 passé composé**	
déjeune	déjeunons	ai déjeuné	avons déjeuné
déjeunes	déjeunez	as déjeuné	avez déjeuné
déjeune	déjeunent	a déjeuné	ont déjeuné
2 imparfait de l'indicatif		**9 plus-que-parfait de l'indicatif**	
déjeunais	déjeunions	avais déjeuné	avions déjeuné
déjeunais	déjeuniez	avais déjeuné	aviez déjeuné
déjeunait	déjeunaient	avait déjeuné	avaient déjeuné
3 passé simple		**10 passé antérieur**	
déjeunai	déjeunâmes	eus déjeuné	eûmes déjeuné
déjeunas	déjeunâtes	eus déjeuné	eûtes déjeuné
déjeuna	déjeunèrent	eut déjeuné	eurent déjeuné
4 futur		**11 futur antérieur**	
déjeunerai	déjeunerons	aurai déjeuné	aurons déjeuné
déjeuneras	déjeunerez	auras déjeuné	aurez déjeuné
déjeunera	déjeuneront	aura déjeuné	auront déjeuné
5 conditionnel		**12 conditionnel passé**	
déjeunerais	déjeunerions	aurais déjeuné	aurions déjeuné
déjeunerais	déjeuneriez	aurais déjeuné	auriez déjeuné
déjeunerait	déjeuneraient	aurait déjeuné	auraient déjeuné
6 présent du subjonctif		**13 passé du subjonctif**	
déjeune	déjeunions	aie déjeuné	ayons déjeuné
déjeunes	déjeuniez	aies déjeuné	ayez déjeuné
déjeune	déjeunent	ait déjeuné	aient déjeuné
7 imparfait du subjonctif		**14 plus-que-parfait du subjonctif**	
déjeunasse	déjeunassions	eusse déjeuné	eussions déjeuné
déjeunasses	déjeunassiez	eusses déjeuné	eussiez déjeuné
déjeunât	déjeunassent	eût déjeuné	eussent déjeuné

Impératif
déjeune
déjeunons
déjeunez

Sentences using this verb and words related to it

Tous les matins je me lève et je prends mon petit déjeuner à sept heures et demie. A midi je déjeune avec mes camarades à l'école. Avec qui déjeunez-vous?

le déjeuner lunch	**rompre le jeûne** to break one's fast
le petit déjeuner breakfast	**un jour de jeûne** a day of fasting
jeûner to fast	**le déjeuner sur l'herbe** picnic lunch (on the
le jeûne fast, fasting	grass)

NOTE: The French tend to say **le petit déjeuner** (breakfast), **le déjeuner** (lunch), and **le dîner** (evening meal) or **le souper** (late evening snack). However, in some French-speaking regions, the meals one eats during the day are **le déjeuner** (breakfast), **le dîner** (lunch), and **le souper** (supper).

The subject pronouns are found on the page facing page 1.   **143**

demander

Part. pr. **demandant**   Part. passé **demandé**

to ask (for), to request

The Seven Simple Tenses		The Seven Compound Tenses	
Singular	Plural	Singular	Plural
1 présent de l'indicatif		**8 passé composé**	
demande	demandons	ai demandé	avons demandé
demandes	demandez	as demandé	avez demandé
demande	demandent	a demandé	ont demandé
2 imparfait de l'indicatif		**9 plus-que-parfait de l'indicatif**	
demandais	demandions	avais demandé	avions demandé
demandais	demandiez	avais demandé	aviez demandé
demandait	demandaient	avait demandé	avaient demandé
3 passé simple		**10 passé antérieur**	
demandai	demandâmes	eus demandé	eûmes demandé
demandas	demandâtes	eus demandé	eûtes demandé
demanda	demandèrent	eut demandé	eurent demandé
4 futur		**11 futur antérieur**	
demanderai	demanderons	aurai demandé	aurons demandé
demanderas	demanderez	auras demandé	aurez demandé
demandera	demanderont	aura demandé	auront demandé
5 conditionnel		**12 conditionnel passé**	
demanderais	demanderions	aurais demandé	aurions demandé
demanderais	demanderiez	aurais demandé	auriez demandé
demanderait	demanderaient	aurait demandé	auraient demandé
6 présent du subjonctif		**13 passé du subjonctif**	
demande	demandions	aie demandé	ayons demandé
demandes	demandiez	aies demandé	ayez demandé
demande	demandent	ait demandé	aient demandé
7 imparfait du subjonctif		**14 plus-que-parfait du subjonctif**	
demandasse	demandassions	eusse demandé	eussions demandé
demandasses	demandassiez	eusses demandé	eussiez demandé
demandât	demandassent	eût demandé	eussent demandé

Impératif
demande
demandons
demandez

Sentences using this verb and words related to it

J'ai demandé à une dame où s'arrête l'autobus. Elle m'a répondu:—Je ne sais pas, monsieur. Demandez à l'agent de police.

une demande   a request
sur demande   on request, on application
faire une demande de   to apply for
Si votre fils demande un morceau de pain, lui
    donnerez-vous une pierre?   If your son
    asks for a piece of bread, will you give him a
    stone? (Matthew 7:9) See "if" clauses, top of
    page 560.

se demander   to wonder
mander   to send word by letter
un mandat   mandate; un mandat-lettre
    letter money order; un mandat-poste   postal
    money order
une demande d'emploi   job application

to reside, to live, to remain, to stay

The Seven Simple Tenses		The Seven Compound Tenses	
Singular	Plural	Singular	Plural
1 présent de l'indicatif		**8 passé composé**	
demeure	demeurons	ai demeuré	avons demeuré
demeures	demeurez	as demeuré	avez demeuré
demeure	demeurent	a demeuré	ont demeuré
2 imparfait de l'indicatif		**9 plus-que-parfait de l'indicatif**	
demeurais	demeurions	avais demeuré	avions demeuré
demeurais	demeuriez	avais demeuré	aviez demeuré
demeurait	demeuraient	avait demeuré	avaient demeuré
3 passé simple		**10 passé antérieur**	
demeurai	demeurâmes	eus demeuré	eûmes demeuré
demeuras	demeurâtes	eus demeuré	eûtes demeuré
demeura	demeurèrent	eut demeuré	eurent demeuré
4 futur		**11 futur antérieur**	
demeurerai	demeurerons	aurai demeuré	aurons demeuré
demeureras	demeurerez	auras demeuré	aurez demeuré
demeurera	demeureront	aura demeuré	auront demeuré
5 conditionnel		**12 conditionnel passé**	
demeurerais	demeurerions	aurais demeuré	aurions demeuré
demeurerais	demeureriez	aurais demeuré	auriez demeuré
demeurerait	demeureraient	aurait demeuré	auraient demeuré
6 présent du subjonctif		**13 passé du subjonctif**	
demeure	demeurions	aie demeuré	ayons demeuré
demeures	demeuriez	aies demeuré	ayez demeuré
demeure	demeurent	ait demeuré	aient demeuré
7 imparfait du subjonctif		**14 plus-que-parfait du subjonctif**	
demeurasse	demeurassions	eusse demeuré	eussions demeuré
demeurasses	demeurassiez	eusses demeuré	eussiez demeuré
demeurât	demeurassent	eût demeuré	eussent demeuré

Impératif
demeure
demeurons
demeurez

Sentences using this verb and words related to it
—**Où demeurez-vous?**
—**Je demeure dans un appartement, rue des Jardins.**

une demeure   dwelling, residence
au demeurant   incidentally
demeurer couché   to stay in bed
demeurer court   to stop short

demeurer à un hôtel   to stay at a hotel
une mise en demeure   injunction
demeurer fidèle   to remain faithful

Going away? Don't forget to check out the practical situations for travelers on pages 568–598.

The subject pronouns are found on the page facing page 1.   **145**

démolir

to demolish

Part. pr. **démolissant**   Part. passé **démoli**

The Seven Simple Tenses		The Seven Compound Tenses	
Singular	Plural	Singular	Plural
1 présent de l'indicatif		**8 passé composé**	
démolis	démolissons	ai démoli	avons démoli
démolis	démolissez	as démoli	avez démoli
démolit	démolissent	a démoli	ont démoli
2 imparfait de l'indicatif		**9 plus-que-parfait de l'indicatif**	
démolissais	démolissions	avais démoli	avions démoli
démolissais	démolissiez	avais démoli	aviez démoli
démolissait	démolissaient	avait démoli	avaient démoli
3 passé simple		**10 passé antérieur**	
démolis	démolîmes	eus démoli	eûmes démoli
démolis	démolîtes	eus démoli	eûtes démoli
démolit	démolirent	eut démoli	eurent démoli
4 futur		**11 futur antérieur**	
démolirai	démolirons	aurai démoli	aurons démoli
démoliras	démolirez	auras démoli	aurez démoli
démolira	démoliront	aura démoli	auront démoli
5 conditionnel		**12 conditionnel passé**	
démolirais	démolirions	aurais démoli	aurions démoli
démolirais	démoliriez	aurais démoli	auriez démoli
démolirait	démoliraient	aurait démoli	auraient démoli
6 présent du subjonctif		**13 passé du subjonctif**	
démolisse	démolissions	aie démoli	ayons démoli
démolisses	démolissiez	aies démoli	ayez démoli
démolisse	démolissent	ait démoli	aient démoli
7 imparfait du subjonctif		**14 plus-que-parfait du subjonctif**	
démolisse	démolissions	eusse démoli	eussions démoli
démolisses	démolissiez	eusses démoli	eussiez démoli
démolît	démolissent	eût démoli	eussent démoli

Impératif
démolis
démolissons
démolissez

Words and expressions related to this verb

une démolition   demolition
un démolisseur, une démolisseuse
   demolisher

se démolir   to fall apart, to fall to pieces
démolir l'estomac   to ruin one's stomach

Grammar putting you in a tense mood? Review the definitions of basic grammatical terms with examples on pages 674–688.

The Seven Simple Tenses		The Seven Compound Tenses	
Singular	Plural	Singular	Plural
1 présent de l'indicatif		8 passé composé	
me dépêche	nous dépêchons	me suis dépêché(e)	nous sommes dépêché(e)s
te dépêches	vous dépêchez	t'es dépêché(e)	vous êtes dépêché(e)(s)
se dépêche	se dépêchent	s'est dépêché(e)	se sont dépêché(e)s
2 imparfait de l'indicatif		9 plus-que-parfait de l'indicatif	
me dépêchais	nous dépêchions	m'étais dépêché(e)	nous étions dépêché(e)s
te dépêchais	vous dépêchiez	t'étais dépêché(e)	vous étiez dépêché(e)(s)
se dépêchait	se dépêchaient	s'était dépêché(e)	s'étaient dépêché(e)s
3 passé simple		10 passé antérieur	
me dépêchai	nous dépêchâmes	me fus dépêché(e)	nous fûmes dépêché(e)s
te dépêchas	vous dépêchâtes	te fus dépêché(e)	vous fûtes dépêché(e)(s)
se dépêcha	se dépêchèrent	se fut dépêché(e)	se furent dépêché(e)s
4 futur		11 futur antérieur	
me dépêcherai	nous dépêcherons	me serai dépêché(e)	nous serons dépêché(e)s
te dépêcheras	vous dépêcherez	te seras dépêché(e)	vous serez dépêché(e)(s)
se dépêchera	se dépêcheront	se sera dépêché(e)	se seront dépêché(e)s
5 conditionnel		12 conditionnel passé	
me dépêcherais	nous dépêcherions	me serais dépêché(e)	nous serions dépêché(e)s
te dépêcherais	vous dépêcheriez	te serais dépêché(e)	vous seriez dépêché(e)(s)
se dépêcherait	se dépêcheraient	se serait dépêché(e)	se seraient dépêché(e)s
6 présent du subjonctif		13 passé du subjonctif	
me dépêche	nous dépêchions	me sois dépêché(e)	nous soyons dépêché(e)s
te dépêches	vous dépêchiez	te sois dépêché(e)	vous soyez dépêché(e)(s)
se dépêche	se dépêchent	se soit dépêché(e)	se soient dépêché(e)s
7 imparfait du subjonctif		14 plus-que-parfait du subjonctif	
me dépêchasse	nous dépêchassions	me fusse dépêché(e)	nous fussions dépêché(e)s
te dépêchasses	vous dépêchassiez	te fusses dépêché(e)	vous fussiez dépêché(e)(s)
se dépêchât	se dépêchassent	se fût dépêché(e)	se fussent dépêché(e)s

Impératif
dépêche-toi; ne te dépêche pas
dépêchons-nous; ne nous dépêchons pas
dépêchez-vous; ne vous dépêchez pas

Sentences using this verb and words related to it
   En me dépêchant pour attraper l'autobus, je suis tombé et je me suis fait mal au genou.
Je me dépêchais de venir chez vous pour vous dire quelque chose de très important.

une dépêche   a telegram, a dispatch
dépêcher   to dispatch
faire les courses en se dépêchant   to do the shopping hurriedly

See also **empêcher.**

Consult the sections on verbs used in idiomatic expressions, verbs with prepositions, and the list of over 1,100 verbs conjugated like model verbs in the back pages.

dépeindre

Part. pr. **dépeignant**   Part. passé **dépeint**

to depict, to describe, to portray

The Seven Simple Tenses		The Seven Compound Tenses	
Singular	Plural	Singular	Plural
1 présent de l'indicatif		**8 passé composé**	
dépeins	dépeignons	ai dépeint	avons dépeint
dépeins	dépeignez	as dépeint	avez dépeint
dépeint	dépeignent	a dépeint	ont dépeint
2 imparfait de l'indicatif		**9 plus-que-parfait de l'indicatif**	
dépeignais	dépeignions	avais dépeint	avions dépeint
dépeignais	dépeigniez	avais dépeint	aviez dépeint
dépeignait	dépeignaient	avait dépeint	avaient dépeint
3 passé simple		**10 passé antérieur**	
dépeignis	dépeignîmes	eus dépeint	eûmes dépeint
dépeignis	dépeignîtes	eus dépeint	eûtes dépeint
dépeignit	dépeignirent	eut dépeint	eurent dépeint
4 futur		**11 futur antérieur**	
dépeindrai	dépeindrons	aurai dépeint	aurons dépeint
dépeindras	dépeindrez	auras dépeint	aurez dépeint
dépeindra	dépeindront	aura dépeint	auront dépeint
5 conditionnel		**12 conditionnel passé**	
dépeindrais	dépeindrions	aurais dépeint	aurions dépeint
dépeindrais	dépeindriez	aurais dépeint	auriez dépeint
dépeindrait	dépeindraient	aurait dépeint	auraient dépeint
6 présent du subjonctif		**13 passé du subjonctif**	
dépeigne	dépeignions	aie dépeint	ayons dépeint
dépeignes	dépeigniez	aies dépeint	ayez dépeint
dépeigne	dépeignent	ait dépeint	aient dépeint
7 imparfait du subjonctif		**14 plus-que-parfait du subjonctif**	
dépeignisse	dépeignissions	eusse dépeint	eussions dépeint
dépeignisses	dépeignissiez	eusses dépeint	eussiez dépeint
dépeignît	dépeignissent	eût dépeint	eussent dépeint

Impératif
dépeins
dépeignons
dépeignez

Words and expressions related to this verb
dépeindre une scène   to depict a scene
peindre   to paint
une peinture à l'huile   oil painting
la peinture   painting

peinturer   to daub
un peintre   painter; **une femme peintre**
  woman artist
repeindre   to repaint

For other words and expressions related to this verb, see **peindre.**

Soak up some verbs used in weather expressions on pages 557 and 558.

to depend (on), to be dependent (on), to take down (something that is hanging)

The Seven Simple Tenses		The Seven Compound Tenses	
Singular	Plural	Singular	Plural
1 présent de l'indicatif		8 passé composé	
dépends	**dépendons**	**ai dépendu**	**avons dépendu**
dépends	**dépendez**	**as dépendu**	**avez dépendu**
dépend	**dépendent**	**a dépendu**	**ont dépendu**
2 imparfait de l'indicatif		9 plus-que-parfait de l'indicatif	
dépendais	**dépendions**	**avais dépendu**	**avions dépendu**
dépendais	**dépendiez**	**avais dépendu**	**aviez dépendu**
dépendait	**dépendaient**	**avait dépendu**	**avaient dépendu**
3 passé simple		10 passé antérieur	
dépendis	**dépendîmes**	**eus dépendu**	**eûmes dépendu**
dépendis	**dépendîtes**	**eus dépendu**	**eûtes dépendu**
dépendit	**dépendirent**	**eut dépendu**	**eurent dépendu**
4 futur		11 futur antérieur	
dépendrai	**dépendrons**	**aurai dépendu**	**aurons dépendu**
dépendras	**dépendrez**	**auras dépendu**	**aurez dépendu**
dépendra	**dépendront**	**aura dépendu**	**auront dépendu**
5 conditionnel		12 conditionnel passé	
dépendrais	**dépendrions**	**aurais dépendu**	**aurions dépendu**
dépendrais	**dépendriez**	**aurais dépendu**	**auriez dépendu**
dépendrait	**dépendraient**	**aurait dépendu**	**auraient dépendu**
6 présent du subjonctif		13 passé du subjonctif	
dépende	**dépendions**	**aie dépendu**	**ayons dépendu**
dépendes	**dépendiez**	**aies dépendu**	**ayez dépendu**
dépende	**dépendent**	**ait dépendu**	**aient dépendu**
7 imparfait du subjonctif		14 plus-que-parfait du subjonctif	
dépendisse	**dépendissions**	**eusse dépendu**	**eussions dépendu**
dépendisses	**dépendissiez**	**eusses dépendu**	**eussiez dépendu**
dépendît	**dépendissent**	**eût dépendu**	**eussent dépendu**

Impératif
dépends
dépendons
dépendez

Common idiomatic expressions using this verb and words related to it

dépendre de   to depend on, to be dependent on

la dépendance   dependence

l'indépendance   independence

être sous la dépendance de   to be dependent on

See also **pendre** (to hang).

Il dépend de vous de + inf.   It depends on you + inf.

indépendamment de   independently of

dépendant de   depending on, subject to

indépendant, indépendante   independent

Cela dépend!   That depends!

Get acquainted with what preposition goes with what verb on pages 543–553.

The subject pronouns are found on the page facing page 1.   **149**

to spend (money)

The Seven Simple Tenses		The Seven Compound Tenses	
Singular	Plural	Singular	Plural
1 présent de l'indicatif		8 passé composé	
dépense	**dépensons**	**ai dépensé**	**avons dépensé**
dépenses	**dépensez**	**as dépensé**	**avez dépensé**
dépense	**dépensent**	**a dépensé**	**ont dépensé**
2 imparfait de l'indicatif		9 plus-que-parfait de l'indicatif	
dépensais	**dépensions**	**avais dépensé**	**avions dépensé**
dépensais	**dépensiez**	**avais dépensé**	**aviez dépensé**
dépensait	**dépensaient**	**avait dépensé**	**avaient dépensé**
3 passé simple		10 passé antérieur	
dépensai	**dépensâmes**	**eus dépensé**	**eûmes dépensé**
dépensas	**dépensâtes**	**eus dépensé**	**eûtes dépensé**
dépensa	**dépensèrent**	**eut dépensé**	**eurent dépensé**
4 futur		11 futur antérieur	
dépenserai	**dépenserons**	**aurai dépensé**	**aurons dépensé**
dépenseras	**dépenserez**	**auras dépensé**	**aurez dépensé**
dépensera	**dépenseront**	**aura dépensé**	**auront dépensé**
5 conditionnel		12 conditionnel passé	
dépenserais	**dépenserions**	**aurais dépensé**	**aurions dépensé**
dépenserais	**dépenseriez**	**aurais dépensé**	**auriez dépensé**
dépenserait	**dépenseraient**	**aurait dépensé**	**auraient dépensé**
6 présent du subjonctif		13 passé du subjonctif	
dépense	**dépensions**	**aie dépensé**	**ayons dépensé**
dépenses	**dépensiez**	**aies dépensé**	**ayez dépensé**
dépense	**dépensent**	**ait dépensé**	**aient dépensé**
7 imparfait du subjonctif		14 plus-que-parfait du subjonctif	
dépensasse	**dépensassions**	**eusse dépensé**	**eussions dépensé**
dépensasses	**dépensassiez**	**eusses dépensé**	**eussiez dépensé**
dépensât	**dépensassent**	**eût dépensé**	**eussent dépensé**

Impératif
dépense
dépensons
dépensez

Sentences using this verb and words related to it

   Mon père m'a dit que je dépense sottement. Je lui ai répondu que je n'ai rien dépensé cette semaine.

dépensier, dépensière extravagant, unthrifty, spendthrift

dépenser sottement to spend money foolishly

aux dépens de quelqu'un at someone's expense

les dépenses du ménage household expenses

How are you doing? Find out with the verb drills and tests with answers explained on pages 622–673.

The Seven Simple Tenses		The Seven Compound Tenses	
Singular	Plural	Singular	Plural

1 présent de l'indicatif		8 passé composé	
déplais	**déplaisons**	**ai déplu**	**avons déplu**
déplais	**déplaisez**	**as déplu**	**avez déplu**
déplaît	**déplaisent**	**a déplu**	**ont déplu**

2 imparfait de l'indicatif		9 plus-que-parfait de l'indicatif	
déplaisais	**déplaisions**	**avais déplu**	**avions déplu**
déplaisais	**déplaisiez**	**avais déplu**	**aviez déplu**
déplaisait	**déplaisaient**	**avait déplu**	**avaient déplu**

3 passé simple		10 passé antérieur	
déplus	**déplûmes**	**eus déplu**	**eûmes déplu**
déplus	**déplûtes**	**eus déplu**	**eûtes déplu**
déplut	**déplurent**	**eut déplu**	**eurent déplu**

4 futur		11 futur antérieur	
déplairai	**déplairons**	**aurai déplu**	**aurons déplu**
déplairas	**déplairez**	**auras déplu**	**aurez déplu**
déplaira	**déplairont**	**aura déplu**	**auront déplu**

5 conditionnel		12 conditionnel passé	
déplairais	**déplairions**	**aurais déplu**	**aurions déplu**
déplairais	**déplairiez**	**aurais déplu**	**auriez déplu**
déplairait	**déplairaient**	**aurait déplu**	**auraient déplu**

6 présent du subjonctif		13 passé du subjonctif	
déplaise	**déplaisions**	**aie déplu**	**ayons déplu**
déplaises	**déplaisiez**	**aies déplu**	**ayez déplu**
déplaise	**déplaisent**	**ait déplu**	**aient déplu**

7 imparfait du subjonctif		14 plus-que-parfait du subjonctif	
déplusse	**déplussions**	**eusse déplu**	**eussions déplu**
déplusses	**déplussiez**	**eusses déplu**	**eussiez déplu**
déplût	**déplussent**	**eût déplu**	**eussent déplu**

Impératif
déplais
déplaisons
déplaisez

Common idiomatic expressions using this verb
Cela me déplaît   I don't like that.
Il me déplaît de + inf.   I don't like + inf.
Plaise à Dieu ...   May God grant that . . .
le plaisir   pleasure
le déplaisir   displeasure
plaire à qqn   to please someone

A Dieu ne plaise!   God forbid!
Plaît-il?   Pardon me? I beg your pardon?
    What did you say?
déplaisant, déplaisante   displeasing, offensive
déplaire à qqn   to displease someone

See also **plaire.**

Use the EE-zee guide to French pronunciation on pages 566 and 567.

déranger

Part. pr. **dérangeant**   Part. passé **dérangé**

to disturb, to derange

The Seven Simple Tenses		The Seven Compound Tenses	
Singular	Plural	Singular	Plural
1 présent de l'indicatif		**8 passé composé**	
dérange	dérangeons	ai dérangé	avons dérangé
déranges	dérangez	as dérangé	avez dérangé
dérange	dérangent	a dérangé	ont dérangé
2 imparfait de l'indicatif		**9 plus-que-parfait de l'indicatif**	
dérangeais	dérangions	avais dérangé	avions dérangé
dérangeais	dérangiez	avais dérangé	aviez dérangé
dérangeait	dérangeaient	avait dérangé	avaient dérangé
3 passé simple		**10 passé antérieur**	
dérangeai	dérangeâmes	eus dérangé	eûmes dérangé
dérangeas	dérangeâtes	eus dérangé	eûtes dérangé
dérangea	dérangèrent	eut dérangé	eurent dérangé
4 futur		**11 futur antérieur**	
dérangerai	dérangerons	aurai dérangé	aurons dérangé
dérangeras	dérangerez	auras dérangé	aurez dérangé
dérangera	dérangeront	aura dérangé	auront dérangé
5 conditionnel		**12 conditionnel passé**	
dérangerais	dérangerions	aurais dérangé	aurions dérangé
dérangerais	dérangeriez	aurais dérangé	auriez dérangé
dérangerait	dérangeraient	aurait dérangé	auraient dérangé
6 présent du subjonctif		**13 passé du subjonctif**	
dérange	dérangions	aie dérangé	ayons dérangé
déranges	dérangiez	aies dérangé	ayez dérangé
dérange	dérangent	ait dérangé	aient dérangé
7 imparfait du subjonctif		**14 plus-que-parfait du subjonctif**	
dérangeasse	dérangeassions	eusse dérangé	eussions dérangé
dérangeasses	dérangeassiez	eusses dérangé	eussiez dérangé
dérangeât	dérangeassent	eût dérangé	eussent dérangé

Impératif
dérange
dérangeons
dérangez

Sentences using this verb and words related to it

Le professeur: Entrez!
L'élève: Excusez-moi, monsieur. Est-ce que je vous dérange?
Le professeur: Non, tu ne me déranges pas. Qu'est-ce que tu veux?
L'élève: Je veux savoir si nous avons un jour de congé demain.
NE PAS DÉRANGER DO NOT DISTURB

dérangé, dérangée upset, out of order, broken down
une personne dérangée a deranged person
un dérangement disarrangement, disorder, inconvenience
se déranger to inconvenience oneself
Je vous en prie, ne vous dérangez pas! I beg you (please), don't disturb yourself!

152

to go down, to descend, to take down, to bring down

The Seven Simple Tenses		The Seven Compound Tenses	
Singular	Plural	Singular	Plural
1 présent de l'indicatif		8 passé composé	
descends	descendons	suis descendu(e)	sommes descendu(e)s
descends	descendez	es descendu(e)	êtes descendu(e)(s)
descend	descendent	est descendu(e)	sont descendu(e)s
2 imparfait de l'indicatif		9 plus-que-parfait de l'indicatif	
descendais	descendions	étais descendu(e)	étions descendu(e)s
descendais	descendiez	étais descendu(e)	étiez descendu(e)(s)
descendait	descendaient	était descendu(e)	étaient descendu(e)s
3 passé simple		10 passé antérieur	
descendis	descendîmes	fus descendu(e)	fûmes descendu(e)s
descendis	descendîtes	fus descendu(e)	fûtes descendu(e)(s)
descendit	descendirent	fut descendu(e)	furent descendu(e)s
4 futur		11 futur antérieur	
descendrai	descendrons	serai descendu(e)	serons descendu(e)s
descendras	descendrez	seras descendu(e)	serez descendu(e)(s)
descendra	descendront	sera descendu(e)	seront descendu(e)s
5 conditionnel		12 conditionnel passé	
descendrais	descendrions	serais descendu(e)	serions descendu(e)s
descendrais	descendriez	serais descendu(e)	seriez descendu(e)(s)
descendrait	descendraient	serait descendu(e)	seraient descendu(e)s
6 présent du subjonctif		13 passé du subjonctif	
descende	descendions	sois descendu(e)	soyons descendu(e)s
descendes	descendiez	sois descendu(e)	soyez descendu(e)(s)
descende	descendent	soit descendu(e)	soient descendu(e)s
7 imparfait du subjonctif		14 plus-que-parfait du subjonctif	
descendisse	descendissions	fusse descendu(e)	fussions descendu(e)s
descendisses	descendissiez	fusses descendu(e)	fussiez descendu(e)(s)
descendît	descendissent	fût descendu(e)	fussent descendu(e)s

Impératif
descends
descendons
descendez

Words and expressions related to this verb
descendre à un hôtel   to stop (stay over) at a hotel
descendre le store   to pull down the window shade
une descente   slope

See also the verb **monter.** Review page viii.

This verb is conjugated with *avoir* when it has a direct object.

Examples: **J'ai descendu l'escalier**   I went down the stairs.
            J'ai descendu les valises   I brought down the suitcases.
BUT: **Elle est descendue vite**   She came down quickly.

The subject pronouns are found on the page facing page 1.   **153**

désirer

to desire

The Seven Simple Tenses		The Seven Compound Tenses	
Singular	Plural	Singular	Plural
1 présent de l'indicatif		**8 passé composé**	
désire	désirons	ai désiré	avons désiré
désires	désirez	as désiré	avez désiré
désire	désirent	a désiré	ont désiré
2 imparfait de l'indicatif		**9 plus-que-parfait de l'indicatif**	
désirais	désirions	avais désiré	avions désiré
désirais	désiriez	avais désiré	aviez désiré
désirait	désiraient	avait désiré	avaient désiré
3 passé simple		**10 passé antérieur**	
désirai	désirâmes	eus désiré	eûmes désiré
désiras	désirâtes	eus désiré	eûtes désiré
désira	désirèrent	eut désiré	eurent désiré
4 futur		**11 futur antérieur**	
désirerai	désirerons	aurai désiré	aurons désiré
désireras	désirerez	auras désiré	aurez désiré
désirera	désireront	aura désiré	auront désiré
5 conditionnel		**12 conditionnel passé**	
désirerais	désirerions	aurais désiré	aurions désiré
désirerais	désireriez	aurais désiré	auriez désiré
désirerait	désireraient	aurait désiré	auraient désiré
6 présent du subjonctif		**13 passé du subjonctif**	
désire	désirions	aie désiré	ayons désiré
désires	désiriez	aies désiré	ayez désiré
désire	désirent	ait désiré	aient désiré
7 imparfait du subjonctif		**14 plus-que-parfait du subjonctif**	
désirasse	désirassions	eusse désiré	eussions désiré
désirasses	désirassiez	eusses désiré	eussiez désiré
désirât	désirassent	eût désiré	eussent désiré

Impératif
désire
désirons
désirez

Sentences using this verb and words related to it

La vendeuse: **Bonjour, monsieur. Vous désirez?**
Le client: **Je désire acheter une cravate.**
La vendeuse: **Bien, monsieur. Vous pouvez choisir. Voici toutes nos cravates.**
un désir   desire, wish; **la désirabilité** desirability

désirable   desirable; **désireux, désireuse**   desirous
indésirable   undesirable
un désir de plaire   a desire to please
laisser à désirer   to leave much to be desired; **le désir de faire qqch**   the desire to do something

Increase your verb power with popular phrases, words, and expressions for travelers on pages 599–621.

to draw, to sketch

The Seven Simple Tenses		The Seven Compound Tenses	
Singular	Plural	Singular	Plural
1 présent de l'indicatif		8 passé composé	
dessine	dessinons	ai dessiné	avons dessiné
dessines	dessinez	as dessiné	avez dessiné
dessine	dessinent	a dessiné	ont dessiné
2 imparfait de l'indicatif		9 plus-que-parfait de l'indicatif	
dessinais	dessinions	avais dessiné	avions dessiné
dessinais	dessiniez	avais dessiné	aviez dessiné
dessinait	dessinaient	avait dessiné	avaient dessiné
3 passé simple		10 passé antérieur	
dessinai	dessinâmes	eus dessiné	eûmes dessiné
dessinas	dessinâtes	eus dessiné	eûtes dessiné
dessina	dessinèrent	eut dessiné	eurent dessiné
4 futur		11 futur antérieur	
dessinerai	dessinerons	aurai dessiné	aurons dessiné
dessineras	dessinerez	auras dessiné	aurez dessiné
dessinera	dessineront	aura dessiné	auront dessiné
5 conditionnel		12 conditionnel passé	
dessinerais	dessinerions	aurais dessiné	aurions dessiné
dessinerais	dessineriez	aurais dessiné	auriez dessiné
dessinerait	dessineraient	aurait dessiné	auraient dessiné
6 présent du subjonctif		13 passé du subjonctif	
dessine	dessinions	aie dessiné	ayons dessiné
dessines	dessiniez	aies dessiné	ayez dessiné
dessine	dessinent	ait dessiné	aient dessiné
7 imparfait du subjonctif		14 plus-que-parfait du subjonctif	
dessinasse	dessinassions	eusse dessiné	eussions dessiné
dessinasses	dessinassiez	eusses dessiné	eussiez dessiné
dessinât	dessinassent	eût dessiné	eussent dessiné

Impératif
dessine
dessinons
dessinez

Words and expressions related to this verb
dessiner au crayon   to draw with a pencil
un dessinateur, une dessinatrice   sketcher;
  — de journal   cartoonist; **— de modes**
dress designer; **— de dessins animés**
cartoonist
une bande dessinée   comic strip
un dessin animé   cartoon

dessiner très vite   to do a quick sketch
se dessiner   to take shape, to stand out
un dessin   drawing, sketch
un dessin à la plume   pen and ink sketch
le dessin assisté par ordinateur   CAD
  (computer-aided design)

Do not confuse **un dessin** (sketch, drawing) with **un dessein** (plan, project, purpose).

détester

Part. pr. **détestant**   Part. passé **détesté**

to detest, to dislike, to hate

The Seven Simple Tenses		The Seven Compound Tenses	
Singular	Plural	Singular	Plural
1 présent de l'indicatif		**8 passé composé**	
déteste	détestons	ai détesté	avons détesté
détestes	détestez	as détesté	avez détesté
déteste	détestent	a détesté	ont détesté
2 imparfait de l'indicatif		**9 plus-que-parfait de l'indicatif**	
détestais	détestions	avais détesté	avions détesté
détestais	détestiez	avais détesté	aviez détesté
détestait	détestaient	avait détesté	avaient détesté
3 passé simple		**10 passé antérieur**	
détestai	détestâmes	eus détesté	eûmes détesté
détestas	détestâtes	eus détesté	eûtes détesté
détesta	détestèrent	eut détesté	eurent détesté
4 futur		**11 futur antérieur**	
détesterai	détesterons	aurai détesté	aurons détesté
détesteras	détesterez	auras détesté	aurez détesté
détestera	détesteront	aura détesté	auront détesté
5 conditionnel		**12 conditionnel passé**	
détesterais	détesterions	aurais détesté	aurions détesté
détesterais	détesteriez	aurais détesté	auriez détesté
détesterait	détesteraient	aurait détesté	auraient détesté
6 présent du subjonctif		**13 passé du subjonctif**	
déteste	détestions	aie détesté	ayons détesté
détestes	détestiez	aies détesté	ayez détesté
déteste	détestent	ait détesté	aient détesté
7 imparfait du subjonctif		**14 plus-que-parfait du subjonctif**	
détestasse	détestassions	eusse détesté	eussions détesté
détestasses	détestassiez	eusses détesté	eussiez détesté
détestât	détestassent	eût détesté	eussent détesté

Impératif
déteste
détestons
détestez

Sentences using this verb and words related to it

Je déteste la médiocrité, je déteste le mensonge, et je déteste la calomnie. Ce sont des choses détestables.

détestable   loathsome, hateful, dreadful
détestablement   detestably

How are you doing? Find out with the verb drills and tests with answers explained on pages 622–673.

to turn aside, to turn away, to divert

The Seven Simple Tenses		The Seven Compound Tenses	
Singular	Plural	Singular	Plural

1 présent de l'indicatif		8 passé composé	
détourne	**détournons**	**ai détourné**	**avons détourné**
détournes	**détournez**	**as détourné**	**avez détourné**
détourne	**détournent**	**a détourné**	**ont détourné**

2 imparfait de l'indicatif		9 plus-que-parfait de l'indicatif	
détournais	**détournions**	**avais détourné**	**avions détourné**
détournais	**détourniez**	**avais détourné**	**aviez détourné**
détournait	**détournaient**	**avait détourné**	**avaient détourné**

3 passé simple		10 passé antérieur	
détournai	**détournâmes**	**eus détourné**	**eûmes détourné**
détournas	**détournâtes**	**eus détourné**	**eûtes détourné**
détourna	**détournèrent**	**eut détourné**	**eurent détourné**

4 futur		11 futur antérieur	
détournerai	**détournerons**	**aurai détourné**	**aurons détourné**
détourneras	**détournerez**	**auras détourné**	**aurez détourné**
détournera	**détourneront**	**aura détourné**	**auront détourné**

5 conditionnel		12 conditionnel passé	
détournerais	**détournerions**	**aurais détourné**	**aurions détourné**
détournerais	**détourneriez**	**aurais détourné**	**auriez détourné**
détournerait	**détourneraient**	**aurait détourné**	**auraient détourné**

6 présent du subjonctif		13 passé du subjonctif	
détourne	**détournions**	**aie détourné**	**ayons détourné**
détournes	**détourniez**	**aies détourné**	**ayez détourné**
détourne	**détournent**	**ait détourné**	**aient détourné**

7 imparfait du subjonctif		14 plus-que-parfait du subjonctif	
détournasse	**détournassions**	**eusse détourné**	**eussions détourné**
détournasses	**détournassiez**	**eusses détourné**	**eussiez détourné**
détournât	**détournassent**	**eût détourné**	**eussent détourné**

Impératif
détourne
détournons
détournez

Words and expressions related to this verb
détourner les yeux to look away
détourner qqn de faire qqch to discourage
  someone from doing something
un chemin détourné side road

se détourner de to turn oneself away from
un détour detour; **faire un détour** to make
  a detour
tourner to turn

See also **retourner** and **tourner**.

Consult the sections on verbs used in idiomatic expressions, verbs with prepositions, and the list
of over 1,100 verbs conjugated like model verbs in the back pages.

The subject pronouns are found on the page facing page 1.   **157**

détruire

to destroy

The Seven Simple Tenses		The Seven Compound Tenses	
Singular	Plural	Singular	Plural

1 présent de l'indicatif		8 passé composé	
détruis	détruisons	ai détruit	avons détruit
détruis	détruisez	as détruit	avez détruit
détruit	détruisent	a détruit	ont détruit

2 imparfait de l'indicatif		9 plus-que-parfait de l'indicatif	
détruisais	détruisions	avais détruit	avions détruit
détruisais	détruisiez	avais détruit	aviez détruit
détruisait	détruisaient	avait détruit	avaient détruit

3 passé simple		10 passé antérieur	
détruisis	détruisîmes	eus détruit	eûmes détruit
détruisis	détruisîtes	eus détruit	eûtes détruit
détruisit	détruisirent	eut détruit	eurent détruit

4 futur		11 futur antérieur	
détruirai	détruirons	aurai détruit	aurons détruit
détruiras	détruirez	auras détruit	aurez détruit
détruira	détruiront	aura détruit	auront détruit

5 conditionnel		12 conditionnel passé	
détruirais	détruirions	aurais détruit	aurions détruit
détruirais	détruiriez	aurais détruit	auriez détruit
détruirait	détruiraient	aurait détruit	auraient détruit

6 présent du subjonctif		13 passé du subjonctif	
détruise	détruisions	aie détruit	ayons détruit
détruises	détruisiez	aies détruit	ayez détruit
détruise	détruisent	ait détruit	aient détruit

7 imparfait du subjonctif		14 plus-que-parfait du subjonctif	
détruisisse	détruisissions	eusse détruit	eussions détruit
détruisisses	détruisissiez	eusses détruit	eussiez détruit
détruisît	détruisissent	eût détruit	eussent détruit

Impératif
détruis
détruisons
détruisez

Words related to this verb
la destruction   destruction
destructif, destructive   destructive
destructeur, destructrice *adj.*   destructive;
   n. destroyer
la destructivité   destructiveness
destructible   destructible

se détruire   to destroy (to do away with)
   oneself
Les drogues ont détruit sa vie   Drugs
   destroyed his/her life.

It's important that you be familiar with the Subjunctive. See pages 560–565.

to develop, to spread out

The Seven Simple Tenses		The Seven Compound Tenses	
Singular	Plural	Singular	Plural
1 présent de l'indicatif		8 passé composé	
développe	développons	ai développé	avons développé
développes	développez	as développé	avez développé
développe	développent	a développé	ont développé
2 imparfait de l'indicatif		9 plus-que-parfait de l'indicatif	
développais	développions	avais développé	avions développé
développais	développiez	avais développé	aviez développé
développait	développaient	avait développé	avaient développé
3 passé simple		10 passé antérieur	
développai	développâmes	eus développé	eûmes développé
développas	développâtes	eus développé	eûtes développé
développa	développèrent	eut développé	eurent développé
4 futur		11 futur antérieur	
développerai	développerons	aurai développé	aurons développé
développeras	développerez	auras développé	aurez développé
développera	développeront	aura développé	auront développé
5 conditionnel		12 conditionnel passé	
développerais	développerions	aurais développé	aurions développé
développerais	développeriez	aurais développé	auriez développé
développerait	développeraient	aurait développé	auraient développé
6 présent du subjonctif		13 passé du subjonctif	
développe	développions	aie développé	ayons développé
développes	développiez	aies développé	ayez développé
développe	développent	ait développé	aient développé
7 imparfait du subjonctif		14 plus-que-parfait du subjonctif	
développasse	développassions	eusse développé	eussions développé
développasses	développassiez	eusses développé	eussiez développé
développât	développassent	eût développé	eussent développé

Impératif
développe
développons
développez

Words related to this verb
un développement   development
un enveloppement   envelopment, wrapping up; **enveloppement sinapisé**   mustard poultice
envelopper   to envelop, to wrap up
une enveloppe   envelope
développer une pellicule   to develop film

Going away? Don't forget to check out the practical situations for travelers on pages 568–598

The subject pronouns are found on the page facing page 1.   **159**

devenir

Part. pr. **devenant**   Part. passé **devenu(e)(s)**

to become

The Seven Simple Tenses		The Seven Compound Tenses	
Singular	Plural	Singular	Plural
1 présent de l'indicatif		**8 passé composé**	
deviens	devenons	suis devenu(e)	sommes devenu(e)s
deviens	devenez	es devenu(e)	êtes devenu(e)(s)
devient	deviennent	est devenu(e)	sont devenu(e)s
2 imparfait de l'indicatif		**9 plus-que-parfait de l'indicatif**	
devenais	devenions	étais devenu(e)	étions devenu(e)s
devenais	deveniez	étais devenu(e)	étiez devenu(e)(s)
devenait	devenaient	était devenu(e)	étaient devenu(e)s
3 passé simple		**10 passé antérieur**	
devins	devînmes	fus devenu(e)	fûmes devenu(e)s
devins	devîntes	fus devenu(e)	fûtes devenu(e)(s)
devint	devinrent	fut devenu(e)	furent devenu(e)s
4 futur		**11 futur antérieur**	
deviendrai	deviendrons	serai devenu(e)	serons devenu(e)s
deviendras	deviendrez	seras devenu(e)	serez devenu(e)(s)
deviendra	deviendront	sera devenu(e)	seront devenu(e)s
5 conditionnel		**12 conditionnel passé**	
deviendrais	deviendrions	serais devenu(e)	serions devenu(e)s
deviendrais	deviendriez	serais devenu(e)	seriez devenu(e)(s)
deviendrait	deviendraient	serait devenu(e)	seraient devenu(e)s
6 présent du subjonctif		**13 passé du subjonctif**	
devienne	devenions	sois devenu(e)	soyons devenu(e)s
deviennes	deveniez	sois devenu(e)	soyez devenu(e)(s)
devienne	deviennent	soit devenu(e)	soient devenu(e)s
7 imparfait du subjonctif		**14 plus-que-parfait du subjonctif**	
devinsse	devinssions	fusse devenu(e)	fussions devenu(e)s
devinsses	devinssiez	fusses devenu(e)	fussiez devenu(e)(s)
devînt	devinssent	fût devenu(e)	fussent devenu(e)s

Impératif
deviens
devenons
devenez

Common idiomatic expressions using this verb

J'ai entendu dire que Claudette est devenue docteur. Et vous, qu'est-ce que vous voulez devenir?

devenir fou, devenir folle   to go mad, crazy; **devenir vieux/grand**   to grow old/tall
Qu'est devenue votre soeur?   What has become of your sister?

See also **convenir, prévenir, revenir, se souvenir,** and **venir.**

Want to learn more idiomatic expressions that contain verbs? Look at pages 530–542.

to have to, must, ought, owe, should

The Seven Simple Tenses		The Seven Compound Tenses	
Singular	Plural	Singular	Plural
1 présent de l'indicatif		8 passé composé	
dois	devons	ai dû	avons dû
dois	devez	as dû	avez dû
doit	doivent	a dû	ont dû
2 imparfait de l'indicatif		9 plus-que-parfait de l'indicatif	
devais	devions	avais dû	avions dû
devais	deviez	avais dû	aviez dû
devait	devaient	avait dû	avaient dû
3 passé simple		10 passé antérieur	
dus	dûmes	eus dû	eûmes dû
dus	dûtes	eus dû	eûtes dû
dut	durent	eut dû	eurent dû
4 futur		11 futur antérieur	
devrai	devrons	aurai dû	aurons dû
devras	devrez	auras dû	aurez dû
devra	devront	aura dû	auront dû
5 conditionnel		12 conditionnel passé	
devrais	devrions	aurais dû	aurions dû
devrais	devriez	aurais dû	auriez dû
devrait	devraient	aurait dû	auraient dû
6 présent du subjonctif		13 passé du subjonctif	
doive	devions	aie dû	ayons dû
doives	deviez	aies dû	ayez dû
doive	doivent	ait dû	aient dû
7 imparfait du subjonctif		14 plus-que-parfait du subjonctif	
dusse	dussions	eusse dû	eussions dû
dusses	dussiez	eusses dû	eussiez dû
dût	dussent	eût dû	eussent dû

Impératif
dois
devons
devez

Common idiomatic expressions using this verb

Hier soir je suis allé au cinéma avec mes amis. Vous auriez dû venir avec nous. Le film était excellent.

Vous auriez dû venir You should have come.
le devoir duty, obligation
les devoirs homework
Cette grosse somme d'argent est due lundi
This large amount of money is due Monday.

faire ses devoirs to do one's homework
Je vous dois cent euros I owe you 100 euros.
J'ai dû attendre deux heures I had to wait two hours.

Taking a trip? Check out the popular words, phrases, and expressions for travelers on pages 599–621.

The subject pronouns are found on the page facing page 1.   **161**

diminuer

Part. pr. **diminuant**   Part. passé **diminué**

to diminish, to decrease, to lessen

The Seven Simple Tenses		The Seven Compound Tenses	
Singular	Plural	Singular	Plural
1 présent de l'indicatif		**8 passé composé**	
diminue	diminuons	ai diminué	avons diminué
diminues	diminuez	as diminué	avez diminué
diminue	diminuent	a diminué	ont diminué
2 imparfait de l'indicatif		**9 plus-que-parfait de l'indicatif**	
diminuais	diminuions	avais diminué	avions diminué
diminuais	diminuiez	avais diminué	aviez diminué
diminuait	diminuaient	avait diminué	avaient diminué
3 passé simple		**10 passé antérieur**	
diminuai	diminuâmes	eus diminué	eûmes diminué
diminuas	diminuâtes	eus diminué	eûtes diminué
diminua	diminuèrent	eut diminué	eurent diminué
4 futur		**11 futur antérieur**	
diminuerai	diminuerons	aurai diminué	aurons diminué
diminueras	diminuerez	auras diminué	aurez diminué
diminuera	diminueront	aura diminué	auront diminué
5 conditionnel		**12 conditionnel passé**	
diminuerais	diminuerions	aurais diminué	aurions diminué
diminuerais	diminueriez	aurais diminué	auriez diminué
diminuerait	diminueraient	aurait diminué	auraient diminué
6 présent du subjonctif		**13 passé du subjonctif**	
diminue	diminuions	aie diminué	ayons diminué
diminues	diminuiez	aies diminué	ayez diminué
diminue	diminuent	ait diminué	aient diminué
7 imparfait du subjonctif		**14 plus-que-parfait du subjonctif**	
diminuasse	diminuassions	eusse diminué	eussions diminué
diminuasses	diminuassiez	eusses diminué	eussiez diminué
diminuât	diminuassent	eût diminué	eussent diminué

Impératif
diminue
diminuons
diminuez

Words and expressions related to this verb

une diminution decrease, diminution, reduction
Le prix du café n'a pas diminué The price of coffee has not gone down.
Votre travail a diminué de moitié Your work has decreased by half.

diminutif, diminutive diminutive
faire diminuer to lower, to decrease
la diminution d'un prix lowering of a price
se diminuer to lower oneself

Increase your verb power with popular phrases, words, and expressions for travelers on pages 599–621.

to dine, to have dinner

The Seven Simple Tenses		The Seven Compound Tenses	
Singular	Plural	Singular	Plural
1 présent de l'indicatif		**8 passé composé**	
dîne	dînons	ai dîné	avons dîné
dînes	dînez	as dîné	avez dîné
dîne	dînent	a dîné	ont dîné
2 imparfait de l'indicatif		**9 plus-que-parfait de l'indicatif**	
dînais	dînions	avais dîné	avions dîné
dînais	dîniez	avais dîné	aviez dîné
dînait	dînaient	avait dîné	avaient dîné
3 passé simple		**10 passé antérieur**	
dînai	dînâmes	eus dîné	eûmes dîné
dînas	dînâtes	eus dîné	eûtes dîné
dîna	dînèrent	eut dîné	eurent dîné
4 futur		**11 futur antérieur**	
dînerai	dînerons	aurai dîné	aurons dîné
dîneras	dînerez	auras dîné	aurez dîné
dînera	dîneront	aura dîné	auront dîné
5 conditionnel		**12 conditionnel passé**	
dînerais	dînerions	aurais dîné	aurions dîné
dînerais	dîneriez	aurais dîné	auriez dîné
dînerait	dîneraient	aurait dîné	auraient dîné
6 présent du subjonctif		**13 passé du subjonctif**	
dîne	dînions	aie dîné	ayons dîné
dînes	dîniez	aies dîné	ayez dîné
dîne	dînent	ait dîné	aient dîné
7 imparfait du subjonctif		**14 plus-que-parfait du subjonctif**	
dînasse	dînassions	eusse dîné	eussions dîné
dînasses	dînassiez	eusses dîné	eussiez dîné
dînât	dînassent	eût dîné	eussent dîné

Impératif
dîne
dînons
dînez

Common idiomatic expressions using this verb
   Lundi j'ai dîné chez des amis. Mardi tu as dîné chez moi. Mercredi nous avons dîné chez Pierre. J'aurais dû dîner seul.

le dîner dinner	**un dîneur** diner
une dînette child's tea party	**donner un dîner** to give a dinner
l'heure du dîner dinner time	**dîner en ville** to dine out
j'aurais dû I should have	**J'aurais dû dîner** I should have had dinner.

Try reading aloud this play on sounds (the letter **d**) as fast as you can:
   Denis a dîné du dos d'un dindon dodu.
   Dennis dined on (ate) the back of a plump turkey.

dire

Part. pr. **disant**   Part. passé **dit**

to say, to tell

The Seven Simple Tenses		The Seven Compound Tenses	
Singular	Plural	Singular	Plural
1 présent de l'indicatif		**8 passé composé**	
dis	disons	ai dit	avons dit
dis	dites	as dit	avez dit
dit	disent	a dit	ont dit
2 imparfait de l'indicatif		**9 plus-que-parfait de l'indicatif**	
disais	disions	avais dit	avions dit
disais	disiez	avais dit	aviez dit
disait	disaient	avait dit	avaient dit
3 passé simple		**10 passé antérieur**	
dis	dîmes	eus dit	eûmes dit
dis	dîtes	eus dit	eûtes dit
dit	dirent	eut dit	eurent dit
4 futur		**11 futur antérieur**	
dirai	dirons	aurai dit	aurons dit
diras	direz	auras dit	aurez dit
dira	diront	aura dit	auront dit
5 conditionnel		**12 conditionnel passé**	
dirais	dirions	aurais dit	aurions dit
dirais	diriez	aurais dit	auriez dit
dirait	diraient	aurait dit	auraient dit
6 présent du subjonctif		**13 passé du subjonctif**	
dise	disions	aie dit	ayons dit
dises	disiez	aies dit	ayez dit
dise	disent	ait dit	aient dit
7 imparfait du subjonctif		**14 plus-que-parfait du subjonctif**	
disse	dissions	eusse dit	eussions dit
disses	dissiez	eusses dit	eussiez dit
dît	dissent	eût dit	eussent dit

Impératif
dis
disons
dites

Common idiomatic expressions using this verb
— **Qu'est-ce que vous avez dit? Je n'ai pas entendu.**
— **J'ai dit que je ne vous ai pas entendu. Parlez plus fort.**

c'est-à-dire   that is, that is to say
entendre dire que   to hear it said that
vouloir dire   to mean

soi-disant   so-called
dire du bien de   to speak well of

See also **contredire, interdire, maudire, médire, prédire** and note the different *vous* form in the *présent de l'indicatif* and the *impératif*.

For more idioms using this verb, see page 534.

164

to discuss, to argue

The Seven Simple Tenses		The Seven Compound Tenses	
Singular	Plural	Singular	Plural

1 présent de l'indicatif		8 passé composé	
discute	discutons	ai discuté	avons discuté
discutes	discutez	as discuté	avez discuté
discute	discutent	a discuté	ont discuté

2 imparfait de l'indicatif		9 plus-que-parfait de l'indicatif	
discutais	discutions	avais discuté	avions discuté
discutais	discutiez	avais discuté	aviez discuté
discutait	discutaient	avait discuté	avaient discuté

3 passé simple		10 passé antérieur	
discutai	discutâmes	eus discuté	eûmes discuté
discutas	discutâtes	eus discuté	eûtes discuté
discuta	discutèrent	eut discuté	eurent discuté

4 futur		11 futur antérieur	
discuterai	discuterons	aurai discuté	aurons discuté
discuteras	discuterez	auras discuté	aurez discuté
discutera	discuteront	aura discuté	auront discuté

5 conditionnel		12 conditionnel passé	
discuterais	discuterions	aurais discuté	aurions discuté
discuterais	discuteriez	aurais discuté	auriez discuté
discuterait	discuteraient	aurait discuté	auraient discuté

6 présent du subjonctif		13 passé du subjonctif	
discute	discutions	aie discuté	ayons discuté
discutes	discutiez	aies discuté	ayez discuté
discute	discutent	ait discuté	aient discuté

7 imparfait du subjonctif		14 plus-que-parfait du subjonctif	
discutasse	discutassions	eusse discuté	eussions discuté
discutasses	discutassiez	eusses discuté	eussiez discuté
discutât	discutassent	eût discuté	eussent discuté

	Impératif	
	discute	
	discutons	
	discutez	

Words and expressions related to this verb
une discussion   discussion
discutable   disputable, questionable
discuter avec   to argue with; **discuter de**   to argue about
un groupe de discussion   newsgroup (Internet)

Get acquainted with what preposition goes with what verb on pages 543–553.

The subject pronouns are found on the page facing page 1.   **165**

disparaître

Part. pr. **disparaissant**   Part. passé **disparu**

to disappear

The Seven Simple Tenses		The Seven Compound Tenses	
Singular	Plural	Singular	Plural
1 présent de l'indicatif		8 passé composé	
disparais	disparaissons	ai disparu	avons disparu
disparais	disparaissez	as disparu	avez disparu
disparaît	disparaissent	a disparu	ont disparu
2 imparfait de l'indicatif		9 plus-que-parfait de l'indicatif	
disparaissais	disparaissions	avais disparu	avions disparu
disparaissais	disparaissiez	avais disparu	aviez disparu
disparaissait	disparaissaient	avait disparu	avaient disparu
3 passé simple		10 passé antérieur	
disparus	disparûmes	eus disparu	eûmes disparu
disparus	disparûtes	eus disparu	eûtes disparu
disparut	disparurent	eut disparu	eurent disparu
4 futur		11 futur antérieur	
disparaîtrai	disparaîtrons	aurai disparu	aurons disparu
disparaîtras	disparaîtrez	auras disparu	aurez disparu
disparaîtra	disparaîtront	aura disparu	auront disparu
5 conditionnel		12 conditionnel passé	
disparaîtrais	disparaîtrions	aurais disparu	aurions disparu
disparaîtrais	disparaîtriez	aurais disparu	auriez disparu
disparaîtrait	disparaîtraient	aurait disparu	auraient disparu
6 présent du subjonctif		13 passé du subjonctif	
disparaisse	disparaissions	aie disparu	ayons disparu
disparaisses	disparaissiez	aies disparu	ayez disparu
disparaisse	disparaissent	ait disparu	aient disparu
7 imparfait du subjonctif		14 plus-que-parfait du subjonctif	
disparusse	disparussions	eusse disparu	eussions disparu
disparusses	disparussiez	eusses disparu	eussiez disparu
disparût	disparussent	eût disparu	eussent disparu

Impératif
disparais
disparaissons
disparaissez

Words and expressions related to this verb

faire disparaître aux regards   to hide from sight

notre cher ami disparu (notre chère amie disparue)   our dear departed friend

la disparition   disappearance, disappearing

disparu, disparue en mer   lost at sea

être porté disparu   to be declared missing

un disparu   missing person

See also **apparaître, paraître,** and **reparaître.**

Grammar putting you in a tense mood? Review the definitions of basic grammatical terms with examples on pages 674–688.

166

The Seven Simple Tenses		The Seven Compound Tenses	
Singular	Plural	Singular	Plural
1 présent de l'indicatif		**8 passé composé**	
donne	donnons	ai donné	avons donné
donnes	donnez	as donné	avez donné
donne	donnent	a donné	ont donné
2 imparfait de l'indicatif		**9 plus-que-parfait de l'indicatif**	
donnais	donnions	avais donné	avions donné
donnais	donniez	avais donné	aviez donné
donnait	donnaient	avait donné	avaient donné
3 passé simple		**10 passé antérieur**	
donnai	donnâmes	eus donné	eûmes donné
donnas	donnâtes	eus donné	eûtes donné
donna	donnèrent	eut donné	eurent donné
4 futur		**11 futur antérieur**	
donnerai	donnerons	aurai donné	aurons donné
donneras	donnerez	auras donné	aurez donné
donnera	donneront	aura donné	auront donné
5 conditionnel		**12 conditionnel passé**	
donnerais	donnerions	aurais donné	aurions donné
donnerais	donneriez	aurais donné	auriez donné
donnerait	donneraient	aurait donné	auraient donné
6 présent du subjonctif		**13 passé du subjonctif**	
donne	donnions	aie donné	ayons donné
donnes	donniez	aies donné	ayez donné
donne	donnent	ait donné	aient donné
7 imparfait du subjonctif		**14 plus-que-parfait du subjonctif**	
donnasse	donnassions	eusse donné	eussions donné
donnasses	donnassiez	eusses donné	eussiez donné
donnât	donnassent	eût donné	eussent donné

Impératif
donne
donnons
donnez

Common idiomatic expressions using this verb and words related to it

donner rendez-vous à qqn   to make an appointment (a date) with someone
donner sur   to look out upon: **La salle à manger donne sur un joli jardin**   The dining room looks out upon (faces) a pretty garden.
donner congé à   to grant leave to

See also **pardonner.**

abandonner   to abandon; **ordonner**   to order; **pardonner**   to pardon
Si votre fils demande un morceau de pain, lui donnerez-vous une pierre?   If your son asks for a piece of bread, will you give him a stone? (*Matthew 7 : 9*) See "if" clauses, top of page 560.
une base de données   database (computer)

Use the EE-zee guide to French pronunciation on pages 566 and 567.

dormir

to sleep

The Seven Simple Tenses		The Seven Compound Tenses	
Singular	Plural	Singular	Plural
1 présent de l'indicatif		**8 passé composé**	
dors	dormons	ai dormi	avons dormi
dors	dormez	as dormi	avez dormi
dort	dorment	a dormi	ont dormi
2 imparfait de l'indicatif		**9 plus-que-parfait de l'indicatif**	
dormais	dormions	avais dormi	avions dormi
dormais	dormiez	avais dormi	aviez dormi
dormait	dormaient	avait dormi	avaient dormi
3 passé simple		**10 passé antérieur**	
dormis	dormîmes	eus dormi	eûmes dormi
dormis	dormîtes	eus dormi	eûtes dormi
dormit	dormirent	eut dormi	eurent dormi
4 futur		**11 futur antérieur**	
dormirai	dormirons	aurai dormi	aurons dormi
dormiras	dormirez	auras dormi	aurez dormi
dormira	dormiront	aura dormi	auront dormi
5 conditionnel		**12 conditionnel passé**	
dormirais	dormirions	aurais dormi	aurions dormi
dormirais	dormiriez	aurais dormi	auriez dormi
dormirait	dormiraient	aurait dormi	auraient dormi
6 présent du subjonctif		**13 passé du subjonctif**	
dorme	dormions	aie dormi	ayons dormi
dormes	dormiez	aies dormi	ayez dormi
dorme	dorment	ait dormi	aient dormi
7 imparfait du subjonctif		**14 plus-que-parfait du subjonctif**	
dormisse	dormissions	eusse dormi	eussions dormi
dormisses	dormissiez	eusses dormi	eussiez dormi
dormît	dormissent	eût dormi	eussent dormi

Impératif
dors
dormons
dormez

Common idiomatic expressions using this verb and words related to it

dormir toute la nuit   to sleep through the night
parler en dormant   to talk in one's sleep
empêcher de dormir   to keep from sleeping
la dormition   dormition (falling asleep)
le dortoir   dormitory
dormir à la belle étoile   to sleep outdoors
dormir sur les deux oreilles   to sleep soundly

endormir   to put to sleep
s'endormir   to fall asleep
avoir envie de dormir   to feel like sleeping
As-tu bien dormi, chéri?   Did you sleep well, darling?
un conte à dormir debout   cock-and-bull story

Taking a trip? Check out the popular words, phrases, and expressions for travelers on pages 599–621.

The Seven Simple Tenses		The Seven Compound Tenses	
Singular	Plural	Singular	Plural
1 présent de l'indicatif		8 passé composé	
doute	doutons	ai douté	avons douté
doutes	doutez	as douté	avez douté
doute	doutent	a douté	ont douté
2 imparfait de l'indicatif		9 plus-que-parfait de l'indicatif	
doutais	doutions	avais douté	avions douté
doutais	doutiez	avais douté	aviez douté
doutait	doutaient	avait douté	avaient douté
3 passé simple		10 passé antérieur	
doutai	doutâmes	eus douté	eûmes douté
doutas	doutâtes	eus douté	eûtes douté
douta	doutèrent	eut douté	eurent douté
4 futur		11 futur antérieur	
douterai	douterons	aurai douté	aurons douté
douteras	douterez	auras douté	aurez douté
doutera	douteront	aura douté	auront douté
5 conditionnel		12 conditionnel passé	
douterais	douterions	aurais douté	aurions douté
douterais	douteriez	aurais douté	auriez douté
douterait	douteraient	aurait douté	auraient douté
6 présent du subjonctif		13 passé du subjonctif	
doute	doutions	aie douté	ayons douté
doutes	doutiez	aies douté	ayez douté
doute	doutent	ait douté	aient douté
7 imparfait du subjonctif		14 plus-que-parfait du subjonctif	
doutasse	doutassions	eusse douté	eussions douté
doutasses	doutassiez	eusses douté	eussiez douté
doutât	doutassent	eût douté	eussent douté

Impératif
doute
doutons
doutez

Common idiomatic expressions using this verb
Je doute que cet homme soit coupable. Il n'y a pas de doute qu'il est innocent.

le doute   doubt
sans doute   no doubt
sans aucun doute   undoubtedly
d'un air de doute   dubiously
redouter   to dread, to fear

ne douter de rien   to doubt nothing, to be too
   credulous
ne se douter de rien   to suspect nothing
se douter de   to suspect
douteux, douteuse   doubtful

It's important that you be familiar with the Subjunctive. See pages 560–565.

to escape, to avoid

The Seven Simple Tenses		The Seven Compound Tenses	
Singular	Plural	Singular	Plural
1 présent de l'indicatif		**8 passé composé**	
échappe	échappons	ai échappé	avons échappé
échappes	échappez	as échappé	avez échappé
échappe	échappent	a échappé	ont échappé
2 imparfait de l'indicatif		**9 plus-que-parfait de l'indicatif**	
échappais	échappions	avais échappé	avions échappé
échappais	échappiez	avais échappé	aviez échappé
échappait	échappaient	avait échappé	avaient échappé
3 passé simple		**10 passé antérieur**	
échappai	échappâmes	eus échappé	eûmes échappé
échappas	échappâtes	eus échappé	eûtes échappé
échappa	échappèrent	eut échappé	eurent échappé
4 futur		**11 futur antérieur**	
échapperai	échapperons	aurai échappé	aurons échappé
échapperas	échapperez	auras échappé	aurez échappé
échappera	échapperont	aura échappé	auront échappé
5 conditionnel		**12 conditionnel passé**	
échapperais	échapperions	aurais échappé	aurions échappé
échapperais	échapperiez	aurais échappé	auriez échappé
échapperait	échapperaient	aurait échappé	auraient échappé
6 présent du subjonctif		**13 passé du subjonctif**	
échappe	échappions	aie échappé	ayons échappé
échappes	échappiez	aies échappé	ayez échappé
échappe	échappent	ait échappé	aient échappé
7 imparfait du subjonctif		**14 plus-que-parfait du subjonctif**	
échappasse	échappassions	eusse échappé	eussions échappé
échappasses	échappassiez	eusses échappé	eussiez échappé
échappât	échappassent	eût échappé	eussent échappé

Impératif
échappe
échappons
échappez

Words and expressions related to this verb
échapper à to avoid; **échapper de** to escape from
l'échapper belle to have a narrow escape; **Je l'ai échappé belle** I had a narrow escape.
Cela m'a échappé I did not notice it.
Cela m'est échappé It slipped my mind (I forgot it).
laisser échapper to let slip, to overlook
s'échapper de to escape from
une échappée de lumière a glimmer of light
l'échappement *m.* exhaust
le pot d'échappement muffler (auto)

Check out the principal parts of some important French verbs on page xii.

170

to fail, to run aground

The Seven Simple Tenses		The Seven Compound Tenses	
Singular	Plural	Singular	Plural

1   présent de l'indicatif

échoue	échouons		
échoues	échouez		
échoue	échouent		

8   passé composé

ai échoué	avons échoué
as échoué	avez échoué
a échoué	ont échoué

2   imparfait de l'indicatif

échouais	échouions
échouais	échouiez
échouait	échouaient

9   plus-que-parfait de l'indicatif

avais échoué	avions échoué
avais échoué	aviez échoué
avait échoué	avaient échoué

3   passé simple

échouai	échouâmes
échouas	échouâtes
échoua	échouèrent

10   passé antérieur

eus échoué	eûmes échoué
eus échoué	eûtes échoué
eut échoué	eurent échoué

4   futur

échouerai	échouerons
échoueras	échouerez
échouera	échoueront

11   futur antérieur

aurai échoué	aurons échoué
auras échoué	aurez échoué
aura échoué	auront échoué

5   conditionnel

échouerais	échouerions
échouerais	échoueriez
échouerait	échoueraient

12   conditionnel passé

aurais échoué	aurions échoué
aurais échoué	auriez échoué
aurait échoué	auraient échoué

6   présent du subjonctif

échoue	échouions
échoues	échouiez
échoue	échouent

13   passé du subjonctif

aie échoué	ayons échoué
aies échoué	ayez échoué
ait échoué	aient échoué

7   imparfait du subjonctif

échouasse	échouassions
échouasses	échouassiez
échouât	échouassent

14   plus-que-parfait du subjonctif

eusse échoué	eussions échoué
eusses échoué	eussiez échoué
eût échoué	eussent échoué

Impératif
échoue
échouons
échouez

Common idiomatic expressions using this verb
échouer à qqch   to fail (flunk) at something
échouer à un examen   to flunk an exam
échouer   to touch bottom (accidentally), to fail
Tous mes espoirs ont échoué   All my hopes have touched bottom (have failed).
Le bateau a échoué sur un banc de sable   The ship ran aground on a shoal.

Consult the sections on verbs used in idiomatic expressions, verbs with prepositions, and the list
of over 1,100 verbs conjugated like model verbs in the back pages.

écouter

Part. pr. écoutant **Part. passé écouté**

to listen (to)

The Seven Simple Tenses		The Seven Compound Tenses	
Singular	Plural	Singular	Plural
1 présent de l'indicatif		8 passé composé	
écoute	écoutons	ai écouté	avons écouté
écoutes	écoutez	as écouté	avez écouté
écoute	écoutent	a écouté	ont écouté
2 imparfait de l'indicatif		9 plus-que-parfait de l'indicatif	
écoutais	écoutions	avais écouté	avions écouté
écoutais	écoutiez	avais écouté	aviez écouté
écoutait	écoutaient	avait écouté	avaient écouté
3 passé simple		10 passé antérieur	
écoutai	écoutâmes	eus écouté	eûmes écouté
écoutas	écoutâtes	eus écouté	eûtes écouté
écouta	écoutèrent	eut écouté	eurent écouté
4 futur		11 futur antérieur	
écouterai	écouterons	aurai écouté	aurons écouté
écouteras	écouterez	auras écouté	aurez écouté
écoutera	écouteront	aura écouté	auront écouté
5 conditionnel		12 conditionnel passé	
écouterais	écouterions	aurais écouté	aurions écouté
écouterais	écouteriez	aurais écouté	auriez écouté
écouterait	écouteraient	aurait écouté	auraient écouté
6 présent du subjonctif		13 passé du subjonctif	
écoute	écoutions	aie écouté	ayons écouté
écoutes	écoutiez	aies écouté	ayez écouté
écoute	écoutent	ait écouté	aient écouté
7 imparfait du subjonctif		14 plus-que-parfait du subjonctif	
écoutasse	écoutassions	eusse écouté	eussions écouté
écoutasses	écoutassiez	eusses écouté	eussiez écouté
écoutât	écoutassent	eût écouté	eussent écouté

Impératif
écoute
écoutons
écoutez

Common idiomatic expressions using this verb and words related to it

Ecoutez-vous le professeur quand il explique la leçon? L'avez-vous écouté ce matin en classe?

aimer à s'écouter parler   to love to hear one's own voice
un écouteur   telephone receiver (earpiece)
être à l'écoute   to be listening in
n'écouter personne   not to heed anyone

savoir écouter   to be a good listener
écouter aux portes   to eavesdrop, to listen secretly
Ecoutez-moi   Listen to me.
Je vous écoute   I'm listening to you.
Parlez donc!   Speak up!

Enjoy verbs in French proverbs on page 559.

The Seven Simple Tenses		The Seven Compound Tenses	
Singular	Plural	Singular	Plural
1 présent de l'indicatif		**8 passé composé**	
écris	écrivons	ai écrit	avons écrit
écris	écrivez	as écrit	avez écrit
écrit	écrivent	a écrit	ont écrit
2 imparfait de l'indicatif		**9 plus-que-parfait de l'indicatif**	
écrivais	écrivions	avais écrit	avions écrit
écrivais	écriviez	avais écrit	aviez écrit
écrivait	écrivaient	avait écrit	avaient écrit
3 passé simple		**10 passé antérieur**	
écrivis	écrivîmes	eus écrit	eûmes écrit
écrivis	écrivîtes	eus écrit	eûtes écrit
écrivit	écrivirent	eut écrit	eurent écrit
4 futur		**11 futur antérieur**	
écrirai	écrirons	aurai écrit	aurons écrit
écriras	écrirez	auras écrit	aurez écrit
écrira	écriront	aura écrit	auront écrit
5 conditionnel		**12 conditionnel passé**	
écrirais	écririons	aurais écrit	aurions écrit
écrirais	écririez	aurais écrit	auriez écrit
écrirait	écriraient	aurait écrit	auraient écrit
6 présent du subjonctif		**13 passé du subjonctif**	
écrive	écrivions	aie écrit	ayons écrit
écrives	écriviez	aies écrit	ayez écrit
écrive	écrivent	ait écrit	aient écrit
7 imparfait du subjonctif		**14 plus-que-parfait du subjonctif**	
écrivisse	écrivissions	eusse écrit	eussions écrit
écrivisses	écrivissiez	eusses écrit	eussiez écrit
écrivît	écrivissent	eût écrit	eussent écrit

Impératif
écris
écrivons
écrivez

Sentences using this verb and words and expressions related to it
Jean: As-tu écrit ta composition pour la classe de français?
Jacques: Non, je ne l'ai pas écrite.
Jean: Ecrivons-la ensemble.

un écrivain writer; **une femme écrivain** woman writer
écriture *f.* handwriting, writing; **par écrit** in writing

écrire un petit mot à qqn to write a note to someone
une machine à écrire a typewriter
réécrire to rewrite

See also **décrire.**

effrayer

Part. pr. **effrayant**   Part. passé **effrayé**

to frighten

The Seven Simple Tenses		The Seven Compound Tenses	
Singular	Plural	Singular	Plural
1 présent de l'indicatif		**8 passé composé**	
effraye	effrayons	ai effrayé	avons effrayé
effrayes	effrayez	as effrayé	avez effrayé
effraye	effrayent	a effrayé	ont effrayé
2 imparfait de l'indicatif		**9 plus-que-parfait de l'indicatif**	
effrayais	effrayions	avais effrayé	avions effrayé
effrayais	effrayiez	avais effrayé	aviez effrayé
effrayait	effrayaient	avait effrayé	avaient effrayé
3 passé simple		**10 passé antérieur**	
effrayai	effrayâmes	eus effrayé	eûmes effrayé
effrayas	effrayâtes	eus effrayé	eûtes effrayé
effraya	effrayèrent	eut effrayé	eurent effrayé
4 futur		**11 futur antérieur**	
effrayerai	effrayerons	aurai effrayé	aurons effrayé
effrayeras	effrayerez	auras effrayé	aurez effrayé
effrayera	effrayeront	aura effrayé	auront effrayé
5 conditionnel		**12 conditionnel passé**	
effrayerais	effrayerions	aurais effrayé	aurions effrayé
effrayerais	effrayeriez	aurais effrayé	auriez effrayé
effrayerait	effrayeraient	aurait effrayé	auraient effrayé
6 présent du subjonctif		**13 passé du subjonctif**	
effraye	effrayions	aie effrayé	ayons effrayé
effrayes	effrayiez	aies effrayé	ayez effrayé
effraye	effrayent	ait effrayé	aient effrayé
7 imparfait du subjonctif		**14 plus-que-parfait du subjonctif**	
effrayasse	effrayassions	eusse effrayé	eussions effrayé
effrayasses	effrayassiez	eusses effrayé	eussiez effrayé
effrayât	effrayassent	eût effrayé	eussent effrayé

Impératif
effraye
effrayons
effrayez

Sentences using this verb and words related to it
   Le tigre a effrayé l'enfant. L'enfant a effrayé le singe. Le singe effraiera le bébé. C'est effrayant!

effrayant, effrayante frightful, awful
effrayé, effrayée frightened
l'effroi *m.* fright, terror

effroyable dreadful, fearful
effroyablement dreadfully, fearfully

Verbs ending in *-ayer* may change *y* to *i* before mute *e* or may keep *y*.

to amuse, to cheer up, to enliven, to entertain

The Seven Simple Tenses		The Seven Compound Tenses	
Singular	Plural	Singular	Plural
1 présent de l'indicatif		**8 passé composé**	
égaye	égayons	ai égayé	avons égayé
égayes	égayez	as égayé	avez égayé
égaye	égayent	a égayé	ont égayé
2 imparfait de l'indicatif		**9 plus-que-parfait de l'indicatif**	
égayais	égayions	avais égayé	avions égayé
égayais	égayiez	avais égayé	aviez égayé
égayait	égayaient	avait égayé	avaient égayé
3 passé simple		**10 passé antérieur**	
égayai	égayâmes	eus égayé	eûmes égayé
égayas	égayâtes	eus égayé	eûtes égayé
égaya	égayèrent	eut égayé	eurent égayé
4 futur		**11 futur antérieur**	
égayerai	égayerons	aurai égayé	aurons égayé
égayeras	égayerez	auras égayé	aurez égayé
égayera	égayeront	aura égayé	auront égayé
5 conditionnel		**12 conditionnel passé**	
égayerais	égayerions	aurais égayé	aurions égayé
égayerais	égayeriez	aurais égayé	auriez égayé
égayerait	égayeraient	aurait égayé	auraient égayé
6 présent du subjonctif		**13 passé du subjonctif**	
égaye	égayions	aie égayé	ayons égayé
égayes	égayiez	aies égayé	ayez égayé
égaye	égayent	ait égayé	aient égayé
7 imparfait du subjonctif		**14 plus-que-parfait du subjonctif**	
égayasse	égayassions	eusse égayé	eussions égayé
égayasses	égayassiez	eusses égayé	eussiez égayé
égayât	égayassent	eût égayé	eussent égayé

Impératif
égaye
égayons
égayez

Words related to this verb

égayant, égayante lively
un égaiement amusement
s'égayer aux dépens de   to amuse oneself at
   someone's expense

gai, gaie gay, cheerful, merry
gaiement   gaily, cheerfully

Verbs ending in -*ayer* may change *y* to *i* before mute *e* or may keep *y*.

Grammar putting you in a tense mood? Review the definitions of basic grammatical terms on pages 674–688.

The subject pronouns are found on the page facing page 1.   **175**

élever

Part. pr. **élevant**   Part. passé **élevé**

to raise, to rear, to bring up

The Seven Simple Tenses		The Seven Compound Tenses	
Singular	Plural	Singular	Plural
1 présent de l'indicatif		**8 passé composé**	
élève	élevons	ai élevé	avons élevé
élèves	élevez	as élevé	avez élevé
élève	élèvent	a élevé	ont élevé
2 imparfait de l'indicatif		**9 plus-que-parfait de l'indicatif**	
élevais	élevions	avais élevé	avions élevé
élevais	éleviez	avais élevé	aviez élevé
élevait	élevaient	avait élevé	avaient élevé
3 passé simple		**10 passé antérieur**	
élevai	élevâmes	eus élevé	eûmes élevé
élevas	élevâtes	eus élevé	eûtes élevé
éleva	élevèrent	eut élevé	eurent élevé
4 futur		**11 futur antérieur**	
élèverai	élèverons	aurai élevé	aurons élevé
élèveras	élèverez	auras élevé	aurez élevé
élèvera	élèveront	aura élevé	auront élevé
5 conditionnel		**12 conditionnel passé**	
élèverais	élèverions	aurais élevé	aurions élevé
élèverais	élèveriez	aurais élevé	auriez élevé
élèverait	élèveraient	aurait élevé	auraient élevé
6 présent du subjonctif		**13 passé du subjonctif**	
élève	élevions	aie élevé	ayons élevé
élèves	éleviez	aies élevé	ayez élevé
élève	élèvent	ait élevé	aient élevé
7 imparfait du subjonctif		**14 plus-que-parfait du subjonctif**	
élevasse	élevassions	eusse élevé	eussions élevé
élevasses	élevassiez	eusses élevé	eussiez élevé
élevât	élevassent	eût élevé	eussent élevé

Impératif
élève
élevons
élevez

Words and expressions related to this verb

un, une élève   pupil, student; **un, une élève professeur**   student teacher
élevage *m.*   breeding, rearing; **occuper une position élevée**   to hold a high position

élévation *f.*   elevation, raising; **La musique élève l'âme**   Music uplifts the soul.
bien élevé   well-bred, well brought up
mal élevé   ill-bred, badly brought up

See also **enlever** and **lever.**

Get acquainted with what preposition goes with what verb on pages 543–553.

to elect, to choose

The Seven Simple Tenses		The Seven Compound Tenses

Singular	Plural	Singular	Plural
1 présent de l'indicatif		8 passé composé	
élis	élisons	ai élu	avons élu
élis	élisez	as élu	avez élu
élit	élisent	a élu	ont élu
2 imparfait de l'indicatif		9 plus-que-parfait de l'indicatif	
élisais	élisions	avais élu	avions élu
élisais	élisiez	avais élu	aviez élu
élisait	élisaient	avait élu	avaient élu
3 passé simple		10 passé antérieur	
élus	élûmes	eus élu	eûmes élu
élus	élûtes	eus élu	eûtes élu
élut	élurent	eut élu	eurent élu
4 futur		11 futur antérieur	
élirai	élirons	aurai élu	aurons élu
éliras	élirez	auras élu	aurez élu
élira	éliront	aura élu	auront élu
5 conditionnel		12 conditionnel passé	
élirais	élirions	aurais élu	aurions élu
élirais	éliriez	aurais élu	auriez élu
élirait	éliraient	aurait élu	auraient élu
6 présent du subjonctif		13 passé du subjonctif	
élise	élisions	aie élu	ayons élu
élises	élisiez	aies élu	ayez élu
élise	élisent	ait élu	aient élu
7 imparfait du subjonctif		14 plus-que-parfait du subjonctif	
élusse	élussions	eusse élu	eussions élu
élusses	élussiez	eusses élu	eussiez élu
élût	élussent	eût élu	eussent élu

Impératif
élis
élisons
élisez

Words and expressions related to this verb
Car il y a beaucoup d'appelés mais peu d'élus   For many are called but few are chosen.
   (*Matthew 22:14*)
une élection   election, choice
le jour des élections   election day
électif, élective   elective
un électeur, une électrice   voter
se rendre aux urnes   to vote, go to the polls

Consult the sections on verbs used in idiomatic expressions, verbs with prepositions, and the list
of over 1,100 verbs conjugated like model verbs in the back pages.

The subject pronouns are found on the page facing page 1.   **177**

to move away, to go away, to withdraw, to step back, to keep back, to keep away

The Seven Simple Tenses		The Seven Compound Tenses	
Singular	Plural	Singular	Plural
1 présent de l'indicatif		**8 passé composé**	
m'éloigne	nous éloignons	me suis éloigné(e)	nous sommes éloigné(e)s
t'éloignes	vous éloignez	t'es éloigné(e)	vous êtes éloigné(e)(s)
s'éloigne	s'éloignent	s'est éloigné(e)	se sont éloigné(e)s
2 imparfait de l'indicatif		**9 plus-que-parfait de l'indicatif**	
m'éloignais	nous éloignions	m'étais éloigné(e)	nous étions éloigné(e)s
t'éloignais	vous éloigniez	t'étais éloigné(e)	vous étiez éloigné(e)(s)
s'éloignait	s'éloignaient	s'était éloigné(e)	s'étaient éloigné(e)s
3 passé simple		**10 passé antérieur**	
m'éloignai	nous éloignâmes	me fus éloigné(e)	nous fûmes éloigné(e)s
t'éloignas	vous éloignâtes	te fus éloigné(e)	vous fûtes éloigné(e)(s)
s'éloigna	s'éloignèrent	se fut éloigné(e)	se furent éloigné(e)s
4 futur		**11 futur antérieur**	
m'éloignerai	nous éloignerons	me serai éloigné(e)	nous serons éloigné(e)s
t'éloigneras	vous éloignerez	te seras éloigné(e)	vous serez éloigné(e)(s)
s'éloignera	s'éloigneront	se sera éloigné(e)	se seront éloigné(e)s
5 conditionnel		**12 conditionnel passé**	
m'éloignerais	nous éloignerions	me serais éloigné(e)	nous serions éloigné(e)s
t'éloignerais	vous éloigneriez	te serais éloigné(e)	vous seriez éloigné(e)(s)
s'éloignerait	s'éloigneraient	se serait éloigné(e)	se seraient éloigné(e)s
6 présent du subjonctif		**13 passé du subjonctif**	
m'éloigne	nous éloignions	me sois éloigné(e)	nous soyons éloigné(e)s
t'éloignes	vous éloigniez	te sois éloigné(e)	vous soyez éloigné(e)(s)
s'éloigne	s'éloignent	se soit éloigné(e)	se soient éloigné(e)s
7 imparfait du subjonctif		**14 plus-que-parfait du subjonctif**	
m'éloignasse	nous éloignassions	me fusse éloigné(e)	nous fussions éloigné(e)s
t'éloignasses	vous éloignassiez	te fusses éloigné(e)	vous fussiez éloigné(e)(s)
s'éloignât	s'éloignassent	se fût éloigné(e)	se fussent éloigné(e)s

Impératif
éloigne-toi; ne t'éloigne pas
éloignons-nous; ne nous éloignons pas
éloignez-vous; ne vous éloignez pas

Words and expressions related to this verb
éloigner de   to keep away from, to keep at a distance
s'éloigner de   to keep one's distance from, to move away from
s'éloigner en courant   to run away, to move away while running
loin   far; **lointain, lointaine**   distant
loin de là, loin de ça   far from it
Loin des yeux, loin du coeur   Out of sight, out of mind.
Eloignez-vous, s'il vous plaît!   Stay back! Keep your distance, please!
l'éloignement *m.*   distance

Going away? Don't forget to check out the practical situations for travelers on pages 568–598.

The Seven Simple Tenses		The Seven Compound Tenses	
Singular	Plural	Singular	Plural
1 présent de l'indicatif		**8 passé composé**	
embrasse	embrassons	ai embrassé	avons embrassé
embrasses	embrassez	as embrassé	avez embrassé
embrasse	embrassent	a embrassé	ont embrassé
2 imparfait de l'indicatif		**9 plus-que-parfait de l'indicatif**	
embrassais	embrassions	avais embrassé	avions embrassé
embrassais	embrassiez	avais embrassé	aviez embrassé
embrassait	embrassaient	avait embrassé	avaient embrassé
3 passé simple		**10 passé antérieur**	
embrassai	embrassâmes	eus embrassé	eûmes embrassé
embrassas	embrassâtes	eus embrassé	eûtes embrassé
embrassa	embrassèrent	eut embrassé	eurent embrassé
4 futur		**11 futur antérieur**	
embrasserai	embrasserons	aurai embrassé	aurons embrassé
embrasseras	embrasserez	auras embrassé	aurez embrassé
embrassera	embrasseront	aura embrassé	auront embrassé
5 conditionnel		**12 conditionnel passé**	
embrasserais	embrasserions	aurais embrassé	aurions embrassé
embrasserais	embrasseriez	aurais embrassé	auriez embrassé
embrasserait	embrasseraient	aurait embrassé	auraient embrassé
6 présent du subjonctif		**13 passé du subjonctif**	
embrasse	embrassions	aie embrassé	ayons embrassé
embrasses	embrassiez	aies embrassé	ayez embrassé
embrasse	embrassent	ait embrassé	aient embrassé
7 imparfait du subjonctif		**14 plus-que-parfait du subjonctif**	
embrassasse	embrassassions	eusse embrassé	eussions embrassé
embrassasses	embrassassiez	eusses embrassé	eussiez embrassé
embrassât	embrassassent	eût embrassé	eussent embrassé

Impératif
embrasse
embrassons
embrassez

Sentences using this verb and words related to it
—**Embrasse-moi. Je t'aime. Ne me quitte pas.**
—**Je t'embrasse. Je t'aime aussi. Je ne te quitte pas. Embrassons-nous.**

le bras arm
un embrassement embracement, embrace
s'embrasser to embrace each other, to hug each other
embrasseur, embrasseuse a person who likes to kiss a lot

How are you doing? Find out with the verb drills and tests with answers explained on pages
622–673.

to lead, to lead away, to take away (persons)

The Seven Simple Tenses		The Seven Compound Tenses	
Singular	Plural	Singular	Plural
1 présent de l'indicatif		**8 passé composé**	
emmène	emmenons	ai emmené	avons emmené
emmènes	emmenez	as emmené	avez emmené
emmène	emmènent	a emmené	ont emmené
2 imparfait de l'indicatif		**9 plus-que-parfait de l'indicatif**	
emmenais	emmenions	avais emmené	avions emmené
emmenais	emmeniez	avais emmené	aviez emmené
emmenait	emmenaient	avait emmené	avaient emmené
3 passé simple		**10 passé antérieur**	
emmenai	emmenâmes	eus emmené	eûmes emmené
emmenas	emmenâtes	eus emmené	eûtes emmené
emmena	emmenèrent	eut emmené	eurent emmené
4 futur		**11 futur antérieur**	
emmènerai	emmènerons	aurai emmené	aurons emmené
emmèneras	emmènerez	auras emmené	aurez emmené
emmènera	emmèneront	aura emmené	auront emmené
5 conditionnel		**12 conditionnel passé**	
emmènerais	emmènerions	aurais emmené	aurions emmené
emmènerais	emmèneriez	aurais emmené	auriez emmené
emmènerait	emmèneraient	aurait emmené	auraient emmené
6 présent du subjonctif		**13 passé du subjonctif**	
emmène	emmenions	aie emmené	ayons emmené
emmènes	emmeniez	aies emmené	ayez emmené
emmène	emmènent	ait emmené	aient emmené
7 imparfait du subjonctif		**14 plus-que-parfait du subjonctif**	
emmenasse	emmenassions	eusse emmené	eussions emmené
emmenasses	emmenassiez	eusses emmené	eussiez emmené
emmenât	emmenassent	eût emmené	eussent emmené

Impératif
emmène
emmenons
emmenez

Sentences using this verb and words related to it

   Quand j'emmène une personne d'un lieu dans un autre, je mène cette personne avec moi. Mon père nous emmènera au cinéma lundi prochain. Samedi dernier il nous a emmenés au théâtre.

Le train m'a emmené à Paris   The train took me to Paris.
Un agent de police a emmené l'assassin   A policeman took away the assassin.

See also **mener** and **amener.**

Want to learn more idiomatic expressions that contain verbs? Look at pages 530–542.

to move, to touch, to excite, to arouse

The Seven Simple Tenses		The Seven Compound Tenses	
Singular	Plural	Singular	Plural
1 présent de l'indicatif		8 passé composé	
émeus	**émouvons**	**ai ému**	**avons ému**
émeus	**émouvez**	**as ému**	**avez ému**
émeut	**émeuvent**	**a ému**	**ont ému**
2 imparfait de l'indicatif		9 plus-que-parfait de l'indicatif	
émouvais	**émouvions**	**avais ému**	**avions ému**
émouvais	**émouviez**	**avais ému**	**aviez ému**
émouvait	**émouvaient**	**avait ému**	**avaient ému**
3 passé simple		10 passé antérieur	
émus	**émûmes**	**eus ému**	**eûmes ému**
émus	**émûtes**	**eus ému**	**eûtes ému**
émut	**émurent**	**eut ému**	**eurent ému**
4 futur		11 futur antérieur	
émouvrai	**émouvrons**	**aurai ému**	**aurons ému**
émouvras	**émouvrez**	**auras ému**	**aurez ému**
émouvra	**émouvront**	**aura ému**	**auront ému**
5 conditionnel		12 conditionnel passé	
émouvrais	**émouvrions**	**aurais ému**	**aurions ému**
émouvrais	**émouvriez**	**aurais ému**	**auriez ému**
émouvrait	**émouvraient**	**aurait ému**	**auraient ému**
6 présent du subjonctif		13 passé du subjonctif	
émeuve	**émouvions**	**aie ému**	**ayons ému**
émeuves	**émouviez**	**aies ému**	**ayez ému**
émeuve	**émeuvent**	**ait ému**	**aient ému**
7 imparfait du subjonctif		14 plus-que-parfait du subjonctif	
émusse	**émussions**	**eusse ému**	**eussions ému**
émusses	**émussiez**	**eusses ému**	**eussiez ému**
émût	**émussent**	**eût ému**	**eussent ému**

Impératif
émeus
émouvons
émouvez

Words and expressions related to this verb
s'émouvoir de   to be moved (touched) by
une émeute   insurrection, insurgency
un émeutier, une émeutière   insurrectionist, insurgent, rioter
être ému(e)   to be moved

émouvant, émouvante   moving, touching
fort émouvant   thrilling
émouvoir la pitié de qqn   to move someone to pity
l'émotion *f.*   feeling

Consult the sections on verbs used in idiomatic expressions, verbs with prepositions, and the list of over 1,100 verbs conjugated like model verbs in the back pages.

empêcher

Part. pr. empêchant   **Part. passé empêché**

to hinder, to prevent

The Seven Simple Tenses		The Seven Compound Tenses	
Singular	Plural	Singular	Plural
1 présent de l'indicatif		**8 passé composé**	
empêche	empêchons	ai empêché	avons empêché
empêches	empêchez	as empêché	avez empêché
empêche	empêchent	a empêché	ont empêché
2 imparfait de l'indicatif		**9 plus-que-parfait de l'indicatif**	
empêchais	empêchions	avais empêché	avions empêché
empêchais	empêchiez	avais empêché	aviez empêché
empêchait	empêchaient	avait empêché	avaient empêché
3 passé simple		**10 passé antérieur**	
empêchai	empêchâmes	eus empêché	eûmes empêché
empêchas	empêchâtes	eus empêché	eûtes empêché
empêcha	empêchèrent	eut empêché	eurent empêché
4 futur		**11 futur antérieur**	
empêcherai	empêcherons	aurai empêché	aurons empêché
empêcheras	empêcherez	auras empêché	aurez empêché
empêchera	empêcheront	aura empêché	auront empêché
5 conditionnel		**12 conditionnel passé**	
empêcherais	empêcherions	aurais empêché	aurions empêché
empêcherais	empêcheriez	aurais empêché	auriez empêché
empêcherait	empêcheraient	aurait empêché	auraient empêché
6 présent du subjonctif		**13 passé du subjonctif**	
empêche	empêchions	aie empêché	ayons empêché
empêches	empêchiez	aies empêché	ayez empêché
empêche	empêchent	ait empêché	aient empêché
7 imparfait du subjonctif		**14 plus-que-parfait du subjonctif**	
empêchasse	empêchassions	eusse empêché	eussions empêché
empêchasses	empêchassiez	eusses empêché	eussiez empêché
empêchât	empêchassent	eût empêché	eussent empêché

Impératif
empêche
empêchons
empêchez

Sentences using this verb and words related to it
Georgette a empêché son frère de finir ses devoirs parce qu'elle jouait des disques en même temps. Le bruit était un vrai empêchement.

un empêchement impediment, hindrance
en cas d'empêchement in case of prevention
empêcher qqn de faire qqch to prevent someone from doing something
empêcher d'entrer to keep from entering

s'empêcher de faire qqch to refrain from doing something
Je n'ai pas pu m'empêcher de rire I couldn't help laughing.

See also **dépêcher.**

Get acquainted with what preposition (if any) goes with what verb on pages 543–553.

182

The Seven Simple Tenses		The Seven Compound Tenses	
Singular	Plural	Singular	Plural
1 présent de l'indicatif		**8 passé composé**	
emploie	employons	ai employé	avons employé
emploies	employez	as employé	avez employé
emploie	emploient	a employé	ont employé
2 imparfait de l'indicatif		**9 plus-que-parfait de l'indicatif**	
employais	employions	avais employé	avions employé
employais	employiez	avais employé	aviez employé
employait	employaient	avait employé	avaient employé
3 passé simple		**10 passé antérieur**	
employai	employâmes	eus employé	eûmes employé
employas	employâtes	eus employé	eûtes employé
employa	employèrent	eut employé	eurent employé
4 futur		**11 futur antérieur**	
emploierai	emploierons	aurai employé	aurons employé
emploieras	emploierez	auras employé	aurez employé
emploiera	emploieront	aura employé	auront employé
5 conditionnel		**12 conditionnel passé**	
emploierais	emploierions	aurais employé	aurions employé
emploierais	emploieriez	aurais employé	auriez employé
emploierait	emploieraient	aurait employé	auraient employé
6 présent du subjonctif		**13 passé du subjonctif**	
emploie	employions	aie employé	ayons employé
emploies	employiez	aies employé	ayez employé
emploie	emploient	ait employé	aient employé
7 imparfait du subjonctif		**14 plus-que-parfait du subjonctif**	
employasse	employassions	eusse employé	eussions employé
employasses	employassiez	eusses employé	eussiez employé
employât	employassent	eût employé	eussent employé

Impératif
emploie
employons
employez

Words and expressions related to this verb
un employé, une employée   employee
un employeur, une employeuse   employer
sans emploi   jobless
un emploi   employment
une demande d'emploi   job application

s'employer à faire qqch   to occupy oneself
   doing something
employer son temps   to spend one's time
un emploi nouveau   a new use

Verbs ending in -*oyer* must change *y* to *i* before mute *e*.

It's important that you use the Subjunctive correctly. See pages 560–565.

The subject pronouns are found on the page facing page 1.   **183**

emprunter

Part. pr. **empruntant**   Part. passé **emprunté**

to borrow

The Seven Simple Tenses		The Seven Compound Tenses	
Singular	Plural	Singular	Plural
1 présent de l'indicatif		**8 passé composé**	
emprunte	empruntons	ai emprunté	avons emprunté
empruntes	empruntez	as emprunté	avez emprunté
emprunte	empruntent	a emprunté	ont emprunté
2 imparfait de l'indicatif		**9 plus-que-parfait de l'indicatif**	
empruntais	empruntions	avais emprunté	avions emprunté
empruntais	empruntiez	avais emprunté	aviez emprunté
empruntait	empruntaient	avait emprunté	avaient emprunté
3 passé simple		**10 passé antérieur**	
empruntai	empruntâmes	eus emprunté	eûmes emprunté
empruntas	empruntâtes	eus emprunté	eûtes emprunté
emprunta	empruntèrent	eut emprunté	eurent emprunté
4 futur		**11 futur antérieur**	
emprunterai	emprunterons	aurai emprunté	aurons emprunté
emprunteras	emprunterez	auras emprunté	aurez emprunté
empruntera	emprunteront	aura emprunté	auront emprunté
5 conditionnel		**12 conditionnel passé**	
emprunterais	emprunterions	aurais emprunté	aurions emprunté
emprunterais	emprunteriez	aurais emprunté	auriez emprunté
emprunterait	emprunteraient	aurait emprunté	auraient emprunté
6 présent du subjonctif		**13 passé du subjonctif**	
emprunte	empruntions	aie emprunté	ayons emprunté
empruntes	empruntiez	aies emprunté	ayez emprunté
emprunte	empruntent	ait emprunté	aient emprunté
7 imparfait du subjonctif		**14 plus-que-parfait du subjonctif**	
empruntasse	empruntassions	eusse emprunté	eussions emprunté
empruntasses	empruntassiez	eusses emprunté	eussiez emprunté
empruntât	empruntassent	eût emprunté	eussent emprunté

Impératif
emprunte
empruntons
empruntez

Words related to this verb

emprunteur, emprunteuse   a person who makes a habit of borrowing
un emprunt   loan, borrowing
emprunter quelque chose à quelqu'un   to borrow something from someone
   Monsieur Leblanc a emprunté de l'argent à mon père   Mr. Leblanc borrowed some money
   from my father.
faire un emprunt pour payer ses dettes de jeu   to take out a loan to pay one's gambling debts

Don't confuse **emprunter** with **prêter** (*to lend*).

The Seven Simple Tenses		The Seven Compound Tenses	
Singular	Plural	Singular	Plural
1 présent de l'indicatif		**8 passé composé**	
encourage	encourageons	ai encouragé	avons encouragé
encourages	encouragez	as encouragé	avez encouragé
encourage	encouragent	a encouragé	ont encouragé
2 imparfait de l'indicatif		**9 plus-que-parfait de l'indicatif**	
encourageais	encouragions	avais encouragé	avions encouragé
encourageais	encouragiez	avais encouragé	aviez encouragé
encourageait	encourageaient	avait encouragé	avaient encouragé
3 passé simple		**10 passé antérieur**	
encourageai	encourageâmes	eus encouragé	eûmes encouragé
encourageas	encourageâtes	eus encouragé	eûtes encouragé
encouragea	encouragèrent	eut encouragé	eurent encouragé
4 futur		**11 futur antérieur**	
encouragerai	encouragerons	aurai encouragé	aurons encouragé
encourageras	encouragerez	auras encouragé	aurez encouragé
encouragera	encourageront	aura encouragé	auront encouragé
5 conditionnel		**12 conditionnel passé**	
encouragerais	encouragerions	aurais encouragé	aurions encouragé
encouragerais	encourageriez	aurais encouragé	auriez encouragé
encouragerait	encourageraient	aurait encouragé	auraient encouragé
6 présent du subjonctif		**13 passé du subjonctif**	
encourage	encouragions	aie encouragé	ayons encouragé
encourages	encouragiez	aies encouragé	ayez encouragé
encourage	encouragent	ait encouragé	aient encouragé
7 imparfait du subjonctif		**14 plus-que-parfait du subjonctif**	
encourageasse	encourageassions	eusse encouragé	eussions encouragé
encourageasses	encourageassiez	eusses encouragé	eussiez encouragé
encourageât	encourageassent	eût encouragé	eussent encouragé

Impératif
encourage
encourageons
encouragez

Words and expressions related to this verb

encourager qqn à faire qqch   to encourage someone to do something
encourageant, encourageante   encouraging;
   des paroles encourageantes   encouraging words
Bon courage!   Good luck! (Take heart!)

l'encouragement *m.*   encouragement
le découragement   discouragement
le courage   courage
décourager   to discourage
se décourager   to become discouraged

Consult the sections on verbs used in idiomatic expressions, verbs with propositions, and the list of over 1,100 verbs conjugated like model verbs in the back pages.

to run away, to slip away, to escape, to flee, to fly away

The Seven Simple Tenses		The Seven Compound Tenses	
Singular	Plural	Singular	Plural
1　présent de l'indicatif		8　passé composé	
m'enfuis	nous enfuyons	me suis enfui(e)	nous sommes enfui(e)s
t'enfuis	vous enfuyez	t'es enfui(e)	vous êtes enfui(e)(s)
s'enfuit	s'enfuient	s'est enfui(e)	se sont enfui(e)s
2　imparfait de l'indicatif		9　plus-que-parfait de l'indicatif	
m'enfuyais	nous enfuyions	m'étais enfui(e)	nous étions enfui(e)s
t'enfuyais	vous enfuyiez	t'étais enfui(e)	vous étiez enfui(e)(s)
s'enfuyait	s'enfuyaient	s'était enfui(e)	s'étaient enfui(e)s
3　passé simple		10　passé antérieur	
m'enfuis	nous enfuîmes	me fus enfui(e)	nous fûmes enfui(e)s
t'enfuis	vous enfuîtes	te fus enfui(e)	vous fûtes enfui(e)(s)
s'enfuit	s'enfuirent	se fut enfui(e)	se furent enfui(e)s
4　futur		11　futur antérieur	
m'enfuirai	nous enfuirons	me serai enfui(e)	nous serons enfui(e)s
t'enfuiras	vous enfuirez	te seras enfui(e)	vous serez enfui(e)(s)
s'enfuira	s'enfuiront	se sera enfui(e)	se seront enfui(e)s
5　conditionnel		12　conditionnel passé	
m'enfuirais	nous enfuirions	me serais enfui(e)	nous serions enfui(e)s
t'enfuirais	vous enfuiriez	te serais enfui(e)	vous seriez enfui(e)(s)
s'enfuirait	s'enfuiraient	se serait enfui(e)	se seraient enfui(e)s
6　présent du subjonctif		13　passé du subjonctif	
m'enfuie	nous enfuyions	me sois enfui(e)	nous soyons enfui(e)s
t'enfuies	vous enfuyiez	te sois enfui(e)	vous soyez enfui(e)(s)
s'enfuie	s'enfuient	se soit enfui(e)	se soient enfui(e)s
7　imparfait du subjonctif		14　plus-que-parfait du subjonctif	
m'enfuisse	nous enfuissions	me fusse enfui(e)	nous fussions enfui(e)s
t'enfuisses	vous enfuissiez	te fusses enfui(e)	vous fussiez enfui(e)(s)
s'enfuît	s'enfuissent	se fût enfui(e)	se fussent enfui(e)s

Impératif
enfuis-toi; ne t'enfuis pas
enfuyons-nous; ne nous enfuyons pas
enfuyez-vous; ne vous enfuyez pas

Common idiomatic expressions using this verb and words related to it

s'enfuir d'un endroit　to flee from a place
prendre la fuite　to take to flight
laid à faire fuir　ugly enough to make you run off
fuir　to flee

faire fuir　to put to flight
la fuite　flight
fuir devant un danger　to run away from danger
Le temps fuit　Time flies.

See also **fuir.**

Taking a trip? Check out the popular words, phrases, and expressions for travelers on pages 599–621.

to carry away, to take away, to remove

The Seven Simple Tenses		The Seven Compound Tenses	
Singular	Plural	Singular	Plural
1 présent de l'indicatif		**8 passé composé**	
enlève	enlevons	ai enlevé	avons enlevé
enlèves	enlevez	as enlevé	avez enlevé
enlève	enlèvent	a enlevé	ont enlevé
2 imparfait de l'indicatif		**9 plus-que-parfait de l'indicatif**	
enlevais	enlevions	avais enlevé	avons enlevé
enlevais	enleviez	avais enlevé	aviez enlevé
enlevait	enlevaient	avait enlevé	avaient enlevé
3 passé simple		**10 passé antérieur**	
enlevai	enlevâmes	eus enlevé	eûmes enlevé
enlevas	enlevâtes	eus enlevé	eûtes enlevé
enleva	enlevèrent	eut enlevé	eurent enlevé
4 futur		**11 futur antérieur**	
enlèverai	enlèverons	aurai enlevé	aurons enlevé
enlèveras	enlèverez	auras enlevé	aurez enlevé
enlèvera	enlèveront	aura enlevé	auront enlevé
5 conditionnel		**12 conditionnel passé**	
enlèverais	enlèverions	aurais enlevé	aurions enlevé
enlèverais	enlèveriez	aurais enlevé	auriez enlevé
enlèverait	enlèveraient	aurait enlevé	auraient enlevé
6 présent du subjonctif		**13 passé du subjonctif**	
enlève	enlevions	aie enlevé	ayons enlevé
enlèves	enleviez	aies enlevé	ayez enlevé
enlève	enlèvent	ait enlevé	aient enlevé
7 imparfait du subjonctif		**14 plus-que-parfait du subjonctif**	
enlevasse	enlevassions	eusse enlevé	eussions enlevé
enlevasses	enlevassiez	eusses enlevé	eussiez enlevé
enlevât	enlevassent	eût enlevé	eussent enlevé

Impératif
enlève
enlevons
enlevez

Sentences using this verb and words related to it

Madame Dubac est entrée dans sa maison. Elle a enlevé son chapeau, son manteau et ses gants. Puis, elle est allée directement au salon pour enlever une chaise et la mettre dans la salle à manger. Après cela, elle a enlevé les ordures.

enlever les ordures   to take the garbage out
un enlèvement   lifting, carrying off, removal
enlèvement d'un enfant   baby snatching, kidnapping
un enlevage   spurt (sports)

See also **élever** and **lever**.

Don't miss orthographically changing verbs on pages 554–556.

to bore, to annoy, to weary

The Seven Simple Tenses		The Seven Compound Tenses	
Singular	Plural	Singular	Plural
1 présent de l'indicatif		8 passé composé	
ennuie	ennuyons	ai ennuyé	avons ennuyé
ennuies	ennuyez	as ennuyé	avez ennuyé
ennuie	ennuient	a ennuyé	ont ennuyé
2 imparfait de l'indicatif		9 plus-que-parfait de l'indicatif	
ennuyais	ennuyions	avais ennuyé	avions ennuyé
ennuyais	ennuyiez	avais ennuyé	aviez ennuyé
ennuyait	ennuyaient	avait ennuyé	avaient ennuyé
3 passé simple		10 passé antérieur	
ennuyai	ennuyâmes	eus ennuyé	eûmes ennuyé
ennuyas	ennuyâtes	eus ennuyé	eûtes ennuyé
ennuya	ennuyèrent	eut ennuyé	eurent ennuyé
4 futur		11 futur antérieur	
ennuierai	ennuierons	aurai ennuyé	aurons ennuyé
ennuieras	ennuierez	auras ennuyé	aurez ennuyé
ennuiera	ennuieront	aura ennuyé	auront ennuyé
5 conditionnel		12 conditionnel passé	
ennuierais	ennuierions	aurais ennuyé	aurions ennuyé
ennuierais	ennuieriez	aurais ennuyé	auriez ennuyé
ennuierait	ennuieraient	aurait ennuyé	auraient ennuyé
6 présent du subjonctif		13 passé du subjonctif	
ennuie	ennuyions	aie ennuyé	ayons ennuyé
ennuies	ennuyiez	aies ennuyé	ayez ennuyé
ennuie	ennuient	ait ennuyé	aient ennuyé
7 imparfait du subjonctif		14 plus-que-parfait du subjonctif	
ennuyasse	ennuyassions	eusse ennuyé	eussions ennuyé
ennuyasses	ennuyassiez	eusses ennuyé	eussiez ennuyé
ennuyât	ennuyassent	eût ennuyé	eussent ennuyé

Impératif
ennuie
ennuyons
ennuyez

Sentences using this verb and words related to it
—**Est-ce que je vous ennuie?**
—**Oui, vous m'ennuyez. Allez-vous-en!**

un ennui   weariness, boredom, ennui
des ennuis   worries, troubles
ennuyeux, ennuyeuse   boring
s'ennuyer de quelqu'un   to miss someone

mourir d'ennui   to be bored to tears
s'ennuyer   to become bored, to get bored
Quel ennui!   What a nuisance!

Verbs ending in -*uyer* must change *y* to *i* before mute *e*.

The Seven Simple Tenses		The Seven Compound Tenses	
Singular	Plural	Singular	Plural

1 présent de l'indicatif
enseigne · enseignons
enseignes · enseignez
enseigne · enseignent

8 passé composé
ai enseigné · avons enseigné
as enseigné · avez enseigné
a enseigné · ont enseigné

2 imparfait de l'indicatif
enseignais · enseignions
enseignais · enseigniez
enseignait · enseignaient

9 plus-que-parfait de l'indicatif
avais enseigné · avions enseigné
avais enseigné · aviez enseigné
avait enseigné · avaient enseigné

3 passé simple
enseignai · enseignâmes
enseignas · enseignâtes
enseigna · enseignèrent

10 passé antérieur
eus enseigné · eûmes enseigné
eus enseigné · eûtes enseigné
eut enseigné · eurent enseigné

4 futur
enseignerai · enseignerons
enseigneras · enseignerez
enseignera · enseigneront

11 futur antérieur
aurai enseigné · aurons enseigné
auras enseigné · aurez enseigné
aura enseigné · auront enseigné

5 conditionnel
enseignerais · enseignerions
enseignerais · enseigneriez
enseignerait · enseigneraient

12 conditionnel passé
aurais enseigné · aurions enseigné
aurais enseigné · auriez enseigné
aurait enseigné · auraient enseigné

6 présent du subjonctif
enseigne · enseignions
enseignes · enseigniez
enseigne · enseignent

13 passé du subjonctif
aie enseigné · ayons enseigné
aies enseigné · ayez enseigné
ait enseigné · aient enseigné

7 imparfait du subjonctif
enseignasse · enseignassions
enseignasses · enseignassiez
enseignât · enseignassent

14 plus-que-parfait du subjonctif
eusse enseigné · eussions enseigné
eusses enseigné · eussiez enseigné
eût enseigné · eussent enseigné

Impératif
enseigne
enseignons
enseignez

Sentences using this verb and words and expressions related to it
J'enseigne aux élèves à lire en français. L'enseignement est une belle profession.

enseigner quelque chose à quelqu'un to teach something to someone
une enseigne sign; **une enseigne lumineuse** neon sign
les enseignements du Christ the teachings of Christ
l'enseignement *m.* teaching

l'enseignement à distance distance education
renseigner qqn de qqch to inform someone about something
se renseigner to get information, to inquire
un renseignement, des renseignements information

The subject pronouns are found on the page facing page 1.   **189**

entendre

Part pr. **entendant**   Part. passé **entendu**

to hear, to understand

The Seven Simple Tenses		The Seven Compound Tenses	
Singular	Plural	Singular	Plural
1 présent de l'indicatif		**8 passé composé**	
entends	entendons	ai entendu	avons entendu
entends	entendez	as entendu	avez entendu
entend	entendent	a entendu	ont entendu
2 imparfait de l'indicatif		**9 plus-que-parfait de l'indicatif**	
entendais	entendions	avais entendu	avions entendu
entendais	entendiez	avais entendu	aviez entendu
entendait	entendaient	avait entendu	avaient entendu
3 passé simple		**10 passé antérieur**	
entendis	entendîmes	eus entendu	eûmes entendu
entendis	entendîtes	eus entendu	eûtes entendu
entendit	entendirent	eut entendu	eurent entendu
4 futur		**11 futur antérieur**	
entendrai	entendrons	aurai entendu	aurons entendu
entendras	entendrez	auras entendu	aurez entendu
entendra	entendront	aura entendu	auront entendu
5 conditionnel		**12 conditionnel passé**	
entendrais	entendrions	aurais entendu	aurions entendu
entendrais	entendriez	aurais entendu	auriez entendu
entendrait	entendraient	aurait entendu	auraient entendu
6 présent du subjonctif		**13 passé du subjonctif**	
entende	entendions	aie entendu	ayons entendu
entendes	entendiez	aies entendu	ayez entendu
entende	entendent	ait entendu	aient entendu
7 imparfait du subjonctif		**14 plus-que-parfait du subjonctif**	
entendisse	entendissions	eusse entendu	eussions entendu
entendisses	entendissiez	eusses entendu	eussiez entendu
entendît	entendissent	eût entendu	eussent entendu

Impératif
entends
entendons
entendez

Sentences using this verb and words and expressions related to it
   —**As-tu entendu quelque chose?**
   —**Non, chéri, je n'ai rien entendu.**
   —**J'ai entendu un bruit . . . de la cuisine . . . silence . . . je l'entends encore.**
   —**Oh! Un cambrioleur!**

un entendement   understanding
sous-entendre   to imply
un sous-entendu   innuendo
une entente   understanding
une mésentente   disagreement
Je m'entends bien avec ma soeur   I get along
   very well with my sister.

bien entendu   of course
C'est entendu!   It's understood! Agreed!
s'entendre avec qqn   to get along with
   someone, to understand each other
s'entendre à merveille   to get along with each
   other marvelously

190

The Seven Simple Tenses		The Seven Compound Tenses

Singular	Plural	Singular	Plural

1   présent de l'indicatif

enterre	enterrons		
enterres	enterrez		
enterre	enterrent		

8   passé composé

ai enterré	avons enterré
as enterré	avez enterré
a enterré	ont enterré

2   imparfait de l'indicatif

enterrais	enterrions
enterrais	enterriez
enterrait	enterraient

9   plus-que-parfait de l'indicatif

avais enterré	avions enterré
avais enterré	aviez enterré
avait enterré	avaient enterré

3   passé simple

enterrai	enterrâmes
enterras	enterrâtes
enterra	enterrèrent

10   passé antérieur

eus enterré	eûmes enterré
eus enterré	eûtes enterré
eut enterré	eurent enterré

4   futur

enterrerai	enterrerons
enterreras	enterrerez
enterrera	enterreront

11   futur antérieur

aurai enterré	aurons enterré
auras enterré	aurez enterré
aura enterré	auront enterré

5   conditionnel

enterrerais	enterrerions
enterrerais	enterreriez
enterrerait	enterreraient

12   conditionnel passé

aurais enterré	aurions enterré
aurais enterré	auriez enterré
aurait enterré	auraient enterré

6   présent du subjonctif

enterre	enterrions
enterres	enterriez
enterre	enterrent

13   passé du subjonctif

aie enterré	ayons enterré
aies enterré	ayez enterré
ait enterré	aient enterré

7   imparfait du subjonctif

enterrasse	enterrassions
enterrasses	enterrassiez
enterrât	enterrassent

14   plus-que-parfait du subjonctif

eusse enterré	eussions enterré
eusses enterré	eussiez enterré
eût enterré	eussent enterré

Impératif
enterre
enterrons
enterrez

Words and expressions related to this verb
enterrer un cadavre   to bury a corpse
s'enterrer   to bury oneself
enterrer une affaire   to abandon a matter
enterrer sa vie de garçon   to hold a
   bachelor's party (for a man about to be
   married)
la terre   earth, soil

enterrer une chose   to bury something, to
   forget about something, to shelve something
un enterrement   burial, interment
s'enterrer dans un endroit   to bury oneself in
   a place, to isolate oneself from the rest of the
   world

Soak up some verbs used in weather expressions on pages 557 and 558.

The subject pronouns are found on the page facing page 1.   **191**

entreprendre

Part. pr. **entreprenant**   Part. passé **entrepris**

to undertake, to engage upon

The Seven Simple Tenses		The Seven Compound Tenses	
Singular	Plural	Singular	Plural
1 présent de l'indicatif		**8 passé composé**	
entreprends	entreprenons	ai entrepris	avons entrepris
entreprends	entreprenez	as entrepris	avez entrepris
entreprend	entreprennent	a entrepris	ont entrepris
2 imparfait de l'indicatif		**9 plus-que-parfait de l'indicatif**	
entreprenais	entreprenions	avais entrepris	avions entrepris
entreprenais	entrepreniez	avais entrepris	aviez entrepris
entreprenait	entreprenaient	avait entrepris	avaient entrepris
3 passé simple		**10 passé antérieur**	
entrepris	entreprîmes	eus entrepris	eûmes entrepris
entrepris	entreprîtes	eus entrepris	eûtes entrepris
entreprit	entreprirent	eut entrepris	eurent entrepris
4 futur		**11 futur antérieur**	
entreprendrai	entreprendrons	aurai entrepris	aurons entrepris
entreprendras	entreprendrez	auras entrepris	aurez entrepris
entreprendra	entreprendront	aura entrepris	auront entrepris
5 conditionnel		**12 conditionnel passé**	
entreprendrais	entreprendrions	aurais entrepris	aurions entrepris
entreprendrais	entreprendriez	aurais entrepris	auriez entrepris
entreprendrait	entreprendraient	aurait entrepris	auraient entrepris
6 présent du subjonctif		**13 passé du subjonctif**	
entreprenne	entreprenions	aie entrepris	ayons entrepris
entreprennes	entrepreniez	aies entrepris	ayez entrepris
entreprenne	entreprennent	ait entrepris	aient entrepris
7 imparfait du subjonctif		**14 plus-que-parfait du subjonctif**	
entreprisse	entreprissions	eusse entrepris	eussions entrepris
entreprisses	entreprissiez	eusses entrepris	eussiez entrepris
entreprît	entreprissent	eût entrepris	eussent entrepris

Impératif
entreprends
entreprenons
entreprenez

Words and expressions related to this verb

entreprendre de faire qqch   to undertake to do something

avoir un esprit entreprenant   to be bold, daring, enterprising

une entreprise   enterprise; **une entreprise rémunératrice**   profitable enterprise

entreprenant, entreprenante   enterprising

un entrepreneur, une entrepreneuse   contractor

une entreprise de déménagement   moving company

See also **apprendre, comprendre, se méprendre, prendre, reprendre,** and **surprendre.**

Consult the sections on verbs used in idiomatic expressions, verbs with prepositions, and the list of over 1,100 verbs conjugated like model verbs in the back pages.

to enter, to come in, to go in

The Seven Simple Tenses		The Seven Compound Tenses	
Singular	Plural	Singular	Plural
1 présent de l'indicatif		8 passé composé	
entre	**entrons**	**suis entré(e)**	**sommes entré(e)s**
entres	**entrez**	**es entré(e)**	**êtes entré(e)(s)**
entre	**entrent**	**est entré(e)**	**sont entré(e)s**
2 imparfait de l'indicatif		9 plus-que-parfait de l'indicatif	
entrais	**entrions**	**étais entré(e)**	**étions entré(e)s**
entrais	**entriez**	**étais entré(e)**	**étiez entré(e)(s)**
entrait	**entraient**	**était entré(e)**	**étaient entré(e)s**
3 passé simple		10 passé antérieur	
entrai	**entrâmes**	**fus entré(e)**	**fûmes entré(e)s**
entras	**entrâtes**	**fus entré(e)**	**fûtes entré(e)(s)**
entra	**entrèrent**	**fut entré(e)**	**furent entré(e)s**
4 futur		11 futur antérieur	
entrerai	**entrerons**	**serai entré(e)**	**serons entré(e)s**
entreras	**entrerez**	**seras entré(e)**	**serez entré(e)(s)**
entrera	**entreront**	**sera entré(e)**	**seront entré(e)s**
5 conditionnel		12 conditionnel passé	
entrerais	**entrerions**	**serais entré(e)**	**serions entré(e)s**
entrerais	**entreriez**	**serais entré(e)**	**seriez entré(e)(s)**
entrerait	**entreraient**	**serait entré(e)**	**seraient entré(e)s**
6 présent du subjonctif		13 passé du subjonctif	
entre	**entrions**	**sois entré(e)**	**soyons entré(e)s**
entres	**entriez**	**sois entré(e)**	**soyez entré(e)(s)**
entre	**entrent**	**soit entré(e)**	**soient entré(e)s**
7 imparfait du subjonctif		14 plus-que-parfait du subjonctif	
entrasse	**entrassions**	**fusse entré(e)**	**fussions entré(e)s**
entrasses	**entrassiez**	**fusses entré(e)**	**fussiez entré(e)(s)**
entrât	**entrassent**	**fût entré(e)**	**fussent entré(e)s**

Impératif
entre
entrons
entrez

Sentences using this verb and words and expressions related to it

Mes parents veulent acheter une nouvelle maison. Nous sommes allés voir quelques maisons à vendre. Nous avons vu une jolie maison et nous y sommes entrés. Ma mère est entrée dans la cuisine pour regarder. Mon père est entré dans le garage pour regarder. Ma soeur est entrée dans la salle à manger et moi, je suis entré dans la salle de bains pour voir s'il y avait une douche.

l'entrée *f.* entrance
entrer par la fenêtre to enter through the window
entrer dans + noun to enter (into) + noun
une entrée gratuite free admission

See also **rentrer**.

Entrez donc! Do come in!
Entrons voir Let's go in and see.
entrer des données to enter/input data (computer)

s'envoler

Part. pr. **s'envolant**   Part. passé **envolé**

to fly off, to fly away, to take flight, to take wing (birds), to take off (airplane)

The Seven Simple Tenses		The Seven Compound Tenses	
Singular	Plural	Singular	Plural
1 présent de l'indicatif		**8 passé composé**	
m'envole	**nous envolons**	**me suis envolé(e)**	**nous sommes envolé(e)s**
t'envoles	**vous envolez**	**t'es envolé(e)**	**vous êtes envolé(e)(s)**
s'envole	**s'envolent**	**s'est envolé(e)**	**se sont envolé(e)s**
2 imparfait de l'indicatif		**9 plus-que-parfait de l'indicatif**	
m'envolais	**nous envolions**	**m'étais envolé(e)**	**nous étions envolé(e)s**
t'envolais	**vous envoliez**	**t'étais envolé(e)**	**vous étiez envolé(e)(s)**
s'envolait	**s'envolaient**	**s'était envolé(e)**	**s'étaient envolé(e)s**
3 passé simple		**10 passé antérieur**	
m'envolai	**nous envolâmes**	**me fus envolé(e)**	**nous fûmes envolé(e)s**
t'envolas	**vous envolâtes**	**te fus envolé(e)**	**vous fûtes envolé(e)(s)**
s'envola	**s'envolèrent**	**se fut envolé(e)**	**se furent envolé(e)s**
4 futur		**11 futur antérieur**	
m'envolerai	**nous envolerons**	**me serai envolé(e)**	**nous serons envolé(e)s**
t'envoleras	**vous envolerez**	**te seras envolé(e)**	**vous serez envolé(e)(s)**
s'envolera	**s'envoleront**	**se sera envolé(e)**	**se seront envolé(e)s**
5 conditionnel		**12 conditionnel passé**	
m'envolerais	**nous envolerions**	**me serais envolé(e)**	**nous serions envolé(e)s**
t'envolerais	**vous envoleriez**	**te serais envolé(e)**	**vous seriez envolé(e)(s)**
s'envolerait	**s'envoleraient**	**se serait envolé(e)**	**se seraient envolé(e)s**
6 présent du subjonctif		**13 passé du subjonctif**	
m'envole	**nous envolions**	**me sois envolé(e)**	**nous soyons envolé(e)s**
t'envoles	**vous envoliez**	**te sois envolé(e)**	**vous soyez envolé(e)(s)**
s'envole	**s'envolent**	**se soit envolé(e)**	**se soient envolé(e)s**
7 imparfait du subjonctif		**14 plus-que-parfait du subjonctif**	
m'envolasse	**nous envolassions**	**me fusse envolé(e)**	**nous fussions envolé(e)s**
t'envolasses	**vous envolassiez**	**te fusses envolé(e)**	**vous fussiez envolé(e)(s)**
s'envolât	**s'envolassent**	**se fût envolé(e)**	**se fussent envolé(e)s**

Impératif
envole-toi; ne t'envole pas
envolons-nous; ne nous envolons pas
envolez-vous; ne vous envolez pas

Words and expressions related to this verb
une envolée   flying off
un envol   flight of a bird; take-off of an airplane
voler   to fly, to steal

le vol   flight, theft
Les paroles s'envolent   Spoken words fly away.

See also **voler.**

Going away? Don't forget to check out the practical situations for travelers on pages 568–598.

The Seven Simple Tenses		The Seven Compound Tenses	
Singular	Plural	Singular	Plural
1 présent de l'indicatif		8 passé composé	
envoie	envoyons	ai envoyé	avons envoyé
envoies	envoyez	as envoyé	avez envoyé
envoie	envoient	a envoyé	ont envoyé
2 imparfait de l'indicatif		9 plus-que-parfait de l'indicatif	
envoyais	envoyions	avais envoyé	avions envoyé
envoyais	envoyiez	avais envoyé	aviez envoyé
envoyait	envoyaient	avait envoyé	avaient envoyé
3 passé simple		10 passé antérieur	
envoyai	envoyâmes	eus envoyé	eûmes envoyé
envoyas	envoyâtes	eus envoyé	eûtes envoyé
envoya	envoyèrent	eut envoyé	eurent envoyé
4 futur		11 futur antérieur	
enverrai	enverrons	aurai envoyé	aurons envoyé
enverras	enverrez	auras envoyé	aurez envoyé
enverra	enverront	aura envoyé	auront envoyé
5 conditionnel		12 conditionnel passé	
enverrais	enverrions	aurais envoyé	aurions envoyé
enverrais	enverriez	aurais envoyé	auriez envoyé
enverrait	enverraient	aurait envoyé	auraient envoyé
6 présent du subjonctif		13 passé du subjonctif	
envoie	envoyions	aie envoyé	ayons envoyé
envoies	envoyiez	aies envoyé	ayez envoyé
envoie	envoient	ait envoyé	aient envoyé
7 imparfait du subjonctif		14 plus-que-parfait du subjonctif	
envoyasse	envoyassions	eusse envoyé	eussions envoyé
envoyasses	envoyassiez	eusses envoyé	eussiez envoyé
envoyât	envoyassent	eût envoyé	eussent envoyé

Impératif
envoie
envoyons
envoyez

Sentences using this verb and words related to it
   **Hier j'ai envoyé une lettre à des amis en France. Demain j'enverrai une lettre à mes amis
en Italie. J'enverrais bien une lettre en Chine mais je ne connais personne dans ce pays.**

envoyer chercher   to send for; **Mon père a
   envoyé chercher le docteur parce que mon
   petit frère est malade.**
un envoi   envoi (poetry), sending

envoyeur, envoyeuse   sender
renvoyer   to send away (back), to discharge
   someone, to sack someone
le renvoi   return, call forwarding

Verbs ending in -*oyer* must change *y* to *i* before mute *e*.

The subject pronouns are found on the page facing page 1.
195

épouser

Part. pr. **épousant**   Part. passé **épousé**

to marry, to wed

The Seven Simple Tenses		The Seven Compound Tenses	
Singular	Plural	Singular	Plural
1 présent de l'indicatif		8 passé composé	
épouse	épousons	ai épousé	avons épousé
épouses	épousez	as épousé	avez épousé
épouse	épousent	a épousé	ont épousé
2 imparfait de l'indicatif		9 plus-que-parfait de l'indicatif	
épousais	épousions	avais épousé	avions épousé
épousais	épousiez	avais épousé	aviez épousé
épousait	épousaient	avait épousé	avaient épousé
3 passé simple		10 passé antérieur	
épousai	épousâmes	eus épousé	eûmes épousé
épousas	épousâtes	eus épousé	eûtes épousé
épousa	épousèrent	eut épousé	eurent épousé
4 futur		11 futur antérieur	
épouserai	épouserons	aurai épousé	aurons épousé
épouseras	épouserez	auras épousé	aurez épousé
épousera	épouseront	aura épousé	auront épousé
5 conditionnel		12 conditionnel passé	
épouserais	épouserions	aurais épousé	aurions épousé
épouserais	épouseriez	aurais épousé	auriez épousé
épouserait	épouseraient	aurait épousé	auraient épousé
6 présent du subjonctif		13 passé du subjonctif	
épouse	épousions	aie épousé	ayons épousé
épouses	épousiez	aies épousé	ayez épousé
épouse	épousent	ait épousé	aient épousé
7 imparfait du subjonctif		14 plus-que-parfait du subjonctif	
épousasse	épousassions	eusse épousé	eussions épousé
épousasses	épousassiez	eusses épousé	eussiez épousé
épousât	épousassent	eût épousé	eussent épousé

Impératif
épouse
épousons
épousez

Sentences using this verb and words related to it

J'ai trois frères. Le premier a épousé une jolie jeune fille française. Le deuxième a épousé une belle jeune fille italienne, et le troisième a épousé une jolie fille espagnole. Elles sont très intelligentes.

un époux husband, spouse	**épouser une grosse fortune** to marry into money
une épouse wife, spouse	**se marier avec quelqu'un** to get married to
les nouveaux mariés the newlyweds	someone

Thinking of eloping? Check out the popular words, phrases, and expressions for travelers on pages 599–621.

to try, to test, to put to the test, to feel, to experience

The Seven Simple Tenses		The Seven Compound Tenses	
Singular	Plural	Singular	Plural
1 présent de l'indicatif		8 passé composé	
éprouve	éprouvons	ai éprouvé	avons éprouvé
éprouves	éprouvez	as éprouvé	avez éprouvé
éprouve	éprouvent	a éprouvé	ont éprouvé
2 imparfait de l'indicatif		9 plus-que-parfait de l'indicatif	
éprouvais	éprouvions	avais éprouvé	avions éprouvé
éprouvais	éprouviez	avais éprouvé	aviez éprouvé
éprouvait	éprouvaient	avait éprouvé	avaient éprouvé
3 passé simple		10 passé antérieur	
éprouvai	éprouvâmes	eus éprouvé	eûmes éprouvé
éprouvas	éprouvâtes	eus éprouvé	eûtes éprouvé
éprouva	éprouvèrent	eut éprouvé	eurent éprouvé
4 futur		11 futur antérieur	
éprouverai	éprouverons	aurai éprouvé	aurons éprouvé
éprouveras	éprouverez	auras éprouvé	aurez éprouvé
éprouvera	éprouveront	aura éprouvé	auront éprouvé
5 conditionnel		12 conditionnel passé	
éprouverais	éprouverions	aurais éprouvé	aurions éprouvé
éprouverais	éprouveriez	aurais éprouvé	auriez éprouvé
éprouverait	éprouveraient	aurait éprouvé	auraient éprouvé
6 présent du subjonctif		13 passé du subjonctif	
éprouve	éprouvions	aie éprouvé	ayons éprouvé
éprouves	éprouviez	aies éprouvé	ayez éprouvé
éprouve	éprouvent	ait éprouvé	aient éprouvé
7 imparfait du subjonctif		14 plus-que-parfait du subjonctif	
éprouvasse	éprouvassions	eusse éprouvé	eussions éprouvé
éprouvasses	éprouvassiez	eusses éprouvé	eussiez éprouvé
éprouvât	éprouvassent	eût éprouvé	eussent éprouvé

Impératif
éprouve
éprouvons
éprouvez

Common idiomatic expressions using this verb and words related to it

éprouver des doutes   to have doubts, to feel doubtful

éprouver qqn   to put someone to the test

mettre qqn à l'épreuve   to put someone to the test

éprouver un regret   to feel a regret

éprouver de la sympathie pour qqn   to feel sympathy for someone

mettre à l'épreuve   to put to the test

une épreuve   test, proof, page proof

une épreuve écrite   written test

une épreuve orale   oral test

éprouver de la honte   to experience shame

How are you doing? Find out with the verb drills and tests with answers explained on pages 622–673.

espérer

Part. pr. **espérant**   Part. passé **espéré**

to hope

The Seven Simple Tenses		The Seven Compound Tenses	
Singular	Plural	Singular	Plural
1 présent de l'indicatif		**8 passé composé**	
espère	espérons	ai espéré	avons espéré
espères	espérez	as espéré	avez espéré
espère	espèrent	a espéré	ont espéré
2 imparfait de l'indicatif		**9 plus-que-parfait de l'indicatif**	
espérais	espérions	avais espéré	avions espéré
espérais	espériez	avais espéré	aviez espéré
espérait	espéraient	avait espéré	avaient espéré
3 passé simple		**10 passé antérieur**	
espérai	espérâmes	eus espéré	eûmes espéré
espéras	espérâtes	eus espéré	eûtes espéré
espéra	espérèrent	eut espéré	eurent espéré
4 futur		**11 futur antérieur**	
espérerai	espérerons	aurai espéré	aurons espéré
espéreras	espérerez	auras espéré	aurez espéré
espérera	espéreront	aura espéré	auront espéré
5 conditionnel		**12 conditionnel passé**	
espérerais	espérerions	aurais espéré	aurions espéré
espérerais	espéreriez	aurais espéré	auriez espéré
espérerait	espéreraient	aurait espéré	auraient espéré
6 présent du subjonctif		**13 passé du subjonctif**	
espère	espérions	aie espéré	ayons espéré
espères	espériez	aies espéré	ayez espéré
espère	espèrent	ait espéré	aient espéré
7 imparfait du subjonctif		**14 plus-que-parfait du subjonctif**	
espérasse	espérassions	eusse espéré	eussions espéré
espérasses	espérassiez	eusses espéré	eussiez espéré
espérât	espérassent	eût espéré	eussent espéré

Impératif
espère
espérons
espérez

Sentences using this verb and words and expressions related to it

J'espère que Paul viendra mais je n'espère pas que son frère vienne.

l'espérance *f.* hope, expectation
plein d'espérance hopeful, full of hope
l'espoir *m.* hope
avoir bon espoir de réussir to have good hopes of succeeding
désespérer de to despair of; **se désespérer** to be in despair
le désespoir despair; **un désespoir d'amour** disappointed love

We hope that you will turn to pages 530–542 to learn more idiomatic expressions that contain verbs.

198

to try, to try on

The Seven Simple Tenses		The Seven Compound Tenses	
Singular	Plural	Singular	Plural

1 présent de l'indicatif

		8 passé composé	
essaye	essayons	ai essayé	avons essayé
essayes	essayez	as essayé	avez essayé
essaye	essayent	a essayé	ont essayé

2 imparfait de l'indicatif

		9 plus-que-parfait de l'indicatif	
essayais	essayions	avais essayé	avions essayé
essayais	essayiez	avais essayé	aviez essayé
essayait	essayaient	avait essayé	avaient essayé

3 passé simple

		10 passé antérieur	
essayai	essayâmes	eus essayé	eûmes essayé
essayas	essayâtes	eus essayé	eûtes essayé
essaya	essayèrent	eut essayé	eurent essayé

4 futur

		11 futur antérieur	
essayerai	essayerons	aurai essayé	aurons essayé
essayeras	essayerez	auras essayé	aurez essayé
essayera	essayeront	aura essayé	auront essayé

5 conditionnel

		12 conditionnel passé	
essayerais	essayerions	aurais essayé	aurions essayé
essayerais	essayeriez	aurais essayé	auriez essayé
essayerait	essayeraient	aurait essayé	auraient essayé

6 présent du subjonctif

		13 passé du subjonctif	
essaye	essayions	aie essayé	ayons essayé
essayes	essayiez	aies essayé	ayez essayé
essaye	essayent	ait essayé	aient essayé

7 imparfait du subjonctif

		14 plus-que-parfait du subjonctif	
essayasse	essayassions	eusse essayé	eussions essayé
essayasses	essayassiez	eusses essayé	eussiez essayé
essayât	essayassent	eût essayé	eussent essayé

Impératif
essaye
essayons
essayez

Sentences using this verb and words related to it

Marcel a essayé d'écrire un essai sur la vie des animaux sauvages mais il n'a pas pu réussir à écrire une seule phrase. Alors, il est allé dans la chambre de son grand frère pour travailler avec lui.

un essai essay		**une salle/un salon d'essayage** fitting room
essayiste essayist		**essayeur, essayeuse** fitter (clothing)
essayer de faire qqch to try to do something		**essayage** *m.* fitting (clothing)

Verbs ending in *-ayer* may change *y* to *i* before mute *e* or may keep *y*.

essuyer

Part. pr. **essuyant**   Part. passé **essuyé**

to wipe

The Seven Simple Tenses		The Seven Compound Tenses	
Singular	Plural	Singular	Plural
1 présent de l'indicatif		**8 passé composé**	
essuie	essuyons	ai essuyé	avons essuyé
essuies	essuyez	as essuyé	avez essuyé
essuie	essuient	a essuyé	ont essuyé
2 imparfait de l'indicatif		**9 plus-que-parfait de l'indicatif**	
essuyais	essuyions	avais essuyé	avions essuyé
essuyais	essuyiez	avais essuyé	aviez essuyé
essuyait	essuyaient	avait essuyé	avaient essuyé
3 passé simple		**10 passé antérieur**	
essuyai	essuyâmes	eus essuyé	eûmes essuyé
essuyas	essuyâtes	eus essuyé	eûtes essuyé
essuya	essuyèrent	eut essuyé	eurent essuyé
4 futur		**11 futur antérieur**	
essuierai	essuierons	aurai essuyé	aurons essuyé
essuieras	essuierez	auras essuyé	aurez essuyé
essuiera	essuieront	aura essuyé	auront essuyé
5 conditionnel		**12 conditionnel passé**	
essuierais	essuierions	aurais essuyé	aurions essuyé
essuierais	essuieriez	aurais essuyé	auriez essuyé
essuierait	essuieraient	aurait essuyé	auraient essuyé
6 présent du subjonctif		**13 passé du subjonctif**	
essuie	essuyions	aie essuyé	ayons essuyé
essuies	essuyiez	aies essuyé	ayez essuyé
essuie	essuient	ait essuyé	aient essuyé
7 imparfait du subjonctif		**14 plus-que-parfait du subjonctif**	
essuyasse	essuyassions	eusse essuyé	eussions essuyé
essuyasses	essuyassiez	eusses essuyé	eussiez essuyé
essuyât	essuyassent	eût essuyé	eussent essuyé

Impératif
essuie
essuyons
essuyez

Words and expressions related to this verb
un essuie-mains   hand towel
un essuie-glace   windshield wiper
l'essuyage *m.*   wiping
un essuie-verres   glass cloth
s'essuyer   to wipe oneself
s'essuyer le front   to wipe one's brow

Verbs ending in *-uyer* must change *y* to *i* before mute *e*.

Soak up some verbs used in weather expressions on pages 557 and 558.

to establish, to set up, to draw up

The Seven Simple Tenses		The Seven Compound Tenses	
Singular	Plural	Singular	Plural
1 présent de l'indicatif		**8 passé composé**	
établis	**établissons**	**ai établi**	**avons établi**
établis	**établissez**	**as établi**	**avez établi**
établit	**établissent**	**a établi**	**ont établi**
2 imparfait de l'indicatif		**9 plus-que-parfait de l'indicatif**	
établissais	**établissions**	**avais établi**	**avions établi**
établissais	**établissiez**	**avais établi**	**aviez établi**
établissait	**établissaient**	**avait établi**	**avaient établi**
3 passé simple		**10 passé antérieur**	
établis	**établîmes**	**eus établi**	**eûmes établi**
établis	**établîtes**	**eus établi**	**eûtes établi**
établit	**établirent**	**eut établi**	**eurent établi**
4 futur		**11 futur antérieur**	
établirai	**établirons**	**aurai établi**	**aurons établi**
établiras	**établirez**	**auras établi**	**aurez établi**
établira	**établiront**	**aura établi**	**auront établi**
5 conditionnel		**12 conditionnel passé**	
établirais	**établirions**	**aurais établi**	**aurions établi**
établirais	**établiriez**	**aurais établi**	**auriez établi**
établirait	**établiraient**	**aurait établi**	**auraient établi**
6 présent du subjonctif		**13 passé du subjonctif**	
établisse	**établissions**	**aie établi**	**ayons établi**
établisses	**établissiez**	**aies établi**	**ayez établi**
établisse	**établissent**	**ait établi**	**aient établi**
7 imparfait du subjonctif		**14 plus-que-parfait du subjonctif**	
établisse	**établissions**	**eusse établi**	**eussions établi**
établisses	**établissiez**	**eusses établi**	**eussiez établi**
établît	**établissent**	**eût établi**	**eussent établi**

Impératif
établis
établissons
établissez

Words related to this verb
rétablir   to reestablish, to restore
s'établir   to settle down, to start a business
se rétablir   to recover one's health
un établissement   establishment
Bon rétablissement!   Get well soon!

Grammar putting you in a tense mood? Review the definitions of basic grammatical terms with examples on pages 674–688.

éteindre

Part. pr. **éteignant**   Part. passé **éteint**

to extinguish, to shut down (computer)

The Seven Simple Tenses		The Seven Compound Tenses	
Singular	Plural	Singular	Plural
1 présent de l'indicatif		**8 passé composé**	
éteins	éteignons	ai éteint	avons éteint
éteins	éteignez	as éteint	avez éteint
éteint	éteignent	a éteint	ont éteint
2 imparfait de l'indicatif		**9 plus-que-parfait de l'indicatif**	
éteignais	éteignions	avais éteint	avions éteint
éteignais	éteigniez	avais éteint	aviez éteint
éteignait	éteignaient	avait éteint	avaient éteint
3 passé simple		**10 passé antérieur**	
éteignis	éteignîmes	eus éteint	eûmes éteint
éteignis	éteignîtes	eus éteint	eûtes éteint
éteignit	éteignirent	eut éteint	eurent éteint
4 futur		**11 futur antérieur**	
éteindrai	éteindrons	aurai éteint	aurons éteint
éteindras	éteindrez	auras éteint	aurez éteint
éteindra	éteindront	aura éteint	auront éteint
5 conditionnel		**12 conditionnel passé**	
éteindrais	éteindrions	aurais éteint	aurions éteint
éteindrais	éteindriez	aurais éteint	auriez éteint
éteindrait	éteindraient	aurait éteint	auraient éteint
6 présent du subjonctif		**13 passé du subjonctif**	
éteigne	éteignions	aie éteint	ayons éteint
éteignes	éteigniez	aies éteint	ayez éteint
éteigne	éteignent	ait éteint	aient éteint
7 imparfait du subjonctif		**14 plus-que-parfait du subjonctif**	
éteignisse	éteignissions	eusse éteint	eussions éteint
éteignisses	éteignissiez	eusses éteint	eussiez éteint
éteignît	éteignissent	eût éteint	eussent éteint

Impératif
éteins
éteignons
éteignez

Sentences using this verb and words and expressions related to it

Il est minuit. Je vais me coucher. Je dois me lever tôt le matin pour aller à l'école. J'éteins la lumière. Bonne nuit!

éteint, éteinte extinct, extinguished	**éteindre le feu** to put out the fire
un éteignoir extinguisher, snuffer	**éteindre la lumière** to turn off the light
s'éteindre to flicker out, to die out, to die	**un extincteur** fire extinguisher

N'oublie pas d'enregistrer (sauver) le document que tu as créé avant d'éteindre ton ordinateur Don't forget to save the document you created before shutting down your computer.

Get acquainted with what preposition goes with what verb on pages 543–553.

202

to stretch oneself, to stretch out, to lie down

The Seven Simple Tenses		The Seven Compound Tenses	
Singular	Plural	Singular	Plural
1 présent de l'indicatif		**8 passé composé**	
m'étends	**nous étendons**	**me suis étendu(e)**	**nous sommes étendu(e)s**
t'étends	**vous étendez**	**t'es étendu(e)**	**vous êtes étendu(e)(s)**
s'étend	**s'étendent**	**s'est étendu(e)**	**se sont étendu(e)s**
2 imparfait de l'indicatif		**9 plus-que-parfait de l'indicatif**	
m'étendais	**nous étendions**	**m'étais étendu(e)**	**nous étions étendu(e)s**
t'étendais	**vous étendiez**	**t'étais étendu(e)**	**vous étiez étendu(e)(s)**
s'étendait	**s'étendaient**	**s'était étendu(e)**	**s'étaient étendu(e)s**
3 passé simple		**10 passé antérieur**	
m'étendis	**nous étendîmes**	**me fus étendu(e)**	**nous fûmes étendu(e)s**
t'étendis	**vous étendîtes**	**te fus étendu(e)**	**vous fûtes étendu(e)(s)**
s'étendit	**s'étendirent**	**se fut étendu(e)**	**se furent étendu(e)s**
4 futur		**11 futur antérieur**	
m'étendrai	**nous étendrons**	**me serai étendu(e)**	**nous serons étendu(e)s**
t'étendras	**vous étendrez**	**te seras étendu(e)**	**vous serez étendu(e)(s)**
s'étendra	**s'étendront**	**se sera étendu(e)**	**se seront étendu(e)s**
5 conditionnel		**12 conditionnel passé**	
m'étendrais	**nous étendrions**	**me serais étendu(e)**	**nous serions étendu(e)s**
t'étendrais	**vous étendriez**	**te serais étendu(e)**	**vous seriez étendu(e)(s)**
s'étendrait	**s'étendraient**	**se serait étendu(e)**	**se seraient étendu(e)s**
6 présent du subjonctif		**13 passé du subjonctif**	
m'étende	**nous étendions**	**me sois étendu(e)**	**nous soyons étendu(e)s**
t'étendes	**vous étendiez**	**te sois étendu(e)**	**vous soyez étendu(e)(s)**
s'étende	**s'étendent**	**se soit étendu(e)**	**se soient étendu(e)s**
7 imparfait du subjonctif		**14 plus-que-parfait du subjonctif**	
m'étendisse	**nous étendissions**	**me fusse étendu(e)**	**nous fussions étendu(e)s**
t'étendisses	**vous étendissiez**	**te fusses étendu(e)**	**vous fussiez étendu(e)(s)**
s'étendît	**s'étendissent**	**se fût étendu(e)**	**se fussent étendu(e)s**

Impératif
étends-toi; ne t'étends pas
étendons-nous; ne nous étendons pas
étendez-vous; ne vous étendez pas

Sentences using this verb and words and expressions related to it
    Ma mère était si fatiguée quand elle est rentrée à la maison après avoir fait du shopping, qu'elle est allée directement au lit et elle s'est étendue.

étendre le linge to hang out the wash   **l'étendue** *f.* area, extent
étendre d'eau to water down   **s'étendre** to stretch
s'étendre sur qqch to dwell on something

Get acquainted with what preposition goes with what verb on pages 543–553.

étonner

Part. pr. **étonnant**   Part. passé **étonné**

to amaze, to astonish, to stun, to surprise

The Seven Simple Tenses		The Seven Compound Tenses	
Singular	Plural	Singular	Plural
1 présent de l'indicatif		**8 passé composé**	
étonne	étonnons	ai étonné	avons étonné
étonnes	étonnez	as étonné	avez étonné
étonne	étonnent	a étonné	ont étonné
2 imparfait de l'indicatif		**9 plus-que-parfait de l'indicatif**	
étonnais	étonnions	avais étonné	avions étonné
étonnais	étonniez	avais étonné	aviez étonné
étonnait	étonnaient	avait étonné	avaient étonné
3 passé simple		**10 passé antérieur**	
étonnai	étonnâmes	eus étonné	eûmes étonné
étonnas	étonnâtes	eus étonné	eûtes étonné
étonna	étonnèrent	eut étonné	eurent étonné
4 futur		**11 futur antérieur**	
étonnerai	étonnerons	aurai étonné	aurons étonné
étonneras	étonnerez	auras étonné	aurez étonné
étonnera	étonneront	aura étonné	auront étonné
5 conditionnel		**12 conditionnel passé**	
étonnerais	étonnerions	aurais étonné	aurions étonné
étonnerais	étonneriez	aurais étonné	auriez étonné
étonnerait	étonneraient	aurait étonné	auraient étonné
6 présent du subjonctif		**13 passé du subjonctif**	
étonne	étonnions	aie étonné	ayons étonné
étonnes	étonniez	aies étonné	ayez étonné
étonne	étonnent	ait étonné	aient étonné
7 imparfait du subjonctif		**14 plus-que-parfait du subjonctif**	
étonnasse	étonnassions	eusse étonné	eussions étonné
étonnasses	étonnassiez	eusses étonné	eussiez étonné
étonnât	étonnassent	eût étonné	eussent étonné

Impératif
étonne
étonnons
étonnez

Words related to this verb
étonnant, étonnante   astonishing
C'est bien étonnant!   It's quite astonishing!
l'étonnement *m.*   astonishment, amazement
s'étonner de   to be astonished at

Cela m'étonne!   That astonishes me!
Cela ne m'étonne pas!   That does not surprise me!

Don't be caught by surprise. Try the verb drills and tests with answers explained on pages 622–673.

to daze, to stun, to make dizzy, to deafen, to bewilder

The Seven Simple Tenses		The Seven Compound Tenses	
Singular	Plural	Singular	Plural
1 présent de l'indicatif		8 passé composé	
étourdis	étourdissons	ai étourdi	avons étourdi
étourdis	étourdissez	as étourdi	avez étourdi
étourdit	étourdissent	a étourdi	ont étourdi
2 imparfait de l'indicatif		9 plus-que-parfait de l'indicatif	
étourdissais	étourdissions	avais étourdi	avions étourdi
étourdissais	étourdissiez	avais étourdi	aviez étourdi
étourdissait	étourdissaient	avait étourdi	avaient étourdi
3 passé simple		10 passé antérieur	
étourdis	étourdîmes	eus étourdi	eûmes étourdi
étourdis	étourdîtes	eus étourdi	eûtes étourdi
étourdit	étourdirent	eut étourdi	eurent étourdi
4 futur		11 futur antérieur	
étourdirai	étourdirons	aurai étourdi	aurons étourdi
étourdiras	étourdirez	auras étourdi	aurez étourdi
étourdira	étourdiront	aura étourdi	auront étourdi
5 conditionnel		12 conditionnel passé	
étourdirais	étourdirions	aurais étourdi	aurions étourdi
étourdirais	étourdiriez	aurais étourdi	auriez étourdi
étourdirait	étourdiraient	aurait étourdi	auraient étourdi
6 présent du subjonctif		13 passé du subjonctif	
étourdisse	étourdissions	aie étourdi	ayons étourdi
étourdisses	étourdissiez	aies étourdi	ayez étourdi
étourdisse	étourdissent	ait étourdi	aient étourdi
7 imparfait du subjonctif		14 plus-que-parfait du subjonctif	
étourdisse	étourdissions	eusse étourdi	eussions étourdi
étourdisses	étourdissiez	eusses étourdi	eussiez étourdi
étourdît	étourdissent	eût étourdi	eussent étourdi

Impératif
étourdis
étourdissons
étourdissez

Words and expressions related to this verb
s'étourdir   to lose one's senses in some kind
  of outlet
une étourderie   thoughtlessness, carelessness
un étourdissement   giddiness; temporary loss
  of one's senses

étourdiment   thoughtlessly
étourdi, étourdie   thoughtless, giddy
par étourderie   by an oversight
étourdissant, étourdissante   staggering,
  deafening

Are you bewildered by the Subjunctive? Read pages 560–565.

to be

The Seven Simple Tenses		The Seven Compound Tenses	
Singular	Plural	Singular	Plural
1 présent de l'indicatif		8 passé composé	
suis	**sommes**	**ai été**	**avons été**
es	**êtes**	**as été**	**avez été**
est	**sont**	**a été**	**ont été**
2 imparfait de l'indicatif		9 plus-que-parfait de l'indicatif	
étais	**étions**	**avais été**	**avions été**
étais	**étiez**	**avais été**	**aviez été**
était	**étaient**	**avait été**	**avaient été**
3 passé simple		10 passé antérieur	
fus	**fûmes**	**eus été**	**eûmes été**
fus	**fûtes**	**eus été**	**eûtes été**
fut	**furent**	**eut été**	**eurent été**
4 futur		11 futur antérieur	
serai	**serons**	**aurai été**	**aurons été**
seras	**serez**	**auras été**	**aurez été**
sera	**seront**	**aura été**	**auront été**
5 conditionnel		12 conditionnel passé	
serais	**serions**	**aurais été**	**aurions été**
serais	**seriez**	**aurais été**	**auriez été**
serait	**seraient**	**aurait été**	**auraient été**
6 présent du subjonctif		13 passé du subjonctif	
sois	**soyons**	**aie été**	**ayons été**
sois	**soyez**	**aies été**	**ayez été**
soit	**soient**	**ait été**	**aient été**
7 imparfait du subjonctif		14 plus-que-parfait du subjonctif	
fusse	**fussions**	**eusse été**	**eussions été**
fusses	**fussiez**	**eusses été**	**eussiez été**
fût	**fussent**	**eût été**	**eussent été**

Impératif
sois
soyons
soyez

Common idiomatic expressions using this verb
être en train de + inf.   to be in the act of + pres. part., to be in the process of, to be busy + pres.
   part.;
   Mon père est en train d'écrire une lettre à mes grands-parents.

être à l'heure   to be on time
être à temps   to be in time
être pressé(e)   to be in a hurry
un être humain   human being
le bien-être   well-being

Je suis à vous   I am at your service.
Je suis d'avis que . . .   I am of the opinion
   that . . .
être ou ne pas être   to be or not to be

For more idiomatic expressions using this verb, consult pages 535 and 536.

206

The Seven Simple Tenses		The Seven Compound Tenses	
Singular	Plural	Singular	Plural
1 présent de l'indicatif		**8 passé composé**	
étudie	étudions	ai étudié	avons étudié
étudies	étudiez	as étudié	avez étudié
étudie	étudient	a étudié	ont étudié
2 imparfait de l'indicatif		**9 plus-que-parfait de l'indicatif**	
étudiais	étudiions	avais étudié	avions étudié
étudiais	étudiiez	avais étudié	aviez étudié
étudiait	étudiaient	avait étudié	avaient étudié
3 passé simple		**10 passé antérieur**	
étudiai	étudiâmes	eus étudié	eûmes étudié
étudias	étudiâtes	eus étudié	eûtes étudié
étudia	étudièrent	eut étudié	eurent étudié
4 futur		**11 futur antérieur**	
étudierai	étudierons	aurai étudié	aurons étudié
étudieras	étudierez	auras étudié	aurez étudié
étudiera	étudieront	aura étudié	auront étudié
5 conditionnel		**12 conditionnel passé**	
étudierais	étudierions	aurais étudié	aurions étudié
étudierais	étudieriez	aurais étudié	auriez étudié
étudierait	étudieraient	aurait étudié	auraient étudié
6 présent du subjonctif		**13 passé du subjonctif**	
étudie	étudiions	aie étudié	ayons étudié
étudies	étudiiez	aies étudié	ayez étudié
étudie	étudient	ait étudié	aient étudié
7 imparfait du subjonctif		**14 plus-que-parfait du subjonctif**	
étudiasse	étudiassions	eusse étudié	eussions étudié
étudiasses	étudiassiez	eusses étudié	eussiez étudié
étudiât	étudiassent	eût étudié	eussent étudié

Impératif
étudie
étudions
étudiez

Sentences using this verb and words related to it

Je connais une jeune fille qui étudie le piano depuis deux ans. Je connais un garçon qui étudie ses leçons à fond. Je connais un astronome qui étudie les étoiles dans le ciel depuis dix ans.

étudier à fond   to study thoroughly
un étudiant, une étudiante   student
l'étude *f.*   study; **les études**   studies
une salle d'études   study hall
faire ses études   to study, to go to school
à l'étude   under consideration, under study

s'étudier   to analyze oneself
étudier qqch de près   to study something closely
s'amuser au lieu d'étudier   to have a good time instead of studying

The subject pronouns are found on the page facing page 1.   **207**

évaluer

Part. pr. **évaluant**　　Part. passé **évalué**

to evaluate, to appraise, to assess, to estimate

The Seven Simple Tenses		The Seven Compound Tenses	
Singular	Plural	Singular	Plural
1　présent de l'indicatif		8　passé composé	
évalue	évaluons	ai évalué	avons évalué
évalues	évaluez	as évalué	avez évalué
évalue	évaluent	a évalué	ont évalué
2　imparfait de l'indicatif		9　plus-que-parfait de l'indicatif	
évaluais	évaluions	avais évalué	avions évalué
évaluais	évaluiez	avais évalué	aviez évalué
évaluait	évaluaient	avait évalué	avaient évalué
3　passé simple		10　passé antérieur	
évaluai	évaluâmes	eus évalué	eûmes évalué
évaluas	évaluâtes	eus évalué	eûtes évalué
évalua	évaluèrent	eut évalué	eurent évalué
4　futur		11　futur antérieur	
évaluerai	évaluerons	aurai évalué	aurons évalué
évalueras	évaluerez	auras évalué	aurez évalué
évaluera	évalueront	aura évalué	auront évalué
5　conditionnel		12　conditionnel passé	
évaluerais	évaluerions	aurais évalué	aurions évalué
évaluerais	évalueriez	aurais évalué	auriez évalué
évaluerait	évalueraient	aurait évalué	auraient évalué
6　présent du subjonctif		13　passé du subjonctif	
évalue	évaluions	aie évalué	ayons évalué
évalues	évaluiez	aies évalué	ayez évalué
évalue	évaluent	ait évalué	aient évalué
7　imparfait du subjonctif		14　plus-que-parfait du subjonctif	
évaluasse	évaluassions	eusse évalué	eussions évalué
évaluasses	évaluassiez	eusses évalué	eussiez évalué
évaluât	évaluassent	eût évalué	eussent évalué

Impératif
évalue
évaluons
évaluez

Words and expressions related to this verb

une évaluation　evaluation, estimate, assessment

de valeur　valuable, of value

valable　valid

mettre en valeur　to emphasize, to enhance

faire évaluer qqch par un expert　to have something appraised by an expert

valablement　validly

valeureusement　valorously

la valeur　value, valor

Consult the sections on verbs used in idiomatic expressions, verbs with prepositions, and the list of over 1,100 verbs conjugated like model verbs in the back pages.

to faint, to lose consciousness, to swoon, to vanish

The Seven Simple Tenses		The Seven Compound Tenses	
Singular	Plural	Singular	Plural
1 présent de l'indicatif		8 passé composé	
m'évanouis	**nous évanouissons**	**me suis évanoui(e)**	**nous sommes évanoui(e)s**
t'évanouis	**vous évanouissez**	**t'es évanoui(e)**	**vous êtes évanoui(e)(s)**
s'évanouit	**s'évanouissent**	**s'est évanoui(e)**	**se sont évanoui(e)s**
2 imparfait de l'indicatif		9 plus-que-parfait de l'indicatif	
m'évanouissais	**nous évanouissions**	**m'étais évanoui(e)**	**nous étions évanoui(e)s**
t'évanouissais	**vous évanouissiez**	**t'étais évanoui(e)**	**vous étiez évanoui(e)(s)**
s'évanouissait	**s'évanouissaient**	**s'était évanoui(e)**	**s'étaient évanoui(e)s**
3 passé simple		10 passé antérieur	
m'évanouis	**nous évanouîmes**	**me fus évanoui(e)**	**nous fûmes évanoui(e)s**
t'évanouis	**vous évanouîtes**	**te fus évanoui(e)**	**vous fûtes évanoui(e)(s)**
s'évanouit	**s'évanouirent**	**se fut évanoui(e)**	**se furent évanoui(e)s**
4 futur		11 futur antérieur	
m'évanouirai	**nous évanouirons**	**me serai évanoui(e)**	**nous serons évanoui(e)s**
t'évanouiras	**vous évanouirez**	**te seras évanoui(e)**	**vous serez évanoui(e)(s)**
s'évanouira	**s'évanouiront**	**se sera évanoui(e)**	**se seront évanoui(e)s**
5 conditionnel		12 conditionnel passé	
m'évanouirais	**nous évanouirions**	**me serais évanoui(e)**	**nous serions évanoui(e)s**
t'évanouirais	**vous évanouiriez**	**te serais évanoui(e)**	**vous seriez évanoui(e)(s)**
s'évanouirait	**s'évanouiraient**	**se serait évanoui(e)**	**se seraient évanoui(e)s**
6 présent du subjonctif		13 passé du subjonctif	
m'évanouisse	**nous évanouissions**	**me sois évanoui(e)**	**nous soyons évanoui(e)s**
t'évanouisses	**vous évanouissiez**	**te sois évanoui(e)**	**vous soyez évanoui(e)(s)**
s'évanouisse	**s'évanouissent**	**se soit évanoui(e)**	**se soient évanoui(e)s**
7 imparfait du subjonctif		14 plus-que-parfait du subjonctif	
m'évanouisse	**nous évanouissions**	**me fusse évanoui(e)**	**nous fussions évanoui(e)s**
t'évanouisses	**vous évanouissiez**	**te fusses évanoui(e)**	**vous fussiez évanoui(e)(s)**
s'évanouît	**s'évanouissent**	**se fût évanoui(e)**	**se fussent évanoui(e)s**

Impératif
évanouis-toi; ne t'évanouis pas
évanouissons-nous; ne nous évanouissons pas
évanouissez-vous; ne vous évanouissez pas

Words and expressions related to this verb
un évanouissement faint, fading
un rêve évanoui vanished dream
tomber évanoui, évanouie to faint, to pass out

évanoui, évanouie unconscious, fainted, in a faint; vanished
revenir d'un évanouissement to come out of a faint

Grammar putting you in a tense mood? Review the definitions of basic grammatical terms with examples on pages 674–688.

The Seven Simple Tenses		The Seven Compound Tenses	
Singular	Plural	Singular	Plural
1 présent de l'indicatif		**8 passé composé**	
évite	évitons	ai évité	avons évité
évites	évitez	as évité	avez évité
évite	évitent	a évité	ont évité
2 imparfait de l'indicatif		**9 plus-que-parfait de l'indicatif**	
évitais	évitions	avais évité	avions évité
évitais	évitiez	avais évité	aviez évité
évitait	évitaient	avait évité	avaient évité
3 passé simple		**10 passé antérieur**	
évitai	évitâmes	eus évité	eûmes évité
évitas	évitâtes	eus évité	eûtes évité
évita	évitèrent	eut évité	eurent évité
4 futur		**11 futur antérieur**	
éviterai	éviterons	aurai évité	aurons évité
éviteras	éviterez	auras évité	aurez évité
évitera	éviteront	aura évité	auront évité
5 conditionnel		**12 conditionnel passé**	
éviterais	éviterions	aurais évité	aurions évité
éviterais	éviteriez	aurais évité	auriez évité
éviterait	éviteraient	aurait évité	auraient évité
6 présent du subjonctif		**13 passé du subjonctif**	
évite	évitions	aie évité	ayons évité
évites	évitiez	aies évité	ayez évité
évite	évitent	ait évité	aient évité
7 imparfait du subjonctif		**14 plus-que-parfait du subjonctif**	
évitasse	évitassions	eusse évité	eussions évité
évitasses	évitassiez	eusses évité	eussiez évité
évitât	évitassent	eût évité	eussent évité

Impératif
évite
évitons
évitez

Words and expressions related to this verb
éviter de faire qqch   to avoid doing something
éviter à qqn la peine de faire qqch   to spare someone the trouble of doing something
évitable   avoidable
inévitable   inevitable, unavoidable
inévitablement   inevitably, unavoidably

Get acquainted with what preposition goes with what verb on pages 543–553.

The Seven Simple Tenses		The Seven Compound Tenses	
Singular	Plural	Singular	Plural

1 présent de l'indicatif		8 passé composé	
excuse	excusons	ai excusé	avons excusé
excuses	excusez	as excusé	avez excusé
excuse	excusent	a excusé	ont excusé

2 imparfait de l'indicatif		9 plus-que-parfait de l'indicatif	
excusais	excusions	avais excusé	avions excusé
excusais	excusiez	avais excusé	aviez excusé
excusait	excusaient	avait excusé	avaient excusé

3 passé simple		10 passé antérieur	
excusai	excusâmes	eus excusé	eûmes excusé
excusas	excusâtes	eus excusé	eûtes excusé
excusa	excusèrent	eut excusé	eurent excusé

4 futur		11 futur antérieur	
excuserai	excuserons	aurai excusé	aurons excusé
excuseras	excuserez	auras excusé	aurez excusé
excusera	excuseront	aura excusé	auront excusé

5 conditionnel		12 conditionnel passé	
excuserais	excuserions	aurais excusé	aurions excusé
excuserais	excuseriez	aurais excusé	auriez excusé
excuserait	excuseraient	aurait excusé	auraient excusé

6 présent du subjonctif		13 passé du subjonctif	
excuse	excusions	aie excusé	ayons excusé
excuses	excusiez	aies excusé	ayez excusé
excuse	excusent	ait excusé	aient excusé

7 imparfait du subjonctif		14 plus-que-parfait du subjonctif	
excusasse	excusassions	eusse excusé	eussions excusé
excusasses	excusassiez	eusses excusé	eussiez excusé
excusât	excusassent	eût excusé	eussent excusé

Impératif
excuse
excusons
excusez

Words and expressions related to this verb

excuser de   to excuse from (for)

excuser qqn de faire qqch   to excuse someone from doing something; to excuse someone's doing something

se faire excuser   to ask to be excused

une excuse   excuse

faire ses excuses à qqn pour qqch   to apologize to someone for something

Mille excuses!   Excuse me! (a thousand pardons)

See also s'**excuser.**

Consult the sections on verbs used in idiomatic expressions, verbs with prepositions, and the list of over 1,100 verbs conjugated like model verbs in the back pages.

to excuse oneself, to apologize

The Seven Simple Tenses		The Seven Compound Tenses	
Singular	Plural	Singular	Plural
1 présent de l'indicatif		8 passé composé	
m'excuse	nous excusons	me suis excusé(e)	nous sommes excusé(e)s
t'excuses	vous excusez	t'es excusé(e)	vous êtes excusé(e)(s)
s'excuse	s'excusent	s'est excusé(e)	se sont excusé(e)s
2 imparfait de l'indicatif		9 plus-que-parfait de l'indicatif	
m'excusais	nous excusions	m'étais excusé(e)	nous étions excusé(e)s
t'excusais	vous excusiez	t'étais excusé(e)	vous étiez excusé(e)(s)
s'excusait	s'excusaient	s'était excusé(e)	s'étaient excusé(e)s
3 passé simple		10 passé antérieur	
m'excusai	nous excusâmes	me fus excusé(e)	nous fûmes excusé(e)s
t'excusas	vous excusâtes	te fus excusé(e)	vous fûtes excusé(e)(s)
s'excusa	s'excusèrent	se fut excusé(e)	se furent excusé(e)s
4 futur		11 futur antérieur	
m'excuserai	nous excuserons	me serai excusé(e)	nous serons excusé(e)s
t'excuseras	vous excuserez	te seras excusé(e)	vous serez excusé(e)(s)
s'excusera	s'excuseront	se sera excusé(e)	se seront excusé(e)s
5 conditionnel		12 conditionnel passé	
m'excuserais	nous excuserions	me serais excusé(e)	nous serions excusé(e)s
t'excuserais	vous excuseriez	te serais excusé(e)	vous seriez excusé(e)(s)
s'excuserait	s'excuseraient	se serait excusé(e)	se seraient excusé(e)s
6 présent du subjonctif		13 passé du subjonctif	
m'excuse	nous excusions	me sois excusé(e)	nous soyons excusé(e)s
t'excuses	vous excusiez	te sois excusé(e)	vous soyez excusé(e)(s)
s'excuse	s'excusent	se soit excusé(e)	se soient excusé(e)s
7 imparfait du subjonctif		14 plus-que-parfait du subjonctif	
m'excusasse	nous excusassions	me fusse excusé(e)	nous fussions excusé(e)s
t'excusasses	vous excusassiez	te fusses excusé(e)	vous fussiez excusé(e)(s)
s'excusât	s'excusassent	se fût excusé(e)	se fussent excusé(e)s

Impératif
excuse-toi; ne t'excuse pas
excusons-nous; ne nous excusons pas
excusez-vous; ne vous excusez pas

Sentences using this verb and words and expressions related to it

L'élève:	**Je m'excuse, madame. Excusez-moi. Je m'excuse de vous déranger.**
	Est-ce que vous m'excusez? Est-ce que je vous dérange?
La maîtresse:	**Oui, je t'excuse. Non, tu ne me déranges pas. Que veux-tu?**
L'élève:	**Est-ce que je peux quitter la salle de classe pour aller aux toilettes?**
La maîtresse:	**Oui, vas-y.**

s'excuser de   to apologize for
Veuillez m'excuser   Please (Be good enough to) excuse me.
Qui s'excuse s'accuse   A guilty conscience needs no accuser.

Enjoy more verbs in French proverbs and sayings on page 559.

212

to demand, to require

The Seven Simple Tenses		The Seven Compound Tenses	
Singular	Plural	Singular	Plural
1 présent de l'indicatif		**8 passé composé**	
exige	exigeons	ai exigé	avons exigé
exiges	exigez	as exigé	avez exigé
exige	exigent	a exigé	ont exigé
2 imparfait de l'indicatif		**9 plus-que-parfait de l'indicatif**	
exigeais	exigions	avais exigé	avions exigé
exigeais	exigiez	avais exigé	aviez exigé
exigeait	exigeaient	avait exigé	avaient exigé
3 passé simple		**10 passé antérieur**	
exigeai	exigeâmes	eus exigé	eûmes exigé
exigeas	exigeâtes	eus exigé	eûtes exigé
exigea	exigèrent	eut exigé	eurent exigé
4 futur		**11 futur antérieur**	
exigerai	exigerons	aurai exigé	aurons exigé
exigeras	exigerez	auras exigé	aurez exigé
exigera	exigeront	aura exigé	auront exigé
5 conditionnel		**12 conditionnel passé**	
exigerais	exigerions	aurais exigé	aurions exigé
exigerais	exigeriez	aurais exigé	auriez exigé
exigerait	exigeraient	aurait exigé	auraient exigé
6 présent du subjonctif		**13 passé du subjonctif**	
exige	exigions	aie exigé	ayons exigé
exiges	exigiez	aies exigé	ayez exigé
exige	exigent	ait exigé	aient exigé
7 imparfait du subjonctif		**14 plus-que-parfait du subjonctif**	
exigeasse	exigeassions	eusse exigé	eussions exigé
exigeasses	exigeassiez	eusses exigé	eussiez exigé
exigeât	exigeassent	eût exigé	eussent exigé

Impératif
exige
exigeons
exigez

Sentences using this verb and words related to it

La maîtresse de français: **Paul, viens ici. Ta composition est pleine de fautes.**
J'exige que tu la refasses. Rends-la-moi dans dix minutes.
L'élève: **Ce n'est pas de ma faute, madame. C'est mon père qui l'a écrite.**
Dois-je la refaire?

exigeant, exigeante exacting   **exiger des soins attentifs** to demand great care
l'exigence *f.* exigency   **les exigences** requirements

Soak up some verbs used in weather expressions on pages 557 and 558.

expliquer

Part. pr. **expliquant**   Part. passé **expliqué**

to explain

The Seven Simple Tenses		The Seven Compound Tenses	
Singular	Plural	Singular	Plural
1 présent de l'indicatif		**8 passé composé**	
explique	expliquons	ai expliqué	avons expliqué
expliques	expliquez	as expliqué	avez expliqué
explique	expliquent	a expliqué	ont expliqué
2 imparfait de l'indicatif		**9 plus-que-parfait de l'indicatif**	
expliquais	expliquions	avais expliqué	avions expliqué
expliquais	expliquiez	avais expliqué	aviez expliqué
expliquait	expliquaient	avait expliqué	avaient expliqué
3 passé simple		**10 passé antérieur**	
expliquai	expliquâmes	eus expliqué	eûmes expliqué
expliquas	expliquâtes	eus expliqué	eûtes expliqué
expliqua	expliquèrent	eut expliqué	eurent expliqué
4 futur		**11 futur antérieur**	
expliquerai	expliquerons	aurai expliqué	aurons expliqué
expliqueras	expliquerez	auras expliqué	aurez expliqué
expliquera	expliqueront	aura expliqué	auront expliqué
5 conditionnel		**12 conditionnel passé**	
expliquerais	expliquerions	aurais expliqué	aurions expliqué
expliquerais	expliqueriez	aurais expliqué	auriez expliqué
expliquerait	expliqueraient	aurait expliqué	auraient expliqué
6 présent du subjonctif		**13 passé du subjonctif**	
explique	expliquions	aie expliqué	ayons expliqué
expliques	expliquiez	aies expliqué	ayez expliqué
explique	expliquent	ait expliqué	aient expliqué
7 imparfait du subjonctif		**14 plus-que-parfait du subjonctif**	
expliquasse	expliquassions	eusse expliqué	eussions expliqué
expliquasses	expliquassiez	eusses expliqué	eussiez expliqué
expliquât	expliquassent	eût expliqué	eussent expliqué

Impératif
explique
expliquons
expliquez

Words related to this verb
explicite explicit
explicitement explicitly
l'explication *f.* explanation
une explication de texte interpretation,
  critical analysis of a text

explicable explainable
explicatif, explicative explanatory
s'expliciter to be explicit

Note the difference in meaning in the following two sentences. See p. xxii (b).

J'ai étudié la leçon que le professeur avait expliquée I studied the lesson that the teacher had explained.

J'avais étudié la leçon que le professeur a expliquée I had studied the lesson that the teacher explained.

The Seven Simple Tenses		The Seven Compound Tenses	
Singular	Plural	Singular	Plural
1 présent de l'indicatif		8 passé composé	
exprime	**exprimons**	**ai exprimé**	**avons exprimé**
exprimes	**exprimez**	**as exprimé**	**avez exprimé**
exprime	**expriment**	**a exprimé**	**ont exprimé**
2 imparfait de l'indicatif		9 plus-que-parfait de l'indicatif	
exprimais	**exprimions**	**avais exprimé**	**avions exprimé**
exprimais	**exprimiez**	**avais exprimé**	**aviez exprimé**
exprimait	**exprimaient**	**avait exprimé**	**avaient exprimé**
3 passé simple		10 passé antérieur	
exprimai	**exprimâmes**	**eus exprimé**	**eûmes exprimé**
exprimas	**exprimâtes**	**eus exprimé**	**eûtes exprimé**
exprima	**exprimèrent**	**eut exprimé**	**eurent exprimé**
4 futur		11 futur antérieur	
exprimerai	**exprimerons**	**aurai exprimé**	**aurons exprimé**
exprimeras	**exprimerez**	**auras exprimé**	**aurez exprimé**
exprimera	**exprimeront**	**aura exprimé**	**auront exprimé**
5 conditionnel		12 conditionnel passé	
exprimerais	**exprimerions**	**aurais exprimé**	**aurions exprimé**
exprimerais	**exprimeriez**	**aurais exprimé**	**auriez exprimé**
exprimerait	**exprimeraient**	**aurait exprimé**	**auraient exprimé**
6 présent du subjonctif		13 passé du subjonctif	
exprime	**exprimions**	**aie exprimé**	**ayons exprimé**
exprimes	**exprimiez**	**aies exprimé**	**ayez exprimé**
exprime	**expriment**	**ait exprimé**	**aient exprimé**
7 imparfait du subjonctif		14 plus-que-parfait du subjonctif	
exprimasse	**exprimassions**	**eusse exprimé**	**eussions exprimé**
exprimasses	**exprimassiez**	**eusses exprimé**	**eussiez exprimé**
exprimât	**exprimassent**	**eût exprimé**	**eussent exprimé**

Impératif
exprime
exprimons
exprimez

Words and expressions related to this verb

exprimer ses voeux   to express (convey) one's wishes

exprimable   expressible

une expression   expression; **expression des sentiments**   expression of feelings

Closing of letter:

Agréez, Monsieur (Madame), l'expression de mes sentiments distingués   Sincerely

s'exprimer   to express oneself

s'exprimer par gestes   to express oneself with gestures

Want to learn more idiomatic expressions that contain verbs? Look at pages 530–542.

se fâcher
Part. pr. **se fâchant**   Part. passé **fâché(e)(s)**

to become angry, to get angry

The Seven Simple Tenses		The Seven Compound Tenses	
Singular	Plural	Singular	Plural
1 présent de l'indicatif		8 passé composé	
me fâche	**nous fâchons**	**me suis fâché(e)**	**nous sommes fâché(e)s**
te fâches	**vous fâchez**	**t'es fâché(e)**	**vous êtes fâché(e)(s)**
se fâche	**se fâchent**	**s'est fâché(e)**	**se sont fâché(e)s**
2 imparfait de l'indicatif		9 plus-que-parfait de l'indicatif	
me fâchais	**nous fâchions**	**m'étais fâché(e)**	**nous étions fâché(e)s**
te fâchais	**vous fâchiez**	**t'étais fâché(e)**	**vous étiez fâché(e)(s)**
se fâchait	**se fâchaient**	**s'était fâché(e)**	**s'étaient fâché(e)s**
3 passé simple		10 passé antérieur	
me fâchai	**nous fâchâmes**	**me fus fâché(e)**	**nous fûmes fâché(e)s**
te fâchas	**vous fâchâtes**	**te fus fâché(e)**	**vous fûtes fâché(e)(s)**
se fâcha	**se fâchèrent**	**se fut fâché(e)**	**se furent fâché(e)s**
4 futur		11 futur antérieur	
me fâcherai	**nous fâcherons**	**me serai fâché(e)**	**nous serons fâché(e)s**
te fâcheras	**vous fâcherez**	**te seras fâché(e)**	**vous serez fâché(e)(s)**
se fâchera	**se fâcheront**	**se sera fâché(e)**	**se seront fâché(e)s**
5 conditionnel		12 conditionnel passé	
me fâcherais	**nous fâcherions**	**me serais fâché(e)**	**nous serions fâché(e)s**
te fâcherais	**vous fâcheriez**	**te serais fâché(e)**	**vous seriez fâché(e)(s)**
se fâcherait	**se fâcheraient**	**se serait fâché(e)**	**se seraient fâché(e)s**
6 présent du subjonctif		13 passé du subjonctif	
me fâche	**nous fâchions**	**me sois fâché(e)**	**nous soyons fâché(e)s**
te fâches	**vous fâchiez**	**te sois fâché(e)**	**vous soyez fâché(e)(s)**
se fâche	**se fâchent**	**se soit fâché(e)**	**se soient fâché(e)s**
7 imparfait du subjonctif		14 plus-que-parfait du subjonctif	
me fâchasse	**nous fâchassions**	**me fusse fâché(e)**	**nous fussions fâché(e)s**
te fâchasses	**vous fâchassiez**	**te fusses fâché(e)**	**vous fussiez fâché(e)(s)**
se fâchât	**se fâchassent**	**se fût fâché(e)**	**se fussent fâché(e)s**

Impératif
fâche-toi; ne te fâche pas
fâchons-nous; ne nous fâchons pas
fâchez-vous; ne vous fâchez pas

Words and expressions related to this verb
fâcher qqn   to anger someone, to offend
   someone
se fâcher contre qqn   to become angry at
   someone

une fâcherie   tiff, quarrel
C'est fâcheux!   It's a nuisance! It's annoying!
fâcheusement   awkwardly, unfortunately
se fâcher tout rouge   to turn red with anger

How are you doing? Find out with the verb drills and tests with answers explained on pages
622–673.

to fail, to almost (do something)

The Seven Simple Tenses		The Seven Compound Tenses	
Singular	Plural	Singular	Plural
1 présent de l'indicatif		**8 passé composé**	
faux	**faillons**	**ai failli**	**avons failli**
faux	**faillez**	**as failli**	**avez failli**
faut	**faillent**	**a failli**	**ont failli**
2 imparfait de l'indicatif		**9 plus-que-parfait de l'indicatif**	
faillais	**faillions**	**avais failli**	**avions failli**
faillais	**failliez**	**avais failli**	**aviez failli**
faillait	**faillaient**	**avait failli**	**avaient failli**
3 passé simple		**10 passé antérieur**	
faillis	**faillîmes**	**eus failli**	**eûmes failli**
faillis	**faillîtes**	**eus failli**	**eûtes failli**
faillit	**faillirent**	**eut failli**	**eurent failli**
4 futur		**11 futur antérieur**	
faillirai or faudrai	**faillirons or faudrons**	**aurai failli**	**aurons failli**
failliras or faudras	**faillirez or faudrez**	**auras failli**	**aurez failli**
faillira or faudra	**failliront or faudront**	**aura failli**	**auront failli**
5 conditionnel		**12 conditionnel passé**	
faillirais or faudrais	**faillirions or faudrions**	**aurais failli**	**aurions failli**
faillirais or faudrais	**failliriez or faudriez**	**aurais failli**	**auriez failli**
faillirait or faudrait	**failliraient or faudraient**	**aurait failli**	**auraient failli**
6 présent du subjonctif		**13 passé du subjonctif**	
faille	**faillions**	**aie failli**	**ayons failli**
failles	**failliez**	**aies failli**	**ayez failli**
faille	**faillent**	**ait failli**	**aient failli**
7 imparfait du subjonctif		**14 plus-que-parfait du subjonctif**	
faillisse	**faillissions**	**eusse failli**	**eussions failli**
faillisses	**faillissiez**	**eusses failli**	**eussiez failli**
faillît	**faillissent**	**eût failli**	**eussent failli**

Impératif
[not in use]

Words and expressions related to this verb

la faillite   bankruptcy, failure
failli, faillie   bankrupt
J'ai failli tomber   I almost fell.
faire faillite   to go bankrupt

défaillir   to weaken, to faint
défaillant, défaillante   feeble
une défaillance   faint (swoon)
être en faillite   to be bankrupt

The conjugated forms of this verb are used most of the time in the **passé simple** and compound tenses. The other tenses are rarely used.

to do, to make

The Seven Simple Tenses		The Seven Compound Tenses	
Singular	Plural	Singular	Plural
1 présent de l'indicatif		8 passé composé	
fais	faisons	ai fait	avons fait
fais	faites	as fait	avez fait
fait	font	a fait	ont fait
2 imparfait de l'indicatif		9 plus-que-parfait de l'indicatif	
faisais	faisions	avais fait	avions fait
faisais	faisiez	avais fait	aviez fait
faisait	faisaient	avait fait	avaient fait
3 passé simple		10 passé antérieur	
fis	fîmes	eus fait	eûmes fait
fis	fîtes	eus fait	eûtes fait
fit	firent	eut fait	eurent fait
4 futur		11 futur antérieur	
ferai	ferons	aurai fait	aurons fait
feras	ferez	auras fait	aurez fait
fera	feront	aura fait	auront fait
5 conditionnel		12 conditionnel passé	
ferais	ferions	aurais fait	aurions fait
ferais	feriez	aurais fait	auriez fait
ferait	feraient	aurait fait	auraient fait
6 présent du subjonctif		13 passé du subjonctif	
fasse	fassions	aie fait	ayons fait
fasses	fassiez	aies fait	ayez fait
fasse	fassent	ait fait	aient fait
7 imparfait du subjonctif		14 plus-que-parfait du subjonctif	
fisse	fissions	eusse fait	eussions fait
fisses	fissiez	eusses fait	eussiez fait
fît	fissent	eût fait	eussent fait

Impératif
fais
faisons
faites

Common idiomatic expressions using this verb
faire beau   to be beautiful weather
faire chaud   to be warm weather
faire froid   to be cold weather
faire de l'autostop, du stop   to hitchhike
faire attention à qqn ou à qqch   to pay
   attention to someone or to something

See also **défaire** and **satisfaire.**

**Madame Reed fait travailler ses élèves dans
la classe de français**   Mrs. Reed makes her
students work in French class.
le savoir-faire   know-how, ability, tact
faire un pèlerinage   to go on a pilgrimage

For more idioms using this verb, see the back pages for the section on verbs used in idiomatic expressions, especially pages 537–539.

218

to be necessary, must, to be lacking to (à), to need

The Seven Simple Tenses		The Seven Compound Tenses	
Singular	Plural	Singular	Plural
1 présent de l'indicatif **il faut**		8 passé composé **il a fallu**	
2 imparfait de l'indicatif **il fallait**		9 plus-que-parfait de l'indicatif **il avait fallu**	
3 passé simple **il fallut**		10 passé antérieur **il eut fallu**	
4 futur **il faudra**		11 futur antérieur **il aura fallu**	
5 conditionnel **il faudrait**		12 conditionnel passé **il aurait fallu**	
6 présent du subjonctif **qu'il faille**		13 passé du subjonctif **qu'il ait fallu**	
7 imparfait du subjonctif **qu'il fallût**		14 plus-que-parfait du subjonctif **qu'il eût fallu**	

Impératif
[not in use]

Common idiomatic expressions using this verb

Il faut que je fasse mes leçons avant de regarder la télé. Il faut me coucher tôt parce qu'il faut me lever tôt. Il faut faire attention en classe, et il faut être sage. Si je fais toutes ces choses, je serai récompensé.

comme il faut   as is proper
agir comme il faut   to behave properly
Il me faut de l'argent   I need some money.

Il faut manger pour vivre   It is necessary to eat in order to live.
Il ne faut pas parler sans politesse   One must not talk impolitely.

This is an impersonal verb and it is used in the tenses given above with the subject *il*.

féliciter

to congratulate

The Seven Simple Tenses		The Seven Compound Tenses	
Singular	Plural	Singular	Plural
1 présent de l'indicatif		**8 passé composé**	
félicite	**félicitons**	**ai félicité**	**avons félicité**
félicites	**félicitez**	**as félicité**	**avez félicité**
félicite	**félicitent**	**a félicité**	**ont félicité**
2 imparfait de l'indicatif		**9 plus-que-parfait de l'indicatif**	
félicitais	**félicitions**	**avais félicité**	**avions félicité**
félicitais	**félicitiez**	**avais félicité**	**aviez félicité**
félicitait	**félicitaient**	**avait félicité**	**avaient félicité**
3 passé simple		**10 passé antérieur**	
félicitai	**félicitâmes**	**eus félicité**	**eûmes félicité**
félicitas	**félicitâtes**	**eus félicité**	**eûtes félicité**
félicita	**félicitèrent**	**eut félicité**	**eurent félicité**
4 futur		**11 futur antérieur**	
féliciterai	**féliciterons**	**aurai félicité**	**aurons félicité**
féliciteras	**féliciterez**	**auras félicité**	**aurez félicité**
félicitera	**féliciteront**	**aura félicité**	**auront félicité**
5 conditionnel		**12 conditionnel passé**	
féliciterais	**féliciterions**	**aurais félicité**	**aurions félicité**
féliciterais	**féliciteriez**	**aurais félicité**	**auriez félicité**
féliciterait	**féliciteraient**	**aurait félicité**	**auraient félicité**
6 présent du subjonctif		**13 passé du subjonctif**	
félicite	**félicitions**	**aie félicité**	**ayons félicité**
félicites	**félicitiez**	**aies félicité**	**ayez félicité**
félicite	**félicitent**	**ait félicité**	**aient félicité**
7 imparfait du subjonctif		**14 plus-que-parfait du subjonctif**	
félicitasse	**félicitassions**	**eusse félicité**	**eussions félicité**
félicitasses	**félicitassiez**	**eusses félicité**	**eussiez félicité**
félicitât	**félicitassent**	**eût félicité**	**eussent félicité**

Impératif
félicite
félicitons
félicitez

Words and expressions related to this verb

féliciter qqn de qqch   to congratulate
  someone for something
Je vous félicite!   I congratulate you!
la félicitation   congratulation

Félicitations!   Congratulations!
se féliciter de qqch   to congratulate oneself
  about something
la félicité   bliss, felicity, happiness

Taking a trip? Check out the popular words, phrases, and expressions for travelers on pages
599–621.

220

to feign, to make believe, to pretend, to simulate

The Seven Simple Tenses		The Seven Compound Tenses	
Singular	Plural	Singular	Plural
1 présent de l'indicatif		**8 passé composé**	
feins	**feignons**	**ai feint**	**avons feint**
feins	**feignez**	**as feint**	**avez feint**
feint	**feignent**	**a feint**	**ont feint**
2 imparfait de l'indicatif		**9 plus-que-parfait de l'indicatif**	
feignais	**feignions**	**avais feint**	**avions feint**
feignais	**feigniez**	**avais feint**	**aviez feint**
feignait	**feignaient**	**avait feint**	**avaient feint**
3 passé simple		**10 passé antérieur**	
feignis	**feignîmes**	**eus feint**	**eûmes feint**
feignis	**feignîtes**	**eus feint**	**eûtes feint**
feignit	**feignirent**	**eut feint**	**eurent feint**
4 futur		**11 futur antérieur**	
feindrai	**feindrons**	**aurai feint**	**aurons feint**
feindras	**feindrez**	**auras feint**	**aurez feint**
feindra	**feindront**	**aura feint**	**auront feint**
5 conditionnel		**12 conditionnel passé**	
feindrais	**feindrions**	**aurais feint**	**aurions feint**
feindrais	**feindriez**	**aurais feint**	**auriez feint**
feindrait	**feindraient**	**aurait feint**	**auraient feint**
6 présent du subjonctif		**13 passé du subjonctif**	
feigne	**feignions**	**aie feint**	**ayons feint**
feignes	**feigniez**	**aies feint**	**ayez feint**
feigne	**feignent**	**ait feint**	**aient feint**
7 imparfait du subjonctif		**14 plus-que-parfait du subjonctif**	
feignisse	**feignissions**	**eusse feint**	**eussions feint**
feignisses	**feignissiez**	**eusses feint**	**eussiez feint**
feignît	**feignissent**	**eût feint**	**eussent feint**

Impératif
feins
feignons
feignez

Words and expressions related to this verb
feint, feinte   feigned, pretended
la feinte   pretense, sham
feinter   to feint, to fake
feindre la colère   to pretend to be angry
feignant, feignante   lazy

fainéant, fainéante   lazy
sans feinte   without pretense
feinter qqn   to fool someone
faire une feinte à qqn   to fool someone

Consult the sections on verbs used in idiomatic expressions, verbs with prepositions, and the list of over 1,100 verbs conjugated like model verbs in the back pages.

fendre

Part. pr. **fendant**   Part. passé **fendu**

to split, to crack, to cleave

The Seven Simple Tenses		The Seven Compound Tenses	
Singular	Plural	Singular	Plural
1 présent de l'indicatif		8 passé composé	
fends	fendons	ai fendu	avons fendu
fends	fendez	as fendu	avez fendu
fend	fendent	a fendu	ont fendu
2 imparfait de l'indicatif		9 plus-que-parfait de l'indicatif	
fendais	fendions	avais fendu	avions fendu
fendais	fendiez	avais fendu	aviez fendu
fendait	fendaient	avait fendu	avaient fendu
3 passé simple		10 passé antérieur	
fendis	fendîmes	eus fendu	eûmes fendu
fendis	fendîtes	eus fendu	eûtes fendu
fendit	fendirent	eut fendu	eurent fendu
4 futur		11 futur antérieur	
fendrai	fendrons	aurai fendu	aurons fendu
fendras	fendrez	auras fendu	aurez fendu
fendra	fendront	aura fendu	auront fendu
5 conditionnel		12 conditionnel passé	
fendrais	fendrions	aurais fendu	aurions fendu
fendrais	fendriez	aurais fendu	auriez fendu
fendrait	fendraient	aurait fendu	auraient fendu
6 présent du subjonctif		13 passé du subjonctif	
fende	fendions	aie fendu	ayons fendu
fendes	fendiez	aies fendu	ayez fendu
fende	fendent	ait fendu	aient fendu
7 imparfait du subjonctif		14 plus-que-parfait du subjonctif	
fendisse	fendissions	eusse fendu	eussions fendu
fendisses	fendissiez	eusses fendu	eussiez fendu
fendît	fendissent	eût fendu	eussent fendu

Impératif
fends
fendons
fendez

Common idiomatic expressions using this verb and words related to it

fendre un mur   to make a crack in a wall
une fente   crack, split, slot
se fendre de chagrin   to feel heartbroken
fendre du bois   to split wood

fendre son coeur   to break one's heart
un fendoir   cleaver
à fendre l'âme   enough to break one's spirit,
   to crush one's heart

Grammar putting you in a tense mood? Review the definitions of basic grammatical terms on pages 674–688.

The Seven Simple Tenses		The Seven Compound Tenses	
Singular	Plural	Singular	Plural
1 présent de l'indicatif		**8 passé composé**	
ferme	fermons	ai fermé	avons fermé
fermes	fermez	as fermé	avez fermé
ferme	ferment	a fermé	ont fermé
2 imparfait de l'indicatif		**9 plus-que-parfait de l'indicatif**	
fermais	fermions	avais fermé	avions fermé
fermais	fermiez	avais fermé	aviez fermé
fermait	fermaient	avait fermé	avaient fermé
3 passé simple		**10 passé antérieur**	
fermai	fermâmes	eus fermé	eûmes fermé
fermas	fermâtes	eus fermé	eûtes fermé
ferma	fermèrent	eut fermé	eurent fermé
4 futur		**11 futur antérieur**	
fermerai	fermerons	aurai fermé	aurons fermé
fermeras	fermerez	auras fermé	aurez fermé
fermera	fermeront	aura fermé	auront fermé
5 conditionnel		**12 conditionnel passé**	
fermerais	fermerions	aurais fermé	aurions fermé
fermerais	fermeriez	aurais fermé	auriez fermé
fermerait	fermeraient	aurait fermé	auraient fermé
6 présent du subjonctif		**13 passé du subjonctif**	
ferme	fermions	aie fermé	ayons fermé
fermes	fermiez	aies fermé	ayez fermé
ferme	ferment	ait fermé	aient fermé
7 imparfait du subjonctif		**14 plus-que-parfait du subjonctif**	
fermasse	fermassions	eusse fermé	eussions fermé
fermasses	fermassiez	eusses fermé	eussiez fermé
fermât	fermassent	eût fermé	eussent fermé

Impératif
ferme
fermons
fermez

Sentences using this verb and words and expressions related to it

Georges est rentré tard hier soir. Il a ouvert la porte, puis il l'a fermée. Il a ouvert la garde-robe pour y mettre son manteau, son chapeau et ses gants et il l'a fermée. Il a ouvert la fenêtre mais il ne l'a pas fermée parce qu'il faisait trop chaud dans sa chambre et il ne peut pas dormir dans une chambre où l'air est lourd.

enfermer to shut in
fermer à clef to lock
fermer au verrou to bolt
Ferme-la! Shut up! Zip it!
fermer le robinet to turn off the tap
fermer un programme to close a program (computer)

renfermer to enclose
Ça sent le renfermé It's musty in here.
une fermeture closing, shutting
une fermeture éclair, une fermeture à glissière zipper
l'heure de fermer closing time

se fier

to depend on, to rely on, to trust in

The Seven Simple Tenses		The Seven Compound Tenses	
Singular	Plural	Singular	Plural
1 présent de l'indicatif		**8 passé composé**	
me fie	**nous fions**	**me suis fié(e)**	**nous sommes fié(e)s**
te fies	**vous fiez**	**t'es fié(e)**	**vous êtes fié(e)(s)**
se fie	**se fient**	**s'est fié(e)**	**se sont fié(e)s**
2 imparfait de l'indicatif		**9 plus-que-parfait de l'indicatif**	
me fiais	**nous fiions**	**m'étais fié(e)**	**nous étions fié(e)s**
te fiais	**vous fiiez**	**t'étais fié(e)**	**vous étiez fié(e)(s)**
se fiait	**se fiaient**	**s'était fié(e)**	**s'étaient fié(e)s**
3 passé simple		**10 passé antérieur**	
me fiai	**nous fiâmes**	**me fus fié(e)**	**nous fûmes fié(e)s**
te fias	**vous fiâtes**	**te fus fié(e)**	**vous fûtes fié(e)(s)**
se fia	**se fièrent**	**se fut fié(e)**	**se furent fié(e)s**
4 futur		**11 futur antérieur**	
me fierai	**nous fierons**	**me serai fié(e)**	**nous serons fié(e)s**
te fieras	**vous fierez**	**te seras fié(e)**	**vous serez fié(e)(s)**
se fiera	**se fieront**	**se sera fié(e)**	**se seront fié(e)s**
5 conditionnel		**12 conditionnel passé**	
me fierais	**nous fierions**	**me serais fié(e)**	**nous serions fié(e)s**
te fierais	**vous fieriez**	**te serais fié(e)**	**vous seriez fié(e)(s)**
se fierait	**se fieraient**	**se serait fié(e)**	**se seraient fié(e)s**
6 présent du subjonctif		**13 passé du subjonctif**	
me fie	**nous fiions**	**me sois fié(e)**	**nous soyons fié(e)s**
te fies	**vous fiiez**	**te sois fié(e)**	**vous soyez fié(e)(s)**
se fie	**se fient**	**se soit fié(e)**	**se soient fié(e)s**
7 imparfait du subjonctif		**14 plus-que-parfait du subjonctif**	
me fiasse	**nous fiassions**	**me fusse fié(e)**	**nous fussions fié(e)s**
te fiasses	**vous fiassiez**	**te fusses fié(e)**	**vous fussiez fié(e)(s)**
se fiât	**se fiassent**	**se fût fié(e)**	**se fussent fié(e)s**

Impératif
fie-toi; ne te fie pas
fions-nous; ne nous fions pas
fiez-vous; ne vous fiez pas

Words and expressions related to this verb
la confiance confidence, trust
avoir confiance en soi to be self-confident
confier à to confide to
se méfier de to mistrust, to distrust, to beware of
fiable reliable, trustworthy

la méfiance mistrust, distrust
se fier à to depend on, to trust in, to rely on
se confier à to trust to, to confide in
Ne vous fiez pas aux apparences Don't trust appearances.

Get acquainted with what preposition goes with what verb on pages 543–553.

to finish, to end, to terminate, to complete

The Seven Simple Tenses		The Seven Compound Tenses	
Singular	Plural	Singular	Plural

1   présent de l'indicatif

finis	finissons	
finis	finissez	
finit	finissent	

8   passé composé

ai fini	avons fini
as fini	avez fini
a fini	ont fini

2   imparfait de l'indicatif

finissais	finissions
finissais	finissiez
finissait	finissaient

9   plus-que-parfait de l'indicatif

avais fini	avions fini
avais fini	aviez fini
avait fini	avaient fini

3   passé simple

finis	finîmes
finis	finîtes
finit	finirent

10   passé antérieur

eus fini	eûmes fini
eus fini	eûtes fini
eut fini	eurent fini

4   futur

finirai	finirons
finiras	finirez
finira	finiront

11   futur antérieur

aurai fini	aurons fini
auras fini	aurez fini
aura fini	auront fini

5   conditionnel

finirais	finirions
finirais	finiriez
finirait	finiraient

12   conditionnel passé

aurais fini	aurions fini
aurais fini	auriez fini
aurait fini	auraient fini

6   présent du subjonctif

finisse	finissions
finisses	finissiez
finisse	finissent

13   passé du subjonctif

aie fini	ayons fini
aies fini	ayez fini
ait fini	aient fini

7   imparfait du subjonctif

finisse	finissions
finisses	finissiez
finît	finissent

14   plus-que-parfait du subjonctif

eusse fini	eussions fini
eusses fini	eussiez fini
eût fini	eussent fini

Impératif
finis
finissons
finissez

Sentences using this verb and words and expressions related to it
finir de + inf.   to finish + pr. part.
J'ai fini de travailler pour aujourd'hui   I have finished working for today.

finir par + inf.   to end up by + pr. part.
Louis a fini par épouser une femme plus âgée que lui   Louis ended up by marrying a woman older than he.

la fin   the end; **la fin de semaine**   weekend; **C'est fini!**   It's all over!
afin de   in order to; **enfin**   finally; **finalement**   finally
mettre fin à   to put an end to; **final, finale**   final; **définir**   to define
la finition   finish (of a piece of work)

The subject pronouns are found on the page facing page 1.   **225**

to found, to establish, to lay the foundation

The Seven Simple Tenses		The Seven Compound Tenses	
Singular	Plural	Singular	Plural
1 présent de l'indicatif		8 passé composé	
fonde	fondons	ai fondé	avons fondé
fondes	fondez	as fondé	avez fondé
fonde	fondent	a fondé	ont fondé
2 imparfait de l'indicatif		9 plus-que-parfait de l'indicatif	
fondais	fondions	avais fondé	avions fondé
fondais	fondiez	avais fondé	aviez fondé
fondait	fondaient	avait fondé	avaient fondé
3 passé simple		10 passé antérieur	
fondai	fondâmes	eus fondé	eûmes fondé
fondas	fondâtes	eus fondé	eûtes fondé
fonda	fondèrent	eut fondé	eurent fondé
4 futur		11 futur antérieur	
fonderai	fonderons	aurai fondé	aurons fondé
fonderas	fonderez	auras fondé	aurez fondé
fondera	fonderont	aura fondé	auront fondé
5 conditionnel		12 conditionnel passé	
fonderais	fonderions	aurais fondé	aurions fondé
fonderais	fonderiez	aurais fondé	auriez fondé
fonderait	fonderaient	aurait fondé	auraient fondé
6 présent du subjonctif		13 passé du subjonctif	
fonde	fondions	aie fondé	ayons fondé
fondes	fondiez	aies fondé	ayez fondé
fonde	fondent	ait fondé	aient fondé
7 imparfait du subjonctif		14 plus-que-parfait du subjonctif	
fondasse	fondassions	eusse fondé	eussions fondé
fondasses	fondassiez	eusses fondé	eussiez fondé
fondât	fondassent	eût fondé	eussent fondé

Impératif
fonde
fondons
fondez

Common idiomatic expressions using this verb and words related to it

se fonder sur   to be based on
un fondateur, une fondatrice   founder
le fond   bottom; background
à fond   thoroughly
du fond du coeur   from the bottom of one's heart
de fond en comble   from top to bottom (from bottom to top)

le fondement   foundation of a building
la fondation   foundation, endowment
bien fondé   well founded; **mal fondé**   ill founded
au fond   in the bottom, in the back, in the rear; at bottom, after all
manquer de fond   to be shallow

Consult the sections on verbs used in idiomatic expressions, verbs with prepositions, and the list of over 1,100 verbs conjugated like model verbs in the back pages.

to melt, to dissolve, to mix colors

The Seven Simple Tenses		The Seven Compound Tenses	
Singular	Plural	Singular	Plural

1 présent de l'indicatif		8 passé composé	
fonds	**fondons**	**ai fondu**	**avons fondu**
fonds	**fondez**	**as fondu**	**avez fondu**
fond	**fondent**	**a fondu**	**ont fondu**

2 imparfait de l'indicatif		9 plus-que-parfait de l'indicatif	
fondais	**fondions**	**avais fondu**	**avions fondu**
fondais	**fondiez**	**avais fondu**	**aviez fondu**
fondait	**fondaient**	**avait fondu**	**avaient fondu**

3 passé simple		10 passé antérieur	
fondis	**fondîmes**	**eus fondu**	**eûmes fondu**
fondis	**fondîtes**	**eus fondu**	**eûtes fondu**
fondit	**fondirent**	**eut fondu**	**eurent fondu**

4 futur		11 futur antérieur	
fondrai	**fondrons**	**aurai fondu**	**aurons fondu**
fondras	**fondrez**	**auras fondu**	**aurez fondu**
fondra	**fondront**	**aura fondu**	**auront fondu**

5 conditionnel		12 conditionnel passé	
fondrais	**fondrions**	**aurais fondu**	**aurions fondu**
fondrais	**fondriez**	**aurais fondu**	**auriez fondu**
fondrait	**fondraient**	**aurait fondu**	**auraient fondu**

6 présent du subjonctif		13 passé du subjonctif	
fonde	**fondions**	**aie fondu**	**ayons fondu**
fondes	**fondiez**	**aies fondu**	**ayez fondu**
fonde	**fondent**	**ait fondu**	**aient fondu**

7 imparfait du subjonctif		14 plus-que-parfait du subjonctif	
fondisse	**fondissions**	**eusse fondu**	**eussions fondu**
fondisses	**fondissiez**	**eusses fondu**	**eussiez fondu**
fondît	**fondissent**	**eût fondu**	**eussent fondu**

Impératif
fonds
fondons
fondez

Words and expressions related to this verb
confondre   to confound, to confuse; **se confondre**   to merge, to mingle
refondre   to recast, to remelt; **se fondre**   to melt, to dissolve
la refonte   recasting, remelting of metal
du beurre fondu   melted butter; **du fromage fondu**   melted cheese
fondre en larmes   to burst into tears

How are you doing? Find out with the verb drills and tests with answers explained on pages 622–673.

The subject pronouns are found on the page facing page 1.   **227**

forcer
to force

Part. pr. **forçant**   Part. passé **forcé**

The Seven Simple Tenses		The Seven Compound Tenses	
Singular	Plural	Singular	Plural
1 présent de l'indicatif		**8 passé composé**	
force	forçons	ai forcé	avons forcé
forces	forcez	as forcé	avez forcé
force	forcent	a forcé	ont forcé
2 imparfait de l'indicatif		**9 plus-que-parfait de l'indicatif**	
forçais	forcions	avais forcé	avions forcé
forçais	forciez	avais forcé	aviez forcé
forçait	forçaient	avait forcé	avaient forcé
3 passé simple		**10 passé antérieur**	
forçai	forçâmes	eus forcé	eûmes forcé
forças	forçâtes	eus forcé	eûtes forcé
força	forcèrent	eut forcé	eurent forcé
4 futur		**11 futur antérieur**	
forcerai	forcerons	aurai forcé	aurons forcé
forceras	forcerez	auras forcé	aurez forcé
forcera	forceront	aura forcé	auront forcé
5 conditionnel		**12 conditionnel passé**	
forcerais	forcerions	aurais forcé	aurions forcé
forcerais	forceriez	aurais forcé	auriez forcé
forcerait	forceraient	aurait forcé	auraient forcé
6 présent du subjonctif		**13 passé du subjonctif**	
force	forcions	aie forcé	ayons forcé
forces	forciez	aies forcé	ayez forcé
force	forcent	ait forcé	aient forcé
7 imparfait du subjonctif		**14 plus-que-parfait du subjonctif**	
forçasse	forçassions	eusse forcé	eussions forcé
forçasses	forçassiez	eusses forcé	eussiez forcé
forçât	forçassent	eût forcé	eussent forcé

Impératif
force
forçons
forcez

Words and expressions related to this verb

forcer la porte de qqn   to force one's way into someone's house
être forcé de faire qqch   to be obliged to do something
se forcer la voix   to strain one's voice
à force de   by dint of, by means of
A force d'essayer, il a réussi   By dint of trying, he succeeded.

la force   strength, force; **avec force** forcefully, with force
forcément   necessarily, inevitably
forcer qqn à faire qqch   to force someone to do something
un forçat   a convict

228

to dig deeply, to excavate, to go deep into, to search

The Seven Simple Tenses		The Seven Compound Tenses	
Singular	Plural	Singular	Plural

1 présent de l'indicatif		8 passé composé	
fouille	fouillons	ai fouillé	avons fouillé
fouilles	fouillez	as fouillé	avez fouillé
fouille	fouillent	a fouillé	ont fouillé

2 imparfait de l'indicatif		9 plus-que-parfait de l'indicatif	
fouillais	fouillions	avais fouillé	avions fouillé
fouillais	fouilliez	avais fouillé	aviez fouillé
fouillait	fouillaient	avait fouillé	avaient fouillé

3 passé simple		10 passé antérieur	
fouillai	fouillâmes	eus fouillé	eûmes fouillé
fouillas	fouillâtes	eus fouillé	eûtes fouillé
fouilla	fouillèrent	eut fouillé	eurent fouillé

4 futur		11 futur antérieur	
fouillerai	fouillerons	aurai fouillé	aurons fouillé
fouilleras	fouillerez	auras fouillé	aurez fouillé
fouillera	fouilleront	aura fouillé	auront fouillé

5 conditionnel		12 conditionnel passé	
fouillerais	fouillerions	aurais fouillé	aurions fouillé
fouillerais	fouilleriez	aurais fouillé	auriez fouillé
fouillerait	fouilleraient	aurait fouillé	auraient fouillé

6 présent du subjonctif		13 passé du subjonctif	
fouille	fouillions	aie fouillé	ayons fouillé
fouilles	fouilliez	aies fouillé	ayez fouillé
fouille	fouillent	ait fouillé	aient fouillé

7 imparfait du subjonctif		14 plus-que-parfait du subjonctif	
fouillasse	fouillassions	eusse fouillé	eussions fouillé
fouillasses	fouillassiez	eusses fouillé	eussiez fouillé
fouillât	fouillassent	eût fouillé	eussent fouillé

Impératif
fouille
fouillons
fouillez

Words and expressions related to this verb
fouiller la maision   to search the house
fouiller dans les poches   to search around
   (to rummage) in one's pockets

fouiller qqn   to frisk (search) someone
la fouille   excavation
un fouilleur, une fouilleuse   searcher

Want to learn more idiomatic expressions that contain verbs? Look at pages 530–542.

fournir

Part. pr. **fournissant**   Part. passé **fourni**

to furnish, to supply

The Seven Simple Tenses		The Seven Compound Tenses	
Singular	Plural	Singular	Plural
1 présent de l'indicatif		**8 passé composé**	
fournis	fournissons	ai fourni	avons fourni
fournis	fournissez	as fourni	avez fourni
fournit	fournissent	a fourni	ont fourni
2 imparfait de l'indicatif		**9 plus-que-parfait de l'indicatif**	
fournissais	fournissions	avais fourni	avions fourni
fournissais	fournissiez	avais fourni	aviez fourni
fournissait	fournissaient	avait fourni	avaient fourni
3 passé simple		**10 passé antérieur**	
fournis	fournîmes	eus fourni	eûmes fourni
fournis	fournîtes	eus fourni	eûtes fourni
fournit	fournirent	eut fourni	eurent fourni
4 futur		**11 futur antérieur**	
fournirai	fournirons	aurai fourni	aurons fourni
fourniras	fournirez	auras fourni	aurez fourni
fournira	fourniront	aura fourni	auront fourni
5 conditionnel		**12 conditionnel passé**	
fournirais	fournirions	aurais fourni	aurions fourni
fournirais	fourniriez	aurais fourni	auriez fourni
fournirait	fourniraient	aurait fourni	auraient fourni
6 présent du subjonctif		**13 passé du subjonctif**	
fournisse	fournissions	aie fourni	ayons fourni
fournisses	fournissiez	aies fourni	ayez fourni
fournisse	fournissent	ait fourni	aient fourni
7 imparfait du subjonctif		**14 plus-que-parfait du subjonctif**	
fournisse	fournissions	eusse fourni	eussions fourni
fournisses	fournissiez	eusses fourni	eussiez fourni
fournît	fournissent	eût fourni	eussent fourni

Impératif
fournis
fournissons
fournissez

Words and expressions related to this verb
fournir qqch à qqn   to supply somebody with something
se fournir de   to provide oneself with
un fournisseur   supplier
fournir à   to provide for; **fournir de**   to furnish with
la fourniture   supplying; **les fournitures**   supplies

Taking a trip? Check out the popular words, phrases, and expressions for travelers on pages 599–621.

to knock, to hit, to frap, to rap, to strike (hit)

The Seven Simple Tenses		The Seven Compound Tenses	
Singular	Plural	Singular	Plural
1 présent de l'indicatif		**8 passé composé**	
frappe	**frappons**	**ai frappé**	**avons frappé**
frappes	**frappez**	**as frappé**	**avez frappé**
frappe	**frappent**	**a frappé**	**ont frappé**
2 imparfait de l'indicatif		**9 plus-que-parfait de l'indicatif**	
frappais	**frappions**	**avais frappé**	**avions frappé**
frappais	**frappiez**	**avais frappé**	**aviez frappé**
frappait	**frappaient**	**avait frappé**	**avaient frappé**
3 passé simple		**10 passé antérieur**	
frappai	**frappâmes**	**eus frappé**	**eûmes frappé**
frappas	**frappâtes**	**eus frappé**	**eûtes frappé**
frappa	**frappèrent**	**eut frappé**	**eurent frappé**
4 futur		**11 futur antérieur**	
frapperai	**frapperons**	**aurai frappé**	**aurons frappé**
frapperas	**frapperez**	**auras frappé**	**aurez frappé**
frappera	**frapperont**	**aura frappé**	**auront frappé**
5 conditionnel		**12 conditionnel passé**	
frapperais	**frapperions**	**aurais frappé**	**aurions frappé**
frapperais	**frapperiez**	**aurais frappé**	**auriez frappé**
frapperait	**frapperaient**	**aurait frappé**	**auraient frappé**
6 présent du subjonctif		**13 passé du subjonctif**	
frappe	**frappions**	**aie frappé**	**ayons frappé**
frappes	**frappiez**	**aies frappé**	**ayez frappé**
frappe	**frappent**	**ait frappé**	**aient frappé**
7 imparfait du subjonctif		**14 plus-que-parfait du subjonctif**	
frappasse	**frappassions**	**eusse frappé**	**eussions frappé**
frappasses	**frappassiez**	**eusses frappé**	**eussiez frappé**
frappât	**frappassent**	**eût frappé**	**eussent frappé**

Impératif
frappe
frappons
frappez

Common idiomatic expressions using this verb and words related to it

se frapper la poitrine   to beat one's chest
le frappage   striking (medals, coins)
une faute de frappe   a typing mistake
frapper à la porte   to knock on the door
frapper du pied   to stamp one's foot
entrer sans frapper   enter without knocking

C'est frappant!   It's striking!
frappé (frappée) de   stricken with
le frappement   beating, striking
frappé à mort   mortally wounded
un lait frappé   milkshake

It's important that you be familiar with the Subjunctive. See pages 560–565.

The subject pronouns are found on the page facing page 1.   **231**

frémir

Part. pr. **frémissant**   Part. passé **frémi**

to shudder, to quiver, to tremble

The Seven Simple Tenses		The Seven Compound Tenses	
Singular	Plural	Singular	Plural
1 présent de l'indicatif		**8 passé composé**	
frémis	frémissons	ai frémi	avons frémi
frémis	frémissez	as frémi	avez frémi
frémit	frémissent	a frémi	ont frémi
2 imparfait de l'indicatif		**9 plus-que-parfait de l'indicatif**	
frémissais	frémissions	avais frémi	avions frémi
frémissais	frémissiez	avais frémi	aviez frémi
frémissait	frémissaient	avait frémi	avaient frémi
3 passé simple		**10 passé antérieur**	
frémis	frémîmes	eus frémi	eûmes frémi
frémis	frémîtes	eus frémi	eûtes frémi
frémit	frémirent	eut frémi	eurent frémi
4 futur		**11 futur antérieur**	
frémirai	frémirons	aurai frémi	aurons frémi
frémiras	frémirez	auras frémi	aurez frémi
frémira	frémiront	aura frémi	auront frémi
5 conditionnel		**12 conditionnel passé**	
frémirais	frémirions	aurais frémi	aurions frémi
frémirais	frémiriez	aurais frémi	auriez frémi
frémirait	frémiraient	aurait frémi	auraient frémi
6 présent du subjonctif		**13 passé du subjonctif**	
frémisse	frémissions	aie frémi	ayons frémi
frémisses	frémissiez	aies frémi	ayez frémi
frémisse	frémissent	ait frémi	aient frémi
7 imparfait du subjonctif		**14 plus-que-parfait du subjonctif**	
frémisse	frémissions	eusse frémi	eussions frémi
frémisses	frémissiez	eusses frémi	eussiez frémi
frémît	frémissent	eût frémi	eussent frémi

Impératif
frémis
frémissons
frémissez

Words and expressions related to this verb
frémir de colère to shake with anger
le frémissement quivering, rustling, shuddering; **le frémissement des feuilles** rustling of leaves
faire frémir qqn to give someone the shivers

une histoire à faire frémir a horror story, a chiller thriller
frémissant, frémissante rustling, quivering, shuddering
de l'eau frémissante simmering water

Consult the sections on verbs used in idiomatic expressions, verbs with prepositions, and the list of over 1,100 verbs conjugated like model verbs in the back pages.

The Seven Simple Tenses		The Seven Compound Tenses	
Singular	Plural	Singular	Plural
1 présent de l'indicatif		8 passé composé	
fris		**ai frit**	**avons frit**
fris		**as frit**	**avez frit**
frit		**a frit**	**ont frit**
		9 plus-que-parfait de l'indicatif	
		avais frit	**avions frit**
		avais frit	**aviez frit**
		avait frit	**avaient frit**
		10 passé antérieur	
		eus frit	**eûmes frit**
		eus frit	**eûtes frit**
		eut frit	**eurent frit**
4 futur		11 futur antérieur	
frirai	**frirons**	**aurai frit**	**aurons frit**
friras	**frirez**	**auras frit**	**aurez frit**
frira	**friront**	**aura frit**	**auront frit**
5 conditionnel		12 conditionnel passé	
frirais	**fririons**	**aurais frit**	**aurions frit**
frirais	**fririez**	**aurais frit**	**auriez frit**
frirait	**friraient**	**aurait frit**	**auraient frit**
		13 passé du subjonctif	
		aie frit	**ayons frit**
		aies frit	**ayez frit**
		ait frit	**aient frit**
		14 plus-que-parfait du subjonctif	
		eusse frit	**eussions frit**
		eusses frit	**eussiez frit**
		eût frit	**eussent frit**

Impératif
fris
faisons frire
faites frire

Words and expressions related to this verb
faire frire   to fry (see note below)
pommes frites   French fries
une friteuse   frying basket
la friture   frying

des pommes de terre frites   fried potatoes
(French style)
un bifteck-frites, un steak-frites   steak with
French fries

This verb is generally used only in the persons and tenses given above. To supply the forms that
are lacking, use the appropriate form of **faire** plus the infinitive **frire**, e.g., the plural of the
present indicative is: **nous faisons frire, vous faites frire, ils font frire**.

The subject pronouns are found on the page facing page 1.

to flee, to fly off, to shun, to leak

The Seven Simple Tenses		The Seven Compound Tenses	
Singular	Plural	Singular	Plural
1 présent de l'indicatif		**8 passé composé**	
fuis	fuyons	ai fui	avons fui
fuis	fuyez	as fui	avez fui
fuit	fuient	a fui	ont fui
2 imparfait de l'indicatif		**9 plus-que-parfait de l'indicatif**	
fuyais	fuyions	avais fui	avions fui
fuyais	fuyiez	avais fui	aviez fui
fuyait	fuyaient	avait fui	avaient fui
3 passé simple		**10 passé antérieur**	
fuis	fuîmes	eus fui	eûmes fui
fuis	fuîtes	eus fui	eûtes fui
fuit	fuirent	eut fui	eurent fui
4 futur		**11 futur antérieur**	
fuirai	fuirons	aurai fui	aurons fui
fuiras	fuirez	auras fui	aurez fui
fuira	fuiront	aura fui	auront fui
5 conditionnel		**12 conditionnel passé**	
fuirais	fuirions	aurais fui	aurions fui
fuirais	fuiriez	aurais fui	auriez fui
fuirait	fuiraient	aurait fui	auraient fui
6 présent du subjonctif		**13 passé du subjonctif**	
fuie	fuyions	aie fui	ayons fui
fuies	fuyiez	aies fui	ayez fui
fuie	fuient	ait fui	aient fui
7 imparfait du subjonctif		**14 plus-que-parfait du subjonctif**	
fuisse	fuissions	eusse fui	eussions fui
fuisses	fuissiez	eusses fui	eussiez fui
fuît	fuissent	eût fui	eussent fui

Impératif
fuis
fuyons
fuyez

Common idiomatic expressions using this verb
faire fuir   to put to flight
la fuite   flight, escape
prendre la fuite   to take to flight
une fuite de gaz   gas leak
s'enfuir de   to flee from, to run away from

See also **s'enfuir.**

fugitif, fugitive   fugitive, fleeting, runaway
fugitivement   fugitively
une fuite d'huile   oil leak
faire une fugue   to run away, to elope

Grammar putting you in a tense mood? Review the definitions of basic grammatical terms with examples on pages 674–688.

The Seven Simple Tenses		The Seven Compound Tenses	
Singular	Plural	Singular	Plural
1 présent de l'indicatif		8 passé composé	
fume	fumons	ai fumé	avons fumé
fumes	fumez	as fumé	avez fumé
fume	fument	a fumé	ont fumé
2 imparfait de l'indicatif		9 plus-que-parfait de l'indicatif	
fumais	fumions	avais fumé	avions fumé
fumais	fumiez	avais fumé	aviez fumé
fumait	fumaient	avait fumé	avaient fumé
3 passé simple		10 passé antérieur	
fumai	fumâmes	eus fumé	eûmes fumé
fumas	fumâtes	eus fumé	eûtes fumé
fuma	fumèrent	eut fumé	eurent fumé
4 futur		11 futur antérieur	
fumerai	fumerons	aurai fumé	aurons fumé
fumeras	fumerez	auras fumé	aurez fumé
fumera	fumeront	aura fumé	auront fumé
5 conditionnel		12 conditionnel passé	
fumerais	fumerions	aurais fumé	aurions fumé
fumerais	fumeriez	aurais fumé	auriez fumé
fumerait	fumeraient	aurait fumé	auraient fumé
6 présent du subjonctif		13 passé du subjonctif	
fume	fumions	aie fumé	ayons fumé
fumes	fumiez	aies fumé	ayez fumé
fume	fument	ait fumé	aient fumé
7 imparfait du subjonctif		14 plus-que-parfait du subjonctif	
fumasse	fumassions	eusse fumé	eussions fumé
fumasses	fumassiez	eusses fumé	eussiez fumé
fumât	fumassent	eût fumé	eussent fumé

Impératif
fume
fumons
fumez

Sentences using this verb and words related to it
Le père: **Je te défends de fumer. C'est une mauvaise habitude.**
Le fils: **Alors, pourquoi fumes-tu, papa?**

Défense de fumer No smoking allowed
la fumée smoke
un rideau de fumée smoke screen
parfumer to perfume
non-fumeur nonsmoking

fumeux, fumeuse smoky
un fume-cigare cigar holder
un fume-cigarette cigarette holder
un fumeur, une fumeuse smoker (person who smokes)

The subject pronouns are found on the page facing page 1.   **235**

gagner

to win, to earn, to gain

The Seven Simple Tenses		The Seven Compound Tenses	
Singular	Plural	Singular	Plural
1 présent de l'indicatif		**8 passé composé**	
gagne	gagnons	ai gagné	avons gagné
gagnes	gagnez	as gagné	avez gagné
gagne	gagnent	a gagné	ont gagné
2 imparfait de l'indicatif		**9 plus-que-parfait de l'indicatif**	
gagnais	gagnions	avais gagné	avions gagné
gagnais	gagniez	avais gagné	aviez gagné
gagnait	gagnaient	avait gagné	avaient gagné
3 passé simple		**10 passé antérieur**	
gagnai	gagnâmes	eus gagné	eûmes gagné
gagnas	gagnâtes	eus gagné	eûtes gagné
gagna	gagnèrent	eut gagné	eurent gagné
4 futur		**11 futur antérieur**	
gagnerai	gagnerons	aurai gagné	aurons gagné
gagneras	gagnerez	auras gagné	aurez gagné
gagnera	gagneront	aura gagné	auront gagné
5 conditionnel		**12 conditionnel passé**	
gagnerais	gagnerions	aurais gagné	aurions gagné
gagnerais	gagneriez	aurais gagné	auriez gagné
gagnerait	gagneraient	aurait gagné	auraient gagné
6 présent du subjonctif		**13 passé du subjonctif**	
gagne	gagnions	aie gagné	ayons gagné
gagnes	gagniez	aies gagné	ayez gagné
gagne	gagnent	ait gagné	aient gagné
7 imparfait du subjonctif		**14 plus-que-parfait du subjonctif**	
gagnasse	gagnassions	eusse gagné	eussions gagné
gagnasses	gagnassiez	eusses gagné	eussiez gagné
gagnât	gagnassent	eût gagné	eussent gagné

Impératif
gagne
gagnons
gagnez

Common idiomatic expressions using this verb and words related to it

gagner sa vie   to earn one's living
gagner du poids   to gain weight
gagner de l'argent   to earn money
gagnable   obtainable
gagner du temps   to save time

regagner   to regain, to recover, to win back
regagner le temps perdu   to make up (to recover) lost time
un gagne-pain   a job
un gagnant, une gagnante   a winner

How are you doing? Find out with the verb drills and tests with answers explained on pages 622–673.

The Seven Simple Tenses		The Seven Compound Tenses	
Singular	Plural	Singular	Plural
1 présent de l'indicatif		8 passé composé	
garde	gardons	ai gardé	avons gardé
gardes	gardez	as gardé	avez gardé
garde	gardent	a gardé	ont gardé
2 imparfait de l'indicatif		9 plus-que-parfait de l'indicatif	
gardais	gardions	avais gardé	avions gardé
gardais	gardiez	avais gardé	aviez gardé
gardait	gardaient	avait gardé	avaient gardé
3 passé simple		10 passé antérieur	
gardai	gardâmes	eus gardé	eûmes gardé
gardas	gardâtes	eus gardé	eûtes gardé
garda	gardèrent	eut gardé	eurent gardé
4 futur		11 futur antérieur	
garderai	garderons	aurai gardé	aurons gardé
garderas	garderez	auras gardé	aurez gardé
gardera	garderont	aura gardé	auront gardé
5 conditionnel		12 conditionnel passé	
garderais	garderions	aurais gardé	aurions gardé
garderais	garderiez	aurais gardé	auriez gardé
garderait	garderaient	aurait gardé	auraient gardé
6 présent du subjonctif		13 passé du subjonctif	
garde	gardions	aie gardé	ayons gardé
gardes	gardiez	aies gardé	ayez gardé
garde	gardent	ait gardé	aient gardé
7 imparfait du subjonctif		14 plus-que-parfait du subjonctif	
gardasse	gardassions	eusse gardé	eussions gardé
gardasses	gardassiez	eusses gardé	eussiez gardé
gardât	gardassent	eût gardé	eussent gardé

Impératif
garde
gardons
gardez

Sentences using this verb and words and expressions related to it

Madame Mimi a mis son enfant chez une gardienne d'enfants parce qu'elle va passer la journée en ville. Elle a besoin d'acheter une nouvelle garde-robe.

se garder   to protect oneself
se garder de tomber   to take care not to fall
un gardien, une gardienne   guardian
prendre garde de   to take care not to
une gardienne d'enfants   babysitter
la garderie   day care
une garde-robe   wardrobe (closet)
un gardien de but   goalie

regarder   to look at, to watch, to consider, to regard
un garde-manger   pantry
un garde-vue   eyeshade (visor)
En garde!   On guard!
Dieu m'en garde!   God forbid!
Garde-à-vous!   Attention! (military)

The subject pronouns are found on the page facing page 1.

gâter

Part. pr. gâtant   **Part. passé gâté**

to spoil, to damage

The Seven Simple Tenses		The Seven Compound Tenses	
Singular	Plural	Singular	Plural
1 présent de l'indicatif		8 passé composé	
gâte	gâtons	ai gâté	avons gâté
gâtes	gâtez	as gâté	avez gâté
gâte	gâtent	a gâté	ont gâté
2 imparfait de l'indicatif		9 plus-que-parfait de l'indicatif	
gâtais	gâtions	avais gâté	avions gâté
gâtais	gâtiez	avais gâté	aviez gâté
gâtait	gâtaient	avait gâté	avaient gâté
3 passé simple		10 passé antérieur	
gâtai	gâtâmes	eus gâté	eûmes gâté
gâtas	gâtâtes	eus gâté	eûtes gâté
gâta	gâtèrent	eut gâté	eurent gâté
4 futur		11 futur antérieur	
gâterai	gâterons	aurai gâté	aurons gâté
gâteras	gâterez	auras gâté	aurez gâté
gâtera	gâteront	aura gâté	auront gâté
5 conditionnel		12 conditionnel passé	
gâterais	gâterions	aurais gâté	aurions gâté
gâterais	gâteriez	aurais gâté	auriez gâté
gâterait	gâteraient	aurait gâté	auraient gâté
6 présent du subjonctif		13 passé du subjonctif	
gâte	gâtions	aie gâté	ayons gâté
gâtes	gâtiez	aies gâté	ayez gâté
gâte	gâtent	ait gâté	aient gâté
7 imparfait du subjonctif		14 plus-que-parfait du subjonctif	
gâtasse	gâtassions	eusse gâté	eussions gâté
gâtasses	gâtassiez	eusses gâté	eussiez gâté
gâtât	gâtassent	eût gâté	eussent gâté

	Impératif
	gâte
	gâtons
	gâtez

Sentences using this verb and words related to it

Marcel est un enfant gâté. Je n'aime pas jouer avec lui. Il gâte tout. Il demande toujours des gâteries.

gâter un enfant   to spoil a child
se gâter   to pamper oneself
faire des dégâts   to cause damage

un enfant gâté   a spoiled child
une gâterie   a treat

Want to learn more idiomatic expressions that contain verbs? Look at pages 530–542.

238

The Seven Simple Tenses

Singular	Plural
1 présent de l'indicatif	
gèle	gelons
gèles	gelez
gèle	gèlent
2 imparfait de l'indicatif	
gelais	gelions
gelais	geliez
gelait	gelaient
3 passé simple	
gelai	gelâmes
gelas	gelâtes
gela	gelèrent
4 futur	
gèlerai	gèlerons
gèleras	gèlerez
gèlera	gèleront
5 conditionnel	
gèlerais	gèlerions
gèlerais	gèleriez
gèlerait	gèleraient
6 présent du subjonctif	
gèle	gelions
gèles	geliez
gèle	gèlent
7 imparfait du subjonctif	
gelasse	gelassions
gelasses	gelassiez
gelât	gelassent

The Seven Compound Tenses

Singular	Plural
8 passé composé	
ai gelé	avons gelé
as gelé	avez gelé
a gelé	ont gelé
9 plus-que-parfait de l'indicatif	
avais gelé	avions gelé
avais gelé	aviez gelé
avait gelé	avaient gelé
10 passé antérieur	
eus gelé	eûmes gelé
eus gelé	eûtes gelé
eut gelé	eurent gelé
11 futur antérieur	
aurai gelé	aurons gelé
auras gelé	aurez gelé
aura gelé	auront gelé
12 conditionnel passé	
aurais gelé	aurions gelé
aurais gelé	auriez gelé
aurait gelé	auraient gelé
13 passé du subjonctif	
aie gelé	ayons gelé
aies gelé	ayez gelé
ait gelé	aient gelé
14 plus-que-parfait du subjonctif	
eusse gelé	eussions gelé
eusses gelé	eussiez gelé
eût gelé	eussent gelé

Impératif
gèle
gelons
gelez

Sentences using this verb and words related to it
   Je ne veux pas sortir aujourd'hui parce qu'il gèle. Quand je me suis levé ce matin, j'ai regardé par la fenêtre et j'ai vu de la gelée partout.

Il gèle! It's freezing!
Qu'il gèle! Let it freeze!
le gel frost, freezing
la gelée frost; jello; jelly
congeler to congeal, to freeze

la congélation congelation, freezing, icing
le point de congélation freezing point
à la gelée jellied
le congélateur freezer

Soak up some verbs used in weather expressions on pages 557 and 558.

The subject pronouns are found on the page facing page 1.   **239**

to bother, to hamper, to constrict, to embarrass, to hinder, to impede, to inconvenience

The Seven Simple Tenses		The Seven Compound Tenses	
Singular	Plural	Singular	Plural
1 présent de l'indicatif		8 passé composé	
gêne	gênons	ai gêné	avons gêné
gênes	gênez	as gêné	avez gêné
gêne	gênent	a gêné	ont gêné
2 imparfait de l'indicatif		9 plus-que-parfait de l'indicatif	
gênais	gênions	avais gêné	avions gêné
gênais	gêniez	avais gêné	aviez gêné
gênait	gênaient	avait gêné	avaient gêné
3 passé simple		10 passé antérieur	
gênai	gênâmes	eus gêné	eûmes gêné
gênas	gênâtes	eus gêné	eûtes gêné
gêna	gênèrent	eut gêné	eurent gêné
4 futur		11 futur antérieur	
gênerai	gênerons	aurai gêné	aurons gêné
gêneras	gênerez	auras gêné	aurez gêné
gênera	gêneront	aura gêné	auront gêné
5 conditionnel		12 conditionnel passé	
gênerais	gênerions	aurais gêné	aurions gêné
gênerais	gêneriez	aurais gêné	auriez gêné
gênerait	gêneraient	aurait gêné	auraient gêné
6 présent du subjonctif		13 passé du subjonctif	
gêne	gênions	aie gêné	ayons gêné
gênes	gêniez	aies gêné	ayez gêné
gêne	gênent	ait gêné	aient gêné
7 imparfait du subjonctif		14 plus-que-parfait du subjonctif	
gênasse	gênassions	eusse gêné	eussions gêné
gênasses	gênassiez	eusses gêné	eussiez gêné
gênât	gênassent	eût gêné	eussent gêné

Impératif
gêne
gênons
gênez

Words and expressions related to this verb
se gêner   to inconvenience oneself
Ne vous gênez pas!   Put yourself at ease!
  Don't trouble yourself!
gêné, gênée   bothered, uncomfortable
un gêneur, une gêneuse   nuisance (person)

C'est gênant!   It's bothersome!
Cela vous gêne?   Does that bother you?
la gêne   embarrassment, discomfort
sans gêne   inconsiderate

Consult the sections on verbs used in idiomatic expressions, verbs with prepositions, and the list of over 1,100 verbs conjugated like model verbs in the back pages.

to lie down, to be lying down

The Seven Simple Tenses		The Seven Compound Tenses	
Singular	Plural	Singular	Plural

1   présent de l'indicatif

gis	**gisons**
gis	**gisez**
gît	**gisent**

2   imparfait de l'indicatif

gisais	**gisions**
gisais	**gisiez**
gisait	**gisaient**

This is a defective verb. It is used only in the two tenses given above.

Words and expressions related to this verb

un gisement   layer, deposit
un gisement de charbon   coal field
Ci-gît . . .   Here lies . . .
Ci-gisent . . .   Here lie . . .

gisant, gisante   lying, fallen, felled
un gîte   lodging, refuge, shelter
gîter   to lodge

This verb is generally used only in the above tenses. It is used primarily in reference to the dead, to sick persons lying down, and to inanimate objects that have been felled.

Consult the sections of verbs used in idiomatic expressions, verbs with prepositions, and the list of over 1,100 verbs conjugated like model verbs in the back pages.

goûter

to taste, to have a snack, to enjoy

The Seven Simple Tenses		The Seven Compound Tenses	
Singular	Plural	Singular	Plural
1 présent de l'indicatif		**8 passé composé**	
goûte	goûtons	ai goûté	avons goûté
goûtes	goûtez	as goûté	avez goûté
goûte	goûtent	a goûté	ont goûté
2 imparfait de l'indicatif		**9 plus-que-parfait de l'indicatif**	
goûtais	goûtions	avais goûté	avions goûté
goûtais	goûtiez	avais goûté	aviez goûté
goûtait	goûtaient	avait goûté	avaient goûté
3 passé simple		**10 passé antérieur**	
goûtai	goûtâmes	eus goûté	eûmes goûté
goûtas	goûtâtes	eus goûté	eûtes goûté
goûta	goûtèrent	eut goûté	eurent goûté
4 futur		**11 futur antérieur**	
goûterai	goûterons	aurai goûté	aurons goûté
goûteras	goûterez	auras goûté	aurez goûté
goûtera	goûteront	aura goûté	auront goûté
5 conditionnel		**12 conditionnel passé**	
goûterais	goûterions	aurais goûté	aurions goûté
goûterais	goûteriez	aurais goûté	auriez goûté
goûterait	goûteraient	aurait goûté	auraient goûté
6 présent du subjonctif		**13 passé du subjonctif**	
goûte	goûtions	aie goûté	ayons goûté
goûtes	goûtiez	aies goûté	ayez goûté
goûte	goûtent	ait goûté	aient goûté
7 imparfait du subjonctif		**14 plus-que-parfait du subjonctif**	
goûtasse	goûtassions	eusse goûté	eussions goûté
goûtasses	goûtassiez	eusses goûté	eussiez goûté
goûtât	goûtassent	eût goûté	eussent goûté

Impératif
goûte
goûtons
goûtez

Common idiomatic expressions using this verb

Quand j'arrive chez moi de l'école l'après-midi, j'ai l'habitude de prendre le goûter à quatre heures.

le goûter snack, bite to eat
goûter sur l'herbe to have a picnic
à chacun son goût To each his own
goûter à to drink or eat only a small quantity
le goût taste
de mauvais goût in bad taste

avoir un goût de to taste like
goûter de to eat or drink something for the first time
dégoûter to disgust
C'est dégoûtant! It's disgusting!

to grow (up, taller), to increase

The Seven Simple Tenses		The Seven Compound Tenses	
Singular	Plural	Singular	Plural
1 présent de l'indicatif		**8 passé composé**	
grandis	grandissons	ai grandi	avons grandi
grandis	grandissez	as grandi	avez grandi
grandit	grandissent	a grandi	ont grandi
2 imparfait de l'indicatif		**9 plus-que-parfait de l'indicatif**	
grandissais	grandissions	avais grandi	avions grandi
grandissais	grandissiez	avais grandi	aviez grandi
grandissait	grandissaient	avait grandi	avaient grandi
3 passé simple		**10 passé antérieur**	
grandis	grandîmes	eus grandi	eûmes grandi
grandis	grandîtes	eus grandi	eûtes grandi
grandit	grandirent	eut grandi	eurent grandi
4 futur		**11 futur antérieur**	
grandirai	grandirons	aurai grandi	aurons grandi
grandiras	grandirez	auras grandi	aurez grandi
grandira	grandiront	aura grandi	auront grandi
5 conditionnel		**12 conditionnel passé**	
grandirais	grandirions	aurais grandi	aurions grandi
grandirais	grandiriez	aurais grandi	auriez grandi
grandirait	grandiraient	aurait grandi	auraient grandi
6 présent du subjonctif		**13 passé du subjonctif**	
grandisse	grandissions	aie grandi	ayons grandi
grandisses	grandissiez	aies grandi	ayez grandi
grandisse	grandissent	ait grandi	aient grandi
7 imparfait du subjonctif		**14 plus-que-parfait du subjonctif**	
grandisse	grandissions	eusse grandi	eussions grandi
grandisses	grandissiez	eusses grandi	eussiez grandi
grandît	grandissent	eût grandi	eussent grandi

Impératif
grandis
grandissons
grandissez

Sentences using this verb and words related to it

Voyez-vous comme Joseph et Joséphine ont grandi? C'est incroyable! Quel âge ont-ils maintenant?

le grandissement growth
grandiose grandiose, grand
grand, grande tall
la grandeur size, greatness, grandeur
grandiosement grandiosely

agrandir to expand, to enlarge
un agrandissement enlargement, extension, aggrandizement
un enfant grandi trop vite a lanky child (grew tall too fast)

Taking a trip? Check out the popular words, phrases, and expressions for travelers on pages 599–621.

The subject pronouns are found on the page facing page 1.   **243**

to grate, to scrape, to scratch

The Seven Simple Tenses		The Seven Compound Tenses	
Singular	Plural	Singular	Plural
1 présent de l'indicatif		8 passé composé	
gratte	**grattons**	**ai gratté**	**avons gratté**
grattes	**grattez**	**as gratté**	**avez gratté**
gratte	**grattent**	**a gratté**	**ont gratté**
2 imparfait de l'indicatif		9 plus-que-parfait de l'indicatif	
grattais	**grattions**	**avais gratté**	**avions gratté**
grattais	**grattiez**	**avais gratté**	**aviez gratté**
grattait	**grattaient**	**avait gratté**	**avaient gratté**
3 passé simple		10 passé antérieur	
grattai	**grattâmes**	**eus gratté**	**eûmes gratté**
grattas	**grattâtes**	**eus gratté**	**eûtes gratté**
gratta	**grattèrent**	**eut gratté**	**eurent gratté**
4 futur		11 futur antérieur	
gratterai	**gratterons**	**aurai gratté**	**aurons gratté**
gratteras	**gratterez**	**auras gratté**	**aurez gratté**
grattera	**gratteront**	**aura gratté**	**auront gratté**
5 conditionnel		12 conditionnel passé	
gratterais	**gratterions**	**aurais gratté**	**aurions gratté**
gratterais	**gratteriez**	**aurais gratté**	**auriez gratté**
gratterait	**gratteraient**	**aurait gratté**	**auraient gratté**
6 présent du subjonctif		13 passé du subjonctif	
gratte	**grattions**	**aie gratté**	**ayons gratté**
grattes	**grattiez**	**aies gratté**	**ayez gratté**
gratte	**grattent**	**ait gratté**	**aient gratté**
7 imparfait du subjonctif		14 plus-que-parfait du subjonctif	
grattasse	**grattassions**	**eusse gratté**	**eussions gratté**
grattasses	**grattassiez**	**eusses gratté**	**eussiez gratté**
grattât	**grattassent**	**eût gratté**	**eussent gratté**

Impératif
gratte
grattons
grattez

Words and expressions related to this verb
le grattement   scratching
un gratte-ciel   skyscraper (**des gratte-ciel**)
un gratte-dos   back scratcher (**des gratte-dos**)
le grattage   scratching, scraping
un grattoir   scraper, grater
se gratter   to scratch oneself

Grammar putting you in a tense mood? Review the definitions of basic grammatical terms on pages 674–688.

to hail (weather)

The Seven Simple Tenses	The Seven Compound Tenses
Singular Plural	Singular Plural
1 présent de l'indicatif **il grêle**	8 passé composé **il a grêlé**
2 imparfait de l'indicatif **il grêlait**	9 plus-que-parfait de l'indicatif **il avait grêlé**
3 passé simple **il grêla**	10 passé antérieur **il eut grêlé**
4 futur **il grêlera**	11 futur antérieur **il aura grêlé**
5 conditionnel **il grêlerait**	12 conditionnel passé **il aurait grêlé**
6 présent du subjonctif **qu'il grêle**	13 passé du subjonctif **qu'il ait grêlé**
7 imparfait du subjonctif **qu'il grêlât**	14 plus-que-parfait du subjonctif **qu'il eût grêlé**

Impératif
Qu'il grêle!   Let it hail!

Words and expressions related to this verb
la grêle   hail (weather)
une averse de grêle   hail storm
un grêlon   hailstone

grêle *adj.*   thin, slender, slim; **un bras grêle**
thin arm; **une voix grêle**   shrill voice

Soak up some verbs used in weather expressions on pages 557 and 558.

grimper

Part. pr. **grimpant**   Part. passé **grimpé**

to climb

The Seven Simple Tenses		The Seven Compound Tenses	
Singular	Plural	Singular	Plural
1 présent de l'indicatif		**8 passé composé**	
grimpe	grimpons	ai grimpé	avons grimpé
grimpes	grimpez	as grimpé	avez grimpé
grimpe	grimpent	a grimpé	ont grimpé
2 imparfait de l'indicatif		**9 plus-que-parfait de l'indicatif**	
grimpais	grimpions	avais grimpé	avions grimpé
grimpais	grimpiez	avais grimpé	aviez grimpé
grimpait	grimpaient	avait grimpé	avaient grimpé
3 passé simple		**10 passé antérieur**	
grimpai	grimpâmes	eus grimpé	eûmes grimpé
grimpas	grimpâtes	eus grimpé	eûtes grimpé
grimpa	grimpèrent	eut grimpé	eurent grimpé
4 futur		**11 futur antérieur**	
grimperai	grimperons	aurai grimpé	aurons grimpé
grimperas	grimperez	auras grimpé	aurez grimpé
grimpera	grimperont	aura grimpé	auront grimpé
5 conditionnel		**12 conditionnel passé**	
grimperais	grimperions	aurais grimpé	aurions grimpé
grimperais	grimperiez	aurais grimpé	auriez grimpé
grimperait	grimperaient	aurait grimpé	auraient grimpé
6 présent du subjonctif		**13 passé du subjonctif**	
grimpe	grimpions	aie grimpé	ayons grimpé
grimpes	grimpiez	aies grimpé	ayez grimpé
grimpe	grimpent	ait grimpé	aient grimpé
7 imparfait du subjonctif		**14 plus-que-parfait du subjonctif**	
grimpasse	grimpassions	eusse grimpé	eussions grimpé
grimpasses	grimpassiez	eusses grimpé	eussiez grimpé
grimpât	grimpassent	eût grimpé	eussent grimpé

Impératif
grimpe
grimpons
grimpez

Words and expressions related to this verb
grimper à l'échelle   to climb a ladder
une plante grimpante   climbing plant
une grimpée, une grimpette   steep climb

un grimpeur, une grimpeuse   climber
grimper aux arbres   to climb trees

Use the EE-zee guide to French pronunciation on pages 566 and 567.

to chide, to reprimand, to scold

The Seven Simple Tenses		The Seven Compound Tenses	
Singular	Plural	Singular	Plural
1 présent de l'indicatif		8 passé composé	
gronde	grondons	ai grondé	avons grondé
grondes	grondez	as grondé	avez grondé
gronde	grondent	a grondé	ont grondé
2 imparfait de l'indicatif		9 plus-que-parfait de l'indicatif	
grondais	grondions	avais grondé	avions grondé
grondais	grondiez	avais grondé	aviez grondé
grondait	grondaient	avait grondé	avaient grondé
3 passé simple		10 passé antérieur	
grondai	grondâmes	eus grondé	eûmes grondé
grondas	grondâtes	eus grondé	eûtes grondé
gronda	grondèrent	eut grondé	eurent grondé
4 futur		11 futur antérieur	
gronderai	gronderons	aurai grondé	aurons grondé
gronderas	gronderez	auras grondé	aurez grondé
grondera	gronderont	aura grondé	auront grondé
5 conditionnel		12 conditionnel passé	
gronderais	gronderions	aurais grondé	aurions grondé
gronderais	gronderiez	aurais grondé	auriez grondé
gronderait	gronderaient	aurait grondé	auraient grondé
6 présent du subjonctif		13 passé du subjonctif	
gronde	grondions	aie grondé	ayons grondé
grondes	grondiez	aies grondé	ayez grondé
gronde	grondent	ait grondé	aient grondé
7 imparfait du subjonctif		14 plus-que-parfait du subjonctif	
grondasse	grondassions	eusse grondé	eussions grondé
grondasses	grondassiez	eusses grondé	eussiez grondé
grondât	grondassent	eût grondé	eussent grondé

Impératif
gronde
grondons
grondez

Sentences using this verb and words related to it
—Victor, pourquoi pleures-tu?
—La maîtresse de mathématiques m'a grondé.
—Pourquoi est-ce qu'elle t'a grondé? Qu'est-ce que tu as fait?
—Ce n'est pas parce que j'ai fait quelque chose. C'est parce que je n'ai rien fait. Je n'ai pas préparé la leçon.
—Alors, tu mérites une gronderie et une réprimande.
—C'est une grondeuse. Elle gronde à chaque instant. C'est une criarde.

une grondeuse   a scolder
une criarde   a nag, nagger

une gronderie   a scolding
à chaque instant   constantly

The subject pronouns are found on the page facing page 1.   **247**

guérir

to cure, to heal, to remedy, to recover

The Seven Simple Tenses		The Seven Compound Tenses	
Singular	Plural	Singular	Plural
1 présent de l'indicatif		**8 passé composé**	
guéris	guérissons	ai guéri	avons guéri
guéris	guérissez	as guéri	avez guéri
guérit	guérissent	a guéri	ont guéri
2 imparfait de l'indicatif		**9 plus-que-parfait de l'indicatif**	
guérissais	guérissions	avais guéri	avions guéri
guérissais	guérissiez	avais guéri	aviez guéri
guérissait	guérissaient	avait guéri	avaient guéri
3 passé simple		**10 passé antérieur**	
guéris	guérîmes	eus guéri	eûmes guéri
guéris	guérîtes	eus guéri	eûtes guéri
guérit	guérirent	eut guéri	eurent guéri
4 futur		**11 futur antérieur**	
guérirai	guérirons	aurai guéri	aurons guéri
guériras	guérirez	auras guéri	aurez guéri
guérira	guériront	aura guéri	auront guéri
5 conditionnel		**12 conditionnel passé**	
guérirais	guéririons	aurais guéri	aurions guéri
guérirais	guéririez	aurais guéri	auriez guéri
guérirait	guériraient	aurait guéri	auraient guéri
6 présent du subjonctif		**13 passé du subjonctif**	
guérisse	guérissions	aie guéri	ayons guéri
guérisses	guérissiez	aies guéri	ayez guéri
guérisse	guérissent	ait guéri	aient guéri
7 imparfait du subjonctif		**14 plus-que-parfait du subjonctif**	
guérisse	guérissions	eusse guéri	eussions guéri
guérisses	guérissiez	eusses guéri	eussiez guéri
guérît	guérissent	eût guéri	eussent guéri

Impératif
guéris
guérissons
guérissez

Sentences using this verb and words related to it

Madame Gérard est tombée dans l'escalier la semaine dernière et elle a reçu une blessure au genou. Elle est allée chez le médecin et maintenant elle est guérie.

une guérison healing, cure
guérisseur, guérisseuse healer
guérissable curable

guérir de to recover from, to cure of
la guérison par la foi faith healing

How are you doing? Find out with the verb drills and tests with answers explained on pages 622–673.

to get dressed, to dress (oneself)

The Seven Simple Tenses		The Seven Compound Tenses	
Singular	Plural	Singular	Plural
1 présent de l'indicatif		8 passé composé	
m'habille	**nous habillons**	**me suis habillé(e)**	**nous sommes habillé(e)s**
t'habilles	**vous habillez**	**t'es habillé(e)**	**vous êtes habillé(e)(s)**
s'habille	**s'habillent**	**s'est habillé(e)**	**se sont habillé(e)s**
2 imparfait de l'indicatif		9 plus-que-parfait de l'indicatif	
m'habillais	**nous habillions**	**m'étais habillé(e)**	**nous étions habillé(e)s**
t'habillais	**vous habilliez**	**t'étais habillé(e)**	**vous étiez habillé(e)(s)**
s'habillait	**s'habillaient**	**s'était habillé(e)**	**s'étaient habillé(e)s**
3 passé simple		10 passé antérieur	
m'habillai	**nous habillâmes**	**me fus habillé(e)**	**nous fûmes habillé(e)s**
t'habillas	**vous habillâtes**	**te fus habillé(e)**	**vous fûtes habillé(e)(s)**
s'habilla	**s'habillèrent**	**se fut habillé(e)**	**se furent habillé(e)s**
4 futur		11 futur antérieur	
m'habillerai	**nous habillerons**	**me serai habillé(e)**	**nous serons habillé(e)s**
t'habilleras	**vous habillerez**	**te seras habillé(e)**	**vous serez habillé(e)(s)**
s'habillera	**s'habilleront**	**se sera habillé(e)**	**se seront habillé(e)s**
5 conditionnel		12 conditionnel passé	
m'habillerais	**nous habillerions**	**me serais habillé(e)**	**nous serions habillé(e)s**
t'habillerais	**vous habilleriez**	**te serais habillé(e)**	**vous seriez habillé(e)(s)**
s'habillerait	**s'habilleraient**	**se serait habillé(e)**	**se seraient habillé(e)s**
6 présent du subjonctif		13 passé du subjonctif	
m'habille	**nous habillions**	**me sois habillé(e)**	**nous soyons habillé(e)s**
t'habilles	**vous habilliez**	**te sois habillé(e)**	**vous soyez habillé(e)(s)**
s'habille	**s'habillent**	**se soit habillé(e)**	**se soient habillé(e)s**
7 imparfait du subjonctif		14 plus-que-parfait du subjonctif	
m'habillasse	**nous habillassions**	**me fusse habillé(e)**	**nous fussions habillé(e)s**
t'habillasses	**vous habillassiez**	**te fusses habillé(e)**	**vous fussiez habillé(e)(s)**
s'habillât	**s'habillassent**	**se fût habillé(e)**	**se fussent habillé(e)s**

Impératif
habille-toi; ne t'habille pas
habillons-nous; ne nous habillons pas
habillez-vous; ne vous habillez pas

Sentences using this verb and words related to it
un habit   costume, outfit
les habits   clothes
habiller qqn   to dress someone
habillement *m.*   garment, wearing apparel
L'habit ne fait pas le moine   Clothes don't make the person (the monk).

See also **vêtir.**

déshabiller   to undress
se déshabiller   to undress oneself, to get undressed
habiller de   to clothe with
l'habit de gala   formal wear
l'habit militaire   military dress

Don't miss the definitions of basic grammatical terms with examples in English and French on pages 674–688.

habiter

Part. pr. **habitant**   Part. passé **habité**

to live (in), to dwell (in), to inhabit

The Seven Simple Tenses		The Seven Compound Tenses	
Singular	Plural	Singular	Plural
1 présent de l'indicatif		**8 passé composé**	
habite	habitons	ai habité	avons habité
habites	habitez	as habité	avez habité
habite	habitent	a habité	ont habité
2 imparfait de l'indicatif		**9 plus-que-parfait de l'indicatif**	
habitais	habitions	avais habité	avions habité
habitais	habitiez	avais habité	aviez habité
habitait	habitaient	avait habité	avaient habité
3 passé simple		**10 passé antérieur**	
habitai	habitâmes	eus habité	eûmes habité
habitas	habitâtes	eus habité	eûtes habité
habita	habitèrent	eut habité	eurent habité
4 futur		**11 futur antérieur**	
habiterai	habiterons	aurai habité	aurons habité
habiteras	habiterez	auras habité	aurez habité
habitera	habiteront	aura habité	auront habité
5 conditionnel		**12 conditionnel passé**	
habiterais	habiterions	aurais habité	aurions habité
habiterais	habiteriez	aurais habité	auriez habité
habiterait	habiteraient	aurait habité	auraient habité
6 présent du subjonctif		**13 passé du subjonctif**	
habite	habitions	aie habité	ayons habité
habites	habitiez	aies habité	ayez habité
habite	habitent	ait habité	aient habité
7 imparfait du subjonctif		**14 plus-que-parfait du subjonctif**	
habitasse	habitassions	eusse habité	eussions habité
habitasses	habitassiez	eusses habité	eussiez habité
habitât	habitassent	eût habité	eussent habité

Impératif
habite
habitons
habitez

Sentences using this verb and words related to it
—**Où habitez-vous?**
—**J'habite 27 rue Duparc dans une petite maison blanche.**
—**Avec qui habitez-vous?**
—**J'habite avec mes parents, mes frères, mes soeurs, et mon chien.**

une habitation dwelling, residence, abode
un habitat habitat
un habitant inhabitant
H.L.M. (habitation à loyer modéré) lodging
at a moderate rental

l' amélioration de l'habitat improvement of
living conditions
habiter à la campagne to live in the country
habiter la banlieue to live in the suburbs

Be careful! **Habitable** means *habitable* or *inhabitable*. But **inhabitable** means *uninhabitable*.

250

The Seven Simple Tenses		The Seven Compound Tenses	
Singular	Plural	Singular	Plural
1 présent de l'indicatif		**8 passé composé**	
hais	haïssons	ai haï	avons haï
hais	haïssez	as haï	avez haï
hait	haïssent	a haï	ont haï
2 imparfait de l'indicatif		**9 plus-que-parfait de l'indicatif**	
haïssais	haïssions	avais haï	avions haï
haïssais	haïssiez	avais haï	aviez haï
haïssait	haïssaient	avait haï	avaient haï
3 passé simple		**10 passé antérieur**	
haïs	haïmes	eus haï	eûmes haï
haïs	haïtes	eus haï	eûtes haï
haït	haïrent	eut haï	eurent haï
4 futur		**11 futur antérieur**	
haïrai	haïrons	aurai haï	aurons haï
haïras	haïrez	auras haï	aurez haï
haïra	haïront	aura haï	auront haï
5 conditionnel		**12 conditionnel passé**	
haïrais	haïrions	aurais haï	aurions haï
haïrais	haïriez	aurais haï	auriez haï
haïrait	haïraient	aurait haï	auraient haï
6 présent du subjonctif		**13 passé du subjonctif**	
haïsse	haïssions	aie haï	ayons haï
haïsses	haïssiez	aies haï	ayez haï
haïsse	haïssent	ait haï	aient haï
7 imparfait du subjonctif		**14 plus-que-parfait du subjonctif**	
haïsse	haïssions	eusse haï	eussions haï
haïsses	haïssiez	eusses haï	eussiez haï
haït	haïssent	eût haï	eussent haï

Impératif
hais
haïssons
haïssez

Sentences using this verb and words related to it
   Je hais le mensonge, je hais la médiocrité, et je hais la calomnie. Ces choses sont haïssables. Je hais Marguerite et Jeanne; elles sont haineuses.

haïssable detestable, hateful	**haïr qqn comme la peste** to hate somebody
la haine hatred, hate	like poison
haineux, haineuse hateful, heinous	**des haines mesquines** petty hatreds

This verb begins with aspirate *h*; make no liaison and use *je* instead of *j'*.

hésiter
to hesitate

Part. pr. **hésitant**   Part. passé **hésité**

The Seven Simple Tenses		The Seven Compound Tenses	
Singular	Plural	Singular	Plural
1 présent de l'indicatif		**8 passé composé**	
hésite	hésitons	ai hésité	avons hésité
hésites	hésitez	as hésité	avez hésité
hésite	hésitent	a hésité	ont hésité
2 imparfait de l'indicatif		**9 plus-que-parfait de l'indicatif**	
hésitais	hésitions	avais hésité	avions hésité
hésitais	hésitiez	avais hésité	aviez hésité
hésitait	hésitaient	avait hésité	avaient hésité
3 passé simple		**10 passé antérieur**	
hésitai	hésitâmes	eus hésité	eûmes hésité
hésitas	hésitâtes	eus hésité	eûtes hésité
hésita	hésitèrent	eut hésité	eurent hésité
4 futur		**11 futur antérieur**	
hésiterai	hésiterons	aurai hésité	aurons hésité
hésiteras	hésiterez	auras hésité	aurez hésité
hésitera	hésiteront	aura hésité	auront hésité
5 conditionnel		**12 conditionnel passé**	
hésiterais	hésiterions	aurais hésité	aurions hésité
hésiterais	hésiteriez	aurais hésité	auriez hésité
hésiterait	hésiteraient	aurait hésité	auraient hésité
6 présent du subjonctif		**13 passé du subjonctif**	
hésite	hésitions	aie hésité	ayons hésité
hésites	hésitiez	aies hésité	ayez hésité
hésite	hésitent	ait hésité	aient hésité
7 imparfait du subjonctif		**14 plus-que-parfait du subjonctif**	
hésitasse	hésitassions	eusse hésité	eussions hésité
hésitasses	hésitassiez	eusses hésité	eussiez hésité
hésitât	hésitassent	eût hésité	eussent hésité

Impératif
hésite
hésitons
hésitez

Words and expressions related to this verb
hésiter à faire qqch to hesitate to do something
une hésitation hesitation
hésitant, hésitante undecided, hesitating
sans hésitation unhesitatingly, without hesitation

Get acquainted with what preposition goes with what verb on pages 543–553.

The Seven Simple Tenses		The Seven Compound Tenses	
Singular	Plural	Singular	Plural
1 présent de l'indicatif		**8 passé composé**	
impose	imposons	ai imposé	avons imposé
imposes	imposez	as imposé	avez imposé
impose	imposent	a imposé	ont imposé
2 imparfait de l'indicatif		**9 plus-que-parfait de l'indicatif**	
imposais	imposions	avais imposé	avions imposé
imposais	imposiez	avais imposé	aviez imposé
imposait	imposaient	avait imposé	avaient imposé
3 passé simple		**10 passé antérieur**	
imposai	imposâmes	eus imposé	eûmes imposé
imposas	imposâtes	eus imposé	eûtes imposé
imposa	imposèrent	eut imposé	eurent imposé
4 futur		**11 futur antérieur**	
imposerai	imposerons	aurai imposé	aurons imposé
imposeras	imposerez	auras imposé	aurez imposé
imposera	imposeront	aura imposé	auront imposé
5 conditionnel		**12 conditionnel passé**	
imposerais	imposerions	aurais imposé	aurions imposé
imposerais	imposeriez	aurais imposé	auriez imposé
imposerait	imposeraient	aurait imposé	auraient imposé
6 présent du subjonctif		**13 passé du subjonctif**	
impose	imposions	aie imposé	ayons imposé
imposes	imposiez	aies imposé	ayez impoé
impose	imposent	ait imposé	aient imposé
7 imparfait du subjonctif		**14 plus-que-parfait du subjonctif**	
imposasse	imposassions	eusse imposé	eussions imposé
imposasses	imposassiez	eusses imposé	eussiez imposé
imposât	imposassent	eût imposé	eussent imposé

Impératif
impose
imposons
imposez

Words and expressions related to this verb
s'imposer   to assert oneself
s'imposer à   to intrude on
imposable   taxable
un impôt   tax; **l'impôt sur le revenu**
   income tax

une imposition   imposition
imposant, imposante   imposing, impressive
imposer le respect   to compel respect
imposer une règle   to lay down a rule

Want to learn more idiomatic expressions that contain verbs? Look at pages 530–542.

The subject pronouns are found on the page facing page 1.   **253**

inclure

Part. pr. **incluyant**   Part. passé **inclus**

to include, to enclose

The Seven Simple Tenses		The Seven Compound Tenses	
Singular	Plural	Singular	Plural
1 présent de l'indicatif		**8 passé composé**	
inclus	incluons	ai inclus	avons inclus
inclus	incluez	as inclus	avez inclus
inclut	incluent	a inclus	ont inclus
2 imparfait de l'indicatif		**9 plus-que-parfait de l'indicatif**	
incluais	incluions	avais inclus	avions inclus
incluais	incluiez	avais inclus	aviez inclus
incluait	incluaient	avait inclus	avaient inclus
3 passé simple		**10 passé antérieur**	
inclus	inclûmes	eus inclus	eûmes inclus
inclus	inclûtes	eus inclus	eûtes inclus
inclut	inclurent	eut inclus	eurent inclus
4 futur		**11 futur antérieur**	
inclurai	inclurons	aurai inclus	aurons inclus
incluras	inclurez	auras inclus	aurez inclus
inclura	incluront	aura inclus	auront inclus
5 conditionnel		**12 conditionnel passé**	
inclurais	inclurions	aurais inclus	aurions inclus
inclurais	incluriez	aurais inclus	auriez inclus
inclurait	incluraient	aurait inclus	auraient inclus
6 présent du subjonctif		**13 passé du subjonctif**	
inclue	incluions	aie inclus	ayons inclus
inclues	incluiez	aies inclus	ayez inclus
inclue	incluent	ait inclus	aient inclus
7 imparfait du subjonctif		**14 plus-que-parfait du subjonctif**	
inclusse	inclussions	eusse inclus	eussions inclus
inclusses	inclussiez	eusses inclus	eussiez inclus
inclût	inclussent	eût inclus	eussent inclus

Impératif
inclus
incluons
incluez

Words and expressions related to this verb
la lettre ci-incluse the letter enclosed
herewith
l'argent ci-inclus the money enclosed
herewith
une inclusion inclusion
inclusif, inclusive inclusive

See also **conclure.**

inclusivement inclusively
service inclus service included (no tip necessary)
exclure to exclude
exclusivement exclusively
exclusif, exclusive exclusive
une exclusion exclusion
exclu, exclue excluded

Consult the sections on verbs used in idiomatic expressions, verbs with prepositions, and the list
of over 1,100 verbs conjugated like model verbs in the back pages.

to indicate, to point out, to show

The Seven Simple Tenses		The Seven Compound Tenses	
Singular	Plural	Singular	Plural
1 présent de l'indicatif		8 passé composé	
indique	indiquons	ai indiqué	avons indiqué
indiques	indiquez	as indiqué	avez indiqué
indique	indiquent	a indiqué	ont indiqué
2 imparfait de l'indicatif		9 plus-que-parfait de l'indicatif	
indiquais	indiquions	avais indiqué	avions indiqué
indiquais	indiquiez	avais indiqué	aviez indiqué
indiquait	indiquaient	avait indiqué	avaient indiqué
3 passé simple		10 passé antérieur	
indiquai	indiquâmes	eus indiqué	eûmes indiqué
indiquas	indiquâtes	eus indiqué	eûtes indiqué
indiqua	indiquèrent	eut indiqué	eurent indiqué
4 futur		11 futur antérieur	
indiquerai	indiquerons	aurai indiqué	aurons indiqué
indiqueras	indiquerez	auras indiqué	aurez indiqué
indiquera	indiqueront	aura indiqué	auront indiqué
5 conditionnel		12 conditionnel passé	
indiquerais	indiquerions	aurais indiqué	aurions indiqué
indiquerais	indiqueriez	aurais indiqué	auriez indiqué
indiquerait	indiqueraient	aurait indiqué	auraient indiqué
6 présent du subjonctif		13 passé du subjonctif	
indique	indiquions	aie indiqué	ayons indiqué
indiques	indiquiez	aies indiqué	ayez indiqué
indique	indiquent	ait indiqué	aient indiqué
7 imparfait du subjonctif		14 plus-que-parfait du subjonctif	
indiquasse	indiquassions	eusse indiqué	eussions indiqué
indiquasses	indiquassiez	eusses indiqué	eussiez indiqué
indiquât	indiquassent	eût indiqué	eussent indiqué

Impératif
indique
indiquons
indiquez

Words and expressions related to this verb
indiquer du doigt   to point out (with one's finger)
indiquer un bon médecin   to recommend a good doctor
une indication   indication
indicatif, indicative   indicative
un indice   index
indicateur, indicatrice   indicator
un indicateur de vitesse   speedometer

How are you doing? Find out with the verb drills and tests with answers explained on pages 622–673.

The subject pronouns are found on the page facing page 1.

s'informer

Part. pr. s'**informant**   Part. passé **informé**

to find out, to inquire, to make inquiries, to inform oneself

The Seven Simple Tenses		The Seven Compound Tenses	
Singular	Plural	Singular	Plural
1 présent de l'indicatif		**8 passé composé**	
m'informe	nous informons	me suis informé(e)	nous sommes informé(e)s
t'informes	vous informez	t'es informé(e)	vous êtes informé(e)(s)
s'informe	s'informent	s'est informé(e)	se sont informé(e)s
2 imparfait de l'indicatif		**9 plus-que-parfait de l'indicatif**	
m'informais	nous informions	m'étais informé(e)	nous étions informé(e)s
t'informais	vous informiez	t'étais informé(e)	vous étiez informé(e)(s)
s'informait	s'informaient	s'était informé(e)	s'étaient informé(e)s
3 passé simple		**10 passé antérieur**	
m'informai	nous informâmes	me fus informé(e)	nous fûmes informé(e)s
t'informas	vous informâtes	te fus informé(e)	vous fûtes informé(e)(s)
s'informa	s'informèrent	se fut informé(e)	se furent informé(e)s
4 futur		**11 futur antérieur**	
m'informerai	nous informerons	me serai informé(e)	nous serons informé(e)s
t'informeras	vous informerez	te seras informé(e)	vous serez informé(e)(s)
s'informera	s'informeront	se sera informé(e)	se seront informé(e)s
5 conditionnel		**12 conditionnel passé**	
m'informerais	nous informerions	me serais informé(e)	nous serions informé(e)s
t'informerais	vous informeriez	te serais informé(e)	vous seriez informé(e)(s)
s'informerait	s'informeraient	se serait informé(e)	se seraient informé(e)s
6 présent du subjonctif		**13 passé du subjonctif**	
m'informe	nous informions	me sois informé(e)	nous soyons informé(e)s
t'informes	vous informiez	te sois informé(e)	vous soyez informé(e)(s)
s'informe	s'informent	se soit informé(e)	se soient informé(e)s
7 imparfait du subjonctif		**14 plus-que-parfait du subjonctif**	
m'informasse	nous informassions	me fusse informé(e)	nous fussions informé(e)s
t'informasses	vous informassiez	te fusses informé(e)	vous fussiez informé(e)(s)
s'informât	s'informassent	se fût informé(e)	se fussent informé(e)s

Impératif
informe-toi; ne t'informe pas
informons-nous; ne nous informons pas
informez-vous; ne vous informez pas

Words and expressions related to this verb

informer   to inform, to advise
Je vous informe que . . .   I am informing you that . . .
les informations *f.*   new items, news bulletins
informatif, informative   informative
informationnel, informationnelle informational
l'informatique *f.*   computer science
s'informer de   to inquire about

prendre des informations sur qqn   to make inquiries about someone
un informateur, une informatrice   informer, informant
une information officielle   official investigation
former   to form
un informaticien, une informaticienne computer scientist

Consult the sections on verbs used in idiomatic expressions, verbs with prepositions, and the list of over 1,100 verbs conjugated like model verbs in the back pages.

to worry, to be upset

The Seven Simple Tenses		The Seven Compound Tenses	
Singular	Plural	Singular	Plural
1 présent de l'indicatif		**8 passé composé**	
m'inquiète	**nous inquiétons**	**me suis inquiété(e)**	**nous sommes inquiété(e)s**
t'inquiètes	**vous inquiétez**	**t'es inquiété(e)**	**vous êtes inquiété(e)(s)**
s'inquiète	**s'inquiètent**	**s'est inquiété(e)**	**se sont inquiété(e)s**
2 imparfait de l'indicatif		**9 plus-que-parfait de l'indicatif**	
m'inquiétais	**nous inquiétions**	**m'étais inquiété(e)**	**nous étions inquiété(e)s**
t'inquiétais	**vous inquiétiez**	**t'étais inquiété(e)**	**vous étiez inquiété(e)(s)**
s'inquiétait	**s'inquiétaient**	**s'était inquiété(e)**	**s'étaient inquiété(e)s**
3 passé simple		**10 passé antérieur**	
m'inquiétai	**nous inquiétâmes**	**me fus inquiété(e)**	**nous fûmes inquiété(e)s**
t'inquiétas	**vous inquiétâtes**	**te fus inquiété(e)**	**vous fûtes inquiété(e)(s)**
s'inquiéta	**s'inquiétèrent**	**se fut inquiété(e)**	**se furent inquiété(e)s**
4 futur		**11 futur antérieur**	
m'inquiéterai	**nous inquiéterons**	**me serai inquiété(e)**	**nous serons inquiété(e)s**
t'inquiéteras	**vous inquiéterez**	**te seras inquiété(e)**	**vous serez inquiété(e)(s)**
s'inquiétera	**s'inquiéteront**	**se sera inquiété(e)**	**se seront inquiété(e)s**
5 conditionnel		**12 conditionnel passé**	
m'inquiéterais	**nous inquiéterions**	**me serais inquiété(e)**	**nous serions inquiété(e)s**
t'inquiéterais	**vous inquiéteriez**	**te serais inquiété(e)**	**vous seriez inquiété(e)(s)**
s'inquiéterait	**s'inquiéteraient**	**se serait inquiété(e)**	**se seraient inquiété(e)s**
6 présent du subjonctif		**13 passé du subjonctif**	
m'inquiète	**nous inquiétions**	**me sois inquiété(e)**	**nous soyons inquiété(e)s**
t'inquiètes	**vous inquiétiez**	**te sois inquiété(e)**	**vous soyez inquiété(e)(s)**
s'inquiète	**s'inquiètent**	**se soit inquiété(e)**	**se soient inquiété(e)s**
7 imparfait du subjonctif		**14 plus-que-parfait du subjonctif**	
m'inquiétasse	**nous inquiétassions**	**me fusse inquiété(e)**	**nous fussions inquiété(e)s**
t'inquiétasses	**vous inquiétassiez**	**te fusses inquiété(e)**	**vous fussiez inquiété(e)(s)**
s'inquiétât	**s'inquiétassent**	**se fût inquiété(e)**	**se fussent inquiété(e)s**

Impératif
inquiète-toi, ne t'inquiète pas
inquiétons-nous; ne nous inquiétons pas
inquiétez-vous; ne vous inquiétez pas

Words related to this verb
s'inquiéter de   to worry about
inquiéter   to trouble, to worry
une inquiétude   restlessness, anxiety, uneasiness
inquiétant, inquiétante   disturbing, alarming
inquiet, inquiète   restless, alarmed, disturbed, worried

Grammar putting you in a tense mood? Review the definitions of basic grammatical terms with examples on pages 674–688.

to insist

The Seven Simple Tenses		The Seven Compound Tenses	
Singular	Plural	Singular	Plural
1 présent de l'indicatif		8 passé composé	
insiste	insistons	ai insisté	avons insisté
insistes	insistez	as insisté	avez insisté
insiste	insistent	a insisté	ont insisté
2 imparfait de l'indicatif		9 plus-que-parfait de l'indicatif	
insistais	insistions	avais insisté	avions insisté
insistais	insistiez	avais insisté	aviez insisté
insistait	insistaient	avait insisté	avaient insisté
3 passé simple		10 passé antérieur	
insistai	insistâmes	eus insisté	eûmes insisté
insistas	insistâtes	eus insisté	eûtes insisté
insista	insistèrent	eut insisté	eurent insisté
4 futur		11 futur antérieur	
insisterai	insisterons	aurai insisté	aurons insisté
insisteras	insisterez	auras insisté	aurez insisté
insistera	insisteront	aura insisté	auront insisté
5 conditionnel		12 conditionnel passé	
insisterais	insisterions	aurais insisté	aurions insisté
insisterais	insisteriez	aurais insisté	auriez insisté
insisterait	insisteraient	aurait insisté	auraient insisté
6 présent du subjonctif		13 passé du subjonctif	
insiste	insistions	aie insisté	ayons insisté
insistes	insistiez	aies insisté	ayez insisté
insiste	insistent	ait insisté	aient insisté
7 imparfait du subjonctif		14 plus-que-parfait du subjonctif	
insistasse	insistassions	eusse insisté	eussions insisté
insistasses	insistassiez	eusses insisté	eussiez insisté
insistât	insistassent	eût insisté	eussent insisté

Impératif
insiste
insistons
insistez

Sentences using this verb and words related to it
Madame Albertine, maîtresse de français, insiste beaucoup sur la discipline dans cette école.

insistant, insistante insistent, persistent
l'insistance f. insistence

insister sur to insist on
inutile d'insister useless to insist

It's important that you be familiar with the Subjunctive. See pages 560–565.

The Seven Simple Tenses		The Seven Compound Tenses	
Singular	Plural	Singular	Plural
1 présent de l'indicatif		8 passé composé	
instruis	**instruisons**	**ai instruit**	**avons instruit**
instruis	**instruisez**	**as instruit**	**avez instruit**
instruit	**instruisent**	**a instruit**	**ont instruit**
2 imparfait de l'indicatif		9 plus-que-parfait de l'indicatif	
instruisais	**instruisions**	**avais instruit**	**avions instruit**
instruisais	**instruisiez**	**avais instruit**	**aviez instruit**
instruisait	**instruisaient**	**avait instruit**	**avaient instruit**
3 passé simple		10 passé antérieur	
instruisis	**instruisîmes**	**eus instruit**	**eûmes instruit**
instruisis	**instruisîtes**	**eus instruit**	**eûtes instruit**
instruisit	**instruisirent**	**eut instruit**	**eurent instruit**
4 futur		11 futur antérieur	
instruirai	**instruirons**	**aurai instruit**	**aurons instruit**
instruiras	**instruirez**	**auras instruit**	**aurez instruit**
instruira	**instruiront**	**aura instruit**	**auront instruit**
5 conditionnel		12 conditionnel passé	
instruirais	**instruirions**	**aurais instruit**	**aurions instruit**
instruirais	**instruiriez**	**aurais instruit**	**auriez instruit**
instruirait	**instruiraient**	**aurait instruit**	**auraient instruit**
6 présent du subjonctif		13 passé du subjonctif	
instruise	**instruisions**	**aie instruit**	**ayons instruit**
instruises	**instruisiez**	**aies instruit**	**ayez instruit**
instruise	**instruisent**	**ait instruit**	**aient instruit**
7 imparfait du subjonctif		14 plus-que-parfait du subjonctif	
instruisisse	**instruisissions**	**eusse instruit**	**eussions instruit**
instruisisses	**instruisissiez**	**eusses instruit**	**eussiez instruit**
instruisît	**instruisissent**	**eût instruit**	**eussent instruit**

Impératif
instruis
instruisons
instruisez

Words and expressions related to this verb
instruit, instruite   educated
instruction *f.*   instruction, teaching
sans instruction   uneducated
instructeur, instructrice   instructor
instructif, instructive   instructive

les instructions   instructions
s'instruire   to teach oneself, to educate oneself
l'instruction publique   public education
bien instruit (instruite), fort instruit
   (instruite)   well educated

Get acquainted with what preposition goes with what verb on pages 543–553.

The subject pronouns are found on the page facing page 1.   **259**

interdire

Part. pr. **interdisant**   Part. passé **interdit**

to forbid, to prohibit

The Seven Simple Tenses		The Seven Compound Tenses	
Singular	Plural	Singular	Plural
1 présent de l'indicatif		**8 passé composé**	
interdis	interdisons	ai interdit	avons interdit
interdis	interdisez	as interdit	avez interdit
interdit	interdisent	a interdit	ont interdit
2 imparfait de l'indicatif		**9 plus-que-parfait de l'indicatif**	
interdisais	interdisions	avais interdit	avions interdit
interdisais	interdisiez	avais interdit	aviez interdit
interdisait	interdisaient	avait interdit	avaient interdit
3 passé simple		**10 passé antérieur**	
interdis	interdîmes	eus interdit	eûmes interdit
interdis	interdîtes	eus interdit	eûtes interdit
interdit	interdirent	eut interdit	eurent interdit
4 futur		**11 futur antérieur**	
interdirai	interdirons	aurai interdit	aurons interdit
interdiras	interdirez	auras interdit	aurez interdit
interdira	interdiront	aura interdit	auront interdit
5 conditionnel		**12 conditionnel passé**	
interdirais	interdirions	aurais interdit	aurions interdit
interdirais	interdiriez	aurais interdit	auriez interdit
interdirait	interdiraient	aurait interdit	auraient interdit
6 présent du subjonctif		**13 passé du subjonctif**	
interdise	interdisions	aie interdit	ayons interdit
interdises	interdisiez	aies interdit	ayez interdit
interdise	interdisent	ait interdit	aient interdit
7 imparfait du subjonctif		**14 plus-que-parfait du subjonctif**	
interdisse	interdissions	eusse interdit	eussions interdit
interdisses	interdissiez	eusses interdit	eussiez interdit
interdît	interdissent	eût interdit	eussent interdit

Impératif
interdis
interdisons
interdisez

Sentences using this verb and words and expressions related to it

Je vous interdis de m'interrompre constamment, je vous interdis d'entrer dans la salle de classe en retard, et je vous interdis de quitter la salle sans permission.

interdire qqch à qqn   to forbid someone something
l'interdit *m.*   interdict; *adj.* **les jeux interdits**   forbidden games
l'interdiction *f.*   interdiction, prohibition
Il est interdit de marcher sur l'herbe   Do not walk on the grass.
interdire à qqn de faire qqch   to forbid someone from doing something
STATIONNEMENT INTERDIT   NO PARKING

See also **contredire, dire, maudire, médire,** and **prédire.**

260

The Seven Simple Tenses		The Seven Compound Tenses	
Singular	Plural	Singular	Plural
1 présent de l'indicatif		**8 passé composé**	
m'intéresse	**nous intéressons**	**me suis intéressé(e)**	**nous sommes intéressé(e)s**
t'intéresses	**vous intéressez**	**t'es intéressé(e)**	**vous êtes intéressé(e)(s)**
s'intéresse	**s'intéressent**	**s'est intéressé(e)**	**se sont intéressé(e)s**
2 imparfait de l'indicatif		**9 plus-que-parfait de l'indicatif**	
m'intéressais	**nous intéressions**	**m'étais intéressé(e)**	**nous étions intéressé(e)s**
t'intéressais	**vous intéressiez**	**t'étais intéressé(e)**	**vous étiez intéressé(e)(s)**
s'intéressait	**s'intéressaient**	**s'était intéressé(e)**	**s'étaient intéressé(e)s**
3 passé simple		**10 passé antérieur**	
m'intéressai	**nous intéressâmes**	**me fus intéressé(e)**	**nous fûmes intéressé(e)s**
t'intéressas	**vous intéressâtes**	**te fus intéressé(e)**	**vous fûtes intéressé(e)(s)**
s'intéressa	**s'intéressèrent**	**se fut intéressé(e)**	**se furent intéressé(e)s**
4 futur		**11 futur antérieur**	
m'intéresserai	**nous intéresserons**	**me serai intéressé(e)**	**nous serons intéressé(e)s**
t'intéresseras	**vous intéresserez**	**te seras intéressé(e)**	**vous serez intéressé(e)(s)**
s'intéressera	**s'intéresseront**	**se sera intéressé(e)**	**se seront intéressé(e)s**
5 conditionnel		**12 conditionnel passé**	
m'intéresserais	**nous intéresserions**	**me serais intéressé(e)**	**nous serions intéressé(e)s**
t'intéresserais	**vous intéresseriez**	**te serais intéressé(e)**	**vous seriez intéressé(e)(s)**
s'intéresserait	**s'intéresseraient**	**se serait intéressé(e)**	**se seraient intéressé(e)s**
6 présent du subjonctif		**13 passé du subjonctif**	
m'intéresse	**nous intéressions**	**me sois intéressé(e)**	**nous soyons intéressé(e)s**
t'intéresses	**vous intéressiez**	**te sois intéressé(e)**	**vous soyez intéressé(e)(s)**
s'intéresse	**s'intéressent**	**se soit intéressé(e)**	**se soient intéressé(e)s**
7 imparfait du subjonctif		**14 plus-que-parfait du subjonctif**	
m'intéressasse	**nous intéressassions**	**me fusse intéressé(e)**	**nous fussions intéressé(e)s**
t'intéressasses	**vous intéressassiez**	**te fusses intéressé(e)**	**vous fussiez intéressé(e)(s)**
s'intéressât	**s'intéressassent**	**se fût intéressé(e)**	**se fussent intéressé(e)s**

Impératif
intéresse-toi; ne t'intéresse pas
intéressons-nous; ne nous intéressons pas
intéressez-vous; ne vous intéressez pas

Words and expressions related to this verb
s'intéresser à qqch   to be interested in something, to concern oneself with
Je m'intéresse aux sports   I am interested in sports.
s'intéresser à qqn   to be interested in someone
Janine s'intéresse à lui   Janine is interested in him.
intéresser qqn à qqch   to interest someone in something
Je m'intéresse à tout   I am interested in everything.
Cela ne m'intéresse pas du tout   That does not interest me at all.
un intérêt   interest
intéressant, intéressante   interesting
Rien ne m'intéresse   Nothing interests me.

The subject pronouns are found on the page facing page 1.   **261**

interroger

Part. pr. interrogeant   **Part. passé** interrogé

to interrogate, to question

The Seven Simple Tenses		The Seven Compound Tenses	
Singular	Plural	Singular	Plural
1 présent de l'indicatif		**8 passé composé**	
interroge	interrogeons	ai interrogé	avons interrogé
interroges	interrogez	as interrogé	avez interrogé
interroge	interrogent	a interrogé	ont interrogé
2 imparfait de l'indicatif		**9 plus-que-parfait de l'indicatif**	
interrogeais	interrogions	avais interrogé	avions interrogé
interrogeais	interrogiez	avais interrogé	aviez interrogé
interrogeait	interrogeaient	avait interrogé	avaient interrogé
3 passé simple		**10 passé antérieur**	
interrogeai	interrogeâmes	eus interrogé	eûmes interrogé
interrogeas	interrogeâtes	eus interrogé	eûtes interrogé
interrogea	interrogèrent	eut interrogé	eurent interrogé
4 futur		**11 futur antérieur**	
interrogerai	interrogerons	aurai interrogé	aurons interrogé
interrogeras	interrogerez	auras interrogé	aurez interrogé
interrogera	interrogeront	aura interrogé	auront interrogé
5 conditionnel		**12 conditionnel passé**	
interrogerais	interrogerions	aurais interrogé	aurions interrogé
interrogerais	interrogeriez	aurais interrogé	auriez interrogé
interrogerait	interrogeraient	aurait interrogé	auraient interrogé
6 présent du subjonctif		**13 passé du subjonctif**	
interroge	interrogions	aie interrogé	ayons interrogé
interroges	interrogiez	aies interrogé	ayez interrogé
interroge	interrogent	ait interrogé	aient interrogé
7 imparfait du subjonctif		**14 plus-que-parfait du subjonctif**	
interrogeasse	interrogeassions	eusse interrogé	eussions interrogé
interrogeasses	interrogeassiez	eusses interrogé	eussiez interrogé
interrogeât	interrogeassent	eût interrogé	eussent interrogé

Impératif
interroge
interrogeons
interrogez

Words and expressions related to this verb
une interrogation interrogation, questioning
un point d'interrogation question mark
un interrogateur, une interrogatrice
  interrogator

interrogatif, interrogative interrogative
interrogativement interrogatively
un interrogatoire interrogation
dérogatoire derogatory

How are you doing? Find out with the verb drills and tests with answers explained on pages 622–673.

The Seven Simple Tenses		The Seven Compound Tenses	
Singular	Plural	Singular	Plural
1 présent de l'indicatif		**8 passé composé**	
interromps	interrompons	ai interrompu	avons interrompu
interromps	interrompez	as interrompu	avez interrompu
interrompt	interrompent	a interrompu	ont interrompu
2 imparfait de l'indicatif		**9 plus-que-parfait de l'indicatif**	
interrompais	interrompions	avais interrompu	avions interrompu
interrompais	interrompiez	avais interrompu	aviez interrompu
interrompait	interrompaient	avait interrompu	avaient interrompu
3 passé simple		**10 passé antérieur**	
interrompis	interrompîmes	eus interrompu	eûmes interrompu
interrompis	interrompîtes	eus interrompu	eûtes interrompu
interrompit	interrompirent	eut interrompu	eurent interrompu
4 futur		**11 futur antérieur**	
interromprai	interromprons	aurai interrompu	aurons interrompu
interrompras	interromprez	auras interrompu	aurez interrompu
interrompra	interrompront	aura interrompu	auront interrompu
5 conditionnel		**12 conditionnel passé**	
interromprais	interromprions	aurais interrompu	aurions interrompu
interromprais	interrompriez	aurais interrompu	auriez interrompu
interromprait	interrompraient	aurait interrompu	auraient interrompu
6 présent du subjonctif		**13 passé du subjonctif**	
interrompe	interrompions	aie interrompu	ayons interrompu
interrompes	interrompiez	aies interrompu	ayez interrompu
interrompe	interrompent	ait interrompu	aient interrompu
7 imparfait du subjonctif		**14 plus-que-parfait du subjonctif**	
interrompisse	interrompissions	eusse interrompu	eussions interrompu
interrompisses	interrompissiez	eusses interrompu	eussiez interrompu
interrompît	interrompissent	eût interrompu	eussent interrompu

Impératif
interromps
interrompons
interrompez

Sentences using this verb and words related to it

—**Maurice, tu m'interromps à chaque instant. Cesse de m'interrompre, s'il te plaît! C'est
une mauvaise habitude et je ne l'aime pas. Est-ce que tu l'aimes quand on t'interrompt
continuellement?**

une interruption interruption
interrompu, interrompue interrupted

un interrupteur, une interruptrice
interrupter
un interrupteur light switch

See also **corrompre** and **rompre**.

Taking a trip? Check out the popular words, phrases, and expressions for travelers on pages
599–621.

introduire

Part. pr. **introduisant**   Part. passé **introduit**

to introduce, to show in

The Seven Simple Tenses		The Seven Compound Tenses	
Singular	Plural	Singular	Plural
1 présent de l'indicatif		**8 passé composé**	
introduis	introduisons	ai introduit	avons introduit
introduis	introduisez	as introduit	avez introduit
introduit	introduisent	a introduit	ont introduit
2 imparfait de l'indicatif		**9 plus-que-parfait de l'indicatif**	
introduisais	introduisions	avais introduit	avions introduit
introduisais	introduisiez	avais introduit	aviez introduit
introduisait	introduisaient	avait introduit	avaient introduit
3 passé simple		**10 passé antérieur**	
introduisis	introduisîmes	eus introduit	eûmes introduit
introduisis	introduisîtes	eus introduit	eûtes introduit
introduisit	introduisirent	eut introduit	eurent introduit
4 futur		**11 futur antérieur**	
introduirai	introduirons	aurai introduit	aurons introduit
introduiras	introduirez	auras introduit	aurez introduit
introduira	introduiront	aura introduit	auront introduit
5 conditionnel		**12 conditionnel passé**	
introduirais	introduirions	aurais introduit	aurions introduit
introduirais	introduiriez	aurais introduit	auriez introduit
introduirait	introduiraient	aurait introduit	auraient introduit
6 présent du subjonctif		**13 passé du subjonctif**	
introduise	introduisions	aie introduit	ayons introduit
introduises	introduisiez	aies introduit	ayez introduit
introduise	introduisent	ait introduit	aient introduit
7 imparfait du subjonctif		**14 plus-que-parfait du subjonctif**	
introduisisse	introduisissions	eusse introduit	eussions introduit
introduisisses	introduisissiez	eusses introduit	eussiez introduit
introduisît	introduisissent	eût introduit	eussent introduit

Impératif
introduis
introduisons
introduisez

Words related to this verb
introducteur, introductrice   introducer, initiator
introductif, introductive   introductory
introduction *f.*   introduction; **les paroles d'introduction**   introductory words

See also **conduire, déduire, produire, réduire, reproduire, séduire,** and **traduire.**

Want to learn more idiomatic expressions that contain verbs? Look at pages 530–542.

The Seven Simple Tenses		The Seven Compound Tenses	
Singular	Plural	Singular	Plural
1 présent de l'indicatif		8 passé composé	
invite	**invitons**	**ai invité**	**avons invité**
invites	**invitez**	**as invité**	**avez invité**
invite	**invitent**	**a invité**	**ont invité**
2 imparfait de l'indicatif		9 plus-que-parfait de l'indicatif	
invitais	**invitions**	**avais invité**	**avions invité**
invitais	**invitiez**	**avais invité**	**aviez invité**
invitait	**invitaient**	**avait invité**	**avaient invité**
3 passé simple		10 passé antérieur	
invitai	**invitâmes**	**eus invité**	**eûmes invité**
invitas	**invitâtes**	**eus invité**	**eûtes invité**
invita	**invitèrent**	**eut invité**	**eurent invité**
4 futur		11 futur antérieur	
inviterai	**inviterons**	**aurai invité**	**aurons invité**
inviteras	**inviterez**	**auras invité**	**aurez invité**
invitera	**inviteront**	**aura invité**	**auront invité**
5 conditionnel		12 conditionnel passé	
inviterais	**inviterions**	**aurais invité**	**aurions invité**
inviterais	**inviteriez**	**aurais invité**	**auriez invité**
inviterait	**inviteraient**	**aurait invité**	**auraient invité**
6 présent du subjonctif		13 passé du subjonctif	
invite	**invitions**	**aie invité**	**ayons invité**
invites	**invitiez**	**aies invité**	**ayez invité**
invite	**invitent**	**ait invité**	**aient invité**
7 imparfait du subjonctif		14 plus-que-parfait du subjonctif	
invitasse	**invitassions**	**eusse invité**	**eussions invité**
invitasses	**invitassiez**	**eusses invité**	**eussiez invité**
invitât	**invitassent**	**eût invité**	**eussent invité**

Impératif
invite
invitons
invitez

Sentences using this verb and words related to it

J'ai reçu une invitation à dîner chez les Martin. C'est pour samedi soir. J'ai accepté avec plaisir et maintenant je vais en ville acheter un cadeau pour eux.

l'invitation *f.*   invitation
les invités   the guests
sur l'invitation de   at the invitation of
sans invitation   without invitation, uninvited

inviter qqn à faire qqch   to invite someone to do something
Elle s'est invitée   She invited herself.
C'est moi qui invite!   My treat!

Going away? Don't forget to check out the practical situations for travelers on pages 568–598.

to throw, to cast

The Seven Simple Tenses		The Seven Compound Tenses	
Singular	Plural	Singular	Plural
1 présent de l'indicatif		**8 passé composé**	
jette	jetons	ai jeté	avons jeté
jettes	jetez	as jeté	avez jeté
jette	jettent	a jeté	ont jeté
2 imparfait de l'indicatif		**9 plus-que-parfait de l'indicatif**	
jetais	jetions	avais jeté	avions jeté
jetais	jetiez	avais jeté	aviez jeté
jetait	jetaient	avait jeté	avaient jeté
3 passé simple		**10 passé antérieur**	
jetai	jetâmes	eus jeté	eûmes jeté
jetas	jetâtes	eus jeté	eûtes jeté
jeta	jetèrent	eut jeté	eurent jeté
4 futur		**11 futur antérieur**	
jetterai	jetterons	aurai jeté	aurons jeté
jetteras	jetterez	auras jeté	aurez jeté
jettera	jetteront	aura jeté	auront jeté
5 conditionnel		**12 conditionnel passé**	
jetterais	jetterions	aurais jeté	aurions jeté
jetterais	jetteriez	aurais jeté	auriez jeté
jetterait	jetteraient	aurait jeté	auraient jeté
6 présent du subjonctif		**13 passé du subjonctif**	
jette	jetions	aie jeté	ayons jeté
jettes	jetiez	aies jeté	ayez jeté
jette	jettent	ait jeté	aient jeté
7 imparfait du subjonctif		**14 plus-que-parfait du subjonctif**	
jetasse	jetassions	eusse jeté	eussions jeté
jetasses	jetassiez	eusses jeté	eussiez jeté
jetât	jetassent	eût jeté	eussent jeté

Impératif
jette
jetons
jetez

Common idiomatic expressions using this verb
jeter un cri   to utter a cry
jeter son argent par la fenêtre   to throw out one's money
se jeter sur (contre)   to throw oneself at (against)
un jeton de téléphone   telephone slug, token
une jetée   jetty
un jet d'eau   fountain
jeter un coup d'oeil à   to glance at; **se jeter au cou de qqn**   to throw oneself at somebody
rejeter   to reject, to throw back; **projeter**   to plan, to project
jetable   disposable

Don't miss orthographically changing verbs on pages 554–556.

266

to join, to contact

The Seven Simple Tenses		The Seven Compound Tenses	
Singular	Plural	Singular	Plural
1 présent de l'indicatif		8 passé composé	
joins	**joignons**	**ai joint**	**avons joint**
joins	**joignez**	**as joint**	**avez joint**
joint	**joignent**	**a joint**	**ont joint**
2 imparfait de l'indicatif		9 plus-que-parfait de l'indicatif	
joignais	**joignions**	**avais joint**	**avions joint**
joignais	**joigniez**	**avais joint**	**aviez joint**
joignait	**joignaient**	**avait joint**	**avaient joint**
3 passé simple		10 passé antérieur	
joignis	**joignîmes**	**eus joint**	**eûmes joint**
joignis	**joignîtes**	**eus joint**	**eûtes joint**
joignit	**joignirent**	**eut joint**	**eurent joint**
4 futur		11 futur antérieur	
joindrai	**joindrons**	**aurai joint**	**aurons joint**
joindras	**joindrez**	**auras joint**	**aurez joint**
joindra	**joindront**	**aura joint**	**auront joint**
5 conditionnel		12 conditionnel passé	
joindrais	**joindrions**	**aurais joint**	**aurions joint**
joindrais	**joindriez**	**aurais joint**	**auriez joint**
joindrait	**joindraient**	**aurait joint**	**auraient joint**
6 présent du subjonctif		13 passé du subjonctif	
joigne	**joignions**	**aie joint**	**ayons joint**
joignes	**joigniez**	**aies joint**	**ayez joint**
joigne	**joignent**	**ait joint**	**aient joint**
7 imparfait du subjonctif		14 plus-que-parfait du subjonctif	
joignisse	**joignissions**	**eusse joint**	**eussions joint**
joignisses	**joignissiez**	**eusses joint**	**eussiez joint**
joignît	**joignissent**	**eût joint**	**eussent joint**

Impératif
joins
joignons
joignez

Common idiomatic expressions using this verb and words related to it

joindre les deux bouts   to make ends meet
les jointures des doigts   knuckles
joint, jointe   joined
les talons joints   heels together
ci-joint   herewith, attached
joindre à   to join to, to add to

rejoindre   to rejoin, to join together
se rejoindre   to meet, to come together again
se joindre à la discussion   to join in the discussion
joindre par téléphone   to reach by telephone

Use the EE-zee guide to French pronunciation on pages 566 and 567.

jouer

to play, to act (in a play), to gamble

The Seven Simple Tenses		The Seven Compound Tenses	
Singular	Plural	Singular	Plural
1 présent de l'indicatif		**8 passé composé**	
joue	jouons	ai joué	avons joué
joues	jouez	as joué	avez joué
joue	jouent	a joué	ont joué
2 imparfait de l'indicatif		**9 plus-que-parfait de l'indicatif**	
jouais	jouions	avais joué	avions joué
jouais	jouiez	avais joué	aviez joué
jouait	jouaient	avait joué	avaient joué
3 passé simple		**10 passé antérieur**	
jouai	jouâmes	eus joué	eûmes joué
jouas	jouâtes	eus joué	eûtes joué
joua	jouèrent	eut joué	eurent joué
4 futur		**11 futur antérieur**	
jouerai	jouerons	aurai joué	aurons joué
joueras	jouerez	auras joué	aurez joué
jouera	joueront	aura joué	auront joué
5 conditionnel		**12 conditionnel passé**	
jouerais	jouerions	aurais joué	aurions joué
jouerais	joueriez	aurais joué	auriez joué
jouerait	joueraient	aurait joué	auraient joué
6 présent du subjonctif		**13 passé du subjonctif**	
joue	jouions	aie joué	ayons joué
joues	jouiez	aies joué	ayez joué
joue	jouent	ait joué	aient joué
7 imparfait du subjonctif		**14 plus-que-parfait du subjonctif**	
jouasse	jouassions	eusse joué	eussions joué
jouasses	jouassiez	eusses joué	eussiez joué
jouât	jouassent	eût joué	eussent joué

Impératif
joue
jouons
jouez

Common idiomatic expressions using this verb

jouer au tennis to play tennis
jouer aux cartes to play cards
jouer du piano to play the piano
jouer un tour à qqn to play a trick on someone
un jouet toy, plaything
joueur, joueuse player, gambler
jouer sur les mots to play with words
déjouer to baffle, to thwart
jouer un rôle to play a part
jouer une partie de qqch to play a game of something

jouer de la flûte to play the flute
se jouer de to make fun of, to deride
un joujou, des joujoux toy, toys (child's language)
jouer gros jeu to play for high stakes
Cela va se jouer ce soir That will be settled tonight.
un jeu a game; **un jeu de cartes** a deck of cards; **un jeu d'outils** a set of tools

The Seven Simple Tenses		The Seven Compound Tenses	
Singular	Plural	Singular	Plural

1 présent de l'indicatif

		8 passé composé	
jouis	jouissons	ai joui	avons joui
jouis	jouissez	as joui	avez joui
jouit	jouissent	a joui	ont joui

2 imparfait de l'indicatif

		9 plus-que-parfait de l'indicatif	
jouissais	jouissions	avais joui	avions joui
jouissais	jouissiez	avais joui	aviez joui
jouissait	jouissaient	avait joui	avaient joui

3 passé simple

		10 passé antérieur	
jouis	jouîmes	eus joui	eûmes joui
jouis	jouîtes	eus joui	eûtes joui
jouit	jouirent	eut joui	eurent joui

4 futur

		11 futur antérieur	
jouirai	jouirons	aurai joui	aurons joui
jouiras	jouirez	auras joui	aurez joui
jouira	jouiront	aura joui	auront joui

5 conditionnel

		12 conditionnel passé	
jouirais	jouirions	aurais joui	aurions joui
jouirais	jouiriez	aurais joui	auriez joui
jouirait	jouiraient	aurait joui	auraient joui

6 présent du subjonctif

		13 passé du subjonctif	
jouisse	jouissions	aie joui	ayons joui
jouisses	jouissiez	aies joui	ayez joui
jouisse	jouissent	ait joui	aient joui

7 imparfait du subjonctif

		14 plus-que-parfait du subjonctif	
jouisse	jouissions	eusse joui	eussions joui
jouisses	jouissiez	eusses joui	eussiez joui
jouît	jouissent	eût joui	eussent joui

Impératif
jouis
jouissons
jouissez

Words and expressions related to this verb
jouir de qqch   to enjoy something
la jouissance   delight, enjoyment
la joie   joy; **la joie de vivre**   joy of living;
  avec joie   gladly
la réjouissance   rejoicing
se réjouir de   to rejoice in, to be delighted at

réjouir   to cheer up, to gladden, to rejoice
réjouir la vue   to be pleasing to the eye
réjouir le coeur   to gladden the heart
réjouissant, réjouissante   entertaining,
  amusing

Consult the sections on verbs used in idiomatic expressions, verbs with prepositions, and the list of over 1,100 verbs conjugated like model verbs in the back pages.

juger

Part. pr. **jugeant**   Part. passé **jugé**

to judge, to deem

The Seven Simple Tenses		The Seven Compound Tenses	
Singular	Plural	Singular	Plural
1 présent de l'indicatif		8 passé composé	
juge	jugeons	ai jugé	avons jugé
juges	jugez	as jugé	avez jugé
juge	jugent	a jugé	ont jugé
2 imparfait de l'indicatif		9 plus-que-parfait de l'indicatif	
jugeais	jugions	avais jugé	avions jugé
jugeais	jugiez	avais jugé	aviez jugé
jugeait	jugeaient	avait jugé	avaient jugé
3 passé simple		10 passé antérieur	
jugeai	jugeâmes	eus jugé	eûmes jugé
jugeas	jugeâtes	eus jugé	eûtes jugé
jugea	jugèrent	eut jugé	eurent jugé
4 futur		11 futur antérieur	
jugerai	jugerons	aurai jugé	aurons jugé
jugeras	jugerez	auras jugé	aurez jugé
jugera	jugeront	aura jugé	auront jugé
5 conditionnel		12 conditionnel passé	
jugerais	jugerions	aurais jugé	aurions jugé
jugerais	jugeriez	aurais jugé	auriez jugé
jugerait	jugeraient	aurait jugé	auraient jugé
6 présent du subjonctif		13 passé du subjonctif	
juge	jugions	aie jugé	ayons jugé
juges	jugiez	aies jugé	ayez jugé
juge	jugent	ait jugé	aient jugé
7 imparfait du subjonctif		14 plus-que-parfait du subjonctif	
jugeasse	jugeassions	eusse jugé	eussions jugé
jugeasses	jugeassiez	eusses jugé	eussiez jugé
jugeât	jugeassent	eût jugé	eussent jugé

	Impératif
	juge
	jugeons
	jugez

Words and expressions related to this verb

juger de   to judge (of); **Jugez de ma joie!**
   You can imagine my joy!
à en juger par . . .   judging by . . .
juger par . . .   to judge by . . .
mal juger qqn   to misjudge someone

juger bon de faire qqch   to think it wise to do
   something
un juge   judge, magistrate; **un juge de paix**
   justice of the peace
un jugement   judgment

Get acquainted with what preposition goes with what verb on pages 543–553.

to swear, to vow

The Seven Simple Tenses		The Seven Compound Tenses	
Singular	Plural	Singular	Plural
1 présent de l'indicatif		**8 passé composé**	
jure	jurons	ai juré	avons juré
jures	jurez	as juré	avez juré
jure	jurent	a juré	ont juré
2 imparfait de l'indicatif		**9 plus-que-parfait de l'indicatif**	
jurais	jurions	avais juré	avions juré
jurais	juriez	avais juré	aviez juré
jurait	juraient	avait juré	avaient juré
3 passé simple		**10 passé antérieur**	
jurai	jurâmes	eus juré	eûmes juré
juras	jurâtes	eus juré	eûtes juré
jura	jurèrent	eut juré	eurent juré
4 futur		**11 futur antérieur**	
jurerai	jurerons	aurai juré	aurons juré
jureras	jurerez	auras juré	aurez juré
jurera	jureront	aura juré	auront juré
5 conditionnel		**12 conditionnel passé**	
jurerais	jurerions	aurais juré	aurions juré
jurerais	jureriez	aurais juré	auriez juré
jurerait	jureraient	aurait juré	auraient juré
6 présent du subjonctif		**13 passé du subjonctif**	
jure	jurions	aie juré	ayons juré
jures	juriez	aies juré	ayez juré
jure	jurent	ait juré	aient juré
7 imparfait du subjonctif		**14 plus-que-parfait du subjonctif**	
jurasse	jurassions	eusse juré	eussions juré
jurasses	jurassiez	eusses juré	eussiez juré
jurât	jurassent	eût juré	eussent juré

Impératif
jure
jurons
jurez

Words and expressions related to this verb
jurer sur la Bible to swear on the Bible
un juriste jurist
la jurisprudence jurisprudence
un jureur swearer
jurer contre to swear against
abjurer to abjure, renounce

un juron curse, oath
un jury jury
un jurisconsulte legal expert
Je vous le jure! I swear it!
dire des jurons to swear, to curse

It's important that you be familiar with the Subjunctive. See pages 560–565.

lâcher

Part. pr. **lâchant**   Part. passé **lâché**

to loosen, to unleash, to let go

The Seven Simple Tenses		The Seven Compound Tenses	
Singular	Plural	Singular	Plural
1 présent de l'indicatif		**8 passé composé**	
lâche	lâchons	ai lâché	avons lâché
lâches	lâchez	as lâché	avez lâché
lâche	lâchent	a lâché	ont lâché
2 imparfait de l'indicatif		**9 plus-que-parfait de l'indicatif**	
lâchais	lâchions	avais lâché	avions lâché
lâchais	lâchiez	avais lâché	aviez lâché
lâchait	lâchaient	avait lâché	avaient lâché
3 passé simple		**10 passé antérieur**	
lâchai	lâchâmes	eus lâché	eûmes lâché
lâchas	lâchâtes	eus lâché	eûtes lâché
lâcha	lâchèrent	eut lâché	eurent lâché
4 futur		**11 futur antérieur**	
lâcherai	lâcherons	aurai lâché	aurons lâché
lâcheras	lâcherez	auras lâché	aurez lâché
lâchera	lâcheront	aura lâché	auront lâché
5 conditionnel		**12 conditionnel passé**	
lâcherais	lâcherions	aurais lâché	aurions lâché
lâcherais	lâcheriez	aurais lâché	auriez lâché
lâcherait	lâcheraient	aurait lâché	auraient lâché
6 présent du subjonctif		**13 passé du subjonctif**	
lâche	lâchions	aie lâché	ayons lâché
lâches	lâchiez	aies lâché	ayez lâché
lâche	lâchent	ait lâché	aient lâché
7 imparfait du subjonctif		**14 plus-que-parfait du subjonctif**	
lâchasse	lâchassions	eusse lâché	eussions lâché
lâchasses	lâchassiez	eusses lâché	eussiez lâché
lâchât	lâchassent	eût lâché	eussent lâché

Impératif
lâche
lâchons
lâchez

Words and expressions related to this verb

lâcher prise to let go
un lâcheur, une lâcheuse quitter
lâche cowardly; **lâchement** in a cowardly way
la lâcheté cowardice
un vêtement lâche flowing, loose garment

un relâche rest, relaxation, respite, temporary closing of a theater
relâcher to abate, to loosen, to relax, to slacken
Lâchez-moi! Let go of me!

Grammar putting you in a tense mood? Review the definitions of basic grammatical terms on pages 674–688.

The Seven Simple Tenses		The Seven Compound Tenses	
Singular	Plural	Singular	Plural
1 présent de l'indicatif		8 passé composé	
laisse	laissons	ai laissé	avons laissé
laisses	laissez	as laissé	avez laissé
laisse	laissent	a laissé	ont laissé
2 imparfait de l'indicatif		9 plus-que-parfait de l'indicatif	
laissais	laissions	avais laissé	avions laissé
laissais	laissiez	avais laissé	aviez laissé
laissait	laissaient	avait laissé	avaient laissé
3 passé simple		10 passé antérieur	
laissai	laissâmes	eus laissé	eûmes laissé
laissas	laissâtes	eus laissé	eûtes laissé
laissa	laissèrent	eut laissé	eurent laissé
4 futur		11 futur antérieur	
laisserai	laisserons	aurai laissé	aurons laissé
laisseras	laisserez	auras laissé	aurez laissé
laissera	laisseront	aura laissé	auront laissé
5 conditionnel		12 conditionnel passé	
laisserais	laisserions	aurais laissé	aurions laissé
laisserais	laisseriez	aurais laissé	auriez laissé
laisserait	laisseraient	aurait laissé	auraient laissé
6 présent du subjonctif		13 passé du subjonctif	
laisse	laissions	aie laissé	ayons laissé
laisses	laissiez	aies laissé	ayez laissé
laisse	laissent	ait laissé	aient laissé
7 imparfait du subjonctif		14 plus-que-parfait du subjonctif	
laissasse	laissassions	eusse laissé	eussions laissé
laissasses	laissassiez	eusses laissé	eussiez laissé
laissât	laissassent	eût laissé	eussent laissé

Impératif
laisse
laissons
laissez

Common idiomatic expressions using this verb

Quand j'ai quitté la maison ce matin pour aller à l'école, j'ai laissé mes livres sur la table dans la cuisine. Dans la classe de français, le professeur m'a demandé où étaient mes livres et je lui ai répondu que je les avais laissés sur la table chez moi. C'était fâcheux.

laissez-faire   do not interfere;   **Laissez-moi faire**   Let me do as I please.
une laisse   a leash; **délaisser**   to abandon, to forsake
laisser entrer   to let in, to allow to enter; **laisser tomber**   to drop
laisser aller   to let go;   **se laisser aller**   to let oneself go
C'était fâcheux!   (See **se fâcher**)

The subject pronouns are found on the page facing page 1.   **273**

lancer

to hurl, to launch, to throw

The Seven Simple Tenses		The Seven Compound Tenses	
Singular	Plural	Singular	Plural
1　présent de l'indicatif		**8　passé composé**	
lance	lançons	ai lancé	avons lancé
lances	lancez	as lancé	avez lancé
lance	lancent	a lancé	ont lancé
2　imparfait de l'indicatif		**9　plus-que-parfait de l'indicatif**	
lançais	lancions	avais lancé	avions lancé
lançais	lanciez	avais lancé	aviez lancé
lançait	lançaient	avait lancé	avaient lancé
3　passé simple		**10　passé antérieur**	
lançai	lançâmes	eus lancé	eûmes lancé
lanças	lançâtes	eus lancé	eûtes lancé
lança	lancèrent	eut lancé	eurent lancé
4　futur		**11　futur antérieur**	
lancerai	lancerons	aurai lancé	aurons lancé
lanceras	lancerez	auras lancé	aurez lancé
lancera	lanceront	aura lancé	auront lancé
5　conditionnel		**12　conditionnel passé**	
lancerais	lancerions	aurais lancé	aurions lancé
lancerais	lanceriez	aurais lancé	auriez lancé
lancerait	lanceraient	aurait lancé	auraient lancé
6　présent du subjonctif		**13　passé du subjonctif**	
lance	lancions	aie lancé	ayons lancé
lances	lanciez	aies lancé	ayez lancé
lance	lancent	ait lancé	aient lancé
7　imparfait du subjonctif		**14　plus-que-parfait du subjonctif**	
lançasse	lançassions	eusse lancé	eussions lancé
lançasses	lançassiez	eusses lancé	eussiez lancé
lançât	lançassent	eût lancé	eussent lancé

Impératif
lance
lançons
lancez

Words and expressions related to this verb
se lancer contre　to throw oneself at, against
un départ lancé　a flying start (sports)
une lance　a spear
le lancement d'un disque, d'un livre, etc.
　ceremony to launch a new record, book, etc.

un lancement　hurling, casting
un lanceur　thrower, pitcher (sports)
lancer un cri　to cry out
une rampe de lancement　launching pad

Want to learn more idiomatic expressions that contain verbs? Look at pages 530–542.

The Seven Simple Tenses		The Seven Compound Tenses	
Singular	Plural	Singular	Plural
1 présent de l'indicatif		**8 passé composé**	
lave	lavons	ai lavé	avons lavé
laves	lavez	as lavé	avez lavé
lave	lavent	a lavé	ont lavé
2 imparfait de l'indicatif		**9 plus-que-parfait de l'indicatif**	
lavais	lavions	avais lavé	avions lavé
lavais	laviez	avais lavé	aviez lavé
lavait	lavaient	avait lavé	avaient lavé
3 passé simple		**10 passé antérieur**	
lavai	lavâmes	eus lavé	eûmes lavé
lavas	lavâtes	eus lavé	eûtes lavé
lava	lavèrent	eut lavé	eurent lavé
4 futur		**11 futur antérieur**	
laverai	laverons	aurai lavé	aurons lavé
laveras	laverez	auras lavé	aurez lavé
lavera	laveront	aura lavé	auront lavé
5 conditionnel		**12 conditionnel passé**	
laverais	laverions	aurais lavé	aurions lavé
laverais	laveriez	aurais lavé	auriez lavé
laverait	laveraient	aurait lavé	auraient lavé
6 présent du subjonctif		**13 passé du subjonctif**	
lave	lavions	aie lavé	ayons lavé
laves	laviez	aies lavé	ayez lavé
lave	lavent	ait lavé	aient lavé
7 imparfait du subjonctif		**14 plus-que-parfait du subjonctif**	
lavasse	lavassions	eusse lavé	eussions lavé
lavasses	lavassiez	eusses lavé	eussiez lavé
lavât	lavassent	eût lavé	eussent lavé

Impératif
lave
lavons
lavez

Sentences using this verb and words related to it

Samedi après-midi j'ai lavé la voiture de mon père et il m'a donné de l'argent pour mon travail.

le lavage   washing
le lavement   enema
la lavette   dish mop
la lavure   dishwater; **un lave-vaisselle** dishwasher
la lessive   laundry detergent

un laveur, une laveuse   washer; **une laverie** launderette
un lave-linge   washing machine
laver en machine   machine wash
laver à la main   hand wash

See also **se laver.**

The subject pronouns are found on the page facing page 1.

275

se laver

Part. pr. se lavant   **Part. passé lavé(e)(s)**

to wash oneself

The Seven Simple Tenses		The Seven Compound Tenses	
Singular	Plural	Singular	Plural
1 présent de l'indicatif		**8 passé composé**	
me lave	nous lavons	me suis lavé(e)	nous sommes lavé(e)s
te laves	vous lavez	t'es lavé(e)	vous êtes lavé(e)(s)
se lave	se lavent	s'est lavé(e)	se sont lavé(e)s
2 imparfait de l'indicatif		**9 plus-que-parfait de l'indicatif**	
me lavais	nous lavions	m'étais lavé(e)	nous étions lavé(e)s
te lavais	vous laviez	t'étais lavé(e)	vous étiez lavé(e)(s)
se lavait	se lavaient	s'était lavé(e)	s'étaient lavé(e)s
3 passé simple		**10 passé antérieur**	
me lavai	nous lavâmes	me fus lavé(e)	nous fûmes lavé(e)s
te lavas	vous lavâtes	te fus lavé(e)	vous fûtes lavé(e)(s)
se lava	se lavèrent	se fut lavé(e)	se furent lavé(e)s
4 futur		**11 futur antérieur**	
me laverai	nous laverons	me serai lavé(e)	nous serons lavé(e)s
te laveras	vous laverez	te seras lavé(e)	vous serez lavé(e)(s)
se lavera	se laveront	se sera lavé(e)	se seront lavé(e)s
5 conditionnel		**12 conditionnel passé**	
me laverais	nous laverions	me serais lavé(e)	nous serions lavé(e)s
te laverais	vous laveriez	te serais lavé(e)	vous seriez lavé(e)(s)
se laverait	se laveraient	se serait lavé(e)	se seraient lavé(e)s
6 présent du subjonctif		**13 passé du subjonctif**	
me lave	nous lavions	me sois lavé(e)	nous soyons lavé(e)s
te laves	vous laviez	te sois lavé(e)	vous soyez lavé(e)(s)
se lave	se lavent	se soit lavé(e)	se soient lavé(e)s
7 imparfait du subjonctif		**14 plus-que-parfait du subjonctif**	
me lavasse	nous lavassions	me fusse lavé(e)	nous fussions lavé(e)s
te lavasses	vous lavassiez	te fusses lavé(e)	vous fussiez lavé(e)(s)
se lavât	se lavassent	se fût lavé(e)	se fussent lavé(e)s

Impératif
lave-toi; ne te lave pas
lavons-nous; ne nous lavons pas
lavez-vous; ne vous lavez pas

Sentences using this verb and words related to it

Tous les matins je me lave. Je me lave le visage, je me lave les mains, le cou et les oreilles. Hier soir je me suis lavé les pieds.

Ma mère m'a demandé:—Henriette, est-ce que tu t'es bien lavée?

Je lui ai répondu:—Oui, maman, je me suis lavée! Je me suis bien lavé les mains!

For words related to **se laver**, see the verb **laver**.

Read the entries in the section on definitions of basic grammatical terms with examples on pages 674–688. In particular, review the entry **agreement of past participle of a reflexive verb with its reflexive pronoun**.

The Seven Simple Tenses		The Seven Compound Tenses

Singular	Plural	Singular	Plural
1 présent de l'indicatif		**8 passé composé**	
lève	**levons**	**ai levé**	**avons levé**
lèves	**levez**	**as levé**	**avez levé**
lève	**lèvent**	**a levé**	**ont levé**
2 imparfait de l'indicatif		**9 plus-que-parfait de l'indicatif**	
levais	**levions**	**avais levé**	**avions levé**
levais	**leviez**	**avais levé**	**aviez levé**
levait	**levaient**	**avait levé**	**avaient levé**
3 passé simple		**10 passé antérieur**	
levai	**levâmes**	**eus levé**	**eûmes levé**
levas	**levâtes**	**eus levé**	**eûtes levé**
leva	**levèrent**	**eut levé**	**eurent levé**
4 futur		**11 futur antérieur**	
lèverai	**lèverons**	**aurai levé**	**aurons levé**
lèveras	**lèverez**	**auras levé**	**aurez levé**
lèvera	**lèveront**	**aura levé**	**auront levé**
5 conditionnel		**12 conditionnel passé**	
lèverais	**lèverions**	**aurais levé**	**aurions levé**
lèverais	**lèveriez**	**aurais levé**	**auriez levé**
lèverait	**lèveraient**	**aurait levé**	**auraient levé**
6 présent du subjonctif		**13 passé du subjonctif**	
lève	**levions**	**aie levé**	**ayons levé**
lèves	**leviez**	**aies levé**	**ayez levé**
lève	**lèvent**	**ait levé**	**aient levé**
7 imparfait du subjonctif		**14 plus-que-parfait du subjonctif**	
levasse	**levassions**	**eusse levé**	**eussions levé**
levasses	**levassiez**	**eusses levé**	**eussiez levé**
levât	**levassent**	**eût levé**	**eussent levé**

Impératif
lève
levons
levez

Words and expressions related to this verb
voter à main levée   to vote by a show of hands
le levage   raising, lifting
faire lever qqn   to get someone out of bed
le levant   the East
le levain   leaven
du pain sans levain   unleavened bread
le lever du soleil   sunrise

se relever   to get up on one's feet
lever la main   to raise one's hand
élever   to raise, to rear, to bring up
enlever   to remove
relever   to raise again, to pick up
La séance est levée   The meeting is adjourned.
prélever   to take a sample, to withdraw

See also **élever**, **enlever**, and **se lever**.

se lever
to get up

Part. pr. **se levant**   Part. passé **levé(e)(s)**

The Seven Simple Tenses		The Seven Compound Tenses	
Singular	Plural	Singular	Plural
1 présent de l'indicatif		**8 passé composé**	
me lève	nous levons	me suis levé(e)	nous sommes levé(e)s
te lèves	vous levez	t'es levé(e)	vous êtes levé(e)(s)
se lève	se lèvent	s'est levé(e)	se sont levé(e)s
2 imparfait de l'indicatif		**9 plus-que-parfait de l'indicatif**	
me levais	nous levions	m'étais levé(e)	nous étions levé(e)s
te levais	vous leviez	t'étais levé(e)	vous étiez levé(e)(s)
se levait	se levaient	s'était levé(e)	s'étaient levé(e)s
3 passé simple		**10 passé antérieur**	
me levai	nous levâmes	me fus levé(e)	nous fûmes levé(e)s
te levas	vous levâtes	te fus levé(e)	vous fûtes levé(e)(s)
se leva	se levèrent	se fut levé(e)	se furent levé(e)s
4 futur		**11 futur antérieur**	
me lèverai	nous lèverons	me serai levé(e)	nous serons levé(e)s
te lèveras	vous lèverez	te seras levé(e)	vous serez levé(e)(s)
se lèvera	se lèveront	se sera levé(e)	se seront levé(e)s
5 conditionnel		**12 conditionnel passé**	
me lèverais	nous lèverions	me serais levé(e)	nous serions levé(e)s
te lèverais	vous lèveriez	te serais levé(e)	vous seriez levé(e)(s)
se lèverait	se lèveraient	se serait levé(e)	se seraient levé(e)s
6 présent du subjonctif		**13 passé du subjonctif**	
me lève	nous levions	me sois levé(e)	nous soyons levé(e)s
te lèves	vous leviez	te sois levé(e)	vous soyez levé(e)(s)
se lève	se lèvent	se soit levé(e)	se soient levé(e)s
7 imparfait du subjonctif		**14 plus-que-parfait du subjonctif**	
me levasse	nous levassions	me fusse levé(e)	nous fussions levé(e)s
te levasses	vous levassiez	te fusses levé(e)	vous fussiez levé(e)(s)
se levât	se levassent	se fût levé(e)	se fussent levé(e)s

Impératif
lève-toi; ne te lève pas
levons-nous; ne nous levons pas
levez-vous; ne vous levez pas

Sentences using this verb

   Caroline est entrée dans le salon. Elle s'est assise, puis elle s'est levée. Après s'être levée, elle a quitté la maison.

See also **élever, enlever,** and **lever.**

Review the entry **agreement of past participle of a reflexive verb with its reflexive pronoun** in the section on definitions of basic grammatical terms with examples on pages 674–688.

The Seven Simple Tenses		The Seven Compound Tenses	
Singular	Plural	Singular	Plural

1 présent de l'indicatif		8 passé composé	
lis	**lisons**	**ai lu**	**avons lu**
lis	**lisez**	**as lu**	**avez lu**
lit	**lisent**	**a lu**	**ont lu**

2 imparfait de l'indicatif		9 plus-que-parfait de l'indicatif	
lisais	**lisions**	**avais lu**	**avions lu**
lisais	**lisiez**	**avais lu**	**aviez lu**
lisait	**lisaient**	**avait lu**	**avaient lu**

3 passé simple		10 passé antérieur	
lus	**lûmes**	**eus lu**	**eûmes lu**
lus	**lûtes**	**eus lu**	**eûtes lu**
lut	**lurent**	**eut lu**	**eurent lu**

4 futur		11 futur antérieur	
lirai	**lirons**	**aurai lu**	**aurons lu**
liras	**lirez**	**auras lu**	**aurez lu**
lira	**liront**	**aura lu**	**auront lu**

5 conditionnel		12 conditionnel passé	
lirais	**lirions**	**aurais lu**	**aurions lu**
lirais	**liriez**	**aurais lu**	**auriez lu**
lirait	**liraient**	**aurait lu**	**auraient lu**

6 présent du subjonctif		13 passé du subjonctif	
lise	**lisions**	**aie lu**	**ayons lu**
lises	**lisiez**	**aies lu**	**ayez lu**
lise	**lisent**	**ait lu**	**aient lu**

7 imparfait du subjonctif		14 plus-que-parfait du subjonctif	
lusse	**lussions**	**eusse lu**	**eussions lu**
lusses	**lussiez**	**eusses lu**	**eussiez lu**
lût	**lussent**	**eût lu**	**eussent lu**

Impératif
lis
lisons
lisez

Words and expressions related to this verb
C'est un livre à lire   It's a book worth
  reading.
lisible   legible, readable
lisiblement   legibly
lecteur, lectrice   reader (a person who reads)
**un lecteur d'épreuves, une lectrice
  d'épreuves**   proofreader
la lecture   reading

lectures pour la jeunesse   juvenile reading
Dans l'espoir de vous lire …   I hope to
  receive a letter from you soon.
lire à haute voix   to read aloud
lire à voix basse   to read in a low voice
lire tout bas   to read to oneself
relire   to reread
la lisibilité   legibility

Can't recognize an irregular verb form? Check out pages 526–529.

louer

Part. pr. **louant**   Part. passé **loué**

to praise, to rent, to rent out

The Seven Simple Tenses		The Seven Compound Tenses	
Singular	Plural	Singular	Plural
1 présent de l'indicatif		**8 passé composé**	
loue	louons	ai loué	avons loué
loues	louez	as loué	avez loué
loue	louent	a loué	ont loué
2 imparfait de l'indicatif		**9 plus-que-parfait de l'indicatif**	
louais	louions	avais loué	avions loué
louais	louiez	avais loué	aviez loué
louait	louaient	avait loué	avaient loué
3 passé simple		**10 passé antérieur**	
louai	louâmes	eus loué	eûmes loué
louas	louâtes	eus loué	eûtes loué
loua	louèrent	eut loué	eurent loué
4 futur		**11 futur antérieur**	
louerai	louerons	aurai loué	aurons loué
loueras	louerez	auras loué	aurez loué
louera	loueront	aura loué	auront loué
5 conditionnel		**12 conditionnel passé**	
louerais	louerions	aurais loué	aurions loué
louerais	loueriez	aurais loué	auriez loué
louerait	loueraient	aurait loué	auraient loué
6 présent du subjonctif		**13 passé du subjonctif**	
loue	louions	aie loué	ayons loué
loues	louiez	aies loué	ayez loué
loue	louent	ait loué	aient loué
7 imparfait du subjonctif		**14 plus-que-parfait du subjonctif**	
louasse	louassions	eusse loué	eussions loué
louasses	louassiez	eusses loué	eussiez loué
louât	louassent	eût loué	eussent loué

Impératif
loue
louons
louez

Words and expressions related to this verb
une place louée   reserved seat
maison à louer   house for rent (to let)
se louer de   to congratulate oneself on
allouer   to allot, to allocate
Dieu soit loué!   God be praised!
la location   rental

un loueur, une loueuse   a person who rents
    something to someone
un loueur de voitures   car rental agent
le louage   renting, hiring out
la louange   praise
le/la locataire   renter

This verb has two very different meanings because it developed from two different Latin verbs:
locāre (to lend) and laudāre (to praise).

to shine, to gleam, to glisten

The Seven Simple Tenses	The Seven Compound Tenses
Singular Plural	Singular Plural
1 présent de l'indicatif **il luit**	8 passé composé **il a lui**
2 imparfait de l'indicatif **il luisait**	9 plus-que-parfait de l'indicatif **il avait lui**
3 passé simple **il luisit**	10 passé antérieur **il eut lui**
4 futur **il luira**	11 futur antérieur **il aura lui**
5 conditionnel **il luirait**	12 conditionnel passé **il aurait lui**
6 présent du subjonctif **qu'il luise**	13 passé du subjonctif **qu'il ait lui**
7 imparfait du subjonctif **qu'il luisît**	14 plus-que-parfait du subjonctif **qu'il eût lui**

Impératif
Qu'il luise!   Let it shine!

Words and expressions related to this verb
la lueur   glimmer, gleam, glow
luisant, luisante   shining
à la lueur d'une bougie   by candlelight
l'espoir luit encore   there is still a glimmer of hope

le lac luisait au soleil du matin   the lake glistened in the morning sunlight
Le soleil luit   The sun is shining.
J'ai le nez qui luit   My nose is shiny.
une lueur d'espoir   a glimmer of hope

Want to learn more verbs used in proverbs and sayings? Take a look at page 559.

The subject pronouns are found on the page facing page 1.

to reduce (one's weight), to grow thin, to lose weight

The Seven Simple Tenses		The Seven Compound Tenses	
Singular	Plural	Singular	Plural
1 présent de l'indicatif		8 passé composé	
maigris	**maigrissons**	**ai maigri**	**avons maigri**
maigris	**maigrissez**	**as maigri**	**avez maigri**
maigrit	**maigrissent**	**a maigri**	**ont maigri**
2 imparfait de l'indicatif		9 plus-que-parfait de l'indicatif	
maigrissais	**maigrissions**	**avais maigri**	**avions maigri**
maigrissais	**maigrissiez**	**avais maigri**	**aviez maigri**
maigrissait	**maigrissaient**	**avait maigri**	**avaient maigri**
3 passé simple		10 passé antérieur	
maigris	**maigrîmes**	**eus maigri**	**eûmes maigri**
maigris	**maigrîtes**	**eus maigri**	**eûtes maigri**
maigrit	**maigrirent**	**eut maigri**	**eurent maigri**
4 futur		11 futur antérieur	
maigrirai	**maigrirons**	**aurai maigri**	**aurons maigri**
maigriras	**maigrirez**	**auras maigri**	**aurez maigri**
maigrira	**maigriront**	**aura maigri**	**auront maigri**
5 conditionnel		12 conditionnel passé	
maigrirais	**maigririons**	**aurais maigri**	**aurions maigri**
maigrirais	**maigririez**	**aurais maigri**	**auriez maigri**
maigrirait	**maigriraient**	**aurait maigri**	**auraient maigri**
6 présent du subjonctif		13 passé du subjonctif	
maigrisse	**maigrissions**	**aie maigri**	**ayons maigri**
maigrisses	**maigrissiez**	**aies maigri**	**ayez maigri**
maigrisse	**maigrissent**	**ait maigri**	**aient maigri**
7 imparfait du subjonctif		14 plus-que-parfait du subjonctif	
maigrisse	**maigrissions**	**eusse maigri**	**eussions maigri**
maigrisses	**maigrissiez**	**eusses maigri**	**eussiez maigri**
maigrît	**maigrissent**	**eût maigri**	**eussent maigri**

Impératif
maigris
maigrissons
maigrissez

Words and expressions related to this verb
maigre   thin
la maigreur   thinness
maigrement   meagerly
se faire maigrir   to slim down one's weight
être au régime pour maigrir   to be on a diet
    to lose weight

s'amaigrir   to lose weight
maigre comme un clou   as thin as a nail
faire maigre   to abstain from meat
un gamin maigrelet   a skinny kid
amaigri, amaigrie   gaunt
amaigrissant   reducing

The Seven Simple Tenses		The Seven Compound Tenses	
Singular	Plural	Singular	Plural

1   présent de l'indicatif

mange	mangeons		
manges	mangez		
mange	mangent		

8   passé composé

ai mangé	avons mangé
as mangé	avez mangé
a mangé	ont mangé

2   imparfait de l'indicatif

mangeais	mangions
mangeais	mangiez
mangeait	mangeaient

9   plus-que-parfait de l'indicatif

avais mangé	avions mangé
avais mangé	aviez mangé
avait mangé	avaient mangé

3   passé simple

mangeai	mangeâmes
mangeas	mangeâtes
mangea	mangèrent

10   passé antérieur

eus mangé	eûmes mangé
eus mangé	eûtes mangé
eut mangé	eurent mangé

4   futur

mangerai	mangerons
mangeras	mangerez
mangera	mangeront

11   futur antérieur

aurai mangé	aurons mangé
auras mangé	aurez mangé
aura mangé	auront mangé

5   conditionnel

mangerais	mangerions
mangerais	mangeriez
mangerait	mangeraient

12   conditionnel passé

aurais mangé	aurions mangé
aurais mangé	auriez mangé
aurait mangé	auraient mangé

6   présent du subjonctif

mange	mangions
manges	mangiez
mange	mangent

13   passé du subjonctif

aie mangé	ayons mangé
aies mangé	ayez mangé
ait mangé	aient mangé

7   imparfait du subjonctif

mangeasse	mangeassions
mangeasses	mangeassiez
mangeât	mangeassent

14   plus-que-parfait du subjonctif

eusse mangé	eussions mangé
eusses mangé	eussiez mangé
eût mangé	eussent mangé

Impératif
mange
mangeons
mangez

Words and expressions related to this verb
le manger   food
gros mangeur   big eater
manger de l'argent   to spend money foolishly
ne pas manger à sa faim   not to have much to eat
manger à sa faim   to eat until filled

manger comme quatre   to eat like a horse
une mangeoire   manger
mangeable   edible, eatable
la mangeaille   disgusting food
immangeable   uneatable, inedible
manger comme un oiseau   to eat like a bird

Retain the *e* in the first person plural (**Nous mangeons**) to keep the soft *g* sound of the verb.

to miss, to lack

The Seven Simple Tenses		The Seven Compound Tenses	
Singular	Plural	Singular	Plural
1 présent de l'indicatif		**8 passé composé**	
manque	manquons	ai manqué	avons manqué
manques	manquez	as manqué	avez manqué
manque	manquent	a manqué	ont manqué
2 imparfait de l'indicatif		**9 plus-que-parfait de l'indicatif**	
manquais	manquions	avais manqué	avions manqué
manquais	manquiez	avais manqué	aviez manqué
manquait	manquaient	avait manqué	avaient manqué
3 passé simple		**10 passé antérieur**	
manquai	manquâmes	eus manqué	eûmes manqué
manquas	manquâtes	eus manqué	eûtes manqué
manqua	manquèrent	eut manqué	eurent manqué
4 futur		**11 futur antérieur**	
manquerai	manquerons	aurai manqué	aurons manqué
manqueras	manquerez	auras manqué	aurez manqué
manquera	manqueront	aura manqué	auront manqué
5 conditionnel		**12 conditionnel passé**	
manquerais	manquerions	aurais manqué	aurions manqué
manquerais	manqueriez	aurais manqué	auriez manqué
manquerait	manqueraient	aurait manqué	auraient manqué
6 présent du subjonctif		**13 passé du subjonctif**	
manque	manquions	aie manqué	ayons manqué
manques	manquiez	aies manqué	ayez manqué
manque	manquent	ait manqué	aient manqué
7 imparfait du subjonctif		**14 plus-que-parfait du subjonctif**	
manquasse	manquassions	eusse manqué	eussions manqué
manquasses	manquassiez	eusses manqué	eussiez manqué
manquât	manquassent	eût manqué	eussent manqué

Impératif
manque
manquons
manquez

Common idiomatic expressions using this verb
manquer à   to lack;   **Le courage lui manque**   He lacks courage.
Elle me manque   I miss her.
Est-ce que je te manque?   Do you miss me?
manquer de qqch   to be lacking something;   **manquer de sucre**   to be out of sugar
Ne manquez pas de venir   Don't fail to come.
un mariage manqué   a broken engagement
un héros manqué   a would-be hero
Il me manque un euro   I am lacking (I need) one euro.

to walk, to march, to run (machine), to function

The Seven Simple Tenses		The Seven Compound Tenses	
Singular	Plural	Singular	Plural
1 présent de l'indicatif		8 passé composé	
marche	marchons	ai marché	avons marché
marches	marchez	as marché	avez marché
marche	marchent	a marché	ont marché
2 imparfait de l'indicatif		9 plus-que-parfait de l'indicatif	
marchais	marchions	avais marché	avions marché
marchais	marchiez	avais marché	aviez marché
marchait	marchaient	avait marché	avaient marché
3 passé simple		10 passé antérieur	
marchai	marchâmes	eus marché	eûmes marché
marchas	marchâtes	eus marché	eûtes marché
marcha	marchèrent	eut marché	eurent marché
4 futur		11 futur antérieur	
marcherai	marcherons	aurai marché	aurons marché
marcheras	marcherez	auras marché	aurez marché
marchera	marcheront	aura marché	auront marché
5 conditionnel		12 conditionnel passé	
marcherais	marcherions	aurais marché	aurions marché
marcherais	marcheriez	aurais marché	auriez marché
marcherait	marcheraient	aurait marché	auraient marché
6 présent du subjonctif		13 passé du subjonctif	
marche	marchions	aie marché	ayons marché
marches	marchiez	aies marché	ayez marché
marche	marchent	ait marché	aient marché
7 imparfait du subjonctif		14 plus-que-parfait du subjonctif	
marchasse	marchassions	eusse marché	eussions marché
marchasses	marchassiez	eusses marché	eussiez marché
marchât	marchassent	eût marché	eussent marché

Impératif
marche
marchons
marchez

Words and expressions related to this verb
la marche march, walking
ralentir sa marche to slow down one's pace
le marché market
le marché aux fleurs flower market
le marché aux puces flea market
à bon marché cheap
faire marcher qqn to put someone on
une démarche gait, walk

faire une démarche to take a step
marcher bien to function (go, run, work) well
marcher sur les pas de qqn to follow in someone's footsteps
faire marcher qqch to make something go (run, function)
Ça ne marche plus It's out of order.
la course et la marche running and walking

maudire

Part. pr. **maudissant** Part. passé **maudit**

to curse

The Seven Simple Tenses		The Seven Compound Tenses	
Singular	Plural	Singular	Plural
1 présent de l'indicatif		**8 passé composé**	
maudis	maudissons	ai maudit	avons maudit
maudis	maudissez	as maudit	avez maudit
maudit	maudissent	a maudit	ont maudit
2 imparfait de l'indicatif		**9 plus-que-parfait de l'indicatif**	
maudissais	maudissions	avais maudit	avions maudit
maudissais	maudissiez	avais maudit	aviez maudit
maudissait	maudissaient	avait maudit	avaient maudit
3 passé simple		**10 passé antérieur**	
maudis	maudîmes	eus maudit	eûmes maudit
maudis	maudîtes	eus maudit	eûtes maudit
maudit	maudirent	eut maudit	eurent maudit
4 futur		**11 futur antérieur**	
maudirai	maudirons	aurai maudit	aurons maudit
maudiras	maudirez	auras maudit	aurez maudit
maudira	maudiront	aura maudit	auront maudit
5 conditionnel		**12 conditionnel passé**	
maudirais	maudirions	aurais maudit	aurions maudit
maudirais	maudiriez	aurais maudit	auriez maudit
maudirait	maudiraient	aurait maudit	auraient maudit
6 présent du subjonctif		**13 passé du subjonctif**	
maudisse	maudissions	aie maudit	ayons maudit
maudisses	maudissiez	aies maudit	ayez maudit
maudisse	maudissent	ait maudit	aient maudit
7 imparfait du subjonctif		**14 plus-que-parfait du subjonctif**	
maudisse	maudissions	eusse maudit	eussions maudit
maudisses	maudissiez	eusses maudit	eussiez maudit
maudît	maudissent	eût maudit	eussent maudit

Impératif
maudis
maudissons
maudissez

Words and expressions related to this verb
maudit, maudite cursed
Quel maudit temps! What rotten weather!
maudire un ennemi to curse an enemy
les maudits the damned

le Maudit Demon
dire to say, to tell; **dire du mal de qqn** to
say something evil about someone

See also **contredire, dire, interdire, médire,** and **prédire.**

Soak up some verbs used in weather expressions on pages 557 and 558.

286

to misjudge, to misunderstand, not to know, not to recognize

The Seven Simple Tenses		The Seven Compound Tenses	
Singular	Plural	Singular	Plural
1 présent de l'indicatif		**8 passé composé**	
méconnais	méconnaissons	ai méconnu	avons méconnu
méconnais	méconnaissez	as méconnu	avez méconnu
méconnaît	méconnaissent	a méconnu	ont méconnu
2 imparfait de l'indicatif		**9 plus-que-parfait de l'indicatif**	
méconnaissais	méconnaissions	avais méconnu	avions méconnu
méconnaissais	méconnaissiez	avais méconnu	aviez méconnu
méconnaissait	méconnaissaient	avait méconnu	avaient méconnu
3 passé simple		**10 passé antérieur**	
méconnus	méconnûmes	eus méconnu	eûmes méconnu
méconnus	méconnûtes	eus méconnu	eûtes méconnu
méconnut	méconnurent	eut méconnu	eurent méconnu
4 futur		**11 futur antérieur**	
méconnaîtrai	méconnaîtrons	aurai méconnu	aurons méconnu
méconnaîtras	méconnaîtrez	auras méconnu	aurez méconnu
méconnaîtra	méconnaîtront	aura méconnu	auront méconnu
5 conditionnel		**12 conditionnel passé**	
méconnaîtrais	méconnaîtrions	aurais méconnu	aurions méconnu
méconnaîtrais	méconnaîtriez	aurais méconnu	auriez méconnu
méconnaîtrait	méconnaîtraient	aurait méconnu	auraient méconnu
6 présent du subjonctif		**13 passé du subjonctif**	
méconnaisse	méconnaissions	aie méconnu	ayons méconnu
méconnaisses	méconnaissiez	aies méconnu	ayez méconnu
méconnaisse	méconnaissent	ait méconnu	aient méconnu
7 imparfait du subjonctif		**14 plus-que-parfait du subjonctif**	
méconnusse	méconnussions	eusse méconnu	eussions méconnu
méconnusses	méconnussiez	eusses méconnu	eussiez méconnu
méconnût	méconnussent	eût méconnu	eussent méconnu

Impératif
méconnais
méconnaissons
méconnaissez

Words related to this verb
méconnaissable unrecognizable
méconnu, méconnue misunderstood

See also **connaître** and **reconnaître.**

la méconnaissance misappreciation
se méconnaître to underrate (underestimate) oneself

Consult the sections on verbs used in idiomatic expressions, verbs with prepositions, and the list of over 1,100 verbs conjugated like model verbs in the back pages.

The Seven Simple Tenses		The Seven Compound Tenses	
Singular	Plural	Singular	Plural
1 présent de l'indicatif		8 passé composé	
médis	médisons	ai médit	avons médit
médis	médisez	as médit	avez médit
médit	médisent	a médit	ont médit
2 imparfait de l'indicatif		9 plus-que-parfait de l'indicatif	
médisais	médisions	avais médit	avions médit
médisais	médisiez	avais médit	aviez médit
médisait	médisaient	avait médit	avaient médit
3 passé simple		10 passé antérieur	
médis	médîmes	eus médit	eûmes médit
médis	médîtes	eus médit	eûtes médit
médit	médirent	eut médit	eurent médit
4 futur		11 futur antérieur	
médirai	médirons	aurai médit	aurons médit
médiras	médirez	auras médit	aurez médit
médira	médiront	aura médit	auront médit
5 conditionnel		12 conditionnel passé	
médirais	médirions	aurais médit	aurions médit
médirais	médiriez	aurais médit	auriez médit
médirait	médiraient	aurait médit	auraient médit
6 présent du subjonctif		13 passé du subjonctif	
médise	médisions	aie médit	ayons médit
médises	médisiez	aies médit	ayez médit
médise	médisent	ait médit	aient médit
7 imparfait du subjonctif		14 plus-que-parfait du subjonctif	
médisse	médissions	eusse médit	eussions médit
médisses	médissiez	eusses médit	eussiez médit
médît	médissent	eût médit	eussent médit

Impératif
médis
médisons
médisez

Words and expressions related to this verb
la médisance   slander
dire des médisances   to say scandalous things

un médisant, une médisante   slanderer
médire de   to speak ill of, to slander

See also **contredire, dire, interdire, maudire,** and **prédire.**

Get acquainted with what preposition goes with what verb on pages 543–553.

288

to beware, to distrust, to mistrust

The Seven Simple Tenses		The Seven Compound Tenses	
Singular	Plural	Singular	Plural

1   présent de l'indicatif

me méfie	nous méfions		
te méfies	vous méfiez		
se méfie	se méfient		

8   passé composé

me suis méfié(e)	nous sommes méfié(e)s
t'es méfié(e)	vous êtes méfié(e)(s)
s'est méfié(e)	se sont méfié(e)s

2   imparfait de l'indicatif

me méfiais	nous méfiions
te méfiais	vous méfiiez
se méfiait	se méfiaient

9   plus-que-parfait de l'indicatif

m'étais méfié(e)	nous étions méfié(e)s
t'étais méfié(e)	vous étiez méfié(e)(s)
s'était méfié(e)	s'étaient méfié(e)s

3   passé simple

me méfiai	nous méfiâmes
te méfias	vous méfiâtes
se méfia	se méfièrent

10   passé antérieur

me fus méfié(e)	nous fûmes méfié(e)s
te fus méfié(e)	vous fûtes méfié(e)(s)
se fut méfié(e)	se furent méfié(e)s

4   futur

me méfierai	nous méfierons
te méfieras	vous méfierez
se méfiera	se méfieront

11   futur antérieur

me serai méfié(e)	nous serons méfié(e)s
te seras méfié(e)	vous serez méfié(e)(s)
se sera méfié(e)	se seront méfié(e)s

5   conditionnel

me méfierais	nous méfierions
te méfierais	vous méfieriez
se méfierait	se méfieraient

12   conditionnel passé

me serais méfié(e)	nous serions méfié(e)s
te serais méfié(e)	vous seriez méfié(e)(s)
se serait méfié(e)	se seraient méfié(e)s

6   présent du subjonctif

me méfie	nous méfiions
te méfies	vous méfiiez
se méfie	se méfient

13   passé du subjonctif

me sois méfié(e)	nous soyons méfié(e)s
te sois méfié(e)	vous soyez méfié(e)(s)
se soit méfié(e)	se soient méfié(e)s

7   imparfait du subjonctif

me méfiasse	nous méfiassions
te méfiasses	vous méfiassiez
se méfiât	se méfiassent

14   plus-que-parfait du subjonctif

me fusse méfié(e)	nous fussions méfié(e)s
te fusses méfié(e)	vous fussiez méfié(e)(s)
se fût méfié(e)	se fussent méfié(e)s

Impératif
méfie-toi; ne te méfie pas
méfions-nous; ne nous méfions pas
méfiez-vous; ne vous méfiez pas

Words and expressions related to this verb
se méfier de   to distrust, to mistrust
Méfiez-vous!   Watch out!
méfiant, méfiante   distrustful
la méfiance   distrust, mistrust
un méfait   misdeed, wrongdoing
Il faut vous méfier   You must be careful.

être sans méfiance   to be completely trusting
Méfiez-vous de lui (d'elle)   Do not trust him (her).
avoir de la méfiance envers quelqu'un   to distrust someone

It's important that you be familiar with the Subjunctive. See pages 560–565.

mener

Part. pr. menant   **Part. passé mené**

to lead, to control

The Seven Simple Tenses		The Seven Compound Tenses	
Singular	Plural	Singular	Plural
1 présent de l'indicatif		**8 passé composé**	
mène	menons	ai mené	avons mené
mènes	menez	as mené	avez mené
mène	mènent	a mené	ont mené
2 imparfait de l'indicatif		**9 plus-que-parfait de l'indicatif**	
menais	menions	avais mené	avions mené
menais	meniez	avais mené	aviez mené
menait	menaient	avait mené	avaient mené
3 passé simple		**10 passé antérieur**	
menai	menâmes	eus mené	eûmes mené
menas	menâtes	eus mené	eûtes mené
mena	menèrent	eut mené	eurent mené
4 futur		**11 futur antérieur**	
mènerai	mènerons	aurai mené	aurons mené
mèneras	mènerez	auras mené	aurez mené
mènera	mèneront	aura mené	auront mené
5 conditionnel		**12 conditionnel passé**	
mènerais	mènerions	aurais mené	aurions mené
mènerais	mèneriez	aurais mené	auriez mené
mènerait	mèneraient	aurait mené	auraient mené
6 présent du subjonctif		**13 passé du subjonctif**	
mène	menions	aie mené	ayons mené
mènes	meniez	aies mené	ayez mené
mène	mènent	ait mené	aient mené
7 imparfait du subjonctif		**14 plus-que-parfait du subjonctif**	
menasse	menassions	eusse mené	eussions mené
menasses	menassiez	eusses mené	eussiez mené
menât	menassent	eût mené	eussent mené

Impératif
mène
menons
menez

Words and expressions related to this verb
un meneur, une meneuse   leader
Cela ne mène à rien   That leads to nothing.
mener qqn par le bout du nez   to lead someone around by the nose
mener une vie vagabonde   to lead a vagabond life
mener tout le monde   to be bossy with everyone
mener la bande   to lead the group
Cela vous mènera loin   That will take you a long way.
malmener   to bully

See also amener, emmener, and promener.

The Seven Simple Tenses		The Seven Compound Tenses	
Singular	Plural	Singular	Plural
1 présent de l'indicatif		8 passé composé	
mens	mentons	ai menti	avons menti
mens	mentez	as menti	avez menti
ment	mentent	a menti	ont menti
2 imparfait de l'indicatif		9 plus-que-parfait de l'indicatif	
mentais	mentions	avais menti	avions menti
mentais	mentiez	avais menti	aviez menti
mentait	mentaient	avait menti	avaient menti
3 passé simple		10 passé antérieur	
mentis	mentîmes	eus menti	eûmes menti
mentis	mentîtes	eus menti	eûtes menti
mentit	mentirent	eut menti	eurent menti
4 futur		11 futur antérieur	
mentirai	mentirons	aurai menti	aurons menti
mentiras	mentirez	auras menti	aurez menti
mentira	mentiront	aura menti	auront menti
5 conditionnel		12 conditionnel passé	
mentirais	mentirions	aurais menti	aurions menti
mentirais	mentiriez	aurais menti	auriez menti
mentirait	mentiraient	aurait menti	auraient menti
6 présent du subjonctif		13 passé du subjonctif	
mente	mentions	aie menti	ayons menti
mentes	mentiez	aies menti	ayez menti
mente	mentent	ait menti	aient menti
7 imparfait du subjonctif		14 plus-que-parfait du subjonctif	
mentisse	mentissions	eusse menti	eussions menti
mentisses	mentissiez	eusses menti	eussiez menti
mentît	mentissent	eût menti	eussent menti

Impératif
mens
mentons
mentez

Words and expressions related to this verb
un mensonge   a lie
dire des mensonges   to tell lies
un menteur, une menteuse   a liar
Elle vit dans le mensonge   Her whole life is a lie.

Ce sont des mensonges   It's all a pack of lies.
Tu mens!   You're a liar!
sans mentir   quite honestly
démentir   to belie, to deny, to falsify, to refute
une menterie   fib

How are you doing? Find out with the verb drills and tests with answers explained on pages 622–673.

se méprendre

Part. pr. se méprenant   **Part. passé mépris(e)(es)**

to be mistaken, to mistake

The Seven Simple Tenses		The Seven Compound Tenses	
Singular	Plural	Singular	Plural
1 présent de l'indicatif		**8 passé composé**	
me méprends	nous méprenons	me suis mépris(e)	nous sommes mépris(es)
te méprends	vous méprenez	t'es mépris(e)	vous êtes mépris(e)(es)
se méprend	se méprennent	s'est mépris(e)	se sont mépris(es)
2 imparfait de l'indicatif		**9 plus-que-parfait de l'indicatif**	
me méprenais	nous méprenions	m'étais mépris(e)	nous étions mépris(es)
te méprenais	vous mépreniez	t'étais mépris(e)	vous étiez mépris(e)(es)
se méprenait	se méprenaient	s'était mépris(e)	s'étaient mépris(es)
3 passé simple		**10 passé antérieur**	
me mépris	nous méprîmes	me fus mépris(e)	nous fûmes mépris(es)
te mépris	vous méprîtes	te fus mépris(e)	vous fûtes mépris(e)(es)
se méprit	se méprirent	se fut mépris(e)	se furent mépris(es)
4 futur		**11 futur antérieur**	
me méprendrai	nous méprendrons	me serai mépris(e)	nous serons mépris(es)
te méprendras	vous méprendrez	te seras mépris(e)	vous serez mépris(e)(es)
se méprendra	se méprendront	se sera mépris(e)	se seront mépris(es)
5 conditionnel		**12 conditionnel passé**	
me méprendrais	nous méprendrions	me serais mépris(e)	nous serions mépris(es)
te méprendrais	vous méprendriez	te serais mépris(e)	vous seriez mépris(e)(es)
se méprendrait	se méprendraient	se serait mépris(e)	se seraient mépris(es)
6 présent du subjonctif		**13 passé du subjonctif**	
me méprenne	nous méprenions	me sois mépris(e)	nous soyons mépris(es)
te méprennes	vous mépreniez	te sois mépris(e)	vous soyez mépris(e)(es)
se méprenne	se méprennent	se soit mépris(e)	se soient mépris(es)
7 imparfait du subjonctif		**14 plus-que-parfait du subjonctif**	
me méprisse	nous méprissions	me fusse mépris(e)	nous fussions mépris(es)
te méprisses	vous méprissiez	te fusses mépris(e)	vous fussiez mépris(e)(es)
se méprît	se méprissent	se fût mépris(e)	se fussent mépris(es)

Impératif
méprends-toi; ne te méprends pas
méprenons-nous; ne nous méprenons pas
méprenez-vous; ne vous méprenez pas

Common idiomatic expressions using this verb
se méprendre sur qqn   to be mistaken about someone; to take someone for someone else

se méprendre au sujet de qqch   to be mistaken about something; to take something for something else

See also **apprendre, comprendre, entreprendre, prendre, reprendre,** and **surprendre.**

Want to learn more idiomatic expressions that contain verbs? Look at pages 530–542.

to merit, to deserve

The Seven Simple Tenses		The Seven Compound Tenses	
Singular	Plural	Singular	Plural
1 présent de l'indicatif		**8 passé composé**	
mérite	méritons	ai mérité	avons mérité
mérites	méritez	as mérité	avez mérité
mérite	méritent	a mérité	ont mérité
2 imparfait de l'indicatif		**9 plus-que-parfait de l'indicatif**	
méritais	méritions	avais mérité	avions mérité
méritais	méritiez	avais mérité	aviez mérité
méritait	méritaient	avait mérité	avaient mérité
3 passé simple		**10 passé antérieur**	
méritai	méritâmes	eus mérité	eûmes mérité
méritas	méritâtes	eus mérité	eûtes mérité
mérita	méritèrent	eut mérité	eurent mérité
4 futur		**11 futur antérieur**	
mériterai	mériterons	aurai mérité	aurons mérité
mériteras	mériterez	auras mérité	aurez mérité
méritera	mériteront	aura mérité	auront mérité
5 conditionnel		**12 conditionnel passé**	
mériterais	mériterions	aurais mérité	aurions mérité
mériterais	mériteriez	aurais mérité	auriez mérité
mériterait	mériteraient	aurait mérité	auraient mérité
6 présent du subjonctif		**13 passé du subjonctif**	
mérite	méritions	aie mérité	ayons mérité
mérites	méritiez	aies mérité	ayez mérité
mérite	méritent	ait mérité	aient mérité
7 imparfait du subjonctif		**14 plus-que-parfait du subjonctif**	
méritasse	méritassions	eusse mérité	eussions mérité
méritasses	méritassiez	eusses mérité	eussiez mérité
méritât	méritassent	eût mérité	eussent mérité

Impératif
mérite
méritons
méritez

Words and expressions related to this verb

un mérite   merit, worthiness
méritant, méritante   deserving (person)
une femme de mérite, un homme de mérite
   a woman, a man of merit

méritoire   meritorious, commendable,
   deserving (things, acts, deeds)
sans mérite   undeserving

Want to learn more verbs in proverbs and sayings? Take a look at page 559.

The subject pronouns are found on the page facing page 1.   **293**

mettre

Part. pr. **mettant**   Part. passé **mis**

to put, to place

The Seven Simple Tenses		The Seven Compound Tenses	
Singular	Plural	Singular	Plural
1 présent de l'indicatif		8 passé composé	
mets	mettons	ai mis	avons mis
mets	mettez	as mis	avez mis
met	mettent	a mis	ont mis
2 imparfait de l'indicatif		9 plus-que-parfait de l'indicatif	
mettais	mettions	avais mis	avions mis
mettais	mettiez	avais mis	aviez mis
mettait	mettaient	avait mis	avaient mis
3 passé simple		10 passé antérieur	
mis	mîmes	eus mis	eûmes mis
mis	mîtes	eus mis	eûtes mis
mit	mirent	eut mis	eurent mis
4 futur		11 futur antérieur	
mettrai	mettrons	aurai mis	aurons mis
mettras	mettrez	auras mis	aurez mis
mettra	mettront	aura mis	auront mis
5 conditionnel		12 conditionnel passé	
mettrais	mettrions	aurais mis	aurions mis
mettrais	mettriez	aurais mis	auriez mis
mettrait	mettraient	aurait mis	auraient mis
6 présent du subjonctif		13 passé du subjonctif	
mette	mettions	aie mis	ayons mis
mettes	mettiez	aies mis	ayez mis
mette	mettent	ait mis	aient mis
7 imparfait du subjonctif		14 plus-que-parfait du subjonctif	
misse	missions	eusse mis	eussions mis
misses	missiez	eusses mis	eussiez mis
mît	missent	eût mis	eussent mis

Impératif
mets
mettons
mettez

Words and expressions related to this verb
mettre la table   to set the table
mettre de côté   to lay aside, to save
mettre en cause   to question
mettre qqn à la porte   to kick somebody out
  the door
remettre   to put back

mettre au courant   to inform
mettre le couvert   to set the table
mettre au point   to make clear
mettre la télé   to turn on the TV
mettre la radio   to turn on the radio
se remettre   to recover

See also **admettre, commettre, se mettre, omettre, permettre, promettre, soumettre,** and **transmettre.**

to begin, to start, to place oneself

The Seven Simple Tenses		The Seven Compound Tenses	
Singular	Plural	Singular	Plural
1 présent de l'indicatif		**8 passé composé**	
me mets	nous mettons	me suis mis(e)	nous sommes mis(es)
te mets	vous mettez	t'es mis(e)	vous êtes mis(e)(es)
se met	se mettent	s'est mis(e)	se sont mis(es)
2 imparfait de l'indicatif		**9 plus-que-parfait de l'indicatif**	
me mettais	nous mettions	m'étais mis(e)	nous étions mis(es)
te mettais	vous mettiez	t'étais mis(e)	vous étiez mis(e)(es)
se mettait	se mettaient	s'était mis(e)	s'étaient mis(es)
3 passé simple		**10 passé antérieur**	
me mis	nous mîmes	me fus mis(e)	nous fûmes mis(es)
te mis	vous mîtes	te fus mis(e)	vous fûtes mis(e)(es)
se mit	se mirent	se fut mis(e)	se furent mis(es)
4 futur		**11 futur antérieur**	
me mettrai	nous mettrons	me serai mis(e)	nous serons mis(es)
te mettras	vous mettrez	te seras mis(e)	vous serez mis(e)(es)
se mettra	se mettront	se sera mis(e)	se seront mis(es)
5 conditionnel		**12 conditionnel passé**	
me mettrais	nous mettrions	me serais mis(e)	nous serions mis(es)
te mettrais	vous mettriez	te serais mis(e)	vous seriez mis(e)(es)
se mettrait	se mettraient	se serait mis(e)	se seraient mis(es)
6 présent du subjonctif		**13 passé du subjonctif**	
me mette	nous mettions	me sois mis(e)	nous soyons mis(es)
te mettes	vous mettiez	te sois mis(e)	vous soyez mis(e)(es)
se mette	se mettent	se soit mis(e)	se soient mis(es)
7 imparfait du subjonctif		**14 plus-que-parfait du subjonctif**	
me misse	nous missions	me fusse mis(e)	nous fussions mis(es)
te misses	vous missiez	te fusses mis(e)	vous fussiez mis(e)(es)
se mît	se missent	se fût mis(e)	se fussent mis(es)

Impératif
mets-toi; ne te mets pas
mettons-nous; ne nous mettons pas
mettez-vous; ne vous mettez pas

Words and expressions related to this verb
se mettre à + inf.   to begin, to start + inf.
se mettre à table   to go sit at the table
se mettre en colère   to get angry
mettable   wearable; **se mettre en grande toilette**   to dress for an occasion;
   se mettre en smoking   to put on a dinner jacket
mettre en scène   to stage; **un metteur en scène**   director of a film

See also **admettre, commettre, mettre, omettre, permettre, promettre, soumettre,** and
transmettre.

Learn more verbs in 30 practical situations for travelers on pages 568–598.

The subject pronouns are found on the page facing page 1.   **295**

mirer

Part. pr. **mirant**   Part. passé **miré**

to mirror

The Seven Simple Tenses		The Seven Compound Tenses	
Singular	Plural	Singular	Plural

1   présent de l'indicatif

		8 passé composé	
mire	mirons	ai miré	avons miré
mires	mirez	as miré	avez miré
mire	mirent	a miré	ont miré

2   imparfait de l'indicatif

		9 plus-que-parfait de l'indicatif	
mirais	mirions	avais miré	avions miré
mirais	miriez	avais miré	aviez miré
mirait	miraient	avait miré	avaient miré

3   passé simple

		10 passé antérieur	
mirai	mirâmes	eus miré	eûmes miré
miras	mirâtes	eus miré	eûtes miré
mira	mirèrent	eut miré	eurent miré

4   futur

		11 futur antérieur	
mirerai	mirerons	aurai miré	aurons miré
mireras	mirerez	auras miré	aurez miré
mirera	mireront	aura miré	auront miré

5   conditionnel

		12 conditionnel passé	
mirerais	mirerions	aurais miré	aurions miré
mirerais	mireriez	aurais miré	auriez miré
mirerait	mireraient	aurait miré	auraient miré

6   présent du subjonctif

		13 passé du subjonctif	
mire	mirions	aie miré	ayons miré
mires	miriez	aies miré	ayez miré
mire	mirent	ait miré	aient miré

7   imparfait du subjonctif

		14 plus-que-parfait du subjonctif	
mirasse	mirassions	eusse miré	eussions miré
mirasses	mirassiez	eusses miré	eussiez miré
mirât	mirassent	eût miré	eussent miré

Impératif
mire
mirons
mirez

Words and expressions related to this verb

la mire   aim, aiming; **point de mire**   point aimed at; **prendre sa mire (viser)**   to take aim
le mirage   mirage; illusion
un miroir   mirror

miroiter   to gleam, glisten, sparkle
se mirer dans   to look at oneself in (a mirror, a pool of water, a shiny surface)
admirer   to admire

See also **admirer.**

Soak up some verbs used in weather expressions on pages 557 and 558.

to go up, to ascend, to take up, to bring up, to mount

The Seven Simple Tenses		The Seven Compound Tenses	
Singular	Plural	Singular	Plural
1 présent de l'indicatif		8 passé composé	
monte	montons	suis monté(e)	sommes monté(e)s
montes	montez	es monté(e)	êtes monté(e)(s)
monte	montent	est monté(e)	sont monté(e)s
2 imparfait de l'indicatif		9 plus-que-parfait de l'indicatif	
montais	montions	étais monté(e)	étions monté(e)s
montais	montiez	étais monté(e)	étiez monté(e)(s)
montait	montaient	était monté(e)	étaient monté(e)s
3 passé simple		10 passé antérieur	
montai	montâmes	fus monté(e)	fûmes monté(e)s
montas	montâtes	fus monté(e)	fûtes monté(e)(s)
monta	montèrent	fut monté(e)	furent monté(e)s
4 futur		11 futur antérieur	
monterai	monterons	serai monté(e)	serons monté(e)s
monteras	monterez	seras monté(e)	serez monté(e)(s)
montera	monteront	sera monté(e)	seront monté(e)s
5 conditionnel		12 conditionnel passé	
monterais	monterions	serais monté(e)	serions monté(e)s
monterais	monteriez	serais monté(e)	seriez monté(e)(s)
monterait	monteraient	serait monté(e)	seraient monté(e)s
6 présent du subjonctif		13 passé du subjonctif	
monte	montions	sois monté(e)	soyons monté(e)s
montes	montiez	sois monté(e)	soyez monté(e)(s)
monte	montent	soit monté(e)	soient monté(e)s
7 imparfait du subjonctif		14 plus-que-parfait du subjonctif	
montasse	montassions	fusse monté(e)	fussions monté(e)s
montasses	montassiez	fusses monté(e)	fussiez monté(e)(s)
montât	montassent	fût monté(e)	fussent monté(e)s

Impératif
monte
montons
montez

This verb is conjugated with *avoir* when it has a direct object.

Examples: **J'ai monté l'escalier**   I went up the stairs.
             J'ai monté les valises   I brought up the suitcases.
BUT: **Elle est montée vite**   She went up quickly.

See also the verb **descendre**. Review page viii.
monter à bicyclette   to ride a bicycle
monter dans un train   to get on a train
monter une pièce de théâtre   to stage a play
monter à cheval   to mount a horse
monter à bord d'un navire   to get on board a ship
monter les prix   to push prices up
remonter   to go up again

montrer

Part. pr. **montrant**   Part. passé **montré**

to show, to display, to exhibit, to point out

The Seven Simple Tenses		The Seven Compound Tenses	
Singular	Plural	Singular	Plural
1 présent de l'indicatif		**8 passé composé**	
montre	montrons	ai montré	avons montré
montres	montrez	as montré	avez montré
montre	montrent	a montré	ont montré
2 imparfait de l'indicatif		**9 plus-que-parfait de l'indicatif**	
montrais	montrions	avais montré	avions montré
montrais	montriez	avais montré	aviez montré
montrait	montraient	avait montré	avaient montré
3 passé simple		**10 passé antérieur**	
montrai	montrâmes	eus montré	eûmes montré
montras	montrâtes	eus montré	eûtes montré
montra	montrèrent	eut montré	eurent montré
4 futur		**11 futur antérieur**	
montrerai	montrerons	aurai montré	aurons montré
montreras	montrerez	auras montré	aurez montré
montrera	montreront	aura montré	auront montré
5 conditionnel		**12 conditionnel passé**	
montrerais	montrerions	aurais montré	aurions montré
montrerais	montreriez	aurais montré	auriez montré
montrerait	montreraient	aurait montré	auraient montré
6 présent du subjonctif		**13 passé du subjonctif**	
montre	montrions	aie montré	ayons montré
montres	montriez	aies montré	ayez montré
montre	montrent	ait montré	aient montré
7 imparfait du subjonctif		**14 plus-que-parfait du subjonctif**	
montrasse	montrassions	eusse montré	eussions montré
montrasses	montrassiez	eusses montré	eussiez montré
montrât	montrassent	eût montré	eussent montré

Impératif
montre
montrons
montrez

Words and expressions related to this verb
une montre a watch, display
une montre-bracelet wristwatch
faire montre de sa richesse to display, to show off one's wealth
Quelle heure est-il à votre montre? What time is it on your watch?

se faire montrer la porte to be put out the door, to be shown out the door
démontrer to demonstrate
se démontrer to be proved
se montrer to show oneself, to appear

Don't miss the definitions of basic grammatical terms with examples in English and French on pages 674–688.

The Seven Simple Tenses		The Seven Compound Tenses	
Singular	Plural	Singular	Plural
1 présent de l'indicatif		8 passé composé	
me moque	**nous moquons**	**me suis moqué(e)**	**nous sommes moqué(e)s**
te moques	**vous moquez**	**t'es moqué(e)**	**vous êtes moqué(e)(s)**
se moque	**se moquent**	**s'est moqué(e)**	**se sont moqué(e)s**
2 imparfait de l'indicatif		9 plus-que-parfait de l'indicatif	
me moquais	**nous moquions**	**m'étais moqué(e)**	**nous étions moqué(e)s**
te moquais	**vous moquiez**	**t'étais moqué(e)**	**vous étiez moqué(e)(s)**
se moquais	**se moquaient**	**s'était moqué(e)**	**s'étaient moqué(e)s**
3 passé simple		10 passé antérieur	
me moquai	**nous moquâmes**	**me fus moqué(e)**	**nous fûmes moqué(e)s**
te moquas	**vous moquâtes**	**te fus moqué(e)**	**vous fûtes moqué(e)(s)**
se moqua	**se moquèrent**	**se fut moqué(e)**	**se furent moqué(e)s**
4 futur		11 futur antérieur	
me moquerai	**nous moquerons**	**me serai moqué(e)**	**nous serons moqué(e)s**
te moqueras	**vous moquerez**	**te seras moqué(e)**	**vous serez moqué(e)(s)**
se moquera	**se moqueront**	**se sera moqué(e)**	**se seront moqué(e)s**
5 conditionnel		12 conditionnel passé	
me moquerais	**nous moquerions**	**me serais moqué(e)**	**nous serions moqué(e)s**
te moquerais	**vous moqueriez**	**te serais moqué(e)**	**vous seriez moqué(e)(s)**
se moquerait	**se moqueraient**	**se serait moqué(e)**	**se seraient moqué(e)s**
6 présent du subjonctif		13 passé du subjonctif	
me moque	**nous moquions**	**me sois moqué(e)**	**nous soyons moqué(e)s**
te moques	**vous moquiez**	**te sois moqué(e)**	**vous soyez moqué(e)(s)**
se moque	**se moquent**	**se soit moqué(e)**	**se soient moqué(e)s**
7 imparfait du subjonctif		14 plus-que-parfait du subjonctif	
me moquasse	**nous moquassions**	**me fusse moqué(e)**	**nous fussions moqué(e)s**
te moquasses	**vous moquassiez**	**te fusses moqué(e)**	**vous fussiez moqué(e)(s)**
se moquât	**se moquassent**	**se fût moqué(e)**	**se fussent moqué(e)s**

Impératif
moque-toi; ne te moque pas
moquons-nous; ne nous moquons pas
moquez-vous; ne vous moquez pas

Words and expressions related to this verb
se moquer de to make fun of, to laugh at
Je m'en moque! I don't give a hoot!
moquer to mock
d'un ton moqueur in a mocking way

une moquerie mockery
un moqueur, une moqueuse mocker
moqueusement mockingly

Consult the sections on verbs used in idiomatic expressions, verbs with prepositions, and the list of over 1,100 verbs conjugated like model verbs in the back pages.

mordre

Part. pr. **mordant**   Part. passé **mordu**

to bite

The Seven Simple Tenses		The Seven Compound Tenses	
Singular	Plural	Singular	Plural
1 présent de l'indicatif		**8 passé composé**	
mords	mordons	ai mordu	avons mordu
mords	mordez	as mordu	avez mordu
mord	mordent	a mordu	ont mordu
2 imparfait de l'indicatif		**9 plus-que-parfait de l'indicatif**	
mordais	mordions	avais mordu	avions mordu
mordais	mordiez	avais mordu	aviez mordu
mordait	mordaient	avait mordu	avaient mordu
3 passé simple		**10 passé antérieur**	
mordis	mordîmes	eus mordu	eûmes mordu
mordis	mordîtes	eus mordu	eûtes mordu
mordit	mordirent	eut mordu	eurent mordu
4 futur		**11 futur antérieur**	
mordrai	mordrons	aurai mordu	aurons mordu
mordras	mordrez	auras mordu	aurez mordu
mordra	mordront	aura mordu	auront mordu
5 conditionnel		**12 conditionnel passé**	
mordrais	mordrions	aurais mordu	aurions mordu
mordrais	mordriez	aurais mordu	auriez mordu
mordrait	mordraient	aurait mordu	auraient mordu
6 présent du subjonctif		**13 passé du subjonctif**	
morde	mordions	aie mordu	ayons mordu
mordes	mordiez	aies mordu	ayez mordu
morde	mordent	ait mordu	aient mordu
7 imparfait du subjonctif		**14 plus-que-parfait du subjonctif**	
mordisse	mordissions	eusse mordu	eussions mordu
mordisses	mordissiez	eusses mordu	eussiez mordu
mordît	mordissent	eût mordu	eussent mordu

Impératif
mords
mordons
mordez

Words and expressions related to this verb

Chien qui aboie ne mord pas A barking dog does not bite; (**aboyer**, to bark)

Tous les chiens qui aboient ne mordent pas All dogs that bark do not bite.

mordre la poussière to bite the dust

se mordre les lèvres to bite one's lips

mordeur, mordeuse biter (one who bites)

mordiller to bite playfully, to nibble

mordant, mordante biting, trenchant

une morsure bite

mordre dans une pomme to bite into an apple

un mordu de l'ordinateur a computer fanatic, buff

C'est un mordu du jazz He's jazz crazy.

Enjoy more verbs in French proverbs and sayings on page 559.

The Seven Simple Tenses		The Seven Compound Tenses	
Singular	Plural	Singular	Plural
1 présent de l'indicatif		**8 passé composé**	
mouds	moulons	ai moulu	avons moulu
mouds	moulez	as moulu	avez moulu
moud	moulent	a moulu	ont moulu
2 imparfait de l'indicatif		**9 plus-que-parfait de l'indicatif**	
moulais	moulions	avais moulu	avions moulu
moulais	mouliez	avais moulu	aviez moulu
moulait	moulaient	avait moulu	avaient moulu
3 passé simple		**10 passé antérieur**	
moulus	moulûmes	eus moulu	eûmes moulu
moulus	moulûtes	eus moulu	eûtes moulu
moulut	moulurent	eut moulu	eurent moulu
4 futur		**11 futur antérieur**	
moudrai	moudrons	aurai moulu	aurons moulu
moudras	moudrez	auras moulu	aurez moulu
moudra	moudront	aura moulu	auront moulu
5 conditionnel		**12 conditionnel passé**	
moudrais	moudrions	aurais moulu	aurions moulu
moudrais	moudriez	aurais moulu	auriez moulu
moudrait	moudraient	aurait moulu	auraient moulu
6 présent du subjonctif		**13 passé du subjonctif**	
moule	moulions	aie moulu	ayons moulu
moules	mouliez	aies moulu	ayez moulu
moule	moulent	ait moulu	aient moulu
7 imparfait du subjonctif		**14 plus-que-parfait du subjonctif**	
moulusse	moulussions	eusse moulu	eussions moulu
moulusses	moulussiez	eusses moulu	eussiez moulu
moulût	moulussent	eût moulu	eussent moulu

Impératif
mouds
moulons
moulez

Words and expressions related to this verb

moudre du café to grind coffee;
  moudre du poivre to grind pepper
un moulin à café coffee mill,
  coffee grinder
un petit moulin à légumes
  vegetable blender

un moulin mill; **un moulin à eau** watermill;
  un moulin à vent windmill; **un moulin**
  rouge red mill
un moulin à paroles person who talks
  constantly without ever stopping; excessively
  talkative; chatterbox

Want to learn more idiomatic expressions that contain verbs? Look at pages 530–542.

mourir

to die

Part. pr. **mourant**   Part. passé **mort(e)(s)**

The Seven Simple Tenses		The Seven Compound Tenses	
Singular	Plural	Singular	Plural
1 présent de l'indicatif		**8 passé composé**	
meurs	mourons	suis mort(e)	sommes mort(e)s
meurs	mourez	es mort(e)	êtes mort(e)(s)
meurt	meurent	est mort(e)	sont mort(e)s
2 imparfait de l'indicatif		**9 plus-que-parfait de l'indicatif**	
mourais	mourions	étais mort(e)	étions mort(e)s
mourais	mouriez	étais mort(e)	étiez mort(e)(s)
mourait	mouraient	était mort(e)	étaient mort(e)s
3 passé simple		**10 passé antérieur**	
mourus	mourûmes	fus mort(e)	fûmes mort(e)s
mourus	mourûtes	fus mort(e)	fûtes mort(e)(s)
mourut	moururent	fut mort(e)	furent mort(e)s
4 futur		**11 futur antérieur**	
mourrai	mourrons	serai mort(e)	serons mort(e)s
mourras	mourrez	seras mort(e)	serez mort(e)(s)
mourra	mourront	sera mort(e)	seront mort(e)s
5 conditionnel		**12 conditionnel passé**	
mourrais	mourrions	serais mort(e)	serions mort(e)s
mourrais	mourriez	serais mort(e)	seriez mort(e)(s)
mourrait	mourraient	serait mort(e)	seraient mort(e)s
6 présent du subjonctif		**13 passé du subjonctif**	
meure	mourions	sois mort(e)	soyons mort(e)s
meures	mouriez	sois mort(e)	soyez mort(e)(s)
meure	meurent	soit mort(e)	soient mort(e)s
7 imparfait du subjonctif		**14 plus-que-parfait du subjonctif**	
mourusse	mourussions	fusse mort(e)	fussions mort(e)s
mourusses	mourussiez	fusses mort(e)	fussiez mort(e)(s)
mourût	mourussent	fût mort(e)	fussent mort(e)s

Impératif
meurs
mourons
mourez

Words and expressions related to this verb
mourir de faim   to starve to death
la mort   death
Elle est mourante   She is dying; **Elle se meurt**   She is dying.
mourir d'ennui   to be bored to tears
mourir de chagrin   to die of a broken heart
mourir de soif   to die of thirst
mourir de rire   to die laughing
mourir d'envie de faire qqch   to be very eager to do something
C'est triste à mourir   It's horribly sad.

Can't recognize an irregular verb form? Check out pages 526–529.

The Seven Simple Tenses		The Seven Compound Tenses	
Singular	Plural	Singular	Plural
1 présent de l'indicatif		**8 passé composé**	
meus	**mouvons**	**ai mû**	**avons mû**
meus	**mouvez**	**as mû**	**avez mû**
meut	**meuvent**	**a mû**	**ont mû**
2 imparfait de l'indicatif		**9 plus-que-parfait de l'indicatif**	
mouvais	**mouvions**	**avais mû**	**avions mû**
mouvais	**mouviez**	**avais mû**	**aviez mû**
mouvait	**mouvaient**	**avait mû**	**avaient mû**
3 passé simple		**10 passé antérieur**	
mus	**mûmes**	**eus mû**	**eûmes mû**
mus	**mûtes**	**eus mû**	**eûtes mû**
mut	**murent**	**eut mû**	**eurent mû**
4 futur		**11 futur antérieur**	
mouvrai	**mouvrons**	**aurai mû**	**aurons mû**
mouvras	**mouvrez**	**auras mû**	**aurez mû**
mouvra	**mouvront**	**aura mû**	**auront mû**
5 conditionnel		**12 conditionnel passé**	
mouvrais	**mouvrions**	**aurais mû**	**aurions mû**
mouvrais	**mouvriez**	**aurais mû**	**auriez mû**
mouvrait	**mouvraient**	**aurait mû**	**auraient mû**
6 présent du subjonctif		**13 passé du subjonctif**	
meuve	**mouvions**	**aie mû**	**ayons mû**
meuves	**mouviez**	**aies mû**	**ayez mû**
meuve	**meuvent**	**ait mû**	**aient mû**
7 imparfait du subjonctif		**14 plus-que-parfait du subjonctif**	
musse	**mussions**	**eusse mû**	**eussions mû**
musses	**mussiez**	**eusses mû**	**eussiez mû**
mût	**mussent**	**eût mû**	**eussent mû**

Impératif
meus
mouvons
mouvez

Words and expressions related to this verb
émouvoir   to move, to affect (emotionally)
s'émouvoir   to be moved, to be touched, to be affected (emotionally)
faire mouvoir   to move, to set in motion
promouvoir   to promote

Do not confuse this verb with **déménager**, which means to move from one dwelling to another or from one city to another.

nager

Part. pr. **nageant**   Part. passé **nagé**

to swim

The Seven Simple Tenses		The Seven Compound Tenses	
Singular	Plural	Singular	Plural
1 présent de l'indicatif		8 passé composé	
nage	nageons	ai nagé	avons nagé
nages	nagez	as nagé	avez nagé
nage	nagent	a nagé	ont nagé
2 imparfait de l'indicatif		9 plus-que-parfait de l'indicatif	
nageais	nagions	avais nagé	avions nagé
nageais	nagiez	avais nagé	aviez nagé
nageait	nageaient	avait nagé	avaient nagé
3 passé simple		10 passé antérieur	
nageai	nageâmes	eus nagé	eûmes nagé
nageas	nageâtes	eus nagé	eûtes nagé
nagea	nagèrent	eut nagé	eurent nagé
4 futur		11 futur antérieur	
nagerai	nagerons	aurai nagé	aurons nagé
nageras	nagerez	auras nagé	aurez nagé
nagera	nageront	aura nagé	auront nagé
5 conditionnel		12 conditionnel passé	
nagerais	nagerions	aurais nagé	aurions nagé
nagerais	nageriez	aurais nagé	auriez nagé
nagerait	nageraient	aurait nagé	auraient nagé
6 présent du subjonctif		13 passé du subjonctif	
nage	nagions	aie nagé	ayons nagé
nages	nagiez	aies nagé	ayez nagé
nage	nagent	ait nagé	aient nagé
7 imparfait du subjonctif		14 plus-que-parfait du subjonctif	
nageasse	nageassions	eusse nagé	eussions nagé
nageasses	nageassiez	eusses nagé	eussiez nagé
nageât	nageassent	eût nagé	eussent nagé

Impératif
nage
nageons
nagez

Words and expressions related to this verb

un nageur, une nageuse   swimmer
la piscine   swimming pool
savoir nager   to know how to swim
la natation   swimming
nager entre deux eaux   to sit on the fence
la nage   swimming; **la nage libre**   free style swimming
se sauver à la nage   to swim to safety

nager sous l'eau   to swim underwater
Il nage dans ses vêtements   His clothes are too big on him.
un maillot de bain   swimsuit
nager comme un poisson   to swim like a fish
nager dans l'opulence   to be rolling in money
aller nager   to go swimming
faire de la natation   to swim

Don't miss orthographically changing verbs on pages 554–556.

The Seven Simple Tenses		The Seven Compound Tenses	
Singular	Plural	Singular	Plural
1 présent de l'indicatif		**8 passé composé**	
nais	**naissons**	**suis né(e)**	**sommes né(e)s**
nais	**naissez**	**es né(e)**	**êtes né(e)(s)**
naît	**naissent**	**est né(e)**	**sont né(e)s**
2 imparfait de l'indicatif		**9 plus-que-parfait de l'indicatif**	
naissais	**naissions**	**étais né(e)**	**étions né(e)s**
naissais	**naissiez**	**étais né(e)**	**étiez né(e)(s)**
naissait	**naissaient**	**était né(e)**	**étaient né(e)s**
3 passé simple		**10 passé antérieur**	
naquis	**naquîmes**	**fus né(e)**	**fûmes né(e)s**
naquis	**naquîtes**	**fus né(e)**	**fûtes né(e)(s)**
naquit	**naquirent**	**fut né(e)**	**furent né(e)s**
4 futur		**11 futur antérieur**	
naîtrai	**naîtrons**	**serai né(e)**	**serons né(e)s**
naîtras	**naîtrez**	**seras né(e)**	**serez né(e)(s)**
naîtra	**naîtront**	**sera né(e)**	**seront né(e)s**
5 conditionnel		**12 conditionnel passé**	
naîtrais	**naîtrions**	**serais né(e)**	**serions né(e)s**
naîtrais	**naîtriez**	**serais né(e)**	**seriez né(e)(s)**
naîtrait	**naîtraient**	**serait né(e)**	**seraient né(e)s**
6 présent du subjonctif		**13 passé du subjonctif**	
naisse	**naissions**	**sois né(e)**	**soyons né(e)s**
naisses	**naissiez**	**sois né(e)**	**soyez né(e)(s)**
naisse	**naissent**	**soit né(e)**	**soient né(e)s**
7 imparfait du subjonctif		**14 plus-que-parfait du subjonctif**	
naquisse	**naquissions**	**fusse né(e)**	**fussions né(e)s**
naquisses	**naquissiez**	**fusses né(e)**	**fussiez né(e)(s)**
naquît	**naquissent**	**fût né(e)**	**fussent né(e)s**

Impératif
nais
naissons
naissez

Words and expressions related to this verb
la naissance   birth
un anniversaire de naissance   a birthday anniversary
donner naissance à   to give birth to; **la naissance du monde**   beginning of the world
Anne est Française de naissance   Anne was born French.
renaître   to be born again
faire naître   to cause, to give rise to
Je ne suis pas né(e) d'hier!   I wasn't born yesterday!
la Nativité   Nativity

Taking a trip? Check out the popular words, phrases, and expressions for travelers on pages 599–621.

The subject pronouns are found on the page facing page 1.   **305**

to snow

The Seven Simple Tenses	The Seven Compound Tenses
Singular Plural	Singular Plural
1 présent de l'indicatif **il neige**	8 passé composé **il a neigé**
2 imparfait de l'indicatif **il neigeait**	9 plus-que-parfait de l'indicatif **il avait neigé**
3 passé simple **il neigea**	10 passé antérieur **il eut neigé**
4 futur **il neigera**	11 futur antérieur **il aura neigé**
5 conditionnel **il neigerait**	12 conditionnel passé **il aurait neigé**
6 présent du subjonctif **qu'il neige**	13 passé du subjonctif **qu'il ait neigé**
7 imparfait du subjonctif **qu'il neigeât**	14 plus-que-parfait du subjonctif **qu'il eût neigé**

Impératif
Qu'il neige!   Let it snow!

Words and expressions related to this verb
la neige   snow
un bonhomme de neige   a snowman
neige fondue   slush
neigeux, neigeuse   snowy
Blanche-Neige   Snow White
une boule de neige   snowball
lancer des boules de neige   to throw
    snowballs
une chute de neige   snowfall
déneiger   to clear the snow

la neige artificielle   artificial snow
la neige poudreuse   dusting of snow
la bataille de boules de neige   snowball fight
être submergé de travail   to be snowed under
    with work
les conditions d'enneigement   snow
    conditions
le bulletin d'enneigement   snow report
un chasse-neige   snowplow

Verbs used in weather expressions are on pages 557 and 558.

The Seven Simple Tenses		The Seven Compound Tenses	
Singular	Plural	Singular	Plural
1 présent de l'indicatif		8 passé composé	
nettoie	**nettoyons**	**ai nettoyé**	**avons nettoyé**
nettoies	**nettoyez**	**as nettoyé**	**avez nettoyé**
nettoie	**nettoient**	**a nettoyé**	**ont nettoyé**
2 imparfait de l'indicatif		9 plus-que-parfait de l'indicatif	
nettoyais	**nettoyions**	**avais nettoyé**	**avions nettoyé**
nettoyais	**nettoyiez**	**avais nettoyé**	**aviez nettoyé**
nettoyait	**nettoyaient**	**avait nettoyé**	**avaient nettoyé**
3 passé simple		10 passé antérieur	
nettoyai	**nettoyâmes**	**eus nettoyé**	**eûmes nettoyé**
nettoyas	**nettoyâtes**	**eus nettoyé**	**eûtes nettoyé**
nettoya	**nettoyèrent**	**eut nettoyé**	**eurent nettoyé**
4 futur		11 futur antérieur	
nettoierai	**nettoierons**	**aurai nettoyé**	**aurons nettoyé**
nettoieras	**nettoierez**	**auras nettoyé**	**aurez nettoyé**
nettoiera	**nettoieront**	**aura nettoyé**	**auront nettoyé**
5 conditionnel		12 conditionnel passé	
nettoierais	**nettoierions**	**aurais nettoyé**	**aurions nettoyé**
nettoierais	**nettoieriez**	**aurais nettoyé**	**auriez nettoyé**
nettoierait	**nettoieraient**	**aurait nettoyé**	**auraient nettoyé**
6 présent du subjonctif		13 passé du subjonctif	
nettoie	**nettoyions**	**aie nettoyé**	**ayons nettoyé**
nettoies	**nettoyiez**	**aies nettoyé**	**ayez nettoyé**
nettoie	**nettoient**	**ait nettoyé**	**aient nettoyé**
7 imparfait du subjonctif		14 plus-que-parfait du subjonctif	
nettoyasse	**nettoyassions**	**eusse nettoyé**	**eussions nettoyé**
nettoyasses	**nettoyassiez**	**eusses nettoyé**	**eussiez nettoyé**
nettoyât	**nettoyassent**	**eût nettoyé**	**eussent nettoyé**

Impératif
nettoie
nettoyons
nettoyez

Words and expressions related to this verb

le nettoyage cleaning; **le nettoyage à sec** dry cleaning
nettoyer à sec to dry clean
une nettoyeuse cleaning machine
un nettoyant cleanser

un nettoyeur de fenêtres window cleaner
Elle refuse nettement She flatly refuses.
se faire nettoyer au jeu to be cleaned out at gambling

Verbs ending in *-oyer* must change *y* to *i* before mute *e*.

to deny

The Seven Simple Tenses		The Seven Compound Tenses	
Singular	Plural	Singular	Plural

1　présent de l'indicatif		8　passé composé	
nie	nions	ai nié	avons nié
nies	niez	as nié	avez nié
nie	nient	a nié	ont nié

2　imparfait de l'indicatif		9　plus-que-parfait de l'indicatif	
niais	niions	avais nié	avions nié
niais	niiez	avais nié	aviez nié
niait	niaient	avait nié	avaient nié

3　passé simple		10　passé antérieur	
niai	niâmes	eus nié	eûmes nié
nias	niâtes	eus nié	eûtes nié
nia	nièrent	eut nié	eurent nié

4　futur		11　futur antérieur	
nierai	nierons	aurai nié	aurons nié
nieras	nierez	auras nié	aurez nié
niera	nieront	aura nié	auront nié

5　conditionnel		12　conditionnel passé	
nierais	nierions	aurais nié	aurions nié
nierais	nieriez	aurais nié	auriez nié
nierait	nieraient	aurait nié	auraient nié

6　présent du subjonctif		13　passé du subjonctif	
nie	niions	aie nié	ayons nié
nies	niiez	aies nié	ayez nié
nie	nient	ait nié	aient nié

7　imparfait du subjonctif		14　plus-que-parfait du subjonctif	
niasse	niassions	eusse nié	eussions nié
niasses	niassiez	eusses nié	eussiez nié
niât	niassent	eût nié	eussent nié

Impératif
nie
nions
niez

Words and expressions related to this verb

nier un fait　to deny a fact
dénier qqch à qqn　to deny someone something, to refuse someone something
un déni　denial; **un déni de justice**　denial of justice
renier　to deny openly, to reject

renier un ami　to reject a friend
renier sa promesse　to go back on, to break one's promise
un renégat, une renégate　renegade
un reniement　denial
indéniable　undeniable

Get acquainted with what preposition goes with what verb on pages 543–553.

The Seven Simple Tenses		The Seven Compound Tenses	
Singular	Plural	Singular	Plural

1 présent de l'indicatif		8 passé composé	
nomme	nommons	ai nommé	avons nommé
nommes	nommez	as nommé	avez nommé
nomme	nomment	a nommé	ont nommé

2 imparfait de l'indicatif		9 plus-que-parfait de l'indicatif	
nommais	nommions	avais nommé	avions nommé
nommais	nommiez	avais nommé	aviez nommé
nommait	nommaient	avait nommé	avaient nommé

3 passé simple		10 passé antérieur	
nommai	nommâmes	eus nommé	eûmes nommé
nommas	nommâtes	eus nommé	eûtes nommé
nomma	nommèrent	eut nommé	eurent nommé

4 futur		11 futur antérieur	
nommerai	nommerons	aurai nommé	aurons nommé
nommeras	nommerez	auras nommé	aurez nommé
nommera	nommeront	aura nommé	auront nommé

5 conditionnel		12 conditionnel passé	
nommerais	nommerions	aurais nommé	aurions nommé
nommerais	nommeriez	aurais nommé	auriez nommé
nommerait	nommeraient	aurait nommé	auraient nommé

6 présent du subjonctif		13 passé du subjonctif	
nomme	nommions	aie nommé	ayons nommé
nommes	nommiez	aies nommé	ayez nommé
nomme	nomment	ait nommé	aient nommé

7 imparfait du subjonctif		14 plus-que-parfait du subjonctif	
nommasse	nommassions	eusse nommé	eussions nommé
nommasses	nommassiez	eusses nommé	eussiez nommé
nommât	nommassent	eût nommé	eussent nommé

Impératif
nomme
nommons
nommez

Common idiomatic expressions using this verb and words related to it

nommément   namely, by name
un pronom   a pronoun
un pseudonyme   pseudonym
un nom de théâtre   stage name
le petit nom   a person's first name
appeler les choses par leur nom   to call a
    spade a spade
anonyme   anonymous

un nom de plume   pen name (a name used by
    an author other than the real name)
un nom de guerre   false (assumed) name
nominalement   nominally
au nom du Père, du Fils, et du Saint-Esprit
    in the name of the Father, the Son, and the
    Holy Spirit
le renom   renown

Want to learn more idiomatic expressions that contain verbs? Look at pages 530–542.

nourrir
to feed, to nourish

Part. pr. nourrissant **Part. passé nourri**

The Seven Simple Tenses		The Seven Compound Tenses	
Singular	Plural	Singular	Plural
1 présent de l'indicatif		**8 passé composé**	
nourris	nourrissons	ai nourri	avons nourri
nourris	nourrissez	as nourri	avez nourri
nourrit	nourrissent	a nourri	ont nourri
2 imparfait de l'indicatif		**9 plus-que-parfait de l'indicatif**	
nourrissais	nourrissions	avais nourri	avions nourri
nourrissais	nourrissiez	avais nourri	aviez nourri
nourrissait	nourrissaient	avait nourri	avaient nourri
3 passé simple		**10 passé antérieur**	
nourris	nourrîmes	eus nourri	eûmes nourri
nourris	nourrîtes	eus nourri	eûtes nourri
nourrit	nourrirent	eut nourri	eurent nourri
4 futur		**11 futur antérieur**	
nourrirai	nourrirons	aurai nourri	aurons nourri
nourriras	nourrirez	auras nourri	aurez nourri
nourrira	nourriront	aura nourri	auront nourri
5 conditionnel		**12 conditionnel passé**	
nourrirais	nourririons	aurais nourri	aurions nourri
nourrirais	nourririez	aurais nourri	auriez nourri
nourrirait	nourriraient	aurait nourri	auraient nourri
6 présent du subjonctif		**13 passé du subjonctif**	
nourrisse	nourrissions	aie nourri	ayons nourri
nourrisses	nourrissiez	aies nourri	ayez nourri
nourrisse	nourrissent	ait nourri	aient nourri
7 imparfait du subjonctif		**14 plus-que-parfait du subjonctif**	
nourrisse	nourrissions	eusse nourri	eussions nourri
nourrisses	nourrissiez	eusses nourri	eussiez nourri
nourrît	nourrissent	eût nourri	eussent nourri

Impératif
nourris
nourrissons
nourrissez

Words and expressions related to this verb
la nourriture nourishment, food
une nourrice wet nurse
bien nourri well fed
mal nourri poorly fed
nourrissant, nourrissante nourishing

un nourrisson infant
nourricier, nourricière nutritious
une mère nourricière foster mother
un père nourricier foster father
se nourrir to feed oneself

Grammar putting you in a tense mood? Review the definitions of basic grammatical terms with examples on pages 674–688.

to harm, to hinder

The Seven Simple Tenses		The Seven Compound Tenses	
Singular	Plural	Singular	Plural
1 présent de l'indicatif		**8 passé composé**	
nuis	nuisons	ai nui	avons nui
nuis	nuisez	as nui	avez nui
nuit	nuisent	a nui	ont nui
2 imparfait de l'indicatif		**9 plus-que-parfait de l'indicatif**	
nuisais	nuisions	avais nui	avions nui
nuisais	nuisiez	avais nui	aviez nui
nuisait	nuisaient	avait nui	avaient nui
3 passé simple		**10 passé antérieur**	
nuisis	nuisîmes	eus nui	eûmes nui
nuisis	nuisîtes	eus nui	eûtes nui
nuisit	nuisirent	eut nui	eurent nui
4 futur		**11 futur antérieur**	
nuirai	nuirons	aurai nui	aurons nui
nuiras	nuirez	auras nui	aurez nui
nuira	nuiront	aura nui	auront nui
5 conditionnel		**12 conditionnel passé**	
nuirais	nuirions	aurais nui	aurions nui
nuirais	nuiriez	aurais nui	auriez nui
nuirait	nuiraient	aurait nui	auraient nui
6 présent du subjonctif		**13 passé du subjonctif**	
nuise	nuisions	aie nui	ayons nui
nuises	nuisiez	aies nui	ayez nui
nuise	nuisent	ait nui	aient nui
7 imparfait du subjonctif		**14 plus-que-parfait du subjonctif**	
nuisisse	nuisissions	eusse nui	eussions nui
nuisisses	nuisissiez	eusses nui	eussiez nui
nuisît	nuisissent	eût nui	eussent nui

Impératif
nuis
nuisons
nuisez

Words and expressions related to this verb
la nuisance nuisance
les nuisances sonores noise pollution
nuisible harmful
nuire à to do harm to, to be injurious to, to be harmful to

Cela peut nuire à la réputation de votre famille That may harm the reputation of your family.

How are you doing? Find out with the verb drills and tests with answers explained on pages 622–673.

obéir

to obey

The Seven Simple Tenses		The Seven Compound Tenses	
Singular	Plural	Singular	Plural
1 présent de l'indicatif		**8 passé composé**	
obéis	obéissons	ai obéi	avons obéi
obéis	obéissez	as obéi	avez obéi
obéit	obéissent	a obéi	ont obéi
2 imparfait de l'indicatif		**9 plus-que-parfait de l'indicatif**	
obéissais	obéissions	avais obéi	avions obéi
obéissais	obéissiez	avais obéi	aviez obéi
obéissait	obéissaient	avait obéi	avaient obéi
3 passé simple		**10 passé antérieur**	
obéis	obéîmes	eus obéi	eûmes obéi
obéis	obéîtes	eus obéi	eûtes obéi
obéit	obéirent	eut obéi	eurent obéi
4 futur		**11 futur antérieur**	
obéirai	obéirons	aurai obéi	aurons obéi
obéiras	obéirez	auras obéi	aurez obéi
obéira	obéiront	aura obéi	auront obéi
5 conditionnel		**12 conditionnel passé**	
obéirais	obéirions	aurais obéi	aurions obéi
obéirais	obéiriez	aurais obéi	auriez obéi
obéirait	obéiraient	aurait obéi	auraient obéi
6 présent du subjonctif		**13 passé du subjonctif**	
obéisse	obéissions	aie obéi	ayons obéi
obéisses	obéissiez	aies obéi	ayez obéi
obéisse	obéissent	ait obéi	aient obéi
7 imparfait du subjonctif		**14 plus-que-parfait du subjonctif**	
obéisse	obéissions	eusse obéi	eussions obéi
obéisses	obéissiez	eusses obéi	eussiez obéi
obéît	obéissent	eût obéi	eussent obéi

Impératif
obéis
obéissons
obéissez

Words and expressions related to this verb
obéir à qqn   to obey someone
désobéir à qqn   to disobey someone
l'obéissance *f.*   obedience

obéissant, obéissante   obedient
désobéissant, désobéissante   disobedient
obéir à ses instincts   to obey one's instincts

Get acquainted with what preposition goes with what verb on pages 543–553.

The Seven Simple Tenses		The Seven Compound Tenses	
Singular	Plural	Singular	Plural

1   présent de l'indicatif

		8 passé composé	
oblige	obligeons	ai obligé	avons obligé
obliges	obligez	as obligé	avez obligé
oblige	obligent	a obligé	ont obligé

2   imparfait de l'indicatif

		9 plus-que-parfait de l'indicatif	
obligeais	obligions	avais obligé	avions obligé
obligeais	obligiez	avais obligé	aviez obligé
obligeait	obligeaient	avait obligé	avaient obligé

3   passé simple

		10 passé antérieur	
obligeai	obligeâmes	eus obligé	eûmes obligé
obligeas	obligeâtes	eus obligé	eûtes obligé
obligea	obligèrent	eut obligé	eurent obligé

4   futur

		11 futur antérieur	
obligerai	obligerons	aurai obligé	aurons obligé
obligeras	obligerez	auras obligé	aurez obligé
obligera	obligeront	aura obligé	auront obligé

5   conditionnel

		12 conditionnel passé	
obligerais	obligerions	aurais obligé	aurions obligé
obligerais	obligeriez	aurais obligé	auriez obligé
obligerait	obligeraient	aurait obligé	auraient obligé

6   présent du subjonctif

		13 passé du subjonctif	
oblige	obligions	aie obligé	ayons obligé
obliges	obligiez	aies obligé	ayez obligé
oblige	obligent	ait obligé	aient obligé

7   imparfait du subjonctif

		14 plus-que-parfait du subjonctif	
obligeasse	obligeassions	eusse obligé	eussions obligé
obligeasses	obligeassiez	eusses obligé	eussiez obligé
obligeât	obligeassent	eût obligé	eussent obligé

Impératif
oblige
obligeons
obligez

Words and expressions related to this verb

obligatoire   obligatory
obligation *f.*   obligation
avoir beaucoup d'obligation à qqn   to be much obliged to someone
obligeant, obligeante   obliging
se montrer obligeant envers qqn   to show kindness to someone

obligé, obligée   obliged
Noblesse oblige   Nobility obliges. (i.e., the moral obligation of a highborn person is to show honorable conduct)

If you want to see a sample English verb fully conjugated in all the tenses, check out pages xiii and xiv.

obtenir

Part. pr. **obtenant**   Part. passé **obtenu**

to obtain, to get

The Seven Simple Tenses		The Seven Compound Tenses	
Singular	Plural	Singular	Plural
1 présent de l'indicatif		**8 passé composé**	
obtiens	obtenons	ai obtenu	avons obtenu
obtiens	obtenez	as obtenu	avez obtenu
obtient	obtiennent	a obtenu	ont obtenu
2 imparfait de l'indicatif		**9 plus-que-parfait de l'indicatif**	
obtenais	obtenions	avais obtenu	avions obtenu
obtenais	obteniez	avais obtenu	aviez obtenu
obtenait	obtenaient	avait obtenu	avaient obtenu
3 passé simple		**10 passé antérieur**	
obtins	obtînmes	eus obtenu	eûmes obtenu
obtins	obtîntes	eus obtenu	eûtes obtenu
obtint	obtinrent	eut obtenu	eurent obtenu
4 futur		**11 futur antérieur**	
obtiendrai	obtiendrons	aurai obtenu	aurons obtenu
obtiendras	obtiendrez	auras obtenu	aurez obtenu
obtiendra	obtiendront	aura obtenu	auront obtenu
5 conditionnel		**12 conditionnel passé**	
obtiendrais	obtiendrions	aurais obtenu	aurions obtenu
obtiendrais	obtiendriez	aurais obtenu	auriez obtenu
obtiendrait	obtiendraient	aurait obtenu	auraient obtenu
6 présent du subjonctif		**13 passé du subjonctif**	
obtienne	obtenions	aie obtenu	ayons obtenu
obtiennes	obteniez	aies obtenu	ayez obtenu
obtienne	obtiennent	ait obtenu	aient obtenu
7 imparfait du subjonctif		**14 plus-que-parfait du subjonctif**	
obtinsse	obtinssions	eusse obtenu	eussions obtenu
obtinsses	obtinssiez	eusses obtenu	eussiez obtenu
obtînt	obtinssent	eût obtenu	eussent obtenu

Impératif
obtiens
obtenons
obtenez

Words and expressions related to this verb
l'obtention obtainment
obtenir de qqn qqch de force to get something out of someone by force
s'obtenir de to be obtained from

See also **contenir, retenir,** and **tenir.**

It's important that you be familiar with the Subjunctive. See pages 560–565.

The Seven Simple Tenses		The Seven Compound Tenses	
Singular	Plural	Singular	Plural
1 présent de l'indicatif		8 passé composé	
occupe	occupons	ai occupé	avons occupé
occupes	occupez	as occupé	avez occupé
occupe	occupent	a occupé	ont occupé
2 imparfait de l'indicatif		9 plus-que-parfait de l'indicatif	
occupais	occupions	avais occupé	avions occupé
occupais	occupiez	avais occupé	aviez occupé
occupait	occupaient	avait occupé	avaient occupé
3 passé simple		10 passé antérieur	
occupai	occupâmes	eus occupé	eûmes occupé
occupas	occupâtes	eus occupé	eûtes occupé
occupa	occupèrent	eut occupé	eurent occupé
4 futur		11 futur antérieur	
occuperai	occuperons	aurai occupé	aurons occupé
occuperas	occuperez	auras occupé	aurez occupé
occupera	occuperont	aura occupé	auront occupé
5 conditionnel		12 conditionnel passé	
occuperais	occuperions	aurais occupé	aurions occupé
occuperais	occuperiez	aurais occupé	auriez occupé
occuperait	occuperaient	aurait occupé	auraient occupé
6 présent du subjonctif		13 passé du subjonctif	
occupe	occupions	aie occupé	ayons occupé
occupes	occupiez	aies occupé	ayez occupé
occupe	occupent	ait occupé	aient occupé
7 imparfait du subjonctif		14 plus-que-parfait du subjonctif	
occupasse	occupassions	eusse occupé	eussions occupé
occupasses	occupassiez	eusses occupé	eussiez occupé
occupât	occupassent	eût occupé	eussent occupé

Impératif
occupe
occupons
occupez

Words and expressions related to this verb
occupation f.   occupation
être occupé(e)   to be busy
occuper qqn   to keep someone busy
occuper trop de place   to take up too much room
occupant, occupante   occupying; **du travail occupant**   engrossing work
occuper l'attention de qqn   to hold someone's attention
préoccuper   to preoccupy; **une préoccupation**   preoccupation
La ligne est occupée   The line is busy.

See also **s'occuper.**

The subject pronouns are found on the page facing page 1.

s'occuper

Part. pr. **s'occupant**   Part. passé **occupé(e)(s)**

to be busy, to keep oneself busy

The Seven Simple Tenses		The Seven Compound Tenses	
Singular	Plural	Singular	Plural
1 présent de l'indicatif		**8 passé composé**	
m'occupe	nous occupons	me suis occupé(e)	nous sommes occupé(e)s
t'occupes	vous occupez	t'es occupé(e)	vous êtes occupé(e)(s)
s'occupe	s'occupent	s'est occupé(e)	se sont occupé(e)s
2 imparfait de l'indicatif		**9 plus-que-parfait de l'indicatif**	
m'occupais	nous occupions	m'étais occupé(e)	nous étions occupé(e)s
t'occupais	vous occupiez	t'étais occupé(e)	vous étiez occupé(e)(s)
s'occupait	s'occupaient	s'était occupé(e)	s'étaient occupé(e)s
3 passé simple		**10 passé antérieur**	
m'occupai	nous occupâmes	me fus occupé(e)	nous fûmes occupé(e)s
t'occupas	vous occupâtes	te fus occupé(e)	vous fûtes occupé(e)(s)
s'occupa	s'occupèrent	se fut occupé(e)	se furent occupé(e)s
4 futur		**11 futur antérieur**	
m'occuperai	nous occuperons	me serai occupé(e)	nous serons occupé(e)s
t'occuperas	vous occuperez	te seras occupé(e)	vous serez occupé(e)(s)
s'occupera	s'occuperont	se sera occupé(e)	se seront occupé(e)s
5 conditionnel		**12 conditionnel passé**	
m'occuperais	nous occuperions	me serais occupé(e)	nous serions occupé(e)s
t'occuperais	vous occuperiez	te serais occupé(e)	vous seriez occupé(e)(s)
s'occuperait	s'occuperaient	se serait occupé(e)	se seraient occupé(e)s
6 présent du subjonctif		**13 passé du subjonctif**	
m'occupe	nous occupions	me sois occupé(e)	nous soyons occupé(e)s
t'occupes	vous occupiez	te sois occupé(e)	vous soyez occupé(e)(s)
s'occupe	s'occupent	se soit occupé(e)	se soient occupé(e)s
7 imparfait du subjonctif		**14 plus-que-parfait du subjonctif**	
m'occupasse	nous occupassions	me fusse occupé(e)	nous fussions occupé(e)s
t'occupasses	vous occupassiez	te fusses occupé(e)	vous fussiez occupé(e)(s)
s'occupât	s'occupassent	se fût occupé(e)	se fussent occupé(e)s

Impératif
occupe-toi; ne t'occupe pas
occupons-nous; ne nous occupons pas
occupez-vous; ne vous occupez pas

Words and expressions related to this verb

s'occuper de ses affaires to mind one's own business
Je m'occupe de mes affaires I mind my own business.
s'occuper des enfants to look after children
s'occuper de to look after, to tend to
s'occuper à to be engaged in

Occupez-vous de vos affaires! Mind your own business!
Ne vous occupez pas de mes affaires! Don't mind my business!
Est-ce qu'on s'occupe de vous? Is someone helping you?

See also the verb **occuper.**

Want to learn more idiomatic expressions that contain verbs? Look at pages 530–542.

The Seven Simple Tenses		The Seven Compound Tenses	
Singular	Plural	Singular	Plural

1 présent de l'indicatif		8 passé composé	
offre	offrons	ai offert	avons offert
offres	offrez	as offert	avez offert
offre	offrent	a offert	ont offert

2 imparfait de l'indicatif		9 plus-que-parfait de l'indicatif	
offrais	offrions	avais offert	avions offert
offrais	offriez	avais offert	aviez offert
offrait	offraient	avait offert	avaient offert

3 passé simple		10 passé antérieur	
offris	offrîmes	eus offert	eûmes offert
offris	offrîtes	eus offert	eûtes offert
offrit	offrirent	eut offert	eurent offert

4 futur		11 futur antérieur	
offrirai	offrirons	aurai offert	aurons offert
offriras	offrirez	auras offert	aurez offert
offrira	offriront	aura offert	auront offert

5 conditionnel		12 conditionnel passé	
offrirais	offririons	aurais offert	aurions offert
offrirais	offririez	aurais offert	auriez offert
offrirait	offriraient	aurait offert	auraient offert

6 présent du subjonctif		13 passé du subjonctif	
offre	offrions	aie offert	ayons offert
offres	offriez	aies offert	ayez offert
offre	offrent	ait offert	aient offert

7 imparfait du subjonctif		14 plus-que-parfait du subjonctif	
offrisse	offrissions	eusse offert	eussions offert
offrisses	offrissiez	eusses offert	eussiez offert
offrît	offrissent	eût offert	eussent offert

Impératif
offre
offrons
offrez

Words and expressions related to this verb

offrir qqch à qqn   to offer (to present)
  something to someone
une offre   an offer, a proposal
une offrande   gift, offering

l'offre et la demande   supply and demand
une offre d'emploi   a job offer
les offres d'emploi   employment opportunities
C'est pour offrir?   Is it to give as a gift?

Get acquainted with what preposition goes with what verb on pages 543–553.

The subject pronouns are found on the page facing page 1.   **317**

omettre

Part. pr. **omettant**   Part. passé **omis**

to omit

The Seven Simple Tenses		The Seven Compound Tenses	
Singular	Plural	Singular	Plural
1 présent de l'indicatif		**8 passé composé**	
omets	omettons	ai omis	avons omis
omets	omettez	as omis	avez omis
omet	omettent	a omis	ont omis
2 imparfait de l'indicatif		**9 plus-que-parfait de l'indicatif**	
omettais	omettions	avais omis	avions omis
omettais	omettiez	avais omis	aviez omis
omettait	omettaient	avait omis	avaient omis
3 passé simple		**10 passé antérieur**	
omis	omîmes	eus omis	eûmes omis
omis	omîtes	eus omis	eûtes omis
omit	omirent	eut omis	eurent omis
4 futur		**11 futur antérieur**	
omettrai	omettrons	aurai omis	aurons omis
omettras	omettrez	auras omis	aurez omis
omettra	omettront	aura omis	auront omis
5 conditionnel		**12 conditionnel passé**	
omettrais	omettrions	aurais omis	aurions omis
omettrais	omettriez	aurais omis	auriez omis
omettrait	omettraient	aurait omis	auraient omis
6 présent du subjonctif		**13 passé du subjonctif**	
omette	omettions	aie omis	ayons omis
omettes	omettiez	aies omis	ayez omis
omette	omettent	ait omis	aient omis
7 imparfait du subjonctif		**14 plus-que-parfait du subjonctif**	
omisse	omissions	eusse omis	eussions omis
omisses	omissiez	eusses omis	eussiez omis
omît	omissent	eût omis	eussent omis

Impératif
omets
omettons
omettez

Words and expressions related to this verb
omettre de faire qqch   to neglect to do something
une omission   an omission
omis, omise   omitted
commettre   to commit

See also **admettre, commettre, mettre, permettre, promettre, remettre, soumettre,** and **transmettre.**

Going away? Don't forget to check out the practical situations for travelers on pages 568–598.

318

The Seven Simple Tenses		The Seven Compound Tenses	
Singular	Plural	Singular	Plural
1 présent de l'indicatif		**8 passé composé**	
ose	osons	ai osé	avons osé
oses	osez	as osé	avez osé
ose	osent	a osé	ont osé
2 imparfait de l'indicatif		**9 plus-que-parfait de l'indicatif**	
osais	osions	avais osé	avions osé
osais	osiez	avais osé	aviez osé
osait	osaient	avait osé	avaient osé
3 passé simple		**10 passé antérieur**	
osai	osâmes	eus osé	eûmes osé
osas	osâtes	eus osé	eûtes osé
osa	osèrent	eut osé	eurent osé
4 futur		**11 futur antérieur**	
oserai	oserons	aurai osé	aurons osé
oseras	oserez	auras osé	aurez osé
osera	oseront	aura osé	auront osé
5 conditionnel		**12 conditionnel passé**	
oserais	oserions	aurais osé	aurions osé
oserais	oseriez	aurais osé	auriez osé
oserait	oseraient	aurait osé	auraient osé
6 présent du subjonctif		**13 passé du subjonctif**	
ose	osions	aie osé	ayons osé
oses	osiez	aies osé	ayez osé
ose	osent	ait osé	aient osé
7 imparfait du subjonctif		**14 plus-que-parfait du subjonctif**	
osasse	osassions	eusse osé	eussions osé
osasses	osassiez	eusses osé	eussiez osé
osât	osassent	eût osé	eussent osé

Impératif
ose
osons
osez

Words and expressions related to this verb
Si j'ose dire . . .   If I may be so bold as to say . . .
Je n'ose le dire   I dare not say so.
oser faire qqch   to dare to do something; to have the courage, audacity to do something
Je n'ose rien dire   I don't dare say anything.
osé, osée   bold, daring

Consult the sections on verbs used in idiomatic expressions, verbs with prepositions, and the list
of over 1,100 verbs conjugated like model verbs in the back pages.

oublier

Part. pr. **oubliant**   Part. passé **oublié**

to forget

The Seven Simple Tenses		The Seven Compound Tenses	
Singular	Plural	Singular	Plural
1 présent de l'indicatif		8 passé composé	
oublie	**oublions**	**ai oublié**	**avons oublié**
oublies	**oubliez**	**as oublié**	**avez oublié**
oublie	**oublient**	**a oublié**	**ont oublié**
2 imparfait de l'indicatif		9 plus-que-parfait de l'indicatif	
oubliais	**oubliions**	**avais oublié**	**avions oublié**
oubliais	**oubliiez**	**avais oublié**	**aviez oublié**
oubliait	**oubliaient**	**avait oublié**	**avaient oublié**
3 passé simple		10 passé antérieur	
oubliai	**oubliâmes**	**eus oublié**	**eûmes oublié**
oublias	**oubliâtes**	**eus oublié**	**eûtes oublié**
oublia	**oublièrent**	**eut oublié**	**eurent oublié**
4 futur		11 futur antérieur	
oublierai	**oublierons**	**aurai oublié**	**aurons oublié**
oublieras	**oublierez**	**auras oublié**	**aurez oublié**
oubliera	**oublieront**	**aura oublié**	**auront oublié**
5 conditionnel		12 conditionnel passé	
oublierais	**oublierions**	**aurais oublié**	**aurions oublié**
oublierais	**oublieriez**	**aurais oublié**	**auriez oublié**
oublierait	**oublieraient**	**aurait oublié**	**auraient oublié**
6 présent du subjonctif		13 passé du subjonctif	
oublie	**oubliions**	**aie oublié**	**ayons oublié**
oublies	**oubliiez**	**aies oublié**	**ayez oublié**
oublie	**oublient**	**ait oublié**	**aient oublié**
7 imparfait du subjonctif		14 plus-que-parfait du subjonctif	
oubliasse	**oubliassions**	**eusse oublié**	**eussions oublié**
oubliasses	**oubliassiez**	**eusses oublié**	**eussiez oublié**
oubliât	**oubliassent**	**eût oublié**	**eussent oublié**

Impératif
oublie
oublions
oubliez

Words and expressions related to this verb

un oubli   oversight; oblivion
tomber dans l'oubli   to be forgotten (over time)
oubliable   forgettable
inoubliable   unforgettable
s'oublier   to forget oneself, to be unmindful of oneself

oublier de faire qqch   to forget to do something
oublieux, oublieuse   oblivious; **oublieux de** unmindful of; forgetful
Nous n'oublierons jamais   We will never forget.

How are you doing? Find out with the verb drills and tests with answers explained on pages 622–673.

The Seven Simple Tenses		The Seven Compound Tenses	
Singular	Plural	Singular	Plural
1 présent de l'indicatif		**8 passé composé**	
ouvre	ouvrons	ai ouvert	avons ouvert
ouvres	ouvrez	as ouvert	avez ouvert
ouvre	ouvrent	a ouvert	ont ouvert
2 imparfait de l'indicatif		**9 plus-que-parfait de l'indicatif**	
ouvrais	ouvrions	avais ouvert	avions ouvert
ouvrais	ouvriez	avais ouvert	aviez ouvert
ouvrait	ouvraient	avait ouvert	avaient ouvert
3 passé simple		**10 passé antérieur**	
ouvris	ouvrîmes	eus ouvert	eûmes ouvert
ouvris	ouvrîtes	eus ouvert	eûtes ouvert
ouvrit	ouvrirent	eut ouvert	eurent ouvert
4 futur		**11 futur antérieur**	
ouvrirai	ouvrirons	aurai ouvert	aurons ouvert
ouvriras	ouvrirez	auras ouvert	aurez ouvert
ouvrira	ouvriront	aura ouvert	auront ouvert
5 conditionnel		**12 conditionnel passé**	
ouvrirais	ouvririons	aurais ouvert	aurions ouvert
ouvrirais	ouvririez	aurais ouvert	auriez ouvert
ouvrirait	ouvriraient	aurait ouvert	auraient ouvert
6 présent du subjonctif		**13 passé du subjonctif**	
ouvre	ouvrions	aie ouvert	ayons ouvert
ouvres	ouvriez	aies ouvert	ayez ouvert
ouvre	ouvrent	ait ouvert	aient ouvert
7 imparfait du subjonctif		**14 plus-que-parfait du subjonctif**	
ouvrisse	ouvrissions	eusse ouvert	eussions ouvert
ouvrisses	ouvrissiez	eusses ouvert	eussiez ouvert
ouvrît	ouvrissent	eût ouvert	eussent ouvert

Impératif
ouvre
ouvrons
ouvrez

Words and expressions related to this verb

ouvert, ouverte   open
ouverture *f.*   opening
ouvrir le gaz   to turn on the gas
ouvrir de force   to force open
un ouvre-boîte (des ouvre-boîtes)   can opener
entrouvert, entrouverte   ajar

un ouvre-bouteille (des ouvre-bouteilles)
   bottle opener
rouvrir   to reopen, to open again
entrouvrir   to open just a bit
s'ouvrir à   to confide in
les heures ouvrables   business hours

Consult the back pages for over 1,100 French verbs conjugated like model verbs among the 501.

The subject pronouns are found on the page facing page 1.   **321**

to appear, to seem

The Seven Simple Tenses		The Seven Compound Tenses	
Singular	Plural	Singular	Plural
1 présent de l'indicatif		8 passé composé	
parais	paraissons	ai paru	avons paru
parais	paraissez	as paru	avez paru
paraît	paraissent	a paru	ont paru
2 imparfait de l'indicatif		9 plus-que-parfait de l'indicatif	
paraissais	paraissions	avais paru	avions paru
paraissais	paraissiez	avais paru	aviez paru
paraissait	paraissaient	avait paru	avaient paru
3 passé simple		10 passé antérieur	
parus	parûmes	eus paru	eûmes paru
parus	parûtes	eus paru	eûtes paru
parut	parurent	eut paru	eurent paru
4 futur		11 futur antérieur	
paraîtrai	paraîtrons	aurai paru	aurons paru
paraîtras	paraîtrez	auras paru	aurez paru
paraîtra	paraîtront	aura paru	auront paru
5 conditionnel		12 conditionnel passé	
paraîtrais	paraîtrions	aurais paru	aurions paru
paraîtrais	paraîtriez	aurais paru	auriez paru
paraîtrait	paraîtraient	aurait paru	auraient paru
6 présent du subjonctif		13 passé du subjonctif	
paraisse	paraissions	aie paru	ayons paru
paraisses	paraissiez	aies paru	ayez paru
paraisse	paraissent	ait paru	aient paru
7 imparfait du subjonctif		14 plus-que-parfait du subjonctif	
parusse	parussions	eusse paru	eussions paru
parusses	parussiez	eusses paru	eussiez paru
parût	parussent	eût paru	eussent paru

Impératif
parais
paraissons
paraissez

Words and expressions related to this verb
apparition *f.*   apparition, appearance
Cela me paraît incroyable   That seems unbelievable to me.
Le jour paraît   Day is breaking.
apparaître   to appear, to come into view
disparaître   to disappear
réapparaître   to reappear
Ce livre vient de paraître   This book has just been published.
la parution   (act of) publication

See also **apparaître, disparaître,** and **reparaître.**

Review the Subjunctive clearly and simply on pages 560–565.

The Seven Simple Tenses		The Seven Compound Tenses	
Singular	Plural	Singular	Plural
1 présent de l'indicatif		**8 passé composé**	
pardonne	pardonnons	ai pardonné	avons pardonné
pardonnes	pardonnez	as pardonné	avez pardonné
pardonne	pardonnent	a pardonné	ont pardonné
2 imparfait de l'indicatif		**9 plus-que-parfaît de l'indicatif**	
pardonnais	pardonnions	avais pardonné	avions pardonné
pardonnais	pardonniez	avais pardonné	aviez pardonné
pardonnait	pardonnaient	avait pardonné	avaient pardonné
3 passé simple		**10 passé antérieur**	
pardonnai	pardonnâmes	eus pardonné	eûmes pardonné
pardonnas	pardonnâtes	eus pardonné	eûtes pardonné
pardonna	pardonnèrent	eut pardonné	eurent pardonné
4 futur		**11 futur antérieur**	
pardonnerai	pardonnerons	aurai pardonné	aurons pardonné
pardonneras	pardonnerez	auras pardonné	aurez pardonné
pardonnera	pardonneront	aura pardonné	auront pardonné
5 conditionnel		**12 conditionnel passé**	
pardonnerais	pardonnerions	aurais pardonné	aurions pardonné
pardonnerais	pardonneriez	aurais pardonné	auriez pardonné
pardonnerait	pardonneraient	aurait pardonné	auraient pardonné
6 présent du subjonctif		**13 passé du subjonctif**	
pardonne	pardonnions	aie pardonné	ayons pardonné
pardonnes	pardonniez	aies pardonné	ayez pardonné
pardonne	pardonnent	ait pardonné	aient pardonné
7 imparfait du subjonctif		**14 plus-que-parfait du subjonctif**	
pardonnasse	pardonnassions	eusse pardonné	eussions pardonné
pardonnasses	pardonnassiez	eusses pardonné	eussiez pardonné
pardonnât	pardonnassent	eût pardonné	eussent pardonné

Impératif
pardonne
pardonnons
pardonnez

Sentences using this verb and words related to it

pardonner à qqn de qqch   to forgive
someone for something
**J'ai pardonné à mon ami d'être arrivé en
retard**   I forgave my friend for having
arrived late.
un pardon   forgiveness, pardon

See also **donner.**

un don   gift
pardonnable   forgivable, pardonable
Pardonnez-moi   Pardon me.
**Marie-Thérèse, ce que vous venez de faire est
impardonnable**   Marie-Thérèse, what you
just did is unforgivable.

Want to learn more verbs used in proverbs and sayings? Take a look at page 559.

The subject pronouns are found on the page facing page 1.

parler

Part. pr. **parlant** Part. passé **parlé**

to talk, to speak

The Seven Simple Tenses		The Seven Compound Tenses	
Singular	Plural	Singular	Plural
1 présent de l'indicatif		8 passé composé	
parle	**parlons**	**ai parlé**	**avons parlé**
parles	**parlez**	**as parlé**	**avez parlé**
parle	**parlent**	**a parlé**	**ont parlé**
2 imparfait de l'indicatif		9 plus-que-parfait de l'indicatif	
parlais	**parlions**	**avais parlé**	**avions parlé**
parlais	**parliez**	**avais parlé**	**aviez parlé**
parlait	**parlaient**	**avait parlé**	**avaient parlé**
3 passé simple		10 passé antérieur	
parlai	**parlâmes**	**eus parlé**	**eûmes parlé**
parlas	**parlâtes**	**eus parlé**	**eûtes parlé**
parla	**parlèrent**	**eut parlé**	**eurent parlé**
4 futur		11 futur antérieur	
parlerai	**parlerons**	**aurai parlé**	**aurons parlé**
parleras	**parlerez**	**auras parlé**	**aurez parlé**
parlera	**parleront**	**aura parlé**	**auront parlé**
5 conditionnel		12 conditionnel passé	
parlerais	**parlerions**	**aurais parlé**	**aurions parlé**
parlerais	**parleriez**	**aurais parlé**	**auriez parlé**
parlerait	**parleraient**	**aurait parlé**	**auraient parlé**
6 présent du subjonctif		13 passé du subjonctif	
parle	**parlions**	**aie parlé**	**ayons parlé**
parles	**parliez**	**aies parlé**	**ayez parlé**
parle	**parlent**	**ait parlé**	**aient parlé**
7 imparfait du subjonctif		14 plus-que-parfait du subjonctif	
parlasse	**parlassions**	**eusse parlé**	**eussions parlé**
parlasses	**parlassiez**	**eusses parlé**	**eussiez parlé**
parlât	**parlassent**	**eût parlé**	**eussent parlé**

Impératif
parle
parlons
parlez

Words and expressions related to this verb

parler à haute voix   to speak in a loud voice;
 parler haut   to speak loudly
parler à voix basse   to speak softly; **parler
 bas**   to speak softly
la parole   spoken word; **parler à**   to talk to;
 parler de   to talk about (of)
selon la parole du Christ   according to
 Christ's words
le don de la parole   the gift of gab

les pourparlers *m.*   negotiations
francophone   French-speaking
parler affaires   to talk business, to talk shop
sans parler de . . .   not to mention . . .
parler pour qqn   to speak for someone;
 parler contre qqn   to speak against
 someone
un parloir   parlor (room where people talk)

Increase your verb power with popular phrases, words, and expressions for travelers on pages
599–621.

The Seven Simple Tenses		The Seven Compound Tenses	
Singular	Plural	Singular	Plural

1 présent de l'indicatif

pars	partons		
pars	partez		
part	partent		

8 passé composé

suis parti(e)		sommes parti(e)s	
es parti(e)		êtes parti(e)(s)	
est parti(e)		sont parti(e)s	

2 imparfait de l'indicatif

partais	partions
partais	partiez
partait	partaient

9 plus-que-parfaît de l'indicatif

étais parti(e)	étions parti(e)s
étais parti(e)	étiez parti(e)(s)
était parti(e)	étaient parti(e)s

3 passé simple

partis	partîmes
partis	partîtes
partit	partirent

10 passé antérieur

fus parti(e)	fûmes parti(e)s
fus parti(e)	fûtes parti(e)(s)
fut parti(e)	furent parti(e)s

4 futur

partirai	partirons
partiras	partirez
partira	partiront

11 futur antérieur

serai parti(e)	serons parti(e)s
seras parti(e)	serez parti(e)(s)
sera parti(e)	seront parti(e)s

5 conditionnel

partirais	partirions
partirais	partiriez
partirait	partiraient

12 conditionnel passé

serais parti(e)	serions parti(e)s
serais parti(e)	seriez parti(e)(s)
serait parti(e)	seraient parti(e)s

6 présent du subjonctif

parte	partions
partes	partiez
parte	partent

13 passé du subjonctif

sois parti(e)	soyons parti(e)s
sois parti(e)	soyez parti(e)(s)
soit parti(e)	soient parti(e)s

7 imparfait du subjonctif

partisse	partissions
partisses	partissiez
partît	partissent

14 plus-que-parfait du subjonctif

fusse parti(e)	fussions parti(e)s
fusses parti(e)	fussiez parti(e)(s)
fût parti(e)	fussent parti(e)s

Impératif
pars
partons
partez

Words and expressions related to this verb
A quelle heure part le train pour Paris?
  At what time does the train for Paris leave?
à partir de maintenant   from now on
à partir d'aujourd'hui   from today on
le départ   departure
partir en voyage   to go on a trip

partir en vacances   to leave for a vacation
repartir   to leave again, to set out again
Le train en partance pour Paris est sur la voie deux   The train leaving for Paris is on track two.
un département   department

Taking a trip? Check out the popular words, phrases, and expressions for travelers on pages 599–621.

The subject pronouns are found on the page facing page 1.   **325**

passer

to pass, to spend (time)

The Seven Simple Tenses		The Seven Compound Tenses	
Singular	Plural	Singular	Plural
1 présent de l'indicatif		**8 passé composé**	
passe	passons	ai passé	avons passé
passes	passez	as passé	avez passé
passe	passent	a passé	ont passé
2 imparfait de l'indicatif		**9 plus-que-parfait de l'indicatif**	
passais	passions	avais passé	avions passé
passais	passiez	avais passé	aviez passé
passait	passaient	avait passé	avaient passé
3 passé simple		**10 passé antérieur**	
passai	passâmes	eus passé	eûmes passé
passas	passâtes	eus passé	eûtes passé
passa	passèrent	eut passé	eurent passé
4 futur		**11 futur antérieur**	
passerai	passerons	aurai passé	aurons passé
passeras	passerez	auras passé	aurez passé
passera	passeront	aura passé	auront passé
5 conditionnel		**12 conditionnel passé**	
passerais	passerions	aurais passé	aurions passé
passerais	passeriez	aurais passé	auriez passé
passerait	passeraient	aurait passé	auraient passé
6 présent du subjonctif		**13 passé du subjonctif**	
passe	passions	aie passé	ayons passé
passes	passiez	aies passé	ayez passé
passe	passent	ait passé	aient passé
7 imparfait du subjonctif		**14 plus-que-parfait du subjonctif**	
passasse	passassions	eusse passé	eussions passé
passasses	passassiez	eusses passé	eussiez passé
passât	passassent	eût passé	eussent passé

	Impératif
	passe
	passons
	passez

This verb is conjugated with **être** to indicate a state.
Example: **Ses soupçons sont passés en certitudes.**
This verb is conjugated with **être** when it means *to pass by, go by:*
Example: **Elle est passée chez moi.**   She came by my house.
BUT: This verb is conjugated with **avoir** when it has a direct object:
Examples: **Elle m'a passé le sel.**   She passed me the salt.
            Elle a passé un examen.   She took an exam.
repasser   to pass again; to iron
dépasser   to protrude, to exceed, to surpass, to pass (a vehicle)
passable   acceptable

See also **repasser** and **se passer.**   Review page viii.

to happen, to take place

The Seven Simple Tenses	The Seven Compound Tenses
Singular Plural	Singular Plural
1 présent de l'indicatif **il se passe**	8 passé composé **il s'est passé**
2 imparfait de l'indicatif **il se passait**	9 plus-que-parfait de l'indicatif **il s'était passé**
3 passé simple **il se passa**	10 passé antérieur **il se fut passé**
4 futur **il se passera**	11 futur antérieur **il se sera passé**
5 conditionnel **il se passerait**	12 conditionnel passé **il se serait passé**
6 présent du subjonctif **qu'il se passe**	13 passé du subjonctif **qu'il se soit passé**
7 imparfait du subjonctif **qu'il se passât**	14 plus-que-parfait du subjonctif **qu'il se fût passé**

Impératif
Qu'il se passe!   Let it happen!

Words and expressions related to this verb
Que se passe-t-il?   What's going on? What's happening?
Qu'est-ce qui se passe?   What's going on? What's happening?
Qu'est-ce qui s'est passé?   What happened?
se passer de qqch   to do without something
Je peux me passer de fumer   I can do without smoking.

See also **passer** and **repasser**.

This verb is impersonal and is generally used in the 3rd person sing. only.

Use the EE-zee guide to French pronunciation on pages 566 and 567.

The subject pronouns are found on the page facing page 1.   **327**

patiner

Part. pr. **patinant**   Part. passé **patiné**

to skate

The Seven Simple Tenses		The Seven Compound Tenses	
Singular	Plural	Singular	Plural
1 présent de l'indicatif		**8 passé composé**	
patine	patinons	ai patiné	avons patiné
patines	patinez	as patiné	avez patiné
patine	patinent	a patiné	ont patiné
2 imparfait de l'indicatif		**9 plus-que-parfait de l'indicatif**	
patinais	patinions	avais patiné	avions patiné
patinais	patiniez	avais patiné	aviez patiné
patinait	patinaient	avait patiné	avaient patiné
3 passé simple		**10 passé antérieur**	
patinai	patinâmes	eus patiné	eûmes patiné
patinas	patinâtes	eus patiné	eûtes patiné
patina	patinèrent	eut patiné	eurent patiné
4 futur		**11 futur antérieur**	
patinerai	patinerons	aurai patiné	aurons patiné
patineras	patinerez	auras patiné	aurez patiné
patinera	patineront	aura patiné	auront patiné
5 conditionnel		**12 conditionnel passé**	
patinerais	patinerions	aurais patiné	aurions patiné
patinerais	patineriez	aurais patiné	auriez patiné
patinerait	patineraient	aurait patiné	auraient patiné
6 présent du subjonctif		**13 passé du subjonctif**	
patine	patinions	aie patiné	ayons patiné
patines	patiniez	aies patiné	ayez patiné
patine	patinent	ait patiné	aient patiné
7 imparfait du subjonctif		**14 plus-que-parfait du subjonctif**	
patinasse	patinassions	eusse patiné	eussions patiné
patinasses	patinassiez	eusses patiné	eussiez patiné
patinât	patinassent	eût patiné	eussent patiné

Impératif
patine
patinons
patinez

Words and expressions related to this verb

patiner sur glace   to skate on ice
une patinette   scooter
un patineur, une patineuse   skater
le patinage   skating
le patinage artistique   figure skating
les patins à roues alignées   inline skates

une patinoire   skating rink
patiner sur roulettes, patiner à roulettes   to roller-skate
le patinage à roulettes   roller-skating
le patinage de vitesse   speed skating

Soak up some verbs used in weather expressions on pages 557 and 558.

The Seven Simple Tenses		The Seven Compound Tenses	
Singular	Plural	Singular	Plural
1 présent de l'indicatif		8 passé composé	
paye	payons	ai payé	avons payé
payes	payez	as payé	avez payé
paye	payent	a payé	ont payé
2 imparfait de l'indicatif		9 plus-que-parfait de l'indicatif	
payais	payions	avais payé	avions payé
payais	payiez	avais payé	aviez payé
payait	payaient	avait payé	avaient payé
3 passé simple		10 passé antérieur	
payai	payâmes	eus payé	eûmes payé
payas	payâtes	eus payé	eûtes payé
paya	payèrent	eut payé	eurent payé
4 futur		11 futur antérieur	
payerai	payerons	aurai payé	aurons payé
payeras	payerez	auras payé	aurez payé
payera	payeront	aura payé	auront payé
5 conditionnel		12 conditionnel passé	
payerais	payerions	aurais payé	aurions payé
payerais	payeriez	aurais payé	auriez payé
payerait	payeraient	aurait payé	auraient payé
6 présent du subjonctif		13 passé du subjonctif	
paye	payions	aie payé	ayons payé
payes	payiez	aies payé	ayez payé
paye	payent	ait payé	aient payé
7 imparfait du subjonctif		14 plus-que-parfait du subjonctif	
payasse	payassions	eusse payé	eussions payé
payasses	payassiez	eusses payé	eussiez payé
payât	payassent	eût payé	eussent payé

Impératif
paye
payons
payez

Words and expressions related to this verb
Payez à la caisse, s'il vous plaît   Pay at the cashier, please.
un payement (or paiement)   payment
avoir de quoi payer   to have the means to pay
payable   payable
se faire payer à dîner par qqn   to get your dinner paid for by someone
payer cher   to pay a lot
payer peu   to pay little
payer comptant   to pay in cash

Verbs ending in -*ayer* may change *y* to *i* before mute *e* or may keep *y*.

to sin, to commit a sin

The Seven Simple Tenses		The Seven Compound Tenses	
Singular	Plural	Singular	Plural
1 présent de l'indicatif		**8 passé composé**	
pèche	péchons	ai péché	avons péché
pèches	péchez	as péché	avez péché
pèche	pèchent	a péché	ont péché
2 imparfait de l'indicatif		**9 plus-que-parfait de l'indicatif**	
péchais	péchions	avais péché	avions péché
péchais	péchiez	avais péché	aviez péché
péchait	péchaient	avait péché	avaient péché
3 passé simple		**10 passé antérieur**	
péchai	péchâmes	eus péché	eûmes péché
péchas	péchâtes	eus péché	eûtes péché
pécha	péchèrent	eut péché	eurent péché
4 futur		**11 futur antérieur**	
pécherai	pécherons	aurai péché	aurons péché
pécheras	pécherez	auras péché	aurez péché
péchera	pécheront	aura péché	auront péché
5 conditionnel		**12 conditionnel passé**	
pécherais	pécherions	aurais péché	aurions péché
pécherais	pécheriez	aurais péché	auriez péché
pécherait	pécheraient	aurait péché	auraient péché
6 présent du subjonctif		**13 passé du subjonctif**	
pèche	péchions	aie péché	ayons péché
pèches	péchiez	aies péché	ayez péché
pèche	pèchent	ait péché	aient péché
7 imparfait du subjonctif		**14 plus-que-parfait du subjonctif**	
péchasse	péchassions	eusse péché	eussions péché
péchasses	péchassiez	eusses péché	eussiez péché
péchât	péchassent	eût péché	eussent péché

Impératif
pèche
péchons
péchez

Words and expressions related to this verb
le péché sin
un pécheur, une pécheresse sinner
à **tout péché miséricorde** forgiveness for
  every sin

commettre, faire un péché to commit sin
vivre dans le péché to lead a sinful life
les sept péchés capitaux the seven deadly
  sins

Do not confuse this verb with **pêcher**, *to fish*.

Want to learn more idiomatic expressions that contain verbs? Check out pages 530–542.

The Seven Simple Tenses		The Seven Compound Tenses	
Singular	Plural	Singular	Plural
1 présent de l'indicatif		**8 passé composé**	
pêche	pêchons	ai pêché	avons pêché
pêches	pêchez	as pêché	avez pêché
pêche	pêchent	a pêché	ont pêché
2 imparfait de l'indicatif		**9 plus-que-parfait de l'indicatif**	
pêchais	pêchions	avais pêché	avions pêché
pêchais	pêchiez	avais pêché	aviez pêché
pêchait	pêchaient	avait pêché	avaient pêché
3 passé simple		**10 passé antérieur**	
pêchai	pêchâmes	eus pêché	eûmes pêché
pêchas	pêchâtes	eus pêché	eûtes pêché
pâcha	pêchèrent	eut pêché	eurent pêché
4 futur		**11 futur antérieur**	
pêcherai	pêcherons	aurai pêché	aurons pêché
pêcheras	pêcherez	auras pêché	aurez pêché
pêchera	pêcheront	aura pêché	auront pêché
5 conditionnel		**12 conditionnel passé**	
pêcherais	pêcherions	aurais pêché	aurions pêché
pêcherais	pêcheriez	aurais pêché	auriez pêché
pêcherait	pêcheraient	aurait pêché	auraient pêché
6 présent du subjonctif		**13 passé du subjonctif**	
pêche	pêchions	aie pêché	ayons pêché
pêches	pêchiez	aies pêché	ayez pêché
pêche	pêchent	ait pêché	aient pêché
7 imparfait du subjonctif		**14 plus-que-parfait du subjonctif**	
pêchasse	pêchassions	eusse pêché	eussions pêché
pêchasses	pêchassiez	eusses pêché	eussiez pêché
pêchât	pêchassent	eût pêché	eussent pêché

Impératif
pêche
pêchons
pêchez

Common idiomatic expressions using this verb

Samedi nous irons à la pêche. Je connais un lac à la campagne où il y a beaucoup de poissons.

aller à la pêche   to go fishing
un pêcheur   fisherman; **une pêcheuse**
un bateau pêcheur   fishing boat
le repêchage   recovery, (act of) fishing out

la pêche au filet   net fishing
un pêcheur de perles   pearl diver
repêcher   to fish out

Do not confuse this verb with **pécher**, *to sin*. And do not confuse **une pêche** (*peach*), which is a fruit, with a verb form of **pêcher** and with the noun **la pêche**, which means *fishing*, the sport.

se peigner

Part. pr. **se peignant**   Part. passé **peigné(e)(s)**

to comb one's hair

The Seven Simple Tenses		The Seven Compound Tenses	
Singular	Plural	Singular	Plural
1 présent de l'indicatif		**8 passé composé**	
me peigne	nous peignons	me suis peigné(e)	nous sommes peigné(e)s
te peignes	vous peignez	t'es peigné(e)	vous êtes peigné(e)(s)
se peigne	se peignent	s'est peigné(e)	se sont peigné(e)s
2 imparfait de l'indicatif		**9 plus-que-parfait de l'indicatif**	
me peignais	nous peignions	m'étais peigné(e)	nous étions peigné(e)s
te peignais	vous peigniez	t'étais peigné(e)	vous étiez peigné(e)(s)
se peignait	se peignaient	s'était peigné(e)	s'étaient peigné(e)s
3 passé simple		**10 passé antérieur**	
me peignai	nous peignâmes	me fus peigné(e)	nous fûmes peigné(e)s
te peignas	vous peignâtes	te fus peigné(e)	vous fûtes peigné(e)(s)
se peigna	se peignèrent	se fut peigné(e)	se furent peigné(e)s
4 futur		**11 futur antérieur**	
me peignerai	nous peignerons	me serai peigné(e)	nous serons peigné(e)s
te peigneras	vous peignerez	te seras peigné(e)	vous serez peigné(e)(s)
se peignera	se peigneront	se sera peigné(e)	se seront peigné(e)s
5 conditionnel		**12 conditionnel passé**	
me peignerais	nous peignerions	me serais peigné(e)	nous serions peigné(e)s
te peignerais	vous peigneriez	te serais peigné(e)	vous seriez peigné(e)(s)
se peignerait	se peigneraient	se serait peigné(e)	se seraient peigné(e)s
6 présent du subjonctif		**13 passé du subjonctif**	
me peigne	nous peignions	me sois peigné(e)	nous soyons peigné(e)s
te peignes	vous peigniez	te sois peigné(e)	vous soyez peigné(e)(s)
se peigne	se peignent	se soit peigné(e)	se soient peigné(e)s
7 imparfait du subjonctif		**14 plus-que-parfait du subjonctif**	
me peignasse	nous peignassions	me fusse peigné(e)	nous fussions peigné(e)s
te peignasses	vous peignassiez	te fusses peigné(e)	vous fussiez peigné(e)(s)
se peignât	se peignassent	se fût peigné(e)	se fussent peigné(e)s

Impératif
peigne-toi; ne te peigne pas
peignons-nous; ne nous peignons pas
peignez-vous; ne vous peignez pas

Sentences using this verb and words related to it

Mon frère a peigné notre petit chien. Ma mère a lavé les cheveux de ma petite soeur et elle l'a peignée. Après cela, elle s'est lavé les cheveux et elle s'est peignée.

peigner qqn to comb someone	**mal peigné(e)(s)**	untidy hair, dishevelled
un peigne a comb	**bien peigné(e)(s)**	well combed
un peignoir dressing gown	**un peignoir de bain**	bathrobe

Review the entry agreement of past participle of a reflexive verb with its reflexive pronoun in the section on definitions of basic grammatical terms with examples on pages 674–675.

to paint, to portray

The Seven Simple Tenses		The Seven Compound Tenses	
Singular	Plural	Singular	Plural

1   présent de l'indicatif

Singular	Plural
peins	peignons
peins	peignez
peint	peignent

8   passé composé

Singular	Plural
ai peint	avons peint
as peint	avez peint
a peint	ont peint

2   imparfait de l'indicatif

Singular	Plural
peignais	peignions
peignais	peigniez
peignait	peignaient

9   plus-que-parfait de l'indicatif

Singular	Plural
avais peint	avions peint
avais peint	aviez peint
avait peint	avaient peint

3   passé simple

Singular	Plural
peignis	peignîmes
peignis	peignîtes
peignit	peignirent

10   passé antérieur

Singular	Plural
eus peint	eûmes peint
eus peint	eûtes peint
eut peint	eurent peint

4   futur

Singular	Plural
peindrai	peindrons
peindras	peindrez
peindra	peindront

11   futur antérieur

Singular	Plural
aurai peint	aurons peint
auras peint	aurez peint
aura peint	auront peint

5   conditionnel

Singular	Plural
peindrais	peindrions
peindrais	peindriez
peindrait	peindraient

12   conditionnel passé

Singular	Plural
aurais peint	aurions peint
aurais peint	auriez peint
aurait peint	auraient peint

6   présent du subjonctif

Singular	Plural
peigne	peignions
peignes	peigniez
peigne	peignent

13   passé du subjonctif

Singular	Plural
aie peint	ayons peint
aies peint	ayez peint
ait peint	aient peint

7   imparfait du subjonctif

Singular	Plural
peignisse	peignissions
peignisses	peignissiez
peignît	peignissent

14   plus-que-parfait du subjonctif

Singular	Plural
eusse peint	eussions peint
eusses peint	eussiez peint
eût peint	eussent peint

Impératif
peins
peignons
peignez

Sentences using this verb and words related to it
—**Qui a peint ce tableau? Mon fils. Il est artiste peintre.**
—**Est-ce que Renoir a jamais peint une reine noire?**

une peinture   painting, picture
un tableau   painting, picture
une peinture à l'huile   oil painting
peintre en bâtiments   house painter
dépeindre   to depict, to describe
PEINTURE FRAÎCHE   WET PAINT

un peintre   painter
un artiste peintre   artist
une femme peintre   woman artist
une palette de peintre   artist's palette
se faire peindre   to have one's portrait painted

See also **dépeindre.**

pendre

Part. pr. **pendant**   Part. passé **pendu**

to hang, to suspend

The Seven Simple Tenses		The Seven Compound Tenses	
Singular	Plural	Singular	Plural
1 présent de l'indicatif		**8 passé composé**	
pends	pendons	ai pendu	avons pendu
pends	pendez	as pendu	avez pendu
pend	pendent	a pendu	ont pendu
2 imparfait de l'indicatif		**9 plus-que-parfait de l'indicatif**	
pendais	pendions	avais pendu	avions pendu
pendais	pendiez	avais pendu	aviez pendu
pendait	pendaient	avait pendu	avaient pendu
3 passé simple		**10 passé antérieur**	
pendis	pendîmes	eus pendu	eûmes pendu
pendis	pendîtes	eus pendu	eûtes pendu
pendit	pendirent	eut pendu	eurent pendu
4 futur		**11 futur antérieur**	
pendrai	pendrons	aurai pendu	aurons pendu
pendras	pendrez	auras pendu	aurez pendu
pendra	pendront	aura pendu	auront pendu
5 conditionnel		**12 conditionnel passé**	
pendrais	pendrions	aurais pendu	aurions pendu
pendrais	pendriez	aurais pendu	auriez pendu
pendrait	pendraient	aurait pendu	auraient pendu
6 présent du subjonctif		**13 passé du subjonctif**	
pende	pendions	aie pendu	ayons pendu
pendes	pendiez	aies pendu	ayez pendu
pende	pendent	ait pendu	aient pendu
7 imparfait du subjonctif		**14 plus-que-parfait du subjonctif**	
pendisse	pendissions	eusse pendu	eussions pendu
pendisses	pendissiez	eusses pendu	eussiez pendu
pendît	pendissent	eût pendu	eussent pendu

Impératif
pends
pendons
pendez

Words and expressions related to this verb

pendre des rideaux   to hang curtains
pendre qqch   to hang something
pendre qqn   to hang someone
se pendre   to hang oneself
dépendre de   to depend on
pendant   during; **pendant que**   while
un pendant   pendant, main piece of a necklace, hanging ornament

See also **dépendre.**

suspendre un lustre   to hang a chandelier (ceiling lighting fixture)
pendu, pendue *adj.*   hung (thing); hanged (person)
un pendule   pendulum
une pendule   clock
un pendant d'oreille   pendant earring, drop earring

For an explanation of meanings and uses of French and English verb tenses and moods, see pages xv–xxvi.

334

The Seven Simple Tenses		The Seven Compound Tenses	
Singular	Plural	Singular	Plural

1   présent de l'indicatif

		8 passé composé	
pense	pensons	ai pensé	avons pensé
penses	pensez	as pensé	avez pensé
pense	pensent	a pensé	ont pensé

2   imparfait de l'indicatif

		9 plus-que-parfait de l'indicatif	
pensais	pensions	avais pensé	avions pensé
pensais	pensiez	avais pensé	aviez pensé
pensait	pensaient	avait pensé	avaient pensé

3   passé simple

		10 passé antérieur	
pensai	pensâmes	eus pensé	eûmes pensé
pensas	pensâtes	eus pensé	eûtes pensé
pensa	pensèrent	eut pensé	eurent pensé

4   futur

		11 futur antérieur	
penserai	penserons	aurai pensé	aurons pensé
penseras	penserez	auras pensé	aurez pensé
pensera	penseront	aura pensé	auront pensé

5   conditionnel

		12 conditionnel passé	
penserais	penserions	aurais pensé	aurions pensé
penserais	penseriez	aurais pensé	auriez pensé
penserait	penseraient	aurait pensé	auraient pensé

6   présent du subjonctif

		13 passé du subjonctif	
pense	pensions	aie pensé	ayons pensé
penses	pensiez	aies pensé	ayez pensé
pense	pensent	ait pensé	aient pensé

7   imparfait du subjonctif

		14 plus-que-parfait du subjonctif	
pensasse	pensassions	eusse pensé	eussions pensé
pensasses	pensassiez	eusses pensé	eussiez pensé
pensât	pensassent	eût pensé	eussent pensé

Impératif
pense
pensons
pensez

Common idiomatic expressions using this verb
—**Robert, tu as l'air pensif; à quoi penses-tu?**
—**Je pense à mon examen de français.**
—**Moi, je pense aux vacances de Noël.**
—**Que penses-tu de cette classe de français?**
—**Je trouve que cette classe est excellente.**
—**Penses-tu continuer à étudier le français l'année prochaine?**
—**Certainement.**

penser à   to think of, to think about; **penser de**   to think about (i.e., to have an opinion about);
  un pense-bête   reminder (e.g., string around one's finger); **repenser**   to rethink

Note: If you want to say that you're making up your mind (reflecting on something) use **réfléchir.**

perdre

to lose

Part. pr. **perdant**   Part. passé **perdu**

The Seven Simple Tenses		The Seven Compound Tenses	
Singular	Plural	Singular	Plural
1 présent de l'indicatif		**8 passé composé**	
perds	perdons	ai perdu	avons perdu
perds	perdez	as perdu	avez perdu
perd	perdent	a perdu	ont perdu
2 imparfait de l'indicatif		**9 plus-que-parfait de l'indicatif**	
perdais	perdions	avais perdu	avions perdu
perdais	perdiez	avais perdu	aviez perdu
perdait	perdaient	avait perdu	avaient perdu
3 passé simple		**10 passé antérieur**	
perdis	perdîmes	eus perdu	eûmes perdu
perdis	perdîtes	eus perdu	eûtes perdu
perdit	perdirent	eut perdu	eurent perdu
4 futur		**11 futur antérieur**	
perdrai	perdrons	aurai perdu	aurons perdu
perdras	perdrez	auras perdu	aurez perdu
perdra	perdront	aura perdu	auront perdu
5 conditionnel		**12 conditionnel passé**	
perdrais	perdrions	aurais perdu	aurions perdu
perdrais	perdriez	aurais perdu	auriez perdu
perdrait	perdraient	aurait perdu	auraient perdu
6 présent du subjonctif		**13 passé du subjonctif**	
perde	perdions	aie perdu	ayons perdu
perdes	perdiez	aies perdu	ayez perdu
perde	perdent	ait perdu	aient perdu
7 imparfait du subjonctif		**14 plus-que-parfait du subjonctif**	
perdisse	perdissions	eusse perdu	eussions perdu
perdisses	perdissiez	eusses perdu	eussiez perdu
perdît	perdissent	eût perdu	eussent perdu

Impératif
perds
perdons
perdez

Sentences using this verb and words related to it

Je n'ai pas d'argent sur moi. Je l'ai laissé à la maison parce que si je l'avais pris avec moi je **sais que je l'aurais perdu dans la rue. Puis-je vous demander deux dollars? Je vous les rendrai la semaine prochaine.**

se perdre   to lose oneself, to lose one's way, to be ruined

perdre son temps   to waste one's time

perdre son chemin   to lose one's way

perdre pied   to lose one's footing

perdre l'esprit   to go out of one's mind

Vous n'avez rien à perdre   You have nothing to lose.

une perte   a loss

perdre de vue   to lose sight of

perdre la raison   to take leave of one's senses

Enjoy verbs in French proverbs on page 559.

The Seven Simple Tenses		The Seven Compound Tenses	
Singular	Plural	Singular	Plural
1 présent de l'indicatif		**8 passé composé**	
péris	**périssons**	**ai péri**	**avons péri**
péris	**périssez**	**as péri**	**avez péri**
périt	**périssent**	**a péri**	**ont péri**
2 imparfait de l'indicatif		**9 plus-que-parfait de l'indicatif**	
périssais	**périssions**	**avais péri**	**avions péri**
périssais	**périssiez**	**avais péri**	**aviez péri**
périssait	**périssaient**	**avait péri**	**avaient péri**
3 passé simple		**10 passé antérieur**	
péris	**pérîmes**	**eus péri**	**eûmes péri**
péris	**pérîtes**	**eus péri**	**eûtes péri**
périt	**périrent**	**eut péri**	**eurent péri**
4 futur		**11 futur antérieur**	
périrai	**périrons**	**aurai péri**	**aurons péri**
périras	**périrez**	**auras péri**	**aurez péri**
périra	**périront**	**aura péri**	**auront péri**
5 conditionnel		**12 conditionnel passé**	
périrais	**péririons**	**aurais péri**	**aurions péri**
périrais	**péririez**	**aurais péri**	**auriez péri**
périrait	**périraient**	**aurait péri**	**auraient péri**
6 présent du subjonctif		**13 passé du subjonctif**	
périsse	**périssions**	**aie péri**	**ayons péri**
périsses	**périssiez**	**aies péri**	**ayez péri**
périsse	**périssent**	**ait péri**	**aient péri**
7 imparfait du subjonctif		**14 plus-que-parfait du subjonctif**	
périsse	**périssions**	**eusse péri**	**eussions péri**
périsses	**périssiez**	**eusses péri**	**eussiez péri**
pérît	**périssent**	**eût péri**	**eussent péri**

Impératif
péris
périssons
périssez

Common idiomatic expressions using this verb
faire périr   to kill
s'ennuyer à périr   to be bored to death
périssable   perishable
périr d'ennui   to be bored to death

péri en mer   lost at sea
périr de froid   to freeze to death
les denrées périssables   perishable foods
impérissable   imperishable, eternal

Want to learn more idiomatic expressions that contain verbs? Look at pages 530–542.

The subject pronouns are found on the page facing page 1.   **337**

permettre

Part. pr. **permettant**   Part. passé **permis**

to permit, to allow, to let

The Seven Simple Tenses		The Seven Compound Tenses	
Singular	Plural	Singular	Plural
1 présent de l'indicatif		**8 passé composé**	
permets	permettons	ai permis	avons permis
permets	permettez	as permis	avez permis
permet	permettent	a permis	ont permis
2 imparfait de l'indicatif		**9 plus-que-parfait de l'indicatif**	
permettais	permettions	avais permis	avions permis
permettais	permettiez	avais permis	aviez permis
permettait	permettaient	avait permis	avaient permis
3 passé simple		**10 passé antérieur**	
permis	permîmes	eus permis	eûmes permis
permis	permîtes	eus permis	eûtes permis
permit	permirent	eut permis	eurent permis
4 futur		**11 futur antérieur**	
permettrai	permettrons	aurai permis	aurons permis
permettras	permettrez	auras permis	aurez permis
permettra	permettront	aura permis	auront permis
5 conditionnel		**12 conditionnel passé**	
permettrais	permettrions	aurais permis	aurions permis
permettrais	permettriez	aurais permis	auriez permis
permettrait	permettraient	aurait permis	auraient permis
6 présent du subjonctif		**13 passé du subjonctif**	
permette	permettions	aie permis	ayons permis
permettes	permettiez	aies permis	ayez permis
permette	permettent	ait permis	aient permis
7 imparfait du subjonctif		**14 plus-que-parfait du subjonctif**	
permisse	permissions	eusse permis	eussions permis
permisses	permissiez	eusses permis	eussiez permis
permît	permissent	eût permis	eussent permis

Impératif
permets
permettons
permettez

Common idiomatic expressions using this verb and words related to it

La maîtresse de français a permis à l'élève de quitter la salle de classe quelques minutes avant la fin de la leçon.

permettre à qqn de faire qqch   to permit (to allow) someone to do something
Vous permettez?   May I? Do you mind?
s'il est permis   if it is allowed, permitted
un permis   permit

un permis de conduire   driving license
la permission   permission
se permettre de faire qqch   to take the liberty to do something; to venture to do something
un permis de construction   building permit

See also **commettre, mettre, omettre, promettre, remettre, soumettre,** and **transmettre.**

to persuade, to convince, to induce

The Seven Simple Tenses		The Seven Compound Tenses	
Singular	Plural	Singular	Plural
1 présent de l'indicatif		8 passé composé	
persuade	persuadons	ai persuadé	avons persuadé
persuades	persuadez	as persuadé	avez persuadé
persuade	persuadent	a persuadé	ont persuadé
2 imparfait de l'indicatif		9 plus-que-parfait de l'indicatif	
persuadais	persuadions	avais persuadé	avions persuadé
persuadais	persuadiez	avais persuadé	aviez persuadé
persuadait	persuadaient	avait persuadé	avaient persuadé
3 passé simple		10 passé antérieur	
persuadai	persuadâmes	eus persuadé	eûmes persuadé
persuadas	persuadâtes	eus persuadé	eûtes persuadé
persuada	persuadèrent	eut persuadé	eurent persuadé
4 futur		11 futur antérieur	
persuaderai	persuaderons	aurai persuadé	aurons persuadé
persuaderas	persuaderez	auras persuadé	aurez persuadé
persuadera	persuaderont	aura persuadé	auront persuadé
5 conditionnel		12 conditionnel passé	
persuaderais	persuaderions	aurais persuadé	aurions persuadé
persuaderais	persuaderiez	aurais persuadé	auriez persuadé
persuaderait	persuaderaient	aurait persuadé	auraient persuadé
6 présent du subjonctif		13 passé du subjonctif	
persuade	persuadions	aie persuadé	ayons persuadé
persuades	persuadiez	aies persuadé	ayez persuadé
persuade	persuadent	ait persuadé	aient persuadé
7 imparfait du subjonctif		14 plus-que-parfait du subjonctif	
persuadasse	persuadassions	eusse persuadé	eussions persuadé
persuadasses	persuadassiez	eusses persuadé	eussiez persuadé
persuadât	persuadassent	eût persuadé	eussent persuadé

Impératif
persuade
persuadons
persuadez

Words and expressions related to this verb
persuader à qqn de faire qqch   to induce
  someone to do something
persuader qqn de qqch   to persuade someone
  of something

dissuader de   to dissuade from
la persuasion   persuasion
persuasif, persuasive   persuasive
persuasivement   persuasively

se persuader de qqch   to persuade (convince) oneself of something

Consult the sections on verbs used in idiomatic expressions, verbs with prepositions, and the list
of over 1,100 verbs conjugated like model verbs in the back pages.

The Seven Simple Tenses		The Seven Compound Tenses	
Singular	Plural	Singular	Plural
1 présent de l'indicatif		**8 passé composé**	
pèse	pesons	ai pesé	avons pesé
pèses	pesez	as pesé	avez pesé
pèse	pèsent	a pesé	ont pesé
2 imparfait de l'indicatif		**9 plus-que-parfait de l'indicatif**	
pesais	pesions	avais pesé	avions pesé
pesais	pesiez	avais pesé	aviez pesé
pesait	pesaient	avait pesé	avaient pesé
3 passé simple		**10 passé antérieur**	
pesai	pesâmes	eus pesé	eûmes pesé
pesas	pesâtes	eus pesé	eûtes pesé
pesa	pesèrent	eut pesé	eurent pesé
4 futur		**11 futur antérieur**	
pèserai	pèserons	aurai pesé	aurons pesé
pèseras	pèserez	auras pesé	aurez pesé
pèsera	pèseront	aura pesé	auront pesé
5 conditionnel		**12 conditionnel passé**	
pèserais	pèserions	aurais pesé	aurions pesé
pèserais	pèseriez	aurais pesé	auriez pesé
pèserait	pèseraient	aurait pesé	auraient pesé
6 présent du subjonctif		**13 passé du subjonctif**	
pèse	pesions	aie pesé	ayons pesé
pèses	pesiez	aies pesé	ayez pesé
pèse	pèsent	ait pesé	aient pesé
7 imparfait du subjonctif		**14 plus-que-parfait du subjonctif**	
pesasse	pesassions	eusse pesé	eussions pesé
pesasses	pesassiez	eusses pesé	eussiez pesé
pesât	pesassent	eût pesé	eussent pesé

Impératif
pèse
pesons
pesez

Words and expressions related to this verb

peser qqch to weigh something; to ponder; to think out, to consider
peser sur to weigh upon
se peser to weigh oneself
pesamment heavily
un pèse-lettre weight scale for letters (des pèse-lettres)

le poids weight (measured)
la pesanteur weight, gravity
pesant, pesante heavy, weighty
poids et mesures weights and measures
perdre du poids to lose weight
un pèse-personne a bathroom scale

Grammar putting you in a tense mood? Review the definitions of basic grammatical terms on pages 674–688.

The Seven Simple Tenses		The Seven Compound Tenses	
Singular	Plural	Singular	Plural
1 présent de l'indicatif		**8 passé composé**	
place	plaçons	ai placé	avons placé
places	placez	as placé	avez placé
place	placent	a placé	ont placé
2 imparfait de l'indicatif		**9 plus-que-parfait de l'indicatif**	
plaçais	placions	avais placé	avions placé
plaçais	placiez	avais placé	aviez placé
plaçait	plaçaient	avait placé	avaient placé
3 passé simple		**10 passé antérieur**	
plaçai	plaçâmes	eus placé	eûmes placé
plaças	plaçâtes	eus placé	eûtes placé
plaça	placèrent	eut placé	eurent placé
4 futur		**11 futur antérieur**	
placerai	placerons	aurai placé	aurons placé
placeras	placerez	auras placé	aurez placé
placera	placeront	aura placé	auront placé
5 conditionnel		**12 conditionnel passé**	
placerais	placerions	aurais placé	aurions placé
placerais	placeriez	aurais placé	auriez placé
placerait	placeraient	aurait placé	auraient placé
6 présent du subjonctif		**13 passé du subjonctif**	
place	placions	aie placé	ayons placé
places	placiez	aies placé	ayez placé
place	placent	ait placé	aient placé
7 imparfait du subjonctif		**14 plus-que-parfait du subjonctif**	
plaçasse	plaçassions	eusse placé	eussions placé
plaçasses	plaçassiez	eusses placé	eussiez placé
plaçât	plaçassent	eût placé	eussent placé

Impératif
place
plaçons
placez

Sentences using this verb and words related to it

Nous pouvons déjeuner maintenant. Ma place est ici près de la fenêtre, ta place est là-bas près de la porte. Marie, place-toi à côté de Pierre. Combien de places y a-t-il? Y a-t-il assez de places pour tout le monde?

une place   a seat, a place
chaque chose à sa place   everything in its place
un placement   placing
un bureau de placement   employment agency
se placer   to place oneself, to take a seat, to find employment
replacer   to replace, put back

See also **remplacer.**

The subject pronouns are found on the page facing page 1.   **341**

plaindre

to pity

Part. pr. **plaignant** Part. passé **plaint**

The Seven Simple Tenses		The Seven Compound Tenses	
Singular	Plural	Singular	Plural
1 présent de l'indicatif		**8 passé composé**	
plains	plaignons	ai plaint	avons plaint
plains	plaignez	as plaint	avez plaint
plaint	plaignent	a plaint	ont plaint
2 imparfait de l'indicatif		**9 plus-que-parfait de l'indicatif**	
plaignais	plaignions	avais plaint	avions plaint
plaignais	plaigniez	avais plaint	aviez plaint
plaignait	plaignaient	avait plaint	avaient plaint
3 passé simple		**10 passé antérieur**	
plaignis	plaignîmes	eus plaint	eûmes plaint
plaignis	plaignîtes	eus plaint	eûtes plaint
plaignit	plaignirent	eut plaint	eurent plaint
4 futur		**11 futur antérieur**	
plaindrai	plaindrons	aurai plaint	aurons plaint
plaindras	plaindrez	auras plaint	aurez plaint
plaindra	plaindront	aura plaint	auront plaint
5 conditionnel		**12 conditionnel passé**	
plaindrais	plaindrions	aurais plaint	aurions plaint
plaindrais	plaindriez	aurais plaint	auriez plaint
plaindrait	plaindraient	aurait plaint	auraient plaint
6 présent du subjonctif		**13 passé du subjonctif**	
plaigne	plaignions	aie plaint	ayons plaint
plaignes	plaigniez	aies plaint	ayez plaint
plaigne	plaignent	ait plaint	aient plaint
7 imparfait du subjonctif		**14 plus-que-parfait du subjonctif**	
plaignisse	plaignissions	eusse plaint	eussions plaint
plaignisses	plaignissiez	eusses plaint	eussiez plaint
plaignît	plaignissent	eût plaint	eussent plaint

Impératif
plains
plaignons
plaignez

Sentences using this verb and words related to it
Pauvre Madame Bayou! Elle a des ennuis et je la plains.

une plainte groan, moan, protest, complaint
porter plainte contre to bring charges against
déposer/faire une plainte to file a complaint
plaintif, plaintive plaintive
plaintivement plaintively, mournfully

Je te plains I feel for you; I feel sorry for
you; I pity you
être à plaindre to be pitied
Elle est à plaindre She is to be pitied.
For additional related words, see **se plaindre.**

Soak up some verbs used in weather expressions on pages 557 and 558.

342

to complain, to lament, to moan

The Seven Simple Tenses		The Seven Compound Tenses	
Singular	Plural	Singular	Plural
1 présent de l'indicatif		8 passé composé	
me plains	**nous plaignons**	**me suis plaint(e)**	**nous sommes plaint(e)s**
te plains	**vous plaignez**	**t'es plaint(e)**	**vous êtes plaint(e)(s)**
se plaint	**se plaignent**	**s'est plaint(e)**	**se sont plaint(e)s**
2 imparfait de l'indicatif		9 plus-que-parfait de l'indicatif	
me plaignais	**nous plaignions**	**m'étais plaint(e)**	**nous étions plaint(e)s**
te plaignais	**vous plaigniez**	**t'étais plaint(e)**	**vous étiez plaint(e)(s)**
se plaignait	**se plaignaient**	**s'était plaint(e)**	**s'étaient plaint(e)s**
3 passé simple		10 passé antérieur	
me plaignis	**nous plaignîmes**	**me fus plaint(e)**	**nous fûmes plaint(e)s**
te plaignis	**vous plaignîtes**	**te fus plaint(e)**	**vous fûtes plaint(e)(s)**
se plaignit	**se plaignirent**	**se fut plaint(e)**	**se furent plaint(e)s**
4 futur		11 futur antérieur	
me plaindrai	**nous plaindrons**	**me serai plaint(e)**	**nous serons plaint(e)s**
te plaindras	**vous plaindrez**	**te seras plaint(e)**	**vous serez plaint(e)(s)**
se plaindra	**se plaindront**	**se sera plaint(e)**	**se seront plaint(e)s**
5 conditionnel		12 conditionnel passé	
me plaindrais	**nous plaindrions**	**me serais plaint(e)**	**nous serions plaint(e)s**
te plaindrais	**vous plaindriez**	**te serais plaint(e)**	**vous seriez plaint(e)(s)**
se plaindrait	**se plaindraient**	**se serait plaint(e)**	**se seraient plaint(e)s**
6 présent du subjonctif		13 passé du subjonctif	
me plaigne	**nous plaignions**	**me sois plaint(e)**	**nous soyons plaint(e)s**
te plaignes	**vous plaigniez**	**te sois plaint(e)**	**vous soyez plaint(e)(s)**
se plaigne	**se plaignent**	**se soit plaint(e)**	**se soient plaint(e)s**
7 imparfait du subjonctif		14 plus-que-parfait du subjonctif	
me plaignisse	**nous plaignissions**	**me fusse plaint(e)**	**nous fussions plaint(e)s**
te plaignisses	**vous plaignissiez**	**te fusses plaint(e)**	**vous fussiez plaint(e)(s)**
se plaignît	**se plaignissent**	**se fût plaint(e)**	**se fussent plaint(e)s**

Impératif
plains-toi; ne te plains pas
plaignons-nous; ne nous plaignons pas
plaignez-vous; ne vous plaignez pas

Common idiomatic expressions using this verb
   Quelle jeune fille! Elle se plaint toujours de tout! Hier elle s'est plainte de son professeur de français, aujourd'hui elle se plaint de ses devoirs, et je suis certain que demain elle se plaindra du temps.

se plaindre du temps   to complain about the weather
se plaindre de qqn ou de qqch   to complain of, to find fault with, someone or something
avoir bonne raison de se plaindre   to have a good reason to complain

For other words related to this verb, see **plaindre.**

It's important that you be familiar with the Subjunctive. See pages 560–565.

The subject pronouns are found on the page facing page 1.   **343**

plaire
to please

Part. pr. **plaisant**   Part. passé **plu**

The Seven Simple Tenses		The Seven Compound Tenses	
Singular	Plural	Singular	Plural
1 présent de l'indicatif		**8 passé composé**	
plais	plaisons	ai plu	avons plu
plais	plaisez	as plu	avez plu
plaît	plaisent	a plu	ont plu
2 imparfait de l'indicatif		**9 plus-que-parfait de l'indicatif**	
plaisais	plaisions	avais plu	avions plu
plaisais	plaisiez	avais plu	aviez plu
plaisait	plaisaient	avait plu	avaient plu
3 passé simple		**10 passé antérieur**	
plus	plûmes	eus plu	eûmes plu
plus	plûtes	eus plu	eûtes plu
plut	plurent	eut plu	eurent plu
4 futur		**11 futur antérieur**	
plairai	plairons	aurai plu	aurons plu
plairas	plairez	auras plu	aurez plu
plaira	plairont	aura plu	auront plu
5 conditionnel		**12 conditionnel passé**	
plairais	plairions	aurais plu	aurions plu
plairais	plairiez	aurais plu	auriez plu
plairait	plairaient	aurait plu	auraient plu
6 présent du subjonctif		**13 passé du subjonctif**	
plaise	plaisions	aie plu	ayons plu
plaises	plaisiez	aies plu	ayez plu
plaise	plaisent	ait plu	aient plu
7 imparfait du subjonctif		**14 plus-que-parfait du subjonctif**	
plusse	plussions	eusse plu	eussions plu
plusses	plussiez	eusses plu	eussiez plu
plût	plussent	eût plu	eussent plu

Impératif
plais
plaisons
plaisez

Common idiomatic expressions using this verb

plaire à qqn to please, to be pleasing to someone; **Son mariage a plu à sa famille** Her (his) marriage pleased her (his) family. **Est-ce que ce cadeau lui plaira?** Will this present please her (him)? Will this gift be pleasing to her (to him)?

se plaire à to take pleasure in; **Robert se plaît à ennuyer son petit frère** Robert takes pleasure in bothering his little brother.

le plaisir delight, pleasure; **complaire à** to please; **déplaire à** to displease

s'il vous plaît; s'il te plaît please (if it is pleasing to you); **avec plaisir** with pleasure

Il a beaucoup plu hier et cela m'a beaucoup plu It rained a lot yesterday and that pleased me a great deal. (See **pleuvoir**)

See also **déplaire**.

Can't recognize an irregular verb form? Check out pages 526–529.

The Seven Simple Tenses | The Seven Compound Tenses

Singular	Plural	Singular	Plural
1 présent de l'indicatif		**8 passé composé**	
plaisante	plaisantons	ai plaisanté	avons plaisanté
plaisantes	plaisantez	as plaisanté	avez plaisanté
plaisante	plaisantent	a plaisanté	ont plaisanté
2 imparfait de l'indicatif		**9 plus-que-parfait de l'indicatif**	
plaisantais	plaisantions	avais plaisanté	avions plaisanté
plaisantais	plaisantiez	avais plaisanté	aviez plaisanté
plaisantait	plaisantaient	avait plaisanté	avaient plaisanté
3 passé simple		**10 passé antérieur**	
plaisantai	plaisantâmes	eus plaisanté	eûmes plaisanté
plaisantas	plaisantâtes	eus plaisanté	eûtes plaisanté
plaisanta	plaisantèrent	eut plaisanté	eurent plaisanté
4 futur		**11 futur antérieur**	
plaisanterai	plaisanterons	aurai plaisanté	aurons plaisanté
plaisanteras	plaisanterez	auras plaisanté	aurez plaisanté
plaisantera	plaisanteront	aura plaisanté	auront plaisanté
5 conditionnel		**12 conditionnel passé**	
plaisanterais	plaisanterions	aurais plaisanté	aurions plaisanté
plaisanterais	plaisanteriez	aurais plaisanté	auriez plaisanté
plaisanterait	plaisanteraient	aurait plaisanté	auraient plaisanté
6 présent du subjonctif		**13 passé du subjonctif**	
plaisante	plaisantions	aie plaisanté	ayons plaisanté
plaisantes	plaisantiez	aies plaisanté	ayez plaisanté
plaisante	plaisantent	ait plaisanté	aient plaisanté
7 imparfait du subjonctif		**14 plus-que-parfait du subjonctif**	
plaisantasse	plaisantassions	eusse plaisanté	eussions plaisanté
plaisantasses	plaisantassiez	eusses plaisanté	eussiez plaisanté
plaisantât	plaisantassent	eût plaisanté	eussent plaisanté

Impératif
plaisante
plaisantons
plaisantez

Words and expressions related to this verb
pour plaisanter   for fun
une plaisanterie   joke, joking
dire des plaisanteries   to crack jokes
en plaisantant   in fun

dire une chose par plaisanterie   to say something in a joking way
prendre bien une plaisanterie   to know how to take a joke

Taking a trip? Check out the popular words, phrases, and expressions for travelers on pages 599–621.

The subject pronouns are found on the page facing page 1.   **345**

to cry, to weep, to mourn

The Seven Simple Tenses		The Seven Compound Tenses	
Singular	Plural	Singular	Plural
1 présent de l'indicatif		8 passé composé	
pleure	pleurons	ai pleuré	avons pleuré
pleures	pleurez	as pleuré	avez pleuré
pleure	pleurent	a pleuré	ont pleuré
2 imparfait de l'indicatif		9 plus-que-parfait de l'indicatif	
pleurais	pleurions	avais pleuré	avions pleuré
pleurais	pleuriez	avais pleuré	aviez pleuré
pleurait	pleuraient	avait pleuré	avaient pleuré
3 passé simple		10 passé antérieur	
pleurai	pleurâmes	eus pleuré	eûmes pleuré
pleuras	pleurâtes	eus pleuré	eûtes pleuré
pleura	pleurèrent	eut pleuré	eurent pleuré
4 futur		11 futur antérieur	
pleurerai	pleurerons	aurai pleuré	aurons pleuré
pleureras	pleurerez	auras pleuré	aurez pleuré
pleurera	pleureront	aura pleuré	auront pleuré
5 conditionnel		12 conditionnel passé	
pleurerais	pleurerions	aurais pleuré	aurions pleuré
pleurerais	pleureriez	aurais pleuré	auriez pleuré
pleurerait	pleureraient	aurait pleuré	auraient pleuré
6 présent du subjonctif		13 passé du subjonctif	
pleure	pleurions	aie pleuré	ayons pleuré
pleures	pleuriez	aies pleuré	ayez pleuré
pleure	pleurent	ait pleuré	aient pleuré
7 imparfait du subjonctif		14 plus-que-parfait du subjonctif	
pleurasse	pleurassions	eusse pleuré	eussions pleuré
pleurasses	pleurassiez	eusses pleuré	eussiez pleuré
pleurât	pleurassent	eût pleuré	eussent pleuré

Impératif
pleure
pleurons
pleurez

Common idiomatic expressions using this verb and words related to it

pleurer toutes les larmes de son corps   to cry one's eyes out

une larme   a tear

un pleur   a tear

pleurard, pleurarde   whimpering person

une pièce pleurnicharde   soap opera

larmoyant, larmoyante   tearful, lachrymose

pleurnicher   to snivel, to whine

un pleurnicheur, une pleurnicheuse   crybaby

How are you doing? Find out with the verb drills and tests with answers explained on pages 622–673.

The Seven Simple Tenses	The Seven Compound Tenses
Singular Plural	Singular Plural
1 présent de l'indicatif **il pleut**	8 passé composé **il a plu**
2 imparfait de l'indicatif **il pleuvait**	9 plus-que-parfait de l'indicatif **il avait plu**
3 passé simple **il plut**	10 passé antérieur **il eut plu**
4 futur **il pleuvra**	11 futur antérieur **il aura plu**
5 conditionnel **il pleuvrait**	12 conditionnel passé **il aurait plu**
6 présent du subjonctif **qu'il pleuve**	13 passé du subjonctif **qu'il ait plu**
7 imparfait du subjonctif **qu'il plût**	14 plus-que-parfait du subjonctif **qu'il eût plu**

Impératif
Qu'il pleuve! Let it rain!

Sentences using this verb and words related to it
Hier il a plu, il pleut maintenant, et je suis certain qu'il pleuvra demain.

la pluie   the rain
pluvieux, pluvieuse   rainy
pleuvoter   to drizzle
bruiner   to drizzle; **un parapluie**   umbrella
Il pleut à seaux   It's raining in buckets.

Il pleut à verse   It's raining hard.
Il a beaucoup plu hier et cela m'a beaucoup plu.   It rained a lot yesterday and that pleased me a great deal. (See **plaire**)

Do not confuse the past part. of this verb with the past part. of **plaire**, which is identical.

Soak up some verbs used in weather expressions on pages 557 and 558.

The subject pronouns are found on the page facing page 1.   **347**

porter

Part. pr. **portant**   Part. passé **porté**

to wear, to carry

The Seven Simple Tenses		The Seven Compound Tenses	
Singular	Plural	Singular	Plural
1 présent de l'indicatif		**8 passé composé**	
porte	portons	ai porté	avons porté
portes	portez	as porté	avez porté
porte	portent	a porté	ont porté
2 imparfait de l'indicatif		**9 plus-que-parfait de l'indicatif**	
portais	portions	avais porté	avions porté
portais	portiez	avais porté	aviez porté
portait	portaient	avait porté	avaient porté
3 passé simple		**10 passé antérieur**	
portai	portâmes	eus porté	eûmes porté
portas	portâtes	eus porté	eûtes porté
porta	portèrent	eut porté	eurent porté
4 futur		**11 futur antérieur**	
porterai	porterons	aurai porté	aurons porté
porteras	porterez	auras porté	aurez porté
portera	porteront	aura porté	auront porté
5 conditionnel		**12 conditionnel passé**	
porterais	porterions	aurais porté	aurions porté
porterais	porteriez	aurais porté	auriez porté
porterait	porteraient	aurait porté	auraient porté
6 présent du subjonctif		**13 passé du subjonctif**	
porte	portions	aie porté	ayons porté
portes	portiez	aies porté	ayez porté
porte	portent	ait porté	aient porté
7 imparfait du subjonctif		**14 plus-que-parfait du subjonctif**	
portasse	portassions	eusse porté	eussions porté
portasses	portassiez	eusses porté	eussiez porté
portât	portassent	eût porté	eussent porté

Impératif
porte
portons
portez

Common idiomatic expressions using this verb and words related to it

porter la main sur qqn   to raise one's hand against someone

porter son âge   to look one's age

se porter   to feel (health); **Comment vous portez-vous aujourd'hui?**   How do you feel today?

apporter   to bring; **rapporter**   to bring back

exporter   to export

importer   to import; to matter, to be of importance

un porte-monnaie   change purse **(des porte-monnaie)**

comporter   to comprise

déporter   to deport

se comporter   to behave

emporter   to carry away; *Autant en emporte le vent* (*Gone With the Wind*)

Elle porte de jolies robes   She wears pretty dresses.

un portable   cell phone, laptop computer

See also **apporter** and **supporter**.

348

to lay, to place, to put, to set, to pose

The Seven Simple Tenses		The Seven Compound Tenses	
Singular	Plural	Singular	Plural
1 présent de l'indicatif		8 passé composé	
pose	posons	ai posé	avons posé
poses	posez	as posé	avez posé
pose	posent	a posé	ont posé
2 imparfait de l'indicatif		9 plus-que-parfait de l'indicatif	
posais	posions	avais posé	avions posé
posais	posiez	avais posé	aviez posé
posait	posaient	avait posé	avaient posé
3 passé simple		10 passé antérieur	
posai	posâmes	eus posé	eûmes posé
posas	posâtes	eus posé	eûtes posé
posa	posèrent	eut posé	eurent posé
4 futur		11 futur antérieur	
poserai	poserons	aurai posé	aurons posé
poseras	poserez	auras posé	aurez posé
posera	poseront	aura posé	auront posé
5 conditionnel		12 conditionnel passé	
poserais	poserions	aurais posé	aurions posé
poserais	poseriez	aurais posé	auriez posé
poserait	poseraient	aurait posé	auraient posé
6 présent du subjonctif		13 passé du subjonctif	
pose	posions	aie posé	ayons posé
poses	posiez	aies posé	ayez posé
pose	posent	ait posé	aient posé
7 imparfait du subjonctif		14 plus-que-parfait du subjonctif	
posasse	posassions	eusse posé	eussions posé
posasses	posassiez	eusses posé	eussiez posé
posât	posassent	eût posé	eussent posé

Impératif
pose
posons
posez

Words and expressions related to this verb
poser une question   to ask a question
poser pour son portrait   to sit for a portrait
  painting
faire poser qqn   to keep someone waiting
déposer   to deposit, to set (put) down
composer   to compose

supposer   to suppose
opposer   to oppose; **s'opposer à**   to be
  opposed to
reposer   to set down again; **se reposer** to rest
exposer   to exhibit, to expose

Going away? Don't forget to check out the practical situations for travelers on pages 568–598.

The subject pronouns are found on the page facing page 1.   **349**

posséder

Part. pr. possédant   **Part. passé possédé**

to possess, to own, to master

The Seven Simple Tenses		The Seven Compound Tenses	
Singular	Plural	Singular	Plural
1 présent de l'indicatif		**8 passé composé**	
possède	possédons	ai possédé	avons possédé
possèdes	possédez	as possédé	avez possédé
possède	possèdent	a possédé	ont possédé
2 imparfait de l'indicatif		**9 plus-que-parfait de l'indicatif**	
possédais	possédions	avais possédé	avions possédé
possédais	possédiez	avais possédé	aviez possédé
possédait	possédaient	avait possédé	avaient possédé
3 passé simple		**10 passé antérieur**	
possédai	possédâmes	eus possédé	eûmes possédé
possédas	possédâtes	eus possédé	eûtes possédé
posséda	possédèrent	eut possédé	eurent possédé
4 futur		**11 futur antérieur**	
posséderai	posséderons	aurai possédé	aurons possédé
posséderas	posséderez	auras possédé	aurez possédé
possédera	posséderont	aura possédé	auront possédé
5 conditionnel		**12 conditionnel passé**	
posséderais	posséderions	aurais possédé	aurions possédé
posséderais	posséderiez	aurais possédé	auriez possédé
posséderait	posséderaient	aurait possédé	auraient possédé
6 présent du subjonctif		**13 passé du subjonctif**	
possède	possédions	aie possédé	ayons possédé
possèdes	possédiez	aies possédé	ayez possédé
possède	possèdent	ait possédé	aient possédé
7 imparfait du subjonctif		**14 plus-que-parfait du subjonctif**	
possédasse	possédassions	eusse possédé	eussions possédé
possédasses	possédassiez	eusses possédé	eussiez possédé
possédât	possédassent	eût possédé	eussent possédé

Impératif
possède
possédons
possédez

Words and expressions related to this verb

se faire posséder to be taken in
la possession possession, ownership
possessif, possessive possessive
se posséder to have control of oneself

un possesseur possessor, owner; **Madame Goulu est possesseur d'un grand château.**
déposséder de to dispossess of (from)
une dépossession dispossession

Want to learn more idiomatic expressions that contain verbs? Look at pages 530–542.

The Seven Simple Tenses		The Seven Compound Tenses	
Singular	Plural	Singular	Plural
1　présent de l'indicatif		8　passé composé	
poursuis	**poursuivons**	**ai poursuivi**	**avons poursuivi**
poursuis	**poursuivez**	**as poursuivi**	**avez poursuivi**
poursuit	**poursuivent**	**a poursuivi**	**ont poursuivi**
2　imparfait de l'indicatif		9　plus-que-parfait de l'indicatif	
poursuivais	**poursuivions**	**avais poursuivi**	**avions poursuivi**
poursuivais	**poursuiviez**	**avais poursuivi**	**aviez poursuivi**
poursuivait	**poursuivaient**	**avait poursuivi**	**avaient poursuivi**
3　passé simple		10　passé antérieur	
poursuivis	**poursuivîmes**	**eus poursuivi**	**eûmes poursuivi**
poursuivis	**poursuivîtes**	**eus poursuivi**	**eûtes poursuivi**
poursuivit	**poursuivirent**	**eut poursuivi**	**eurent poursuivi**
4　futur		11　futur antérieur	
poursuivrai	**poursuivrons**	**aurai poursuivi**	**aurons poursuivi**
poursuivras	**poursuivrez**	**auras poursuivi**	**aurez poursuivi**
poursuivra	**poursuivront**	**aura poursuivi**	**auront poursuivi**
5　conditionnel		12　conditionnel passé	
poursuivrais	**poursuivrions**	**aurais poursuivi**	**aurions poursuivi**
poursuivrais	**poursuivriez**	**aurais poursuivi**	**auriez poursuivi**
poursuivrait	**poursuivraient**	**aurait poursuivi**	**auraient poursuivi**
6　présent du subjonctif		13　passé du subjonctif	
poursuive	**poursuivions**	**aie poursuivi**	**ayons poursuivi**
poursuives	**poursuiviez**	**aies poursuivi**	**ayez poursuivi**
poursuive	**poursuivent**	**ait poursuivi**	**aient poursuivi**
7　imparfait du subjonctif		14　plus-que-parfait du subjonctif	
poursuivisse	**poursuivissions**	**eusse poursuivi**	**eussions poursuivi**
poursuivisses	**poursuivissiez**	**eusses poursuivi**	**eussiez poursuivi**
poursuivît	**poursuivissent**	**eût poursuivi**	**eussent poursuivi**

Impératif
poursuis
poursuivons
poursuivez

Words and expressions related to this verb
se poursuivre　to pursue each other
poursuivre qqn en justice　to sue someone, to prosecute
poursuivre ses études　to carry on one's studies

une poursuite　pursuit
à la poursuite de　in pursuit of
poursuivre son chemin　to continue on one's way

See also **suivre.**

Want to learn more verbs used in proverbs and sayings? Take a look at page 559.

pousser

Part. pr. poussant   **Part. passé poussé**

to push, to grow

The Seven Simple Tenses		The Seven Compound Tenses	
Singular	Plural	Singular	Plural
1 présent de l'indicatif		8 passé composé	
pousse	poussons	ai poussé	avons poussé
pousses	poussez	as poussé	avez poussé
pousse	poussent	a poussé	ont poussé
2 imparfait de l'indicatif		9 plus-que-parfait de l'indicatif	
poussais	poussions	avais poussé	avions poussé
poussais	poussiez	avais poussé	aviez poussé
poussait	poussaient	avait poussé	avaient poussé
3 passé simple		10 passé antérieur	
poussai	poussâmes	eus poussé	eûmes poussé
poussas	poussâtes	eus poussé	eûtes poussé
poussa	poussèrent	eut poussé	eurent poussé
4 futur		11 futur antérieur	
pousserai	pousserons	aurai poussé	aurons poussé
pousseras	pousserez	auras poussé	aurez poussé
poussera	pousseront	aura poussé	auront poussé
5 conditionnel		12 conditionnel passé	
pousserais	pousserions	aurais poussé	aurions poussé
pousserais	pousseriez	aurais poussé	auriez poussé
pousserait	pousseraient	aurait poussé	auraient poussé
6 présent du subjonctif		13 passé du subjonctif	
pousse	poussions	aie poussé	ayons poussé
pousses	poussiez	aies poussé	ayez poussé
pousse	poussent	ait poussé	aient poussé
7 imparfait du subjonctif		14 plus-que-parfait du subjonctif	
poussasse	poussassions	eusse poussé	eussions poussé
poussasses	poussassiez	eusses poussé	eussiez poussé
poussât	poussassent	eût poussé	eussent poussé

Impératif
pousse
poussons
poussez

Common idiomatic expressions using this verb

une poussée   a push, a thrust
pousser qqn à faire qqch   to egg someone on to do something
Robert pousse une barbe   Robert is growing a beard.
pousser un cri   to utter a cry; **pousser un soupir**   to heave a sigh

repousser   to repulse, to drive back; to grow in again, to grow back in
se pousser   to push oneself; to push each other
un pousse-pousse   rickshaw
pousser qqn à bout   to corner someone
une poussette   a stroller

Going away? Don't forget to check out the practical situations for travelers on pages 568–598.

The Seven Simple Tenses		The Seven Compound Tenses	
Singular	Plural	Singular	Plural
1 présent de l'indicatif		**8 passé composé**	
peux *or* **puis**	**pouvons**	**ai pu**	**avons pu**
peux	**pouvez**	**as pu**	**avez pu**
peut	**peuvent**	**a pu**	**ont pu**
2 imparfait de l'indicatif		**9 plus-que-parfait de l'indicatif**	
pouvais	**pouvions**	**avais pu**	**avions pu**
pouvais	**pouviez**	**avais pu**	**aviez pu**
pouvait	**pouvaient**	**avait pu**	**avaient pu**
3 passé simple		**10 passé antérieur**	
pus	**pûmes**	**eus pu**	**eûmes pu**
pus	**pûtes**	**eus pu**	**eûtes pu**
put	**purent**	**eut pu**	**eurent pu**
4 futur		**11 futur antérieur**	
pourrai	**pourrons**	**aurai pu**	**aurons pu**
pourras	**pourrez**	**auras pu**	**aurez pu**
pourra	**pourront**	**aura pu**	**auront pu**
5 conditionnel		**12 conditionnel passé**	
pourrais	**pourrions**	**aurais pu**	**aurions pu**
pourrais	**pourriez**	**aurais pu**	**auriez pu**
pourrait	**pourraient**	**aurait pu**	**auraient pu**
6 présent du subjonctif		**13 passé du subjonctif**	
puisse	**puissions**	**aie pu**	**ayons pu**
puisses	**puissiez**	**aies pu**	**ayez pu**
puisse	**puissent**	**ait pu**	**aient pu**
7 imparfait du subjonctif		**14 plus-que-parfait du subjonctif**	
pusse	**pussions**	**eusse pu**	**eussions pu**
pusses	**pussiez**	**eusses pu**	**eussiez pu**
pût	**pussent**	**eût pu**	**eussent pu**

Impératif
[not in use]

Common idiomatic expressions using this verb and words related to it

si l'on peut dire   if one may say so
se pouvoir: Cela se peut   That may be.
le pouvoir   power
la course au pouvoir   the race for power
avoir du pouvoir sur soi-même   to have self control
la puissance   power

n'y pouvoir rien   not to be able to do anything about it; **Que me voulez-vous?**   What do you want from me? **Je n'y peux rien** I can't help it; I can't do anything about it.
Puis-je entrer? Est-ce que je peux entrer? May I come in?

Can't recognize an irregular verb form? Check out pages 526–529.

prédire

Part. pr. **prédisant**   Part. passé **prédit**

to predict, to foretell

The Seven Simple Tenses		The Seven Compound Tenses	
Singular	Plural	Singular	Plural
1 présent de l'indicatif		8 passé composé	
prédis	prédisons	ai prédit	avons prédit
prédis	prédisez	as prédit	avez prédit
prédit	prédisent	a prédit	ont prédit
2 imparfait de l'indicatif		9 plus-que-parfait de l'indicatif	
prédisais	prédisions	avais prédit	avions prédit
prédisais	prédisiez	avais prédit	aviez prédit
prédisait	prédisaient	avait prédit	avaient prédit
3 passé simple		10 passé antérieur	
prédis	prédîmes	eus prédit	eûmes prédit
prédis	prédîtes	eus prédit	eûtes prédit
prédit	prédirent	eut prédit	eurent prédit
4 futur		11 futur antérieur	
prédirai	prédirons	aurai prédit	aurons prédit
prédiras	prédirez	auras prédit	aurez prédit
prédira	prédiront	aura prédit	auront prédit
5 conditionnel		12 conditionnel passé	
prédirais	prédirions	aurais prédit	aurions prédit
prédirais	prédiriez	aurais prédit	auriez prédit
prédirait	prédiraient	aurait prédit	auraient prédit
6 présent du subjonctif		13 passé du subjonctif	
prédise	prédisions	aie prédit	ayons prédit
prédises	prédisiez	aies prédit	ayez prédit
prédise	prédisent	ait prédit	aient prédit
7 imparfait du subjonctif		14 plus-que-parfait du subjonctif	
prédisse	prédissions	eusse prédit	eussions prédit
prédisses	prédissiez	eusses prédit	eussiez prédit
prédît	prédissent	eût prédit	eussent prédit

Impératif
prédis
prédisons
prédisez

Words related to this verb
une prédiction   prediction
prédire l'avenir   to predict the future

See also **contredire, dire, interdire, maudire,** and **médire.**

Compare (**vous**) **prédisez** with (**vous**) **dites** of **dire** on page 164.

Consult the back pages for sections on verbs used in idiomatic expressions, verbs with prepositions, French proverbs using verbs, weather expressions using verbs, and over 1,100 verbs conjugated like model verbs.

The Seven Simple Tenses		The Seven Compound Tenses	
Singular	Plural	Singular	Plural
1 présent de l'indicatif		8 passé composé	
préfère	préférons	ai préféré	avons préféré
préfères	préférez	as préféré	avez préféré
préfère	préfèrent	a préféré	ont préféré
2 imparfait de l'indicatif		9 plus-que-parfait de l'indicatif	
préférais	préférions	avais préféré	avions préféré
préférais	préfériez	avais préféré	aviez préféré
préférait	préféraient	avait préféré	avaient préféré
3 passé simple		10 passé antérieur	
préférai	préférâmes	eus préféré	eûmes préféré
préféras	préférâtes	eus préféré	eûtes préféré
préféra	préférèrent	eut préféré	eurent préféré
4 futur		11 futur antérieur	
préférerai	préférerons	aurai préféré	aurons préféré
préféreras	préférerez	auras préféré	aurez préféré
préférera	préféreront	aura préféré	auront préféré
5 conditionnel		12 conditionnel passé	
préférerais	préférerions	aurais préféré	aurions préféré
préférerais	préféreriez	aurais préféré	auriez préféré
préférerait	préféreraient	aurait préféré	auraient préféré
6 présent du subjonctif		13 passé du subjonctif	
préfère	préférions	aie préféré	ayons préféré
préfères	préfériez	aies préféré	ayez préféré
préfère	préfèrent	ait préféré	aient préféré
7 imparfait du subjonctif		14 plus-que-parfait du subjonctif	
préférasse	préférassions	eusse préféré	eussions préféré
préférasses	préférassiez	eusses préféré	eussiez préféré
préférât	préférassent	eût préféré	eussent préféré

Impératif
préfère
préférons
préférez

Sentences using this verb and words related to it
—**Qu'est-ce que vous préférez faire ce soir?**
—**Je préfère aller voir un bon film. Et vous?**
—**Je préfère rester à la maison. Ne préféreriez-vous pas rester ici avec moi?**

une préférence   a preference
préférentiel, préférentielle   preferential
préférable   preferable
préférablement   preferably
de préférence à   in preference to

Je n'ai pas de préférence   I have no preference.
par ordre de préférence   in order of preference

Don't miss orthographically changing verbs on pages 554–556.

The subject pronouns are found on the page facing page 1.   **355**

The Seven Simple Tenses		The Seven Compound Tenses	
Singular	Plural	Singular	Plural
1 présent de l'indicatif		**8 passé composé**	
prends	prenons	ai pris	avons pris
prends	prenez	as pris	avez pris
prend	prennent	a pris	ont pris
2 imparfait de l'indicatif		**9 plus-que-parfait de l'indicatif**	
prenais	prenions	avais pris	avions pris
prenais	preniez	avais pris	aviez pris
prenait	prenaient	avait pris	avaient pris
3 passé simple		**10 passé antérieur**	
pris	prîmes	eus pris	eûmes pris
pris	prîtes	eus pris	eûtes pris
prit	prirent	eut pris	eurent pris
4 futur		**11 futur antérieur**	
prendrai	prendrons	aurai pris	aurons pris
prendras	prendrez	auras pris	aurez pris
prendra	prendront	aura pris	auront pris
5 conditionnel		**12 conditionnel passé**	
prendrais	prendrions	aurais pris	aurions pris
prendrais	prendriez	aurais pris	auriez pris
prendrait	prendraient	aurait pris	auraient pris
6 présent du subjonctif		**13 passé du subjonctif**	
prenne	prenions	aie pris	ayons pris
prennes	preniez	aies pris	ayez pris
prenne	prennent	ait pris	aient pris
7 imparfait du subjonctif		**14 plus-que-parfait du subjonctif**	
prisse	prissions	eusse pris	eussions pris
prisses	prissiez	eusses pris	eussiez pris
prît	prissent	eût pris	eussent pris

Impératif
prends
prenons
prenez

Sentences using this verb and words related to it
—Qui a pris les fleurs qui étaient sur la table?
—C'est moi qui les ai prises.

à tout prendre   on the whole, all in all
un preneur, une preneuse   taker, purchaser
s'y prendre   to go about it, to handle it, to set about it
Je ne sais comment m'y prendre   I don't know how to go about it.

C'est à prendre ou à laisser   Take it or leave it.
prendre à témoin   to call to witness
la prise   seizure, capture; **La Prise de la Bastille**   The Storming of the Bastille (July 14, 1789)

See also **apprendre, comprendre, entreprendre, se méprendre, reprendre,** and **surprendre.**

Can't recognize an irregular verb form? Check out pages 526–529.

The Seven Simple Tenses		The Seven Compound Tenses	
Singular	Plural	Singular	Plural

1   présent de l'indicatif

prépare	préparons	ai préparé	avons préparé
prépares	préparez	as préparé	avez préparé
prépare	préparent	a préparé	ont préparé

2   imparfait de l'indicatif   9   plus-que-parfait de l'indicatif

préparais	préparions	avais préparé	avions préparé
préparais	prépariez	avais préparé	aviez préparé
préparait	préparaient	avait préparé	avaient préparé

3   passé simple   10   passé antérieur

préparai	préparâmes	eus préparé	eûmes préparé
préparas	préparâtes	eus préparé	eûtes préparé
prépara	préparèrent	eut préparé	eurent préparé

4   futur   11   futur antérieur

préparerai	préparerons	aurai préparé	aurons préparé
prépareras	préparerez	auras préparé	aurez préparé
préparera	prépareront	aura préparé	auront préparé

5   conditionnel   12   conditionnel passé

préparerais	préparerions	aurais préparé	aurions préparé
préparerais	prépareriez	aurais préparé	auriez préparé
préparerait	prépareraient	aurait préparé	auraient préparé

6   présent du subjonctif   13   passé du subjonctif

prépare	préparions	aie préparé	ayons préparé
prépares	prépariez	aies préparé	ayez préparé
prépare	préparent	ait préparé	aient préparé

7   imparfait du subjonctif   14   plus-que-parfait du subjonctif

préparasse	préparassions	eusse préparé	eussions préparé
préparasses	préparassiez	eusses préparé	eussiez préparé
préparât	préparassent	eût préparé	eussent préparé

Impératif
prépare
préparons
préparez

Sentences using this verb and words related to it

Si Albert avait préparé sa leçon, il aurait reçu une bonne note. Il prépare toujours ses leçons, mais, cette fois, il ne les a pas préparées.

la préparation   preparation
les préparatifs *m.*   preparations
préparatoire   preparatory
se préparer   to prepare oneself
préparer un examen   to study for an exam

Get acquainted with what preposition goes with what verb on pages 543–553.

The subject pronouns are found on the page facing page 1.   **357**

présenter

Part. pr. **présentant**   Part. passé **présenté**

to present, to introduce

The Seven Simple Tenses		The Seven Compound Tenses	
Singular	Plural	Singular	Plural
1 présent de l'indicatif		**8 passé composé**	
présente	présentons	ai présenté	avons présenté
présentes	présentez	as présenté	avez présenté
présente	présentent	a présenté	ont présenté
2 imparfait de l'indicatif		**9 plus-que-parfait de l'indicatif**	
présentais	présentions	avais présenté	avions présenté
présentais	présentiez	avais présenté	aviez présenté
présentait	présentaient	avait présenté	avaient présenté
3 passé simple		**10 passé antérieur**	
présentai	présentâmes	eus présenté	eûmes présenté
présentas	présentâtes	eus présenté	eûtes présenté
présenta	présentèrent	eut présenté	eurent présenté
4 futur		**11 futur antérieur**	
présenterai	présenterons	aurai présenté	aurons présenté
présenteras	présenterez	auras présenté	aurez présenté
présentera	présenteront	aura présenté	auront présenté
5 conditionnel		**12 conditionnel passé**	
présenterais	présenterions	aurais présenté	aurions présenté
présenterais	présenteriez	aurais présenté	auriez présenté
présenterait	présenteraient	aurait présenté	auraient présenté
6 présent du subjonctif		**13 passé du subjonctif**	
présente	présentions	aie présenté	ayons présenté
présentes	présentiez	aies présenté	ayez présenté
présente	présentent	ait présenté	aient présenté
7 imparfait du subjonctif		**14 plus-que-parfait du subjonctif**	
présentasse	présentassions	eusse présenté	eussions présenté
présentasses	présentassiez	eusses présenté	eussiez présenté
présentât	présentassent	eût présenté	eussent présenté

Impératif
présente
présentons
présentez

Common idiomatic expressions using this verb
présenter qqn à qqn   to introduce someone to someone
Je vous présente à mon professeur de français.   May I introduce you to my French teacher?
un présentateur, une présentatrice   newscaster, announcer
se présenter   to introduce oneself
Permettez-moi de me présenter   Allow me to introduce myself.
présenter bien   to make a good impression
présenter mal   to make a bad impression
un présentoir   display

Want to learn more idiomatic expressions that contain verbs? Look at pages 530–542.

358

to press, to squeeze

The Seven Simple Tenses		The Seven Compound Tenses	
Singular	Plural	Singular	Plural
1 présent de l'indicatif		8 passé composé	
presse	pressons	ai pressé	avons pressé
presses	pressez	as pressé	avez pressé
presse	pressent	a pressé	ont pressé
2 imparfait de l'indicatif		9 plus-que-parfait de l'indicatif	
pressais	pressions	avais pressé	avions pressé
pressais	pressiez	avais pressé	aviez pressé
pressait	pressaient	avait pressé	avaient pressé
3 passé simple		10 passé antérieur	
pressai	pressâmes	eus pressé	eûmes pressé
pressas	pressâtes	eus pressé	eûtes pressé
pressa	pressèrent	eut pressé	eurent pressé
4 futur		11 futur antérieur	
presserai	presserons	aurai pressé	aurons pressé
presseras	presserez	auras pressé	aurez pressé
pressera	presseront	aura pressé	auront pressé
5 conditionnel		12 conditionnel passé	
presserais	presserions	aurais pressé	aurions pressé
presserais	presseriez	aurais pressé	auriez pressé
presserait	presseraient	aurait pressé	auraient pressé
6 présent du subjonctif		13 passé du subjonctif	
presse	pressions	aie pressé	ayons pressé
presses	pressiez	aies pressé	ayez pressé
presse	pressent	ait pressé	aient pressé
7 imparfait du subjonctif		14 plus-que-parfait du subjonctif	
pressasse	pressassions	eusse pressé	eussions pressé
pressasses	pressassiez	eusses pressé	eussiez pressé
pressât	pressassent	eût pressé	eussent pressé

Impératif
presse
pressons
pressez

Words and expressions related to this verb

presser qqn   to hurry someone
la pression   pressure
un presse-bouton   push button
  (**presse-bouton** *adj. pl.*)
un presse-papiers   paperweight
  (**des presse-papiers**)
un pressoir   press
un presseur, une presseuse   press worker

presser qqn de se décider   to urge someone to
  make a decision
être sous pression   to be under pressure
un presse-citron   lemon squeezer (**des
  presse-citrons**)
faire le coup du presse-citron à qqn   to put
  the squeeze on someone
le pressing   steam pressing (dry cleaner's)

Get acquainted with what preposition (if any) goes with what verb on pages 543–553.

The subject pronouns are found on the page facing page 1.   **359**

se presser

Part. pr. se pressant   **Part. passé pressé(e)(s)**

to be in a hurry, to make haste, to rush, to crowd

The Seven Simple Tenses		The Seven Compound Tenses	
Singular	Plural	Singular	Plural
1 présent de l'indicatif		**8 passé composé**	
me presse	nous pressons	me suis pressé(e)	nous sommes pressé(e)s
te presses	vous pressez	t'es pressé(e)	vous êtes pressé(e)(s)
se presse	se pressent	s'est pressé(e)	se sont pressé(e)s
2 imparfait de l'indicatif		**9 plus-que-parfait de l'indicatif**	
me pressais	nous pressions	m'étais pressé(e)	nous étions pressé(e)s
te pressais	vous pressiez	t'étais pressé(e)	vous étiez pressé(e)(s)
se pressait	se pressaient	s'était pressé(e)	s'étaient pressé(e)s
3 passé simple		**10 passé antérieur**	
me pressai	nous pressâmes	me fus pressé(e)	nous fûmes pressé(e)s
te pressas	vous pressâtes	te fus pressé(e)	vous fûtes pressé(e)(s)
se pressa	se pressèrent	se fut pressé(e)	se furent pressé(e)s
4 futur		**11 futur antérieur**	
me presserai	nous presserons	me serai pressé(e)	nous serons pressé(e)s
te presseras	vous presserez	te seras pressé(e)	vous serez pressé(e)(s)
se pressera	se presseront	se sera pressé(e)	se seront pressé(e)s
5 conditionnel		**12 conditionnel passé**	
me presserais	nous presserions	me serais pressé(e)	nous serions pressé(e)s
te presserais	vous presseriez	te serais pressé(e)	vous seriez pressé(e)(s)
se presserait	se presseraient	se serait pressé(e)	se seraient pressé(e)s
6 présent du subjonctif		**13 passé du subjonctif**	
me presse	nous pressions	me sois pressé(e)	nous soyons pressé(e)s
te presses	vous pressiez	te sois pressé(e)	vous soyez pressé(e)(s)
se presse	se pressent	se soit pressé(e)	se soient pressé(e)s
7 imparfait du subjonctif		**14 plus-que-parfait du subjonctif**	
me pressasse	nous pressassions	me fusse pressé(e)	nous fussions pressé(e)s
te pressasses	vous pressassiez	te fusses pressé(e)	vous fussiez pressé(e)(s)
se pressât	se pressassent	se fût pressé(e)	se fussent pressé(e)s

Impératif
presse-toi; ne te presse pas
pressons-nous; ne nous pressons pas
pressez-vous; ne vous pressez pas

Words and expressions related to this verb

se presser contre qqn   to press oneself against someone
se presser de faire qqch   to hurry to do something
se presser en foule   to press against each other in a crowd

presser   to press, to squeeze
presser le pas   to walk more quickly
presser qqn   to urge someone, to hurry someone
une pression   pressure
faire pression sur qqn   to exert pressure on someone

Hurry up and get acquainted with what preposition goes with what verb on pages 543–553.

to pretend, to claim, to lay claim, to maintain

The Seven Simple Tenses		The Seven Compound Tenses	
Singular	Plural	Singular	Plural
1　présent de l'indicatif		**8　passé composé**	
prétends	prétendons	ai prétendu	avons prétendu
prétends	prétendez	as prétendu	avez prétendu
prétend	prétendent	a prétendu	ont prétendu
2　imparfait de l'indicatif		**9　plus-que-parfait de l'indicatif**	
prétendais	prétendions	avais prétendu	avions prétendu
prétendais	prétendiez	avais prétendu	aviez prétendu
prétendait	prétendaient	avait prétendu	avaient prétendu
3　passé simple		**10　passé antérieur**	
prétendis	prétendîmes	eus prétendu	eûmes prétendu
prétendis	prétendîtes	eus prétendu	eûtes prétendu
prétendit	prétendirent	eut prétendu	eurent prétendu
4　futur		**11　futur antérieur**	
prétendrai	prétendrons	aurai prétendu	aurons prétendu
prétendras	prétendrez	auras prétendu	aurez prétendu
prétendra	prétendront	aura prétendu	auront prétendu
5　conditionnel		**12　conditionnel passé**	
prétendrais	prétendrions	aurais prétendu	aurions prétendu
prétendrais	prétendriez	aurais prétendu	auriez prétendu
prétendrait	prétendraient	aurait prétendu	auraient prétendu
6　présent du subjonctif		**13　passé du subjonctif**	
prétende	prétendions	aie prétendu	ayons prétendu
prétendes	prétendiez	aies prétendu	ayez prétendu
prétende	prétendent	ait prétendu	aient prétendu
7　imparfait du subjonctif		**14　plus-que-parfait du subjonctif**	
prétendisse	prétendissions	eusse prétendu	eussions prétendu
prétendisses	prétendissiez	eusses prétendu	eussiez prétendu
prétendît	prétendissent	eût prétendu	eussent prétendu

Impératif
prétends
prétendons
prétendez

Words and expressions related to this verb
prétendre savoir qqch　to claim to know
　something
prétentieux, prétentieuse　pretentious
un prétendu spécialiste　self-styled specialist
prétendre à　to lay claim to

la prétention　pretention
sans prétentions　unpretentious,
　unpretentiously
prétentieusement　pretentiously

How are you doing? Find out with the verb drills and tests with answers explained on pages 622–673.

The subject pronouns are found on the page facing page 1.　　　　　**361**

prêter

to lend

Part. pr. **prêtant**   Part. passé **prêté**

The Seven Simple Tenses		The Seven Compound Tenses	
Singular	Plural	Singular	Plural
1 présent de l'indicatif		**8 passé composé**	
prête	prêtons	ai prêté	avons prêté
prêtes	prêtez	as prêté	avez prêté
prête	prêtent	a prêté	ont prêté
2 imparfait de l'indicatif		**9 plus-que-parfait de l'indicatif**	
prêtais	prêtions	avais prêté	avions prêté
prêtais	prêtiez	avais prêté	aviez prêté
prêtait	prêtaient	avait prêté	avaient prêté
3 passé simple		**10 passé antérieur**	
prêtai	prêtâmes	eus prêté	eûmes prêté
prêtas	prêtâtes	eus prêté	eûtes prêté
prêta	prêtèrent	eut prêté	eurent prêté
4 futur		**11 futur antérieur**	
prêterai	prêterons	aurai prêté	aurons prêté
prêteras	prêterez	auras prêté	aurez prêté
prêtera	prêteront	aura prêté	auront prêté
5 conditionnel		**12 conditionnel passé**	
prêterais	prêterions	aurais prêté	aurions prêté
prêterais	prêteriez	aurais prêté	auriez prêté
prêterait	prêteraient	aurait prêté	auraient prêté
6 présent du subjonctif		**13 passé du subjonctif**	
prête	prêtions	aie prêté	ayons prêté
prêtes	prêtiez	aies prêté	ayez prêté
prête	prêtent	ait prêté	aient prêté
7 imparfait du subjonctif		**14 plus-que-parfait du subjonctif**	
prêtasse	prêtassions	eusse prêté	eussions prêté
prêtasses	prêtassiez	eusses prêté	eussiez prêté
prêtât	prêtassent	eût prêté	eussent prêté

Impératif
prête
prêtons
prêtez

Common idiomatic expressions using this verb

prêter à intérêt to lend at interest
prêter attention à qqn ou à qqch to pay attention to someone or something
un prêteur sur gages pawnbroker
prêter la main à qqn to give a helping hand to someone

prêter secours à qqn to go to someone's rescue (help)
apprêter to prepare, to get (something) ready
s'apprêter to get oneself ready
prêter l'oreille to listen, to lend an ear

NOTE: Don't confuse **prêter** with **emprunter** (to borrow).

362

to warn, to forestall, to ward off

The Seven Simple Tenses		The Seven Compound Tenses	
Singular	Plural	Singular	Plural
1 présent de l'indicatif		**8 passé composé**	
préviens	**prévenons**	**ai prévenu**	**avons prévenu**
préviens	**prévenez**	**as prévenu**	**avez prévenu**
prévient	**préviennent**	**a prévenu**	**ont prévenu**
2 imparfait de l'indicatif		**9 plus-que-parfait de l'indicatif**	
prévenais	**prévenions**	**avais prévenu**	**avions prévenu**
prévenais	**préveniez**	**avais prévenu**	**aviez prévenu**
prévenait	**prévenaient**	**avait prévenu**	**avaient prévenu**
3 passé simple		**10 passé antérieur**	
prévins	**prévînmes**	**eus prévenu**	**eûmes prévenu**
prévins	**prévîntes**	**eus prévenu**	**eûtes prévenu**
prévint	**prévinrent**	**eut prévenu**	**eurent prévenu**
4 futur		**11 futur antérieur**	
préviendrai	**préviendrons**	**aurai prévenu**	**aurons prévenu**
préviendras	**préviendrez**	**auras prévenu**	**aurez prévenu**
préviendra	**préviendront**	**aura prévenu**	**auront prévenu**
5 conditionnel		**12 conditionnel passé**	
préviendrais	**préviendrions**	**aurais prévenu**	**aurions prévenu**
préviendrais	**préviendriez**	**aurais prévenu**	**auriez prévenu**
préviendrait	**préviendraient**	**aurait prévenu**	**auraient prévenu**
6 présent du subjonctif		**13 passé du subjonctif**	
prévienne	**prévenions**	**aie prévenu**	**ayons prévenu**
préviennes	**préveniez**	**aies prévenu**	**ayez prévenu**
prévienne	**préviennent**	**ait prévenu**	**aient prévenu**
7 imparfait du subjonctif		**14 plus-que-parfait du subjonctif**	
prévinsse	**prévinssions**	**eusse prévenu**	**eussions prévenu**
prévinsses	**prévinssiez**	**eusses prévenu**	**eussiez prévenu**
prévînt	**prévinssent**	**eût prévenu**	**eussent prévenu**

Impératif
préviens
prévenons
prévenez

Words and expressions related to this verb
Mieux vaut prévenir que guérir   Prevention
  is better than cure.
la prévenance   considerateness, kindness
la prévention   prevention

prévenant, prévenante   considerate, kind,
  thoughtful
entourer qqn de prévenances   to shower
  someone with kindness, attention

See also **convenir, devenir, revenir, venir,** and **se souvenir.**

Want to learn more verbs used in proverbs and sayings? Take a look at page 559.

The subject pronouns are found on the page facing page 1.   **363**

to foresee

The Seven Simple Tenses		The Seven Compound Tenses	
Singular	Plural	Singular	Plural
1 présent de l'indicatif		8 passé composé	
prévois	**prévoyons**	**ai prévu**	**avons prévu**
prévois	**prévoyez**	**as prévu**	**avez prévu**
prévoit	**prévoient**	**a prévu**	**ont prévu**
2 imparfait de l'indicatif		9 plus-que-parfait de l'indicatif	
prévoyais	**prévoyions**	**avais prévu**	**avions prévu**
prévoyais	**prévoyiez**	**avais prévu**	**aviez prévu**
prévoyait	**prévoyaient**	**avait prévu**	**avaient prévu**
3 passé simple		10 passé antérieur	
prévis	**prévîmes**	**eus prévu**	**eûmes prévu**
prévis	**prévîtes**	**eus prévu**	**eûtes prévu**
prévit	**prévirent**	**eut prévu**	**eurent prévu**
4 futur		11 futur antérieur	
prévoirai	**prévoirons**	**aurai prévu**	**aurons prévu**
prévoiras	**prévoirez**	**auras prévu**	**aurez prévu**
prévoira	**prévoiront**	**aura prévu**	**auront prévu**
5 conditionnel		12 conditionnel passé	
prévoirais	**prévoirions**	**aurais prévu**	**aurions prévu**
prévoirais	**prévoiriez**	**aurais prévu**	**auriez prévu**
prévoirait	**prévoiraient**	**aurait prévu**	**auraient prévu**
6 présent du subjonctif		13 passé du subjonctif	
prévoie	**prévoyions**	**aie prévu**	**ayons prévu**
prévoies	**prévoyiez**	**aies prévu**	**ayez prévu**
prévoie	**prévoient**	**ait prévu**	**aient prévu**
7 imparfait du subjonctif		14 plus-que-parfait du subjonctif	
prévisse	**prévissions**	**eusse prévu**	**eussions prévu**
prévisses	**prévissiez**	**eusses prévu**	**eussiez prévu**
prévît	**prévissent**	**eût prévu**	**eussent prévu**

Impératif
prévois
prévoyons
prévoyez

Words and expressions related to this verb
la prévision forecast
en prévision de in anticipation of
prévisible foreseeable; **visible** visible
la prévoyance foresight
une avant-première preview

prévoir le temps to forecast the weather
les prévisions météorologiques weather
  forecasts
voir to see
prévoyant, prévoyante provident

See also **voir.**

Soak up some verbs used in weather expressions on pages 557 and 558.

to pray, to supplicate, to entreat, to beg, to request

The Seven Simple Tenses		The Seven Compound Tenses	
Singular	Plural	Singular	Plural

1 présent de l'indicatif		8 passé composé	
prie	prions	ai prié	avons prié
pries	priez	as prié	avez prié
prie	prient	a prié	ont prié

2 imparfait de l'indicatif		9 plus-que-parfait de l'indicatif	
priais	priions	avais prié	avions prié
priais	priiez	avais prié	aviez prié
priait	priaient	avait prié	avaient prié

3 passé simple		10 passé antérieur	
priai	priâmes	eus prié	eûmes prié
prias	priâtes	eus prié	eûtes prié
pria	prièrent	eut prié	eurent prié

4 futur		11 futur antérieur	
prierai	prierons	aurai prié	aurons prié
prieras	prierez	auras prié	aurez prié
priera	prieront	aura prié	auront prié

5 conditionnel		12 conditionnel passé	
prierais	prierions	aurais prié	aurions prié
prierais	prieriez	aurais prié	auriez prié
prierait	prieraient	aurait prié	auraient prié

6 présent du subjonctif		13 passé du subjonctif	
prie	priions	aie prié	ayons prié
pries	priiez	aies prié	ayez prié
prie	prient	ait prié	aient prié

7 imparfait du subjonctif		14 plus-que-parfait du subjonctif	
priasse	priassions	eusse prié	eussions prié
priasses	priassiez	eusses prié	eussiez prié
priât	priassent	eût prié	eussent prié

	Impératif
	prie
	prions
	priez

Words and expressions related to this verb

prier qqn de faire qqch   to beg (entreat, request) someone to do something

Je vous en prie!   You're welcome! I beg of you!

On vous prie de + inf.   You are requested + inf.

prier qqn à faire qqch   to invite someone to do something

une prière   prayer; **Prière d'entrer sans frapper**   Please enter without knocking.

Prière de ne pas fumer   You are requested not to smoke.

Puis-je entrer?   May I come in?—**Je vous en prie!**   Please do! (I beg you to do so)

vouloir se faire prier   to desire to be urged; **Madame Duchemin veut toujours se faire prier**   Mrs. Duchemin always wants to be urged.

sans se faire prier   willingly

The subject pronouns are found on the page facing page 1.   **365**

produire
to produce

Part. pr. **produisant**   Part. passé **produit**

The Seven Simple Tenses		The Seven Compound Tenses	
Singular	Plural	Singular	Plural
1 présent de l'indicatif		**8 passé composé**	
produis	produisons	ai produit	avons produit
produis	produisez	as produit	avez produit
produit	produisent	a produit	ont produit
2 imparfait de l'indicatif		**9 plus-que-parfait de l'indicatif**	
produisais	produisions	avais produit	avions produit
produisais	produisiez	avais produit	aviez produit
produisait	produisaient	avait produit	avaient produit
3 passé simple		**10 passé antérieur**	
produisis	produisîmes	eus produit	eûmes produit
produisis	produisîtes	eus produit	eûtes produit
produisit	produisirent	eut produit	eurent produit
4 futur		**11 futur antérieur**	
produirai	produirons	aurai produit	aurons produit
produiras	produirez	auras produit	aurez produit
produira	produiront	aura produit	auront produit
5 conditionnel		**12 conditionnel passé**	
produirais	produirions	aurais produit	aurions produit
produirais	produiriez	aurais produit	auriez produit
produirait	produiraient	aurait produit	auraient produit
6 présent du subjonctif		**13 passé du subjonctif**	
produise	produisions	aie produit	ayons produit
produises	produisiez	aies produit	ayez produit
produise	produisent	ait produit	aient produit
7 imparfait du subjonctif		**14 plus-que-parfait du subjonctif**	
produisisse	produisissions	eusse produit	eussions produit
produisisses	produisissiez	eusses produit	eussiez produit
produisît	produisissent	eût produit	eussent produit

Impératif
produis
produisons
produisez

Words related to this verb
un produit product
la production production
productible producible
productif, productive productive
le produit national brut the gross national product

la productivité productivity
se produire to happen, to occur, to be brought about
les produits alimentaires food products
se produire en public to appear in public

See also **conduire, déduire, introduire, réduire, reproduire, séduire,** and **traduire.**

Get acquainted with what preposition goes with what verb on pages 543–553.

The Seven Simple Tenses		The Seven Compound Tenses	
Singular	Plural	Singular	Plural
1 présent de l'indicatif		8 passé composé	
me promène	nous promenons	me suis promené(e)	nous sommes promené(e)s
te promènes	vous promenez	t'es promené(e)	vous êtes promené(e)(s)
se promène	se promènent	s'est promené(e)	se sont promené(e)s
2 imparfait de l'indicatif		9 plus-que-parfait de l'indicatif	
me promenais	nous promenions	m'étais promené(e)	nous étions promené(e)s
te promenais	vous promeniez	t'étais promené(e)	vous étiez promené(e)(s)
se promenait	se promenaient	s'était promené(e)	s'étaient promené(e)s
3 passé simple		10 passé antérieur	
me promenai	nous promenâmes	me fus promené(e)	nous fûmes promené(e)s
te promenas	vous promenâtes	te fus promené(e)	vous fûtes promené(e)(s)
se promena	se promenèrent	se fut promené(e)	se furent promené(e)s
4 futur		11 futur antérieur	
me promènerai	nous promènerons	me serai promené(e)	nous serons promené(e)s
te promèneras	vous promènerez	te seras promené(e)	vous serez promené(e)(s)
se promènera	se promèneront	se sera promené(e)	se seront promené(e)s
5 conditionnel		12 conditionnel passé	
me promènerais	nous promènerions	me serais promené(e)	nous serions promené(e)s
te promènerais	vous promèneriez	te serais promené(e)	vous seriez promené(e)(s)
se promènerait	se promèneraient	se serait promené(e)	se seraient promené(e)s
6 présent du subjonctif		13 passé du subjonctif	
me promène	nous promenions	me sois promené(e)	nous soyons promené(e)s
te promènes	vous promeniez	te sois promené(e)	vous soyez promené(e)(s)
se promène	se promènent	se soit promené(e)	se soient promené(e)s
7 imparfait du subjonctif		14 plus-que-parfait du subjonctif	
me promenasse	nous promenassions	me fusse promené(e)	nous fussions promené(e)s
te promenasses	vous promenassiez	te fusses promené(e)	vous fussiez promené(e)(s)
se promenât	se promenassent	se fût promené(e)	se fussent promené(e)s

Impératif
promène-toi; ne te promène pas
promenons-nous; ne nous promenons pas
promenez-vous; ne vous promenez pas

Common idiomatic expressions using this verb

Je me promène tous les matins   I take a walk every morning.

Cette promenade est merveilleuse   This walk is marvelous.

Janine et Robert se sont promenés dans le parc   Janine and Robert took a walk in the park.

faire une promenade   to take a walk

faire une promenade en voiture   to go for a drive

promener son chien   to take one's dog out for a walk

promener ses regards sur   to cast one's eyes on, to look over

un promenoir   indoor mall for walking, strolling

See also **amener, emmener,** and **mener.**

The subject pronouns are found on the page facing page 1.   **367**

promettre

Part. pr. **promettant**   Part. passé **promis**

to promise

The Seven Simple Tenses		The Seven Compound Tenses	
Singular	Plural	Singular	Plural
1 présent de l'indicatif		**8 passé composé**	
promets	promettons	ai promis	avons promis
promets	promettez	as promis	avez promis
promet	promettent	a promis	ont promis
2 imparfait de l'indicatif		**9 plus-que-parfait de l'indicatif**	
promettais	promettions	avais promis	avions promis
promettais	promettiez	avais promis	aviez promis
promettait	promettaient	avait promis	avaient promis
3 passé simple		**10 passé antérieur**	
promis	promîmes	eus promis	eûmes promis
promis	promîtes	eus promis	eûtes promis
promit	promirent	eut promis	eurent promis
4 futur		**11 futur antérieur**	
promettrai	promettrons	aurai promis	aurons promis
promettras	promettrez	auras promis	aurez promis
promettra	promettront	aura promis	auront promis
5 conditionnel		**12 conditionnel passé**	
promettrais	promettrions	aurais promis	aurions promis
promettrais	promettriez	aurais promis	auriez promis
promettrait	promettraient	aurait promis	auraient promis
6 présent du subjonctif		**13 passé du subjonctif**	
promette	promettions	aie promis	ayons promis
promettes	promettiez	aies promis	ayez promis
promette	promettent	ait promis	aient promis
7 imparfait du subjonctif		**14 plus-que-parfait du subjonctif**	
promisse	promissions	eusse promis	eussions promis
promisses	promissiez	eusses promis	eussiez promis
promît	promissent	eût promis	eussent promis

Impératif
promets
promettons
promettez

Common idiomatic expressions using this verb
promettre de faire qqch   to promise to do something
une promesse   promise
tenir sa promesse   to keep one's promise
promettre à qqn de faire qqch   to promise someone to do something
Ça promet!   It looks promising!
se promettre   to promise oneself
compromettre   to compromise

See also **commettre, permettre, mettre, se mettre, omettre, remettre, soumettre,** and **transmettre.**

to pronounce, to declare

The Seven Simple Tenses		The Seven Compound Tenses	
Singular	Plural	Singular	Plural
1 présent de l'indicatif		8 passé composé	
prononce	prononçons	ai prononcé	avons prononcé
prononces	prononcez	as prononcé	avez prononcé
prononce	prononcent	a prononcé	ont prononcé
2 imparfait de l'indicatif		9 plus-que-parfait de l'indicatif	
prononçais	prononcions	avais prononcé	avions prononcé
prononçais	prononciez	avais prononcé	aviez prononcé
prononçait	prononçaient	avait prononcé	avaient prononcé
3 passé simple		10 passé antérieur	
prononçai	prononçâmes	eus prononcé	eûmes prononcé
prononças	prononçâtes	eus prononcé	eûtes prononcé
prononça	prononcèrent	eut prononcé	eurent prononcé
4 futur		11 futur antérieur	
prononcerai	prononcerons	aurai prononcé	aurons prononcé
prononceras	prononcerez	auras prononcé	aurez prononcé
prononcera	prononceront	aura prononcé	auront prononcé
5 conditionnel		12 conditionnel passé	
prononcerais	prononcerions	aurais prononcé	aurions prononcé
prononcerais	prononceriez	aurais prononcé	auriez prononcé
prononcerait	prononceraient	aurait prononcé	auraient prononcé
6 présent du subjonctif		13 passé du subjonctif	
prononce	prononcions	aie prononcé	ayons prononcé
prononces	prononciez	aies prononcé	ayez prononcé
prononce	prononcent	ait prononcé	aient prononcé
7 imparfait du subjonctif		14 plus-que-parfait du subjonctif	
prononçasse	prononçassions	eusse prononcé	eussions prononcé
prononçasses	prononçassiez	eusses prononcé	eussiez prononcé
prononçât	prononçassent	eût prononcé	eussent prononcé

Impératif
prononce
prononçons
prononcez

Words and expressions related to this verb
prononcer un discours   to deliver a speech
la prononciation   pronunciation
prononçable   pronounceable
se prononcer pour   to decide in favor of
énoncer   to enunciate

See also **annoncer**.

annoncer   to announce
dénoncer   to denounce
se prononcer   to declare, to be pronounced
   (as a word)
se prononcer contre   to decide against

Don't miss orthographically changing verbs on pages 554–556.

Use the EE-zee guide to French pronunciation on pages 566 and 567.

to prove

The Seven Simple Tenses		The Seven Compound Tenses	
Singular	Plural	Singular	Plural
1　présent de l'indicatif		**8　passé composé**	
prouve	prouvons	ai prouvé	avons prouvé
prouves	prouvez	as prouvé	avez prouvé
prouve	prouvent	a prouvé	ont prouvé
2　imparfait de l'indicatif		**9　plus-que-parfait de l'indicatif**	
prouvais	prouvions	avais prouvé	avions prouvé
prouvais	prouviez	avais prouvé	aviez prouvé
prouvait	prouvaient	avait prouvé	avaient prouvé
3　passé simple		**10　passé antérieur**	
prouvai	prouvâmes	eus prouvé	eûmes prouvé
prouvas	prouvâtes	eus prouvé	eûtes prouvé
prouva	prouvèrent	eut prouvé	eurent prouvé
4　futur		**11　futur antérieur**	
prouverai	prouverons	aurai prouvé	aurons prouvé
prouveras	prouverez	auras prouvé	aurez prouvé
prouvera	prouveront	aura prouvé	auront prouvé
5　conditionnel		**12　conditionnel passé**	
prouverais	prouverions	aurais prouvé	aurions prouvé
prouverais	prouveriez	aurais prouvé	auriez prouvé
prouverait	prouveraient	aurait prouvé	auraient prouvé
6　présent du subjonctif		**13　passé du subjonctif**	
prouve	prouvions	aie prouvé	ayons prouvé
prouves	prouviez	aies prouvé	ayez prouvé
prouve	prouvent	ait prouvé	aient prouvé
7　imparfait du subjonctif		**14　plus-que-parfait du subjonctif**	
prouvasse	prouvassions	eusse prouvé	eussions prouvé
prouvasses	prouvassiez	eusses prouvé	eussiez prouvé
prouvât	prouvassent	eût prouvé	eussent prouvé

Impératif
prouve
prouvons
prouvez

Words and expressions related to this verb
une preuve　proof
comme preuve　by way of proof
prouvable　provable
une épreuve　test, proof
faire la preuve de qqch　to prove something
éprouver　to test, to try, to experience

éprouver de la sympathie pour　to feel sympathy for
mettre à l'épreuve　to put to the test
avoir la preuve de　to have proof of
désapprouver　to disapprove of

See also **approuver** and **éprouver**.

It's important that you be familiar with the Subjunctive. See pages 560–565.

The Seven Simple Tenses

Singular	Plural

1 présent de l'indicatif

pue	**puons**
pues	**puez**
pue	**puent**

2 imparfait de l'indicatif

puais	**puions**
puais	**puiez**
puait	**puaient**

4 futur

puerai	**puerons**
pueras	**puerez**
puera	**pueront**

5 conditionnel

puerais	**puerions**
puerais	**pueriez**
puerait	**pueraient**

Words and expressions related to this verb
puant, puante   stinking; conceited
la puanteur   stink, foul smell
Robert est un type puant   Robert is a stinker.
Cet ivrogne pue l'alcool; je me bouche le nez   This drunkard stinks of alcohol; I'm plugging my nose.
Joseph, ta chambre pue la porcherie   Joseph, your room smells like a pigsty.

This verb is used mainly in the above tenses.

If you have the need to use this verb in all the 14 tenses and the imperative, the forms are the same as for the verb **tuer** among the 501 verbs. Just replace the letter **t** with the letter **p**.

See the summary of sequence of tenses with **si** (*if*) clauses on page 560.

The subject pronouns are found on the page facing page 1.

punir

Part. pr. **punissant**   Part. passé **puni**

to punish

The Seven Simple Tenses		The Seven Compound Tenses	
Singular	Plural	Singular	Plural
1 présent de l'indicatif		**8 passé composé**	
punis	punissons	ai puni	avons puni
punis	punissez	as puni	avez puni
punit	punissent	a puni	ont puni
2 imparfait de l'indicatif		**9 plus-que-parfait de l'indicatif**	
punissais	punissions	avais puni	avions puni
punissais	punissiez	avais puni	aviez puni
punissait	punissaient	avait puni	avaient puni
3 passé simple		**10 passé antérieur**	
punis	punîmes	eus puni	eûmes puni
punis	punîtes	eus puni	eûtes puni
punit	punirent	eut puni	eurent puni
4 futur		**11 futur antérieur**	
punirai	punirons	aurai puni	aurons puni
puniras	punirez	auras puni	aurez puni
punira	puniront	aura puni	auront puni
5 conditionnel		**12 conditionnel passé**	
punirais	punirions	aurais puni	aurions puni
punirais	puniriez	aurais puni	auriez puni
punirait	puniraient	aurait puni	auraient puni
6 présent du subjonctif		**13 passé du subjonctif**	
punisse	punissions	aie puni	ayons puni
punisses	punissiez	aies puni	ayez puni
punisse	punissent	ait puni	aient puni
7 imparfait du subjonctif		**14 plus-que-parfait du subjonctif**	
punisse	punissions	eusse puni	eussions puni
punisses	punissiez	eusses puni	eussiez puni
punît	punissent	eût puni	eussent puni

Impératif
punis
punissons
punissez

Words and expressions related to this verb

punisseur, punisseuse   punisher
punissable   punishable
punition *f.*   punishment
punitif, punitive   punitive

échapper à la punition   to escape punishment
la peine capitale   capital punishment
en punition   as a punishment

Grammar putting you in a tense mood? Review the definitions of basic grammatical terms with examples on pages 674–688.

The Seven Simple Tenses		The Seven Compound Tenses

Singular	Plural	Singular	Plural

1 présent de l'indicatif

quitte	quittons	
quittes	quittez	
quitte	quittent	

8 passé composé

ai quitté	avons quitté
as quitté	avez quitté
a quitté	ont quitté

2 imparfait de l'indicatif

quittais	quittions
quittais	quittiez
quittait	quittaient

9 plus-que-parfait de l'indicatif

avais quitté	avions quitté
avais quitté	aviez quitté
avait quitté	avaient quitté

3 passé simple

quittai	quittâmes
quittas	quittâtes
quitta	quittèrent

10 passé antérieur

eus quitté	eûmes quitté
eus quitté	eûtes quitté
eut quitté	eurent quitté

4 futur

quitterai	quitterons
quitteras	quitterez
quittera	quitteront

11 futur antérieur

aurai quitté	aurons quitté
auras quitté	aurez quitté
aura quitté	auront quitté

5 conditionnel

quitterais	quitterions
quitterais	quitteriez
quitterait	quitteraient

12 conditionnel passé

aurais quitté	aurions quitté
aurais quitté	auriez quitté
aurait quitté	auraient quitté

6 présent du subjonctif

quitte	quittions
quittes	quittiez
quitte	quittent

13 passé du subjonctif

aie quitté	ayons quitté
aies quitté	ayez quitté
ait quitté	aient quitté

7 imparfait du subjonctif

quittasse	quittassions
quittasses	quittassiez
quittât	quittassent

14 plus-que-parfait du subjonctif

eusse quitté	eussions quitté
eusses quitté	eussiez quitté
eût quitté	eussent quitté

Impératif
quitte
quittons
quittez

Words and expressions related to this verb
une quittance acquittance, discharge
quitter son chapeau to take off one's hat
se quitter to separate, to leave each other
Ne quittez pas, s'il vous plaît Hold the line, please! (on the phone)
être quitte to be free of an obligation
Elle a quitté son mari She left her husband.

acquitter to acquit
s'acquitter de to fulfill
un acquittement acquittal, payment
Je vous ai payé la dette; maintenant nous sommes quittes! I paid you the debt; now we're even!
Il a quitté sa femme He left his wife.

Going away? Don't forget to check out the practical situations for travelers on pages 568–598.

The subject pronouns are found on the page facing page 1.   **373**

raconter   Part. pr. **racontant**   Part. passé **raconté**

to relate, to tell about, to tell (a story)

The Seven Simple Tenses		The Seven Compound Tenses	
Singular	Plural	Singular	Plural
1 présent de l'indicatif		8 passé composé	
raconte	racontons	ai raconté	avons raconté
racontes	racontez	as raconté	avez raconté
raconte	racontent	a raconté	ont raconté
2 imparfait de l'indicatif		9 plus-que-parfait de l'indicatif	
racontais	racontions	avais raconté	avions raconté
racontais	racontiez	avais raconté	aviez raconté
racontait	racontaient	avait raconté	avaient raconté
3 passé simple		10 passé antérieur	
racontai	racontâmes	eus raconté	eûmes raconté
racontas	racontâtes	eus raconté	eûtes raconté
raconta	racontèrent	eut raconté	eurent raconté
4 futur		11 futur antérieur	
raconterai	raconterons	aurai raconté	aurons raconté
raconteras	raconterez	auras raconté	aurez raconté
racontera	raconteront	aura raconté	auront raconté
5 conditionnel		12 conditionnel passé	
raconterais	raconterions	aurais raconté	aurions raconté
raconterais	raconteriez	aurais raconté	auriez raconté
raconterait	raconteraient	aurait raconté	auraient raconté
6 présent du subjonctif		13 passé du subjonctif	
raconte	racontions	aie raconté	ayons raconté
racontes	racontiez	aies raconté	ayez raconté
raconte	racontent	ait raconté	aient raconté
7 imparfait du subjonctif		14 plus-que-parfait du subjonctif	
racontasse	racontassions	eusse raconté	eussions raconté
racontasses	racontassiez	eusses raconté	eussiez raconté
racontât	racontassent	eût raconté	eussent raconté

Impératif
raconte
racontons
racontez

Sentences using this verb and words related to it

Mon professeur de français aime nous raconter des anecdotes en français dans la classe de français. C'est un bon raconteur.

un raconteur, une raconteuse   storyteller
Qu'est-ce que vous racontez?   What are you talking about?

See also **conter.**

Want to learn more idiomatic expressions that contain verbs? Look at pages 530–542.	If you don't know the French verb for an English verb you have in mind, try the index on pages 503–514.

to set (put) in order, to tidy up

The Seven Simple Tenses		The Seven Compound Tenses	
Singular	Plural	Singular	Plural
1 présent de l'indicatif		8 passé composé	
range	**rangeons**	**ai rangé**	**avons rangé**
ranges	**rangez**	**as rangé**	**avez rangé**
range	**rangent**	**a rangé**	**ont rangé**
2 imparfait de l'indicatif		9 plus-que-parfait de l'indicatif	
rangeais	**rangions**	**avais rangé**	**avions rangé**
rangeais	**rangiez**	**avais rangé**	**aviez rangé**
rangeait	**rangeaient**	**avait rangé**	**avaient rangé**
3 passé simple		10 passé antérieur	
rangeai	**rangeâmes**	**eus rangé**	**eûmes rangé**
rangeas	**rangeâtes**	**eus rangé**	**eûtes rangé**
rangea	**rangèrent**	**eut rangé**	**eurent rangé**
4 futur		11 futur antérieur	
rangerai	**rangerons**	**aurai rangé**	**aurons rangé**
rangeras	**rangerez**	**auras rangé**	**aurez rangé**
rangera	**rangeront**	**aura rangé**	**auront rangé**
5 conditionnel		12 conditionnel passé	
rangerais	**rangerions**	**aurais rangé**	**aurions rangé**
rangerais	**rangeriez**	**aurais rangé**	**auriez rangé**
rangerait	**rangeraient**	**aurait rangé**	**auraient rangé**
6 présent du subjonctif		13 passé du subjonctif	
range	**rangions**	**aie rangé**	**ayons rangé**
ranges	**rangiez**	**aies rangé**	**ayez rangé**
range	**rangent**	**ait rangé**	**aient rangé**
7 imparfait du subjonctif		14 plus-que-parfait du subjonctif	
rangeasse	**rangeassions**	**eusse rangé**	**eussions rangé**
rangeasses	**rangeassiez**	**eusses rangé**	**eussiez rangé**
rangeât	**rangeassent**	**eût rangé**	**eussent rangé**

Impératif
range
rangeons
rangez

Words and expressions related to this verb
un rang   row; rank
sortir du rang   to rise from the ranks
une rangée d'arbres   a line of trees
déranger   to disturb
se déranger   to inconvenience oneself
de premier rang   first-rate

se mettre sur les rangs   to join the ranks
se ranger   to stand back (out of the way)
arranger   to arrange; **s'arranger avec**   to come to terms with, to come to an agreement with; to manage

Consult the sections on verbs used in idiomatic expressions, verbs with prepositons, and the list of over 1,100 verbs conjugated like model verbs in the back pages.

The subject pronouns are found on the page facing page 1.

rappeler

Part. pr. **rappelant**   Part. passé **rappelé**

to call again, to call back, to recall, to remind

The Seven Simple Tenses		The Seven Compound Tenses	
Singular	Plural	Singular	Plural
1 présent de l'indicatif		**8 passé composé**	
rappelle	rappelons	ai rappelé	avons rappelé
rappelles	rappelez	as rappelé	avez rappelé
rappelle	rappellent	a rappelé	ont rappelé
2 imparfait de l'indicatif		**9 plus-que-parfait de l'indicatif**	
rappelais	rappelions	avais rappelé	avions rappelé
rappelais	rappeliez	avais rappelé	aviez rappelé
rappelait	rappelaient	avait rappelé	avaient rappelé
3 passé simple		**10 passé antérieur**	
rappelai	rappelâmes	eus rappelé	eûmes rappelé
rappelas	rappelâtes	eus rappelé	eûtes rappelé
rappela	rappelèrent	eut rappelé	eurent rappelé
4 futur		**11 futur antérieur**	
rappellerai	rappellerons	aurai rappelé	aurons rappelé
rappelleras	rappellerez	auras rappelé	aurez rappelé
rappellera	rappelleront	aura rappelé	auront rappelé
5 conditionnel		**12 conditionnel passé**	
rappellerais	rappellerions	aurais rappelé	aurions rappelé
rappellerais	rappelleriez	aurais rappelé	auriez rappelé
rappellerait	rappelleraient	aurait rappelé	auraient rappelé
6 présent du subjonctif		**13 passé du subjonctif**	
rappelle	rappelions	aie rappelé	ayons rappelé
rappelles	rappeliez	aies rappelé	ayez rappelé
rappelle	rappellent	ait rappelé	aient rappelé
7 imparfait du subjonctif		**14 plus-que-parfait du subjonctif**	
rappelasse	rappelassions	eusse rappelé	eussions rappelé
rappelasses	rappelassiez	eusses rappelé	eussiez rappelé
rappelât	rappelassent	eût rappelé	eussent rappelé

Impératif
rappelle
rappelons
rappelez

Sentences using this verb and words related to it
—**Je ne peux pas vous parler maintenant. Rappelez-moi demain.**
—**D'accord. Je vous rappellerai demain.**

un rappel   recall, call back, recalling
rappeler à la vie   to restore to life
Rappelez-moi votre nom   Remind me of your name.
rappeler qqn à l'ordre   to call someone to order

See also **appeler, s'appeler,** and **se rappeler.**

Don't miss orthographically changing verbs on pages 554–556.

376

to remember, to recall, to recollect

The Seven Simple Tenses		The Seven Compound Tenses	
Singular	Plural	Singular	Plural

1   présent de l'indicatif

me rappelle	nous rappelons		
te rappelles	vous rappelez		
se rappelle	se rappellent		

8   passé composé

me suis rappelé(e)		nous sommes rappelé(e)s	
t'es rappelé(e)		vous êtes rappelé(e)(s)	
s'est rappelé(e)		se sont rappelé(e)s	

2   imparfait de l'indicatif

me rappelais	nous rappelions
te rappelais	vous rappeliez
se rappelait	se rappelaient

9   plus-que-parfait de l'indicatif

m'étais rappelé(e)	nous étions rappelé(e)s
t'étais rappelé(e)	vous étiez rappelé(e)(s)
s'était rappelé(e)	s'étaient rappelé(e)s

3   passé simple

me rappelai	nous rappelâmes
te rappelas	vous rappelâtes
se rappela	se rappelèrent

10   passé antérieur

me fus rappelé(e)	nous fûmes rappelé(e)s
te fus rappelé(e)	vous fûtes rappelé(e)(s)
se fut rappelé(e)	se furent rappelé(e)s

4   futur

me rappellerai	nous rappellerons
te rappelleras	vous rappellerez
se rappellera	se rappelleront

11   futur antérieur

me serai rappelé(e)	nous serons rappelé(e)s
te seras rappelé(e)	vous serez rappelé(e)(s)
se sera rappelé(e)	se seront rappelé(e)s

5   conditionnel

me rappellerais	nous rappellerions
te rappellerais	vous rappelleriez
se rappellerait	se rappelleraient

12   conditionnel passé

me serais rappelé(e)	nous serions rappelé(e)s
te serais rappelé(e)	vous seriez rappelé(e)(s)
se serait rappelé(e)	se seraient rappelé(e)s

6   présent du subjonctif

me rappelle	nous rappelions
te rappelles	vous rappeliez
se rappelle	se rappellent

13   passé du subjonctif

me sois rappelé(e)	nous soyons rappelé(e)s
te sois rappelé(e)	vous soyez rappelé(e)(s)
se soit rappelé(e)	se soient rappelé(e)s

7   imparfait du subjonctif

me rappelasse	nous rappelassions
te rappelasses	vous rappelassiez
se rappelât	se rappelassent

14   plus-que-parfait du subjonctif

me fusse rappelé(e)	nous fussions rappelé(e)
te fusses rappelé(e)	vous fussiez rappelé(e)(s)
se fût rappelé(e)	se fussent rappelé(e)s

Impératif
rappelle-toi; ne te rappelle pas
rappelons-nous; ne nous rappelons pas
rappelez-vous; ne vous rappelez pas

Sentences using this verb and words related to it
   Je me rappelle bien le premier jour où j'ai vu la belle Hélène. C'était un jour inoubliable.

See also **appeler, s'appeler,** and **rappeler.**

How are you doing? Find out with the verb drills and tests with answers explained on pages 622–673.

recevoir

to receive, to get

Part. pr. **recevant**   Part. passé **reçu**

The Seven Simple Tenses		The Seven Compound Tenses	
Singular	Plural	Singular	Plural
1 présent de l'indicatif		**8 passé composé**	
reçois	recevons	ai reçu	avons reçu
reçois	recevez	as reçu	avez reçu
reçoit	reçoivent	a reçu	ont reçu
2 imparfait de l'indicatif		**9 plus-que-parfait de l'indicatif**	
recevais	recevions	avais reçu	avions reçu
recevais	receviez	avais reçu	aviez reçu
recevait	recevaient	avait reçu	avaient reçu
3 passé simple		**10 passé antérieur**	
reçus	reçûmes	eus reçu	eûmes reçu
reçus	reçûtes	eus reçu	eûtes reçu
reçut	reçurent	eut reçu	eurent reçu
4 futur		**11 futur antérieur**	
recevrai	recevrons	aurai reçu	aurons reçu
recevras	recevrez	auras reçu	aurez reçu
recevra	recevront	aura reçu	auront reçu
5 conditionnel		**12 conditionnel passé**	
recevrais	recevrions	aurais reçu	aurions reçu
recevrais	recevriez	aurais reçu	auriez reçu
recevrait	recevraient	aurait reçu	auraient reçu
6 présent du subjonctif		**13 passé du subjonctif**	
reçoive	recevions	aie reçu	ayons reçu
reçoives	receviez	aies reçu	ayez reçu
reçoive	reçoivent	ait reçu	aient reçu
7 imparfait du subjonctif		**14 plus-que-parfait du subjonctif**	
reçusse	reçussions	eusse reçu	eussions reçu
reçusses	reçussiez	eusses reçu	eussiez reçu
reçût	reçussent	eût reçu	eussent reçu

Impératif
reçois
recevons
recevez

Words and expressions related to this verb
réceptif, réceptive receptive
une réception reception, welcome
un, une réceptionniste receptionist
un reçu a receipt

au reçu de on receipt of
recevable receivable
un receveur, une receveuse receiver
être reçu à un examen to pass an exam

Don't miss the definitions of basic grammatical terms with examples in English and French on pages 674–688.

to recognize, to acknowledge

The Seven Simple Tenses		The Seven Compound Tenses	
Singular	Plural	Singular	Plural
1 présent de l'indicatif		**8 passé composé**	
reconnais	reconnaissons	ai reconnu	avons reconnu
reconnais	reconnaissez	as reconnu	avez reconnu
reconnaît	reconnaissent	a reconnu	ont reconnu
2 imparfait de l'indicatif		**9 plus-que-parfait de l'indicatif**	
reconnaissais	reconnaissions	avais reconnu	avions reconnu
reconnaissais	reconnaissiez	avais reconnu	aviez reconnu
reconnaissait	reconnaissaient	avait reconnu	avaient reconnu
3 passé simple		**10 passé antérieur**	
reconnus	reconnûmes	eus reconnu	eûmes reconnu
reconnus	reconnûtes	eus reconnu	eûtes reconnu
reconnut	reconnurent	eut reconnu	eurent reconnu
4 futur		**11 futur antérieur**	
reconnaîtrai	reconnaîtrons	aurai reconnu	aurons reconnu
reconnaîtras	reconnaîtrez	auras reconnu	aurez reconnu
reconnaîtra	reconnaîtront	aura reconnu	auront reconnu
5 conditionnel		**12 conditionnel passé**	
reconnaîtrais	reconnaîtrions	aurais reconnu	aurions reconnu
reconnaîtrais	reconnaîtriez	aurais reconnu	auriez reconnu
reconnaîtrait	reconnaîtraient	aurait reconnu	auraient reconnu
6 présent du subjonctif		**13 passé du subjonctif**	
reconnaisse	reconnaissions	aie reconnu	ayons reconnu
reconnaisses	reconnaissiez	aies reconnu	ayez reconnu
reconnaisse	reconnaissent	ait reconnu	aient reconnu
7 imparfait du subjonctif		**14 plus-que-parfait du subjonctif**	
reconnusse	reconnussions	eusse reconnu	eussions reconnu
reconnusses	reconnussiez	eusses reconnu	eussiez reconnu
reconnût	reconnussent	eût reconnu	eussent reconnu

Impératif
reconnais
reconnaissons
reconnaissez

Words and expressions related to this verb

la reconnaissance gratitude, gratefulness, recognition

être reconnaissant à qqn de to be grateful (thankful, obliged) to someone for

See also **connaître** and **méconnaître**.

la reconnaissance vocale speech/voice recognition (computer)

se reconnaître to recognize oneself, to recognize each other

reconnaissable recognizable

Consult the sections on verbs used in idiomatic expressions, verbs with prepositions, and the list of over 1,100 verbs conjugated like model verbs in the back pages.

The subject pronouns are found on the page facing page 1. **379**

recueillir

Part. pr. **recueillant**   Part. passé **recueilli**

to collect, to gather, to harvest

The Seven Simple Tenses		The Seven Compound Tenses	
Singular	Plural	Singular	Plural
1 présent de l'indicatif		8 passé composé	
recueille	recueillons	ai recueilli	avons recueilli
recueilles	recueillez	as recueilli	avez recueilli
recueille	recueillent	a recueilli	ont recueilli
2 imparfait de l'indicatif		9 plus-que-parfait de l'indicatif	
recueillais	recueillions	avais recueilli	avions recueilli
recueillais	recueilliez	avais recueilli	aviez recueilli
recueillait	recueillaient	avait recueilli	avaient recueilli
3 passé simple		10 passé antérieur	
recueillis	recueillîmes	eus recueilli	eûmes recueilli
recueillis	recueillîtes	eus recueilli	eûtes recueilli
recueillit	recueillirent	eut recueilli	eurent recueilli
4 futur		11 futur antérieur	
recueillerai	recueillerons	aurai recueilli	aurons recueilli
recueilleras	recueillerez	auras recueilli	aurez recueilli
recueillera	recueilleront	aura recueilli	auront recueilli
5 conditionnel		12 conditionnel passé	
recueillerais	recueillerions	aurais recueilli	aurions recueilli
recueillerais	recueilleriez	aurais recueilli	auriez recueilli
recueillerait	recueilleraient	aurait recueilli	auraient recueilli
6 présent du subjonctif		13 passé du subjonctif	
recueille	recueillions	aie recueilli	ayons recueilli
recueilles	recueilliez	aies recueilli	ayez recueilli
recueille	recueillent	ait recueilli	aient recueilli
7 imparfait du subjonctif		14 plus-que-parfait du subjonctif	
recueillisse	recueillissions	eusse recueilli	eussions recueilli
recueillisses	recueillissiez	eusses recueilli	eussiez recueilli
recueillît	recueillissent	eût recueilli	eussent recueilli

Impératif
recueille
recueillons
recueillez

Words and expressions related to this verb

recueillir le fruit de son travail   to reap the fruit of one's labor

un recueil   collection; **un recueil de contes**   collection of stories

le recueillement   meditation, contemplation

See aslo **accueillir** and **cueillir**.

se recueillir   to meditate, to collect one's thoughts

Avez-vous jamais lu le poème *Recueillement* de Charles Baudelaire?   Have you ever read the poem *Recueillement* by Charles Baudelaire?

Want to learn more idiomatic expressions that contain verbs? Look at pages 530–542.

to reduce, to decrease, to diminish

The Seven Simple Tenses		The Seven Compound Tenses	
Singular	Plural	Singular	Plural

1   présent de l'indicatif

		8 passé composé	
réduis	réduisons	ai réduit	avons réduit
réduis	réduisez	as réduit	avez réduit
réduit	réduisent	a réduit	ont réduit

2   imparfait de l'indicatif

		9 plus-que-parfait de l'indicatif	
réduisais	réduisions	avais réduit	avions réduit
réduisais	réduisiez	avais réduit	aviez réduit
réduisait	réduisaient	avait réduit	avaient réduit

3   passé simple

		10 passé antérieur	
réduisis	réduisîmes	eus réduit	eûmes réduit
réduisis	réduisîtes	eus réduit	eûtes réduit
réduisit	réduisirent	eut réduit	eurent réduit

4   futur

		11 futur antérieur	
réduirai	réduirons	aurai réduit	aurons réduit
réduiras	réduirez	auras réduit	aurez réduit
réduira	réduiront	aura réduit	auront réduit

5   conditionnel

		12 conditionnel passé	
réduirais	réduirions	aurais réduit	aurions réduit
réduirais	réduiriez	aurais réduit	auriez réduit
réduirait	réduiraient	aurait réduit	auraient réduit

6   présent du subjonctif

		13 passé du subjonctif	
réduise	réduisions	aie réduit	ayons réduit
réduises	réduisiez	aies réduit	ayez réduit
réduise	réduisent	ait réduit	aient réduit

7   imparfait du subjonctif

		14 plus-que-parfait du subjonctif	
réduisisse	réduisissions	eusse réduit	eussions réduit
réduisisses	réduisissiez	eusses réduit	eussiez réduit
réduisît	réduisissent	eût réduit	eussent réduit

Impératif
réduis
réduisons
réduisez

Words and expressions related to this verb
une réduction   reduction, decrease
réductible   reducible
une tête réduite   shrunken head

la réductibilité   reductibility
se réduire à   to be reduced to
à prix réduit   at a reduced price

See also **conduire, déduire, introduire, produire, reproduire, séduire,** and **traduire.**

Consult the back pages for over 1,100 verbs conjugated like model verbs among the 501 in this book.

How are you doing? Find out with the verb drills and tests with answers explained on pages 622–673.

réfléchir

Part. pr. **réfléchissant**   Part. passé **réfléchi**

to think, to meditate, to reflect, to ponder

The Seven Simple Tenses		The Seven Compound Tenses	
Singular	Plural	Singular	Plural
1 présent de l'indicatif		**8 passé composé**	
réfléchis	réfléchissons	ai réfléchi	avons réfléchi
réfléchis	réfléchissez	as réfléchi	avez réfléchi
réfléchit	réfléchissent	a réfléchi	ont réfléchi
2 imparfait de l'indicatif		**9 plus-que-parfait de l'indicatif**	
réfléchissais	réfléchissions	avais réfléchi	avions réfléchi
réfléchissais	réfléchissiez	avais réfléchi	aviez réfléchi
réfléchissait	réfléchissaient	avait réfléchi	avaient réfléchi
3 passé simple		**10 passé antérieur**	
réfléchis	réfléchîmes	eus réfléchi	eûmes réfléchi
réfléchis	réfléchîtes	eus réfléchi	eûtes réfléchi
réfléchit	réfléchirent	eut réfléchi	eurent réfléchi
4 futur		**11 futur antérieur**	
réfléchirai	réfléchirons	aurai réfléchi	aurons réfléchi
réfléchiras	réfléchirez	auras réfléchi	aurez réfléchi
réfléchira	réfléchiront	aura réfléchi	auront réfléchi
5 conditionnel		**12 conditionnel passé**	
réfléchirais	réfléchirions	aurais réfléchi	aurions réfléchi
réfléchirais	réfléchiriez	aurais réfléchi	auriez réfléchi
réfléchirait	réfléchiraient	aurait réfléchi	auraient réfléchi
6 présent du subjonctif		**13 passé du subjonctif**	
réfléchisse	réfléchissions	aie réfléchi	ayons réfléchi
réfléchisses	réfléchissiez	aies réfléchi	ayez réfléchi
réfléchisse	réfléchissent	ait réfléchi	aient réfléchi
7 imparfait du subjonctif		**14 plus-que-parfait du subjonctif**	
réfléchisse	réfléchissions	eusse réfléchi	eussions réfléchi
réfléchisses	réfléchissiez	eusses réfléchi	eussiez réfléchi
réfléchît	réfléchissent	eût réfléchi	eussent réfléchi

Impératif
réfléchis
réfléchissons
réfléchissez

Sentences using this verb and expressions related to it
Mathide: Yvette, vas-tu au bal samedi soir?
Yvette: Je ne sais pas si j'y vais. Je demande à réfléchir.
Mathilde: Bon, alors, réfléchis avant de me donner ta réponse.

réfléchir à qqch   to think over (ponder) something
Il faut que j'y réfléchisse   I must think it over.
réfléchir avant de parler   to think before speaking
La mer réfléchit le ciel   The sea reflects the sky.
un reflet   reflection
tout bien réfléchi   after careful thought

Review the Subjunctive clearly and simply on pages 560–565.

The Seven Simple Tenses		The Seven Compound Tenses	
Singular	Plural	Singular	Plural
1 présent de l'indicatif		**8 passé composé**	
refuse	refusons	ai refusé	avons refusé
refuses	refusez	as refusé	avez refusé
refuse	refusent	a refusé	ont refusé
2 imparfait de l'indicatif		**9 plus-que-parfait de l'indicatif**	
refusais	refusions	avais refusé	avions refusé
refusais	refusiez	avais refusé	aviez refusé
refusait	refusaient	avait refusé	avaient refusé
3 passé simple		**10 passé antérieur**	
refusai	refusâmes	eus refusé	eûmes refusé
refusas	refusâtes	eus refusé	eûtes refusé
refusa	refusèrent	eut refusé	eurent refusé
4 futur		**11 futur antérieur**	
refuserai	refuserons	aurai refusé	aurons refusé
refuseras	refuserez	auras refusé	aurez refusé
refusera	refuseront	aura refusé	auront refusé
5 conditionnel		**12 conditionnel passé**	
refuserais	refuserions	aurais refusé	aurions refusé
refuserais	refuseriez	aurais refusé	auriez refusé
refuserait	refuseraient	aurait refusé	auraient refusé
6 présent du subjonctif		**13 passé du subjonctif**	
refuse	refusions	aie refusé	ayons refusé
refuses	refusiez	aies refusé	ayez refusé
refuse	refusent	ait refusé	aient refusé
7 imparfait du subjonctif		**14 plus-que-parfait du subjonctif**	
refusasse	refusassions	eusse refusé	eussions refusé
refusasses	refusassiez	eusses refusé	eussiez refusé
refusât	refusassent	eût refusé	eussent refusé

Impératif
refuse
refusons
refusez

Sentences using this verb and words related to it

Je refuse absolument de vous écouter. Sortez, s'il vous plaît! Si vous refusez, vous le regretterez.

refuser de faire qqch   to refuse to do something
se refuser qqch   to deny oneself something
refusable   refusable
un refus   refusal

refuser l'entrée à qqn   to turn someone away
refuser la vie routinière   to refuse a routine life
Elle a été refusée   She was refused.

Use the EE-zee guide to French pronunciation on pages 566 and 567.

regarder

Part. pr. regardant   Part. passé **regardé**

to look (at), to watch

The Seven Simple Tenses		The Seven Compound Tenses	
Singular	Plural	Singular	Plural
1 présent de l'indicatif		**8 passé composé**	
regarde	regardons	ai regardé	avons regardé
regardes	regardez	as regardé	avez regardé
regarde	regardent	a regardé	ont regardé
2 imparfait de l'indicatif		**9 plus-que-parfait de l'indicatif**	
regardais	regardions	avais regardé	avions regardé
regardais	regardiez	avais regardé	aviez regardé
regardait	regardaient	avait regardé	avaient regardé
3 passé simple		**10 passé antérieur**	
regardai	regardâmes	eus regardé	eûmes regardé
regardas	regardâtes	eus regardé	eûtes regardé
regarda	regardèrent	eut regardé	eurent regardé
4 futur		**11 futur antérieur**	
regarderai	regarderons	aurai regardé	aurons regardé
regarderas	regarderez	auras regardé	aurez regardé
regardera	regarderont	aura regardé	auront regardé
5 conditionnel		**12 conditionnel passé**	
regarderais	regarderions	aurais regardé	aurions regardé
regarderais	regarderiez	aurais regardé	auriez regardé
regarderait	regarderaient	aurait regardé	auraient regardé
6 présent du subjonctif		**13 passé du subjonctif**	
regarde	regardions	aie regardé	ayons regardé
regardes	regardiez	aies regardé	ayez regardé
regarde	regardent	ait regardé	aient regardé
7 imparfait du subjonctif		**14 plus-que-parfait du subjonctif**	
regardasse	regardassions	eusse regardé	eussions regardé
regardasses	regardassiez	eusses regardé	eussiez regardé
regardât	regardassent	eût regardé	eussent regardé

Impératif
regarde
regardons
regardez

Sentences using this verb and words related to it
—**Qu'est-ce que tu regardes, Bernard?**
—**Je regarde le ciel. Il est beau et clair.**
—**Pourquoi ne me regardes-tu pas?**

regarder qqch   to look at (to watch) something;   **regarder la télé**   to watch TV
un regard   glance, look;   **au regard de**   compared to, with regard to

Consult page 553 for the section on verbs that do not require a preposition.

384

The Seven Simple Tenses		The Seven Compound Tenses	
Singular	Plural	Singular	Plural

1 présent de l'indicatif		8 passé composé	
regrette	regrettons	ai regretté	avons regretté
regrettes	regrettez	as regretté	avez regretté
regrette	regrettent	a regretté	ont regretté

2 imparfait de l'indicatif		9 plus-que-parfait de l'indicatif	
regrettais	regrettions	avais regretté	avions regretté
regrettais	regrettiez	avais regretté	aviez regretté
regrettait	regrettaient	avait regretté	avaient regretté

3 passé simple		10 passé antérieur	
regrettai	regrettâmes	eus regretté	eûmes regretté
regrettas	regrettâtes	eus regretté	eûtes regretté
regretta	regrettèrent	eut regretté	eurent regretté

4 futur		11 futur antérieur	
regretterai	regretterons	aurai regretté	aurons regretté
regretteras	regretterez	auras regretté	aurez regretté
regrettera	regretteront	aura regretté	auront regretté

5 conditionnel		12 conditionnel passé	
regretterais	regretterions	aurais regretté	aurions regretté
regretterais	regretteriez	aurais regretté	auriez regretté
regretterait	regretteraient	aurait regretté	auraient regretté

6 présent du subjonctif		13 passé du subjonctif	
regrette	regrettions	aie regretté	ayons regretté
regrettes	regrettiez	aies regretté	ayez regretté
regrette	regrettent	ait regretté	aient regretté

7 imparfait du subjonctif		14 plus-que-parfait du subjonctif	
regrettasse	regrettassions	eusse regretté	eussions regretté
regrettasses	regrettassiez	eusses regretté	eussiez regretté
regrettât	regrettassent	eût regretté	eussent regretté

Impératif
regrette
regrettons
regrettez

Common idiomatic expressions using this verb and words related to it
regretter d'avoir fait qqch   to regret (to be sorry for) having done something
regrettable   regrettable; **Il est regrettable que + subjunctive**   It is regrettable (It is a pity)
   that . . .
Je ne regrette rien   I regret nothing.
un regret   regret; **avoir regret de qqch**   to regret something, to feel sorry about something

It's important that you be familiar with the Subjunctive. See pages 560–565.

relire

Part. pr. **relisant**   Part. passé **relu**

to read again, to reread

The Seven Simple Tenses		The Seven Compound Tenses	
Singular	Plural	Singular	Plural
1 présent de l'indicatif		**8 passé composé**	
relis	relisons	ai relu	avons relu
relis	relisez	as relu	avez relu
relit	relisent	a relu	ont relu
2 imparfait de l'indicatif		**9 plus-que-parfait de l'indicatif**	
relisais	relisions	avais relu	avions relu
relisais	relisiez	avais relu	aviez relu
relisait	relisaient	avait relu	avaient relu
3 passé simple		**10 passé antérieur**	
relus	relûmes	eus relu	eûmes relu
relus	relûtes	eus relu	eûtes relu
relut	relurent	eut relu	eurent relu
4 futur		**11 futur antérieur**	
relirai	relirons	aurai relu	aurons relu
reliras	relirez	auras relu	aurez relu
relira	reliront	aura relu	auront relu
5 conditionnel		**12 conditionnel passé**	
relirais	relirions	aurais relu	aurions relu
relirais	reliriez	aurais relu	auriez relu
relirait	reliraient	aurait relu	auraient relu
6 présent du subjonctif		**13 passé du subjonctif**	
relise	relisions	aie relu	ayons relu
relises	relisiez	aies relu	ayez relu
relise	relisent	ait relu	aient relu
7 imparfait du subjonctif		**14 plus-que-parfait du subjonctif**	
relusse	relussions	eusse relu	eussions relu
relusses	relussiez	eusses relu	eussiez relu
relût	relussent	eût relu	eussent relu

Impératif
relis
relisons
relisez

Words and expressions related to this verb
lire to read
la lecture reading; reading selection
la relecture rereading

relire une composition en vue de la corriger
to reread a composition for the purpose of
correcting it

For other words related to this verb see **lire.**

Grammar putting you in a tense mood? Review the definitions of basic grammatical terms on
pages 674–688.

to remark, to notice, to observe, to distinguish

The Seven Simple Tenses		The Seven Compound Tenses	
Singular	Plural	Singular	Plural
1 présent de l'indicatif		8 passé composé	
remarque	remarquons	ai remarqué	avons remarqué
remarques	remarquez	as remarqué	avez remarqué
remarque	remarquent	a remarqué	ont remarqué
2 imparfait de l'indicatif		9 plus-que-parfait de l'indicatif	
remarquais	remarquions	avais remarqué	avions remarqué
remarquais	remarquiez	avais remarqué	aviez remarqué
remarquait	remarquaient	avait remarqué	avaient remarqué
3 passé simple		10 passé antérieur	
remarquai	remarquâmes	eus remarqué	eûmes remarqué
remarquas	remarquâtes	eus remarqué	eûtes remarqué
remarqua	remarquèrent	eut remarqué	eurent remarqué
4 futur		11 futur antérieur	
remarquerai	remarquerons	aurai remarqué	aurons remarqué
remarqueras	remarquerez	auras remarqué	aurez remarqué
remarquera	remarqueront	aura remarqué	auront remarqué
5 conditionnel		12 conditionnel passé	
remarquerais	remarquerions	aurais remarqué	aurions remarqué
remarquerais	remarqueriez	aurais remarqué	auriez remarqué
remarquerait	remarqueraient	aurait remarqué	auraient remarqué
6 présent du subjonctif		13 passé du subjonctif	
remarque	remarquions	aie remarqué	ayons remarqué
remarques	remarquiez	aies remarqué	ayez remarqué
remarque	remarquent	ait remarqué	aient remarqué
7 imparfait du subjonctif		14 plus-que-parfait du subjonctif	
remarquasse	remarquassions	eusse remarqué	eussions remarqué
remarquasses	remarquassiez	eusses remarqué	eussiez remarqué
remarquât	remarquassent	eût remarqué	eussent remarqué

Impératif
remarque
remarquons
remarquez

Words and expressions related to this verb

une remarque   remark, observation, comment;
  marquer   to mark
faire remarquer qqch à qqn   to bring
  something to someone's attention, to point
  out something to someone

se faire remarquer   to make oneself noticed,
  draw attention
remarquable   remarkable

Want to learn more idiomatic expressions that contain verbs? Look at pages 530–542.

The subject pronouns are found on the page facing page 1.

to thank

The Seven Simple Tenses		The Seven Compound Tenses	
Singular	Plural	Singular	Plural
1　présent de l'indicatif		**8　passé composé**	
remercie	remercions	ai remercié	avons remercié
remercies	remerciez	as remercié	avez remercié
remercie	remercient	a remercié	ont remercié
2　imparfait de l'indicatif		**9　plus-que-parfait de l'indicatif**	
remerciais	remerciions	avais remercié	avions remercié
remerciais	remerciiez	avais remercié	aviez remercié
remerciait	remerciaient	avait remercié	avaient remercié
3　passé simple		**10　passé antérieur**	
remerciai	remerciâmes	eus remercié	eûmes remercié
remercias	remerciâtes	eus remercié	eûtes remercié
remercia	remercièrent	eut remercié	eurent remercié
4　futur		**11　futur antérieur**	
remercierai	remercierons	aurai remercié	aurons remercié
remercieras	remercierez	auras remercié	aurez remercié
remerciera	remercieront	aura remercié	auront remercié
5　conditionnel		**12　conditionnel passé**	
remercierais	remercierions	aurais remercié	aurions remercié
remercierais	remercieriez	aurais remercié	auriez remercié
remercierait	remercieraient	aurait remercié	auraient remercié
6　présent du subjonctif		**13　passé du subjonctif**	
remercie	remerciions	aie remercié	ayons remercié
remercies	remerciiez	aies remercié	ayez remercié
remercie	remercient	ait remercié	aient remercié
7　imparfait du subjonctif		**14　plus-que-parfait du subjonctif**	
remerciasse	remerciassions	eusse remercié	eussions remercié
remerciasses	remerciassiez	eusses remercié	eussiez remercié
remerciât	remerciassent	eût remercié	eussent remercié

Impératif
remercie
remercions
remerciez

Common idiomatic expressions using this verb and words related to it

remercier qqn de qqch　to thank someone for something;　**Je vous remercie de votre aimable invitation**　I thank you for your kind invitation.

un remerciement　acknowledgment, thanks

Merci!　Thank you!
Merci bien!　Thank you very much!
sans merci　without mercy, mercilessly
être à la merci de　to be at the mercy of;
　la merci　mercy, good will

Taking a trip? Check out the popular words, phrases, and expressions for travelers on pages 599–621.

to put (on) again, to replace, to put back, to give back, to postpone

The Seven Simple Tenses		The Seven Compound Tenses	
Singular	Plural	Singular	Plural
1 présent de l'indicatif		**8 passé composé**	
remets	remettons	ai remis	avons remis
remets	remettez	as remis	avez remis
remet	remettent	a remis	ont remis
2 imparfait de l'indicatif		**9 plus-que-parfait de l'indicatif**	
remettais	remettions	avais remis	avions remis
remettais	remettiez	avais remis	aviez remis
remettait	remettaient	avait remis	avaient remis
3 passé simple		**10 passé antérieur**	
remis	remîmes	eus remis	eûmes remis
remis	remîtes	eus remis	eûtes remis
remit	remirent	eut remis	eurent remis
4 futur		**11 futur antérieur**	
remettrai	remettrons	aurai remis	aurons remis
remettras	remettrez	auras remis	aurez remis
remettra	remettront	aura remis	auront remis
5 conditionnel		**12 conditionnel passé**	
remettrais	remettrions	aurais remis	aurions remis
remettrais	remettriez	aurais remis	auriez remis
remettrait	remettraient	aurait remis	auraient remis
6 présent du subjonctif		**13 passé du subjonctif**	
remette	remettions	aie remis	ayons remis
remettes	remettiez	aies remis	ayez remis
remette	remettent	ait remis	aient remis
7 imparfait du subjonctif		**14 plus-que-parfait du subjonctif**	
remisse	remissions	eusse remis	eussions remis
remisses	remissiez	eusses remis	eussiez remis
remît	remissent	eût remis	eussent remis

Impératif
remets
remettons
remettez

Sentences using this verb and words and expressions related to it
—**Où avez-vous remis les fleurs que je vous ai données?**
—**Je les ai remises là-bas. Ne les voyez-vous pas?**

se remettre de   to recover from
se remettre à faire qqch   to start to do
   something again
s'en remettre à   to depend on, to rely on

Remettez-vous!   Pull yourself together!
une remise   remittance, postponement,
   discount

See also **commettre, mettre, se mettre, omettre, permettre, promettre, soumettre,** and
transmettre.

remplacer

Part. pr. **remplaçant**   Part. passé **remplacé**

to replace

The Seven Simple Tenses		The Seven Compound Tenses	
Singular	Plural	Singular	Plural
1 présent de l'indicatif		**8 passé composé**	
remplace	remplaçons	ai remplacé	avons remplacé
remplaces	remplacez	as remplacé	avez remplacé
remplace	remplacent	a remplacé	ont remplacé
2 imparfait de l'indicatif		**9 plus-que-parfait de l'indicatif**	
remplaçais	remplacions	avais remplacé	avions remplacé
remplaçais	remplaciez	avais remplacé	aviez remplacé
remplaçait	remplaçaient	avait remplacé	avaient remplacé
3 passé simple		**10 passé antérieur**	
remplaçai	remplaçâmes	eus remplacé	eûmes remplacé
remplaças	remplaçâtes	eus remplacé	eûtes remplacé
remplaça	remplacèrent	eut remplacé	eurent remplacé
4 futur		**11 futur antérieur**	
remplacerai	remplacerons	aurai remplacé	aurons remplacé
remplaceras	remplacerez	auras remplacé	aurez remplacé
remplacera	remplaceront	aura remplacé	auront remplacé
5 conditionnel		**12 conditionnel passé**	
remplacerais	remplacerions	aurais remplacé	aurions remplacé
remplacerais	remplaceriez	aurais remplacé	auriez remplacé
remplacerait	remplaceraient	aurait remplacé	auraient remplacé
6 présent du subjonctif		**13 passé du subjonctif**	
remplace	remplacions	aie remplacé	ayons remplacé
remplaces	remplaciez	aies remplacé	ayez remplacé
remplace	remplacent	ait remplacé	aient remplacé
7 imparfait du subjonctif		**14 plus-que-parfait du subjonctif**	
remplaçasse	remplaçassions	eusse remplacé	eussions remplacé
remplaçasses	remplaçassiez	eusses remplacé	eussiez remplacé
remplaçât	remplaçassent	eût remplacé	eussent remplacé

Impératif
remplace
remplaçons
remplacez

Words and expressions related to this verb

remplacer par to replace with
un remplacement replacement (thing)
un remplaçant, une remplaçante
 replacement (person), substitute

remplaçable replaceable; **irremplaçable**
 irreplaceable
en remplacement de in place of

See also **placer.**

Use the EE-zee guide to French pronunciation on pages 566 and 567.

to fill, to fulfill, to fill in, to fill out

The Seven Simple Tenses		The Seven Compound Tenses	
Singular	Plural	Singular	Plural
1 présent de l'indicatif		8 passé composé	
remplis	remplissons	ai rempli	avons rempli
remplis	remplissez	as rempli	avez rempli
remplit	remplissent	a rempli	ont rempli
2 imparfait de l'indicatif		9 plus-que-parfait de l'indicatif	
remplissais	remplissions	avais rempli	avions rempli
remplissais	remplissiez	avais rempli	aviez rempli
remplissait	remplissaient	avait rempli	avaient rempli
3 passé simple		10 passé antérieur	
remplis	remplîmes	eus rempli	eûmes rempli
remplis	remplîtes	eus rempli	eûtes rempli
remplit	remplirent	eut rempli	eurent rempli
4 futur		11 futur antérieur	
remplirai	remplirons	aurai rempli	aurons rempli
rempliras	remplirez	auras rempli	aurez rempli
remplira	rempliront	aura rempli	auront rempli
5 conditionnel		12 conditionnel passé	
remplirais	remplirions	aurais rempli	aurions rempli
remplirais	rempliriez	aurais rempli	auriez rempli
remplirait	rempliraient	aurait rempli	auraient rempli
6 présent du subjonctif		13 passé du subjonctif	
remplisse	remplissions	aie rempli	ayons rempli
remplisses	remplissiez	aies rempli	ayez rempli
remplisse	remplissent	ait rempli	aient rempli
7 imparfait du subjonctif		14 plus-que-parfait du subjonctif	
remplisse	remplissions	eusse rempli	eussions rempli
remplisses	remplissiez	eusses rempli	eussiez rempli
remplît	remplissent	eût rempli	eussent rempli

Impératif
remplis
remplissons
remplissez

Words and expressions related to this verb

remplir de   to fill with
remplir qqch de qqch   to fill something with
  something
se remplir   to fill up
un remplissage   filling up
emplir   to fill

remplir des conditions   to fulfill
  requirements, conditions
remplir une tâche   to carry out (perform) a
  task
remplir quelqu'un d'admiration   to fill
  someone with admiration

Grammar putting you in a tense mood? Review the definitions of basic grammatical terms on pages 674–688.

to meet, to encounter

The Seven Simple Tenses		The Seven Compound Tenses	
Singular	Plural	Singular	Plural
1 présent de l'indicatif		**8 passé composé**	
rencontre	rencontrons	ai rencontré	avons rencontré
rencontres	rencontrez	as rencontré	avez rencontré
rencontre	rencontrent	a rencontré	ont rencontré
2 imparfait de l'indicatif		**9 plus-que-parfait de l'indicatif**	
rencontrais	rencontrions	avais rencontré	avions rencontré
rencontrais	rencontriez	avais rencontré	aviez rencontré
rencontrait	rencontraient	avait rencontré	avaient rencontré
3 passé simple		**10 passé antérieur**	
rencontrai	rencontrâmes	eus rencontré	eûmes rencontré
rencontras	rencontrâtes	eus rencontré	eûtes rencontré
rencontra	rencontrèrent	eut rencontré	eurent rencontré
4 futur		**11 futur antérieur**	
rencontrerai	rencontrerons	aurai rencontré	aurons rencontré
rencontreras	rencontrerez	auras rencontré	aurez rencontré
rencontrera	rencontreront	aura rencontré	auront rencontré
5 conditionnel		**12 conditionnel passé**	
rencontrerais	rencontrerions	aurais rencontré	aurions rencontré
rencontrerais	rencontreriez	aurais rencontré	auriez rencontré
rencontrerait	rencontreraient	aurait rencontré	auraient rencontré
6 présent du subjonctif		**13 passé du subjonctif**	
rencontre	rencontrions	aie rencontré	ayons rencontré
rencontres	rencontriez	aies rencontré	ayez rencontré
rencontre	rencontrent	ait rencontré	aient rencontré
7 imparfait du subjonctif		**14 plus-que-parfait du subjonctif**	
rencontrasse	rencontrassions	eusse rencontré	eussions rencontré
rencontrasses	rencontrassiez	eusses rencontré	eussiez rencontré
rencontrât	rencontrassent	eût rencontré	eussent rencontré

Impératif
rencontre
rencontrons
rencontrez

Words and expressions related to this verb
se rencontrer to meet each other
une rencontre encounter, meeting
aller à la rencontre de qqn to go to meet someone
rencontrer par hasard to meet someone by chance (bump into)

une rencontre au sommet summit meeting
faire une rencontre inattendue to have an unexpected encounter
de mauvaises rencontres the wrong sort of people

Going away? Don't forget to check out the practical situations for travelers on pages 568–598.

to give back, to return (something), to render; to vomit

The Seven Simple Tenses		The Seven Compound Tenses	
Singular	Plural	Singular	Plural
1 présent de l'indicatif		**8 passé composé**	
rends	**rendons**	**ai rendu**	**avons rendu**
rends	**rendez**	**as rendu**	**avez rendu**
rend	**rendent**	**a rendu**	**ont rendu**
2 imparfait de l'indicatif		**9 plus-que-parfait de l'indicatif**	
rendais	**rendions**	**avais rendu**	**avions rendu**
rendais	**rendiez**	**avais rendu**	**aviez rendu**
rendait	**rendaient**	**avait rendu**	**avaient rendu**
3 passé simple		**10 passé antérieur**	
rendis	**rendîmes**	**eus rendu**	**eûmes rendu**
rendis	**rendîtes**	**eus rendu**	**eûtes rendu**
rendit	**rendirent**	**eut rendu**	**eurent rendu**
4 futur		**11 futur antérieur**	
rendrai	**rendrons**	**aurai rendu**	**aurons rendu**
rendras	**rendrez**	**auras rendu**	**aurez rendu**
rendra	**rendront**	**aura rendu**	**auront rendu**
5 conditionnel		**12 conditionnel passé**	
rendrais	**rendrions**	**aurais rendu**	**aurions rendu**
rendrais	**rendriez**	**aurais rendu**	**auriez rendu**
rendrait	**rendraient**	**aurait rendu**	**auraient rendu**
6 présent du subjonctif		**13 passé du subjonctif**	
rende	**rendions**	**aie rendu**	**ayons rendu**
rendes	**rendiez**	**aies rendu**	**ayez rendu**
rende	**rendent**	**ait rendu**	**aient rendu**
7 imparfait du subjonctif		**14 plus-que-parfait du subjonctif**	
rendisse	**rendissions**	**eusse rendu**	**eussions rendu**
rendisses	**rendissiez**	**eusses rendu**	**eussiez rendu**
rendît	**rendissent**	**eût rendu**	**eussent rendu**

Impératif
rends
rendons
rendez

Words and expressions related to this verb
un rendez-vous appointment, date
un compte rendu report, account
se rendre à to surrender to, to go to
se rendre compte de to realize
rendre un service à qqn to do someone a favor
rendre qqn + adj. to make someone + adj.
Elle a rendu tout ce qu'elle a mangé She vomited everything she ate.
J'ai rendu le livre à la bibliothèque I returned the book to the library.

fixer un rendez-vous to make an appointment, a date
rendre grâce à qqn to give thanks to someone
rendre service à qqn to be of service to someone
rendre compte de qqch to give an account of something
rendre justice to uphold justice
rendre qqch to return something
se rendre aux urnes to vote

The subject pronouns are found on the page facing page 1.

rentrer

Part. pr. **rentrant**   Part. passé **rentré(e)(s)**

to return

The Seven Simple Tenses		The Seven Compound Tenses	
Singular	Plural	Singular	Plural
1 présent de l'indicatif		**8 passé composé**	
rentre	rentrons	suis rentré(e)	sommes rentré(e)s
rentres	rentrez	es rentré(e)	êtes rentré(e)(s)
rentre	rentrent	est rentré(e)	sont rentré(e)s
2 imparfait de l'indicatif		**9 plus-que-parfait de l'indicatif**	
rentrais	rentrions	étais rentré(e)	étions rentré(e)s
rentrais	rentriez	étais rentré(e)	étiez rentré(e)(s)
rentrait	rentraient	était rentré(e)	étaient rentré(e)s
3 passé simple		**10 passé antérieur**	
rentrai	rentrâmes	fus rentré(e)	fûmes rentré(e)s
rentras	rentrâtes	fus rentré(e)	fûtes rentré(e)(s)
rentra	rentrèrent	fut rentré(e)	furent rentré(e)s
4 futur		**11 futur antérieur**	
rentrerai	rentrerons	serai rentré(e)	serons rentré(e)s
rentreras	rentrerez	seras rentré(e)	serez rentré(e)(s)
rentrera	rentreront	sera rentré(e)	seront rentré(e)s
5 conditionnel		**12 conditionnel passé**	
rentrerais	rentrerions	serais rentré(e)	serions rentré(e)s
rentrerais	rentreriez	serais rentré(e)	seriez rentré(e)(s)
rentrerait	rentreraient	serait rentré(e)	seraient rentré(e)s
6 présent du subjonctif		**13 passé du subjonctif**	
rentre	rentrions	sois rentré(e)	soyons rentré(e)s
rentres	rentriez	sois rentré(e)	soyez rentré(e)(s)
rentre	rentrent	soit rentré(e)	soient rentré(e)s
7 imparfait du subjonctif		**14 plus-que-parfait du subjonctif**	
rentrasse	rentrassions	fusse rentré(e)	fussions rentré(e)s
rentrasses	rentrassiez	fusses rentré(e)	fussiez rentré(e)(s)
rentrât	rentrassent	fût rentré(e)	fussent rentré(e)s

Impératif
rentre
rentrons
rentrez

Words and expressions related to this verb

rentrer chez soi   to go back home
rentrer les enfants   to take the children home
rentrer ses larmes   to hold back one's tears

la rentrée   return, homecoming
la rentrée des classes   back to school

See also **entrer.** Review page viii.

> This verb is conjugated with **avoir** when it has a direct object.
>
> Example: **Elle a rentré le chat dans la maison**   She brought (took) the cat into the house.
> BUT: **Elle est rentrée tôt**   She returned home early.

to spread, to scatter, to spill

The Seven Simple Tenses		The Seven Compound Tenses	
Singular	Plural	Singular	Plural
1 présent de l'indicatif		**8 passé composé**	
répands	**répandons**	**ai répandu**	**avons répandu**
répands	**répandez**	**as répandu**	**avez répandu**
répand	**répandent**	**a répandu**	**ont répandu**
2 imparfait de l'indicatif		**9 plus-que-parfait de l'indicatif**	
répandais	**répandions**	**avais répandu**	**avions répandu**
répandais	**répandiez**	**avais répandu**	**aviez répandu**
répandait	**répandaient**	**avait répandu**	**avaient répandu**
3 passé simple		**10 passé antérieur**	
répandis	**répandîmes**	**eus répandu**	**eûmes répandu**
répandis	**répandîtes**	**eus répandu**	**eûtes répandu**
répandit	**répandirent**	**eut répandu**	**eurent répandu**
4 futur		**11 futur antérieur**	
répandrai	**répandrons**	**aurai répandu**	**aurons répandu**
répandras	**répandrez**	**auras répandu**	**aurez répandu**
répandra	**répandront**	**aura répandu**	**auront répandu**
5 conditionnel		**12 conditionnel passé**	
répandrais	**répandrions**	**aurais répandu**	**aurions répandu**
répandrais	**répandriez**	**aurais répandu**	**auriez répandu**
répandrait	**répandraient**	**aurait répandu**	**auraient répandu**
6 présent du subjonctif		**13 passé du subjonctif**	
répande	**répandions**	**aie répandu**	**ayons répandu**
répandes	**répandiez**	**aies répandu**	**ayez répandu**
répande	**répandent**	**ait répandu**	**aient répandu**
7 imparfait du subjonctif		**14 plus-que-parfait du subjonctif**	
répandisse	**répandissions**	**eusse répandu**	**eussions répandu**
répandisses	**répandissiez**	**eusses répandu**	**eussiez répandu**
répandît	**répandissent**	**eût répandu**	**eussent répandu**

Impératif
répands
répandons
répandez

Words and expressions related to this verb
répandre l'effroi to spread fear
une personne répandue widely known
person
une opinion répandue widely accepted
opinion

répandre du sang to shed blood
répandre une nouvelle to spread news
se répandre en injures to pour out insults
répandre la joie to spread joy

Consult the sections on verbs used in idiomatic expressions, verbs with prepositions, and the list
of over 1,100 verbs conjugated like model verbs in the back pages.

The subject pronouns are found on the page facing page 1.

reparaître

to reappear, to appear again

The Seven Simple Tenses		The Seven Compound Tenses	
Singular	Plural	Singular	Plural
1 présent de l'indicatif		**8 passé composé**	
reparais	reparaissons	ai reparu	avons reparu
reparais	reparaissez	as reparu	avez reparu
reparaît	reparaissent	a reparu	ont reparu
2 imparfait de l'indicatif		**9 plus-que-parfait de l'indicatif**	
reparaissais	reparaissions	avais reparu	avions reparu
reparaissais	reparaissiez	avais reparu	aviez reparu
reparaissait	reparaissaient	avait reparu	avaient reparu
3 passé simple		**10 passé antérieur**	
reparus	reparûmes	eus reparu	eûmes reparu
reparus	reparûtes	eus reparu	eûtes reparu
reparut	reparurent	eut reparu	eurent reparu
4 futur		**11 futur antérieur**	
reparaîtrai	reparaîtrons	aurai reparu	aurons reparu
reparaîtras	reparaîtrez	auras reparu	aurez reparu
reparaîtra	reparaîtront	aura reparu	auront reparu
5 conditionnel		**12 conditionnel passé**	
reparaîtrais	reparaîtrions	aurais reparu	aurions reparu
reparaîtrais	reparaîtriez	aurais reparu	auriez reparu
reparaîtrait	reparaîtraient	aurait reparu	auraient reparu
6 présent du subjonctif		**13 passé du subjonctif**	
reparaisse	reparaissions	aie reparu	ayons reparu
reparaisses	reparaissiez	aies reparu	ayez reparu
reparaisse	reparaissent	ait reparu	aient reparu
7 imparfait du subjonctif		**14 plus-que-parfait du subjonctif**	
reparusse	reparussions	eusse reparu	eussions reparu
reparusses	reparussiez	eusses reparu	eussiez reparu
reparût	reparussent	eût reparu	eussent reparu

Impératif
reparais
reparaissons
reparaissez

Words related to this verb
paraître   to appear, to seem
réapparaître   to appear again, to reappear
la réapparition   reappearance

disparaître   to disappear
apparaître   to appear, to come into view

See also **apparaître, disparaître,** and **paraître.**

Going away? Don't forget to check out the practical situations for travelers on pages 568–598.

The Seven Simple Tenses | The Seven Compound Tenses

Singular	Plural		Singular	Plural

1 présent de l'indicatif
répare	réparons
répares	réparez
répare	réparent

8 passé composé
ai réparé	avons réparé
as réparé	avez réparé
a réparé	ont réparé

2 imparfait de l'indicatif
réparais	réparions
réparais	répariez
réparait	réparaient

9 plus-que-parfait de l'indicatif
avais réparé	avions réparé
avais réparé	aviez réparé
avait réparé	avaient réparé

3 passé simple
réparai	réparâmes
réparas	réparâtes
répara	réparèrent

10 passé antérieur
eus réparé	eûmes réparé
eus réparé	eûtes réparé
eut réparé	eurent réparé

4 futur
réparerai	réparerons
répareras	réparerez
réparera	répareront

11 futur antérieur
aurai réparé	aurons réparé
auras réparé	aurez réparé
aura réparé	auront réparé

5 conditionnel
réparerais	réparerions
réparerais	répareriez
réparerait	répareraient

12 conditionnel passé
aurais réparé	aurions réparé
aurais réparé	auriez réparé
aurait réparé	auraient réparé

6 présent du subjonctif
répare	réparions
répares	répariez
répare	réparent

13 passé du subjonctif
aie réparé	ayons réparé
aies réparé	ayez réparé
ait réparé	aient réparé

7 imparfait du subjonctif
réparasse	réparassions
réparasses	réparassiez
réparât	réparassent

14 plus-que-parfait du subjonctif
eusse réparé	eussions réparé
eusses réparé	eussiez réparé
eût réparé	eussent réparé

Impératif
répare
réparons
réparez

Words and expressions related to this verb
faire réparer ses chaussures to have one's shoes repaired
un réparateur, une réparatrice repairer
réparable reparable
irréparable irreparable

réparer une maison to restore a house
la réparation repair, repairing; **en réparation** in repair, under repair
réparer une offense to correct an offense
irréparablement irreparably

How are you doing? Find out with the verb drills and tests with answers explained on pages 622–673.

The subject pronouns are found on the page facing page 1.

to iron, to pass again, to pass by again

The Seven Simple Tenses		The Seven Compound Tenses	
Singular	Plural	Singular	Plural
1　présent de l'indicatif		8　passé composé	
repasse	repassons	ai repassé	avons repassé
repasses	repassez	as repassé	avez repassé
repasse	repassent	a repassé	ont repassé
2　imparfait de l'indicatif		9　plus-que-parfait de l'indicatif	
repassais	repassions	avais repassé	avions repassé
repassais	repassiez	avais repassé	aviez repassé
repassait	repassaient	avait repassé	avaient repassé
3　passé simple		10　passé antérieur	
repassai	repassâmes	eus repassé	eûmes repassé
repassas	repassâtes	eus repassé	eûtes repassé
repassa	repassèrent	eut repassé	eurent repassé
4　futur		11　futur antérieur	
repasserai	repasserons	aurai repassé	aurons repassé
repasseras	repasserez	auras repassé	aurez repassé
repassera	repasseront	aura repassé	auront repassé
5　conditionnel		12　conditionnel passé	
repasserais	repasserions	aurais repassé	aurions repassé
repasserais	repasseriez	aurais repassé	auriez repassé
repasserait	repasseraient	aurait repassé	auraient repassé
6　présent du subjonctif		13　passé du subjonctif	
repasse	repassions	aie repassé	ayons repassé
repasses	repassiez	aies repassé	ayez repassé
repasse	repassent	ait repassé	aient repassé
7　imparfait du subjonctif		14　plus-que-parfait du subjonctif	
repassasse	repassassions	eusse repassé	eussions repassé
repassasses	repassassiez	eusses repassé	eussiez repassé
repassât	repassassent	eût repassé	eussent repassé

Impératif
repasse
repassons
repassez

Common idiomatic expressions using this verb and words related to it

une planche à repasser　ironing board
un fer à repasser　flat iron (for ironing clothes)
passer un examen　to take (sit for) an exam
repasser un examen　to take an exam over again

repasser un couteau, des ciseaux　to sharpen a knife, scissors
repasser une leçon　to review a lesson
repasser une chemise　to iron a shirt
repasser un autre jour　to stop in again another day
du linge à repasser　laundry to iron

See also **passer.**

Taking a trip? Check out the popular words, phrases, and expressions for travelers on pages 599–621.

to repeat, to rehearse

The Seven Simple Tenses		The Seven Compound Tenses	
Singular	Plural	Singular	Plural
1 présent de l'indicatif		**8 passé composé**	
répète	répétons	ai répété	avons répété
répètes	répétez	as répété	avez répété
répète	répètent	a répété	ont répété
2 imparfait de l'indicatif		**9 plus-que-parfait de l'indicatif**	
répétais	répétions	avais répété	avions répété
répétais	répétiez	avais répété	aviez répété
répétait	répétaient	avait répété	avaient répété
3 passé simple		**10 passé antérieur**	
répétai	répétâmes	eus répété	eûmes répété
répétas	répétâtes	eus répété	eûtes répété
répéta	répétèrent	eut répété	eurent répété
4 futur		**11 futur antérieur**	
répéterai	répéterons	aurai répété	aurons répété
répéteras	répéterez	auras répété	aurez répété
répétera	répéteront	aura répété	auront répété
5 conditionnel		**12 conditionnel passé**	
répéterais	répéterions	aurais répété	aurions répété
répéterais	répéteriez	aurais répété	auriez répété
répéterait	répéteraient	aurait répété	auraient répété
6 présent du subjonctif		**13 passé du subjonctif**	
répète	répétions	aie répété	ayons répété
répètes	répétiez	aies répété	ayez répété
répète	répètent	ait répété	aient répété
7 imparfait du subjonctif		**14 plus-que-parfait du subjonctif**	
répétasse	répétassions	eusse répété	eussions répété
répétasses	répétassiez	eusses répété	eussiez répété
répétât	répétassent	eût répété	eussent répété

Impératif
répète
répétons
répétez

Words and expressions related to this verb

répéter une pièce de théâtre   to rehearse a play

une répétition   repetition

La pièce est en répétition   The play is in rehearsal.

se répéter   to repeat oneself; to recur

Soak up some verbs used in weather expressions on pages 557 and 558.

The subject pronouns are found on the page facing page 1.

répondre

Part. pr. **répondant**   Part. passé **répondu**

to respond, to reply, to answer

The Seven Simple Tenses		The Seven Compound Tenses	
Singular	Plural	Singular	Plural
1 présent de l'indicatif		**8 passé composé**	
réponds	répondons	ai répondu	avons répondu
réponds	répondez	as répondu	avez répondu
répond	répondent	a répondu	ont répondu
2 imparfait de l'indicatif		**9 plus-que-parfait de l'indicatif**	
répondais	répondions	avais répondu	avions répondu
répondais	répondiez	avais répondu	aviez répondu
répondait	répondaient	avait répondu	avaient répondu
3 passé simple		**10 passé antérieur**	
répondis	répondîmes	eus répondu	eûmes répondu
répondis	répondîtes	eus répondu	eûtes répondu
répondit	répondirent	eut répondu	eurent répondu
4 futur		**11 futur antérieur**	
répondrai	répondrons	aurai répondu	aurons répondu
répondras	répondrez	auras répondu	aurez répondu
répondra	répondront	aura répondu	auront répondu
5 conditionnel		**12 conditionnel passé**	
répondrais	répondrions	aurais répondu	aurions répondu
répondrais	répondriez	aurais répondu	auriez répondu
répondrait	répondraient	aurait répondu	auraient répondu
6 présent du subjonctif		**13 passé du subjonctif**	
réponde	répondions	aie répondu	ayons répondu
répondes	répondiez	aies répondu	ayez répondu
réponde	répondent	ait répondu	aient répondu
7 imparfait du subjonctif		**14 plus-que-parfait du subjonctif**	
répondisse	répondissions	eusse répondu	eussions répondu
répondisses	répondissiez	eusses répondu	eussiez répondu
répondît	répondissent	eût répondu	eussent répondu

Impératif
réponds
répondons
répondez

Words and expressions related to this verb

répondre à qqn   to answer someone; to reply to someone

répondre de qqn   to be responsible for, to vouch for someone

répondre de qqch   to vouch for something, to guarantee something

une réponse   answer, reply; **en réponse à votre lettre . . .**   in reply to your letter . . .

pour répondre à la question de . . .   in answer to the question of . . .

un répondeur téléphonique   telephone answering machine

Elle m'a répondu en claquant la porte   She answered me by slamming the door.

Get acquainted with what preposition goes with what verb on pages 543–553.

The Seven Simple Tenses		The Seven Compound Tenses	
Singular	Plural	Singular	Plural
1 présent de l'indicatif		**8 passé composé**	
me repose	nous reposons	me suis reposé(e)	nous sommes reposé(e)s
te reposes	vous reposez	t'es reposé(e)	vous êtes reposé(e)(s)
se repose	se reposent	s'est reposé(e)	se sont reposé(e)s
2 imparfait de l'indicatif		**9 plus-que-parfait de l'indicatif**	
me reposais	nous reposions	m'étais reposé(e)	nous étions reposé(e)s
te reposais	vous reposiez	t'étais reposé(e)	vous étiez reposé(e)(s)
se reposait	se reposaient	s'était reposé(e)	s'étaient reposé(e)s
3 passé simple		**10 passé antérieur**	
me reposai	nous reposâmes	me fus reposé(e)	nous fûmes reposé(e)s
te reposas	vous reposâtes	te fus reposé(e)	vous fûtes reposé(e)(s)
se reposa	se reposèrent	se fut reposé(e)	se furent reposé(e)s
4 futur		**11 futur antérieur**	
me reposerai	nous reposerons	me serai reposé(e)	nous serons reposé(e)s
te reposeras	vous reposerez	te seras reposé(e)	vous serez reposé(e)(s)
se reposera	se reposeront	se sera reposé(e)	se seront reposé(e)s
5 conditionnel		**12 conditionnel passé**	
me reposerais	nous reposerions	me serais reposé(e)	nous serions reposé(e)s
te reposerais	vous reposeriez	te serais reposé(e)	vous seriez reposé(e)(s)
se reposerait	se reposeraient	se serait reposé(e)	se seraient reposé(e)s
6 présent du subjonctif		**13 passé du subjonctif**	
me repose	nous reposions	me sois reposé(e)	nous soyons reposé(e)s
te reposes	vous reposiez	te sois reposé(e)	vous soyez reposé(e)(s)
se repose	se reposent	se soit reposé(e)	se soient reposé(e)s
7 imparfait du subjonctif		**14 plus-que-parfait du subjonctif**	
me reposasse	nous reposassions	me fusse reposé(e)	nous fussions reposé(e)s
te reposasses	vous reposassiez	te fusses reposé(e)	vous fussiez reposé(e)(s)
se reposât	se reposassent	se fût reposé(e)	se fussent reposé(e)s

Impératif
repose-toi; ne te repose pas
reposons-nous; ne nous reposons pas
reposez-vous; ne vous reposez pas

Words and expressions related to this verb

reposer   to put down again; **reposer la tête sur**   to rest one's head on; **reposer sur** to be based on

le repos   rest, repose; **Au repos!**   At ease!

se reposer sur qqn, qqch   to put one's trust in someone, something

un repose-pied   footrest; **un repose-bras** armrest

Je suis fatigué; je vais me reposer.   I'm tired; I'm going to rest.

Taking a trip? Check out the popular words, phrases, and expressions for travelers on pages 599–621.

reprendre

Part. pr. **reprenant**   Part. passé **repris**

to take again, to take back, to recover, to resume

The Seven Simple Tenses		The Seven Compound Tenses	
Singular	Plural	Singular	Plural
1 présent de l'indicatif		**8 passé composé**	
reprends	reprenons	ai repris	avons repris
reprends	reprenez	as repris	avez repris
reprend	reprennent	a repris	ont repris
2 imparfait de l'indicatif		**9 plus-que-parfait de l'indicatif**	
reprenais	reprenions	avais repris	avions repris
reprenais	repreniez	avais repris	aviez repris
reprenait	reprenaient	avait repris	avaient repris
3 passé simple		**10 passé antérieur**	
repris	reprîmes	eus repris	eûmes repris
repris	reprîtes	eus repris	eûtes repris
reprit	reprirent	eut repris	eurent repris
4 futur		**11 futur antérieur**	
reprendrai	reprendrons	aurai repris	aurons repris
reprendras	reprendrez	auras repris	aurez repris
reprendra	reprendront	aura repris	auront repris
5 conditionnel		**12 conditionnel passé**	
reprendrais	reprendrions	aurais repris	aurions repris
reprendrais	reprendriez	aurais repris	auriez repris
reprendrait	reprendraient	aurait repris	auraient repris
6 présent du subjonctif		**13 passé du subjonctif**	
reprenne	reprenions	aie repris	ayons repris
reprennes	repreniez	aies repris	ayez repris
reprenne	reprennent	ait repris	aient repris
7 imparfait du subjonctif		**14 plus-que-parfait du subjonctif**	
reprisse	reprissions	eusse repris	eussions repris
reprisses	reprissiez	eusses repris	eussiez repris
reprît	reprissent	eût repris	eussent repris

Impératif
reprends
reprenons
reprenez

Words and expressions related to this verb
reprendre froid   to catch cold again
reprendre ses esprits   to recover one's senses
reprendre le dessus   to regain the upper hand
reprendre ses forces   to recover one's strength

se reprendre   to take hold of oneself, to recover oneself
une reprise   resumption, renewal, repetition (*music*)
à maintes reprises   over and over again

See also **apprendre, comprendre, entreprendre, se méprendre, prendre,** and **surprendre.**

Want to learn more idiomatic expressions that contain verbs? Look at pages 530–542.

The Seven Simple Tenses		The Seven Compound Tenses	
Singular	Plural	Singular	Plural
1 présent de l'indicatif		8 passé composé	
réprimande	**réprimandons**	**ai réprimandé**	**avons réprimandé**
réprimandes	**réprimandez**	**as réprimandé**	**avez réprimandé**
réprimande	**réprimandent**	**a réprimandé**	**ont réprimandé**
2 imparfait de l'indicatif		9 plus-que-parfait de l'indicatif	
réprimandais	**réprimandions**	**avais réprimandé**	**avions réprimandé**
réprimandais	**réprimandiez**	**avais réprimandé**	**aviez réprimandé**
réprimandait	**réprimandaient**	**avait réprimandé**	**avaient réprimandé**
3 passé simple		10 passé antérieur	
réprimandai	**réprimandâmes**	**eus réprimandé**	**eûmes réprimandé**
réprimandas	**réprimandâtes**	**eus réprimandé**	**eûtes réprimandé**
réprimanda	**réprimandèrent**	**eut réprimandé**	**eurent réprimandé**
4 futur		11 futur antérieur	
réprimanderai	**réprimanderons**	**aurai réprimandé**	**aurons réprimandé**
réprimanderas	**réprimanderez**	**auras réprimandé**	**aurez réprimandé**
réprimandera	**réprimanderont**	**aura réprimandé**	**auront réprimandé**
5 conditionnel		12 conditionnel passé	
réprimanderais	**réprimanderions**	**aurais réprimandé**	**aurions réprimandé**
réprimanderais	**réprimanderiez**	**aurais réprimandé**	**auriez réprimandé**
réprimanderait	**réprimanderaient**	**aurait réprimandé**	**auraient réprimandé**
6 présent du subjonctif		13 passé du subjonctif	
réprimande	**réprimandions**	**aie réprimandé**	**ayons réprimandé**
réprimandes	**réprimandiez**	**aies réprimandé**	**ayez réprimandé**
réprimande	**réprimandent**	**ait réprimandé**	**aient réprimandé**
7 imparfait du subjonctif		14 plus-que-parfait du subjonctif	
réprimandasse	**réprimandassions**	**eusse réprimandé**	**eussions réprimandé**
réprimandasses	**réprimandassiez**	**eusses réprimandé**	**eussiez réprimandé**
réprimandât	**réprimandassent**	**eût réprimandé**	**eussent réprimandé**

Impératif
réprimande
réprimandons
réprimandez

Words and expressions related to this verb
une réprimande   reprimand, rebuke
faire des réprimandes   to make rebukes

réprimandable   blameworthy
prononcer une réprimande   to issue a reprimand

If you want to see a sample English verb fully conjugated in all the tenses, check out pages xiii and xiv.

reproduire

Part. pr. reproduisant   **Part. passé reproduit**

to reproduce

The Seven Simple Tenses		The Seven Compound Tenses	
Singular	Plural	Singular	Plural
1 présent de l'indicatif		**8 passé composé**	
reproduis	reproduisons	ai reproduit	avons reproduit
reproduis	reproduisez	as reproduit	avez reproduit
reproduit	reproduisent	a reproduit	ont reproduit
2 imparfait de l'indicatif		**9 plus-que-parfait de l'indicatif**	
reproduisais	reproduisions	avais reproduit	avions reproduit
reproduisais	reproduisiez	avais reproduit	aviez reproduit
reproduisait	reproduisaient	avait reproduit	avaient reproduit
3 passé simple		**10 passé antérieur**	
reproduisis	reproduisîmes	eus reproduit	eûmes reproduit
reproduisis	reproduisîtes	eus reproduit	eûtes reproduit
reproduisit	reproduisirent	eut reproduit	eurent reproduit
4 futur		**11 futur antérieur**	
reproduirai	reproduirons	aurai reproduit	aurons reproduit
reproduiras	reproduirez	auras reproduit	aurez reproduit
reproduira	reproduiront	aura reproduit	auront reproduit
5 conditionnel		**12 conditionnel passé**	
reproduirais	reproduirions	aurais reproduit	aurions reproduit
reproduirais	reproduiriez	aurais reproduit	auriez reproduit
reproduirait	reproduiraient	aurait reproduit	auraient reproduit
6 présent du subjonctif		**13 passé du subjonctif**	
reproduise	reproduisions	aie reproduit	ayons reproduit
reproduises	reproduisiez	aies reproduit	ayez reproduit
reproduise	reproduisent	ait reproduit	aient reproduit
7 imparfait du subjonctif		**14 plus-que-parfait du subjonctif**	
reproduisisse	reproduisissions	eusse reproduit	eussions reproduit
reproduisisses	reproduisissiez	eusses reproduit	eussiez reproduit
reproduisît	reproduisissent	eût reproduit	eussent reproduit

Impératif
reproduis
reproduisons
reproduisez

Words and expressions related to this verb

se reproduire to reproduce itself, to multiply, to recur, to happen again

une reproduction reproduction; **les droits de reproduction** copyright

reproductif, reproductive reproductive

reproductible reproductible

le clonage cloning

cloner to clone

See also **conduire, déduire, introduire, produire, réduire, séduire,** and **traduire.**

Grammar putting you in a tense mood? Review the definitions of basic grammatical terms with examples on pages 674–688.

The Seven Simple Tenses		The Seven Compound Tenses	
Singular	Plural	Singular	Plural
1 présent de l'indicatif		**8 passé composé**	
résous	**résolvons**	**ai résolu**	**avons résolu**
résous	**résolvez**	**as résolu**	**avez résolu**
résout	**résolvent**	**a résolu**	**ont résolu**
2 imparfait de l'indicatif		**9 plus-que-parfait de l'indicatif**	
résolvais	**résolvions**	**avais résolu**	**avions résolu**
résolvais	**résolviez**	**avais résolu**	**aviez résolu**
résolvait	**résolvaient**	**avait résolu**	**avaient résolu**
3 passé simple		**10 passé antérieur**	
résolus	**résolûmes**	**eus résolu**	**eûmes résolu**
résolus	**résolûtes**	**eus résolu**	**eûtes résolu**
résolut	**résolurent**	**eut résolu**	**eurent résolu**
4 futur		**11 futur antérieur**	
résoudrai	**résoudrons**	**aurai résolu**	**aurons résolu**
résoudras	**résoudrez**	**auras résolu**	**aurez résolu**
résoudra	**résoudront**	**aura résolu**	**auront résolu**
5 conditionnel		**12 conditionnel passé**	
résoudrais	**résoudrions**	**aurais résolu**	**aurions résolu**
résoudrais	**résoudriez**	**aurais résolu**	**auriez résolu**
résoudrait	**résoudraient**	**aurait résolu**	**auraient résolu**
6 présent du subjonctif		**13 passé du subjonctif**	
résolve	**résolvions**	**aie résolu**	**ayons résolu**
résolves	**résolviez**	**aies résolu**	**ayez résolu**
résolve	**résolvent**	**ait résolu**	**aient résolu**
7 imparfait du subjonctif		**14 plus-que-parfait du subjonctif**	
résolusse	**résolussions**	**eusse résolu**	**eussions résolu**
résolusses	**résolussiez**	**eusses résolu**	**eussiez résolu**
résolût	**résolussent**	**eût résolu**	**eussent résolu**

Impératif
résous
résolvons
résolvez

Words and expressions related to this verb
se résoudre à to make up one's mind to
résoudre qqn à faire qqch to induce someone to do something
résoudre un problème mathématique to solve a math problem
une résolution resolution

See also **absoudre**.

être résolu(e) à faire qqch to be resolved to doing something
Le feu a résous le bois en cendres The fire has changed the wood into ashes. (The past part. **résous** is used for things that have undergone a physical change.)

Soak up some verbs used in weather expressions on pages 557 and 558.

ressembler

Part. pr. **ressemblant**   Part. passé **ressemblé**

to resemble, to be like, to look like

The Seven Simple Tenses		The Seven Compound Tenses	
Singular	Plural	Singular	Plural
1 présent de l'indicatif		**8 passé composé**	
ressemble	ressemblons	ai ressemblé	avons ressemblé
ressembles	ressemblez	as ressemblé	avez ressemblé
ressemble	ressemblent	a ressemblé	ont ressemblé
2 imparfait de l'indicatif		**9 plus-que-parfait de l'indicatif**	
ressemblais	ressemblions	avais ressemblé	avions ressemblé
ressemblais	ressembliez	avais ressemblé	aviez ressemblé
ressemblait	ressemblaient	avait ressemblé	avaient ressemblé
3 passé simple		**10 passé antérieur**	
ressemblai	ressemblâmes	eus ressemblé	eûmes ressemblé
ressemblas	ressemblâtes	eus ressemblé	eûtes ressemblé
ressembla	ressemblèrent	eut ressemblé	eurent ressemblé
4 futur		**11 futur antérieur**	
ressemblerai	ressemblerons	aurai ressemblé	aurons ressemblé
ressembleras	ressemblerez	auras ressemblé	aurez ressemblé
ressemblera	ressembleront	aura ressemblé	auront ressemblé
5 conditionnel		**12 conditionnel passé**	
ressemblerais	ressemblerions	aurais ressemblé	aurions ressemblé
ressemblerais	ressembleriez	aurais ressemblé	auriez ressemblé
ressemblerait	ressembleraient	aurait ressemblé	auraient ressemblé
6 présent du subjonctif		**13 passé du subjonctif**	
ressemble	ressemblions	aie ressemblé	ayons ressemblé
ressembles	ressembliez	aies ressemblé	ayez ressemblé
ressemble	ressemblent	ait ressemblé	aient ressemblé
7 imparfait du subjonctif		**14 plus-que-parfait du subjonctif**	
ressemblasse	ressemblassions	eusse ressemblé	eussions ressemblé
ressemblasses	ressemblassiez	eusses ressemblé	eussiez ressemblé
ressemblât	ressemblassent	eût ressemblé	eussent ressemblé

Impératif
ressemble
ressemblons
ressemblez

Words and expressions related to this verb
ressembler à qqn   to resemble someone
Paulette ressemble beaucoup à sa mère
   Paulette looks very much like her mother.
se ressembler   to resemble each other, to look
   alike
Qui se ressemble s'assemble   Birds of a
   feather flock together.

sembler   to seem, to appear
une ressemblance   resemblance
Cela ne te ressemble pas!   That's not like
   you!
Ils se ressemblent comme deux gouttes d'eau
   They are as alike as two peas in a pod (like
   two drops of water).

Want to learn more verbs used in proverbs and sayings? Take a look at page 559.

to remain, to stay; to be left (over)

The Seven Simple Tenses		The Seven Compound Tenses	
Singular	Plural	Singular	Plural

1   présent de l'indicatif

reste	restons	
restes	restez	
reste	restent	

8   passé composé

suis resté(e)	sommes resté(e)s
es resté(e)	êtes resté(e)(s)
est resté(e)	sont resté(e)s

2   imparfait de l'indicatif

restais	restions
restais	restiez
restait	restaient

9   plus-que-parfait de l'indicatif

étais resté(e)	étions resté(e)s
étais resté(e)	étiez resté(e)(s)
était resté(e)	étaient resté(e)s

3   passé simple

restai	restâmes
restas	restâtes
resta	restèrent

10   passé antérieur

fus resté(e)	fûmes resté(e)s
fus resté(e)	fûtes resté(e)(s)
fut resté(e)	furent resté(e)s

4   futur

resterai	resterons
resteras	resterez
restera	resteront

11   futur antérieur

serai resté(e)	serons resté(e)s
seras resté(e)	serez resté(e)(s)
sera resté(e)	seront resté(e)s

5   conditionnel

resterais	resterions
resterais	resteriez
resterait	resteraient

12   conditionnel passé

serais resté(e)	serions resté(e)s
serais resté(e)	seriez resté(e)(s)
serait resté(e)	seraient resté(e)s

6   présent du subjonctif

reste	restions
restes	restiez
reste	restent

13   passé du subjonctif

sois resté(e)	soyons resté(e)s
sois resté(e)	soyez resté(e)(s)
soit resté(e)	soient resté(e)s

7   imparfait du subjonctif

restasse	restassions
restasses	restassiez
restât	restassent

14   plus-que-parfait du subjonctif

fusse resté(e)	fussions resté(e)s
fusses resté(e)	fussiez resté(e)(s)
fût resté(e)	fussent resté(e)s

Impératif
reste
restons
restez

Words and expressions related to this verb

Combien d'argent vous reste-t-il?   How much money do you have left (over)?
   Il me reste deux cents euros   I have two hundred euros left.
Restez là; je reviens tout de suite   Stay there; I'll be right back.

Simone est restée au lit toute la journée   Simone stayed in bed all day.
les restes   leftovers; **le reste du temps** the rest of the time
le restant   remainder
rester au lit   to stay in bed

Going away? Don't forget to check out the practical situations for travelers on pages 568–598.

The subject pronouns are found on the page facing page 1.   **407**

retenir

Part. pr. retenant   **Part. passé retenu**

to retain, to keep, to detain, to hold back

The Seven Simple Tenses		The Seven Compound Tenses	
Singular	Plural	Singular	Plural
1 présent de l'indicatif		**8 passé composé**	
retiens	retenons	ai retenu	avons retenu
retiens	retenez	as retenu	avez retenu
retient	retiennent	a retenu	ont retenu
2 imparfait de l'indicatif		**9 plus-que-parfait de l'indicatif**	
retenais	retenions	avais retenu	avions retenu
retenais	reteniez	avais retenu	aviez retenu
retenait	retenaient	avait retenu	avaient retenu
3 passé simple		**10 passé antérieur**	
retins	retînmes	eus retenu	eûmes retenu
retins	retîntes	eus retenu	eûtes retenu
retint	retinrent	eut retenu	eurent retenu
4 futur		**11 futur antérieur**	
retiendrai	retiendrons	aurai retenu	aurons retenu
retiendras	retiendrez	auras retenu	aurez retenu
retiendra	retiendront	aura retenu	auront retenu
5 conditionnel		**12 conditionnel passé**	
retiendrais	retiendrions	aurais retenu	aurions retenu
retiendrais	retiendriez	aurais retenu	auriez retenu
retiendrait	retiendraient	aurait retenu	auraient retenu
6 présent du subjonctif		**13 passé du subjonctif**	
retienne	retenions	aie retenu	ayons retenu
retiennes	reteniez	aies retenu	ayez retenu
retienne	retiennent	ait retenu	aient retenu
7 imparfait du subjonctif		**14 plus-que-parfait du subjonctif**	
retinsse	retinssions	eusse retenu	eussions retenu
retinsses	retinssiez	eusses retenu	eussiez retenu
retînt	retinssent	eût retenu	eussent retenu

Impératif
retiens
retenons
retenez

Words and expressions related to this verb

retenir au lit to confine to bed
retenir qqn to detain someone
se retenir to restrain oneself

retenir une chambre to reserve a room
retenir une place to reserve a place, a seat
une rétention retention

See also **contenir, obtenir,** and **tenir.**

Want to learn more idiomatic expressions that contain verbs? Look at pages 530–542.

The Seven Simple Tenses		The Seven Compound Tenses	
Singular	Plural	Singular	Plural
1 présent de l'indicatif		8 passé composé	
retire	retirons	ai retiré	avons retiré
retires	retirez	as retiré	avez retiré
retire	retirent	a retiré	ont retiré
2 imparfait de l'indicatif		9 plus-que-parfait de l'indicatif	
retirais	retirions	avais retiré	avions retiré
retirais	retiriez	avais retiré	aviez retiré
retirait	retiraient	avait retiré	avaient retiré
3 passé simple		10 passé antérieur	
retirai	retirâmes	eus retiré	eûmes retiré
retiras	retirâtes	eus retiré	eûtes retiré
retira	retirèrent	eut retiré	eurent retiré
4 futur		11 futur antérieur	
retirerai	retirerons	aurai retiré	aurons retiré
retireras	retirerez	auras retiré	aurez retiré
retirera	retireront	aura retiré	auront retiré
5 conditionnel		12 conditionnel passé	
retirerais	retirerions	aurais retiré	aurions retiré
retirerais	retireriez	aurais retiré	auriez retiré
retirerait	retireraient	aurait retiré	auraient retiré
6 présent du subjonctif		13 passé du subjonctif	
retire	retirions	aie retiré	ayons retiré
retires	retiriez	aies retiré	ayez retiré
retire	retirent	ait retiré	aient retiré
7 imparfait du subjonctif		14 plus-que-parfait du subjonctif	
retirasse	retirassions	eusse retiré	eussions retiré
retirasses	retirassiez	eusses retiré	eussiez retiré
retirât	retirassent	eût retiré	eussent retiré

Impératif
retire
retirons
retirez

Words and expressions related to this verb

retirer qqch à qqn   to take something back
from someone
retirer qqn de   to take someone out of, to
withdraw someone from
retirer une promesse   to take back a promise

retirer ses chaussures   to take off one's shoes
retirer qqch de   to take something out of
retirer ses paroles   to withdraw, to take back
one's words

See also **attirer, se retirer,** and **tirer.**

How are you doing? Find out with the verb drills and tests with answers explained on pages
622–673.

se retirer

Part. pr. se retirant   Part. passé **retiré(e)(s)**

to retire, to withdraw

The Seven Simple Tenses		The Seven Compound Tenses	
Singular	Plural	Singular	Plural
1 présent de l'indicatif		**8 passé composé**	
me retire	nous retirons	me suis retiré(e)	nous sommes retiré(e)s
te retires	vous retirez	t'es retiré(e)	vous êtes retiré(e)(s)
se retire	se retirent	s'est retiré(e)	se sont retiré(e)s
2 imparfait de l'indicatif		**9 plus-que-parfait de l'indicatif**	
me retirais	nous retirions	m'étais retiré(e)	nous étions retiré(e)s
te retirais	vous retiriez	t'étais retiré(e)	vous étiez retiré(e)(s)
se retirait	se retiraient	s'était retiré(e)	s'étaient retiré(e)s
3 passé simple		**10 passé antérieur**	
me retirai	nous retirâmes	me fus retiré(e)	nous fûmes retiré(e)s
te retiras	vous retirâtes	te fus retiré(e)	vous fûtes retiré(e)(s)
se retira	se retirèrent	se fut retiré(e)	se furent retiré(e)s
4 futur		**11 futur antérieur**	
me retirerai	nous retirerons	me serai retiré(e)	nous serons retiré(e)s
te retireras	vous retirerez	te seras retiré(e)	vous serez retiré(e)(s)
se retirera	se retireront	se sera retiré(e)	se seront retiré(e)s
5 conditionnel		**12 conditionnel passé**	
me retirerais	nous retirerions	me serais retiré(e)	nous serions retiré(e)s
te retirerais	vous retireriez	te serais retiré(e)	vous seriez retiré(e)(s)
se retirerait	se retireraient	se serait retiré(e)	se seraient retiré(e)s
6 présent du subjonctif		**13 passé du subjonctif**	
me retire	nous retirions	me sois retiré(e)	nous soyons retiré(e)s
te retires	vous retiriez	te sois retiré(e)	vous soyez retiré(e)(s)
se retire	se retirent	se soit retiré(e)	se soient retiré(e)s
7 imparfait du subjonctif		**14 plus-que-parfait du subjonctif**	
me retirasse	nous retirassions	me fusse retiré(e)	nous fussions retiré(e)s
te retirasses	vous retirassiez	te fusses retiré(e)	vous fussiez retiré(e)(s)
se retirât	se retirassent	se fût retiré(e)	se fussent retiré(e)s

Impératif
retire-toi; ne te retire pas
retirons-nous; ne nous retirons pas
retirez-vous; ne vous retirez pas

Words and expressions related to this verb
se retirer des affaires to retire from business
retraité, retraitée retired, pensioned off
un officier en retraite retired officer
une retraite retreat, retirement; **vivre à la retraite** to live in retirement

un retrait withdrawal; **en retrait** set back; out of line; **un mur en retrait** recess of a wall.

See also **attirer, retirer,** and **tirer.**

It's important that you be familiar with the Subjunctive. See pages 560–565.

The Seven Simple Tenses		The Seven Compound Tenses	
Singular	Plural	Singular	Plural
1 présent de l'indicatif		**8 passé composé**	
retourne	retournons	suis retourné(e)	sommes retourné(e)s
retournes	retournez	es retourné(e)	êtes retourné(e)(s)
retourne	retournent	est retourné(e)	sont retourné(e)s
2 imparfait de l'indicatif		**9 plus-que-parfait de l'indicatif**	
retournais	retournions	étais retourné(e)	étions retourné(e)s
retournais	retourniez	étais retourné(e)	étiez retourné(e)(s)
retournait	retournaient	était retourné(e)	étaient retourné(e)s
3 passé simple		**10 passé antérieur**	
retournai	retournâmes	fus retourné(e)	fûmes retourné(e)s
retournas	retournâtes	fus retourné(e)	fûtes retourné(e)(s)
retourna	retournèrent	fut retourné(e)	furent retourné(e)s
4 futur		**11 futur antérieur**	
retournerai	retournerons	serai retourné(e)	serons retourné(e)s
retourneras	retournerez	seras retourné(e)	serez retourné(e)(s)
retournera	retourneront	sera retourné(e)	seront retourné(e)s
5 conditionnel		**12 conditionnel passé**	
retournerais	retournerions	serais retourné(e)	serions retourné(e)s
retournerais	retourneriez	serais retourné(e)	seriez retourné(e)(s)
retournerait	retourneraient	serait retourné(e)	seraient retourné(e)s
6 présent du subjonctif		**13 passé du subjonctif**	
retourne	retournions	sois retourné(e)	soyons retourné(e)s
retournes	retourniez	sois retourné(e)	soyez retourné(e)(s)
retourne	retournent	soit retourné(e)	soient retourné(e)s
7 imparfait du subjonctif		**14 plus-que-parfait du subjonctif**	
retournasse	retournassions	fusse retourné(e)	fussions retourné(e)s
retournasses	retournassiez	fusses retourné(e)	fussiez retourné(e)(s)
retournât	retournassent	fût retourné(e)	fussent retourné(e)s

Impératif
retourne
retournons
retournez

Words and expressions related to this verb
retourner une chaussette to turn a sock inside out
retourner un matelas to turn over a mattress
retourner qqn to change someone's mind
se retourner to turn around; **se retourner sur le dos** to turn over on one's back

un retour return; **un billet de retour** return ticket
un billet d'aller et retour a round trip ticket
être de retour to be back; **Madame Dupin sera de retour demain.**

See also **détourner** and **tourner.**

Taking a trip? Check out the popular words, phrases, and expressions for travelers on pages 599–621.

The subject pronouns are found on the page facing page 1.   **411**

réussir

Part. pr. réussissant   **Part. passé réussi**

to succeed, to result

The Seven Simple Tenses		The Seven Compound Tenses	
Singular	Plural	Singular	Plural
1 présent de l'indicatif		8 passé composé	
réussis	réussissons	ai réussi	avons réussi
réussis	réussissez	as réussi	avez réussi
réussit	réussissent	a réussi	ont réussi
2 imparfait de l'indicatif		9 plus-que-parfait de l'indicatif	
réussissais	réussissions	avais réussi	avions réussi
réussissais	réussissiez	avais réussi	aviez réussi
réussissait	réussissaient	avait réussi	avaient réussi
3 passé simple		10 passé antérieur	
réussis	réussîmes	eus réussi	eûmes réussi
réussis	réussîtes	eus réussi	eûtes réussi
réussit	réussirent	eut réussi	eurent réussi
4 futur		11 futur antérieur	
réussirai	réussirons	aurai réussi	aurons réussi
réussiras	réussirez	auras réussi	aurez réussi
réussira	réussiront	aura réussi	auront réussi
5 conditionnel		12 conditionnel passé	
réussirais	réussirions	aurais réussi	aurions réussi
réussirais	réussiriez	aurais réussi	auriez réussi
réussirait	réussiraient	aurait réussi	auraient réussi
6 présent du subjonctif		13 passé du subjonctif	
réussisse	réussissions	aie réussi	ayons réussi
réussisses	réussissiez	aies réussi	ayez réussi
réussisse	réussissent	ait réussi	aient réussi
7 imparfait du subjonctif		14 plus-que-parfait du subjonctif	
réussisse	réussissions	eusse réussi	eussions réussi
réussisses	réussissiez	eusses réussi	eussiez réussi
réussît	réussissent	eût réussi	eussent réussi

Impératif
réussis
réussissons
réussissez

Words and expressions related to this verb
réussir à qqch   to succeed in something
réussir à un examen   to pass an exam
une réussite   success; **une réussite sociale**
social success
réussir   to result; **Le projet a mal réussi**
The plan turned out badly; **Le projet a bien
réussi**   The plan turned out well.

une soirée réussie   a successful evening
réussir dans la vie   to succeed in life
Les fritures ne me réussissent pas   Fried
food doesn't agree with me.

Get acquainted with what preposition goes
with what verb on pages 543–553.

Enjoy more verbs in French proverbs and
sayings on page 559.

412

The Seven Simple Tenses		The Seven Compound Tenses	
Singular	Plural	Singular	Plural
1 présent de l'indicatif		**8 passé composé**	
me réveille	**nous réveillons**	**me suis réveillé(e)**	**nous sommes réveillé(e)s**
te réveilles	**vous réveillez**	**t'es réveillé(e)**	**vous êtes réveillé(e)(s)**
se réveille	**se réveillent**	**s'est réveillé(e)**	**se sont réveillé(e)s**
2 imparfait de l'indicatif		**9 plus-que-parfait de l'indicatif**	
me réveillais	**nous réveillions**	**m'étais réveillé(e)**	**nous étions réveillé(e)s**
te réveillais	**vous réveilliez**	**t'étais réveillé(e)**	**vous étiez réveillé(e)(s)**
se réveillait	**se réveillaient**	**s'était réveillé(e)**	**s'étaient réveillé(e)s**
3 passé simple		**10 passé antérieur**	
me réveillai	**nous réveillâmes**	**me fus réveillé(e)**	**nous fûmes réveillé(e)s**
te réveillas	**vous réveillâtes**	**te fus réveillé(e)**	**vous fûtes réveillé(e)(s)**
se réveilla	**se réveillèrent**	**se fut réveillé(e)**	**se furent réveillé(e)s**
4 futur		**11 futur antérieur**	
me réveillerai	**nous réveillerons**	**me serai réveillé(e)**	**nous serons réveillé(e)s**
te réveilleras	**vous réveillerez**	**te seras réveillé(e)**	**vous serez réveillé(e)(s)**
se réveillera	**se réveilleront**	**se sera réveillé(e)**	**se seront réveillé(e)s**
5 conditionnel		**12 conditionnel passé**	
me réveillerais	**nous réveillerions**	**me serais réveillé(e)**	**nous serions réveillé(e)s**
te réveillerais	**vous réveilleriez**	**te serais réveillé(e)**	**vous seriez réveillé(e)(s)**
se réveillerait	**se réveilleraient**	**se serait réveillé(e)**	**se seraient réveillé(e)s**
6 présent du subjonctif		**13 passé du subjonctif**	
me réveille	**nous réveillions**	**me sois réveillé(e)**	**nous soyons réveillé(e)s**
te réveilles	**vous réveilliez**	**te sois réveillé(e)**	**vous soyez réveillé(e)(s)**
se réveille	**se réveillent**	**se soit réveillé(e)**	**se soient réveillé(e)s**
7 imparfait du subjonctif		**14 plus-que-parfait du subjonctif**	
me réveillasse	**nous réveillassions**	**me fusse réveillé(e)**	**nous fussions réveillé(e)s**
te réveillasses	**vous réveillassiez**	**te fusses réveillé(e)**	**vous fussiez réveillé(e)(s)**
se réveillât	**se réveillassent**	**se fût réveillé(e)**	**se fussent réveillé(e)s**

Impératif
réveille-toi; ne te réveille pas
réveillons-nous; ne nous réveillons pas
réveillez-vous; ne vous réveillez pas

Words and expressions related to this verb
le réveillon   Christmas or New Year's Eve
   party
faire réveillon   to see the New Year in, to see
   Christmas in on Christmas eve
un réveille-matin   alarm clock
éveiller (réveiller) qqn   to wake up, awaken
   someone; **éveiller**   implies to awaken or
   wake up gently; **réveiller**   suggests with
   some effort

veiller   to stay awake; **veiller à**   to look after
veiller sur   to watch over; **surveiller**   to keep
   an eye on
la veille de Noël   Christmas Eve
La tempête a réveillé le chien   The storm
   woke up the dog.
Marie s'est réveillée à six heures   Mary woke
   up at six o'clock.

The subject pronouns are found on the page facing page 1.   **413**

to come back

The Seven Simple Tenses		The Seven Compound Tenses	
Singular	Plural	Singular	Plural
1 présent de l'indicatif		**8 passé composé**	
reviens	**revenons**	**suis revenu(e)**	**sommes revenu(e)s**
reviens	**revenez**	**es revenu(e)**	**êtes revenu(e)(s)**
revient	**reviennent**	**est revenu(e)**	**sont revenu(e)s**
2 imparfait de l'indicatif		**9 plus-que-parfait de l'indicatif**	
revenais	**revenions**	**étais revenu(e)**	**étions revenu(e)s**
revenais	**reveniez**	**étais revenu(e)**	**étiez revenu(e)(s)**
revenait	**revenaient**	**était revenu(e)**	**étaient revenu(e)s**
3 passé simple		**10 passé antérieur**	
revins	**revînmes**	**fus revenu(e)**	**fûmes revenu(e)s**
revins	**revîntes**	**fus revenu(e)**	**fûtes revenu(e)(s)**
revint	**revinrent**	**fut revenu(e)**	**furent revenu(e)s**
4 futur		**11 futur antérieur**	
reviendrai	**reviendrons**	**serai revenu(e)**	**serons revenu(e)s**
reviendras	**reviendrez**	**seras revenu(e)**	**serez revenu(e)(s)**
reviendra	**reviendront**	**sera revenu(e)**	**seront revenu(e)s**
5 conditionnel		**12 conditionnel passé**	
reviendrais	**reviendrions**	**serais revenu(e)**	**serions revenu(e)s**
reviendrais	**reviendriez**	**serais revenu(e)**	**seriez revenu(e)(s)**
reviendrait	**reviendraient**	**serait revenu(e)**	**seraient revenu(e)s**
6 présent du subjonctif		**13 passé du subjonctif**	
revienne	**revenions**	**sois revenu(e)**	**soyons revenu(e)s**
reviennes	**reveniez**	**sois revenu(e)**	**soyez revenu(e)(s)**
revienne	**reviennent**	**soit revenu(e)**	**soient revenu(e)s**
7 imparfait du subjonctif		**14 plus-que-parfait du subjonctif**	
revinsse	**revinssions**	**fusse revenu(e)**	**fussions revenu(e)s**
revinsses	**revinssiez**	**fusses revenu(e)**	**fussiez revenu(e)(s)**
revînt	**revinssent**	**fût revenu(e)**	**fussent revenu(e)s**

Impératif
reviens
revenons
revenez

Words and expressions related to this verb
le revenu revenue, income
à revenu fixe fixed interest
revenir d'une erreur to realize one's mistake
revenir au même to amount to the same thing
revenir sur ses pas to retrace one's steps
revenir sur le sujet to get back to the subject
revenir sur sa parole to go back on one's word

Tout revient à ceci . . . It all boils down to this . . .
Il/Elle s'appelle "reviens" Make sure you return it (*m.* or *f.* object that is being lent to someone). (Literally: Its name is "come back.")

See also **convenir, devenir, prévenir, se souvenir,** and **venir.**

The Seven Simple Tenses		The Seven Compound Tenses	
Singular	Plural	Singular	Plural
1 présent de l'indicatif		**8 passé composé**	
rêve	rêvons	ai rêvé	avons rêvé
rêves	rêvez	as rêvé	avez rêvé
rêve	rêvent	a rêvé	ont rêvé
2 imparfait de l'indicatif		**9 plus-que-parfait de l'indicatif**	
rêvais	rêvions	avais rêvé	avions rêvé
rêvais	rêviez	avais rêvé	aviez rêvé
rêvait	rêvaient	avait rêvé	avaient rêvé
3 passé simple		**10 passé antérieur**	
rêvai	rêvâmes	eus rêvé	eûmes rêvé
rêvas	rêvâtes	eus rêvé	eûtes rêvé
rêva	rêvèrent	eut rêvé	eurent rêvé
4 futur		**11 futur antérieur**	
rêverai	rêverons	aurai rêvé	aurons rêvé
rêveras	rêverez	auras rêvé	aurez rêvé
rêvera	rêveront	aura rêvé	auront rêvé
5 conditionnel		**12 conditionnel passé**	
rêverais	rêverions	aurais rêvé	aurions rêvé
rêverais	rêveriez	aurais rêvé	auriez rêvé
rêverait	rêveraient	aurait rêvé	auraient rêvé
6 présent du subjonctif		**13 passé du subjonctif**	
rêve	rêvions	aie rêvé	ayons rêvé
rêves	rêviez	aies rêvé	ayez rêvé
rêve	rêvent	ait rêvé	aient rêvé
7 imparfait du subjonctif		**14 plus-que-parfait du subjonctif**	
rêvasse	rêvassions	eusse rêvé	eussions rêvé
rêvasses	rêvassiez	eusses rêvé	eussiez rêvé
rêvât	rêvassent	eût rêvé	eussent rêvé

Impératif
rêve
rêvons
rêvez

Common idiomatic expressions using this verb and words related to it

rêver de to dream of, to dream about, to yearn for

J'ai rêvé de toi toute la nuit I dreamt of you all night long.

rêver tout éveillé(e) to daydream

rêver à to imagine, to think vaguely about something, to daydream

Janine, tu ne fais pas attention! A quoi rêves-tu? Janine, you are not paying attention! What are you dreaming about?

un rêveur, une rêveuse dreamer

une rêverie reverie, meditation

un rêve dream

Use the EE-zee guide to French pronunciation on pages 566 and 567.

to see again, to see once more

The Seven Simple Tenses		The Seven Compound Tenses	
Singular	Plural	Singular	Plural
1 présent de l'indicatif		8 passé composé	
revois	revoyons	ai revu	avons revu
revois	revoyez	as revu	avez revu
revoit	revoient	a revu	ont revu
2 imparfait de l'indicatif		9 plus-que-parfait de l'indicatif	
revoyais	revoyions	avais revu	avions revu
revoyais	revoyiez	avais revu	aviez revu
revoyait	revoyaient	avait revu	avaient revu
3 passé simple		10 passé antérieur	
revis	revîmes	eus revu	eûmes revu
revis	revîtes	eus revu	eûtes revu
revit	revirent	eut revu	eurent revu
4 futur		11 futur antérieur	
reverrai	reverrons	aurai revu	aurons revu
reverras	reverrez	auras revu	aurez revu
reverra	reverront	aura revu	auront revu
5 conditionnel		12 conditionnel passé	
reverrais	reverrions	aurais revu	aurions revu
reverrais	reverriez	aurais revu	auriez revu
reverrait	reverraient	aurait revu	auraient revu
6 présent du subjonctif		13 passé du subjonctif	
revoie	revoyions	aie revu	ayons revu
revoies	revoyiez	aies revu	ayez revu
revoie	revoient	ait revu	aient revu
7 imparfait du subjonctif		14 plus-que-parfait du subjonctif	
revisse	revissions	eusse revu	eussions revu
revisses	revissiez	eusses revu	eussiez revu
revît	revissent	eût revu	eussent revu

Impératif
revois
revoyons
revoyez

Words and expressions related to this verb

au revoir good-bye, see you again, until we meet again

se revoir to see each other again

une revue review, magazine

un, une revuiste a writer of reviews

une révision revision; **à revoir** to be revised

See also **prévoir** and **voir**.

Going away? Don't forget to check out the practical situations for travelers on pages 568–598.

416

to laugh

The Seven Simple Tenses		The Seven Compound Tenses	
Singular	Plural	Singular	Plural
1 présent de l'indicatif		**8 passé composé**	
ris	rions	ai ri	avons ri
ris	riez	as ri	avez ri
rit	rient	a ri	ont ri
2 imparfait de l'indicatif		**9 plus-que-parfait de l'indicatif**	
riais	riions	avais ri	avions ri
riais	riiez	avais ri	aviez ri
riait	riaient	avait ri	avaient ri
3 passé simple		**10 passé antérieur**	
ris	rîmes	eus ri	eûmes ri
ris	rîtes	eus ri	eûtes ri
rit	rirent	eut ri	eurent ri
4 futur		**11 futur antérieur**	
rirai	rirons	aurai ri	aurons ri
riras	rirez	auras ri	aurez ri
rira	riront	aura ri	auront ri
5 conditionnel		**12 conditionnel passé**	
rirais	ririons	aurais ri	aurions ri
rirais	ririez	aurais ri	auriez ri
rirait	riraient	aurait ri	auraient ri
6 présent du subjonctif		**13 passé du subjonctif**	
rie	riions	aie ri	ayons ri
ries	riiez	aies ri	ayez ri
rie	rient	ait ri	aient ri
7 imparfait du subjonctif		**14 plus-que-parfait du subjonctif**	
risse	rissions	eusse ri	eussions ri
risses	rissiez	eusses ri	eussiez ri
rît	rissent	eût ri	eussent ri

Impératif
ris
rions
riez

Words and expressions related to this verb
éclater de rire to burst out laughing; **rire de** to laugh at
dire qqch pour rire to say something just for a laugh
rire au nez de qqn to laugh in someone's face

rire de bon coeur to laugh heartily
le rire laughter; **un sourire** smile; **risible** laughable
le fou rire fit of laughter, giggles

See also **sourire.**

Grammar putting you in a tense mood? Review the definitions of basic grammatical terms on pages 674–688.

The subject pronouns are found on the page facing page 1.   **417**

rompre

Part. pr. **rompant**   Part. passé **rompu**

to break, to burst, to shatter, to break off

The Seven Simple Tenses		The Seven Compound Tenses	
Singular	Plural	Singular	Plural
1 présent de l'indicatif		**8 passé composé**	
romps	rompons	ai rompu	avons rompu
romps	rompez	as rompu	avez rompu
rompt	rompent	a rompu	ont rompu
2 imparfait de l'indicatif		**9 plus-que-parfait de l'indicatif**	
rompais	rompions	avais rompu	avions rompu
rompais	rompiez	avais rompu	aviez rompu
rompait	rompaient	avait rompu	avaient rompu
3 passé simple		**10 passé antérieur**	
rompis	rompîmes	eus rompu	eûmes rompu
rompis	rompîtes	eus rompu	eûtes rompu
rompit	rompirent	eut rompu	eurent rompu
4 futur		**11 futur antérieur**	
romprai	romprons	aurai rompu	aurons rompu
rompras	romprez	auras rompu	aurez rompu
rompra	rompront	aura rompu	auront rompu
5 conditionnel		**12 conditionnel passé**	
romprais	romprions	aurais rompu	aurions rompu
romprais	rompriez	aurais rompu	auriez rompu
romprait	rompraient	aurait rompu	auraient rompu
6 présent du subjonctif		**13 passé du subjonctif**	
rompe	rompions	aie rompu	ayons rompu
rompes	rompiez	aies rompu	ayez rompu
rompe	rompent	ait rompu	aient rompu
7 imparfait du subjonctif		**14 plus-que-parfait du subjonctif**	
rompisse	rompissions	eusse rompu	eussions rompu
rompisses	rompissiez	eusses rompu	eussiez rompu
rompît	rompissent	eût rompu	eussent rompu

Impératif
romps
rompons
rompez

Common idiomatic expressions using this verb and words related to it

rompu de fatigue   worn out
rompu aux affaires   experienced in
   business
se rompre à   to get used to
se rompre la tête   to rack one's brains
une rupture de contrat   breach of contract

corrompre   to corrupt
interrompre   to interrupt
une rupture   rupture, bursting
un rupteur   circuit breaker
rompre avec qqn   to have a falling out with
   someone

See also **corrompre** and **interrompre**.

How are you doing? Find out with the verb drills and tests with answers explained on pages 622–673.

The Seven Simple Tenses		The Seven Compound Tenses	
Singular	Plural	Singular	Plural

1 présent de l'indicatif		8 passé composé	
rougis	**rougissons**	**ai rougi**	**avons rougi**
rougis	**rougissez**	**as rougi**	**avez rougi**
rougit	**rougissent**	**a rougi**	**ont rougi**

2 imparfait de l'indicatif		9 plus-que-parfait de l'indicatif	
rougissais	**rougissions**	**avais rougi**	**avions rougi**
rougissais	**rougissiez**	**avais rougi**	**aviez rougi**
rougissait	**rougissaient**	**avait rougi**	**avaient rougi**

3 passé simple		10 passé antérieur	
rougis	**rougîmes**	**eus rougi**	**eûmes rougi**
rougis	**rougîtes**	**eus rougi**	**eûtes rougi**
rougit	**rougirent**	**eut rougi**	**eurent rougi**

4 futur		11 futur antérieur	
rougirai	**rougirons**	**aurai rougi**	**aurons rougi**
rougiras	**rougirez**	**auras rougi**	**aurez rougi**
rougira	**rougiront**	**aura rougi**	**auront rougi**

5 conditionnel		12 conditionnel passé	
rougirais	**rougirions**	**aurais rougi**	**aurions rougi**
rougirais	**rougiriez**	**aurais rougi**	**auriez rougi**
rougirait	**rougiraient**	**aurait rougi**	**auraient rougi**

6 présent du subjonctif		13 passé du subjonctif	
rougisse	**rougissions**	**aie rougi**	**ayons rougi**
rougisses	**rougissiez**	**aies rougi**	**ayez rougi**
rougisse	**rougissent**	**ait rougi**	**aient rougi**

7 imparfait du subjonctif		14 plus-que-parfait du subjonctif	
rougisse	**rougissions**	**eusse rougi**	**eussions rougi**
rougisses	**rougissiez**	**eusses rougi**	**eussiez rougi**
rougît	**rougissent**	**eût rougi**	**eussent rougi**

Impératif
rougis
rougissons
rougissez

Words and expressions related to this verb
faire rougir qqn to make someone blush
le rouge red; **rougeâtre** reddish
un rouge-gorge robin redbreast;
  (des rouges-gorges)
rougir de qqn to feel shame for someone
la rougeole measles

rougeaud, rougeaude ruddy complexion
le rouge à lèvres lipstick; **le rouge à joues**
  rouge (for cheeks)
voir rouge to see red
une jeune mariée rougissante a blushing
  bride

Consult the sections on verbs used in idiomatic expressions, verbs with prepositions, and the list of over 1,100 verbs conjugated like model verbs in the back pages.

The subject pronouns are found on the page facing page 1.

rouler

Part. pr. roulant   **Part. passé roulé**

to roll, to roll along, to drive (a car), to ride along

The Seven Simple Tenses		The Seven Compound Tenses	
Singular	Plural	Singular	Plural
1 présent de l'indicatif		**8 passé composé**	
roule	roulons	ai roulé	avons roulé
roules	roulez	as roulé	avez roulé
roule	roulent	a roulé	ont roulé
2 imparfait de l'indicatif		**9 plus-que-parfait de l'indicatif**	
roulais	roulions	avais roulé	avions roulé
roulais	rouliez	avais roulé	aviez roulé
roulait	roulaient	avait roulé	avaient roulé
3 passé simple		**10 passé antérieur**	
roulai	roulâmes	eus roulé	eûmes roulé
roulas	roulâtes	eus roulé	eûtes roulé
roula	roulèrent	eut roulé	eurent roulé
4 futur		**11 futur antérieur**	
roulerai	roulerons	aurai roulé	aurons roulé
rouleras	roulerez	auras roulé	aurez roulé
roulera	rouleront	aura roulé	auront roulé
5 conditionnel		**12 conditionnel passé**	
roulerais	roulerions	aurais roulé	aurions roulé
roulerais	rouleriez	aurais roulé	auriez roulé
roulerait	rouleraient	aurait roulé	auraient roulé
6 présent du subjonctif		**13 passé du subjonctif**	
roule	roulions	aie roulé	ayons roulé
roules	rouliez	aies roulé	ayez roulé
roule	roulent	ait roulé	aient roulé
7 imparfait du subjonctif		**14 plus-que-parfait du subjonctif**	
roulasse	roulassions	eusse roulé	eussions roulé
roulasses	roulassiez	eusses roulé	eussiez roulé
roulât	roulassent	eût roulé	eussent roulé

Impératif
roule
roulons
roulez

Words and expressions related to this verb
rouler les *r*   to roll one's r's
rouler sur l'or   to be rolling in dough (money)
se rouler   to roll over
dérouler   to unroll
un rouleau   roll; **un rouleau de papier peint**
  roll of wallpaper

un rouleau de pièces de monnaie   a roll of
  coins
un rouleau de pellicule   roll of film
un rouleau à pâtisserie   rolling pin
se dérouler   to take place, to develop, to
  unfold

Review the Subjunctive clearly and simply on pages 560–565.

to seize, to grasp, to comprehend

The Seven Simple Tenses		The Seven Compound Tenses	
Singular	Plural	Singular	Plural
1 présent de l'indicatif		**8 passé composé**	
saisis	saisissons	ai saisi	avons saisi
saisis	saisissez	as saisi	avez saisi
saisit	saisissent	a saisi	ont saisi
2 imparfait de l'indicatif		**9 plus-que-parfait de l'indicatif**	
saisissais	saisissions	avais saisi	avions saisi
saisissais	saisissiez	avais saisi	aviez saisi
saisissait	saisissaient	avait saisi	avaient saisi
3 passé simple		**10 passé antérieur**	
saisis	saisîmes	eus saisi	eûmes saisi
saisis	saisîtes	eus saisi	eûtes saisi
saisit	saisirent	eut saisi	eurent saisi
4 futur		**11 futur antérieur**	
saisirai	saisirons	aurai saisi	aurons saisi
saisiras	saisirez	auras saisi	aurez saisi
saisira	saisiront	aura saisi	auront saisi
5 conditionnel		**12 conditionnel passé**	
saisirais	saisirions	aurais saisi	aurions saisi
saisirais	saisiriez	aurais saisi	auriez saisi
saisirait	saisiraient	aurait saisi	auraient saisi
6 présent du subjonctif		**13 passé du subjonctif**	
saisisse	saisissions	aie saisi	ayons saisi
saisisses	saisissiez	aies saisi	ayez saisi
saisisse	saisissent	ait saisi	aient saisi
7 imparfait du subjonctif		**14 plus-que-parfait du subjonctif**	
saisisse	saisissions	eusse saisi	eussions saisi
saisisses	saisissiez	eusses saisi	eussiez saisi
saisît	saisissent	eût saisi	eussent saisi

Impératif
saisis
saisissons
saisissez

Words and expressions related to this verb
un saisissement shock
saisissable seizable
saisissant, saisissante thrilling, piercing
une saisie seizure
saisir des données to input data (comp.)
la saisie de données data input (comp.)

saisir l'occasion to seize the opportunity
saisi de joie overcome with joy
saisir la signification de qqch to grasp the
  meaning of something
insaisissable elusive
se saisir de to take possession of

Seize the opportunity! Read pages 560–565 and grasp the basics of the Subjunctive.

The subject pronouns are found on the page facing page 1.

salir
to soil, to dirty

Part. pr. **salissant**   Part. passé **sali**

The Seven Simple Tenses		The Seven Compound Tenses	
Singular	Plural	Singular	Plural
1 présent de l'indicatif		**8 passé composé**	
salis	salissons	ai sali	avons sali
salis	salissez	as sali	avez sali
salit	salissent	a sali	ont sali
2 imparfait de l'indicatif		**9 plus-que-parfait de l'indicatif**	
salissais	salissions	avais sali	avions sali
salissais	salissiez	avais sali	aviez sali
salissait	salissaient	avait sali	avaient sali
3 passé simple		**10 passé antérieur**	
salis	salîmes	eus sali	eûmes sali
salis	salîtes	eus sali	eûtes sali
salit	salirent	eut sali	eurent sali
4 futur		**11 futur antérieur**	
salirai	salirons	aurai sali	aurons sali
saliras	salirez	auras sali	aurez sali
salira	saliront	aura sali	auront sali
5 conditionnel		**12 conditionnel passé**	
salirais	salirions	aurais sali	aurions sali
salirais	saliriez	aurais sali	auriez sali
salirait	saliraient	aurait sali	auraient sali
6 présent du subjonctif		**13 passé du subjonctif**	
salisse	salissions	aie sali	ayons sali
salisses	salissiez	aies sali	ayez sali
salisse	salissent	ait sali	aient sali
7 imparfait du subjonctif		**14 plus-que-parfait du subjonctif**	
salisse	salissions	eusse sali	eussions sali
salisses	salissiez	eusses sali	eussiez sali
salît	salissent	eût sali	eussent sali

Impératif
salis
salissons
salissez

Words and expressions related to this verb

sale dirty, soiled
salement disgustingly
la saleté filth
dire des saletés to use filthy language

les mains sales soiled hands
une réputation salie a tarnished reputation
Avez-vous jamais lu ou vu la pièce de théâtre
   Les Mains sales **de Jean-Paul Sartre?**

How are you doing? Find out with the verb drills and tests with answers explained on pages 622–673.

The Seven Simple Tenses		The Seven Compound Tenses	
Singular	Plural	Singular	Plural

1 présent de l'indicatif		8 passé composé	
satisfais	satisfaisons	ai satisfait	avons satisfait
satisfais	satisfaites	as satisfait	avez satisfait
satisfait	satisfont	a satisfait	ont satisfait

2 imparfait de l'indicatif		9 plus-que-parfait de l'indicatif	
satisfaisais	satisfaisions	avais satisfait	avions satisfait
satisfaisais	satisfaisiez	avais satisfait	aviez satisfait
satisfaisait	satisfaisaient	avait satisfait	avaient satisfait

3 passé simple		10 passé antérieur	
satisfis	satisfîmes	eus satisfait	eûmes satisfait
satisfis	satisfîtes	eus satisfait	eûtes satisfait
satisfit	satisfirent	eut satisfait	eurent satisfait

4 futur		11 futur antérieur	
satisferai	satisferons	aurai satisfait	aurons satisfait
satisferas	satisferez	auras satisfait	aurez satisfait
satisfera	satisferont	aura satisfait	auront satisfait

5 conditionnel		12 conditionnel passé	
satisferais	satisferions	aurais satisfait	aurions satisfait
satisferais	satisferiez	aurais satisfait	auriez satisfait
satisferait	satisferaient	aurait satisfait	auraient satisfait

6 présent du subjonctif		13 passé du subjonctif	
satisfasse	satisfassions	aie satisfait	ayons satisfait
satisfasses	satisfassiez	aies satisfait	ayez satisfait
satisfasse	satisfassent	ait satisfait	aient satisfait

7 imparfait du subjonctif		14 plus-que-parfait du subjonctif	
satisfisse	satisfissions	eusse satisfait	eussions satisfait
satisfisses	satisfissiez	eusses satisfait	eussiez satisfait
satisfît	satisfissent	eût satisfait	eussent satisfait

Impératif
satisfais
satisfaisons
satisfaites

Words and expressions related to this verb
satisfaire sa faim   to satisfy one's hunger;
   satisfaire sa soif   to satisfy one's thirst
satisfaisant, satisfaisante   satisfying
la satisfaction   satisfaction

demander satisfaction à   to demand
   satisfaction from
être satisfait (satisfaite) de   to be satisfied
   with

See also **défaire** and **faire.**

Consult the sections on verbs used in idiomatic expressions, verbs with prepositions, and the list of over 1,100 verbs conjugated like model verbs in the back pages.

The subject pronouns are found on the page facing page 1.

to jump, to leap

The Seven Simple Tenses		The Seven Compound Tenses	
Singular	Plural	Singular	Plural
1 présent de l'indicatif		**8 passé composé**	
saute	sautons	ai sauté	avons sauté
sautes	sautez	as sauté	avez sauté
saute	sautent	a sauté	ont sauté
2 imparfait de l'indicatif		**9 plus-que-parfait de l'indicatif**	
sautais	sautions	avais sauté	avions sauté
sautais	sautiez	avais sauté	aviez sauté
sautait	sautaient	avait sauté	avaient sauté
3 passé simple		**10 passé antérieur**	
sautai	sautâmes	eus sauté	eûmes sauté
sautas	sautâtes	eus sauté	eûtes sauté
sauta	sautèrent	eut sauté	eurent sauté
4 futur		**11 futur antérieur**	
sauterai	sauterons	aurai sauté	aurons sauté
sauteras	sauterez	auras sauté	aurez sauté
sautera	sauteront	aura sauté	auront sauté
5 conditionnel		**12 conditionnel passé**	
sauterais	sauterions	aurais sauté	aurions sauté
sauterais	sauteriez	aurais sauté	auriez sauté
sauterait	sauteraient	aurait sauté	auraient sauté
6 présent du subjonctif		**13 passé du subjonctif**	
saute	sautions	aie sauté	ayons sauté
sautes	sautiez	aies sauté	ayez sauté
saute	sautent	ait sauté	aient sauté
7 imparfait du subjonctif		**14 plus-que-parfait du subjonctif**	
sautasse	sautassions	eusse sauté	eussions sauté
sautasses	sautassiez	eusses sauté	eussiez sauté
sautât	sautassent	eût sauté	eussent sauté

Impératif
saute
sautons
sautez

Words and expressions related to this verb
un saut   leap, jump
une sauterelle   grasshopper
sautiller   to skip, to hop
sauter à la corde   to jump (skip) rope

sauter au bas du lit   to jump out of bed
faire sauter une crêpe   to toss a pancake
Cela saute aux yeux   That's obvious.
sursauter   to jump, start

Want to learn more verbs used in proverbs and sayings? Take a look at page 559.

to rescue, to save

The Seven Simple Tenses		The Seven Compound Tenses	
Singular	Plural	Singular	Plural

1   présent de l'indicatif

sauve	**sauvons**	
sauves	**sauvez**	
sauve	**sauvent**	

8   passé composé

ai sauvé	**avons sauvé**
as sauvé	**avez sauvé**
a sauvé	**ont sauvé**

2   imparfait de l'indicatif

sauvais	**sauvions**
sauvais	**sauviez**
sauvait	**sauvaient**

9   plus-que-parfait de l'indicatif

avais sauvé	**avions sauvé**
avais sauvé	**aviez sauvé**
avait sauvé	**avaient sauvé**

3   passé simple

sauvai	**sauvâmes**
sauvas	**sauvâtes**
sauva	**sauvèrent**

10   passé antérieur

eus sauvé	**eûmes sauvé**
eus sauvé	**eûtes sauvé**
eut sauvé	**eurent sauvé**

4   futur

sauverai	**sauverons**
sauveras	**sauverez**
sauvera	**sauveront**

11   futur antérieur

aurai sauvé	**aurons sauvé**
auras sauvé	**aurez sauvé**
aura sauvé	**auront sauvé**

5   conditionnel

sauverais	**sauverions**
sauverais	**sauveriez**
sauverait	**sauveraient**

12   conditionnel passé

aurais sauvé	**aurions sauvé**
aurais sauvé	**auriez sauvé**
aurait sauvé	**auraient sauvé**

6   présent du subjonctif

sauve	**sauvions**
sauves	**sauviez**
sauve	**sauvent**

13   passé du subjonctif

aie sauvé	**ayons sauvé**
aies sauvé	**ayez sauvé**
ait sauvé	**aient sauvé**

7   imparfait du subjonctif

sauvasse	**sauvassions**
sauvasses	**sauvassiez**
sauvât	**sauvassent**

14   plus-que-parfait du subjonctif

eusse sauvé	**eussions sauvé**
eusses sauvé	**eussiez sauvé**
eût sauvé	**eussent sauvé**

Impératif
sauve
sauvons
sauvez

Words and expressions related to this verb
sauvegarder   to safeguard
le sauvetage   life-saving, rescue
sauve-qui-peut   run for your life
sauver les apparences   to preserve
  appearances

se sauver   to run away, to escape, to rush off
sauver la vie à qqn   to save someone's life
une échelle de sauvetage   fire escape
un gilet de sauvetage   a life jacket

See also **se sauver.**

Grammar putting you in a tense mood? Review the definitions of basic grammatical terms on
pages 674–688.

se sauver

Part. pr. se sauvant   **Part. passé sauvé(e)(s)**

to run away, to rush off, to escape

The Seven Simple Tenses		The Seven Compound Tenses	
Singular	Plural	Singular	Plural
1 présent de l'indicatif		**8 passé composé**	
me sauve	nous sauvons	me suis sauvé(e)	nous sommes sauvé(e)s
te sauves	vous sauvez	t'es sauvé(e)	vous êtes sauvé(e)(s)
se sauve	se sauvent	s'est sauvé(e)	se sont sauvé(e)s
2 imparfait de l'indicatif		**9 plus-que-parfait de l'indicatif**	
me sauvais	nous sauvions	m'étais sauvé(e)	nous étions sauvé(e)s
te sauvais	vous sauviez	t'étais sauvé(e)	vous étiez sauvé(e)(s)
se sauvait	se sauvaient	s'était sauvé(e)	s'étaient sauvé(e)s
3 passé simple		**10 passé antérieur**	
me sauvai	nous sauvâmes	me fus sauvé(e)	nous fûmes sauvé(e)s
te sauvas	vous sauvâtes	te fus sauvé(e)	vous fûtes sauvé(e)(s)
se sauva	se sauvèrent	se fut sauvé(e)	se furent sauvé(e)s
4 futur		**11 futur antérieur**	
me sauverai	nous sauverons	me serai sauvé(e)	nous serons sauvé(e)s
te sauveras	vous sauverez	te seras sauvé(e)	vous serez sauvé(e)(s)
se sauvera	se sauveront	se sera sauvé(e)	se seront sauvé(e)s
5 conditionnel		**12 conditionnel passé**	
me sauverais	nous sauverions	me serais sauvé(e)	nous serions sauvé(e)s
te sauverais	vous sauveriez	te serais sauvé(e)	vous seriez sauvé(e)(s)
se sauverait	se sauveraient	se serait sauvé(e)	se seraient sauvé(e)s
6 présent du subjonctif		**13 passé du subjonctif**	
me sauve	nous sauvions	me sois sauvé(e)	nous soyons sauvé(e)s
te sauves	vous sauviez	te sois sauvé(e)	vous soyez sauvé(e)(s)
se sauve	se sauvent	se soit sauvé(e)	se soient sauvé(e)s
7 imparfait du subjonctif		**14 plus-que-parfait du subjonctif**	
me sauvasse	nous sauvassions	me fusse sauvé(e)	nous fussions sauvé(e)s
te sauvasses	vous sauvassiez	te fusses sauvé(e)	vous fussiez sauvé(e)(s)
se sauvât	se sauvassent	se fût sauvé(e)	se fussent sauvé(e)s

Impératif
sauve-toi; ne te sauve pas
sauvons-nous; ne nous sauvons pas
sauvez-vous; ne vous sauvez pas

Words and expressions related to this verb
se sauver de prison to get out of prison
sauvegarder to safeguard
le sauvetage life-saving, rescue
sauve-qui-peut run for your life

sauver to rescue, to save
sauver la vie à qqn to save someone's life
vendre à la sauvette to peddle in the streets
une vente à la sauvette street peddling

See also **sauver**.

Get acquainted with what preposition goes with what verb on pages 543–553.

The Seven Simple Tenses		The Seven Compound Tenses	
Singular	Plural	Singular	Plural
1 présent de l'indicatif		**8 passé composé**	
sais	**savons**	**ai su**	**avons su**
sais	**savez**	**as su**	**avez su**
sait	**savent**	**a su**	**ont su**
2 imparfait de l'indicatif		**9 plus-que-parfait de l'indicatif**	
savais	**savions**	**avais su**	**avions su**
savais	**saviez**	**avais su**	**aviez su**
savait	**savaient**	**avait su**	**avaient su**
3 passé simple		**10 passé antérieur**	
sus	**sûmes**	**eus su**	**eûmes su**
sus	**sûtes**	**eus su**	**eûtes su**
sut	**surent**	**eut su**	**eurent su**
4 futur		**11 futur antérieur**	
saurai	**saurons**	**aurai su**	**aurons su**
sauras	**saurez**	**auras su**	**aurez su**
saura	**sauront**	**aura su**	**auront su**
5 conditionnel		**12 conditionnel passé**	
saurais	**saurions**	**aurais su**	**aurions su**
saurais	**sauriez**	**aurais su**	**auriez su**
saurait	**sauraient**	**aurait su**	**auraient su**
6 présent du subjonctif		**13 passé du subjonctif**	
sache	**sachions**	**aie su**	**ayons su**
saches	**sachiez**	**aies su**	**ayez su**
sache	**sachent**	**ait su**	**aient su**
7 imparfait du subjonctif		**14 plus-que-parfait du subjonctif**	
susse	**sussions**	**eusse su**	**eussions su**
susses	**sussiez**	**eusses su**	**eussiez su**
sût	**sussent**	**eût su**	**eussent su**

Impératif
sache
sachons
sachez

Words and expressions related to this verb
le savoir   knowledge
le savoir-faire   know-how, tact, ability
avoir le savoir-vivre   to be well-mannered, well-bred
faire savoir   to inform
Pas que je sache   Not to my knowledge.

savoir faire qqch   to know how to do something; **Savez-vous jouer du piano?**
Autant que je sache . . .   As far as I know . . .
C'est à savoir   That remains to be seen.
sans le savoir   without knowing it

Pronounce out loud this tongue twister as fast as you can: Le chasseur, sachant chasser sans son chien, chassera. (The hunter, knowing how to hunt without his dog, will hunt.)

The subject pronouns are found on the page facing page 1.   **427**

to shake, to shake down (off)

The Seven Simple Tenses		The Seven Compound Tenses	
Singular	Plural	Singular	Plural
1 présent de l'indicatif		8 passé composé	
secoue	secouons	ai secoué	avons secoué
secoues	secouez	as secoué	avez secoué
secoue	secouent	a secoué	ont secoué
2 imparfait de l'indicatif		9 plus-que-parfait de l'indicatif	
secouais	secouions	avais secoué	avions secoué
secouais	secouiez	avais secoué	aviez secoué
secouait	secouaient	avait secoué	avaient secoué
3 passé simple		10 passé antérieur	
secouai	secouâmes	eus secoué	eûmes secoué
secouas	secouâtes	eus secoué	eûtes secoué
secoua	secouèrent	eut secoué	eurent secoué
4 futur		11 futur antérieur	
secouerai	secouerons	aurai secoué	aurons secoué
secoueras	secouerez	auras secoué	aurez secoué
secouera	secoueront	aura secoué	auront secoué
5 conditionnel		12 conditionnel passé	
secouerais	secouerions	aurais secoué	aurions secoué
secouerais	secoueriez	aurais secoué	auriez secoué
secouerait	secoueraient	aurait secoué	auraient secoué
6 présent du subjonctif		13 passé du subjonctif	
secoue	secouions	aie secoué	ayons secoué
secoues	secouiez	aies secoué	ayez secoué
secoue	secouent	ait secoué	aient secoué
7 imparfait du subjonctif		14 plus-que-parfait du subjonctif	
secouasse	secouassions	eusse secoué	eussions secoué
secouasses	secouassiez	eusses secoué	eussiez secoué
secouât	secouassent	eût secoué	eussent secoué

Impératif
secoue
secouons
secouez

Words and expressions related to this verb
secouer la tête   to shake one's head
le secouement   shaking

secouer la poussière   to shake off the dust
une secousse   jolt; **sans secousse**   smoothly

Taking a trip? Check out the popular words, phrases, and expressions for travelers on pages 599–621.

to help, to relieve, to succor

The Seven Simple Tenses		The Seven Compound Tenses	
Singular	Plural	Singular	Plural
1 présent de l'indicatif		8 passé composé	
secours	secourons	ai secouru	avons secouru
secours	secourez	as secouru	avez secouru
secourt	secourent	a secouru	ont secouru
2 imparfait de l'indicatif		9 plus-que-parfait de l'indicatif	
secourais	secourions	avais secouru	avions secouru
secourais	secouriez	avais secouru	aviez secouru
secourait	secouraient	avait secouru	avaient secouru
3 passé simple		10 passé antérieur	
secourus	secourûmes	eus secouru	eûmes secouru
secourus	secourûtes	eus secouru	eûtes secouru
secourut	secoururent	eut secouru	eurent secouru
4 futur		11 futur antérieur	
secourrai	secourrons	aurai secouru	aurons secouru
secourras	secourrez	auras secouru	aurez secouru
secourra	secourront	aura secouru	auront secouru
5 conditionnel		12 conditionnel passé	
secourrais	secourrions	aurais secouru	aurions secouru
secourrais	secourriez	aurais secouru	auriez secouru
secourrait	secourraient	aurait secouru	auraient secouru
6 présent du subjonctif		13 passé du subjonctif	
secoure	secourions	aie secouru	ayons secouru
secoures	secouriez	aies secouru	ayez secouru
secoure	secourent	ait secouru	aient secouru
7 imparfait du subjonctif		14 plus-que-parfait du subjonctif	
secourusse	secourussions	eusse secouru	eussions secouru
secourusses	secourussiez	eusses secouru	eussiez secouru
secourût	secourussent	eût secouru	eussent secouru

Impératif
secours
secourons
secourez

Common idiomatic expressions using this verb and words related to it

le secours help, assistance
Au secours! Help!
crier au secours to shout for help
une roue de secours spare wheel
une sortie de secours emergency exit
secourir qqn contre un ennemi to help someone from an enemy

aller au secours de qqn to go to someone's aid
prêter secours à qqn to go to someone's rescue, assistance
une équipe de secours rescue squad
courir to run

Increase your verb power with popular phrases, words, and expressions on pages 599–621.

séduire

to seduce

The Seven Simple Tenses		The Seven Compound Tenses	
Singular	Plural	Singular	Plural
1 présent de l'indicatif		8 passé composé	
séduis	séduisons	ai séduit	avons séduit
séduis	séduisez	as séduit	avez séduit
séduit	séduisent	a séduit	ont séduit
2 imparfait de l'indicatif		9 plus-que-parfait de l'indicatif	
séduisais	séduisions	avais séduit	avions séduit
séduisais	séduisiez	avais séduit	aviez séduit
séduisait	séduisaient	avait séduit	avaient séduit
3 passé simple		10 passé antérieur	
séduisis	séduisîmes	eus séduit	eûmes séduit
séduisis	séduisîtes	eus séduit	eûtes séduit
séduisit	séduisirent	eut séduit	eurent séduit
4 futur		11 futur antérieur	
séduirai	séduirons	aurai séduit	aurons séduit
séduiras	séduirez	auras séduit	aurez séduit
séduira	séduiront	aura séduit	auront séduit
5 conditionnel		12 conditionnel passé	
séduirais	séduirions	aurais séduit	aurions séduit
séduirais	séduiriez	aurais séduit	auriez séduit
séduirait	séduiraient	aurait séduit	auraient séduit
6 présent du subjonctif		13 passé du subjonctif	
séduise	séduisions	aie séduit	ayons séduit
séduises	séduisiez	aies séduit	ayez séduit
séduise	séduisent	ait séduit	aient séduit
7 imparfait du subjonctif		14 plus-que-parfait du subjonctif	
séduisisse	séduisissions	eusse séduit	eussions séduit
séduisisses	séduisissiez	eusses séduit	eussiez séduit
séduisît	séduisissent	eût séduit	eussent séduit

Impératif
séduis
séduisons
séduisez

Words related to this verb
séduisant, séduisante   fascinating, seductive, attractive
un séducteur, une séductrice   tempter (temptress), seducer (seductress)
une séduction   seduction, enticement

See also **conduire, déduire, introduire, produire, réduire, reproduire,** and **traduire.**

Soak up some verbs used in weather expressions on pages 557–558.

to sojourn, to live somewhere temporarily

The Seven Simple Tenses		The Seven Compound Tenses	
Singular	Plural	Singular	Plural
1 présent de l'indicatif		**8 passé composé**	
séjourne	séjournons	ai séjourné	avons séjourné
séjournes	séjournez	as séjourné	avez séjourné
séjourne	séjournent	a séjourné	ont séjourné
2 imparfait de l'indicatif		**9 plus-que-parfait de l'indicatif**	
séjournais	séjournions	avais séjourné	avions séjourné
séjournais	séjourniez	avais séjourné	aviez séjourné
séjournait	séjournaient	avait séjourné	avaient séjourné
3 passé simple		**10 passé antérieur**	
séjournai	séjournâmes	eus séjourné	eûmes séjourné
séjournas	séjournâtes	eus séjourné	eûtes séjourné
séjourna	séjournèrent	eut séjourné	eurent séjourné
4 futur		**11 futur antérieur**	
séjournerai	séjournerons	aurai séjourné	aurons séjourné
séjourneras	séjournerez	auras séjourné	aurez séjourné
séjournera	séjourneront	aura séjourné	auront séjourné
5 conditionnel		**12 conditionnel passé**	
séjournerais	séjournerions	aurais séjourné	aurions séjourné
séjournerais	séjourneriez	aurais séjourné	auriez séjourné
séjournerait	séjourneraient	aurait séjourné	auraient séjourné
6 présent du subjonctif		**13 passé du subjonctif**	
séjourne	séjournions	aie séjourné	ayons séjourné
séjournes	séjourniez	aies séjourné	ayez séjourné
séjourne	séjournent	ait séjourné	aient séjourné
7 imparfait du subjonctif		**14 plus-que-parfait du subjonctif**	
séjournasse	séjournassions	eusse séjourné	eussions séjourné
séjournasses	séjournassiez	eusses séjourné	eussiez séjourné
séjournât	séjournassent	eût séjourné	eussent séjourné

Impératif
séjourne
séjournons
séjournez

Words and expressions related to this verb
séjourner à un hôtel   to stay (stop) at a hotel
un séjour   sojourn, stay
faire un séjour à la campagne   to stay in the
   country

séjourner chez des amis   to stay with friends
le jour   day
une salle de séjour   living room
un bref séjour   a brief stay

Going away? Don't forget to check out the practical situations for travelers on pages 568–598.

The subject pronouns are found on the page facing page 1.   **431**

sembler

Part. pr. [not in use]   **Part. passé semblé**

to seem

The Seven Simple Tenses		The Seven Compound Tenses	
Singular	Plural	Singular	Plural
1 présent de l'indicatif **il semble**		8 passé composé **il a semblé**	
2 imparfait de l'indicatif **il semblait**		9 plus-que-parfait de l'indicatif **il avait semblé**	
3 passé simple **il sembla**		10 passé antérieur **il eut semblé**	
4 futur **il semblera**		11 futur antérieur **il aura semblé**	
5 conditionnel **il semblerait**		12 conditionnel passé **il aurait semblé**	
6 présent du subjonctif **qu'il semble**		13 passé du subjonctif **qu'il ait semblé**	
7 imparfait du subjonctif **qu'il semblât**		14 plus-que-parfait du subjonctif **qu'il eût semblé**	

Impératif
[not in use]

Words and expressions related to this verb

Il me semble difficile   It seems difficult to me.

Il me semble que . . .   It seems to me that . . .

Il semble bon   It seems good.

Il semble inutile   It seems useless.

à ce qu'il me semble . . .   to my mind . . .

C'est ce qui me semble   That's what it looks like to me.

> This verb has regular forms in all the tenses (like **ressembler** among the 501 verbs in this book) but much of the time it is used impersonally in the forms given above with **il** (*it*) as the subject.

to feel, to smell, to perceive

The Seven Simple Tenses		The Seven Compound Tenses	
Singular	Plural	Singular	Plural
1 présent de l'indicatif		**8 passé composé**	
sens	sentons	ai senti	avons senti
sens	sentez	as senti	avez senti
sent	sentent	a senti	ont senti
2 imparfait de l'indicatif		**9 plus-que-parfait de l'indicatif**	
sentais	sentions	avais senti	avions senti
sentais	sentiez	avais senti	aviez senti
sentait	sentaient	avait senti	avaient senti
3 passé simple		**10 passé antérieur**	
sentis	sentîmes	eus senti	eûmes senti
sentis	sentîtes	eus senti	eûtes senti
sentit	sentirent	eut senti	eurent senti
4 futur		**11 futur antérieur**	
sentirai	sentirons	aurai senti	aurons senti
sentiras	sentirez	auras senti	aurez senti
sentira	sentiront	aura senti	auront senti
5 conditionnel		**12 conditionnel passé**	
sentirais	sentirions	aurais senti	aurions senti
sentirais	sentiriez	aurais senti	auriez senti
sentirait	sentiraient	aurait senti	auraient senti
6 présent du subjonctif		**13 passé du subjonctif**	
sente	sentions	aie senti	ayons senti
sentes	sentiez	aies senti	ayez senti
sente	sentent	ait senti	aient senti
7 imparfait du subjonctif		**14 plus-que-parfait du subjonctif**	
sentisse	sentissions	eusse senti	eussions senti
sentisses	sentissiez	eusses senti	eussiez senti
sentît	sentissent	eût senti	eussent senti

Impératif
sens
sentons
sentez

Words and expressions related to this verb
un sentiment   feeling, sense, impression
sentimental, sentimentale   sentimental
la sentimentalité   sentimentality
sentir le chagrin   to feel sorrow
se sentir + adj.   to feel + adj.; **Je me sens
   malade.**   I feel sick.
ressentir   to feel
un sentiment d'appartenance   feeling of
   membership, belonging

See also **consentir.**

sentir bon   to smell good
sentir mauvais   to smell bad
faire sentir qqch à qqn   to make someone feel
   something
se faire sentir   to make itself felt
ne se sentir pas bien   not to feel well; **Je ne
   me sens pas bien**   I don't feel well.

The subject pronouns are found on the page facing page 1.   **433**

seoir   Part. pr. **seyant**   Part. passé [not in use]

to be becoming, to suit

The Seven Simple Tenses

Singular	Plural

1   présent de l'indicatif
il sied   **ils siéent**

2   imparfait de l'indicatif
il seyait   **ils seyaient**

4   futur
il siéra   **ils siéront**

5   conditionnel
il siérait   **ils siéraient**

6   présent du subjonctif
qu'il siée   **qu'ils siéent**

This verb is defective and it is generally used only in the above persons and tenses.
Cela vous sied   That suits you well.
Ce chapeau te sied si bien!   That hat looks so good on you!
Connaissez-vous la pièce *Le Deuil sied à Electre* **d'Eugene O'Neill?**   Do you know the play
    Mourning Becomes Electra by Eugene O'Neill?
seoir à   to be becoming to

See also **s'asseoir.**

Consult the sections on verbs used in idiomatic expressions, verbs with prepositions, and the list
of over 1,100 verbs conjugated like model verbs in the back pages.

The form **séant** is used as an adj.: **Il n'est pas séant de faire cela**   It's unbecoming to do that.

434

The Seven Simple Tenses		The Seven Compound Tenses	
Singular	Plural	Singular	Plural
1 présent de l'indicatif		**8 passé composé**	
sépare	séparons	ai séparé	avons séparé
sépares	séparez	as séparé	avez séparé
sépare	séparent	a séparé	ont séparé
2 imparfait de l'indicatif		**9 plus-que-parfait de l'indicatif**	
séparais	séparions	avais séparé	avions séparé
séparais	sépariez	avais séparé	aviez séparé
séparait	séparaient	avait séparé	avaient séparé
3 passé simple		**10 passé antérieur**	
séparai	séparâmes	eus séparé	eûmes séparé
séparas	séparâtes	eus séparé	eûtes séparé
sépara	séparèrent	eut séparé	eurent séparé
4 futur		**11 futur antérieur**	
séparerai	séparerons	aurai séparé	aurons séparé
sépareras	séparerez	auras séparé	aurez séparé
séparera	sépareront	aura séparé	auront séparé
5 conditionnel		**12 conditionnel passé**	
séparerais	séparerions	aurais séparé	aurions séparé
séparerais	sépareriez	aurais séparé	auriez séparé
séparerait	sépareraient	aurait séparé	auraient séparé
6 présent du subjonctif		**13 passé du subjonctif**	
sépare	séparions	aie séparé	ayons séparé
sépares	sépariez	aies séparé	ayez séparé
sépare	séparent	ait séparé	aient séparé
7 imparfait du subjonctif		**14 plus-que-parfait du subjonctif**	
séparasse	séparassions	eusse séparé	eussions séparé
séparasses	séparassiez	eusses séparé	eussiez séparé
séparât	séparassent	eût séparé	eussent séparé

Impératif
sépare
séparons
séparez

Words and expressions related to this verb
séparer de   to sever from, to separate from
Les Pyrénées séparent la France et l'Espagne
France is separated from Spain by the
Pyrenees.

se séparer de   to be separated from, to
separate oneself from
Madame Dubois se sépare de son mari
Mrs. Dubois is separating from her husband.
une séparation   separation, parting

Get acquainted with what preposition goes with what verb on pages 543–553.

serrer

serrer   Part. pr. **serrant**   Part. passé **serré**

to grasp, to press, to squeeze, to shake (hands)

The Seven Simple Tenses		The Seven Compound Tenses	
Singular	Plural	Singular	Plural
1 présent de l'indicatif		8 passé composé	
serre	serrons	ai serré	avons serré
serres	serrez	as serré	avez serré
serre	serrent	a serré	ont serré
2 imparfait de l'indicatif		9 plus-que-parfait de l'indicatif	
serrais	serrions	avais serré	avions serré
serrais	serriez	avais serré	aviez serré
serrait	serraient	avait serré	avaient serré
3 passé simple		10 passé antérieur	
serrai	serrâmes	eus serré	eûmes serré
serras	serrâtes	eus serré	eûtes serré
serra	serrèrent	eut serré	eurent serré
4 futur		11 futur antérieur	
serrerai	serrerons	aurai serré	aurons serré
serreras	serrerez	auras serré	aurez serré
serrera	serreront	aura serré	auront serré
5 conditionnel		12 conditionnel passé	
serrerais	serrerions	aurais serré	aurions serré
serrerais	serreriez	aurais serré	auriez serré
serrerait	serreraient	aurait serré	auraient serré
6 présent du subjonctif		13 passé du subjonctif	
serre	serrions	aie serré	ayons serré
serres	serriez	aies serré	ayez serré
serre	serrent	ait serré	aient serré
7 imparfait du subjonctif		14 plus-que-parfait du subjonctif	
serrasse	serrassions	eusse serré	eussions serré
serrasses	serrassiez	eusses serré	eussiez serré
serrât	serrassent	eût serré	eussent serré

Impératif
serre
serrons
serrez

Words and expressions related to this verb

serrer la main à qqn   to shake hands with
  someone
serrer un noeud   to tighten a knot
un serre-livres   book end; **(des serre-livres)**
serrer les rangs   to close up ranks

serrer le coeur   to wring one's heart
serrés comme des harengs   packed like
  sardines
une serrure   lock; **le trou de la serrure**
  keyhole

Grammar putting you in a tense mood? Review the definitions of basic grammatical terms on pages 674–688.

The Seven Simple Tenses		The Seven Compound Tenses	
Singular	Plural	Singular	Plural
1 présent de l'indicatif		8 passé composé	
sers	servons	ai servi	avons servi
sers	servez	as servi	avez servi
sert	servent	a servi	ont servi
2 imparfait de l'indicatif		9 plus-que-parfait de l'indicatif	
servais	servions	avais servi	avions servi
servais	serviez	avais servi	aviez servi
servait	servaient	avait servi	avaient servi
3 passé simple		10 passé antérieur	
servis	servîmes	eus servi	eûmes servi
servis	servîtes	eus servi	eûtes servi
servit	servirent	eut servi	eurent servi
4 futur		11 futur antérieur	
servirai	servirons	aurai servi	aurons servi
serviras	servirez	auras servi	aurez servi
servira	serviront	aura servi	auront servi
5 conditionnel		12 conditionnel passé	
servirais	servirions	aurais servi	aurions servi
servirais	serviriez	aurais servi	auriez servi
servirait	serviraient	aurait servi	auraient servi
6 présent du subjonctif		13 passé du subjonctif	
serve	servions	aie servi	ayons servi
serves	serviez	aies servi	ayez servi
serve	servent	ait servi	aient servi
7 imparfait du subjonctif		14 plus-que-parfait du subjonctif	
servisse	servissions	eusse servi	eussions servi
servisses	servissiez	eusses servi	eussiez servi
servît	servissent	eût servi	eussent servi

Impératif
sers
servons
servez

Words and expressions related to this verb
le serveur   waiter
la serveuse   waitress
le service   service
une serviette   napkin
un serviteur   servant
la servitude   servitude
desservir   to clear off the table
un serveur   server (computer)

se servir   to serve oneself, to help oneself
se servir de qqch   to use something, to avail oneself of something, to make use of something
servir à qqch   to be of some use
servir à rien   to be of no use; Cela ne sert à rien   That serves no purpose.

See also se **servir**.

The subject pronouns are found on the page facing page 1.

437

se servir   Part. pr. **se servant**   Part. passé **servi(e)(s)**

se servir
to serve oneself, to help oneself (to food and drink)

The Seven Simple Tenses		The Seven Compound Tenses	
Singular	Plural	Singular	Plural
1 présent de l'indicatif		**8 passé composé**	
me sers	nous servons	me suis servi(e)	nous sommes servi(e)s
te sers	vous servez	t'es servi(e)	vous êtes servi(e)(s)
se sert	se servent	s'est servi(e)	se sont servi(e)s
2 imparfait de l'indicatif		**9 plus-que-parfait de l'indicatif**	
me servais	nous servions	m'étais servi(e)	nous étions servi(e)s
te servais	vous serviez	t'étais servi(e)	vous étiez servi(e)(s)
se servait	se servaient	s'était servi(e)	s'étaient servi(e)s
3 passé simple		**10 passé antérieur**	
me servis	nous servîmes	me fus servi(e)	nous fûmes servi(e)s
te servis	vous servîtes	te fus servi(e)	vous fûtes servi(e)(s)
se servit	se servirent	se fut servi(e)	se furent servi(e)s
4 futur		**11 futur antérieur**	
me servirai	nous servirons	me serai servi(e)	nous serons servi(e)s
te serviras	vous servirez	te seras servi(e)	vous serez servi(e)(s)
se servira	se serviront	se sera servi(e)	se seront servi(e)s
5 conditionnel		**12 conditionnel passé**	
me servirais	nous servirions	me serais servi(e)	nous serions servi(e)s
te servirais	vous serviriez	te serais servi(e)	vous seriez servi(e)(s)
se servirait	se serviraient	se serait servi(e)	se seraient servi(e)s
6 présent du subjonctif		**13 passé du subjonctif**	
me serve	nous servions	me sois servi(e)	nous soyons servi(e)s
te serves	vous serviez	te sois servi(e)	vous soyez servi(e)(s)
se serve	se servent	se soit servi(e)	se soient servi(e)s
7 imparfait du subjonctif		**14 plus-que-parfait du subjonctif**	
me servisse	nous servissions	me fusse servi(e)	nous fussions servi(e)s
te servisses	vous servissiez	te fusses servi(e)	vous fussiez servi(e)(s)
se servît	se servissent	se fût servi(e)	se fussent servi(e)s

Impératif
sers-toi; ne te sers pas
servons-nous; ne nous servons pas
servez-vous; ne vous servez pas

Words and expressions related to this verb
un serviteur servant
la servitude servitude
le serveur waiter
la serveuse waitress
le service service
une serviette napkin

See also **servir.**

se servir de qqch to use something, to make use of something
Servez-vous, je vous en prie! Help yourself, please!
Est-ce qu'on se sert seul dans ce restaurant?—Oui, c'est un restaurant self-service.

Want to learn more verbs used in proverbs and sayings? Take a look at page 559.

to whistle, to hiss, to boo

The Seven Simple Tenses		The Seven Compound Tenses	
Singular	Plural	Singular	Plural
1 présent de l'indicatif		**8 passé composé**	
siffle	sifflons	ai sifflé	avons sifflé
siffles	sifflez	as sifflé	avez sifflé
siffle	sifflent	a sifflé	ont sifflé
2 imparfait de l'indicatif		**9 plus-que-parfait de l'indicatif**	
sifflais	sifflions	avais sifflé	avions sifflé
sifflais	siffliez	avais sifflé	aviez sifflé
sifflait	sifflaient	avait sifflé	avaient sifflé
3 passé simple		**10 passé antérieur**	
sifflai	sifflâmes	eus sifflé	eûmes sifflé
sifflas	sifflâtes	eus sifflé	eûtes sifflé
siffla	sifflèrent	eut sifflé	eurent sifflé
4 futur		**11 futur antérieur**	
sifflerai	sifflerons	aurai sifflé	aurons sifflé
siffleras	sifflerez	auras sifflé	aurez sifflé
sifflera	siffleront	aura sifflé	auront sifflé
5 conditionnel		**12 conditionnel passé**	
sifflerais	sifflerions	aurais sifflé	aurions sifflé
sifflerais	siffleriez	aurais sifflé	auriez sifflé
sifflerait	siffleraient	aurait sifflé	auraient sifflé
6 présent du subjonctif		**13 passé du subjonctif**	
siffle	sifflions	aie sifflé	ayons sifflé
siffles	siffliez	aies sifflé	ayez sifflé
siffle	sifflent	ait sifflé	aient sifflé
7 imparfait du subjonctif		**14 plus-que-parfait du subjonctif**	
sifflasse	sifflassions	eusse sifflé	eussions sifflé
sifflasses	sifflassiez	eusses sifflé	eussiez sifflé
sifflât	sifflassent	eût sifflé	eussent sifflé

Impératif
siffle
sifflons
sifflez

Words and expressions related to this verb
un sifflet   whistle
un sifflet d'alarme   alarm whistle
un siffleur, une siffleuse   whistler, booer, hisser

le sifflet d'un agent de police   policeman's whistle
le sifflement   whistling, hissing

Consult the sections on verbs used in idiomatic expressions, verbs with prepositions, and the list of over 1,100 verbs conjugated like model verbs in the back pages.

The subject pronouns are found on the page facing page 1.   **439**

signaler

Part. pr. signalant **Part. passé signalé**

to point out, to signal

The Seven Simple Tenses		The Seven Compound Tenses	
Singular	Plural	Singular	Plural
1 présent de l'indicatif		**8 passé composé**	
signale	signalons	ai signalé	avons signalé
signales	signalez	as signalé	avez signalé
signale	signalent	a signalé	ont signalé
2 imparfait de l'indicatif		**9 plus-que-parfait de l'indicatif**	
signalais	signalions	avais signalé	avions signalé
signalais	signaliez	avais signalé	aviez signalé
signalait	signalaient	avait signalé	avaient signalé
3 passé simple		**10 passé antérieur**	
signalai	signalâmes	eus signalé	eûmes signalé
signalas	signalâtes	eus signalé	eûtes signalé
signala	signalèrent	eut signalé	eurent signalé
4 futur		**11 futur antérieur**	
signalerai	signalerons	aurai signalé	aurons signalé
signaleras	signalerez	auras signalé	aurez signalé
signalera	signaleront	aura signalé	auront signalé
5 conditionnel		**12 conditionnel passé**	
signalerais	signalerions	aurais signalé	aurions signalé
signaierais	signaleriez	aurais signalé	auriez signalé
signalerait	signaleraient	aurait signalé	auraient signalé
6 présent du subjonctif		**13 passé du subjonctif**	
signale	signalions	aie signalé	ayons signalé
signales	signaliez	aies signalé	ayez signalé
signale	signalent	ait signalé	aient signalé
7 imparfait du subjonctif		**14 plus-que-parfait du subjonctif**	
signalasse	signalassions	eusse signalé	eussions signalé
signalasses	signalassiez	eusses signalé	eussiez signalé
signalât	signalassent	eût signalé	eussent signalé

Impératif
signale
signalons
signalez

Words and expressions related to this verb
se signaler   to distinguish oneself
un signal   signal
le signal d'alarme   alarm signal
les signaux de route   road signs
signaliser   to mark with signs

le signal de détresse   distress signal
tirer le signal d'alarme   to pull the alarm
les moyens de signalisation   means of
   signaling

Taking a trip? Check out the popular words, phrases, and expressions for travelers on pages 599–621.

The Seven Simple Tenses		The Seven Compound Tenses	
Singular	Plural	Singular	Plural
1 présent de l'indicatif		**8 passé composé**	
signe	signons	ai signé	avons signé
signes	signez	as signé	avez signé
signe	signent	a signé	ont signé
2 imparfait de l'indicatif		**9 plus-que-parfait de l'indicatif**	
signais	signions	avais signé	avions signé
signais	signiez	avais signé	aviez signé
signait	signaient	avait signé	avaient signé
3 passé simple		**10 passé antérieur**	
signai	signâmes	eus signé	eûmes signé
signas	signâtes	eus signé	eûtes signé
signa	signèrent	eut signé	eurent signé
4 futur		**11 futur antérieur**	
signerai	signerons	aurai signé	aurons signé
signeras	signerez	auras signé	aurez signé
signera	signeront	aura signé	auront signé
5 conditionnel		**12 conditionnel passé**	
signerais	signerions	aurais signé	aurions signé
signerais	signeriez	aurais signé	auriez signé
signerait	signeraient	aurait signé	auraient signé
6 présent du subjonctif		**13 passé du subjonctif**	
signe	signions	aie signé	ayons signé
signes	signiez	aies signé	ayez signé
signe	signent	ait signé	aient signé
7 imparfait du subjonctif		**14 plus-que-parfait du subjonctif**	
signasse	signassions	eusse signé	eussions signé
signasses	signassiez	eusses signé	eussiez signé
signât	signassent	eût signé	eussent signé

Impératif
signe
signons
signez

Words and expressions related to this verb

se signer   to cross oneself (to make the sign of the Cross)
un signe   gesture, sign; **un signe de tête**   nod
faire le signe de la Croix   to make the sign of the Cross
la signature   signature, signing
assigner   to assign

consigner   to deposit (money); to consign (merchandise)
la consignation   consignment, deposit
le, la consignataire   consignee
le, la signataire   signer
les signes de vie   signs of life

If you don't know the French verb for an English verb you have in mind, try the index on pages 503–514.

The subject pronouns are found on the page facing page 1.   **441**

to dream, to think

The Seven Simple Tenses		The Seven Compound Tenses	
Singular	Plural	Singular	Plural
1 présent de l'indicatif		**8 passé composé**	
songe	songeons	ai songé	avons songé
songes	songez	as songé	avez songé
songe	songent	a songé	ont songé
2 imparfait de l'indicatif		**9 plus-que-parfait de l'indicatif**	
songeais	songions	avais songé	avions songé
songeais	songiez	avais songé	aviez songé
songeait	songeaient	avait songé	avaient songé
3 passé simple		**10 passé antérieur**	
songeai	songeâmes	eus songé	eûmes songé
songeas	songeâtes	eus songé	eûtes songé
songea	songèrent	eut songé	eurent songé
4 futur		**11 futur antérieur**	
songerai	songerons	aurai songe	aurons songé
songeras	songerez	auras songé	aurez songé
songera	songeront	aura songé	auront songé
5 conditionnel		**12 conditionnel passé**	
songerais	songerions	aurais songé	aurions songé
songerais	songeriez	aurais songé	auriez songé
songerait	songeraient	aurait songé	auraient songé
6 présent du subjonctif		**13 passé du subjonctif**	
songe	songions	aie songé	ayons songé
songes	songiez	aies songé	ayez songé
songe	songent	ait songé	aient songé
7 imparfait du subjonctif		**14 plus-que-parfait du subjonctif**	
songeasse	songeassions	eusse songé	eussions songé
songeasses	songeassiez	eusses songé	eussiez songé
songeât	songeassent	eût songé	eussent songé

Impératif
songe
songeons
songez

Words and expressions related to this verb
un songe   dream
un songeur, une songeuse   dreamer
songer à l'avenir   to think of the future
faire un songe   to have a dream

songer à   to think of something, to give
   thought to something
Songez-y bien!   Think it over carefully!
songer à faire qqch   to contemplate doing
   something

Get acquainted with what preposition goes with what verb on pages 543–553.

442

The Seven Simple Tenses		The Seven Compound Tenses

Singular	Plural	Singular	Plural
1 présent de l'indicatif		8 passé composé	
sonne	**sonnons**	**ai sonné**	**avons sonné**
sonnes	**sonnez**	**as sonné**	**avez sonné**
sonne	**sonnent**	**a sonné**	**ont sonné**
2 imparfait de l'indicatif		9 plus-que-parfait de l'indicatif	
sonnais	**sonnions**	**avais sonné**	**avions sonné**
sonnais	**sonniez**	**avais sonné**	**aviez sonné**
sonnait	**sonnaient**	**avait sonné**	**avaient sonné**
3 passé simple		10 passé antérieur	
sonnai	**sonnâmes**	**eus sonné**	**eûmes sonné**
sonnas	**sonnâtes**	**eus sonné**	**eûtes sonné**
sonna	**sonnèrent**	**eut sonné**	**eurent sonné**
4 futur		11 futur antérieur	
sonnerai	**sonnerons**	**aurai sonné**	**aurons sonné**
sonneras	**sonnerez**	**auras sonné**	**aurez sonné**
sonnera	**sonneront**	**aura sonné**	**auront sonné**
5 conditionnel		12 conditionnel passé	
sonnerais	**sonnerions**	**aurais sonné**	**aurions sonné**
sonnerais	**sonneriez**	**aurais sonné**	**auriez sonné**
sonnerait	**sonneraient**	**aurait sonné**	**auraient sonné**
6 présent du subjonctif		13 passé du subjonctif	
sonne	**sonnions**	**aie sonné**	**ayons sonné**
sonnes	**sonniez**	**aies sonné**	**ayez sonné**
sonne	**sonnent**	**ait sonné**	**aient sonné**
7 imparfait du subjonctif		14 plus-que-parfait du subjonctif	
sonnasse	**sonnassions**	**eusse sonné**	**eussions sonné**
sonnasses	**sonnassiez**	**eusses sonné**	**eussiez sonné**
sonnât	**sonnassent**	**eût sonné**	**eussent sonné**

Impératif
sonne
sonnons
sonnez

Words and expressions related to this verb
une sonnerie   ringing, chiming
une sonnette   house bell, doorbell
une sonnette électrique   electric bell
le son   sound, ringing
une sonnette de nuit   night bell
sonner creux   to sound hollow

une sonnette d'alarme   alarm bell
faire sonner un mot   to emphasize a word
une clochette   hand bell
la sonnerie du téléphone   the ringing of the
   telephone

Use the EE-zee guide to French pronunciation on pages 566 and 567.

sortir

Part. pr. **sortant**   Part. passé **sorti(e)(s)**

to go out, to leave

The Seven Simple Tenses		The Seven Compound Tenses	
Singular	Plural	Singular	Plural
1 présent de l'indicatif		**8 passé composé**	
sors	sortons	suis sorti(e)	sommes sorti(e)s
sors	sortez	es sorti(e)	êtes sorti(e)(s)
sort	sortent	est sorti(e)	sont sorti(e)s
2 imparfait de l'indicatif		**9 plus-que-parfait de l'indicatif**	
sortais	sortions	étais sorti(e)	étions sorti(e)s
sortais	sortiez	étais sorti(e)	étiez sorti(e)(s)
sortait	sortaient	était sorti(e)	étaient sorti(e)s
3 passé simple		**10 passé antérieur**	
sortis	sortîmes	fus sorti(e)	fûmes sorti(e)s
sortis	sortîtes	fus sorti(e)	fûtes sorti(e)(s)
sortit	sortirent	fut sorti(e)	furent sorti(e)s
4 futur		**11 futur antérieur**	
sortirai	sortirons	serai sorti(e)	serons sorti(e)s
sortiras	sortirez	seras sorti(e)	serez sorti(e)(s)
sortira	sortiront	sera sorti(e)	seront sorti(e)s
5 conditionnel		**12 conditionnel passé**	
sortirais	sortirions	serais sorti(e)	serions sorti(e)s
sortirais	sortiriez	serais sorti(e)	seriez sorti(e)(s)
sortirait	sortiraient	serait sorti(e)	seraient sorti(e)s
6 présent du subjonctif		**13 passé du subjonctif**	
sorte	sortions	sois sorti(e)	soyons sorti(e)s
sortes	sortiez	sois sorti(e)	soyez sorti(e)(s)
sorte	sortent	soit sorti(e)	soient sorti(e)s
7 imparfait du subjonctif		**14 plus-que-parfait du subjonctif**	
sortisse	sortissions	fusse sorti(e)	fussions sorti(e)s
sortisses	sortissiez	fusses sorti(e)	fussiez sorti(e)(s)
sortît	sortissent	fût sorti(e)	fussent sorti(e)s

Impératif
sors
sortons
sortez

Words and expressions related to this verb
ressortir   to go out again
une sortie   exit;
   une sortie de secours   emergency exit
sortir du lit   to get out of bed

se sortir d'une situation   to get oneself out of
   a situation
sortir d'une bonne famille   to come from a
   good family

This verb is conjugated with **avoir** when it has a direct object. Review p. viii.

Example: **Elle a sorti son mouchoir**   She took out her handkerchief.
BUT: **Elle est sortie hier soir**   She went out last night.

to blow, to pant, to prompt (an actor/actress with a cue)

The Seven Simple Tenses		The Seven Compound Tenses	
Singular	Plural	Singular	Plural
1 présent de l'indicatif		8 passé composé	
souffle	soufflons	ai soufflé	avons soufflé
souffles	soufflez	as soufflé	avez soufflé
souffle	soufflent	a soufflé	ont soufflé
2 imparfait de l'indicatif		9 plus-que-parfait de l'indicatif	
soufflais	soufflions	avais soufflé	avions soufflé
soufflais	souffliez	avais soufflé	aviez soufflé
soufflait	soufflaient	avait soufflé	avaient soufflé
3 passé simple		10 passé antérieur	
soufflai	soufflâmes	eus soufflé	eûmes soufflé
soufflas	soufflâtes	eus soufflé	eûtes soufflé
souffla	soufflèrent	eut soufflé	eurent soufflé
4 futur		11 futur antérieur	
soufflerai	soufflerons	aurai soufflé	aurons soufflé
souffleras	soufflerez	auras soufflé	aurez soufflé
soufflera	souffleront	aura soufflé	auront soufflé
5 conditionnel		12 conditionnel passé	
soufflerais	soufflerions	aurais soufflé	aurions soufflé
soufflerais	souffleriez	aurais soufflé	auriez soufflé
soufflerait	souffleraient	aurait soufflé	auraient soufflé
6 présent du subjonctif		13 passé du subjonctif	
souffle	soufflions	aie soufflé	ayons soufflé
souffles	souffliez	aies soufflé	ayez soufflé
souffle	soufflent	ait soufflé	aient soufflé
7 imparfait du subjonctif		14 plus-que-parfait du subjonctif	
soufflasse	soufflassions	eusse soufflé	eussions soufflé
soufflasses	soufflassiez	eusses soufflé	eussiez soufflé
soufflât	soufflassent	eût soufflé	eussent soufflé

Impératif
souffle
soufflons
soufflez

Words and expressions related to this verb
le souffle   breath, breathing
à bout de souffle   out of breath
retenir son souffle   to hold one's breath
couper le souffle à qqn   to take someone's
   breath away

un soufflé au fromage   cheese soufflé
souffler le verre   to blow glass
le souffle cardiaque   heart murmur
une souffleuse   snowblower

Want to learn more idiomatic expressions that contain verbs? Look at pages 530–542.

The subject pronouns are found on the page facing page 1.   **445**

souffrir

Part. pr **souffrant**   Part. passé **souffert**

to suffer, to endure

The Seven Simple Tenses		The Seven Compound Tenses	
Singular	Plural	Singular	Plural
1 présent de l'indicatif		**8 passé composé**	
souffre	souffrons	ai souffert	avons souffert
souffres	souffrez	as souffert	avez souffert
souffre	souffrent	a souffert	ont souffert
2 imparfait de l'indicatif		**9 plus-que-parfait de l'indicatif**	
souffrais	souffrions	avais souffert	avions souffert
souffrais	souffriez	avais souffert	aviez souffert
souffrait	souffraient	avait souffert	avaient souffert
3 passé simple		**10 passé antérieur**	
souffris	souffrîmes	eus souffert	eûmes souffert
souffris	souffrîtes	eus souffert	eûtes souffert
souffrit	souffrirent	eut souffert	eurent souffert
4 futur		**11 futur antérieur**	
souffrirai	souffrirons	aurai souffert	aurons souffert
souffriras	souffrirez	auras souffert	aurez souffert
souffrira	souffriront	aura souffert	auront souffert
5 conditionnel		**12 conditionnel passé**	
souffrirais	souffririons	aurais souffert	aurions souffert
souffrirais	souffririez	aurais souffert	auriez souffert
souffrirait	souffriraient	aurait souffert	auraient souffert
6 présent du subjonctif		**13 passé du subjonctif**	
souffre	souffrions	aie souffert	ayons souffert
souffres	souffriez	aies souffert	ayez souffert
souffre	souffrent	ait souffert	aient souffert
7 imparfait du subjonctif		**14 plus-que-parfait du subjonctif**	
souffrisse	souffrissions	eusse souffert	eussions souffert
souffrisses	souffrissiez	eusses souffert	eussiez souffert
souffrît	souffrissent	eût souffert	eussent souffert

Impératif
souffre
souffrons
souffrez

Words and expressions related to this verb

la souffrance suffering
souffrant, souffrante ailing, sick
souffreteux, souffreteuse sickly, feeble

souffrir le froid to withstand the cold
Cela me fait souffrir That hurts me.

Increase your verb power with popular phrases, words, and expressions for travelers on pages 599–621.

The Seven Simple Tenses		The Seven Compound Tenses	
Singular	Plural	Singular	Plural
1 présent de l'indicatif		**8 passé composé**	
souhaite	souhaitons	ai souhaité	avons souhaité
souhaites	souhaitez	as souhaité	avez souhaité
souhaite	souhaitent	a souhaité	ont souhaité
2 imparfait de l'indicatif		**9 plus-que-parfait de l'indicatif**	
souhaitais	souhaitions	avais souhaité	avions souhaité
souhaitais	souhaitiez	avais souhaité	aviez souhaité
souhaitait	souhaitaient	avait souhaité	avaient souhaité
3 passé simple		**10 passé antérieur**	
souhaitai	souhaitâmes	eus souhaité	eûmes souhaité
souhaitas	souhaitâtes	eus souhaité	eûtes souhaité
souhaita	souhaitèrent	eut souhaité	eurent souhaité
4 futur		**11 futur antérieur**	
souhaiterai	souhaiterons	aurai souhaité	aurons souhaité
souhaiteras	souhaiterez	auras souhaité	aurez souhaité
souhaitera	souhaiteront	aura souhaité	auront souhaité
5 conditionnel		**12 conditionnel passé**	
souhaiterais	souhaiterions	aurais souhaité	aurions souhaité
souhaiterais	souhaiteriez	aurais souhaité	auriez souhaité
souhaiterait	souhaiteraient	aurait souhaité	auraient souhaité
6 présent du subjonctif		**13 passé du subjonctif**	
souhaite	souhaitions	aie souhaité	ayons souhaité
souhaites	souhaitiez	aies souhaité	ayez souhaité
souhaite	souhaitent	ait souhaité	aient souhaité
7 imparfait du subjonctif		**14 plus-que-parfait du subjonctif**	
souhaitasse	souhaitassions	eusse souhaité	eussions souhaité
souhaitasses	souhaitassiez	eusses souhaité	eussiez souhaité
souhaitât	souhaitassent	eût souhaité	eussent souhaité

	Impératif	
	souhaite	
	souhaitons	
	souhaitez	

Words and expressions related to this verb

un souhait   a wish
à souhait   to one's liking
souhaits de bonne année   New Year's greetings
souhaiter bon voyage à qqn   to wish someone a good trip

souhaiter la bienvenue à qqn   to welcome someone
souhaiter le bonjour à qqn   to greet someone
souhaitable   desirable

Don't miss the definitions of basic grammatical terms with examples in English and French on pages 674–688.

souiller

Part. pr. souillant   **Part. passé souillé**

to dirty, to muddy, to soil

The Seven Simple Tenses		The Seven Compound Tenses	
Singular	Plural	Singular	Plural
1 présent de l'indicatif		**8 passé composé**	
souille	souillons	ai souillé	avons souillé
souilles	souillez	as souillé	avez souillé
souille	souillent	a souillé	ont souillé
2 imparfait de l'indicatif		**9 plus-que-parfait de l'indicatif**	
souillais	souillions	avais souillé	avions souillé
souillais	souilliez	avais souillé	aviez souillé
souillait	souillaient	avait souillé	avaient souillé
3 passé simple		**10 passé antérieur**	
souillai	souillâmes	eus souillé	eûmes souillé
souillas	souillâtes	eus souillé	eûtes souillé
souilla	souillèrent	eut souillé	eurent souillé
4 futur		**11 futur antérieur**	
souillerai	souillerons	aurai souillé	aurons souillé
souilleras	souillerez	auras souillé	aurez souillé
souillera	souilleront	aura souillé	auront souillé
5 conditionnel		**12 conditionnel passé**	
souillerais	souillerions	aurais souillé	aurions souillé
souillerais	souilleriez	aurais souillé	auriez souillé
souillerait	souilleraient	aurait souillé	auraient souillé
6 présent du subjonctif		**13 passé du subjonctif**	
souille	souillions	aie souillé	ayons souillé
souilles	souilliez	aies souillé	ayez souillé
souille	souillent	ait souillé	aient souillé
7 imparfait du subjonctif		**14 plus-que-parfait du subjonctif**	
souillasse	souillassions	eusse souillé	eussions souillé
souillasses	souillassiez	eusses souillé	eussiez souillé
souillât	souillassent	eût souillé	eussent souillé

Impératif
souille
souillons
souillez

Sentences using this verb and words related to it

Monsieur Beauregard dîne seul dans un restaurant. Le garçon lui apporte du poisson et après quelques minutes il demande au monsieur.

   —**Eh bien, monsieur. Comment trouvez-vous le poisson? Il est bon, n'est-ce pas?**
   —**Non, je le trouve dégoûtant. Ce poisson salé est souillé. Emportez-le!**

dégoûtant, dégoûtante disgusting
salé, salée salty
Comment trouvez-vous le poisson? How do
  you like the fish?

souillé, souillée dirty, soiled
Emportez-le! Take it away!
un, une souillon filthy slob
une souillure spot, stain

The Seven Simple Tenses		The Seven Compound Tenses	
Singular	Plural	Singular	Plural

1 présent de l'indicatif		8 passé composé	
soumets	soumettons	ai soumis	avons soumis
soumets	soumettez	as soumis	avez soumis
soumet	soumettent	a soumis	ont soumis

2 imparfait de l'indicatif		9 plus-que-parfait de l'indicatif	
soumettais	soumettions	avais soumis	avions soumis
soumettais	soumettiez	avais soumis	aviez soumis
soumettait	soumettaient	avait soumis	avaient soumis

3 passé simple		10 passé antérieur	
soumis	soumîmes	eus soumis	eûmes soumis
soumis	soumîtes	eus soumis	eûtes soumis
soumit	soumirent	eut soumis	eurent soumis

4 futur		11 futur antérieur	
soumettrai	soumettrons	aurai soumis	aurons soumis
soumettras	soumettrez	auras soumis	aurez soumis
soumettra	soumettront	aura soumis	auront soumis

5 conditionnel		12 conditionnel passé	
soumettrais	soumettrions	aurais soumis	aurions soumis
soumettrais	soumettriez	aurais soumis	auriez soumis
soumettrait	soumettraient	aurait soumis	auraient soumis

6 présent du subjonctif		13 passé du subjonctif	
soumette	soumettions	aie soumis	ayons soumis
soumettes	soumettiez	aies soumis	ayez soumis
soumette	soumettent	ait soumis	aient soumis

7 imparfait du subjonctif		14 plus-que-parfait du subjonctif	
soumisse	soumissions	eusse soumis	eussions soumis
soumisses	soumissiez	eusses soumis	eussiez soumis
soumît	soumissent	eût soumis	eussent soumis

Impératif
soumets
soumettons
soumettez

Words and expressions related to this verb
se **soumettre à**   to give in to, to comply with
se **soumettre à une décision**   to comply with a decision
la soumission   submission

See also **commettre, mettre, se mettre, permettre, promettre, remettre, soumettre,** and **transmettre.**

It's important that you be familiar with the Subjunctive. See pages 560–565.

sourire   Part. pr. **souriant**   Part. passé **souri**

to smile

The Seven Simple Tenses		The Seven Compound Tenses	
Singular	Plural	Singular	Plural
1 présent de l'indicatif		**8 passé composé**	
souris	sourions	ai souri	avons souri
souris	souriez	as souri	avez souri
sourit	sourient	a souri	ont souri
2 imparfait de l'indicatif		**9 plus-que-parfait de l'indicatif**	
souriais	souriions	avais souri	avions souri
souriais	souriiez	avais souri	aviez souri
souriait	souriaient	avait souri	avaient souri
3 passé simple		**10 passé antérieur**	
souris	sourîmes	eus souri	eûmes souri
souris	sourîtes	eus souri	eûtes souri
sourit	sourirent	eut souri	eurent souri
4 futur		**11 futur antérieur**	
sourirai	sourirons	aurai souri	aurons souri
souriras	sourirez	auras souri	aurez souri
sourira	souriront	aura souri	auront souri
5 conditionnel		**12 conditionnel passé**	
sourirais	souririons	aurais souri	aurions souri
sourirais	souririez	aurais souri	auriez souri
sourirait	souriraient	aurait souri	auraient souri
6 présent du subjonctif		**13 passé du subjonctif**	
sourie	souriions	aie souri	ayons souri
souries	souriiez	aies souri	ayez souri
sourie	sourient	ait souri	aient souri
7 imparfait du subjonctif		**14 plus-que-parfait du subjonctif**	
sourisse	sourissions	eusse souri	eussions souri
sourisses	sourissiez	eusses souri	eussiez souri
sourît	sourissent	eût souri	eussent souri

Impératif
souris
sourions
souriez

Words and expressions related to this verb
un sourire a smile
Gardez le sourire! Keep smiling!
un large sourire a broad smile
le rire laughter
sourire à to favor, to be favorable to, to smile on; **Claudine est heureuse; la vie lui sourit.**

See also **rire**.

faire un sourire à qqn to give someone a smile
Souris à la vie, et la vie te sourira. Smile at life and life will smile at you.

Want to learn more verbs used in proverbs and sayings? Take a look at page 559.

450

The Seven Simple Tenses		The Seven Compound Tenses	
Singular	Plural	Singular	Plural
1 présent de l'indicatif		8 passé composé	
me souviens	**nous souvenons**	**me suis souvenu(e)**	**nous sommes souvenu(e)s**
te souviens	**vous souvenez**	**t'es souvenu(e)**	**vous êtes souvenu(e)(s)**
se souvient	**se souviennent**	**s'est souvenu(e)**	**se sont souvenu(e)s**
2 imparfait de l'indicatif		9 plus-que-parfait de l'indicatif	
me souvenais	**nous souvenions**	**m'étais souvenu(e)**	**nous étions souvenu(e)s**
te souvenais	**vous souveniez**	**t'étais souvenu(e)**	**vous étiez souvenu(e)(s)**
se souvenait	**se souvenaient**	**s'était souvenu(e)**	**s'étaient souvenu(e)s**
3 passé simple		10 passé antérieur	
me souvins	**nous souvînmes**	**me fus souvenu(e)**	**nous fûmes souvenu(e)s**
te souvins	**vous souvîntes**	**te fus souvenu(e)**	**vous fûtes souvenu(e)(s)**
se souvint	**se souvinrent**	**se fut souvenu(e)**	**se furent souvenu(e)s**
4 futur		11 futur antérieur	
me souviendrai	**nous souviendrons**	**me serai souvenu(e)**	**nous serons souvenu(e)s**
te souviendras	**vous souviendrez**	**te seras souvenu(e)**	**vous serez souvenu(e)(s)**
se souviendra	**se souviendront**	**se sera souvenu(e)**	**se seront souvenu(e)s**
5 conditionnel		12 conditionnel passé	
me souviendrais	**nous souviendrions**	**me serais souvenu(e)**	**nous serions souvenu(e)s**
te souviendrais	**vous souviendriez**	**te serais souvenu(e)**	**vous seriez souvenu(e)(s)**
se souviendrait	**se souviendraient**	**se serait souvenu(e)**	**se seraient souvenu(e)s**
6 présent du subjonctif		13 passé du subjonctif	
me souvienne	**nous souvenions**	**me sois souvenu(e)**	**nous soyons souvenu(e)s**
te souviennes	**vous souveniez**	**te sois souvenu(e)**	**vous soyez souvenu(e)(s)**
se souvienne	**se souviennent**	**se soit souvenu(e)**	**se soient souvenu(e)s**
7 imparfait du subjonctif		14 plus-que-parfait du subjonctif	
me souvinsse	**nous souvinssions**	**me fusse souvenu(e)**	**nous fussions souvenu(e)s**
te souvinsses	**vous souvinssiez**	**te fusses souvenu(e)**	**vous fussiez souvenu(e)(s)**
se souvînt	**se souvinssent**	**se fût souvenu(e)**	**se fussent souvenu(e)s**

Impératif
souviens-toi; ne te souviens pas
souvenons-nous; ne nous souvenons pas
souvenez-vous; ne vous souvenez pas

Words and expressions related to this verb

un souvenir   souvenir, remembrance
Je m'en souviendrai!   I'll remember that!
   I won't forget that!
se souvenir de qqn ou de qqch   to remember
   someone or something
conserver le souvenir de qqch   to retain the
   memory of something

raconter des souvenirs d'enfance   to recount
   memories of one's childhood
les souvenirs   memoirs
en souvenir de   in remembrance of
Je me souviens   I remember. (Motto of the
   Province of Québec)

See also **convenir, devenir, prévenir, revenir,** and **venir.**

The subject pronouns are found on the page facing page 1.   **451**

to suck

The Seven Simple Tenses		The Seven Compound Tenses	
Singular	Plural	Singular	Plural
1 présent de l'indicatif		8 passé composé	
suce	suçons	ai sucé	avons sucé
suces	sucez	as sucé	avez sucé
suce	sucent	a sucé	ont sucé
2 imparfait de l'indicatif		9 plus-que-parfait de l'indicatif	
suçais	sucions	avais sucé	avions sucé
suçais	suciez	avais sucé	aviez sucé
suçait	suçaient	avait sucé	avaient sucé
3 passé simple		10 passé antérieur	
suçai	suçâmes	eus sucé	eûmes sucé
suças	suçâtes	eus sucé	eûtes sucé
suça	sucèrent	eut sucé	eurent sucé
4 futur		11 futur antérieur	
sucerai	sucerons	aurai sucé	aurons sucé
suceras	sucerez	auras sucé	aurez sucé
sucera	suceront	aura sucé	auront sucé
5 conditionnel		12 conditionnel passé	
sucerais	sucerions	aurais sucé	aurions sucé
sucerais	suceriez	aurais sucé	auriez sucé
sucerait	suceraient	aurait sucé	auraient sucé
6 présent du subjonctif		13 passé du subjonctif	
suce	sucions	aie sucé	ayons sucé
suces	suciez	aies sucé	ayez sucé
suce	sucent	ait sucé	aient sucé
7 imparfait du subjonctif		14 plus-que-parfait du subjonctif	
suçasse	suçassions	eusse sucé	eussions sucé
suçasses	suçassiez	eusses sucé	eussiez sucé
suçât	suçassent	eût sucé	eussent sucé

Impératif
suce
suçons
sucez

Words and expressions related to this verb
une sucette lollipop; **une sucette de bébé**
  teething ring
sucer le jus d'une orange to suck the juice of
  an orange
un suceur, une suceuse sucker;
  suceur de sang bloodsucker

suçoter to suck away on a candy;
  toujours à sucer des bonbons always
  sucking candies
un suçon hickey

Don't miss the definitions of basic grammatical terms with examples in English and French on
pages 674–688.

to suffice, to be sufficient, to be enough

The Seven Simple Tenses	The Seven Compound Tenses
Singular Plural	Singular Plural
1 présent de l'indicatif **il suffit**	8 passé composé **il a suffi**
2 imparfait de l'indicatif **il suffisait**	9 plus-que-parfait de l'indicatif **il avait suffi**
3 passé simple **il suffit**	10 passé antérieur **il eut suffi**
4 futur **il suffira**	11 futur antérieur **il aura suffi**
5 conditionnel **il suffirait**	12 conditionnel passé **il aurait suffi**
6 présent du subjonctif **qu'il suffise**	13 passé du subjonctif **qu'il ait suffi**
7 imparfait du subjonctif **qu'il suffît**	14 plus-que-parfait du subjonctif **qu'il eût suffi**

Impératif
Qu'il suffise!

Words and expressions related to this verb
la suffisance   sufficiency
suffisamment   sufficiently
Cela suffit!   That's quite enough!
Suffit!   Enough! Stop it!
Ma famille suffit à mon bonheur   My family
   is enough for my happiness.

Ça ne te suffit pas?   That's not enough for
   you?
Y a-t-il suffisamment à manger?   Is there
   enough to eat?

This verb is generally impersonal and is used in the third person singular as given in the above
tenses.

suivre

Part. pr. **suivant**   Part. passé **suivi**

to follow

The Seven Simple Tenses		The Seven Compound Tenses	
Singular	Plural	Singular	Plural
1 présent de l'indicatif		**8 passé composé**	
suis	suivons	ai suivi	avons suivi
suis	suivez	as suivi	avez suivi
suit	suivent	a suivi	ont suivi
2 imparfait de l'indicatif		**9 plus-que-parfait de l'indicatif**	
suivais	suivions	avais suivi	avions suivi
suivais	suiviez	avais suivi	aviez suivi
suivait	suivaient	avait suivi	avaient suivi
3 passé simple		**10 passe antérieur**	
suivis	suivîmes	eus suivi	eûmes suivi
suivis	suivîtes	eus suivi	eûtes suivi
suivit	suivirent	eut suivi	eurent suivi
4 futur		**11 futur antérieur**	
suivrai	suivrons	aurai suivi	aurons suivi
suivras	suivrez	auras suivi	aurez suivi
suivra	suivront	aura suivi	auront suivi
5 conditionnel		**12 conditionnel passé**	
suivrais	suivrions	aurais suivi	aurions suivi
suivrais	suivriez	aurais suivi	auriez suivi
suivrait	suivraient	aurait suivi	auraient suivi
6 présent du subjonctif		**13 passé du subjonctif**	
suive	suivions	aie suivi	ayons suivi
suives	suiviez	aies suivi	ayez suivi
suive	suivent	ait suivi	aient suivi
7 imparfait du subjonctif		**14 plus-que-parfait du subjonctif**	
suivisse	suivissions	eusse suivi	eussions suivi
suivisses	suivissiez	eusses suivi	eussiez suivi
suivît	suivissent	eût suivi	eussent suivi

Impératif
suis
suivons
suivez

Words and expressions related to this verb
suivant   according to
suivant que . . .   according as . . .
la suite   continuation
à la suite de   coming after
de suite   in succession, right away
à suivre   to be continued

le jour suivant   on the following day
les questions suivantes   the following questions
tout de suite   immediately
suivre un cours   to take a course

See also **poursuivre**.

Taking a trip? Check out the popular words, phrases, and expressions for travelers on pages 599–621.

to beg, to beseech, to implore, to supplicate

The Seven Simple Tenses		The Seven Compound Tenses	
Singular	Plural	Singular	Plural

1   présent de l'indicatif

supplie	supplions	
supplies	suppliez	
supplie	supplient	

8   passé composé

ai supplié	avons supplié	
as supplié	avez supplié	
a supplié	ont supplié	

2   imparfait de l'indicatif

suppliais	suppliions
suppliais	suppliiez
suppliait	suppliaient

9   plus-que-parfait de l'indicatif

avais supplié	avions supplié
avais supplié	aviez supplié
avait supplié	avaient supplié

3   passé simple

suppliai	suppliâmes
supplias	suppliâtes
supplia	supplièrent

10   passé antérieur

eus supplié	eûmes supplié
eus supplié	eûtes supplié
eut supplié	eurent supplié

4   futur

supplierai	supplierons
supplieras	supplierez
suppliera	supplieront

11   futur antérieur

aurai supplié	aurons supplié
auras supplié	aurez supplié
aura supplié	auront supplié

5   conditionnel

supplierais	supplierions
supplierais	supplieriez
supplierait	supplieraient

12   conditionnel passé

aurais supplié	aurions supplié
aurais supplié	auriez supplié
aurait supplié	auraient supplié

6   présent du subjonctif

supplie	suppliions
supplies	suppliiez
supplie	supplient

13   passé du subjonctif

aie supplié	ayons supplié
aies supplié	ayez supplié
ait supplié	aient supplié

7   imparfait du subjonctif

suppliasse	suppliassions
suppliasses	suppliassiez
suppliât	suppliassent

14   plus-que-parfait du subjonctif

eusse supplié	eussions supplié
eusses supplié	eussiez supplié
eût supplié	eussent supplié

Impératif
supplie
supplions
suppliez

Words and expressions related to this verb
une supplique   request, petition
suppliant, suppliante   imploring, supplicating
supplicier   to torture
un supplice   torture

une supplication   supplication, plea
supplier qqn à genoux   to beg someone on hands and knees

Try the verb drills and verb tests with answers explained on pages 622–673.

supporter   Part. pr. **supportant**   Part. passé **supporté**

to hold up, to prop up, to support, to endure, to tolerate

The Seven Simple Tenses		The Seven Compound Tenses	
Singular	Plural	Singular	Plural
1 présent de l'indicatif		8 passé composé	
supporte	supportons	ai supporté	avons supporté
supportes	supportez	as supporté	avez supporté
supporte	supportent	a supporté	ont supporté
2 imparfait de l'indicatif		9 plus-que-parfait de l'indicatif	
supportais	supportions	avais supporté	avions supporté
supportais	supportiez	avais supporté	aviez supporté
supportait	supportaient	avait supporté	avaient supporté
3 passé simple		10 passé antérieur	
supportai	supportâmes	eus supporté	eûmes supporté
supportas	supportâtes	eus supporté	eûtes supporté
supporta	supportèrent	eut supporté	eurent supporté
4 futur		11 futur antérieur	
supporterai	supporterons	aurai supporté	aurons supporté
supporteras	supporterez	auras supporté	aurez supporté
supportera	supporteront	aura supporté	auront supporté
5 conditionnel		12 conditionnel passé	
supporterais	supporterions	aurais supporté	aurions supporté
supporterais	supporteriez	aurais supporté	auriez supporté
supporterait	supporteraient	aurait supporté	auraient supporté
6 présent du subjonctif		13 passé du subjonctif	
supporte	supportions	aie supporté	ayons supporté
supportes	supportiez	aies supporté	ayez supporté
supporte	supportent	ait supporté	aient supporté
7 imparfait du subjonctif		14 plus-que-parfait du subjonctif	
supportasse	supportassions	eusse supporté	eussions supporté
supportasses	supportassiez	eusses supporté	eussiez supporté
supportât	supportassent	eût supporté	eussent supporté

Impératif
supporte
supportons
supportez

Words and expressions related to this verb
supportable endurable, bearable, supportable
porter to carry
insupportable unbearable, insufferable
un support support, prop
un support-chaussette elastic band support (for socks) (**des supports-chaussettes**)

See also **apporter** and **porter.**

Grammar putting you in a tense mood? Review the definitions of basic grammatical terms on pages 674–688.

The Seven Simple Tenses		The Seven Compound Tenses	
Singular	Plural	Singular	Plural

1 présent de l'indicatif		8 passé composé	
surprends	surprenons	ai surpris	avons surpris
surprends	surprenez	as surpris	avez surpris
surprend	surprennent	a surpris	ont surpris

2 imparfait de l'indicatif		9 plus-que-parfait de l'indicatif	
surprenais	surprenions	avais surpris	avions surpris
surprenais	surpreniez	avais surpris	aviez surpris
surprenait	surprenaient	avait surpris	avaient surpris

3 passé simple		10 passé antérieur	
surpris	surprîmes	eus surpris	eûmes surpris
surpris	surprîtes	eus surpris	eûtes surpris
surprit	surprirent	eut surpris	eurent surpris

4 futur		11 futur antérieur	
surprendrai	surprendrons	aurai surpris	aurons surpris
surprendras	surprendrez	auras surpris	aurez surpris
surprendra	surprendront	aura surpris	auront surpris

5 conditionnel		12 conditionnel passé	
surprendrais	surprendrions	aurais surpris	aurions aurpris
surprendrais	surprendriez	aurais surpris	auriez surpris
surprendrait	surprendraient	aurait surpris	auraient surpris

6 présent du subjonctif		13 passé du subjonctif	
surprenne	surprenions	aie surpris	ayons surpris
surprennes	surpreniez	aies surpirs	ayez surpris
surprenne	surprennent	ait surpris	aient surpris

7 imparfait du subjonctif		14 plus-que-parfait du subjonctif	
surprisse	surprissions	eusse surpris	eussions surpris
surprisses	surprissiez	eusses surpris	eussiez surpris
surprît	surprissent	eût surpris	eussent surpris

Impératif
surprends
surprenons
surprenez

Words and expressions related to this verb

surprendre qqn chez soi   to surprise someone
at home
une surprise   surprise
surprenant, surprenante   surprising
une boîte à surprise   jack-in-the-box
surpris par qqn   surprised by someone

surpris par qqch   surprised by something
par surprise   by surprise
à ma grande surprise   to my great surprise
une surprise partie (une surprise-party)
surprise party; **des surprises-parties**

See also **apprendre, comprendre, entreprendre, se méprendre, prendre,** and **reprendre.**

Going away? Don't forget to check out the practical situations for travelers on pages 568–598.

The subject pronouns are found on the page facing page 1.   **457**

survivre

to survive

The Seven Simple Tenses		The Seven Compound Tenses	
Singular	Plural	Singular	Plural
1 présent de l'indicatif		**8 passé composé**	
survis	survivons	ai survécu	avons survécu
survis	survivez	as survécu	avez survécu
survit	survivent	a survécu	ont survécu
2 imparfait de l'indicatif		**9 plus-que-parfait de l'indicatif**	
survivais	survivions	avais survécu	avions survécu
survivais	surviviez	avais survécu	aviez survécu
survivait	survivaient	avait survécu	avaient survécu
3 passé simple		**10 passé antérieur**	
survécus	survécûmes	eus survécu	eûmes survécu
survécus	survécûtes	eus survécu	eûtes survécu
survécut	survécurent	eut survécu	eurent survécu
4 futur		**11 futur antérieur**	
survivrai	survivrons	aurai survécu	aurons survécu
survivras	survivrez	auras survécu	aurez survécu
survivra	survivront	aura survécu	auront survécu
5 conditionnel		**12 conditionnel passé**	
survivrais	survivrions	aurais survécu	aurions survécu
survivrais	survivriez	aurais survécu	auriez survécu
survivrait	survivraient	aurait survécu	auraient survécu
6 présent du subjonctif		**13 passé du subjonctif**	
survive	survivions	aie survécu	ayons survécu
survives	surviviez	aies survécu	ayez survécu
survive	survivent	ait survécu	aient survécu
7 imparfait du subjonctif		**14 plus-que-parfait du subjonctif**	
survécusse	survécussions	eusse survécu	eussions survécu
survécusses	survécussiez	eusses survécu	eussiez survécu
survécût	survécussent	eût survécu	eussent survécu

Impératif
survis
survivons
survivez

Words and expressions related to this verb
survivre à qqn to survive someone
survivant, survivante surviving; survivor
la survivance survival
se survivre to live on

survivre à l'humiliation to survive humiliation
la survie survival

See also **vivre**.

For an explanation of meanings and uses of French and English verb tenses and moods, see pages xv–xxvi.

The Seven Simple Tenses		The Seven Compound Tenses	
Singular	Plural	Singular	Plural
1 présent de l'indicatif		8 passé composé	
survole	survolons	ai survolé	avons survolé
survoles	survolez	as survolé	avez survolé
survole	survolent	a survolé	ont survolé
2 imparfait de l'indicatif		9 plus-que-parfait de l'indicatif	
survolais	survolions	avais survolé	avions survolé
survolais	survoliez	avais survolé	aviez survolé
survolait	survolaient	avait survolé	avaient survolé
3 passé simple		10 passé antérieur	
survolai	survolâmes	eus survolé	eûmes survolé
survolas	survolâtes	eus survolé	eûtes survolé
survola	survolèrent	eut survolé	eurent survolé
4 futur		11 futur antérieur	
survolerai	survolerons	aurai survolé	aurons survolé
survoleras	survolerez	auras survolé	aurez survolé
survolera	survoleront	aura survolé	auront survolé
5 conditionnel		12 conditionnel passé	
survolerais	survolerions	aurais survolé	aurions survolé
survolerais	survoleriez	aurais survolé	auriez survolé
survolerait	survoleraient	aurait survolé	auraient survolé
6 présent du subjonctif		13 passé du subjonctif	
survole	survolions	aie survolé	ayons survolé
survoles	survoliez	aies survolé	ayez survolé
survole	survolent	ait survolé	aient survolé
7 imparfait du subjonctif		14 plus-que-parfait du subjonctif	
survolasse	survolassions	eusse survolé	eussions survolé
survolasses	survolassiez	eusses survolé	eussiez survolé
survolât	survolassent	eût survolé	eussent survolé

Impératif
survole
survolons
survolez

Words and expressions related to this verb
le survol   flying over
voler   to fly, to steal
le vol   flight, theft
faire un survol à basse altitude   to make a low flight

See also **voler.**

> If you want to see a sample English verb fully conjugated in all the tenses, check out pages xiii and xiv.

se taire

to be silent, to be quiet, not to speak

The Seven Simple Tenses		The Seven Compound Tenses	
Singular	Plural	Singular	Plural
1 présent de l'indicatif		8 passé composé	
me tais	nous taisons	me suis tu(e)	nous sommes tu(e)s
te tais	vous taisez	t'es tu(e)	vous êtes tu(e)(s)
se tait	se taisent	s'est tu(e)	se sont tu(e)s
2 imparfait de l'indicatif		9 plus-que-parfait de l'indicatif	
me taisais	nous taisions	m'étais tu(e)	nous étions tu(e)s
te taisais	vous taisiez	t'étais tu(e)	vous étiez tu(e)(s)
se taisait	se taisaient	s'était tu(e)	s'étaient tu(e)s
3 passé simple		10 passé antérieur	
me tus	nous tûmes	me fus tu(e)	nous fûmes tu(e)s
te tus	vous tûtes	te fus tu(e)	vous fûtes tu(e)(s)
se tut	se turent	se fut tu(e)	se furent tu(e)s
4 futur		11 futur antérieur	
me tairai	nous tairons	me serai tu(e)	nous serons tu(e)s
te tairas	vous tairez	te seras tu(e)	vous serez tu(e)(s)
se taira	se tairont	se sera tu(e)	se seront tu(e)s
5 conditionnel		12 conditionnel passé	
me tairais	nous tairions	me serais tu(e)	nous serions tu(e)s
te tairais	vous tairiez	te serais tu(e)	vous seriez tu(e)(s)
se tairait	se tairaient	se serait tu(e)	se seraient tu(e)s
6 présent du subjonctif		13 passé du subjonctif	
me taise	nous taisions	me sois tu(e)	nous soyons tu(e)s
te taises	vous taisiez	te sois tu(e)	vous soyez tu(e)(s)
se taise	se taisent	se soit tu(e)	se soient tu(e)s
7 imparfait du subjonctif		14 plus-que-parfait du subjonctif	
me tusse	nous tussions	me fusse tu(e)	nous fussions tu(e)s
te tusses	vous tussiez	te fusses tu(e)	vous fussiez tu(e)(s)
se tût	se tussent	se fût tu(e)	se fussent tu(e)s

Impératif
tais-toi; ne te tais pas
taisons-nous; ne nous taisons pas
taisez-vous; ne vous taisez pas

—Marie, veux-tu te taire! Tu es trop bavarde. Et toi, Hélène, tais-toi aussi.
Les deux élèves ne se taisent pas. La maîtresse de chimie continue:
—Taisez-vous, je vous dis, toutes les deux; autrement, vous resterez dans cette salle après la classe.
Les deux jeunes filles se sont tues.

See also **bavarder** and **cesser.**

For an explanation of meanings and uses of French and English verb tenses and moods, see pages xv–xxvi.

The Seven Simple Tenses		The Seven Compound Tenses	
Singular	Plural	Singular	Plural
1 présent de l'indicatif		8 passé composé	
teins	**teignons**	**ai teint**	**avons teint**
teins	**teignez**	**as teint**	**avez teint**
teint	**teignent**	**a teint**	**ont teint**
2 imparfait de l'indicatif		9 plus-que-parfait de l'indicatif	
teignais	**teignions**	**avais teint**	**avions teint**
teignais	**teigniez**	**avais teint**	**aviez teint**
teignait	**teignaient**	**avait teint**	**avaient teint**
3 passé simple		10 passé antérieur	
teignis	**teignîmes**	**eus teint**	**eûmes teint**
teignis	**teignîtes**	**eus teint**	**eûtes teint**
teignit	**teignirent**	**eut teint**	**eurent teint**
4 futur		11 futur antérieur	
teindrai	**teindrons**	**aurai teint**	**aurons teint**
teindras	**teindrez**	**auras teint**	**aurez teint**
teindra	**teindront**	**aura teint**	**auront teint**
5 conditionnel		12 conditionnel passé	
teindrais	**teindrions**	**aurais teint**	**aurions teint**
teindrais	**teindriez**	**aurais teint**	**auriez teint**
teindrait	**teindraient**	**aurait teint**	**auraient teint**
6 présent du subjonctif		13 passé du subjonctif	
teigne	**teignions**	**aie teint**	**ayons teint**
teignes	**teigniez**	**aies teint**	**ayez teint**
teigne	**teignent**	**ait teint**	**aient teint**
7 imparfait du subjonctif		14 plus-que-parfait du subjonctif	
teignisse	**teignissions**	**eusse teint**	**eussions teint**
teignisses	**teignissiez**	**eusses teint**	**eussiez teint**
teignît	**teignissent**	**eût teint**	**eussent teint**

Impératif
teins
teignons
teignez

Words and expressions related to this verb

déteindre   to fade, to lose color, to remove the color
faire teindre qqch   to have something dyed
la teinture   dyeing
un teinturier, une teinturière   dyer
des cheveux teints   dyed hair

teindre en noir   to dye black
le teint   color, dye; complexion
teinter   to tint
la teinturerie   cleaning and dyeing
des lunettes à verres teintés   tinted eyeglasses
se teindre les cheveux   to dye one's hair

Use the EE-zee guide to French pronunciation on pages 566 and 567.

téléphoner

Part. pr. **téléphonant**   Part. passé **téléphoné**

to telephone

The Seven Simple Tenses		The Seven Compound Tenses	
Singular	Plural	Singular	Plural
1 présent de l'indicatif		**8 passé composé**	
téléphone	téléphonons	ai téléphoné	avons téléphoné
téléphones	téléphonez	as téléphoné	avez téléphoné
téléphone	téléphonent	a téléphoné	ont téléphoné
2 imparfait de l'indicatif		**9 plus-que-parfait de l'indicatif**	
téléphonais	téléphonions	avais téléphoné	avions téléphoné
téléphonais	téléphoniez	avais téléphoné	aviez téléphoné
téléphonait	téléphonaient	avait téléphoné	avaient téléphoné
3 passé simple		**10 passé antérieur**	
téléphonai	téléphonâmes	eus téléphoné	eûmes téléphoné
téléphonas	téléphonâtes	eus téléphoné	eûtes téléphoné
téléphona	téléphonèrent	eut téléphoné	eurent téléphoné
4 futur		**11 futur antérieur**	
téléphonerai	téléphonerons	aurai téléphoné	aurons téléphoné
téléphoneras	téléphonerez	auras téléphoné	aurez téléphoné
téléphonera	téléphoneront	aura téléphoné	auront téléphoné
5 conditionnel		**12 conditionnel passé**	
téléphonerais	téléphonerions	aurais téléphoné	aurions téléphoné
téléphonerais	téléphoneriez	aurais téléphoné	auriez téléphoné
téléphonerait	téléphoneraient	aurait téléphoné	auraient téléphoné
6 présent du subjonctif		**13 passé du subjonctif**	
téléphone	téléphonions	aie téléphoné	ayons téléphoné
téléphones	téléphoniez	aies téléphoné	ayez téléphoné
téléphone	téléphonent	ait téléphoné	aient téléphoné
7 imparfait du subjonctif		**14 plus-que-parfait du subjonctif**	
téléphonasse	téléphonassions	eusse téléphoné	eussions téléphoné
téléphonasses	téléphonassiez	eusses téléphoné	eussiez téléphoné
téléphonât	téléphonassent	eût téléphoné	eussent téléphoné

Impératif
téléphone
téléphonons
téléphonez

Words and expressions related to this verb

le téléphone   telephone
téléphonique   telephonic
téléphoniquement   telephonically (by
  telephone)
un, une téléphoniste   telephone operator
téléphoner à qqn   to telephone someone

Marie? Je lui ai téléphoné hier   Mary?
  I telephoned her yesterday.
le téléphone rouge   hot line
un téléphone cellulaire, un portable   cell
  phone

Check out the principal parts of some important French verbs on page xii.

to strain, to stretch, to tighten, to tend

The Seven Simple Tenses		The Seven Compound Tenses	
Singular	Plural	Singular	Plural
1 présent de l'indicatif		8 passé composé	
tends	**tendons**	**ai tendu**	**avons tendu**
tends	**tendez**	**as tendu**	**avez tendu**
tend	**tendent**	**a tendu**	**ont tendu**
2 imparfait de l'indicatif		9 plus-que-parfait de l'indicatif	
tendais	**tendions**	**avais tendu**	**avions tendu**
tendais	**tendiez**	**avais tendu**	**aviez tendu**
tendait	**tendaient**	**avait tendu**	**avaient tendu**
3 passé simple		10 passé antérieur	
tendis	**tendîmes**	**eus tendu**	**eûmes tendu**
tendis	**tendîtes**	**eus tendu**	**eûtes tendu**
tendit	**tendirent**	**eut tendu**	**eurent tendu**
4 futur		11 futur antérieur	
tendrai	**tendrons**	**aurai tendu**	**aurons tendu**
tendras	**tendrez**	**auras tendu**	**aurez tendu**
tendra	**tendront**	**aura tendu**	**auront tendu**
5 conditionnel		12 conditionnel passé	
tendrais	**tendrions**	**aurais tendu**	**aurions tendu**
tendrais	**tendriez**	**aurais tendu**	**auriez tendu**
tendrait	**tendraient**	**aurait tendu**	**auraient tendu**
6 présent du subjonctif		13 passé du subjonctif	
tende	**tendions**	**aie tendu**	**ayons tendu**
tendes	**tendiez**	**aies tendu**	**ayez tendu**
tende	**tendent**	**ait tendu**	**aient tendu**
7 imparfait du subjonctif		14 plus-que-parfait du subjonctif	
tendisse	**tendissions**	**eusse tendu**	**eussions tendu**
tendisses	**tendissiez**	**eusses tendu**	**eussiez tendu**
tendît	**tendissent**	**eût tendu**	**eussent tendu**

Impératif
tends
tendons
tendez

Words and expressions related to this verb

tendre la main à qqn   to hold out one's hand
    to someone
attendre   to wait (for)
détendre   to slacken
se détendre   to bend, to relax
étendre   to extend, to spread
une détente   relaxing, slackening, release of
    tension

s'attendre à   to expect
entendre   to hear, to understand
s'entendre avec qqn   to get along with
    someone, to understand each other, to agree
s'étendre   to stretch out, to lie down
tendre l'autre joue   to turn the other cheek
tendre l'oreille   to prick up one's ears
tendre un piège   to set a trap

See the summary of sequence of tenses with *si* (if) clauses on page 560.

The subject pronouns are found on the page facing page 1.   **463**

tenir

to hold, to grasp

The Seven Simple Tenses		The Seven Compound Tenses	
Singular	Plural	Singular	Plural
1 présent de l'indicatif		**8 passé composé**	
tiens	tenons	ai tenu	avons tenu
tiens	tenez	as tenu	avez tenu
tient	tiennent	a tenu	ont tenu
2 imparfait de l'indicatif		**9 plus-que-parfait de l'indicatif**	
tenais	tenions	avais tenu	avions tenu
tenais	teniez	avais tenu	aviez tenu
tenait	tenaient	avait tenu	avaient tenu
3 passé simple		**10 passé antérieur**	
tins	tînmes	eus tenu	eûmes tenu
tins	tîntes	eus tenu	eûtes tenu
tint	tinrent	eut tenu	eurent tenu
4 futur		**11 futur antérieur**	
tiendrai	tiendrons	aurai tenu	aurons tenu
tiendras	tiendrez	auras tenu	aurez tenu
tiendra	tiendront	aura tenu	auront tenu
5 conditionnel		**12 conditionnel passé**	
tiendrais	tiendrions	aurais tenu	aurions tenu
tiendrais	tiendriez	aurais tenu	auriez tenu
tiendrait	tiendraient	aurait tenu	auraient tenu
6 présent du subjonctif		**13 passé du subjonctif**	
tienne	tenions	aie tenu	ayons tenu
tiennes	teniez	aies tenu	ayez tenu
tienne	tiennent	ait tenu	aient tenu
7 imparfait du subjonctif		**14 plus-que-parfait du subjonctif**	
tinsse	tinssions	eusse tenu	eussions tenu
tinsses	tinssiez	eusses tenu	eussiez tenu
tînt	tinssent	eût tenu	eussent tenu

Impératif
tiens
tenons
tenez

Words and expressions related to this verb

tenir de qqn   to take after (to favor) someone;
  Robert tient de son père   Robert takes after
  his father.
tenir de bonne source   to have on good
  authority
tenir à qqch   to cherish something
tenir le pari   to take on the bet
tenir les bras levés   to keep one's arms up

See also **contenir, obtenir,** and **retenir.**

tenir les yeux fermés   to keep one's eyes
  closed
tenir un chien en laisse   to keep a dog on a
  leash
Cette maîtresse tient bien sa classe   This
  teacher controls her class well.
Tiens! Voilà Bob!   Look! There's Bob!
Tiens, tiens!   Well, well! Fancy that!
maintenir   to maintain

Check out the principal parts of some important French verbs on page xii.

The Seven Simple Tenses		The Seven Compound Tenses	
Singular	Plural	Singular	Plural
1 présent de l'indicatif		8 passé composé	
tente	tentons	ai tenté	avons tenté
tentes	tentez	as tenté	avez tenté
tente	tentent	a tenté	ont tenté
2 imparfait de l'indicatif		9 plus-que-parfait de l'indicatif	
tentais	tentions	avais tenté	avions tenté
tentais	tentiez	avais tenté	aviez tenté
tentait	tentaient	avait tenté	avaient tenté
3 passé simple		10 passé antérieur	
tentai	tentâmes	eus tenté	eûmes tenté
tentas	tentâtes	eus tenté	eûtes tenté
tenta	tentèrent	eut tenté	eurent tenté
4 futur		11 futur antérieur	
tenterai	tenterons	aurai tenté	aurons tenté
tenteras	tenterez	auras tenté	aurez tenté
tentera	tenteront	aura tenté	auront tenté
5 conditionnel		12 conditionnel passé	
tenterais	tenterions	aurais tenté	aurions tenté
tenterais	tenteriez	aurais tenté	auriez tenté
tenterait	tenteraient	aurait tenté	auraient tenté
6 présent du subjonctif		13 passé du subjonctif	
tente	tentions	aie tenté	ayons tenté
tentes	tentiez	aies tenté	ayez tenté
tente	tentent	ait tenté	aient tenté
7 imparfait du subjonctif		14 plus-que-parfait du subjonctif	
tentasse	tentassions	eusse tenté	eussions tenté
tentasses	tentassiez	eusses tenté	eussiez tenté
tentât	tentassent	eût tenté	eussent tenté

Impératif
tente
tentons
tentez

Words and expressions related to this verb
se laisser tenter to allow oneself to be tempted
une tentative attempt
tenter sa chance to try one's luck

un tentateur, une tentatrice tempter, temptress
tenter de faire qqch to try, to attempt to do something
tentant, tentante tempting, inviting

Use the EE-zee guide to French pronunciation on pages 566 and 567.

terminer
Part. pr. **terminant**   Part. passé **terminé**

to terminate, to finish, to end

The Seven Simple Tenses		The Seven Compound Tenses	
Singular	Plural	Singular	Plural
1 présent de l'indicatif		**8 passé composé**	
termine	terminons	ai terminé	avons terminé
termines	terminez	as terminé	avez terminé
termine	terminent	a terminé	ont terminé
2 imparfait de l'indicatif		**9 plus-que-parfait de l'indicatif**	
terminais	terminions	avais terminé	avions terminé
terminais	terminiez	avais terminé	aviez terminé
terminait	terminaient	avait terminé	avaient terminé
3 passé simple		**10 passé antérieur**	
terminai	terminâmes	eus terminé	eûmes terminé
terminas	terminâtes	eus terminé	eûtes terminé
termina	terminèrent	eut terminé	eurent terminé
4 futur		**11 futur antérieur**	
terminerai	terminerons	aurai terminé	aurons terminé
termineras	terminerez	auras terminé	aurez terminé
terminera	termineront	aura terminé	auront terminé
5 conditionnel		**12 conditionnel passé**	
terminerais	terminerions	aurais terminé	aurions terminé
terminerais	termineriez	aurais terminé	auriez terminé
terminerait	termineraient	aurait terminé	auraient terminé
6 présent du subjonctif		**13 passé du subjonctif**	
termine	terminions	aie terminé	ayons terminé
termines	terminiez	aies terminé	ayez terminé
termine	terminent	ait terminé	aient terminé
7 imparfait du subjonctif		**14 plus-que-parfait du subjonctif**	
terminasse	terminassions	eusse terminé	eussions terminé
terminasses	terminassiez	eusses terminé	eussiez terminé
terminât	terminassent	eût terminé	eussent terminé

Impératif
termine
terminons
terminez

Words and expressions related to this verb

terminal, terminale terminal
la terminaison ending, termination
terminable terminable
interminable interminable, endless
exterminer to exterminate
terminer la journée chez un ami to end the day at a friend's house

J'attends qu'elle termine le travail I'm waiting for her to finish the work.
Les vacances de Noël se terminent demain Christmas vacation ends tomorrow.
se terminer to end (itself)
se terminer en to end in; **un verbe qui se termine en** *er . . .* a verb that ends in *er . . .*
terminer un repas to finish a meal

Check out the principal parts of some important French verbs on page xii.

to draw out, to shoot, to pull

The Seven Simple Tenses		The Seven Compound Tenses	
Singular	Plural	Singular	Plural
1 présent de l'indicatif		**8 passé composé**	
tire	tirons	ai tiré	avons tiré
tires	tirez	as tiré	avez tiré
tire	tirent	a tiré	ont tiré
2 imparfait de l'indicatif		**9 plus-que-parfait de l'indicatif**	
tirais	tirions	avais tiré	avions tiré
tirais	tiriez	avais tiré	aviez tiré
tirait	tiraient	avait tiré	avaient tiré
3 passé simple		**10 passé antérieur**	
tirai	tirâmes	eus tiré	eûmes tiré
tiras	tirâtes	eus tiré	eûtes tiré
tira	tirèrent	eut tiré	eurent tiré
4 futur		**11 futur antérieur**	
tirerai	tirerons	aurai tiré	aurons tiré
tireras	tirerez	auras tiré	aurez tiré
tirera	tireront	aura tiré	auront tiré
5 conditionnel		**12 conditionnel passé**	
tirerais	tirerions	aurais tiré	aurions tiré
tirerais	tireriez	aurais tiré	auriez tiré
tirerait	tireraient	aurait tiré	auraient tiré
6 présent du subjonctif		**13 passé du subjonctif**	
tire	tirions	aie tiré	ayons tiré
tires	tiriez	aies tiré	ayez tiré
tire	tirent	ait tiré	aient tiré
7 imparfait du subjonctif		**14 plus-que-parfait du subjonctif**	
tirasse	tirassions	eusse tiré	eussions tiré
tirasses	tirassiez	eusses tiré	eussiez tiré
tirât	tirassent	eût tiré	eussent tiré

Impératif
tire
tirons
tirez

Words and expressions related to this verb

tirer une affaire au clair   to clear up a matter

tirer parti de   to take advantage of, to make the best of

un tireur, une tireuse   marksman, markswoman

un tire-bouchon   corkscrew (**des tire-bouchons**)

s'en tirer   to pull through

s'en tirer bien   to get off well, to come through well

tirer sur   to fire (shoot) at

un tiroir   drawer (of a desk, etc.)

se tirer d'affaire   to get out of a jam

un tire-clou   nail puller (**des tire-clous**)

See also **attirer, retirer,** and **se retirer.**

For more idioms, see pages 530–542.

tomber

Part. pr. **tombant**   Part. passé **tombé(e)(s)**

to fall

The Seven Simple Tenses		The Seven Compound Tenses	
Singular	Plural	Singular	Plural
1 présent de l'indicatif		**8 passé composé**	
tombe	tombons	suis tombé(e)	sommes tombé(e)s
tombes	tombez	es tombé(e)	êtes tombé(e)(s)
tombe	tombent	est tombé(e)	sont tombé(e)s
2 imparfait de l'indicatif		**9 plus-que-parfait de l'indicatif**	
tombais	tombions	étais tombé(e)	étions tombé(e)s
tombais	tombiez	étais tombé(e)	étiez tombé(e)(s)
tombait	tombaient	était tombé(e)	étaient tombé(e)s
3 passé simple		**10 passé antérieur**	
tombai	tombâmes	fus tombé(e)	fûmes tombé(e)s
tombas	tombâtes	fus tombé(e)	fûtes tombé(e)(s)
tomba	tombèrent	fut tombé(e)	furent tombé(e)s
4 futur		**11 futur antérieur**	
tomberai	tomberons	serai tombé(e)	serons tombé(e)s
tomberas	tomberez	seras tombé(e)	serez tombé(e)(s)
tombera	tomberont	sera tombé(e)	seront tombé(e)s
5 conditionnel		**12 conditionnel passé**	
tomberais	tomberions	serais tombé(e)	serions tombé(e)s
tomberais	tomberiez	serais tombé(e)	seriez tombé(e)(s)
tomberait	tomberaient	serait tombé(e)	seraient tombé(e)s
6 présent du subjonctif		**13 passé du subjonctif**	
tombe	tombions	sois tombé(e)	soyons tombé(e)s
tombes	tombiez	sois tombé(e)	soyez tombé(e)(s)
tombe	tombent	soit tombé(e)	soient tombé(e)s
7 imparfait du subjonctif		**14 plus-que-parfait du subjonctif**	
tombasse	tombassions	fusse tombé(e)	fussions tombé(e)s
tombasses	tombassiez	fusses tombé(e)	fussiez tombé(e)(s)
tombât	tombassent	fût tombé(e)	fussent tombé(e)s

Impératif
tombe
tombons
tombez

Words and expressions using this verb

tomber amourex (amoureuse) de qqn   to fall
  in love with someone
tomber sur   to run into, to come across
laisser tomber   to drop
tomber malade   to fall sick

faire tomber   to knock down
retomber   to fall again
tomber en panne   to break down
tomber dans les pommes   to pass out

Review p. viii.

Want to learn more verbs used in proverbs and sayings? Take a look at page 559.

The Seven Simple Tenses	The Seven Compound Tenses
Singular Plural	Singular Plural
1 présent de l'indicatif **il tonne**	8 passé composé **il a tonné**
2 imparfait de l'indicatif **il tonnait**	9 plus-que-parfait de l'indicatif **il avait tonné**
3 passé simple **il tonna**	10 passé antérieur **il eut tonné**
4 futur **il tonnera**	11 futur antérieur **il aura tonné**
5 conditionnel **il tonnerait**	12 conditionnel passé **il aurait tonné**
6 présent du subjonctif **qu'il tonne**	13 passé du subjonctif **qu'il ait tonné**
7 imparfait du subjonctif **qu'il tonnât**	14 plus-que-parfait du subjonctif **qu'il eût tonné**

Impératif
Qu'il tonne!   Let it thunder!

Common idiomatic expressions using this verb and words related to it
le tonnerre   thunder
Tonnerre!   By thunder!
C'est du tonnerre!   That's terrific!

un coup de tonnerre   a clap of thunder
un tonnerre d'acclamations   thundering
applause

This verb is impersonal and is used in the third person singular.

Soak up some verbs used in weather expressions on pages 557 and 558.

toquer

Part. pr. **toquant**   Part. passé **toqué**

to rap, to tap, to knock

The Seven Simple Tenses		The Seven Compound Tenses	
Singular	Plural	Singular	Plural
1 présent de l'indicatif		**8 passé composé**	
toque	toquons	ai toqué	avons toqué
toques	toquez	as toqué	avez toqué
toque	toquent	a toqué	ont toqué
2 imparfait de l'indicatif		**9 plus-que-parfait de l'indicatif**	
toquais	toquions	avais toqué	avions toqué
toquais	toquiez	avais toqué	aviez toqué
toquait	toquaient	avait toqué	avaient toqué
3 passé simple		**10 passé antérieur**	
toquai	toquâmes	eus toqué	eûmes toqué
toquas	toquâtes	eus toqué	eûtes toqué
toqua	toquèrent	eut toqué	eurent toqué
4 futur		**11 futur antérieur**	
toquerai	toquerons	aurai toqué	aurons toqué
toqueras	toquerez	auras toqué	aurez toqué
toquera	toqueront	aura toqué	auront toqué
5 conditionnel		**12 conditionnel passé**	
toquerais	toquerions	aurais toqué	aurions toqué
toquerais	toqueriez	aurais toqué	auriez toqué
toquerait	toqueraient	aurait toqué	auraient toqué
6 présent du subjonctif		**13 passé du subjonctif**	
toque	toquions	aie toqué	ayons toqué
toques	toquiez	aies toqué	ayez toqué
toque	toquent	ait toqué	aient toqué
7 imparfait du subjonctif		**14 plus-que-parfait du subjonctif**	
toquasse	toquassions	eusse toqué	eussions toqué
toquasses	toquassiez	eusses toqué	eussiez toqué
toquât	toquassent	eût toqué	eussent toqué

Impératif
toque
toquons
toquez

Sentences using this verb and words and expressions related to it

Je suis allé voir Madame Dutour, notre voisine qui est un peu toquée. J'ai toqué à la porte de l'index (with my index finger) **trois fois mais il n'y avait pas de réponse. Sa fille a une toquade pour mon fils et je voulais lui en parler.**

toquer à la porte to knock (tap) on the door
se toquer to go crazy; **se toquer de** to go mad about (over)
une toque cap (worn on head)
être toqué(e) to be tetched (in the head), to be a little crazy, nuts, batty, daft

une toquante ticker
une toquade infatuation, craze; **avoir une toquade pour qqn** to fall for someone, to become infatuated with someone
une toque de cuisinier chef's hat

Consult the sections on verbs used in idiomatic expressions, verbs with prepositions, and the list of over 1,100 verbs conjugated like model verbs in the back pages.

The Seven Simple Tenses | | The Seven Compound Tenses

Singular	Plural	Singular	Plural

1 présent de l'indicatif
tords | **tordons**
tords | **tordez**
tord | **tordent**

8 passé composé
ai tordu | **avons tordu**
as tordu | **avez tordu**
a tordu | **ont tordu**

2 imparfait de l'indicatif
tordais | **tordions**
tordais | **tordiez**
tordait | **tordaient**

9 plus-que-parfait de l'indicatif
avais tordu | **avions tordu**
avais tordu | **aviez tordu**
avait tordu | **avaient tordu**

3 passé simple
tordis | **tordîmes**
tordis | **tordîtes**
tordit | **tordirent**

10 passé antérieur
eus tordu | **eûmes tordu**
eus tordu | **eûtes tordu**
eut tordu | **eurent tordu**

4 futur
tordrai | **tordrons**
tordras | **tordrez**
tordra | **tordront**

11 futur antérieur
aurai tordu | **aurons tordu**
auras tordu | **aurez tordu**
aura tordu | **auront tordu**

5 conditionnel
tordrais | **tordrions**
tordrais | **tordriez**
tordrait | **tordraient**

12 conditionnel passé
aurais tordu | **aurions tordu**
aurais tordu | **auriez tordu**
aurait tordu | **auraient tordu**

6 présent du subjonctif
torde | **tordions**
tordes | **tordiez**
torde | **tordent**

13 passé du subjonctif
aie tordu | **ayons tordu**
aies tordu | **ayez tordu**
ait tordu | **aient tordu**

7 imparfait du subjonctif
tordisse | **tordissions**
tordisses | **tordissiez**
tordît | **tordissent**

14 plus-que-parfait du subjonctif
eusse tordu | **eussions tordu**
eusses tordu | **eussiez tordu**
eût tordu | **eussent tordu**

Impératif
tords
tordons
tordez

Words and expressions related to this verb
tordre le cou à qqn   to twist someone's neck
tordu, tordue   twisted
tortueux   twisting
être tordu (tordue)   to be crazy
une rue tortueuse   winding street

se tordre les mains   to wring one's hands
se tordre de rire   to split one's sides laughing
avoir la gueule tordue   to have an ugly puss (face)
avoir l'esprit tordu   to have a twisted mind

How are you doing? Find out with the verb drills and tests with answers explained on pages 622–673.

toucher

Part. pr. **touchant**   Part. passé **touché**

to touch, to affect

The Seven Simple Tenses		The Seven Compound Tenses	
Singular	Plural	Singular	Plural
1 présent de l'indicatif		**8 passé composé**	
touche	touchons	ai touché	avons touché
touches	touchez	as touché	avez touché
touche	touchent	a touché	ont touché
2 imparfait de l'indicatif		**9 plus-que-parfait de l'indicatif**	
touchais	touchions	avais touché	avions touché
touchais	touchiez	avais touché	aviez touché
touchait	touchaient	avait touché	avaient touché
3 passé simple		**10 passé antérieur**	
touchai	touchâmes	eus touché	eûmes touché
touchas	touchâtes	eus touché	eûtes touché
toucha	touchèrent	eut touché	eurent touché
4 futur		**11 futur antérieur**	
toucherai	toucherons	aurai touché	aurons touché
toucheras	toucherez	auras touché	aurez touché
touchera	toucheront	aura touché	auront touché
5 conditionnel		**12 conditionnel passé**	
toucherais	toucherions	aurais touché	aurions touché
toucherais	toucheriez	aurais touché	auriez touché
toucherait	toucheraient	aurait touché	auraient touché
6 présent du subjonctif		**13 passé du subjonctif**	
touche	touchions	aie touché	ayons touché
touches	touchiez	aies touché	ayez touché
touche	touchent	ait touché	aient touché
7 imparfait du subjonctif		**14 plus-que-parfait du subjonctif**	
touchasse	touchassions	eusse touché	eussions touché
touchasses	touchassiez	eusses touché	eussiez touché
touchât	touchassent	eût touché	eussent touché

Impératif
touche
touchons
touchez

Words and expressions related to this verb

Une personne qui touche à tout
  a meddlesome person
Touchez là! Put it there! Shake!
toucher à qqch to touch something
N'y touchez pas! Don't touch!
retoucher to touch up

le toucher touch, feeling, sense of touch
toucher de l'argent to get some money
Cela me touche profondément That touches
  me deeply.
un, une touche-à-tout meddler

Increase your verb power with popular phrases, words, and expressions for travelers on pages 599–621.

The Seven Simple Tenses		The Seven Compound Tenses	
Singular	Plural	Singular	Plural
1 présent de l'indicatif		**8 passé composé**	
tourne	tournons	ai tourné	avons tourné
tournes	tournez	as tourné	avez tourné
tourne	tournent	a tourné	ont tourné
2 imparfait de l'indicatif		**9 plus-que-parfait de l'indicatif**	
tournais	tournions	avais tourné	avions tourné
tournais	tourniez	avais tourné	aviez tourné
tournait	tournaient	avait tourné	avaient tourné
3 passé simple		**10 passé antérieur**	
tournai	tournâmes	eus tourné	eûmes tourné
tournas	tournâtes	eus tourné	eûtes tourné
tourna	tournèrent	eut tourné	eurent tourné
4 futur		**11 futur antérieur**	
tournerai	tournerons	aurai tourné	aurons tourné
tourneras	tournerez	auras tourné	aurez tourné
tournera	tourneront	aura tourné	auront tourné
5 conditionnel		**12 conditionnel passé**	
tournerais	tournerions	aurais tourné	aurions tourné
tournerais	tourneriez	aurais tourné	auriez tourné
tournerait	tourneraient	aurait tourné	auraient tourné
6 présent du subjonctif		**13 passé du subjonctif**	
tourne	tournions	aie tourné	ayons tourné
tournes	tourniez	aies tourné	ayez tourné
tourne	tournent	ait tourné	aient tourné
7 imparfait du subjonctif		**14 plus-que-parfait du subjonctif**	
tournasse	tournassions	eusse tourné	eussions tourné
tournasses	tournassiez	eusses tourné	eussiez tourné
tournât	tournassent	eût tourné	eussent tourné

Impératif
tourne
tournons
tournez

Words and expressions related to this verb
se tourner to turn around
tourner qqn en ridicule to ridicule someone
un tourne-disque record player
(**des tourne-disques**)
un tournevis screwdriver
retourner to return

tourner l'estomac à qqn to turn someone's stomach
faire une tournée to go on a tour
tourner autour du pot to beat around the bush

See also **détourner** and **retourner.**

If you don't know the French verb for an English verb you have in mind, try the index on pages 503–514.

tousser   Part. pr. **toussant**   Part. passé **toussé**

to cough

The Seven Simple Tenses		The Seven Compound Tenses	
Singular	Plural	Singular	Plural
1 présent de l'indicatif		**8 passé composé**	
tousse	toussons	ai toussé	avons toussé
tousses	toussez	as toussé	avez toussé
tousse	toussent	a toussé	ont toussé
2 imparfait de l'indicatif		**9 plus-que-parfait de l'indicatif**	
toussais	toussions	avais toussé	avions toussé
toussais	toussiez	avais toussé	aviez toussé
toussait	toussaient	avait toussé	avaient toussé
3 passé simple		**10 passé antérieur**	
toussai	toussâmes	eus toussé	eûmes toussé
toussas	toussâtes	eus toussé	eûtes toussé
toussa	toussèrent	eut toussé	eurent toussé
4 futur		**11 futur antérieur**	
tousserai	tousserons	aurai toussé	aurons toussé
tousseras	tousserez	auras toussé	aurez toussé
toussera	tousseront	aura toussé	auront toussé
5 conditionnel		**12 conditionnel passé**	
tousserais	tousserions	aurais toussé	aurions toussé
tousserais	tousseriez	aurais toussé	auriez toussé
tousserait	tousseraient	aurait toussé	auraient toussé
6 présent du subjonctif		**13 passé du subjonctif**	
tousse	toussions	aie toussé	ayons toussé
tousses	toussiez	aies toussé	ayez toussé
tousse	toussent	ait toussé	aient toussé
7 imparfait du subjonctif		**14 plus-que-parfait du subjonctif**	
toussasse	toussassions	eusse toussé	eussions toussé
toussasses	toussassiez	eusses toussé	eussiez toussé
toussât	toussassent	eût toussé	eussent toussé

Impératif
tousse
toussons
toussez

Words and expressions related to this verb

une toux   cough; **une toux grasse**   crackling cough, heavy cough; **une toux sèche**   dry cough

une toux nerveuse   nervous cough

toussoter   to have a minor, slight cough
un tousseur, une tousseuse   cougher
un toussotement   slight cough

How are you doing? Find out with the verb drills and tests with answers explained on pages 622–673.

The Seven Simple Tenses		The Seven Compound Tenses	
Singular	Plural	Singular	Plural

1   présent de l'indicatif

traduis	traduisons	
traduis	traduisez	
traduit	traduisent	

8   passé composé

ai traduit	avons traduit
as traduit	avez traduit
a traduit	ont traduit

2   imparfait de l'indicatif

traduisais	traduisions
traduisais	traduisiez
traduisait	traduisaient

9   plus-que-parfait de l'indicatif

avais traduit	avions traduit
avais traduit	aviez traduit
avait traduit	avaient traduit

3   passé simple

traduisis	traduisîmes
traduisis	traduisîtes
traduisit	traduisirent

10   passé antérieur

eus traduit	eûmes traduit
eus traduit	eûtes traduit
eut traduit	eurent traduit

4   futur

traduirai	traduirons
traduiras	traduirez
traduira	traduiront

11   futur antérieur

aurai traduit	aurons traduit
auras traduit	aurez traduit
aura traduit	auront traduit

5   conditionnel

traduirais	traduirions
traduirais	traduiriez
traduirait	traduiraient

12   conditionnel passé

aurais traduit	aurions traduit
aurais traduit	auriez traduit
aurait traduit	auraient traduit

6   présent du subjonctif

traduise	traduisions
traduises	tradusiez
traduise	traduisent

13   passé du subjonctif

aie traduit	ayons traduit
aies traduit	ayez traduit
ait traduit	aient traduit

7   imparfait du subjonctif

traduisisse	traduisissions
traduisisses	traduisissiez
traduisît	traduisissent

14   plus-que-parfait du subjonctif

eusse traduit	eussions traduit
eusses traduit	eussiez traduit
eût traduit	eussent traduit

Impératif
traduis
traduisons
traduisez

Words and expressions related to this verb
un traducteur, une traductrice   translator
une traduction   a translation
traduisible   translatable
une traduction littérale   a literal translation
une traduction libre   a free translation
traduire du français en anglais   to translate from French to English

se traduire   to be translated; **Cette phrase se traduit facilement**   This sentence is easily translated.
une traduction fidèle   a faithful translation
traduire de l'anglais en français   to translate from English to French

See also **conduire, déduire, introduire, produire, réduire, reproduire,** and **séduire.**

trahir

Part. pr. **trahissant**   Part. passé **trahi**

to betray

The Seven Simple Tenses		The Seven Compound Tenses	
Singular	Plural	Singular	Plural
1 présent de l'indicatif		**8 passé composé**	
trahis	trahissons	ai trahi	avons trahi
trahis	trahissez	as trahi	avez trahi
trahit	trahissent	a trahi	ont trahi
2 imparfait de l'indicatif		**9 plus-que-parfait de l'indicatif**	
trahissais	trahissions	avais trahi	avions trahi
trahissais	trahissiez	avais trahi	aviez trahi
trahissait	trahissaient	avait trahi	avaient trahi
3 passé simple		**10 passé antérieur**	
trahis	trahîmes	eus trahi	eûmes trahi
trahis	trahîtes	eus trahi	eûtes trahi
trahit	trahirent	eut trahi	eurent trahi
4 futur		**11 futur antérieur**	
trahirai	trahirons	aurai trahi	aurons trahi
trahiras	trahirez	auras trahi	aurez trahi
trahira	trahiront	aura trahi	auront trahi
5 conditionnel		**12 conditionnel passé**	
trahirais	trahirions	aurais trahi	aurions trahi
trahirais	trahiriez	aurais trahi	auriez trahi
trahirait	trahiraient	aurait trahi	auraient trahi
6 présent du subjonctif		**13 passé du subjonctif**	
trahisse	trahissions	aie trahi	ayons trahi
trahisses	trahissiez	aies trahi	ayez trahi
trahisse	trahissent	ait trahi	aient trahi
7 imparfait du subjonctif		**14 plus-que-parfait du subjonctif**	
trahisse	trahissions	eusse trahi	eussions trahi
trahisses	trahissiez	eusses trahi	eussiez trahi
trahît	trahissent	eût trahi	eussent trahi

Impératif
trahis
trahissons
trahissez

Words and expressions related to this verb

se trahir to give oneself away, to betray each
other, to deceive each other
traîtreusement treacherously
la trahison betrayal, treason

la haute trahison high treason
un traître traitor, betrayer
une traîtresse traitress, betrayer

Don't miss the definitions of basic grammatical terms with examples in English and French on
pages 674–688.

to treat, to negotiate

The Seven Simple Tenses		The Seven Compound Tenses	
Singular	Plural	Singular	Plural
1 présent de l'indicatif		**8 passé composé**	
traite	traitons	ai traité	avons traité
traites	traitez	as traité	avez traité
traite	traitent	a traité	ont traité
2 imparfait de l'indicatif		**9 plus-que-parfait de l'indicatif**	
traitais	traitions	avais traité	avions traité
traitais	traitiez	avais traité	aviez traité
traitait	traitaient	avait traité	avaient traité
3 passé simple		**10 passé antérieur**	
traitai	traitâmes	eus traité	eûmes traité
traitas	traitâtes	eus traité	eûtes traité
traita	traitèrent	eut traité	eurent traité
4 futur		**11 futur antérieur**	
traiterai	traiterons	aurai traité	aurons traité
traiteras	traiterez	auras traité	aurez traité
traitera	traiteront	aura traité	auront traité
5 conditionnel		**12 conditionnel passé**	
traiterais	traiterions	aurais traité	aurions traité
traiterais	traiteriez	aurais traité	auriez traité
traiterait	traiteraient	aurait traité	auraient traité
6 présent du subjonctif		**13 passé du subjonctif**	
traite	traitions	aie traité	ayons traité
traites	traitiez	aies traité	ayez traité
traite	traitent	ait traité	aient traité
7 imparfait du subjonctif		**14 plus-que-parfait du subjonctif**	
traitasse	traitassions	eusse traité	eussions traité
traitasses	traitassiez	eusses traité	eussiez traité
traitât	traitassent	eût traité	eussent traité

Impératif
traite
traitons
traitez

Words and expressions related to this verb

traiter qqn mal   to treat someone badly;
   traiter qqn bien   to treat someone well
maltraiter   to maltreat, to mistreat; **traiter de**
   to deal with
traiter qqn de qqch   to call someone
   something; **traiter qqn de menteur**   to call
   someone a liar

un traitement   treatment; salary
un traité   treatise; treaty
boire d'une seule traite   to drink in one
   gulp
le traitement de texte   word processing

Want to learn more idiomatic expressions that contain verbs? Look at pages 530–542.

The subject pronouns are found on the page facing page 1.

to transmit, to transfer

The Seven Simple Tenses		The Seven Compound Tenses	
Singular	Plural	Singular	Plural
1 présent de l'indicatif		**8 passé composé**	
transmets	transmettons	ai transmis	avons transmis
transmets	transmettez	as transmis	avez transmis
transmet	transmettent	a transmis	ont transmis
2 imparfait de l'indicatif		**9 plus-que-parfait de l'indicatif**	
transmettais	transmettions	avais transmis	avions transmis
transmettais	transmettiez	avais transmis	aviez transmis
transmettait	transmettaient	avait transmis	avaient transmis
3 passé simple		**10 passé antérieur**	
transmis	transmîmes	eus transmis	eûmes transmis
transmis	transmîtes	eus transmis	eûtes transmis
transmit	transmirent	eut transmis	eurent transmis
4 futur		**11 futur antérieur**	
transmettrai	transmettrons	aurai transmis	aurons transmis
transmettras	transmettrez	auras transmis	aurez transmis
transmettra	transmettront	aura transmis	auront transmis
5 conditionnel		**12 conditionnel passé**	
transmettrais	transmettrions	aurais transmis	aurions transmis
transmettrais	transmettriez	aurais transmis	auriez transmis
transmettrait	transmettraient	aurait transmis	auraient transmis
6 présent du subjonctif		**13 passé du subjonctif**	
transmette	transmettions	aie transmis	ayons transmis
transmettes	transmettiez	aies transmis	ayez transmis
transmette	transmettent	ait transmis	aient transmis
7 imparfait du subjonctif		**14 plus-que-parfait du subjonctif**	
transmisse	transmissions	eusse transmis	eussions transmis
transmisses	transmissiez	eusses transmis	eussiez transmis
transmît	transmissent	eût transmis	eussent transmis

Impératif
transmets
transmettons
transmettez

Words and expressions related to this verb

transmettre une maladie   to transmit an illness

transmettre un message   to relay, to transmit a message

transmettre son autorité   to transfer one's authority

transmettre une lettre   to forward a letter

une transmission   transmission

transmissible   transmissible, transferable

une maladie transmissible   contagious disease

Le SIDA est une maladie transmissible   AIDS is a transmittable disease.

See also **commettre, mettre, se mettre, omettre, permettre, promettre, remettre,** and **soumettre.**

The Seven Simple Tenses		The Seven Compound Tenses	
Singular	Plural	Singular	Plural
1 présent de l'indicatif		**8 passé composé**	
travaille	travaillons	ai travaillé	avons travaillé
travailles	travaillez	as travaillé	avez travaillé
travaille	travaillent	a travaillé	ont travaillé
2 imparfait de l'indicatif		**9 plus-que-parfait de l'indicatif**	
travaillais	travaillions	avais travaillé	avions travaillé
travaillais	travailliez	avais travaillé	aviez travaillé
travaillait	travaillaient	avait travaillé	avaient travaillé
3 passé simple		**10 passé antérieur**	
travaillai	travaillâmes	eus travaillé	eûmes travaillé
travaillas	travaillâtes	eus travaillé	eûtes travaillé
travailla	travaillèrent	eut travaillé	eurent travaillé
4 futur		**11 futur antérieur**	
travaillerai	travaillerons	aurai travaillé	aurons travaillé
travailleras	travaillerez	auras travaillé	aurez travaillé
travaillera	travailleront	aura travaillé	auront travaillé
5 conditionnel		**12 conditionnel passé**	
travaillerais	travaillerions	aurais travaillé	aurions travaillé
travaillerais	travailleriez	aurais travaillé	auriez travaillé
travaillerait	travailleraient	aurait travaillé	auraient travaillé
6 présent du subjonctif		**13 passé du subjonctif**	
travaille	travaillions	aie travaillé	ayons travaillé
travailles	travailliez	aies travaillé	ayez travaillé
travaille	travaillent	ait travaillé	aient travaillé
7 imparfait du subjonctif		**14 plus-que-parfait du subjonctif**	
travaillasse	travaillassions	eusse travaillé	eussions travaillé
travaillasses	travaillassiez	eusses travaillé	eussiez travaillé
travaillât	travaillassent	eût travaillé	eussent travaillé

Impératif
travaille
travaillons
travaillez

Words and expressions related to this verb

travailleur, travailleuse industrious, worker

être sans travail to be out of work

faire travailler son argent to put one's money to work (to earn interest)

Madame Reed fait travailler ses élèves dans la classe de français Mrs. Reed makes her students work in French class.

le travail work, labor, travail (**les travaux**)

les travaux publics public works

les vêtements de travail work clothes

Consult the entry *causative* **faire** (page 676) in the section on definitions of basic grammatical terms with examples in the back pages.

The subject pronouns are found on the page facing page 1.   **479**

to traverse, to cross

The Seven Simple Tenses		The Seven Compound Tenses	
Singular	Plural	Singular	Plural
1 présent de l'indicatif		**8 passé composé**	
traverse	traversons	ai traversé	avons traversé
traverses	traversez	as traversé	avez traversé
traverse	traversent	a traversé	ont traversé
2 imparfait de l'indicatif		**9 plus-que-parfait de l'indicatif**	
traversais	traversions	avais traversé	avions traversé
traversais	traversiez	avais traversé	aviez traversé
traversait	traversaient	avait traversé	avaient traversé
3 passé simple		**10 passé antérieur**	
traversai	traversâmes	eus traversé	eûmes traversé
traversas	traversâtes	eus traversé	eûtes traversé
traversa	traversèrent	eut traversé	eurent traversé
4 futur		**11 futur antérieur**	
traverserai	traverserons	aurai traversé	aurons traversé
traverseras	traverserez	auras traversé	aurez traversé
traversera	traverseront	aura traversé	auront traversé
5 conditionnel		**12 conditionnel passé**	
traverserais	traverserions	aurais traversé	aurions traversé
traverserais	traverseriez	aurais traversé	auriez traversé
traverserait	traverseraient	aurait traversé	auraient traversé
6 présent du subjonctif		**13 passé du subjonctif**	
traverse	traversions	aie traversé	ayons traversé
traverses	traversiez	aies traversé	ayez traversé
traverse	traversent	ait traversé	aient traversé
7 imparfait du subjonctif		**14 plus-que-parfait du subjonctif**	
traversasse	traversassions	eusse traversé	eussions traversé
traversasses	traversassiez	eusses traversé	eussiez traversé
traversât	traversassent	eût traversé	eussent traversé

Impératif
traverse
traversons
traversez

Words and expressions related to this verb
la traversée the crossing
à travers through
de travers askew, awry, crooked

une traversée de voie railroad crossing
marcher de travers to stagger

Check out the principal parts of some important French verbs on page xii.

480

The Seven Simple Tenses		The Seven Compound Tenses	
Singular	Plural	Singular	Plural
1 présent de l'indicatif		8 passé composé	
triche	trichons	ai triché	avons triché
triches	trichez	as triché	avez triché
triche	trichent	a triché	ont triché
2 imparfait de l'indicatif		9 plus-que-parfait de l'indicatif	
trichais	trichions	avais triché	avions triché
trichais	trichiez	avais triché	aviez triché
trichait	trichaient	avait triché	avaient triché
3 passé simple		10 passé antérieur	
trichai	trichâmes	eus triché	eûmes triché
trichas	trichâtes	eus triché	eûtes triché
tricha	trichèrent	eut triché	eurent triché
4 futur		11 futur antérieur	
tricherai	tricherons	aurai triché	aurons triché
tricheras	tricherez	auras triché	aurez triché
trichera	tricheront	aura triché	auront triché
5 conditionnel		12 conditionnel passé	
tricherais	tricherions	aurais triché	aurions triché
tricherais	tricheriez	aurais triché	auriez triché
tricherait	tricheraient	aurait triché	auraient triché
6 présent du subjonctif		13 passé du subjonctif	
triche	trichions	aie triché	ayons triché
triches	trichiez	aies triché	ayez triché
triche	trichent	ait triché	aient triché
7 imparfait du subjonctif		14 plus-que-parfait du subjonctif	
trichasse	trichassions	eusse triché	eussions triché
trichasses	trichassiez	eusses triché	eussiez triché
trichât	trichassent	eût triché	eussent triché

Impératif
triche
trichons
trichez

Words and expressions related to this verb
une tricherie cheating
gagner par tricherie to win by cheating
une triche cheating

un tricheur, une tricheuse cheater
tricher aux cartes to cheat at cards

If you want to see a sample English verb fully conjugated in all the tenses, check out pages xiii and xiv.

se tromper

to be mistaken, to be wrong (about something)

The Seven Simple Tenses		The Seven Compound Tenses	
Singular	Plural	Singular	Plural
1 présent de l'indicatif		**8 passé composé**	
me trompe	nous trompons	me suis trompé(e)	nous sommes trompé(e)s
te trompes	vous trompez	t'es trompé(e)	vous êtes trompé(e)(s)
se trompe	se trompent	s'est trompé(e)	se sont trompé(e)s
2 imparfait de l'indicatif		**9 plus-que-parfait de l'indicatif**	
me trompais	nous trompions	m'étais trompé(e)	nous étions trompé(e)s
te trompais	vous trompiez	t'étais trompé(e)	vous étiez trompé(e)(s)
se trompait	se trompaient	s'était trompé(e)	s'étaient trompé(e)s
3 passé simple		**10 passé antérieur**	
me trompai	nous trompâmes	me fus trompé(e)	nous fûmes trompé(e)s
te trompas	vous trompâtes	te fus trompé(e)	vous fûtes trompé(e)(s)
se trompa	se trompèrent	se fut trompé(e)	se furent trompé(e)s
4 futur		**11 futur antérieur**	
me tromperai	nous tromperons	me serai trompé(e)	nous serons trompé(e)s
te tromperas	vous tromperez	te seras trompé(e)	vous serez trompé(e)(s)
se trompera	se tromperont	se sera trompé(e)	se seront trompé(e)s
5 conditionnel		**12 conditionnel passé**	
me tromperais	nous tromperions	me serais trompé(e)	nous serions trompé(e)s
te tromperais	vous tromperiez	te serais trompé(e)	vous seriez trompé(e)(s)
se tromperait	se tromperaient	se serait trompé(e)	se seraient trompé(e)s
6 présent du subjonctif		**13 passé du subjonctif**	
me trompe	nous trompions	me sois trompé(e)	nous soyons trompé(e)s
te trompes	vous trompiez	te sois trompé(e)	vous soyez trompé(e)(s)
se trompe	se trompent	se soit trompé(e)	se soient trompé(e)s
7 imparfait du subjonctif		**14 plus-que-parfait du subjonctif**	
me trompasse	nous trompassions	me fusse trompé(e)	nous fussions trompé(e)s
te trompasses	vous trompassiez	te fusses trompé(e)	vous fussiez trompé(e)(s)
se trompât	se trompassent	se fût trompé(e)	se fussent trompé(e)s

Impératif
trompe-toi; ne te trompe pas
trompons-nous; ne nous trompons pas
trompez-vous; ne vous trompez pas

Words and expressions related to this verb
tromper to cheat, to deceive
détromper to free from deception, to set a matter straight
se laisser tromper to be taken in (fooled, deceived)

un trompeur, une trompeuse deceiver
se détromper to see the truth about a matter
se tromper de chemin to take the wrong route
une tromperie deceit, deception

For an explanation of meanings and uses of French and English verb tenses and moods, see pages xv to xxvi.

The Seven Simple Tenses		The Seven Compound Tenses	
Singular	Plural	Singular	Plural
1 présent de l'indicatif		**8 passé composé**	
trouve	trouvons	ai trouvé	avons trouvé
trouves	trouvez	as trouvé	avez trouvé
trouve	trouvent	a trouvé	ont trouvé
2 imparfait de l'indicatif		**9 plus-que-parfait de l'indicatif**	
trouvais	trouvions	avais trouvé	avions trouvé
trouvais	trouviez	avais trouvé	aviez trouvé
trouvait	trouvaient	avait trouvé	avaient trouvé
3 passé simple		**10 passé antérieur**	
trouvai	trouvâmes	eus trouvé	eûmes trouvé
trouvas	trouvâtes	eus trouvé	eûtes trouvé
trouva	trouvèrent	eut trouvé	eurent trouvé
4 futur		**11 futur antérieur**	
trouverai	trouverons	aurai trouvé	aurons trouvé
trouveras	trouverez	auras trouvé	aurez trouvé
trouvera	trouveront	aura trouvé	auront trouvé
5 conditionnel		**12 conditionnel passé**	
trouverais	trouverions	aurais trouvé	aurions trouvé
trouverais	trouveriez	aurais trouvé	auriez trouvé
trouverait	trouveraient	aurait trouvé	auraient trouvé
6 présent du subjonctif		**13 passé du subjonctif**	
trouve	trouvions	aie trouvé	ayons trouvé
trouves	trouviez	aies trouvé	ayez trouvé
trouve	trouvent	ait trouvé	aient trouvé
7 imparfait du subjonctif		**14 plus-que-parfait du subjonctif**	
trouvasse	trouvassions	eusse trouvé	eussions trouvé
trouvasses	trouvassiez	eusses trouvé	eussiez trouvé
trouvât	trouvassent	eût trouvé	eussent trouvé

Impératif
trouve
trouvons
trouvez

Words and expressions related to this verb

J'ai une nouvelle voiture; comment la trouvez-vous? I have a new car; how do you like it?

trouver un emploi to find a job

trouver bon de faire qqch to think fit to do something

retrouver to find again, to recover, to retrieve

trouver porte close not to find anyone answering the door after knocking

une trouvaille a discovery, a find

les retrouvailles *f.* reunion, rediscovery

See also **se trouver.**

Review the Subjunctive clearly and simply on pages 560–565.

The subject pronouns are found on the page facing page 1.   **483**

to be located, to be situated

The Seven Simple Tenses		The Seven Compound Tenses	
Singular	Plural	Singular	Plural
1 présent de l'indicatif		8 passé composé	
me trouve	nous trouvons	me suis trouvé(e)	nous sommes trouvé(e)s
te trouves	vous trouvez	t'es trouvé(e)	vous êtes trouvé(e)(s)
se trouve	se trouvent	s'est trouvé(e)	se sont trouvé(e)s
2 imparfait de l'indicatif		9 plus-que-parfait de l'indicatif	
me trouvais	nous trouvions	m'étais trouvé(e)	nous étions trouvé(e)s
te trouvais	vous trouviez	t'étais trouvé(e)	vous étiez trouvé(e)(s)
se trouvait	se trouvaient	s'était trouvé(e)	s'étaient trouvé(e)s
3 passé simple		10 passé antérieur	
me trouvai	nous trouvâmes	me fus trouvé(e)	nous fûmes trouvé(e)s
te trouvas	vous trouvâtes	te fus trouvé(e)	vous fûtes trouvé(e)(s)
se trouva	se trouvèrent	se fut trouvé(e)	se furent trouvé(e)s
4 futur		11 futur antérieur	
me trouverai	nous trouverons	me serai trouvé(e)	nous serons trouvé(e)s
te trouveras	vous trouverez	te seras trouvé(e)	vous serez trouvé(e)(s)
se trouvera	se trouveront	se sera trouvé(e)	se seront trouvé(e)s
5 conditionnel		12 conditionnel passé	
me trouverais	nous trouverions	me serais trouvé(e)	nous serions trouvé(e)s
te trouverais	vous trouveriez	te serais trouvé(e)	vous seriez trouvé(e)(s)
se trouverait	se trouveraient	se serait trouvé(e)	se seraient trouvé(e)s
6 présent du subjonctif		13 passé du subjonctif	
me trouve	nous trouvions	me sois trouvé(e)	nous soyons trouvé(e)s
te trouves	vous trouviez	te sois trouvé(e)	vous soyez trouvé(e)(s)
se trouve	se trouvent	se soit trouvé(e)	se soient trouvé(e)s
7 imparfait du subjonctif		14 plus-que-parfait du subjonctif	
me trouvasse	nous trouvassions	me fusse trouvé(e)	nous fussions trouvé(e)s
te trouvasses	vous trouvassiez	te fusses trouvé(e)	vous fussiez trouvé(e)(s)
se trouvât	se trouvassent	se fût trouvé(e)	se fussent trouvé(e)s

Impératif
trouve-toi; ne te trouve pas
trouvons-nous; ne nous trouvons pas
trouvez-vous; ne vous trouvez pas

Words and expressions related to this verb
Où se trouve le bureau de poste? Where is the post office located?
Trouve-toi dans ce café à huit heures ce soir Be in this café at 8 o'clock tonight.

See also **trouver.**

Vous avez été malade; allez-vous mieux maintenant?—Oui, je me trouve mieux, merci! You have been sick; are you feeling better now?—Yes, I'm feeling better, thank you!

Use the EE-zee guide to French pronunciation on pages 566 and 567.

The Seven Simple Tenses

The Seven Compound Tenses

Singular	Plural	Singular	Plural
1　présent de l'indicatif		8　passé composé	
tue	**tuons**	**ai tué**	**avons tué**
tues	**tuez**	**as tué**	**avez tué**
tue	**tuent**	**a tué**	**ont tué**
2　imparfait de l'indicatif		9　plus-que-parfait de l'indicatif	
tuais	**tuions**	**avais tué**	**avions tué**
tuais	**tuiez**	**avais tué**	**aviez tué**
tuait	**tuaient**	**avait tué**	**avaient tué**
3　passé simple		10　passé antérieur	
tuai	**tuâmes**	**eus tué**	**eûmes tué**
tuas	**tuâtes**	**eus tué**	**eûtes tué**
tua	**tuèrent**	**eut tué**	**eurent tué**
4　futur		11　futur antérieur	
tuerai	**tuerons**	**aurai tué**	**aurons tué**
tueras	**tuerez**	**auras tué**	**aurez tué**
tuera	**tueront**	**aura tué**	**auront tué**
5　conditionnel		12　conditionnel passé	
tuerais	**tuerions**	**aurais tué**	**aurions tué**
tuerais	**tueriez**	**aurais tué**	**auriez tué**
tuerait	**tueraient**	**aurait tué**	**auraient tué**
6　présent du subjonctif		13　passé du subjonctif	
tue	**tuions**	**aie tué**	**ayons tué**
tues	**tuiez**	**aies tué**	**ayez tué**
tue	**tuent**	**ait tué**	**aient tué**
7　imparfait du subjonctif		14　plus-que-parfait du subjonctif	
tuasse	**tuassions**	**eusse tué**	**eussions tué**
tuasses	**tuassiez**	**eusses tué**	**eussiez tué**
tuât	**tuassent**	**eût tué**	**eussent tué**

Impératif
tue
tuons
tuez

Words and expressions related to this verb
tuer le temps　to kill time
Ce travail me tue!　This work is killing me!
se tuer　to kill oneself; to get killed
un tueur, une tueuse　killer
une tuerie　slaughter
La drogue tue　Drugs kill.

un tue-mouche　fly swatter (**des tue-mouches**)
crier à tue-tête　to shout at the top of one's voice.
chanter à tue-tête　to sing at the top of one's voice

If you don't know the French verb for an English verb you have in mind, try the index on pages 503–514.

to unite, to join

The Seven Simple Tenses		The Seven Compound Tenses	
Singular	Plural	Singular	Plural
1 présent de l'indicatif		**8 passé composé**	
unis	unissons	ai uni	avons uni
unis	unissez	as uni	avez uni
unit	unissent	a uni	ont uni
2 imparfait de l'indicatif		**9 plus-que-parfait de l'indicatif**	
unissais	unissions	avais uni	avions uni
unissais	unissiez	avais uni	aviez uni
unissait	unissaient	avait uni	avaient uni
3 passé simple		**10 passé antérieur**	
unis	unîmes	eus uni	eûmes uni
unis	unîtes	eus uni	eûtes uni
unit	unirent	eut uni	eurent uni
4 futur		**11 futur antérieur**	
unirai	unirons	aurai uni	aurons uni
uniras	unirez	auras uni	aurez uni
unira	uniront	aura uni	auront uni
5 conditionnel		**12 conditionnel passé**	
unirais	unirions	aurais uni	aurions uni
unirais	uniriez	aurais uni	auriez uni
unirait	uniraient	aurait uni	auraient uni
6 présent du subjonctif		**13 passé du subjonctif**	
unisse	unissions	aie uni	ayons uni
unisses	unissiez	aies uni	ayez uni
unisse	unissent	ait uni	aient uni
7 imparfait du subjonctif		**14 plus-que-parfait du subjonctif**	
unisse	unissions	eusse uni	eussions uni
unisses	unissiez	eusses uni	eussiez uni
unît	unissent	eût uni	eussent uni

Impératif
unis
unissons
unissez

Words and expressions related to this verb
s'unir to join together, to marry
réunir to reunite; **se réunir** to meet together
les Etats-Unis the United States
les Nations-Unies (l'ONU) the United Nations

une union union, alliance
un trait d'union hyphen
unisexe unisex
unir ses forces to combine one's forces
chanter à l'unisson to sing in unison

Increase your verb power with popular phrases, words, and expressions for travelers on pages 599–621.

to utilize, to use, to make use of, to put to use

The Seven Simple Tenses		The Seven Compound Tenses	
Singular	Plural	Singular	Plural
1 présent de l'indicatif		8 passé composé	
utilise	utilisons	ai utilisé	avons utilisé
utilises	utilisez	as utilisé	avez utilisé
utilise	utilisent	a utilisé	ont utilisé
2 imparfait de l'indicatif		9 plus-que-parfait de l'indicatif	
utilisais	utilisions	avais utilisé	avions utilisé
utilisais	utilisiez	avais utilisé	aviez utilisé
utilisait	utilisaient	avait utilisé	avaient utilisé
3 passé simple		10 passé antérieur	
utilisai	utilisâmes	eus utilisé	eûmes utilisé
utilisas	utilisâtes	eus utilisé	eûtes utilisé
utilisa	utilisèrent	eut utilisé	eurent utilisé
4 futur		11 futur antérieur	
utiliserai	utiliserons	aurai utilisé	aurons utilisé
utiliseras	utiliserez	auras utilisé	aurez utilisé
utilisera	utiliseront	aura utilisé	auront utilisé
5 conditionnel		12 conditionnel passé	
utiliserais	utiliserions	aurais utilisé	aurions utilisé
utiliserais	utiliseriez	aurais utilisé	auriez utilisé
utiliserait	utiliseraient	aurait utilisé	auraient utilisé
6 présent du subjonctif		13 passé du subjonctif	
utilise	utilisions	aie utilisé	ayons utilisé
utilises	utilisiez	aies utilisé	ayez utilisé
utilise	utilisent	ait utilisé	aient utilisé
7 imparfait du subjonctif		14 plus-que-parfait du subjonctif	
utilisasse	utilisassions	eusse utilisé	eussions utilisé
utilisasses	utilisassiez	eusses utilisé	eussiez utilisé
utilisât	utilisassent	eût utilisé	eussent utilisé

Impératif
utilise
utilisons
utilisez

Words and expressions related to this verb

utile   useful
inutile   useless
une utilité   utility, usefulness
un utilisateur, une utilisatrice   user

utilitaire   utilitarian
une utilisation   utilization
Il est utile de + inf.   It is useful + inf.
utilement   usefully

Get acquainted with what preposition (if any) goes with what verb on pages 543–553.

The subject pronouns are found on the page facing page 1.   **487**

vaincre

Part. pr. **vainquant**   Part. passé **vaincu**

to vanquish, to conquer

The Seven Simple Tenses		The Seven Compound Tenses	
Singular	Plural	Singular	Plural
1 présent de l'indicatif		**8 passé composé**	
vaincs	vainquons	ai vaincu	avons vaincu
vaincs	vainquez	as vaincu	avez vaincu
vainc	vainquent	a vaincu	ont vaincu
2 imparfait de l'indicatif		**9 plus-que-parfait de l'indicatif**	
vainquais	vainquions	avais vaincu	avions vaincu
vainquais	vainquiez	avais vaincu	aviez vaincu
vainquait	vainquaient	avait vaincu	avaient vaincu
3 passé simple		**10 passé antérieur**	
vainquis	vainquîmes	eus vaincu	eûmes vaincu
vainquis	vainquîtes	eus vaincu	eûtes vaincu
vainquit	vainquirent	eut vaincu	eurent vaincu
4 futur		**11 futur antérieur**	
vaincrai	vaincrons	aurai vaincu	aurons vaincu
vaincras	vaincrez	auras vaincu	aurez vaincu
vaincra	vaincront	aura vaincu	auront vaincu
5 conditionnel		**12 conditionnel passé**	
vaincrais	vaincrions	aurais vaincu	aurions vaincu
vaincrais	vaincriez	aurais vaincu	auriez vaincu
vaincrait	vaincraient	aurait vaincu	auraient vaincu
6 présent du subjonctif		**13 passé du subjonctif**	
vainque	vainquions	aie vaincu	ayons vaincu
vainques	vainquiez	aies vaincu	ayez vaincu
vainque	vainquent	ait vaincu	aient vaincu
7 imparfait du subjonctif		**14 plus-que-parfait du subjonctif**	
vainquisse	vainquissions	eusse vaincu	eussions vaincu
vainquisses	vainquissiez	eusses vaincu	eussiez vaincu
vainquît	vainquissent	eût vaincu	eussent vaincu

Impératif
vaincs
vainquons
vainquez

Words and expressions related to this verb

convaincre qqn de qqch   to convince, to persuade someone of something

vainqueur   victor, victorious; conqueror, conquering

convaincant, convaincante   convincing

vaincu   defeated

See also **convaincre.**

How are you doing? Find out with the verb drills and tests with answers explained on pages 622–673.

to be worth, to be as good as, to deserve, to merit, to be equal to

The Seven Simple Tenses		The Seven Compound Tenses	
Singular	Plural	Singular	Plural
1 présent de l'indicatif		**8 passé composé**	
vaux	**valons**	**ai valu**	**avons valu**
vaux	**valez**	**as valu**	**avez valu**
vaut	**valent**	**a valu**	**ont valu**
2 imparfait de l'indicatif		**9 plus-que-parfait de l'indicatif**	
valais	**valions**	**avais valu**	**avions valu**
valais	**valiez**	**avais valu**	**aviez valu**
valait	**valaient**	**avait valu**	**avaient valu**
3 passé simple		**10 passé antérieur**	
valus	**valûmes**	**eus valu**	**eûmes valu**
valus	**valûtes**	**eus valu**	**eûtes valu**
valut	**valurent**	**eut valu**	**eurent valu**
4 futur		**11 futur antérieur**	
vaudrai	**vaudrons**	**aurai valu**	**aurons valu**
vaudras	**vaudrez**	**auras valu**	**aurez valu**
vaudra	**vaudront**	**aura valu**	**auront valu**
5 conditionnel		**12 conditionnel passé**	
vaudrais	**vaudrions**	**aurais valu**	**aurions valu**
vaudrais	**vaudriez**	**aurais valu**	**auriez valu**
vaudrait	**vaudraient**	**aurait valu**	**auraient valu**
6 présent du subjonctif		**13 passé du subjonctif**	
vaille	**valions**	**aie valu**	**ayons valu**
vailles	**valiez**	**aies valu**	**ayez valu**
vaille	**vaillent**	**ait valu**	**aient valu**
7 imparfait du subjonctif		**14 plus-que-parfait du subjonctif**	
valusse	**valussions**	**eusse valu**	**eussions valu**
valusses	**valussiez**	**eusses valu**	**eussiez valu**
valût	**valussent**	**eût valu**	**eussent valu**

Impératif
vaux
valons
valez

Words and expressions related to this verb
la valeur   value, worth
valeureusement   valorously
valeureux, valeureuse   valorous
la validation   validation
valide   valid
Mieux vaut tard que jamais   Better late than never.

Cela vaut la peine   It's worth the trouble.
faire valoir   to make the most of, to invest one's money
valoir cher   to be worth a lot
valoir de l'argent   to be worth money

Can't recognize an irregular verb form? Check out pages 526–529.

The subject pronouns are found on the page facing page 1.   **489**

to sell

The Seven Simple Tenses		The Seven Compound Tenses	
Singular	Plural	Singular	Plural
1 présent de l'indicatif		**8 passé composé**	
vends	vendons	ai vendu	avons vendu
vends	vendez	as vendu	avez vendu
vend	vendent	a vendu	ont vendu
2 imparfait de l'indicatif		**9 plus-que-parfait de l'indicatif**	
vendais	vendions	avais vendu	avions vendu
vendais	vendiez	avais vendu	aviez vendu
vendait	vendaient	avait vendu	avaient vendu
3 passé simple		**10 passé antérieur**	
vendis	vendîmes	eus vendu	eûmes vendu
vendis	vendîtes	eus vendu	eûtes vendu
vendit	vendirent	eut vendu	eurent vendu
4 futur		**11 futur antérieur**	
vendrai	vendrons	aurai vendu	aurons vendu
vendras	vendrez	auras vendu	aurez vendu
vendra	vendront	aura vendu	auront vendu
5 conditionnel		**12 conditionnel passé**	
vendrais	vendrions	aurais vendu	aurions vendu
vendrais	vendriez	aurais vendu	auriez vendu
vendrait	vendraient	aurait vendu	auraient vendu
6 présent du subjonctif		**13 passé du subjonctif**	
vende	vendions	aie vendu	ayons vendu
vendes	vendiez	aies vendu	ayez vendu
vende	vendent	ait vendu	aient vendu
7 imparfait du subjonctif		**14 plus-que-parfait du subjonctif**	
vendisse	vendissions	eusse vendu	eussions vendu
vendisses	vendissiez	eusses vendu	eussiez vendu
vendît	vendissent	eût vendu	eussent vendu

Impératif
vends
vendons
vendez

Words and expressions related to this verb

un vendeur, une vendeuse salesperson
une vente a sale
maison à vendre house for sale
revendre to resell
en vente on sale
une salle des ventes salesroom
vendre à bon marché to sell at a reasonably
  low price (a good buy)

vendre la peau de l'ours avant de l'avoir tué
  to count one's chickens before they're
  hatched
une vente aux enchères auction sale
vendre au rabais to sell at a discount
On vend des livres ici Books are sold here.
vendre à la sauvette to peddle on the streets
une vente à la sauvette street peddling

The Seven Simple Tenses		The Seven Compound Tenses

Singular	Plural	Singular	Plural
1 présent de l'indicatif		**8 passé composé**	
venge	vengeons	ai vengé	avons vengé
venges	vengez	as vengé	avez vengé
venge	vengent	a vengé	ont vengé
2 imparfait de l'indicatif		**9 plus-que-parfait de l'indicatif**	
vengeais	vengions	avais vengé	avions vengé
vengeais	vengiez	avais vengé	aviez vengé
vengeait	vengeaient	avait vengé	avaient vengé
3 passé simple		**10 passé antérieur**	
vengeai	vengeâmes	eus vengé	eûmes vengé
vengeas	vengeâtes	eus vengé	eûtes vengé
vengea	vengèrent	eut vengé	eurent vengé
4 futur		**11 futur antérieur**	
vengerai	vengerons	aurai vengé	aurons vengé
vengeras	vengerez	auras vengé	aurez vengé
vengera	vengeront	aura vengé	auront vengé
5 conditionnel		**12 conditionnel passé**	
vengerais	vengerions	aurais vengé	aurions vengé
vengerais	vengeriez	aurais vengé	auriez vengé
vengerait	vengeraient	aurait vengé	auraient vengé
6 présent du subjonctif		**13 passé du subjonctif**	
venge	vengions	aie vengé	ayons vengé
venges	vengiez	aies vengé	ayez vengé
venge	vengent	ait vengé	aient vengé
7 imparfait du subjonctif		**14 plus-que-parfait du subjonctif**	
vengeasse	vengeassions	eusse vengé	eussions vengé
vengeasses	vengeassiez	eusses vengé	eussiez vengé
vengeât	vengeassent	eût vengé	eussent vengé

Impératif
venge
vengeons
vengez

Words and expressions related to this verb
se venger   to avenge oneself
venger son honneur   to avenge one's honor
par vengeance   out of revenge
un vengeur, une vengeresse   avenger

se venger de   to avenge oneself for
la vengeance   vengeance, revenge
la vengeance divine   divine vengeance

Don't miss orthographically changing verbs on pages 554–556.

venir

Part. pr. venant   Part. passé **venu(e)(s)**

to come

The Seven Simple Tenses		The Seven Compound Tenses	
Singular	Plural	Singular	Plural
1 présent de l'indicatif		**8 passé composé**	
viens	venons	suis venu(e)	sommes venu(e)s
viens	venez	es venu(e)	êtes venu(e)(s)
vient	viennent	est venu(e)	sont venu(e)s
2 imparfait de l'indicatif		**9 plus-que-parfait de l'indicatif**	
venais	venions	étais venu(e)	étions venu(e)s
venais	veniez	étais venu(e)	étiez venu(e)(s)
venait	venaient	était venu(e)	étaient venu(e)s
3 passé simple		**10 passé antérieur**	
vins	vînmes	fus venu(e)	fûmes venu(e)s
vins	vîntes	fus venu(e)	fûtes venu(e)(s)
vint	vinrent	fut venu(e)	furent venu(e)s
4 futur		**11 futur antérieur**	
viendrai	viendrons	serai venu(e)	serons venu(e)s
viendras	viendrez	seras venu(e)	serez venu(e)(s)
viendra	viendront	sera venu(e)	seront venu(e)s
5 conditionnel		**12 conditionnel passé**	
viendrais	viendrions	serais venu(e)	serions venu(e)s
viendrais	viendriez	serais venu(e)	seriez venu(e)(s)
viendrait	viendraient	serait venu(e)	seraient venu(e)s
6 présent du subjonctif		**13 passé du subjonctif**	
vienne	venions	sois venu(e)	soyons venu(e)s
viennes	veniez	sois venu(e)	soyez venu(e)(s)
vienne	viennent	soit venu(e)	soient venu(e)s
7 imparfait du subjonctif		**14 plus-que-parfait du subjonctif**	
vinsse	vinssions	fusse venu(e)	fussions venu(e)s
vinsses	vinssiez	fusses venu(e)	fussiez venu(e)(s)
vînt	vinssent	fût venu(e)	fussent venu(e)s

Impératif
viens
venons
venez

Words and expressions related to this verb

venir de faire qqch   to have just done something
Je viens de manger   I have just eaten.
venir à + inf.   to happen to; **Si je viens à devenir riche . . .**   If I happen to become rich . . .
s'en venir   to come

faire venir   to send for
venir chercher   to call for, to come to get
D'où vient cela?   Where does that come from?
Venons-en au fait   Let's get to the point.
le va et vient   coming and going (people, cars, etc.)
parvenir à   to reach, succeed

See also **convenir, devenir, prévenir, revenir,** and **se souvenir.**

Can't recognize an irregular verb form? Check out pages 526–529.

The Seven Simple Tenses		The Seven Compound Tenses	
Singular	Plural	Singular	Plural
1 présent de l'indicatif		8 passé composé	
verse	**versons**	**ai versé**	**avons versé**
verses	**versez**	**as versé**	**avez versé**
verse	**versent**	**a versé**	**ont versé**
2 imparfait de l'indicatif		9 plus-que-parfait de l'indicatif	
versais	**versions**	**avais versé**	**avions versé**
versais	**versiez**	**avais versé**	**aviez versé**
versait	**versaient**	**avait versé**	**avaient versé**
3 passé simple		10 passé antérieur	
versai	**versâmes**	**eus versé**	**eûmes versé**
versas	**versâtes**	**eus versé**	**eûtes versé**
versa	**versèrent**	**eut versé**	**eurent versé**
4 futur		11 futur antérieur	
verserai	**verserons**	**aurai versé**	**aurons versé**
verseras	**verserez**	**auras versé**	**aurez versé**
versera	**verseront**	**aura versé**	**auront versé**
5 conditionnel		12 conditionnel passé	
verserais	**verserions**	**aurais versé**	**aurions versé**
verserais	**verseriez**	**aurais versé**	**auriez versé**
verserait	**verseraient**	**aurait versé**	**auraient versé**
6 présent du subjonctif		13 passé du subjonctif	
verse	**versions**	**aie versé**	**ayons versé**
verses	**versiez**	**aies versé**	**ayez versé**
verse	**versent**	**ait versé**	**aient versé**
7 imparfait du subjonctif		14 plus-que-parfait du subjonctif	
versasse	**versassions**	**eusse versé**	**eussions versé**
versasses	**versassiez**	**eusses versé**	**eussiez versé**
versât	**versassent**	**eût versé**	**eussent versé**

Impératif
verse
versons
versez

Common idiomatic expressions using this verb and words related to it
verser des larmes   to shed tears
verser de l'argent   to deposit money
verser des fonds   to invest capital
un versement   deposit, payment

verser du sang   to shed blood
verser à boire à qqn   to pour someone a drink
pleuvoir à verse   to rain hard

Soak up some verbs used in weather expressions on pages 557 and 558.

The subject pronouns are found on the page facing page 1.   **493**

vêtir

Part. pr. vêtant   **Part. passé vêtu**

to clothe, to dress

The Seven Simple Tenses		The Seven Compound Tenses	
Singular	Plural	Singular	Plural
1 présent de l'indicatif		**8 passé composé**	
vêts	vêtons	ai vêtu	avons vêtu
vêts	vêtez	as vêtu	avez vêtu
vêt	vêtent	a vêtu	ont vêtu
2 imparfait de l'indicatif		**9 plus-que-parfait de l'indicatif**	
vêtais	vêtions	avais vêtu	avions vêtu
vêtais	vêtiez	avais vêtu	aviez vêtu
vêtait	vêtaient	avait vêtu	avaient vêtu
3 passé simple		**10 passé antérieur**	
vêtis	vêtîmes	eus vêtu	eûmes vêtu
vêtis	vêtîtes	eus vêtu	eûtes vêtu
vêtit	vêtirent	eut vêtu	eurent vêtu
4 futur		**11 futur antérieur**	
vêtirai	vêtirons	aurai vêtu	aurons vêtu
vêtiras	vêtirez	auras vêtu	aurez vêtu
vêtira	vêtiront	aura vêtu	auront vêtu
5 conditionnel		**12 conditionnel passé**	
vêtirais	vêtirions	aurais vêtu	aurions vêtu
vêtirais	vêtiriez	aurais vêtu	auriez vêtu
vêtirait	vêtiraient	aurait vêtu	auraient vêtu
6 présent du subjonctif		**13 passé du subjonctif**	
vête	vêtions	aie vêtu	ayons vêtu
vêtes	vêtiez	aies vêtu	ayez vêtu
vête	vêtent	ait vêtu	aient vêtu
7 imparfait du subjonctif		**14 plus-que-parfait du subjonctif**	
vêtisse	vêtissions	eusse vêtu	eussions vêtu
vêtisses	vêtissiez	eusses vêtu	eussiez vêtu
vêtît	vêtissent	eût vêtu	eussent vêtu

Impératif
vêts
vêtons
vêtez

Words and expressions related to this verb
un vêtement garment, wearing apparel;
  des vêtements clothes
les vêtements de dessus outerwear
les sous-vêtements underwear
vêtir un enfant to dress a child
dévêtir to undress
mettre sur soi un vêtement to put on clothing
les vêtements de deuil mourning clothes

le vestiaire coatroom
les vêtements de travail work clothes
se vêtir to dress oneself
se dévêtir to undress oneself
être bien vêtu (vêtue) to be well dressed;
  mal vêtu badly dressed;
  à demi-vêtu half dressed

See also **s'habiller.**

to grow old, to become old, to age

The Seven Simple Tenses		The Seven Compound Tenses	
Singular	Plural	Singular	Plural

1 présent de l'indicatif		8 passé composé	
vieillis	**vieillissons**	**ai vieilli**	**avons vieilli**
vieillis	**vieillissez**	**as vieilli**	**avez vieilli**
vieillit	**vieillissent**	**a vieilli**	**ont vieilli**
2 imparfait de l'indicatif		9 plus-que-parfait de l'indicatif	
vieillissais	**vieillissions**	**avais vieilli**	**avions vieilli**
vieillissais	**vieillissiez**	**avais vieilli**	**aviez vieilli**
vieillissait	**vieillissaient**	**avait vieilli**	**avaient vieilli**
3 passé simple		10 passé antérieur	
vieillis	**vieillîmes**	**eus vieilli**	**eûmes vieilli**
vieillis	**vieillîtes**	**eus vieilli**	**eûtes vieilli**
vieillit	**vieillirent**	**eut vieilli**	**eurent vieilli**
4 futur		11 futur antérieur	
vieillirai	**vieillirons**	**aurai vieilli**	**aurons vieilli**
vieilliras	**vieillirez**	**auras vieilli**	**aurez vieilli**
vieillira	**vieilliront**	**aura vieilli**	**auront vieilli**
5 conditionnel		12 conditionnel passé	
vieillirais	**vieillirions**	**aurais vieilli**	**aurions vieilli**
vieillirais	**vieilliriez**	**aurais vieilli**	**auriez vieilli**
vieillirait	**vieilliraient**	**aurait vieilli**	**auraient vieilli**
6 présent du subjonctif		13 passé du subjonctif	
vieillisse	**vieillissions**	**aie vieilli**	**ayons vieilli**
vieillisses	**vieillissiez**	**aies vieilli**	**ayez vieilli**
vieillisse	**vieillissent**	**ait vieilli**	**aient vieilli**
7 imparfait du subjonctif		14 plus-que-parfait du subjonctif	
vieillisse	**vieillissions**	**eusse vieilli**	**eussions vieilli**
vieillisses	**vieillissiez**	**eusses vieilli**	**eussiez vieilli**
vieillît	**vieillissent**	**eût vieilli**	**eussent vieilli**

Impératif
vieillis
vieillissons
vieillissez

Words related to this verb
vieux, vieil, vieille   old
  un vieux chapeau   an old hat
  un vieil arbre   an old tree
  un vieil homme   an old man
  deux vieux hommes   two old men
  une vieille dame   an old lady

la vieillesse   old age
un vieillard   old man
une vieille   old woman
vieillissant, vieillissante *adj.*   aging
le vieillissement   aging, growing old

Want to learn more idiomatic expressions that contain verbs? Look at pages 530–542.

visiter

Part. pr. **visitant**   Part. passé **visité**

to visit

The Seven Simple Tenses		The Seven Compound Tenses	
Singular	Plural	Singular	Plural
1 présent de l'indicatif		**8 passé composé**	
visite	visitons	ai visité	avons visité
visites	visitez	as visité	avez visité
visite	visitent	a visité	ont visité
2 imparfait de l'indicatif		**9 plus-que-parfait de l'indicatif**	
visitais	visitions	avais visité	avions visité
visitais	visitiez	avais visité	aviez visité
visitait	visitaient	avait visité	avaient visité
3 passé simple		**10 passé antérieur**	
visitai	visitâmes	eus visité	eûmes visité
visitas	visitâtes	eus visité	eûtes visité
visita	visitèrent	eut visité	eurent visité
4 futur		**11 futur antérieur**	
visiterai	visiterons	aurai visité	aurons visité
visiteras	visiterez	auras visité	aurez visité
visitera	visiteront	aura visité	auront visité
5 conditionnel		**12 conditionnel passé**	
visiterais	visiterions	aurais visité	aurions visité
visiterais	visiteriez	aurais visité	auriez visité
visiterait	visiteraient	aurait visité	auraient visité
6 présent du subjonctif		**13 passé du subjonctif**	
visite	visitions	aie visité	ayons visité
visites	visitiez	aies visité	ayez visité
visite	visitent	ait visité	aient visité
7 imparfait du subjonctif		**14 plus-que-parfait du subjonctif**	
visitasse	visitassions	eusse visité	eussions visité
visitasses	visitassiez	eusses visité	eussiez visité
visitât	visitassent	eût visité	eussent visité

Impératif
visite
visitons
visitez

Words and expressions related to this verb

rendre visite à qqn   to visit someone, to pay a call
un visiteur, une visiteuse   visitor, caller
une visite guidée   a guided tour

rendre une visite à qqn   to return a visit
les heures de visite   visiting hours
une visitation   visitation

Taking a trip? Check out the popular words, phrases, and expressions for travelers on pages 599–621.

496

The Seven Simple Tenses		The Seven Compound Tenses	
Singular	Plural	Singular	Plural
1 présent de l'indicatif		**8 passé composé**	
vis	vivons	ai vécu	avons vécu
vis	vivez	as vécu	avez vécu
vit	vivent	a vécu	ont vécu
2 imparfait de l'indicatif		**9 plus-que-parfait de l'indicatif**	
vivais	vivions	avais vécu	avions vécu
vivais	viviez	avais vécu	aviez vécu
vivait	vivaient	avait vécu	avaient vécu
3 passé simple		**10 passé antérieur**	
vécus	vécûmes	eus vécu	eûmes vécu
vécus	vécûtes	eus vécu	eûtes vécu
vécut	vécurent	eut vécu	eurent vécu
4 futur		**11 futur antérieur**	
vivrai	vivrons	aurai vécu	aurons vécu
vivras	vivrez	auras vécu	aurez vécu
vivra	vivront	aura vécu	auront vécu
5 conditionnel		**12 conditionnel passé**	
vivrais	vivrions	aurais vécu	aurions vécu
vivrais	vivriez	aurais vécu	auriez vécu
vivrait	vivraient	aurait vécu	auraient vécu
6 présent du subjonctif		**13 passé du subjonctif**	
vive	vivions	aie vécu	ayons vécu
vives	viviez	aies vécu	ayez vécu
vive	vivent	ait vécu	aient vécu
7 imparfait du subjonctif		**14 plus-que-parfait du subjonctif**	
vécusse	vécussions	eusse vécu	eussions vécu
vécusses	vécussiez	eusses vécu	eussiez vécu
vécût	vécussent	eût vécu	eussent vécu

Impératif
vis
vivons
vivez

Words and expressions related to this verb
revivre to relive, to revive
survivre à to survive
Vive la France! Long live France!
avoir de quoi vivre to have enough to live on
vivre de to subsist on
savoir-vivre to be well-mannered

See also **survivre.**

Vivent les Etats-Unis! Long live the United States!
le vivre et le couvert room and board
vivre largement to live well
Nous vivons des temps troublés We are living in troubled times.

Can't recognize an irregular verb form? Check out pages 526–529.

Grammar putting you in a tense mood? Review the definitions of basic grammatical terms with examples on pages 674–688.

voir

to see

The Seven Simple Tenses		The Seven Compound Tenses	
Singular	Plural	Singular	Plural
1 présent de l'indicatif		**8 passé composé**	
vois	voyons	ai vu	avons vu
vois	voyez	as vu	avez vu
voit	voient	a vu	ont uv
2 imparfait de l'indicatif		**9 plus-que-parfait de l'indicatif**	
voyais	voyions	avais vu	avions vu
voyais	voyiez	avais vu	aviez vu
voyait	voyaient	avait vu	avaient vu
3 passé simple		**10 passé antérieur**	
vis	vîmes	eus vu	eûmes vu
vis	vîtes	eus vu	eûtes vu
vit	virent	eut vu	eurent vu
4 futur		**11 futur antérieur**	
verrai	verrons	aurai vu	aurons vu
verras	verrez	auras vu	aurez vu
verra	verront	aura vu	auront vu
5 conditionnel		**12 conditionnel passé**	
verrais	verrions	aurais vu	aurions vu
verrais	verriez	aurais vu	auriez vu
verrait	verraient	aurait vu	auraient vu
6 présent du subjonctif		**13 passé du subjonctif**	
voie	voyions	aie vu	ayons vu
voies	voyiez	aies vu	ayez vu
voie	voient	ait vu	aient vu
7 imparfait du subjonctif		**14 plus-que-parfait du subjonctif**	
visse	vissions	eusse vu	eussions vu
visses	vissiez	eusses vu	eussiez vu
vît	vissent	eût vu	eussent vu

Impératif
vois
voyons
voyez

Words and expressions related to this verb
revoir   to see again
faire voir   to show
voir la vie en rose   to see the bright side of life
Voyez vous-même!   See for yourself!

entrevoir   to catch a glimpse, to glimpse
C'est à voir   It remains to be seen.
Cela se voit   That's obvious.
Voyons!   See here now!
Voir c'est croire   Seeing is believing.

See also **prévoir** and **revoir.**

Can't recognize an irregular verb form? Check out pages 526–529.

Get acquainted with what preposition goes with what verb on pages 543–553.

498

The Seven Simple Tenses		The Seven Compound Tenses	
Singular	Plural	Singular	Plural
1 présent de l'indicatif		**8 passé composé**	
vole	volons	ai volé	avons volé
voles	volez	as volé	avez volé
vole	volent	a volé	ont volé
2 imparfait de l'indicatif		**9 plus-que-parfait de l'indicatif**	
volais	volions	avais volé	avions volé
volais	voliez	avais volé	aviez volé
volait	volaient	avait volé	avaient volé
3 passé simple		**10 passé antérieur**	
volai	volâmes	eus volé	eûmes volé
volas	volâtes	eus volé	eûtes volé
vola	volèrent	eut volé	eurent volé
4 futur		**11 futur antérieur**	
volerai	volerons	aurai volé	aurons volé
voleras	volerez	auras volé	aurez volé
volera	voleront	aura volé	auront volé
5 conditionnel		**12 conditionnel passé**	
volerais	volerions	aurais volé	aurions volé
volerais	voleriez	aurais volé	auriez volé
volerait	voleraient	aurait volé	auraient volé
6 présent du subjonctif		**13 passé du subjonctif**	
vole	volions	aie volé	ayons volé
voles	voliez	aies volé	ayez volé
vole	volent	ait volé	aient volé
7 imparfait du subjonctif		**14 plus-que-parfait du subjonctif**	
volasse	volassions	eusse volé	eussions volé
volasses	volassiez	eusses volé	eussiez volé
volât	volassent	eût volé	eussent volé

Impératif
vole
volons
volez

Words and expressions related to this verb
un vol flight, theft
le voleur thief
à vol d'oiseau as the crow flies
vol de nuit night flying (airplane), night flight
New York à vol d'oiseau bird's eye view of New York
survoler to fly over

le volant steering wheel
se mettre au volant to take the (steering) wheel
voler un baiser à qqn to steal a kiss from someone
voler dans les bras de qqn to fly into someone's arms

See also **s'envoler** and **survoler.**

The subject pronouns are found on the page facing page 1.

vouloir

Part. pr. **voulant**   Part. passé **voulu**

to want

The Seven Simple Tenses		The Seven Compound Tenses	
Singular	Plural	Singular	Plural
1 présent de l'indicatif		**8 passé composé**	
veux	voulons	ai voulu	avons voulu
veux	voulez	as voulu	avez voulu
veut	veulent	a voulu	ont voulu
2 imparfait de l'indicatif		**9 plus-que-parfait de l'indicatif**	
voulais	voulions	avais voulu	avions voulu
voulais	vouliez	avais voulu	aviez voulu
voulait	voulaient	avait voulu	avaient voulu
3 passé simple		**10 passé antérieur**	
voulus	voulûmes	eus voulu	eûmes voulu
voulus	voulûtes	eus voulu	eûtes voulu
voulut	voulurent	eut voulu	eurent voulu
4 futur		**11 futur antérieur**	
voudrai	voudrons	aurai voulu	aurons voulu
voudras	voudrez	auras voulu	aurez voulu
voudra	voudront	aura voulu	auront voulu
5 conditionnel		**12 conditionnel passé**	
voudrais	voudrions	aurais voulu	aurions voulu
voudrais	voudriez	aurais voulu	auriez voulu
voudrait	voudraient	aurait voulu	auraient voulu
6 présent du subjonctif		**13 passé du subjonctif**	
veuille	voulions	aie voulu	ayons voulu
veuilles	vouliez	aies voulu	ayez voulu
veuille	veuillent	ait voulu	aient voulu
7 imparfait du subjonctif		**14 plus-que-parfait du subjonctif**	
voulusse	voulussions	eusse voulu	eussions voulu
voulusses	voulussiez	eusses voulu	eussiez voulu
voulût	voulussent	eût voulu	eussent voulu

Impératif
veuille
veuillons
veuillez

Words and expressions related to this verb

un voeu a wish
meilleurs voeux best wishes
Vouloir c'est pouvoir Where there's a will there's a way.
vouloir dire to mean; **Qu'est-ce que cela veut dire?** What does that mean?
vouloir bien faire qqch to be willing to do something

sans le vouloir without meaning to, unintentionally
en temps voulu in due time
en vouloir à qqn to bear a grudge against someone
Que voulez-vous dire par là? What do you mean by that remark?
Dieu le veuille! May God will it! God willing!

Can't recognize an irregular verb form? Check out pages 526–529.

500

The Seven Simple Tenses		The Seven Compound Tenses	
Singular	Plural	Singular	Plural
1 présent de l'indicatif		**8 passé composé**	
voyage	voyageons	ai voyagé	avons voyagé
voyages	voyagez	as voyagé	avez voyagé
voyage	voyagent	a voyagé	ont voyagé
2 imparfait de l'indicatif		**9 plus-que-parfait de l'indicatif**	
voyageais	voyagions	avais voyagé	avions voyagé
voyageais	voyagiez	avais voyagé	aviez voyagé
voyageait	voyageaient	avait voyagé	avaient voyagé
3 passé simple		**10 passé antérieur**	
voyageai	voyageâmes	eus voyagé	eûmes voyagé
voyageas	voyageâtes	eus voyagé	eûtes voyagé
voyagea	voyagèrent	eut voyagé	eurent voyagé
4 futur		**11 futur antérieur**	
voyagerai	voyagerons	aurai voyagé	aurons voyagé
voyageras	voyagerez	auras voyagé	aurez voyagé
voyagera	voyageront	aura voyagé	auront voyagé
5 conditionnel		**12 conditionnel passé**	
voyagerais	voyagerions	aurais voyagé	aurions voyagé
voyagerais	voyageriez	aurais voyagé	auriez voyagé
voyagerait	voyageraient	aurait voyagé	auraient voyagé
6 présent du subjonctif		**13 passé du subjonctif**	
voyage	voyagions	aie voyagé	ayons voyagé
voyages	voyagiez	aies voyagé	ayez voyagé
voyage	voyagent	ait voyagé	aient voyagé
7 imparfait du subjonctif		**14 plus-que-parfait du subjonctif**	
voyageasse	voyageassions	eusse voyagé	eussions voyagé
voyageasses	voyageassiez	eusses voyagé	eussiez voyagé
voyageât	voyageassent	eût voyagé	eussent voyagé

Impératif
voyage
voyageons
voyagez

Words and expressions related to this verb
un voyage   a trip
faire un voyage   to take a trip
un voyageur, une voyageuse   traveler
une agence de voyages   tourist agency
Bon voyage!   Have a good trip!

Bon voyage et bon retour!   Have a good trip and a safe return!
Les Voyages de Gulliver   *Gulliver's Travels*
les frais de voyage   travel expenses
un voyage d'affaires   business trip
un voyage d'agrément   pleasure trip

Don't miss orthographically changing verbs on pages 554–556.

Going away? Don't forget to check out the practical situations for travelers on pages 568–598.

The subject pronouns are found on the page facing page 1.

Appendixes

English-French verb index

The purpose of this index is to give you instantly the French verb for the English verb you have in mind to use. This saves you time if you do not have at your fingertips a standard English-French word dictionary.

If the French verb you want is reflexive (*e.g.*, **s'appeler** or **se lever**), you will find it listed alphabetically under the first letter of the verb and not under the reflexive pronoun *s'* or *se*.

When you find the French verb you need through the English verb, look up its verb forms in this book, where all verbs are listed alphabetically at the top of each page. If it is not among the 501 verbs in this book, consult the list of over 1,100 French verbs conjugated like model verbs among the 501, which begins at the end of this index.

A

abandon **abandonner**
able, be **pouvoir**
abolish **abolir**
absolve **absoudre**
abstain **s'abstenir**
abstract **abstraire**
accept **accepter**
acclaim **acclamer**
accompany **accompagner**
accuse **accuser**
achieve **achever**
acknowledge **convenir, reconnaître**
acquainted with, be **connaître**
acquire **acquérir**
act **agir**, act (in a play) **jouer**
add **ajouter**
add more **rajouter**
address **adresser**
adjoin **adjoindre**
adjourn **ajourner**
admire **admirer**
admit **accorder, admettre**
adore **adorer**
advance **avancer**
advise **conseiller**
affect **toucher,** (emotionally) **émouvoir**
afraid, be **craindre**
age **vieillir**
agree **consentir, convenir**
aid **aider**
aim (at) **viser (à)**

allow **laisser, permettre**
allure **attirer**
amaze **étonner**
amuse **amuser, égayer**
amuse oneself **s'amuser**
angry, become **se fâcher**
announce **annoncer**
annoy **agacer, ennuyer**
answer **répondre**
apologize **s'excuser**
appeal **appeler**
appear **apparaître, paraître**
appear again **reparaître**
appease **adoucir**
applaud **acclamer**
appoint **nommer**
appraise **évaluer**
approach **approcher**
appropriate, be **convenir**
approve (of) **approuver**
argue **discuter**
arouse **émouvoir**
arrange **arranger**
arrest **arrêter**
arrive **arriver**
arrive at **gagner**
ascend **monter**
ascertain **constater**
ask (for) **demander, réclamer**
assess **évaluer**
assist **aider**
assist (at) **assister**
assure **assurer**
assure oneself **s'assurer**

astonish **étonner**
attain **atteindre**
attempt **tenter**
attend **assister (à)**
attest **certifier**
attract **attirer**
augment **augmenter**
avenge **venger**
avoid **échapper, éviter**

B

babble **bavarder**
balance **balancer**
be **être**
be a matter of **s'agir de**
be a question of **s'agir de**
be able **pouvoir**
be acquainted with **connaître**
be afraid **craindre**
be appropriate **convenir**
be as good as **valoir**
be becoming (in appearance) **seoir**
be born **naître**
be busy **s'occuper**
be dependent on **dépendre**
be enough **suffire**
be equal **valoir**
be in a hurry **se presser**
be interested **s'intéresser**
be lacking **falloir, manquer**
be left (over) **rester**
be like **ressembler**
be located **se trouver**
be mistaken **se méprendre, se tromper**
be named **s'appeler**
be necessary **falloir**
be present (at) **assister (à)**
be quiet **se taire**
be silent **se taire**
be situated **se trouver**
be sufficient **suffire**
be suitable **convenir**
be the matter **s'agir**
be upset **s'inquiéter**
be worth **valoir**
bear **apporter, porter, subir**
beat **battre**

become **devenir**
become angry **se fâcher**
become old **vieillir**
becoming, be (in appearance) **seoir**
beg **prier, supplier**
begin **commencer, se mettre**
behave **agir, se comporter**
believe **croire**
belong **appartenir**
beseech **supplier**
bet **parier**
betray **trahir**
beware **se méfier**
bewilder **abasourdir, étourdir**
bite **mordre**
blame **blâmer**
blaspheme **blasphémer**
bless **bénir**
blow **souffler**
blush **rougir**
boil **bouillir**
boo **siffler, huer**
boot up (comp.) **démarrer, amorcer**
bore **ennuyer**
born, be **naître**
borrow **emprunter**
bother **gêner, déranger**
break **casser, se casser, rompre**
breakfast (have) **déjeuner**
bring **amener, apporter**
bring back **rapporter**
bring down **descendre**
bring near **approcher**
bring up (raise) **élever**
bring up (take up) **monter**
brush **brosser**
brush oneself **se brosser**
budge **bouger**
build **bâtir, construire**
bully **malmener**
burden **charger**
burn **brûler**
burst **rompre**
bury **enterrer**
busy, be **s'occuper**
buy **acheter**

C

call **appeler**
call again **rappeler**
call back **rappeler**
call oneself **s'appeler**
can (be able) **pouvoir**
carry **porter**
carry away **enlever, emporter**
cast **jeter**
catch **attraper**
cause **causer**
cease **cesser**
cede **céder**
certify **certifier, constater**
change **changer**
charge **charger**
chase **chasser**
chat **bavarder, causer**
chatter **bavarder**
cheat **tricher**
check in (a hotel) **enregistrer**
cheer **acclamer**
cheer up **égayer**
cherish **chérir**
chide **gronder**
choose **choisir, élire**
claim **prétendre**
class **classer**
classify **classer**
clean **nettoyer**
clear (snow) **déneiger**
cleave **fendre**
climb **grimper**
clip **tailler**
clone **cloner**
close **fermer**
clothe **vêtir**
coat **enduire**
collect **recueillir**
comb one's hair **se peigner**
combat **combattre**
come **venir**
come back **revenir**
come (go) running to **accourir**
come in **entrer**
come near **approcher**
come to pass **advenir, survenir**
command **commander**

commence **commencer**
commit **commettre**
commit sin **pécher**
compare **comparer**
compel **contraindre**
complain **se plaindre**
complete **achever, finir**
comprehend **comprendre, saisir**
compromise **compromettre**
conceive **concevoir**
conclude **conclure**
concur **concourir**
condescend **s'abaisser**
conduct **conduire**
congratulate **féliciter**
conquer **conquérir, vaincre**
consecrate **bénir, consacrer**
consent **consentir**
constrain **contraindre**
constrict **gêner**
construct **construire, bâtir**
contact **joindre, contacter**
contain **contenir**
continue **continuer**
contradict **contredire**
control **mener**
convince **convaincre, persuader**
cook **cuire, cuisiner**
correct **corriger**
corrupt **corrompre**
cost **coûter**
cough **tousser**
counsel **conseiller**
count **compter**
cover **couvrir**
crack **fendre**
crash (comp.) **tomber en panne**
create **créer**
criticize **critiquer, décrier**
cross **traverser**
crowd **se presser**
cry **pleurer**
cry out **crier**
cure **guérir**
curse **maudire**
cut **couper**
cut down **abattre**
cut (out) **tailler**

D

damage **gâter**
dance **danser**
dare **oser**
daze **abasourdir, étourdir**
deafen **abasourdir, étourdir**
deceive **décevoir**
decide **décider**
declare **prononcer, déclarer**
decrease **décroître, diminuer, réduire**
deduce **déduire**
deduct **déduire**
deem **juger**
defend **défendre**
delete **effacer**
demand **exiger, réclamer**
demolish **démolir**
deny **nier**
depart **partir**
depend on **dépendre, se fier**
dependent, be **dépendre**
depict **dépeindre**
derange **déranger**
descend **descendre**
describe **décrire, dépeindre**
desert **abandonner**
deserve **mériter, valoir**
desire **désirer**
destroy **détruire**
detain **retenir**
detest **détester**
develop **développer**
die **mourir, périr**
dig deeply **fouiller**
diminish **décroître, diminuer, réduire**
dine **dîner**
dirty **salir, souiller**
disappear **disparaître**
disappoint **décevoir**
discourse **discourir**
discover **découvrir**
discuss **discuter**
dishearten **abattre**
disinfect **désinfecter**
dislike **détester**
display **montrer**
displease **déplaire**
dissolve **fondre**

dissuade **dissuader**
distinguish **remarquer**
distrust **se méfier**
disturb **déranger**
divert **détourner**
divest **dévêtir**
do **faire**
do away with **abolir**
doubt **douter**
download **télécharger, charger**
draw (sketch) **dessiner**
draw (out) **tirer**
draw (out) again **retirer**
draw up **établir**
dream **rêver, songer**
dress **vêtir**
dress oneself **s'habiller**
drift **voguer**
drink **boire**
drive **conduire**
drive (a car) **conduire, rouler**
drive out **chasser**
drool **baver**
dwell (in) **habiter**
dye **teindre**

E

earn **gagner**
eat **manger**
elect **élire**
embarrass **gêner**
embrace **étreindre, embrasser**
employ **employer**
enclose **inclure**
encounter **rencontrer**
encourage **encourager**
end **achever, finir, terminer**
endure **souffrir, supporter**
engage upon **entreprendre**
enjoy **goûter, jouir**
enjoy oneself **s'amuser**
enlarge **accroître**
enliven **égayer**
enough, be **suffire**
ensure **assurer**
enter **entrer**
entertain **amuser, égayer**
entreat **prier**

escape **échapper, s'enfuir, se sauver**
establish **établir, fonder**
estimate **évaluer**
evaluate **évaluer**
excavate **fouiller**
excite **émouvoir**
exclude **exclure**
excuse **excuser**
excuse oneself **s'excuser**
exhibit **montrer**
expect **attendre**
expect to **compter**
experience **éprouver**
explain **expliquer**
express **exprimer**
extinguish **éteindre**

forbid **défendre, interdire**
force **forcer**
foresee **prévoir**
forestall **prévenir**
foretell **prédire**
forget **oublier**
forgive **pardonner**
found (establish) **fonder**
frap **frapper**
freeze **geler**
freeze again **regeler**
frighten **effrayer**
fry **frire**
fulfill **remplir**
function **marcher**
furnish **fournir**

F

fail **échouer, faillir**
faint **s'évanouir**
fake **truquer**
fall **tomber**
fall asleep **s'endormir**
fax **télécopier**
fear **craindre**
feed **nourrir**
feed oneself **se nourrir**
feel **sentir, ressentir**
feel (experience) **éprouver**
feign **feindre**
fight **se battre, combattre**
fill, fill in, fill out **remplir**
fill up **emplir**
find **trouver**
find out **s'informer**
finish **achever, finir, terminer**
fish **pêcher**
fish out **repêcher**
flatten **coucher**
flatter **flatter**
flee **s'enfuir, fuir**
float **flotter**
fly **s'enfuir, fuir, voler**
fly away **s'enfuir, s'envoler**
fly off **s'envoler, fuir**
fly over **survoler**
fold **plier**
follow **suivre**

G

gain **gagner**
gamble **jouer**
gather **cueillir, recueillir**
get **obtenir, recevoir**
get angry **se fâcher**
get dressed **s'habiller**
get up **se lever**
give **donner**
give back **remettre, rendre**
go **aller**
go away **s'éloigner, s'en aller**
go back **retourner**
go deeply into **fouiller**
go down **descendre**
go forward **avancer**
go in **entrer**
go out **sortir**
go to bed **se coucher**
go up **monter**
go up (cost) **renchérir**
gossip **bavarder**
grant **accorder**
grasp **saisir, serrer**
greet **accueillir**
grind **moudre**
grip **étreindre**
grow **croître, pousser**
grow old **vieillir**
grow thin **maigrir**
grow (up, grow taller) **grandir**

guarantee **assurer, certifier**
guard **garder**
guide **guider**

H

hack (comp.) **pirater**
hail (weather) **grêler**
hamper **gêner, empêcher**
hang **accrocher, pendre**
hang on **s'accrocher**
hang up **raccrocher**
happen **advenir, se passer, arriver**
harm **blesser, nuire**
harvest **recueillir**
hasten **se dépêcher**
hate **détester, haïr**
have **avoir**
have (hold) **tenir**
have a good time **s'amuser**
have a snack **goûter**
have dinner **dîner**
have lunch **déjeuner**
have supper **souper**
have to **devoir**
heal **guérir**
hear **entendre**
help **aider, assister, secourir**
help (each other) **s'entraider**
help oneself (to food and drink)
　　se servir
hesitate **hésiter**
hide **cacher**
hide oneself **se cacher**
hinder **arrêter, empêcher, gêner, nuire**
hire **engager**
hiss **siffler**
hit **battre, taper, frapper**
hit (target) **atteindre**
hold **tenir**
hold back **retenir**
hold up **supporter**
hook **accrocher**
hope **espérer**
humble **abaisser**
humble oneself **s'abaisser**
humiliate **abaisser**
hunt **chasser**
hurl **lancer**

hurry **se dépêcher**
hurry (be in a hurry) **se presser**
hurt **blesser**
hurt oneself **se blesser**

I

impede **gêner**
implore **supplier**
impose **imposer**
include **inclure**
inconvenience **gêner**
increase **accroître, augmenter,**
　　croître, grandir
indicate **indiquer**
induce **persuader**
infer **déduire**
inform **informer**
inform oneself **s'informer**
inhabit **habiter**
injure **blesser**
injure oneself **se blesser**
inquire **s'informer**
insist **insister**
instruct **instruire**
insure **assurer**
insure oneself **s'assurer**
intend **compter**
interrogate **interroger**
interrupt **interrompre**
introduce **introduire**
introduce (a person) **présenter**
invent **inventer**
invite **inviter**
iron **repasser**
irritate **agacer**

J

join **joindre, unir**
joke **plaisanter**
judge **juger**
jump **sauter**

K

keep **garder, retenir**
keep away **s'éloigner**
keep back **s'éloigner**

keep oneself busy **s'occuper**
kill **tuer**
kiss **embrasser**
knock **frapper, toquer**
knock down **abattre**
know **connaître**
know (how) **savoir**
know, not to **méconnaître**

L

lace **lacer**
lack **manquer**
lament **se plaindre**
laugh **rire**
launch **lancer**
lay **coucher, poser**
lay claim **prétendre**
lay the foundation **fonder**
lead **amener, conduire, guider, mener**
lead away **emmener**
leak **fuir**
leap **sauter**
learn **apprendre**
leave **laisser, partir, quitter, sortir**
leave hold **lâcher**
lend **prêter**
lessen **diminuer**
let **laisser, permettre**
let go **lâcher**
lick **lécher**
lie dead **gésir**
lie down **s'étendre, se coucher, gésir**
lie ill **gésir**
lie, tell a **mentir**
lift **lever**
like **aimer**
listen (to) **écouter**
live **vivre**
live (reside) **demeurer**
live (in) **habiter**
live somewhere temporarily **séjourner**
load **charger**
located, be **se trouver**
look (at) **regarder**
look for **chercher**
look like **ressembler**
loosen **lâcher**
lose **perdre**

lose consciousness **s'évanouir**
lose weight **maigrir**
love **aimer**
lower **abaisser, baisser**
lower oneself **s'abaisser**
lunch **déjeuner**
lying down **s'étendre, se coucher, gésir**

M

maintain **maintenir, prétendre, soutenir**
make **faire**
make believe **feindre**
make dizzy **étourdir**
make fun **se moquer**
make greater **accroître**
make haste **se presser**
make inquiries **s'informer**
make sure **s'assurer**
make the acquaintance **connaître**
make use of **utiliser**
manage **conduire**
march **marcher**
marry **épouser**
matter, be the **s'agir**
meditate **méditer, réfléchir**
meet **rencontrer**
melt **fondre**
merit **mériter, valoir**
mill **moudre**
misjudge **méconnaître**
miss **manquer, regretter**
mistaken, be **(se) méprendre, se tromper**
mistrust **se méfier**
misunderstand **méconnaître**
mix (colors) **fondre**
moan **se plaindre**
mount **monter**
mourn **pleurer**
move **émouvoir, mouvoir**
move away **s'éloigner**
move (budge) **bouger**
move forward **avancer**
move out (change residence) **déménager**
muddy **souiller**

murmur **murmurer**
must **devoir, falloir**
mutter **murmurer**

N

name **appeler, nommer**
named, be **s'appeler**
narrate **conter, narrer, raconter**
necessary, be **falloir**
need **falloir**
negotiate **traiter**
not to know **méconnaître**
not to recognize **méconnaître**
not to speak **se taire**
notice **remarquer**
nourish **nourrir**

O

obey **obéir**
oblige **obliger**
observe **constater, remarquer**
obtain **acquérir, obtenir**
occupy **occuper**
occur **advenir**
offend **blesser, offenser**
offer **offrir**
omit **omettre**
open **ouvrir**
order **commander**
ought **devoir**
overtake **gagner**
owe **devoir**
own **posséder**

P

paint **peindre**
pant **souffler**
pardon **pardonner**
park (a car) **stationner**
pass **passer**
pass again **repasser**
pass away **décéder**
pass by again **repasser**
pause **s'arrêter**
pay **payer**
perceive **apercevoir, sentir**

perish **périr**
permit **permettre**
persuade **persuader**
pertain **appartenir**
pester **agacer**
pet **flatter**
pick (choose) **choisir**
pick (gather) **cueillir**
pity **plaindre**
place **mettre, placer, poser**
place oneself **se mettre**
play **jouer**
please **plaire**
plug in **brancher**
point out **indiquer, montrer, signaler**
ponder **réfléchir**
portray **dépeindre, peindre**
pose **poser**
possess **posséder**
postpone **remettre**
pour **verser**
praise **louer**
pray **prier**
predict **prédire**
prefer **préférer**
prepare **préparer**
prescribe (medicine) **ordonner**
present **présenter**
present (at), be **assister (à)**
press **presser, serrer**
pretend **feindre, prétendre**
prevent **empêcher**
produce **produire**
prohibit **défendre, interdire**
promise **promettre**
promote **avancer, promouvoir**
prompt (an actor/actress with a cue) **souffler**
pronounce **prononcer**
prop up **supporter**
prosecute **poursuivre**
prove **prouver**
pull **tirer**
pull again **retirer**
pull up, pull out **arracher**
punch (ticket) **composter**
punish **punir**
purchase **acheter**

pursue **chasser, poursuivre, pourchasser**
push **pousser**
put **mettre, placer, poser**
put back **remettre, replacer**
put forward **avancer**
put in order **ranger**
put (on) again **remettre**
put to bed **coucher**
put to the test **éprouver**
put to use **utiliser**

Q

question **interroger**
question (be a question of) **s'agir**
quiet, be **se taire**
quiver **frémir**

R

race **courir**
rain **pleuvoir**
raise (bring up) **élever**
raise (lift) **lever**
rap **frapper, taper, toquer**
reach **atteindre**
react **réagir**
read **lire**
read again **relire**
reappear **reparaître**
rear **élever**
rebuild **rebâtir**
rebuke **réprimander**
recall **rappeler, se rappeler, se souvenir**
receive **recevoir**
recognize **reconnaître**
recognize, not to **méconnaître**
recollect **se rappeler**
recommend **conseiller**
reconcile **accorder**
recover **guérir, reprendre, se remettre**
redden **rougir**
reduce **abaisser, réduire**
reduce (one's weight) **maigrir**
reflect **réfléchir**
refuse **refuser**
regret **regretter**

rehearse **répéter**
relate **conter, raconter**
relieve **secourir**
rely on **se fier**
remain **demeurer, rester**
remark **remarquer**
remedy **guérir**
remember **se rappeler, se souvenir**
remind **rappeler**
remove **enlever**
rend **déchirer**
render **rendre**
rent **louer**
repaint **repeindre**
repair **réparer**
repeat **répéter**
replace **remettre, remplacer**
reply **répondre**
reprimand **gronder, réprimander**
reproduce **reproduire**
request **demander, prier**
require **exiger**
reread **relire**
rescue **sauver**
resemble **ressembler**
reside **demeurer**
resolve **résoudre**
respond **répondre**
rest **se reposer**
restrain **contraindre**
result **résulter, réussir**
resume **reprendre**
retain **garder, retenir**
rethink **repenser**
retire **se retirer**
return **rentrer, retourner**
return (something) **rendre**
rewrite **réécrire**
ride along **rouler**
ridicule **ridiculiser**
ring **sonner**
rip **déchirer**
roll **rouler**
roll along **rouler**
rouse **émouvoir**
row **voguer**
run **courir**
run (machine) **marcher**
run aground **échouer**

run away   s'enfuir, se sauver
run to   accourir
run up to   accourir
rush   se presser
rush off   se sauver

S

sail   voguer
sample   prélever
satisfy   satisfaire
save (money)   épargner
save (rescue)   sauver
say   dire
scatter   répandre
scold   gronder
scrape   gratter
scratch   gratter
search   chercher, fouiller
seduce   séduire
see   apercevoir, voir
see again   revoir
see once more   revoir
see someone out   raccompagner
seek   chercher
seem   paraître, sembler
seize   saisir
select   choisir
sell   vendre
send   envoyer
sense   percevoir, sentir
separate   séparer
serve   servir
serve oneself   se servir
set   poser
set in order   ranger
set up   établir
sew   coudre
shake   secouer
shake down (off)   secouer
shake (hands)   serrer
shatter   rompre
shine   luire
shoot   tirer
should   devoir
shout   crier
show   indiquer, montrer
show in   introduire
shudder   frémir

shun   fuir
shut down (computer)   éteindre
sigh   soupirer
sign   signer
silent, be   se taire
simulate   feindre
sin   pécher
sing   chanter
sink   baisser
sit down   s'asseoir
skate   patiner
sketch   dessiner
slander   médire
slaughter   abattre
sleep   dormir
slip away   s'enfuir
slope   s'abaisser
smack   taper
smell   sentir
smile   sourire
smoke   fumer
smooth   adoucir
snow   neiger
soften   adoucir
soil   salir, souiller
sojourn   séjourner
solve   résoudre
sort   classer
speak   parler
speak, not to   se taire
spend (money)   dépenser
spend (time)   passer
split   fendre
spoil   gâter
spread   répandre, enduire
squeeze   presser, serrer
start   commencer, se mettre
station   stationner
stay   demeurer, rester
steal   voler
steam   fumer
step back   s'éloigner
stink   puer
stir   émouvoir
stitch   coudre
stoop to   s'abaisser à
stop (oneself)   s'arrêter
stop (someone or something)   arrêter
straighten up   redresser

strain **tendre**
stretch **tendre**
stretch (oneself) **s'étendre**
stretch out (oneself) **s'étendre**
strike (beat) **battre**
strike down **abattre**
strike (hit) **battre, frapper, taper**
strip **dévêtir**
stroll **se balader**
study **étudier**
stun **abasourdir, étonner, étourdir**
stupefy **abasourdir**
submit **soumettre**
succeed **réussir, parvenir à**
succor **secourir**
suck **sucer**
suffer **souffrir**
suffice **suffire**
sufficient, be **suffire**
suit **convenir, seoir**
suitable, be **convenir**
sup **souper**
supplicate **prier, supplier**
supply **fournir**
support **supporter**
suppose **supposer**
surf **surfer**, (Internet) **naviguer**
surprise **étonner, surprendre**
survive **survivre**
suspend **pendre**
swallow **avaler**
sway **balancer**
swear **jurer**
sweep **balayer**
swell **s'enfler**
swim **nager**
swing **balancer**
switch off **couper**
swoon **s'évanouir**

T

take **prendre**
take a walk **se promener**
take again **reprendre**
take away **enlever, emmener** (for persons)
take back **reprendre**
take down **descendre**

take down (something that is hanging) **dépendre**
take effect **agir**
take flight **s'envoler**
take for a walk **promener**
take off (airplane) **s'envoler**
take place **se passer**
take up (carry up) **monter**
take wing **s'envoler**
talk **parler**
tap **taper, toquer**
taste **goûter**
teach **enseigner**
tear **déchirer**
telephone **téléphoner**
tell **dire**
tell a lie **mentir**
tell (a story) **raconter**
tell about **raconter**
tell lies **mentir**
tempt **tenter**
tend **tendre**
terminate **finir, terminer**
test **éprouver**
thank **remercier**
thaw **dégeler**
think **penser, réfléchir, songer**
throw **jeter, lancer**
thunder **tonner**
tidy up **ranger**
tighten **tendre**
time **chronométrer**
tolerate **supporter, tolérer**
touch **émouvoir, toucher**
touch up **retoucher**
transfer **transmettre**
translate **traduire**
transmit **transmettre**
travel **voyager**
traverse **traverser**
treat **traiter** (to a meal), **inviter**
tremble **frémir, trembler**
trick **tricher**
trim **tailler**
trust **se fier**
try **éprouver, essayer, tenter**
try on **essayer**
turn **tourner**
turn again **retourner**

turn aside **détourner**
turn (oneself) aside, away **se détourner**
turn away **détourner**
turn to (for help) **recourir à**
twist **tordre**

U

uncover **découvrir**
understand **comprendre, entendre**
undertake **entreprendre**
undo **défaire**
unite **unir**
unlace **délacer**
unleash **lâcher**
unload **décharger**
unsew **découdre**
unstitch **découdre**
untie **défaire**
upload **charger**
uproot **arracher**
use **employer, utiliser**
utilize **utiliser**

V

validate **composter**
vanish **s'évanouir**
vanquish **vaincre**
vex **agacer**
visit **visiter**
vomit **rendre**
vow **jurer**

W

wager **parier**
wait (for) **attendre**

wake up **se réveiller**
walk **marcher**
walk, take a **se promener**
wander **voguer**
want **vouloir**
ward off **prévenir**
warn **prévenir**
wash **laver**
wash oneself **se laver**
watch **regarder**
water **arroser,** (animal) **abreuver**
wear **porter**
weary **ennuyer**
wed **épouser**
weep **pleurer**
weigh **balancer, peser**
welcome **accueillir**
whisper **chuchoter**
whistle **siffler**
whiten **blanchir**
win **gagner**
wipe **essuyer**
wish **souhaiter**
withdraw **s'éloigner, se retirer**
withhold **refuser**
wonder **se demander**
work **travailler**
worry **s'inquiéter**
worship **adorer**
worth, be **valoir**
wound **blesser**
wound oneself **se blesser**
write **écrire**

Y

yield **céder**

The number after each verb is the page number in this book where a model verb is shown fully conjugated. At times there are two page references; for example, **abréger** is conjugated like **céder** on p. 85 because **é** changes to **è**, and like **manger** on p. 283 because **abréger** and **manger** are both **-ger** type verbs.

If the French verb you want is reflexive (*e.g.*, **s'appeler** or **se lever**), you will find it listed alphabetically under the first letter of the verb. The reflexive pronoun **s'** or **se** is given in parentheses after the verb, *e.g.*, **appeler (s'), lever (se).**

A

abandonner to abandon   167
abhorrer to abhor, loathe   29
abîmer to damage, spoil   29
abjurer to abjure, renounce   145
abominer to abominate, loathe   466
abonder en to abound in   28
abonner (s') à to subscribe to   81, 167
abonner à to subscribe for someone to   167
aborder to accost, approach   28
abouter to join tip to tip   169
aboutir à/dans to succeed, end up in   225
aboyer to bark   183
abréger to shorten, abridge   85, 283
abreuver to water (animals)   28
abriter de/contre to shelter from   250
abrutir to exhaust   225
absenter (s') de to absent oneself from   28
absorber to absorb   384
abuser de qqch to abuse, misuse   34
accabler to overwhelm   406
accéder à to get to, attain   85
accélérer to accelerate   355
accentuer to accentuate, stress   112
accommoder to accommodate   144
accomplir to accomplish   391

accoster to accost   156
accoucher de to give birth to   119
accoupler to couple   29
accoutumer to get used to   235
accréditer to accredit   250
accrocher (s') to hang on, collide   13
accroupir (s') to squat   209
acculer to corner somebody   79
accumuler to accumulate   79
accuser (s') to accuse oneself   16, 35
acharner (s') contre qqn to dog someone   35
acheminer to direct towards   466
acquitter de to release from   373
actionner to activate   167
activer to speed up, pep up   28
actualiser to bring up to date   16
adapter à to fit, adapt to   8
additionner to add up   167
adhérer à to adhere to   85
adjoindre à to associate with   267
adjuger to award   283
adjurer to implore, beg   271
administrer to administer   28
adopter to adopt   8
adoucir to soften, sweeten   225
aduler to adulate, flatter   29

aérer to air, aerate   85
affaiblir to weaken   225
affamer to starve   223
affecter de to pretend to   8
affectionner to have a liking for   167
affermer to lease, rent   223
affermir to strengthen   225
afficher to display   91
affirmer to affirm   223
affliger de to afflict with   117
affluer to abound   112
affranchir to set free; to stamp (frank)   71
affronter to confront   111
agenouiller (s') to kneel   229
aggraver to aggravate, make worse   275
agiter to wag, wave, shake   250
agrandir to enlarge   243
agréer to accept   127
agrémenter de to embellish with   59
agresser to attack   23
ahurir to astound, stun   225
aigrir to sour   225
ajourner to postpone   431
ajuster to adjust   30
alarmer to alarm   309
alerter de to warn about   169
aligner to align   28
alimenter de to feed with   59
allonger to stretch out   442
allouer to allocate, grant   280

allumer to light, turn on 235

alourdir de to weigh down 225

altérer to alter, spoil 85

amaigrir to make thin 282

amasser to amass, pile up 90

ambitionner de to aspire to 167

améliorer to improve 22

américaniser to Americanize 34

amoindrir to lessen 225

amorcer to boot (comp.), start 341

amplifier de to amplify with/by 320

amputer to amputate 250

analyser to analyze 34

anéantir to annihilate 225

angoisser to cause anguish, distress 23

animer to animate 29

applaudir de to applaud for 225

appliquer to apply 214

apprécier to appreciate 388

apprêter (s') à qqch to get oneself ready for 49, 362

apprêter to get ready, prepare 362

approcher (s') to approach, come near 35, 44

approfondir to deepen 225

approprier (s') to appropriate 81, 207

appuyer to lean, press 188

armer to arm 235

arranger (s') to come to an agreement 35, 47

articuler to articulate 79

aspirer to inhale 21

assassiner to murder, assassinate 155

assembler to assemble 406

assigner to assign 441

associer qqch à to link something with 207

attacher to tie up 80

attaquer to attack 214

attarder to delay 237

attendre (s') à to expect 56, 203

atterrir to land 225

attester to testify 156

attribuer à to attribute to 112

autoriser to authorize 16

avaler to swallow 29

avancer (s') to advance (oneself) 35, 60

aventurer to venture 145

avertir de to warn about 225

aviser to notify 34; **aviser (s')** to notice, become aware 34

avouer to admit 268

B

babiller sur to gossip about 29

bachoter to cram for an exam 94

bâcler to botch up 445

badiner to exchange banter, jest 163

bafouer qqn to flout, scorn 268

bafouiller to stammer 229

bâfrer to guzzle 80

bagarrer to wrangle, argue 435

baigner to bathe 10

bâiller to yawn 479

baiser to kiss, have intercourse 29

balader to take for a walk 28

balader (se) to stroll 28

balbutier to stammer 207

bannir de to banish from 225

baptiser to baptize 34

barbouiller de to daub with 479

barrer to bar 21

batailler to battle 479

bâtonner to beat with a stick 167

baver to drool, dribble 275

bégayer to stammer 175

bénéficier de to profit from/by 388

bercer to rock 97

beurrer to butter 28

bivouaquer to bivouac 214

blaguer to joke 284

blaser (se) de to become indifferent to 35

blasphémer to blaspheme 355

blêmir to become pale 225

bleuir to turn blue 225

bloquer to block up 214

bluffer to bluff 28

boiter to limp 28

bombarder to bombard 384

bondir to leap 225

border to border 247

boucher to block up 472

boucler to buckle 472

bouder to sulk 237

bouffer to gobble up 231

bougonner to grumble 167

bouillonner to bubble 167

bouler to roll 28

bouleverser to overwhelm 493

bourdonner to buzz 167

bourrer to stuff 22

boursoufler to bloat, puff up 445

bousculer to shove, bump 79

boutonner to button 167

boxer to box 28

boycotter to boycott 373

brancher sur to connect to, plug into 91

branler to shake 499

briller to shine 479

briser to break, smash 34

bronzer to bronze, tan 133

broyer to crush, grind 183

bruiner to drizzle 469

brunir to brown 225

brusquer to rush, hasten 214

buriner to engrave 466

C

cacheter to seal   266
cajoler to cajole, coax   29
calculer to calculate   79
calmer to calm   29
calmer (se) to calm down   29
calomnier to slander, libel   207
cambrioler to break into, burglarize   28
camoufler to camouflage   445
camper to camp   231
canaliser to channel, funnel   28
canoniser to canonize   493
canoter to go boating, rowing   28
cantonner to station, billet   167
capitaliser to capitalize   493
capituler to capitulate, surrender   28
captiver to captivate   163
capturer to capture   29
caractériser to characterize   493
caresser to caress   352
caricaturer to caricature   21
castrer to castrate   29
cataloguer to catalog   284
cautionner to guarantee   167
ceindre de to encircle with   333
célébrer to celebrate   355
celer to conceal   17
censurer to censure   53
centraliser to centralize   493
cercler de to encircle with   29
certifier to certify   207
chagriner to grieve, distress   328
chahuter to create an uproar   8
chaîner to chain   163
chanceler to stagger   40
chantonner to sing to oneself   167
chaperonner to chaperon   167

charmer to charm   235
châtier to punish   207
chatouiller to tickle   229
chauffer to warm up, heat up   231
chausser to put on shoes   77
cheminer to walk along   466
chicaner to haggle, quibble   144
chiffonner to crumple   167
chiper to pinch, steal   29
chloroformer to chloroform   223
chômer to be unemployed   29
choquer to shock   470
chronométrer to time   85
chuter to fall, flop   30
circuler to circulate   79
citer to quote   250
civiliser to civilize   493
clapper (de la langue) to click one's tongue   231
claquer to bang   470
clarifier to clarify   207
classer to classify   90
classifier to classify   207
cligner to blink   10
clignoter to blink, flash, twinkle   29
climatiser to air-condition   493
cliquer to click   214
cloner to clone   462
clouer to nail, tack down   268
cocher to check off   119
coder to code   28
codifier to codify   28
coexister to coexist   258
cogner to hit   10
coiffer qqn to do someone's hair   443
collaborer to collaborate   22
collectionner to collect   167
coller à to stick to   445
colleter to grab by the collar   266
coloniser to colonize, settle   493
colorer to color   22

colorier to color (in)   207
colporter to peddle   348
combiner to combine   328
combler de to fill up with   406
commémorer to commemorate   22
commercer avec to trade with   97
commercialiser to commercialize   493
communier to receive communion   388
communiquer to communicate   214
comparaître to appear before court   322
compiler to compile   250
complaire à to try to please   344
compléter to complete   85
complimenter to compliment   59
compliquer to complicate   214
comploter to plot   348
comporter (se) to behave   78, 348
comporter to comprise   348
composer to compose   349
compromettre to compromise   294
compulser to consult   34
concasser to crush   82
concéder to concede   85
concentrer (se) sur to concentrate (oneself) on   78, 298
concentrer sur to concentrate on   298
concilier to reconcile   207
concorder avec to agree with   11
concourir avec to compete with   123
condamner to condemn   96
conditionner to condition   167
confesser to confess   72
confier to entrust   207
configurer to configure   29

confirmer to confirm 223

confisquer to confiscate 214

confondre to confound 227

confronter to confront 111

congédier to dismiss 207

congeler to deep freeze 239

conjoindre to join in marriage 267

conjuguer to conjugate 214

considérer to consider 85

consoler to console 29

conspirer to conspire 21

constater to make a statement of fact 238

constituer to constitute 485

consulter to consult 374

contenter to content 465

contester to dispute 156

contrefaire to counterfeit 218

contribuer to contribute 112

contrôler to control 79

converser to converse 493

convertir to convert 225

convoquer to summon 214

coopérer to cooperate 355

copier to copy 207

correspondre to correspond 400

cotiser to contribute 34

couler to flow 79

courber to bend 483

cracher to spit 80

craquer to crack 214

créditer de to credit with 250

creuser to dig 34

crever de to burst with 277

critiquer to criticize 214

crocheter to pick, to crochet 17

croiser to cross 84

croquer to crunch 214

crouler to collapse, crumble 79

crucifier to crucify 207

cuisiner to cook 328

culbuter to somersault, tumble 30

cultiver to cultivate 328

D

dactylographier to type 365

daigner to deign, condescend 10

damner to damn 236

dater de to date from 238

débarquer de to disembark from 214

débarrasser to clear off 179

débiter to debit, to sell retail 250

déboguer to debug (comp.) 397

déborder to overflow 28

déboutonner to unbutton 167

débrouiller to disentangle 229

décapiter to decapitate 250

décerner to award 473

déchanter to become disillusioned 88

décharger to unload 89

déchausser (se) to take off one's shoes 78

déclamer to declaim 70

déclarer to declare 68

décliner to decline 466

décoiffer qqn to mess up someone's hair 443

décolérer to be in a temper 355

décoller to unstick, to take off (airplane) 384

décolorer to decolorize, to bleach 22

décommander to cancel an order 96

déconseiller to advise against 107

décorer de to decorate with 22

découcher to spend the night away from one's house 119

découdre to unstitch 121

découper to cut up 122

décourager de to discourage from 304

décrier to decry 128

décrocher to unhook 80

dédaigner to disdain 10

dédicacer à to dedicate to (a book) 341

dédier à to dedicate to 207

défaillir to weaken, to faint 217

défier to challenge 207

définir to define 225

défoncer to push the bottom out 369

déformer to deform 223

dégager de to release from 304

dégeler to thaw 239

dégoûter to disgust 242

dégoutter to drip 242

dégriser to sober up 493

déguster to taste, sample food 52

déjouer to foil, thwart 268

délacer to unlace 341

délaisser to abandon, quit 273

délibérer to deliberate 355

délier to untie 388

délivrer to set free 21

déloger to dislodge, move out 304

demander (se) to wonder 120, 144

démanger to feel an itch 283

démarrer to boot (comp.), start 29

déménager to move belongings from one residence to another 304

démentir to deny, refute 291

démériter de to show oneself unworthy of 293

démettre to dislocate 294

démissionner de to resign from 167

démonter qqch (with avoir) to dismantle something 297

démontrer to demonstrate 298

dénigrer to denigrate 21

dénoncer to denounce 369

dénoter to denote 499

dénouer to untie   268

dépasser to go past, beyond   326

dépêcher to dispatch   147

déplacer to move, shift, displace   341

déplier to unfold   388

déplorer to deplore   22

déporter to deport   348

déposer to put down, set down, deposit   349

déprimer to depress   215

déraciner to uproot   155

dérouler to unwind, roll out, unroll   420

dérouter to divert, reroute   169

désapprouver to disapprove of   45

désarmer to disarm   235

déserter to desert, abandon   42

désespérer to despair   198

déshabiller (se) to undress oneself   249

déshonorer to dishonor   22

désister (se) de to withdraw (**en faveur de qqn**) (in someone's favor)   52

désobéir à to disobey   312

dessécher to dry out   85

desservir to clear away (**la table**/the table); to provide a service   437

déteindre to take out the color   202

détendre to loosen, slacken   463

détenir to detain   464

détourner (se) to turn oneself away from   120, 157

détromper (se) to see the truth about a matter   482

détromper de to disabuse   315

devancer to arrive ahead of, precede, anticipate   60

dévaster to devastate   258

dévêtir (se) to undress oneself   249, 494

dévêtir to undress   494

dévider to unwind, reel off   250

deviner to guess   328

diagnostiquer to diagnose   214

dialoguer to converse; **avec un ordinateur** to interact with a computer   214

dicter to dictate   252

diffamer to defame, slander   70

différer to differ, defer   198

digérer to digest   198

diriger to direct   117

discontinuer to discontinue   112

discourir sur to expatiate on, discourse   123

discriminer to distinguish   466

disjoindre to separate   267

disperser to disperse   480

disposer to arrange   349

disputer de qqch to dispute something   424

disqualifier to disqualify   207

disséminer to disseminate, scatter   466

dissuader de to dissuade from   339

distinguer to distinguish   284

distribuer to distribute   112

diviser en to divide into   34

documenter to document   59

dorer to gild   22

doubler to double, to pass   483

douter (se) to suspect   120, 169

dresser to draw up   23

duper to dupe   315

durer to last   271

E

ébaucher to sketch   472

éblouir to dazzle   225

écarter to separate, spread apart   68

échanger to exchange   87

écharper to tear to pieces   58

échauffer to overheat   167

éclaircir to clear up   225

éclairer to light   21

éclater en to burst into   172

écraser to crush   179

éditer to publish   250

effacer to efface, erase   341

effectuer to effect, bring about   112

égaler to equal   324

élargir to widen   225

élider to elide   250

éliminer to eliminate   466

éloigner de to move, keep away from   189

élucider to elucidate   28

embarquer to embark   214

embarrasser to embarrass   82

émettre to emit   294

émigrer to emigrate   21

emporter to carry away   348

empresser (s') to make haste   360

enchanter to enchant   88

encourir to incur   123

endommager to damage   304

endormir (s') to fall asleep   168

enfermer to shut away, lock up   223

enfler (s') to swell   445

enfoncer to plunge in   369

engager (s') to commit oneself to do   304, 316

engager to engage, start up, to hire   304

enjamber to stride, step over   237

enjoindre à qqn de faire to charge someone to do   267

enlacer to entwine   341

ennuyer (s') to be bored   54, 188

énoncer to state, express   369

enregistrer to record, register   392

enrichir to enrich   225
entamer to begin, start   70
entourer de to surround with   21
entraîner to carry away   29
entrecouper de to intersperse, interrupt with   122
entrelacer to intertwine, interlace   341
entretenir to maintain, support   464
entrevoir to catch a glimpse   498
entrouvrir to half open   321
énumérer to enumerate   355
envahir to invade   225
envelopper to envelope, wrap up   231
envier to envy   207
envisager to envisage   304
épargner to save, economize   10
épeler to spell   40
épicer to spice up   341
épier to spy on   207
éponger to sponge   283
épuiser to exhaust   34
équiper de to equip with   58
ériger to erect   117
errer to wander   21
escompter to discount   101
espionner to spy on   167
esquisser to sketch   179
étaler to spread out, display   324
étendre to roll out, spread out   463
éternuer to sneeze   112
étirer to stretch; **s'étirer** to stretch oneself   467
étrangler to strangle   324
étreindre to embrace, hug   333
évacuer to evacuate   112
évader (s') de to escape from   28
éveiller (with **avoir**) to awaken   413
évoquer to evoke   214
exagérer to exaggerate   355
examiner to examine   466

exciter to excite   250
exclure to exclude   103
exécuter to execute, carry out   165
exister to exist   348
exploiter to exploit   250
exporter to export   348
exposer to expose   349
exterminer to exterminate   466

F

fabriquer to manufacture   214
fabuler to fantasize   79
fâcher qqn (with **avoir**) to annoy, offend, anger someone   80, 216
faciliter to facilitate   220
façonner to shape, fashion   167
facturer to bill   21
faiblir to weaken   391
falsifier to falsify   207
farcir de to stuff with   225
farder (se) to apply makeup on one's own face   81, 237
farder to apply makeup, paint on a face   237
fasciner to fascinate   466
fatiguer (se) to get tired, tire oneself   120
fatiguer to tire, weary   387
favoriser to favor   34
filer to spin, dash off, run off   29
filmer to film   223
filtrer to filter   298
fixer to fix   8
flâner to stroll   443
flanquer to fling   387
flatter to flatter   82
fléchir to bend, flex   382
flirter to flirt   424
flotter to float   77
foncer to dash along, run along   369
formater to format (comp.)   172
former to form   223
fouetter to whip   447

fouler to press, trample on   420
franchir to clear, cross   382
fredonner to hum   167
fréquenter to frequent   59
friser to curl   493
frissonner to shiver   167
froncer to wrinkle   36
frotter to rub   77
fuser to burst forth   34
fusiller to shoot   479

G

gâcher to spoil   80
gambader to gambol, leap about   28
garantir to guarantee   225
garer to park   435
gargariser (se) to gargle   34
garnir de to garnish, provide with   225
gaspiller to waste   479
gazouiller to chirp, warble   229
gémir to groan   225
glisser to glide, slide   72
gonfler to inflate   445
grelotter to shiver   77
griffonner to scribble   167
grimacer to grimace (one's face)   341
grincer to creak, grind   97
griser to intoxicate, make tipsy   493
grogner to growl, grumble   10
grossir to get bigger, put on weight   282
grouper to group   122
guider to guide   28

H

NOTE: The mark * in front of the letter *h* denotes that it is aspirate; make no liaison and use *je* instead of *j'*; *me*, not *m'*.

habiliter to authorize   250
habiller qqn, qqch (with **avoir**) to dress someone, something   249

habituer (s') to accustom oneself, get used to   35

habituer to accustom   485

*****haleter** to pant   17

*****hanter** to haunt   88

*****harasser** to exhaust   179

*****harceler** to harass   17

*****hasarder** to hazard, risk   237

*****hâter (se)** to hurry oneself   73, 238

*****hâter** to hasten   238

*****hausser** to raise   90

hériter to inherit   293

*****hisser** to hoist   82

*****hululer, ululer** to hoot, screech   79

*****hurler** to howl   324

hypothéquer to mortgage   85

I

identifier to identify   207

idolâtrer to idolize   298

ignorer to be unaware of, not to know   22

illuminer to illuminate   466

illustrer to illustrate   298

imaginer to imagine   328

imbiber to soak   68

imiter to imitate   250

immatriculer to register   79

immerger to immerse   89

immigrer to immigrate   91

immoler to immolate   79

immuniser to immunize   34

impliquer to imply, implicate   214

implorer to implore   22

importer to import; to matter   348

impressionner to impress   167

imprimer to print   215

improviser to improvise   34

incarcérer to imprison   85

incinérer to incinerate   355

inciter to incite   250

incliner (s') devant to bow before   35

incliner to incline   163

incorporer à to incorporate in   22

induire à to induce to   104

infecter de to infect with   111

inférer de to infer from   355

infester de to infest with   258

infiltrer (s') dans to infiltrate, filter into   298

infliger à to inflict on   213

influencer to influence   97

informer to inform   223, 256

initier à to initiate into   388

injecter to inject   8

injurier to abuse   388

inquiéter qqn (with **avoir**) to worry, disturb someone   257

inscrire to inscribe   173

insérer to insert   85

insinuer to insinuate   112

inspecter to inspect   111

inspirer to inspire, to inhale   250

installer to install   29

instituer to institute   112

insulter to insult   172

intercéder to intercede   85

intéresser qqn à qqch (with **avoir**) to interest someone in something   261

interpoler to interpolate   324

interposer entre to interpose between   349

interpréter to interpret   85

intervenir to intervene   492

interviewer to interview   29

intimider par to intimidate by   265

invalider to invalidate   265

inventer to invent   88

invoquer to invoke   214

irradier to irradiate, radiate   388

irriter to irritate   265

isoler de to isolate from   324

J

jacasser to chatter, jabber   82

jaillir to gush forth, spurt out   422

japper to yap, yelp   231

jardiner to garden   163

jargonner to jabber   167

jaser to chatter, prattle   82

jauger to gauge, size up   75

jaunir to yellow, turn yellow   225

javelliser to chlorinate   250

jeûner to fast, go without food   143

joncher qqch de to strew something with   91

jongler to juggle   324

jucher sur to perch on   472

justifier to justify   388

K

kidnapper to kidnap   231

klaxonner to hoot, toot, sound a horn   167

L

labourer to plow   483

lacer to lace   341

lacérer to lacerate   355

lamenter (se) sur qqch to lament, moan over something   59

languir to languish   225

lécher to lick   85

légiférer to legislate   85

libérer de to free from   85

lier to tie   128

limiter to limit   250

lisser to smooth down   72

livrer à to deliver to   29

loger dans to live in, **loger chez** to live with, at   262

lustrer to shine, make shiny   298

lutter to struggle   424

M

mâcher to chew   285

mâchurer to stain black, blacken, blur   346

maintenir to maintain   464

malmener to handle roughly   290

maltraiter to abuse, misuse, handle roughly   477

mander to command, summon   144

manier to handle   207

manifester to show, demonstrate   298

manipuler to manipulate   30

manoeuvrer to operate a machine, manipulate a person   28

manufacturer to manufacture   21

maquiller (se) to put makeup on one's face   120

marchander to haggle, bargain over   144

marier (se) à/avec qqn to get married to someone   120

marier to marry (someone to someone)   388

marquer de to mark with   214

masquer à to mask, conceal from   214

massacrer to massacre   298

mastiquer to chew   214

matelasser to pad   273

méditer to meditate   250

mélanger to mix   283

mêler (se) à to join in, meddle with, get mixed up in   81

mêler à/avec to mix with   80

menacer de to threaten with   341

ménager to be sparing in the use of   304

mentionner to mention   167

mépriser to despise, scorn   34

mesurer to measure   53

meubler de to furnish with   29

mimer to mime   29

moderniser to modernize   34

modifier to modify   388

moduler to modulate   79

molester to molest   156

mollir to soften   225

mortifier to mortify   388

motiver to motivate   28

moucher (se) to blow one's nose   120

mouiller (se) to get oneself wet   81, 229

mouiller to wet   229

munir de to supply with   225

murmurer to murmur   53

mutiler to mutilate   29

N

napper de to coat, top with   58

narrer to narrate   22

naviguer to navigate, sail, to surf (Internet)   214

négocier to negotiate   388

neutraliser to neutralize   34

noircir to blacken   225

noter to note   172

notifier to notify   320

nouer to tie   268

noyer (se) to drown   120, 183

O

objecter to make an objection   156

oblitérer to obliterate   355

observer to observe   483

obstiner (s') à to persist in   316

offenser to offend   335

ombrager to shade   185

opérer to operate   355

opposer to oppose   349

oppresser to weigh down, suffocate   359

opprimer to oppress   29

opter pour to opt for   111

ordonner to arrange, organize, order, to prescribe (medical)   167

organiser to organize   34

orienter vers to direct towards   111

orner de to decorate with   473

ôter to take off, remove   499

outrager to outrage   304

P

pacifier to pacify   388

pâlir to turn pale   422

palpiter to palpitate   250

paniquer to panic   214

panser to bandage   133

parachuter to parachute   424

parcourir to travel through   123

parer to adorn   435

parfumer to perfume   235

parier sur to bet on   128

parodier to parody   207

partager to share   501

participer à to participate in   250

parvenir à to get to, reach   492

patienter to be patient, wait   28

patronner to sponsor, patronize   167

peler to peel   239

pencher (se) to lean over   120

pencher to tilt, tip up   91

pénétrer to penetrate   355

percer to pierce   274

percevoir to perceive   378

percher to perch   91

percuter to strike, smash into   165

perfectionner to perfect   167

perforer to perforate   22

perpétrer to perpetrate   355

persister to persist   258

personnifier to personify   388

photocopier to photocopy   207

photographier to photograph   207

piger to catch on, understand   304

piloter to pilot   30

pincer to pinch   97

piquer to prick, sting, to steal   214

pirater to pirate, hack (comp.)   30

plagier to plagiarize 388
plaider to plead 28
planer sur to hover over 70
planter to plant 88
plier en to fold into 128
plisser to pleat, crease 72
plonger to plunge, dive 442
polir to polish 422
polluer de to pollute with 112
pomper to pump 58
ponctuer to punctuate 485
porter (se) to feel well/unwell 120, 348
pourchasser to pursue 90
pratiquer to practice 214
précéder to precede 85
prêcher to preach 331
préciser to specify 34
prédisposer to predispose 349
prédominer sur to prevail over 466
préméditer to premeditate 250
prénommer to give a first name 309
préoccuper to preoccupy 315
préposer à to appoint to 349
prescrire to prescribe 173
préserver de to preserve from 425
présumer to presume 235
présupposer to presuppose 349
prévaloir sur to prevail over 489
procéder de to arise, proceed from 85
proclamer to proclaim 70
procurer qqch à qqn to get something for someone 53
professer to profess 72
profiter de to profit from 250
programmer to program 70
progresser to progress 72
projeter to project 266

prolonger de to prolong by 442
promener to take for a walk 290
proposer to propose 349
proscrire to proscribe, ban, outlaw 173
prospérer to prosper 198
prostituer (se) to prostitute oneself 120, 485
protéger to protect 85, 283
protester to protest 156
provenir de to result from 492
provoquer to provoke 214
psychanalyser to psychoanalyze 34
publier to publish 207

Q

quereller (se) to quarrel with each other 120, 479
quereller to scold 479
questionner to question 167
quêter to collect (money); to seek after 48

R

rabaisser to reduce, decrease 62
rabattre to pull down 66
raccommoder to mend 144
raccorder à to connect to, link up 11
raccourcir to shorten 93
raccrocher to hang up 472
racheter to buy back 17
rafraîchir to cool, refresh 382
rager to rage 304
raisonner to reason 443
rajouter to add more 30
ralentir to slow down 93
rallonger to lengthen 442
rallumer to light again 235
ramasser to pick up 90
ramener to bring back 33
ramer to row 29
ranimer to revive 29
râper to grate 58
rapporter to bring back 42

rapprendre, réapprendre to learn again, relearn 43
rapprocher de to bring closer to 44
raser (se) to shave oneself 84, 120
raser to shave 84
rassembler to assemble 406
rassurer to reassure 53
rater to miss, fail 30
rationner to ration 167
rattacher to attach again 80
rattraper to catch up 58
ravir to delight 421
rayer to cross out 329
réagir to react 26
réaliser to carry out, realize 34
réapparaître to reappear 322
recharger to reload, refill 89
rechercher to search, hunt for 91
réciter to recite 250
réclamer to ask for, reclaim 70
recommander to recommend; to register (a letter) 96
recommencer to begin again 97
réconcilier to reconcile 207
reconstruire to reconstruct 109
recoucher (se) to go back to bed 120
recoudre to sew up again 121
recouper to cut again 122
rectifier to rectify, correct 388
reculer to step back 53
rédiger to edit 304
redire to say again, repeat 164
redonner to give again, give back 167
redouter de to dread, fear 169
référer (se) à to refer to, consult 120, 355

refléter to reflect   85
refroidir to cool   225
réfuter to refute   424
regagner to regain, win back, get back   236
regeler to freeze again   239
régler to regulate, settle   85
réitérer to reiterate   355
rejeter to reject, vomit, spew   266
rejoindre to rejoin   267
réjouir to delight, gladden   269
relever to raise again   277
remonter to go up again   297
remuer to move, stir   112
renfermer to enclose, shut again, contain   223
renoncer to renounce, give up   369
renseigner to inform   189
renverser to knock over, turn upside down   493
renvoyer to send back   195
répercuter sur to pass on to   165
replacer to replace, put back   341
replier to fold again   128
répliquer to retort, reply   214
reporter to carry forward, postpone   348
reposer to put back   349
repousser to push away   352
représenter to represent   59
réprimer to repress   215
reprocher qqch à qqn to blame, reproach someone for something   44
résister to resist   258
respirer to breathe   467
ressentir to feel, experience   433
restituer to return, restore   485
résumer to summarize   235
rétablir to reestablish   201
retomber to fall again   468

retrouver to find (again)   483
réunir à to reunite with   486
réveiller to wake up (someone asleep)   413, 479
révéler to reveal   355
revendiquer to claim   255
revendre to resell   490
réviser to revise   34
revivre to live again, come alive again   497
révolutionner to revolutionize   167
ridiculiser to ridicule   34
rincer to rinse   97
risquer to risk   214
ronfler to snore   445
rouvrir to reopen   321
ruiner to ruin   328

S

sacrifier to sacrifice   207
saliver to salivate   425
saluer to greet, salute   112
sangloter to sob   319
scanner to scan (image)   167
sécher to dry   85
sélectionner to select   167
semer to sow   277
sermonner to lecture   167
signifier to mean, signify   207
simplifier to simplify   207
simuler to simulate   79
skier to ski   128
soigner qqn to take care of, look after someone   10
sommeiller to doze   479
soulager de to relieve of   304
soulever to raise   277
souligner to underline   10
soupçonner de to suspect of   167
souper to have supper   122
soupirer to sigh   21
souscrire à to subscribe to   173
soutenir to support   464
spécifier to specify   207
stationner to park   167

stériliser to sterilize   34
stimuler to stimulate   79
stipuler to stipulate   79
subir to undergo   93
subsister de to live on   52
substituer à to substitute for   485
subvenir à to provide for   492
succéder à to succeed   85
sucrer to sweeten   21
suer to sweat   485
suffoquer de to suffocate, choke with   214
suggérer to suggest   355
supposer to suppose   349
supprimer to suppress   215
surgir to loom up, spring up   225
sursauter to jump, give a start   424
suspecter de to suspect of   111
suspendre to suspend   334
sympathiser avec to get on well with   34
synchroniser to synchronize   34

T

tacher de to stain with   80
tâcher to try   80
tailler to cut, sharpen, trim   479
tamponner to dab, mop up, plug   167
tanner qqn to badger, pester someone   167
tapper to tap, type, strike, slap   231
taquiner to tease   163
tarder to delay   237
tâter to feel by touching   238
tâtonner to grope   167
tatouer to tattoo   171
télécharger to download   89
télécopier to fax   207
télégraphier to telegraph   207
téléviser to televise   34
témoigner to testify   10

terrifier to terrify   207
tester to test   156
tisser to weave   72
tolérer to tolerate   355
torturer to torture   53
totaliser to total   34
tournoyer to whirl   307
tracasser to bother, worry   82
tracer to trace   341
traîner to drag   163
trancher to slice   472
transcrire to transcribe   173
transférer to transfer   355
transformer en to transform into   223
trembler de to tremble with   406
tresser to plait, braid   72
tromper to deceive   122
troquer to swap, trade   214
trouer to make a hole in   268
truquer to fake, rig   214
tutoyer to use the **tu** form with someone   183
tyranniser to tyrannize   34
ulcérer to ulcerate   85

U

ululer, hululer to hoot, screech   79
unifier to unify   207
uniformiser to make uniform, standardize   34
urbaniser to urbanize   34
uriner to urinate   466
user to wear out, use up   34

V

vacciner contre to vaccinate against   328
vaciller to sway, stagger   479
vagabonder to wander   247
vaguer to roam, wander   284
valider to validate   250
valser to waltz   493
vanter to vaunt, praise   88
vaporiser to spray   34
varier to vary   128
végéter to vegetate   355
veiller to stay up, keep watch   479
vénérer to venerate   355
ventiler to ventilate   265
verbaliser to verbalize   34

vérifier to verify   207
vernir to varnish   225
vexer to annoy, offend, upset   29
vider to empty   250
violer to rape, violate   499
virer to turn direction of a vehicle   21
viser à to aim at   34
visser to screw on   34
voguer to sail   284
vomir to vomit   225
voter pour/contre to vote for/against   30
vouer à to dedicate to, to vow   268
vouvoyer to use the **vous** form with someone   183
vriller to spin, whirl   479
vulgariser to vulgarize, popularize   34

Z

zébrer de to streak, stripe with   85
zézayer to lisp   329
zigzaguer to zigzag   284
zipper to zip up   231

Index of common irregular French verb forms identified by infinitive

The purpose of this index is to help you identify those verb forms that cannot be readily identified because they are irregular in some way. For example, if you come across the verb form *fut* (which is very common) in your French readings, this index will tell you that *fut* is a form of **être**. Then you look up **être** in this book and you will find that verb form on the page where all the forms of **être** are given.

Verb forms whose first few letters are the same as the infinitive have not been included because they can easily be identified by referring to the alphabetical listing of the 501 verbs in this book.

After you find the verb of an irregular verb form, if it is not among the 501 verbs, consult the list of over 1,100 French verbs conjugated like model verbs, which begins on page 515.

A

a **avoir**
ai **avoir**
aie **avoir**
aient **avoir**
aies **avoir**
aille **aller**
ait **avoir**
as **avoir**
asseyais, *etc.* **asseoir**
assieds **asseoir**
assiérai, *etc.* **asseoir**
assis **asseoir**
assoie **asseoir**
assoirai, *etc.* **asseoir**
assoyais, *etc.* **asseoir**
aurai, *etc.* **avoir**
avaient **avoir**
avais **avoir**
avait **avoir**
avez **avoir**
aviez **avoir**
avions **avoir**
avons **avoir**
ayant **avoir**
ayons, *etc.* **avoir**

B

bats **battre**
bois **boire**

boivent **boire**
bu **boire**
bûmes **boire**
burent **boire**
bus, bût **boire**
busse, *etc.* **boire**
but **boire**
bûtes **boire**
buvant **boire**
buvez **boire**
buvons **boire**

C

connu **connaître**
craignis, *etc.* **craindre**
crois **croire**
croîs **croître**
croissais, *etc.* **croître**
croit **croire**
croît **croître**
croyais, *etc.* **croire**
cru **croire**
crû, crue **croître**
crûmes **croire, croître**
crurent **croire**
crûrent **croître**
crus **croire**
crûs **croître**
crûsse, *etc.* **croître**
crût **croire, croître**

D

devais, *etc.* **devoir**
dîmes **dire**
dis, disais, *etc.* **dire**
disse, *etc.* **dire**
dit, dît **dire**
dois, *etc.* **devoir**
doive, *etc.* **devoir**
dors, *etc.* **dormir**
dû, due **devoir**
dûmes **devoir**
dus, dussent **devoir**
dut, dût, dûtes **devoir**

E

es **être**
est **être**
étais, *etc.* **être**
été **être**
êtes **être**
étiez **être**
eu **avoir**
eûmes **avoir**
eurent **avoir**
eus **avoir**
eusse, *etc.* **avoir**
eut, eût **avoir**
eûtes **avoir**

F

faille **faillir, falloir**
fais, *etc.* **faire**
fallut, *etc.* **falloir**
fasse, *etc.* **faire**
faudra **faillir, falloir**
faudrait **faillir, falloir**
faut **faillir, falloir**
faux **faillir**
ferai, *etc.* **faire**
fîmes **faire**
firent **faire**
fis, *etc.* **faire**
font **faire**
fûmes **être**
furent **être**
fus, *etc.* **être**

fut, fût **être**
fuyais, *etc.* **fuir**

G

gis, gisons, *etc.* **gésir**
gît **gésir**

I

ira, irai, iras, *etc.* **aller**

L

lis, *etc.* **lire**
lu **lire**
lus, *etc.* **lire**

M

mens **mentir**
mets **mettre**
meure, *etc.* **mourir**
meus, *etc.* **mouvoir**
mîmes **mettre**
mirent **mettre, mirer**
mis **mettre**
misses, *etc.* **mettre**
mit **mettre**
mort **mourir**
moulons, *etc.* **moudre**
moulu **moudre**
mû, mue **mouvoir**
mussent **mouvoir**
mut **mouvoir**

N

nais, *etc.* **naître**
naquîmes, *etc.* **naître**
né **naître**
nuis, nuit, *etc.* **nuire**

O

offert **offrir**
omis **omettre**
ont **avoir**

P

paie (paye) **payer**
pars **partir**
paru, *etc.* **paraître**
peignis, *etc.* **peindre**
peins, *etc.* **peindre**
pendant **pendre**
peuvent **pouvoir**
peut, *etc.* **pouvoir**
plaigne, *etc.* **plaindre**
plu **plaire, pleuvoir**
plurent **plaire**
plut, plût, *etc.* **plaire, pleuvoir**
plûtes **plaire**
pourrai, *etc.* **pouvoir**
prenne, *etc.* **prendre**
prîmes **prendre**
prirent **prendre**
pris **prendre**
prisse, *etc.* **prendre**
pu **pouvoir**
puis **pouvoir**
puisse, *etc.* **pouvoir**
pûmes, *etc.* **pouvoir**
purent **pouvoir**
pus **pouvoir**
pusse **pouvoir**
put, pût **pouvoir**

R

reçois, *etc.* **recevoir**
reçûmes, *etc.* **recevoir**
relu **relire**
résolu, *etc.* **résoudre**
reviens, *etc.* **revenir**
revins, *etc.* **revenir**
ri, rie, riant, *etc.* **rire**
riiez **rire**
ris, *etc.* **rire**

S

sache, *etc.* **savoir**
sais, *etc.* **savoir**
saurai, *etc.* **savoir**
séant **seoir**
sens, *etc.* **sentir**

serai, *etc.* **être**
sers, *etc.* **servir**
seyant **seoir**
sied **seoir**
siéent **seoir**
siéra, *etc.* **seoir**
sois, *etc.* **être**
sommes **être**
sont **être**
sors, *etc.* **sortir**
soyez **être**
soyons **être**
su **savoir**
suis **être, suivre**
suit **suivre**
sûmes **savoir**
surent **savoir**
survécu **survivre**
sus, susse, *etc.* **savoir**
sut, sût **savoir**

T

tais, *etc.* **se taire**
teigne, *etc.* **teindre**
tiendrai, *etc.* **tenir**
tienne, *etc.* **tenir**
tînmes **tenir**
tins, *etc.* **tenir**
trayant **traire**
tu **se taire**
tûmes **se taire**
turent **se taire**
tus **se taire**
tusse, *etc.* **se taire**
tut, tût **se taire**

V

va **aller**
vaille **valoir**
vainque, *etc.* **vaincre**
vais **aller**
vas **aller**
vaudrai, *etc.* **valoir**
vaux, *etc.* **valoir**
vécu, *etc.* **vivre**
vécûmes, *etc.* **vivre**
verrai, *etc.* **voir**

veuille, *etc.* **vouloir**
veulent **vouloir**
veut, *etc.* **vouloir**
viendrai, *etc.* **venir**
vienne, *etc.* **venir**
viens, *etc.* **venir**
vîmes **voir**
vînmes **venir**
vinrent **venir**
vins, *etc.* **venir**
virent **voir**

vis **vivre, voir**
visse, *etc.* **voir**
vit **vivre, voir**
vît **voir**
vîtes **voir**
voie, *etc.* **voir**
vont **aller**
voudrai, *etc.* **vouloir**
voulu, *etc.* **vouloir**
voyais, *etc.* **voir**
vu **voir**

Verbs used in idiomatic expressions

On the pages containing 501 verbs in this book, you can find simple sentences using verbs and idiomatic expressions. They can help build your French vocabulary and knowledge of French idioms.

When you look up the verb forms of a particular verb in this book, consult the following list so that you may learn some common idiomatic expressions. Consulting this list will save you time because you will not have to use a standard French-English word dictionary to find out what the verbal idiom means. Also, if you do this, you will learn two things at the same time: the verb forms for a particular verb and verbal idioms.

Remember that all verbs in the French language are not used in idioms. Those given below are used very frequently in French readings and in conversation. Some of the following entries contain words, usually nouns, that are related to the verb entry. This, too, will help build your vocabulary. A few proverbs containing verbs are also included because they are interesting, colorful, useful, and they help build your knowledge of French words and idiomatic expressions.

accuser, s'accuser   to accuse, to accuse oneself
    accuser réception de qqch   to acknowledge receipt of something
    Qui s'excuse, s'accuse.   A guilty conscience needs no accuser.

acheter   to buy, to purchase
    acheter qqch à qqn   to buy something from someone

achever   to achieve, to finish
    achever de faire qqch   to complete (finish) doing something

adresser   to address
    adresser la parole à   to speak to, to direct your words to

agir   to act, to behave
    agir à la légère   to act thoughtlessly

aider, s'aider   to help, to help oneself
    Aide-toi, le ciel t'aidera.   Heaven helps those who help themselves.

aimer   to like
    aimer (à) faire qqch   to like doing something
    aimer mieux   to prefer

aller   to go
    to feel (health)   **Comment allez-vous?**   How are you?   **Je vais bien.**   I'm fine.   **Je vais mal.**   I'm not well.   **Je vais mieux maintenant.**   I'm feeling better now.
    aller à quelqu'un   to be becoming, to fit, to suit someone
    Cette robe lui va bien.   This dress suits her fine.   **La barbe de Paul ne lui va pas bien.**   Paul's beard does not look good on him.
    aller à la pêche   to go fishing
    aller à la rencontre de quelqu'un   to go to meet someone

aller à pied   to walk, to go on foot

aller au-devant de quelqu'un   to go to meet someone

aller au fond des choses   to get to the bottom of things

aller avec qqch   to match something

aller chercher   to go get

aller de pair avec . . .   to go hand in hand with . . .

aller en voiture   to ride in a car

aller sans dire   to go without saying   **Ça va sans dire.**   That goes without saying.

Allez-y!   Go to it! Go ahead!

allons donc!   nonsense! come, now! come on, now!

Just for the fun of it, try reading aloud this play on words as fast as you can:

Un ver vert va vers un verre vert. (A green worm is going toward a green glass.)

appeler   to call

être appelé à qqch   to be destined for something, to have a calling (vocation, career)

apprendre   to learn

apprendre par coeur   to memorize

arriver   to arrive

to happen   **Qu'est-ce qui est arrivé?**   What happened?   **Qu'est-ce qui arrive?** What's happening? What's going on?

Quoi qu'il arrive . . .   Come what may . . .

assister   to assist

assister à   to attend, to be present at   **Hier soir, j'ai assisté à la conférence des musiciens.**   Last night I attended the meeting of musicians.

avoir   to have

to have something the matter   **Qu'est-ce que vous avez?**   What's the matter with you?   **Qu'est-ce qu'il y a?**   What's the matter?

avoir . . . ans   to be . . . years old   **Quel âge avez-vous?**   How old are you? **J'ai seize ans.**   I'm sixteen.

avoir à + inf.   to have to, to be obliged to + inf.   **J'ai quelque chose à vous dire.** I have something to tell you.

avoir affaire à quelqu'un   to deal with someone

avoir beau + inf.   to be useless + inf., to do something in vain   **Vous avez beau parler; je ne vous écoute pas.**   You are talking in vain (uselessly); I'm not listening to you.

avoir besoin de   to need, to have need of   **Vous avez l'air fatigué; vous avez besoin de repos.**   You look tired; you need some rest.

avoir bonne mine   to look well, to look good (persons) **Joseph a bonne mine aujourd'hui, ne trouvez-vous pas?**   Joseph looks good today, don't you think so?

avoir chaud   to be (feel) warm (persons)   **J'ai chaud; ouvrez la fenêtre, s'il vous plaît.**   I feel warm; open the window please.

avoir congé   to have a day off, a holiday from work or school   **Demain nous avons congé et nous allons à la plage.**   Tomorrow we have the day off and we're going to the beach.

avoir de la chance   to be lucky   **Ah! Tu as trouvé une pièce de monnaie?!
Tu as de la chance!**   Ah! You found a coin?! You're lucky!

avoir de quoi + inf.   to have the material, means, enough + inf.   **As-tu de quoi
manger?**   Have you something (enough) to eat?

avoir des nouvelles   to receive news, to hear (from someone)

avoir droit à   to be entitled to

avoir du savoir-faire   to have tact

avoir du savoir-vivre   to have good manners, etiquette

avoir envie de + inf.   to feel like, to have a desire to   **Madame Loisel a
toujours envie de danser.**   Mrs. Loisel always feels like dancing.

avoir faim   to be (feel) hungry   **As-tu faim, Fifi? Bon, alors je vais te donner à
manger.**   Are you hungry, Fifi? Good, then I'm going to give you something to
eat.

avoir froid   to be (feel) cold (persons)   **J'ai froid; fermez la fenêtre, s'il vous
plaît.**   I feel cold; close the window, please.

avoir hâte   to be in a hurry;   **avoir hâte de faire qqch**   to be anxious to do
something, to look forward to doing something

avoir honte   to be (to feel) ashamed

avoir l'air + adj.   to seem, to appear, to look + adj.   **Vous avez l'air malade;
asseyez-vous.**   You look sick; sit down.

avoir l'air de + inf.   to appear + inf.   **Vous avez l'air d'être malade;
couchez-vous.**   You appear to be sick; lie down.

avoir l'habitude de + inf.   to be accustomed to, to be in the habit of   **J'ai
l'habitude de faire mes devoirs avant le dîner.**   I'm in the habit of doing my
homework before dinner.

avoir l'idée de + inf.   to have a notion + inf.

avoir l'impression   to be under the impression

avoir l'intention de + inf.   to intend + inf.

avoir l'occasion de + inf.   to have the opportunity + inf.

avoir l'oeil au guet   to be on the look-out, on the watch

avoir la bonté de + inf.   to have the kindness + inf.

avoir la langue bien pendue   to have the gift of gab

avoir la parole   to have the floor (to speak)

avoir le cafard   to feel downhearted (downcast), to have the blues

avoir le coeur gros   to be heartbroken

avoir le droit de faire qqch   to be entitled (have the right) to do something

avoir le temps de + inf.   to have (the) time + inf.

avoir lieu   to take place   **Le match aura lieu demain.**   The game will take
place tomorrow.

avoir l'occasion de faire qqch   to have the opportunity to do something

avoir mal   to feel sick   **Qu'est-ce que tu as, Robert?**   What's the matter,
Robert?   **J'ai mal.**   I feel sick.   **avoir mal au coeur**   to feel nauseous

avoir mal à + (place where it hurts)   to have a pain or ache in . . .   **J'ai mal à la
jambe.**   My leg hurts.   **J'ai mal à la tête.**   I have a headache.

avoir mauvaise mine   to look ill, not to look well   **Qu'est-ce que tu as, Janine?**
What's the matter, Janine?   **Tu as mauvaise mine.**   You don't look well.

avoir peine à + inf.   to have difficulty in + pres. part.

avoir peur de   to be afraid of

avoir pitié de   to take pity on

avoir qqn   to get the better of someone   **Je t'ai eu!**   I got you!

avoir raison   to be right (persons)

avoir recours à   to resort to

avoir rendez-vous avec qqn   to have a date (appointment) with someone

avoir soif   to be thirsty

avoir soin de faire qqch   to take care of doing something

avoir sommeil   to be sleepy

avoir son mot à dire   to have one's way

avoir tendance à faire qqch   to tend to do something

avoir tort   to be wrong (persons)

avoir trait à qqch   to have to do with something

avoir une faim de loup   to be starving

en avoir assez   to have enough of it

en avoir marre   to be fed up, to be bored stiff, to be sick and tired of something
   J'en ai marre!   I'm fed up! I've had it!

en avoir par-dessus la tête   to have enough of it, to be sick and tired of it, to have
   it up to here   **J'en ai par-dessus la tête!**   I've had it up to here!

en avoir plein le casque   to have enough of it

en avoir plein le dos   to be sick and tired of it

il y a . . .   there is . . . , there are . . .

il y avait . . . , il y a eu . . .   there was . . . , there were . . .

il y aura . . .   there will be . . .

il y aurait . . .   there would be . . .

il y a + length of time   ago   **Madame Duclos est partie il y a un mois.**   Mrs.
   Duclos left a month ago.

Il y a dix minutes que j'attends l'autobus   I have been waiting for the bus for ten
   minutes.

Il y a lieu de croire que . . .   There is reason to believe that . . .

Il n'y a pas de quoi.   You're welcome.

boire   to drink

boire à la bouteille   to drink right out of the bottle

boire à sa soif   to drink to one's heart's content

briller   to shine, to glitter

Tout ce qui brille n'est pas or.   All that glitters is not gold.

casser, se casser   to break

casser la tête à qqn   to pester someone

casser les oreilles à qqn   to bore someone stiff (by talking too much)

casser les pieds à qqn   to be a pain in the neck to someone

se casser +   a part of one's body   **Janine s'est cassé la jambe.**   Janine broke
   her leg.

se casser la tête   to rack one's brains

changer   to change

changer d'avis   to change one's mind, one's opinion;   **changer de route**   to
   take another road;   **changer de train**   to change trains;   **changer de
   vêtements**   to change clothes

Plus ça change plus c'est la même chose.   The more it changes the more it remains the same.

chanter   to sing
   faire chanter qqn   to blackmail someone
   Mais qu'est-ce que vous chantez là?   What are you talking about?

chercher   to look for
   envoyer chercher   to send for   **Je vais envoyer chercher le médecin.**   I am going to send for the doctor.

combler   to fill up, to fill in
   pour comble de malheur   to make matters worse
   le comble de ...   the height of ... ;   **le comble de la stupidité**   the height of stupidity

comprendre   to understand, to comprise
   y compris   including;   **y compris la taxe**   tax included;   **service compris, y compris le service**   service included

craindre   to fear
   Chat échaudé craint l'eau froide.   A burnt child dreads the fire. (Literally, the French proverb refers to a cat but to a child in English.)

croire   to believe
   Je crois que oui.   I think so.   **Je crois que non.**   I don't think so.

dire   to say, to tell
   à ce qu'on dit ...   according to what they say ...
   à vrai dire   to tell the truth
   c'est-à-dire   that is, that is to say
   dire du bien de   to speak well of;   **dire du mal de**   to speak ill of
   entendre dire que   to hear it said that, to hear tell that   **J'entends dire que Tina s'est mariée avec Alexandre.**   I hear that Tina married Alexander.
   vouloir dire   to mean   **Que veut dire ce mot?**   What does this word mean?
   Dis-moi ce que tu manges et je te dirai ce que tu es.   Tell me what you eat and I will tell you what you are.
   Qui l'aurait dit?   Who would have thought so?

disposer   to dispose
   L'homme propose mais Dieu dispose.   Man proposes but God disposes.

donner   to give
   donner à boire à qqn   to give someone something to drink
   donner à manger à qqn   to feed someone
   donner congé à   to grant leave to
   donner du chagrin à qqn   to give someone grief
   donner rendez-vous à qqn   to make an appointment (a date) with someone
   donner sur   to look out upon   **La salle à manger donne sur le jardin.**
      The dining room looks out upon (faces) the garden.
   donner un cours   to give a course, to lecture

dormir   to sleep
  dormir à la belle étoile   to sleep outdoors
  dormir sur les deux oreilles   to sleep soundly

éclater   to burst
  éclater de rire, rire aux éclats   to burst out laughing, to roar with laughter
  éclater en applaudissements   to burst into applause

écouter   to listen (to)
  être aux écoutes   to be on the watch, to eavesdrop

écrire   to write
  de quoi écrire   something to write with

égaler   to equal, to be equal to, to match
  Cela est égal.   It's all the same; It doesn't matter; It makes no difference.
  Cela m'est égal; ça m'est égal.   It doesn't matter to me; it's all the same to me.

endommager   to damage
  C'est dommage!   It's too bad! It's a pity!

entendre   to hear
  bien entendu   of course
  C'est entendu!   It's agreed! It's understood!
  entendre dire que   to hear it said that, to hear tell that   **J'ai entendu dire qu'on mange bien dans ce restaurant.**   I've heard that a person can have a good meal in this restaurant.
  Qu'entendez-vous par là!   What do you mean by that!
  laisser entendre   to hint
  entendre raison   to listen to reason
  ne pas entendre malice   not to mean any harm

entendre parler de   to hear about, to hear of   **J'ai entendu parler d'un grand changement dans l'administration de cette école.**   I've heard about a big change in the administration of this school.

envoyer   to send
  envoyer chercher   to send for   **Je vais envoyer chercher le docteur.**   I am going to send for the doctor.

être   to be
  Ainsi soit-il!   So be it!
  être à qqn   to belong to someone   **A qui est ce livre?**   Whose book is this?
  Ce livre est à moi.   This book is mine.
  être à l'heure   to be on time
  être à temps   to be in time   **Nous sommes arrivés juste à temps.**   We arrived just in time.
  être au courant de   to be informed about   **Madame Beaupuy parle toujours au téléphone avec ses amies; elle est au courant de tout.**   Mrs. Beaupuy talks on the telephone all the time with her friends; she is informed about everything.
  être bien   to be comfortable   **Est-ce que vous êtes bien dans cette chaise?**   Are you comfortable in this chair?
  être bien aise (de)   to be very glad, happy (to)

être bien mis (mise)   to be well dressed   **Madame Paquet est toujours bien mise.**   Mrs. Paquet is always well dressed.

être d'accord avec   to agree with

être dans son assiette   to feel up to par   **Je ne suis pas dans mon assiette aujourd'hui.**   I'm not feeling up to par (quite myself) today.

être de bonne (mauvaise) humeur   to be in a good (bad) mood

être de retour   to be back   **A quelle heure ta mère sera-t-elle de retour?**   At what time will your mother be back?

être en bonne forme   to be in good shape

être en état de + inf.   to be able + inf.   **Mon père est très malade; il n'est pas en état de vous parler maintenant.**   My father is very sick; he's not able to talk to you now.

être en panne   to be broken-down, out of order (machine, auto)   **La voiture de mon père est toujours en panne.**   My father's car always has a breakdown. **Mon ordinateur est en panne!**   My computer has crashed!

être en retard   to be late, not to be on time   **Le train est en retard.**   The train is late.

être en train de + inf.   to be in the act of + pres. part., to be in the process of, to be busy + pres. part.   **Mon père est en train de réparer le téléviseur.**   My father is busy repairing the television set.

être en vacances   to be on vacation

être en vie   to be alive

être enrhumé   to have a cold, to be sick with a cold

être hors de soi   to be beside oneself, to be upset, to be furious, to be irritated, annoyed   **Je suis hors de moi parce que je n'ai pas reçu de bonnes notes dans mes études.**   I'm upset because I did not receive good grades in my studies.

être le bienvenu (la bienvenue)   to be welcome   **On est toujours le bienvenu dans cet hôtel.**   One is always welcome in this hotel.

être pressé(e)   to be in a hurry

être sur le point de + inf.   to be about + inf.   **Dépêchons-nous parce que le train est sur le point de partir.**   Let's hurry because the train is about to leave.

être temps de + inf.   to be time to + inf.   **Il est temps de partir.**   It is time to leave.

De quelle couleur est (sont) . . .   What color is (are) . . . ?   **De quelle couleur est votre nouvelle voiture?**   What color is your new car?

Il était une fois . . .   Once upon a time there was . . .

Quelle heure est-il?   What time is it?   **Il est une heure.**   It is one o'clock. **Il est trois heures.**   It is three o'clock.

y être   to be there, to understand it, to get it   **Ah! J'y suis!**   Ah, I get it! I understand it!   **Ça y est!**   That's it!

c'est ça!   That's right!

étudier   to study

à l'étude   under study   **Le dossier de Monsieur Pompier est à l'étude.**   Mr. Pompier's file is under study.

faire ses études à   to study at;   **Gervaise fait ses études à l'Université de Paris.**   Gervaise is studying at the University of Paris.

Depuis combien de temps étudiez-vous le français?   How long have you been studying French?

J'étudie le français depuis deux ans.   I have been studying French for two years.

excuser, s'excuser   to excuse, to excuse oneself

Qui s'excuse, s'accuse   A guilty conscience needs no accuser.

faillir   to fail, to miss

faillir + inf.   to almost do something   **Le bébé a failli tomber.**   The baby almost fell.

faire   to do, to make

aussitôt dit aussitôt fait (aussitôt dit que fait)   no sooner said than done

Cela ne fait rien.   That doesn't matter; That makes no difference.

Comment se fait-il . . . ?   How come . . . ?

en faire autant   to do the same, to do as much

faire + inf.   to have something done   **Ma mère a fait faire une jolie robe.** My mother had a pretty dress made.   **Mon père a fait bâtir une nouvelle maison.**   My father had a new house built. (See **causative faire**, page 676.)

faire à sa tête   to have one's way

faire attention (à)   to pay attention (to)

faire beau   to be pleasant, nice weather   **Il fait beau aujourd'hui.**   It's nice weather today.   **faire mauvais**   to be bad weather

faire bon accueil   to welcome

faire chaud   to be warm (weather)   **Il a fait très chaud hier.**   It was very warm yesterday.

faire comme chez soi   to make oneself at home   **Faites comme chez vous!** Make yourself at home!

faire d'une pierre deux coups   to kill two birds with one stone

faire de l'autostop, faire du pouce   to hitchhike

faire de la peine à qqn   to hurt someone (morally, emotionally)

faire de son mieux   to do one's best

faire des châteaux en Espagne   to build castles in the air

faire des cours   to give courses, to lecture

faire des emplettes, faire des courses, faire des achats, faire du shopping   to do or to go shopping

faire des progrès   to make progress

faire du bien à qqn   to do good for someone   **Cela lui fera du bien.**   That will do her (him) some good.

faire du ski   to ski

faire du sport   to play sports

faire du vélo   to ride a bike

faire exprès   to do on purpose

faire face à   to oppose

faire faire   to have something made (done)   **Mon père fait peindre la maison.** My father is having the house painted. (See **causative faire**, page 676.)

faire fi   to scorn

faire froid   to be cold (weather)   **Il fait très froid ce matin.**   It's very cold this morning.

faire jour   to be daylight

faire la bête   to act like a fool

faire la connaissance de qqn   to make the acquaintance of someone, to meet someone for the first time, to become acquainted with someone   **Hier soir au bal Michel a fait la connaissance de beaucoup de jeunes filles.**   Last night at the dance Michael met many girls.

faire la cuisine   to do the cooking

faire la grasse matinée   to sleep late in the morning

faire la lessive   to do the laundry

faire la malle   to pack the trunk

faire la queue   to line up, to get in line, to stand in line

faire la sourde oreille   to turn a deaf ear, to pretend not to hear

faire la vaisselle   to do (wash) the dishes

faire le ménage   to do housework

faire le tour de   to take a stroll, to go around   **Faisons le tour du parc.**   Let's go around the park.

faire les bagages   to pack the baggage, luggage

faire les valises   to pack the suitcases, valises

faire mal à qqn   to hurt, to harm someone   **Ce grand garçon-là a fait mal à mon petit frère.**   That big boy hurt my little brother.

faire mon affaire   to suit me, to be just the thing for me

faire nuit   to be night(time)

faire part à qqn   to inform someone

faire part de qqch à qqn   to let someone know about something, to inform, to notify someone of something   **Je leur ai fait part du mariage de mon fils.**   I notified them of the marriage of my son.

faire partie de   to be a part of

faire peur à qqn   to frighten someone

faire plaisir à qqn   to please someone

faire sa toilette   to wash up

faire savoir qqch à qqn   to inform someone of something

faire semblant de + inf.   to pretend + inf.

faire ses adieux   to say good-bye

faire ses amitiés à qqn   to give one's regards to someone

faire ses études à   to study at   **Ma fille fait ses études à l'Université de Paris.**   My daughter is studying at the University of Paris.

faire son lit   to make one's bed

faire son possible   to do one's best (utmost)

faire suivre   to forward mail   **Faites suivre mes lettres, s'il vous plaît.**   Forward my letters please.

faire un cours   to give a course, to lecture

faire un tour   to go for a stroll

faire un voyage   to take a trip

faire une malle   to pack a trunk

faire une partie de   to play a game of

faire une promenade   to take a walk

faire une promenade en voiture   to go for a drive

faire une question   to ask (to pose) a question

faire une réclamation   to make a complaint

faire une visite   to pay a visit

faire venir qqn   to have someone come   **Mon père a fait venir le médecin parce que ma mère est malade.**   My father had the doctor come because my mother is sick.

faire venir l'eau à la bouche   to make one's mouth water

Faites comme chez vous!   Make yourself at home!

Que faire?   What is to be done?

Quel temps fait-il?   What's the weather like?

se faire faire   to have something made (done) for oneself   **Ma mère se fait faire une belle robe.**   My mother is having a beautiful dress made.

falloir   to be necessary, must, to be lacking

Il faut . . .   It is necessary; one must . . .

Il ne faut pas . . .   One must not . . .

Comme il faut . . .   As it ought to be . . .

Peu s'en faut . . .   It takes only a little . . .

s'en falloir   to be lacking

Il s'en faut de beaucoup . . .   It takes a lot . . .

féliciter   to congratulate

féliciter qqn de qqch   to congratulate someone for (on) something   **Je vous félicite de votre succès.**   I congratulate you on your success.

fermer   to close

fermer à clef   to lock

fermer au verrou   to bolt

hâter, se hâter   to hasten

en toute hâte   in all possible speed, in great haste

importer   to matter, to be of importance

Cela n'importe.   That doesn't matter.

jeter   to throw

jeter l'argent par la fenêtre   to waste money

manger   to eat

de quoi manger   something to eat   **Y a-t-il de quoi manger?**   Is there something to eat?

manquer   to lack, to fail, to be missing

manquer de + inf.   to fail to, to almost do something   **J'ai manqué de tomber.** I almost fell.   **Paul a manqué de venir.**   Paul failed to come.

manquer à sa parole   to go back on one's word

mettre   to put, to place

mettre   to put on (clothing)   **Mimi a mis ses souliers blancs.**   Mimi put on her white shoes.

mettre au courant de   to inform about   **Tu ne me mets jamais au courant de rien!**   You never inform me about anything!

mettre de côté   to lay aside, to save

mettre en cause   to question

mettre en pièces   to tear to pieces, to break into pieces   **Roger était si fâché**

contre Julie qu'il a mis sa lettre en morceaux.   Roger was so angry at Julie that he tore her letter to pieces.

mettre fin à qqch   to put an end to something

mettre la table, mettre le couvert   to set the table

se mettre à table   to sit down at the table   **La cuisinière a mis la table et a annoncé: Venez, tout le monde; mettez-vous à table!**   The cook set the table and announced: Come, everybody; sit down at the table!

montrer   to show

montrer du doigt   to point out, to show, to indicate by pointing

parler   to talk, to speak

à proprement parler   strictly speaking

adresser la parole à   to speak to, to direct one's words at   **Ecoutez, le professeur va nous adresser la parole.**   Listen, the professor is going to speak to us.

entendre parler de   to hear about;   **Avez-vous jamais entendu parler de cela?**   Have you ever heard of that?

Il est bon de parler et meilleur de se taire.   Speech is silver; silence is golden.

Ce n'est qu'une façon de parler.   It's just a way of speaking.

partir   to leave

à partir de   from now on, beginning with   **A partir de cet instant, tu vas faire tes devoirs tous les soirs** *avant de* **regarder la télévision.**   From this moment on, you are going to do your homework every evening *before* watching television.

passer   to pass, to pass by

passer un examen   to take an exam

passer chez qqn   to drop in on someone

passer un coup de fil à qqn   to give someone a ring (a telephone call)

plaire   to please

s'il vous plaît (s'il te plaît)   please

Plaît-il?   What did you say? Would you repeat that please?

pleuvoir   to rain

pleuvoir à verse   to rain hard

pouvoir   to be able (to)

n'en pouvoir plus   to be unable to go on any longer, to be exhausted   **Je n'en peux plus.**   I can't go on any longer.

Cela se peut.   That may be.

prendre   to take

prendre garde de + inf.   to avoid + pres. part., to take care not + inf.   **Prenez garde de tomber.**   Avoid falling.   **Prenez garde de ne pas tomber.**   Take care not to fall.

prendre le parti de + inf.   to decide + inf.

prendre un billet   to buy a ticket

Qu'est-ce qui vous prend?   What's got into you?

profiter   to profit

profiter de   to take advantage of

proposer   to propose
   L'homme propose mais Dieu dispose.   Man proposes but God disposes.

regarder   to look (at), to watch
   Cela ne vous regarde pas.   That's none of your business.

rendre   to render, to return (something)
   rendre hommage à qqn   to pay someone homage
   rendre visite à   to pay a visit to

reprendre   to take up again
   reprendre la parole   to go on speaking, to resume speaking
   reprendre ses esprits   to regain one's senses

retourner   to return, to go back
   être de retour   to be back   **Madame Duval sera de retour aujourd'hui.**   Mrs. Duval will be back today.

revoir   to see again
   au revoir   good-bye

rire   to laugh
   rire au nez de qqn   to laugh in someone's face
   rire aux éclats   to roar with laughter

risquer   to risk
   Qui ne risque rien, n'a rien.   Nothing ventured, nothing gained.

sauter   to leap, to jump
   sauter aux yeux   to be evident, self-evident

savoir   to know
   savoir bon gré à qqn   to be thankful, grateful to someone

servir   to serve
   Cela ne sert à rien.   That serves no purpose.
   se servir de   to use, to make use of   **Ma mère se sert d'un lave-vaisselle pour faire la vaisselle.**   My mother uses a dishwasher to do the dishes.

suivre   to follow
   suivre un cours   to take a course   **Je vais suivre un cours de français cet été.**   I'm going to take a course in French this summer.
   suivre un régime   to be on a diet
   à suivre   to be continued

tomber   to fall
   tomber à la renverse   to fall backward
   Cela tombe bien!   That's fortunate!

traverser   to cross, to traverse
   à travers   across, through

trouver   to find
   Ne trouvez-vous pas?   Don't you think so?
   trouver visage de bois   not to find anyone answering the door after knocking

tuer   to kill

   à tue-tête   at the top of one's voice, as loud as possible   **Pour attraper l'autobus qui était en train de partir, Monsieur Duval a crié à tue-tête.** To catch the bus which was about to leave, Mr. Duval shouted at the top of his voice.

valoir   to be worth

   valoir mieux   to be better (worth more), to be preferable   **Mieux vaut tard que jamais.**   Better late than never.

venir   to come

   venir à   to happen to   **Si nous venons à nous voir en ville, nous pouvons prendre une tasse de café ensemble.**   If we happen to see each other downtown, we can have a cup of coffee together.
   venir à bout de + inf.   to manage, to succeed + inf.
   venir de + inf.   to have just done something   **Je viens de manger.**   I just ate. **Tina Marie venait de sortir avec Alexandre quand le téléphone a sonné.**   Tina Marie had just gone out with Alexander when the telephone rang.

vivre   to live

   de quoi vivre   something (enough) to live on   **Je vais apporter du pain et du beurre chez les Duval parce qu'ils n'ont pas de quoi vivre.**   I'm going to bring some bread and butter to the Duvals because they don't have enough to live on.

voir   to see

   à vue d'oeil   visibly
   voir de loin   to be farsighted
   voir tout en rose   to see the bright side of things, to be optimistic

vouloir   to wish, to want

   en vouloir à qqn   to bear a grudge against someone
   vouloir dire   to mean   **Que voulez-vous dire?**   What do you mean?
   vouloir du bien à qqn   to wish someone well
   Que voulez-vous?!   What do you expect?!
   Veuillez agréer, Monsieur (Madame), mes sincères salutations.   Literally: Please be good enough to accept my sincere greetings. (This is one of many possible closing statements in correspondence. Of course, in English we simply say: Sincerely.)

Verbs with prepositions

French verbs are used with certain prepositions or no preposition at all. At times, the preposition used with a particular verb changes the meaning entirely, *e.g.*, **se passer** means *to happen* and **se passer de** means *to do without*.

When you look up a verb among the 501 to find its verb forms (or in the section of over 1,100 verbs), also consult the following categories so that you will learn what preposition that verb requires, if any.

Consult all the categories that are given below; *e.g.*, verbs that take **à** + noun, verbs that take **à** + inf., verbs that take **de** + noun, verbs that take **de** + inf., verbs that take **à** + noun + **de** + inf., verbs that take prepositions other than **à** or **de**, verbs that require no preposition, and verbs that do not require any preposition in French whereas in English a preposition is used.

The following are used frequently in French readings and in conversation.

A. *The following verbs take* à + *noun*

assister à qqch (à une assemblée, à une réunion, à un spectacle, *etc.***)** to attend a gathering, a meeting, a theatrical presentation, *etc.*, or to be present at: **Allez-vous assister à la conférence du professeur Godard?** Are you going to attend (to be present at) Prof. Godard's lecture? **Oui, je vais y assister.** Yes, I am going to attend it.

convenir à qqn ou à qqch to please (to be pleasing to), to suit (to be suitable to): **Cette robe ne convient pas à la circonstance.** This dress does not suit the occasion. **Cela ne convient pas à mon père.** That is not suitable to my father.

demander à qqn to ask someone: **Demandez à la dame où s'arrête l'autobus.** Ask the lady where the bus stops.

déplaire à qqn to displease someone, to be displeasing to someone: **Cet homme-là déplaît à ma soeur.** That man is displeasing to my sister. **Cet homme-là lui déplaît.** That man is displeasing to her.

désobéir à qqn to disobey someone: **Ce chien ne désobéit jamais à son maître.** This dog never disobeys his master. **Il ne lui désobéit jamais.** He never disobeys him.

être à qqn to belong to someone: **Ce livre est à Victor.** This book belongs to Victor. [Note this special possessive meaning when you use **être** + **à**.]

faire attention à qqn ou à qqch to pay attention to someone or to something: **Faites attention au professeur.** Pay attention to the professor. **Faites attention aux marches.** Pay attention to the steps.

se fier à qqn to trust someone: **Je me fie à mes parents.** I trust my parents. **Je me fie à eux.** I trust them.

goûter à qqch to taste a little, to sample a little something: **Goûtez à ce gâteau; il**

est **délicieux et vous m'en direz des nouvelles.**   Taste a little of this cake; it is delicious and you will rave about it.   **Goûtez-y!**   Taste it!

s'habituer à qqn ou à qqch   to get used to someone or something: **Je m'habitue à mon nouveau professeur.**   I am getting used to my new teacher.   **Je m'habitue à lui.**   I am getting used to him.   **Je m'habitue à ce travail.**   I am getting used to this work.   **Je m'y habitue.**   I am getting used to it.

s'intéresser à qqn ou à qqch   to be interested in someone or something: **Je m'intéresse aux sports.**   I am interested in sports.

jouer à   to play (a game or sport):   **Il aime bien jouer à la balle.**   He likes to play ball.   **Elle aime bien jouer au tennis.**   She likes to play tennis.

manquer à qqn   to miss someone (because of an absence):   **Vous me manquez.**   I miss you.   **Ses enfants lui manquent.**   He (or She) misses his (or her) children.

se mêler à qqch   to mingle with, to mix with, to join in: **Il se mêle à tous les groupes à l'école.**   He mixes with all the groups at school.

nuire à qqn ou à qqch   to harm someone or something: **Ce que vous faites peut nuire à la réputation de votre famille.**   What you are doing may harm the reputation of your family.

obéir à qqn   to obey someone: **Une personne honorable obéit à ses parents.**   An honorable person obeys his (her) parents.

s'opposer à qqn ou à qqch   to oppose someone or something: **Je m'oppose aux idées du président.**   I am opposed to the president's ideas.

penser à qqn ou à qqch   to think of (about) someone or something: **Je pense à mes amis.**   I am thinking of my friends.   **Je pense à eux.**   I am thinking of them.   **Je pense à mon travail.**   I am thinking about my work.   **J'y pense.**   I am thinking about it. BUT: **Que pensez-vous de cela?**   What do you think of that?

plaire à qqn   to please, to be pleasing to someone: **Mon mariage plaît à ma famille.**   My marriage pleases my family.   **Mon mariage leur plaît.**   My marriage pleases them (is pleasing to them).

réfléchir à qqch   to think over something

répondre à qqn ou à qqch   to answer someone or something: **J'ai répondu au professeur.**   I answered the teacher.   **Je lui ai répondu.**   I answered him.   **J'ai répondu à la lettre.**   I answered the letter.   **J'y ai répondu.**   I answered it.

résister à qqn ou à qqch   to resist someone or something: **Le criminel a résisté à l'agent de police.**   The criminal resisted the police officer.

ressembler à qqn   to resemble someone: **Il ressemble beaucoup à sa mère.**   He resembles his mother a lot.

réussir à qqch   to succeed in something.   **réussir à un examen**   to pass an examination: **Il a réussi à l'examen.**   He passed the exam.

serrer la main à qqn   to shake hands with someone: **Bobby, va serrer la main à la dame.**   Bobby, go shake hands with the lady.

songer à qqn ou à qqch   to dream (to think) of someone or something: **Je songe aux grandes vacances.**   I'm dreaming of the summer vacation.

survivre à qqn ou à qqch   to survive someone or something: **Il a survécu à l'ouragan.**   He survived the hurricane.

téléphoner à qqn   to telephone someone: **Marie a téléphoné à Paul.**   Marie telephoned Paul.   **Elle lui a téléphoné.**   She telephoned him.

B. *The following verbs take à + inf.*

aider à   to help: **Roger aide son petit frère à faire sa leçon de mathématiques.** Roger is helping his little brother do the math lesson.

aimer à   to like: **J'aime à lire.**   I like to read. [Note that **aimer à + inf.** is used primarily in literary style; ordinarily, use **aimer + inf.**]

s'amuser à   to amuse oneself, to enjoy, to have fun: **Il y a des élèves qui s'amusent à mettre le professeur en colère.**   There are pupils who have fun making the teacher angry.

apprendre à   to learn: **J'apprends à lire.**   I am learning to read.

s'apprêter à   to get ready: **Je m'apprête à aller au bal.**   I am getting ready to go to the dance.

arriver à   to succeed in: **Jacques arrive à comprendre le subjonctif.**   Jack is succeeding in learning the subjunctive.

s'attendre à   to expect: **Je m'attendais à trouver une salle de classe vide.**   I was expecting to find an empty classroom.

autoriser à   to authorize, to allow: **Je vous autorise à quitter cette salle de classe tout de suite.**   I authorize you to leave this classroom immediately.

avoir à   to have, to be obliged (to do something):   **J'ai à faire mes devoirs ce soir.** I have to do my homework tonight.

commencer à   to begin: **Il commence à pleuvoir.**   It is beginning to rain. [Note that **commencer de + inf.** is also correct.]

consentir à   to consent: **Je consens à venir chez vous après le dîner.**   I consent (agree) to come to your house after dinner.

continuer à   to continue: **Je continue à étudier le français.**   I am continuing to study French. [Note that **continuer de + inf.** is also correct.]

décider qqn à   to persuade someone: **J'ai décidé mon père à me prêter quelques euros.**   I persuaded my father to lend me a few euros.

se décider à   to make up one's mind: **Il s'est décidé à l'épouser.**   He made up his mind to marry her.

demander à   to ask, to request: **Elle demande à parler.**   She asks to speak. [Note that here the subjects are the same—she is the one who is asking to speak. If the subjects are different, use **demander de**: **Je vous demande de parler.**   I am asking you to talk.]

encourager à   to encourage: **Je l'ai encouragé à suivre un cours de français.**   I encouraged him to take a course in French.

s'engager à   to get oneself around (to doing something):   **Je ne peux pas m'engager à accepter ses idées frivoles.**   I can't get myself around to accepting his (her) frivolous ideas.

enseigner à   to teach: **Je vous enseigne à lire en français.**   I am teaching you to read in French.

s'habituer à   to get used (to):   **Je m'habitue à parler français couramment.**   I am getting used to speaking French fluently.

hésiter à   to hesitate: **J'hésite à répondre à sa lettre.**   I hesitate to reply to her (his) letter.

inviter à   to invite: **Monsieur et Madame Boivin ont invité les Béry à dîner chez eux.**   Mr. and Mrs. Boivin invited the Bérys to have dinner at their house.

se mettre à   to begin: **L'enfant se met à rire.**   The child is beginning to laugh.

parvenir à   to succeed: **Elle est parvenue à devenir docteur.**   She succeeded in becoming a doctor.

persister à   to persist: **Je persiste à croire que cet homme est innocent.**   I persist in believing that this man is innocent.

se plaire à   to take pleasure in: **Il se plaît à taquiner ses amis.**   He takes pleasure in teasing his friends.

recommencer à   to begin again: **Il recommence à pleuvoir.**   It is beginning to rain again.

résister à   to resist: **Je résiste à croire qu'il est malhonnête.**   I resist believing that he is dishonest.

réussir à   to succeed in: **Henri a réussi à me convaincre.**   Henry succeeded in convincing me.

songer à   to dream, to think: **Elle songe à trouver un millionnaire.**   She is dreaming of finding a millionaire.

tarder à   to delay: **Mes amis tardent à venir.**   My friends are late in coming.

tenir à   to insist, to be anxious: **Je tiens absolument à voir mon enfant cet instant.**   I am very anxious to see my child this instant.

venir à   to happen (to):   **Si je viens à voir mes amis en ville, je vous le dirai.**   If I happen to see my friends downtown, I will tell you (so).

s'agir de   to be a question of, to be a matter of: **Il s'agit de l'amour.**   It is a matter of love.

s'approcher de   to approach: **La dame s'approche de la porte et elle l'ouvre.**   The lady approaches the door and opens it.

changer de   to change: **Je dois changer de train à Paris.**   I have to change trains in Paris.

dépendre de   to depend on: **Je veux sortir avec toi mais cela dépend des circonstances.**   I want to go out with you but that depends on the circumstances.

douter de   to doubt: **Je doute de la véracité de ce que vous dites.**   I doubt the veracity of what you are saying.

se douter de   to suspect: **Je me doute de ses actions.**   I suspect his (her) actions.

féliciter de   to congratulate on: **Je vous félicite de vos progrès.**   I congratulate you on your progress.

jouer de   to play (a musical instrument):   **Je sais jouer du piano.**   I know how to play the piano.

jouir de   to enjoy: **Mon père jouit d'une bonne santé.**   My father enjoys good health.

manquer de   to lack: **Cette personne manque de politesse.**   This person lacks courtesy.   **Mon frère manque de bon sens.**   My brother lacks common sense.

se méfier de   to distrust, to mistrust, to beware of: **Je me méfie des personnes que je ne connais pas.**   I distrust persons whom I do not know.

se moquer de   to make fun of: **Les enfants aiment se moquer d'un singe.**   Children like to make fun of a monkey.

s'occuper de   to be busy with: **Madame Boulanger s'occupe de son mari infirme.**   Mrs. Boulanger is busy with her disabled husband.   **Je m'occupe de mes affaires.**   I mind my own business.   **Occupez-vous de vos affaires!**   Mind your own business!

partir de   to leave: **Il est parti de la maison à 8 h.**   He left the house at 8 o'clock.

se passer de   to do without: **Je me passe de sel.**   I do without salt.

se plaindre de   to complain about: **Il se plaint toujours de son travail.**   He always complains about his work.

remercier de   to thank: **Je vous remercie de votre bonté.**   I thank you for your kindness. [Use **remercier de** + **an abstract noun** or + **inf.**; Use **remercier pour** + **a concrete object**; *e.g.*,   **Je vous remercie pour le cadeau.**   I thank you for the present.]

se rendre compte de   to realize: **Je me rends compte de la condition de cette personne.**   I realize the condition of this person.

rire de   to laugh at;   **Tout le monde rit de cette personne.**   Everybody laughs at this person.

se servir de   to employ, to use, to make use of: **Je me sers d'un stylo quand j'écris une lettre.**   I use a pen when I write a letter.

se soucier de   to care about, to be concerned about: **Marc se soucie de ses amis.**   Marc cares about his friends.

se souvenir de   to remember: **Oui, je me souviens de Gervaise.**   Yes, I remember Gervaise.   **Je me souviens de lui.**   I remember him.   **Je me souviens d'elle.** I remember her.   **Je me souviens de l'été passé.**   I remember last summer.   **Je m'en souviens.**   I remember it.

tenir de   to take after (to resemble):   **Julie tient de sa mère.**   Julie takes after her mother.

D. *Verbs that take* de + *inf.*

s'agir de   to be a question of, to be a matter of: **Il s'agit de faire les devoirs tous les jours.**   It is a matter of doing the homework every day.

avoir peur de   to be afraid of: **Le petit garçon a peur de traverser la rue seul.**   The little boy is afraid of crossing the street alone.

cesser de   to stop, to cease: **Il a cessé de pleuvoir.**   It has stopped raining.

commencer de   to begin: **Il a commencé de pleuvoir.**   It has started to rain. [Note that **commencer à + inf.** is also correct.]

continuer de   to continue: **Il continue de pleuvoir.**   It's still raining OR It's continuing to rain. [Note that **continuer à + inf.** is also correct.]

convenir de faire qqch   to agree to do something: **Nous avons convenu de venir chez vous.**   We agreed to coming to your place.

craindre de   to be afraid of, to fear: **La petite fille craint de traverser la rue seule.**   The little girl is afraid of crossing the street alone.

décider de   to decide: **J'ai décidé de partir tout de suite.**   I decided to leave immediately.   **Il a décidé d'acheter la maison.**   He decided to buy the house.

demander de   to ask, to request: **Je vous demande de parler.**   I am asking you to speak. [Note that here the subjects are different: I am asking you to speak; whereas, when the subjects are the same, use **damander à**:   **Elle demande à parler.**   She is asking to speak.   **Je demande à parler.**   I am asking to speak.]

se dépêcher de   to hurry: **Je me suis dépêché de venir chez vous pour vous dire quelque chose.**   I hurried to come to your place in order to tell you something.

empêcher de to keep from, to prevent: **Je vous empêche de sortir.** I prevent you from going out.

s'empresser de to hurry: **Je m'empresse de venir chez toi.** I am hurrying to come to your place.

essayer de to try: **J'essaye d'ouvrir la porte mais je ne peux pas.** I'm trying to open the door but I can't.

féliciter de to congratulate: **On m'a félicité d'avoir gagné le prix.** I was congratulated on having won the prize.

finir de to finish: **J'ai fini de travailler sur cette composition.** I have finished working on this composition.

gronder de to scold: **La maîtresse a grondé l'élève d'avoir fait beaucoup de fautes dans le devoir.** The teacher scolded the pupil for having made many errors in the homework.

se hâter de to hurry: **Je me hâte de venir chez toi.** I am hurrying to come to your house.

manquer de to neglect to, to fail to, to forget to: **Guy a manqué de compléter sa leçon de français.** Guy neglected to complete his French lesson.

offrir de to offer: **J'ai offert d'écrire une lettre pour elle.** I offered to write a letter for her.

oublier de to forget: **J'ai oublié de vous donner la monnaie.** I forgot to give you the change.

persuader de to persuade: **J'ai persuadé mon père de me prêter quelques euros.** I persuaded my father to lend me a few euros.

prendre garde de to take care not to: **Prenez garde de tomber.** Be careful not to fall.

prendre le parti de faire qqch to decide to do something: **Théodore n'a pas hésité à prendre le parti de voter pour elle.** Theodore did not hesitate to decide to vote for her.

prier de to beg: **Je vous prie d'arrêter.** I beg you to stop.

promettre de to promise: **J'ai promis de venir chez toi à 8 h.** I promised to come to your place at 8 o'clock.

refuser de to refuse: **Je refuse de le croire.** I refuse to believe it.

regretter de to regret, to be sorry: **Je regrette d'être obligé de vous dire cela.** I am sorry to be obliged to tell you that.

remercier de to thank: **Je vous remercie d'être venu si vite.** I thank you for coming (having come) so quickly. [Use **remercier de + inf.** or **+ abstract noun**. Use **remercier pour + concrete object**.]

se souvenir de to remember: **Tu vois? Je me suis souvenu de venir chez toi.** You see? I remembered to come to your house.

tâcher de   to try: **Tâche de finir tes devoirs avant de sortir.**   Try to finish your homework before going out.

venir de   to have just (done something):   **Je viens de manger.**   I have just eaten *or* I just ate.

E. *The following verbs commonly take* à + *noun* + de + *inf.*

The model to follow is: **J'ai conseillé à Robert de suivre un cours de français.**   I advised Robert to take a course in French.

conseiller à   to advise: **J'ai conseillé à Jeanne de se marier.**   I advised Joan to get married.

défendre à   to forbid: **Mon père défend à mon frère de fumer.**   My father forbids my brother to smoke.

demander à   to ask, to request: **J'ai demandé à Marie de venir.**   I asked Mary to come.

dire à   to say, to tell: **J'ai dit à Charles de venir.**   I told Charles to come.

interdire à   to forbid: **Mon père interdit à mon frère de fumer.**   My father forbids my brother to smoke.

ordonner à   to order: **J'ai ordonné au chauffeur de ralentir.**   I ordered the driver to slow down.

permettre à   to permit: **J'ai permis à l'étudiant de partir quelques minutes avant la fin de la classe.**   I permitted the student to leave a few minutes before the end of class.

promettre à   to promise: **J'ai promis à mon ami d'arriver à l'heure.**   I promised my friend to arrive on time.

téléphoner à   to telephone: **J'ai téléphoné à Marcel de venir me voir.**   I phoned Marcel to come to see me.

F. *Verb* + *other prepositions*

commencer par + **inf.**   to begin by + present participle: **La présidente a commencé par discuter les problèmes de la société.**   The president began by discussing the problems in society.

continuer par + **inf.**   to continue by + pres. part.:   **La maîtresse a continué la conférence par lire un poème.**   The teacher continued the lecture by reading a poem.

entrer dans + **noun**   to enter, to go in: **Elle est entrée dans le restaurant.**   She went in the restaurant.

être en colère contre qqn   to be angry with someone: **Monsieur Laroche est toujours en colère contre ses voisins.**   Mr. Laroche is always angry with his neighbors.

finir par + inf.   to end up by + pres part.:   **Clément a fini par épouser une femme plus âgée que lui.**   Clement ended up marrying a woman older than he.

s'incliner devant qqn   to bow to someone: **La princesse s'incline devant la reine.**   The princess is bowing to the queen.

insister pour + inf.   to insist on, upon: **J'insiste pour obtenir tous mes droits.**   I insist on obtaining all my rights.

se marier avec qqn   to marry someone: **Elle va se marier avec lui.**   She is going to marry him.

se mettre en colère   to become angry, upset: **Monsieur Leduc se met en colère facilement.**   Mr. Leduc gets angry easily.

se mettre en route   to start out, to set out: **Ils se sont mis en route dès l'aube.**   They started out at dawn.

remercier pour + a concrete noun   to thank for: **Je vous remercie pour le joli cadeau.**   I thank you for the pretty present. [Remember to use **remercier pour + a concrete object**; use **remercier de + an abstract noun** or + **inf.**   **Je vous remercie de votre bonté.**   I thank you for your kindness.   **Je vous remercie d'être venue si vite.**   I thank you for coming so quickly.]

G. *Verb + NO PREPOSITION + inf.*

adorer + inf.   to adore, to love: **Madame Morin adore mettre tous ses bijoux avant de sortir.**   Mrs. Morin loves to put on all her jewelry before going out.

aimer + inf.   to like: **J'aime lire.**   I like to read. [You may also say: **J'aime à lire**, but **aimer + à + inf.** is used primarily in literary style.]

aimer mieux + inf.   to prefer: **J'aime mieux rester ici.**   I prefer to stay here.

aller + inf.   to go: **Je vais faire mes devoirs maintenant.**   I am going to do my homework now.

apercevoir + inf.   to perceive: **J'aperçois avancer l'ouragan.**   I notice the hurricane advancing. [This is a verb of perception. You may also say: **J'aperçois l'ouragan qui s'avance.**]

compter + inf.   to intend: **Je compte aller en France l'été prochain.**   I intend to go to France next summer.

croire + inf.   to believe: **Il croit être innocent.**   He believes he is innocent.

désirer + inf.   to desire, to wish: **Je désire prendre une tasse de café.**   I desire to have a cup of coffee.

devoir + inf.   to have to, ought to: **Je dois faire mes devoirs avant de sortir.**   I have to do my homework before going out.

écouter + inf. to listen to: **J'écoute chanter les enfants.** I am listening to the children singing. [This is a verb of perception. You may also say: **J'écoute les enfants qui chantent.**]

entendre + inf. to hear: **J'entends chanter les enfants.** I hear the children singing. [This is a verb of perception. You may also say: **J'entends les enfants qui chantent.**]

espérer + inf. to hope: **J'espère aller en France.** I hope to go to France.

faire + inf. to cause, to make, to have something done by someone: **Le professeur fait travailler les élèves dans la salle de classe.** The teacher has the pupils work in the classroom. (See **causative faire**, page 676.)

falloir + inf. to be necessary: **Il faut être honnête.** One must be honest.

laisser + inf. to let, to allow: **Je vous laisse partir.** I am letting you go.

oser + inf. to dare: **Ce garçon ose dire n'importe quoi.** This boy dares to say anything.

paraître + inf. to appear, to seem: **Elle paraît être capable.** She appears to be capable.

penser + inf. to think, to plan, to intend: **Je pense aller à Paris.** I intend to go to Paris.

pouvoir + inf. to be able, can: **Je peux marcher mieux maintenant après l'accident.** I can walk better now after the accident.

préférer + inf. to prefer: **Je préfère manger maintenant.** I prefer to eat now.

regarder + inf. to look at: **Je regarde voler les oiseaux.** I am looking at the birds flying. [This is a verb of perception. You may also say: **Je regarde les oiseaux qui volent.**]

savoir + inf. to know, to know how: **Je sais nager.** I know how to swim.

sentir + inf. to feel: **Je sens s'approcher l'ouragan.** I feel the hurricane approaching. [This is a verb of perception. You can also say: **Je sens l'ouragan qui s'approche.**]

sentir + inf. to smell: **Je sens venir une odeur agréable du jardin.** I smell a pleasant fragrance coming from the garden. [This is another verb of perception. You may also say: **Je sens une odeur agréable qui vient du jardin.**]

valoir mieux + inf. to be better: **Il vaut mieux être honnête.** It is better to be honest.

venir + inf. to come: **Gérard vient voir ma nouvelle voiture.** Gerard is coming to see my new car.

voir + inf. to see: **Je vois courir les enfants.** I see the children running. [This is another verb of perception. You may also say: **Je vois les enfants qui courent.**]

vouloir + inf. to want: **Je veux venir chez vous.** I want to come to your house.

H. *Verbs that do not require a preposition, whereas in English a preposition is used*

approuver   to approve of: **J'approuve votre décision.**   I approve of your decision.

attendre   to wait for: **J'attends l'autobus depuis vingt minutes.**   I have been waiting for the bus for twenty minutes.

chercher   to look for: **Je cherche mon livre.**   I'm looking for my book.

demander   to ask for: **Je demande une réponse.**   I am asking for a reply

écouter   to listen to: **J'écoute la musique.**   I am listening to the music.   **J'écoute le professeur.**   I am listening to the teacher.

envoyer chercher   to send for: **J'ai envoyé chercher le docteur.**   I sent for the doctor.

essayer   to try on: **Elle a essayé une jolie robe.**   She tried on a pretty dress.

habiter   to live in: **J'habite cette maison.**   I live in this house.

ignorer   to be unaware of: **J'ignore ce fait.**   I am unaware of this fact.

mettre   to put on: **Elle a mis la robe rouge.**   She put on the red dress.

payer   to pay for: **J'ai payé le dîner.**   I paid for the dinner.

pleurer   to cry about, to cry over: **Elle pleure la perte de son petit chien.**   She is crying over the loss of her little dog.

prier   to pray to: **Elle prie le ciel.**   She is praying to the heavens.   **Elle prie la Vierge.**   She is praying to the Holy Mother.

puer   to stink of: **Cet ivrogne pue l'alcool.**   This drunkard stinks of alcohol.

regarder   to look at: **Je regarde le ciel.**   I am looking at the sky.

sentir   to smell of: **Robert, ta chambre sent la porcherie.**   Robert, your room smells like a pigsty (pigpen).

soigner   to take care of: **Cette personne soigne les pauvres.**   This person takes care of (cares for) poor people.

Orthographically changing verbs— verb forms that change in spelling

Verbs that end in **–cer** in the infinitive form change **c** to **ç** when in front of the vowels **a, o** or **u** in order to keep the **s** sound in the infinitive form and retain its identity. That little mark under the **c** (**ç**) is called **une cédille.** Actually it is the lower part of the letter **s** which is used in order to tell the reader that the **ç** should be pronounced as an **s**. Without that mark, the letter **c** in front of the vowels **a, o** and **u** must be pronounced as a **k** sound. Since the **c** in the ending **–cer** is pronounced like an **s**, the same sound must be retained in all its forms.

(1) Some common verbs that end in **–cer** in the infinitive form are:

annoncer / to announce	**lancer** / to launch, to hurl
avancer / to advance	**menacer** / to threaten
commencer / to begin, to start	**placer** / to place, to set
divorcer / to divorce	**prononcer** / to pronounce
effacer / to erase, to efface	**remplacer** / to replace

(2) Examples of when this change occurs:

    Present indicative: nous annonçons, nous avançons, nous commençons, nous divorçons, nous effaçons, nous lançons, nous menaçons, nous prononçons, nous remplaçons.

    Imperfect indicative: j'annonçais, tu annonçais, il (elle, on) annonçait; ils (elles) annonçaient [You do the same for the other **–cer** type verbs given above in (1).]

    Passé simple: j'annonçai, tu annonças, il (elle, on) annonça; nous annonçâmes, vous annonçâtes [You do the same for the other **–cer** type verbs given above in (1).]

    Imperfect subjunctive: que j'annonçasse, que tu annonçasses, qu'il (qu'elle, qu'on) annonçât; que nous annonçassions, que vous annonçassiez, qu'ils (qu'elles) annonçassent [Now you do the same for the other **–cer** type verbs given above in (1).]

(3) Verbs that end in **–ger** in the infinitive form change **g** to **ge** in front of the vowels **a, o** or **u** in order to keep the soft sound of **g** in the infinitive form and retain its identity; otherwise, **g** in front of **a, o** or **u** is normally pronounced hard, as in **go.**

(4) Some common verbs that end in **–ger** in the infinitive form are:

arranger / to arrange	**obliger** / to oblige
changer / to change	**partager** / to divide, to share
corriger / to correct	**plonger** / to dive, to plunge
déranger / to disturb	**ranger** / to arrange by row, put in order
manger / to eat	
nager / to swim	**songer** / to think, to dream
neiger / to snow	**voyager** / to travel

(5) Examples of when this change occurs:

    Present indicative: nous arrangeons, nous changeons, nous corrigeons, nous dérangeons [Now you do the same for the other **–ger** type verbs given above in (4).]

Imperfect indicative: j'arrangeais, tu arrangeais, il (elle, on) arrangeait; ils (elles) arrangeaient [Now you do the same for the other –ger type verbs given above in (4).]

Passé simple: j'arrangeai, tu arrangeas, il (elle, on) arrangea; nous arrangeâmes, vous arrangeâtes [Now you do the same for the other –ger type verbs given above in (4).]

Imperfect subjunctive: que j'arrangeasse, que tu arrangeasses, qu'il (qu'elle, qu'on) arrangeât; que nous arrangeassions, que vous arrangeassiez, qu'ils (qu'elles) arrangeassent [Just for the fun of it, do the same for the other –ger type verbs given above.]

(6) Verbs that end in **–oyer** or **–uyer** in the infinitive form must change **y** to **i** in front of mute **e.**

(7) Common verbs that end in **–oyer** or **–uyer** in the infinitive form are:

–OYER	**–UYER**
choyer / to fondle, to coddle	**ennuyer** / to bore, to annoy
employer / to employ, to use	**essuyer** / to wipe
envoyer / to send	
nettoyer / to clean	

(8) Verbs that end in **–AYER** in the infinitive form may change **y** to **i** or may keep **y** in front of mute **e.**

Two common verbs that end in **–ayer** in the infinitive form are: **essayer** / to try, to try on; and **payer** / to pay, to pay for.

(9) Examples of when this change occurs:

Present indicative: j'emploie, tu emploies, il (elle, on) emploie; ils (elles) emploient.

Future: j'emploierai, tu emploieras, il (elle, on) emploiera; nous emploierons, vous emploierez, ils (elles) emploieront.

Conditional: j'emploierais, tu emploierais, il (elle, on) emploierait; nous emploierions, vous emploieriez, ils (elles) emploieraient.

Present subjunctive: que j'emploie, que tu emploies, qu'il (qu'elle, qu'on) emploie; qu'ils (qu'elles) emploient.

(10) Verbs that contain a mute **e** in the syllable before the infinitive ending **–er:**

acheter / to buy	lever / to raise, to lift
achever / to complete	se lever / to get up
amener / to bring, to lead	mener / to lead
élever / to raise	peser / to weigh
emmener / to lead away, to take away	promener / to walk (a person or an animal)
enlever / to remove, to take off	se promener / to take a walk (for yourself)
geler / to freeze	

(11) These verbs, given above in (10), change mute **e** to **è** when, in a verb form, the syllable after it contains another mute **e.**

(12) This change occurs because that mute **e** in the stem of the infinitive now becomes pronounced clearly in some verb forms. Examples:

Present indicative: j'achète, tu achètes, il (elle, on) achète; ils (elles) achètent.

Future: j'achèterai, tu achèteras, il (elle, on) achètera; nous achèterons, vous achèterez, ils (elles) achèteront.

Conditional: j'achèterais, tu achèterais, il (elle, on) achèterait; nous achèterions, vous achèteriez, ils (elles) achèteraient.

Present subjunctive: que j'achète, que tu achètes, qu'il (qu'elle, qu'on) achète; qu'ils (qu'elles) achètent.

(13) Instead of changing like the verbs above in (10)–(12) the following verbs double the consonant in the syllable that contains the mute **e** in the stem:

appeler / to call	jeter / to throw
rappeler / to recall	rejeter / to throw again, to throw back
se rappeler / to remember	

Examples of when this spelling change occurs:

Present indicative: je m'appelle, tu t'appelles, il (elle, on) s'appelle; ils (elles) s'appellent.

Future: je m'appellerai, tu t'appelleras, il (elle, on) s'appellera; nous nous appellerons, vous vous appellerez, ils (elles) s'appelleront

Conditional: je m'appellerais, tu t'appellerais, il (elle, on) s'appellerait; nous nous appellerions, vous vous appelleriez, ils (elles) s'appelleraient.

Present subjunctive: que je m'appelle, que tu t'appelles, qu'il (qu'elle, qu'on) s'appelle; qu'ils (qu'elles) s'appellent.

(14) Verbs that contain **é** in the syllable before the infinitive ending **–er:**

céder / to cede, to yield, to give up	posséder / to possess, to own
célébrer / to celebrate	préférer / to prefer
concéder / to concede, to give up	protéger / to protect
considérer / to consider	répéter / to repeat
espérer / to hope	suggérer / to suggest

(15) These verbs, given above in (14), change **é** to **è** when, in a verb form, the syllable after it contains mute **e**.

Examples of when this spelling change occurs:

Present indicative: je préfère, tu préfères, il (elle, on) préfère: ils (elles) préfèrent.

Present subjunctive: que je préfère, que tu préfères, qu'il (qu'elle, qu'on) préfère; qu'ils (qu'elles) préfèrent.

Verbs used in weather expressions
Quel temps fait-il? / What's the weather like?

(a) With **Il fait . . .**

Il fait beau / The weather is fine; The weather is beautiful.
Il fait beau temps / The weather is beautiful.
Il fait bon / It's nice; It's good.
Il fait brumeux / It's misty.
Il fait chaud / It's warm.
Il fait clair / It is clear.
Il fait de l'orage / It's storming; there is a thunderstorm.
Il fait des éclairs / There's lightning.
Il fait doux / It's mild.
Il fait du soleil / It's sunny.
Il fait du tonnerre / It's thundering. (You can also say: **Il tonne.**)
Il fait du vent / It's windy.
Il fait frais / It is cool.
Il fait froid / It's cold.
Il fait glissant / It is slippery.
Il fait humide / It's humid.
Il fait jour / It is daylight.
Il fait lourd / The weather is sultry.
Il fait mauvais / The weather is bad.
Il fait nuit / It is dark.
Il fait sec / It's dry.
Il fait une chaleur épouvantable / It's awfully (frightfully) hot.

(b) With **Il fait un temps . . .**

Il fait un temps affreux / The weather is frightful.
Il fait un temps calme / The weather is calm.
Il fait un temps couvert / The weather is cloudy.
Il fait un temps de saison / The weather is seasonal.
Il fait un temps épouvantable / The weather is frightful.
Il fait un temps lourd / It's muggy.
Il fait un temps magnifique / The weather is magnificent.
Il fait un temps pourri / The weather is rotten.
Il fait un temps serein / The weather is serene.
Il fait un temps superbe / The weather is superb.

(c) With **Le temps + verb . . .**

Le temps menace / The weather is threatening.
Le temps s'éclaircit / The weather is clearing up.
Le temps se couvre / The sky is overcast.
Le temps se gâte / The weather is getting bad.
Le temps se met au beau / The weather is getting beautiful.
Le temps se met au froid / It's getting cold.
Le temps se radoucit / The weather is getting nice again.
Le temps se rafraîchit / The weather is getting cold.
Le temps se remet / The weather is clearing up.

Verbs used in weather expressions 557

(d) With **Le ciel est . . .**
   Le ciel est bleu / The sky is blue.
   Le ciel est calme / The sky is calm.
   Le ciel est couvert / The sky is cloudy.
   Le ciel est gris / The sky is gray.
   Le ciel est serein / The sky is serene.

(e) With other verbs
   Il gèle / It's freezing.
   Il grêle / It's hailing.
   Il neige / It's snowing.
   Il pleut / It's raining.
   Il pleut à verse / It's raining hard.
   Il tombe de la grêle / It's hailing.
   Il va grêler / It's going to hail.
   Il tonne / It's thundering.
   Je sors par tous les temps / I go out in all kinds of weather.
   Quelle est la prévision scientifique du temps? Quelle est la météo? / What is the
      weather forecast?

Verbs used in French proverbs and sayings

1. **Le chat parti, les souris dansent.** (When the cat is away, the mice will play.)
2. **L'appétit vient en mangeant.** (The more you have, the more you want) *i.e.,* Appetite comes while eating.
3. **Bien faire et laisser dire.** (Do your work well and never mind the critics.)
4. **Il n'y a pas de fumée sans feu.** (Where there's smoke, there's fire.)
5. **Mieux vaut tard que jamais.** (Better late than never.)
6. **Les murs ont des oreilles.** (Walls have ears.)
7. **Tout est bien qui finit bien.** (All's well that ends well.)
8. **Qui se ressemble s'assemble.** (Birds of a feather flock together.)
9. **Qui ne risque rien n'a rien.** (Nothing ventured, nothing gained.)
10. **Vouloir, c'est pouvoir.** (Where there's a will, there's a way.)
11. **Qui vivra verra.** (Time will tell.)
12. **L'habit ne fait pas le moine.** (Clothes don't make the person.)
13. **Rira bien qui rira le dernier.** (Whoever laughs last laughs best.)
14. **Aide-toi, le ciel t'aidera.** (Heaven helps those who help themselves.)
15. **Quand on parle du loup, on en voit la queue!** (Speak of the devil!)
16. **Sauve qui peut!** (Run for your life!)
17. **L'argent ne fait pas le bonheur.** (Money can't buy happiness.)
18. **Qui se marie à la hâte se repent à loisir.** (Marry in haste, repent later.)
19. **Plus ça change, plus c'est la même chose.** (The more it changes, the more it remains the same.)
20. **Les apparences sont souvent trompeuses.** (Appearances are often deceiving.)
21. **Qui s'excuse, s'accuse.** (A guilty conscience needs no accuser.)
22. **Tout ce qui brille n'est pas or.** (All that glitters is not gold.)
23. **Il est bon de parler et meilleur de se taire.** (Speech is silver, silence is golden.)
24. **Chien qui aboie ne mord pas.** (A barking dog does not bite.) [**aboyer,** to bark]
25. **Oignez vilain, il vous poindra; poignez vilain, il vous oindra.** (Bless a villain and he will curse you; curse a villain and he will bless you; or, Anoint a villain and he will sting you; sting a villain and he will annoint you; or, you must treat a rough person roughly if you expect respect.) The verb forms **oignez** and **oindra** are from **oindre,** to anoint; **poignez** and **poindra** are from **poindre,** to sting.

A summary of sequence of verb tenses—Si clauses

WHEN THE VERB IN THE
SI CLAUSE IS:

THE VERB IN THE MAIN OR RESULT CLAUSE IS:

(a) present indicative   present indicative, or future, or imperative
(b) imperfect indicative   conditional
(c) pluperfect indicative   conditional perfect

NOTE: By **si** we mean *if*. Sometimes **si** can mean *whether,* and in that case this summary of what tenses are used does not apply. When **si** means *whether,* there are no restrictions about the tenses. By the way, the sequence of tenses with a **si** clause in French is the same as it is in English with an *if* clause.

Example:
    (a) Si elle arrive, je pars.   If she arrives, I'm leaving.
          Si elle arrive, je partirai.   If she arrives, I will leave.
          Si elle arrive, partez!   If she arrives, leave!

    (b) Si elle arrivait, je partirais.   If she arrived, I would leave.

    (c) Si elle était arrivée, je serais parti.   If she had arrived, I would have left.

The Subjunctive

The subjunctive is not a tense; it is a mood, or mode. Usually, when we speak in French or English, we use the indicative mood. We use the subjunctive mood in French for certain reasons. The following are the principal reasons.

After certain conjunctions
When the following conjunctions introduce a new clause, the verb in that new clause is normally in the subjunctive mood:

à condition que   on condition that; **Je vous prêterai l'argent à condition que vous me le rendiez le plutôt possible.**
à moins que   unless; **Je pars à six heures précises à moins qu'il (n') y ait un orage.** [Expletive **ne** is optional]
afin que   in order that, so that; **Je vous explique clairement afin que vous compreniez.**
attendre que   to wait until; **Attendez que je finisse mon dîner.**
au cas que   in case; **Au cas qu'il vienne, je pars tout de suite.**
autant que   **Autant que je le sache ...**   As far as I know . . .
avant que   before; **Ne me dites rien avant qu'il vienne.** [Expletive **ne** is optional]
bien que   although; **Bien que Madame Cartier soit malade, elle a toujours bon appétit.**
de crainte que   for fear that; **La mère a dit à sa petite fille de rester dans la maison de crainte qu'elle ne se fasse mal dans la rue.** [Expletive **ne** is required]
de façon que   so that, in a way that, in such a way that; **Barbara étudie de façon qu'elle puisse réussir.**
de manière que   so that, in a way that, in such a way that; **Joseph travaille dans la salle de classe de manière qu'il puisse réussir.**

de peur que   for fear that; **Je vous dis de rester dans la maison aujourd'hui de peur que vous ne glissiez sur la glace.** [Expletive **ne** is required]

de sorte que   so that, in a way that, in such a way that; **Nettoyez la chambre de sorte que tout soit propre.**

en attendant que   until; **Nous allons rester ici en attendant qu'elle vienne.**

jusqu'à ce que   until; **Je vais attendre jusqu'à ce que vous finissiez.**

malgré que   although; **Malgré que Madame Cartier soit malade, elle a toujours bon appétit.** (NOTE: prefer to use **bien que,** as in the example given with **bien que** above on this list)

pour autant que   as far as, as much as; **Pour autant que je me souvienne . . .** As far as I remember (NOTE: prefer to use **autant que,** as in the example given with **autant que** above on this list)

pour que   in order that, so that; **Expliquez-vous mieux, s'il vous plaît, pour que je comprenne.**

pourvu que   provided that; **Vous pouvez parler librement pourvu que vous me laissiez faire de même.**

que . . . ou non   whether . . . or not; **Qu'il vienne ou non, cela m'est égal.**

quoique   although; **Quoiqu'il soit vieux, il a l'agilité d'un jeune homme.**

sans que . . . ou que   whether . . . or; either . . . or; **Soit qu'elle comprenne ou qu'elle ne comprenne pas, cela m'est égal.**

soit que . . . soit que   whether . . . or whether; **Soit que vous le fassiez, soit que vous ne le fassiez pas, cela m'est égal.**

tâcher que   to try to, to attempt to; **Tâchez que le bébé soit bien nourri.**

veiller à ce que   to see to it that; **Veillez à ce que la porte soit fermée à clef pendant mon absence.**

After indefinite expressions

où que   wherever; **Où que vous alliez, cela ne m'importe pas.**

quel que   whatever; **Je vous aiderai, quelles que soient vos ambitions** / I will help you, whatever your ambitions may be. (NOTE that the appropriate form of **quel** is needed in this indefinite expression because you are dealing with a noun (**ambitions**) and **quel** functions as an adjective)

qui que   whoever; **Qui que vous soyez, je ne veux pas vous écouter** / Whoever you are (Whoever you may be), I don't want to listen to you.

quoi que   whatever, no matter what; **Quoi que cet homme dise, je ne le crois pas** / No matter what this man says, I do not believe him.

Si + adj. + que   however; **Si bavarde qu'elle soit, elle ne dit jamais de bêtises** / However talkative she may be, she never says anything stupid.

After an indefinite antecedent

The reason why the subjunctive is needed after an indefinite antecedent is that the person or thing desired may possibly not exist; or, if it does exist, you may never find it.

(a) **Je cherche une personne qui soit honnête** / I am looking for a person who is honest.

(b) **Je cherche un appartement qui ne soit pas trop cher** / I am looking for an apartment that is not too expensive.

(c) **Connaissez-vous quelqu'un qui puisse réparer mon téléviseur une fois pour toutes?** / Do you know someone who can repair my TV set once and for all?

(d) **Y a-t-il un élève qui comprenne le subjonctif?** / Is there a student who understands the subjunctive?

BUT IF THE PERSON OR THING YOU ARE LOOKING FOR DOES EXIST, USE THE INDICATIVE MOOD:

(a) **J'ai trouvé une personne qui est honnête.**

(b) **J'ai un appartement qui n'est pas trop cher.**

(c) **Je connais une personne qui peut réparer votre téléviseur.**

After a superlative expressing an opinion

Those superlatives expressing an opinion are commonly: **le seul, la seule** (the only), **le premier, la première** (the first), **le dernier, la dernière** (the last), **le plus petit, la plus petite** (the smallest), **le plus grand, la plus grande,** *etc.*

(a) **A mon avis, Marie est la seule étudiante qui comprenne le subjonctif parfaitement.**

(b) **A mon opinion, Henriette est la plus jolie élève que j'aie jamais vue.**

After **Que,** meaning *let* or *may* to express a wish, an order, a command in the 3rd person singular or plural

(a) **Qu'il parte!** / Let him leave!

(b) **Que Dieu nous pardonne!** / May God forgive us! (NOTE that the form *pardonne* is the same in the 3rd pers. subjunctive as in the indicative)

(c) **Qu'ils s'en aillent!** / Let them go away!
NOTE that what is understood in front of **Que** here is **(Je veux) que . . .**

After certain impersonal expressions

c'est dommage que   it's a pity that; it's too bad that; **C'est dommage qu'elle soit morte.**

il est à souhaiter que   it is to be desired that; **Il est à souhaiter qu'elle soit guérie.**

il est bizarre que   it is odd that; **Il est bizarre qu'il soit parti sans rien dire.**

il est bon que   it is good that; **Il est bon que vous restiez au lit.**

il est convenable que   it is fitting (proper) that; **Il est convenable qu'il vienne me voir.**

il est douteux que   it is doubtful that; **Il est douteux qu'il soit présent au concert ce soir.**

il est essentiel que   it is essential that; **Il est essentiel que vous veniez me voir le plus tôt possible.**

il est étonnant que it is astonishing that; **Il est étonnant qu'elle soit sortie sans rien dire.**

il est étrange que it is strange that; **Il est étrange qu'il n'ait pas répondu à ta lettre.**

il est faux que it is false (it is not true) that; **Il est faux que vous ayez vu ma soeur dans ce cabaret.**

il est heureux que it is fortunate that; **Il est très heureux que Madame Piquet soit guérie.**

il est honteux que it is shameful (a shame) that; **Il est honteux que vous trichiez.**

il est important que it is important that; **Il est important que vous arriviez à l'heure.**

il est impossible que it is impossible that; **Il est impossible que je sois chez vous avant trois heures.**

il est juste que it is right that; **Il est juste que le criminel soit puni pour son crime.**

il est naturel que it is natural that; **Il est naturel qu'on ait peur dans un moment dangereux.**

il est nécessaire que it is necessary that; **Il est nécessaire que tu finisses la leçon de français avant d'aller au cinéma.**

il est possible que it is possible that; **Il est possible que Madame Paquet soit déjà partie.**

il est rare que it is rare that; **Il est rare qu'elle sorte.**

il est regrettable que it is regrettable that; **Il est regrettable que cet homme riche ait perdu tout au jeu.**

il est surprenant que it is surprising that; **Il est surprenant que tu n'aies pas fait ton devoir aujourd'hui.**

il est temps que it is time that; **Il est temps que tu fasses tes devoirs tous les jours.**

il est urgent que it is urgent that; **Il est urgent que le docteur vienne immédiatement.**

il faut que it is necessary that; **Il faut que tu sois ici à neuf heures précises.**

il importe que it is important that; **Il importe que tu me dises toute la vérité.**

il se peut que it may be that; **Il se peut qu'elle soit sortie.**

il semble que it seems that, it appears that; **Il semble que Madame Gervaise soit déjà partie.**

il suffit que it is enough that, it suffices that; **Il suffit qu'il soit informé tout simplement.**

il vaut mieux que it is better that; **Il vaut mieux que vous soyez présent quand le docteur est ici.**

After the following impersonal expressions (in English, the subject is *It*) used in the negative or interrogative because they suggest some kind of doubt, uncertainty, hesitation . . .

Il ne me semble pas que . . .	**Il ne paraît pas que** . . .
Me semble-t-il que . . . ?	**Paraît-il que** . . . ?
Il n'est pas clair que . . .	**Il n'est pas vrai que** . . .
Est-il clair que . . . ?	**Est-il vrai que** . . . ?

Il n'est pas évident que . . .
Est-il évident que . . . ?

Il n'est pas sûr que . . .
Est-il sûr que . . . ?

Il n'est pas certain que . . .
Est-il certain que . . . ?

Il n'est pas probable que . . .
Est-il probable que . . . ?

After certain verbs expressing doubt, emotion, wishing

aimer que . . .
to like that . . .
aimer mieux que . . .
to prefer that . . .
s'attendre à ce que . . .
to expect that . . .
avoir peur que . . .
to be afraid that . . .
[expletive **ne** is required]
craindre que . . .
to fear that . . .
[expletive **ne** is required]
défendre que . . .
to forbid that . . .
désirer que . . .
to desire that . . .
douter que . . .
to doubt that . . .
empêcher que . . .
to prevent that . . .
s'étonner que . . .
to be astonished that . . .
s'étonner de ce que . . .
to be astonished at the fact that . . .
être bien aise que . . .
to be pleased that . . .
être content que . . .
to be glad that . . .
être désolé que . . .
to be distressed that . . .
être étonné que . . .
to be astonished that . . .

être heureux que . . .
to be happy that . . .
être joyeux que . . .
to be joyful that . . .
être malheureux que . . .
to be unhappy that . . .
être ravi que . . .
to be delighted that . . .
être surpris que . . .
to be surprised that . . .
être triste que . . .
to be sad that . . .
exiger que . . .
to demand that . . .
se fâcher que . . .
to be angry that . . .
ordonner que . . .
to order that . . .
préférer que . . .
to prefer that . . .
regretter que . . .
to regret that . . .
souhaiter que . . .
to wish that . . .
tenir à ce que . . .
to insist upon . . .
trembler que . . .
to tremble that . . .
[expletive **ne** is required]
vouloir que . . .
to want that . . .

SOME EXAMPLES:
J'aimerais que vous restiez ici / I would like you to stay here.
J'aime mieux que vous restiez ici / I prefer that you stay here.
Je m'attends à ce qu'elle vienne immédiatement / I expect her to come
immediately.
J'ai peur qu'il ne soit malade / I am afraid that he may be sick. [expletive **ne**
is required]

Je crains qu'elle ne soit gravement malade / I fear that she may be seriously ill. [expletive **ne** is required]

Je m'étonne qu'elle ne soit pas venue me voir / I am astonished that she has not come to see me.

Je m'étonne de ce qu'il ne soit pas parti / I am astonished (at the fact that) he has not left.

Ta mère est contente que tu sois heureux / Your mother is glad that you are happy.

Madame Poulet est désolée que son mari ait perdu toute sa fortune / Mrs. Poulet is distressed that her husband has lost his entire fortune.

After verbs of believing and thinking, such as **croire, penser, trouver** (meaning *to think, to have an impression*), and **espérer** when used in the negative OR interrogative but not when both interrogative AND negative . . .

EXAMPLES:

Je ne pense pas qu'il soit coupable / I don't think that he is guilty. **Croyez-vous qu'il dise la vérité?** / Do you believe he is telling the truth?

BUT: **Ne croyez-vous pas qu'il dit la vérité?** / Don't you think that he is telling the truth?

Trouvez-vous qu'il y ait beaucoup de crimes dans la société d'aujourd'hui? Do you find (think) that there are many crimes in today's society?

BUT: **Ne trouvez-vous pas que ce livre est intéressant?** / Don't you think (*or:* Don't you find) that this book is interesting?

Note: The subjunctive forms in Tense No. 6 (**présent du subjonctif**), Tense No. 7 (**imparfait du subjonctif**), Tense No. 13 (**passé du subjonctif**), and Tense No. 14 (**plus-que-parfait du subjonctif**) of any verb are normally preceded by **que** (that); for example, **que je sois** / that I may be, **que tu ailles** / that you may go.

EE-zee guide to French pronunciation

The purpose of the guide on page 567 is to help you pronounce French words as correctly as possible. However, the best way to improve your pronunciation is to imitate spoken French that you hear from speakers who pronounce French accurately. To accomplish this, you may want to consult the Barron's book *Pronounce It Perfectly in French*, which comes with two audiocassettes that give you practice, during pauses, in imitating French spoken by French speakers.

In French there are several spellings for the same sound; for example, the following spellings are all pronounced **ay**, as in the English word *say*.

et (j')**ai** (parl)**é** (av)**ez** (all)**er** (l)**es**

The system of transcription of French sounds used here is English letters in italics. As soon as you catch on to this system, you will find it EE-zee. At first, you will have to refer to the list repeatedly until it is fixed in your mind. The sounds are arranged alphabetically in transcription form. This is the easiest way for you to find the transcription as you read the English letters next to the French words.

Consonant sounds are approximately the same in French and English. Any variations in the pronunciation of some French consonants are found in the sound transcriptions. When speaking French, you must raise your voice slightly on the last transcription sound when there is more than one in a group; for example, in pronouncing **s'il vous plaît** (please), raise your voice slightly on *pleh* in *seel-voo-pleh*.

There are only four nasal vowel sounds in French. They are expressed in the following catchy phrase, which means "a good white wine."

un	**bon**	**vin**	**blanc**
uh	*boh*	*veh*	*blah*

The straight line over the two letters means that the vowel is nasalized. How do you nasalize a vowel in French? Instead of letting breath (air) out your mouth, you must push it up your nose so that it does not come out your mouth.

Now, become familiar with the EE-zee guide to French pronunciation. Remember, the transcriptions in italics serve only as a guide to pronouncing the French. Practice pronouncing each sound first and then try it out by reading aloud some of the words and expressions on the pages that follow.

Approximate pronunciation

TRANSCRIPTION LETTERS	ENGLISH WORD	FRENCH WORD	TRANSCRIPTION SOUNDS
a	lollipop	la	*la*
ah	**ah**!	pas	*pah*
ay	s**ay**	**ai**	*ay*
e	the	le	*le*
ee	s**ee**	**ici**	*ee-see*
eh	egg	m**è**re	*mehr*
ew	f**ew**	l**u**	*lew*
ew-ee	**you eat**	h**ui**t	*ew-eet*
ny	can**y**on	monta**gne**	*moh̄-ta-ny*
o	als**o**	h**ô**tel	*o-tehl*
oh	**oh**	ch**o**se	*sh-oh-z*
oo	t**oo**	**ou**	*oo*
sh	**sh**ip	**ch**ose	*sh-oh-z*
ss	ki**ss**	ce**ss**e	*seh-ss*
u	b**u**n	b**o**nne	*bun*
uh	p**u**dding	p**eux**	*puh*
ur	p**ur**ple	h**eu**re	*ur*
y	**y**es	jo**y**eux	*zh-wah-yuh*
z	**z**ero	**z**éro	*zay-roh*
zh	mea**s**ure	**j**e	*zhe*

Nasal vowels

ūh	s**u**ng	**un**	*ūh*
ōh	s**o**ng	b**on**	*bōh*
ēh	s**a**ng	**vin**	*vēh*
āh	**yo**nder	bl**anc**	*blāh*

Thirty practical situations for travelers

The purpose of this feature is to give you useful basic verbs, expressions, and words for thirty practical situations you may find yourself in while visiting France or any French-speaking country or region of the world.

On each page where a situation is given, for example, in a restaurant or hotel, a few basic statements and questions are also included to help you communicate your thoughts effectively in the spoken language.

For the convenience of the traveler who cannot read or speak French, next to the French words there is a transcription of French sounds in italicized English letters. They are not words either in French or English and the hyphens, therefore, do not represent a division of words into syllables. They are merely sound transcriptions, and the hyphens indicate very short pauses or breath groups for about one second between sounds. In this way, the hyphens set apart the different transcriptions of sounds as listed in the EE-zee Guide to French Pronunciation on the preceding page. Study that page to become familiar with the simple system of transcription of sounds. Also, consult the Guide to Thirty Practical Situations below, where you can quickly find the page number of the situation that is of interest to you.

If there are other verbs you need to use, besides the ones given in this section, consult those in the main part of this book between pages 1 and 501.

Bon voyage! *boh vwah-yah-zh*   Have a good trip!

GUIDE TO THIRTY PRACTICAL SITUATIONS

Basic verbs, expressions, and words useful in this situation:

aller   *a-lay*   to go
quelle heure   *kehl ur*   what time
arriver   *a-ree-vay*   to arrive
s'il vous plaît   *seel-voo-pleh*   please
attendre   *a-tāh-dre*   to wait (for)
où   *oo*   where
dire   *deer*   to say, to tell
pour Paris   *poor pah-ree*   for Paris
être   *eh-tre*   to be
voyager   *vwah-yah-zh-ay*   to travel
faire un voyage   *fehr ūh vwah-yah-zh*   to take a trip
à la douane   *a la dwahn*   to customs
déclarer   *day-kla-ray*   to declare
un billet électronique   *ūh bee-yay ay-lekh-trun-eek*   electronic ticket
une pièce d'identité   *ewn p-yeh-s deed-āh-tee-tay*   ID card
l'heure *f.* **de départ**   *lur de day-pahr*   departure time
HPA (heure *f.* **prévue d'arrivée)**   *ash-pay-ah (ur pray-vew da-ree-vay)*   ETA (estimated time of arrival)
une carte d'embarquement   *ewn kart dāh-bark-māh*   boarding pass
partir   *par-teer*   to leave

l'avion (*m.*)   *la-vee-ōh*   the airplane
plaire   *plehr*   to please
dites-moi   *deet-mwah*   tell me
pouvoir   *poo-vwahr*   to be able, can
merci   *mehr-see*   thank you
savoir   *sa-vwahr*   to know
je peux   *zhe puh*   I can
vouloir   *vool-wahr*   to want
la salle d'attente   *la sal da-tāht*   waiting room
un billet aller-retour   *ūh bee-yay a-lay retoor*   a round-trip ticket
la délivrance/la livraison des bagages   *la day-leevr-āh-ss/la lee-vray-zōh day ba-ga-zh*   baggage claim
le guichet d'enregistrement   *le kee-shay dah re-zh-ees-tre-māh*   check-in counter
le bureau/l'aire *f.* **de renseignements**   *le bew-roh/lehr de-rāh-sehn-y-māh*   information desk
le vol de correspondance   *le vul de kor-ehs-poh-dāhss*   connecting flight
le poste de contrôle de sécurité   *le pust de kōh-trohl de say-kew-ree-tay*   security checkpoint
le bureau d'objets trouvés   *le bew-roh dub-zh-ay troo-vay*   lost and found

Basic statements and questions useful in this situation:

1. **Je voudrais savoir à quelle heure l'avion va partir pour Paris.**
   zhe voo-dreh sa-vwahr a kehl ur la-vee-ōh va par-teer poor pah-ree.
   I would like to know at what time the airplane is going to leave for Paris.

2. **À quelle heure est-ce que l'avion arrive à Paris?**
   a kehl ur ehs-ke la-vee-ōh a-reev a pah-ree?
   At what time does the airplane arrive in Paris?

3. **Dites-moi, s'il vous plaît, où je peux attendre. Merci beaucoup.**
   deet-mwah, seel-voo-pleh, oo zhe puh a-tāh-dre. mehr-see boh-koo.
   Tell me, please, where I can wait. Thank you very much.

Expressions you may hear:

4. **Veuillez éteindre vos portables/téléphones cellulaires.**
   vuy-yay ayt-ēh-dr voh por-tabl/tay-lay-fun sehl-ew-lehr.
   Please turn off your cell phones.

5. **Veuillez attacher votre ceinture de sécurité et relever le dos de votre siège.**
   vuh-yay ata-shay vutr sēh-tewr de say-kew-ree-tay ay re-le-vay le doh de vutr syeh-zh.
   Please fasten your safety belt and place your seat in an upright position.

For more verbs, expressions, and popular words commonly used, consult page 599.

Basic verbs, expressions, and words useful in this situation:

réserver   *ray-zehr-vay*   to reserve
payer   *pay-yay*   to pay
monter   *moh-tay*   to go up
descendre   *day-sah-dre*   to go down
arriver   *a-ree-vay*   to arrive
une chambre   *ewn shah-bre*   room
un lit   *uh lee*   bed
un grand lit   *uh grah lee*   large bed
deux lits   *duh lee*   two beds
une serviette   *ewn sehr-vee-eht*   a towel
du savon   *dew sa-voh*   some soap
y a-t-il . . . ?   *ee-a-teel*   is there . . . ? are there . . . ?
la sortie de secours   *la sorteed skoor*   emergency exit
la minuterie   *la mee-new-tree*   one-minute timed light switch in hall or stairwell

pas cher   *pah shehr*   not expensive
pas de bruit   *pahd brew-ee*   no noise
pour une nuit   *poor ewn new-ee*   for one night
pour deux nuits   *poor duh new-ee*   for two nights
une baignoire   *ewn beh-ny-wahr*   bathtub
une douche   *ewn doosh*   a shower
un lavabo   *uh la-va-boh*   a washstand
mes bagages   *may ba-gazh*   my luggage
une semaine   *ewn smen*   one week
une télé   *ewn tay-lay*   a TV
au rez de chaussée   *oh rayd sho-say*   on the ground (first) floor
au premier étage   *oh prem-yay ayta-zh*   on the second floor

Basic statements and questions useful in this situation:

1. **Bonjour. Je voudrais une chambre pour une nuit, s'il vous plaît.**
   boh-zhoor. zhe voo-dreh ewn shah-bre poor ewn new-ee, seel-voo-pleh.
   Hello. I would like a room for one night, please.

2. **J'ai mon passeport. Le voici. Tout est en ordre?**
   zhay moh pahs-pohr. le vwah-see. too teh ah nurdre?
   I have my passport. Here it is. Is everything in order?

3. **Acceptez-vous des cartes bancaires?**
   ah-ksehp-tay voo day kart b-ah-kehr?
   Do you accept credit cards?

4. **Je préfère monter l'escalier. Je n'aime pas les ascenseurs!**
   zhe pray-fehr moh-tay lehs-ka-lee-ay. zhe nehm pah lay za-sah-sur!
   I prefer to walk up the stairs. I don't like elevators!

Expressions you may hear:

5. **Prière de rendre la clé de la chambre avant de partir.**
   pree-yeh-r de rah-dr la klayd la sh-ah-br av-ah de parteer
   Please return the room key before leaving. (When going out for the day or checking out.)

6. **Veuillez libérer la chambre avant midi.**
   vuy-yay lee-bay-ray la sh-ah-br av-ah mee-dee
   Please check out before noon.

For more verbs, expressions, and popular words commonly used, consult page 599.

Basic verbs, expressions, and words useful in this situation:

faire du shopping *fehr dew shup-een*   to go shopping

acheter *ash-tay*   to buy, to purchase

chercher *shehr-shay*   to look for

jouer aux jeux vidéo *zhoo-ay oh zhuh vee-day-oh*   to play video games

aimer *ay-may*   to like

payer en espèces/comptant *pay-yay $\overline{ah}$ nehs-pehs/k-$\overline{oh}$-t-$\overline{ah}$*   to pay in cash

la musique de jazz, le jazz *la mew-zeek de zh-az, le zh-az*   jazz music

un jouet *$\overline{uh}$ zhoo-ay*   a toy

un achat *$\overline{uh}$ na-sha*   a purchase

un reçu *$\overline{uh}$ res-ew*   receipt

un parfum *$\overline{uh}$ par-f$\overline{uh}$*   perfume

une eau de toilette *ewn oh de twah-leht* (a light fragrance that does not last long)

pour une femme *poor ewn fahm*   for a woman

les cassettes *lay ka-seht*   cassettes

les disques *lay deesk*   records, recordings

le "flipper" *le flee-pehr*   popular word for video game

une carte de crédit/bancaire *ewn kart de kray-dee/b-$\overline{ah}$-kehr*   a credit card

une cassette vidéo *ewn ka-seht vee-day-oh*   videocassette

sur quel étage? *sewr kehl ay-tazh*   on what floor?

au rez-de-chaussée *oh rayd shoh-say*   on the main (ground) floor

pour un homme *poor $\overline{uh}$ num*   for a man

désirer *day-zee-ray*   to desire, want

du maquillage *dew ma-kee-yah-zh*   facial make-up

Basic statements and questions useful in this situation:

1. **Pouvez-vous me dire où se trouvent les grands magasins?**
   poo-vay-voo me deer oo stroov lay gr$\overline{ah}$ ma-ga-z$\overline{eh}$?
   Can you tell me where the big department stores are located?

2. **Il y a beaucoup de grands magasins près de l'Opéra.**
   eel-ee-a boh-koo de gr$\overline{ah}$ ma-ga-z$\overline{eh}$ prehd loh-pay-ra.
   There are many big department stores near the Opera.

3. **Pardonnez-moi. Pouvez-vous m'aider, s'il vous plaît? Je cherche . . .**
   par-dun-ay mwah. poo-vay-voo may-day, seel-voo-pleh? zhe shehrsh . . .
   Pardon me. Can you help me, please? I'm looking for . . .

4. **Je voudrais acheter des jouets. Où vend-on des jouets?**
   zhe vood-reh ash-tay day zhoo-ay. oo v$\overline{ah}$-t$\overline{oh}$ day zhoo-ay?
   I would like to buy some toys. Where do they sell toys?

5. **C'est pour offrir.** *seh poor uf-reer.*   It's to give as a present.

6. **J'ai besoin de rouge à lèvres.**
   zhay be-zw$\overline{eh}$ de roo-zh a leh-vre.
   I need some lipstick.

7. **Je pense que c'est tout. Merci beaucoup. Au revoir.**
   zhe p$\overline{ah}$-ss ke seh too. mehr-see boh-koo. u-re-vwahr.
   I think that's all. Thank you very much. Good-bye.

For more verbs, expressions, and popular words commonly used, consult page 599.

Basic verbs, expressions, and words useful in this situation:

lire   *leer*   to read
écrire   *ay-kreer*   to write
un livre   *uh leevre*   a book
art (*m.*)   *ahr*   art
histoire (*f.*)   *ees-twahr*   history
un dictionnaire   *uh deek-see-un-ehr*
   dictionary
une enveloppe   *une ah-vlup*   envelope
un stylo   *uh stee-loh*   pen
un crayon   *uh kray-oh*   pencil
un bloc de papier   *uh bluk de pap-ee-ay*
   writing pad
avec lignes   *a-vehk lee-ny*   with lines
papier à dessin   *pap-ee-ay a day-seh*
   drawing paper

sans lignes   *sah lee-ny*   without lines
trop cher   *troh shehr*   too expensive
à bon marché   *a boh mar-shay*   inexpensive
moins cher   *mweh shehr*   less expensive
livres d'occasion   *leevre duk-a-zee-oh*   used
   books
une gomme   *ewn gum*   eraser
un stylo à bille   *uh stee-loh a bee-y*
   ballpoint pen
crayons de couleur   *kray-oh de koo-lur*
   color pencils
le papier quadrillé   *le pap-yay ka-dree-yay*
   graph paper

Basic statements and questions useful in this situation:

1. **Bonjour! Je désire acheter un livre d'art, s'il vous plaît.**
   boh-zhoor! zhe day-zeer ash-tay uh leevre dahr, seel-voo-pleh.
   Hello! I would like to buy an art book, please.

2. **Les livres d'art sont au fond du magasin, là-bas.**
   lay leevre dahr soh oh foh dew ma-ga-zeh, lah-bah.
   Books on art are in the rear of the store, over there.

3. **Je voudrais acheter, aussi, des trombones, des élastiques et de la ficelle.**
   zhe voo-dreh ash-tay, oh-see, day troh-bun, day zay-las-teek ay de la fee-sehl.
   I would like to buy, also, some paper clips, rubber bands, and some string.

4. **Je pense que c'est tout. Voici l'argent. Merci beaucoup. Au revoir!**
   zhe pah-ss ke seh too. vwah-see lar-zhah. mehr-see boh-koo. u-re-vwahr!
   I think that's all. Here is the money. Thank you very much. Good-bye!

For more verbs, expressions, and popular words commonly used, consult page 599.

Basic verbs, expressions, and words useful in this situation:

appeler *ap-lay* to call

téléphoner *tay-lay-fun-ay* to telephone

composer le numéro *koh-poh-zay le new-may-roh* to dial the number

le bottin *le but-eh* phone book

téléphoner en direct *tay-lay-fun-ay ah dee-rehkt* to telephone direct

la ligne est occupée *la lee-ny eh tuk-ew-pay* the line is busy

j'ai été coupé *zhay ay-tay-koo-pay* I was cut off

j'écoute *zhay koot* I'm listening

je le regrette *zhel re-greht* I'm sorry

un numéro privé *uh new-may-roh pree-vay* an unlisted number

une carte à puce *ewn kart a pew-ss* plastic card with a microchip for financial or other information

un téléphone sans fil *uh tay-lay-fun sah feel* cordless phone

parler *par-lay* to talk, to speak

une cabine téléphonique *ewn ka-been tay-lay-fun-eek* telephone booth

le/la téléphoniste *le/la tay-lay-fun-eest* telephone operator

mon numéro est . . . *moh new-may-roh eh* my number is . . .

le mauvais numéro *le mu-veh new-may-roh* the wrong number

allô *a-loh* hello (when answering a telephone call)

un appel en P.C.V. *uh na-pehl ah pay say vay* a collect call

un télécopieur *uh tay-lay-kup-yur* fax machine

une télécopie *ewn tay-lay-kup-ee* fax

un téléphone cellulaire/portable *uh tay-lay-fun sehl-ew-lehr/por-tabl* cell phone

une pagette/un pager *ewn pa-zh-eht/uh pa-zh-ur* pager

Basic statements and questions useful in this situation:

1. **Allô. Allô. Qui est à l'appareil, s'il vous plaît?**
   a-loh. a-loh. kee eh ta-la-pa-ray, seel-voo-pleh?
   Hello. Hello. Who is on the phone, please?

2. **Je ne peux pas vous entendre. Parlez plus fort, s'il vous plaît.**
   zhe ne puh pah voo zah-tah-dre. par-lay plew fohr, seel-voo-pleh.
   I can't hear you. Speak more loudly, please.

3. **Ne quittez pas la ligne.** *ne kee-tay pah la lee-ny.* Don't hang up.

4. **Pardonnez-moi. Pouvez-vous m'aider à faire un appel téléphonique?**
   par-dun-ay mwah. poo-vay voo may-day a fehr uh na-pehl tay-lay-fun-eek?
   Pardon me. Can you help me make a telephone call?

5. **Je voudrais téléphoner en P.C.V.** *zhe voo-dreh tay-lay-fun-ay ah pay say vay.*
   I would like to make a collect call.

For more verbs, expressions, and popular words commonly used, consult page 599.

Basic verbs, expressions, and words useful in this situation:

laver *la-vay* to wash
combien de minutes *koh-bee-eh de mee-newt* how many minutes
sécher *say-shay* to dry
le javel *le zha-vehl* bleach
eau de javel *oh de zha-vehl* liquid bleach
un jeton *uh zhe-toh* a token
la monnaie *la mun-ay* change (coins)
savon en poudre *sa-voh ah poo-dre* powdered soap
aidez-moi, s'il vous plaît *ay-day-mwah, seel-voo-pleh* help me, please
faire laver *fehr la-vay* to have (something) washed
repasser *re-pah-say* to iron
avec javel *a-vehk zha-vehl* with bleach
sans amidon *sah-za-mee-doh* without starch

une machine à laver *ewn ma-sheen a la-vay* washing machine
il faut attendre *eel-foh a-tah-dre* it is necessary to wait
sans javel *sah zha-vehl* without bleach
amidon *a-mee-doh* starch
beaucoup *boh-koo* much, a lot, many
très peu *treh-puh* very little
la lessive *la leh-seev* laundry (soiled clothing to wash)
un séchoir automatique *uh say-shwahr u-toh-ma-teek* an automatic drying machine
coudre *koo-dre* to sew
la fermeture à glissière/la fermeture éclair *la fehrm-tewr a glee-see-ehr/la fehrm-tewr ay-klehr* zipper
une chemise *ewn shmeez* shirt
une blouse *ewn blooz* blouse

Basic statements and questions useful in this situation:

1. **Excusez-moi. Pouvez-vous m'aider, s'il vous plaît?**
   ehks-kew-zay-mwah. poo-vay-voo may-day, seel-voo-pleh?
   Excuse me. Can you help me, please?

2. **Comment est-ce que ces machines marchent?**
   kum-mah ehs-ke say ma-sheen marsh?
   How do these machines operate?

3. **J'ai besoin de pièces de monnaie?**
   zhay be-zweh de pee-ehs de mun-ay?
   Do I need coins?

4. **Vous êtes bien aimable. Je vous remercie beaucoup.**
   voo-zeht bee-eh ay-mah-ble. zhe voo re-mehr-see boh-koo.
   You are very kind. I thank you very much.

5. **Je voudrais faire laver quelque chose.** *zhe voo-dreh fehr la-vay kehl-ke-sh-ohz.* I would like to have something washed.

6. **Quand est-ce que je peux revenir?** *kah tehs-ke zhe puh re-vneer?* When may I come back?

7. **Cela va me coûter combien, s'il vous plaît?** *slah vahm koo-tay koh-bee-eh, seel-voo-pleh?* That is going to cost me how much, please?

For more verbs, expressions, and popular words commonly used, consult page 599.

Dans une pharmacie   *daH zewn far-ma-see*   In a pharmacy

Basic verbs, expressions, and words useful in this situation:

chercher   *shehr-shay*   to look for
j'ai besoin d'aspirines   *zhay be-zweH das-pee-reen*   I need (some) aspirin
c'est urgent   *seh tewr-zhaH*   it's urgent, it's an emergency
revenir   *re-vneer*   to come back, to return
j'ai un mal de dents   *zhay uH mahl de daH*   I have a toothache
le sirop contre la toux   *le see-roh koH-tre la too*   cough syrup
un antiseptique   *uH nah-tee-sehp-teek*   an antiseptic
teinture d'iode   *teH-tewr dee-ud*   iodine
crème à raser   *krehm a rah-zay*   shaving cream
un comprimé   *uH k-oH-pree-may*   tablet
une pilule   *ewn pee-lewl*   pill
une vitamine   *ewn vee-ta-meen*   vitamin

avoir besoin de . . .   *a-vwahr be-zweH de*   to need . . . , to have need of . . .
puis-je . . . ?   *pew-ee-zh*   may I . . . ?
du savon   *dew-sa-voH*   some soap
pastilles contre la toux   *pa-stee-y koH-tre la too*   cough drops
un laxatif léger   *uH laks-a-teef lay-zhay*   mild laxative
une brûlure   *ewn brew-lewr*   burn
la diarrhée   *la dee-a-ray*   diarrhea
une brosse à dents   *ewn bruss a daH*   toothbrush
dentifrice au fluor   *daH-tee-frees oh flew-ohr*   toothpaste with fluoride
un sparadrap   *uH spa-ra-drah*   adhesive strip
un antiacide   *uH nah-tee-a-seed*   antacid

Basic statements and questions useful in this situation:

1. **J'ai besoin de quelque chose pour une brûlure. Et une solution pour bain de bouche.**
   zhay be-zweH de kehl-ke shohz poor ewn brew-lewr. ay ewn sul-ew-see-oH poor beH de boosh.
   I need something for a burn. And a mouthwash solution.

2. **Quelle est la posologie? Combien de comprimés par jour?**
   kehl eh la pu-su-lu-zhee? koH-bee-eH de koH-pree-may pahr zhoor?
   What is the dosage? How many tablets a day?

3. **Avez-vous quelque chose pour une démangeaison?**
   a-vay-voo kehl-ke shohz poor ewn day-maH-zhay-zoH
   Have you something for an itch?

4. **Puis-je revenir dans une heure? Cet après-midi?**
   pew-ee-zh re-vneer daH zewn ur? seht a-preh mee-dee?
   May I come back in an hour? This afternoon?

For more verbs, expressions, and popular words commonly used, consult page 599.

Basic verbs, expressions, and words useful in this situation:

être malade   *eh-tre ma-lad*   to be sick

j'ai mal ici . . .   *zhay mal ee-see*   It hurts here . . .

je suis malade   *zhe swee ma-lahd*   I'm sick

j'ai le vertige   *zhayl vehr-teezh*   I feel dizzy

quelques semaines   *kehl-ke smen*   a few weeks

une douleur ici . . .   *ewn doo-lur ee-see*   a pain here . . .

restez au lit   *reh-stay oh lee*   stay in bed

pour une semaine   *poor ewn smen*   for a week

le pansement   *le pahs-mah*   bandage

le médicament   *le may-de-kam-ah*   medicine

une radiographie   *ewn rad-yoh-gra-fee*   X-ray

vomir   *vu-meer*   to vomit

depuis combien de temps?   *de-pew-ee koh-bee-eh de tah*   for how long a time?

s'évanouir   *ay-va-noo-eer*   to faint

la tension artérielle   *la tah-see-oh ar-tay-ree-ehl*   blood pressure

je suis enceinte   *zhe swee ah-seh-t*   I'm pregnant

quelques jours   *kehl-ke zhoor*   a few days

c'est grave?   *seh grahv*   is it serious?

une ordonnance   *ewn ur-dun-ahs*   a prescription

une piqûre   *ewn peek-ewr*   shot, injection

se faire examiner   *se fehr ehg-za-mee-nay*   to get examined

un mal de gorge   *uh mal de gor-zh*   sore throat

Basic statements and questions useful in this situation:

1. **Je suis diabétique. Aujourd'hui j'ai des douleurs et de la fièvre.**
   zhe swee dee-a-bay-teek. oh-zhoor-dwee zhay day doo-lur ay dla fee-eh-vre.
   I am diabetic. Today I have pains and a fever.

2. **Bonjour, docteur. Je suis malade. Aidez-moi. Je vous en prie.**
   boh-zhoor, duk-tur. zhe swee ma-lad. ay-day mwah. zhe voo zah pree.
   Hello, doctor. I am sick. Help me. I beg you.

3. **Où est-ce que vous avez mal?**   *oo ehs-ke voo zavay mal?*
   Where do you feel sick?

4. **Montrez-moi.**   *moh-tray mwah.*   Show me.   **Toussez!**   *too-say!*   Cough!

5. **Tirez la langue.**   *tee-ray la lah-g.*   Stick out your tongue.

6. **Je me sens mal.**
   jem-sah-mal.   I feel bad.

7. **J'ai mal à la gorge.**
   zh-ay mal a la gor-zh.   I have a sore throat.

For more verbs, expressions, and popular words commonly used, consult page 599.

Basic verbs, expressions, and words useful in this situation:

conclure un accord/un marché *kōh-klewr uh̄ nak-or/uh̄ mar-shay* to close a deal

un/une collègue *uh̄/ewn kul-ehg* work associate

le directeur/la directrice *le dee-rehk-tur/la dee-rehk-treess* manager

la publicité *la pew-blee-see-tay* advertising

un employé/une employée *uh̄ nah̄-plwa-yay/ewn ah̄-plwa-yay* employee

une société commerciale *ewn suss-yay-tay kum-ehr-syal* company

une photocopie *ewn futoh-kupee* fax

un calendrier *uh̄ kal-ah̄-dree-yay* calendar

un agenda *uh̄ na-zh-ah̄-da* appointment book

le droit international *le drwa ēh-tehr-na-see-yun-al* international law

la signature *la see-ny-a-tewr* signature

un dossier *uh̄ dos-yay* file

un homme/une femme d'affaires *uh̄ num/ewn fahm daf-ehr* businessman, businesswoman

le P-DG (président-directeur général) *le pay day zh-ay (pray-zeed-ah̄-dee-rehk-tur zh-ay-nay-ral)* CEO (Chief Executive Officer)

une visioconférence *ewn veez-yoh-kōh-fay-rah̄-ss* videoconference

la gestion *la zh-ehst-yoh̄* management

les actions *lay zaks-yoh̄* shares

les actionnaires *lay zaks-yun-ehr* shareholders

un avocat, une avocate *uh̄ navokah, ewn avokaht* lawyer

un comptable *uh̄ kōh-tabl* accountant

Basic statements and questions useful in this situation:

1. **Permettez-moi de me présenter. Je m'appelle . . .**
   pehr-mehtay-mwad me prayzah̄tay. zhe mapehl . . .
   Please allow me to introduce myself. My name is . . .

2. **Pouvez-vous, s'il vous plaît, traduire cette phrase?**
   poovay voo, seel voo pleh, tra-dew-eer seht frahz?
   Could you please translate this sentence?

3. **Veuillez signer le document ici.**
   vuy-yay seen-yay le duk-ew-mah̄ ee-see.
   Please sign the document here.

Note: This page is intended to help you feel a little more comfortable in a business situation. However, there is nothing that can replace a thorough study of business French if you would like to even the playing field. In any case, keep studying and practicing your French! Your clients will appreciate the effort and they will meet you halfway!

For more verbs, expressions, and popular words commonly used, consult page 599.

Basic verbs, expressions, and words useful in this situation:

vouloir *vool-wahr* to want

je voudrais *zhe voo-dreh* I would like

du vin *dew vēh* some wine

monsieur *me-sy-uh* sir; waiter

mademoiselle *mad-mwah-zehl* miss; waitress

les toilettes *lay-twah-leht* restrooms

la spécialité *la spay-see-a-lee-tay* the specialty, the special

la bière *la bee-ehr* beer

au lait *oh-leh* with milk

un steak-frites/un bifteck frites *ūh stehk-freet/ūh beef-tehk freet* steak with French fries

saignant *say-ny-āh* rare (meat)

prix net/service compris *pree neht/sehr-vees kōh-pree* tip included, no tip necessary

s'il vous plaît *seel-voo-pleh* please

les desserts *lay day-sehr* desserts

une table *ewn ta-ble* table

un menu *ūh me-new* menu

commander *kum-āh-day* to order

madame *ma-dahm* madam; waitress

pour moi *poor mwah* for me

payer l'addition *pay-yay la-dee-sy-ōh* to pay for the check

une gazeuse *ewn ga-zuh-z* soda drink

un café *ūh ka-fay* coffee

bien cuit *bee-ēh kew-ee* well done (meat)

à point *a-pwēh* medium (meat)

Basic statements and questions useful in this situation:

1. **Nous voudrions une table pour quatre près de la fenêtre, s'il vous plaît.**
   noo voo-dree-ōh ewn ta-ble poor ka-tre prehd la fneh-tre, seel-voo-pleh.
   We would like a table for four near the window, please.

2. **Moi, je préfère un steak à point et des frites, s'il vous plaît.**
   mwah, zhe pray-fehr ūh stehk a pwēh ay day freet, seel-voo-pleh.
   As for me, I prefer a steak medium and some French fries, please.

3. **Apportez-nous une bouteille de vin rouge, s'il vous plaît.**
   a-pohr-tay-noo ewn boo-tay de vēh roo-zh, seel-voo-pleh.
   Bring us a bottle of red wine, please.

4. **Il y a une mouche dans ma soupe!**
   eel-ee-a ewn moosh dāh ma soop!
   There is a fly in my soup!

5. **Où sont les toilettes?** *oo sōh lay twah-leht?* Where are the restrooms?

For more verbs, expressions, and popular words commonly used, consult page 599.

Basic verbs, expressions, and words useful in this situation:

l'inscription *f.*   *leh-skreeps-yoh*
registration

le campus   *le kah-pewss*   campus

une résidence universitaire, un dortoir   *ewn ray-zeed-ah-ss ew-nee-vehr-see-tehr, uh dortwar*   dormitory

le couvre-feu   *le koovr-fuh*   curfew

la laverie   *la lavree*   laundry (room)

le loyer   *le lwa-yay*   rent

le gymnase   *le zh-eem-nahz*   gym

le restaurant universitaire   *le restur-ah ew-nee-vehr-see-tehr*   campus cafeteria

la salle de bains   *la sal de beh*   bathroom

la bibliothèque   *la beeblee-yut-ehk*   library

la salle de classe   *la sal de klass*   classroom

un cours pour débutants   *uh koor poor day-bewt-ah*   beginner's course

une manifestation/une manif   *ewn maneef-ehst-ass-yoh/ewn maneef*   demonstration

Basic statements and questions useful in this situation:

1. **Je cherche le pavillon . . .**
   zhe sh-ehr-sh le pavee-yoh . . .
   I am looking for the . . . building.

2. **Pardonnez-moi, où est le restaurant universitaire?**
   pardun-ay-mwa, oo eh le restur-ah ew-nee-vehr-see-tehr?
   Excuse me, where is the cafeteria?

For more verbs, expressions, and popular words commonly used, consult page 599.

Basic verbs, expressions, and words useful in this situation:

quel film?   *kehl feelm*   which film (movie)?

un billet   *uh bee-yay*   ticket

quelle séance?   *kehl say-ah-s*   which showing?

le spectacle   *le spehk-tak-le*   show

où sont les toilettes?   *oo soh lay twah-leht* where are the restrooms?

combien d'heures?   *koh-bee-eh dur*   how many hours?

une place   *ewn plahs*   one seat

y a-t-il un balcon?   *ee-a-teel uh bal-koh* is there a balcony?

en anglais?   *ah nah-gleh*   in English?

les sous-titres *(m. pl.)*   *lay soo-teetr* subtitles

donnez-moi   *dun-nay mwah*   give me

à quelle heure?   *a kehl ur*   at what time?

commencer   *kum-ah-say*   to begin

bon   *boh*   good

mauvais   *mu-veh*   bad

amusant   *a-mew-zah*   amusing, funny

drôle   *drohl*   funny

deux places   *duh plahs*   two seats

en français?   *ah frah-seh*   in French?

c'est doublé?   *seh doo-blay*   is it dubbed?

où est l'entrée?   *oo eh lah-tray*   where is the entrance?

version originale   *vehr-see-oh u-ree-zh-ee-nal*   original version

avec sous-titrage   *av-ehk soo-teet-ra-zh* subtitled

Basic statements and questions useful in this situation:

1. **Deux places, s'il vous plaît, pour le film de trois heures.**
   duh plahs, seel-voo-pleh, poor le feelm de trwah zur.
   Two seats, please, for the movie at three o'clock.

2. **C'est combien?**   *seh koh-bee-eh?*   It's how much?

3. **C'est par quelle porte pour entrer dans le cinéma?**
   seh pahr kehl pohrt poor ah-tray dahl see-nay-ma?
   It's through which door to go into the cinema?

4. **Où sont les toilettes pour dames? Pour hommes?**
   oo soh lay twah-leht poor dahm?   poor um?
   Where are the restrooms for ladies? For men?

5. **Merci beaucoup.**   *mehr-see boh-koo.*   Thank you very much.

For more verbs, expressions, and popular words commonly used, consult page 599.

Basic verbs, expressions, and words useful in this situation:

un billet $\overline{uh}$ *bee-yay*   ticket
un ticket $\overline{uh}$ *tee-kay*   ticket
faire la queue *fehr la kuh*   to stand in line,
  to queue up
retourner *re-toor-nay*   to return
le train *le tr$\overline{eh}$*   train
l'autobus (m.) *loh-toh-bewss*   city bus
aller simple *a-lay s$\overline{eh}$-ple*   one-way
aller-retour *a-lay re-toor*   round-trip
le prochain *le pru-sh-$\overline{eh}$*   the next
quelle porte? *kehl poh-rt*   what gate?
quelle voie? *kehl vwah*   what track?
le buffet *le bew-fay*   snack bar
le TGV (train à grande vitesse) *le tay zhay
  vay (tr-$\overline{eh}$ a gr-$\overline{ah}$-d veet-ehss)*   high-speed
  train
composter *k$\overline{oh}$-puss-tay*   to validate, to
  punch

avoir *av-wahr*   to have
acheter *ash-tay*   to buy, to purchase
vouloir *vool-wahr*   to want
aller *a-lay*   to go
en première classe *$\overline{ah}$ pre-mee-ehr klahss*
  in first class
en seconde classe *$\overline{ah}$ se-g$\overline{oh}$-d klahss*   in
  second class
l'autocar (m.) *loh-toh-kahr*   long-distance
  bus
désirer *day-zee-ray*   to desire
à quelle heure? *a kehl ur*   at what time?
la sortie *la sohr-tee*   exit
une place réservée *ewn plass rayz-ehr-vay*
  reserved seat

Basic statements and questions useful in this situation:

1. **Je voudrais un billet aller-retour pour Cannes, s'il vous plaît.**
   zhe voo-dreh $\overline{uh}$ bee-yay a-lay re-toor poor kahn, seel-voo-pleh.
   I would like a round-trip ticket for Cannes, please.

2. **A quelle heure part le prochain train? Donnez-moi un horaire, s'il vous plaît.**
   a kehl ur pahr le pru-sh-$\overline{eh}$ tr$\overline{eh}$? dun-nay mwah $\overline{uh}$ nu-rehr, seel-voo-pleh.
   At what time does the next train leave? Give me a time schedule, please.

3. **Sur quelle voie, s'il vous plaît? Quel est le numéro de ma voiture?**
   sewr kehl vwah, seel-voo-pleh? kehl ehl new-may-rohd ma vwah-tewr?
   On what track, please? What is the number of my (train) car?

4. **Combien ça coûte? Quel est le tarif?**
   k$\overline{oh}$-bee-$\overline{eh}$ sah koot? kehl eh le ta-reef?
   How much does it cost? What is the fare?

For more verbs, expressions, and popular words commonly used, consult page 599.

Basic verbs, expressions, and words useful in this situation:

acheter   *ash-tay*   to buy, to purchase
aimer   *ay-may*   to like
coûter   *koo-tay*   to cost
un éclair   *uh nay-klehr*   eclair
une tarte aux fraises   *ewn tart oh freh-z*   strawberry tart
croustillant   *kroo-stee-yah*   crispy, crunchy
une barquette   *ewn bar-keht*   boat-shaped pastry with fruit filling
aux fruits   *oh frew-ee*   with fruits
un millefeuilles   *uh meel-fuh-y*   napoleon
un chou à crème   *uh shoo a krehm*   cream puff
un gâteau au chocolat   *uh ga-toh oh sh-u-ku-lah*   chocolate cake

devoir   *de-vwahr*   to owe
donner   *dun-nay*   to give
vouloir   *vool-wahr*   to want
un gâteau   *uh gah-toh*   cake
un feuilletté aux pommes   *uh fu-yeht-ay oh pum*   apple strudel
un flan   *uh flah*   baked custard
une tourte   *ewn toort*   layer cake
crème Chantilly   *krehm sh-ah-tee-yee*   whipped cream
aux abricots   *oh za-bree-koh*   with apricots
aux pommes   *oh pum*   with apples
des madeleines *(f. pl.)*   *day mad-lehn*   spongy plain cake
aux fraises   *oh frehz*   with strawberries

Basic statements and questions useful in this situation:

1. **Je voudrais acheter quelques pâtisseries.**
   zhe voo-dreh ash-tay kehl-ke pah-tee-sree.
   I would like to buy some pastries.

2. **Donnez-moi, s'il vous plaît, cet éclair et deux beignets aux pommes.**
   dun-nay mwah, seel-voo-pleh, seht ay-klehr ay duh beh-ny-ay oh pum.
   Give me, please, this eclair and two apple fritters.

3. **Et avec ça, j'aimerais ce grand gâteau au chocolat. J'ai grand faim!**
   ay ah-vehk sah, zhem-reh se grah gah-toh oh shu-ku-la. zhay grah feh!
   And with that, I would like this big chocolate cake. I'm very hungry!

4. **Ça coûte combien pour tout? Combien je vous dois?**
   sah koot koh-bee-eh poor too? koh-bee-eh zhe voo dwah?
   That costs how much for everything? How much do I owe you?

For more verbs, expressions, and popular words commonly used, consult page 599.

Basic verbs, expressions, and words useful in this situation:

un journal $\overline{uh}$ *zh-oor-nal* newspaper
un magazine $\overline{uh}$ *ma-ga-zeen* magazine
un plan $\overline{uh}$ *pla͞h* map
un plan de cette ville $\overline{uh}$ *pla͞h de seht veel*
  a map of this city
donnez-moi, s'il vous plaît *dun-nay mwah,*
  seel-voo-pleh give me, please
c'est combien pour ce numéro? *seh ko͞h-*
  bee-e͞h poor se new-may-roh how much is
  it for this issue?
en italien *a͞h nee-ta-lee-e͞h* in Italian
une revue scientifique *ewn re-vew see-ya͞h-*
  tee-feek science magazine
une bande dessinée *ewn ba͞hd day-see-nay*
  comic book
une revue de mode *ewn re-vew de mud*
  fashion magazine

des cartes postales (de vues) *day kart*
  pus-tal (de vew) (picture) postcards
un guide touristique $\overline{uh}$ *geed too-ree-steek*
  tourist guidebook
un télé guide $\overline{uh}$ *tay-lay geed* TV guide
avez-vous la monnaie de cent euros? *a-vay*
  voo la mun-nay de sa͞h uh-ro have you
  change for one hundred euros?
en français *a͞h fra͞h-seh* in French
en anglais *a͞h na͞h-gleh* in English
en allemand *a͞h nal-ma͞h* in German
les mots croisés *lay moh krwa-zay* crossword puzzle
un quotidien $\overline{uh}$ *kut-eed-ye͞h* daily
  newspaper

Basic statements and questions useful in this situation:

1. **Avez-vous des journaux américains? anglais? allemands? italiens?**
   a-vay voo day zh-oor-noh a-may-ree-ke͞h? a͞h-gleh? al-ma͞h? ee-ta-lee-e͞h?
   Have you any American newspapers? English? German? Italian?

2. **J'achète ce journal, ce télé guide et ce magazine.**
   zh-a-sh-eht se zh-oor-nal, se tay-lay geed ay se ma-ga-zeen.
   I'm buying this newspaper, this TV guide, and this magazine.

3. **Quand est-ce que vous aurez le prochain numéro?**
   ka͞h tehs-ke voo zu-ray le prush-e͞h new-may-roh?
   When will you have the next issue?

4. **Voici l'argent. Merci beaucoup, monsieur (madame).**
   vwah-see lar-zh-a͞h. mehr-see boh-koo, me-sy-uh (ma-dahm).
   Here is the money. Thank you very much, sir (madam).

For more verbs, expressions, and popular words commonly used, consult page 599.

Le pressing et le nettoyage à sec   *le prehs-een ay le neh-twah-yah-zh a sehk*
Pressing and dry cleaning

Basic verbs, expressions, and words useful in this situation:

nettoyage a sec   *neh-twah-yah-zh a sehk*
  dry cleaning
repasser   *re-pah-say*   to iron, to press
réparer   *ray-pah-ray*   to repair, to mend
prêt   *preh*   ready
une robe   *ewn rub*   dress
un complet   *uh koh-pleh*   suit
un manteau   *uh mah-toh*   overcoat
une chemise   *ewn shmeez*   shirt
des gants (*m.*)   *day gah*   gloves
la teinture   *la teh-tewr*   dyeing
une ceinture   *ewn seh-tewr*   belt
cet imperméable   *seht eh-pehr-may-ah-ble*
  this raincoat, mackintosh

les vêtements   *lay veht-mah*   clothes
sale   *sahl*   soiled, dirty
déchiré   *day-shee-ray*   torn
bientôt   *bee-eh-toh*   soon
un pantalon   *uh pah-ta-loh*   pants, trousers
une blouse   *ewn blooz*   blouse
une écharpe   *ewn ay-sharp*   scarf
une jupe   *ewn zh-ewp*   skirt
ce costume   *se kus-tewm*   this suit
les boutons   *lay boo-toh*   buttons
cette cravate   *seht kra-vaht*   this necktie
coudre   *koo-dre*   to sew

Basic statements and questions useful in this situation:

1. **Je cherche un magasin de pressing et nettoyage à sec.**
   zhe sh-ehr-sh uh ma-ga-zeh de prehs-een ay neh-twah-yah-zh a sehk.
   I am looking for a pressing and dry cleaning store.

2. **Y a-t-il un magasin ici dans ce quartier?**
   ee-a-teel uh ma-ga-zeh ee-see dah ce kar-tee-ay?
   Is there a store here in this neighborhood?

3. **Est-ce que vous faites des teintures?**
   ehs-ke voo feht day teh-tewr?
   Do you do any dyeing?

4. **Oui, nous faisons des teintures. Quelle couleur préférez-vous?**
   wee, noo fe-zoh day teh-tewr. kehl koo-lur pray-fay-ray voo?
   Yes, we do dyeing. What color do you prefer?

For more verbs, expressions, and popular words commonly used, consult page 599.

Chez le coiffeur masculin-féminin *shayl kwah-fur mas-kew-lēh fay-mee-nēh*
At the hair stylist for men and women

Basic verbs, expressions, and words useful in this situation:

couper *koo-pay* to cut
laver *la-vay* to wash
brosser *brus-say* to brush
raser *rah-zay* to shave
un shampooing *ūh sh-āh-pwēh* shampoo
une coiffure folle *ewn kwah-fewr ful*
a crazy, wild hair style
les cheveux courts *lay sh-vuh koor* short
hair
ce modèle *se mud-ehl* this style, type
élégant *ay-lay-gāh* elegant
mouillé *moo-yay* wet, moist
éblouissant *ay-bloo-ee-sāh* dazzling

une nouvelle coiffure *ewn noo-vehl kwah-fewr* a new hair style
un coiffeur *ūh kwah-fur* hair stylist (man);
barber
une coiffeuse *ewn kwah-fuh-z* hair stylist
(f.)
une coiffure sage *ewn kwah-fewr sah-zh*
a simple, plain hair style
les cheveux longs *lay sh-vuh lōh* long
hair
sec *sehk* dry
une permanente *ewn perman-āh-t*
permanent

Basic statements and questions useful in this situation:

1. **Je voudrais une coiffure folle, s'il vous plaît.**
   zhe voo-dreh ewn kwah-fewr ful, seel-voo-pleh.
   I would like a crazy, wild hair style, please.

2. **Non, excusez-moi, je pense que je préfère une coiffure sage et simple.**
   nōh, eks-kew-zay mwah, zhe pāh-ss ke zhe pray-fehr ewn kwah-fewr sah-zh ay sēh-ple.
   No, excuse me, I think I prefer a simple, plain hair style.

3. **D'abord, un shampooing, s'il vous plaît.**
   da-bu-r, ūh sh-āh-pwēh, seel-voo-pleh.
   First of all, a shampoo, please.

For more verbs, expressions, and popular words commonly used, consult page 599.

Basic verbs, expressions, and words useful in this situation:

désirer *day-zee-ray* to desire, to want

toucher un chèque *too-shay uh sh-ehk* to cash a check

un chèque de voyage *uh sh-ehk de vwah-yah-zh* traveler's check

changer de l'argent *sh-ah-zh-ay de lar-zh-ah* to exchange some money

devoir *de-vwahr* ought to, must

francs français *frah frah-seh* French francs

dollars américains *dul-ahr a-may-ree-keh* American dollars

voici mon passeport *vwah-see moh pas-pohr* here is my passport

un eurodollar, un euro *uh nuh-ro dular, uh nuh-ro* eurodollar, euro

le guichet *le kee-shay* teller's window

le guichet automatique *le kee-shay o-tu-ma-teek* ATM

la carte de retrait *la kart de re-treh* debit card

payer *pay-yay* to pay

recevoir *re-se-vwahr* to receive, to get

avoir besoin de *a-vwahr be-zweh de* to need, to have need of

le bureau de change *le bew-roh de sh-ah-zh* money exchange desk (office)

faire la queue *fehr la kuh* to stand in line, to queue up

francs suisses *frah swees* Swiss francs

francs belges *frah behl-zh* Belgian francs

dollars canadiens *dul-ahr ka-na-dee-eh* Canadian dollars

la carte bancaire *la kart b-ah-kehr* credit card

le NIP (le numéro d'identité personnel) *le ehn-ee-pay, le neep (le new-may-ro deed-ah-tee-tay pehr-sun-ehl)* PIN (personal identification number)

Basic statements and questions useful in this situation:

1. **Bonjour. Je désire changer de l'argent.**
   boh-zhoor. zhe day-zeer sh-ah-zh-ay de lar-zh-ah.
   Hello. I would like to exchange some money.

2. **Avez-vous des dollars américains? Des livres anglaises?**
   a-vay-voo day dul-ahr a-may-ree-keh? day lee-vre ah-glehz?
   Have you any American dollars? English pounds?

3. **Combien désirez-vous changer?**
   koh-bee-eh day-zee-ray voo sh-ah-zh-ay?
   How much do you want to exchange?

4. **J'attends de l'argent des Etats-Unis (de l'Angleterre).**
   zh-a-tah de lar-zh-ah day zay-ta-zew-nee (de lah-gle-tehr)
   I'm expecting some money from the United States (from England).

For more verbs, expressions, and popular words commonly used, consult page 599.

Basic verbs, expressions, and words useful in this situation:

louer *loo-ay* to rent, to hire

aller *a-lay* to go

traverser *trah-verhr-say* to cross, to go across

une auto(mobile) *ewn u-toh (mu-beel)* an automobile, car

une grande voiture *ewn grah-d vwah-tewr* a big car

sens unique *sah-ss ew-neek* one-way street

essence (f.) *ay-sah-ss* gasoline, petrol

la circulation *la seer-kew-la-sy-oh* traffic

le stationnement *le stah-see-un-mah* parking

conduire *koh-dew-eer* to drive (a motor vehicle)

arrêter *a-reh-tay* to stop

un taxi *uh tak-see* taxi

un autocar *uh nu-toh-kahr* (a long-distance bus)

un autobus *uh nu-toh-bewss* a city bus

mon permis *moh pehr-mee* my permit, (driver's) license

les feux rouges *lay fuh roo-zh* traffic lights

l'autoroute *lu-toh-root* highway, freeway

le métro *le may-troh* subway (tube)

une voiture *ewn vwah-tewr* car

Basic statements and questions useful in this situation:

1. **Je voudrais louer une voiture, s'il vous plaît, pour une semaine.**
   zhe voo-dreh loo-ay ewn vwah-tewr, seel-voo-pleh, poor ewn smehn.
   I would like to rent (hire) a car, please, for one week.

2. **Quelle est la direction pour aller à . . . ?**
   kehl eh la dee-rehk-see-oh poor a-lay a . . . ?
   What is the direction to go to . . . ?

3. **Pouvez-vous me dire si c'est loin d'ici?**
   poo-vay voom deer see seh lweh dee-see?
   Can you tell me if it's far from here?

4. **Est-ce que je vais tout droit pour arriver à . . . ?**
   ehs-ke zhe veh too drwah poor a-ree-vay a . . . ?
   Do I go straight ahead to arrive at . . . ?

For more verbs, expressions, and popular words commonly used, consult page 599.

Basic verbs, expressions, and words useful in this situation:

aller *a-lay* to go

changer *sh-ah-zh-ay* to change

un billet *uh bee-yay* ticket

un carnet de billets *uh kar-nay de bee-yay*
booklet of tickets

quelle direction pour . . . ? *kehl dee-rehk-see-oh poor* what direction for . . . ?

je descends *zhe day-sah* I'm getting off

la sortie *la sor-tee* exit

l'escalier mécanique *lehs-kal-yay may-ka-neek* escalator

aidez-moi, s'il vous plaît *ay-day mwah, seel-voo-pleh* help me, please

composter *koh-puss-tay* to validate, to punch

une carte hebdomadaire *ewn kart ehb-do-ma-dehr* weekly card (ticket)

arriver *a-ree-vay* to arrive

la correspondance *la ku-rehs-poh-dah-ss*
transfer, connection, change of trains

quelle ligne? *kehl lee-ny* what line?

excusez-moi *ehks-kew-zay mwah* excuse me

à la prochaine station *a la pru-sh-ehn sta-see-oh* at the next station stop

par où? *pahr oo* which way?

allez tout droit *a-lay too drwah* go straight ahead

montez l'escalier *moh-tay lehs-kal-yay* go up the stairs

Basic statements and questions useful in this situation:

1. **Pardonnez-moi. Pouvez-vous m'aider, s'il vous plaît, pour aller à l'Opéra?**
   par-dun-nay mwah. poo-vay voo may-day, seel-voo-pleh, poor a-lay a loh-pay-rah
   Pardon me. Can you help me, please, to go to the Opera?

2. **Où est l'entrée pour le métro? Ici, ou là-bas?**
   oo-eh lah-tray poor le may-troh? ee-see, oo la-bah?
   Where is the entrance to the subway (tube)? Here, or over there?

3. **Est-il nécessaire de faire la correspondance? Dans quelle direction?**
   eh-teel nay-say-sehr de fehr la ku-rehs-poh-dah-ss? dah kehl dee-rehk-see-oh?
   Is it necessary to transfer (change trains)? In what direction?

4. **Dites-moi comment ouvrir cette porte, s'il vous plaît. Montrez-moi.**
   deet-mwah kum-ah oo-vreer seht pohrt, seel-voo-pleh. moh-tray mwah.
   Tell me how to open this door, please. Show me.

For more verbs, expressions, and popular words commonly used, consult page 599.

Basic verbs, expressions, and words useful in this situation:

envoyer *ah-vwah-yay* to send

mettre à la poste *meh-tre a la pust* to mail, post

poste restante *pust rehs-tah-t* general delivery

poste aérienne *pust a-ay-ree-ehn* airmail

le poids *le pwah* weight

lourd *loor* heavy

léger *lay-zh-ay* light (in weight)

coupon-réponse international *koo-poh-ray-poh-ss eh-tehr-na-see-un-al* international postage reply coupon

le tarif *le ta-reef* rate

moins (plus) cher *mweh (plew) sh-ehr* less (more) expensive

l'expéditeur *m.*, **l'expéditrice** *f.* *leh-x-pay-dee-tur, leh-x-pay-dee-treess* sender

par avion *par av-yoh* air mail

une lettre *ewn leh-tre* letter

un colis *uh kul-ee* a package, parcel

un mandat *uh mah-dah* money order

un avis de réception *uh na-veed ray-sehp-see-oh* return receipt requested

un timbre-poste *uh teh-bre pust* postage stamp

une lettre recommandée *ewn leh-tre re-kum-ah-day* a registered letter

peser *pe-zay* to weigh

poste ordinaire (surface) *pust ohr-dee-nehr (sewr-fahss)* ordinary surface mail

imprimés *eh-pree-may* printed matter

par exprès *par eks-prehss* express delivery

le guichet *le kee-shay* clerk's window

le/la destinataire *le/la dehs-tee-na-tehr* addressee

Basic statements and questions useful in this situation:

1. **Je voudrais des timbres-poste par avion pour envoyer ces lettres aux Etats-Unis.**
   zhe voo-dreh day teh-bre pust par a-vee-oh poor ah-vwah-yay say leh-tre oh zay-ta-zew-nee.
   I would like some airmail postage stamps to send these letters to the United States.

2. **J'ai, aussi, quelques cartes postales pour envoyer en Angleterre, au Canada et en Australie.**
   zh-ay, oh-see, kehl-ke kart pus-tal poor ah-vwah-yay ah nah-gle-tehr, oh ka-na-da ay ah nus-tra-lee.
   I have, also, a few postcards to send to England, Canada, and Australia.

3. **Il y a des livres dans ce colis. C'est un cadeau pour un ami (une amie).**
   eel-ee-a day lee-vre dah se kul-ee. seh tuh ka-doh poor uh na-mee (ewn a-mee).
   There are books in this package. It's a present for a friend.

For more verbs, expressions, and popular words commonly used, consult page 599.

Basic verbs, expressions, and words useful in this situation:

prendre des photos   *prāh-dre day foto*   to take pictures

développer des films   *day-vlup-ay day feelm*   to develop films

combien coûte . . . ?   *kōh-bee-ēh koot*   how much does it cost . . . ?

sur papier mat   *sewr pa-pee-ay mat*   on a matte finish

une cartouche   *ewn kar-toosh*   one pack (of film)

vite   *veet*   quickly, fast

quel numéro?   *kehl new-may-roh*   what number?

un appareil photo   *ūh na-pa-reh-y fut-o*   camera

une caméra vidéo   *ewn ka-may-ra vee-day-o*   video camera

en couleur   *āh koo-lur*   in color

en noir et blanc   *āh nwahr ay blāh*   in black and white

une épreuve   *ewn ay-pruhv*   print

sur papier brillant   *sewr pa-pee-ay bree-y-ah*   on glossy finish

dans une heure   *dāh zewn ur*   in one hour

une pellicule   *ewn pehl-ee-kewl*   a roll of film

film négatif couleur   *feelm nay-ga-teef koo-lur*   color negative film

une photo(graphie)   *ewn fut-o(graf-ee)*   photo(graph)

un rouleau de film   *ūh roo-lohd feelm*   a roll of film

Basic statements and questions useful in this situation:

1. **Je voudrais faire développer ce rouleau de film, s'il vous plaît.**
   zhe voo-dreh fehr day-vlup-ay se roo-lohd feelm, seel-voo-pleh.
   I would like to have this roll of film developed, please.

2. **En couleur ou en noir et blanc?**
   āh koo-lur oo āh nwahr ay blāh?
   In color or in black and white?

3. **Sur papier mat ou sur papier brillant?**
   sewr pa-pee-ay mat oo sewr pa-pee-ay bree-y-āh
   On a matte finish or on glossy paper?

4. **Puis-je revenir dans une heure, cet après-midi, ou ce soir? Demain?**
   pew-ee-zh re-vneer dāh zewn ur, seht a-preh-mee-dee, oo se swahr? de-mēh?
   May I come back in one hour, this afternoon, or this evening? Tomorrow?

5. **Les photos seront prêtes dans une heure?**
   lay foto srōh preht dāh zewn ur?
   Will the photos be ready in one hour?

For more verbs, expressions, and popular words commonly used, consult page 599.

Dans un magasin de vêtements   *dah zuh ma-ga-zeh de veht-mah*
In a clothing store

Basic verbs, expressions, and words useful in this situation:

essayer *eh-say-yay* to try on

acheter *ash-tay* to buy, to purchase

payer à la caisse *pay-yay a la kehss* to pay at the cashier's desk

une robe *ewn rub* dress

une robe de soirée *ewn rub de swa-ray* an evening dress (gown)

un corset *uh kohr-seh* girdle

petite taille *pteet tah-y* small size

un peignoir *uh peh-ny-wahr* a dressing gown, robe

une chemise de nuit *ewn shmeez de new-ee* nightgown

des chaussures *(f.)* *day sh-oh-sewr* shoes

une salle d'esssayage *ewn sal day-seh-ya-zh* fitting room

raccourcir *ra-koor-seer* to shorten

une chemise *ewn shmeez* shirt

un costume *uh kus-tewm* suit

un slip *uh sleep* briefs, underwear

un tee-shirt *uh tee-sh-eert* T-shirt

prendre *prah-dre* to take

une taille moyenne *ewn tah-y mwah-yehn* medium size

une taille grande *ewn tah-y grah-d* large size

une culotte *ewn kew-lut* panties

un soutien-gorge *uh soot-y-eh gohr-zh* bra (brassiere)

une jupe *ewn zh-ewp* skirt

un jupon *uh zh-ew-poh* half-slip

pur coton *pewr kut-oh* pure cotton

les collants *(m.)* *lay kul-ah* tights, leotards

un fond de robe *uh foh de rub* full slip

un pyjama *uh pee-zha-ma* pajamas

un manteau *uh mah-toh* overcoat

une ceinture *ewn seh-tewr* belt

un pantalon *uh pah-ta-loh* trousers

la fermeture à glissière/la fermeture éclair *la fehrm-tewr a glee-see-ehr/la fehrm-tewr ay-klehr* zipper

une cravate *ewn kra-vat* necktie

Basic statements and questions useful in this situation:

1. **J'aimerais acheter quelques vêtements. Pouvez-vous m'aider, s'il vous plaît?**
   zh-ehm-reh ash-tay kehl-ke veht-mah. poo-vay-voo may-day, seel-voo-pleh?
   I would like to buy some clothes. Can you help me, please?

2. **Puis-je essayer cette robe? C'est une taille moyenne?**
   pew-ee-zh eh-say-yay seht rub? seh tewn tah-y mwah-yehn?
   May I try on this dress? Is it a medium size?

3. **Je préfère les couleurs rose, rouge, bleu et jaune.**
   zhe pray-fehr lay koo-lur rohz, roo-zh, bluh ay zh-ohn.
   I prefer the colors pink, red, blue, and yellow.

4. **Merci beaucoup, madame! Passez une bonne journée! Au revoir!**
   mehr-see boh-koo, ma-dahm! pah-say ewn bun zh-oor-nay! u-re-vwahr!
   Thank you very much, madam! Have a nice day! Good-bye!

5. **Bonjour, monsieur. Pouvez-vous m'aider, s'il vous plaît?**
   boh-zhoor, me-sy-uh. poo-vay-voo may-day, seel-voo-pleh?
   Hello, sir. Can you help me, please?

6. **En quels coloris avez-vous les slips et les tee-shirts?**
   ah kehl kul-u-ree a-vay-voo lay sleep ay lay tee-sh-eert?
   In what colors do you have briefs and T-shirts?

For more verbs, expressions, and popular words commonly used, consult page 599.

Dans un magasin d'ordinateurs ou un cybercafé *dah-zuh ma-gaz-eh dor-dee-na-tur oo uh see-behr-ka-fay* In a computer store or an Internet café

Basic verbs, expressions, and words useful in this situation:

démarrer *day-ma-ray* to boot

tomber en panne *t-oh-bay ah pahn* to crash

ouvrir une session *oo-vreer ewn sehss-yoh* to log on

terminer une session *tehr-mee-nay ewn sehss-yoh* to log off

le mot de passe *le moh de pahss* password

télécharger *tay-lay-sh-ar-zh-ay* to download

éteindre *ayt-eh-dr* to turn off, to shut down

le courrier électronique *le koo-ree-yay ay-lehk-trun-eek* e-mail

une adresse électronique *ewn ad-rehss ay-lehk-trun-eek* e-mail address

le traitement de texte *le treht-mah de tehxt* word processing

le Web *le wehb* the World Wide Web

un moteur de recherche *uh mut-ur de re-sh-ehr-sh* search engine

un fureteur *uh fewr-tur* web browser

une page web *ewn pa-zh wehb* web page

la souris *la soo-ree* mouse

une copie de secours *ewn kup-ee de skoor* backup copy

un scanner *uh skan-ehr* scanner

chargez du papier *shar-zhay dew papyay* load some paper

soulevez le capot *sool-vay le kap-oh* lift the cover

enregistrer/sauvegarder *ah-re-zh-ees-tray/sov-gar-day* to save

un ordinateur *uh nor-dee-na-tur* computer

un logiciel *uh lu-zh-ee-sy-ehl* program

naviguer *na-vee-gay* to navigate, to surf

un modem *uh mud-ehm* modem

causer *ko-zay* to chat

un virus *uh veer-ewss* virus

Basic statements and questions useful in this situation:

1. **Où est-ce que je peux envoyer un courrier électronique?**
   oo ehs-ke zhe puh ah-vwa-yay uh koor-ee-yay ay-lehk-trun-eek?
   Where can I send an e-mail?

2. **Il me faut envoyer un message instantané.**
   eel me foh ah-vwa-yay uh mess-azh eh-st-ah-ta-nay.
   I have to send an instant message.

3. **J'aimerais causer avec ma petite amie (mon petit ami).**
   zh-ehm-reh ko-zay a-vehk ma pteet a-mee (m-oh ptee a-mee).
   I would like to chat with my girlfriend (boyfriend).

4. **Je voudrais installer ce logiciel. Pouvez-vous m'aider?**
   zhe vood-reh eh-stal-ay se lu-zh-ee-sy-ehl. poovay voo may-day?
   I would like to install this program. Can you help me?

For more verbs, expressions, and popular words commonly used, consult page 599.

Basic verbs, expressions, and words useful in this situation:

goûter *goo-tay* to taste
manger *mah-zh-ay* to eat
aimer *ay-may* to like
vouloir *vool-wahr* to want
du sucre *dew sew-kre* some sugar
chaud *sh-oh* hot
du chocolat *dew sh-u-ku-lah* some chocolate
un sandwich au fromage *uh s-ah-dweetch oh frum-azh* a cheese sandwich
prix net/service compris *pree neht/sehr-veess k-oh-pree* tip included (no tip necessary)
un café crème *uh ka-fay krehm* coffee with hot milk

prendre *prah-dre* to take
davantage *da-vah-tah-zh* some more; plenty
s'il vous plaît *seel-voo-pleh* please
pas beaucoup *pah-boh-koo* not much
très chaud *treh sh-oh* very hot
tiède *tee-ehd* warm
des madeleines (*f.*) *day mad-lehn* spongy plain cake
la spécialité de la maison *la spay-see-a-lee-tay de la may-zoh* the shop's specialty
un (café) express *uh (ka-fay) ex-preh-ss* espresso
un (café) allongé *uh (ka-fay) al-oh-zh-ay* coffee with extra water

Basic statements and questions useful in this situation:

1. **Bonjour! Une table pour moi (pour deux personnes), s'il vous plaît.**
   boh-zhoor   ewn ta-ble poor mwah (poor duh pehr-sun), seel-voo-pleh.
   Hello! A table for me (for two persons), please.

2. **J'aimerais avoir une tasse de thé très chaud et la spécialité de la maison.**
   zh-em-reh a-vwahr ewn tah-ss de tay treh sh-oh ay la spay-see-a-lee-tay de la may-zoh.
   I would like to have a very hot cup of tea and the shop's specialty.

3. **Moi, je préfère du citron. Pour mon ami(e) du lait avec le thé.**
   mwah, zhe pray-fehr dew see-troh. poor mun-a-mee, dew lay a-vehk le tay.
   As for me, I prefer some lemon. For my friend, some milk with the tea.

4. **Donnez-moi l'addition, s'il vous plaît. Le service est compris? Merci.**
   dun-nay-mwah la-dee-s-y-oh, seel-voo-pleh. le sehr-veess eh koh-pree? mehr-see.
   Give me the check, please. The service (tip) is included? Thank you.

Note: When ordering in a restaurant or café it is not necessary to use the partitive (**du café**). Instead, you may say "**J'aimerais un café, s'il vous plaît.**" (I would like a coffee, please.) But you may still use the partitive when you want to add **du sucre** (some sugar).

For more verbs, expressions, and popular words commonly used, consult page 599.

Basic verbs, expressions, and words useful in this situation:

il fait doux *eel feh doo* the weather is nice

il fait (du) soleil *eel feh (dew) sul-ay* it's sunny

il gèle *eel zh-ehl* it's freezing

il grêle *eel grehl* it's hailing

il neige *eel neh-zh* it's snowing

il pleut *eel pluh* it's raining

il va neiger *eel va neh-zhay* it's going to snow

il va pleuvoir *eel va pl-uh-vwahr* it's going to rain

la poudrerie *la pood-re-ree* snow flurry

une tempête de neige *ewn t-ah-peht de neh-zh* snowstorm

le ciel est beau *le see-ehl eh boh* the sky is beautiful

le ciel est bleu *le see-ehl eh bluh* the sky is blue

le temps menace *le tah me-nahss* the weather is threatening

le temps s'éclaircit *le tah say-klehr-see* the weather is clearing up

le temps se gâte *le tah se gaht* the weather is getting bad

le temps se met au beau *le tah se meh toh boh* the weather is getting beautiful

un blizzard *uh bleez-ar* blizzard

Basic statements and questions useful in this situation:

1. **Quel temps fait-il aujourd'hui?**
   kehl tah feh-teel oh-zh-oor-dwee?
   What's the weather like today?

2. **Savez-vous quel temps il fera demain?**
   sah-vay voo kehl tah eel frah de-meh?
   Do you know what the weather will be like tomorrow?

3. **Il pleut à verse.** *eel pluh a vehr-ss.* It's raining hard.

4. **J'ai besoin d'un parapluie.** *zh-ay be-zweh duh pa-ra-plew-ee.* I need an umbrella.

5. **Je sors par tous les temps.** *zhe su-r pahr too lay tah.* I go out in all kinds of weather.

6. **Quel sale temps!** *kehl sahl tah!* What awful weather!

7. **Il fait un temps superbe aujourd'hui, n'est-ce pas?**
   eel feh uh tah sew-pehrb oh-zh-oor-dwee, neh-spah?
   The weather is superb today, isn't it?

For more verbs, expressions, and popular words commonly used, consult page 599.

Basic verbs, expressions, and words useful in this situation:

désirer *day-zee-ray* to desire
vouloir *vool-wahr* to want
aimer *ay-may* to like
choisir *sh-wah-zeer* to choose
préférer *pray-fay-ray* to prefer
acheter *ash-tay* to buy, to purchase
joli *zh-ul-ee* pretty
faire envoyer *fehr ah-vwah-yay* to send, to deliver
œillet (m.) *uh-yay* carnation
géranium (m.) *zh-ay-ra-nee-um* geranium

une botte de fleurs *ewn but de flur* bunch of flowers
une plante *ewn plah-t* plant
quelques roses *kehl-ke rohz* some roses
offrir *uf-reer* to offer
c'est pour offrir *seh poor uf-reer* it's to give as a gift
pas trop cher *pah troh sh-ehr* not too expensive
un ruban *uh rew-bah* ribbon
prendre *prah-dre* to take
glaïeul (m.) *gla-ee-ul* gladioli

Basic statements and questions useful in this situation:

1. **Je désire acheter quelques fleurs pour des amis.**
   zhe day-zeer ash-tay kehl-ke flur poor day za-mee.
   I'd like to buy some flowers for some friends.

2. **Je préfère les jolies couleurs, comme rouge, rose, blanc, bleu clair.**
   zhe pray-fehr lay zh-ul-ee koo-lur, kum roo-zh, rohz, blah, bluh klehr.
   I prefer the pretty colors, like red, pink, white, light blue.

3. **Je vais prendre cette botte de roses jaunes.**
   zhe vay prah-dre seht but de rohz zh-oh-n.
   I'm going to take this bunch of yellow roses.

4. **J'aime beaucoup cette plante rouge. Elle est très jolie. C'est combien?**
   zh-ehm boh-koo seht plah-t roo-zh. ehl eh treh zh-ul-ee. seh koh-bee-eh?
   I like this red plant very much. It is very pretty. How much is it?

5. **Je la prends avec moi tout de suite.**
   zhe la prah ah-vehk mwah tood sweet.
   I'll take it with me right away.

For more verbs, expressions, and popular words commonly used, consult page 599.

Basic verbs, expressions, and words useful in this situation:

nager   *na-zh-ay*   to swim

plonger   *ploh-zh-ay*   to dive

faire du ski nautique   *fehr dew skee nu-teek* to water-ski

prendre un bain de soleil   *prah-dre uh behd sul-ay*   to sunbathe

se bronzer   *se broh-zay*   to get a suntan

une piscine   *ewn pee-seen*   swimming pool

une limonade   *ewn lee-mun-ahd*   lemonade

les vagues   *lay vahg*   waves

un maillot de bain   *uh ma-yohd beh*   a swimsuit

un sauveteur   *uh sov-tur*   lifeguard

la réanimation cardio-pulmonaire   *la ray-anee-mas-y-oh kard-yo pewl-mun-ehr*   CPR (cardiopulmonary resuscitation)

acheter   *ash-tay*   to buy, to purchase

louer   *loo-ay*   to rent, to hire

prendre   *prah-dre*   to take

boire   *bwahr*   to drink

dans la mer   *dah la mehr*   in the sea

l'eau   *loh*   water

une lotion solaire   *ewn lu-see-oh sul-ehr*   suntan lotion

salé   *sa-lay*   salty

le sable   *le sa-ble*   sand

apprendre à nager   *a-prah-dre a na-zh-ay* to learn to swim

une gazeuse   *ewn ga-zuh-z*   carbonated drink

la crème solaire   *la krehm sul-ehr*   suntan lotion

Basic statements and questions useful in this situation:

1. **Je voudrais passer quelques jours à la plage à Cannes.**
   zhe voo-dreh pah-say kehl-ke zh-oor a la plah-zh a kahn.
   I would like to spend a few days at the beach at Cannes.

2. **J'ai pris assez de soleil. Je vais nager maintenant. Tu viens avec moi?**
   zh-ay pree a-sayd sul-ay. zhe veh na-zh-ay meh-te-nah. tew vee-eh a-vehk mwah?
   I've had enough sun. I'm going to swim now. Are you coming with me?

3. **Je voudrais louer un parasol parce que le soleil est très fort aujourd'hui.**
   zhe voo-dreh loo-ay uh pa-ra-sul pahr-se-ke le sul-ay eh treh fu-r oh-zh-oor-dwee.
   I would like to rent a beach umbrella because the sun is very strong today.

For more verbs, expressions, and popular words commonly used, consult page 599.

Basic verbs, expressions, and words useful in this situation:

partir *pahr-teer* to leave

régler mon compte *ray-glay mõh kõh-t* to pay (for) my bill

je dois partir *zhe dwah pahr-teer* I must leave

nous devons partir *nood võh pahr-teer* we must leave

combien je vous dois? *kõh-bee-eh zhe voo dwah?* how much do I owe you?

payer *pay-ay* to pay

un reçu *uh re-sew* receipt

ce soir *se swahr* this evening

mes bagages *may ba-ga-zh* my luggage

demain matin *de-mẽh ma tẽh* tomorrow morning

tôt *toh* early

avant midi *avãh mee-dee* before noon

tout est en règle? *too teh tãh reh-gle* everything is accounted for?

mon séjour *mõh say-zh-oor* my stay

très bien *treh bee-eh* very fine

très agréable *treh za-gray-abl* very pleasant

appelez un taxi, s'il vous plaît *a-play uh tak-see, seel-voo-pleh* call a taxi, please

Basic statements and questions useful in this situation:

1. **Je vais partir demain matin avant midi.**
   zhe veh pahr-teer de-mẽh ma-tẽh avãh mee-dee.
   I'm going to leave tomorrow morning before noon.

2. **Avant quelle heure dois-je quitter la chambre?**
   avãh kehl ur dwah-zh keè-tay la sh-ãh-bre?
   Before what time must I leave the room?

3. **Mon séjour dans votre hôtel a été très agréable.**
   mõh say-zh-oor dãh vut-re oh-tehl a ay-tay treh za-gray-abl.
   My stay in your hotel has been very pleasant.

4. **Je voudrais régler mon compte tout de suite, s'il vous plaît.**
   zhe voo-dreh ray-glay mõh kõh-t tood sweet, seel-voo-pleh.
   I would like to pay for my bill right away, please.

5. **Aidez-moi à descendre mes bagages, s'il vous plaît.**
   ay-day mwah a day-sãh-dre may ba-ga-zh seel-voo-pleh.
   Help me bring down my luggage, please.

For more verbs, expressions, and popular words commonly used, consult page 599.

Basic verbs, expressions, and words useful in this situation:

contrôler *kōh-troh-lay* to control
présenter *pray-zāh-tay* to present
je ne sais pas *zhe ne seh pah* I don't know
excusez-moi *ehks-kew-zay mwah* excuse me
je ne comprends pas *zhe ne kōh-prāh pah* I don't understand
déclarer *day-kla-ray* to declare
un voyage d'affaires *ūh vwah-y-ahzh da-fehr* a business trip
je rentre chez moi *zhe rāh-tre shay mwah* I'm returning home

voici . . . *vwah-see* here is (are) . . .
donner *dun-nay* to give
je le regrette *zhe le re-greht* I'm sorry
oui, je parle français *wee, zhe parl frāh-seh* yes I speak French
je comprends *zhe kōh-prāh* I understand
un peu *ūh puh* a little
parlez lentement, s'il vous plaît *par-lay lāh-te-māh, seel-voo-pleh* speak slowly, please
rien *ree-ēh* nothing
usage personnel *ew-zah-zh pehr-sun-ehl* personal use

Basic statements and questions useful in this situation:

1. **Voici mon passeport et voici mes bagages.**
   vwah-see mōh pahs-pu-r ay vwah-see may ba-ga-zh.
   Here is my passport and here are my suitcases (my luggage).

2. **Je vais ouvrir mes bagages. Je cherche mes clefs.**
   zhe veh oo-vreer may ba-ga-zh. zhe sh-ehr-sh may klay.
   I'm going to open my luggage. I'm looking for my keys.

3. **Je n'ai rien à déclarer. J'ai seulement des articles d'usage personnel.**
   zhe nay ree-ēh a day-kla-ray. zhay sul-māh day zar-tee-kle dew-zah-zh pehr-sun-ehl.
   I have nothing to declare. I have only articles for personal use.

4. **J'ai passé un séjour très agréable dans votre pays! Au revoir!**
   zhay pah-say ūh say-zh-oor treh za-gray-abl dāh vut-re pay-ee! u-re-vwahr!
   I spent a very pleasant stay in your country! Good-bye!

For more verbs, expressions, and popular words commonly used, consult page 599.

Popular phrases, words, and expressions for travelers

This feature provides you with many popular phrases, words, expressions, abbreviations, signs, and notices that you will most likely need to understand when you hear them or when you see them posted in many public places in France or any French-speaking country or region of the world. There are also many you will need to use yourself when speaking French.

All the entries in English and French are given in one alphabetical listing. It is more convenient to look in one place instead of two for an entry. One listing also prevents you from looking inadvertently in a French listing for an English word or in an English listing for a French word. Also, cognates and near-cognates in both languages are reduced to a single entry. French words are printed in boldface letters. After the French phrase or word, you are given an approximate sound so you may pronounce the French as well as possible to communicate effectively. Consult the *EE-zee* guide to French pronunciation on page 566.

If you do not find the word or phrase you have in mind, perhaps it is given in the thirty situations that precede this section. Be sure to consult the guide to situations on page 568. Also, if there is a French verb you wish to use that is not given in this section, consult the 501 verbs in this book and the English-French verb index that begins on page 503.

A

a, an, **un** *uh;* **une** *ewn;* **un crayon** *uh kray-yoh* a pencil;
une orange *ewn u-rah-zh* an orange

A DROITE *a-drwaht* TO THE RIGHT

A GAUCHE *a-goh-sh* TO THE LEFT
a little **un peu** *uh-puh*
a lot **beaucoup** *boh-koo*

A LOUER *a-loo-ay* FOR RENT (HIRE)

A VENDRE *a-vah-dre* FOR SALE

ACCES AUX QUAIS *ak-seh-oh-keh* TO PLATFORMS
advertisement **une réclame** *ewn-ray-klahm*
advise **conseiller** *koh-say-ay*
after me **après moi** *a-pray-mwah*
agneau *(m.)* *a-ny-oh* lamb

AIDS **SIDA** *see-dah* (sexually transmitted infectious disease)
air **air** *ehr*
air conditioned **climatisé** *klee-ma-tee-zay*
airmail **par avion** *pahr a-vee-oh*
airplane **un avion** *uh na-vee-oh*
airport **aéroport** *(m.)* *a-ay-roh-pohr*
alone **seul** *sul*
also **aussi** *oh-see*
always **toujours** *too-zh-oor*
amandine *ah-mah-deen* with almonds

ambulance   **une ambulance**   *ewn $\overline{ah}$-bew-$\overline{lah}$-ss*

American, I am   **je suis américain** *(m.)*   *zhe swee a-may-ree-$\overline{keh}$;*   **je suis américaine**
   (f.)   *zhe swee a-may-ree-kehn*

American Hospital of Paris   **l'Hôpital Américain de Paris**   *loh-pee-tal a-may-ree-$\overline{keh}$*
   de pah-ree (located in Neuilly, a suburb of Paris, about 20 minutes by taxi from the Arc
   de Triomphe)

and   **et**   *ay*

and you?   **et vous?**   *ay-voo*

andouille *(f.)*   *$\overline{ah}$-doo-y*   pork sausage

apple   **une pomme**   *ewn-pum*

appuyez sur le bouton   *a-pew-ee-ay sewr le boo-$\overline{toh}$*   press the button

April   **avril**   *a-vreel*

are there . . .?   **y a-t-il . . .?**   *ee-a-teel*

ASCENSEUR   *a-$\overline{sah}$-sur*   ELEVATOR (LIFT)

ashtray   **un cendrier**   *$\overline{uh}$ $\overline{sah}$-dree-ay*

ask for   **demander**   *de-$\overline{mah}$-day*

assure   **assurer**   *a-sewr-ay*

at   **à**   *a;*   at all costs   **à tout prix**   *a-too-pree*

ATTENDEZ   *a-$\overline{tah}$-day*   WAIT

ATTENTION   *a-$\overline{tah}$-see-$\overline{oh}$*   CAUTION

ATTENTION AU CHIEN MECHANT   *a-$\overline{tah}$-see-$\overline{oh}$ oh shee-$\overline{eh}$ may-sh-$\overline{ah}$*   BEWARE OF
   THE DOG

ATTENTION AUX MARCHES   *a-$\overline{tah}$-see-$\overline{oh}$ oh marsh*   WATCH OUT FOR THE STEPS

au jus   *oh-zh-ew*   in clear gravy (natural juices)

aubergine *(f.)*   *oh-behr-zh-een*   eggplant

August   **août**   *oot* (*oo* is also correct)

Australia   **Australie**   *us-tra-lee*

Australian, I am   **je suis australien** *(m.)*   *zhe swee us-tra-lee-$\overline{eh}$;*   **je suis australienne**
   (f.)   *zhe swee us-tra-lee-ehn*

auto   **une auto**   *ewn u-toh;* automobile   **une automobile**   *ewn u-toh-mu-beel*

automatic   **automatique**   *u-toh-ma-teek*

AVIS   *a-vee*   NOTICE

awful   **épouvantable**   *ay-poo-$\overline{vah}$-table*

B

baby   **un bébé**   *$\overline{uh}$ bay-bay;*   baby bottle   **un biberon**   *$\overline{uh}$ beeb-$\overline{roh}$*

bad   **mauvais**   *mu-veh;*   **mal**   *mahl*

baggage   **les bagages** *(m. pl.)*   *lay ba-ga-zh*

baggage cart   **un chariot**   *$\overline{uh}$ shah-ree-oh*

baggage checking room   **la consigne**   *la $\overline{koh}$-see-ny*

bakery   **une boulangerie**   *ewn boo-$\overline{lah}$-zh-ree*

band-aid   **un pansement**   *$\overline{uh}$ $\overline{pah}$-smah;*   **un bandage**   *$\overline{uh}$ $\overline{bah}$-dah-zh*

bank   **une banque**   *ewn $\overline{bah}$-k*

bar of chocolate   **une tablette de chocolat**   *ewn tah-bleht de shu-ku-lah* bargain **soldes** *suld*

bath, to take a **prendre un bain** *prah-dre uh beh*

bathroom **une salle de bains** *ewn sal de beh*

beat it! (get away from me!) **fichez-moi le camp!** *fee-shay mwahl kah*

bed **un lit** *uh lee;* bed and board **logement et nourriture** *lu-zh-mah ay noo-ree-tewr*

bed bug **une punaise** *ewn pew-neh-z* (also the word for thumbtack)

bedpan **un bassin de lit** *uh ba-sehd lee*

bedspread **un dessus de lit** *uh de-sewd-lee*

beef **le boeuf** *le buf*

beer **une bière** *ewn bee-ehr;* **un demi** *uh dmee* (glass of beer)

behind **derrière** *deh-ree-ehr*

believe me **croyez-moi** *krwah-yay mwah*

bib (for baby) **une bavette (pour le bébé)** *ewn bah-veht (poor le bay-bay)*

bicycle **une bicyclette** *ewn bee-see-kleht;* bike **un vélo** *uh vay-loh*

black **noir** *nwahr;* black coffee **un café noir** *uh ka-fay nwahr*

bless you! **salut!** *sa-lew*

blood **le sang** *le sah*

blue **bleu** *bluh*

boarding pass (on ship) **la carte d'embarquement** *la kart dah-bark-mah;* (on plane) **la carte d'accès à bord** *la kart dak-seh a bu-r*

boat **un bateau** *uh ba-toh*

boeuf *buf* beef

BON MARCHE *boh mar-shay* INEXPENSIVE

boss **le patron** *le pa-troh;* **la patronne** *la pa-trun*

bottle **une bouteille** *ewn boo-tay*

bottle opener **un ouvre-bouteille** *uh noo-vre boo-tay*

bottled water **de l'eau en bouteille** *de loh ah boo-tay*

boudin *boo-deh* thick dark sausage made of inner parts of pig

bourguignon *boor-gee-ny-oh* beef stew braised in red wine

bread **le pain** *le peh;* some bread **du pain** *dew peh*

breakdown (vehicle, machine) **en panne** *ah-pahn*

breakfast **un petit déjeuner** *uh ptee day-zh-uh-nay*

bring it here! **apportez-le ici!** *a-pohr-tay-le ee-see;* **apportez-la ici!** *a-pohr-tay-la ee-see;* bring them here! **apportez-les ici!** *a-pohr-tay-lay ee-see*

bring me . . . , please **apportez-moi . . . , s'il vous plaît** *a-pohr-tay-mwah seel-voo-pleh*

brochette *(f.)* *brush-eht* chunks of meat and vegetables skewered and grilled, like a shish kabob

brown **brun** *bruh*

BUFFET *bew-fay* SNACK BAR

bulb (electric light) **une ampoule** *ewn ah-pool*

BUREAU DE CHANGE *bew-rohd sh-ah-zh* MONEY EXCHANGE OFFICE

business **les affaires** *lay-za-fehr*

but **mais** *meh*

butter **le beurre** *le bur;* some butter **du beurre** *dew bur*

C

CAISSE *keh-ss* CASHIER'S DESK

calculator **une calculatrice** *ewn kal-kew-la-treess*

call an ambulance! **appelez une ambulance!** *ap-lay ewn āh-bew-lāh-ss*

call me **appelez-moi** *ap-lay-mwah;* call me (phone me) **téléphonez-moi** *tay-lay-fun-nay mwah*

call the police! **appelez la police!** *ap-lay la pul-eess*

can I . . .? **puis-je . . .?** *pew-ee-zh . . .*

can opener **un ouvre-boîte** *uh noo-vre bwaht*

Canadian, I am **je suis canadien** *(m.)* *zhe swee ka-na-dee-ēh;* **je suis canadienne** *(f.)* *zhe swee ka-na-dee-ehn*

canard *(m.)* *ka-nahr* duck

candy **bonbons** *(m. pl.)* *bōh-boh*

car (auto) **une voiture** *ewn vwah-tewr;* **une auto** *ewn u-toh*

cart **un chariot** *uh shah-ree-oh*

cashier's desk **la caisse** *la keh-ss*

CEDEZ *say-day* YIELD

celebrate **fêter** *feh-tay;* **célébrer** *say-lay-bray*

celebration **une célébration** *ewn say-lay-brah-see-ōh*

CHANGE *sh-āh-zh* MONEY EXCHANGE

CHAUD *sh-oh* HOT

check (to pay, as in a restaurant) **l'addition** *la-dee-see-ōh*

check (the baggage) **faire enregistrer les bagages** *fehr āh-re-zh-eess-tray lay ba-ga-zh*

cheese **le fromage** *le frum-ah-zh*

cheese sandwich **un sandwich au fromage** *uh sāh-dwee-sh oh frum-ah-zh*

CHEMIN PRIVE *sh-mēh pree-vay* PRIVATE ROAD

chest (human body) **la poitrine** *la pwah-treen*

chicken **le poulet** *le poo-leh*

child **enfant** *āh-fāh;* sick child **enfant malade** *āh-fāh mal-ahd*

children **les enfants** *lay zāh-fāh*

chocolate **le chocolat** *le shu-ku-lah*

choose **choisir** *sh-wa-zeer*

cigarette lighter **un briquet** *uh bree-kay*

citron *(m.)* *see-trōh* lemon; **au citron** *oh see-trōh* lemon flavor

clean **propre** *pru-pre*

CLIMATISE *klee-ma-tee-zay* AIR CONDITIONED

close the door, please **fermez la porte, s'il vous plaît** *fehr-may la pohrt, seel-voo-pleh*

close the window **fermez la fenêtre** *fehr-may laf-neh-tre*

clothes, clothing **les vêtements** *lay veht-māh*

coat (overcoat) **le manteau** *le māh-toh*

cockroach **un cafard** *uh ka-far,* **une blatte** *ewn blaht*

coffee **le café** *le ka-fay*

coffee with lots of milk **un café au lait** *uh ka-fay oh leh*

cold **froid** *fr-wah;* I feel cold **j'ai froid** *zhay fr-wah;* it's cold in my room
il fait froid dans ma chambre *eel feh fr-wah dah ma sh-ah-bre*

comic strips **les bandes dessinées** *lay bah-d day-see-nay*

COMPLET *koh-pleh* FULL (NO ROOM, NO VACANCIES, NO SEATS)

computer **un ordinateur** *uh nu-r-dee-na-tur*

concert **un concert** *uh koh-sehr*

connect me with . . . (on phone) **passez-moi . . .** *pah-say mwah*

CONSIGNE *koh-see-ny* BAGGAGE CHECK

contrary, on the **au contraire** *oh koh-trehr*

cool! swell! great! neat! **chouette!** *sh-weht!*

cork **un bouchon** *uh boo-sh-oh;* corkscrew **un tire-bouchon** *uh teer boo-sh-oh*

corner **le coin** *le kw-eh*

CORRESPONDANCE *ku-rehs-poh-dah-ss* transfer, connection, change trains

counter **le comptoir** *le koh-twahr*

cream **la crème** *la krehm;* with cream **avec crème** *a-vehk krehm;* without cream **sans crème** *sah krehm*

creamed soup **la soupe purée** *la soop pew-ray*

credit card **la carte de crédit** *la kart de kray-dee,* **la carte bancaire** *la kart b-ah-kehr*

croque-madame *(m.)* *kruk-ma-dahm* grilled cheese sandwich with ham

croque-monsieur *(m.)* *kruk-me-sy-uh* grilled cheese sandwich

cut (hair) **couper les cheveux** *koo-pay lay sh-vuh*

D

DAMES *dahm* LADIES

DANGER DE MORT *dah-zhay de mu-r* DANGER OF DEATH

dangerous, it's **c'est dangereux** *seh dah-zh-ruh*

dark (color) **foncé** *foh-say*

day **le jour** *le zh-oor*

dead **mort** *(m.)* *mu-r;* **morte** *(f.)* *mu-rt*

dear me! **ma foi!** *ma fwah*

decaffeinated **décaféiné** *day-kah-fay-een-ay*

December **décembre** *day-sah-bre*

DEFENDU *day-fah-dew* FORBIDDEN

DEFENSE DE . . . *day-fah-ss de* NO . . . ALLOWED

DEFENSE D'AFFICHER *day-fah-ss da-fee-shay* POST NO BILLS (SIGNS)

DEFENSE DE FUMER *day-fah-ss de few-may* NO SMOKING

DEFENSE D'ENTRER *day-fah-ss dah-tray* KEEP OUT

DEVIATION *day-vee-a-see-oh* DETOUR

diamond **un diamant** *uh dee-ah-mah*

Popular phrases, words, and expressions for travelers **603**

dinde *(f.)* *dēh-d* turkey; **dindon** *(m.)* *dēh-doh*

dining room **la salle à manger** *la sal a māh-zh-ay*

dirty **sale** *sahl;* dirty water **de l'eau sale** *de loh sahl*

disease **une maladie** *ewn ma-la-dee*

dizziness **le vertige** *le vehr-tee-zh*

do **faire** *fehr*

do you speak English? **parlez-vous anglais?** *par-lay voo āh-gleh;* German? **allemand?** *al-māh;* Greek? **grec?** *gr-eh-k;* Italian? **italien?** *ee-ta-lee-ēh;* Spanish? **espagnol?** *ess-pa-ny-ul*

don't mention it? (you're welcome!) **de rien** *de ree-ēh;* **il n'y a pas de quoi** *eel-nee-a-pahd-kwah;* **je vous en prie** *zhe voo-zāh-pree*

don't tell me! **ne me dites pas!** *nem deet-pah*

DOUANE *dwahn* CUSTOMS

double lock the door **fermez la porte à clef, à double tour** *fehr-may la pohrt a klay, a doo-bluh toor*

dozen **une douzaine** *ewn doo-zehn*

dress **une robe** *ewn rub*

drink *(v.)* **boire** *bwahr;* drink *(n.)* **une boisson** *ewn bwah-soh*

drugstore **une pharmacie** *ewn far-ma-see*

Dutch, I am **je suis hollandais** *(m.)* *zhe swee ul-āh-deh;* **je suis hollandaise** *(f.)* *zhe swee ul-āh-deh-z*

E

early **tôt** *toh;* **de bonne heure** *de bun ur*

eat **manger** *māh-zh-ay*

EAU NON POTABLE *oh nōh put-ah-ble* DO NOT DRINK THIS WATER

EAU POTABLE *oh put-ah-ble* DRINKING WATER

egg **un oeuf** *uh nuf* (sounds very much like the English word enough)

eight **huit** *ew-eet*

eighteen **dix-huit** *deez-ew-eet*

eighth **huitième** *ew-eet-ee-ehm*

eighty **quatre-vingts** *katre-vēh*

eighty-one **quatre-vingt-un** *katre-vēh-ūh*

eighty-two **quatre-vingt-deux** *katre-vēh-duh*

electricity **électricité** *(f.)* *ay-lehk-tree-see-tay*

eleven **onze** *ōh-z*

embassy **ambassade** *(f.)* *āh-bah-sahd*

emergency **urgence** *(f.)* *ewr-zh-āh-s*

émincé *ay-mēh-say* sliced thinly (meat)

EMPORTER *āh-pohr-tay* FOOD CARRY-OUT

EN PANNE *āh-pahn* OUT OF ORDER, OUT OF SERVICE

England **l'Angleterre** *lāh-gle-tehr*

English, I am **je suis anglais** *(m.)* *zhe swee āh-gleh;* **je suis anglaise** *(f.)* *zhe swee āh-gleh-z*

enough **assez** *ah-say;* not enough **pas assez** *pah-zah-say*

entrecôte (f.) *ah-tre-koht* sirloin or rib steak

ENTREE *ah-tray* ENTRANCE

ENTREE INTERDITE *ah-tray eh-tehr-deet* KEEP OUT, DO NOT ENTER

ENTREE LIBRE *ah-tray lee-bre* FREE ADMISSION

ENTREZ SANS FRAPPER *ah-tray sah fra-pay* ENTER WITHOUT KNOCKING

envelope **une enveloppe** *ewn ah-vlup*

error **une erreur** *ewn ehr-ur*

exasperated **outré** *oo-tray*

excuse me **excusez-moi** *ehks-kew-zay-mwah*

F

facing the courtyard **donnant sur la cour** *dun-ah sewr la koor;* the garden **le jardin** *le zh-ar-deh;* the street **la rue** *la rew*

family **une famille** *ewn fah-mee*

far from **loin de** *lweh de*

faucet **un robinet** *uh rub-ee-nay*

fault **une faute** *ewn foh-t*

February **février** *fay-vree-ay*

FEMMES *fahm* WOMEN

FERME *fehr-may* CLOSED

fever **fièvre** (f.) *la fee-eh-vre*

fifteen **quinze** *keh-z*

fifth **cinquième** *seh-kee-ehm*

fifty **cinquante** *seh-kah-t*

filet (m.) *fee-leh* boneless meat or fish

find **trouver** *troo-vay*

fine! **bien!** *bee-eh*

finish **finir** *fee-neer*

fire **feu** (m.) *le fuh*

first **premier** *pre-mee-ay;* **première** *pre-mee-ehr*

fish **poisson** (m.) *le pwah-ssoh*

five **cinq** *seh-k*

flag **un drapeau** *uh drah-poh;* French flag **le tricolore** *le tree-ku-lu-r*

flambé *flah-bay* brandy or liqueur in a flame over food

flan (m.) *flah* baked custard

flea **une puce** *ewn pew-ss;* flea market **le marché aux puces** *le mar-shay oh pew-ss*

flight (airplane) **le vol** *le vul*

florentine *flu-rah-teen* cooked with spinach

fly (n.) **une mouche** *ewn moosh*

fly (v.) **voler** *vul-ay*

follow **suivre** *swee-vre;* why are you following me?
pourquoi me suivez-vous? *poor-kwah me swee-vay voo?*

food **alimentation** *(f.)* *a-lee-mah̄-ta-see-oh̄*
foot **pied** *(m.)* *le pee-ay*
for **pour** *poor;* for me **pour moi** *poor mwah*
fork **une fourchette** *ewn foor-sh-eht*
forty **quarante** *ka-rah̄-t*
forty-one **quarante et un** *ka-rah̄-t ay uh̄*
forty-two **quarante-deux** *ka-rah̄-t duh*
four **quatre** *katre*
fourteen **quatorze** *ka-torz*
fourth **quatrième** *ka-tree-ehm*
francophone *frah̄-koh-fun* French-speaking
Friday **vendredi** *vah̄-dre-dee*
frites *(f.)* *freet* French fries

FROID *fr-wah* COLD
front **devant** *de-vah̄*

FUMEURS *few-mur* SMOKING PERMITTED
funny **drôle** *drohl*

G

game **le jeu** *le zh-uh;* games **les jeux** *lay-zh-uh*
gasoline (petrol) **essence** *(f.)* *ay-sah-ss*

GAZON *ga-zoh̄* LAWN; **NE MARCHEZ PAS SUR LE GAZON** *ne mar-shay pah sewr le ga-zoh̄* DO NOT WALK ON THE GRASS (LAWN)
German, I am **je suis allemand** *(m.)* *zhe swee al-mah̄;* **je suis allemande** *(f.)* *zhe swee al-mah̄-d*
Germany **Allemagne** *al-ma-ny*
get a doctor **appelez un médecin** *ap-lay uh̄ mayd-seh̄*
get away from me! **fichez-moi le camp!** *fee-shay mwahl kah̄*
get help right away! **à l'aide tout de suite!** *a-lehd tood sweet*
get something, to **chercher quelque chose** *sh-ehr-shay kehl-ke sh-oh-z*
gift **un cadeau** *uh̄ ka-doh;* **un don** *uh̄ doh̄*
give me **donnez-moi** *dun-nay mwah;* give us **donnez-nous** *dun-nay noo*
glass (for drinking) **un verre** *uh̄ vehr*
go away! **allez-vous en!** *a-lay voo-zah̄;* **filez!** *fee-lay*
go by **passer** *pah-say*
go down the stairs **descendre l'escalier** *day-sah̄-dre lay-ska-lee-ay*
go out **sortir** *sor-teer*
go up the stairs **monter l'escalier** *moh̄-tay lay-ska-lee-ay*
God **Dieu** *dee-uh*
good! **bon!** *boh̄*
good afternoon **bonjour** *boh̄-zhoor*
good-bye **au revoir** *u-re-vwahr*
good day **bonjour** *boh̄-zhoor*
good evening **bonsoir** *boh̄-swahr*
good idea! **bonne idée!** *bun ee-day*
good morning **bonjour** *boh̄-zhoor*

good news **bonnes nouvelles** *bun noo-vehl*

good night **bonsoir** *bōh-swahr;* (when going to sleep) **bonne nuit** *bun new-ee*

good trip! **bon voyage!** *bōh vwah-yah-zh*

good work **bon travail** *bōh tra-vah-y*

Great Britain **la Grande Bretagne** *la grāh-d bre-ta-ny*

Greek, I am **je suis grec** *(m.)* *zhe swee gr-eh-k;* **je suis grecque** *(f.)* *zhe swee gr-eh-k*

green **vert** *vehr*

H

hair **les cheveux** *lay sh-vuh*

haircut **une coupe de cheveux** *ewn koop de sh-vuh*

half **la moitié** *la mwah-tee-ay*

ham sandwich **un sandwich au jambon** *uh sāh-dwee-sh oh zh-āh-bōh*

handbag **un sac à main** *uh sak-a-mēh*

hang up! (on telephone) **raccrochez!** *ra-krush-ay*

happy **content** *kōh-tāh*

happy anniversary! **bon anniversaire!** *bun-a-nee-vehr-sehr* (same French expression for happy birthday)

HAUTE TENSION *oh-t tāh-see-ōh* HIGH VOLTAGE

have a nice day! **passez une bonne journée!** *pah-say ewn bun zh-oor-nay*

he **il** *eel*

headache **un mal de tête** *uh mal de teht*

heat **la chaleur** *la sh-a-lur*

heating **le chauffage** *le sh-oh-fah-zh*

hello! **bonjour!** *bōh-zhoor;* (on the phone) **allô** *a-loh*

help! **au secours!** *oh-skoor*

help me! **aidez-moi!** *ay-day mwah*

here **ici** *ee-see*

here I am! **me voici!** *me vwah-see*

here it is! **le voici!** *le vwah-see*

hold on, please (on the phone) **ne quittez pas, s'il vous plaît** *ne keet-ay pah, seel-voo-pleh*

HOMMES *um* MEN

HORS SERVICE *or sehr-veess* OUT OF SERVICE

hospital **l'hôpital** *(m.)* *loh-pee-tal*

hot **chaud** *sh-oh;* I feel hot **j'ai chaud** *zhay sh-oh;* it's too hot in my room **il fait trop chaud dans ma chambre** *eel feh troh sh-oh dāh ma sh-āh-bre*

hot chocolate **un chocolat chaud** *uh shu-ku-lah sh-oh*

hour **heure** *(f.)* *ur*

how **comment** *kem-māh*

how are things? **ça va?** *sah-vah*

how are you? **comment allez-vous?** *kum-māh tal-ay-voo*

how do you say . . . ? **comment dit-on . . . ?** *kum-māh deet-ōh*

how far? **à quelle distance?** *a kehl dee-stāh-ss*

how long? (time) **combien de temps?** *kōh-bee-ēh de tāh*

how long? (length) **quelle longueur?** *kehl lōh-gur*

how many? how much? **combien?** *kōh-bee-ēh*

how much does this cost? **combien coûte ceci?** *kōh-bee-ēh koot se-see*

HUIS CLOS *ew-ee kloh* NO EXIT

hundred **cent** *sah*

hurry, in a **pressé** *preh-say*

hurry up! **dépêchez-vous!** *day-peh-shay-voo*

husband **le mari** *ma-ree*

I

I **je** *zhe*

I assure you **je vous assure** *zhe voo za-sewr*

I beg your pardon **pardonnez-moi, je vous en prie** *par-dun-ay-mwah, zhe voo-zāh-pree*

I don't know **je ne sais pas** *zhen seh pah*

I don't like . . . **je n'aime pas . . .** *zhe nehm pah*

I don't understand **je ne comprends pas** *zhen kōh-prāh pah*

I don't want . . . **je ne veux pas . . .** *zhen vuh pah*

I hate it **je le déteste** *zhel day-tehst*

I have a problem **j'ai un problème** *zhay ūh pru-blehm*

I have no money **je n'ai pas d'argent** *zhe nay pah dar-zh-āh*

I like **j'aime** *zh-ehm;* I like it **je l'aime** *zhe lehm*

I love it **je l'adore** *zhe la-du-r*

I love you **je vous aime** *zhe voo zehm* (If you know the person intimately, you can say: **je t'aime** *zhe tehm*)

I speak a little French **je parle un peu français** *zhe parl ūh puh frāh-seh*

I understand **je comprends** *zhe kōh-prāh*

I visited . . . **j'ai visité . . .** *zhay vee-zee-tay*

I went . . . **je suis allé(e) . . .** *zhe swee za-lay*

ice cream **la glace (à la crème)** *la glahss a la krehm*

ice cubes (chips) **des glaçons** *day glah-soh*

iced water **de l'eau glacée** *de loh glah-say*

I'd like . . . **je voudrais . . .** *zhe voo-dreh*

if **si** *see*

I'm afraid **j'ai peur** *zhay pur*

I'm bleeding **je saigne** *zhe seh-ny*

I'm broke (I have no money) **je suis fauché** *zhe swee foh-shay*

I'm going . . . **je vais . . .** *zhe veh*

I'm going to have . . . **je vais avoir . . .** *zhe veh za-vwahr*

I'm hungry **j'ai faim** *zhay fēh*

I'm married **je suis marié(e)** *zhe swee ma-ree-ay*

I'm resting **je me repose** *zhem re-pohz*

I'm sad **je suis triste** *zhe swee treest*

I'm single (unmarried) **je suis célibataire** *zhe swee say-lee-ba-tehr*

I'm sleepy **j'ai sommeil** *zhay sum-ay*

I'm thirsty **j'ai soif** *zhay swahf*

I'm tired **je suis fatigué(e)** *zhe swee fa-tee-gay*

I'm wounded **je suis blessé(e)** *zhe swee bleh-say*
immediately **immédiatement** *ee-may-dee-at-mah;* **tout de suite** *tood sweet*

IMPASSE *eh-pahss* DEAD END
in **dans** *dah;* **en** *ah*
in a minute **dans une minute** *dah zewn mee-newt*
in English **en anglais** *ah nah-gleh*
in French **en français** *ah frah-seh*
in front of me **devant moi** *de-vah mwah*
included **compris** *koh-pree;* **inclus** *eh-klew*
infant **un bébé** *uh bay-bay*
information **renseignements** *rah-seh-ny-mah*
insect **un insecte** *uh neh-sehkt*
inside **dedans** *de-dah*

INTERDIT *eh-tehr-dee* FORBIDDEN
introduce **présenter** *pray-zah-tay;* this is Mr. . . . , Mrs. . . . , Miss . . . **je vous présente Monsieur . . . , Madame . . . , Mademoiselle . . .** *zhe voo pray-zah-t me-sy-uh . . . , ma-dahm . . . , mad-mwah-zehl . . .*
Ireland **Irlande** *eer-lah-d*
Irish, I am **je suis irlandais** *(m.)* *zhe swee eer-lah-deh;* **je suis irlandaise** *(f.)* *zhe swee eer-lah-dehz*
iron (press) **repasser** *re-pah-say*
is it closed? **c'est fermé?** *seh fehr-may*
is it correct? **c'est correct?** *seh ku-reh-kt*
is it necessary? **faut-il?** *foh-teel;* **est-il nécessaire?** *eh-teel nay-say-sehr*
is it open? **c'est ouvert?** *seh too-vehr*
is there . . . ? **y a-t-il . . . ?** *ee-a-teel*
isn't that so? **n'est-ce pas?** *neh-spah*
it doesn't matter **ça ne fait rien** *sahn feh ree-eh;* **n'importe** *neh-pohrt*
Italian, I am **je suis italien** *(m.)* *zhe swee ee-ta-lee-eh;* **je suis italienne** *(f.)* *zhe swee ee-ta-lee-ehn*
Italy **Italie** *ee-ta-lee*
it's . . . **c'est . . .** *seh*
it's a pleasure **c'est un plaisir** *seh tuh play-zeer*
it's for me **c'est pour moi** *seh poor mwah*
it's for us **c'est pour nous** *seh poor noo*
it's for you **c'est pour vous** *seh poor voo*
it's funny **c'est drôle** *seh drohl*
it's impossible **c'est impossible** *seh teh-pus-ee-ble*
it's my fault **c'est ma faute** *seh ma foht*
it's possible **c'est possible** *seh pus-ee-ble*
it's your fault **c'est votre faute** *seh vut-re foht*

J

jam (preserves) **la confiture** *la koh-fee-tewr*
jambon *zh-ah-boh* ham
January **janvier** *zh-ah-vee-ay*

jewelry **les bijoux** *lay bee-zh-oo;* jewelry shop **une bijouterie** *ewn bee-zh-oo-tree*

joke **plaisanter** *play-zah̄-tay;* you're joking! **vous plaisantez!** *voo play-zah̄-tay*

juice **un jus** *uh̄ zh-ew*

julienne *zh-ew-lee-ehn* vegetables cut in thin strips

July **juillet** *zh-ew-ee-ay*

June **juin** *zh-weh̄*

just a minute, please **une minute, s'il vous plaît** *ewn mee-newt, seel-voo-pleh*

K

keep it! **gardez-le!** *gar-day-le;* **gardez-la!** *gar-day-la*

key **une clef** *ewn klay*

knife **un couteau** *uh̄ koo-toh*

knock **frapper** *fra-pay;* (you) knock on the door **frappez à la porte** *fra-pay a la pohrt*

L

laitue *leh-tew* lettuce

land (airplane) **atterrir** *a-tehr-eer*

landing card **une carte de débarquement** *ewn kart de day-bark-mah̄*

large **grand** *grah̄;* larger **plus grand** *plew grah̄*

later **plus tard** *plew tar*

leather **le cuir** *le kew-eer*

leave me alone! **laissez-moi tranquille!** *lay-say mwah trah̄-keel*

LENT *lah̄* SLOW

let me get by, please **laissez-moi passer, s'il vous plaît** *lay-say mwah pah-say, seel-voo-pleh*

letter **une lettre** *ewn leh-tre*

LIBRE *lee-bre* VACANT, UNOCCUPIED

light (color) **clair** *klehr;* light (in weight) **léger** *lay-zh-ay;* light (opposite of darkness) **la lumière** *la lew-mee-ehr*

lightbulb **une ampoule** *ewn ah̄-pool*

listen! **écoutez!** *ay-koo-tay*

LOCATIONS *luk-a-see-oh̄* RENTALS

locker (for baggage) **un casier** *uh̄ ka-zee-ay*

lollipop **une sucette** *ewn sew-seht*

look! **regardez!** *re-gar-day*

look out! **attention!** *a-tah̄-see-oh̄*

lost and found office **le bureau des objets trouvés** *le bew-roh day zub-zh-ay troo-vay*

lost, I'm **je me suis perdu(e)** *zhem swee pehr-dew*

lunch **le déjeuner** *le day-zh-uh-nay;* to lunch **prendre le déjeuner** *prah̄-dre le day-zh-uh-nay*

M

machine does not work **la machine ne marche pas** *la ma-sheen ne marsh pah*
madam **madame** *ma-dahm* (abbreviation: **Mme**)
man **un homme** *ūh num*
manager **le gérant** *le zhay-rāh*
many **beaucoup** *boh-koo;* many things **beaucoup de choses** *boh-kood sh-oh-z*
March **mars** *marss.*

MARCHE AUX PUCES *mar-shay oh pew-ss* FLEA MARKET
mashed (whipped) potatoes **purée de pommes de terre** *pew-rayd-pum-de-tehr*
match **une allumette** *ewn a-lew-meht*
may I . . . ? **puis-je. . . ?** *pew-ee-zh*
May **mai** *may*
maybe **peut-être** *puh-teh-tre*
meal **un repas** *ūh re-pah*
message **un message** *ūh mehs-ah-zh*
milk **le lait** *le leh*
mind your own business **occupez-vous de vos affaires** *u-kew-pay vood voh za-fehr*
miss **mademoiselle** *mad-mwah-zehl* (abbreviation: **Mlle**)
mistake **une faute** *ewn foht*
mister **monsieur** *me-sy-uh* (abbreviation: **M.**)

M.M. LADIES AND GENTLEMEN
Monday **lundi** *lūh-dee*
money **argent** *(m.)* *ar-zh-āh*
more **plus** *plew;* more slowly **plus lentement** *plew lāht-māh*
mousse *(f.)* **au chocolat** *mooss oh shu-ku-lah* chocolate pudding
much **beaucoup** *boh-koo*
museum **un musée** *ūh mew-zay*
my child **mon enfant** *mun āh-fāh;* my children **mes enfants** *may-zāh-fāh*
my daughter **ma fille** *ma fee-y*
my family **ma famille** *ma fa-mee-y*
my friend **mon ami(e)** *mun a-mee;* my friends **mes ami(e)s** *may-za-mee*
my God! **mon Dieu!** *mōh dee-uh*
my husband **mon mari** *mōh ma-ree*
my money **mon argent** *mun ar-za-āh*
my, oh, my! **oh! là! là!** *oh-lah-lah*
my purse **mon sac à main** *mōh sak a meh*
my son **mon fils** *mōh feess*
my wallet **mon portefeuille** *mōh pohrt-fu-y*
my wife **ma femme** *ma fahm*
my word! **ma foi!** *ma fwah*
my wristwatch **ma montre** *ma mōh-tre*

N

napkin **une serviette** *ewn sehr-vee-eht*
nationality **la nationalité** *la na-see-un-a-lee-tay*
naturally **naturellement** *na-tewr-ehl-māh*

NE CUEILLEZ PAS LES FLEURS   *ne kuh-yay pah lay flur*   DO NOT PICK THE FLOWERS

NE JAMAIS LAISSER A LA PORTEE DES ENFANTS   *ne zh-a-meh lay-say a la pohrt-ay day zah-fah*   KEEP OUT OF REACH OF CHILDREN

NE JETEZ RIEN PAR LA FENETRE   *ne zh-eht-ay ree-eh pahr la fneh-tre*   DO NOT THROW ANYTHING OUT THE WINDOW

NE MARCHEZ PAS SUR LE GAZON   *ne marsh-ay pah sewr le ga-zoh*   KEEP OFF THE GRASS

NE PAS DERANGER   *ne pah day-rah-zhay*   DO NOT DISTURB

NE PAS TOUCHER   *ne pah too-shay;*   **NE TOUCHEZ PAS**   *ne too-shay pah*   DO NOT TOUCH

near   **près**   *preh;*   **proche**   *prush*

never   **jamais**   *zh-a-meh*

never open   **n'ouvrez jamais**   *noo-vray zh-a-meh*

next to   **à côté de**   *a koh-tay de*

nice day, have a   **passez une bonne journée!**   *pah-say ewn bun zh-oor-nay*

night   **la nuit**   *la new-ee;*   during the night   **pendant la nuit**   *pah-dah la new-ee*

nightclub   **une boîte de nuit**   *ewn bwaht de new-ee*

nine   **neuf**   *nuf*

nineteen   **dix-neuf**   *deez-nuf*

ninety   **quatre-vingt-dix**   *ka-tre-veh-deess*

ninety-one   **quatre-vingt-onze**   *ka-tre-veh-ohz*

ninety-two   **quatre-vingt-douze**   *ka-tre-veh-dooz*

ninth   **neuvième**   *nuh-vee-ehm*

no   **non**   *noh*

no cold water   **pas d'eau froide**   *pahd oh frwahd*

no harm   **pas de mal**   *pahd mahl*

no hot water   **pas d'eau chaude**   *pahd oh sh-oh-d*

no noise   **pas de bruit**   *pahd brew-ee*

no problem   **pas de problème**   *pahd pru-blehm*

no towels   **pas de serviettes**   *pahd sehr-vee-eht*

no water   **pas d'eau**   *pahd-oh*

no way   **pas moyen**   *pah mwah-y-eh*

noodles   **les nouilles** (f.)   *lay noo-y*

not bad   **pas mal**   *pah mahl;*   **pas mauvais**   *pah muv-eh*

November   **novembre**   *nuv-ah-bre*

O

OCCUPE   *u-kew-pay*   OCCUPIED, IN USE

October   **octobre**   *uk-tub-re*

of course   **bien sûr**   *bee-eh sewr*

OK (okay)   **d'accord**   *dak-or;*   **okay**   *u-kay*

on   **sur**   *sewr*

on a business trip   **en voyage d'affaires**   *ah vwah-yah-zh da-fehr*

on a visit   **en visite**   *ah vee-zeet*

ON PARLE ANGLAIS *oh parl ah̄-gleh* ENGLISH IS SPOKEN
on the contrary **au contraire** *oh koh-trehr*
on vacation **en vacances** *ah̄-va-kah̄-ss*
once **une fois** *ewn fwah*
one **un** *uh̄;* **une** *ewn*
one hundred **cent** *sah̄*
only **seulement** *sul-mah̄*
out of order **en panne** *ah̄-pahn*
outside **dehors** *de-or*

OUVERT DE. . .A. . . *oo-vehr de. . .a. . .* OPEN FROM . . . TO . . .
over there **là-bas** *lah-bah*
overcoat **un manteau** *uh̄ mah̄-toh*

P

pain **une douleur** *ewn doo-lur;* I have a pain in my chest **j'ai une douleur dans la poitrine** *zhay ewn doo-lur dah̄ la pwah-treen;* I have a pain in my neck **j'ai une douleur dans le cou** *zhay ewn doo-lur dah̄l koo*
pardon me, please **pardonnez-moi, s'il vous plaît** *pahr-dun-ay-mwah, seel-voo-pleh*
park, public **un parc public** *uh̄ park pew-bleek*
parking (vehicle) lot **un stationnement de voitures** *uh̄ sta-see-un-mah̄ de vwah tewr*
party **une fête** *ewn feht*

PASSAGE SOUTERRAIN *pah-sa-zh soot-reh̄* UNDERGROUND PASSAGE
passenger **un passager** *(m.)* *uh̄ pah-sa-zhay;* **une passagère** *(f.)* *ewn pah-sa-zh-ehr*
passport, lost **passeport perdu** *pahs-pohr pehr-dew*

PEINTURE FRAICHE *peh̄-tewr freh-sh* WET PAINT
percent **pour cent** *poor-sah̄*
perhaps **peut-être** *puh-teh-tre*
peroxide **le peroxyde** *le peh-ruks-eed*
petrol (gasoline) **essence** *(f.)* *ay-sah̄-ss*
phone me **téléphonez-moi** *tay-lay-fun-ay-mwah*

PIETONS *pee-ay-toh̄* PEDESTRIANS
pig **un cochon** *uh̄ kush-oh̄*
pill **une pilule** *ewn pee-lewl*

PISTE POUR CYCLISTES *peest poor see-kleest* BICYCLE ROUTE
please **s'il vous plaît** *seel-voo-pleh*
pleased to meet you **c'est mon plaisir** *seh moh̄ play-zeer*
plumbing **la plomberie** *la ploh̄-bree*
pocket **une poche** *ewn pu-sh*
poison **le poison** *le pwa-zoh̄*
police **la police** *la pul-eess;* I'm going to call the police **je vais appeler la police** *zhe veh ap-lay la pul-eess*
police headquarters **la préfecture de police** *la pray-fehk-tewr de pul-eess*
porter **un porteur** *uh̄ pohr-tur*
potatoes **les pommes de terre** *lay pum-de-tehr*

pot-au-feu *(m.)* *pu-toh-fuh* stew
poulet *(m.)* *poo-leh* chicken

POUSSEZ *poo-say* PUSH
present (gift) **un cadeau** *uh ka-doh*
preserves (jam) **la confiture** *la koh-fee-tewr*
press (iron) **repasser** *re-pah-say*
price **le prix** *le pree*

PRIERE DE. . . *pree-ehr de* YOU ARE REQUESTED . . .
priest **un prêtre** *uh preh-tre*
private bathroom **une salle de bains privée** *ewn sal de beh pree-vay*

PRIVE *pree-vay* PRIVATE
pull **tirez** *tee-ray*
purple **pourpre** *poor-pre,* **violet** *vee-oh-lay*
purse **un sac à main** *uh sak-a-meh*
push **poussez** *poo-say*
put this thing here **mettez cette chose ici** *meht-ay seht sh-oh-z ee-see*
put this thing there **mettez cette chose là** *meht-ay seht sh-oh-z lah*

Q

QUAIS *kay* PLATFORMS (TRAINS)
question **une question** *ewn kehs-tee-oh*
quick, quickly **vite** *veet*
quiet **tranquille** *trah-keel*
quite enough **assez** *ah-say*

R

RABAIS *rah-beh* BARGAINS (SALE, REDUCED PRICES)
ragoût *(m.)* *rah-goo* stew
rain **la pluie** *la plew-ee*

RALENTIR *ra-lah-teer* SLOW DOWN

R.A.T.P. **Régie Autonome des Transports Parisiens** *ray-zh-ee u-tun-um day trah-spohr pah-ree-zee-eh* PARIS TRANSPORT AUTHORITY
razor (electric) **rasoir électrique** *ra-zwahr ay-lehk-treek;* razor blade **une lame** *ewn lahm*
rear, to the **à l'arrière** *a-la-ree-ehr*
receipt **un reçu** *uh re-sew*
red **rouge** *roo-zh*
remain (stay) **rester** *reh-stay*

RENSEIGNEMENTS *rah-seh-ny-mah* INFORMATION
rent (hire) **louer** *loo-ay*
repair **réparer** *ray-pah-ray*

repeat, please **répétez, s'il vous plaît** *ray-pay-tay, seel-voo-pleh*
reservation **réservation** *ray-zehr-va-see-oh*

RESERVE *ray-zehr-vay* **RESERVED**

rest **se reposer** *se re-poh-zay;* I'd like to take a rest **je voudrais me reposer** *zhe voo-dreh me re-poh-zay*
restrooms (toilets) **les toilettes** *lay twa-leht;* **W.C.** (Water Closet) *doo-ble-vay-say*
right away **tout de suite** *tood-sweet*

R.N. **Route Nationale** *root na-see-un-al* national highway
roulade (*f.*) *roo-lahd* rolled slices of meat with a tasty filling

R.S.V.P. **répondez, s'il vous plaît** *ray-poh-day, seel-voo-pleh* answer, please

S

sur *sewr* on
sales slip **une fiche** *ewn feesh*

SALLE D'ATTENTE *sal da-taht* WAITING ROOM
salty **salé** *sal-ay*
Saturday **samedi** *sahm-dee*
seat **une place** *ewn plahss;* **un siège** *uh see-eh-zh*
second floor **deuxième étage** *duh-zee-ehm ay-tah-zh*
security control **le contrôle de sécurité** *le koh-trohl de say-kew-ree-tay*
see you later **à tout à l'heure** *a toot a lur*
see you next week **à la semaine prochaine** *a la smehn prush-ehn*
see you soon **à bientôt** *a bee-eh-toh*
see you tomorrow **à demain** *ad-meh*
see you tonight **à ce soir** *a se swahr*

SENS UNIQUE *sah-ss ew-neek* ONE-WAY STREET
September **septembre** *sehp-tah-bre*

SERREZ A DROITE *seh-ray a drwaht* SQUEEZE TO THE RIGHT

SERREZ A GAUCHE *seh-ray a goh-sh* SQUEEZE TO THE LEFT
service is included? **le service est compris?** *le sehr-veess eh koh-pree*
seven **sept** *seht*
seventeen **dix-sept** *dee-seht*
seventh **septième** *seht-ee-ehm*
seventy **soixante-dix** *swah-saht-deess*
seventy-one **soixante et onze** *swah-saht-ay-oh-z*
seventy-two **soixante-douze** *swah-saht-dooz*
she **elle** *ehl*
show me **montrez-moi** *moh-tray-mwah*
shower (bath) **une douche** *ewn doosh*
shut the door **fermez la porte** *fehr-may la pohrt*
shut the window **fermez la fenêtre** *fehr-may la fneh-tre*
shut your mouth! **fermez la bouche!** *fehr-may la boosh*
sick **malade** *ma-lahd;* I am sick **je suis malade** *zhe swee ma-lahd*
sir **monsieur** *me-sy-uh*

six **six** *seess*

sixteen **seize** *sehz* (sounds exactly like the English word "says")

sixth **sixième** *see-zee-ehm*

sixty **soixante** *swah-sāht*

sixty-one **soixante et un** *swah-sāht-ay-ūh*

sixty-two **soixante-deux** *swah-sāht-duh*

slice **une tranche** *ewn trāh-sh*

slowly **lentement** *lāht-māh*

small **petit** *ptee;* smaller **plus petit** *plew-ptee*

smelling salts **les sels volatils** *lay sehl vul-a-teel*

smoke **fumer** *few-may;* smoking area **pour fumeurs** *poor few-mur*

snack bar **un buffet** *ūh bew-fay;* **un snack bar** *ūh snak-bahr*

S.N.C.F. Société Nationale des Chemins de Fer *su-see-ay-tay na-see-un-al day sh-mēhd fehr* French National Railroads

so sorry to hear that! **je suis désolé!** *zhe swee day-zul-ay*

soap **le savon** *le sa-vōh*

SOLDES *suld* SALE (BARGAINS)

SONNEZ *sun-ay* RING THE BELL

sooner or later **tôt ou tard** *toh-oo-tar*

sorbet *sohr-beh* sherbet

SORTIE *sohr-tee* EXIT

SORTIE DE SECOURS *sohr-tee de skoor* EMERGENCY EXIT

Spain **Espagne** *ehs-pay-ny*

Spanish, I am **je suis espagnol** *(m.)* *zhe swee ehs-pah-ny-ul;* **je suis espagnole** *(f.)* *zhe swee ehs-pay-ny-ul*

spirits of ammonia **essence ammoniaque** *ay-sāh-ss a-mun-ee-ahk*

spoon **une cuillère** *ewn kew-ee-ehr*

sports **les sports** *lay spohr*

spray **un spray** *ūh spray*

STATIONNEMENT INTERDIT *stah-see-un-māh ēh-tehr-dee* NO PARKING

steak *stehk* steak

steal **voler** *vul-ay*

sticker (label) **une étiquette** *ewn ay-tee-keht*

stolen items **des objets volés** *day zub-zhay vul-ay*

stop! **arrêtez!** *a-reht-ay*

stop her! **arrêtez-la!** *a-reht-ay-la*

stop him! **arrêtez-le!** *a-reht-ay-le*

stop that person! **arrêtez cette personne-là!** *a-reht-ay seht pehr-sun lah*

stop the noise! **arrêtez le bruit!** *a-reht-ayl brew-ee*

stop them! **arrêtez-les!** *a-reht-ay lay*

stop thief! **au voleur!** *oh vul-ur*

straight ahead **tout droit** *too-drwah*

straight away **tout de suite** *tood sweet*

stranger **un étranger** *(m.)* *ūh nay-trāh-zhay;* **une étrangère** *(f.)* *ewn ay-trāh-zh-ehr*

strawberry **une fraise** *ewn frehz*

street **la rue** *la rew*
subtitles (at the movies, cinema) **les sous-titres** *(m. pl.) lay soo-tee-tre*
subway (tube) **le métro** *le may-troh*
sugar **le sucre** *le sew-kre;* with sugar **avec sucre** *a-vehk sew-kre;* without sugar
sans sucre *sah̄ sew-kre*
suitcase **une valise** *ewn va-leez*
Sunday **dimanche** *dee-mah̄-sh*
sure **sûr** *sewr;* surely **bien sûr** *bee-ēh sewr*
surprise party **une surprise-partie** *ewn sewr-preez pahr-tee*

S.V.P. s'il vous plaît *seel-voo-pleh* please
syphilis **la syphilis** *la see-fee-leess*

T

TABAC *ta-ba* TOBACCO SHOP (you can also buy postage stamps at a *ta-ba*)
tablet (of paper) **un bloc de papier** *ūh bluk de pa-pee-ay*
tablet (pill) **un comprimé** *ūh koh̄-pree-may*
tap (faucet) **un robinet** *ūh rub-ee-nay*
tea **un thé** *ūh tay;* plain tea **un thé nature** *ūh tay-na-tewr;* tea with cream
un thé à crème *ūh tay-a-krehm;* tea with lemon **un thé au citron** *ūh tay-oh-see-
troh̄;* tea with milk **un thé au lait** *ūh tay-oh-leh*
telegram **un télégramme** *ūh tay-lay-grahm*
television **la télévision** *la tay-lay-vee-zee-ōh;* TV set **le téléviseur** *le tay-lay-vee-
zur*
tell me **dites-moi** *deet-mwah*
telly (TV) **la télé** *la tay-lay*
ten **dix** *deess*

TENEZ VOTRE DROITE *te-nay vut-re drwaht* KEEP TO YOUR RIGHT
tenth **dixième** *dee-zee-ehm*

T.G.V. *tay-zhay-vay* **Train à Grande Vitesse** *trēh-a-grah̄-d vee-tehss* high-speed
train
thank you **merci** *mehr-see;* thank you very much **merci beaucoup** *mehr-see
boh-koo*
that's a good idea **c'est une bonne idée** *seh tewn bun ee-day*
that's all right **ça va** *sah-vah*
that's right **c'est ça** *seh-sah*
theft **un vol** *ūh vul;* (same word for flight)
there! **là!** *lah!*
there are . . . , there is . . . **il y a. . .** *eel-ee-a*
there it is! **le voilà!** *le vwah-lah!* **la voilà** *la vwah-lah;* there they are! **les voilà!**
lay vwah-lah; there you are! **vous voilà!** *voo-vwah-lah*
thermometer **un thermomètre** *ūh tehr-mum-eh-tre*
they **ils** *(m.) eel;* **elles** *(f.) ehl*
thing **une chose** *ewn sh-oh-z*
third **troisième** *trwa-zee-ehm*
thirteen **treize** *trehz*

thirty **trente** *trah-t*

thirty-one **trente et un** *trah-tay-uh*

thirty-two **trente-deux** *trah-t duh*

this evening **ce soir** *se swahr*

thousand **mil (mille)** *meel*

three **trois** *trwah*

three hundred **trois cents** *trwah-sah*

thumb **le pouce** *le pooss*

Thursday **jeudi** *zh-uh-dee*

ticket **un billet** *uh bee-yay;* **un ticket** *uh tee-keh*

ticket window **un guichet** *uh geesh-eh*

time (hour) **heure** *ur;* what time is it? **quelle heure est-il?** *kehl ur eh-teel* at
what time? **à quelle heure?** *a kehl ur*

tip (gratuity) **un pourboire** *uh poor-bwahr*

tired **fatigué** *fa-tee-gay*

TIREZ *tee-ray* PULL; **TIREZ ICI** *tee-ray ee-see* PULL HERE

to the left **à gauche** *a goh-sh*

to the right **à droite** *a drwaht*

today **aujourd'hui** *oh-zhoor-dwee*

toilet **les toilettes** *lay twa-leht;* **W.C.** *doo-ble-vay-say* (Water Closet)

toilet paper (tissue) **le papier hygiénique** *le pa-pee-ay eezh-yay-neek*

tomorrow **demain** *de-meh*

tonight **ce soir** *se swahr*

too (also) **aussi** *oh-see*

too bad **tant pis** *tah-pee*

too big **trop grand** *troh grah*

too cold **trop froid** *troh frwah*

too hot **trop chaud** *troh sh-oh*

too little **trop peu** *troh puh*

too much **trop** *troh*

too much noise **trop de bruit** *trohd brew-ee*

too salty **trop salé** *troh sal-ay*

too small **trop petit** *troh ptee*

tourist **touriste** *toor-eest;* I'm a tourist **je suis touriste** *zhe swee toor-eest*

tournedos *(m.)* *toorn-doh* tender slices of beef

towel **une serviette** *ewn sehr-vee-eht*

traffic **la circulation** *la seer-kew-la-see-oh*

train **un train** *uh treh*

TRAVERSER *tra-vehr-say* CROSS THE STREET

tray **un plateau** *uh pla-toh*

trip, to take a **faire un voyage** *fehr uh vwah-yah-zh*

tube (subway) **le métro** *le may-troh*

Tuesday **mardi** *mar-dee*

turn off the lights! **éteignez la lumière!** *ay-tay-ny-ay la lew-mee-ehr;* turn on the
lights! **allumez la lumière!** *a-lew-may la lew-mee-ehr*

TV **la télé** *la tay-lay;* TV set **le téléviseur** *le tay-lay-vee-zur*

T.V.A. **Taxes à la Valeur Ajoutée** *taks-a-la-val-ur ah-zh-oo-tay* VAT (Value Added Tax)

twelve **douze** *dooz*

twenty **vingt** *veh̄*

twenty-one **vingt et un** *veh̄-tay-uh̄*

twenty-two **vingt-deux** *veh̄-duh*

twice **deux fois** *duh fwah*

two **deux** *duh*

typewriter **une machine à écrire** *ewn ma-sheen a ay-kreer*

U

umbrella **un parapluie** *uh̄ pa-ra-plew-ee*

under **sous** *soo*

understood **compris** *koh̄-pree;* **entendu** *ah̄-tah̄-dew;* **d'accord** *dak-or*

United States **les Etats-Unis** *lay-zay-ta-zew-nee;* from the United States **des Etats-Unis** *day-zay-ta-zew-nee;* to the United States **aux Etats-Unis** *oh-zay-ta-zew-nee*

urgent **urgent** *ewr-zh-ah̄*

V

vacant room **une chambre libre** *ewn sh-ah̄-bre lee-bre*

valuables **les valables** *lay va-la-ble*

value **la valeur** *la va-lur*

vanilla **à la vanille** *a-la-va-nee-y*

veau *(m.)* *voh* veal

very fine **très bien** *treh bee-eh̄*

very little (not much) **très peu** *treh-puh*

very much **beaucoup** *boh-koo*

very well **très bien** *treh bee-eh̄*

VITESSE *vee-tehss* SPEED

VOITURE NUMERO (NO.) *vwah-tewr new-may-roh* TRAIN CAR NUMBER

vomit **vomir** *vum-eer*

VOYAGEURS *vwah-yah-zh-ur* TRAVELERS

W

wait! **attendez!** *a-tah̄-day;* wait a minute! **attendez une minute!** *a-tah̄-day ewn mee-newt*

waiter **un serveur** *uh̄ sehr-vuhr*

waiting room **la salle d'attente** *la sal da-tah̄t*

waitress **une serveuse** *ewn sehr-vuhz*

wake me up! **réveillez-moi!** *ray-vay-yay-mwah*

walk **aller à pied** *a-lay a pee-ay;* **marcher** *marsh-ay*

wallet, my **mon portefeuille** *moh̄ pohrt-fu-y*

want **vouloir** *vool-wahr;* **désirer** *day-zee-ray*

warm **chaud** *sh-oh;* it's warm today **il fait chaud aujourd'hui** *eel-feh sh-oh oh-zhoor-dwee;* warm (lukewarm, moderately warm) **tiède** *tee-ehd;* **la soupe est tiède, pas chaude** *la soop eh tee-ehd, pah sh-ohd* the soup is warm, not hot

wash **laver** *la-vay;* to wash oneself **se laver** *se la-vay;* I must wash myself **je dois me laver** *zhe dwahm la-vay*

watch (wrist) **une montre** *ewn mōh-tre*

water, some **de l'eau** *de-loh*

watermelon **la pastèque** *la pas-tehk*

w.c. (water closet) toilet *doo-ble-vay-say*

we **nous** *noo*

Wednesday **mercredi** *mehr-kre-dee*

week **une semaine** *ewn smehn*

well **bien** *bee-ēh*

what? **pardon?** *pahr-dōh*

what are you saying? **qu'est-ce que vous dites?** *kehs-ke voo deet*

what did you say? **comment?** *kum-māh*

what does that mean? **que veut dire cela?** *ke vuh deer sla;* what does this mean? **que veut dire ceci?** *ke vuh deer se-see*

what time? **quelle heure?** *kehl ur;* at what time? **à quelle heure?** *a kehl ur*

what time is it? **quelle heure est-il?** *kehl ur eh-teel*

what's that? **qu'est-ce que c'est?** *kehs-ke seh*

what's your name? **quel est votre nom?** *kehl eh vut-re nōh*

when **quand** *kāh*

when does it close? **quand ferme-t-il?** *kāh fehrm-teel*

when does it open? **quand ouvre-t-il?** *kāh oo-vre-teel*

where **où** *oo*

where are . . . ? **où sont. . . ?** *oo sōh;* where is . . . ? **où est. . . ?** *oo eh*

where are the women? **où sont les femmes?** *oo sōh lay fahm;* where are the children? **où sont les enfants?** *oo sōh lay zāh-fāh*

where can I find . . . ? **où puis-je trouver . . . ?** *oo pew-ee-zh troo-vay*

which? **lequel?** *(m.)* *le-kehl;* **laquelle?** *(f.)* *la-kehl*

which way? **par où** *pahr-oo*

white **blanc** *blāh*

who **qui** *kee*

who are you? **qui êtes-vous?** *kee eht-voo*

who is it? **qui est-ce?** *kee-ehss*

who is there? **qui est là** *kee eh-lah*

why? **pourquoi?** *poor-kwah;* why not? **pourquoi pas?** *poor-kwah pah*

wide **large** *lar-zh*

wife, my **ma femme** *ma-fahm*

willingly **volontiers** *vu-lōh-tee-ay*

wine **un vin** *ūh vēh*

with **avec** *a-vehk*

with a balcony **avec balcon** *a-vehk bal-kōh*

with bath **avec bain** *a-vehk bēh*

with breakfast only **avec petit déjeuner seulement** *a-vehk ptee day-zh-uh-nay sul-māh*

with meals **avec repas** *a-vehk re-pah*
with shower **avec douche** *a-vehk doosh*
without **sans** *sah*
woman **une femme** *ewn fahm*
word (spoken) **une parole** *ewn pa-rul;* word (written) **un mot** *uh moh*
would you please . . . **voulez-vous, s'il vous plaît. . .** *voo-lay-voo, seel-voo-pleh*
wow! **Oh! là! là!** *oh-lah-lah*
write to me **écrivez-moi** *ay-kree-vay-mwah*

Y

yes **oui** *wee*
yesterday **hier** *ee-yehr*
you **vous** *voo* (sing. & pl., polite); **tu** *tew* (sing., fam.)
you don't say! **ne me dites pas!** *nem deet-pah*
you're joking! **vous plaisantez!** *voo-play-zah-tay*
you're welcome **de rien** *de-ree-eh;* **je vous en prie** *zhe voo-zah-pree;* **il n'y a pas de quoi** *eel-nee-a-pahd-kwah*

Z

zipper **une fermeture à glissière** *ewn fehrm-tewr-a-glee-see-ehr,* **une fermeture éclair** *ewn fehrm-tewr ay-klehr*
zut! *zewt* darn it!

The hundreds of verb forms in this part of the book will immerse you in the practice and improvement of your knowledge of French verb forms, tenses, and uses. You will find a variety of types of questions to make your experience interesting, challenging, and rewarding. All verb forms used in the drills and tests are found in the preliminary pages, among the 501 verbs, and in the back pages of this book.

The answers and explanations begin on page 653. The explanations are brief and to the point, including references to pages in this book for study and review.

Tips: To figure out the correct verb form of the required tense, examine each sentence carefully. Take a good look at the subject of the verb. Is it 1st, 2d, or 3d person? Is it singular or plural? Is it masculine or feminine? Look for a possible preceding noun or pronoun direct object, agreement on the past participle if necessary, and key elements that precede or follow the verb to determine the verb form and tense.

Also, look for other key words, such as yesterday, last week, today, at this moment, tomorrow, next year, certain conjunctions, and other key elements that indicate the need for the indicative or subjunctive moods in the required tense. The correct verb form depends on the sense and grammatical structure of the sentence. The best way to learn irregular forms in the seven simple tenses is from study, practice, and experience. For the formation of present and past participles, including irregulars, consult page ix. As for the formation of regular verb forms, consult pages xxvii to xxx. From time to time study and review pages xv to xxvi.

Verb Test 1

SENTENCE COMPLETION

Directions: Each of the following sentences contains a missing verb form. From the choices given, select the verb form of the tense that is required, according to the sense of the sentence, and write the letter of your choice on the line. At times, only the infinitive form is needed or a present or past participle. Answers and explanations begin on page 653.

1. Hier, Marguerite _____ allée au théâtre avec ses amis.
   A. a   B. est   C. avait   D. était

2. Madame Céléstine ne _____ pas lire parce qu'elle a besoin de ses lunettes.
   A. pouvons   B. peuvent   C. peux   D. peut

3. Quand j'étais enfant, j' _____ beaucoup de camarades à l'école.
   A. ai   B. eus   C. avais   D. aurai

4. La petite fille _____ parce qu'elle est heureuse.
   A. sourit   B. souris   C. ait souri   D. eût souri

5. Hier soir, j'ai bien ri pendant que je _____ un film comique à la télé.
   A. regardait B. regardais   C. ai regardé   D. regarderais

6. À cause du grand bruit qui vient de la rue, je ne peux pas _____ .
   A. dormir   B. dors   C. dormant   D. dormirai

7. Asseyez-vous, s'il vous plaît. Le docteur _____ d'arriver.
   A. viens   B. vient   C. est venu   D. était venu

8. Robert, je te demande de _____ ta chambre parce qu'elle est bien sale.
   A. nettoie   B. nettoyant   C. nettoyer   D. nettoyez

9. Le tonnerre va _____ peur aux enfants.
   A. faire   B. faisant   C. fait   D. font

10. Il commence à pleuvoir et Hélène a _____ son parapluie.
   A. oublié   B. oubliée   C. oublie   D. oublia

11. Chéri, aimes-tu les chaussures que j'ai _____ aujourd'hui?
   A. acheté   B. achetée   C. achetés   D. achetées

12. La semaine prochaine j' _____ en France.
   A. irai   B. alla   C. allais   D. irais

13. Si j'avais assez d'argent, j' _____ en Italie.
   A. irai   B. irais   C. allais   D. aille

14. Si j'ai assez d'argent, j' _____ au Canada.
   A. irai   B. irais   C. allais   D. aille

15. Ce matin Paulette _____ .
   A. s'est lavé   B. s'est lavée   C. se sont lavés   D. se sont lavées

16. Ce matin Gertrude _____ les cheveux.
   A. s'est lavé   B. s'est lavée   C. se sont lavés   D. se sont lavées

17. Je _____ à l'école en ce moment.
   A. suis allé   B. étais allé   C. vais   D. serais allé

18. Je _____ à la bibliothèque tous les jours.
   A. vais   B. étais allé   C. serai allé   D. serais allé

19. Deux et deux _____ quatre.
   A. fait   B. font   C. feraient   D. faisaient

20. Depuis combien de temps êtes-vous ici? Moi? Je _____ ici depuis dix minutes.
   A. étais   B. serai   C. serais   D. suis

DIALOGUE

Directions: *In the following dialogue there are blank spaces indicating missing verb forms. Select the appropriate verb form according to the sense of what the speakers are saying and write the letter of your choice on the line. The situation is given below. First, read the entire selection once. During the second reading, make your choices.*

Situation: You just got off an airplane. You go to the baggage room to claim your suitcase but you can't find it. An employee talks to you.

L'employé: Y a-t-il quelque chose qui ne va pas, mademoiselle?
Vous: Je ne _____ pas ma valise.

  1. A. trouve   B. trouverai   C. trouverais   D. trouvais

L'employé: Donnez-moi votre ticket de bagages, s'il vous plaît.
Vous: Une seconde, s'il vous plaît. _____ qu'il est dans ma poche.

  2. A. J'ai cru   B. Je croirai   C. Je croirais   D. Je crois

L'employé: Une minute. Je vais voir ce qui se passe.
Vous: J' _____ que ma valise n'est pas perdue!

  3. A. espère   B. espérer   C. espères   D. espérais

L'employé: Votre valise est dans l'avion qui arrive cet après-midi.
Vous: _____ bien contente.

  4. A. J'ai été   B. J'avais été   C. J'aurais été   D. Je suis

L'employé: Votre valise sera ici vers cinq heures, mademoiselle.
Vous: Je _____ la chercher. Merci bien, monsieur.

  5. A. viendrai   B. suis venue   C. suis venu   D. viendrais

PATTERN RESPONSES

Directions: Answer the following questions in French in complete sentences in the affirmative, using a pronoun for the subject. Add **aussi** (also).

Model: **François apprend bien. Et vos frères?**
You write: **Ils apprennent bien aussi.**

1. Pierre comprend bien. Et vos frères?

_____

2. Robert écrit bien. Et vos soeurs?

_____

3. Anne va bien. Et ses amis?

_____

4. Juliette lit un livre dans le lit. Et toi?

_____

5. Catherine voit bien. Et tes amis?

_____

6. Richard est allé au cinéma. Et Suzanne?

_____

7. Jean a bien mangé. Et nous?

_____

8 Jeanne s'est assise. Et les autres jeunes filles?

_____

9. Monsieur Dufy s'est lavé. Et sa femme?

_____

10. Monsieur Durand s'est lavé les cheveux. Et sa femme?

_____

11. Tu as rougi. Et les enfants?

_____

12. Monsieur Bertrand choisit une auto. Et Monsieur et Madame Duval?

_____

13. Tu finis la leçon. Et Pierre?

_____

14. Les enfants ont fait les devoirs. Et toi?

_____

15. Ce soldat défend la patrie. Et les autres soldats?

_____

16. Vous répondez à la question. Et Jacques?

_____

17. Vous vous couchez à dix heures. Et vos parents?

_____

18. Les enfants se sont amusés. Et Marie?

_____

19. Jacqueline s'est reposée. Et vous?

_____

20. Annie s'est levée tôt. Et nous?

_____

Verb Test 4

SENTENCE COMPLETION

Directions: *Each of the following sentences contains a missing verb form. From the choices given, select the verb form of the tense that is required, according to the sense of the sentence, and write the letter of your choice on the line.*

1. Je partirai quand mon amie _____ .
    A. arrive   B. arrivera   C. est arrivé   D. est arrivée

2. Je voudrais vous _____ ces fleurs.
    A. donnez   B. donner   C. donnerais   D. donnerez

3. Avez-vous lu les deux livres que je vous ai _____ la semaine dernière?
    A. donner   B. donné   C. donnés   D. donnez

4. Voici la lettre que _____ hier.
    A. je reçois   B. j'ai reçu   C. je recevrais   D. j'ai reçue

5. Hier _____ une lettre à des amis en France.
    A. j'ai envoyé   B. j'ai envoyée   C. j'enverrai   D. j'enverrais

6. J'irais en France si _____ assez d'argent.
    A. j'ai   B. j'aurais   C. j'aurai   D. j'avais

7. J'irai en France quand _____ assez d'argent.
    A. j'aurai   B. j'aurais   C. j'ai eu   D. j'avais

8 J'insiste que tu _____ ici avant cinq heures.
    A. es   B. sois   C. soit   D. soyez

9. Quand un enfant grandit, cela _____ dire qu'il devient plus grand.
   A. veuille   B. voulût   C. veux   D. veut

10. Pour bien apprendre dans la classe de français, _____ faire attention.
   A. il faut   B. il est   C. il pleut   D. il fend

11. Mon frère lisait pendant que j' _____ .
   A. écris   B. écrive   C. ai écrit   D. écrivais

12. Les étudiants lisaient quand _____ dans la salle de classe.
   A. je suis entré   B. j'entre   C. j'étais entré   D. j'entrerai

13. Quand j'étais petit, ma famille et moi _____ à la plage en été.
   A. allons   B. allions   C. allaient   D. irons

14. Richard _____ triste quand je l'ai vu.
   A. est   B. sera   C. était   D. serait

15. Quand ma mère était jeune, elle _____ jolie.
   A. était   B. est   C. a été   D. serait

16. À minuit, Pierre _____ et il a dit à son frère: "Lève-toi!"
   A. se réveille   B. s'est réveillé   C. s'est réveillée   D. se réveillera

17. J'entends _____ quelqu'un en bas dans la salle à manger!
   A. marchant   B. marché   C. marcher   D. a marché

18. En général, on _____ froid en hiver.
   A. est   B. fait   C. tient   D. a

19. L'année dernière nous _____ en France.
   A. est allé   B. est allée   C. sommes allés   D. irons

20. Voici les livres que vous avez _____ .
   A. désiré   B. désirée   C. désirés   D. désirer

Verb Test 5

DIALOGUE

Directions: *In the following dialogue there are blank spaces indicating missing verb forms. Select the appropriate verb form according to the sense of what the speakers are saying and write the letter of your choice on the line. The conversation is taking place at the present time. First, read the entire selection once. During the second reading, make your choices.*

Situation: It's the morning of the year-end French exam in school. You and Jeanne are talking about the exams and your plans for summer vacation.

Jeanne: Il me reste encore un examen pour demain, puis les vacances vont commencer.
Vous: Mon dernier examen _____ lieu après-demain.

1. A. est   B. sera   C. aura   D. avait

Jeanne: J'espère réussir à tous mes examens.
Vous: Il n'y _____ rien à craindre. Tu reçois toujours de bonnes notes.

2. A. ait   B. soit   C. a eu   D. a

Jeanne: Ma famille et moi nous allons faire un voyage à Québec en juillet.
Vous: Moi, je devrai _____ ici à travailler.

3. A. reste   B. rester   C. restera   D. resterai

Jeanne: L'été passé nous sommes allés dans les montagnes.
Vous: Alors, tu _____ faire un voyage tous les étés!

4. A. pouvez   B. puis   C. peux   D. put

Jeanne: Alors, je te souhaite bonne chance dans tes examens.
Vous: Merci. Et je te _____ la même chose!

5. A. souhaite   B. souhaites   C. souhaité   D. souhaitai

Verb Test 6

CHANGING FROM ONE VERB TO ANOTHER

Directions: The verb forms in the following statements are all in the imperative. Change each sentence by replacing the verb with the proper form of the verb in parentheses, keeping the imperative form. The verb form you write must be in the same person as the one you are replacing. In other words, you must recognize if the given verb form is 2d person singular (tu), 1st person plural (nous), or 2d person plural, polite singular (vous). See page 526 for irregular verb forms that you cannot identify.

Model: **Prononcez le mot. (écrire)**

You write: Écrivez le mot.

1. Lisez la phrase. (dire)

_____

2. Prends le lait. (boire)

_____

3. Venez tout de suite. (partir)

_____

4. Ouvre la fenêtre. (fermer)

_____

5. Mets la valise là-bas. (prendre)

6. Lisons la lettre. (écrire)

7. Apprenez le poème. (lire)

8. Partons maintenant. (sortir)

9. Soyez à l'heure! (revenir)

10. Voyons la leçon. (faire)

11. Asseyez-vous, s'il vous plaît. (se lever)

12. Accepte l'argent. (refuser)

13. Vends le vélo. (acheter)

14. Venez à l'heure. (être)

15. Reste dans la maison. (aller)

16. Lave-toi. (se lever)

17. Cachons-nous. (se dépêcher)

18. Arrête-toi. (s'amuser)

19. Vends la maison. (acheter)

20. Mange. (venir)

CHANGING FROM ONE TENSE TO ANOTHER

Directions: The following verb forms are all in the ***future tense***. Change them to the ***conditional***, keeping the same subject. See page 526 for irregular verb forms that you cannot identify.

Model: J'aurai　　**You write: J'aurais**

1. J'irai _____
2. Je partirai _____
3. J'aurai _____
4. Je serai _____
5. Tu aimeras _____
6. Tu feras _____
7. Il aura _____
8. Il sera _____
9. Il ira _____
10. On dira _____
11. Vous serez _____
12. Elle lira _____
13. J'ouvrirai _____
14. Nous saurons _____
15. Ils viendront _____

16. On boira _____
17. Ils courront _____
18. Ils liront _____
19. Elle mettra _____
20. Il apprendra _____
21. Je couvrirai _____
22. Il deviendra _____
23. Nous devrons _____
24. Vous direz _____
25. Vous irez _____
26. J'aimerai _____
27. Il faudra _____
28. Ils seront _____
29. Elles feront _____
30. On choisira _____

PATTERN RESPONSES

Directions: Answer the following questions in the negative in complete French sentences. In answer (a), use **non**. In answer (b), use **non plus** (either). Study models (a) and (b) carefully. Use a pronoun as subject in your answers. Place **non plus** at the end of the sentence.

Models: (a) **Est-ce que vous dansez?**
 (Do you dance?)

You write: (a) **Non, je ne danse pas.**
 (No, I don't dance.)

 (b) **Et Charles?**
 (And Charles?)

You write: (b) **Il ne danse pas non plus.**
 (He doesn't dance either.)

1. (a) Est-ce que vous travaillez?

_____

 (b) Et Paul?

_____

2. (a) Est-ce que Jacqueline étudie?

_____

 (b) Et les grands garçons?

_____

3. (a) Est-ce qu'Anne va au match?

_____

 (b) Et toi?

_____

4. (a) Est-ce que les enfants crient?

_____

 (b) Et toi et tes amis?

_____

5. (a) Est-ce que l'avion arrive?

_____

 (b) Et les trains?

_____

6. (a) Est-ce que tu es occupé?

_____

 (b) Et tes parents?

_____

7. (a) As-tu fermé la fenêtre?

_____

(b) Et Pierre?

_____

8. (a) Avez-vous assisté à la conférence?

_____

(b) Et vos amis?

_____

9. (a) Monsieur Durand est-il allé au supermarché?

_____

(b) Et sa femme?

_____

10. (a) Madame Coty est-elle allée à la piscine?

_____

(b) Et les enfants?

_____

Verb Test 9

DIALOGUE

Directions: *In the following dialogue there are blank spaces indicating missing verb forms. Select the appropriate verb form according to the sense of what the speakers are saying and write the letter of your choice on the line. The situation is given below. The conversation is taking place at the present time. First, read the entire selection once. During the second reading, make your choices.*

Situation: You are seated in a train about to leave for Paris. A young man approaches and asks if he can sit next to you.

Le jeune homme: Vous permettez?
Vous: Mais, bien sûr! Je vous en _____ .

1.   A. prie   B. priez   C. pries   D. prions

Le jeune homme: J'espère que nous _____ un voyage agréable.

2.   A. faisons   B. fassions   C. avons fait   D. ferons

Vous: Je l' _____ bien aussi.

3.   A. espérer   B. ai espéré   C. avais espéré D. espère

Le jeune homme: Savez-vous à quelle heure le train _____ à Paris?

4.   A. est arrivé B. arriverait   C. arrivera   D. arrivait

632   Verb drills and tests

| Vous: | Vers une heure et quart. |
| Le jeune homme: | Il semble qu'il _____ beau temps. |

5.   A. a fait   B. va faire   C. faisait   D. fasse

Vous: Oui, on _____ une belle journée pour aujourd'hui.

6.   A. prévoit   B. prévois   C. prévoira   D. prévoie

Le jeune homme: Je suppose que le train _____ bientôt.

7.   A. est parti   B. sera parti   C. va partir   D. partir

Vous: En effet, je _____ que nous sommes déjà en route.

8.   A. crus   B. croit   C. croyais   D. crois

Verb Test 10

SENTENCE COMPLETION

Directions: *Each of the following sentences contains a missing verb form. From the choices given, select the verb form of the tense that is required, according to the sense of the sentence, and write the letter of your choice on the line. At times, only the infinitive form is needed or a present or past participle.*

1. J'ai besoin de _____ mais je n'ai pas de savon.
   A. laver   B. se laver   C. me laver   D. me laverai

2. Quand Lisa _____ dans le salon, elle a vu un vase de jolies fleurs.
   A. entre   B. entrera   C. est entré   D. est entrée

3. Si j'ai le temps, _____ le travail.
   A. j'ai fait   B. je ferai   C. je ferais   D. je faisais

4. Si j'avais le temps, _____ le travail.
   A. je ferais   B. je ferai   C. j'aurais fait   D. j'ai fait

5. Si j'avais eu le temps, _____ le travail.
   A. j'ai fait   B. j'aurai fait   C. j'aurais fait   D. je faisais

6. Mademoiselle, un café pour mon ami, s'il vous plaît. Moi, _____ un thé.
   A. j'aimerais   B. j'ai aimé   C. j'aimai   D. j'aimais

7. À quelle heure pourriez-vous venir? Je _____ venir après le dîner.
   A. pouvais   B. pourrais   C. pouvons   D. puisse

8. Si j'étais vous, je ne le _____ pas.

    A. ferai   B. ferais   C. faisais   D. fasse

9. Je doute que Jeanne _____ ce soir.

    A. viendra   B. vienne   C. viendrait   D. vient

10. J'ai peur qu'il ne _____ malade.

    A. sois   B. soit   C. sera   D. serait

11. Je regrette que tu _____ malade.

    A. es   B. est   C. soit   D. sois

12. Je partirai à moins qu'il ne _____ .

    A. vienne   B. viennent   C. viendra   D. vient

13. Quoiqu'elle _____ belle, il ne l'aime pas.

    A. est   B. soit   C. serait   D. sera

14. Je le lui explique pour qu'elle _____ .

    A. comprendra   B. comprenne   C. comprennent   D. comprend

15. Je partirai dès qu'elle _____ .

    A. arrive   B. arrivera   C. arriverait   D. est arrivée

16. Il est urgent que vous _____ .

    A. pars   B. partez   C. partiez   D. partirez

17. Tout d'un coup, je me suis rappelé que _____ de le lui dire.

    A. j'ai oublié   B. j'oublie   C. j'oublierai   D. j'avais oublié

18. J'étais fatigué ce matin parce que _____ dormi.

    A. je n'ai pas   B. je n'aurai pas   C. je n'avais pas   D. j'ai

19. Je suis fatigué maintenant parce que _____ dormi.

    A. j'ai   B. je n'ai pas   C. je vais   D. je n'avais pas

20. Quand elle arrivera demain _____ le travail.

    A. j'aurai fini   B. j'ai fini   C. j'avais fini   D. je finisse

CHANGING FROM ONE TENSE TO ANOTHER

Directions: *The following verb forms are all in the present indicative tense. Change them to the **passé composé**, keeping the same subject. Consult page 526 for irregular verb forms that you cannot identify. Keep in mind that to form the **passé composé** you need to use the present indicative tense of either **avoir** or **être** (depending on which of the two helping verbs is required) plus the past participle of the verb you are working with. If you feel uncertain about this, consult page viii about when to use **avoir** or **être** as a helping verb.*

Model: **Elle mange.**

You write: **Elle a mangé.**

1. Elle va. _____
2. Il a. _____
3. Je m'assieds. _____
4. Ils ont. _____
5. Tu es. _____
6. Il va. _____
7. Nous allons. _____
8. Nous avons. _____
9. Je parle. _____
10. Elles viennent. _____
11. Je bois. _____
12. Ils boivent. _____
13. Vous buvez. _____
14. Je crois. _____
15. Tu dis. _____

16. Je peux. _____
17. Il faut. _____
18. Vous lisez. _____
19. Vous dites. _____
20. Tu mets. _____
21. Elle naît. _____
22. Elle meurt. _____
23. Elle vend. _____
24. Ils s'amusent. _____
25. Elle entre. _____
26. On finit. _____
27. Elles courent. _____
28. Ils prennent. _____
29. On apprend. _____
30. Elles arrivent. _____

COMPLETION OF VERB FORMS
(in the Seven Simple Tenses)

Directions: Complete each verb form in the tenses indicated by writing the correct letter or letters on the blank lines.

Présent de l'indicatif (Tense No. 1)

1. (aimer) J'aim ____
2. (chanter) Tu chant ____
3. (étudier)Il/elle/on étudi ____
4. (choisir) Janine chois ____
5. (entendre) J'entend ____

6. (attendre) Nous attend ____
7. (manger) Vous mang ____
8. (vendre) Ils/elles vend ____
9. (finir) Richard et moi fin ____
10. (donner) Marie et Jeanne donn ____

Imparfait de l'indicatif (Tense No. 2)

1. (parler) Je parl ____
2. (finir) Tu finiss ____
3. (vendre) Il/elle/on vend ____
4. (être) Madeleine ét ____
5. (avoir) Il/elle/on av ____

6. (venir) Nous ven ____
7. (faire) Vous fais ____
8. (aller) Ils/elles all ____
9. (jouer) Paul et Henri jou ____
10. (donner) Tu donn ____

Passé simple (Tense No. 3)
(*This tense is not used in conversation. It is used in literary style.*)

1. (parler) Je parl ____
2. (finir) Tu fin ____
3. (vendre) Il/elle/on vend ____
4. (écrire) Catherine écriv ____
5. (aller) Ils/elles all ____

6. (donner) Nous donn ____
7. (choisir) Vous chois ____
8. (comprendre) Ils/elles compr ____
9. (désirer) Hélène et Raymond désir ____
10. (danser) Il/elle/on dans ____

Futur (Tense No. 4)

1. (manger) Je manger ____
2. (finir) Tu finir ____
3. (vendre) Il/elle/on vendr ____
4. (écrire) La femme écrir ____
5. (aller) J'ir ____

6. (donner) Nous donner ____
7. (choisir) Vous choisir ____
8. (comprendre) Ils/elles comprendr ____
9. (jouer) Les garçons jouer ____
10. (avoir) J'aur ____

Conditionnel (Tense No. 5)

1. (aller) J'ir ____
2. (finir) Tu finir ____
3. (faire) Il/elle/on fer ____
4. (manger) Je manger ____
5. (pouvoir) Vous pourr ____

6. (parler) Nous parler ____
7. (être) Vous ser ____
8. (avoir) Ils/elles aur ____
9. (prendre) Je prendr ____
10. (dîner) Vous dîner ____

Présent du subjonctif (Tense No. 6)

1. (parler) que je parl ____
2. (donner) que tu donn ____
3. (oser) qu'il/elle/on os ____
4. (choisir) que je choisiss ____
5. (manger) que tu mang ____

6. (partir) que nous part ____
7. (vendre) que vous vend ____
8. (prendre) qu'ils/elles prenn ____
9. (finir) que nous finiss ____
10. (fermer) qu'il/elle/on ferm ____

Imparfait du subjonctif (Tense No. 7)

1. (parler) que je parl ____
2. (donner) que tu donn ____
3. (ouvrir) qu'il/elle/on ouvr ____

4. (partir) que nous part ____
5. (vouloir) que vous voul ____
6. (finir) qu'ils/elles fin ____

Verb Test 13

PAST PARTICIPLES

Directions: In this crossword puzzle (**mots-croisés**) write the past participle for each of the verbs given below. Most of them are irregular. Past participles are important to know because they are needed to form the seven compound tenses, for example, the **passé composé**.

Horizontalement
1. donner
5. pouvoir
7. fuir
8. rire
9. devoir (*backwards*)
10. taire
11. savoir
13. lire
15. savoir
18. naître
19. rire (*backwards*)
21. taire
22. tuer

Verticalement
1. devoir
2. naître
3. lire
4. vendre
5. prendre
6. dire
7. falloir
12. user
14. finir
16. mourir
17. être
20. avoir

Verb Test 14

DRILLING THE VERB *AVOIR*
(in the Seven Simple Tenses)

Note: You definitely must know the verb **avoir** in the seven simple tenses because they are needed to form the seven compound tenses of verbs conjugated with **avoir,** for example, the **passé composé** (Tense No. 8), as in **j'ai mangé** (I have eaten). Practice these by writing them every day until you know them thoroughly. If you don't know them, see page 61. Also, read about **avoir** verbs on page viii. Review pages xxviii to xxx.

Directions: *Write the verb forms of* **avoir** *in the seven simple tenses indicated.*

1. Présent de l'indicatif (Tense No. 1)

<table>
<tr><td colspan="2" align="center">Singular</td><td colspan="2" align="center">Plural</td></tr>
<tr><td>j'</td><td>_____</td><td>nous</td><td>_____</td></tr>
<tr><td>tu</td><td>_____</td><td>vous</td><td>_____</td></tr>
<tr><td>il/elle/on/(or a noun)</td><td>_____</td><td>ils/elles/(or a noun)</td><td>_____</td></tr>
</table>

2. Imparfait de l'indicatif (Tense No. 2)

<table>
<tr><td>j'</td><td>_____</td><td>nous</td><td>_____</td></tr>
<tr><td>tu</td><td>_____</td><td>vous</td><td>_____</td></tr>
<tr><td>il/elle/on/(or a noun)</td><td>_____</td><td>ils/elles/(or a noun)</td><td>_____</td></tr>
</table>

3. Passé simple (Tense No. 3)

<table>
<tr><td>j'</td><td>_____</td><td>nous</td><td>_____</td></tr>
<tr><td>tu</td><td>_____</td><td>vous</td><td>_____</td></tr>
<tr><td>il/elle/on/(or a noun)</td><td>_____</td><td>ils/elles/(or a noun)</td><td>_____</td></tr>
</table>

4. Futur (Tense No. 4)

<table>
<tr><td>j'</td><td>_____</td><td>nous</td><td>_____</td></tr>
<tr><td>tu</td><td>_____</td><td>vous</td><td>_____</td></tr>
<tr><td>il/elle/on/(or a noun)</td><td>_____</td><td>ils/elles/(or a noun)</td><td>_____</td></tr>
</table>

5. Conditionnel (Tense No. 5)

<table>
<tr><td>j'</td><td>_____</td><td>nous</td><td>_____</td></tr>
<tr><td>tu</td><td>_____</td><td>vous</td><td>_____</td></tr>
<tr><td>il/elle/on/(or a noun)</td><td>_____</td><td>ils/elles/(or a noun)</td><td>_____</td></tr>
</table>

6. Présent du subjonctif (Tense No. 6)

<table>
<tr><td>que j'</td><td>_____</td><td>que nous</td><td>_____</td></tr>
<tr><td>que tu</td><td>_____</td><td>que vous</td><td>_____</td></tr>
<tr><td>qu'il/elle/on/(or a noun)</td><td>_____</td><td>qu'ils/elles/(or a noun)</td><td>_____</td></tr>
</table>

7. Imparfait du subjonctif (Tense No. 7)

<table>
<tr><td>que j'</td><td>_____</td><td>que nous</td><td>_____</td></tr>
<tr><td>que tu</td><td>_____</td><td>que vous</td><td>_____</td></tr>
<tr><td>qu'il/elle/on/(or a noun)</td><td>_____</td><td>qu'ils/elles/(or a noun)</td><td>_____</td></tr>
</table>

DRILLING THE VERB *ÊTRE*
(in the Seven Simple Tenses)

Note: You must know the verb **être** in the seven simple tenses because they are needed to form the seven compound tenses of verbs conjugated with **être**, for example, the **passé composé** (Tense No. 8), as in **elle est arrivée** (she has arrived). Practice these by writing them every day until you know them thoroughly. If you don't know them, see page 206. Also, read about **être** verbs on page viii. Review pages xxviii to xxx.

*Directions: Write the verb forms of **être** in the seven simple tenses indicated.*

1. Présent de l'indicatif (Tense No. 1)

        <u>Singular</u>   <u>Plural</u>

je ———————————— nous ————————————
tu ———————————— vous ————————————
il/elle/on/(*or a noun*) —————— ils/elles/(*or a noun*) ——————

2. Imparfait de l'indicatif (Tense No. 2)

j' ———————————— nous ————————————
tu ———————————— vous ————————————
il/elle/on/(*or a noun*) —————— ils/elles/(*or a noun*)——————

3. Passé simple (Tense No. 3)

je ———————————— nous ————————————
tu ———————————— vous ————————————
il/elle/on/(*or a noun*) —————— ils/elles/(*or a noun*)——————

4. Futur (Tense No. 4)

je ———————————— nous ————————————
tu ———————————— vous ————————————
il/elle/on/(*or a noun*) —————— ils/elles/(*or a noun*)——————

5. Conditionnel (Tense No. 5)

je ———————————— nous ————————————
tu ———————————— vous ————————————
il/elle/on/(*or a noun*) —————— ils/elles/(*or a noun*)——————

6. Présent du subjonctif (Tense No. 6)

que je _____   que nous _____

que tu _____   que vous _____

qu'il/elle/on/(*or a noun*) _____   qu'ils/elles/(*or a noun*) _____

7. Imparfait du subjonctif (Tense No. 7)

que je _____   que nous _____

que tu _____   que vous _____

qu'il/elle/on/(*or a noun*) _____   qu'ils/elles/(*or a noun*) _____

Verb Test 16

CHANGING FROM ONE TENSE TO ANOTHER

*Directions: The following verb forms are all in the **passé composé** (Tense No. 8). Change them to the **plus-que-parfait de l'indicatif** (Tense No. 9), keeping the same subject. Keep in mind that to form the **plus-que-parfait de l'indicatif** you need to use the imperfect indicative tense of either **avoir** or **être** (depending on which of the two helping verbs is required) plus the past participle of the verb you are working with. If you feel uncertain about this, consult page viii about when to use **avoir** or **être** as a helping verb. Review the formation of the past participles on page ix. Also, review Verb Tests 14 and 15.*

<table>
<tr><td colspan="2" align="center">Passé composé</td><td colspan="2" align="center">Plus-que-parfait de l'indicatif</td></tr>
<tr><td>Model:</td><td>Elle a mangé.
(She has eaten.)
Elle est arrivée.
(She has arrived.)</td><td>You write:</td><td>Elle avait mangé.
(She had eaten.)
Elle était arrivée.
(She had arrived.)</td></tr>
</table>

1. Elle est allée.	_____	**16.** J'ai pu.	_____
2. Il a eu.	_____	**17.** Il a fallu.	_____
3. Je me suis assis.	_____	**18.** Vous avez lu.	_____
4. Ils ont eu.	_____	**19.** Vous avez dit.	_____
5. Tu as été.	_____	**20.** Tu as mis.	_____
6. Il est allé.	_____	**21.** Elle est née.	_____
7. Nous sommes allés.	_____	**22.** Elle est morte.	_____
8. Nous avons eu.	_____	**23.** Elle s'est lavée.	_____
9. J'ai parlé.	_____	**24.** Elles se sont lavées.	_____
10. Elle est venue.	_____	**25.** Je suis entré.	_____
11. J'ai bu.	_____	**26.** On a parlé.	_____
12. Ils se sont tus.	_____	**27.** Ils ont couru.	_____
13. J'ai fait.	_____	**28.** Ils ont pris.	_____
14. Tu as dû.	_____	**29.** On a dit.	_____
15. Vous avez dit.	_____	**30.** J'ai compris.	_____

SENTENCE COMPLETION

Directions: *Each of the following sentences contains a missing verb form. From the choices given, select the verb form of the tense that is required, according to the sense of the sentence, and write the letter of your choice on the line. At times only the infinitive form is needed or a present or past participle.*

1. Il est possible qu'elle _____ partie.
   A. est   B. soit   C. a   D. ait

2. Je doute que Laurent _____ fait cela.
   A. a   B. est   C. ait   D. soit

3. Je ne peux pas _____ maintenant parce qu'il fait un temps affreux.
   A. sort   B. sortant   C. sortir   D. sors

4. Joséphine est tombée en _____ dans la cuisine.
   A. entrer   B. entrant   C. entrée   D. entre

5. Simone a _____ la table.
   A. essuyer   B. essuyé   C. essuyée   D. essuyant

6. Françoise s'est _____ à écrire une lettre à sa tante.
   A. mis   B. mise   C. mettre   D. mettant

7. Les enfants _____ dire bonsoir aux invités.
   A. vouloir   B. voulu   C. voulus   D. veulent

8. Voici les fleurs que j'ai _____ .
   A. acheté   B. achetés   C. achetées   D. acheter

9. Quand Raymond eut mangé, il _____ .
   A. partit   B. partis   C. partir   D. partira

10. J' _____ fait le travail si j'avais eu le temps.
   A. aurait   B. aurais   C. avais   D. ai

PRESENT PARTICIPLES

Directions: In this word puzzle, find the present participle of each of the verbs listed below and draw a line around each one. To get you started, the first verb on the list (***aller***), whose present participle is ***allant***, is already done. The present participles are written horizontally, vertically, or backwards.

aller
avoir
chanter
choisir
croire
dire
être
faire
finir

lire
naître
oser
prendre
tenir
vendre
venir
voir

C	H	A	N	T	A	N	T	A	T
H	F	Y	T	N	V	E	A	P	N
O	A	A	N	A	E	F	V	R	A
I	I	N	A	N	A	I	E	E	Y
S	S	T	Y	E	N	N	N	N	O
I	A	A	O	T	T	I	D	A	V
S	N	N	R	D	I	S	A	N	T
S	T	T	C	T	E	S	N	T	N
A	L	L	A	N	T	A	T	O	A
N	A	I	S	S	A	N	T	S	N
T	N	O	S	A	N	T	F	A	E
L	I	S	A	N	T	T	A	N	V

DIALOGUE

Directions: In the following dialogue there are blank spaces indicating missing verb forms. Select the appropriate verb form according to the sense of what the speakers are saying and write the letter of your choice on the line. The situation is given below.

Situation: You are a tourist in Paris. You are talking with the desk clerk in a hotel about a room.

L'employé: Bonjour. Vous désirez une chambre?
Vous: Oui, je désire _____ une petite chambre avec salle de bains.
1.   A. louer   B. loué   C. louée   D. louant

L'employé: C'est pour combien de personnes, s'il vous plaît?
Vous: _____ pour moi seulement.
2.   A. C'était   B. C'est   C. Ce fut   D. Ce fût

L'employé: Il me reste seulement une chambre à 150 euros la nuit, petit déjeuner compris.
Vous: D'accord. Je la _____ .
3.   A. prend   B. prends   C. pris   D. prenne

L'employé:	C'est pour combien de temps?			
Vous:	Probablement pour une semaine, je _____ .			
4.	A. croit	B. crus	C. croie	D. crois

L'employé:	Bon. Signez ici et _____-moi votre passeport, s'il vous plaît.			
5.	A. montres	B. montez	C. montrez	D. montrerez

Verb Test 20

CHANGING FROM ONE VERB TO ANOTHER

*Directions: The verb forms in the following statements are all in the **passé composé**. Change each sentence by replacing the verb in the sentence with the proper form of the verb in parentheses. Keep the **passé composé**, of course. Rewrite the statement in French.*

Models: Madeleine *est arrivée.* (partir)   **You write:** Madeleine *est partie.*
           Simone *a mangé* le gâteau. (faire)   Simone *a fait* le gâteau.

1. Richard *a appris* la leçon. (écrire)

_____

2. Elle *s'est assise.* (se lever)

_____

3. J'*ai écrit* la lettre. (lire)

_____

4. Elle *a fermé* la fenêtre. (ouvrir)

_____

5. Hélène *est arrivée.* (mourir)

_____

6. *Avez-vous acheté* un cadeau? (offrir)

_____

7. Marguerite *est sortie.* (venir)

_____

8. *Nous avons écouté* l'histoire. (croire)

_____

9. *Ils ont visité* Paris. (voir)

_____

10. Les enfants *ont pleuré.* (rire)

_____

11. *As-tu commandé* les frites? (prendre)

_____

12. *Ils sont allés* à Paris. (rester)

_____

13. L'étudiant *n'a pas compris* la réponse. (savoir)

_____

14. L'enfant *a mangé* un bon repas. (avoir)

_____

15. J'*ai envoyé* la lettre. (recevoir)

_____

16. *Avez-vous voyagé* en France? (être)

_____

17. *A-t-il ouvert* la boîte? (couvrir)

_____

18. Les enfants *se sont lavés*. (se taire)

_____

19. Louise *a désiré* venir chez moi. (vouloir)

_____

20. Qui *a entendu* le bruit? (faire)

_____

Verb Test 21

TRANSLATING VERB FORMS OF *ALLER*

Directions: Translate the following verb forms of **aller** *with their subjects into English. Keep in mind that some verb tenses can be translated into English in more than one way. For example, depending on the thought expressed in a particular situation,* **Je vais** *can mean I go, I do go, or I am going.*

1. Nous allons	_____	**8.** Elle est allée	_____
2. Tu allais	_____	**9.** Elles étaient allées	_____
3. Il alla	_____	**10.** Nous fûmes allés	_____
4. Nous irons	_____	**11.** Tu seras allé	_____
5. Vous iriez	_____	**12.** Vous seriez allé	_____
6. Que j'aille	_____	**13.** Qu'il soit allé	_____
7. Que j'allasse	_____	**14.** Qu'elle fût allée	_____

Now, let's try a few other verbs. The infinitive form is given in parentheses in case you do not recognize the verb form. Remember that all verb forms used in these drills and tests are in this book among the 501 French verbs, in the preliminary pages, and in the back pages.

15. (savoir) Je sais _____   **23.** (faire) Nous ferons _____
16. (être) Il fut _____   **24.** (venir) Je serais venu _____
17. (avoir) Elle aura _____   **25.** (s'en aller) Allez-vous-en! _____
18. (avoir) Nous aurions _____   **26.** (vendre) Vous avez vendu _____
19. (être) que je sois _____   **27.** (finir) Nous aurons fini _____
20. (avoir) Il eut _____   **28.** (boire) Tu avais bu _____
21. (avoir) J'ai eu _____   **29.** (monter) Elle est montée _____
22. (mettre) J'ai mis _____   **30.** (rester) Nous sommes restés _____

Verb Test 22

PRESENT INDICATIVE

Directions: *In this word puzzle, find the verb form in the present indicative tense for each infinitive given in parentheses in the sentences below. When you find them, draw a line around each one. The verb form in the present tense of **faire** in the first statement given below is **faites**. It has already been done to get you started. The words are written horizontally, vertically, diagonally, or backwards.*

- Que (**faire**)-vous ce soir?
- Que me (**dire**)-vous?
- J' (**aimer**) danser.
- Moi, je (**aller**) chez moi.
- Les garçons (**avoir**)-ils assez d'argent pour aller au cinéma?
- Nous (**aller**) en France l'été prochain.
- Quand (**partir**)-tu?
- Et vous, (**être**)-vous heureux?
- Tes parents (**pouvoir**)-ils venir avec nous?
- Que (**devoir**)-tu faire maintenant?
- Pourquoi (**courir**)-tu?
- (**Vendre**)-ils leur maison?
- Est-ce que nous (**finir**) le travail aujourd'hui?

A	I	M	E	B	A	L	I	T	A
C	D	A	L	O	S	E	T	I	D
O	O	E	F	I	O	A	E	G	I
U	I	E	A	A	L	L	O	N	S
R	S	V	S	I	O	U	E	A	U
S	A	I	R	E	U	Ê	T	E	S
I	L	N	A	P	S	U	V	L	O
A	E	I	P	E	U	V	E	N	T
E	O	N	T	N	E	D	N	E	V
L	U	I	A	L	L	E	Z	O	N
F	A	T	E	Z	V	A	V	A	I
F	I	N	I	S	S	O	N	S	S

Verb drills and tests   645

TRANSLATING VERB FORMS
(from English into French)

Directions: Translate the following verb forms with their subjects into French. In Test 21 you did the opposite. This is good practice because it helps you to master verb forms in French and English.

1. We are going

2. You (*tu*) were going

3. He went (*Tense No 3*)

4. We will go

5. You (*vous*) would go

6. that I may go

7. that I might go (*Tense No. 7*)

8. She has gone

9. They (*fem.*) had gone

10. We had gone (*Tense No. 10*)

11. You (*tu*) will have gone

12. You (*vous*) would have gone

13. that he may have gone

14. that she might have gone (*Tense No. 14*)

15. I know (*savoir*)

16. He was (*Tense No. 3*)

17. She will have

18. We would have

19. that I may be

20. He had (*Tense No. 3*)

21. I have had

22. I have put

23. We will do

24. I would have come

25. Go away! (*vous*)

26. You (*vous*) sold

27. We will have finished

28. You (*tu*) had drunk

29. She went up

30. We stayed

DRILLING THE VERB *AVOIR* AGAIN
(in the Seven Simple Tenses)

Note: In Test 14 you drilled the verb **avoir** in the seven simple tenses. Now, do it again here because you must know them in order to form the seven compound tenses of verbs conjugated with **avoir**. Practice these by writing them every day until you know them thoroughly. If you don't know them yet, see page 61. Also, read about **avoir** verbs on page viii. Review pages xxviii to xxx again.

Directions: Write the verb forms of **avoir** in the tenses indicated.

<u>Singular</u>   <u>Plural</u>

1. Présent de l'indicatif (Tense No. 1)

j' _____   nous _____
tu _____   vous _____
il/elle/on/(*or a noun*) _____   ils/elles/(*or a noun*) _____

2. Imparfait de l'indicatif (Tense No. 2)

j' _____   nous _____
tu _____   vous _____
il/elle/on/(*or a noun*) _____   ils/elles/(*or a noun*) _____

3. Passé simple (Tense No. 3)

j' _____   nous _____
tu _____   vous _____
il/elle/on/(*or a noun*) _____   ils/elles/(*or a noun*) _____

4. Futur (Tense No. 4)

j' _____   nous _____
tu _____   vous _____
il/elle/on/(*or a noun*) _____   ils/elles/(*or a noun*) _____

5. Conditionnel (Tense No. 5)

j' _____   nous _____
tu _____   vous _____
il/elle/on/(*or a noun*) _____   ils/elles/(*or a noun*) _____

6. Présent du subjonctif (Tense No. 6)

que j' _____ que nous _____
que tu _____ que vous _____
qu'il/elle/on/(*or a noun*) _____ qu'ils/elles/(*or a noun*) _____

7. Imparfait du subjonctif (Tense No. 7)

que j' _____ que nous _____
que tu _____ que vous _____
qu'il/elle/on/(*or a noun*) _____ qu'ils/elles/(*or a noun*) _____

Verb Test 25

DRILLING THE VERB *ÊTRE* AGAIN
(in the Seven Simple Tenses)

Note: In Test 15 you drilled the verb **être** in the seven simple tenses. We would like you to do it again here because you must know them in order to form the seven compound tenses of verbs conjugated with **être**. Practice these by writing them every day until you know them thoroughly. If you don't know them yet, see page 206. Also, read the statement about **être** verbs on page viii. Review again pages xxviii to xxx.

Directions: Write the verb forms of **être** *in the tenses indicated.*

1. Présent de l'indicatif (Tense No. 1)

<u>Singular</u>   <u>Plural</u>

je _____ nous _____
tu _____ vous _____
il/elle/on/(*or a noun*) _____ ils/elles/(*or a noun*) _____

2. Imparfait de l'indicatif (Tense No. 2)

j' _____ nous _____
tu _____ vous _____
il/elle/on/(*or a noun*) _____ ils/elles/(*or a noun*) _____

3. **Passé simple** (Tense No. 3)

je _____   nous _____

tu _____   vous _____

il/elle/on/(*or a noun*) _____   ils/elles/(*or a noun*) _____

4. **Futur** (Tense No. 4)

je _____   nous _____

tu _____   vous _____

il/elle/on/(*or a noun*) _____   ils/elles/(*or a noun*) _____

5. **Conditionnel** (Tense No. 5)

je _____   nous _____

tu _____   vous _____

il/elle/on/(*or a noun*) _____   ils/elles/(*or a noun*) _____

6. **Présent du subjonctif** (Tense No. 6)

que je _____   que nous _____

que tu _____   que vous _____

qu'il/elle/on/(*or a noun*) _____   qu'ils/elles/(*or a noun*) _____

7. **Imparfait du subjonctif** (Tense No. 7)

que je _____   que nous _____

que tu _____   que vous _____

qu'il/elle/on/(*or a noun*) _____   qu'ils/elles/(*or a noun*) _____

LE PASSÉ COMPOSÉ

Directions: This crossword puzzle *(mots-croisés)* tests your knowledge of the **passé composé**. The missing words in the sentences below are the present tense of **avoir** or **être**, or the correct form of the past participle, or a subject pronoun.

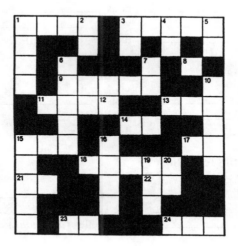

Horizontalement

1. Hier, je ____ allé au cinéma.
3. Marie est ____ (aller) à Paris.
8. Pierre ____ lu un livre.
9. Ils ont ____ (vouloir) partir.
11. ____ avez bien parlé.
13. La lettre? Je l'ai ____ (lire).
14. Paul s'est ____ (taire).
15. J'ai ____ (mettre) du sucre dans le café.
17. J'ai ____ (devoir) (*backwards*) partir.
18. Les lettres? Je les ai ____ (mettre) sur le bureau.
21. Nous avons bien ____ (rire).
22. Avez-vous ____ (savoir) la réponse?
23. Victor a-t- ____ compris?
24. Qu'a-t-elle ____ (dire)?

Verticalement

1. Je ____ tombé en montant l'escalier.
2. J'ai ____ (savoir) la réponse.
3. Hier soir, j' ____ beaucoup mangé.
4. Simone a ____ (lire) un livre.
5. Ce matin j'ai ____ (avoir) un petit accident.
6. Nous ____ pris le train.
7. Les enfants ont ____ (pouvoir) venir.
10. Nous avons ____ (vendre) la maison.
12. A-t-il ____ (savoir) (*backwards*) la réponse?
15. Madame Durand est ____ (mourir) hier soir.
16. Tu as ____ (finir) la leçon?
19. Jacqueline ____ restée à la maison.
20. Tu as ____ (savoir) cela, n'est-ce pas?

IDENTIFYING VERB FORMS
(in a Passage from French Literature)

*Directions: Read the following literary passage twice. Then, identify the verb forms with their subjects printed in **bold face** by giving (a) the infinitive of the verb form, (b) the name of the tense in French, and (c) the person and number of the verb form.*

Example: je vois   You write: (a) voir
(b) présent de l'indicatif
(c) 1st person singular

Pourquoi donc ne vous **vois-je** pas, mon cher ami? **Je suis** inquiète de vous. **Vous** m'**aviez** tant **promis** de ne faire qu'aller et venir de l'Hermitage ici! Sur cela **je** vous **ai laissé** libre; et point du tout, **vous laissez** passer huit jours. Si **on** ne m'**avait** pas **dit** que **vous étiez** en bonne santé, **je** vous **croirais** malade. **Je** vous **attendais** avant-hier ou hier, et **je** ne vous **vois** point arriver.

Mon Dieu! qu'**avez-vous** donc? **Vous** n'**avez** point d'affaires; **vous** n'**avez** pas non plus de chagrins, car **je me flatte** que **vous seriez venu** sur-le-champ me les confier. **Vous êtes** donc malade! **Tirez**-moi d'inquiétude bien vite, **je** vous en **prie**. Adieu, mon cher ami.

Lettre de Madame d'Épinay à Jean-Jacques Rousseau,
Selection from *Les Confessions* by Jean-Jacques Rousseau

1. vois-je

(a) _____

(b) _____

(c) _____

2. je suis

(a) _____

(b) _____

(c) _____

3. vous aviez promis

(a) _____

(b) _____

(c) _____

4. j'ai laissé

(a) _____

(b) _____

(c) _____

5. vous laissez

(a) _____

(b) _____

(c) _____

6. on avait dit

(a) _____

(b) _____

(c) _____

7. vous étiez

(a) _____

(b) _____

(c) _____

8. je croirais

(a) _____

(b) _____

(c) _____

9. vous avez

(a) _____

(b) _____

(c) _____

10. j'attendais

(a) _____

(b) _____

(c) _____

11. je vois

(a) _____

(b) _____

(c) _____

12. avez-vous

(a) _____

(b) _____

(c) _____

13. vous avez

(a) _____

(b) _____

(c) _____

14. je me flatte

(a) _____

(b) _____

(c) _____

15. vous seriez venu

(a) _____

(b) _____

(c) _____

16. vous êtes

(a) _____

(b) _____

(c) _____

17. tirez

(a) _____

(b) _____

(c) _____

18. je prie

(a) _____

(b) _____

(c) _____

Answers to Verb Tests with Explanations

Test 1

1. B   The verb **aller** is conjugated with **être** to form a compound tense. Review page viii. A and C are not correct because they are forms of **avoir**. You need the *passé composé* because of **hier**/yesterday. In D, **était** is imperfect indicative, which makes the verb form **était allée** pluperfect indicative. Review the uses of the *passé composé* on page xxi and the *plus-que-parfait de l'indicatif* on pages xxi to xxii. Review **aller** on page 31.

2. D   The subject is 3d person sing. In D, **peut** is 3d person sing. A, B, and C are not 3d person sing. Review **pouvoir** on page 353.

3. C   The tenses of **avoir** in A, B, and D would not make sense here because you need the imperfect indicative, which is in C. Review the imperfect tense on pages xvi and xvii. Review **avoir** on page 61.

4. A   You need the 3d person sing., present tense, of **sourire** because the subject is 3d person sing. The tenses in C and D do not make any sense here because there is nothing in the sentence to require the subjunctive. The verb form in B is not 3d person sing. Review **sourire** on page 450.

5. B   The tenses of **regarder** in C and D would not make sense here because you need the imperfect indicative, which is in B. The verb form in A is 3d person sing. and you are dealing with the subject **je**, which is 1st person, sing. Besides, C is not a good choice because **je** would be **j'** in front of **ai regardé**. Review the uses of the imperfect indicative tense on pages xvi and xvii. Review **regarder** on page 384.

6. A   You need the infinitive form **dormir** because it is right after the verb form **peux** in **je ne peux pas** (I am not able to sleep). The forms in B, C, and D would make no sense. Review those forms of **dormir** on page 168.

7. B   The situation is in the present. The subject, **le docteur**, is 3d person sing. and so is **vient** in B. In A, **viens** is not 3d person sing. C and D are not in the present tense. Review **venir** on page 492 and **venir de** on the bottom of that page. Also review *Verbs with prepositions* beginning on page 543, specifically at the top of page 550 where **venir de + inf.** is given.

8. C   The infinitive **nettoyer** is needed because of the preposition **de** in front of it. Review *Verbs with prepositions* beginning on page 543, specifically on page 548 where **demander de + inf.** is listed. Review the other forms of **nettoyer** in A, B, and D on page 307.

9. A   The infinitive **faire** is needed because **va** (a form of **aller**) precedes it. Review **aller + inf.** on page 551 and the other forms of **faire** in B, C, and D on page 218.

10. A   You need the past participle to complete the *passé composé* where you see the helping verb **a** in front of the blank space. The past participle in B is feminine but there is no preceding feminine direct object. Review the forms of **oublier** in C and D on page 320.

11. D   You need the fem. pl. form of the past participle (**achetées**) because there is a preceding fem. pl. direct object noun (**les chaussures**). The other past participles are masc. sing. in A, fem. sing. in B, and masc. pl. in C.

12. A   The subject is 1st pers. sing. **j'** and it requires **irai**, the future of **aller**. **La semaine prochaine** indicates future time. Review the other tenses of **aller** in B, C, and D on page 31.

13. B You need the 1st pers. sing. conditional of **aller** because the subordinate clause begins with **si** (if) and the verb in that clause is imperfect indicative (**j'avais**). Review **si** clauses, a summary of sequence of verb tenses at the top of page 560 where there are examples. Review the other tenses of **aller** in A, C, and D on page 31. Study, practice, and experience will help you recognize French verb forms and tenses.

14. A You need the 1st pers. sing. future of **aller** because the subordinate clause begins with **si** (if) and the verb in that clause is present indicative (**j'ai**). Review **si** clauses, a summary of sequence of verb tenses at the top of page 560 where there are examples. Review the other tenses of **aller** in B, C, and D on page 31.

15. B You need the fem. sing. form of the past participle (**lavée**) because the verb is reflexive (**se laver**/to wash oneself) and the fem. sing. agreement on the past participle is made with the reflexive pronoun **s'** (herself). We know it's fem. because the subject is **Paulette**. The reflexive pronoun **s'** in this sentence serves as a preceding direct object because Paulette washed *herself*. However, if there were a direct object *after* the verb, e.g., her feet, hair (as in sentence 16 below), there would be no agreement on the past participle. The other past participles in this sentence are masc. sing. in A, masc. pl. in C, and fem. pl. in D. Review also page viii.

16. A You need the masc. sing. form of the past participle (**lavé**) because in this sentence the reflexive pronoun **s'** in **s'est lavé** is an indirect object, not a direct object. A past participle never agrees in gender (masc. or fem.) or number (sing. or. pl.) with an indirect object. In other words, Gertrude washed her hair (**les cheveux**), which is *on herself*. Compare this sentence with number 15 above.

17. C You need the present indicative of **aller** because the sentence states **en ce moment**/at this moment. Review the other tenses of **aller** in A, B, and D on page 31. Review the uses of the present indicative tense and the examples on pages xv and xvi.

18. A You need the present indicative of **aller** because the sentence states **tous les jours** (every day), which is habitual action. Review the uses of the present indicative tense and the examples on page xv, in particular, the example in (b) at the top of page xvi.

19. B You need the present tense, 3d person pl. of **faire** because the subject is 3d person pl. Review the examples in (c) at the top of page xvi. Also, review the other tenses of **faire** in A, C, and D on page 218.

20. D You need the present tense, 1st person sing. of **être** because the subject is 1st person sing. Review the examples in (f) on page xvi. Also, review the other tenses of **être** in A, B, and C on page 206.

Test 2

1. A The situation is in the present. Review the other tenses of **trouver** in B, C, and D on page 483.

2. D You need the present tense because the action is going on in the present. Do you recognize the other tenses in A, B, and C? Review **croire** on page 129.

3. A Again, the present tense. Review the forms of **espérer** on page 198.

4. D If you cannot identify the tenses, review **être** on page 206.

5. A You need the future tense of **venir** because the clerk says that the suitcase will be available around five o'clock. You will come to get it at that time. Review the tenses of **venir** on page 492.

Test 3

1. **Ils comprennent bien aussi.** Study the forms of **comprendre** on page 100.
2. **Elles écrivent bien aussi.** Study the forms of **écrire** on page 173.
3. **Ils vont bien aussi.** Study the forms of **aller** on page 31.
4. **Je lis un livre dans le lit aussi.** Study the forms of **lire** on page 279.
5. **Ils voient bien aussi.** Study the forms of **voir** on page 498.
6. **Elle est allée au cinéma aussi.** You need to add **e** on the past participle for fem. agreement with the subject **elle**. Study the non-reflexive verbs conjugated with **être** to form the compound tenses on page viii. Also, study the forms of **aller** on page 31.
7. **Nous avons bien mangé aussi.** Study the *passé composé* of **manger** on page 283.
8. **Elles se sont assises aussi.** You need the fem. pl. agreement on the past participle of this reflexive verb **s'asseoir** because the reflexive pronoun **se** is a preceding direct object and the subject is **elles**. In other words, they *sat themselves*. Review the explanation in number 15 in Test 1. Review the forms of **s'asseoir** on page 51.
9. **Elle s'est lavée aussi.** Review the explanation in number 15 in Test 1. It's the same idea here. Review the *passé composé* of **se laver** on page 276.
10. **Elle s'est lavé les cheveux aussi.** Review the explanation in number 16 in Test 1. It's the same idea here.
11. **Ils ont rougi aussi.** Review the *passé composé* of **rougir** on page 419.
12. **Ils choisissent une auto aussi.** Study the present tense of **choisir** on page 93.
13. **Il finit la leçon aussi.** Study the present tense of **finir** on page 225.
14. **J'ai fait les devoirs aussi.** Study the *passé composé* of **faire** on page 218.
15. **Ils défendent la patrie aussi.** Study the present tense of **défendre** on page 142.
16. **Il répond à la question aussi.** Study the present tense of **répondre** on page 400 and **répondre à** + noun, page 544.
17. **Ils se couchent à dix heures aussi.** Study the forms of the reflexive verb **se coucher** on page 120.
18. **Elle s'est amusée aussi.** She amused *herself*. Review the explanation in number 15 in Test 1. It's the same idea here. Also, study the *passé composé* of the reflexive verb **s'amuser** on page 35.
19. **Je me suis reposé(e) aussi. Je** tells you if it is fem. or masc., depending on the context. If **me** (myself) is fem., add **e** to the past participle for fem. agreement with it. The idea here is the same as in the explanation in number 15 in Test 1. Study the *passé composé* of **se reposer** on page 401.
20. **Nous nous sommes levés tôt aussi.** Same idea here as in number 19 above. Review **se lever** on page 278.

Test 4

1. B   You need the future tense because **quand** introduces the clause and the verb in the main clause is future tense. Review the uses and examples of the future tense on page xviii and the formation of the future on page xxvii. On page 50 study the verb forms of **arriver** in A, C, and D.
2. B   You need the infinitive form because there is no subject preceding the blank space. Here, **vous** is an indirect object pronoun meaning *to you* (I would like to give these flowers to you.) On page 167 study the verb forms of **donner** in A, C, and D.

3. C You need the masc. pl. form of the past participle because **donner** is conjugated with **avoir** to form the *passé composé*, a compound tense, and it must agree with the preceding direct object **livres**. Here, **que** is a relative pronoun (*that* or *which*) and it refers to **les deux livres**. In other words, *Did you read the two books that I gave (to) you last week?*

4. D Same idea here as in number 3 above. Do you think you understand this construction by now? You need the fem. sing. form of the past participle because it refers to **que**, which relates to **la lettre**. In other words, *Here is the letter that I received yesterday.* Review the forms of **recevoir** on page 378.

5. A You need the *passé composé* because the sentence begins with **hier**/yesterday. In B the past participle is fem. because of the added **e**. There is no need for a fem. past participle because there is no *preceding* fem. direct object. The direct object is **une lettre**, which comes *after* the verb. Review the verb forms in C and D of **envoyer** on page 195.

6. D The clause where a verb form is needed begins with **si**/if. The verb in the main clause is conditional (**j'irais**/I would go). For those two reasons you need the imperfect indicative in D. Review **si** clauses where there are examples at the top of page 560. If you reversed the two clauses, the idea would be the same: **Si j'avais assez d'argent j'irais en France**/If I had enough money I would go to France. Review the verb forms in A, B, and C of **avoir** on page 61.

7. A You need the future tense of **avoir** because **quand** (when) precedes the required verb form and the verb in the main clause is future (**j'irai**). Review the uses and examples of the future on page xviii, in particular, example (d) at the top of the page. Also, review the other forms of **avoir** in B, C, and D on page 61.

8. B You need the present subjunctive of **être** (**que tu *sois***) because the verb in the preceding main clause is **j'insiste**. Here, the need for the subjunctive is the same in English, too, when we say: *I insist that you be here before five o'clock.* Review the uses and examples of the present subjunctive on page xix, especially example (c). Study the other forms of **être** in A, C, and D on page 206.

9. D You need the 3d person sing. present tense **veut** because the subject (**cela**/that) is 3d person sing. The form **veux** in C is 1st or 2d person sing. present tense of **vouloir.** There is nothing in the sentence to require the present subjunctive in A or the imperfect subjunctive in B. Review the forms of **vouloir** on page 500.

10. A You must know the impersonal expression **il faut**/it is necessary. Review the forms of **falloir** on page 219 and the expressions on the bottom of that page. Also, review the section on verbs with prepositions beginning on page 543, in particular, **falloir** + inf. on page 552. In B review **être** on page 206. In C review **il pleut (pleuvoir)** on page 347 and the examples on the bottom of that page. In D review **il fend (fendre)** on page 222.

11. D The conjunction **pendant que** (while) precedes the subject and required verb form. This indicates that two actions were going on at the same time in the past: *My brother was reading while I was writing.* For that reason the imperfect indicative is needed. Review the imperfect tense on pages xvi and xvii, especially example (a). Also, review the other forms of **écrire** in A, B, and C on page 173. See page xxvii for the regular formation of the imperfect.

12. A An action was going on in the past when another action occurred: *The students were reading when I entered the classroom.* Review the imperfect tense on pages xvi and xvii, especially example (b). Review the other forms of **entrer** in B, C, and D on page 193.

13. **B** You need the imperfect indicative tense because a habitual action took place in the past: *When I was little, my family and I used to go to the beach in the summer.* Review the imperfect tense on pages xvi and xvii, especially example (c). Review the other forms of **aller** in A, C, and D on page 31.

14. **C** You need the imperfect indicative tense because the sentence contains a description in the past: *Richard was sad when I saw him.* Review the imperfect tense on pages xvi and xvii, especially example (d). Also, review the other forms of **être** in A, B, and D on page 206.

15. **A** The reason for the imperfect indicative tense here is the same as in no. 14 above. Do you think you understand this construction now?

16. **B** You need the *passé composé* because the action took place in the past: *At midnight, Peter woke up and said to his brother: "Get up!"* In C the past participle is fem. sing., but there is no need for it because the subject is masc. Review agreement on the past participle of a reflexive verb in nos. 15 and 16, Test 1. Review the other forms of **se réveiller** in A, C, and D on page 413.

17. **C** You need the infinitive form **marcher** because it is right after the verb **entendre**. Review **entendre** + inf. on page 552. Review the other forms of **marcher** in A, B, and D on page 285.

18. **D** You are dealing with **avoir froid**/to feel cold. Review the section on verbs used in idiomatic expressions, beginning on page 530, especially **avoir froid** on page 532. Review the forms of **avoir** on page 61 and the examples on the bottom of that page. In A review **être** on page 206, **faire** in B on page 218, **tenir** in C on page 464, and the idiomatic expressions on the bottom of those pages.

19. **C** The subject of the verb is **nous**, 1st person pl. You need the *passé composé* because of **l'année dernière**/last year. The plural **s** is needed on **allés** because it is conjugated with **être** and the subject is plural. Review the other forms of **aller** in A, B, and D on page 31. Also, review page viii.

20. **C** The explanation here is the same as in nos. 3 and 4 above in this test.

Test 5

1. **C** You are dealing with **avoir lieu**/to take place. Review the section on verbs used in idiomatic expressions, beginning on page 530, especially **avoir lieu** near the bottom of page 532. You need the future of **avoir** because the exam will take place after tomorrow. Review **avoir** on page 61 and the forms of **être** in A and B on page 206.

2. **D** You are dealing with **avoir** in the idiomatic expression **il y a**/there is . . ., there are: *There is nothing to fear.* Review the section on verbs used in idiomatic expressions, beginning on page 530, especially **il y a** in the middle of page 533. Review the other forms of **avoir** in A and C on page 61. Review also **être** on page 206 for **soit** in B.

3. **B** You need the infinitive form **rester** because it is right after the verb **devrai** (devoir). Review **devoir** on page 161 and **devoir** + inf. on page 551. See **rester** on page 407 for the other forms in A, C, and D.

4. **C** Review **pouvoir** on page 353 for the forms in A, B, C, and D.

5. **A** Review **souhaiter** on page 447 for the forms in A, B, C, and D.

Test 6

Note: In this test, the verb form you are given in each sentence is the imperative (command) mood. Review the *impératif* on pages xxv and xxvi. The forms of the imperative are given near the bottom of each page among the 501 verbs fully conjugated in all the tenses in this book. They are the *tu*, *nous*, and *vous* forms; for example: **donne!**/give! (*tu* understood), **donnons!**/let's give! (*nous* understood), **donnez!**/give! (*vous* understood). You have to look at the ending of the verb form to see if the subject understood is 2d person sing. (*tu*), 1st person pl. (*nous*), or 2d person pl., polite sing. (*vous*).

In the imperative, **er** verbs, like **donner**, drop the **s** in the 2d person sing. (*tu* form) of the present indicative, for example: **Marie, donne-moi le chocolat!**/Marie, give me the chocolate! But the **s** remains if the word that follows is **en** or **y** to facilitate a liaison in pronunciation, making the **s** sound as **z**, for example: **Robert, donnes-en aux enfants!**/Robert, give some to the children! If you need to improve your pronunciation of French—in particular, verb forms—consult Barron's book *Pronounce It Perfectly in French*.

1. **Dites la phrase.** Study the forms of **lire** on page 279 and **dire**, page 164.
2. **Bois le lait.** Study the forms of **prendre** on page 356 and **boire**, page 74.
3. **Partez tout de suite.** Study the forms of **venir** on page 492 and **partir**, page 325.
4. **Ferme la fenêtre.** Study the forms of **ouvrir** on page 321 and **fermer**, page 223.
5. **Prends la valise là-bas.** Study the forms of **mettre** on page 294 and **prendre**, page 356.
6. **Écrivons la lettre.** Study the forms of **lire** on page 279 and **écrire**, page 173.
7. **Lisez le poème.** Study the forms of **apprendre** on page 43 and **lire**, page 279.
8. **Sortons maintenant.** Study the forms of **partir** on page 325 and **sortir**, page 444.
9. **Revenez à l'heure!** Study the forms of **être** (for *soyez*) on page 206 and **revenir**, page 414. Note that in the imperative **être** uses the forms of the present subjunctive. See example (d) at the bottom of page xxv.
10. **Faisons la leçon.** Study the forms of **voir** on page 498 and **faire**, page 218.
11. **Levez-vous, s'il vous plaît.** Study the forms of the reflexive verb **s'asseoir** on page 51 and **se lever**, page 278. Note that when you use a reflexive verb in the imperative, drop the subject pronoun, of course, but keep the reflexive pronoun **nous** or **vous**, placing it after the verb with a hyphen. **Tu** changes to **toi** in the affirmative imperative; for example: **Lève-toi!**/Get up! Under the *Impératif* on pages 51 and 278 note where the reflexive pronoun is placed when the imperative is negative.
12. **Refuse l'argent.** Study the forms of **accepter** on page 8 and **refuser**, page 383.
13. **Achète le vélo.** Study the forms of **vendre** on page 490 and **acheter**, page 17. Read the note above for an explanation of when **s** drops or is kept on **er** verbs in the *tu* form of the imperative.
14. **Soyez à l'heure.** Study the forms of **venir** on page 492 and **être** (for *soyez*) on page 206. Note that in the imperative **être** uses the forms of the present subjunctive. See example (d) at the bottom of page xxv.
15. **Va dans la maison.** Study the forms of **aller** on page 31 and **rester**, page 407. Note that **s** drops in the 2d person sing. (*tu* form) of the present indicative of **aller** when used in the imperative. But the **s** remains if the word that follows is **y** to facilitate a liaison in pronunciation, making the **s** sound as **z**, for example: **Robert, vas-y!**/Robert, go to it!
16. **Lève-toi.** Study the forms of **se laver** in the imperative on page 276 and **se lever**, page 278. Read our note of explanation in sentence no. 11 above.

17. **Dépêchons-nous.** Study the forms of the imperative of **se cacher** on page 81 and **se dépêcher**, page 147.

18. **Amuse-toi.** Study the forms of the imperative of **s'arrêter** on page 49 and **s'amuser**, page 35. Read the explanation about reflexive verbs in the imperative, affirmative, and negative, above in no. 11.

19. **Achète la maison.** Study the forms of the imperative of **vendre** on page 490 and **acheter**, page 17. Review the explanation in no. 13 above.

20. **Viens.** Study the imperative of **manger**, page 283 and **venir**, page 492.

Test 7

Note: For all verb forms in this test, review the uses and examples of the future and conditional on page xviii. For the formation of the future and conditional of regular verbs, review page xxvii.

Also, review the future and conditional on the page numbers given below.

1. **J'irais.** See **aller**, page 31.
2. **Je partirais.** See **partir**, page 325.
3. **J'aurais.** See **avoir**, page 61.
4. **Je serais.** See **être**, page 206.
5. **Tu aimerais.** See **aimer**, page 29.
6. **Tu ferais.** See **faire**, page 218.
7. **Il aurait.** See **avoir**, page 61.
8. **Il serait.** See **être**, page 206.
9. **Il irait.** See **aller**, page 31.
10. **On dirait.** See **dire**, page 164.
11. **Vous seriez.** See **être**, page 206.
12. **Elle lirait.** See **lire**, page 279.
13. **J'ouvrirais.** See **ouvrir**, page 321.
14. **Nous saurions.** See **savoir**, page 427.
15. **Ils viendraient.** See **venir**, page 492.
16. **On boirait.** See **boire**, page 74.

17. **Ils courraient.** See **courir**, page 123.
18. **Ils liraient.** See **lire**, page 279.
19. **Elle mettrait.** See **mettre**, page 294.
20. **Il apprendrait.** See **apprendre**, page 43.
21. **Je couvrirais.** See **couvrir**, page 125.
22. **Il deviendrait.** See **devenir**, page 160.
23. **Nous devrions.** See **devoir**, page 161.
24. **Vous diriez.** See **dire**, page 164.
25. **Vous iriez.** See **aller**, page 31.
26. **J'aimerais.** See **aimer**, page 29.
27. **Il faudrait.** See **falloir**, page 219.
28. **Ils seraient.** See **être**, page 206.
29. **Elles feraient.** See **faire**, page 218.
30. **On choisirait.** See **choisir**, page 93.

Test 8

Note: For the formation of the present indicative tense of regular verbs, review page xxvii. For the formation of the *passé composé* and other compound tenses, review pages xxviii to xxx. Note the position of **ne** and **pas** in the following negative sentences.

1. (a) **Non, je ne travaille pas.** (b) **Il ne travaille pas non plus.**
   Review the present indicative of **travailler** on page 479.
2. (a) **Non, elle n'étudie pas.** (b) **Ils n'étudient pas non plus.**
   Review the present indicative of **étudier** on page 207.
3. (a) **Non, elle ne va pas au match.** (b) **Je ne vais pas au match non plus.**
   Review the present indicative of **aller** on page 31.
4. (a) **Non, ils ne crient pas.** (b) **Nous ne crions pas non plus.**
   Review the present indicative of **crier** on page 128.
5. (a) **Non, il n'arrive pas.** (b) **Ils n'arrivent pas non plus.**
   Review the present indicative of **arriver** on page 50.

6. (a) **Non, je ne suis pas occupé.** (b) **Ils ne sont pas occupés non plus.**
   Review the present indicative of **être** on page 206. Note the expression **être occupé**
   (to be busy) on the bottom of page 315. Note also that **occupés** contains **s** to make it
   masc. pl. because it is an adjective that describes the subject **ils**, which is masc. plural.
   If the subject were **elles**, the sentence would be **elles ne sont pas occupées non plus.**

7. (a) **Non, je n'ai pas fermé la fenêtre.** (b) **Il n'a pas fermé la fenêtre non plus.**
   Review the *passé composé* of **fermer** on page 223. Note the position of **ne** and **pas** in
   a compound tense.

8. (a) **Non, je n'ai pas assisté à la conférence.** (b) **Ils n'ont pas assisté à la
   conférence non plus.**
   Review the *passé composé* of **assister** on page 52. On the bottom of that page, note
   the expression **assister à**. Note also the position of **ne** and **pas** in a compound tense.
   Also review the use of **assister à** on page 531.

9. (a) **Non, il n'est pas allé au supermarché.** (b) **Elle n'est pas allée au supermarché
   non plus.**
   Review the *passé composé* of **aller** on page 31. Note the need for the addition of **e** on
   the past participle **allée**. The fem. sing. agreement must be made on it because **aller**
   is conjugated with **être** to form a compound tense. The agreement is made with the
   subject, which is **elle**, fem. sing. Review page viii.

10. (a) **Non, elle n'est pas allée à la piscine.** (b) **Ils ne sont pas allés à la piscine non plus.**
   Read the explanation in no. 9 above. It's the same idea here.

Test 9

Note: From time to time practice the formation of the seven simple tenses for regular
verbs on pages xxvii and xxviii and the formation of the seven compound tenses on
pages xxviii to xxx.

1. A   The subject is **je**; therefore, you need the 1st person sing. of **prier**. Review the
      forms of **prier** in the present indicative tense on page 365 and the words and
      expressions related to that verb on the bottom of that page.

2. D   You need the 1st person pl. of **faire** because the subject is **nous**. The future tense
      is needed because of the sense of the statement. The other verb forms in A, B, and
      C would not make any sense here. If you do not recognize those forms, review
      faire on page 218.

3. D   You need the 1st person sing. of **espérer** because the subject is **je**. The tenses of
      espérer in B and C would make no sense here. In A the infinitive form of the verb
      cannot be used here because there is a subject. Review **espérer** on page 198. If
      you want to know why the *accent aigu* on **espérer** sometimes changes to *accent
      grave*, as in **j'espère**, review the section on orthographically changing verbs (those
      that change in spelling) on pages 554–556, in particular, examples (14) and (15)
      on page 556.

4. C   You need the 3d person sing. because the subject is **le train**, 3d person sing. The
      future tense is needed because the tenses in A, B, and D would make no sense. A
      is the *passé composé*. B is the conditional. D is the imperfect indicative. Can you
      recognize those tenses from the endings of the verb forms? If not, review them on
      pages xxvii, xxviii, and 50. Also, if you are not sure of how they are translated
      into English, review pages xiii and xiv where you will find English translations of
      all the tenses using the verb *to go* as an example. Just substitute the verb *to arrive*
      in place of *to go*.

5. B The only sensible verb tense here is in B: *It seems that it is going to be beautiful weather*. A is the *passé composé* of **faire** but the speakers are not talking about what the weather was like in the past. C is the imperfect indicative of **faire** but the speakers are not talking about what the weather was like at any particular time in the past. D is the present subjunctive of **faire** and there is nothing in the sentence that requires the subjunctive. Review the tenses of **faire** on page 218 and the expressions regarding weather on the bottom of that page. Also review the section on verbs used in idiomatic expressions, in particular with **faire** on page 537.

6. A The subject is **on**, 3d person sing. The verb form in A is also 3d person sing. As for the tenses of the verb forms in B, C, and D, review the verb **prévoir** on page 364.

7. C You cannot use the infinitive form in D because **le train**, 3d person sing., is the subject. As for the tenses of the verb forms in A and B, review the verb **partir** on page 325. The speaker supposes that the train *is going to leave* soon.

8. D You need the 1st person sing. of **croire** because the subject is **je**. B is 3d person sing. A is the *passé simple*, which is not used in conversation. C is the imperfect indicative of **croire**, which is a past tense, and the speakers are talking about things happening now. Review the verb forms of **croire** on page 129.

Test 10

1. C You need the infinitive form of the reflexive verb **se laver** because the preposition **de** is in front of the blank space where a verb form is required. For that reason, D is not a correct choice because it is not an infinitive. In C the form *me laver* (to wash myself) is needed because the subject is **je**. A is not a reflexive verb. B is reflexive but you cannot use **se laver** because the subject is **je**. When you use a reflexive verb, its pronoun (**me, te, se, nous, vous, se**) must agree with the subject; for example: **je me . . . , tu te . . . , il se . . .** and so on. Review the forms of **se laver** on page 276. Also, review **avoir besoin de** on the bottom of page 61.

2. D You need the *passé composé* of **entrer** because of the sense of the statement and the use of **a vu** (*passé composé* of **voir**) in the sentence. When Lisa entered the living room, she saw a vase of pretty flowers. In D the past participle **entrée** is fem. sing. because the verb is conjugated with **être** and the subject is fem. sing. Review page viii. In C the past participle **entré** is masc. sing. A is the present tense and B is the future, neither of which makes any sense from the point of view of time because the action is in the past. Review the forms of **entrer** on page 193.

3. B The sentence means *If I have the time, I will do the work*. Review the verb tenses in **si** (if) clauses at the top of page 560, example (a). Review the verb **faire** on page 218 where you will find the *passé composé* in choice A, the future in B, the conditional in C, and the imperfect indicative in D.

4. A The sentence means *If I had the time, I would do the work*. Review the verb tenses in **si** (if) clauses at the top of page 560, example (b). Review the verb **faire** on page 218 where you will find the conditional in A, the future in B, the conditional perfect in C, and the *passé composé* in D.

5. C The sentence means *If I had had the time, I would have done the work*. Review the verb tenses in **si** (if) clauses at the top of page 560, example (c). Review the verb **faire** on page 218 where you will find the *passé composé* in A, the future perfect in B, the conditional perfect in C, and the imperfect indicative in D. Also, see page xxiii, example (b) on the bottom of the page where the uses of the conditional perfect are explained with examples.

6. A This is the conditional of courtesy. See page xviii, example (b) on the bottom of the page where the uses of the conditional are explained with examples. Review the verb **aimer** on page 29 where you will find the conditional in A, the *passé composé* in B, the *passé simple* in C, and the imperfect indicative in D.

7. B At what time *would you be able* to come? The reply to the question contains the same verb (**pouvoir**) in the same tense. Review the English translation of the conditional on page xiii. See also the explanation on the bottom of page xviii in note (2) with the example. Study the verb forms of **pouvoir** on page 353.

8. B The verb in the **si** (if) clause is imperfect indicative of **être**; for that reason, the verb form in the other clause must be conditional. See the note in example (b) on page xix. See also example (b) at the top of page 560. Review **faire** on page 218 for the other forms in A, C, and D.

9. B **Je doute** expresses doubt and it requires the subjunctive of **venir** in the clause that follows. Review the subjunctive that begins in the middle of page 560, specifically **douter que** on page 564. Review **venir** on page 492 for the other forms in A, C, and D.

10. B **Avoir peur** expresses fear and it requires the subjunctive of **être** in the clause that follows. Review the subjunctive that begins in the middle of page 560, specifically **avoir peur que** on page 564, and the last example on the bottom of that page. Review **être** on page 206 for the other forms in A, C, and D. Review idiomatic expressions with **avoir** on pages 531 to 533.

11. D **Je regrette** expresses regret and it requires the subjunctive of the verb in the following clause. Review the subjunctive that begins in the middle of page 560, specifically **regretter que** on page 564. Review **être** on page 206 for the other forms in A, B, and C.

12. A The conjunction **à moins que** (unless) requires the subjunctive of the verb in the clause it introduces. Review the subjunctive that begins in the middle of page 560, specifically **à moins que** listed under certain conjunctions on that page. Review **venir** on page 492 for the other forms in B, C, and D.

13. B The conjunction **quoique** (although) requires the subjunctive of the verb in the clause it introduces. Review the subjunctive that begins in the middle of page 560, specifically **quoique** listed under certain conjunctions on page 561. Review **être** on page 206 for the other forms in A, C, and D.

14. B The conjunction **pour que** (in order that, so that) requires the subjunctive of the verb in the clause it introduces. Review the subjunctive that begins in the middle of page 560, specifically **pour que** listed under certain conjunctions on page 561. Review **comprendre** on page 100 for the other forms in A, C, and D.

15. B The conjunction **dès que** requires the future of the verb in the clause it introduces, provided that the verb in the main clause implies future time. In this sentence, **je partirai** is future. Review the future tense on page xviii and the example in (c). Review **arriver** on page 50 for the forms in A, B, C, and D.

16. C The impersonal expression **il est urgent que . . .** (it is urgent that . . .) requires the subjunctive of the verb in the clause it introduces. Review the subjunctive that begins in the middle of page 560, specifically **il est urgent que** on page 563. Review **partir** on page 325 for the forms in A, B, C, and D.

17. D You need the pluperfect indicative tense of **oublier** because this past action occurred *before* the other past action in the sentence (*I remembered that I had forgotten*). Review the explanation and uses of the pluperfect indicative tense on

the bottom of page xxi to page xxii. Review **oublier** on page 320 for the forms in A, B, C, and D. Also, review **se rappeler** on page 377.

18. C You need the pluperfect indicative tense of **dormir**. Review, again, the explanation and uses of the pluperfect indicative tense on the bottom of page xxi to page xxii. Review **dormir** on page 168.

19. B You need the *passé composé* of **dormir**. You are saying that you are tired *now* (**maintenant**) because you did not sleep. Review the explanation and uses of the *passé composé* with examples on page xxi.

20. A You need the future perfect of **finir** because the verb in the other clause is in the future (**elle arrivera**) and it is introduced by the conjunction **quand** (when). Both actions will take place in the future. The action that will happen in the future *before* another future action is in the future perfect tense. Review the explanation and uses of the future perfect, with examples, on page xxiii. Review the verb forms of **finir** on page 225. If you did not recognize **arrivera** as future, review **arriver** on page 50.

Test 11

Note: For all verb forms in this test, review the uses and examples of the present indicative on pages xv and xvi and the *passé composé* on page xxi. For the formation of the present indicative of regular verbs, review page xxvii. For the formation of the *passé composé*, review the bottom of page xxviii and Tense No. 8 at the top of page xxix.

For the formation of regular and irregular past participles, see page ix.

Also, review the present indicative and the *passé composé* on the page numbers given below.

1. **Elle est allée.**
   See **aller**, page 31.
2. **Il a eu.**
   See **avoir**, page 61.
3. **Je me suis assis.**
   See **s'asseoir**, page 51.
4. **Ils ont eu.**
   See **avoir**, page 61.
5. **Tu as été.**
   See **être**, page 206.
6. **Il est allé.**
   See **aller**, page 31.
7. **Nous sommes allés.**
   See **aller**, page 31.
8. **Nous avons eu.**
   See **avoir**, page 61.
9. **J'ai parlé.**
   See **parler**, page 324.
10. **Elles sont venues.**
    See **venir**, page 492.

11. **J'ai bu.**
    See **boire**, page 74.
12. **Ils ont bu.**
    See **boire**, page 74.
13. **Vous avez bu.**
    See **boire**, page 74.
14. **J'ai cru.**
    See **croire**, page 129.
15. **Tu as dit.**
    See **dire**, page 164.
16. **J'ai pu.**
    See **pouvoir**, page 353.
17. **Il a fallu.**
    See **falloir**, page 219.
18. **Vous avez lu.**
    See **lire**, page 279.
19. **Vous avez dit.**
    See **dire**, page 164.
20. **Tu as mis.**
    See **mettre**, page 294.

21. **Elle est née.**
    See **naître**, page 305.
22. **Elle est morte.**
    See **mourir**, page 302.
23. **Elle a vendu.**
    See **vendre**, page 490.
24. **Ils se sont amusés.**
    See **s'amuser**, page 35.
25. **Elle est entrée.**
    See **entrer**, page 193.
26. **On a fini.**
    See **finir**, page 225.
27. **Elles ont couru.**
    See **courir**, page 123.
28. **Ils ont pris.**
    See **prendre**, page 356.
29. **On a appris.**
    See **apprendre**, page 43.
30. **Elles sont arrivées.**
    See **arriver**, page 50.

Test 12

Note: This test is a good exercise to practice the formation of the seven simple tenses by using the required endings for regular **-er, -ir,** and **-re** verbs. The explanations and endings are on pages xxvii and xxviii. For irregular verbs, see the verbs arranged alphabetically at the top of each page among the 501 verbs fully conjugated in all the tenses in this book.

Présent de l'indicatif (Tense No. 1)
1. J'aime.
2. Tu chantes.
3. Il/elle/on étudie.
4. Janine choisit.
5. J'entends.
6. Nous attendons.
7. Vous mangez.
8. Ils/elles vendent.
9. Richard et moi finissons.
10. Marie et Jeanne donnent.

Imparfait de l'indicatif (Tense No. 2)
1. Je parlais.
2. Tu finissais.
3. Il/elle/on vendait.
4. Madeleine était.
5. Il/elle/on avait.
6. Nous venions.
7. Vous faisiez.
8. Ils/elles allaient.
9. Paul et Henri jouaient.
10. Tu donnais.

Passé simple (Tense No. 3)
1. Je parlai.
2. Tu finis.
3. Il/elle/on vendit.
4. Catherine écrivit.
5. Ils/elles allèrent.
6. Nous donnâmes.
7. Vous choisîtes.
8. Ils/elles comprirent.
9. Hélène et Raymond désirèrent.
10. Il/elle/on dansa.

Futur (Tense No. 4)
1. Je mangerai.
2. Tu finiras.
3. Il/elle/on vendra.
4. La femme écrira.
5. J'irai.
6. Nous donnerons.
7. Vous choisirez.
8. Ils/elles comprendront.
9. Les garçons joueront.
10. J'aurai.

Conditionnel (Tense No. 5)
1. J'irais.
2. Tu finirais.
3. Il/elle/on ferait.
4. Je mangerais.
5. Vous pourriez.
6. Nous parlerions.
7. Vous seriez.
8. Ils/elles auraient.
9. Je prendrais.
10. Vous dîneriez.

Présent du subjonctif (Tense No. 6)
1. que je parle
2. que tu donnes
3. qu'il/elle/on ose
4. que je choisisse
5. que tu manges
6. que nous partions
7. que vous vendiez
8. qu'ils/elles prennent
9. que nous finissions
10. qu'il/elle/on ferme

Imparfait du subjonctif (Tense No. 7)

1. que je parlasse
2. que tu donnasses
3. qu'il/elle/on ouvrît

4. que nous partissions
5. que vous voulussiez
6. qu'ils/elles finissent

Test 13

Note: Review the regular and irregular past participles on page ix.

Test 14

Note: You must know the verb **avoir** in the seven simple tenses because they are needed to form the seven compound tenses of verbs conjugated with **avoir**. If you did not do well on this test, study them on page 61 and write them for practice until you are sure that you know them. Review the seven compound tenses of a verb conjugated with **avoir**, for example, **parler** on page 324. If you drop the past participle **parlé**, you will see that what is left is the verb **avoir** in the seven simple tenses.

1. Présent de l'indicatif
(Tense No. 1)

j'ai	nous avons
tu as	vous avez
il/elle/on a	ils/elles ont

2. Imparfait de l'indicatif
(Tense No. 2)

j'avais	nous avions
tu avais	vous aviez
il/elle/on avait	ils/elles avaient

3. Passé simple
(Tense No. 3)

j'eus	nous eûmes
tu eus	vous eûtes
il/elle/on eut	ils/elles eurent

4. Futur
(Tense No. 4)

j'aurai	nous aurons
tu auras	vous aurez
il/elle/on aura	ils/elles auront

5. Conditionnel
(Tense No. 5)

j'aurais	nous aurions
tu aurais	vous auriez
il/elle/on aurait	ils/elles auraient

7. Imparfait du subjonctif
(Tense No. 7)

que j'eusse	que nous eussions
que tu eusses	que vous eussiez
qu'il/elle/on eût	qu'ils/elles eussent

6. Présent du subjonctif
(Tense No. 6)

que j'aie	que nous ayons
que tu aies	que vous ayez
qu'il/elle/on ait	qu'ils/elles aient

Test 15

Note: You must know the verb **être** in the seven simple tenses because they are needed to form the seven compound tenses of verbs conjugated with **être**. If you did not do well on this test, study them on page 206 and write them for practice until you are sure that you know them. Review the seven compound tenses of a verb conjugated with **être**, for example, **aller** on page 31. If you drop the past participle **allé**, you will see that what is left is the verb **être** in the seven simple tenses.

1. Présent de l'indicatif
(Tense No. 1)

je suis	nous sommes
tu es	vous êtes
il/elle/on est	ils/elles sont

5. Conditionnel
(Tense No. 5)

je serais	nous serions
tu serais	vous seriez
il/elle/on serait	ils/elles seraient

2. Imparfait de l'indicatif
(Tense No. 2)

j'étais	nous étions
tu étais	vous étiez
il/elle/on était	ils/elles étaient

6. Présent du subjonctif
(Tense No. 6)

que je sois	que nous soyons
que tu sois	que vous soyez
qu'il/elle/on soit	qu'ils/elles soient

3. Passé simple
(Tense No. 3)

je fus	nous fûmes
tu fus	vous fûtes
il/elle/on fut	ils/elles furent

7. Imparfait du subjonctif
(Tense No. 7)

que je fusse	que nous fussions
que tu fusses	que vous fussiez
qu'il/elle/on fût	qu'ils/elles fussent

4. Futur
(Tense No. 4)

je serai	nous serons
tu seras	vous serez
il/elle/on sera	ils/elles seront

Test 16

Note: This test is another example to show that it is very important for you to know the present indicative of **avoir** and **être** so that you can form the *passé composé*. It also shows that you must know the imperfect indicative of **avoir** and **être** so that you can form the pluperfect indicative (*le plus-que-parfait de l'indicatif*). For the English translations of both these tenses, review the *passé composé* and the *plus-que-parfait de l'indicatif* on pages xxi to xxii, where you will find explanations and examples in French and English.

Review the *passé composé* and the *plus-que-parfait de l'indicatif* on the page numbers given below.

1. **Elle était allée.**
   See **aller**, page 31.
2. **Il avait eu.**
   See **avoir**, page 61.
3. **Je m'étais assis.**
   See **s'asseoir**, page 51.
4. **Ils avaient eu.**
   See **avoir**, page 61.
5. **Tu avais été.**
   See **être**, page 206.
6. **Il était allé.**
   See **aller**, page 31.
7. **Nous étions allés.**
   See **aller**, page 31.
8. **Nous avions eu.**
   See **avoir**, page 61.
9. **J'avais parlé.**
   See **parler**, page 324.
10. **Elle était venue.**
    See **venir**, page 492.
11. **J'avais bu.**
    See **boire**, page 74.
12. **Ils s'étaient tus.**
    See **se taire**, page 460.
13. **J'avais fait.**
    See **faire**, page 218.
14. **Tu avais dû.**
    See **devoir**, page 161.
15. **Vous aviez dit.**
    See **dire**, page 164.
16. **J'avais pu.**
    See **pouvoir**, page 353.
17. **Il avait fallu.**
    See **falloir**, page 219.
18. **Vous aviez lu.**
    See **lire**, page 279.
19. **Vous aviez dit.**
    See **dire**, page 164.
20. **Tu avais mis.**
    See **mettre**, page 294.
21. **Elle était née.**
    See **naître**, page 305.
22. **Elle était morte.**
    See **mourir**, page 302.
23. **Elle s'était lavée.**
    See **se laver**, page 276.
24. **Elles s'étaient lavées.**
    See **se laver**, page 276.
25. **J'étais entré.**
    See **entrer**, page 193.
26. **On avait parlé.**
    See **parler**, page 324.
27. **Ils avaient couru.**
    See **courir**, page 123.
28. **Ils avaient pris.**
    See **prendre**, page 356.
29. **On avait dit.**
    See **dire**, page 164.
30. **J'avais compris.**
    See **comprendre**, page 100.

Test 17

1. **B** **Partir** is conjugated with **être** to form a compound tense, so C and D are not appropriate choices because they are forms of **avoir**. You need the present subjunctive of **être** in B because of the impersonal expression **il est possible que** in the beginning of the sentence. Review the section on the uses of the subjunctive that begins in the middle of page 560, in particular, **il est possible que** on page 563. Review also **partir** in the *passé du subjonctif* (Tense No. 13), page 325. Refresh your memory by reading about the *passé du subjonctif* with explanations and examples in French and English on page xxiv.

2. **C** **Faire** is conjugated with **avoir** to form a compound tense; so B and D are not appropriate choices because they are forms of **être**. You need the present subjunctive of **avoir** in C because the verb in the main clause is **douter**. Review the section on the uses of the subjunctive that begins in the middle of page 560, in particular, **douter que** on page 564. Review also **faire** in the *passé du subjonctif* (Tense No. 13), page 218. Refresh your memory by reading about the *passé du subjonctif* with explanations and examples in French and English on page xxiv.

3. C   In front of the blank space there is a verb form (**je ne peux pas**/I can't). That is why you need the infinitive form in C (*I am not able to go out*). Review **pouvoir** + inf. on page 552. Review the other forms of sortir in A, B, and D on page 444. As for **il fait un temps affreux**, review verbs used in weather expressions on pages 557 and 558, specifically (b) on page 557.

4. B   You need the present participle **entrant** because it is preceded by **en**. Josephine fell *while entering* (*en entrant*) the kitchen. Review regular and irregular present participles on page ix. Review the other forms of **entrer** in A, C, and D on page 193.

5. B   Simone wiped the table. You need the past participle **essuyé** to complete the *passé composé*. There is no need for the fem. agreement in C because there is no fem. sing. direct object that *precedes* the verb. A is the infinitive form. D is the present participle. Review **essuyer** on page 200.

6. B   To complete the *passé composé* you need **mise**, which is fem. sing. because the reflexive pronoun **s'** (*se*/herself) serves as the preceding direct object pronoun and it refers to **Françoise**, the subject, which is fem. sing. Review **se mettre à** + inf. on page 546. Review the forms of **se mettre** on page 295 and the examples on the bottom of that page.

7. D   The subject, **les enfants**, is 3d person pl. The only verb form that is also 3d person pl. among the choices is in D. Review the forms of **vouloir** on page 500.

8. C   To complete the *passé composé* you need **achetées**, which is fem. pl. because the relative pronoun **que** (which or that) refers to the preceding direct object, **les fleurs**, which is fem. pl. The past participle in A is masc. sing. In B it is masc. pl. The infinitive in D cannot be used because you must complete the *passé composé*. Review **acheter** on page 17 and the examples on the bottom of that page.

9. A   The verb form in the clause beginning with **quand** is in the *passé antérieur* (past anterior), which is used in literary style. Review the explanation and examples of that tense on page xxii. Since that tense is used in the subordinate clause, you need to use the *passé simple* in the main clause, which is in choice A. You need the 3d person sing. (**partit**) because the subject (**il**) is 3d person sing. Review the uses and explanation of the *passé simple* on page xvii and the examples in French and English. Also, review the *passé antérieur* (Tense No. 10) of **manger** on page 283 and the *passé simple* (Tense No. 3) of **partir** as well as the other forms in the choices on page 325. Remember that the *passé simple* and the *passé antérieur* are literary tenses. They are not normally used in conversational French. These two tenses are occasionally used in these tests so you can become aware of them when reading French literature.

10. B   To complete the *conditionnel passé* (Tense No. 12) of **faire**, you need the conditional (Tense No. 5) of **avoir**, which is **aurais**, 1st person sing., since the subject **je** is 1st person sing. As for **j'aurais fait** (I would have done), review the uses and explanation of the *conditionnel passé* on page xxiii and the examples in French and English, as well as Tense No. 12 of **faire** on page 218. As for **j'avais eu** (I had had) review the *plus-que-parfait de l'indicatif* (Tense No. 9) on pages xxi, xxii, and 61. Also, review **si** (if) clauses at the top of page 560.

Test 18

Note: Review the regular and irregular present participles on page ix.

```
C H A N T A N T A T
H F Y T N V E A P N
O A A N A E F V R A
I I N A N A I E E Y
S S T Y E N N N N O
I A A O T T I D A V
S N N R D I S A N T
S T T C T É S N T N
A L L A N T A T O A
N A I S S A N T S N
T N O S A N T F A E
L I S A N T T A N V
```

Test 19

Note: From time to time practice the formation of the seven simple tenses for regular verbs on pages xxvii and xxviii and the formation of the seven compound tenses on pages xxviii to xxx.

1. A The infinitive form is needed because the blank space is preceded by a verb form and a subject (**Je désire**). Review **désirer** + inf. on page 551. In B, **loué** is a masc. sing. past participle. In C, **louée** is a fem. sing. past participle. There is no need for a past participle here because there is no helping verb in the sentence to require the completion of a compound tense. In D, **louant** is a present participle and there is no need for that because it would make no sense. Review **louer** on page 280.

2. B You need the present indicative tense (**C'est**/It is) because the conversation is taking place right now. Review the other forms of **être** in A, C, and D on page 206.

3. B By now we hope that you are able to recognize the ending of a verb form that agrees with the subject in person (1st, 2d, or 3d) and number (sing. or pl.). For example: **je prends, tu prends, il prend**, and so forth. There is nothing in the sentence to require the present subjunctive **prenne**. Review the verb forms and tenses of **prendre** on page 356.

4. D Same here. The ending of a verb form agrees with the subject in person and number. See no. 3 above. There is nothing in the sentence to require the present subjunctive **croie**. Review the verb forms and tenses of **croire** on page 129.

5. C The clerk at the hotel desk started the conversation by using the polite **vous** form while talking to you. That is why you need the **vous** form, **montrez**, in C. The clerk also tells you **"Signez"** in the same statement. You are dealing with the imperative (command) because he is telling you to do something. In the imperative the subject is not stated. Review the imperative on pages xxv and xxvi. In B the infinitive of the verb form **montez** is **monter**/to go up, which is on page 297. Review the forms of **montrer** on page 298.

Test 20

Note: Review page viii. Review regular and irregular past participles on page ix. Study the formation and uses of the *passé composé* with examples in French and English on page xxi. Also, review the *passé composé* on the pages given after each answer.

1. **Richard a écrit la leçon.** Review **apprendre**, page 43 and **écrire**, page 173.
2. **Elle s'est levée.** Review **s'asseoir**, page 51 and **se lever**, page 278.
3. **J'ai lu la lettre.** Review **écrire**, page 173 and **lire**, page 279.
4. **Elle a ouvert la fenêtre.** Review **fermer**, page 223 and **ouvrir**, page 321.
5. **Hélène est morte.** Review **arriver**, page 50 and **mourir**, page 302.
6. **Avez-vous offert un cadeau?** Review **acheter**, page 17 and **offrir**, page 317.
7. **Marguerite est venue.** Review **sortir**, page 444 and **venir**, page 492.
8. **Nous avons cru l'histoire.** Review **écouter**, page 172 and **croire**, page 129.
9. **Ils ont vu Paris.** Review **visiter**, page 496 and **voir**, page 498.
10. **Les enfants ont ri.** Review **pleurer**, page 346 and **rire**, page 417.
11. **As-tu pris les frites?** Review **commander**, page 96 and **prendre**, page 356.
12. **Ils sont restés à Paris.** Review **aller**, page 31 and **rester**, page 407.
13. **L'étudiant n'a pas su la réponse.** Review **comprendre**, page 100 and **savoir**, page 427.
14. **L'enfant a eu un bon repas.** Review **manger**, page 283 and **avoir**, page 61.
15. **J'ai reçu la lettre.** Review **envoyer**, page 195 and **recevoir**, page 378.
16. **Avez-vous été en France?** Review **voyager**, page 501 and **être**, page 206.
17. **A-t-il couvert la boîte?** Review **ouvrir**, page 321 and **couvrir**, page 125.
18. **Les enfants se sont tus.** Review **se laver**, page 276 and **se taire**, page 460.
19. **Louise a voulu venir chez moi.** Review **désirer**, page 154 and **vouloir**, page 500.
20. **Qui a fait le bruit?** Review **entendre**, page 190 and **faire**, page 218.

Test 21

Note: Review the two-page spread on pages xiii and xiv to be sure you can translate into English the seven simple tenses, the seven compound tenses, and the imperative. The model verb on those two pages is *to go* (***aller***). Keep those two pages open flat and flip back and forth to page 31, where you see all the forms in all the tenses of **aller**. Compare the forms in English and French. As a guide, follow the tense No. and the name of the tense in both languages as you make your comparison. For practice, you can apply this procedure to other verbs by merely substituting an English verb for a French one, e.g., *to drink* (***boire***), which is on page 74.

The asterisks in front of each of the English verb forms below designate the following:
*The French verb forms in Tense No. 3 (*le passé simple*) are used in literary style, formal writing. In French conversation and informal writing use the *passé composé* (Tense No. 8) instead of this tense.
**The French verb forms in Tense No. 7 (*l'imparfait du subjonctif*) are used in literary style, formal writing. In French conversation and informal writing use the *présent du subjonctif* (Tense No. 6) instead of this tense.
***The French verb forms in Tense No. 10 (*le passé antérieur*) are used in literary style, formal writing. In French conversation and informal writing, use *le plus-que-parfait de l'indicatif* (Tense No. 9) instead of this tense.

****The French verb forms in Tense No. 14 (*le plus-que-parfait du subjonctif*) are used in literary style, formal writing. In French conversation and informal writing, use *le passé du subjonctif* (Tense No. 13) instead of this tense.

1. we go, we do go, we are going
2. you were going, you went, you used to go
*3. he went, he did go
4. we shall go, we will go
5. you would go
6. that I may go
**7. that I might go
8. she has gone, she went, she did go
9. they had gone
***10. we had gone
11. you will have gone

12. you would have gone
13. that he may have gone
****14. that she might have gone

15. I know, I do know

*16. he was
17. she will have

18. we would have
19. that I may be
*20. he had
21. I have had, I had, I did have
22. I put, I have put, I did put
23. we will do, we will make
24. I would have come
25. Go away!
26. You have sold, you sold, you did sell
27. We will have finished
28. You had drunk
29. She has gone up, she went up, she did go up
30. We have stayed, we stayed, we did stay

Test 22

Note: Verify the verb forms in the present indicative tense by looking up the verbs in this test on the pages where they appear among the 501 verbs in this book.

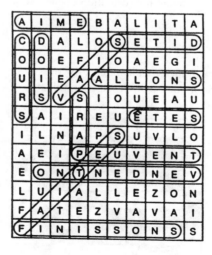

Test 23

Note: In Test 21 you translated verb forms in a variety of tenses from French to English. In this test you are translating English verb forms in a variety of tenses back into French.

<table>
<tr><td>1. Nous allons</td><td>16. Il fut</td></tr>
<tr><td>2. Tu allais</td><td>17. Elle aura</td></tr>
<tr><td>3. Il alla</td><td>18. Nous aurions</td></tr>
<tr><td>4. Nous irons</td><td>19. Que je sois</td></tr>
<tr><td>5. Vous iriez</td><td>20. Il eut</td></tr>
<tr><td>6. Que j'aille</td><td>21. J'ai eu</td></tr>
<tr><td>7. Que j'allasse</td><td>22. J'ai mis</td></tr>
<tr><td>8. Elle est allée</td><td>23. Nous ferons</td></tr>
<tr><td>9. Elles étaient allées</td><td>24. Je serais venu</td></tr>
<tr><td>10. Nous fûmes allés</td><td>25. Allez-vous-en!</td></tr>
<tr><td>11. Tu seras allé</td><td>26. Vous avez vendu</td></tr>
<tr><td>12. Vous seriez allé</td><td>27. Nous aurons fini</td></tr>
<tr><td>13. Qu'il soit allé</td><td>28. Tu avais bu</td></tr>
<tr><td>14. Qu'elle fût allée</td><td>29. Elle est montée</td></tr>
<tr><td>15. Je sais</td><td>30. Nous sommes restés</td></tr>
</table>

Test 24

Note: This is a repeat of Test 14 because you must know thoroughly the verb forms of **avoir** in the seven simple tenses. They are needed to form the seven compound tenses. Go to Test 14 in this answers section and correct your work. Also, review page 61 where you will find them all. Review again the formation of the seven compound tenses on pages xxviii to xxx.

Test 25

Note: This is a repeat of Test 15 because you must know thoroughly the verb forms of **être** in the seven simple tenses. They are needed to form the seven compound tenses. Go to Test 15 in this answers section and correct your work. Also, review page 206 where you will find them all. Review again the formation of the seven compound tenses on pages xxviii to xxx.

Test 26

Note: Verify the verb forms in the *passé composé* by looking up the verbs in this test on the pages where they appear among the 501 verbs in this book.

Test 27

1. (a) **voir**
   (b) **présent de l'indicatif**
   (c) 1st pers., sing.
2. (a) **être**
   (b) **présent de l'indicatif**
   (c) 1st pers., sing.
3. (a) **promettre**
   (b) **plus-que-parfait de l'indicatif**
   (c) 2d pers., pl.
4. (a) **laisser**
   (b) **passé composé**
   (c) 1st pers., sing.
5. (a) **laisser**
   (b) **présent de l'indicatif**
   (c) 2d pers., pl.
6. (a) **dire**
   (b) **plus-que-parfait de l'indicatif**
   (c) 3d pers., sing.
7. (a) **être**
   (b) **imparfait de l'indicatif**
   (c) 2d pers., pl.
8. (a) **croire**
   (b) **conditionnel**
   (c) 1st pers., sing.
9. (a) **avoir**
   (b) **présent de l'indicatif**
   (c) 2d pers., pl.
10. (a) **attendre**
    (b) **imparfait de l'indicatif**
    (c) 1st pers., sing.
11. (a) **voir**
    (b) **présent de l'indicatif**
    (c) 1st pers., sing.
12. (a) **avoir**
    (b) **présent de l'indicatif**
    (c) 2d pers., pl.
13. (a) **avoir**
    (b) **présent de l'indicatif**
    (c) 2d pers., pl.
14. (a) **se flatter**
    (b) **présent de l'indicatif**
    (c) 1st pers., sing.
15. (a) **venir**
    (b) **conditionnel passé**
    (c) 2d pers., pl.
16. (a) **être**
    (b) **présent de l'indicatif**
    (c) 2d pers., pl.
17. (a) **tirer**
    (b) **impératif**
    (c) 2d pers., pl.
18. (a) **prier**
    (b) **présent de l'indicatif**
    (c) 1st pers., sing.

active voice   When we speak or write in the active voice, the subject of the verb performs the action. The action falls on the direct object.

*Everyone loves Janine / **Tout le monde aime Janine.***

The subject is *everyone*. The verb is *loves*. The direct object is *Janine*. See also *passive voice* in this list. Compare the above sentence with the example in the passive voice.

adjective   An adjective is a word that modifies a noun or a pronoun. In grammar, to modify a word means to describe, limit, expand, or make the meaning particular.

*a beautiful garden / **un beau jardin;** she is pretty / **elle est jolie.***

The adjective *beautiful/**beau*** modifies the noun *garden/**jardin***. The adjective *pretty/**jolie*** modifies the pronoun *she/**elle***. In French there are different kinds of adjectives. *See also* comparative adjective, demonstrative adjective, descriptive adjective, interrogative adjective, limiting adjective, possessive adjective, superlative adjective.

adverb   An adverb is a word that modifies a verb, an adjective, or another adverb. An adverb says something about how, when, where, to what extent, or in what way.

*Jane runs swiftly / **Jeanne court rapidement.***

The adverb *swiftly/**rapidement*** modifies the verb *runs/**court***. The adverb shows *how* she runs.

*Jack is a very good friend / **Jacques est un très bon ami.***

The adverb *very/**très*** modifies the adjective *good/**bon***. The adverb shows *how good* a friend he is.

*The boy is eating too fast now / **Le garçon mange trop vite maintenant.***

The adverb *too/**trop*** modifies the adverb *fast/**vite***. The adverb shows *to what extent* he is eating *fast*. The adverb *now/**maintenant*** tells us *when*.

*The post office is there / **Le bureau de poste est là.***

The adverb *there/**là*** modifies the verb *is/**est***. It tells us *where* the post office is.

*Mary writes carefully / **Marie écrit soigneusement.***

The adverb *carefully/**soigneusement*** modifies the verb *writes/**écrit***. It tells us *in what way* she writes.

affirmative statement, negative statement   A statement in the affirmative is expressed positively. To negate an affirmative statement is to make it negative.

Affirmative: *I like chocolate ice cream / **J'aime la glace au chocolat.***

Negative: *I do not like chocolate ice cream / **Je n'aime pas la glace au chocolat.***

agreement of adjective with noun   Agreement is made on the adjective with the noun it modifies in gender (masculine or feminine) and number (singular or plural).

*a white house / **une maison blanche.***

The adjective **blanche** is feminine singular because the noun **une maison** is feminine singular.

*two white houses / **deux maisons blanches.***

The adjective **blanches** is feminine plural because the noun **maisons** is feminine plural.

agreement of past participle of a reflexive verb with its reflexive pronoun
Agreement is made on the past participle of a reflexive verb with its reflexive pronoun in gender (masculine or feminine) and number (singular or plural) if that pronoun is the *direct object* of the verb. The agreement is determined by looking at the subject to see

its gender and number, which is the same as its reflexive pronoun. If the reflexive pronoun is the *indirect object*, an agreement is *not* made. *See* **se laver** *on page 276 and* **se lever** *on page 278.*

*She washed herself / **Elle s'est lavée.***

There is a feminine agreement on the past participle **lavée** (added **e**) with the reflexive pronoun **se** (here, **s'**) because it serves as a direct object pronoun. What or whom did she wash? Herself, which is expressed in **se (s')**.

But:

*She washed her hair / **Elle s'est lavé les cheveux.***

There is no feminine agreement on the past participle **lavé** here because the reflexive pronoun (**se**, here, **s'**) serves as an *indirect object*. The direct object is **les cheveux** and it is stated *after* the verb. What did she wash? She washed her hair *on herself (s')*. *See also* reflexive pronoun and reflexive verb.

agreement of past participle with its direct object   Agreement is made on the past participle with its direct object in gender (masculine or feminine) and number (singular or plural) when the verb is conjugated with **avoir** in the compound tenses. Agreement is made when the direct object, if there is one, *precedes* the verb.

*Where are the little cakes? Paul ate them / **Où sont les petits gâteaux?***
Paul les a mangés.

The verb **a mangés** is in the *passé composé*; **manger** is conjugated with **avoir**. There is a plural agreement on the past participle **mangés** (added **s**) because the *preceding* direct object *them/les* is masculine plural, referring to *les petits gâteaux*, which is masculine plural.

*Who wrote the letters? Robert wrote them / **Qui a écrit les lettres?***
Robert les a écrites.

The verb **a écrites** is in the *passé composé*; **écrire** is conjugated with **avoir**. There is a feminine plural agreement on the past participle **écrites** (added **e** and **s**) because the *preceding*-direct object *them/les* is feminine plural, referring to *les lettres*, which is feminine plural. A past participle functions as an adjective.

An agreement in gender and number is *not* made with *an indirect object*. *See* indirect object noun, indirect object pronoun. Review the regular formation of past participles and irregular past participles on page ix. *See also* direct object noun, direct object pronoun.

agreement of past participle with the subject   Agreement is made on the past participle with the subject in gender (masculine or feminine) and number (singular or plural) when the verb is conjugated with **être** in the compound tenses.

*She went to Paris / **Elle est allée à Paris.***

The verb **est allée** is in the *passé composé*; **aller** is conjugated with **être**. There is a feminine agreement on the past participle **allée** (added **e**) because the subject **elle** is feminine singular.

*The boys have arrived / **Les garçons sont arrivés.***

The verb **sont arrivés** is in the *passé composé*; **arriver** is conjugated with **être**. There is a plural agreement on the past participle **arrivés** (added **s**) because the subject **les garçons** is masculine plural.

Review page viii to find out about verbs conjugated with either **avoir** or **être** to form the seven compound tenses. *See* **aller** *on page 31 and* **arriver** *on page 50. See also* past participle and subject.

agreement of verb with its subject   A verb agrees in person (1st, 2d, or 3d) and in number (singular or plural) with its subject.

*Does he always tell the truth? / **Dit-il toujours la vérité?***

The verb **dit** (of **dire**) is 3d person singular because the subject *il/he* is 3d person singular.

*Where are they going? / **Où vont-ils?***

The verb **vont** (of **aller**) is 3d person plural because the subject *ils/they* is 3d person plural. For subject pronouns in the singular and plural, review the page facing page 1.

antecedent   An antecedent is a word to which a relative pronoun refers. It comes *before* the pronoun.

The girl who is laughing over there is my sister /
La jeune fille qui rit là-bas est ma soeur.

The antecedent is *girl/la jeune fille*. The relative pronoun *who/qui* refers to the girl.

*The car that I bought is expensive / **La voiture que j'ai achetée est chère.***

The antecedent is *car/la voiture*. The relative pronoun *that/que* refers to the car. Note also that the past participle ***achetée*** is fem. sing. because it refers to ***la voiture*** (fem. sing.), which precedes the verb. Review **acheter** on page 17 and **rire** on page 417. *See also* relative pronoun.

auxiliary verb   An auxiliary verb is a helping verb. In English grammar it is *to have*. In French grammar it is **avoir** (to have) or **être** (to be). An auxiliary verb is used to help form the seven compound tenses.

*I have eaten /**J'ai mangé;** she has left / **elle est partie.***

Review page viii to find out about verbs conjugated with **avoir** or **être** as helping verbs. Also, review **manger** on page 283 and **partir** on page 325.

cardinal number   A cardinal number is a number that expresses an amount, such as *one*, *two*, *three*, and so on. *See also* ordinal number.

causative faire   In English grammar a causative verb causes something to be done. In French grammar the idea is the same. The subject of the verb causes the action expressed in the verb to be carried out by someone else.

Mrs. Roth makes her students work in French class /
Madame Roth fait travailler ses élèves dans la classe de français.

*Mr. Smith is having a house built / **Monsieur Smith fait construire une maison.***

Review **construire** on page 109, **faire** on page 218, and **travailler** on page 479.

clause   A clause is a group of words that contains a subject and a predicate. A predicate may contain more than one word. A conjugated verb form is revealed in the predicate.

Mrs. Coty lives in a small apartment /
Madame Coty demeure dans un petit appartement.

The subject is *Mrs. Coty/Madame Coty*. The predicate is *lives in a small apartment/demeure dans un petit appartement*. The verb is *lives/demeure*. *See also* dependent clause, independent clause.

comparative adjective   When making a comparison between two persons or things, an adjective is used to express the degree of comparison in the following ways.
Same degree of comparison:

*Raymond is as tall as his father / **Raymond est aussi grand que son père.***

Lesser degree of comparison:

*Monique is less intelligent than her sister / **Monique est moins intelligente que sa soeur.***

Higher degree of comparison:

This apple is more delicious than that apple /
Cette pomme-ci est plus délicieuse que cette pomme-là.

See also superlative adjective.

comparative adverb   An adverb is compared in the same way as an adjective is compared. *See* comparative adjective.

Same degree of comparison:

Mr. Bernard speaks as fast as Mr. Claude /
Monsieur Bernard parle aussi vite que Monsieur Claude.

Lesser degree of comparison:

Alice studies less seriously than her sister /
Alice étudie moins sérieusement que sa soeur.

Higher degree of comparison:

Albert works more slowly than his brother /
Albert travaille plus lentement que son frère.

See also superlative adverb.

complex sentence   A complex sentence contains one independent clause and one or more dependent clauses.

One independent clause and one dependent clause:

Jack is handsome but his brother isn't / **Jacques est beau mais son frère ne l'est pas.**
The independent clause is *Jack is handsome*. It makes sense when it stands alone because it expresses a complete thought. The dependent clause is *but his brother isn't*. The dependent clause, which is introduced by the conjunction *but*, does not make complete sense when it stands alone because it *depends* on the thought expressed in the independent clause.

One independent clause and two dependent clauses:

Mary gets good grades in school because she studies but her sister never studies /
**Marie reçoit de bonnes notes à l'école parce
qu'elle étudie mais sa soeur n'étudie jamais.**

The independent clause is *Mary gets good grades in school*. It makes sense when it stands alone because it expresses a complete thought. The first dependent clause is *because she studies*. This dependent clause, which is introduced by the conjunction *because*, does not make complete sense when it stands alone because it *depends* on the thought expressed in the independent clause. The second dependent clause is *but her sister never studies*. That dependent clause, which is introduced by the conjunction *but*, does not make complete sense either when it stands alone because it *depends* on the thought expressed in the independent clause. *See also* dependent clause, independent clause.

compound sentence   A compound sentence contains two or more independent clauses.

*Mrs. Dubois went to the supermarket, she bought some groceries, and then
she returned home* / **Madame Dubois est allée au supermarché, elle a acheté des
provisions, et puis elle est rentrée chez elle.**

This compound sentence contains three independent clauses. They are independent because they make sense when they stand alone. Review the *passé composé* on page xxi. *See also* independent clause.

conditional perfect tense   In French grammar the conditional used to be considered a mood. Grammarians now regard it as a tense of the indicative mood. This tense is defined with examples on pages xxiii and xxiv.

Definitions of basic grammatical terms with examples   677

conditional present tense In French grammar the conditional used to be considered a mood. Grammarians now regard it as a tense of the indicative mood. This tense is defined with examples on page xviii.

conjugation The conjugation of a verb is the fixed order of all its forms showing their inflections (changes) in the three persons of the singular and plural in a particular tense.

conjunction A conjunction is a word that connects words or groups of words.
*and/**et**, or/**ou**, but/**mais***
*You and I are going downtown / **Toi et moi, nous allons en ville.***
You can stay home or you can come with us /
Tu peux rester à la maison ou tu peux venir avec nous.

declarative sentence A declarative sentence makes a statement.
*I have finished the work / **J'ai fini le travail.***
Review **finir** on page 225.

definite article The definite article in French has four forms and they all mean *the*.
They are: **le, la, l', les**, as in:
le livre/the book, la maison/the house, l'école/the school,
les enfants/the children
The definite articles are also used as direct object pronouns. *See* direct object pronoun.

demonstrative adjective A demonstrative adjective is an adjective that points out. It is placed in front of a noun.
*this book/**ce livre**; this hotel/**cet hôtel**; this child/**cet enfant**; this house/**cette maison**;*
*these flowers/**ces fleurs***

demonstrative pronoun A demonstrative pronoun is a pronoun that points out. It takes the place of a noun. It agrees in gender and number with the noun it replaces.
I have two apples; do you prefer this one or that one?
J'ai deux pommes; préférez-vous celle-ci ou celle-là?
*Sorry, but I prefer those / **Je regrette, mais je préfère celles-là.***
*Do you like the ones that are on the table? / **Aimez-vous celles qui sont sur la table?***
For demonstrative pronouns that are neuter, *see* neuter.

dependent clause A dependent clause is a group of words that contains a subject and a predicate. It does not express a complete thought when it stands alone. It is called *dependent* because it depends on the independent clause for a complete meaning. Subordinate clause is another term for dependent clause.
Mary is absent today because she is sick /
Marie est absente aujourd'hui parce qu'elle est malade.
The independent clause is *Mary is absent today*. The dependent clause is *because she is sick*.
See also clause, independent clause.

descriptive adjective A descriptive adjective is an adjective that describes a person, place, or thing.
*a pretty girl/**une jolie jeune fille**; a handsome boy/**un beau garçon**;*
*a small house/**une petite maison**; a big city/**une grande ville**;*
*an expensive car/**une voiture chère**.*
See also adjective.

direct object noun   A direct object noun receives the action of the verb *directly*. That is why it is called a direct object, as opposed to an indirect object. A direct object noun is normally placed *after* the verb.

> *I am writing a letter* / ***J'écris une lettre.***

The subject is *I/Je*. The verb is *am writing/écris*. The direct object is the noun *letter/une lettre*. *See also* direct object pronoun.

direct object pronoun   A direct object pronoun receives the action of the verb *directly*. It takes the place of a direct object noun. In French a pronoun that is a direct object of a verb is ordinarily placed *in front of* the verb.

> *I am reading it [the letter]* / ***Je la lis.***

A direct object pronoun is placed *after* the verb and joined with a hyphen *in the affirmative imperative*.

> *Write it [the letter] now* / ***Écrivez-la maintenant.***

The direct object pronouns are:

Person	Singular	Plural
1st	*me (m')* me	*nous* us
2d	*te (t')* you (fam.)	*vous* you (sing. polite or pl.)
3d	*le (l')* him, it (person or thing)	*les* them (persons or things)
	la (l') her, it (person or thing)	

Review **écrire** on page 173 and **lire** on page 279. *See also* imperative.

disjunctive pronoun   In French grammar a disjunctive pronoun is a pronoun that is stressed; in other words, emphasis is placed on it.

> *I speak well; he does not speak well* / ***Moi, je parle bien; lui, il ne parle pas bien.***
> *Talk to me* / ***Parlez-moi.***

A disjunctive pronoun is also object of a preposition:

> *She is talking with me* / ***Elle parle avec moi.***
> *I always think of you* / ***Je pense toujours à toi.***

The disjunctive pronouns are:

Person	Singular	Plural
1st	*moi* me, I	*nous* us, we
2d	*toi* you (fam.)	*vous* you (sing. polite or pl.)
3d	*soi* oneself	
	lui him, he	*eux* them, they (m.)
	elle her, she	*elles* them, they (f.)

ending of a verb   In French grammar the ending of a verb form changes according to the person and number of the subject and the tense of the verb.

For example, to form the present indicative tense of a regular **-er** type verb like **parler**, drop **er** of the infinitive and add the following endings: **-e, -es, -e** for the 1st, 2d, and 3d persons of the singular; **-ons, -ez, -ent** for the 1st, 2d, and 3d persons of the plural. You then get:

je parle, tu parles, il (elle, on) parle;
nous parlons, vous parlez, ils (elles) parlent

Review pages xxvii and xxviii. *See also* stem of a verb.

feminine   In French grammar the gender of a noun, pronoun, or adjective is feminine or masculine, not male or female.

Masculine			Feminine		
noun	pronoun	adjective	noun	pronoun	adjective
le garçon	*il*	*grand*	*la femme*	*elle*	*grande*
the boy	he	tall	the woman	she	tall
le livre	*il*	*petit*	*la voiture*	*elle*	*petite*
the book	it	small	the car	it	small

See also gender.

future perfect tense   This tense is defined with examples on page xxiii.

future tense   This tense is defined with examples on page xviii.

gender   In French grammar gender means masculine or feminine.

Masculine: *the boy/le garçon; he, it/il; the rooster/le coq; the book/le livre*
Feminine; *the girl/la jeune fille; she, it/elle;*
the hen/la poule; the house/la maison

gerund   In English grammar a gerund is a word formed from a verb. It ends in *ing*. Actually, it is the present participle of a verb. But it is not used as a verb. It is used as a noun.

Seeing is believing / Voir c'est croire.

However, in French grammar the infinitive form of the verb is used, as in the above example, when the verb is used as a noun. In French, *seeing is believing* is expressed as *to see is to believe.*

The French gerund is also a word formed from a verb. It ends in ***ant***. It is also the present participle of a verb. As a gerund, it is normally preceded by the preposition **en**.

En partant, il a fait ses excuses / *While leaving, he made his excuses.*
See also present participle.

***if* (si) clause**   An "if" clause is defined with examples at the top of page 560. *See also* clause.

imperative   The imperative is a mood, not a tense. It is used to express a command. In French it is used in the 2d person of the singular (**tu**), the 2d person of the plural (**vous**), and in the 1st person of the plural (**nous**). Review the imperative with examples on pages xxv and xxvi. Also review the three imperative forms of **donner** on page 167. *See also* person (1st, 2d, 3d).

imperfect indicative tense   This tense is defined with examples on pages xvi and xvii.

imperfect subjunctive tense   This tense is defined with examples on pages xx and xxi.

indefinite article   In English the indefinite articles are *a, an*, as in *a book, an apple*. They are indefinite because they do not refer to any definite or particular noun.

In French there are two indefinite articles in the singular: one in the masculine form (**un**) and one in the feminine form (**une**).

Masculine singular: ***un ami**/a friend*
Feminine singular: ***une pomme**/an apple*

In French they both change to **des** in the plural.

*I have a brother/**J'ai un frère**; I have brothers/**J'ai des frères**.*
*I have a sister/**J'ai une soeur**; I have sisters/**J'ai des soeurs**.*
*I have an apple/**J'ai une pomme**; I have apples/**J'ai des pommes**.*

See also definite article.

indefinite pronoun   An indefinite pronoun is a pronoun that does not refer to any definite or particular noun.

*something/**quelque chose**; someone, somebody/**quelqu'un**, **quelqu'une**;*
*each one/**chacun**, **chacune**; anything/**n'importe quoi***

independent clause   An independent clause is a group of words that contains a subject and a predicate. It expresses a complete thought when it stands alone.

*The cat is sleeping under the bed / **Le chat dort sous le lit**.*

See also clause, dependent clause, predicate.

indicative mood   The indicative mood is used in sentences that make a statement or ask a question. The indicative mood is used most of the time when we speak or write in English or French.

*I am going home now/**Je vais chez moi maintenant**.*
*Where are you going?/**Où allez-vous?***

indirect object noun   An indirect object noun receives the action of the verb *indirectly*.
*I am writing a letter to Mary or I am writing Mary a letter / **J'écris une lettre à Marie**.*
The subject is *I/**Je***. The verb is *am writing/**écris***. The direct object noun is *a letter/**une lettre***. The indirect object noun is *Mary/**Marie**.* An agreement is not made with an indirect object noun. *See also* indirect object pronoun, direct object noun, direct object pronoun.

indirect object pronoun   An indirect object pronoun takes the place of an indirect object noun. It receives the action of the verb *indirectly*. In French a pronoun that is the indirect object of a verb is ordinarily placed *in front of* the verb.

*I am writing a letter to her or I am writing her a letter / **Je lui écris une lettre**.*
The indirect object pronoun is *(to) her/**lui***. An agreement is not made with an indirect object pronoun.

An indirect object pronoun is placed *after* the verb and joined with a hyphen *in the affirmative imperative*.

*Write to her now / **Écris-lui maintenant**.*

The indirect object pronouns are:

Person	Singular	Plural
1st	*me* (*m'*) *to me*	*nous* *to us*
2d	*te* (*t'*) *to you (fam.)*	*vous* *to you (sing. polite or pl.)*
3d	*lui* *to him, to her*	*leur* *to them*

See also indirect object noun.

infinitive   An infinitive is a verb form. In English it is normally stated with the preposition *to*, as in *to talk, to finish, to sell*. In French the infinitive form of a verb consists of three major types: those of the 1st conjugation that end in **-er**, those of the 2d conjugation that end in **-ir**, and those of the 3d conjugation that end in **-re**.
> *parler*/*to talk, to speak*; *finir*/*to finish*; *vendre*/*to sell*

All the verbs in this book on pages 1 to 501 are given in the infinitive form at the top of each page where they are arranged alphabetically.

interjection   An interjection is a word that expresses emotion, a feeling of joy, of sadness, an exclamation of surprise, and other exclamations consisting of one or two words.
> *Ah!*/*Ah! Oh!*/*Oh! Darn it!*/*Zut! Whew!*/*Ouf! My God!*/*Mon Dieu!*

interrogative adjective   An interrogative adjective is an adjective that is used in a question. It agrees in gender and number with the noun it modifies.
> *What book do you want?* / *Quel livre désirez-vous?*
> *What time is it?* / *Quelle heure est-il?*

interrogative adverb   An interrogative adverb is an adverb that introduces a question. As an adverb, it modifies the verb.
> *How are you?* / *Comment allez-vous?*
> *How much does this book cost?* / *Combien coûte ce livre?*
> *When will you arrive?* / *Quand arriverez-vous?*

interrogative pronoun   An interrogative pronoun is a pronoun that asks a question. There are interrogative pronouns that refer to persons and those that refer to things.
> *Who is on the phone?* / *Qui est à l'appareil?*
> *What are you saying?* / *Que dites-vous?*

interrogative sentence   An interrogative sentence asks a question.
> *What are you doing?* / *Que faites-vous?*

intransitive verb   An intransitive verb is a verb that does not take a direct object.
> *The professor is talking loudly* / *Le professeur parle fort.*

An intransitive verb takes an indirect object.
> *The professor is talking to us* / *Le professeur nous parle.*

See also indirect object pronoun.

irregular verb   An irregular verb is a verb that does not follow a fixed pattern in its conjugation in the various verb tenses.

Basic irregular verbs in French:

aller/to go   *avoir*/to have   *être*/to be   *faire*/to do, to make

Review these verbs on pages 31, 61, 206, and 218. *See also* conjugation, regular verb.

limiting adjective   A limiting adjective is an adjective that limits a quantity.

three tickets/*trois billets*; *a few candies*/*quelques bonbons*

main clause   Main clause is another term for independent clause. *See* independent clause.

masculine   In French grammar the gender of a noun, pronoun, or adjective is masculine or feminine, not male or female. *See also* gender.

mood of verbs   Some grammarians use the term *the mode* instead of *the mood* of a verb. Either term means *the manner or way* a verb is expressed. In English and in French grammar a verb expresses an action or state of being in the following three moods (modes, *ways*): the indicative mood, the imperative mood, and the subjunctive mood. In French grammar there is also the infinitive mood when the whole infinitive is used, *e.g.*, **voir**, **croire**, as in **Voir c'est croire**/*Seeing is believing (to see is to believe)*. Most of the time, in English and French, we speak and write in the indicative mood.

negative statement, affirmative statement
   see **affirmative statement, negative statement**

neuter   A word that is neuter is neither masculine nor feminine. Common neuter demonstrative pronouns are **ce (c')**/*it*, **ceci**/*this*, **cela**/*that*, **ça**/*that*. They are invariable, which means they do not change in gender and number.

It's not true/*Ce n'est pas vrai*; *it is true*/*c'est vrai*; *this is true*/*ceci est vrai*; *that is true*/*cela est vrai*; *what is that?*/*qu'est-ce que c'est que ça?*

For demonstrative pronouns that are not neuter, *see* demonstrative pronoun. There is also the neuter pronoun **le**, as in: *Je le crois / I believe it*; *Je le pense / I think so*.

noun   A noun is a word that names a person, animal, place, thing, condition or state, or quality.

the man/*l'homme*, *the woman*/*la femme*, *the horse*/*le cheval*, *the house*/*la maison*
the book/*le livre*, *happiness*/*le bonheur*, *excellence*/*l'excellence* (fem.)

In French the noun **le nom** is the word for name and noun.

number   In English and French grammar, number means singular or plural.
Masc. sing.:

the boy/*le garçon*; *the arm*/*le bras*; *the eye*/*l'oeil*

Masc. pl.:

the boys/*les garçons*; *the arms*/*les bras*; *the eyes*/*les yeux*

Fem. sing.:

the girl/*la jeune fille*; *the house*/*la maison*; *the hen*/*la poule*

Fem. pl.:

the girls/*les jeunes filles*; *the houses*/*les maisons*; *the hens*/*les poules*

ordinal number   An ordinal number is a number that expresses position in a series, such as *first, second, third*, and so on. In English and French grammar we talk about 1st person, 2d person, 3d person singular or plural regarding subjects and verbs. *See also* cardinal number and person (1st, 2d, 3d).

orthographical changes in verb forms An orthographical change in a verb form is a change in spelling.

The second letter **c** in the verb *commencer/to begin* changes to **ç** if the letter after it is **a**, **o**, or **u**, as in *nous commençons/we begin*. The reason for this spelling change is to preserve the sound of **s** as it is pronounced in the infinitive form **commencer**. When **a**, **o**, or **u** follow the letter **c**, the **c** is pronounced as in the sound of **k**. The mark under the letter **ç** is called *une cédille/cedilla*. Some linguists say it is the lower part of the letter **s** and it tells you to pronounce **ç** as an **s** sound. Other linguists say that **ç** was borrowed from the Greek alphabet, which represents the sound of **s** when it is the last letter of a Greek word.

The verb *s'appeler/to call oneself, to be named* contains a single **l**. When a verb form is stressed on the syllable containing one **l**, it doubles, as in *je m'appelle . . ./I call myself . . . , my name is . . . .*

partitive In French grammar the partitive denotes a *part* of a whole. In English we express the partitive by saying *some* or *any* in front of the noun. In French we use the following partitive forms in front of the noun:

Masculine singular: **du** or **de l'**   Feminine singular: **de la** or **de l'**
Masculine or feminine plural: **des**
I have some coffee / J'ai du café.
I'd like some water / J'aimerais de l'eau.
I'd like some meat / J'aimerais de la viande.
Do you have any candies? / Avez-vous des bonbons?

In the negative, these partitive forms change to **de** or **d'**:
I don't have any coffee / Je n'ai pas de café.
I don't want any water / Je ne veux pas d'eau.
I wouldn't like any meat / Je n'aimerais pas de viande.
No, I don't have any candies / Non, je n'ai pas de bonbons.

passive voice When we speak or write in the active voice and change to the passive voice, the direct object becomes the subject, the subject becomes the object of a preposition, and the verb becomes *to be* plus the past participle of the active verb. The past participle functions as an adjective.

Janine is loved by everyone / Janine est aimée de tout le monde.

The subject is *Janine*. The verb is *is/est*. The object of the preposition *by/de* is *everyone/tout le monde*. *See also* active voice. Compare the above sentence with the example in the active voice.

past anterior tense This tense is defined with examples on page xxii.

past definite or simple past tense This tense is defined with examples on page xvii. In French it is the *passé simple*.

past indefinite tense This tense is defined with examples on page xxi. In French it is the *passé composé*.

past participle A past participle is derived from a verb. It is used to form the compound tenses. Its auxiliary verb in English is *to have*. In French the auxiliary verb is **avoir**/to have or **être**/to be. It is part of the verb tense.

With **avoir** as the auxiliary verb: *Elle a mangé / She has eaten.*

The subject is *elle*/she. The verb is *a mangé*/has eaten. The tense of the verb is the *passé composé*. The auxiliary verb is *a*/has. The past participle is *mangé*/eaten.

With **être** as the auxiliary verb: *Elle est arrivée / She has arrived.*
The verb is *est arrivée*/has arrived. The tense of the verb is the *passé composé*.
The auxiliary verb is *est*. The past participle is *arrivée*/arrived.

Review page ix for the regular formation of a past participle and a list of basic irregular past participles. Review page viii to find out about verbs conjugated with either **avoir** or **être**. *See also* auxiliary verb and agreement of past participle with the subject.

past perfect tense   This tense is also called the pluperfect indicative tense. Review pages xxi and xxii for a definition with examples.

past simple tense   This tense is defined with examples on page xvii. It is also called the simple past tense or past definite tense. In French it is the *passé simple*.

past subjunctive tense   This tense is also called the perfect subjunctive tense. It is defined with examples on page xxiv.

person (1st, 2d, 3d)   Verb forms in a particular tense are learned systematically according to person (1st, 2d, 3d) and number (singular, plural).
Present indicative tense of the verb **aller**/to go:

Singular	Plural
1st person: *je vais*	1st person: *nous allons*
2d person: *tu vas*	2d person: *vous allez*
3d person: *il, elle, on va*	3d person: *ils, elles vont*

personal pronoun   A personal pronoun refers to a person. The pronoun *it*/*il* or *elle* is in this category. Review the subject pronouns on the page facing page 1. For examples of other types of pronouns, *see also* demonstrative pronoun, direct object pronoun, disjunctive pronoun, indefinite pronoun, indirect object pronoun, interrogative pronoun, possessive pronoun, reflexive pronoun, relative pronoun.

pluperfect indicative tense   This tense is also called the past perfect indicative tense. It is defined with examples on pages xxi and xxii.

pluperfect subjunctive tense   This tense is also called the past perfect subjunctive tense. It is defined with examples on pages xxiv and xxv.

plural   Plural means more than one. *See also* person (1st, 2d, 3d) and singular.

possessive adjective   A possessive adjective is an adjective that is placed in front of a noun to show possession. In French their forms change in gender (masculine or feminine) and number (singular or plural) to agree with the noun they modify.
my book/**mon livre**   *my books*/**mes livres**   *my dress*/**ma robe**

possessive pronoun   A possessive pronoun is a pronoun that shows possession. It takes the place of a possessive adjective with the noun. Its form agrees in gender (masculine or feminine) and number (singular or plural) with what it is replacing.

English:

mine, yours, his, hers, its, ours, theirs

Definitions of basic grammatical terms with examples   685

French:

Possessive adjective	Possessive pronoun
my book/**mon livre**	mine/**le mien**
my dress/**ma robe**	mine/**la mienne**
my shoes/**mes chaussures**	mine/**les miennes**

predicate   The predicate is that part of the sentence that tells us something about the subject. The main word of the predicate is the verb.

The tourists are waiting for the tour bus / ***Les touristes attendent l'autocar***.
The subject is *the tourists/**les touristes***. The predicate is *are waiting for the tour bus/**attendent l'autocar***. The verb is *are waiting/**attendent***. The direct object is *the tour bus/**l'autocar***.

preposition   A preposition is a word that establishes a rapport between words.
English:

with, in, on, at, between

French:

*with me/**avec moi**   in the drawer/**dans le tiroir**   on the table/**sur la table**
at six o'clock/**à six heures**   between him and her/**entre lui et elle***
Review verbs with prepositions beginning on page 543.

present indicative tense   This tense is defined with examples on pages xv and xvi.

present participle   A present participle is derived from a verb form. In French it is regularly formed like this: take the **nous** form of the present indicative tense of the verb you have in mind, then drop the ending **ons** and add **ant.** In English a present participle ends in *ing*.

Infinitive	Present Indicative **nous** form	Present participle
chanter	***nous chantons***	***chantant***
to sing	*we sing*	*singing*
finir	***nous finissons***	***finissant***
to finish	*we finish*	*finishing*
vendre	***nous vendons***	***vendant***
to sell	*we sell*	*selling*

For the regular formation of present participles and to find out what the three common irregular present participles are, review page ix.

present subjunctive tense   This tense is defined with examples on pages xix and xx.

pronoun   A pronoun is a word that takes the place of a noun.

l'homme/il	***la femme/elle***	***l'arbre/il***	***la voiture/elle***
the man/he	*the woman/she*	*the tree/it*	*the car/it*

reflexive pronoun and reflexive verb   In English a reflexive pronoun is a personal pronoun that contains *self* or *selves*. In French and English a reflexive pronoun is used with a verb that is called reflexive because the action of the verb falls on the reflexive pronoun.

In French there is a required set of reflexive pronouns for a reflexive verb.

se laver	***Je me lave.***	***Se blesser***	***Elle s'est blessée.***
to wash oneself	*I wash myself.*	*to hurt oneself*	*She hurt herself.*

In French a reflexive verb is conjugated with **être** to form the compound tenses. The French term for a reflexive verb is **un verbe pronominal** because a pronoun goes with the verb. Review the reflexive verbs **s'appeler** on page 41, **se blesser** on page 73, **se laver** on page 276, and **se lever** on page 278. *See also* agreement of past participle of a reflexive verb with its reflexive pronoun.

regular verb   A regular verb is a verb that is conjugated in the various tenses according to a fixed pattern. For examples, review pages xxvii to xxx. *See also* conjugation, irregular verb.

relative pronoun   A relative pronoun is a pronoun that refers to its antecedent.
> *The girl who is laughing over there is my sister /*
> **La jeune fille qui rit là-bas est ma soeur.**

The antecedent is *girl/la jeune fille*. The relative pronoun *who/qui* refers to the girl. *See also* antecedent.

sentence   A sentence is a group of words that contains a subject and a predicate. The verb is contained in the predicate. A sentence expresses a complete thought.
> *The train leaves from the North Station at two o'clock in the afternoon /*
> **Le train part de la Gare du Nord à deux heures de l'après-midi.**

The subject is *train/le train.* The predicate is *leaves from the North Station at two o'clock in the afternoon/part de la Gare du Nord à deux heures de l'après-midi.* The verb is *leaves/part. See also* complex sentence, compound sentence, simple sentence.

simple sentence   A simple sentence is a sentence that contains one subject and one predicate. The verb is the core of the predicate. The verb is the most important word in a sentence because it tells us what the subject is doing.
> *Mary is eating an apple from her garden /* **Marie mange une pomme de son jardin.**

The subject is *Mary/***Marie.** The predicate is *is eating an apple from her garden/mange une pomme de son jardin.* The verb is *is eating/mange.* The direct object is *an apple/une pomme. From her garden/de son jardin* is an adverbial phrase. It tells you from where the apple came. *See also* complex sentence, compound sentence.

singular   Singular means one. *See also* plural.

stem of a verb   The stem of a verb is what is left after we drop the ending of its infinitive form. It is necessary to add to it the required endings of a regular verb in a particular verb tense.

Infinitive	Ending of infinitive	Stem
donner/to give	**er**	***donn***
choisir/to choose	**ir**	***chois***
vendre/to sell	**re**	***vend***

See also ending of a verb.

subject   A subject is that part of a sentence that is related to its verb. The verb says something about the subject.
> *Clara and Isabel are beautiful /* **Clara et Isabel sont belles.**

subjunctive mood   The subjunctive mood is the mood of a verb that is used in specific cases, *e.g.*, after certain verbs expressing a wish, doubt, emotion, fear, joy, uncertainty, an indefinite expression, an indefinite antecedent, certain conjunctions, and others. The subjunctive mood is used more frequently in French than in English. Review the uses of the subjunctive mood with examples on pages 560 to 565. *See also* mood of verbs.

subordinate clause   Subordinate clause is another term for dependent clause. *See* dependent clause.

superlative adjective   A superlative adjective is an adjective that expresses the highest degree when making a comparison of more than two persons or things.

Adjective	Comparative	Superlative
bon/good	*meilleur*/better	*le meilleur*/best
mauvais/bad	*plus mauvais*/worse	*le plus mauvais*/worst

See also comparative adjective.

superlative adverb   A superlative adverb is an adverb that expresses the highest degree when making a comparison of more than two persons or things.

Adverb	Comparative	Superlative
vite/quickly	*plus vite*/more quickly	*le plus vite*/most quickly
	moins vite/less quickly	*le moins vite*/least quickly

See also comparative adverb.

tense of verb   In English and French grammar, tense means time. The tense of the verb indicates the time of the action or state of being. The three major segments of time are past, present, and future. In French there are fourteen verb tenses, of which seven are simple tenses and seven are compound. Review pages xxvi and xxviii for the names of the fourteen tenses in French and English.

transitive verb   A transitive verb is a verb that takes a direct object.
*I am closing the window/ **Je ferme la fenêtre.***
The subject is *I*/**Je.** The verb is *am closing / **ferme.*** The direct object is *the window/**la fenêtre.***
See also intransitive verb.

verb   A verb is a word that expresses action or a state of being.
Action: ***Les oiseaux volent** / The birds are flying.*
The verb is ***volent**/are flying.*
State of being: ***La jeune fille est heureuse** / The girl is happy.*
The verb is ***est**/is.*